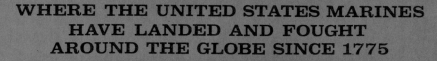

WHERE THE UNITED STATES MARINES HAVE LANDED AND FOUGHT AROUND THE GLOBE SINCE 1775

Iceland 1941

Whitehaven 1778

Moscow 1934

EUROPE

Belleau Wood 1918 • Argonne 1918

MERICA

Penobscot 1779
Valcour I. 1776 • Boston 1833
Baltimore 1814 • New York 1863
Ferry 1859 • Princeton 1777
Il Run 1861 • Trenton 1777
Bladensburg 1814
Fort Fisher 1865

Azores 1918

Ionian Islands 1953
Cyprus 1974
Beirut 1958
Jerusalem 1956

Agadir 1960

Tripoli 1803

Derna 1805

Alexandria 1882

1862
1815
ay 1864

Fort Brooke 1836
Nassau 1776
Guantanamo 1898
Puerto Plata 1800
Haiti 1915 • Fajardo 1824
Dominican Republic 1916, 1965
Curaçao 1800
Trinidad 1895

AFRICA

Addis Ababa 1903

1924
1912, 1927
Panama 1901

ATLANTIC

Cape Palmas 1843

OCEAN

INDIAN

Lima 1835

SOUTH

AMERICA

OCEAN

Paraguay 1855

Valparaiso · 1814
Buenos Aires 1852 • Montevideo 1855, 1868

Falkland Islands 1832

BOOKS BY J. ROBERT MOSKIN

Morality in America
Turncoat
The Decline of the American Male (co-author)

J. Robert Moskin

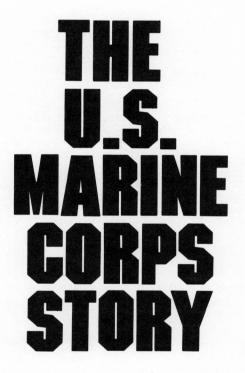

THE U.S. MARINE CORPS STORY

McGRAW-HILL BOOK COMPANY
New York   St. Louis   San Francisco
Toronto   Düsseldorf   Mexico   Panama

Photo essays designed by A Good Thing, Inc.

Maps by George Buctel.

Copyright © 1977 by J. Robert Moskin.
All rights reserved.
Printed in the United States of America.
No part of this publication may
be reproduced, stored in a retrieval
system, or transmitted,
in any form or by any means,
electronic, mechanical, photocopying,
recording or otherwise, without the prior written
permission of the publisher.

123456789 KPKP 7987

Library of Congress Cataloging in Publication Data
Moskin, J Robert.
   The U.S. Marine Corps story.
   Bibliography: p.
   Includes index.
   1. United States. Marine Corps—History. I. Title.
VE23.M64   359.9'6'0973   75-14213
ISBN 0-07-043453-0

Dedicated to the men and women
who lived this story—
and those who died for it

CONTENTS

CONTENTS

III

Archibald Henderson and the Indian Wars
1817–1842

IV

The Mexican War
1842–1847

V

The Civil War
1857–1865

CONTENTS

VI

Sweep Toward Empire
1848–1894

VII

The Four-Month War with Spain
1898   301

VIII

On Imperial Duty
1899–1902

ix

IX

Imperialism in the Caribbean
1901–1934

X

World War I
1914–1919

XI

Getting Ready
1919–1941

XII

World War II
1941–1949

XIII

The Korean War
1946–1953

XIV

Tumultuous Times
1953–1965

XV

The Vietnam War
1954–1975

XVI

"In Step and Smartly"
1975–   915

Foreword

The story of the U.S. Marine Corps is, first of all, the story of men in battle—the story of individual courage—of men who risked everything to do what had to be done. Although no Marine ever started a war, the Marines have been ready when called. Trained to kill, they are, in Stephen Crane's words, members of "a mysterious fraternity born of smoke and the danger of death."

This is also the story of what America is really like: how it has thrust its power outward around the globe—spearheaded repeatedly by United States Marines. It is, obviously, the story of American imperialism. Some of this story is praiseworthy; some of it is ugly. All of it must be told—unvarnished.

The reader will discover here a mainstream of the nation's story. From the Marines who fought at Princeton, New Orleans, Harpers Ferry, Peking, Haiti, Belleau Wood, Iwo Jima, the Chosin Reservoir and Khe Sanh, the reader will gain a fresh understanding of the meaning and uses—and the price—of more than 200 years of American power.

The reader who has been or is now a Marine will find here the true story of the Corps to which he looks with pride. He will see its story whole, in a way he has not before. He will read of Marines who have fought in his country's every war: John Trevett in the Revolution, Presley O'Bannon at Tripoli, Samuel Miller in the War of 1812, Archibald Henderson in the Indian wars, George Terrett in the Mexican War, Louis Fagan in the Civil War, John Quick in the War with Spain, Tony Waller in the Philippine Insurrection, Dan Daly in World War I, William Deane Hawkins and John Basilone in World War II, Chesty Puller in Korea, Lewis Walt in Vietnam. They were men—Marines—worth reading about.

The Marine Corps' story fascinates me because it mirrors the entire violent sweep of American history. When I was an editor with *Look* Magazine, assignments enabled me to report on Marines who fought and served at Da Nang, Inchon, Guantanamo, Chapultepec and Okinawa, and across the United States from Parris Island to Camp Pendleton. I had to be impressed with the effectiveness and pride I saw. Those Marines were by no means all supermen; they had to conquer the fear that hides in every man. But the *esprit* of their Corps, their code of comradeship made them special and drove them, when their country needed them, to move forward in battle where men kill and are killed.

The American Marines were born in 1775—before the nation. The need was there, as it still is today, more than two centuries later. Elmer Davis, the World War II director of the U.S. Office of War Information, put it baldly: "This will remain the land of the free only so long as it is the home of the brave." The Marines will be needed as long as the nation must be defended.

By the year of American Independence, nearly three million people had stepped onto these western shores of the Atlantic. They multiplied to two hundred million, strode across the continent and manned outposts around the globe. They became the most powerful people on earth, now at the height—and limit—of their expansion.

What spurred them on? They were propelled by the desire to escape tyrannies and wars, by hunger for freedom and land and economic well-being, and by faith in a self-appointed mission to spread civilization and God's word—in their own image.

The U.S. Marine Corps acquired, over time, the bloody duty of carrying the flag of empire, until this elite professional corps won an unerasable place in America's history and heritage. The Marine Corps both paced and symbolized the global destiny that the nation chose for itself.

This thrust pushed beyond the continent, through the islands of the Caribbean and the Pacific, and grabbed for footholds on the mainland of Asia. There, it met forces that proved unmovable; and the limits of expansion were learned slowly and painfully.

When the American Heritage Press division of the McGraw-Hill Book Company first decided to publish this book, United States Marines were still fighting and dying in Vietnam—the latest in the long parade of wars Marines have fought for their country.

The U.S. Marine Corps Story is the first totally independent history of this cavalcade ever written. It is the candid and unofficial story of the nation's growth to maturity and self-realization and of the Marines who led the way. And finally, like most stories worth telling, it is a story of love—of men's love for country and for those with whom they share the battle and the dying.

MAPS

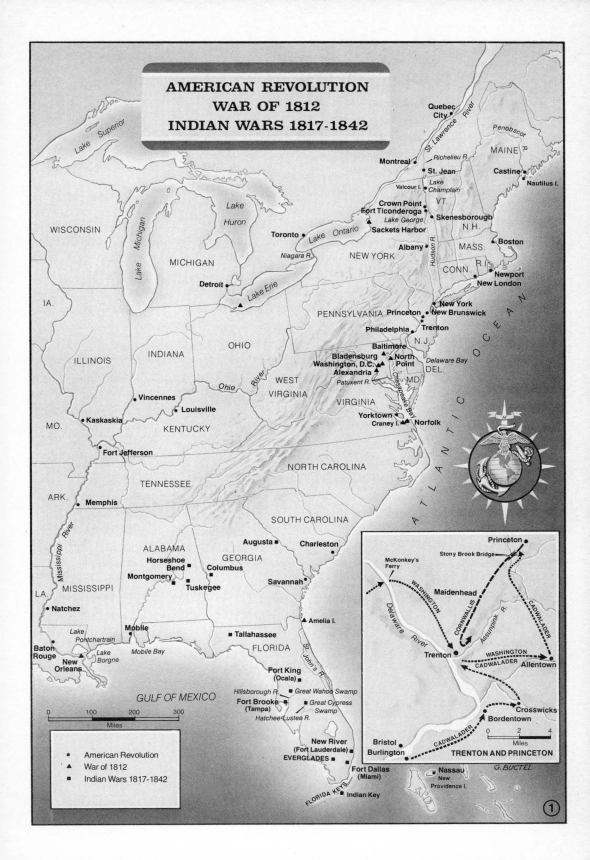

AMERICAN REVOLUTION
WAR OF 1812
INDIAN WARS 1817-1842

Lake Superior

Lake Huron

Lake Michigan

WISCONSIN

MICHIGAN

IA.

Quebec City

Penobscot R.

MAINE

Montreal

St. Lawrence River

Richelieu R.

Castine

St. Jean

Nautilus I.

Valcour I.

Lake Champlain

Crown Point

VT.

Fort Ticonderoga

Lake George

Skenesborough

N.H.

Sackets Harbor

Toronto

Lake Ontario

Albany

MASS.

Boston

Niagara R.

NEW YORK

Hudson R.

CONN.

R.I.

Newport

Detroit

Lake Erie

New London

New York

PENNSYLVANIA

Princeton

New Brunswick

Trenton

Philadelphia

N.J.

OHIO

Baltimore

Bladensburg

North Point

Washington, D.C.

Delaware Bay

DEL.

Alexandria

Patuxent R.

MD.

ILLINOIS

INDIANA

Ohio River

WEST VIRGINIA

Chesapeake Bay

Vincennes

Louisville

VIRGINIA

Yorktown

Norfolk

MO.

Kaskaskia

KENTUCKY

Craney I.

Fort Jefferson

ARK.

TENNESSEE

NORTH CAROLINA

Memphis

ATLANTIC OCEAN

SOUTH CAROLINA

Augusta

Charleston

ALABAMA

GEORGIA

Horseshoe Bend

Columbus

Montgomery

Savannah

MISSISSIPPI

Tuskegee

LA.

Natchez

Amelia I.

Mobile

Tallahassee

Lake Pontchartrain

Mobile Bay

FLORIDA

Baton Rouge

New Orleans

Lake Borgne

St. John's R.

Fort King (Ocala)

GULF OF MEXICO

Hillsborough R.

Great Wahoo Swamp

Fort Brooke (Tampa)

Great Cypress Swamp

Hatchee Lustee R.

New River (Fort Lauderdale)

EVERGLADES

Fort Dallas (Miami)

FLORIDA KEYS

Indian Key

0   100   200   300
Miles

● American Revolution
▲ War of 1812
■ Indian Wars 1817-1842

TRENTON AND PRINCETON

McKonkey's Ferry

WASHINGTON

Princeton

Stony Brook Bridge

Maidenhead

CADWALADER

Delaware River

CORNWALLIS

Assunpink R.

WASHINGTON

CADWALADER

Trenton

Allentown

Crosswicks

Bordentown

CADWALADER

0   2   4
Miles

Bristol

Burlington

Nassau
New Providence I.

G. BUCTEL

①

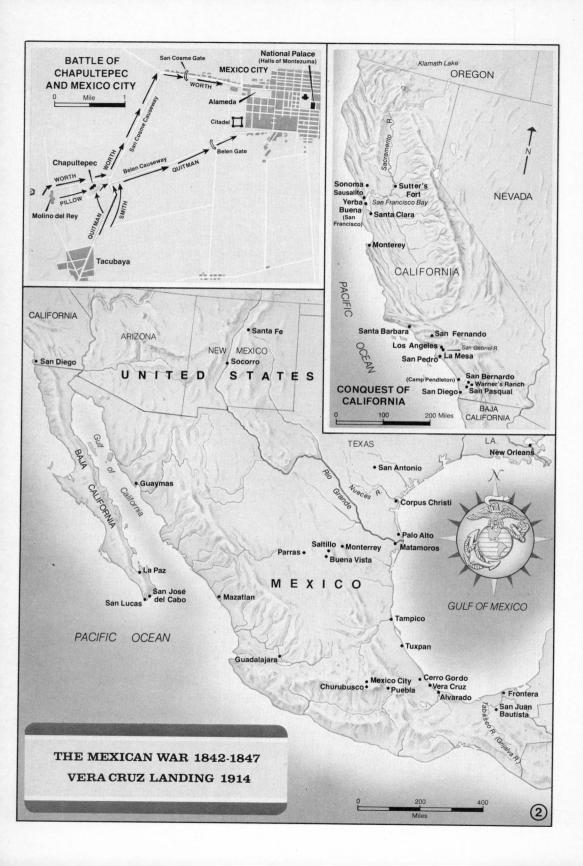

BATTLE OF CHAPULTEPEC AND MEXICO CITY

0 —— Mile —— 1

San Cosme Gate

National Palace
(Halls of Montezuma)

MEXICO CITY

WORTH

San Cosme Causeway

Alameda

Citadel

Chapultepec

WORTH

Belen Causeway

Belen Gate

PILLOW

WORTH

QUITMAN

Molino del Rey

QUITMAN

SMITH

Tacubaya

Klamath Lake

OREGON

Sacramento R.

NEVADA

Sonoma
Sausalito
Yerba Buena (San Francisco)

Sutter's Fort

San Francisco Bay

Santa Clara

Monterey

CALIFORNIA

PACIFIC OCEAN

Santa Barbara

San Fernando

Los Angeles

San Gabriel R.

San Pedro

La Mesa

San Bernardo
Warner's Ranch

(Camp Pendleton)

San Diego

San Pasqual

CONQUEST OF CALIFORNIA

0 —— 100 —— 200 Miles

BAJA CALIFORNIA

CALIFORNIA

ARIZONA

Santa Fe

NEW MEXICO

Socorro

San Diego

U N I T E D   S T A T E S

TEXAS

L.A.

New Orleans

San Antonio

Rio Grande

Nueces R.

Corpus Christi

BAJA CALIFORNIA

Gulf of California

Guaymas

Palo Alto

Saltillo

Monterrey

Matamoros

Parras

Buena Vista

La Paz

M E X I C O

GULF OF MEXICO

San José del Cabo

Mazatlan

San Lucas

PACIFIC OCEAN

Tampico

Tuxpan

Guadalajara

Cerro Gordo

Mexico City

Vera Cruz

Churubusco

Puebla

Alvarado

Frontera

San Juan Bautista

Tabasco R. (Grijalva R.)

THE MEXICAN WAR 1842-1847

VERA CRUZ LANDING 1914

0 —— 200 —— 400

Miles

②

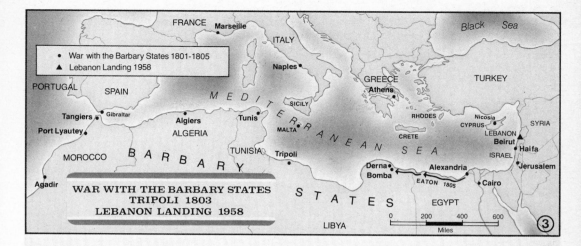

**WAR WITH THE BARBARY STATES
TRIPOLI 1803
LEBANON LANDING 1958**

FRANCE · Marseille

ITALY

Black Sea

Naples

GREECE
Athens

TURKEY

PORTUGAL · SPAIN

M E D I T E R R A N E A N

SICILY

RHODES

Nicosia
CYPRUS

SYRIA

Tangiers · Gibraltar

Algiers

Tunis

MALTA

CRETE

LEBANON
Beirut ▲

Haifa

Port Lyautey

ALGERIA

TUNISIA

Tripoli

S E A

ISRAEL

Jerusalem

MOROCCO

B A R B A R Y

Derna
Bomba

Alexandria

Cairo

Agadir

S T A T E S

EATON 1805

EGYPT

LIBYA

0   200   400   600
Miles

③

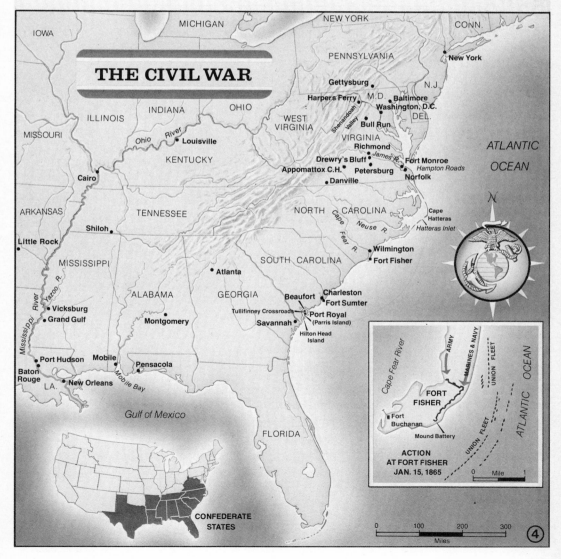

THE CIVIL WAR

IOWA

MICHIGAN

NEW YORK

CONN.

PENNSYLVANIA

New York

Gettysburg

N.J.

ILLINOIS

INDIANA

OHIO

WEST
VIRGINIA

Harpers Ferry

M.D.

Baltimore

Washington, D.C.

DEL.

MISSOURI

Ohio   River

Louisville

KENTUCKY

Shenandoah Valley

Bull Run

VIRGINIA

Richmond

James R.

Fort Monroe

Hampton Roads

ATLANTIC

OCEAN

Cairo

Drewry's Bluff

Appomattox C.H.

Petersburg

Norfolk

ARKANSAS

TENNESSEE

Danville

N

Shiloh

NORTH CAROLINA

Cape Fear R.

Neuse R.

Cape
Hatteras

Hatteras Inlet

Little Rock

MISSISSIPPI

SOUTH CAROLINA

Wilmington

Fort Fisher

Yazoo R.

Atlanta

Vicksburg

Grand Gulf

ALABAMA

GEORGIA

Montgomery

Beaufort

Charleston

Fort Sumter

Tullifinney Crossroads

Port Royal
(Parris Island)

Mississippi River

Port Hudson

Mobile

Pensacola

Savannah

Hilton Head
Island

Baton
Rouge

LA.

New Orleans

Mobile Bay

Gulf of Mexico

FLORIDA

**CONFEDERATE
STATES**

Cape Fear River

ARMY

MARINES & NAVY

UNION FLEET

FORT
FISHER

Fort
Buchanan

Mound Battery

UNION FLEET

ATLANTIC OCEAN

**ACTION
AT FORT FISHER
JAN. 15, 1865**

0   Mile   1

0   100   200   300
Miles

④

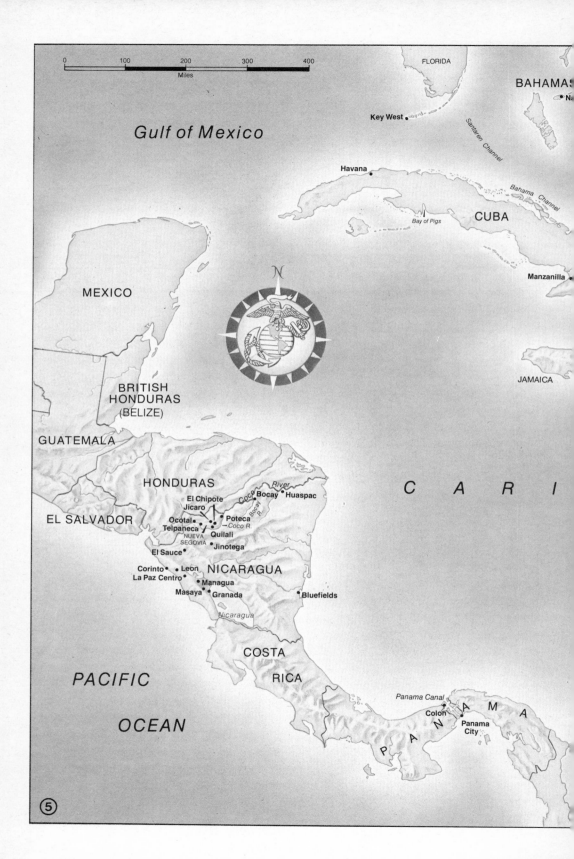

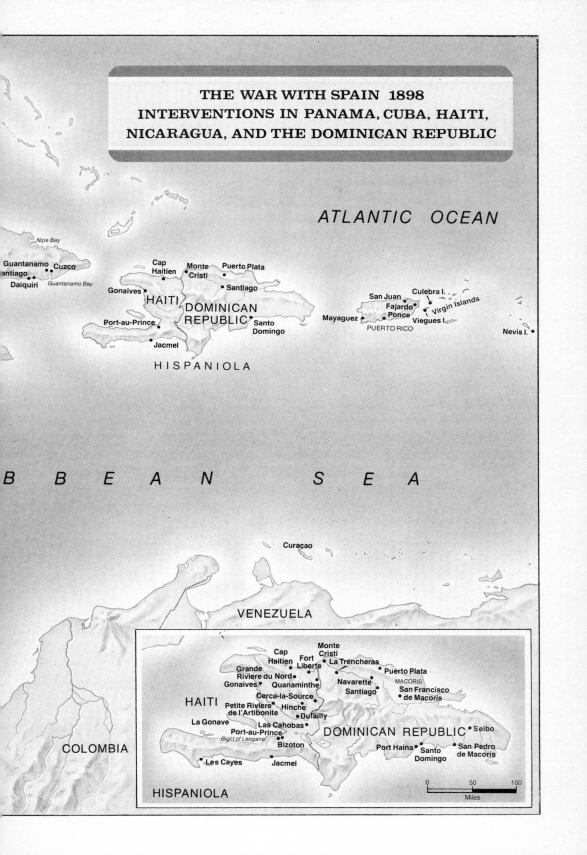

THE WAR WITH SPAIN 1898
INTERVENTIONS IN PANAMA, CUBA, HAITI, NICARAGUA, AND THE DOMINICAN REPUBLIC

ATLANTIC OCEAN

Nipe Bay

Guantanamo
Santiago   • Cuzco
Daiquiri   *Guantanamo Bay*

Cap
Haitien   Monte
Cristi   Puerto Plata

Gonaives   • Santiago

HAITI   DOMINICAN
REPUBLIC   San Juan   Culebra I.
Fajardo   Virgin Islands

Port-au-Prince   Santo
Domingo   Mayaguez   Ponce   Viegues I.

PUERTO RICO   Nevis I. •

Jacmel

HISPANIOLA

B B E A N   S E A

Curaçao

VENEZUELA

Monte
Cristi
Cap   Fort   La Trencheras
Haitien   Liberte
Grande   Puerto Plata
Riviere du Nord   Navarette   MACORIS
Gonaives   Quanaminthe   Santiago   San Francisco
Cerca-la-Source   de Macoris
HAITI   Petite Riviere   Hinche
de l'Artibonite   Dufailly
La Gonave   Las Cahobas   DOMINICAN REPUBLIC   • Seibo
Port-au-Prince
Bight of Leogane   Bizoton   Port Haina   San Pedro
Santo   de Macoris
Domingo
Les Cayes   Jacmel

COLOMBIA

0   50   100
Miles

HISPANIOLA

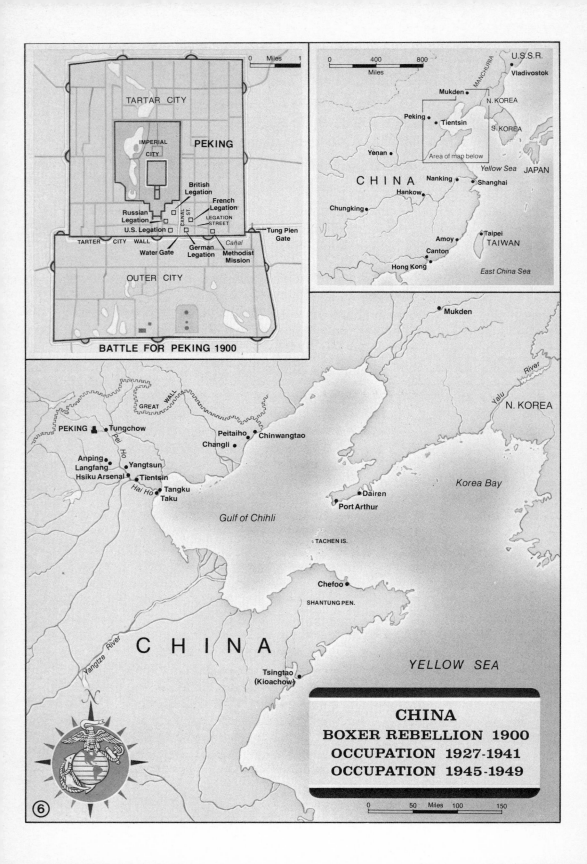

BATTLE FOR PEKING 1900

Peking inset labels:
TARTAR CITY
PEKING
IMPERIAL CITY
British Legation
French Legation
Russian Legation
CANAL ST.
LEGATION STREET
U.S. Legation
Tung Pien Gate
TARTER CITY WALL
Water Gate
German Legation
Methodist Mission
Canal
OUTER CITY

Regional inset labels:
U.S.S.R.
MANCHURIA
Vladivostok
Mukden
N. KOREA
Peking
Tientsin
S. KOREA
Yenan
JAPAN
Yellow Sea
CHINA
Nanking
Shanghai
Hankow
Chungking
Area of map below
Amoy
Taipei
TAIWAN
Canton
Hong Kong
East China Sea

Main map labels:
Mukden
Yalu River
N. KOREA
GREAT WALL
PEKING
Tungchow
Peitaiho
Chinwangtao
Changli
Anping
Langfang
Yangtsun
Hsiku Arsenal
Tientsin
Pei Ho
Hai Ho
Tangku
Taku
Korea Bay
Dairen
Port Arthur
Gulf of Chihli
TACHEN IS.
Chefoo
SHANTUNG PEN.
CHINA
Yangtze River
YELLOW SEA
Tsingtao (Kioachow)

CHINA
BOXER REBELLION 1900
OCCUPATION 1927-1941
OCCUPATION 1945-1949

0   50   Miles   100   150

⑥

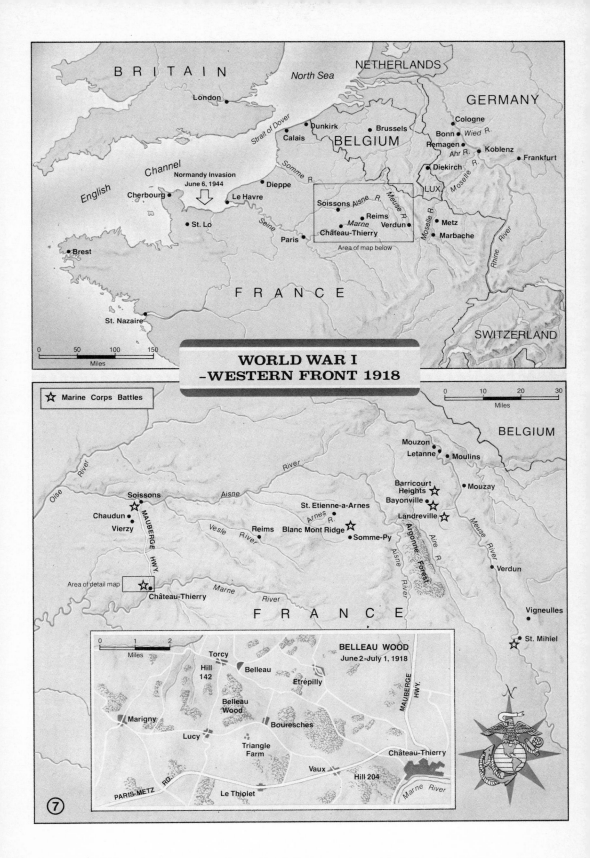

B R I T A I N

North Sea

NETHERLANDS

GERMANY

London

Dunkirk
Calais
Brussels
Cologne
Bonn
Wied R.
Remagen
Ahr R.
Koblenz
Diekirch
Frankfurt

BELGIUM

Strait of Dover

Somme R.

LUX.

Moselle R.

Moselle R.

Channel

Normandy Invasion
June 6, 1944

Dieppe

Le Havre

Soissons
Aisne R.
Meuse R.

Metz

English

Cherbourg

St. Lo

Seine

Reims
Marne
Château-Thierry
Verdun

Marbache

Paris

Area of map below

Rhine River

Brest

F R A N C E

SWITZERLAND

St. Nazaire

0   50   100   150
Miles

WORLD WAR I
–WESTERN FRONT 1918

0   10   20   30
Miles

☆ Marine Corps Battles

BELGIUM

Oise River

River

Mouzon
Letanne
Moulins

Aisne

Barricourt
Heights
Bayonville
Mouzay

Soissons

St. Etienne-a-Arnes

Chaudun
Vierzy

MAUBERGE HWY.

Arnes R.

Landreville

Vesle River

Reims

Blanc Mont Ridge
Somme-Py

Argonne Forest

Aire R.

Aisne River

Verdun

Area of detail map

Marne River

Vigneulles

Château-Thierry

F R A N C E

St. Mihiel

N

BELLEAU WOOD
June 2-July 1, 1918

0   1   2
Miles

Torcy

Belleau

MAUBERGE HWY.

Hill 142

Etrépilly

Belleau Wood

Marigny

Boûresches

Lucy

Triangle Farm

Château-Thierry

Vaux

Hill 204

PARIS-METZ RD.

Le Thiolet

Marne River

⑦

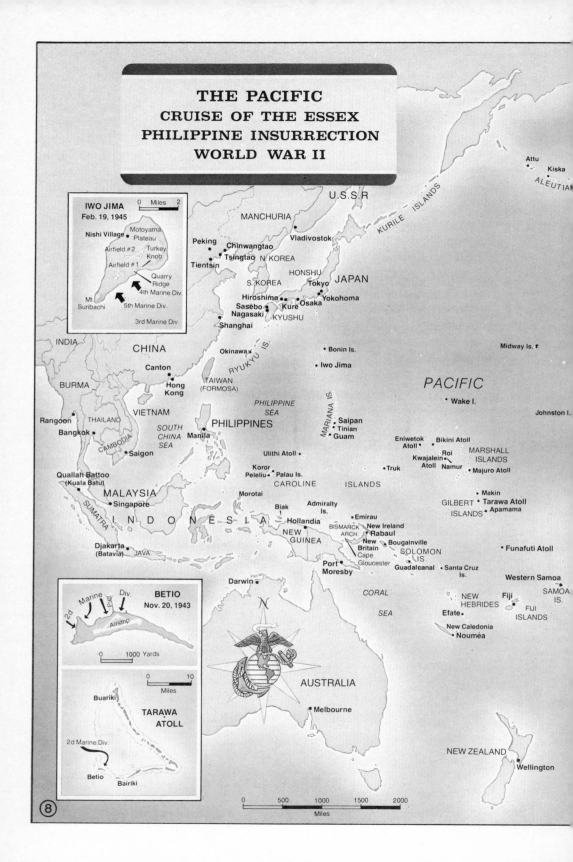

THE PACIFIC
CRUISE OF THE ESSEX
PHILIPPINE INSURRECTION
WORLD WAR II

IWO JIMA
Feb. 19, 1945

0 — Miles — 2

Nishi Village • Motoyama
Plateau
Airfield #2 • Turkey
Knob
Airfield #1
Quarry
Ridge
4th Marine Div.
Mt. Suribachi
5th Marine Div.
3rd Marine Div.

U.S.S.R

MANCHURIA

Peking • Vladivostok
Chinwangtao
Tsingtao • N. KOREA
Tientsin
S. KOREA
HONSHU
Tokyo • JAPAN
Yokohoma
Hiroshima • Osaka
Sasebo • Kure
Nagasaki • KYUSHU
Shanghai

KURILE ISLANDS

Attu
Kiska
ALEUTIA

INDIA
CHINA
Canton
BURMA
Hong Kong
Rangoon
THAILAND
VIETNAM
Bangkok
CAMBODIA
Saigon
Quallah Battoo
(Kuala Batu)
MALAYSIA
Singapore
SUMATRA
I N D O N E S I A
Djakarta
(Batavia) JAVA

Okinawa
RYUKYU IS.
TAIWAN
(FORMOSA)
SOUTH
CHINA
SEA
PHILIPPINE
SEA
PHILIPPINES
Manila

• Bonin Is.
• Iwo Jima

Midway Is.

PACIFIC

• Wake I.

Johnston I.

MARIANA IS.
Saipan
Tinian
Guam

Ulithi Atoll •
Koror
Peleliu • Palau Is.
• Truk
CAROLINE   ISLANDS
Morotai
Biak
Admiralty
Is.
Hollandia
• Emirau
BISMARCK New Ireland
ARCH. • Rabaul
NEW
GUINEA
New
Britain
Cape
Gloucester
Port
Moresby

Eniwetok
Atoll
Bikini Atoll
Roi
Kwajalein
Atoll Namur
MARSHALL
ISLANDS
• Majuro Atoll

• Makin
GILBERT • Tarawa Atoll
ISLANDS • Apamama

• Funafuti Atoll

SOLOMON
IS.
Bougainville
Guadalcanal • Santa Cruz
Is.

Western Samoa

SAMOA
IS.

Darwin •

N

CORAL

SEA

NEW
HEBRIDES
Efate •
New Caledonia
• Nouméa

Fiji
FIJI
ISLANDS

BETIO
Nov. 20, 1943

2d Marine Div.
Pier
Airstrip

0 — 1000 Yards

0 — 10
Miles

**TARAWA
ATOLL**

Buariki

2d Marine Div.

Betio
Bairiki

AUSTRALIA
• Melbourne

NEW ZEALAND
• Wellington

0   500   1000   1500   2000
Miles

⑧

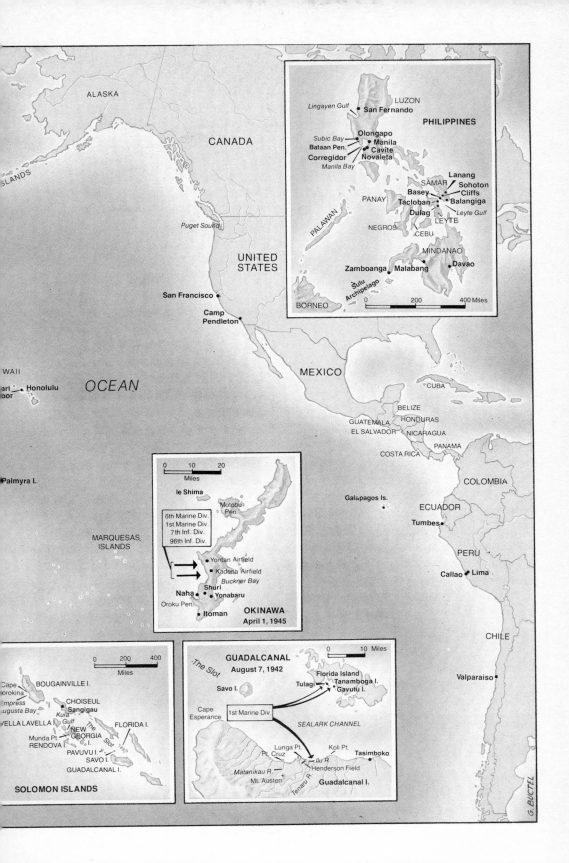

ALASKA

CANADA

PHILIPPINES

Lingayen Gulf • San Fernando — LUZON

Olongapo
Subic Bay • Manila
Bataan Pen. • Cavite
Corregidor • Novaleta
Manila Bay

Lanang
Sohoton
SAMAR • Cliffs
Basey • Balangiga
PANAY Tacloban • *Leyte Gulf*
Dulag
LEYTE

PALAWAN

NEGROS • CEBU

MINDANAO

Zamboanga • Malabang • Davao

Sulu
Archipelago
0   200   400 Miles

BORNEO

Puget Sound

UNITED
STATES

San Francisco •
Camp
Pendleton •

MEXICO

CUBA

BELIZE
GUATEMALA • HONDURAS
EL SALVADOR • NICARAGUA
COSTA RICA • PANAMA

WAII

OCEAN

arl • Honolulu
oor

COLOMBIA

Galapagos Is. •
ECUADOR
Tumbes •

Palmyra I. •

MARQUESAS
ISLANDS

PERU
Callao • Lima

0   10   20
Miles

le Shima

Motobu
Pen.

6th Marine Div.
1st Marine Div.
7th Inf. Div.
96th Inf. Div.

• Yontan Airfield
• Kadena Airfield
Buckner Bay
Shuri
Naha • • Yonabaru
Oroku Pen.
• Itoman

OKINAWA
April 1, 1945

CHILE

Valparaiso •

0   200   400
Miles

Cape
orokina • BOUGAINVILLE I.
Empress
ugusta Bay
CHOISEUL
Sangigau
Kula
Gulf
VELLA LAVELLA I.
FLORIDA I.
Munda Pt. NEW
GEORGIA
RENDOVA I. I.
PAVUVU I.
SAVO I.
GUADALCANAL I.

SOLOMON ISLANDS

GUADALCANAL
August 7, 1942

The Slot

0   10 Miles

Florida Island
Savo I. Tulagi • Tanamboga I.
• Gavutu I.

Cape
Esperance
1st Marine Div.

SEALARK CHANNEL

Lunga Pt. Koli Pt.
Pt. Cruz • Tasimboko
Matanikau R. *Ilu R.*
Mt. Austen Henderson Field
Tenaru R. Guadalcanal I.

G. BUCTEL

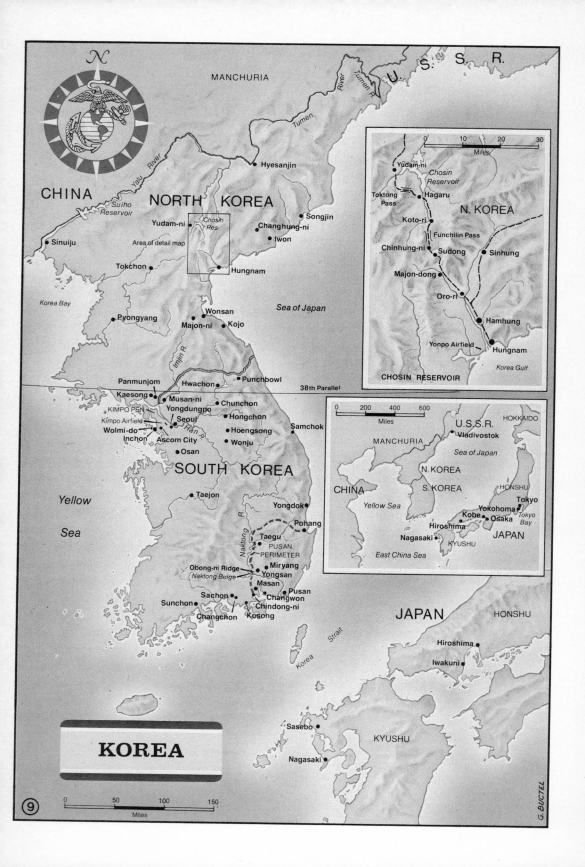

KOREA

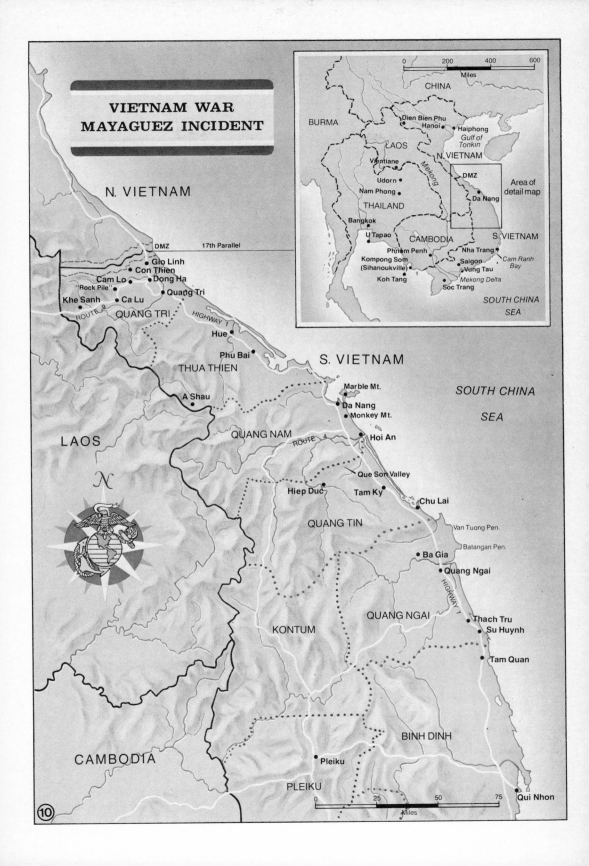

VIETNAM WAR
MAYAGUEZ INCIDENT

N. VIETNAM

Inset map labels:
CHINA
BURMA
Dien Bien Phu
Hanoi
Haiphong
Gulf of Tonkin
LAOS
N. VIETNAM
Vientiane
DMZ
Udorn
Nam Phong
Da Nang
THAILAND
Area of detail map
Bangkok
U Tapao
CAMBODIA
Phnom Penh
Nha Trang
Kompong Som
(Sihanoukville)
Saigon
Vung Tau
Koh Tang
Mekong Delta
Soc Trang
S. VIETNAM
Cam Ranh Bay
SOUTH CHINA SEA
Mekong

0   200   400   600
Miles

Main map labels:
DMZ   17th Parallel
Gio Linh
Con Thien
Cam Lo   Dong Ha
"Rock Pile"
Khe Sanh   Ca Lu   Quang Tri
ROUTE 9   QUANG TRI   HIGHWAY 1
Hue
Phu Bai   S. VIETNAM
THUA THIEN
A Shau
Marble Mt.
Da Nang
Monkey Mt.
QUANG NAM   ROUTE 4
Hoi An
LAOS
Que Son Valley
Hiep Duc   Tam Ky
Chu Lai
QUANG TIN
Van Tuong Pen.
Batangan Pen.
Ba Gia
Quang Ngai
KONTUM
HIGHWAY 1
QUANG NGAI
Thach Tru
Su Huynh
Tam Quan
BINH DINH
CAMBODIA
Pleiku
PLEIKU   0   25   50   75
Miles
Qui Nhon

SOUTH CHINA

SEA

⑩

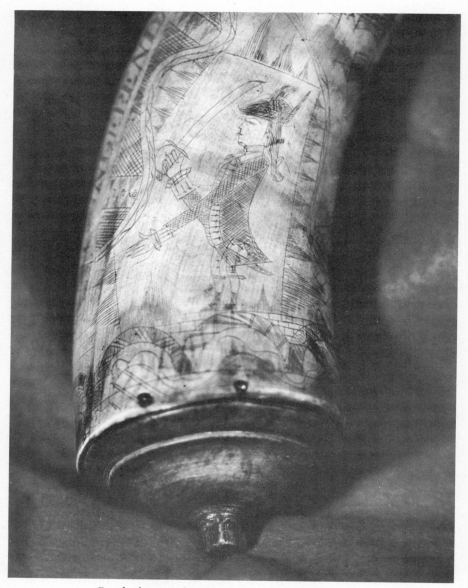

Powder horn used in the American Revolution depicts
a Continental Marine of Alfred in 1776.
Museums Branch, USMC

SEMPER FIDELIS

I
THE
CONTINENTAL
MARINES
1775-1784

1
The Marines Land for the First Time

The story began on the seacoast—Americans have been an amphibious people from the beginning. The Revolutionary War started when the colonists gathered to throw the British army out of Boston seaport. It was won when Maj. Gen. Charles Cornwallis, hoping to be resupplied by the British Navy, retreated to the sea at Yorktown, Virginia, and was cut off by the French fleet. Rather than starve, the British army marched out and laid down its arms. Between those two events, the story of American independence was repeatedly shaped by the sea and the wilderness waterways.

In the fall of 1775, seven months after the first gunfire at Lexington and Concord, George Washington commanded the Colonial Army and, although desperately short of guns and gunpowder, ringed Maj. Gen. Thomas Gage's Boston troops in an uneasy siege. At Philadelphia, the new-born Continental Navy was organizing its first excursion to sea. The Thirteen Colonies were fighting for their liberty, and young Americans were making up their minds about entering the fight.

In that crisis, John Trevett stepped ashore at Philadelphia from the 75–ton sloop *Katy* with a number of other volunteers. Trevett was twenty-eight, a Rhode Islander of a seafaring family—with courage, level-headed intelligence and a quiet New England sense of humor. He believed earnestly in the Revolution: "We are engaged in a good cause," he wrote later in his journal, "and are fighting the Lord's battles."[1]

John Trevett was one of the first men to serve as an American Marine. On November 10, shortly before he reached Philadelphia, the Second Continental Congress, in session there, had resolved that two battalions of American Marines "be

[For the location of places in the American Revolution see Map No. 1 in the map section.—*Au.*]

inlisted and commissioned to serve for and during the present war between Great Britain and the colonies."[2] The two battalions, intended as part of an expedition to bring Nova Scotia into the revolution, were never raised; General Washington did not want men taken from his army. But on November 28, the Congress commissioned Capt. Samuel Nicholas, a Quaker and blacksmith's son, as the first Marine officer. The American Marines were born.

The Congress had already begun to pull together a Continental Navy and appointed a longtime merchant sea captain, Esek Hopkins of Rhode Island, as commander-in-chief of the fleet. "Though antiquated in figure," General Henry Knox wrote his wife of Hopkins, "he is shrewd and sensible."[3] Commodore Hopkins promptly recruited a hundred men in his home state. Abraham Whipple brought some of them to Philadelphia in *Katy*, which then joined the Continental Navy as the 12-gun *Providence*. John Trevett was one of these volunteers, arriving in Philadelphia on December 5. It is possible that Trevett was signed up in Robert Mullan's Tun Tavern on the east side of King (now South Water) Street at the corner of Tun (now Wilcox's) Alley, which led down to the Delaware River. As Trevett wrote in his diary, "I went aboard the Ship Columbus as first lieutenant of Marines." His formal commission was dated February 13, 1776, by which time he was already on board.

While the winter ice imprisoned Hopkins' eight ships in Delaware Bay, he prepared his fleet and his officers enlisted 234 men to serve as Marines. Captain Nicholas was aboard the 24-gun flagship *Alfred* with Lt. Matthew Parke, son of a prominent British family, and Lt. John Fitzpatrick. Also on *Alfred* was a young naval officer, John Paul Jones. John Trevett was lieutenant of Marines on the next largest ship, the 20-gun *Columbus*, with Marine Capt. Joseph Shoemaker and Captain Whipple in command. Isaac Craig, an Irish-born carpenter, was lieutenant of Marines on the brig *Andrea Doria*. Capt. John Welsh, also Irish-born, led the Marines on the brig *Cabot*. Lt. Henry Dayton commanded the 20 Marines on *Providence*. On February 17, the ice freed the squadron.

Hopkins' orders were to tackle the British men-of-war off the Virginia and Carolina coasts. He decided to use his discretion; he had a better idea. Knowing that General Washington was practically out of gunpowder, Hopkins planned to seize a supply of it from the enemy's naval depot in the Bahamas.

On March 1, the little American fleet rendezvoused off Great Abaco Island in the Bahamas. Hopkins organized a landing force of the Marines under Captain Nicholas and 50 sailors led by Lt. Thomas Weaver of *Cabot*. Hopkins ordered them to sail, in *Providence* and two small captured sloops, to Nassau on the island of New Providence, where, he had heard, they would find 600 barrels of gunpowder.

Speeding ahead to surprise the British, the sloops with the landing force were spotted from the shore. The fort fired an alarm signal. Lt. John Paul Jones described the landing: "We then ran in and anchored at a small key three leagues to windward of the town, and from thence the Commodore despatched the marines, with the sloop *Providence* and schooner *Wasp* to cover their landing. They landed without opposition."[4] They went ashore in whaleboats two miles east of Fort Montagu.

At 2 P.M. on Sunday, March 3, 1776, American Marines had landed for the first time.

Lieutenant Trevett played a key role in the events that followed.

> I took command of one of the companies and marched to the first fort [he wrote in his journal]. They fired a few 18 pound shot, but did no damage. We saw an officer coming and I went up to him to know what he wanted. He informed me that Gov. [Montfort] Brown[e] would wish to know who we were, and what our business was. We soon gave him his answer and the first fort [Fort Montagu] stopped firing, and that night we lodged in the fort.[5]

At daybreak, Nicholas marched the mile to the edge of town. There he demanded the keys to the second fort, Fort Nassau, and hauled down the British colors. It was as simple as that. But Nicholas' decision to spend the night at Fort Montagu—and Hopkins' failure to blockade the harbor—had been fatal to the success of the expedition. During the night, Governor Browne had sent off the bulk of the gunpowder—162 casks—to safety in Florida by two ships that sailed past Hopkins' squadron.

With the landing force in possession of the forts, Hopkins

brought *Alfred* into the harbor and came ashore. Trevett was assigned to take a detachment of 32 Marines and guard the governor in his house on the hill until they could bring him back to the mainland a prisoner.

The Americans found only 24 casks of powder. They also took 46 cannon from Fort Nassau, 12 smaller guns from Fort Montagu, and 15 mortars. After loading this booty and assorted ammunition, they set sail on March 17, bringing with them three ships recaptured from the British and Governor Browne and two other officials as prisoners.

On the return cruise, Hopkins' fleet met the 20-gun *Glasgow* off Block Island. At 2 A.M. on April 6, his ships engaged the lone frigate in a battle that opened when a Marine on *Cabot* tossed a grenade down on *Glasgow's* deck. The fight raged for one and a half hours. Among the 11 American dead were Marine 2d Lt. John Hood Wilson and two enlisted Marines of *Cabot*, which met the enemy first, and Marine 2d Lt. Fitzpatrick of *Alfred*. Fitzpatrick was standing next to Captain Nicholas on the quarter-deck when he was struck in the head by a musket ball. The damaged *Glasgow* hightailed it to Newport, Rhode Island; and Hopkins' ships put in at New London. There were only one dead and three wounded on the British ship, all shot by the Marines' muskets.

News of the expedition stirred excitement in the Colonies. Commodore Hopkins was congratulated by John Hancock, president of the Continental Congress; and on April 23 General Washington, on his way from Cambridge to New York, stopped at New London and honored *Alfred* with a visit. But later Hopkins was dismissed from the service on charges brought by a group of officers led by Marine Capt. John Grannis.

Historians call the gunpowder expedition "the first fight in the records of the Regular Navy."[6] John Trevett was paid off in Continental dollars—which, he noted, would pay him the equivalent of one pair of shoes for five months' work—but he did not complain. He wrote cheerfully, "A grand cruise and I am glad it ended so well."

2
Fighting with
Benedict Arnold

During the sweltering summer of 1775, before Nicholas and Trevett became Continental Marines, the first act was being played out in a drama that would go far in deciding the outcome of the Revolution. A few colonists served as marines in a campaign that would, in the long run, mean much more than Commodore Hopkins' abortive raid.

The key man in this drama was Benedict Arnold. Although in 1779 he would become America's most infamous traitor, in the early years of the war Arnold was a hero. He was a swarthy little man with a violent temper and a monumental vanity; but he had daring and courage.

Arnold plotted to seize the cannon at Fort Ticonderoga for General Washington. On May 2, 1775, he wangled a Massachusetts colonel's commission authorizing him to raise 400 men and attack Ticonderoga. Meanwhile, backwoodsmen in the Green Mountains of Vermont, led by a tough giant named Ethan Allen, were already assembling to capture Ticonderoga and drive the British from Lake Champlain and Lake George.

The fresh-water northern lakes were links of a crucial lifeline in colonial America, a land virtually without roads. This water route ran westward up the St. Lawrence River, south along the north-flowing Richelieu River, along the 107 miles of Lake Champlain, across the short portage guarded by Fort Ticonderoga into Lake George and over the watershed to the Hudson River, which flows south past Saratoga and Albany to New York. If the British controlled this waterway, they could cut the Colonies in two; if the Americans grabbed it, they could drive into Canada.

Ethan Allen had mobilized 160 mountain men in a tavern at

Castleton east of Lake Champlain on Monday, May 8, and had just decided to attack Fort Ticonderoga on Wednesday—when up rode Benedict Arnold, resplendent in a red and gold uniform, and announced that he was in command.

Tempers flared. The Green Mountain Boys would not follow some little stranger from the cities; they would obey Allen. So Arnold tagged along while Allen led 83 men across the lake in a galley and a scow. Just before dawn they stormed the fort. The Americans outnumbered the sleeping garrison two to one, and tradition has it that the fortress was ordered to surrender "in the name of the great Jehovah and the Continental Congress." Washington would have his cannon and would be able to force the British out of Boston.

In the next couple of days, Colonel Arnold's men began to arrive from Massachusetts. Arnold took command of a new 40-ton schooner, renamed *Liberty*, that Allen's men had captured farther south on Lake Champlain at Skenesborough (now Whitehall); put aboard some 50 men to serve as sailors and marines, and set out on May 16 to grab a British armed sloop at the northern end of the lake. They found the sloop at St. Jean, captured her crew of seven and imprisoned St. Jean's tiny garrison. Arnold renamed the sloop *Enterprize*. With her he commanded the lake and the water route between Montreal and New York.

The payroll of *Enterprize* for July 1, 1775, is one of the oldest documents marking the existence of American marines. It includes the name of Lt. James Watson of marines and 17 marines, crediting some of the men with Continental pay from May 3, the day on which Arnold had set out on his journey to Vermont.

As there was still no American Navy, the ships on the lake and the men aboard them were made part of the Continental Army under Washington's overall command. Lieutenant Watson and his men were soldiers acting as marines. But the boldness they exhibited in the summer of 1775 and the courage with which they would fight the next year are part of the tradition of American Marines.

As Capt. Alfred T. Mahan, the American naval historian, said later of Arnold's and Allen's action in seizing the fort and *Enterprize*: "By such trifling means two active officers had secured the temporary control of the lake itself and of the

8

approaches to it from the south. There being no roads, the British, debarred from the water line, were unable to advance."[7]

That fall, Allen made a dashing raid on Montreal and was captured. Gen. Richard Montgomery and an American army took Montreal on November 13. Arnold led a force through the Maine wilderness and joined Montgomery in a futile attack on Quebec. Montgomery was killed and Arnold was shot through the leg. In the spring, the British and Hessians drove the Americans south; and by early July 1776, they were back at Fort Ticonderoga for the second act of the drama of the lakes.

That second summer, while Washington was fighting on Long Island, the northern lakes witnessed a frenzy of shipbuilding. At Skenesborough, Benedict Arnold directed the creation of an American fleet. He had *Enterprize*, *Liberty* and the British schooner *Royal Savage*, which Montgomery had captured. Carpenters and blacksmiths, assembled with promises of high wages, built the small schooner *Revenge* and a squadron of round-bottomed, 70-foot-long row galleys and smaller flat-bottomed gondolas. This miniature fleet was about to change the course of history.

The British plan was to chase the Americans south through the lakes and down the Hudson and split the rebellious Colonies. But Arnold's fleet was in the way. So the British settled down at St. Jean to build their own fleet.

Calling on the resources of their navy in the St. Lawrence, the British built a superior squadron of 53 vessels with more than 90 guns. On October 4, 1776, the British Commander, Sir Guy Carleton, was ready to fight. Arnold had already taken a position he thought he could hold between two-mile-long Valcour Island and the nearby western shore of Lake Champlain, below where Plattsburgh, New York, stands today. There, Arnold figured, Carleton could not bring all his power to bear simultaneously.

Arnold had little faith in his men. He wrote Gen. Horatio Gates: "We have a wretched, motley crew in the fleet, the marines, the refuse of every regiment and the seamen few of them ever wet with salt water."[8]

Carleton confidently moved his ships southward; in one broadside his guns could throw nearly twice as much metal as could the Americans'. On October 11, a clear cold day with snow on the Adirondack Mountains, the British fleet sailed past the

Americans hidden at anchor behind heavily-wooded Valcour Island. Two miles beyond the island, Carleton sighted Arnold's ships and had to come back in the teeth of the wind.

By 11 A.M. the battle was joined. The Americans took a pounding all day; every American ship was hit. *Royal Savage* was lost. But at five o'clock the British ceased firing and set up a picket line across the channel leading south.

The next morning, when the heavy mountain fog lifted, Arnold and his fleet were gone. During the night, they had stolen silently around the pickets and escaped. The British gave chase. The crippled galley *Washington,* covering the retreat, was forced to surrender. Marine Lt. Heathcote Muirson was captured. In all, 11 vessels were destroyed. Arnold's flagship, the galley *Congress,* was beached and burned 10 miles above Crown Point. Arnold and the 46 remaining men of *Congress'* crew of 73 fled to the outpost there. They burned the fort's buildings and retreated south to Fort Ticonderoga to prepare a defense against the advancing British.

Carleton never came. The American force on the lake had been almost totally destroyed; but the British, seeing winter approaching rapidly, returned to St. Jean.

The British had won the battle, but they had lost the war. When they drove south the next summer under Gen. John Burgoyne, the Americans were mobilized. On October 17, 1777, Burgoyne surrendered his sword at Saratoga.

Arnold's fleet had made that victory possible. Captain Mahan wrote, "That the Americans were strong enough to impose the capitulation of Saratoga was due to the invaluable year of delay secured to them in 1776 by their little navy on Lake Champlain. . . ."[9]

The American sailors and marines on the lake had fought a tiny battle—"a strife of pigmies for the prize of a continent"[10]— but its results were momentous. As Mahan points out, "The surrender of Burgoyne determined the intervention of France, in 1778; the intervention of France the accession of Spain thereto, in 1779 . . . . How great a matter a little fire kindleth!"[11]

The road from the boatyard at Skenesborough and the cove at Valcour Island led directly to Yorktown. American marines fought in no more significant naval campaign during the Revolution.

3
"For the Defence of American Liberty"

November 10 is celebrated as the birthday of the U.S. Marine Corps at posts and stations around the globe. Whenever possible—and sometimes when it would seem impossible—there is a birthday cake.

November 10 is celebrated because on that date in 1775 the Continental Congress passed the following resolution:

> *Resolved*, That two Battalions of marines be raised, consisting of one Colonel, two Lieutenant Colonels, two Majors, and other officers as usual in other regiments; that they consist of an equal number of privates with other battalions; that particular care be taken that no persons be appointed to offices, or inlisted into said Battalions, but such as are good seamen, or so acquainted with maritime affairs as to be able to serve to advantage by sea when required; that they be inlisted and commissioned to serve for and during the present war between Great Britain and the colonies, unless dismissed by order of Congress; that they be distinguished by the names of the first and second battalions of American Marines.[12]

This resolution was written by a special five-man Congressional Committee that had been established only a week before and, well supplied with Jamaican rum, met evenings in a public house in Philadelphia. The committee had not intended to create a separate unit of marines but to transfer soldiers from Washington's Continental Army. When the general objected (the first but not the last case of interservice rivalry between Ameri-

11

can soldiers and Marines), the Congress agreed to recruit Marines independently.

The wording of the resolution of November 10 indicates that the Founding Fathers had a less than crystal-clear idea of what marines were supposed to be. The battalions are ordered to accept only "such as are good seamen, or so acquainted with maritime affairs as to be able to serve to advantage by sea when required." But marines are not specialized sailors; they are a totally different breed of fighter. In fact, the British Marines, on whom the American establishment was based, were specifically exempted from sea duties. Since 1775, the role of American Marines has evolved in various forms as their country's needs have demanded; but they have not served as sailors. The committee's language hung over from the original intention to use as marines those of Washington's soldiers who had had some sea experience.

In 1775, the British Marines were only 111 years old. But at least as far back as a thousand years before the birth of Christ, men on ships of war were divided into rowers and fighters (sailors and marines). Marines in the fleet of Ramses III helped keep hordes of northern invaders out of ancient Egypt. The Greek ships that attacked Troy and of which Homer sang carried marines who fought on a forward deck. At the battle of Salamis in 480 B.C., when the Greek city states defeated mighty Persia, marines (*epibatai*) from Athens and Corinth played a vital part in a naval battle that changed history.

When Rome ruled the seas, her men-of-war carried a powerful force of marines (*milites classici*). These warriors helped defeat the naval power of Carthage in 260 B.C. At the crucial battle of Mylae off Sicily, the Romans had 120 marines aboard each of their ships to control the rowers and board the enemy. This victory began the Roman navy's mastery of the Mediterranean Sea.

As the historian of ancient sea warfare, Lionel Casson, says of those early marines, "Without such fighters to rake the opponent's deck during the approach or to stand by to repel boarders after the impact [of ramming], the attacked vessel's marines could grapple, board, and stand a fair chance of taking over the attacker."[13]

The British Marines were originally ordered raised by King Charles II on October 28, 1664, during the Second Dutch War, which turned New Amsterdam into New York. They were called the Admiral's Regiment and reputedly were the first unit to be armed with firelocks rather than muskets. A detachment of the regiment, dressed in yellow coats and red breeches, was sent to Virginia to keep the peace in 1676. A few of them stayed and became colonists. By 1741, three regiments of Marines were ordered raised in the American colonies under Col. Alexander Spotswood of Virginia. One regiment, commanded by Virginia's lieutenant governor, Col. William Gooch—and known as Gooch's Marines—fought in the Caribbean against Spain. British Marines helped capture the French base of Louisburg on Cape Breton Island in 1745, and they aided James Wolfe capture Quebec in 1759. Wolfe himself was first commissioned in the Marines, as was John Churchill, who became the Duke of Marlborough.

On that morning of April 19, 1775, British Marines participated in the first shots heard round the world. Maj. John Pitcairn, who led the advance guard sent to seize the colonists' military stores at Concord, was a Marine. It was his contingent that killed Minute Men on snow-covered Lexington green. After the skirmish later that morning at Concord, the 1st British Marine Battalion formed a hollow square at Lexington to give a breathing spell to the Redcoats returning from Concord under a hail of Colonial bullets.

Two months later, on June 17, the 1st Marine Battalion charged on the left flank in the assault against the hastily constructed American entrenchments on Breed's Hill. Twice, the British moved up the hill and were thrown back. Major Pitcairn, at the head of his men, was twice wounded. Maj. Gen. Gage, the British commander in America, ordered a third assault. The story is told that when a British army battalion in this third attack was held up by heavy Colonial fire, it was enjoined to "Break, then, and let the Marines pass through you!"[14]

The Americans on the hilltop finally ran out of gunpowder and, after fighting with musket butts and stones, fled from the British bayonets. The British Marines were the first to penetrate the American lines. Major Pitcairn was killed; but in this "Battle of Bunker Hill," for the first time, Colonials had stood up to a frontal assault by British regulars.

British Marines fought in many sea battles and coastal raids during the Revolution. They helped throw Arnold and the Americans back from Quebec in the spring of 1776. They fought Americans hand-to-hand to prevent them from recapturing Savannah in October 1779. The following spring they helped seize Fort Moultrie in Charleston harbor. And Marines were in the force which Cornwallis surrendered at Yorktown on October 19, 1781. (At Yorktown, French marines helped blockade Col. Balastre Tarleton, who was holding open an escape route for Cornwallis.)

In 1802, George III declared the British Marines to be "The Royal Marines." Admiral Horatio Nelson, England's greatest sea fighter, wrote that "Every fleet should have a perfect battalion of Marines and, commanded by experienced officers, they would be prepared to make a serious impression on the enemy's coast."[15]

The Royal and American Marines began as enemies, but over the years after the War of 1812 they became comrades. They were blooded together in the Boxer Rebellion, World War II and Korea. They share many traditions. The Royal Marines wear a badge showing the eastern hemisphere of the globe; U.S. Marines wear one with the western hemisphere.

By 1775, the British Marines were already used by the Navy to provide a landing force, to keep order aboard warships and in sea battles to fire their muskets "from the tops" of the masts and often to man "the great guns."

The Continental Marines were another story. From time to time they performed these same jobs, but it is difficult to conceive of them as a corps during the Revolution. Continental Marines were usually recruited to serve in particular ships or squadrons. Various colonies had their own marines. Washington manned ships with sailors and marines to attack British shipping. Benedict Arnold commanded his own fleet. Oliver Pollock at New Orleans created a naval force. A number of officials could commission Continental Marines (those Marines authorized directly by the Continental Congress), including the committee of Congress running naval affairs, the Navy Boards, Continental agents, the Commissioners in Paris and commercial agents stationed outside the thirteen states.

Americans first served as marines in the navies of the individual states and on privateers, the privately owned armed ships commissioned by the Congress or the states. At one time or another during the Revolution, every state except New Jersey and Delaware had its own navy. The earliest was probably that created in June 1775, when the citizens of Machias, Massachusetts (now Maine), captured two British ships and killed British Marines in the process. These two ships, commanded by Jeremiah O'Brien, were the seed of the Massachusetts navy.

Connecticut, Pennsylvania and Maryland also formed navies early in the war to defend their coasts. The largest Connecticut ship was the 20-gun *Oliver Cromwell*. On April 13, 1778, aided by *Defence*, she fought the 18-gun *Admiral Keppel* and the 16-gun *Cygnus*. Marine Capt. James Day of *Oliver Cromwell* was mortally wounded, dying the next day. At various times, 78 state marines served aboard *Oliver Cromwell*, including five Negro privates.

The two most important Southern state navies were those of Virginia and South Carolina. South Carolina's navy was especially active. It was created in the fall of 1775 with one 10-gun schooner, *Defence*, to which were assigned 35 marines. The most crucial event in the history of the South Carolina navy was the sea battle between the Continental frigate *Randolph*, 32 guns, commanded by able, twenty-eight-year-old Capt. Nicholas Biddle, and the British ship-of-the-line *Yarmouth*, 64 guns. Captain Biddle had taken aboard his flagship 52 South Carolina soldiers to serve with Capt. Samuel Shaw and his detachment of Continental Marines. *Randolph* was accompanied by four ships of the South Carolina navy. On March 7, 1778, Biddle encountered *Yarmouth* east of Barbados. After a running night battle that lasted but 15 minutes, an enemy shot exploded *Randolph's* powder magazine. Of the frigate's crew of 305, only four seamen survived.

Although the first Continental Marines joined Hopkins' fleet in the autumn of 1775, Congress did not organize the Marines fully because of the scarcity of ships and men. Finally, on June 25, 1776, Samuel Nicholas, the senior Marine captain who had led the amphibious landing on New Providence, was appointed major of Marines, the highest Marine rank created during the war. He was ordered to organize four Marine companies for the Continental frigates then being built. The Board of Admiralty later ruled that a major of Marines should serve at sea only aboard a ship-of-the-line; and since the United States Navy never put to sea anything larger than a frigate during the Revolution, Major Nicholas was compelled to serve on land. Like many an officer chained to a desk, he chafed; and on August 10, 1781, he asked Congress to recompense him for the prize money and other advantages he might have had at sea.

This first leader of the Continental Marines, a round-faced Quaker of thirty-two, had studied at the academy that later became the University of Pennsylvania. He was a Masonic lodge brother of Benjamin Franklin and a member of the best hunting and fishing clubs in Philadelphia. He had made a voyage to Canton as a supercargo. It is said that one of his grandfathers was a mayor of Philadelphia; the other, a lawyer. Before and after the war, Samuel Nicholas was reputedly an innkeeper, running the Conestogoe Waggon on Market Street between 4th and 5th Streets. He died on August 27, 1790, at the age of forty-six.

Nicholas had signed up early to fight in the cause of liberty. His original commission was signed by John Hancock, President of the Continental Congress, and appointed Nicholas "to be Captain of Marines in the Service of the Thirteen United Colonies of North-America, fitted out for the defence of American Liberty, and for repelling every hostile Invasion thereof."

Although Nicholas never went to sea again as a Marine once he was promoted to major, he fought with Washington at Trenton and Princeton. And he helped safeguard the money that would pay the army at Yorktown. In 1781, Benjamin Franklin had arranged for a loan of more than two and a half million livres from France. The silver, so urgently needed to pay the army, was sent over on the French frigate *La Resolve*, which was blown off course and finally made port in Boston. In September, Robert Morris organized a secret mission—with Tench Francis, a husky Philadelphia merchant, and Samuel Nicholas in command—to bring most of the silver down to Philadelphia. They safely conducted the money to the capital in oxcarts.

At the same time that Nicholas was promoted to major in June 1776, six captains (Andrew Porter, Joseph Hardy, Samuel Shaw, Benjamin Dean, Robert Mullan and John Stewart) and a number of lieutenants were also designated. Late in the year, three more Marine captains and five additional lieutenants were also commissioned.

Four companies of Marines had been formed for the New Providence expedition, and now four more were organized. Dr. Benjamin Rush, a signer of the Declaration of Independence, took care of their health. Some payroll and muster records have survived from Captain Mullan's company, one of this second group. They show that on November 24, 1776, Pvt. Henry Hassan was sentenced by court-martial to 50 lashes for desertion and 21 lashes for quitting his guard post—"on his bare Back well laid on at the head of his Company."[16]

On September 5, Congress authorized a special Marine officer uniform: "A Green Coat faced with white, Round Cuffs, Slash'd Sleeves and Pockets; with Buttons round the Cuff, Silver Epaulett on the right Shoulder—Skirts turn'd back, Buttons to suit the Faceing. White waistcoat and Brieches edged with Green, Black Gaiters & Garters." Green was the special color for Marines. The enlisted men were to wear green shirts "if they can be procured."

Recruiting was always highly competitive against both the Continental Army and the more profitable sea service aboard the privateers. Many times, Continental ships were unable to sail because of the shortage of seamen and Marines. Marines were promised prize money shares, enlistment bounties, rations and grog. The first pay table gave an enlisted Marine $6.67 a month, the same as that given an able seaman. A corporal was to receive $7.33, the same as a drummer; sergeants would receive $8 a month. In December 1775, a private's pay was raised to $8 monthly and other adjustments were made. By the end of 1776, the Continental Marines numbered more than 600 men.

Continental regulations made naval officers superior to Marine officers. "All sea officers of the same denomination shall take rank [over] the officers of the Marines," they stated. And this distinction was reflected on the pay table. A Marine captain was given $26.67 a month, between a naval lieutenant's $20 and a naval captain's $32. A Marine lieutenant received $18 against the naval lieutenant's $20. During the next year, a Marine captain's pay was raised to $30 and a lieutenant's to $20.

Throughout the Revolution, the method of running the Continental Navy and Marines changed. In the beginning, under the democratic idealism of the Revolutionary movement, all decisions were made by committee; a Congressional committee (the Marine Committee) administered the Navy and Marines. Then, this responsibility was given to a board that included some non-Congressmen who had more permanent tenure: The Board of Admiralty. Finally, under pressure for decisions while fighting a war, control was given to an individual (though still responsible to the legislature directly).

No one knows exactly how many Marines served in the Continental Navy during the Revolution. Probably not more than 3,000 seamen and Marines served at any one time. The best figures suggest that the Marines had, all told, one major, 30 captains and approximately 100 lieutenants—a total of about 131 commissioned officers—and no more than 2,000 enlisted men. By contrast, the British Navy in 1775 had 18,000 seamen and Marines and by 1783 had grown to 110,000 men.

4
Helping Washington's Army

Before 1776 was over, the newly organized Continental Marines fought in their first land campaign, side by side with the soldiers of Washington's army. The British army that had shoved Washington off Long Island and through Manhattan, White Plains and Peekskill was now chasing him across New Jersey. Philadelphia was threatened, and the Marines stationed there and on the ships in the Delaware River were called out to help stem the Redcoated tide.

Major Nicholas was ordered to organize a "battalion" of 131 men from the Marine companies assigned to the Continental frigates being built around Philadelphia. The companies were commanded by Captains Andrew Porter, Robert Mullan and Benjamin Dean. Capt. Samuel Shaw's company stayed on board the new frigate *Randolph*, which was getting ready to sail.

At the same time, William Shippin commanded the Pennsylvania marines on the armed galley *Hancock*, a privateer, in the Delaware. Before the war, Shippin had run a butcher shop at Philadelphia's Market Street wharf. He knew something about boats and the water. Early in December 1776, now twenty-six years old, he led his marines on a raid to hunt Tories and Hessians hiding in the Burlington, New Jersey, area.

General Washington called urgently for more men. Congress ordered out the volunteer Philadelphia Associators under Col. John Cadwalader, a polished aristocrat, a brave soldier and reputedly the deadliest duelist in Patriot ranks. On December 2, Nicholas' Marine battalion was ordered to join Cadwalader, and Nicholas led it up to the Delaware by gondola to help the army. Isaac Craig from *Andrea Doria* served as Nicholas' adjutant. William Brown and his men from *Montgomery* served as artil-

19

lerymen. William Shippin's marines marched with Cadwalader's second battalion.

While Congress fled to Baltimore, Washington turned on his tormentors. He wanted to strike before his army's enlistments expired at year-end. He proposed to cross back over the ice-littered Delaware on Christmas night and hit the Hessians guarding Trenton before dawn on Thursday, December 26. Cadwalader's division of 1,800 men was to cross downriver near Bristol, Pennsylvania, and create a diversion. Brig. Gen. James Ewing was to cross the river just below Trenton and block the Hessians' escape route to the south. Washington's own division would cross above Trenton and attack the town from the north. Afterwards, the three corps would tackle the British detachments at Princeton and New Brunswick.

Everyone knows the story of Washington's crossing of the river at McKonkey's Ferry in boats manned by the Marblehead seamen of Col. John Glover's amphibious regiment. (They had enabled the army to escape from Long Island to Manhattan the previous August.) Although Glover's tough fishermen were not Marines but soldiers and boatmen, they are regarded as precursors of today's Marines.

Only Washington's corps crossed the river. Cadwalader's and Ewing's did not make it. Cadwalader's advance party crossed and was ready to protect the main body; but, partly because he could not carry over his two field pieces when the tide rose and piled ice on the New Jersey shore, Cadwalader cautiously withdrew.

Washington's men—most of them in summer clothing and many with rags wrapped around their feet—trudged the frozen roads through the darkness toward Trenton. Hail and freezing rain pummeled them. The bloody footprints they left in the snow are part of America's heritage. Early Thursday morning, in total surprise, they attacked Trenton, killed 22 and wounded 92 and took 948 prisoners. Only four Americans were killed. But lacking Ewing's and Cadwalader's support, Washington had to retreat across the river.

Cadwalader finally got his corps over the Delaware by 11 A.M. on Friday. Then, he learned that Washington had recrossed the river. Faced with rebellion by his men, some of whom had now crossed the river three times, he marched on toward

Burlington but found no enemy of consequence. On a patrol, Major Nicholas discovered that some 70 Loyalists were at Monmouth Courthouse; he urged Cadwalader to disperse them. But Cadwalader refused and on Saturday marched his corps to Bordentown on the river.

Washington planned another bold stroke. He crossed the river again and marched into Trenton. Maj. Gen. Cornwallis moved swiftly south against him with 8,000 men. On New Year's Day, Washington sent Col. Edward Hand with a unit of Pennsylvania riflemen to delay the British advance and give the Americans one day of grace. Colonel Hand's men fought at Maidenhead, northeast of Trenton, and then retreated slowly toward Trenton. The Marines were among the troops delaying the British at Assunpink Creek. They helped give Washington the extra day he needed. He made good use of it.

That night the two armies faced each other across their strings of campfires. Figuring Washington was trapped between the British army and the river, Cornwallis thought he would wipe out the Americans in the morning. But Washington slipped away, leaving 400 men behind to keep the campfires burning through the night. He circled Cornwallis' left flank and lit out through the severely cold night for Princeton.

Washington detached Brig. Gen. Hugh Mercer's brigade and Cadwalader's Associators, including Nicholas' Marines, to hold a stone bridge two miles below Princeton on the Princeton-Trenton road. Just as Mercer's advance guard was emerging from a wood toward the bridge, it ran head on into Lt. Col. Charles Mawhood and two British regiments marching for Trenton. The Americans advanced through a nearby orchard on high commanding ground, and the British opened fire from behind a bank. The British 17th Regiment charged with bayonets; Brig. Gen. Mercer was mortally wounded; the Americans broke.

Cadwalader came out of the wood. His soldiers and the Marines on his right flank tried to make a stand. Washington galloped between the opposing forces to rally the Americans. Then reinforcements arrived and the tide turned. Cadwalader's men stood firm. Mawhood was routed and fled toward Trenton with his 17th Regiment. The 55th British Regiment retreated to Princeton, where it surrendered.

21

The action against Mawhood took only about 20 minutes. The British casualties numbered 273. The Americans lost about 40 killed and 100 wounded. Among the American dead were seven officers. One of them was the Aberdeen-born physician, Brig. Gen. Hugh Mercer; another was the little ex-butcher, Pennsylvania Marine Captain William Shippin.

Washington's bottom-of-the-barrel victories at Trenton and Princeton kept the British out of Philadelphia for the time being. They retreated north. Washington, with great new prestige, went into winter quarters at Morristown, New Jersey. Nicholas and 80 Marines stayed with Washington and filled in for artillerymen whose enlistments had expired. Mullan and his Marines took 25 British prisoners back to Philadelphia late in February, and Dean led his company back in April. Porter's company stayed with the army as artillerymen. The Marines' first land campaign was over.

The following September, after defeating Washington at Brandywine, the British finally captured the American capital. Attempting to control the Delaware River, the Continental frigate *Delaware* grounded and was boarded by British Marines. Marine Capt. Robert Mullan and most of the crew were captured; but Marine Lt. Alexander Neilson, who had served as a Marine sergeant on the first expedition to New Providence, escaped with one group of men. By the end of 1777, the British controlled the Delaware from Philadelphia to the sea.

5
On the Western Frontier

A few Marines fought on the Western frontier beyond the Appalachians, over the vast territory from New Orleans to the Illinois country. At the southern end of the frontier, the Spanish controlled the entrance to the Mississippi. In the north, the British based at Detroit aroused the Indian tribes to attack American settlers.

The leader of the American war effort in the West was a tall, red-headed, twenty-three-year-old Indian fighter named George Rogers Clark. One of his chief concerns was to stop the British-incited Indians from massacring the settlers in Kentucky. On June 26, 1778, Clark set out from Louisville with 175 men to attack Kaskaskia in the Illinois country, and, if possible, Detroit. After traveling 1,200 miles through trackless wilderness, they captured Kaskaskia and two satellite forts on July 4th, almost without firing a shot.

In the meantime, the Commerce Committee of Congress had directed twenty-seven-year-old Capt. James Willing to raise a company of Marines, seize British property along the Mississippi River, carry dispatches to New Orleans and return with supplies. Young Willing came from a prominent Philadelphia family and had been a merchant and a hard-drinking playboy in Natchez before the Revolution. On January 10, 1778, he started from Fort Pitt with a crew of about 35 men in an old boat he called *Rattletrap.*

Willing and his Marines captured several ships on their way down the Ohio and Mississippi and occupied Natchez. Much of the time, Marine Lt. Robert George scouted ahead of the expedition in a canoe. Willing then proceeded down the river, destroying the crops and stock of the British planters, burning their houses and carrying off their slaves. His force grew; and when he arrived at Spanish-held New Orleans in the first week of March, he had 100 men. He had swept aside Britain's hold on the Mississippi.

At New Orleans, Continental Agent Oliver Pollock, who has been justly called the "financer of the Revolution in the West," installed 24 guns on a British sloop that Willing's Marines, led by Lt. Richard Harrison, had captured on the Mississippi. Pollock renamed her *Morris* for Robert Morris and commissioned Robert Elliott as her captain of Marines and Daniel Longstreet as lieutenant. (This was an example of the various authorities who commissioned Continental Marine officers during the Revolution.) But before *Morris* could protect American commerce or sail against British ships, a hurricane sank her and drowned 11 of her crew.

With Spain by now at war with Britain, the Spanish governor of Louisiana gave Pollock an armed schooner. On September 10, 1779, she defeated an armed British sloop on Lake Pontchartrain after a hot fight. Lieutenant Longstreet and a party of seamen and Marines captured several British settlements on the north side of the lake. The Americans commanded the lake for the rest of the year.

While Pollock had been preparing *Morris* for action, he had trouble with Willing's men. Not only did they cost Pollock money, but they were insubordinate and unruly. Many deserted. And they thoroughly aroused Loyalist resistance to the American cause. A British official called them "a horde of brigands."[17] By midsummer 1778, Pollock was demanding that they leave New Orleans. Willing, carrying messages back to Congress, sailed for Philadelphia and was captured at sea and imprisoned in New York. In August 1778, 60 of his men, led by Marine Lieutenants Robert George and Richard Harrison, headed north from New Orleans to join George Rogers Clark in the Illinois country. They carried supplies from Pollock that Clark needed badly.

By the following June, George and his party reached Clark at Kaskaskia. There, the Marines were disbanded; some enlisted in a new artillery company commanded by George, now a militia captain. A Virginian and distant relative of Clark, George was a skilled artilleryman.

On February 24, 1779, Clark recaptured Vincennes from the British and won control of the Illinois country and the West. He established a fort—which he named after Thomas Jefferson—five miles south of the Ohio River's mouth. That summer, while Clark was leading a force against the Shawnee Indians, Fort Jefferson was attacked by Chickasaw and Choctaw warriors. The fort's 30-man garrison commanded by Captain George fought desperately for six days and nights. They were exhausted and just about out of ammunition and supplies when reinforcements from Kaskaskia arrived and saved the fort.

Clark played a major role in the bitter Indian fighting that went on long after the victory at Yorktown. Although records preserve little information about the part that the former Marines played in helping Clark, their often-forgotten participation on the Mississippi and in the Illinois country helped make it possible for the nation to expand westward toward the Pacific.

6
The First Landing
under Fire

After Esek Hopkins' gunpowder expedition to New Providence in 1776, the Continental Marines participated in one more major amphibious operation during the Revolution. This second landing—on the coast of Maine—was their first in the face of enemy fire and the first in which they tried to hold the ground they seized.

In both operations the Marines did their share. But if their first effort was less than wholly successful (partly because Marine Captain Nicholas had given the British time to ship out most of their gunpowder), the Maine expedition was a disaster.

By 1778, the British had their hands full trying to protect the many Loyalists who had refused to join the Rebels. General Sir Henry Clinton, then commander-in-chief in America, was directed to create a colony for the displaced Loyalists near the Penobscot River in what is now Maine but was then part of Massachusetts. In early June 1779, Clinton fitted out from Halifax an expedition of 650 soldiers under Brig. Gen. Francis MacLean to build a fort at the mouth of the Penobscot, near where Castine, Maine, now stands.

The British expedition alarmed the Massachusetts authorities. A powerful counterexpedition was assembled including three Continental warships: the frigate *Warren*, the brig *Diligent* and the same sloop *Providence* in which John Trevett had shipped earlier, although that Marine officer decided against joining this dubious enterprise. In addition, one ship was contributed by New Hampshire and three brigs by the Massachusetts state navy, plus 10 privateers that were taken into the Massachusetts service. Dudley Saltonstall, a forty-year-old New Londoner, was in command of the naval force. Leading some

900 Massachusetts militiamen and 300 marines from the ships (about half of them Continental Marines and the rest from the state navies) was Brig. Gen. Solomon Lovell of the Massachusetts militia. Lt. Col. Paul Revere commanded the artillery, and Marine Capt. John Welsh of *Warren* led the Continental Marines under Lovell. Welsh had commanded the Marines on the brig *Cabot* in the first expedition against New Providence three years earlier. He had twice been captured by the enemy; once he was released and once he escaped from the prison at Portsmouth, England.

The American expeditionary force arrived off the Penobscot on the afternoon of July 25, 1779. American security was dreadful. Brig. Gen. MacLean had heard of their approach four days earlier, and he rushed to complete his log fortifications.

The next day, the British and American warships fought for two hours. Then the British fleet retired up the Penobscot, and the Marines from *Providence* led by Captain Welsh landed on Nautilus Island, which commands the harbor. The 20 British Marines on the island quickly fled, leaving their flag flying. The Americans installed a battery of two 18-pound cannon and one 12-pounder on the island. This battery, assisted by *Warren*, forced the British ships farther up the harbor.

At dawn on July 28, Captain Welsh and his Marines, together with the militia, assaulted the mainland peninsula where the British were building their fort. The Americans landed at the foot of a steep bluff that rose almost perpendicular from the water. They landed under fire in three divisions, the Marines on the right. Two ships and three brigs laid down a steady fire until the men reached shore. As they inched up the steep hill and finally advanced into thick woods, they met a guard of British regulars and drove them back into the main fortification.

Lt. Col. Paul Revere, who landed with his artillery in the center division, later wrote:

> The enemy's greatest strength lay upon our right, where the marines landed; they had three hundred in the woods. As soon as the right [the Marine division] landed they were briskly attacked. The enemy had the most advantageous place I ever saw; it is a bank above three

27

hundred feet high and so steep that no person can get up it but by pushing himself up by bushes and trees, with which it is covered. In less than 20 minutes the enemy gave way and we pursued them.[18]

Captain Welsh was killed in the assault. The British also killed eight Continental Marine privates from *Warren*. Marine Lt. William Hamilton was mortally wounded at the base of the cliff.

Instead of pressing the attack, Brig. Gen. Lovell laid cautious siege to the British fort. While the superior American force was stalled in front of the isolated and outnumbered enemy garrison, a British squadron under Sir George Collier sailed from New York. As soon as it appeared off the Penobscot on the afternoon of August 13, the Americans panicked. Captain Saltonstall refused to stay. Lovell began loading his force on the transports at one o'clock the next morning. By dawn, men and ships were fleeing up river. The British pursued immediately.

Rather than fight, Saltonstall ran his ships ashore and set fire to all but three, which were captured. The Americans escaped overland through the forests, as Sir Henry Clinton put it, "under every circumstance of mortification and disgrace."[19]

The Massachusetts navy had been virtually wiped out. Captain Saltonstall was courtmartialed and dismissed. Penobscot became a permanent British base for the rest of the war.

But the Marines had performed gallantly at Penobscot. For the first time in history, they had landed from the sea in force against enemy fire. Until timid superior officers slowed down the attack and ran when the enemy brought up reinforcements, the Marines had had everything well in hand.

7
Deadly Duels
at Sea

The Americans fought a hit-and-run naval war during the Revolution. In a Navy so hopelessly outnumbered and outgunned by the British, individual ships usually fought alone.

In the many sea battles, Marines fought from the rigging, where, with muskets and grenades, they picked off enemy officers and gunners. Sometimes they served as artillerymen. They formed boarding parties to fight hand-to-hand on enemy ships and raiding parties to carry the battle onto the enemy shores. When not in battle, they were responsible for keeping discipline among the crew.

Victory in eighteenth-century sea duels of ship against ship depended on three elements. First was sailing, in which the captain's position, speed and maneuvering ability were all-important. Second was gunnery, in which accurate and rapid fire were crucial. Equally important in a close-in duel was the small-arms fire, especially from "the tops" of the masts. Third was the courage and determination of the Marines and sailors who boarded the enemy or repelled his boarders.

In January 1778, Capt. John Trevett, the Marine who had led a company ashore at New Providence in the spring of 1776, participated in a single-ship amphibious operation. This was one of the more successful raids to which Marines contributed. It was a second voyage to New Providence, inspired by word that the 16-gun British brig *Mary*, which the previous summer had fought *Providence* off New York, had put in there in distress. As Trevett said, "We thought the time of retaliation had come, and we had a notion of killing two birds with one stone."[20] The Americans planned to seize both Fort Nassau and *Mary*.

Since the first raid on New Providence, Trevett had a new reason for wanting to fight the British. His brother, Constant Church Trevett, had been captured while commanding a merchant vessel and imprisoned in the infamous prison ship *Old Jersey* at New York. Trevett had hurried to obtain a British captain to exchange for his brother; "but it was too late," Trevett wrote bitterly, "for before the British Captain arrived he died with hard treatment from the British pirates. . . . I had rather be taken by the Turks!"[21]

Arriving at New Providence at midnight of January 27 with the sloop *Providence's* guns hidden and all men out of sight, Trevett took 26 Marines ashore. They landed about a mile from Fort Nassau. Trevett's journal tells the story:

> We took nothing with us to eat or drink but filled our pockets with ball cartridges. We landed about a mile from the Fort, and got our scaling ladder and all things ready. I recollected that when I was at the taking of New Providence with Com. Hopkins, I left out one of the pickets [in the wooden fence] of the fort, and I thought this might prove fortunate if it had not been replaced. So I left my men and went myself to see, and found it as I left it, still out. I went through, and near the embrazures I heard talking in the fort, and instantly one of the sentinels came to the corner of the fort and cried "all is well!" . . . and was answered from the other end of the fort, "all is well!" The ship that lay near the fort—her sentinel also cried "all is well!" I lay still a few moments, as I supposed the sentinels were going their rounds. I then went back, and we came on with the scaling ladder, and lay down near the fort until the sentry should come round again, for I expected they gave the cry every half hour, and so it was. We had been but a short time there before they came round and cried "all is well!" I waited a few minutes and then placed the scaling ladder near one of the embrazures and went over, every man following me. I gave positive orders not to fire a pistol or make any noise, as I knew it would instantly alarm the town. I went on, and as I was turning round the corner of the barracks

I met one of the British sentinels full but. I seized him by the collar, and ordered him in the first barrack door; he was much frightened, and exclaimed, "for God's sake, what have I done!" One of our men, in despite of my orders, fired a pistol over my shoulders at the sentinel. I had hold of it, but it did no damage. I spoke a soft word, and went into the barracks and examined the prisoner, and found there was only one more sentinel, and he at the other end of the Fort. I soon put him into another barrack-room and examined them apart; they both told me one story, and said that Gov. [John] Gambier had sent into the fort every article necessary, about three weeks before we made them this friendly visit. I asked them the reason of having only two sentinels in the fort in time of war; they said if they had only time to fire one or two guns, that in less than ten minutes they would have more than five hundred fighting men in the fort.[22]

Trevett and his men trained the fort's cannon on the streets of the town and the ships in the harbor. At daybreak they hoisted the American flag, and Marine Lt. Michael Molton and two men were sent to take Fort Montagu four miles to the east. They met no opposition and spiked the fort's guns. The Americans also seized *Mary* without a shot fired. They put both forts out of commission, released 30 American prisoners and took with them *Mary*, other freed ships and a substantial amount of gunpowder. Trevett sailed *Mary* to Nantucket as prize master and then to Old Town. The ship was later burned by Loyalists at Wood's Hole, at the foot of Cape Cod.

John Trevett served briefly as a spy in British-held Newport, Rhode Island, his home town, and fought in several sea battles. In 1780 he sailed on the first cruise of the 28-gun *Trumbull*, the last of the Continental Navy's original 13 frigates. Off Bermuda on June 1, *Trumbull* met the 36-gun British letter of marque *Watt*. Starting at one in the afternoon, the fight became a bruising, bitter slugging match at close quarters for two and a half hours. The ships were never more than 100 yards apart; at times their yards touched. The Marines fought vigorously; they killed or drove below deck *Watts'* Marines and the men in her tops, and then they manned the quarterdeck guns. John Trevett lost his right eye. Marine Lieutenants David Bill, Jabez Smith, Jr., and Daniel Starr and Sgt. Ezekial Hyatt were killed.

The captain of about 30 Marines on *Trumbull*, Gilbert Saltonstall, a Harvard graduate, wrote his father:

> It is beyond my power to give an adequate idea of the carnage, slaughter, havoc and destruction that ensued. Let your imagination do its best, it will fall short. We were literally cut all to pieces. . . . I had eleven different wounds from my shoulder to my hip; some with buck shot, others with splinters of the quarter deck gun [the after quarterdeck gun had a foot of its muzzle shot away]. I had one shot through the brim of my hat, but was not so disabled as to quit the quarter deck till after the engagement and am now as well as ever. Have one buck shot in my hip.

The fight of *Trumbull* and *Watt* was "one of the most hotly contested engagements fought at sea during the Revolution."[23] *Trumbull* was badly damaged, but *Watt* more so. After *Trumbull* broke off the action, *Watt* fled to New York (and the following September was sunk at Montauk Point). In a second letter home, Marine Captain Saltonstall summed up the battle: "Upon the whole there has not been a more close, obstinate and bloody engagement since the war. I hope it won't be treason if I don't except even Paul Jones'—all things considered we may dispute titles with him."[24]

Another young Marine officer left a journal of his experiences in the Revolution. William Jennison, Jr., had graduated from Harvard College in 1774 at the age of sixteen and was appointed a lieutenant of Marines aboard the new frigate *Warren* in April 1776. Unable to recruit his alloted 25 Marines, he resigned his commission. He fought with the army around New York and rejoined the Continental Marines as an enlisted man in February 1777 and by the year's end was made a lieutenant. Serving now on *Boston*, Jennison fought in several battles, helped take John Adams to France and, when *Boston* was refitting, signed aboard a privateer. He was captured by the British in 1779, imprisoned at Halifax and finally exchanged. Returning to

Boston, he was taken prisoner again at Charleston, South Carolina, in 1780. After all these escapades, Jennison became a teacher and died in Boston on the day before Christmas, 1843, at the age of eighty-six.

The greatest of the American sea duelists was John Paul Jones, the courageous, violent-tempered little Scot whose willingness to fight and whose flair for publicity have made his the best-known name in American naval history. In May 1776, shortly after he served as lieutenant on the expedition to New Providence, Jones gained his first command: *Providence,* on which John Trevett had sailed to New Providence. In July 1777, Jones took command of the new 18-gun sloop of war *Ranger* and was ordered to France where Benjamin Franklin was boldly organizing American attacks on British merchant shipping.

Continental Marines played an important part in all Jones' battles from the moment he arrived in European waters. Initially, his captain of Marines was Matthew Parke, an old friend and the only one of his officers who had served with the Navy. Samuel Wallingford, a New Hampshire militia officer, was his lieutenant of Marines.

Jones' first significant engagement was a raid on the British Isles. He sailed *Ranger* from Brest and on April 22, 1778, made a hit-and-run landing at Whitehaven, where he was familiar with the waters of the Irish Sea. At midnight, the 30-man landing party cast off in two small boats, Jones commanding one and Wallingford, the other. (Captain Parke had left the ship at Brest in a dispute over prize money.) Both boats carried "the necessary combustibles" to set fire to the ships in Whitehaven harbor.

Just before daybreak on the 23rd, Wallingford reached the north side of the harbor; Jones, the south. One account says that Wallingford and his men headed for the nearest tavern. Jones and his party scaled the wall of the fort guarding the southern end of the harbor, found the four guards asleep, locked them in the guard house and spiked the cannon. Jones later reported:

> On my return from this business, I naturally expected to see the fire of the ships on the north side, as well as to find my own party with everything in readiness to set fire to the shipping in the south. Instead of this, I found the boat under the direction of Mr. [Midshipman Benjamin]

33

Hill and Mr. Wallingsford [sic] returned and the party in some confusion, their light having burnt out at the instant when it became necessary. By the strangest fatality my own party were in the same situation, the candles being all burnt out.

As dawn approached, Jones moved rapidly. He brazenly obtained a light for his torches from a public house situated apart from the town and set a fire in the hold of a large ship closely surrounded by what Jones estimated to be nearly 100 other vessels. Since he did not have time to fire a number of ships, he poured tar on the flames of this one to make certain she burned.

Seeing the flames, the townspeople ran to the scene. Jones wrote: "I stood between them and the ship on fire with a pistol in my hand and ordered them to retire, which they did with precipitation. The flames had already caught the rigging and began to ascend the mainmast. The sun was a full hour's march above the horizon and as sleep no longer ruled the world, it was time to retire."[25] Jones and his men escaped without suffering injury—or causing any—and Jones gloated over the disappointment the populace must have felt on dashing to the fort to fire on *Ranger* and finding the guns useless.

That same morning, Jones made a second landing, on St. Mary's Isle across Solway Firth, to capture the Earl of Selkirk to use for exchange. But Selkirk was away from home. Afterwards, his wife wrote the earl: "Of the two officers, one [Wallingford] was a civil young man in a green uniform, an anchor on his buttons, which were white. He came to the house in a blue greatcoat." The raiders seized the family silver. Later, Jones bought the plate from his men and gallantly returned it to the earl.

The next day, April 24, off the northeast coast of Ireland near Belfast, Jones forced a fight with the British 20-gun sloop of war *Drake*. In an hour, the British ship, manned by a green crew, had 25 men killed or wounded, including the captain, who was hit by a Marine musket ball. Jones had six wounded and three killed. One of the dead, shot through the head by a British Marine early in the action, was his commander of Marines, the "civil young man," Lt. Wallingford. Marine Sgt. John Ricker took command of the Marine detachment until Lt. William Morris joined *Ranger* at Brest.

By the following year (1779), both France and Spain were allies of the United States. Benjamin Franklin and the Marquis de Lafayette planned an expedition directly against England and gave Jones command of an ancient, slow French merchantman, *Le Duc de Duras*. The plan never came off; but Jones renamed his ship *Bonhomme Richard* in honor of his patron Franklin, manned her in part with exchanged American prisoners and collected a five-ship fleet.

In addition to *Bonhomme Richard*, 42 guns, Commodore Jones had the swift new frigate *Alliance*, 36 guns, under Pierre Landais, the only Frenchman to command an American naval vessel; the French frigate *Pallas*, 26 guns; the cutter *Le Cerf*, 18 guns, and the brig *Vengeance*, 12 guns. *Alliance* was the squadron's only ship that was originally American; and Congress' trust in the delicate-featured Landais, an experienced officer who had sailed around the world with Sieur de Bougainville in 1767, would prove a terrible mistake.

In January 1779, Landais and *Alliance* had sailed from Boston to bring Lafayette to Brest. While at sea on February 2, a mutiny was uncovered among British and Irish sailors in the crew. The mutiny was led by the sergeant-at-arms, John Savage, and the sergeant of Marines, William Murray. Murray confessed that they planned to seize *Alliance* and sail her to England or Ireland. They intended to put Landais in the ship's cutter without food, bring Lafayette as a prisoner to England, make the ship's lieutenants who would not cooperate walk the plank and hang and quarter the Marine officers aboard. Thirty-eight of the mutineers were seized and jailed.

When Jones' squadron sailed from L'Orient on August 14, it was amply manned by Marines, chiefly Irish infantrymen uniformed in red and white. Lt. Edward Stack commanded the 137 Marines aboard *Bonhomme Richard* with Lieutenants Eugene MacCarthy and James O'Kelly. Under Landais on *Alliance* were Marine Captain Parke and Lieutenants James Warren, Jr., and Thomas Elwood. Capt. Maurice O'Connell was the Marine officer on *Pallas*.

Stack, MacCarthy and O'Kelly were officers in the Irish Regiment of the French Army who had taken leaves of absence to fight the British with Jones and were commissioned as American Marines. The twenty-three-year-old Stack was a tall, thin Irish adventurer with elegant manners and a passion for fighting. After this cruise, he would return to his regiment, fight under several flags and eventually rise to the rank of general in the British Army.

Early in the afternoon of September 23, Jones, sailing in the North Sea, sighted a convoy of 41 British merchantmen rounding England's Flamborough Head. Escorting them were *Serapis*, a new frigate with 50 guns, and the 20-gun sloop of war *Countess of Scarborough*. The merchantmen fled, and the two British war ships sailed confidently for Jones' ships. (*Cerf* was separated from the squadron.) Landais, failing to obey Jones' signal, kept *Alliance* out of the fray. And *Vengeance* did not engage. *Bonhomme Richard* tackled *Serapis*, and *Pallas* took on *Countess of Scarborough*.

Jones stood on the quarterdeck. On the poop were Lieutenant O'Kelly and 20 Marines. Lt. Richard Dale commanded the 12-pound guns. Lieutenant Stack led four sailors and 15 Marines in the main top. The men in the "tops" were armed with swivel guns, coehorns (small mortars that hurled grenades) and muskets. Their orders were to clear *Serapis'* tops and then her decks.

Seven o'clock marked the beginning of one of the most dramatic sea fights in history. Jones, at close range, fired a starboard broadside into *Serapis*. His main guns were quickly put out of action by the enemy. But by eight o'clock the Marines had cleared *Serapis'* tops, and Jones had the two ships lashed together stern to bow, their guns almost touching as they poured fire into each other. The Marines in the rigging could scramble from their tops to the enemy's. The aged *Bonhomme Richard* was pierced repeatedly and in danger of sinking.

Two things saved the ship and turned the tide of battle: Jones and the Marines. Jones' own story is vivid:

> I had now only two pieces of cannon, 9-pounders, on the quarter-deck that were not silenced, and not one of the heavier cannon was fired during the rest of the action. The purser, Mr. Mease, who commanded the guns on the quarter-deck, being dangerously wounded in the head, I

was obliged to fill his place, and with great difficulty rallied a few men, and shifted over one of the lee quarter-deck guns, so that we afterward played three pieces of 9-pounders upon the enemy. The tops alone seconded the first of this little battery and held out bravely during the whole of the action; expecially the main top, where [Marine] Lieutenant Stack commanded. I directed the fire of one of the three cannon against the main-mast, with double-headed shot, while the other two were exceedingly well served with grape and canister shot to silence the enemy's musketry, and clear her decks, which was at last effected. The enemy were, as I have since understood, on the instant of calling for quarter, when the cowardice or treachery of three of my under-officers induced them to call to the enemy. The English commodore asked me if I demanded quarter, and I having answered him in the most determined negative, they renewed the battle with double fury. They were unable to stand the deck; but the fire of their cannon, especially the lower battery, which was entirely formed of ten-pounders, was incessant; both ships were set on fire in various places, and the scene was dreadful beyond the reach of language.

The British tried to board *Bonhomme Richard* and were repelled. When the outlook seemed darkest, the British captain asked Jones if he had surrendered. Then came the famous reply: "I have not yet begun to fight!"

The Marines turned the tide. With the British driven out of their own tops, the Marines climbed into *Serapis'* rigging, now tangled with that of the American ship. They kept *Serapis'* deck cleared of defenders. Then a seaman who had crossed to the enemy's maintop administered the coup de grâce—a grenade that bounced into *Serapis'* open hatch, blew up the powder among the cannon and started a chain reaction among the cartridges. The explosions and fire killed all 20 men behind the main mast (leaving some with only their collars on their bodies), disorganized the British crew and put a sizable number of *Serapis'* guns out of action.

The grenade had done its job just in time. Jones continues:

My situation was really deplorable; the *Bon Homme Richard* received various shots under the water from *Alliance* [Landais fired three broadsides at the ships lashed together, damaging *Bonhomme Richard*, killing several men and mortally wounding Marine Lieutenant O'Kelly]; the leak gained on the pumps, and the fire increased much on board both ships. Some officers persuaded me to strike, of whose courage and good sense I entertain a high opinion. My treacherous master-at-arms let loose all my prisoners without my knowledge, and my prospects became gloomy indeed. I would not, however, give up the point. The enemy's mainmast began to shake, their firing decreased fast, ours rather increased, and the British colours were struck at half an hour past ten o'clock.[26]

In the meantime, *Pallas* had more easily conquered *Countess of Scarborough*. When *Serapis* struck her flag, *Bonhomme Richard* was afire with five feet of water in her hold. She sank on the morning of the 25th, her flag still flying. In this, the single greatest sea fight of the war, the Marines had helped ensure Jones' victory.

In May, 1781, *Alliance*, now commanded by Capt. John Barry, engaged two British warships; Marine Lt. Samuel Pritchard was mortally wounded; Lt. James Warren, Jr., lost his right leg, and Sgt. David Brewer was killed.

The Continental Marines were to fight in one more major battle. Unlike their triumphant performance with Jones, this swan song was to be both a defensive action and a defeat.

Late in the war, Sir Henry Clinton attempted a new strategy. He would seek victory in the southern colonies, where Loyalist sympathies promised to make the job easier. It is sufficient to say that this British plan ended at Yorktown. But the road to Yorktown was a dismal one for the Americans.

By 1779, the British, following their new strategy, had captured Savannah; and in February, 1780, Clinton and Cornwallis led a force from New York to attack the Americans at Charleston, South Carolina. On May 6, British Marines and seamen forced the surrender of Fort Moultrie; and on the night of May 9, Clinton opened the final attack with a heavy bombardment. Three days later, Gen. Benjamin Lincoln surrendered the American defenders. More than 5,000 men, including seven generals, were taken prisoner. The British lost only 268 killed and wounded. It was Clinton's greatest triumph on the way to final disaster.

Throughout the defense of Charleston, the American naval squadron's Continental Marines under Capts. Richard Palmes, Edmund Arrowsmith and William Jones (later governor of Rhode Island) fought bravely but futilely—reputedly under the youthful Colonel John Laurens, a former aide of Washington and a veteran of Valley Forge who was to distinguish himself at Yorktown.

Yorktown in October 1781 was the climactic British defeat. But the war went on and on, with the British victorious at sea against France and Spain while retracting their lines in America to the seaports. Finally, a tentative peace treaty was signed on the last day of November 1782.

By late 1781, the American Navy was down to 61 officers; only 5 captains and 7 lieutenants remained on active duty. The Continental Marines were reduced to 12 captains and 12 lieutenants, with three of each on active duty. Only the Marine detachments on the frigates *Alliance* and *Deane* were still in position to fight. The Marines on the former were commanded by Captain Parke and on the latter by Captain Palmes.

Lt. Thomas Elwood of Fairfield, Connecticut, the last Continental Marine officer, was discharged in September 1783. *Alliance*, the last ship in the Continental Navy, was auctioned off in 1785. The first chapter of the American Marines was closed.

The story of the American Marines in the Revolution is a mixture of heroism and amateurishness. They came from a seafaring, coastal people eager to fight for liberty in the manner they knew best. They had no traditions, no esprit de corps, no professionalism. They had little sea-fighting experience and less organization. They fought, one might say, as civilians in uniform. Yet they fought a crucial delaying action at Valcour Island. They seized Fort Nassau with boldness. They helped the army courageously at Princeton. They did their job, though surrounded by incompetency, at the Penobscot. They fought magnificently in the sea duels of John Paul Jones. Because they were allowed to be cornered, they lost at Charleston. They fought the kind of war that people always have to fight for freedom against masters who can outgun and outman them: retreat and counterpunch and stay alive to fight again.

The Marines did their share on the long, bleeding road to victory and the establishment of their nation. The names of Nicholas and Trevett and Stack and the others have been too long neglected. And the names of the men who fought with them have been sadly forgotten. The glory of the Corps was yet to come, but the service and honor were there from the beginning.

*A corporal in the U.S. Marine Corps, shortly after it was
established on July 11, 1798. From watercolor
by Col. John H. Magruder III.
© Marine Corps Association.*

SEMPER FIDELIS

II
ESTABLISHING
THE
CORPS
1798-1815

1
A Tough and Fancy Corps

As Marines tell it, when the fighting of the Revolution was over and the nation's military forces were disbanded, all that remained was a corps of mules and two battalions of Marines. The army and the navy tossed a coin to determine who would take the mules and who, the Marines. The army, according to the story, won the toss—and took the mules.

Only the first part of the anecdote can be authenticated: When the Revolution was won, the new nation quickly gave up its military establishment. Americans had reason to fear a standing armed force in tyrannical hands; one of the purposes of the war had been to free the United States from British military power. Throughout the decade of the 1780s, when even the form of the new government was undecided, many thinking people worried that someone might use the military to establish a homegrown monarchy. In 1789, the Constitution pronounced it the duty of the Federal government to "provide for the common defense"; it also confirmed the rights of individual states to maintain their own militias and of individual citizens to bear arms.

But ten years after the last Continental Marine had been discharged, fears of a military establishment had given way to the realization that a nation unable to protect itself was prey to every bully. As the new kid on the block, the young United States would have to fight to win respect. In the next three decades, it took on three bullies: the piratical Barbary states on the north shore of Africa, then France and finally England.

Because the United States consisted primarily of a strip of settlements on the far edge of the Atlantic, these three wars were in great part fought on the seas. In all three, the seizure of

American merchant ships and sailors was a major issue. Not until the critical 30 years were over was independence truly won.

A mob stormed the Paris Bastille in 1789. Europe was at war by 1792, a struggle that would be settled only by the Duke of Wellington's victory at Waterloo 21 years later. By 1794, the United States had been violated by both England and France; attacked by British-paid Indians on the western frontier, and forced to pay humiliating tribute to the Barbary powers. There was neither safety nor honor in weakness.

On March 27, 1794, Congress ordered the building of six naval frigates and the enlistment of seamen and Marines to man them. Ostensibly, the frigates would fight the Barbary states; but they were also intended to protect American shipping, ports and seamen against France and England. In June, Congress announced the United States' neutrality from the European war.

The nation was bitterly divided over the naval bill. New England and the port cities of the South, dependent on overseas commerce, favored it; the inland sections vigorously opposed it, warning that it would drag the country into Europe's wars. The Federalists, led by Washington, advocated the construction of the frigates. In the end, after peace was temporarily signed with Algiers, only three of the ships—*United States, Constitution* and *Constellation*—were launched in 1797. Their Marines were commanded respectively by Capt. Franklin Wharton, a future Commandant of the Corps; Lt. Lemuel Clark, and Lt. Philip Edwards. (The first acting Marine officer on *United States* was Lt. William MacRae. And because Edwards was late in reporting, Army Lt. James Triplett made the first cruise of *Constellation* as acting lieutenant of Marines.) Each officer was authorized to enlist his own detachment. There was no Marine Corps.

The next year, on July 11, 1798, a congressional act provided for "establishing and organizing a Marine Corps," and the Corps as it is known today was born. The Marine Corps act provided for 881 men: 1 major, 4 captains, 16 first lieutenants, 12 second lieutenants, 48 sergeants, 48 corporals, 32 drummers and fifers, and 720 privates. Enlistments would be for three years, and the United States Senate would appoint all officers, except when the President acted in the Senate's absence. Whenever

Marines were massed to serve with the Army, all specialists such as adjutants, paymasters and quartermasters would be appointed by the Commandant from within the Corps. From the beginning, the principle was established that still holds today: Every Marine is a fighter first and a specialist second.

The Marines would keep discipline aboard ship, lead boarding parties and amphibious landings, fight with muskets in short-range naval battles and, if the captain wished, work some of the ship's long guns. They would also man coastal installations and forts, "or any other duty ashore, as the President, at his discretion, shall direct." Privates would receive $6 a month and one ration (worth 15 to 17 cents) per day; a second lieutenant $25 a month and two rations per day; a first lieutenant $30 and three rations; a captain $40 and three rations; and the major $50 a month and four rations. A ration consisted of a pound and a half of beef or a pound of pork or salt fish; a pound of bread; a pound of peas, rice or potatoes; cheese or butter; and a half pint of spirits or a quart of beer.

No Negroes, mulattoes, or Indians could be enlisted under the original rules, and the foreign-born, even if naturalized, could not make up more than one-fourth of the Corps.

At least three blacks had served in the Continental Marines during the Revolution and an estimated ten others served in the Connecticut, Massachusetts and Pennsylvania state navies. The first black Continental Marine was John Martin or "Keto," a slave of William Marshall of Wilmington, Delaware; he was recruited without Marshall's knowledge by Marine Captain Miles Pennington in April 1776. John Martin served on *Reprisal* and was killed when the brig foundered off the Newfoundland Banks in October 1777. The two other known black Continental Marines were members of Capt. Robert Mullan's company: "Isaac Walker (Negro)" enlisted on August 27, 1776, and "Orange . . . Negro" enlisted on October 1. They were still on the rolls on April 1, 1777, and presumably served at the Battle of Princeton and at Morristown. As far as is known, these were the first black American Marines; and, officially, they were the last until World War II. (There is one reference to an American Indian serving as a Marine private in Nicaragua in 1928.)

From the beginning, it was a tough Corps. Discipline was modeled on the British Navy's. A man could be flogged. A commanding officer could order 12 lashes and a general court martial could decree that a man receive 100 lashes with a cat-o'-nine tails—actually a death sentence. A man could also have his head shaved, be assigned to hard labor with ball and chain, be drummed out of his unit or even have his rum ration taken away.

And it was a fancy Corps. Uniforms quickly became elaborate. The early Marine officer wore a long blue coat with red lapels and lining, a red vest and blue breeches. His uniform was decorated with many buttons bearing a fouled (rope-entwined) anchor and the American eagle. His epaulets denoted his rank: lieutenants wore one and captains and the major two. Enlisted men wore a blue coat and trousers trimmed with red; a cocked hat, and the black leather collar that kept their heads erect, protected them against saber slashes and powder burns and gave them the lasting name of "Leathernecks."

President John Adams had named Benjamin Stoddert of Maryland as Secretary of the Navy in May 1798. (Adams himself had fought briefly as a marine aboard *Boston* when she engaged *Martha* while carrying him to France in 1778.) On July 12, the day after Adams approved the act of Congress creating the Corps, Stoddert appointed the Corps' senior officer: William Ward Burrows, a lawyer and a Southerner.

Burrows commanded the Marine Corps for nearly six years. His main job was to recruit Marines for the ships of the rapidly growing Navy. Recruiting was difficult because the demand for Marines increased rapidly and because the Army, expanding simultaneously, was authorized to offer eager young men recruiting bonuses, a luxury denied the Marine Corps. On March 2, 1799, the Corps' authorized strength was increased by 204. Marines had to be posted on each of 26 naval vessels built, purchased or captured from the French in the next two years. *Ganges* was the first to put to sea, with Lt. Daniel Carmick and 24 Marines aboard.

Surprisingly little is known about the Corps' first leader. Burrows was born in Charleston, South Carolina, on January 16, 1758, the son of a well-to-do lawyer. He studied law in England, and it is believed that during the Revolution he served in the South Carolina militia. At the time of his appointment, he was forty years old, short, stocky, popular and in the words of Washington Irving "a gentleman of accomplished mind and polished manner."

One recorded episode suggests Burrows' character. In 1800, a Navy lieutenant insulted and struck Lt. Henry Caldwell, one of the Corps' first officers. Burrows sent the young Marine a letter calling the incident an affair of honor and urging him to fight a duel with the Navy officer. Burrows said:

> A Blow ought never to be forgiven, and without you wipe away this Insult offered to the Marine Corps, you cannot expect to join our officers . . . don't let me see you 'till you have wiped away this Disgrace. It is my duty to support my Officers and I will do it with my life, but they must deserve it.

This was the spirit Burrows sought to instill in the new Marine Corps as he led it through the quasi-war with France and the troubles with the Barbary powers. He also sought a larger share of prize money for Marine officers. And he tried to give second lieutenants the same ration that first lieutenants received, noting that it was "no great object as to the expense to the U.S. but is of serious import to the 2nd Lieuts."

Burrows first set up headquarters in Philadelphia on August 23, 1798. (A Marine detachment had been at the navy yard there since March.) In June 1800, he moved headquarters to Washington. After bivouacking briefly on Prospect Hill, Georgetown, the Washington camp was established on the site of the present Naval hospital. The next year, the Marine Barracks was begun at "Eighth and Eye"—it is the Corps' oldest post. Burrows founded the famous Marine Corps Band; under Drum Major William Farr, it played at the Executive Mansion as early as New Year's Day 1801.

In April 1800, Burrows became the Corps' first Commandant with the title of "Lieutenant Colonel Commandant." By 1804, Commandant Burrows was ready to resign. His wife had died, and he was in poor health. He was also totally out of sympathy with the Jefferson Administration, which wanted to restrict the Navy to flotillas of gunboats capable only of protecting U.S. harbors. Burrows was a staunch and lifelong Federalist—not an unimportant fact in his appointment to lead the Corps.

On March 6, 1804, Jefferson's Secretary of the Navy, Robert Smith, accepted Burrows' resignation with a chilly note sent to him in Charleston containing a barely disguised order: "as there is a large balance to your debit on the books of this department it is expected that you will without delay repair to this place for the purpose of settling this balance."

The question of the Commandant's accounts brought on a Congressional investigation. The committee checking into the matter found that the Marine Corps, which had received $353,573.53 by that time, was overdrawn by $9,428. The size of this discrepancy can be seen when compared to Burrows' pay: only $1,100 a year plus "subsistence and forage." But today there is no explanation of how Burrows, who for a time served also as Paymaster of the Corps, had gotten himself into this financial trouble. The Congressional committee finally recommended that in the future the Marine Corps be required to make monthly or quarterly accountings of its expenditures, but nothing more seems to have come of the matter.

Exactly a year to the day after he resigned, William Ward Burrows was dead. He was buried in the Presbyterian Cemetery in Georgetown, and in 1892 his body was moved to Arlington National Cemetery.

2
"The Men Went on Board Like Devils"

When William Burrows took command of the Corps, the seeds of the two conflicts in which his men would fight were already sown. The French, who had been gallant allies at Yorktown just 17 years earlier, had overthrown their monarchy and were now displaying contempt for the new nation. Their navy was impressing large numbers of United States merchantmen on the high seas, and French privateers were venturing smack into American harbors to grab defenseless shipping.

War was never declared in the vicious little scrap with the French. But Congress ordered the Navy to seize armed French vessels acting belligerently in American waters and to recapture stolen American ships. In a disconnected series of sea battles, most of them fought in West Indian waters, the U.S. Navy seized more than 85 French ships in the next couple of years; but incidents of navy ships fighting navy ships were rare.

The first action occurred off Egg Harbor, New Jersey, in July 1798, when the 20-gun *Delaware* captured the 14-gun French privateer *Croyable*. On the afternoon of February 9, the next year, France's *L'Insurgente* met *Constellation*, 38 guns vs. 36. In an hour's battle off the West Indian island of Nevis, the French frigate suffered 70 casualties from devastating hull-aimed American broadsides and surrendered. Almost exactly a year later—on February 1 and 2, 1800—*Constellation* engaged the 52-gun frigate *Vengeance* in a five-hour night battle at pistol range. *Vengeance* finally fled in the darkness just as *Constellation* lost its mainmast. In both these fights, *Constellation's* Marine detachment was led by Lt. Bartholomew Clinch. Navy Capt. Thomas Truxtun's report of the action with *Vengeance* specifically praised the Marines.

[For the location of places in this section see map No. 5 in the map section.—*Au.*]

When the badly damaged *Vengeance* reached Curaçao, the Dutch refused its captain credit to make repairs. Angry at this lack of hospitality, the French in July sent 1,400 men from Guadaloupe to take the Dutch island. The French landed, laid siege to the town and threatened to seize American property to pay for the repairs. In September, the American consul called for help. The Navy sent *Merrimack* and *Patapsco*, which arrived on September 22 while the French were demanding the town's surrender. That night, the French dueled with *Patapsco* in the harbor; and at 2 A.M., Marine 2d Lt. James Middleton led a 70-man landing party ashore to reinforce the Dutch batteries. In the face of American support, the French withdrew from the island. The Marines had helped save Curaçao.

The war went on in small, bitter fights, which settled little but taught the French that the Americans were not pushovers. The United States attempted to strike a more telling blow against the French by aiding Toussaint L'Ouverture, the self-educated slave who was leading the Negroes' fight for freedom on the island of Haiti. L'Ouverture was battling Hyacinthe Rigaud, who had allied himself with the French.

On New Year's Day, 1800, the swift new U.S. Navy schooner *Experiment* was convoying four merchantmen through the Bight of Leogane off Haiti. She was commanded by Lt. William Maley, with young David Porter second in command. The crew of 70 included 14 Marines.

The five ships were becalmed in the bight. Suddenly out from the shore swarmed 10 barges loaded with some 400 of Rigaud's men, who preyed on hapless merchantmen deserted by the wind in those narrow waters. *Experiment* remained buttoned up, looking like another merchantman. When the barges opened fire, the convoy's guns replied with grape and small-arms fire. The aim of the sailors and Marines was good; the surprise complete. The pirates retreated and regrouped. Their second attack was more shrewdly planned. Twelve barges surrounded *Experiment*, seeking to destroy the convoy's sole protector. The Americans had oars out so that they could turn the ship, and they had created strong points of fire by concentrating the Marines and sailors with muskets on the forecastle and quarterdeck. *Experiment's* large guns kept the barges at bay; her musket fire was deadly.

Pirates from several barges seized one of the merchantmen and murdered her captain. *Experiment* poured fire into the captured vessel until the enemy deserted her. As the day wore on, two of the convoy's vessels drifted beyond *Experiment's* protective reach and were abandoned. The enemy boarded them and towed them off. Captain Maley's three remaining ships were finally able to make port.

The following month, the frigate *General Greene*, 28 guns, carrying Marines commanded by Lt. James Weaver, blockaded and bombarded the city of Jacmel on Haiti's southern coast while L'Ouverture attacked by land and captured the town from Rigaud. On March 11, the new frigate *Boston*, with 36 Marines under Lt. Jonathan Church, was becalmed, as *Experiment* had been, in the Bight of Leogane. For five hours the Marines helped fight off Rigaud's barges.

In the spring of 1800, the Navy set out to capture the British ship *Sandwich*, held by the French on the north coast of Santo Domingo. A landing party was formed of Marines and sailors from *Constitution*. The Marines were commanded by Capt. Daniel Carmick (one of the first four captains commissioned in the re-established Corps). Ninety men piled into a sloop named *Sally*; all but half a dozen were hidden in the hold. On May 12, they sailed into Puerto Plata harbor and boarded the unsuspecting *Sandwich*. Carmick and Lt. William Amory then led the Marines ashore through neck-high water. They captured the fort and spiked its cannon. Later, Captain Carmick said in a letter that "It put me in mind of the wooden horse at Troy . . . The men went on board like devils." This first landing by the young Marine Corps was daring and expertly executed; but it violated the neutrality of the Spanish port, and the United States had to give up the prize.

Marines fought in numerous sea duels during that war, but others had less glamorous duty. One of the Corps' important jobs was to transfer and guard the prisoners taken from captured ships to several concentration camps, the most prominent being at Frederick, Maryland, and Lancaster, Pennsylvania.

Finally, in February 1801, prolonged negotiations with Napoleon ended the "war." Many of the American claims against the French were included in the purchase price of the Louisiana territory, which was bought from France in 1803. But in that year, war broke out once more in Europe; and neutral American shipping was again unsafe. During the decade after 1801, the French seized more than 500 American ships and the British more than 900.

Immediately after the French war, Congress passed the Peace Establishment Act, drastically reducing the armed forces. On May 12, 1802, President Jefferson ordered all Marines discharged except the men on the ships and a 17-man detail at each of the Navy yards (at Boston, New York, Philadelphia, Washington and Norfolk). By February 1803, there were only 453 enlisted Marines on the rolls; and by November the Corps' officer strength was down to 23. The Corps remained at about that level for the next six years.

3
To the Shores
of Tripoli

The Marine Corps hymn sings the praises of only two actions of the Corps: in the halls of Montezuma and on the shores of Tripoli. Looking back from the perspective of Tarawa, Iwo Jima and the Chosin Reservoir, it is easy to lose sight of the courage of those few men who fought and died in an earlier age: the Marines in Africa with William Osborne of *Philadelphia* and Presley O'Bannon in Eaton's army, and the Marines with Samuel Watson in Mexico.

The glory of the "shores of Tripoli" began in disgrace. By gaining independence, the United States had lost the security that Great Britain gave to maritime commerce under her flag. Within two years after winning freedom from England, the young nation had to deal with the pirates of the Barbary states. These rapacious little political entities on the coast of North Africa, made up in good part of Moors who had been forced out of Spain, existed as "nations" by preying on unarmed Mediterranean shipping. The Barbary states—Algiers, Tunis, Morocco and Tripoli—forced the European powers to pay tribute to minimize attacks on their ships and citizens. Algiers began seizing American merchant ships and enslaving their crews in 1785; by the turn of the century the United States had bought treaties from all of the Barbary states.

The Barbary pirates were aided and abetted by Great Britain. She was the world's foremost shipping power; but when she was fighting the French, the added war risk discouraged merchants from using her bottoms. The Barbary corsairs made English vessels appear more attractive by endangering the ships of neutral powers, including the United States.

The nub of the American troubles with Algiers was a treaty

[For the location of places in this section see map No. 2 in the map section.—*Au.*]

signed between that state and Portugal in 1793 allowing Algerian warships to operate in the Atlantic. This treaty, arranged by
the British, meant that more American ships would be seized;
and it led directly to the building of the first U.S. frigates and the
creation of the permanent American Navy. At the time of the
Naval Bill of 1794, Algiers held 13 American ships and 119
American prisoners. Because the United States were not prepared to fight, the next year the Senate ratified a treaty with
Algiers by which the U.S. government ignominiously paid
nearly a million dollars in tribute and ransoms. It was a
tremendous sum, given the limited resources of the young
nation.

In 1800, the 24-gun *George Washington* had the honor of
being the first American warship in the Mediterranean—and the
dishonor of carrying tribute to the Dey of Algiers. *George
Washington*'s skipper, twenty-six-year-old William Bainbridge,
unfortunately brought his ship under the Dey's guns; and that
potentate forced him to carry the Dey's presents to the Sultan of
Turkey. The Dey even required Bainbridge to fly the Algerian
flag—on an American warship—until he had cleared the harbor
and could safely pull it down.

Meanwhile, the Pasha of Tripoli, the weakest of the Barbary
powers, was growing restless. He had received tributes totaling
at least $100,000; but by the spring of 1800, egged on by a
British agent, he felt that his deal was not as good as those
extorted by Algiers and Tunis. He wanted more money.

The Pasha's timing was terrible. The Navy, which had been
cut back after the United States bought peace from Algiers, had
been built up again during the sea war with France. And when
that trouble was settled early in 1801, President Jefferson felt
strong enough to send a squadron of four ships to the Mediterranean under Commodore Richard Dale, who had fought as
John Paul Jones' first lieutenant on *Bonhomme Richard* when
she beat *Serapis*. Jefferson wrote the Pasha of Tripoli: "We mean
to rest the safety of our commerce on the resources of our own
strength and bravery, in every sea. . . ."[1]

By the time Dale reached Gibraltar on June 30, he found
that the Pasha had declared war on the United States. This was
another mistake, for Dale carried with him a gift of $10,000 to
sweeten Jefferson's letter.

Dale's squadron was too weak to press the issue. Early in 1802, however, Congress gave the President war powers; and on Dale's return to the United States, a stronger fleet of 10 ships was sent to the Mediterranean under the easygoing, less than competent Capt. Richard V. Morris. The most memorable event of his tour occurred on May 22, 1802, when several of his ships chased a group of Tripolitanian merchantmen into the harbor. The enemy hauled their vessels onto the shore and built a crude breastwork to protect them. Lt. David Porter led a party of Marines and sailors ashore, drove the enemy away and burned the Tripolitanian ships. But Captain Morris proved incapable of ending the war promptly and was dismissed from the Navy.

In the summer of 1803, Capt. Edward Preble took a third squadron to the Mediterranean. Preble was a different kind of man. He was a tough New Englander, a disciplinarian with a violent temper and ulcers. All the ship commanders in his squadron were under thirty; Captain Preble, forty-two, called them his "school boys." He taught them how to fight and instilled in them a sense of professionalism that began to make the Navy an effective fighting force.

In October, Preble paraded a show of strength off Tangiers, Morocco, where the Emperor had issued orders to seize American ships. Preble's mission there was successful. But behind him blockading Tripoli he had left *Philadelphia*, captained by the unfortunate William Bainbridge, and the tiny *Vixen*. On Monday morning, October 31, while Captain Bainbridge was chasing a small Tripolitan ship, he grounded his fast frigate on the uncharted shoals of Kaliusa Reef. A mosquito fleet of Tripolitan gun boats came out to fight the stranded American giant. They peppered away at her for four hours. Trying to lighten his ship and free her from the reef, Bainbridge ordered everything—even the guns—thrown overboard. Still stuck on the reef and with no defenses left, Bainbridge struck his flag. Not a man was wounded; 308 Americans, including the 43 Marines commanded by 1st Lt. William S. Osborne, were herded ashore and imprisoned for 19 months. The officers were treated reasonably well, but the crewmen were forced to work at hard labor and were frequently beaten. News of the frigate's shocking capture compelled the nation to face the realities of the Barbary problem. The government ordered all possible ships to the Mediterranean. They included 400 Marines—four-fifths of the enlisted strength of the Corps.

One of the Marines on the captured *Philadelphia* was Pvt. William Ray, who had enlisted only the previous June. Ray had been a schoolteacher, storekeeper, poet and newspaper editor. At thirty-one, he was a bitter, unsuccessful man, deeply in debt. When he had reached Philadelphia that spring, he was without a job and had become a heavy drinker. "Commanded by imperious necessity," as he put it, he joined the Marines.

Private Ray became "ship's writer" on *Philadelphia* and kept an account of his adventures and his months in prison. His story, which he called *Horrors of Slavery, or The American Tars in Tripoli*, is one of the few records of what it was like to be an enlisted Marine in the early Corps.

Ray writes impassionedly of the bad feeling between sailor and Marine aboard ship, in which the Marine "is made the miserable object of incessant contumely and querulous abuse— reprehended or corrected for the omission of duties which are out of his power to perform; and . . . lashed to the bone for not understanding what he has never been taught, and never had an opportunity to learn."[2] He describes in detail several floggings given Marines aboard *Philadelphia* for minor offenses, often ordered by midshipmen only twelve or fourteen years old, and often without the victim being told what his offense had been.

When *Philadelphia* surrendered, the Tripolitans stripped Ray and the other men of everything except their shirts, trousers and hats. The Americans were made to swim ashore and pass down a row of armed men to the castle gate. They were spat upon and led into a marble hall and the enthroned presence of the Pasha of Tripoli, Yusuf Karamanli, who wore gold-mounted pistols, a saber with a gold hilt, a white beribboned turban and a beard that reached to his chest. Crowded into damp cold cells the men were not fed for two days; and then each was given only a 12-ounce loaf of bread. Later, this was increased to two loaves a day; and they were allowed to retrieve some of their supplies from *Philadelphia*.

Ray was put in a work gang that ran errands about town, carrying pig iron, copper kettles, and bundles of faggots. Always under guard, the men were let out to work at sunup and locked in their cells again at sundown. Ray had no shoes; most of the men were half-dressed, "naked as the natives of Pellew" as Ray described them.[3] They were infested with vermin and could bathe or wash their clothes only by plunging into the surf.

The Tripolitans freed *Philadelphia* from the reef and brought her under the guns of the castle. Captain Preble decided to destroy the frigate before the enemy could fit her out and sail against his own ships. The job went to Navy Lt. Stephen Decatur. On the night of February 16, 1804, Decatur and 74 volunteers, including eight Marines led by Sgt. Solomon Wren (and Navy Lt. James Lawrence and Midshipman Thomas Macdonough, both of whom would survive to win glory in the War of 1812) stole into the harbor in a captured 70-ton Tripolitan ketch, which they had renamed *Intrepid*.

The daring venture had been carefully planned and rehearsed. A half-dozen men were dressed as Maltese; the rest kept out of sight. After announcing that they had lost their anchors in the last gale, the "Maltese" received permission to tie up alongside *Philadelphia* in the dark. Once in position, Decatur shouted "Board!" and his men dashed forward with a yell. They quickly killed or captured all the enemy aboard *Philadelphia*, except two who fled and raised the alarm. The Americans hoisted combustibles aboard and set the ship afire. The whole operation took about 20 minutes. The flames brought the shore batteries into action; but the ketch escaped to the harbor's edge, where she was taken in tow by the brig *Siren*. Not a man was hurt. British Admiral Horatio Nelson, then blockading the French fleet across the Mediterranean at Toulon, called it "the most bold and daring act of the age."[4]

Private Ray wrote that at 11 P.M. on the night of Decatur's deed there was tumult and confusion in the town and castle and that he hoped that the Americans had landed to liberate them. But the next morning their captors beat them and spat on them. Their workload was increased and their bread withheld. The prisoners were put to work trying, without success, to free the fire-gutted hulk of the frigate from the rocks onto which it had drifted.

On July 28, Commodore Preble's squadron appeared again off Tripoli. At noon on August 3, when the winds shifted, Preble sent in his gunboats. They attacked through a shower of grapeshot in two divisions headed by Navy Lt. Richard Somers and

Decatur. *Constitution* bombarded the castle at longer range. The Marines of *Constitution* handled six long 26-pounders on the spar deck, and were later commended for their gunnery.

At 2:45, the gunboats hurled shells into the town and the small-craft fleet in the harbor. The hand-to-hand fighting in the small boats was epic, and the Marines were in the middle in it. Lt. John Trippe, USN, boarded a larger Tripolitan boat with a midshipman and nine men who included several Marines. The odds were 36 to 11 against the Americans. As Trippe fought hand-to-hand with one enemy, another aimed a blow at him from behind; Marine Sgt. John Meredith bayoneted the second Tripolitan. The small party of Americans cleared the deck, killed 14 of the enemy and took the boat. Trippe received 11 saber wounds; one sailor and two Marines were also wounded.

Decatur and a boarding party captured an enemy boat after a vicious battle. Leaving some men aboard the prize, Decatur and his nine remaining men chased another enemy vessel. When they closed, the 10 Americans and 24 of the enemy struggled hand-to-hand. Decatur's Sergeant of Marines Solomon Wren was wounded. The enemy boat surrendered only after 21 of her men were killed. At 4:30, the gunboats retired under *Constitution's* covering fire.

During that summer, Preble hammered away at Tripoli's shipping and fortifications. The gunboats, many of which had Marines aboard, made five raids into the harbor. Sergeant Meredith and Pvt. Nathanial Holmes were killed attacking the shore batteries on August 7. On September 3, Lieutenant Somers and a volunteer crew took *Intrepid*, loaded with explosives, and tried to blow up the enemy's gunboats nestled under the castle's walls. *Intrepid* exploded prematurely and all aboard were killed.

Shortly afterwards, Commodore Samuel Barron arrived to take over the squadron from Preble. Although there had been much heroism, Preble had not won a decision. Tripoli's offers to settle the affair by ransoming Ray and his fellows at a bargain price were stubbornly and repeatedly rejected.

The captured Americans now endured a period of hunger. Food was short in Tripoli, and the American blockade cut off supplies. By December, even bread was denied the prisoners for days at a time. On December 10, the men refused to fall out for work; the Pasha ordered them to be given bread, and the crisis passed. During the winter months, the American squadron disappeared to safer waters. In the spring of 1805 it returned and an expedition was organized to overthrow the Pasha and seat his brother on the throne.

This expedition brought on the scene the greatest Marine hero of the Tripolitan war, a very young lieutenant from the Blue Ridge Mountains, Presley Neville O'Bannon. He participated in the war's final campaign, one fought overland and of such grandiose concept that it would sound like a wild-eyed dream if it had not come within inches of success.

The dream was not O'Bannon's but that of a Revolutionary Army captain, William Eaton. Eaton was an independent, fearless, fiery-tempered man, a graduate of Dartmouth College and a schoolteacher who had served since 1797 as consul at Tunis. Early in the war, Eaton and the American consul at Tripoli, James L. Cathcart (a former sailor who had been a slave in Algiers for 10 years), cooked up a scheme to overthrow Tripoli's Pasha, who had so brazenly challenged the United States. The Pasha, Yusuf Karamanli, had won the throne by murdering his oldest brother and banishing his second brother, Hamet. Eaton and Cathcart thought they could rally a native force around Hamet and dethrone Yusuf.

President Jefferson and Congress had their doubts about the whole idea, but they permitted Eaton to try. Eaton, now a "naval agent" to the Barbary states, set out for Egypt to persuade Hamet to lead an expedition against his brother. Eaton sailed for Alexandria in November, 1804, aboard the swift 16-gun brig *Argus*; her captain, Lt. Isaac Hull, would later win fame in the War of 1812. Commanding *Argus'* Marine detachment was Lieutenant O'Bannon.

O'Bannon, who had joined the Marines three years earlier at age seventeen, was now on his second tour in the Mediterranean. On November 29, he landed at Alexandria with Eaton and a sergeant and six privates of Marines. Hamet was not there. Eaton, O'Bannon and a party of 18 men went up the Nile to Cairo, searching for him. Finally, in February 1805, they arranged a meeting in the desert. Face to face with Eaton's fervor, Hamet agreed to the scheme. On the morning of March 8, they set out with 500 men and 107 camels to conquer Tripoli by marching across the desert along the route that years later would be followed by the mechanized armies of Montgomery and Rommel.

Eaton's expedition became a nightmare. The native drivers mutinied repeatedly; Eaton had to bribe them to stay with the party. He depended on O'Bannon and his handful of Marines to keep discipline. At one point, the camel drivers deserted and the Arab warriors threatened to leave. Eaton dissuaded them by ordering the Marines to seize the food supply and facing the rebels with starvation in the desert. They marched on. The rabble army attracted many local tribesmen and grew to 1,200, including 700 fighting men. Then, Hamet himself seized the provisions and deserted. On that and many another occasion, he was brought around by Eaton's persuasiveness and O'Bannon's cool courage.

On April 15, they arrived at Bomba, where they were supposed to rendezvous with *Argus* and *Hornet*. They had marched with almost no food and water for days. They found the harbor empty. But that night, the ships, which had sailed away the day before, spotted Eaton's signal fires and returned. Eaton's column rested at Bomba for a week and then pressed on.

At the seaport of Derna, 600 miles from Eaton's starting point and about halfway to Tripoli, *Argus* was to meet the expedition again with supplies and, Eaton hoped, reinforcements. Before leaving Alexandria, he had written the Secretary of the Navy requesting 100 Marines.

On April 25, Eaton's army camped on a hill overlooking Derna; and the following day, Eaton sent a flag of truce. The governor, with 800 men eager to fight the invaders, sent back a message: "My head or yours!"

Argus, *Hornet* and *Nautilus* arrived, and on the morning of April 27 the little squadron bombarded Derna. At two o'clock, Eaton ordered a general attack. In the center, O'Bannon led the Marines, 36 Greeks, 24 cannoneers with one gun, and a few Arabs. O'Bannon's attack was stopped cold and the gun knocked out of action when the gunners shot away their rammer. Eaton rushed up his reserve to assist the Marine lieutenant. Together, they pressed into the city. Eaton was shot through the left wrist. O'Bannon and his Marines and Midshipman George Mann, USN, led the charge with the bayonet, racing through the city to the harbor fort in a shower of bullets. They advanced so swiftly that they found the fort's guns loaded and even primed. They turned them on the castle; and at 3:30, O'Bannon raised the American flag over the fort—the first time the Stars and Stripes had been raised in battle in the Eastern Hemisphere.

The capture of the fort ended the fight. Hamet took the castle, the city surrendered and Hamet's horsemen pursued the fleeing defenders into the hills.

Among the casualties were three of the six Marine privates. One was wounded, Pvt. John Whitten was killed and Pvt. Edward Steward died later of his wounds.

Eaton organized the defense of the city. On May 13, Yusuf's forces from Tripoli struck. It required a six-hour struggle in the streets, during which Hamet was nearly captured, to throw back the counterattack. The enemy laid siege to the city. Almost daily skirmishes followed, and on June 10 Yusuf's soldiers attacked again. This time, Hamet led the troops and, after a four-and-a-half-hour battle, totally defeated his brother's men.

The very next day *Constitution* arrived in the harbor with the news that the Americans had made peace with the Pasha of Tripoli. Yusuf, threatened by Eaton's and O'Bannon's approach, had sued for peace. The State Department's agent Tobias Lear had agreed to a treaty that provided a $60,000 ransom for the captives from *Philadelphia*. The prisoners had already been freed on June 3, and the treaty signed on the 10th, the very day Yusuf's troops had been decisively beaten. With the American Navy off Tripoli in force and Eaton's army advancing to overthrow the frightened Pasha, the ransom-bought end of the war was disgraceful.

When released, Marine Lieutenant Osborne went aboard *President* with Bainbridge and reached the United States on August 6. Private Ray returned on the frigate *Essex*. Back in the United States, Ray left the Corps and tried storekeeping in Essex County in northern New York state. His enterprise failed; he then established the first newspaper in the county, but it failed also. During the War of 1812, Ray served with state troops at Plattsburgh, and afterwards he worked in several northern New York state towns as a druggist, local editor and justice of the peace. He died at Auburn, New York, in 1827, a son of misfortune whose highest adventure was his experience as a Marine on the shores of Tripoli.

Eaton was ordered to evacuate Derna, and on June 12, Marines were put ashore to cover the withdrawal. Eaton, O'Bannon and the Marines were the last to leave. The men who had made up Eaton's army woke to find themselves deserted; they fled the city. Hamet was taken to safety at Syracuse. Eaton and O'Bannon went home heroes.

Eaton recommended George Farquhar, a young English adventurer who had accompanied him, for the highest reward he could think of—a commission in the U.S. Marine Corps. And Eaton praised O'Bannon as an "intrepid, judicious and enterprising officer." Historians credit the heroism of O'Bannon and his Marines on the desert march and in the assault on Derna for making possible what success the expedition did win.

Legend has it that O'Bannon was given Hamet's jeweled sword with its 32$\frac{1}{8}$-inch blade and that it was the model for the "Mameluke sword" that Marine officers still carry today. The state of Virginia presented O'Bannon a gold sword. But the Marine Corps gave him neither a promotion nor a brevet (an honorary raise in rank); and on March 6, 1807, Lieutenant O'Bannon resigned from the Corps. He went west to Kentucky, married and settled down into obscurity. When he died, he was buried in a small cemetery at Russellville, Logan County, in western Kentucky. In 1920, his body was removed to Frankfort, the state capital.

The Navy's show of force and Tobias Lear's treaty, which included provisions that no future tribute would be paid and captives would be treated as prisoners of war rather than as slaves, quieted the Barbary states for a time. But they resumed their depredations during the War of 1812; and despite their defeats by Stephen Decatur's squadron in 1815, they were not completely subdued until France occupied Algeria in 1830.

The war with Tripoli had ended without honor for the United States. The Navy had proved unable to defeat the weakest of the Barbary powers; the United States had rescued its imprisoned sailors and Marines by ransoming them. But the war did demonstrate that the United States would fight, and it served as a training ground for young naval officers who in a few years would be the captains in the greater struggle with Great Britain. A professional service was begun; men were tested under fire, and this war, like all American wars, produced a few Marine heroes.

4
The War of 1812
at Sea

The War of 1812 was an affair of courtesies and atrocities, chivalrous duels and wanton raids, heroism and trafficking with the enemy. It was a war in which Englishmen fought the descendants of Englishmen only one generation after American independence.

The United States had two reasons for going to war on June 18, 1812. Americans were itching to expand; some still dreamt of bringing Canada into the Union, and others hoped to grab fertile lands to the south. They also wanted to stop the impressment of American sailors whom the British Navy claimed were British-born subjects of the king. Thousands of Americans had been seized on the seas. On June 21, 1807, three American seamen were actually taken by force from the hapless U.S. Navy frigate *Chesapeake.*

Expansion was by far the stronger reason behind the war. Unlike the naval wars with France and Tripoli, which were supported most vigorously on the Atlantic seaboard, the War of 1812 was most popular among inland people: The maritime sections did not want their growing ocean trade interrupted by a major naval war. Congress authorized enlarging the regular Army by 25,000 men but empowered the Navy only to repair three frigates. A proposal was made to build a strong Navy with 25 ships-of-the-line (heavy warships with two or three gun decks) and 40 frigates (faster, lighter ships with only one gun deck); it lost by three votes. The expansionists were in the saddle, preparing for a land war.

When the United States declared war, England was busy fighting Napoleon. To those who wanted to stretch American borders, it seemed like a good moment to strike. Only after Napoleon's temporary exile to Elba in April 1814 could Great

Britain finally turn her full attention to the United States. Then came the climactic battles at Washington and Baltimore and on Lake Champlain in the north, and at New Orleans in the south. By that time the United States had acquired enough strength and skill to win the last three encounters and settle the war at a standoff.

But in 1812 the United States was unprepared to fight. Its military leadership was incompetent, its militia undependable. The United States was without a single ship-of-the-line, and had only three frigates rated at 44 guns, three with 38 guns, *Essex* with 32 and *Adams* with 28. It had only 16 vessels with 21 guns or more. In contrast, the British, when their fleet was freed from the Napoleonic conflict in 1814, had 219 huge ships-of-the-line and 296 swift frigates. Even in early 1813, the British sent against the United States a fleet headed by 16 ships-of-the-line.

President Jefferson had put his faith in gunboats. He felt they were ideal for a people whose prime military interest was self-defense and could not in any case match the British Navy. At the beginning of the war with Great Britain, the United States still had more than 250 of Jefferson's gunboats. Each was 71 feet long and carried two officers, 16 sailors and 5 Marines. The gunboats were to prove worthless.

Fortunately, each of the young nation's three 44-gun frigates, although it could never tackle a ship-of-the-line, was superior to any British frigate. (As they came to learn this, the British ordered their frigate commanders to fight the American frigates only on a two-to-one basis.) Even more fortunately, the U.S. Navy was skillful and aggressive from the beginning. Unlike the untried Army, the Navy, as a result of the French and Barbary wars, had the core of a professional service with esprit de corps; and early in this war it won a series of dramatic victories.

Those victories hung on a thread. They only came about because two Navy captains went to Washington and fought the Navy's case. They were the brilliant, red-headed Charles Stewart and William Bainbridge, who had commanded *Philadelphia* and been captured at Tripoli. They urged Secretary of the Navy Paul Hamilton to get more ships for the Navy and give it a chance to sail against the British. The Navy's opponents argued that it was foolhardy to risk the tiny U.S. fleet in ship-to-ship combat. President Madison, pressed by the two determined captains, finally agreed on a compromise: the American frigates could go out on one cruise as an experiment. As a result, *Constitution* met *Guerriere* and *United States* met *Macedonian.*

One point the two captains made in arguing the Navy's ability to fight the British was that American frigates carried United States Marines, many of whom were backwoodsmen— among the best marksmen in the world. Posted high in the rigging to pick off the officers and gunners on an enemy's decks, their fire was deadly.

At the start of the war, according to Theodore Roosevelt's history of the conflict, the Marine Corps had 42 officers and 1,523 men, less than either its authorized strength (46 officers and 1,823 men) or the number that would soon be needed. The Corps was never able to solve its recruiting problem during the war. Although it offered the attraction of prize money for lucky sea-going Marines, it was still not permitted to offer enlistment bonuses as was the Army. It was a national service, and many men preferred to join their state militia. And the Corps had little reputation. By September 1812, it had only 37 officers and 1,294 enlisted men.

Lt. Col. Franklin Wharton, a heavy-jowled, wealthy, forty-five-year-old Philadelphian, had succeeded William Burrows as Commandant of the Marine Corps in 1804. President Jefferson appointed him as a matter of seniority. Wharton had served as commander of the Marine detachment on *United States* in the French war. He was most interested in discipline, neatness and the Marine Band. When the rum ration was increased in 1805, he prudently ordered it diluted and issued twice a day to reduce drunkenness; that did not increase his popularity. He was devoted to the Corps and as the wealthiest Marine of his era, spent his own funds on it. But the War of 1812 would bring him personal disgrace.

The first Marines to see action were the 51 aboard *Constitution,* which on the cloudy afternoon of August 19, 1812, was sailing 750 miles east of Boston. She had left that port without orders 17 days before, to avoid being blockaded. Now a sail was sighted, and *Constitution's* captain, Isaac Hull, gave chase.

At about 5 o'clock, the pudgy Hull, one of the Navy's most

experienced and able officers, opened fire on the frigate *Guerriere*. The two ships fought at close range, exchanging broadside for broadside. American gunnery proved superior, and *Guerriere's* mizzenmast (third mast) was shot away as Hull twice crossed the enemy's bow.

Despite the heavy seas, the Marines' musket fire was highly effective. The British captain, James Dacres, was hit. When the ships locked momentarily, both commanders prepared boarding parties. Marine Lt. William S. Bush rallied *Constitution's* boarders and leapt onto the rail. Shot through the head by a British Marine, he fell back dead on *Constitution's* deck.

After the ships separated, *Guerriere's* two other masts went over the side; and she lay rolling wildly, a defenseless hulk. When *Constitution* reached Boston on August 30, news of the victory spread quickly; the nation cheered. A British warship had been outsailed, outfought and conquered.

As the sea duels continued, the American frigates won spectacular victories. But soon the British blockade of the Atlantic coast bottled up most of the American warships, and the British policy of fighting U.S. frigates not ship for ship but strength for strength turned the tide in Britain's favor.

Whenever ships fought at close range, the Marines played a vital role. On December 29, *Constitution*, Bainbridge now in command, met *Java* off Brazil. The swifter *Java*, commanded by James Lambert, overtook *Constitution*. Bainbridge handled his ship brilliantly. *Constitution* shot away *Java's* bowsprit and jibboom. The ships closed, and the Americans in the tops did heavy damage. Commanded by 1st Lt. John Contee and 2d Lt. William H. Freeman, the Marines proved they were sharpshooters that afternoon. Lambert ordered boarders readied and tried to lead them with cutlass in hand. A Marine's bullet wounded him mortally. The Americans' small-arms fire broke the attempt to board *Constitution*. The slaughter on *Java's* open decks was dreadful. Under the Americans' cool and precise gunnery, *Java's* foremast went. Thinking the enemy had struck their colors, Bainbridge ceased fire; then *Java's* mainmast fell, leaving the ship a hulk. *Java* surrendered. The Americans suffered 12 killed (including Marine Thomas Hanson) and 22 wounded (including Marines Anthony Reaver, Michael Chesly and John Elwell); the British had 48 killed and 102 wounded.

This battle had an unexpected consequence. *Constitution*

had planned to rendezvous with *Essex*, commanded by David Porter, and together to wreak havoc in the British sea lanes to the Indies. The damage done by *Java* wiped out that possibility, and Porter went on to adventures of his own—a tale that has a special place in the Marine Corps story.

On June 1, 1813, *Chesapeake* met *Shannon* outside Boston harbor. *Shannon*, one of two British frigates blockading Boston, was momentarily alone on station when Capt. James Lawrence decided—recklessly, as it proved—to take out *Chesapeake* and do battle. Except for the 44 Marines aboard, his crew was inexperienced and untried.

The fight began with broadside against broadside at close range as the ships raced along together. Then a grenade from *Shannon* blew up an arms chest on *Chesapeake's* quarterdeck. *Shannon's* Capt. Philip Broke immediately ordered the ships lashed together and called for boarders. Lawrence, who had been second in command to Decatur when *Intrepid* blew up the captured *Philadelphia*, was shot through the body by a British Marine. Carried below fatally wounded, he gave his famous order: "Don't give up the ship!"

Broke himself led the boarders onto *Chesapeake's* quarterdeck and along the gangways. The green American crew panicked. Only the remaining Marines and a handful of sailors held fast and rallied on the forecastle. The British came at them. The Marines in the tops who tried to stop them were silenced by one of *Shannon's* guns and by her topmen, who ran along the yards into *Chesapeake's* rigging, killed their opponents and fired on the defenders below. Broke cut down one man and then was badly wounded by a cutlass stroke to his head. The Marines fought at bay with clubbed muskets. For an instant their defense was so stubborn that the battle hung in the balance; but the British, now reinforced, stormed forward again and cut down the defenders to the last man.

Five minutes after Broke had set foot on *Chesapeake*, the bloodbath was over. In a fight that lasted just 15 minutes, almost half of *Chesapeake's* crew were casualties; most of the others had fled below decks. Of the Marines, 14, including 1st Lt. James Broom and Cpl. William Dixon, were dead and 18, including Sergeants Twin and Harris, were wounded. Only one corporal and nine privates remained unscathed.

A year later, a sea duel occurred in which Marines (according to some accounts they were seamen serving as Marines) had better luck in repelling boarders and moving to the attack themselves. The brand-new sloop of war *Wasp* had run the blockade and was seizing British merchant prizes in the very mouth of the English Channel. Before dawn on June 28, 1814, she met the British brig-sloop *Reindeer*. The two captains, *Wasp's* Master Commandant Johnston Blakely and *Reindeer's* Capt. William Manners, jockeyed for hours in a skillful display of sailing. *Reindeer* opened fire first; and for ten minutes, the two ships sailed 20 yards apart, firing into each other. *Wasp's* Marines commanded by Sgt. William D. Barnes picked off the British officers; Manners, though shot in both thighs, called for boarders and pulled himself into the rigging to lead them. Two more balls from *Wasp's* maintop struck him in the head, killing him.

Blakely had summoned his 16 Marines to the point at which the two ships touched. The Americans and British hacked at each other through the portholes; and when Manners fell, Blakely gave the command to board. Shouting, the Americans swarmed onto *Reindeer*. There was a brief bloody struggle, and the British were driven below decks or killed.

These sea fights—*Constitution* vs. *Guerriere, Constitution* vs. *Java, Chesapeake* vs. *Shannon* and *Wasp* vs. *Reindeer*—were four in which Marines played a major role. Several others in which Marines fought, ironically enough, occurred after peace had been signed but before the word could reach the scattered ships at sea. Marine Lt. Levi Twiggs distinguished himself when *President*, Decatur in command, beat *Endymion* on January 15, 1815, off New York. Twiggs would die in battle 31 years later—still a Marine. On February 20, *Constitution*, now commanded by Charles Stewart, beat the two smaller corvettes *Cyane* and *Levant* in a 40-minute battle off Portugal. *Constitution's* 44 Marines, commanded by Capt. Archibald Henderson, were constantly engaged; two were killed and three wounded. Because of the Marines' accurate fire, the dead on both British ships exceeded the wounded. Henderson received special mention in the official report of that action. More would be heard of him.

5
Caught
Shorthanded

While none of the ocean battles between single ships could be called decisive, the campaigns on Lake Erie and Lake Champlain shaped the outcome of the War of 1812. To fight on the lakes, Marines had to be recruited out of the frontier wilderness and soldiers converted into "acting marines."

When the war started in June 1812, the only Marines on Lake Ontario were the few on the brig *Oneida.* On November 2, 60 more under Capt. Richard Smith arrived from New York, and by year's end there were 100 Marines on the lake. The following year, Capt. Robert D. Wainwright, who later would become a special Marine Corps hero, brought 125 more Marines to Sackets Harbor at the eastern end of the lake. On May 27, 1813, the Americans assaulted and took Fort George on the Canadian side of the Niagara River. The Marines helped pursue the enemy.

The struggle for Lake Ontario settled down to a seesaw series of encounters with neither side willing to risk a decision. Fortunately, this northern front in the spring of 1813 gained a fighting naval commander: Oliver Hazard Perry, then twenty eight years old. Perry had a difficult time building ships on Lake Erie and gathering men for them. His sole Marine officer was Lt. John Brooks, the handsome son of the governor of Massachusetts. To his force of 12 Marines, Brooks added Pennsylvania and Kentucky woodsmen in fringed hunting jackets; they served as Marines on Perry's flagship *Lawrence.*

At dawn on Friday, September 10, Perry brought out his superior little fleet. The British approached his squadron in tight formation; and 15 minutes before noon, their flagship *Detroit* fired the first shot. For 20 minutes, Perry's flagship took violent punishment. Its sand-strewn decks ran with blood. Of the 102

[For the location of places in this section see map No. 1 in the map section.—*Au.*]

men aboard who were fit for duty, 83 were killed or wounded. A cannon ball mortally wounded Lieutenant Brooks.

Young Perry survived and transferred to fight from *Niagara*. A half hour later, the British struck their flag. The battle was won. In addition to Brooks, Marine Cpl. Philip Sharbley and Pvts. Jesse Harland and Abner Williams had been killed.

The battle ended British and Indian attacks on the western frontier and opened the Northwest to American expansion. The Americans recaptured Detroit and kept control of Lake Erie.

Exactly a year and a day after Perry's victory came the crucial battle of the War of 1812. Napoleon had been defeated on the Continent and had abdicated on April 11, 1814; England could now turn her attention to the impudent United States. Regulars from the Duke of Wellington's army, 28,000 strong, were shipped to Canada.

The British repeated their plan of the Revolutionary War: to slice down the Lake Champlain–Hudson River valley and split the Americans in two. But they failed to reckon with thirty-one-year-old Thomas Macdonough. As a midshipman, he had helped Decatur fire *Philadelphia* at Tripoli and had been one of the last to leave the burning frigate.

On Lake Champlain, Macdonough had no men from the Marine Corps. Some 200 infantrymen served as marines; their prime duty was to repel any enemy attempts to board Macdonough's ships. On Sunday, September 11, 1814, the decisive battle of Lake Champlain was won. Casualties on both sides were heavy. Among the Americans, seven of the acting marines were killed and 10 wounded. But the great invasion by the flower of Wellington's army was defeated. Word of the American victory reached London on October 21. Two weeks later, Wellington himself was offered the command in America. He declined on November 9 and urged that peace be signed. Six weeks later it was.

6
Courage and Disgrace

That Sunday, September 11, 1814, marked high tide for the British. While on Lake Champlain they were poised to invade the United States from the north, on the Atlantic coast, another expeditionary force, having burned Washington, sailed to attack Baltimore. But by Wednesday night, the Americans had taken the heart out of the enemy.

The attack on Baltimore was preceded by a 16-month campaign, under the command of Sir George Cockburn, to blockade the east coast of the United States. Cockburn's goal was to choke off America's shipping; and in the spring of 1813, he launched a series of swift raids up Chesapeake Bay. They were so frightening that the Secretary of the Navy ordered Commandant Wharton to raise a battalion of Marines to help meet the danger.

The 38-gun American frigate *Constellation* was trapped in the Chesapeake by the British blockade. Charles Stewart, her commander, anchored near Norfolk and placed some of his ship's guns on Craney Island; the British would have to pass them if they tried to take the frigate. Late in June, Cockburn was ready to make the attempt. On the 20th, his squadron, headed by three 74-gun ships-of-the-line, paraded off Craney Island. The determined Americans had a battery of 18-pounders manned by *Constellation's* 100 sailors and 50 Marines under Lt. Henry B. Breckinridge.

The British landed on the mainland and tried to flank the battery on the island. The sailors and Marines shifted their guns and stopped the landing attempt. A second assault was aimed directly at the American strongpoint on the island by 1,500 British sailors and Marines in a flotilla of barges. American

[For the location of places in this section see map No. 1 in the map section.—*Au.*]

71

gunnery sank three barges, and the British failed to put their force ashore. By midmorning they had lost 91 men and given up the effort. The battle of Craney Island was won; *Constellation* was saved.

The year 1814 brought, in a very real sense, a new war. England, freed from the scourge of Napoleon, mounted three expeditions: one down Lake Champlain, another against New Orleans and the third at the American homeland directly from the Atlantic. The targets of the mass of British ships that assembled in the Chesapeake: Washington and Baltimore.

The naval defense of the bay was assigned to Joshua Barney, a tough fifty-four-year-old veteran of the Revolution. His force consisted mainly of barges, with a few sloops and schooners. He could do little more than attack individual British ships whenever given the chance and retire to shallow water when things grew too hot.

After a number of skirmishes during June, Barney was blockaded up the Patuxent River. A few regulars and Marines under Marine Capt. Samuel Miller cooperated with Barney from the shore. On June 26, this combined force drove off the two frigates that had kept the American "fleet" bottled up; and Barney brought his small, persistent command back into the bay. The Marines fought well, and a Court of Enquiry later called Captain Miller "cool, collected and intrepid . . . brave, vigilant, judicious and enterprising."

The British buildup in the Chesapeake finally aroused President Madison to establish an organization under Brig. Gen. Henry Winder that could, if necessary, defend Washington. By mid-August, when a British expeditionary force led by Maj. Gen. Robert Ross and Vice Adm. Sir Alexander Cochrane reached Chesapeake Bay, some 4,000 men were on hand to invade the United States.

Barney could not face this strength. His 503 Marines and sailors retreated again to the Patuxent River, according to plan. The British sent an approximately equal force in after him. The two flotillas locked horns, and both sides suffered severely before the British withdrew to their ships. That was the first round.

The second came when Captain Miller joined Barney again with three artillery pieces and 100 Marines from Washington.

They attempted a joint operation like the one that had been successful in June. But this time, although the Marines and the Army troops with them exhausted their ammunition, Barney could not break out. He was trapped.

The British, undecided about whether to attack Washington or Baltimore, chose to follow Barney up the Patuxent, wipe him out and keep the American army uncertain about their final objective until it would be too late. They entered the Patuxent on August 17. Barney retreated upriver as far as he could and then prepared to fight on land. On Friday, August 19, the British led by Maj. Gen. Ross landed unopposed at the head of navigation at Benedict, Maryland. As they advanced, Barney's men blew up their own boats.

The British started marching the 40 miles to Washington. Barney with 400 of his men joined Brig. Gen. Winder early Monday afternoon, August 22. He found that Captain Miller had arrived from Washington on Sunday noon with 110 Marines and five pieces of artillery. Miller reported his men for duty with Barney.

Tuesday afternoon, Ross' advance guard began to probe the American outposts. Winder's command retreated to the capital, leaving militia troops to guard the road at Bladensburg, four miles northeast of Washington, where a bridge crossed the Eastern Branch of the Potomac. Barney's men, including the Marines, spent the night in the Marine Barracks in panic-stricken Washington.

On Wednesday morning, the British army could be heard nearing Bladensburg. Its route of march was finally committed. Winder marched quickly out of Washington to support the militiamen he had posted and the rest of the assembling army. Barney was told to stay behind and use his guns to guard Washington's Eastern Branch Bridge (now the John Philip Sousa Bridge). With great reluctance, he left most of his flotilla men and the Marines at the barracks and positioned his battery. At the bridge he met President Madison, stormed over to him and had his assignment changed. The bridge was blown up; and Barney, his sailors and Marines took their guns to the Battle of Bladensburg.

The Americans had drawn up three lines deep along heights on the Washington side of the river, across from Bladensburg.

Just as the battle was beginning, Barney reached the Maryland–District of Columbia line. It was nearly 100 degrees under the August sun. Ordering his men up "in a trot," Barney placed his battery on a rise in the center, commanding the bridge and the road along which the British would come. To his right stretched 114 Marines and then the 370 flotilla men, all serving as infantry. Barney supervised the battery; Miller and Marine Capt. Alexander Sevier, the infantry.

Barney's five guns were zeroed in on the road. As the British crossed the bridge, they were met by the sailors' accurate fire: Gunnery on dry land was a lot easier than firing from a ship's pitching deck. Barney's gunners, with well-aimed 18-pound shot, destroyed the first enemy company to cross. Twice again the British tried to advance up the fire-swept road over their comrades' bodies and were hurled back by the gunners. Then the enemy extended through the fields to the left and moved forward until they met the sailors and Marines. Miller used his three 12-pounders effectively; the Americans charged—the Marines with bayonets, the sailors with cutlasses—and broke the men of the 4th and 85th Regiments and chased them into a ravine.

But the American militia could not stand against the British regulars. By now Barney was on foot, his horse having been killed. Miller went down in "a shower of musket-balls," badly wounded in the arm and out of action. Marine Lt. Benjamin Richardson, commanding the right flank, went to help him. Most of the American army had retreated. Ross, whose men had been pressed back almost to the river's edge by the sailors and Marines, sent his troops wide; the men of the 44th Regiment forded the river. Barney turned his guns to meet them, but the British fired rockets to terrify the green civilian troops and cut through the remaining militia. The second brigade crossed the river and overwhelmed the Americans.

The field and road in front of Barney's men were strewn with dead British soldiers and horses, but the Americans were surrounded. Barney was wounded severely in the thigh. His men stood by their guns. Those serving as infantrymen stepped in to replace fallen gunners. Some were bayoneted with fuses still in their hands. Barney gave the order to retreat; and the sailors and Marines, now standing alone against the enemy, retired in order, leaving most of their dead and wounded. Both Barney and Miller were captured.

That evening, the British marched unopposed into Washington. Government officials, the Army and even the Commandant of the Marine Corps had fled.

Wharton's flight from the city scandalized the Marine Corps. He had seen the doctors dress Captain Sevier's wound and then, with Capt. John Crabb, had gone to the Marine Barracks. He led the barracks guard to the Navy Yard, and at sunset he and Crabb took a small boat to Georgetown and went by wagon to Frederick, Maryland. Ross ordered the Marine barracks burned and then countermanded the order when told the fire would endanger the neighborhood. Wharton wrote later, "While the enemy was in the city, I was with the paymaster at Fredricktown. . . . the events of the past days seem as a bad dream."[5] He stayed there until the British went back to their ships.

The defense of Washington had been a shameful affair. There had been little preparation to hold the city. And when the British finally came, there was more running than fighting. The battle became known as "the Bladensburg races." But Barney's sailors and the Marines had given a superb account of themselves. Despite the numbers involved, American casualties were estimated at only 10 to 12 killed and 40 wounded; the Marines alone had 8 killed and 14 wounded.

Miller and Sevier were breveted majors after the battle. "Both sailors and marines did nobly," wrote Theodore Roosevelt in his history of the war, "inflicting most of the loss the British suffered."[6] Maj. Gen. Ross wrote the next day of Barney, "Had half your army been composed of such men as your commodore commanded, with the advantage you had in choosing your position, we should never have got to your city."[7]

After two nights in Washington, during which the British burned most of the public buildings, Ross began his withdrawal; and by August 29 he was loading his transports. That same day, Alexandria, Virginia, surrendered to a second British squadron that had struggled up the Potomac. On their way back downstream, the British had to duel 13 guns manned by sailors and Marines on the bluff at White House, Virginia.

On that fateful Sunday, September 11, while Macdonough

was triumphing on Lake Champlain, Ross' army showed up in front of Baltimore. Its arrival at the Patapsco River was no surprise. Ten thousand men had gathered to build earthworks and defend the city, the nation's third largest. Marines rushed in. One hundred and seventy arrived from Newcastle with Commodore John Rodgers. Commodore David Porter brought a detachment from New York, including some from the former *Essex*. Capt. Alfred Grayson commanded the Baltimore detachment. A thousand sailors and Marines were formed into a brigade under Rodgers' command. Commodore Oliver Hazard Perry led one of the brigade's two regiments, which by the time the British attacked included the Marines from Bladensburg under Capt. Samuel Bacon. The 51 Marines from *Guerriere* served under Lt. Joseph L. Kuhn and Lt. John Harris, a future Commandant of the Corps. They were posted across the river's Northwest Branch from Fort McHenry, where Patterson Park is today.

Before dawn on Monday, September 12, the British landed at North Point, 14 miles from the city. The defenders were pushed back nearly 10 miles but not broken. Ross rode forward supervising the British advance. A militiaman's bullet struck him in the chest. His death stalled the British; the spark of leadership had been extinguished. The army halted and waited for the navy to turn the American flank. For 24 hours, the ships bombarded Fort McHenry. Bur when dawn came the huge Star-Spangled Banner still waved above the fort, and Baltimore was safe. The British army pulled back to its ships on Wednesday, and the terrifying raids in Chesapeake Bay were over. On two of three fronts the invaders had been stopped.

7
Florida and
New Orleans

On September 11, 1814 (that Sunday again), a party of Marines from the detachment at New Orleans commanded by Maj. Daniel Carmick sailed aboard the schooner *Carolina* to attack the settlement of pirates at Barataria Bay on the western side of the Mississippi delta. The pirates, led by the infamous brothers Jean and Pierre Lafitte, had been urged by the British to fight against the Americans. The pirates had delayed giving the British an answer and had reported the offer to the authorities at New Orleans. Despite this remarkable loyalty, Master Commandant Daniel T. Patterson, commanding the New Orleans Naval Station, mounted the expedition against them.

On September 16, *Carolina*, seven gunboats, and a tender stood off Grand Terre Island from which the "gentry of the coast" conducted their smuggling, piracy and slave trade. Eight hundred pirates in ten ships lined up for battle. Patterson attacked; the pirates fled. The Marines and the men from the 44th U.S. Infantry landed and destroyed the pirate stronghold. This was one small Gulf Coast prelude to the great conflict of arms to come.

Spain, hoping to secure her hold on the Floridas, had signed the Treaty of San Lorenzo (Pinckney's Treaty) with the United States in 1795. It set the northern boundary between Spanish West Florida and the United States along the 31st Parallel and gave the United States the right to deposit goods at New Orleans. Five years later, Spain had turned over to France the vast Louisiana Territory; and in 1803, President Jefferson had purchased it from Napoleon, who needed the cash.

Early in 1804, Captain Carmick took 105 Marines to reinforce the new naval station at New Orleans. Carmick had begun his Marine career in 1798 as captain of the detachment on *Ganges*, the first of the new Navy's ships to get to sea, and had led the Marines in the cutting out of *Sandwich* during the naval war with the French. When the Marine detachment at New Orleans was enlarged in 1807 and 1808, Carmick, who had been replaced by Lt. Samuel Baldwin, returned to command it. He came back to fight and die there.

American desire to possess the warm and fertile Gulf lands was almost irresistible; and long before war was declared officially in Washington, it was a fact in East Florida—as it was in the Northwest (the Battle of Tippecanoe had been fought in Ohio on November 7, 1811). One southern trouble center was Amelia Island, part of the Atlantic coastline at the mouth of the St. Mary's River, which divided American Georgia from Spanish East Florida. On the excuse that the island was a smugglers' den, Navy ships with Marines aboard had aided a force of armed Georgia "patriots" that seized the island on March 17, 1812. The Spanish commander immediately surrendered, and the Army and a Marine detachment under Capt. John Williams, a forty-six-year-old Virginian, went ashore the next day. Williams' 35 Marines occupied the island; and the Georgians and Army "volunteers" under Lt. Col. Thomas A. Smith, USA, marched to St. Augustine. The Marines convoyed wagon trains from Davis Creek (now Bayard) to the advanced positions. Commandant Wharton ordered Williams to withdraw from this "adventure"; but the captain wrote, "If I evacuate this post all supplies would be immediately cut off from Colonel Smith." During the summer, the Americans pulled back to the line of the St. John's River in East Florida. Davis Creek became an advanced position.

On September 12, Captain Williams led a party of about 20 Marines and volunteers from Milledgeville, Georgia, to escort a wagon train. At dusk they entered Twelve Mile Swamp, 12 miles from St. John's. Indians and Negroes who had escaped American slavery lay in wait for them. They walked right into the ambush. The enemy shrewdly fired first at the horses of the wagon train; the wagons blocked the narrow trail, and the Americans had to stand and fight the unseen enemy against heavy odds. Williams was shot immediately but stayed in command. He was hit again and again. The fight was furious and the enemy attacked with tomahawks; the Marines charged and drove them off. One Marine was killed and eight were wounded; Williams had been hit eight times. A few men stayed to guard the wounded, and the rest retreated to the blockhouse on Davis Creek for help. The next morning a relief party came out and brought in the wounded.

Two days later Williams wrote Wharton that the men from the blockhouse "found me, wounded, my right leg is Broke, my right hand Shot through, a Ball in my left thigh near the groin, another through the Bottom of my Belly, which renders me altogether helpless. . . . You may expect that I am in a dreadful situation, tho I yet hope I shall recover in a few months." Two weeks later he was dead.

Williams' command fell to Lt. Alexander Sevier, who avenged his death by destroying the village of the attacking Indians. The next spring, Sevier and his Marines returned to Washington and a year later fought at Bladensburg.

Once Napoleon had been exiled to Elba, the British took the offensive along the Gulf of Mexico, as everywhere else. They hoped to seize the Gulf Coast, New Orleans and the lower Mississippi before the peace treaty, already in the offing, was signed and ratified.

After Ross' death at Baltimore, the British command was given to Sir Edward Pakenham, Wellington's wife's brother and a brave if inept soldier. Joined by the men from Ross' army, Pakenham sailed from Jamaica for New Orleans on November 26, 1814, with 9,000 soldiers. On December 11, his main convoy anchored off Lake Borgne, which is actually not a lake at all but a long arm of the Gulf of Mexico stretching westward to within six miles of what was then New Orleans.

Only nine days before the enemy arrived, a tall, gaunt, shabbily dressed officer with iron gray hair had ridden into the city. Maj. Gen. Andrew Jackson found New Orleans and its 20,000 inhabitants almost defenseless; the few local troops could never stand off a full-scale attack by Great Britain's best.

Navy Lt. Thomas ap Catesby Jones, commanding a tiny flotilla of five gunboats with 147 sailors and 35 Marines, was ordered to hold Lake Borgne. The presence of even this tiny American naval force would slow the British—and time was what Jackson needed most. The British sent a thousand men in 45 barges, with guns in their bows, to meet Jones. On the morning of December 14, the battle was joined on the northern edge of the lake. Jones and his few men fought gallantly. They delayed inevitable defeat throughout the morning and took a toll of more than 300 British. Jones was severely wounded and captured. Three Marines were killed and two wounded on his "flagship," Gunboat No. 156. By 12:40, the last of the gunboats had surrendered. The British swept through and touched land at Bayou Bienvenue.

New Orleans was in panic. Women carried daggers; the British war cry was said to be "Beauty and Booty." Jackson declared martial law; and everyone who could bear arms, except those of English birth, was ordered to defend the city.

But Pakenham moved ponderously, and Jackson used every precious moment to bolster the strength and spirit of the American defenders. On Sunday, December 18, a brilliant balmy southern winter's day, Jackson reviewed his troops, including Major Carmick's company of Marines. In the next few days, John Coffee, Jackson's cavalry leader, arrived with 800 mounted Tennesseans; and William Carroll brought a regiment of Jackson's veteran militia. While the British tarried, the Americans were gaining strength.

On the afternoon of Friday, December 23, Jackson received word that 1,700 enemy soldiers had marched within nine miles of New Orleans. He promptly moved against them with the army of 2,000 he had pulled together—the Tennesseans under Coffee, the best of the Creole militia, the regulars of the 7th Infantry and 55 Marines under Lt. Francis B. de Bellevue. Carroll's militiamen were the reserve.

The Americans marched at dusk. "We must fight them tonight," Jackson said. After 7 P.M., the guns of the schooner *Carolina*, which had sailed opposite the British camp, opened the battle in the darkness. Jackson, advancing close to the river, drove in the surprised British outposts. The enemy's counterattack was halted by two cannon. British reinforcements came up to seize the guns from the artillerymen and the supporting Marines. The horses with the cannon were hit; the Marines were forced back. Jackson dashed forward, roaring at his men to save the guns. He rallied the Marines until a company of the 7th Infantry came up and dragged off the guns.

Slowly, the American army pushed the British back. In the

darkness, Coffee's men fought with long knives against British bayonets. A thick fog rolled in across the blazing battlefield. Men fired blindly in the confusion. Finally, Jackson called a halt. In a couple of hours, the British had lost 247 men and the Americans, 213.

Now the shape of things to come was clear: The British would advance on the city between the river and a cypress swamp. Jackson was determined to draw a line the enemy could not cross. He retreated to the Rodriquez Canal, a shallow dry ditch—20 feet wide and four deep—that ran at right angles to the British advance, at the narrowest point between river and swamp. There he began to build his line.

The two armies faced each other the next morning, December 24. On that day across the world at Ghent, Belgium, peace was signed. The American dreams of conquest had long been lost; the issue of impressment of sailors was not even mentioned in the treaty. But it was an honorable peace and with it the United States' independence achieved respect. The men in front of New Orleans did not know the war was over; their battle would go on.

Jackson left the British with one immediate problem: *Carolina* kept peppering them from the river. It took them until the 27th to mount a battery of five guns, which in half an hour set the schooner on fire and blew her up. Her crew—some say it included Marines—escaped to shore to continue the fight. Again, the enemy had been delayed, and delay would make the difference.

Jackson organized his 12 guns into batteries and posted them and the motley units of his army behind the mile-long canal. He accepted the services of Lafitte's controversial pirates and formed a battalion of volunteers under the Creole Maj. Jean B. Plauché. Major Carmick and his Marines joined Plauché.

On Christmas Day, Pakenham arrived to take personal command. He massed 8,000 men; and on the night after *Carolina* was destroyed, they moved within 600 yards of the American army strung out along the canal. The next morning, in two columns in close formation and under an umbrella of artillery fire and rockets, the British attacked.

Jackson's artillerymen mowed down the solid advancing columns. *Louisiana*, the only remaining American ship, fired

800 rounds in support. The guns stopped the British infantry. While the infantrymen waited in the ditches, the Americans outdueled the British artillery. By noon, Pakenham's army was in retreat. Major Carmick was among the casualties, struck in the forehead by a rocket fragment and thrown from his horse. Both his arms were injured and he lost a thumb. Almost two years later, Carmick died, apparently from his wounds.

Then came three days of waiting while the British brought up naval guns to blast the Americans out from behind their parapets of cotton bales. On New Year's Day, 1815, the enemy opened an artillery duel with 30 guns handled by navy gunners. But men from *Carolina*, the pirates and artillerymen of the regular Army outshot them. The British Army was again forced to pull back.

During the next week, as the deadlock continued, Pakenham prepared for a final assault. He brought up 2,000 more reinforcements and ordered a canal dug so that boats could be brought over to the Mississippi. Fifteen hundred men were shifted to the west bank of the river under Col. William Thornton, who had fought at Bladensburg. Pakenham himself would lead the main attack on the east bank.

Meanwhile, the Americans had strengthened their breastworks. Jackson now had about 5,000 troops; he transferred 800 across the river so that Thornton could not simply march past him into New Orleans. The right flank of Jackson's main line on the east bank was anchored on the river by the regulars of the 7th Infantry. Plauché's men held the center; to their left stood Carroll and a thousand Tennessee veterans. On the dangerous far left flank were Coffee and 500 men. For days, Coffee's frontiersmen lived in the swamp itself on rafts tied to cypress trees.

One unit of 15 Marines under Lieutenant de Bellevue was posted just east of Battery No. 7 and formed the link between the 7th Infantry and Plauché's militia. In Carroll's sector stood two more guns manned by Marines.

Pakenham proposed to march his men across the open plain directly at the Americans entrenched behind the ditch and breastwork. It would be a classic example of military imbecility.

Early on January 8, the British army moved forward. As the fog lifted, the Americans saw the enemy coming in two great gleaming columns of white and red. The veterans of Wellington's army had beaten the finest in Europe; they advanced confidently. One column moved against the American left flank held by the Tennesseans. The other approached the 7th Infantry at the right end of the American line. The battlefield was almost silent; there was a sense of climax in the bright, chilly morning. Batteries 6, 7 and 8 on the left ripped the British lines. The holes were filled; the British came on. When they were but 200 yards from the canal, Carroll's backwoodsmen opened fire. They aimed for the officers and almost wiped them out.

The British 44th Regiment had been assigned to bring up scaling ladders and fascines of sugar cane to fill the canal, but at the vital moment they were not there. The British halted at the ditch. They could not be started forward again in the face of the American fire. Pakenham rode up, trying to bring on the 44th. A shot shattered his right arm; another killed his horse. The British retreated out of range to throw off their heavy knapsacks and regroup. Then, supported by the Highlanders of the 93rd Regiment with bagpipes skirling, they surged forward again. Pakenham was killed and two other generals were hit. Many men faltered; but the Highlanders, with incredible braveness, moved within 100 yards of the flaming parapet. Five hundred of their regiment were shot down. They finally broke and fled.

At the other end of the American line, where the British met the regulars, the decision came even faster. The enemy advanced and were routed by murderous fire—all within 25 minutes. The British advance in the face of such fire, against men they could not hit, was blindly heroic and almost insane.

On the field in front of the Rodriquez Canal lay 2,100 British dead and wounded. In some places there was no room to walk between them. Five hundred British soldiers had been captured. The Americans had suffered only 71 casualties. Jackson knew the limitations of his men and did not order them to pursue. Behind their parapets, they had fought with superb effectiveness; on the open field, it might be a different story. The British buried 700 dead. On January 18, prisoners were exchanged; and that night, the British returned to their ships. The next day, the bloody plain was empty.

On February 11, word reached New York that peace had been signed in December.

The British attack on New Orleans was carried out with grand stupidity and defeated with determination and doggedness. The Marines in the struggle were few in number (as they were everywhere in this war), but they were highly commended by Jackson. On Washington's Birthday, Congress passed a resolution: "Resolved, That Congress entertain a high sense of the valor and good conduct of Major Daniel Carmick, of the officers, noncommissioned officers, and Marines under his command, in the defence of the said city, on the late memorable occasion."

8
"Spirits Different from Other Men"

An epic story of the United States Marines began in October 1812, when the 32-gun frigate *Essex* sailed from the Delaware. Among the 319 men aboard were 32 Marines: 1st Lt. John Marshall Gamble, commanding; Sgts. Abraham Van Deezer and Pierce G. Small, two corporals, one drummer, one fifer and 25 privates. It was still early in the war as *Essex* set out to join Captain Bainbridge and *Constitution* in the South Atlantic and cut England's ocean trade by intercepting East Indies merchantmen returning home heavily laden. *Essex's* captain, David Porter, was fated for one of the great sea adventures of history, and Lieutenant Gamble was destined to become the leading Marine hero of the War of 1812.

Gamble, who had received his lieutenant's commission two years earlier at the age of seventeen, was a handsome daredevil with wild black hair, deep piercing eyes, a high forehead and an air of smiling alertness. He came from a fighting family. His father had been a major in the American Revolution; his three brothers were all to die in the naval service.

Essex, a fast sailer, had been the first American warship to round the Cape of Good Hope. Soon after the War of 1812 began, she captured the first British warship taken in the war, the 20-gun *Alert*. In September, David Porter received his orders to join Bainbridge.

Porter was an exceptional man: daring, able, imaginative, literate, short-tempered and stubborn. He was now only thirty-two, small and delicate of build, but he had seen a lot of action. Porter had adopted James Farragut, who went with him on this voyage as an eleven-year-old midshipman. After this cruise, he would take the first name of his adoptive father; as David Farragut, he would become the United States' first admiral.

[For the location of places in this section see map No. 8 in the map section.—*Au.*]

When Porter arrived for his rendezvous with Bainbridge, there was no sign of *Constitution*. Then, Porter heard three pieces of bad news: *Constitution's* fight with *Java* on December 29 had forced Bainbridge to head north; the British were assembling a large fleet in the southern Atlantic, and the blockade of the American ports was being tightened. It looked like the end of an unsuccessful cruise.

But before leaving the United States, Porter had convinced the Secretary of the Navy and Captain Bainbridge to approve a bold alternative plan. This was to sail *Essex* around Cape Horn into the Pacific and destroy the British whaling fleet, which had been harassing the many American whalers in those waters. Herman Melville was to call this cruise "the strangest and most stirring to be found in the history of the American navy."

On February 3, 1813, Captain Porter addressed a message to his crew:

> Sailors and Marines:
>
> A large increase of the enemy's force compels us to abandon a coast, that will neither afford us security nor supplies; nor are there any inducements for a long continuance there. We will, therefore, proceed to annoy them, where we are least expected. What was never performed by a single ship, we will attempt. The Pacific Ocean affords us many friendly ports. The unprotected British commerce, on the coast of Chili [sic], Peru, and Mexico will give you an abundant supply of wealth; and the girls of the Sandwich islands, shall reward you for your sufferings during the passage around Cape Horn.
>
> D. Porter[8]

In a stormy passage, *Essex* rounded the Cape on March 5. For the first time in American history, United States Marines were in the great ocean to fight on shores where so many of them would die in years to come.

From Valparaiso, Chile, Porter wrote Bainbridge: "I have as complete power in the Pacific as the whole British Navy can have in the Atlantic." He reprovisioned, sailed again promptly, took several prizes and headed north to the Galapagos Islands, a British whaling base. On April 29, the Americans chased a becalmed fleet of British whalers by putting out boats and rowing. Marine Lieutenant Gamble commanded the gig in this assault by open boat. They caught two of the whalers.

A month later, Porter seized his sixth prize, the 10-gun whaler *Greenwich*. He was beginning to find it difficult to supply prize crews and wrote in his journal: ". . . for want of sea officers, I put lieutenant Gamble of the marines in charge of the *Greenwich*. I had much confidence in the discretion of this gentleman; and, to make up for his want of nautical knowledge, I put two expert seamen with him as mates, one of whom is a good navigator."[9]

In June, at Tumbes, Peru, Gamble's ship was made into an armed store ship for the little fleet. Even young Farragut was given command of a prize. Then they returned to the waters around the Galapagos.

On the morning of July 12, they sighted three ships. *Essex* quickly took *Charlton*, and *Greenwich* chased the 14-gun *Seringapatam*, the finest British ship in those waters. Chewing tobacco and with a spyglass to his eye, Porter watched Gamble's attack from *Essex*. The enemy tacked and Porter said "Now, Mr. Gamble, if you'll only stand five minutes and then tack, I'll make you a Prince." Almost as if to Porter's command, Gamble held fast, avoiding raking fire from *Seringapatam*. Porter then said, "Now is your time!" As though he had heard, Gamble tacked, raked the enemy and damaged her badly. Porter put his spyglass under his arm and walked aft with a smile. Gamble was wounded, but the Marine lieutenant had won his naval battle.

On August 10, Gamble went ashore on James Island (now called San Salvador) and fought a duel with Midshipman and Acting Navy Lt. John S. Cowan. Each man fired three times, and young Cowan fell dead.

By autumn, the American "squadron" had cleared the seas of the British whaling fleet, which Porter figured was worth two and a half million dollars. In addition to *Essex*, Porter now had *Seringapatam*, *Essex Junior* (formerly *Atlantic*), *Greenwich*, *New Zealander* and *Sir Andrew Hammond*. The former three carried 20 guns or more each; the latter two, 10 apiece.

Word was received that the British were collecting a force to deal with the American raiders. So Porter sailed westward to the Marquesas Islands. They arrived on October 23, just about a year after sailing from New York, and established a base on Nukuhiva, which Porter renamed Madison Island. Porter loaded four boats with Marines and went ashore. The natives fled. The Americans found three white men on the island, one of whom was an Englishman named Wilson who had lived in the islands for a long time and whom Porter eventually began to use as an interpreter.

Slowly the natives reappeared. To impress them, Porter put the Marines through their paces and had them fire their muskets out over the bay. Porter wrote, "The drum appeared to give them much pleasure; and the regular movements of the marines occasioned much astonishment. They said they were spirits or beings of a class different from other men."[10]

The native women immediately attracted the Americans' attention. Porter described them as

> handsome and well formed; their skins were remarkably soft and smooth, and their complexions no darker than many brunetts in America celebrated for their beauty . . . if they suffered themselves to be presented naked to strangers, may it not be in compliance with a custom which teached them to sacrifice to hospitality all that is most estimable. . . .[11]

Porter soon became involved in the native wars on the island. He had landed in the home area of the Tayees tribe, whose breadfruit grove was being pilfered by the neighboring Happahs. Porter led the Marines and sailors from *Essex* over a nearby mountain, killed five Happahs with musket fire and stormed their stockade with a shouting charge. That stopped the breadfruit thefts.

In mid-November, Porter discovered a plot among some of the many British prisoners who had been captured on the whalers. They planned to seize *Sir Andrew Hammond* by getting the crew drunk. Porter placed the rum casks on the gun deck under a Marine guard, but two of the Marines helped the British steal the rum. Porter punished the guards and warned the Marine detachment that the next neglect of duty would be severely punished—if necessary with the death penalty.

The very next night, Porter, lying on his bed, failed to hear the Marine guard give an "All's well" at 10:30. He wrote:

> I was determined that the safety of the whole should not be hazarded by the neglect of the marines. I therefore seized my pistol, and followed by the sergeant and a guard preceeded for the bake-house, where we found the culprit fast asleep, his musket lying beside him. I directed him to be seized, and at the same moment he was wounded through the fleshy part of the thigh; this example had a proper effect, and rendered every person more vigilant, particularly the marines.[12]

On November 19, with appropriate ceremony, Porter raised the American flag over the fort he had built above the native village he called Madisonville and took possession of the island for the United States. The declaration of possession was signed by Porter and witnessed by fourteen men, including "John M. Gamble, lieutenant U.S. marines." (Later the claim was rejected in Washington, but Porter has been called the first imperialist among American naval officers.)

Ten days later, Porter and Gamble led an expedition of small boats and canoes against the warlike Typee tribe. They landed in the face of a barrage of stones and spears from the brush. As they advanced, Lt. John Downes' left leg was broken by a stone. Four men accompanied Porter's wounded first lieutenant back to the beach, leaving Porter to pursue the Typees with 24 men and a contingent of natives. Porter and Gamble stood together behind a tree and fired at the Typees as they rose to throw their rocks. Cartridges ran low, and Porter sent Gamble and four men back to the ships for more ammunition. Porter started retreating and reached the beach just as Gamble returned with the ammunition.

Porter was resolved not to let the defeat stand. The following night, he marched 200 men overland to the Typee country. It rained heavily. After waiting a day for their ammunition to dry, they attacked the Typees' fortified village. Several of the enemy were killed and three Americans were wounded. Porter burned the villages of these "unhappy and heroic people," as he called them. After three nights' absence, the party returned to Madisonville. Several of the men were laid up with fatigue, and two days later Marine Cpl. Andrew Mahon died. An exchange of gifts, including 400 hogs, was arranged; and peace was restored to the island.

Once *Essex* was ready, Porter sailed on December 9 for the Pacific coast of South America to seek battle with the British warships that had been sent out after him. As they prepared to leave, Porter confined his men to their ships. The native women lined the beach, dipping their fingers in the sea and touching them to their eyes and threatening to kill themselves.

Porter left three prizes, *Seringapatam, Sir Andrew Hammond* and *Greenwich*, at the island so that he would have a base if he found his fight and needed repairs. The ships were placed in charge of Marine Lieutenant Gamble, accompanied by Midshipman William W. Feltus and 21 "volunteers," including four Marines and six prisoners of war. If Gamble had not heard from Porter after five and a half months, he was to sail for Valparaiso.

Essex and *Essex, Jr.*, reached Valparaiso on February 3, 1814. While Porter stood safely in the neutral harbor, two British ships—*Phoebe*, 36 guns, and *Cherub*, 18 guns—arrived. On March 28, Porter decided to make a dash for it. The two British ships gave chase. *Essex* lost her top mainmast in a squall, and Porter had to put in at a small bay three miles from Valparaiso. Seeing *Essex* disabled, *Phoebe* and *Cherub* closed in and raked the American ship. Porter had three 12-pounders dragged to the stern and drove off the British. They stayed out of Porter's range and bombarded him. *Essex* was helpless. Porter tried to close; the British kept their distance. In desperation, his ship a wreck, Porter tried to beach; the wind shifted, and he could not make it. Half his crew were casualties. Porter gave others permission to swim ashore. At 6:20, with *Essex* in flames, he surrendered. As Theodore Roosevelt wrote, "throughout the war no ship was so desperately defended as the *Essex*."[13]

The total British loss was five killed and ten wounded. Of *Essex's* 255 men, 58 were killed, 66 were wounded and 31 drowned. Only 76 remained unwounded. Three Marines were missing and one was wounded. Porter gave special praise to a Mr. Samuel B. Johnson, who had been in the service of the Chilean government. Porter wrote that Johnson, "who had joined me the day before, and acted as marine officer [in Gamble's absence], conducted himself with great bravery, and exerted himself in assisting at the long guns; the musketry after the first half hour being useless, from our great distance."[14] Johnson was later commissioned in the U.S. Marine Corps.

Porter, Midshipman Farragut and 137 other Americans, including nine remaining Marines (Sergeant Small and eight privates), were sent home in *Essex, Jr.*, Porter returned in time to participate in the defense of the Potomac. The British kept the fast-sailing *Essex*; in the 1830s, she served as a convict ship at Kingston, Jamaica.

Meanwhile, back in the Marquesas Islands, Gamble was having troubles of his own. On the night of March 18, four men, one of whom had been punished for theft and another who had been flogged for desertion, stole an open boat, loaded it with arms and supplies and fled after smashing the only other boat that could pursue them.

In mid-April, Gamble started rigging the ships for sea. Mutiny began to build up among the prisoners and the foreign-born members of *Essex* crew. On the afternoon of May 7, when Gamble ordered work done aboard *Seringapatam*, the men refused to obey; one drew a knife. Gamble tried to escape to a boat alongside, but he was grabbed by a half-dozen men, thrown to the deck, his hands and legs bound. Then he was dropped below decks. Midshipman Feltus and Acting Midshipman Clapp were also seized and thrown into the hold. The mutineers raised the British flag with a cheer. They sent out parties to spike the guns of the fort and *Greenwich*, on which Gamble had made his headquarters.

The mutineers numbered 13. The officers and eight men—including Marines Benjamin Bispham, Peter Caddington and John Pittenger—did not join them. (Gamble's fourth Marine, John Wetter, had meanwhile been drowned while swimming in the surf.)

That night the mutineers sailed *Seringapatam* out of the bay. A prisoner of war who was guarding the captives shot Gamble through the left foot. The shot aroused the other men, and for a tense moment several muskets pointed at the three prisoners through the skylight. At sea, the mutineers decided to get rid of their prisoners. They put Gamble, Feltus, Clapp and two seamen, William Worth and Richard Sansbury, into a leaking boat. Gamble argued with the mutineers and was finally given two muskets and a keg of cartridges. Clapp bailed; Gamble, in great pain, steered, and the other three rowed. After two hours they reached *Greenwich*.

The next day Gamble transferred supplies to the smaller *Hammond*. Then Worth and Marine Peter Caddington set out to find the Englishman Wilson, whom they believed had inspired the mutiny. Wilson fled; and when a larger party was sent to seize supplies Wilson had taken, the natives became aroused. A battle erupted on the beach and in the surf as the party tried to retreat to the ships. The natives killed Feltus. Worth and Caddington swam to *Hammond*; the Marine was severely wounded in the head and bleeding profusely. Midshipman Clapp, Sansbury and Marine Benjamin Bispham put out in a boat to help the two men. Gamble, alone on *Hammond*, hobbled from gun to gun, firing them at the shore, and succeeded in scaring off the natives.

Then a boat brought over to *Hammond* Marine John Pittenger, who had an injured leg and had been singlehandedly guarding *Greenwich*. Gamble had *Greenwich* set afire. At 4 o'clock on May 9, the little party aboard *Hammond* sailed from the bay. Gamble had seven men in his crew. He himself was wounded and feverish. Marine Caddington had been wounded in the head, and Pittenger was crippled. Of the three seamen, Worth had a fractured leg, Sansbury suffered from rheumatism and Joseph Burnham was an old man just recovering from scurvy. Only Midshipman Clapp and Marine Bispham were in sound health. They had no compass, no spyglass, no maps; only six cartridges were left. When they tried to pull up the boat, it broke in two; and they had to cut away their only anchor. They decided to do the one thing they could: run with the tradewinds. On May 23, after sailing for 15 days, they sighted the Hawaiian Islands and made land, exhausted, at Waikiki Bay on May 31.

On June 11, *Hammond*, her crew filled out with nine Hawaiians, set out to carry 40 natives to visit their king. At dawn on the 13th, Gamble sighted a strange sail directly ahead. The unknown ship hoisted American colors, which by the tactics of those days convinced him she was an enemy. But he could not escape. By nine o'clock, the ship had closed, raised the British flag and fired a shot at *Hammond*. In the face of the larger enemy, Gamble fired a shot to leeward signalling surrender and a boarding party came over. Their captor was the British *Cherub*, which had helped take *Essex*. For the next three months, Gamble was held aboard *Cherub* as she visited various ports and islands. *Cherub* put in to Rio de Janiero at the end of November; in February they learned that the war had ended.

Gamble, his health broken, was permitted to sail for home in a Swedish ship. Transferred to the American ship *Oliver Ellsworth*, he reached New York City on August 28, 1815. He had been gone two years and ten months. Two days later, he wrote to Captain Porter: "I am at present unable to travel, and shall therefore await either your orders or the Commandant of the Marine Corps at this place."[15]

Gamble received the recognition he deserved from the Corps. He was commissioned a captain as of June 18, 1814. In later years, he was brevetted first a major and then a lieutenant colonel. He was given the honor of commanding the Marines Barracks at Philadelphia, the oldest station in the Corps. The handsome Marine married Hannah Letitia Lang, the beautiful daughter of the editor of the *New York Observer.* In October 1824, he was a host to Lafayette when he visited Philadelphia. Gamble served at Portsmouth for several years and then commanded the Marines in New York. But he was still suffering from the ravages of his epic cruise in the Pacific, and after a year's illness he died in Brooklyn on September 11, 1836, at the age of 46.

In its obituary, the *New York American* said:

> In feelings, manners and character, Col. Gamble was thoroughly a gentleman. As an officer, amiable, gentle, yet firm, he knew how to conciliate the authority of command, with due consideration for the feeling of all subordinate to him. As a member of the Episcopal church, he was strictly, yet unostentatiously observant of his religious duties. In his private relations he was exemplary.[16]

Captain Porter wrote to the Navy Department of the Marine hero: "No Marine officer in the service ever had such strong claims as Captain Gamble . . . none have been placed in such conspicuous and critical situations, and . . . none could have extricated themselves from them more to their honor."

In the War of 1812, the Marine Corps was already a national service; but its esprit and its professionalism were in their infancy. Throughout the war there were never enough Marines to fill their assignments, and their Commandant hardly ranked with the Corps' great leaders. They made their most important contribution as sharpshooters on the American warships, picking off enemy officers, including Captains Dacres of *Guerriere*, Lambert of *Java* and Manners of *Reindeer*. There, their work often turned the tide of battle.

And yet, such an interpretation tells only half the story. As important to victory as Perry's preparation on Lake Erie or Macdonough's planning on Lake Champlain was the Marines' willingness to stand and fight when the odds appeared insurmountable and the outcome bleak. The whole story must tell of the Marines who stayed and fought at Bladensburg, and Marines who stood on *Chesapeake's* deck when she was overrun by *Shannon's* men, the Marines who stood with Jackson against the seemingly invincible Redcoated legion at New Orleans. The men of the Corps—men like Bush of *Constitution*, Brooks on Lake Erie, Carmick, Miller, Sevier, Williams and Gamble—showed the new nation that it could fight.

Archibald Henderson served as Commandant of the
Marine Corps for thirty-eight years,
longer than any other man.
Private Collection, Courtesy of Museums Branch, USMC

SEMPER FIDELIS

III
ARCHIBALD
HENDERSON
AND THE
INDIAN WARS
1817–1842

1
Whiskey and Politics

Two years after the War of 1812 ended, Marine Capt. Archibald Henderson brought charges against the Commandant of the Marine Corps. Henderson attacked Lt. Col. Franklin Wharton's conduct during the British assault on Washington: The Commandant had "sent" the Marines to fight the enemy at Bladensburg, rather than leading them himself; he had fled the capital, rather than helping to defend it. Henderson, ambitious for both the Corps and himself, charged that Wharton refused "to take any effectual measures to put a stop to reports so highly injurious to his own character, and of great disadvantage to the Corps under his command."[1]

A court, composed of Marine Captains Anthony Gale and John M. Gamble and Navy Captains Charles Stewart, Jacob Jones and Lewis Warrington, decided that it did not have jurisdiction because the Marines ashore were subject to the Articles of War. So an Army court was convened. But it refused to hear testimony, and President Monroe approved that decision on September 22, 1817.

Although Wharton remained as Commandant, the stain of his conduct during the raid on Washington clung to him. Less than a year later, he became ill and visited Saratoga Springs and Ballston Spa in New York state "for the waters." On his way home, he died in New York City on September 1, 1818, at the age of fifty-one, and was buried in the Old Trinity Church Yard.

If the policy by which Wharton had become Commandant was to be followed again, Brevet Maj. Anthony Gale, now the senior officer of the Corps, should succeed him. But there were many Marines—Henderson and Samuel Miller in particular— who felt earnestly that Gale was not fit to hold the post. For the

97

next two years, the Corps was torn by the bitter battle among these three men.

Anthony Gale was a tragic figure, the victim of his own weaknesses and the ambitions of stronger men. Irish born, he was commissioned in 1798, almost as soon as the Corps was established. In November 1799, he had killed Lt. Allen McKenzie, USN, the second lieutenant of *Ganges*, in a duel. McKenzie had put one of Gale's men in irons without consulting the Marine officer; when Gale inquired about the incident, McKenzie had called him a rascal. After the duel, Commandant Burrows supported Gale, saying, "It is hoped that this may be a lesson to the Navy officers to treat the Marines as well as their Officers with some more Respect."[2]

Gale served at sea during the French war and in the Mediterranean from 1804 to 1806. In 1815, while he was in charge of the Marine Barracks in Philadelphia, a post of distinction, he became involved in a dispute with Commandant Wharton over the construction of new buildings there. Wharton had been accused of overspending on the project, and he in turn charged Gale with building extravagant officers' quarters. Gale finally appealed to the Secretary of the Navy, asserting that he had been given no specific plans and that Wharton had known what was being done. A court of inquiry cleared him, but he was transferred to a less desirable command in New Orleans.

Gale began to drink heavily. On February 1, 1817, Henderson—at about the same time he was bringing charges against Commandant Wharton—also wrote the Secretary of the Navy saying that officers had "frequently seen Major Gale intoxicated at New Orleans, and that his associates were of such a description and his habits of such a nature as to prevent the respectable officers on that station from having any social or friendly intercourse with him."[3]

Henderson's hearsay accusations may have been encouraged by his own desire to succeed Wharton, but there was truth to his charges. A year later, Daniel T. Patterson, commander of the New Orleans Naval Station, wrote the Secretary of the Navy:

> It is reluctantly and with extreme regret that I have again [to] address you relative to the Marines of this station, but longer to remain silent would be to neglect my duty.

> The non-commissioned officers and Privates, are without exception the most depraved, abandoned, and Drunken set of men ever collected together and in whom not the smallest confidence can be placed. The only thefts that have been committed from the Public Stores, have invariably been traced to the very men who were placed to guard them. . . . Major Gale has his Marine Quarters at Tchifonti where he retains Lt. Brown, with only a Sergeants Guard, while the Marine Barracks and the largest part of his command is left here with only one commissioned officer.[4]

Gale's conduct was clearly vulnerable to attack; and when Wharton died, the scramble for the Commandant's job began.

Samuel Miller ardently sought the assignment. He was now forty-three years old and a hero of Bladensburg. He had joined the Corps in 1808 and ever since May 1809 had served in Washington as adjutant of the Corps; he was a Headquarters Marine. Miller pushed his case in Washington's political circles. Letters were written to President Monroe urging that he be appointed. Congressman Joseph Desha of Kentucky, the father of the paymaster of the Marine Corps, wrote Monroe: "I have, from his gentlemanly conduct, capacity & tried courage, long considered him as the life of the Corps."[5]

When Wharton died, Gale was still stationed in New Orleans. Henderson, the next in line after Gale, took charge of the Corps' affairs until a new Commandant could be selected. Using Miller's self-seeking as a base, Henderson mounted his own campaign. He had already tried to oust Wharton and defame Gale. Now, he wrote to the President on November 18, 1818:

> It never had been *my* wish since I entered the service, to rise over the heads of meritorious officers, it is very far from being so now, but I cannot but be of opinion, if the Government decide that the present Senior Officer [Gale] is incompetent to discharge the duties of the Command of the Corps, that my claim is the only just one for the Command.
>
> That claim is founded in the first place, on my being

99

the next senior officer and in the second, on the active and honourable service which it was my good fortune to be employed on during the period of my professional career in which my country was at War with great Britain.[6]

If Gale was rejected as "incompetent," Henderson did not want Miller to grab the job.

In the meantime, another round of trouble lay ahead for Anthony Gale. Lt. Robert M. Desha, the paymaster whose Congressman father was supporting Miller for Commandant, accused Gale of misappropriating $4,000 intended for the payment of his men in New Orleans. Desha, whose serious charge seems also based on hearsay evidence, became Gale's enemy.

In that same fall of 1818, Desha was involved in another unpleasant affair. He served as second in one of the most notorious duels in Marine Corps history.

Commodore Oliver Perry, the hero of Lake Erie, had commanded *Java* in the Mediterranean in the summer of 1816. He became thoroughly annoyed with the commander of his Marine detachment, Capt. John Heath, a stout man with little military bearing and an enthusiasm for creature comforts. Perry's aggravation boiled over when, at Messina, Sicily, on September 16, two of Heath's Marines jumped overboard to swim to shore. Perry called for Heath, who sent a reply that he was in his stateroom indisposed. Perry angrily commanded him to appear and muster his Marines. Heath did it too sloppily for Perry's taste. He was relieved from duty and sent below. Heath remained in his room for two days and then sent a note to Perry, saying,

> Sir,
> On the evening of the sixteenth instant I was ordered below by you from the quarter-deck, with these words, or to that effect: "I have no farther use for your services on board this ship." I have waited till this moment to know why I have been thus treated, and, being ignorant of the cause, request my arrest and charges.
> Very respectfully, etc.
> John Heath[7]

Furious at what he unreasonably regarded as Heath's insolence, Perry sent for him and when he arrived in the captain's cabin had Marine Lt. Parke G. Howle take Heath's sword. Perry said to Heath, "Consider yourself under arrest." Heath said, "Very well, sir." Perry ordered him to be silent. Heath replied again, "Very well, sir." And as Perry later admitted, "Passion became predominant and I gave him a blow."

Perry immediately regretted what he had done. He sent Heath a note offering to apologize. But word of the incident swiftly spread through the squadron. The Marine officers from all the ships came aboard *Java* and vigorously lectured Heath that the Corps' honor was at stake. They urged him to refuse the offer of an apology and to demand legal justice. As a result, both men were tried. Heath was found guilty of neglect of duty and disrespect; Perry was found guilty of striking an officer. Both men were sentenced to be reprimanded in private and were restored to duty. Even Perry's biographer, who was serving on *Java* at the time, felt that Perry "should have been more severely dealt with" for striking a fellow officer.

When *Java* returned to the United States, the affair became a sensation in the newspapers. Heath, egged on by Marine officers, demanded a duel. On January 18, 1818, Perry wrote his friend Capt. Stephen Decatur that he would give Heath satisfaction but "I cannot consent to return his fire, as the meeting, on my part, will be entirely an atonement for the violated rules of the service." The civil authorities tried to prevent the duel; but the two men finally met on October 19 near Hoboken, New Jersey, where Burr had killed Hamilton. With Perry came Decatur; Heath's second was Desha. Perry and Heath stood back to back. At a signal, they took five paces on count and wheeled. Heath fired—and missed. Perry refused to fire. Then Decatur stepped forward and announced that it had been Perry's decision not to return the Marine's fire and received from Desha agreement that Heath's honor was now satisfied.

Secretary of the Navy Smith Thompson called a court of inquiry to determine whether Henderson's and Desha's charges against Gale had foundation. The court would decide who was to be the next Commandant. On February 20, 1819, the court met at Strother's Hotel in Washington, officially at Gale's request, "to examine into the truth of certain reports injurious to

101

your character." Gale was brought up from New Orleans; the witnesses included Henderson, Miller, Gamble and Desha. President of the court was Col. Jacob Hindman, USA. Gale was found not guilty; and on March 5, Secretary Thompson notified him that the President of the United States had appointed him Lieutenant Colonel Commandant of the Marine Corps.

The slate was wiped clean—but Gale's troubles were by no means over. He fought a running battle with the Secretary Thompson over the prerogatives of the Commandant. This dispute reached a climax in August 1820. On August 8, Gale wrote Thompson, complaining that the Secretary had given long furloughs to men whom Gale had assigned to duty away from headquarters. Politely but firmly, he suggested that the Secretary should give his orders through the Commandant, not directly to Marine officers under him, and that he should establish rules of operation but leave their application to Gale. Eight days later, Gale was notified that the Secretary had granted a four-week leave to Captain Gamble and had suspended Gale's order sending Captain DeBellevue to the Mediterranean. The Commandant's orders were being countermanded.

On August 29, Benjamin Homans of the Navy Department wrote Captain Miller, adjutant of the Corps:

> The conduct of Lieut. Col. A. Gale, commandant of Marines, has for some time past been so notoriously improper, and unbecoming the character of the Office & Gentleman that it is indispensable necessary [sic] that a Court Martial be immediately ordered for his trial, and you are, therefore required to relieve Lt. Col. Gale from duty; place him under arrest. . . .

Miller, Gale's old enemy, now became acting commandant, his official prosecutor and the man assigned to draw up the charges against him. Miller arrested Gale that same day and confined him to quarters. On September 7, General Orders announced that the court, headed by Brig. Gen. Thomas S. Jesup of the Army, would convene at the Marine Barracks on Monday, September 18.

The charges, which were dated September 11, make strange reading when the date of Homans' letter ordering Gale's arrest is kept in mind—August 29.

There were four charges. The first was that Gale was publicly intoxicated in the city of Washington on six specified dates during August, including August 31—after his arrest was already ordered.

The second charge was of conduct unbecoming an officer and gentleman. There were three specifications. First, that Gale had visited a house of prostitution near the Marine Barracks "in open and disgraceful manner" on that same August 31 (after his arrest). Second, that he had on September 1 (after his arrest) called the paymaster, Lieutenant Desha—who was Miller's partisan and had earlier charged Gale with misappropriation—"a damned rascal, liar and coward and threatening him with personal chastisement unless he would immediately challenge and fight him." And finally, that he had declared in the street in front of the Marine Barracks "that he did not care a damn for the President, Jesus Christ or God Almighty!"

The third charge was that Gale had signed a false certificate that said he had not used a Marine for personal services when in fact he had had a man assigned as waiter and coachman from October 17, 1819, until June 3, 1820.

The fourth charge was that Gale had broken arrest "at sundry times" between September 1 and 8 while he was confined to quarters—after he had been arrested.

These sound like thin charges on which to courtmartial the Commandant of the Marine Corps. Most of them occurred after the courtmartial was already ordered. The rest amount to five acts of drunkenness, cursing in public and denying that he had had a man assigned to act as his waiter. Chances are that today Gale would be regarded as an alcoholic, and that he was not the most competent of men. But it also seems clear that vicious headquarters politics were involved here and that the cards were stacked against Anthony Gale.

When his trial opened, Gale requested permission of the court to go and collect witnesses on his own behalf. The court replied that he would have to obtain permission from the Navy Department, which had him under arrest. Gale asked Homans for this permission and was told the court would have to give him permission. The buck was passed back and forth, and Gale apparently never was allowed to gather the witnesses he desired.

The outcome was predictable. The court found the Commandant guilty as charged. President Monroe approved its

103

findings; and on October 18, 1820, Gale was cashiered—the only Commandant in the history of the Marine Corps to be so disgraced.

Afterwards, Gale appealed to the President, seeking $5,000 he felt was owed him from his 22 years of service. He moved to central Kentucky, and in 1835 established his mental derangement to obtain a pension, first of $15 a month and later $25. On October 8, 1840, his wife Catharine wrote the Commissioner of Pensions asking that his pension be sent directly to her because "he is so deranged at times." Three years later, Gale died at Stanford, Kentucky, in another man's house. He was probably a pauper. No trace of his grave exists today. And Anthony Gale is the only Commandant of whom the Marine Corps does not have a portrait to hang in its headquarters.

2
Henderson Takes Command

The man who in 1820 became Commandant of the Corps was thirty-seven years old, with a distinguished record in the War of 1812. He had climbed to the top, and now he would stay there for 38 years—until his death. His would be the longest term as Commandant in all Marine Corps history. Fortunately for the Corps, Archibald Henderson became one of the Marines' great Commandants: able, jealous of the Corps' status and reputation and quick to seize any opportunity to give the Marines a wider role in the nation's destiny.

The portrait of Henderson that hangs in the U.S. Naval Academy shows a young man with a long aristocratic face, a high forehead and a large nose—alert and determined. He is wearing the long sideburns of the day and his head is stiff, almost awkward, in a collar that reaches nearly to his earlobes.

Henderson was a proper Virginian. He had been born at Colchester, Virginia, on January 21, 1783. His father, Alexander, who had come over from Scotland about 30 years before, was a merchant and belonged to the same church as did George Washington. When he was twenty-three, Archibald Henderson joined the Marine Corps, and by the time the war with Great Britain began, had risen to the rank of captain. Most of his wartime service was on *Constitution*; when she fought *Cyane* and *Levant* early in 1815, he was honored by both Congress and his native state. During the following five years, he served at Marine Corps stations at Boston; Portsmouth, New Hampshire; Washington, and New Orleans.

A young man who came to see him about a commission liked the new Commandant. Robert C. Caldwell, who became a Marine officer and served until his death, wrote, "Col. Henderson I find to be a very plain and familiar man, entirely easy in his manners and very gentlemanly in his friendship,—has nothing of the cold and withering fronths of ceremony about him."

One of Henderson's first acts as Commandant was to get Samuel Miller out of headquarters. Henderson removed him as adjutant of the Corps—a post Miller had held for more than 11 years. Some of the most respected officers of the Corps—Richard Smith, Robert Wainwright, John Gamble, Samuel Watson and John Harris—signed a letter to Henderson urging that Miller "be removed to a station, where his intrigues and selfish examples may be less destructive to the prosperity of a service, in which we have all so deep an interest." Miller was succeeded by Lt. Parke G. Howle, another Virginian and an ally of Henderson, who would have the job until his death 36 years later.

In 1822, Henderson ordered Miller to duty on the West India station where the Corps was helping to wipe out the local pirates. But Miller's order was reversed by President Monroe. Henderson wrote to defend himself and point out that Miller had never had sea duty since joining the Corps in 1808. He admitted his antagonism toward Miller, saying:

> In 1818, he took every possible means to raise himself to the command of the Corps. The degraded character of the late Commandant [Gale] it was thought would have prevented his elevation to that rank and every possible measure was used by Major Miller to establish the position in case Major Gale was passed over, his claim tho he was the sixth officer was equal to mine who was the second. It is this circumstance in Major Miller's course of conduct which has made so deep an impression on my mind that I cannot forget it. It was this circumstance that made me reject his proffered services in the Staff.

As late as 1825, Henderson was writing to the Secretary of the Navy, trying to transfer Miller to New Hampshire.

Samuel Miller stayed on in the Corps until his death on December 9, 1855, at the age of eighty. He was twice found guilty by general courts-martial and each time suspended from duty for three months. But he also served with honor in the Indian wars and did long service in command of the Marine station in Philadelphia. When he was seventy, he offered to serve actively in the Mexican War.

Partly because of such headquarters politicking, morale in the Marine Corps was low when Henderson took over. Its authorized strength was down to 988 officers and men. He entered on a long battle to give the Corps independence and to establish it as a military force with peacetime responsibilities broader than simply maintaining discipline on Navy ships and guarding Navy shipyards. To prepare for more extensive duties, Henderson kept at headquarters a skeletonized battalion training in infantry tactics and the use of artillery. And he sought to commission as Marine officers West Point graduates who could not find places in the peacetime Army.

The Corps' mission was already a continuing problem. On March 17, 1820, Henderson had written the Secretary of the Navy that "our isolated Corps, with the Army on one side and the Navy on the other (neither friendly), has been struggling ever since its establishment, for its very existence." The Navy Commissioners wanted the Marines broken up into small detachments. And in 1830, Capt. Lewis Warrington, USN, then a Navy Commissioner, recommended the Corps' abolishment, because, he said, a police force aboard ship was necessary only in the British Navy, where seamen were impressed into service. President Andrew Jackson recommended that the Corps be absorbed into the Army. But finally, after hearings in 1830, the idea died in Congress. It would come up again—over and over—whenever the nation relaxed in peace.

Exactly what the Marine Corps was to be and what its relationship was to both the Navy and the Army had to be settled. As far back as 1812, Capt. Robert D. Wainwright had had a dispute over the right of an Army general to give orders to Marines. He appealed to headquarters, and the Secretary of the Navy ruled that since a Marine is "for the purpose of performing Naval Services, he is not liable to the orders of any Army officer whatsoever. . . ."[8]

The Corps' relationship with its parent body, the Navy, also had to be hammered out. On shipboard, Marines were not directly under the Commandant's rule but responsible to the

Navy officer commanding the warship. The question now arose: Were Marines in navy yards under the Commandant or the naval officer commanding the yard? The President detached Marines in the Navy yards from the Commandant's control and put them on the same status as Marines aboard warships. Henderson lost that round. It would take him 15 years to win this argument.

By 1834, all these unresolved questions stimulated the passage by Congress, on June 30, of "an act for the better organization of the United States 'Marine Corps.'" This was the first major act dealing with the Marines since the 1798 law establishing the Corps. The most vital part of the act in the eyes of the Corps was Section Two, which stated in part ". . . the said corps shall, at all times, be subject to, and under the laws and regulations which are, or may hereafter be, established for the better government of the navy, except when detached for service with the army by order of the President of the United States."

The parallel section in the act of 1798, Section Six, read "That the Marine corps, established by this act, shall, at any time, be liable to do duty in the forts and garrisons of the United States, on the seacoast, or any other duty ashore, as the President, at his discretion, shall direct."

The difference was subtle but enormously important. The Marine Corps was now clearly responsible to the Navy except on the "order" of the President. This meant that Marine officers were not responsible to Army officers—and also that the Corps could serve with the Army in many new ways. Just two years later, this possibility would become a reality.

However, the act did not supply all the answers to the Corps' relationship to the Navy. Henderson continued his fight to define the Corps as a separate military entity. In the fall of 1835, he wrote the Secretary of the Navy: "The Corps of Marines by Law is not included in the Navy proper but is an independent Corps under Naval Law . . . the Act of 30th June 1834 fully recognizes the Corps as a Military Body. . . ."[9]

The act of 1834 also dealt with many other aspects of Marine Corps service. Enlistments were to be for four years. In 1798 they had been set at three years, and had been increased to five years in 1809; the longer tour had not made the recruiting problem any easier. The act made Marine Corps pay parallel to Army pay and rank the same as Army rank. And it ruled that no

Marine officer shall "exercise command over any navy yard or vessel of the United States." (For this reason, it is believed that John Gamble on the cruise of *Essex* was the last and probably the only Marine Corps officer to command a ship of war.)

The act also increased the strength of the Corps. It would be headed by one "Colonel Commandant," and Henderson was promoted to that rank on July 1. And the Corps would expand to 1,287 officers and men from the 988 officers and men authorized by the Peace Establishment Act of 1817.

For the Marine private, the twenty years after the War of 1812 had little glamour. His pay ranged from $6 to $10 a month. He could still be lashed with the cat-o'-nine-tails for minor offenses (in 1835, Miller wrote Henderson that he opposed lashing but found it difficult to discipline by other means men who had been punished on shipboard with the cat). There are numerous instances in Marine Corps records of Marines (or their wives) writing to headquarters claiming that they had been enlisted while they were drunk. The Marines' main jobs were still what they had been from the beginning: maintaining discipline aboard ship; keeping the gun crews at their jobs in combat; boarding and repelling boarders; and fighting from the tops and in the waist, the warships' most exposed and dangerous areas.

3
A Prison and Pirates

A riot broke out in the Massachusetts State Prison at Boston on March 12, 1824. Three prisoners who were to be flogged seized a guard and took him as a hostage into the prison dining room. Word of their rebellion sped swiftly. Prisoners ran from the workshops and details, arming themselves with whatever weapons they could find. The riot grew until the prison authorities sent a call for help to the Marines at the Boston Navy Yard. Brevet Maj. Robert D. Wainwright led a detachment to the prison. He was asked to fire powder alone at first and, if that did not disperse the prisoners, to fire ball.

Wainwright refused. With 30 Marines, he entered the large locked dining room and tried to reason with the mob of more than 280 prisoners. They refused to surrender, shouting that they would not be flogged. Wainwright told his men to hold up their bullets so that the prisoners could see them, and then load their pieces. Then, the major stepped forward again and ordered the rioters to disperse. When his order was not obeyed, Wainwright took out his watch and told the prisoners they had three minutes to leave the room or he would order his men to fire.

The seconds ticked away in silence. If the prisoners had been willing to risk the first volley, they could have slaughtered the outnumbered Marines before they could reload. For two long minutes, no one moved. Then a few of the prisoners nearest the rear door sneaked out. More drifted away; and as the last seconds ran out, the rest broke for the door.

The courage of Wainwright and his men avoided casualties and stemmed the riot. Word of their bravery spread throughout the nation. The story, repeated in the widely used McGuffey Readers, was taught to generations of school children, adding to

110

the esteem of the Corps. And the affair became an important precedent for calling on the Corps in moments of civilian disorder.

In this same period, the Marines had their most dramatic overseas encounter with pirates in the far-off East Indies. American merchant ships were now sailing all the world—to China for silks and tea, to Ceylon and the East Indies for spices, to Hawaii for sandalwood. They fell prey to many marauders. On February 7, 1831, when *Friendship*, out of Salem, Massachusetts, was loading a cargo of pepper at Quallah Battoo on the island of Sumatra, pirates killed the mate and two seamen and plundered the ship.

Commodore John Downes, who had been with David Porter on the cruise of *Essex*, sailed from New York on August 21 in the frigate *Potomac* to punish the pirates. He rounded the Cape of Good Hope and reached Sumatra on February 4, 1832. *Potomac* was disguised as a merchantman; her gunports were closed and hammock cloths covered the guns on the spar deck. Most of the men were kept below and only one sail was worked at a time, in merchant-ship fashion. As the frigate approached Quallah Battoo, a Danish flag was raised.

Standing three miles offshore, the Americans could see a village on an attractive beach, guarded at each end by a fort. At midnight on February 7, a landing party of 286 sailors and Marines was mustered under Navy Lt. Irvine Shubrick. The boats were rowed with muffled oars. It was a brilliant tropical night, calm and clear; the sky was filled with stars. A large meteor whipped across the sky, and the men took it as an omen of success. At dawn, they landed a mile north of the town in a heavy surf.

The Marines with Brevet Capt. Alvin Edson and Lt. George H. Terrett were in the van. As they advanced along the beach, they rounded a point of land and were spotted by the natives. Quickly, the Americans attacked the nearest fort and subdued it. Edson's Marines and a division of sailors turned inland to attack the two forts behind the village. They marched through the bazaars and were shot at by natives but did not return the fire. Another division of sailors attacked the main fort alongside a river in the center of the town.

111

Edson stormed his fort by seizing the drawbridge and forcing an entrance. The defenders would not surrender; all who did not flee were killed.

Then, the Marines turned back to help the sailors who were attacking the center fort. The whole American force assaulted this point—the local rajah's stronghold. The natives fought back with guns, javelins and spears. The Marines were on the river side, pouring in a deadly crossfire. The battle went on for two hours, according to Assistant Surgeon Jonathan M. Foltz of *Potomac*, who was on the scene and wrote in his journal, "we received a reenforcement from the Marine Corps, whose aim was generally fatal, but so desperate and savage are these people that quarter is unknown to them, and they fought until every man was killed."[10]

Finally, the royal magazine exploded; and the native defenders fell back and rallied in the jungle behind the town. There, the battle went on, the enemy now firing from cover. Marine Privates Benjamin T. Brown and Daniel H. Cole were shot through the chest at almost the same moment. Brown was killed and Cole mortally wounded. Edson and Pvt. James A. Huster were slightly wounded. The natives pressed forward, and the Marines formed a rear guard as the landing party moved out to their boats. All the houses in the village had been destroyed and the town's forts wrecked. A fort on the far side of the river fired on the small boats but managed only several near misses. By 10 o'clock that morning, the Americans were back aboard *Potomac*. The next day, the frigate fired on the remaining fort across the river until a white flag was raised.

4
"In the First Hour of Danger"

An often repeated legend in the Marine Corps says that on May 23, 1836, there was nailed to the door of Marine headquarters in Washington this notice:

> Have gone to Florida to fight Indians. Will be back when the war is over.
>
> A. Henderson, Commandant.[11]

All along the frontier the Indians had risen to fight the government's plan to force them to move from their traditional homes, now coveted by white settlers and land speculators, to the wilderness west of the Mississippi River. The Army, scattered along the inland edge of the nation and numbering only about 4,000 soldiers, needed help. Colonel Henderson volunteered the Marine Corps, and President Jackson accepted with alacrity. This was a historic event for the Corps—the first time under the broader ruling of the act of 1834 that the Marines would go on detached service "by order of the President of the United States."

On May 21, the Army posted General Order 33, which said in part:

> 1. The Colonel of the Marines having tendered the services of his Corps for duty in the field, the President accordingly has been pleased to direct that all the disposable Marines be withdrawn from their respective stations, leaving at each a Sergeant's guard, and that the Corps, under the direction of the Commandant be organized and forthwith proceed in two detachments from the

[For the location of places in thé Indian wars see map No. 1 in the map section.—*Au.*]

New York and Norfolk stations, via Charleston and Augusta for Fort Mitchell, and there report to the Commanding General for active duty with the Army in the field.[12]

Henderson moved with vigor. His instructions to take the field went out to the commanders of the Marine detachments in Boston, Washington, Norfolk, Philadelphia and New York. In charge of headquarters he left Lt. Col. Wainwright and a handful of crippled or older men.

On June 2, the *National Intelligencer* in Washington reported the Marine Corps departure with breathless amazement:

> In the present emergency it did not wait even an intimation that its services would be acceptable, but promptly came forth, through its commanding officer, in the first hour of danger, and voluntarily offered to leave their comfortable quarters, and within one week from the offer, we see a strong and well-appointed detachment of fine-looking men bidding farewell to families and friends, and taking up the line of march to seek a savage and treacherous foe in a distant land and in an inhospitable climate. . . .[13]

On June 23, Henderson reported 462 men to Gen. Winfield Scott at Columbus, Georgia, on the Alabama border across from Fort Mitchell. They had marched the 224 miles across the state from Augusta in 14 days. The next day, 160 additional Marines, who had sailed from New York under Lt. Col. William H. Freeman, reached Milledgeville, Georgia, in the center of the state and headed south to Florida.

The story behind the presence of the Marines in Georgia and Florida is one of horror and tragedy. The "wars" against the Creeks and Seminoles were born out of fear and fraud, intimidation and injustice—on both sides.

Land was the disputed prize. As America's population grew, the frontier pushed outward. Where Indians stood in the way, they were shoved aside or killed. North of the Ohio River, the Indian tribes were relatively weak; but on the Old Southwest frontier, the way west was blocked by four powerful tribes—the

Creeks and Cherokees and further west the Chickasaws and Choctaws. They stood more or less together against the white man's advance.

These southern Indians were people who cultivated the land, raised herds and crops, laid out roads and sometimes sent their children to missionary schools. They loved their land and their ancestral homes. But the guerrilla warfare between them and the white people stretched far back in time and was filled with ingrained bitterness. Eventually, 60,000 southern Indians were expelled from their homelands by the whites.

The idea to "remove" the Indians west of the Mississippi was originally Thomas Jefferson's. Apparently his great democratic ideals did not extend in their purest form to the Indian; Jefferson advocated furnishing the Indian with goods, letting him get in debt and then persuading him to surrender his lands to pay off these debts.

A major civil war erupted among the Creeks at about the time the United States entered the War of 1812. This civil war was a reaction to efforts to "civilize" the southern tribes under the leadership of Indian agent Benjamin Hawkins. Hawkins hoped by developing an agricultural economy to reduce the Indians' need for huge land holdings and to make great tracts available for white settlers.

His reforms split the Creeks. The conservative faction, the Red Sticks, opposed Hawkins' reforms and looked to the Shawnee chief Tecumseh, who opposed adoption of the white men's ways and the cession of Indian lands. His "prophets" fired up the people into a civil war that led directly to the massacre at Fort Mims on August 30, 1813. In that massacre, more than 300 men, women and children were slaughtered. It converted the civil war into a war against the United States and led to Andrew Jackson destroying the strength of the Creeks in the famous Battle at Horseshoe Bend in Alabama on March 27, 1814. Of 1,000 Creek warriors only 70 escaped. Not one surrendered. The Creek survivors fled to join the Seminole tribe in Spanish Florida; and on August 9, a handful of minor Creek chiefs signed a treaty with Jackson ceding two-thirds of all the tribe's lands—20 million acres known as the Hickory Ground.

Now, events moved toward all-out war and the intercession of the Marines.

Jackson invaded Spanish Florida in April 1818. Although deplored in Washington, this so-called First Seminole War was popular in the West and the following February precipitated the acquisition of East Florida from Spain (West Florida had already been seized during the War of 1812). Settlers and land speculators poured into Florida; and Jackson, by this time its military governor, proposed consolidating the Seminoles in one place. The result was the shameful Treaty of Camp Moultrie in which the Seminoles agreed to move into a reservation. The treaty, signed in September 1823, was obtained by bribery and intimidation, and has been called "one of the worst in all history."[14] The Seminoles, unable to feed themselves in their swampy new home, resorted to stealing cattle and murdering.

Jackson also forced treaties on the Cherokees by supplementing "open intimidation with wholesale hidden bribery";[15] on the Chickasaws, by much the same means, and in 1825 on the Creeks.

In 1829, Jackson, the Indians' great enemy, reached the White House. And on May 27, 1830, after prolonged and violent debate, Congress passed a Removal Act providing for an exchange of land with the Indians. Under the threat that this was their last chance to be compensated for lands the white man was determined to take, the Chickasaws agreed provisionally to removal on September 1; and the Choctaws succumbed by the end of the month.

The Cherokees, the best organized of the tribes, carried their case to the United States Supreme Court, where the majority, led by Chief Justice John Marshall, denied their appeal because they were not a "foreign nation" but a "domestic dependent nation." As a result, part of the Cherokees eventually agreed to go West; a quarter of the tribe perished on the way.

Jackson was also determined to move out the Creeks and the Seminoles. His policy again led to war. In the Upper Mississippi Valley, Chief Black Hawk threw the Sauk and Fox against the United States Army. In Florida, Osceola roused his Seminole warriors to violent resistance. The charismatic son of an English trader named William Powell and a Creek mother, Osceola would become the Marines' great Indian opponent.

In the autumn of 1835, the able Indian agent Wiley Thompson began to gather the Seminoles at Tampa Bay to ship them westward by sea. On the morning of December 28, Osceola struck back. A large Seminole war party ambushed Maj. Francis L. Dade and 109 soldiers marching to Fort King, where Ocala, Florida, stands today. Dade and all but three of his men were massacred.

That same afternoon at Fort King, Wiley Thompson was ambushed 300 yards from the Indian Agency office. There were 14 bullets in his body and he had been scalped. Osceola himself apparently led the party that murdered him. The war was on; the whole Florida peninsula was shaken by fear.

Three days after Dade and Thompson were killed, Osceola attacked a group of 500 regulars and militiamen under the command of Gen. Duncan L. Clinch as they crossed the Withlacoochee River. The Indians threw them back across the river; Osceola's tactics were brilliantly executed.

The Seminoles now on the warpath were mostly Creeks who had moved south, many of them after the Battle of Horseshoe Bend. Ever since the Treaty of Payne's Landing on May 9, 1832, the 5,000 Seminoles had expected to be transported west. Because of the impending emigration, they had failed to plant crops; even the peaceful members of the tribe had to steal to survive.

The tension between the two races was increased by the presence of Negro slaves who had escaped from Southern plantations and taken refuge with the Seminoles. The runaways were hunted down by their former white owners and by speculators who wanted to resell them on the American market. The Negroes living with the Seminoles joined the Indians in fighting the white man.

A leading historian of the tribe has written: "As long as Andrew Jackson was President, the United States could be depended upon to place the property rights of voters ahead of treaty rights of American Indians. But the Seminoles were not inclined to submit tamely to long-continued injustices."[16]

In answer to the massacre of Dade, the murder of Thompson and the defeat of Clinch, the Navy's West India Squadron under Commodore A. J. Dallas was ordered to Florida to help suppress the Indians. A detachment of several officers, a half-dozen sailors and 57 Marines under 1st Lt. Nathaniel S. Waldron of *Constellation* was landed on January 22, 1836, at Fort Brooke (on the site of present-day Tampa). These were the first Marines to join the Second Seminole War. Waldron and his men stayed at Fort Brooke, while other ships' detachments scurried up and down the coast in answer to frantic pleas for help from white settlers.

On February 10, Gen. Edmund P. Gaines arrived with 1,100 troops from New Orleans and set off after the Seminoles, leaving Waldron's detachment and a few soldiers to hold Fort Brooke. Gaines' expedition failed, and he was soon replaced by Gen. Winfield Scott, who spent the spring futilely chasing his elusive foe. Waldron's Marines participated in several inconclusive skirmishes. The Indians raided behind Scott's lines, attacked weak points and avoided any showdown.

Soon, Scott headed north to fight the Creeks, who had risen in Alabama; and his unfinished Florida business was turned over to Governor Robert K. Call, commander of the volunteers in Clinch's controversial defeat. On July 3, Commodore Dallas wrote the Secretary of the Navy: "The Marines which I detached from this ship [*Constellation*], have been marching and countermarching, have done their duty with credit to themselves and the Corps, and are still detained at Fort Brooke."[17] Lieutenant Waldron and his men would stay at Tampa Bay until August. By then, it would be a new war.

However just their cause, the Creeks were now attacking white settlements, especially around Columbus, Georgia, destroying property and murdering whites. Settlers were fleeing into Columbus for protection. On May 19, the United States government ordered that the whole tribe—those who were peaceful as well as those on the warpath—be removed west. It would take 11,000 troops, including 1,800 friendly Creeks, to subdue 1,500 hostile Indians.

The Marines led into the Creek country by Henderson encamped 15 miles below Columbus on the west side of the Chattahoochee River. Their camp was named after their Commandant.

> Their location being in the most exposed part of the enemy's country [reported the Columbus, Georgia, *Sentinel* on July 1], their camp has been for two successive nights roused by Indians lurking about, and approaching the picket sentinels within a few yards, when they were

fired on and pursuit immediately given, but no traces of them could be found. Last night, after the roll of the drum had ceased, a whoop was distinctly heard up the river, which no doubt was a signal to a party above. . . .[18]

On June 24, the very day after they arrived in the Creek country, Marine Captains Levi Twiggs and William Dulany led their companies, joined by a company of Georgia militia, in pursuit of a party of Creeks. At the Indians' deserted camp, fires were still burning, meat still cooking. The troops captured some horses and other property belonging to the Indians and returned to Camp Henderson.

The Marines in the Creek country had left behind their frock coats and high caps. They wore white fatigues, and most of them were armed with old-fashioned muskets. A few had new Colt rifles, which had a nasty tendency to blow up if kept loaded for several days. Commandant Henderson carried the gold cane that was a souvenir of the fight with *Cyane* and *Levant*.

Lt. Col. Samuel Miller took his First Battalion on patrols; but more often, the Marines' efforts were company-size. Through the remainder of the summer, the Marines guarded the mail road from Columbus west to Tuskegee, Alabama, and supervised the concentration camp at Talessee, Alabama, one of several in which the Creeks were being collected for removal.

The march of the 15,000 Creeks to today's Oklahoma began early in July. The Indians called it "the Trail of Tears." The first group of 1,600 was guarded by soldiers. The Indians, chained together in double file, walked along slowly and sullenly. The children, the aged and the sick followed in wagons. They trudged west to the Alabama River at Montgomery, where they were jammed into barges and towed downstream to Mobile on the Gulf. Eighty-one died on the way, including fifty children.

The fifth detachment of Creeks was in charge of Marine 2d Lt. John T. Sprague, an able and sensitive twenty-six-year-old native of Newburyport, Massachusetts, the son of an Army surgeon. Apparently well educated, he read poetry in the field and wrote extensively and well about his experiences. He had joined the Corps in 1834; and in 1837 he would resign to accept a commission in the Army. During the Civil War, Sprague served as Florida's military governor.

On August 10, 1836, following his orders, Lieutenant

Sprague reached his detachment of Creek Indians. He assembled all the chiefs and explained the removal arrangements. His talk was met with utter silence.

> The necessity of their leaving the country immediately was evident to every one; although wretchedly poor they were growing more so every day they remained. A large number of whitemen were prowling about, robbing them of their horses and cattle and carrying among them liquors which kept up an alarming state of intoxication.[19]

On September 5, Sprague and his long line of hopeless, humiliated charges started out from the eastern edge of Alabama. The first goal was Memphis, on the Mississippi. In the train were 1,984 Indians, 45 wagons for the children and the sick and 500 ponies. Some 150 actively hostile Indians who had hidden in the swamps joined the line in the night. The Indians drove a herd of cattle before them for fresh beef. Each day corn was distributed, and every second day the rest of a meager ration was handed out.

Sprague pushed to get out of the area where whites "preyed upon them without mercy," seizing their horses and even their clothes. He feared the Indians would be roused to violence. But they were beaten in spirit. The long line moved an average of 12 miles a day for 20 days. Sprague had increasing trouble with stragglers; and finally, persuaded by the heat and weariness, he planned a halt. The civilian wagon contractors opposed the delay; it would eat up their profits, they protested. But the Marine lieutenant told them he intended to bring the Indians west in good condition. On September 24, his detachment rested for the day.

When they set out again, Sprague sped up the pace. They moved as much as 20 miles a day. Water was scarce. Some of the wagoners would start in the morning whether their Indian passengers were ready or not; children and old people then had to walk. Many stragglers came into the nightly camp long after dark. Sometimes, Sprague would hire the wagons to go back and bring them in.

By October 9, they were near Memphis. Here, Sprague's tenuous control broke down. Rations could not be distributed fairly. Frequently, the Indians got drunk. "If any white-man broke in upon these bacchanals he did it at the imminent hazard of his life," wrote Sprague.

By October 27, some 13,000 Indians had congregated at Memphis to cross the Mississippi River. Liquor was prohibited, and rations were issued in more orderly fashion. The Indians rested and recouped their strength.

Sprague's group was the third to cross the Mississippi. He organized 500 men to ride their ponies through the huge 50-mile-wide Mississippi Swamp. And he arranged for the bulk of his party, some 1,500, to take the steamboat *John Nelson* and two flatboats up the Arkansas River directly to Little Rock. It was good judgment, and Sprague wrote later, ". . . it put us ahead of all the parties, secured us an abundant supply of provisions, and avoided a tedious journey of one hundred and fifty miles on foot."

While the men on horseback were being escorted by an assistant, Sprague went with the main group by boat. This group had to be divided, some 900 waiting for the steamboat's second trip. The first party on *John Nelson* arrived at Little Rock on November 3. Most of those who had come through the swamp joined them the next day. But some of the Indians did not show up. They had found a refuge in the swamp, where game was plentiful and the white man was nonexistent.

On November 14, the steamboat carrying the second party arrived at Lewisburg, where Morrilton, Arkansas, is today. Lieutenant Sprague put the sick, feeble and aged aboard the boat and sent them to Fort Gibson, the final rendezvous, in what is now Oklahoma. They arrived there on November 22.

The agents who were rounding up the stragglers rejoined Sprague by November 17. They had failed to bring in some of the Indians who had hidden in the swamp. The weather was growing more severe, and Sprague ordered the advance to proceed at once. The governor of Arkansas sent 100 militiamen to drive the Indians out of the swamp. They fled toward Fort Gibson.

The main party was also having its troubles. Sprague wrote: "The sufferings of the Indians at this period were intense. With nothing more than a cotton garment thrown over them, their feet bare, they were compelled to encounter cold, sleeting storms and to travel over hard frozen ground. Frequent appeals were made to me to clothe their nakedness and to protect their lacerated feet." There was little Sprague could do, despite his real sympathy for his hapless charges. They suffered frostbite, waded barefoot in cold mud and stumbled over frozen ground. The dead were devoured by wolves. Sprague drove them on; "delay only made our condition worse."

The steamboat returning from Fort Gibson found them camped near where the Spadra River enters the Arkansas. On November 24, Sprague put aboard 1,600 Indians, almost all those who had been advancing by foot; the rest were mounted on horses or put in wagons. Six days later, the boat grounded; and the people aboard had to continue overland. Now the Creeks were able to get whiskey from other Indians living in the area. They repeatedly got drunk. "The artifices of both combined no man could detect," Sprague commented sadly.

When at last Sprague's contingent reached Fort Gibson, a count was made; there were 2,237 Indians present, more than Sprague had started out with. The column had been increased by the previously hostile Indians who had sneaked into the line of march and whom Sprague had never been able to enroll. The lieutenant shook his head and wondered how they had survived without rations. Their friends and families had apparently shared the little they had.

Each Indian was given "a blanket and a homespun frock," in accordance with the treaty; and then they moved on to the country assigned to them. Sprague went along. "Thirty five miles beyond Fort Gibson I encamped them upon a prairie and they soon after scattered in every direction, seeking a desirable location for their new homes. . . ."

Although Sprague's detachment was the fifth to set out, he brought it in second. Sprague and his chargs had traveled 1,225 miles in 96 days, 800 miles by land and 425 by water. On the way, 29 had died—14 children and, as Sprague put it, the "aged, feeble and intemperate."

Looking back at his experience, John Sprague said of the Indians he had brought west:

> They were poor, wretchedly, and depravedly poor, many of them without a garment to cover their nakedness. . . .

They were in a deplorable condition when they left their homes, and a journey upwards of a thousand miles could not certainly have improved it. . . . The situation of the officers of the Government, at the head of these parties, was peculiarly responsible and embarrassing. . . . Had a few thousand dollars been placed at the disposal of the officer which he could have expended at his discretion, the great sufferings which all ages, particularly the young, were subjected to, might have been in a measure avoided. But as it was, the officer was obliged to listen to their complaints without any means of redress.

The Indians under Sprague's care had been fortunate to have the Marine lieutenant in charge. Some of them realized this; they wrote to Sprague, thanking him for his kindness. And they added:

You have been with us many moons. . . . You have heard the cries of our women and children . . . our road has been a long one . . . and on it we have laid the bones of our men, women, and children. When we left our homes the great [Brigadier] General [Thomas S.] Jesup told us that we could get to our country as we wanted to. We wanted to gather our crops, and we wanted to go in peace and friendship. Did we? No! We were drove off like wolves . . . lost our crops . . . and our peoples' feet were bleeding with long marches. . . . Tell General Jackson if the white man will let us we will live in peace and friendship . . . but tell him these agents [emigrating contractors] came not to treat us well, but make money and tell our people not to be drove off like dogs. We are men . . . we have women and children, and why should we come like wild horses?[20]

The last piteous cry from a tragic people.

5
Fighting
the Seminoles

Late in that same summer of 1836, Colonel Henderson marched his Marine battalion south. The war with the Creeks had been won; the Seminoles remained unconquered. By the end of August, most of the Marine unit was at Tallahassee. Henderson joined Lt. Col. Freeman's battalion, which had gone directly into Florida, and proceeded via Apalachicola to Fort Brooke on Tampa Bay. On October 28 Henderson took command at Fort Brooke.

The two battalions now were reorganized into one regiment of six companies, comprising more than half the strength of the entire Corps. They were joined by 750 Creek volunteers, men who had not taken up arms against United States forces. The Indians wore white turbans to distinguish them from the enemy in battle. Marine officers commanded some of the Creek units; this was the Corps' first experience leading "native troops" (unless one counts O'Bannon's adventure in North Africa).

On November 1, Florida's Governor Call led 1,000 men into the Great Wahoo Swamp and was defeated. On November 18, he entered the swamp with a scouting force of Tennessee volunteers. This time, the Seminoles were driven back, leaving 25 dead on the field. At dawn three days later, the army again plunged into Wahoo Swamp. Meeting the Indians, the troops charged forward, whooping and yelling, and in a heavy fire fight forced the Seminoles to retreat.

The allied Creeks led the pursuit. The enemy strongly positioned on the far side of the main stream of the Withlacoochee River. Army Maj. David Moniac, a thirty-four-year-old Creek who had graduated from West Point in 1822, bravely entered the river and was killed. The enemy fire was intense.

Marine 1st Lt. Andrew Ross (who held the rank of captain in the Creek unit) tried to cross and was shot. With nightfall near and ammunition low, the Army did not try to cross again.

Lieutenant Ross was carried to Fort Heileman near Jacksonville, where he died on December 11 of his wounds. He was the first Marine officer to be killed in action since the end of the War of 1812.

Governor Call was now replaced by Brig. Gen. Jesup, who had led the war against the Creeks in Alabama. Jesup, an experienced commander, came to respect the hardy, courageous Seminoles with whom he now did battle.

Jesup organized the Army of the South into two brigades and on January 8, 1937, gave Colonel Henderson command of the Second Brigade. It contained the Marines, the 4th U.S. Infantry, two artillery regiments, the Georgia Volunteers and one battalion of Creeks. On April 26, the Army of the South would be reorganized into two departments; and Henderson would receive command of one.

The order of January 8 also detailed men from both brigades to guard convoys moving between Tampa Bay and the Army's depots on the military road north to Fort King. Marine Lt. Col. Samuel Miller was given this responsibility and command of the depots with A Company of the Marines, headquarters troops and whatever convalescents could not accompany the Army into the interior. Miller was instructed to wait at Tampa Bay until a naval garrison from Commodore Dallas' squadron and the 6th Infantry arrived; then he was to march with the infantry to rejoin Jesup.

Jesup ordered the Army to travel light and issued axes to a dozen men in each company, designating them as pioneers. They would be needed when the Army tried to flush the Indians out of the swamps. The Army advanced to Fort Armstrong, which Jesup had built on the site of the Dade massacre. On January 23 near Lake Ahapopka, a detachment including Captain John Harris' company of mounted Marines ("Horse Marines") fought a large body of Indians.

Five days later, Colonel Henderson led a force into the Great Cypress Swamp in the center of the peninsula to search out the main concentration of Seminoles. With him went the mounted Alabama Volunteers, a unit of artillery regulars and the

Marines. The company of Creeks was to follow in support. Early in the morning, Henderson probed a mile into the swamp. The main force of Seminoles retreated, and a group of Creeks pushed into the swamp after them. It was now nearly noon. Soon, firing could be heard ahead; and Henderson ordered the Marines into the battle, followed by the regulars and Alabama Volunteers. Advancing 500 yards in the dense swamp, the Marines came to the Hatchee-Lustee River, a deep, 20-yard-wide stream. The Creeks were engaging the Seminoles across the water.

The Marines and the soldiers extended right and left along the creek bank to lay in a crossfire. The enemy's fire slackened, and the troops plunged over the creek, swimming or crossing on logs. Marine Captain Harris was one of the first across. The enemy fell back. Marine Pvt. Joel Wright was killed in the crossing and three others were wounded.

Henderson's force pursued the enemy into an even more difficult part of the swamp. The Marines and volunteers were now in the center and the Creeks on the flanks. They advanced a half mile through the roughest kind of terrain before the Seminoles made another stand. A fire fight began. Marine Drummer Thomas P. Peterson of B Company was killed and Cpl. Leonard Stevens was wounded. The enemy retreated again, and the Army gave chase. The Seminoles made scattered stands, but Henderson's force could never catch up to their main body. Henderson pursued until dark and then returned to camp.

The Battle of the Hatchee-Lustee was the Marines' largest engagement of the Second Seminole War. It was a crucial battle and led directly to a conference on February 18 between Brig. Gen. Jesup and Seminole Chiefs Abraham, Jumper and Alligator. After prolonged negotiations, an armistice was signed on March 6. The Indians agreed to assemble for removal; it looked deceptively as though the war was over.

For his part in the Indian campaigns, Henderson was promoted to brevet brigadier general, making him the first Marine to hold general officer rank. Captains William Dulany and Harris were made brevet majors. Corporal Stevens was promoted to sergeant and Pvt. Josiah Whitcomb to corporal for their gallantry in action. Six Marines had been killed in action or died later of their wounds.

The Indians now began to concentrate at Tampa Bay. Lt. Col. Miller had his hands full providing for them, guarding those taken in battle and keeping away whites hunting Negroes they claimed to own. In camp seven miles from Tampa, Colonel Henderson wrote in his journal on April 13:

> The Indians come in slowly, but such is their characteristic, & I doubt not they will all be in this month or early in the next. We expect the first emigrating party to start the last of this week. So soon as this takes place, I shall ask orders to return to Washington. I did not wish to be premature in this request, & thereby do away any of the character which the Corps or myself has acquired on this service. I am anxious to leave Florida & our connection with the Army, without the shadow of a˙stain on our escutcheon, & that the Corps shall return to its stations with an untarnished character. . . .[21]

On May 22, Henderson was free to return to Washington; he was accompanied by Captain Howle. Brevet Lt. Col. Miller was left in command of the troops south of the Hillsborough River. His force included 189 Marines at Tampa Bay. Indians continued to trickle into the camp site selected for them near Fort Brooke; 20 vessels waited in the harbor to carry them to New Orleans. All the units in Florida had been stripped to skeleton strength. Everyone was convinced that the Battle of the Hatchee-Lustee, in which the Marines had played so important a role, had finished the war.

Then, at midnight on June 2, in a daring raid at Tampa Bay, Osceola recaptured the more compliant chiefs who had agreed to emigrate, including the aged principal chief Micanopy, and forced them and all their 700 followers to leave the Marine-guarded encampment before dawn. Suddenly, progress toward removing the tribe had been destroyed, and the war again begun. It would go on for five more years.

Jesup was discouraged and bitter. On June 10, he ordered the militia built up once more and wrote the Secretary of War, "If the war be carried on it must necessarily be one of extermination. We have, at no former period in our history, had to contend with so formidable an enemy. No Seminole proves false to his country, nor has a single instance ever occurred of a first rate warrior having surrendered."[22] Jesup also wrote the adjutant general, asking to be relieved of his command. "I have the honor to report that this campaign, so far as relates to Indian emigration has entirely failed," he said. "The Indians, generally, would prefer death to removal from the country, and nothing short of extermination will free us from them."[23]

Miller wrote Henderson on June 15, ". . . The Seminoles encamped in this vicinity, have de-camped, and taken French leave."[24] Henderson was in a quandry. His men had been away from their normal posts for a year; they had endured the hardship of a rugged campaign in a disease-ridden climate. On June 24, he wrote Jesup at the request of the Secretary of the Navy, asking that the Marines be returned to their home stations. On the fourth of July, Jesup replied, "There is nothing within my power which I would not do to serve your Corps—I owe too many obligations to be indifferent to its interests, or even to its wishes . . .[but] . . . The number of troops composing the Corps cannot be abstracted from service here without endangering the peace and security of the frontier. . . . "[25]

The Marines in Florida were already alerted and prepared for action. Jesup headed north to inspect his outlying bases, leaving Miller in command at Fort Brooke with orders to send out patrols of friendly Indians to search for the Seminoles. Finally, on July 18, Miller was ordered to proceed to Washington with Jesup's thanks for his services. Command of the Marines remaining at Tampa Bay was turned over to Brevet Maj. William Dulany.

A week later, Jesup received a critical letter from Secretary of War Joel R. Poinsett, insisting that the policy of removal be continued. Poinsett said firmly:

> To abandon the settled policy of the Government because the Seminoles have proved themselves to be good warriors, and rely for the protection of our frontier upon the faith of treaties with a people who have given such repeated proofs of treachery, would be unwise and

> impolitic. . . . I am persuaded that this obligation [to the citizens of Florida] can be fulfilled without seeking to exterminate the Seminoles . . .[26]

The effort to remove the Seminoles to the West continued. The summer passed without decision; and in October, Osceola offered to parlay under a flag of truce. During the meeting, he was seized and brought in a prisoner. Jesup was widely condemned for violating the truce flag, but some analysts have argued that his action was justified in this guerrilla war. Osceola was taken to Fort Moultrie at Charleston where he died, probably of malaria. He was thirty-three, and as Marine Lt. John Sprague called him, "the master-spirit of the war."[27]

The Seminoles continued to resist removal under Chief Coacoochee (Wild Cat), who said, "I would rather be killed by a white man in Florida than die in Arkansas."[28]

The field command in the fall of 1837 was turned over to Col. Zachary Taylor, who had fought the Indians in the Northwest. On Christmas Day, Taylor's army units fought the last big battle of the war at Lake Okeechobee. But it was not decisive; the Indians crept back into the Everglade swamps.

There were still 190 Marines serving with the Army in Florida on December 1, and Secretary of War Poinsett wrote Congress: "Part of the Marine Corps, which volunteered its services in Florida, and distinguished itself during the last campaign, still remains there; and it is hoped that they may be permitted to continue their valuable services to the Army of the South until the close of the war."[29]

On January 24, 1838, Brig. Gen. Jesup was wounded in the face; and, on May 15, he returned to Washington. Before he left Florida, he wrote a candid letter to the Secretary of War:

> In regard to the Seminoles, we have committed the error of attempting to remove them when their lands were not required for agricultural purposes; when they were not in the way of the white inhabitants; and when the greater portion of their country was an unexplored wilderness, of the interior of which we were as ignorant as of the interior of China.[30]

The general had gained in wisdom in Florida. He came to see the injustice of the Seminole removal to benefit land speculators and slave hunters. The war went on long after Jesup had left. Many of the Indians were forceably moved beyond the Mississippi; others holed up in the virtually impenetrable swamps. The fighting and dying continued, but the Seminoles were really never conquered.

In all, 30 Marines of the regiment had died in Florida. That seven died as the result of enemy action and 23 of disease documents the rigors of this campaign.

When the Marine Corps' duty with the Army was over in the summer of 1838, the Colonel Commandant was perfectly justified in telling his men that their services against the Indians had "elevated their Ancient Corps in the estimation of the Country."[31] But Marines in smaller numbers followed the two tragic trails down which the war now sped.

6
With the Mosquito Fleet

While the Marine regiment was serving with the Army in Florida, other members of the Corps were fighting there with the Navy. For six years, these Marines waged a guerrilla war from the sea and up the rivers leading into the swampy interior. Like the men of the regiment, they suffered more from disease than from the enemy.

When Henderson and his men first arrived at Fort Brooke in the fall of 1836, they freed Lt. Nathaniel Waldron's Marine detachment to return to the ships of Commodore Dallas' West India Squadron based at Key West. On October 12, an expedition, led by Navy Lt. L. M. Powell and including 95 Marines under Waldron, attempted to surprise the Indians in the area where Miami stands today but found the Indians' settlements abandoned. Lieutenant Powell organized a more ambitious expedition to hunt Seminoles along the New River in the vicinity of present-day Fort Lauderdale. This lengthy, tiring search also failed. Waldron and the last element of his Marines finally returned to their ships on December 23.

In the summer of 1838, a special force was organized under Navy Lt. John T. McLaughlin to round up the Seminoles who had fled into the Everglades. Working with small schooners, a tiny steamer, a few barges and 140 canoes, this novel unit won the nickname "Mosquito Fleet." It started out with 160 sailors and Marines and by 1841 totaled 622 men, including 130 Marines. In November 1839, the force was joined by two companies of Marines, led by 1st Lt. George H. Terrett and 2d Lts. Isaac R. Wilson and Robert D. Taylor. Terrett had fought the pirates at Quallah Battoo and would later win renown outside the halls of Montezuma. He was succeeded in command

131

of the Mosquito Fleet Marines after a year by 1st Lt. Thomas T. Sloan.

The Mosquito Fleet, based on Indian Key, made innumerable sorties into the Everglades. Detachments lived in canoes for weeks at a time. On one of their largest expeditions, McLaughlin set out from Fort Dallas on the Miami River on November 3, 1841, with two companies of the 3rd Field Artillery and 150 sailors and Marines. They entered the Caloosahatchee River where Fort Myers now stands. Paddling upriver in canoes, they skirmished with the enemy deep in the interior near Lake Thompson, picked their way through the Everglades and finally arrived back at Fort Dallas. On their 22-day patrol they had explored a wilderness never before seen by white men.

When the war ended in July 1842, the Marines with the Mosquito Fleet returned North. Eighteen had died of disease and other causes, and one, Acting Cpl. William Smith, had been killed in combat.

In the entire Florida war, a staggering total of 1,466 men of the Regular Army and 61 men of the Marine Corps lost their lives to the enemy and to tropical disease. The war had also cost the United States $30 million—when it was over, Seminoles remained in the Everglades.

By the end of 1838, approximately 15,400 Seminoles had been "removed." Perhaps 2,000 more still defied the United States in the Everglade fastness. A number of Marines, including Terrett and Sloan, played significant roles in moving the bulk of the tribe beyond the Mississippi. In the judgment of a leading historian, "the worst of the removal hardships were endured by the Seminoles."[32]

Early in 1838, 1st Lt. John G. Reynolds was assigned to bring a large party of Seminoles and their slaves to the West. Reynolds, who would command the Marines at Bull Run in the Civil War, had been born in New Jersey in 1801. He had dropped out of West Point in his third year and joined the Marine Corps as a second lieutenant in 1824.

In obeying his orders to escort the Indians, Reynolds became embroiled in one of the major problems of the Seminole war: the Negroes residing with the Indians. Three parties were vying for control of the unfortunate Negroes then held by the Army: the Seminoles who regarded them as their property, the Creek warriors who had captured them in Florida and claimed possession of them, and the white men who sought to reenslave them on the plantations of the South.

Reynolds and 29 men sailed from Charleston on February 22 with 220 Seminoles, picked up the Negroes being held at Tampa Bay and took them to New Orleans, where the Indians were confined at Fort Pike. Two months later, Reynolds brought a second party of Indians and Negroes from Tampa to New Orleans, where 1,160 now awaited transportation to their new homes. Reynolds kept the Seminoles and their Negroes together, in compliance with his orders.

Reynolds was caught in a crossfire between the Indian Office and Secretary of War Poinsett, who apparently was advising Georgians to bid on the Seminoles' Negroes for quick profits. The Marine lieutenant moved swiftly to escape the slave traders and their lawyers, who sought to prevent the movement of the Negroes into Indian territory.

A slave dealer succeeded in buying the Negroes from the Indians for $15,000. Reynolds refused to recognize the purchase, regarding the Negroes as prisoners of war whom he had been instructed to escort safely to Fort Gibson. He began the movement of 1,127 people—200 of whom were Negroes—up the Mississippi in two steamboats. The slave dealer who had bought the Negroes pursued them; but on June 12, Reynolds delivered to Fort Gibson all of the large party except 54 who died en route.

Later, the slave traders filed a claim in Congress, and a vigorous debate ensued. As a historian of the removal has said, "It . . . became clear that the war in Florida was conducted largely as a slave catching enterprise for the benefit of the citizens of Georgia and Florida."[33]

In the spring of 1838, Brig. Gen. Jesup was ordered west to put down trouble that had erupted with the Cherokees. Marine Captain Dulany and his D and E Companies were sent to Baton Rouge to assist him. Lieutenants Terrett and Caldwell went with the detachment, which was the last of the Marine regiment to leave Florida. Some 15,000 Cherokees had refused to carry out their removal agreement. When the Army massed a sizable force to compel them, the Cherokees capitulated and moved peaceably. Dulany's Marines stayed in the West only a short time; on July 23, 1838, they reported to Marine Corps headquarters in Washington.

This was the last assignment performed by the Marine

regiment that had been volunteered to fight the Indians. Its service with the Army marked one of the turning points in Marine Corps history—for the first time, a Marine expeditionary force had fought a sustained campaign ashore to extend the power of the United States. It pointed the way to Belleau Wood, Okinawa and the Chosin Reservoir.

*Center design of flag given to the Marine Corps after the
Mexican War by the citizens of Washington, D.C.
Reputedly, this is the first time the phrase "From Tripoli
to the Halls of the Montezumas" was used.
Museums Branch, USMC*

SEMPER FIDELIS

IV
THE
MEXICAN
WAR
1842-1847

1
The Button
on the Mainmast

On the rolling South Atlantic in the autumn of 1844, a bearded ordinary seaman aboard the frigate *United States*, returning from a long voyage into the South Pacific, was called before the mast for being absent from his sailing station. He was ordered flogged with the cat-o'-nine tails. "My blood seemed clotting in my veins," the young sailor remembered later. "I felt icy cold at the tips of my fingers, and a dimness was before my eyes. But through that dimness the boatswain's mate, a scourge in hand, loomed like a giant."[1]

Suddenly, a corporal of Marines stepped forward and declared that the seaman had been absent from his post only because he had not been told his assignment. "Seldom or never before had a marine dared to speak to the Captain of a frigate in behalf of a seaman at the mast." The sailor's immediate superior, the captain of the maintop, mustered his courage and also defended him. The warship's captain released the sailor without a lashing.

This threatened flogging and a Marine's courage have not drifted unrecorded into the limbo of time past because the seaman was Herman Melville, who would one day write *Moby Dick*.

Melville had gone to the Pacific on a whaler and jumped ship in the Marquesas Islands (where Porter and Gamble had stopped 30 years earlier). Eventually reaching Tahiti, he signed aboard *United States*, heading home around Cape Horn. He later wrote *White Jacket*, a book depicting life aboard the American man-of-war.

Descriptions of Marines of the distant past are rare. Melville's vivid writing about the Marines on *United States* (which he camouflaged as *USS Neversink*) is a unique account of U.S. Marines of that day. He termed them "bronzed marines" and remembered that "The marine sergeants are generally tall fellows with unyielding spines and stiff upper lips, and very exclusive in their tastes and predilections."

He sat across from

> one of the marine messes, mustering the aristocracy of the marine corps—the two corporals, the drummer and fifer, and some six or eight rather gentlemanly privates, native-born Americans, who had served in the Seminole campaigns in Florida; and they now enlivened their salt fare with stories of wild ambushes in the Everglades; and one of them related a surprising tale of his hand-to-hand encounter with Osceola, the Indian chief, whom he fought one morning from daybreak till breakfast time. This slashing private also boasted that he could take a chip from between your teeth at twenty paces; he offered to bet any amount on it; and as he could get no one to hold the chip, his boast remained forever good.[2]

Melville portrayed the Marines' duties and role aboard the warship with a sailor's antagonistic eye (he never saw the Marines in action against an emeny):

> Our marines had no other than martial duty to perform; excepting that, at sea, they stood watches like sailors, and now and then lazily assisted in pulling the ropes. But they never put foot in rigging or hand in tarbucket.
>
> . . . What, then, were they for? Let us see. When a ship is running into action, her marines generally lie flat on their faces behind the bulwarks (the sailors are sometimes ordered to do the same), and when the vessel is fairly engaged, they are usually drawn up in the ship's waist—like a company reviewing in the Park. At close quarters, their muskets may pick off a seaman or two in the rigging, but at long-run distance they must passively stand in their ranks and be decimated at the enemy's leisure. Only in one case in ten—that is, when their vessel is attempted to be boarded by a large party, are these

marines of any essential service as fighting men; with their bayonets they are then called upon to "repel!"

If comparatively so useless as soldiers, why have marines at all in the Navy? Know, then, that what standing armies are to nations, what turnkeys are to jails, these marines are to the seamen in all large men-of-war. Their muskets are their keys. With those muskets they stand guard over the fresh water; over the grog, when doled; over the provisions, when being served out by the Master's mate; over the "brig" or jail; at the Commodore's and Captain's cabin doors; and, in port, at both the gangways and forecastle. . . .

It must be evident that the man-of-war's-man casts by an evil eye on a marine. To call a man a 'horse-marine,' is, among seamen, one of the greatest terms of contempt.

But the mutual contempt, and even hatred, subsisting between these two bodies of men—both clinging to one keel, both lodged in one household—is held by most Navy officers as the height of the perfection of Navy discipline. It is regarded as the button that caps the uttermost point on their main-mast.

Thus they reason: Secure of this antagonism between the marine and the sailor, we can always rely upon it, that if the sailor mutinies, it needs no great incitement for the marine to thrust his bayonet through his heart; if the marine revolts, the pike of the sailor is impatient to charge. Checks and balances, blood against blood, *that* is the cry and the argument.[3]

In time, Melville became more appreciative of the Marine guard's separateness aboard warships.

In the last year of his life, he wrote *Billy Budd, Foretopman* about an incident in the great mutinies in the British Navy back in 1797. Explaining the mutinies, Melville wrote, "Final suppression, however, there was; but only made possible perhaps by the unswerving loyalty of the marine corps, and a voluntary resumption of loyalty among influential sections of the crews."[4]

The absence of such a Marine guard made possible the most famous mutiny in the American Navy. This conspiracy was uncovered late in 1842 while the 10-gun brig *Somers* was returning to New York after carrying dispatches to an American squadron off Africa. On December 1, three men were hung from *Somers'* yardarm. One was Acting Midshipman Philip Spencer, the young playboy son of the Secretary of War. Before his death, Spencer and one conspirator confessed their guilt; their execution quieted the angry crew and saved the ship.

The *Somers* mutiny became one of the most controversial incidents in American naval history. Although the ship's captain, Commander Alexander Slidell Mackenzie, was acquitted by both a court of inquiry and a courtmartial, naval officers quarreled bitterly over the case for years afterward.

At his courtmartial, Mackenzie asserted that his ship had been jeopardized by the lack of a Marine detachment "to form a counterpoise and check to the turbulent spirits of the common seamen."

In fact, one Marine had been aboard *Somers*: Sgt. Michael H. Garty was a passenger being invalided home and served as the ship's master-at-arms. Mackenzie later wrote the Secretary of the Navy that Garty had been ill and confined to his hammock but "at the moment when the conspiracy was discovered, he rose upon his feet a well man." Garty supported the captain in the crisis, and Mackenzie recommended him for a commission as a Marine second lieutenant, a reward Garty was never granted.

2
The Thrust
Outward

By 1840, the United States had expanded to 17 million people and 26 states. The young nation's thrust outward was not only transcontinental; it was global. Three widely separated stories of the Pacific, Africa and China illustrate the variety and range of this early overseas drive, in which the U.S. Marine Corps participated.

In the summer of 1838, the six ships of the Wilkes Exploring Expedition began one of the most remarkable voyages in American history. Into the Pacific with Navy Lt. Charles Wilkes sailed 33 enlisted Marines, led by Quartermaster Sgt. Simeon Stearns. These were the first United States Marines to see Tarawa, Wake and Makin—a century before Pearl Harbor.

By the time the surviving men and ships returned nearly four years later, they had explored the Antarctic, surveyed 208 Pacific islands and 800 miles of the northwest coast of North America and circumnavigated the globe. At Little Malolo in the Fiji Islands and Tabiteuea in the Gilberts, landing parties of Marines and sailors went ashore and fought hostile natives and destroyed their villages. The expedition visited Tarawa Atoll in the Gilberts on April 19, 1841. Wilkes was surprised at Tarawa's isolation, which was confirmed by the natives' ignorance of tobacco, so highly prized in the other islands, and by their failure to bring out women in their canoes, as visiting whalers usually taught the islanders. When Marines came back to Tarawa in 1943, they used the charts Wilkes had made.

At the end of April, the expedition visited Makin Atoll, which was thickly populated with well-fed, peaceful people. Wilkes learned that the local kings and chiefs monopolized all

[For the location of places in the Pacific see map No. 8 in the map section.—*Au.*]

the women. As Wilkes reported in his most impersonal style: "The consequences of this state of society may readily be imagined to produce illicit intercourse among the lower classes."[5]

Wilkes' ships stopped at Wake Atoll on December 19, 1841, but a landing party found neither coconut trees nor fresh water. (Exactly 100 years later, a Marine battalion was desperately defending this atoll. When the Japanese finally landed, the last Marines to surrender were on the atoll's Wilkes Island.)

On to Manila, past Corregidor, then to Singapore, round the Cape of Good Hope and home to New York: It was a tremendous feat of men and sailing ships. Four Marines lost their lives on the historic expedition. And Marines had seen for the first time some of the tiny Pacific islands that would loom so large in their story.

As the nation stretched its commercial arms around the globe, the Navy became responsible for protecting American interests abroad. Marines were ordered ashore on distant coasts to prevent interference with American commerce and to guard—or avenge the loss of—American lives and property. When Marines were no longer needed to snipe from warships' tops and to repel boarders, they would find a new job: to go ashore and clean up the mess. It is still their job.

In 1842, the United States agreed to establish an 80-gun squadron off Africa to seize American ships in the slave trade and to protect those in legitimate commerce. The Webster-Ashburton Treaty required that American warships make sure merchantmen flying the American flag were not carrying slaves and that British warships search slave ships flying the Union Jack. The British had wanted mutual right of search, but Americans trafficking in human beings raised a "patriotic" hue and cry against foreign inspection of U.S. merchantmen. The British Navy was able to control the British slave trade; and, shamefully, the American flag came to fly over more and more slave ships.

In 1843, Commodore Matthew Calbraith Perry took a squadron to the African coast to meet the American treaty commitment. Matthew Perry was Oliver Hazard "Lake Erie" Perry's kid brother—if one can refer so flippantly to the pompous, dictatorial, slow-moving but brilliant commodore. He was the most important man in the American Navy between Decatur and Farragut; a decade later, he would open Japan to the world. On this cruise in 1843, he would find no slavers, but he would find trouble.

Perry, aboard *USS Macedonian*, visited Liberia, on Africa's Atlantic bulge, where a rash of clashes had erupted between white merchants and the natives. Although he recognized that much of the tension was caused by the traders' high-handed and often brutal actions, one tribe appeared to deserve punishment—the Fishmen, ruled by a giant king called Ben Crack-O. They had seized a portion of shoreline that gave them control over trade with tribes in the interior. Perry was told that the Fishmen had obscenely tortured and killed the crew of the American schooner *Mary Carver*.

At Sino on the southern edge of Liberia, Perry went ashore on November 29 with 75 Marines and sailors. The Marines were commanded by 1st Lt. Jabez C. Rich of *Macedonian* and 2d Lt. Isaac T. Doughty of *Saratoga*. (These two young officers would fight on opposing sides 20 years later.) The landing party occupied the Fishmen's village, and a palaver was held. But nothing came of the meeting, and the Americans marched back to their ships. Later, they landed again and tore down the village.

On December 11, Perry reached Cape Palmas, further south, and took a landing party ashore to deal with King Ben Crack-O himself. Stationing Marines at the gates of Ben Crack-O's palisaded village, Perry met with the huge king, who wore a gorgeous robe and carried a meat cleaver. He denied he had had anything to do with the fate of the crew of the *Mary Carver*.

Two days later, there was another palaver. Perry took 200 men with him. He and the king sat in the center of a pavilion inside the palisade. Behind the American delegation stood Marines; behind the king, a group of native guards. They eyed each other tensely. Through a native interpreter, Ben Crack-O denied everything—and then added that the captain of *Mary Carver* had been killed for murdering two tribesmen.

Suddenly, Perry was on his feet, red with anger. He strode over to the interpreter and charged that he was lying. The terrified man fled. The king leaped at Perry and tried to drag the commodore to where he had left an iron spear. Someone jumped on Ben Crack-O, stripping his robe from him. The naked giant strode on with the proud commodore tucked under his arm. Perry shouted for help. The Marines were already moving into the melee. A sergeant shot Ben Crack-O; two other Marines bayonetted him. Despite his wounds, the king fought viciously. Three men leaped on him; he tore loose and lunged at another officer. He was shot again, stabbed repeatedly and finally overpowered. The Marines fired into the crowd of natives, who scattered immediately. Perry, bruised but not hurt, organized a retreat to the beach, taking the bleeding king with him. The Marines laid down a sharp covering fire.

The Marines then burned the village. Later, they landed and destroyed three other villages, despite sporadic fire from natives hidden in the brush. In the villages they found the flag and other relics from *Mary Carver*. Ben Crack-O died the next day aboard *Macedonian*. Apparently he harbored no grudge; he willed Commodore Perry his seven wives.

On the other side of the globe in June of 1844, Marines were summoned to safeguard Americans from Chinese mobs attacking the British and American compounds on Whampoa Island near Canton. The Chinese had recently been defeated by the British in the infamous Opium Wars. The British, who insisted on the right to import opium into China, had then imposed the Treaty of Nanking, by which they grabbed the island of Hong Kong and opened five ports to British commerce.

The United States sent Caleb Cushing, a Massachusetts politician, to negotiate a similar treaty. On June 15, 1844, rioting broke out again at the British compound. A mob forced the British, who had no ammunition, to flee onto the river in their boats. The next day, several Americans walking in the garden of the United States compound were approached by a menacing mob. Other Americans, who had been sailing on the river, returned; and the embattled group fired into the mob, killing a thirty-year-old Chinese named Hsu A-man. Forty-four Marines and sailors from the sloop of war *St. Louis*, one of Cushing's ships, went ashore armed with muskets and cutlasses to guard the Americans.

On July 3, Cushing signed the Treaty of Wanghia, giving Americans rights equal to those the British had won in the

Opium War. Refusing Chinese demands that he hand over the Americans who had killed Hsu A-man, Cushing formed an American jury, which decided that the shots had been fired in self-defense. The Chinese had to accept the decision and the doctrine of "extraterritoriality," which gave foreigners the right to try their own citizens. The Marines remained to guard American lives and property for another month until the crisis blew over.

3
California
Kick-Off

September 1842. Portent of things to come:

Commodore Thomas ap Catesby Jones—the gunboat hero at New Orleans back in 1814—sits with his East Pacific Squadron at Callao, Peru, and nervously keeps an eye on a British squadron in the harbor. The two nations are tense over the fate of the wild Oregon territory far to the north. There has also been disturbing news about anti-American Mexican officials up in California. And reports that the United States will annex Texas have stirred anger in Mexico. War seems to be just over the horizon.

The British sail from Callao—their destination unknown. Commodore Jones sniffs a fact here and a rumor there. He concludes that the British expect war between the United States and Mexico and have sailed to seize California. With his fastest ships, the frigate *United States* and the sloop *Cyane*, he races for Monterey, the capital of Mexico's Upper California in the center of the coast of what is today the State of California.

On October 19, Jones arrives at Monterey. The British are nowhere in sight. Jones figures proudly that he has won the race and saved California for the United States.

His guns shotted, his decks sanded for action, Jones gives the Mexican governor 18 hours to surrender or he will blast the little 14-gun fort to kingdom come. The governor, a practical man, surrenders. Jones' force looks much larger than his, and anyway he has not heard of any war between their two countries.

Just before noon the next day, Jones sends 150 Marines and seamen to seize the fort and replace the governor's white flag with the Stars and Stripes. The Marines are led by 1st Lt. George W. Robbins from the flagship and Orderly Sgt. John Robinson

[For the location of places in California see map No. 4 in the map section.—*Au.*]

from *Cyane.* As the American flag is hoisted, the landing party gives three cheers "which was returned by the Squadron."[6]

The morning after: The Mexicans and American Consul Thomas O. Larkin show Commodore Jones newspapers and dispatches and finally convince him that his imagination had gotten the better of his information: there is no war. After 30 hours on foreign soil, Jones recalls his men, restores the Mexican flag and repays twofold the powder the fort expended saluting him. He is embarrassed.

It all sounds like farce, except that Jones had an idea Americans were buying; he was just four years too early.

4
Secret Mission
to California

At the White House on the night of Thursday, October 30, 1845, a young Marine lieutenant is conducted into the presence of President James K. Polk for a secret meeting of the greatest import to the United States. First Lt. Archibald H. Gillespie receives confidential instructions and a letter from Secretary of State James Buchanan to deliver to the American consul in the Mexican province of California.

Lieutenant Gillespie is to travel in disguise; no one is to know his destination or his mission. The President wants California for the United States if war should break out with Mexico, and the Marine officer has been chosen as his courier to see that his wishes are carried out. Gillespie steps out of the Presidential mansion into the dark night and one of the most exciting assignments in Marine Corps annals.

Back at his desk, the President writes in his diary:

> I held a confidential conversation with Lieut. Gillespie of the Marine Corps, about eight o'clock P.M., on the subject of the secret mission on which he was about to go to California. His secret instructions and the letter to Mr. Larkin, United States consul at Monterey, in the Department of State, will explain the object of his mission.[7]

Polk did not trust the purpose of Gillespie's assignment even to his private journal.

This was the situation:

Expansion was Polk's ambition. He intended to acquire California and to stretch the boundary of Texas, which had, on the previous July 4, accepted admittance as a state of the Union.

148

And he was determined to keep every European power—England especially—out of North America.

The torturous struggle for Texas independence had been raging for ten years. In 1835, the American settlers in that northern province of Mexico tried to overthrow the dictator Antonio Lopez de Santa Anna. The following March, the Mexicans under Santa Anna smashed the Texans holed up in a fortified mission across the river from San Antonio. They massacred every man in the garrison, and gave Texans a symbol and a rallying cry: They would remember the Alamo.

Texas now declared its independence from Mexico. Sam Houston and his Texas sharpshooters surprised and captured Santa Anna near the mouth of the San Jacinto River.

The American South wanted Texas annexed, fearing that an independent Texas would give England another source for cotton. Northern leaders dreaded that annexation would expand slavery into the new territory, upset the Compromise of 1820 and endanger the Union. Finally in January, 1845, after Polk's election, Congress passed a joint resolution inviting Texas to become a state. The Republic of Texas voted to join the United States.

Mexico asserted that Texas extended only as far south as the Nueces River, some 120 miles north of the Rio Grande. Polk wanted Texas to reach to the Rio Grande. In July and August 1845, the veteran Indian fighter Zachary Taylor, on orders, took an army to Corpus Christi, a smugglers' den at the mouth of the Nueces. Brig. Gen. Taylor was poised to jump into the disputed area between the rivers when given the signal. By October, Taylor commanded 4,000 men—half the Regular U.S. Army. Off both coasts of Mexico stood American naval squadrons. Polk hoped the pressure would pay off without bloodshed; but if Mexico wanted to fight, he was ready. First, he needed to communicate with his Pacific squadron and his consul in California. Enter Marine Lieutenant Gillespie.

Why Gillespie? His judgment would prove not always the wisest, but he was courageous and dependable, tough and cool-headed, and he spoke Spanish fluently. Born in New York State in 1812, Gillespie had served in the Corps briefly as an enlisted man in 1830. Then he had resigned and had been commissioned a second lieutenant late in October 1832—13

149

years before his secret meeting with the President. During the years before Commandant Henderson ordered him to Washington and the fateful meeting, Gillespie had made three cruises in the Pacific (he had been in China in 1844). Navy Secretary George Bancroft years later remembered him as "an accomplished and most trustworthy officer."[8]

The day after the Presidential meeting, Gillespie hurried to New York. He carried dispatches for Commodore John D. Sloat, who commanded the Pacific squadron at Mazatlan on the Mexican west coast, and for Thomas O. Larkin, a local merchant serving as the American consul at Monterey in Mexico's California. He also carried personal letters for Army Lt. John C. Frémont, who was exploring areas of the Far West for the Army's Topographical Corps. The letters were from Frémont's wife and his father-in-law, Senator Thomas Hart Benton. Gillespie was to deliver his dispatches to Sloat and Larkin, and then find Frémont and inform him of Larkin's instructions.

On December 10, a whiskey salesman arrived at Vera Cruz, Mexico, on the brig *Petersburgh* out of New York. With him was his Negro servant, Ben. If anyone had cared enough to notice, he would have seen the salesman spend three days sightseeing and devote an inordinate amount of his time inspecting the city's fortifications and troops. He didn't seem to sell any whiskey. But in his "cover" as a salesman, Lieutenant Gillespie learned a good deal about the defenses of Vera Cruz, where 15 months later the U.S. Army and Marines would make the largest American amphibious landing up to that time.

Then the "commercial traveller" moved on to Mexico City, and stayed there a month, spying out defenses and troop strength. By now he had memorized and destroyed his dispatches. On January 21, 1846, he set out via Guadalajara for Mazatlan and Commodore Sloat. He was far from the Mexican capital when, in March, Polk ordered General Taylor to advance the Army to the Rio Grande—from the Mexican view, to invade their country.

At Mazatlan, Gillespie found the commodore with seven warships and passed on to him his orders to occupy California if war came. Since a British squadron lay in the harbor, "Mr." Gillespie let word get around that he was on his way to China. He sailed on the swift sloop of war *Cyane* for Hawaii. On shipboard, Gillespie wrote out again the dispatches he had memorized. He surely revealed to 2d Lt. William A. T. Maddox, commanding *Cyane's* Marine guard, that he too was a Marine Corps officer. They would meet soon again.

On April 17, Gillespie finally arrived at Monterey—five months and a day out of New York—and gave Consul Larkin his orders. Secretary of State Buchanan had written Larkin that the United States government had two immediate objectives in California: (1) to prevent a foreign power from seizing control of the area, and (2) to support any local independence movement to break away from Mexico—a la Texas. "Whilst I repeat," Buchanan wrote, "that this Government does not, under existing circumstances, intend to interfere between Mexico and California, it would vigorously interpose to prevent the latter from becoming a British or French colony."[9] Was this a veiled hint that the United States would intervene when the right time came? In any case, Larkin now knew that his undercover role was to support any effort by the American settlers in California to set up their own republic.

Buchanan's dispatch made Larkin a confidential agent and said of Gillespie: "He is a gentlemen in whom the President reposes entire confidence. He has seen these instructions and will cooperate as a confidential agent with you in carrying them into execution."

Gillespie set off to find the Army explorer Frémont, who had been ordered out of the province by the Mexican commandante, General José Castro. Frémont was riding slowly north into Oregon, which was still the subject of dispute between the United States and England. At sunset on May 9, Gillespie and Frémont met in a snow-patched glade at the southern tip of Klamath Lake. The Marine showed Frémont a copy of Larkin's instructions and gave him the letters from his wife and Senator Benton. It was the first news from the East that Frémont had received in nearly a year. Frémont later wrote:

> From the [official] letter I learned nothing, but it was intelligibly explained to me by my previous knowledge, by the letter from Senator Benton, and by communications from Lieutenant Gillespie. . . .[10] We had talked late, but now, tired out, Gillespie was asleep. I sat far into

the night, alone, reading my home letters by the fire and thinking I saw the way opening clear before me, and a grand opportunity was now presented to realize fully the farsighted views which would make the Pacific Ocean the western boundary of the United States.[11]

This thirty-three-year-old man, musing alone by the fire, was a strange, flamboyant, ambitious character and one of the most controversial figures in American history. Born a bastard, the handsome young Frémont had won powerful friends and eloped with Jessie Benton, the sixteen-year-old daughter of one of the most important expansionists in the nation—over the senator's violent objections. But Senator Benton had been won over by his daring, often foolhardy son-in-law, and he was now Frémont's staunchest ally. Frémont's account of his earlier explorations, amplified by his wife's literary imagination, had caused a sensation and stimulated Frémont's appetite for glory.

Now, during the night by the campfire under the Oregon pines, Frémont envisioned his "grand opportunity." The government's barely suppressed desire to gain California was a signal to him. Senator Benton's letter was a "trumpet giving no uncertain note." He rejected the specific orders to conciliate the native Californians and work with them toward independence from Mexico: "This idea was no longer practicable, as actual war was inevitable and immediate; moreover, it was in conflict with our own instructions. We dropped this idea from our minds, but falling on others less informed, it came dangerously near to losing us California."[12] That night he changed the whole direction of his government's intent to fit his own ambitions and desires.

What did Frémont mean by "our own instructions?" Did Gillespie bring him separate instructions to act independently of Larkin? What did Gillespie mean when, years later, he referred under oath to himself as "bringing Frémont into the country"?[13] Ever since, historians have debated these questions; at least one has said outright that Frémont was a liar. Today, most historians think that there were no additional orders, but only Frémont's eagerness to turn black into white if that would light the road to fame. As one historian put it, "Though no one knew it, Polk least of all, the conquest of California had begun."[14] Although his very presence in California would be regarded as hostile by General Castro, Frémont decided to return south.

Excited by his visions, Frémont went to sleep without making the most basic preparations against an Indian attack. No guards were posted, and even his veteran scout Kit Carson slept with his gun unloaded. Toward dawn, hostile Indians, who had trailed Gillespie to the camp, struck. They tomahawked three of Frémont's men, and the shooting continued until dawn.

Frémont's men spent the next several days seeking revenge. They killed some Indians and burned a village. Then, led by the two young officers—they were the same age—they headed south to California.

Note this date: Saturday, May 9, 1846. It was the pivotal day.

Scene: Klamath Lake. Late this day Lieutenant Gillespie had caught up with Frémont and set him on the road to participation in the conquest of California, high office, wealth and the first Republican nomination for President of the United States.

Scene: The White House. President Polk met with his Cabinet. War with Mexico was inevitable, they agreed. How could they make it a reality? Should the President go ahead and ask Congress to declare war now, or should he wait for a hostile act? The President ordered preparation of a message to Congress recommending war. The meeting broke up.

At six o'clock the same evening, a dispatch was brought to the President from Brig. Gen. Taylor on the Mexican border: On April 25, two companies of Army dragoons, patrolling in the disputed territory on the Texas side of the Rio Grande, had been surprised by the Mexicans. Sixteen Americans had been killed and 47 captured. Polk had his hostile act. The Cabinet gathered again at 7:30 that night; and at noon on Monday, Polk urged Congress to recognize that "war exists." It did so—and the Mexican War officially began.

Scene: The Rio Grande. On Friday afternoon, May 8, a Mexican army had met Taylor's army at Palo Alto and been badly mauled by the Americans' mobile light artillery. The Mexicans retreated; and on Saturday afternoon, Taylor routed them at the Resaca de la Palma, a dry former bed of the Rio

Grande. The United States won its first fight against a real army since the Battle of New Orleans. Ten days later, Taylor crossed the Rio Grande—thus invading what even the United States recognized as Mexican territory—and occupied Matamoros, the first foreign city captured by American troops.

By the end of that pivotal May 9, the lines of history had converged: The conquest of California was launched, the decision to declare war was made and the first battle of the new war was fought.

One more converging line in Polk's plan to push the nation's boundaries to the Pacific: In the following weeks, the Army of the West was formed at Fort Leavenworth, Kansas, under Col. Stephen Watts Kearny. He had overt orders to march to Mexican-held Santa Fe. His secret orders: Conquer California.

In California, events were moving rapidly. Frémont and Gillespie rode south with rugged companions wearing buckskin and fur caps and carrying rifles and long hunting knives. Many American settlers, increasingly fearful of and angry at California's Mexican authorities, rode in to join them. Frémont was close-mouthed about the instructions Gillespie had brought him, but he encouraged his men to believe that his actions were backed by the power of the United States government.

Gillespie went ahead to San Francisco Bay to obtain arms and supplies from Commander John B. Montgomery aboard the sloop *Portsmouth* at Sausalito. He told Montgomery that Frémont was nearly destitute, living on horse meat, and needed the supplies for an exploring trip. This seemed a legitimate request from an American officer who signed himself "First Lieutenant, U.S. Marine Corps, and special and confidential Agent for California."[15] So Montgomery gave Gillespie a keg of powder, 8,000 percussion caps and enough lead to make 9,000 bullets—a lot of ammunition for an exploring expedition.

Gillespie would soon have use for it. While he was at San Francisco Bay, a dozen roughneck American settlers seized 170 horses being herded to General Castro; they feared that Castro was preparing to throw the Americans out of California. After they led the horses to Sutter's Fort on the Sacramento River, 35 men rode to Sonoma, a tiny settlement 15 miles north of San Francisco Bay, captured a sleeping Mexican general and on June

15 proclaimed the California Republic—the Bear Flag Republic. Consul Larkin and Commander Montgomery disavowed the act as outlawry.

Gillespie heard of this escapade while returning to Frémont in a Navy launch. He dashed off a penciled note to Montgomery:

> I am of the opinion that the settlers have obtained decided proof of Castro's intention to have their crops burned to warrant the course they have pursued. The bearer hereof says he heard a messenger to Captain Sutter state that they had acted under advice from Captain Frémont. If such is the fact, which I very much doubt, there is positive cause for hostility on the part of the settlers.[16]

Whether Frémont instigated the Bear Flag revolt has never been proved. In any case, he took charge of the military force of the "one-village nation" and chased the local Mexicans through the Bay area. Kit Carson murdered a couple of captured Mexicans, and Frémont stormed a deserted fort at Yerba Buena (San Francisco). On June 28, Gillespie was back on *Portsmouth* telling Montgomery—the only officer thereabouts who could legally act in the name of the United States—that Lieutenant Frémont, USA, had joined the Bears.

Gillespie returned to Sonoma and took the title of "major" in the Bear battalion, serving as Frémont's executive and operations officer in charge of training the Bear Flag "army." He drilled the strange collection of trappers, ranchers and scouts for long hours. Apparently, he instilled some semblance of discipline; the battalion committed no more outrages. "Col. Frémont being entirely ignorant of military matters, his attention having been always occupied with subjects of science,"[17] as Gillespie later wrote of the Secretary of the Navy, the Marine officer took over the responsibility for turning Frémont's growing force of bearded, buckskin-garbed frontiersmen into effective fighters.

5
West Coast
Conquest

On July 2, 1846, elderly Commodore Sloat arrived at Monterey, the seat of Mexican power in the north, to blockade the California ports. He alone had the authority to make war in California. But remembering Catesby Jones' fiasco at Monterey four years earlier—and Jones' subsequent recall—Sloat hesitated for five days. Finally, his knowledge that hostilities had begun on the Rio Grande and the reports of Frémont's activity against the Mexicans decided him. In the faith that Frémont was acting under orders from Washington, at 10 A.M. on July 7, Sloat invaded California for the United States.

He sent Capt. William Mervine, USN, ashore at Monterey with 165 sailors and 85 Marines. Capt. Ward Marston and 2d Lt. Henry W. Queen led the Marines from flagship *Savannah*; 2d Lt. William A. T. Maddox, those from *Cyane*; and Orderly Sgt. McCabe, the 15 Marines from *Levant*. The invasion force marched to the customs house where a proclamation was read and the American flag raised, followed by three cheers and a 21-gun salute from the ships' guns. By 11 A.M., everyone except a Marine detachment under Lieutenant Maddox went back to the ships. The Marines stayed ashore as a garrison—the West Coast's first Marine Corps post.

Sloat also ordered Commander Montgomery to seize Yerba Buena and Sonoma for the United States, and the next day formed a mounted company of 35 Marines and sailors to keep communications open between Yerba Buena and Monterey. This unit quickly became known after its commanding officer, as "Fauntleroy's Dragoons."

On July 9, the Bear Flag Republic became American, and Frémont's and Gillespie's little war was transformed into a legitimate part of the war between Mexico and the United States.

Early that same morning, Montgomery put an occupation force ashore at Yerba Buena. Second Lt. Henry B. Watson led 14 Marines. Preceded by drum and fife playing "Yankee Doodle," the force marched to the plaza and formed a hollow square for the flag-raising, cheers and salute from the ships. Lieutenant Watson was named military commander of the town and began dating his reports from "Marine Barracks, Yerba Buena." Montgomery set a battery on the top of Telegraph Hill and sent the Marines out on patrol.

The tale is told that Lieutenant Watson would return to town from his patrols late at night and pause at Brown's Tavern. He would rouse the proprietor, the apparently amiable John H. Brown, with the signal "The Mexicans are in the brush." Brown would come drowsily to the door and give the Marine lieutenant a quick nightcap. One night, very late, Watson could not wake Brown. In thirsty exasperation, he finally shouted the signal and fired his pistol angrily into the air. The entire sleepy garrison rushed out in alarmed confusion and began firing into the darkness. A landing party even set out from *Portsmouth* before the flustered Watson could set matters straight.[18]

On July 19, Frémont and Gillespie rode into Monterey at the head of 160 mounted irregulars. They looked like a cutthroat crew. Gillespie was delighted to see U.S. Marines parading in the streets in full uniform. Frémont and Gillespie reported to Sloat aboard *Savannah* and sought his support for their efforts. Frémont later reported:

> After a few words he [Sloat] informed me that he had applied to Lieutenant Gillespie, whom he knew to be an agent of the Government, for his authority; but it had been declined. He then asked to see my instructions. . . .
>
> I informed him that I had been expected to act, and had acted, largely on my own responsibility, and without written authority from the Government to justify hostilities.
>
> He was greatly disturbed by this, and distinctly told me that in raising the flag at Monterey he had acted upon the faith of my operations in the north.
>
> He had expected to find that I had been acting under

such *written* authority as would support his action in raising the flag. He was so discouraged and offended that he terminated the interview abruptly, quitting the cabin and leaving me. . . . He declined to see me again; and, as a much younger officer, I could not urge myself upon one of his rank and present command.[19]

"Obviously," says his most respected biographer, "Frémont had here no authority for hostile action."[20] Neither had his companion from the Marine Corps.

But Frémont was not one to let an aged naval commander interfere with his plans. He visited Commodore Robert F. Stockton aboard *Congress*, and found a more receptive man. Stockton was a politician, energetic and almost as hungry for fame as Frémont. At the moment, his hands were tied; he was second in command to Sloat. But he advised Frémont to wait; Sloat was about to go home to retire, and then they would see what could be arranged. Frémont camped on a hill behind the town and waited. On July 23, Stockton took over.

The very next day Stockton made a deal. If Frémont would place himself and his men under Stockton's command, the Commodore would recognize his irregulars as the "California Navy Battalion of Mounted Riflemen." He would "commission" Frémont as major and give him command of the battalion and make Gillespie "captain" and second in command. They promptly accepted.

Stockton squeezed the battalion aboard *Cyane*, captained by Samuel F. DuPont, and sent it south to San Diego to cut off Castro, who was now operating near Los Angeles. The battalion, along with Lieutenant Maddox and some 80 Marines, landed at San Diego on the afternoon of July 30 and raised the American flag.

Stockton followed on *Congress*. En route, a party including forty-year-old 1st Lt. Jacob Zeilin and his Marine detachment raised the flag at Santa Barbara. (He would be an important man: Zeilin.) Leaving 10 Marines at Santa Barbara, Stockton sailed to San Pedro, the port of Los Angeles, and occupied it in the name of the United States. The plan: Stockton and Frémont would converge on the remaining center of Mexican resistance—Los Angeles.

But first there were some essentials to be learned for a land campaign. Stockton described the San Pedro camp later: "We were in the midst of our preparations, learning how to form line and to form squares, of which the only man in the whole concern that knew anything, as I am aware, was Lieutenant Zeilin, of the marine corps, and perhaps the men who were with him."[21]

On August 11, Stockton massed 360 Marines and sailors for the 18-mile march on Los Angeles. Frémont joined him with 120 horsemen, leaving Gillespie behind to hold San Diego with 48 men. Consul Larkin, who had come down with Stockton, went ahead and entered Los Angeles on August 12. Stockton's force arrived the next day, preceded by a brass band. Los Angeles was occupied without a shot fired. Castro had fled into Mexico. As far as Commodore Stockton could see, California had been bloodlessly conquered. He sent Kit Carson overland with the great news.

On October 6 near Socorro, in what is today New Mexico, the little mountain man—quite by chance—met Stephen Kearny, now a brevet brigadier general and the vanquisher of Santa Fe—also bloodlessly—marching to California. On hearing Carson's news of victory, the general ordered 200 of his mule-mounted First Dragoons to return eastward. With only 110 men—and with a reluctant Carson ordered to guide him—Kearny rode on to the newly won territory of California. He was in for unpleasant surprises.

Meanwhile, Gillespie was in trouble. With California apparently secure, Stockton had dreamt a new dream. He would build a force in California, sail to Acapulco on the Pacific coast and then march to Mexico City to link up with General Taylor and win the war. It would be magnificent.

First, he had to place California in reliable hands. On August 24, he named Frémont as Military Governor of California and ordered him to go north and raise men for the expedition to Mexico City. Stockton named Gillespie as Commandant of the Southern District, the center of Mexican influence. On his way north to San Francisco, Stockton appointed Marine Lieutenant Maddox Commandant of the Middle Department.

"Commandant" Gillespie came up from San Diego and established his headquarters at Los Angeles. He had 48 men to hold all of southern California. Now, the lack of discipline, the readiness to get drunk and the tactless frontier roughness of the volunteers proved disastrous. The townspeople, already antagonistic toward the Americans, soon grew to detest the small band of conquerers. Gillespie tried to rule Los Angeles with an iron hand. He prohibited the people from gathering in the streets, ordered that no liquor be sold without his permission, searched homes for weapons and arrested civilians on mere suspicion. His harshness betrayed his weakness.

As anti-American feeling rose in Los Angeles, Gillespie sent to Stockton and Frémont for more men. The messenger carried his requests straight to a Mexican guerrilla chief, who was overjoyed to learn of the Americans' small numbers.

> Upon the morning of [September] the 23rd at 3 o'clock [Gillespie wrote later], I was suddenly aroused by the sharp report of fire arms upon the front and rear of the quarters. Our small force was soon under arms and upon the roof, replying to the fire. We only numbered twenty one. The Enemy was soon driven off, and as we discovered in the morning, with the loss of two killed or wounded.[22]

A mile outside the town, Capt. José María Flores of the Mexican army marshalled 400 hard-riding Californians. The next night, Gillespie wrote in a tiny hand on the inside of a cigar paper: "Believe the bearer," marked the paper with his seal and with this credential sent off one Juan Flaco, paying him $30, to get help from Stockton and Frémont. Flaco made a heroic ride, covering more than 400 miles through enemy territory in four days, and gave out the news of the threat at Los Angeles.

The next morning, September 25, Gillespie and his small band—now 72 strong, counting every servant, Indian and camp follower—were under siege. "The men who had conducted themselves badly, were amongst the first when any duty was ordered, and showed most conclusively, that when not idle and restrained from drinking, good service could be performed by them."[23] The garrison lived on dried beef, for, as Gillespie reported, "I was without supplies of any kind. I had no artillery when attacked in the Government House. After much labor I

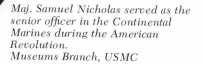

Maj. Samuel Nicholas served as the senior officer in the Continental Marines during the American Revolution.
Museums Branch, USMC

Marines fight in the tops high above the deck of the Continental frigate Alliance *in 1781, as painted by Maj. Charles H. Waterhouse.*
Museums Branch, USMC

Sailors and Marines aboard the ketch
Intrepid *set fire to the captured*
frigate Philadelphia *in the harbor of*
Tripoli on the night of February 16,
1804.
Olds Collection, New York Historical
Society

Lt. Presley Neville O'Bannon led
seven Marines with Eaton's army to
Derna, Tripoli, in 1805.
Contemporary miniature by an
unknown artist.
Museums Branch, USMC

O'Bannon's Marines march behind William Eaton on the long trek from Alexandria, Egypt, to Derna.
Museums Branch, USMC

Maj. John Marshall Gamble commanded the Marines on the epic cruise of Essex, *1812–1815.*
Museums Branch, USMC

Portrait of a U.S. Marine Corps officer in 1819.
Museums Branch, USMC

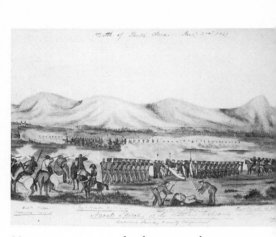

Capt. George H. Terrett was a Marine
hero of the battle for Mexico City in
1847 and later joined the Confederate
States Marine Corps.
Private collection; courtesy Museums
Branch, USMC

Marines, in center with white crossed
belts, fight Mexicans in the battle of
Santa Clara, near San Francisco, in
1847. The Marines were led by Capt.
Ward Marston and 2d Lt. Robert
Tansill.
Franklin D. Roosevelt Library

U.S. soldiers and Marines storm the Hill of Chapultepec.
Maj. Levi Twiggs was killed in the assault while leading
the Marines, who dashed ahead to the gates of Mexico City.
Marine Corps Photo, National Archives

The army of Maj. Gen. Winfield Scott enters the Grand Plaza of Mexico City. Scott is the mounted figure waving his hat in this engraving. Behind him march the ranks of Marines.
Marine Corps Photo, National Archives

Early muskets and rifles carried by U.S. Marines: top to bottom, Hall Model 1819 breech-loading rifle; U.S. Model 1842 musket; U.S. Model 1855 rifled musket.
National Rifle Association Firearms Museum; courtesy Museums Branch, USMC

Three famous nineteenth-century Marine Corps swords. Top to bottom, the sword of Commandant Jacob Zeilin; the sword of Commandant Franklin Wharton; and the sword presented to Lt. Presley Neville O'Bannon by the State of Virginia on his return from Tripoli.
Museums Branch, USMC

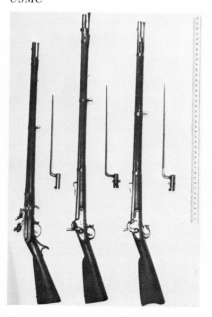

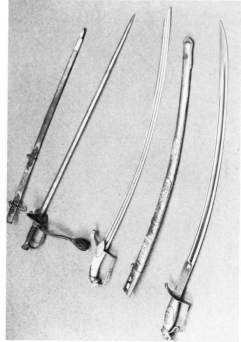

On October 18, 1859, U.S. Marines storm the engine
house at Harpers Ferry in which the abolitionist John
Brown and his men had barricaded themselves. Marine
Pvt. Luke Quinn lies mortally wounded in the foreground.
Museums Branch, USMC

In 1864, Maj. Jacob Zeilin, Jr., was
selected over four of his seniors as
Commandant of the Corps. He
became the first Marine to gain
regular general officer rank.
Museums Branch, USMC

Col. Lloyd J. Beall, a West Point friend of Jefferson Davis and veteran of thirty years in the U.S. Army, commanded the Confederate States Marine Corps during the Civil War. Some of the best Marine officers of the period joined the CSMC.
Museums Branch, USMC

United States Marines as portrayed by Japanese at the time of Commodore Matthew C. Perry's visit in Tokyo Bay in 1854.
U.S. Navy

U.S. Marines, on the right, line up for Commodore
Perry's ceremonial landing in Japan near present-day
Yokohama.
Marine Corps Photo, National Archives

John Philip Sousa, standing on platform, and the U.S.
Marine Corps Band he made world-famous. Sousa led
the band from 1880 to 1892 and wrote many marches,
including Semper Fidelis. *Picture was taken about 1890.*
Marine Corps Photo, National Archives

succeeded in clearing, and mounted upon the Axels of Ox Carts, three old pieces of (Iron) artillery and made shot and grape from the lead of distillery pipes, which I found in the vineyard close at hand."[24]

On the 28th, he led his men to a hilltop—a strong position, but without water. Gillespie's situation grew hopeless. On the 30th, outnumbered 10 to 1, he was permitted by Flores to march out with his arms and with his flags flying. He and his men reached San Pedro that evening; and under the watchful eyes of 300 Mexicans, they went aboard the merchant vessel *Vandalia* in the harbor. A detachment of the California Battalion, besieged at San Diego, was all that remained of the conquest of southern California.

Consul Larkin was vehemently critical of Gillespie's "harshness" at Los Angeles, writing that had "any proper and prudent person been left here by the Commodore, all this disturbance would not have happened."[25]

When Stockton heard of the uprising against the Marine lieutenant, he angrily ordered Navy Captain Mervine to take *Savannah* posthaste to San Pedro. Mervine moved promptly and at daylight on October 7 led ashore 310 sailors and Marines, plus Gillespie and his men, to recapture Los Angeles.

Marines under Capt. Ward Marston, a veteran of 27 years in the Corps, led the march on foot. At 2 P.M., the exhausted Americans halted at Domingo Ranch, "not one man among us accustomed to walking any distance," Gillespie admitted. That night they were attacked by swift-striking riders. Captain Mervine sent off parties on foot in several directions in the darkness, "acting [according to Gillespie] more like an insane man . . . to overtake some of the best horsemen in the world mounted upon fleet horses."[26]

The next morning, the Americans attacked 200 of the enemy in the face of fire from an artillery piece. Seven men were wounded. Mervine ordered a retreat. Harassed by enemy horsemen, the Americans reached the harbor at 3 P.M., and left San Pedro again in enemy hands. All told, nine Americans had been wounded; two of them died during the retreat and a third afterward. The expedition had been a failure.

"The Sailors and Marines are as brave a crew as ever trod the deck of a ship of war, but I do feel that their Commander

[Mervine] truly merits the severest reproach of his country," Gillespie wrote. He had begged Mervine to take guns and more ammunition and to provide care for possible casualties, but Mervine had not heeded the Marine. With understandable exaggeration, Gillespie called the result "one of the most disgraceful defeats our arms have ever sustained."

Late in October, Stockton himself arrived at San Pedro, landed sailors and Marines and sent Gillespie down to San Diego with his own men and 20 Marines. Those two ports could be held by the warships' guns. It took Gillespie well into November to round up enough horses and push Flores back so that he no longer menaced San Diego.

Further north, native guerrillas drove the 10 Marines out of Santa Barbara. The Marines held off the enemy horsemen, marched through the mountains and after the greatest hardship reached Monterey on November 10.

Then, Stockton received word that Kearny and his dragoons had entered California. Guided by Kit Carson, Kearny had painfully crossed the mountains and the desert that is now the irrigated Imperial Valley. On December 2, they reached Warner's Ranch in Agua Caliente, 60 miles from San Diego. Fearing that his worn-out men were too weakened to fight through to Stockton, Kearny sent a message ahead, asking the Commodore for reinforcements. Stockton sent Gillespie and 39 volunteers, all he had horses for, to meet Kearny's troop.

Without waiting, Kearny started for San Diego on the 4th. Gillespie and his men rode through a hard, cold rain and found the exhausted soldiers near Witch Creek.

A hundred Mexicans commanded by Andrés Pico held the road near an Indian hamlet called San Pasqual. In the cold dawn, despite the ragged condition of his men and mounts, Kearny attacked. The Battle of San Pasqual was a disorganized tussle. With ammunition wet and useless, it became a wild struggle between Mexican lances and American sabers. The Americans took the worst of it. The men in the heart of the action were lanced again and again. Kearny was lanced twice and out of the action. The swift-riding Mexicans attacked one group of dragoons, killed its leader and forced the soldiers to give way. Gillespie later described what happened next:

I came up just at this moment, attended by Capt. Gibson

162

and three of my men. I dashed forward sword in hand not seeing an officer near the Dragoons, crying, "Rally, men, Rally, for God sake Rally, shove a front, don't turn your backs, face them, face them!" But all to no purpose, they retired slowly, as if panic stricken, and passed me upon my left hand, and I fell in upon the Enemy's centre, when I was instantly recognized and surrounded. Four lances were dashed at me quick as thought, & when leaning over the neck of my horse, to parry a lance coming full tilt to me, I received a blow from behind, which threw me from my saddle upon the ground. As I attempted to rise, another blow from behind struck me under the left arm upon the ribs, cutting through to the lungs, and as I looked for this last who struck me in the mouth, cutting my upper lip and breaking off a front tooth in the jaw, before I could disengage my sword arm from the ground. I now rose and cut my way to the rear, and blood gushing in a torrent from my wound.[27]

The wounded Gillespie fired one of Kearny's mountain howitzers "with my segar machero." Gillespie always believed that his cannon shot frightened off the Mexican lancers; perhaps he was right. The Mexicans rode away. Although the Americans held the battlefield and could now march on toward the coast, they had in fact been badly beaten. Of the no more than 50 Americans who had actually closed with the Mexicans, 18 were dead and 20 wounded.

Army Surgeon John S. Griffin dressed the wounds of the bleeding Gillespie and the others. The story is told that the Mexican commander, Pico, invited Gillespie, whom he knew, to his camp for medical treatment. It is said that Gillespie accepted the humane invitation and then returned freely to his own camp. Repeatedly, the California Mexicans treated the Americans with generosity.

On December 7, Kearny was able to resume command and led a 10-mile march to a ranch at San Bernardo, where there was some food for the wounded and water for the animals. The able-bodied men ate mule meat and their besieged camp won the name of Mule Hill.

Commodore Stockton sent Navy Lt. Andrew Gray with 100 soldiers and 80 Marines under Lieutenant Zeilin to escort the general and his men toward San Diego. Gillespie reported to Washington: "The credit of the march is due to Captain [then 1st Lt.] Zeilin of the Marines, without whom the force would have been in a sad condition."[28] And Andrés Pico would say years later that only the arrival of the Marines saved Kearny at the end of his historic march.

In the north, Marine Capt. Ward Marston led 101 men, including 34 Marines commanded by 2d Lt. Robert Tansill, out from Yerba Buena to recover a Navy lieutenant who had been captured by the enemy. On the morning of January 2, 1847, they spotted 80 well-mounted Mexicans on the plains of Santa Clara, 50 miles from the Bay. Marston prepared to fight. Tansill and his Marines held the center. They advanced through a marsh, knee-deep in mud. A fire fight blazed for an hour; one Marine was wounded in the head. At last, the enemy turned their horses and headed toward the mountains.

The Mexican leader, Francisco Sanchez, reappeared under a flag of truce. With him he brought the missing Navy lieutenant. Sanchez said his men had no quarrel with the American Army but were fighting the irregulars who had stolen Mexicans' horses and saddles and turned women and children out of their homes. He asked that the irregulars be controlled and that the local Mexicans be recompensed by the U.S. government for their losses. The Marine captain agreed to an armistice.

Mervine furiously condemned Marston for allowing Sanchez to go free without parole and for agreeing to an armistice with men he called "outlaws." Marston believed his policy had restored quiet to the countryside. He eventually was vindicated and received a major's brevet for his work in California.

Meanwhile, Commodore Stockton still planned to recapture Los Angeles. When Kearny's men recuperated from their thousand-mile ordeal, Stockton organized a battalion of 440 sailors and Marines, 57 of Kearny's Dragoons and 60 mounted men of the Volunteer Battalion under Gillespie. On December 29, 1846, they set out from San Diego on the 140-mile march. Seven miles from Los Angeles, the enemy made a stand on bluffs behind the San Gabriel River. Five hundred Californians led by Captain Flores, who had forced Gillespie out of Los Angeles in September, commanded the ford of the river. Their artillery was in place on the heights. At 2 P.M., the Americans formed a square, their baggage in the center. Zeilin and his Marines held the right flank; Gillespie commanded the rear guard. It was January 8, 1847, the anniversary of the Battle of New Orleans, and that provided the Americans rallying cry.

They waded the knee-deep river in the face of fire from sharpshooters and small guns and pushed the enemy before them. The American artillery plunged into the water under fire, bogged down, was pulled free and started to hammer the enemy. Having crossed the river, the Americans charged, bayonets fixed. The enemy in front of them fled, but the Californian horsemen struck both their flanks. The sailors on the left and the Marines on the right beat them off. The enemy swung wide and attacked the rear guard. Gillespie was ready. "I gave them such a warm reception," he said, "the guard of the day delivering a beautiful fire, they turned and fled."[29] Now, the Americans formed in line; and with the right wing—which included the Marines—in the front, they charged the enemy on the bluffs. The Californians were driven off. It was quickly over. One American had been killed; among the nine wounded was Marine Pvt. William Scott. It was the Marine Corps' largest battle in California.

The next afternoon, at La Mesa, three miles from the white walls of Los Angeles, in what today is Vernon, the enemy made another stand across the road. These superb Californian horsemen were a colorful sight with brilliant serapes draped over their shoulders. Their units were festooned with flags and colored handkerchiefs tied to their raised lances. They were accompanied by trumpeters and buglers and even guitars and fiddlers. Some were armed with carbines, rifles and pistols, but most carried only a short lance with a long blade—a deadly weapon at close quarters. An eyewitness called them "the best horsemen, probably, in the world."[30]

The Americans formed a square with their artillery pieces at the corners. The enemy charged; the Americans opened fire. Men and horses tumbled, but the enemy retired in order. Twice more they charged the American square—first at its front, where the Marines and Kearny's dragoons fought, and then at the flanks defended by the sailors. They were cut down with accurate fire at close range. At last, the Mexicans wheeled and rode off to the mountains, leaving the road to Los Angeles open.[31] No Americans were killed; but Gillespie was among the wounded, struck in the hip by a carbine ball.

This engagement—exactly eight months after Gillespie and Frémont had met on Klamath Lake—ended armed resistance in California. On January 10, with the band playing, Stockton and Kearny led their men into Los Angeles. Gillespie raised the flag over his earlier headquarters.

The enemy retreated north. At San Fernando, they met Frémont (who still had never fought a battle), and he negotiated the Treaty of Cahuenga with them. Frémont gave the enemy generous terms that Stockton had previously rejected. After seven months of fighting and blundering, California was finally conquered.

For the battles of San Gabriel and La Mesa, Lieutenant Zeilin was jumped a rank and made a brevet major. Maddox was named a brevet captain. For his stand at Santa Clara, Marston was given a major's brevet. Gillespie was made a brevet captain for his defense at Los Angeles and later was promoted to brevet major for his gallantry at San Pasqual.

There were messy aftermaths to the story. Kearny and Stockton got into a terrible row over which of them was to govern California. It was partly Army versus Navy, partly personal. Kearny was the man authorized by Washington to do the job, but he did not have the manpower to enforce his claim. The ambitious Stockton refused to recognize Kearny's right and denied him command of either sailors or Marines. Frémont, named governor by Stockton, sided with his sponsor and, though an Army officer, refused to obey Kearny's orders.

Late in January, the Mormon Battalion of 350 men arrived. Gillespie was dispatched to escort them in, and the battalion camped north of San Diego, near where the Marines' Camp Pendleton is today. Commodore Shubrick came out to replace Stockton and immediately recognized Kearny as governor. But Frémont continued to oppose Kearny; and the general, having had his fill of insubordination, ordered him home. Kearny also relieved Gillespie, who had been serving as major of the Battalion of California Volunteers, from his detached service, and ordered him to report to Marine Corps headquarters in Washington.

In May, a tall, red-headed Army lieutenant named William Tecumseh Sherman, serving as Kearny's aide, brought Gillespie a message from Commodore James Biddle, who had taken over command from Shubrick. On Kearny's request, Biddle ordered Gillespie not to leave Monterey. Gillespie gave his word of honor not to stir up the people against Kearny and prepared for the long journey home. As Kearny testified at Frémont's trial, "There was at no time any difference between Lieutenant Gillespie and myself. Whenever we met we exchanged salutations as between gentlemen; there was nothing further between us."[32] By December 4, Gillespie was back in Washington. His servant Ben was still with him.

Kearny put Frémont under arrest and ordered him to report for trial. His courtmartial opened in Washington on November 2 and became one of the most famous trials in American history, filled with histrionics, bad temper and personal abuse. Frémont defended himself as much in the newspapers as in the courtroom. On January 31, 1848, the court found Frémont guilty of mutiny, disobedience of orders and conduct prejudicial to good order and discipline. He was sentenced to be dismissed from the Army. President Polk approved the court's decision. But to allay Senator Benton's anger, he remitted the penalty and restored Frémont to duty. Frémont resigned anyway and was named senator from California in 1850 and nominated for the Presidency in 1856.

Gillespie testified for Frémont at his courtmartial, but, surprisingly, opposed his friend for President. On October 14, 1854, Gillespie resigned from the Corps as a captain and brevet major, and returned to California. For a couple of years, he farmed on Battle Creek in Shasta County; then he moved to Sacramento. On August 14, 1873, at the age of sixty-one, he died in San Francisco.

Archibald Gillespie was one of the most romantic figures in the Marine Corps story. Although he stepped over the border of legitimate authority, his boldness and courage were repeatedly important to the conquest of California: in carrying the President's instruction to California on the eve of war, in getting arms from the Navy for Frémont, in the battles of San Pasqual and San Gabriel. He was not much of a military governor in Los Angeles, but he was a hell of a fighter.

The conquest of California was a primitive adventure in imperialism. In hindsight, it contained one lesson: If the United

States wanted to extend its territory on hostile shores, it would need amphibious forces to put ashore. California was finally won from Mexico when the United States could land a force strong enough to hold.

This lesson was evident again when, after California was conquered, the Navy pushed the war down into Lower California and along the Pacific coast of Mexico. In the spring of 1847, the Marines helped seize San Jose del Cabo and San Lucas at the tip of Lower California, and La Paz slightly further north. That fall, the entire Pacific squadron sailed south to blockade the west coast ports of the Mexican mainland. On October 20, Lt. Henry B. Watson and a party of Marines occupied Guaymas, the first important mainland target. When a Mexican force reentered the town on November 17, 65 sailors and Marines went ashore from *USS Dale* and engaged them.

The Navy wanted to establish a base on the strategic end of the Lower California peninsula; and on November 8, 1847, 20 enlisted Marines and four midshipman, commanded by Navy Lt. Charles Heywood (father of a future Marine Corps Commandant), occupied San Jose there. The next day, their ships sailed off, and Heywood set up a defensive position in a ramshackle mission house on a hill north of the town. Twenty Californians joined them.

On the morning of November 19, 150 Mexicans approached and ordered the Americans to surrender. They refused. At 10 P.M. that night, a Marine sentry heard a noise, challenged and fired. He was answered by a hail of ball as the enemy stormed the mission house, front and back. The defenders held off the onslaught the rest of the night. The following night the enemy struck again and fought their way into the rear of the mission house. The Marines, almost overwhelmed, battled desperately. When the Mexican leader was mortally wounded, the attack disintegrated.

In January, 1848, the Mexicans again laid siege to the San Jose garrison. The defenders—27 Marines, 10 sailors and 20 Californians—had to care for 50 women and children who had taken refuge with the Americans. By February 10, the Mexicans controlled the town; two days later they seized the Americans' water supply. Just as the situation looked hopeless, *Cyane* appeared and landed a strong force. Together, the Marines and the relief party drove the Mexicans from the town.

Meanwhile, one other important landing—the largest of all—was made without opposition at Mazatlan, the mainland port where Gillespie had found Commodore Sloat in March 1846. Now, on November 11, 1847, Commodore Shubrick put ashore 600 sailors and Marines in an exceptionally well-executed landing. The newly promoted Captain Zeilin led 36 Marines from *Congress*, 2d Lt. William W. Russell commanded 50 from *Independence* and Sergeant Forrest headed 11 from *Cyane*. The Americans aggressively pursued the enemy, and the Marines garrisoned Mazatlan until the end of the war.

In all, 402 Marines served on the Pacific Coast in the Mexican War. Commodore Shubrick reported to Washington:

> The Marines have behaved with the fidelity and constancy which characterizes that valuable Corps, and I embrace this opportunity respectfully to recommend that ships coming to this station be allowed as large a complement of these valuable men as possible. The service would be greatly benefited by doubling the number allowed to each ship, and reducing the same extent, if necessary, the complement of landsmen and ordinary seamen. The want of Marines is strongly felt in all operations on shore.[33]

6
Mission for the Future: Amphibious Warfare

Seventy ships loaded with more than 12,000 soldiers, sailors and Marines stood off Vera Cruz, Mexico's largest port, in March of 1847, for the first major D-Day in American history. It was, said the Secretary of the Navy proudly, "the largest squadron, it is believed, which has ever been assembled under the American flag."[34] Ready to land in the first wave was a battalion of Marines commanded by Capt. Alvin Edson. This would be the first step to the Halls of Montezuma.

Alvin Edson was no longer a youngster. He had led the Marines against the pirates at Quallah Battoo and commanded E Company of Colonel Henderson's regiment in the Seminole War. Now he was the senior Marine officer of the Home Squadron in the Gulf of Mexico.

Edson had been in this war since the beginning. On May 7, 1846, his twenty-fourth anniversary in the Corps, he led the Marines in a 500-man naval force that garrisoned the Army's base at Point Isabel, just north of the mouth of the Rio Grande. They had freed Brig. Gen. Taylor's soldiers to attack the Mexicans at Palo Alto.

With the war begun, the Marine Corps—its authorized strength at 1,283 officers and men—acquired a new job: amphibious warfare. Alvin Edson and his men would point the way for the U.S. Marine Corps of the future.

Since there was no significant Mexican navy to fight, the American commanders blockading the Mexican coasts made a series of amphibious sorties on the enemy's ports. Of course, U.S. Marines had repeatedly attacked shore targets from the sea; their very first operation, at New Providence in the Revolution, had been amphibious. But now one more step was taken toward

[For the location of places in Mexico see map No. 4 in the map section.—*Au.*]

170

modern amphibious doctrine: For the first time, U.S. Marines were brought together from the shipboard detachments scattered throughout a naval squadron and ordered to fight together as a unit for a period of time.

The U.S. Navy of 1846 lacked the essentials for amphibious operations. It had no shallow-water craft, no gunboats to cover a landing, no steamers to bring up rowed boats, no landing equipment. It had to make-do. The first two landings attempted on the Gulf coast in the fall of 1846 were at Alvarado, through which the Mexican army was obtaining supplies; they both failed because the Navy had no boats able to enter the river. But by the time of the climactic assault at Vera Cruz the following March, it had made two successful landings and was prepared to launch a competent major amphibious attack.

By the end of 1846, the new Secretary of the Navy, the expansionist John Y. Mason, was preaching greater use of Marines in amphibious warfare—the destiny of the Corps. In a bellwether report, Mason said:

> I am strongly impressed with the opinion that an increase of the rank and file of the corps would greatly promote the efficiency of our ships in their operations against Mexico. With light pieces, prepared as field artillery, on board each ship, the expeditions, which must include operations on shore, would derive important aid from increased guards of marines.[35]

Mason's support was aroused by an enthusiast for amphibious attacks against the enemy coast: Matthew Perry. Perry joined the squadron off the east coast of Mexico in September 1846 as second in command to Commodore David Conner. Like the Marines aboard the cramped and crowded ships, Perry saw no hope of glory in the endless, blazing hot days of sailing on deadly-dull blockade duty. To fill the vacuum of inactivity, Perry planned amphibious raids.

On October 23, a seven-ship flotilla under Perry's command arrived off the Tabasco (Grijalva) River in the south to seek a base for the Army. Captain Edson commanded 200 Marines whom Perry had ordered assembled as a battalion. A landing party dashed ashore at Frontera, Tabasco's port, seized the town and captured several Mexican steamers. Perry used them to tow his men upriver against the heavy current. At 3 P.M. on the 25th, they approached the provincial capital of San Juan Bautista, 72 miles from the coast. Perry fired a few shots at a fort at the "Devil's Bend," a turn in the river below the town, and then ordered Edson and his Marines ashore to attack this strong point. But it was getting dark; and before they could take the fort, Perry recalled them to the boats. The next morning, Navy gunners dueled the city's batteries; when a landing was ordered, the city surrendered. Edson took his Marines ashore and after a minor skirmish occupied the plaza. Perry was furious. He had hoped for a battle.

The Americans did not have enough manpower to garrison the city. They grabbed two small steamers and seven sailing vessels—which could be useful in future shallow-water operations—and returned to Frontera. The Mexicans grandiloquently claimed they had forced the Americans out. But the operation on the river did make Perry a hero. It was the first dramatic event in all the months of the Navy's blockade and did wonders for the morale of the Home Squadron and its Marines.

Perry and Conner brought a naval force north to Tampico, Mexico's second largest port, halfway between Vera Cruz and Texas. Their purpose was to protect the left flank of Maj. Gen. Taylor's army. On the morning of November 16, Edson's Marines landed and took Tampico without firing a shot. The Navy captured five small vessels and left a Marine garrison until the Army arrived.

In the meantime, Taylor had advanced to Monterrey—the largest Mexican city in the north—and on September 20, he opened a bloody, five-day battle through the city's forts and streets. Brig. Gen. William J. Worth's division, with Texans out to avenge the Alamo, led the attack. The Mississippi Rifles commanded by Col. Jefferson Davis won the crucial redoubt. Taylor settled down at Monterrey; and in November, Polk took the initiative away from him. Polk decided to invade Mexico from the sea at Vera Cruz. He gave the command of this campaign to the head of the Army, Maj. Gen. Winfield Scott, and told him to take from Taylor all the men he needed. Scott, then sixty years old, was a giant of a man, over six feet four, proud, stuffy, courageous and a brilliant leader. His men called him "Old Fuss and Feathers."

Meanwhile, the exiled former dictator Santa Anna, whom Polk had foolishly allowed to return to Mexico, raised an army that heavily outnumbered Taylor's. The two forces met in the mountains at Buena Vista on Washington's Birthday, 1847. Again, Jefferson Davis' regiment saved the day. His men turned almost certain defeat into a standoff, which Taylor reported back home as a great victory. The battle, in a strange way, helped make two men "president": Zachary Taylor and Jefferson Davis.

Santa Anna's strategy had failed. He had gone north to Buena Vista believing that by attacking Taylor he could force Scott to give up his amphibious assault and come to Taylor's aid. Taylor's squeak-through victory meant that Santa Anna could not be at the beaches of Vera Cruz to meet Scott's landing.

The invasion at Vera Cruz was the turning point of the war and the United States' first really important amphibious operation—the largest until World War II.

Maj. Gen. Scott hurried to land and advance inland before the terrible yellow fever season began on the coast. On March 6, his army joined the Navy at the anchorage of Anton Lizardo, 16 miles south of the invasion port.

For the landing, Scott and his staff selected the beach of Collado, two and a half miles south of Vera Cruz, opposite Sacrificios Island and out of range of the guns of the giant island fortress, San Juan de Ulúa.

For the first time, special landing craft had been built to specifications for an American amphibious operation. These "surf boats" were pointed at both ends so they could move in either direction. They were to be rowed by sailors and steered by an officer in the stern. They were designed to be shipped in nests of three. The largest of each set was 40 feet long and 12 feet wide and carried 90 men; each of the other two boats was progressively a bit smaller. The Navy had ordered 141 surf boats (at $795 each), but only 64 arrived in time for the landing.

The squadron's Marine battalion was reformed under Captain Edson and assigned to the van of the assault. Edson and his 180 men were attached to the First Brigade led by Brig. Gen. Worth, the vain, impatient hero of Monterrey.

The morning of March 9 was clear and torridly hot, the sea smooth. By 11 A.M., the expeditionary force was under way. The men spent the afternoon at Sacrificios Island, transferring from ships to surf boats for the final dash to the beach. Each man carried 40 cartridges and bread and cooked meat enough for two days' rations.

At 6 P.M., a signal gun from Scott's command ship, the steamer *Massachusetts*, fired the order to land. Gunboats sprayed the landing area with grape. The surf boats were led in; they cast off their towlines and raced in "with colors displayed, bands playing, and loud cheers from the fleet."[36] As soon as each boat dropped its load, it was rowed back for more men. A few of the boats grounded in the shallow water; and the men, holding their bayoneted muskets high, waded through the waist-deep water.

When they reached the beach, Edson quickly led his Marines to the crest of the first row of sand dunes and formed a line of skirmishers, ready to fight. But not a shot was fired—the beach was empty.

By 10 P.M., more than 10,000 men were ashore. The Navy and Army had cooperated beautifully; not a man had been lost. The gunboats chased off some enemy cavalry hovering in the distance. In the morning, Scott came ashore with 2,000 more men.

Edson's Marines dug in with the 3rd Artillery Regiment, which held the right wing, nearest the sea south of the city. The Army rapidly worked its way north under enemy artillery fire until it touched the sea above the city and completely encircled brick-walled Vera Cruz with a seven-mile-long line of trenches and strong points.

The men fought enemy snipers, the suffocating heat, vicious sand fleas and a series of northers that cut them off from their ships for most of the week. On the 13th, Maj. Gen. Scott sent his report on the landing to the Secretary of War. He included the accolade: "A handsome detachment of marines under Captain Edson, of the corps, landed with the first line, and is doing duty with the army."[37]

Heavy guns, including a Navy battery of six large shell-throwing cannon, laid siege to the fortified city. On March 24, the city's defenders sued for terms; and on March 29, 5,000 enemy soldiers marched out to the Plain of Cocos south of the city and piled their arms between files of American soldiers, sailors and Marines. Scott marched into Vera Cruz to the strains of "Yankee Doodle." He had executed his invasion and captured Vera Cruz with the loss of only 19 men—one a Marine.

Perry, who had replaced the aging Commodore Conner as commander of the Home Squadron, now set out to make amphibious war. He created a Naval Brigade of 2,500 sailors and Marines with 10 pieces of artillery and on April 18 sent 1,500 men against Tuxpan, north of Vera Cruz. The squadron's Marines, at last part of a semipermanent amphibious force, were again under Edson's command. The forts at Tuxpan laid down a heavy fire against the Naval Brigade's small ships. But when the landing parties (which included Marine 2d Lt. William F. Perry, the commodore's son) came ashore, resistance faded.

In June, Commodore Perry took the Brigade down to the Tabasco River, where he had been too weak to establish a garrison the previous October. The river was still being used to bring supplies to the Mexican army from Central America. Edson's unit of 150 Marines was assigned to small sailing craft and ships' boats. Four steamers towed 1,084 men and seven guns upstream. On the 14th, enemy infantrymen shot at them from the jungle along the banks. The next day, at the Devil's Bend, a fire fight developed; the sailors and Marines in the boats scattered the enemy.

The next morning, the invasion force struck obstacles placed in the river channel; and the enemy fired from the shore. Perry led the way up the steep bluff and planted his broad pennant on top. The men following him—including the Marines—cheered. It was a rare sight to see a Navy commander-in-chief ashore with sword in hand, eager to fight on land.

The Marines, following immediately after the force's scouts, marched for a half hour and then were attacked by some 100 of the enemy. They dispersed the Mexicans with field guns and musket fire. The rest of the force in the boats finally blew a passage through the river obstructions with dynamite, moved upstream and took Fort Itúrbide, which guarded the city of San Juan Bautista. When Perry's column arrived three hours later, the American flag was flying over the fort. Escorted by Edson and a guard of Marines, Perry strode up the steep street to the plaza at the head of his men. He garrisoned the town with 70 Marines under Brevet Capt. William B. Slack.

Late that night, the Marines were attacked by 200 of the enemy and drove them off with three guns that Slack had set up in the plaza. Perry reinforced the garrison with 105 men, including 55 Marines; but the Mexicans continued to attack the city at night. Yellow fever now struck down half the men in the American garrison; and on July 22, Perry withdrew the men to the squadron. He praised the Marines in the Naval Brigade: "I repeat what I have often said, that this distinguished and veteran corps is one of the most effective and valuable arms of the service."[38]

This second invasion of the Tabasco was the last notable naval operation of the war in the Gulf of Mexico and the final action in which the Marines served with the high-spirited Naval Brigade.

Maj. Gen. Scott, who had marched swiftly inland from Vera Cruz, defeated Santa Anna in the mountain pass at Cerro Gordo on April 18, the same day the Marines had landed at Tuxpan. Scott then advanced to Puebla, a prosperous city in the mountains, and settled down for the summer.

By this time, the enlistments in the Army's old volunteer regiments were running out. Few men were willing to reenlist; they had seen enough of tropical war, with its disease, inescapable heat and death. Of 3,700 volunteers in Scott's army, those who reenlisted filled only a single company.

By May, Scott was down to less than 6,000 men. Santa Anna's army outnumbered his, and he had to wait until hard-to-come-by replacements could be sent to him. Every possible man was assigned to him. In Washington, the Secretary of the Navy and Marine Commandant Henderson told President Polk that six companies of Marines were available to serve with Scott. The President gave his permission, and these Marines were organized to fight with the Army. They would write one of the most dramatic chapters in Marine Corps history.

Perry was instructed to give up to Scott some of the Marines in his Naval Brigade, but Captain Edson was not destined to go with his men. On July 15, he died aboard the frigate *Raritan*, reportedly of an accidental gunshot wound. In 25 years of service, Alvin Edson had done his share of fighting and had seen the Marine Corps become a truly amphibious force.

7
The Halls
of Montezuma

The politicians who brewed this war figured that it would be over quickly. They whipped up the nation's martial spirit; and young men, bubbling with enthusiasm, flocked to volunteer: three months of excitement and glory and they would return home soldier-heroes. They had little thought of dysentery or yellow fever or dying; no worry that the enemy too could fight.

Scott's invasion at Vera Cruz was a reluctant admission in Washington that Taylor's rowdy volunteers had failed to win the war swiftly or easily. It was evidence that the Mexican peasant-soldier, though forced into uniform and stupidly led, would fight for his homeland with courage and tenacity. It testified that Americans could be bumblers when it came to bullying anyone tougher to conquer than the frontier Indians.

By the spring of 1847, new men were needed to fill the ranks when the short-termers who had seen enough of glory went home. Ten new volunteer Army regiments were authorized. And the Marine Corps' strength was almost doubled by the addition of 12 officers and 1,000 enlisted men.

On May 21, a year after war had been declared, the Secretary of the Navy (who actually believed this new increase gave the Marine Corps more officers than it required) ordered the Marine regiment formed for duty with Scott. In command were two veterans of the War of 1812, surprisingly antique for field duty in the tropics. They typified how Commandant Henderson's generation had aged. Lt. Col. Samuel E. Watson, the regiment's commander, had been a Marine for 35 years. Back in 1814, when *Adams* had been trapped by the British in the Penobscot River, Watson had led the ship's Marines overland on the 200-mile retreat to Portland, Maine. Maj. Levi Twiggs, second in command of the new regiment, was an aggressive, heavy, full-faced Georgian, born in 1793. In the War of 1812, he had distinguished himself aboard *President* when she was defeated by *Endymion* and her consorts. He had fought in the Creek and Seminole campaigns. Both Watson and Twiggs would die in Mexico.

The 314-man regiment was constructed of raw recruits, who enlisted that April and May, and seasoned with a sprinkling of experienced noncoms. As he had for the Indian wars, Commandant Henderson cut shipboard and navy yard Marine detachments to sergeants' guards to free enough men to fill out the unit.

The Marine regiment sailed from Fort Hamilton, New York, landed at Vera Cruz in the beginning of July and camped on the beach just north of the city. It was seriously understrength. But Perry insisted he could not spare Marines who were garrisoning enemy ports and finally sent Lt. Col. Watson only 52 men from the ships in the harbor at Vera Cruz.

Watson attached the regiment to a large contingent being taken inland to Scott by Brig. Gen. Franklin Pierce. (Five years later, Pierce, a popular New Hampshire Democratic politician, would defeat Scott for the Presidency of the United States.) Pierce and 2,400 recruits set out for Puebla through 200 miles of guerrilla-infested mountains. The Marines, now reorganized more realistically as a battalion, served as the rear guard of the poorly disciplined column. The march was a nightmare. Repeatedly the column was attacked by small bands of Mexicans, who kept it in a constant state of trembling alert. For days, tropical rains soaked the recruits. Fifteen hundred men were stricken with dysentery. The line stretched out; guerrillas and wolves attacked the stragglers. Many of the Marines threw away their equipment on the hot climb through the mountains. This was tough on-the-job training.

Pierce finally reached Scott on August 6. These were the last of Scott's replacements, and he now had 14,000 men on his muster rolls. Even though most of his men were recruits and 2,500 were sick, Scott prepared to march immediately.

Four divisions were organized. Brig. Gen. Worth, the egotist-hero of Monterrey and Vera Cruz, and hulking, Georgia-born, 57-year old Brig. Gen. David E. Twiggs—both of them intrepid and impetuous regulars—commanded the first and second divisions. Gideon J. Pillow, a Tennessee politician who had been President Polk's law partner and was a less-than-competent military commander, led the third. The Marines were assigned to the fourth division commanded by John A. Quitman, a rich, New York–born Mississippi sugar planter, a loyal Democrat—and a pretty fair officer. Command of the second brigade of Quitman's division—consisting of the Second Pennsylvania Volunteers and the Marine battalion, which now numbered 360 men—was given to Marine Lt. Col. Watson. One observer said the Marines in Quitman's division were "decidedly the finest looking corps the gallant Mississippian had under his command."[39]

On August 7, the day after the Marines arrived at Puebla, flags were uncased, the bands struck up a march and the army started for the City of Mexico. Leaving behind a 500-man garrison and 1,800 sick soldiers, Scott boldly broke off from his supply route to the coast. It was a do-or-die stroke.

Scott took with him about 11,000 men under arms. Quitman's division with the Marines was the second to go, five hours' march behind Twiggs. After the fighting men trailed the wagon train and a motley of camp followers from printers to prostitutes. Between Scott's army and Mexico City waited Santa Anna with a new army—30,000 strong.

The Americans struggled for four days through the snow-topped mountains that form the backbone of the country. Then they entered the Valley of Mexico. Below them stretched a vast panorama of lakes and marshes, and—glittering in the distance, framed by the walls Cortes had built—the ancient, bustling city that was their goal.

The assault on Mexico City had two phases. The Marine battalion did not fight in the first. Quitman's division was held in reserve at San Agustin, where it guarded the wagon train, the supplies and the hospital. Scott called Quitman's assignment "the post of honor," because the army, now isolated deep in enemy territory, had no other resources. But the Marines chafed in their white tents.

In this first half of the campaign, Scott entered the valley from the southeast and sidestepped to the west around Santa Anna's army. Capt. Robert E. Lee found a shortcut that placed

Scott's army between two elements of the Mexican army. At dawn on August 19, the Americans attacked and sent one Mexican force fleeing in disorder. Then they turned and attacked the desperately defended town and fortress of Churubusco, taking it with the bayonet at the cost of 1,000 casualties. A third of Santa Anna's army had been either killed or captured; and on August 22 he asked for an armistice. Scott agreed. His army encamped at the foot of the mountains south of Mexico City. The Marines had not yet been blooded, but it would not be long now.

The armistice lasted exactly two weeks. Scott soon realized that Santa Anna was only using the pause to refresh his army and strengthen his defenses. The Mexican commander intended to fight it out.

At noon on September 7, Scott reopened the war. The first order of business was to seize an ancient mill, Molino del Rey, less than a mile west of the Hill of Chapultepec, the strong point dominating the plain west of the city. Worth's Regulars attacked at dawn of the 8th and met a murderous fire from the fortified mill. Worth arrogantly ordered a bayonet charge at terrible cost. After two hours, the Americans took the mill and then withdrew. More than 750 Americans had been killed or wounded—almost one in every four who fought there. Scott and Worth argued bitterly over the fiasco. This bloody battle, which Lt. Ulysses S. Grant later called "wholly unnecessary,"[40] brought Quitman's division and the Marines to battle.

Scott's problem: Should he attack Mexico City from the south or from the west? The western approach was guarded by the steep, ominous Hill of Chapultepec. It rose lone and sheer from the plain, 600 yards long and 200 feet high, surrounded at its base by a 12-foot wall and topped by a gray-walled palace that was now a military school. The Hill was a fearsome objective to assault. Santa Anna expected Scott to avoid Chapultepec and had massed most of his army on the southern approach and flooded the fields between the Americans and the city's southern gates.

Scott called a council of war. Most of his generals voted to attack the city from the south. Lee agreed. Scott and Twiggs favored the western approach, believing that once Chapultepec

fell the war would be won. Then young Lt. Pierre G. T. Beauregard of the Engineers, who one day would order Fort Sumter
fired on, spoke up and argued brilliantly for an attack from the
west. He asserted that the Mexicans' southern defenses were
now even stronger than those that had cost so many American
lives at Churubusco. Once Chapultepec was taken, he said, the
army could move swiftly along the two western causeways to the
so-called gates of Belen and San Cosme. (These gates were
actually blockhouses and served the defenders as strongpoints.) Beauregard's argument changed Pierce's vote, and Scott
decided: Chapultepec.

Quitman's division, including the Marines, was brought up
to strengthen the wounded army. On Saturday, September 11,
just before the final attack, the division advanced in front of the
southern gates to deceive the Mexicans. As soon as darkness fell,
it marched two miles northwest to Tacubaya, south of the Hill.

This was now Scott's plan: Twiggs would stage a diversion
in front of the southern gate to hold Santa Anna there. Pillow's
volunteers, supported by Worth's battered division, would reoccupy Molino del Rey and attack Chapultepec's west side, the
Hill's most gradual slope but covered by enemy batteries.
Quitman, plus one of Twigg's brigades, would assault the
southern side of Chapultepec. Once the Hill was taken, Quitman would veer to the right along the southwest causeway to the
Belen gate. Worth would move north of the Hill and, wheeling
to his right, attack up the more northerly causeway leading to the
San Cosme gate.

The bombardment to soften the target began on Sunday.
Marine Major Twiggs led a reconnaissance of 40 volunteers to
scout Chapultepec's southern slope and locate the enemy's
guns. As they completed their mission and fell back, they were
pursued by the enemy. Twiggs was wounded; the party was
almost surrounded. The men panicked. Two companies of
Pennsylvania volunteers from Watson's brigade dashed up and
halted the enemy attack. The Americans suffered 11 casualties.

Monday, September 13, 1847, is the most famous date in the
Marine Corps' first hundred years. At daylight, the artillery
resumed its pounding of Chapultepec. The Marines were on the
division's right or east flank, nearest the city. At 8 A.M. the attack
started.

Almost as soon as they began to advance, the Marines were pinned down by heavy fire from the Hill and from a battery in the road that ran north just east of the Hill. Three hundred yards shy of the Hill, the Marines were forced to seek cover among the pulque bushes in the fields to the right of the road. They rose to fire and ducked down again to reload. The bushes made poor shelter; Marines were being hit at close range. They could not advance.

Quitman had organized three storming parties to pass through the Marine battalion and cut a path up the Hill. They carried ladders, crowbars and picks. Army Capt. Silas Casey of the Second Infantry led one large party. Major Twiggs commanded a group of 120 hand-picked soldiers and Marines. Marine Capt. John G. Reynolds, a veteran of the Florida war, led 40 Marine and Army volunteers. When the Marine battalion was stopped, Reynolds laid two ladders over a ditch and tried to advance with seven or eight men. On the open ground beyond the ditch, they came under fire from the enemy gun in the road ahead and had to fall back to the ditch.

Impatient at the delay, Major Twiggs, carrying his double-barrelled fowling piece, recklessly stood up in the middle of the road to call to Reynolds and gather his own storming party. A musket ball struck him in the chest. He sighed once and fell dead.

Over on the west side of the Hill, Pillow's men were halted in the open and absorbed heavy fire for 15 terrible minutes until their scaling ladders were brought up. Supported by some of Worth's troops, they then clawed their way up the Hill. The fighting was fierce. Pillow went down, wounded. Capt. Joe Hooker (who in the Civil War would command the Union's Army of the Potomac) now led the attack. Many of the Mexican defenders, including the boy-cadets of the academy, fought to the death. Others fled to the city. The fire from the castle atop Chapultepec slackened.

On the still strongly defended southern slope, the Marines struggled forward, fighting hand-to-hand with bayonets and clubbed rifles; Cpl. Hugh Graham and five Marine privates were killed. Americans on both sides of the Hill reached the castle simultaneously. From the south, the Marines and a New York army company, hard hit by the enemy, led the attack. Marine

Lieutenants Daniel J. Sutherland and Augustus S. Nicholson (who was serving as Quitman's aide) were among the first to enter the castle. At 9:30, Army Lt. George E. Pickett of the Fourth Infantry seized a bullet-ripped flag from Army Lt. James Longstreet, just as Longstreet was hit, and raised it over the fortress of Chapultepec. A wild yell rolled through the army.

Maj. Gen. Scott gave expansive credit to Quitman's Marines and volunteers, who had been "delayed with their division by the hot engagement below, [and] arrived just in time to participate in the assault of the heights."[41] At the summit of Chapultepec, Brig. Gen. Quitman turned to Capt. D. D. Baker, the adjutant of the Marine battalion and veteran of the Florida war, and said, "Adjutant, your marines behaved nobly. But we must now push on for the Belen."[42]

The push was already on. While Chapultepec was being attacked, Capt. George H. Terrett, USMC, commanding C Company on the left flank of the Marine battalion, was moving swiftly. Virginia-born Terrett had fought the pirates at Quallah Battoo and the Indians in Florida. With him now were 1st Lt. John D. Simms, 2d Lt. Charles A. Henderson (the son of the Commandant) and 36 men. Terrett led a rush on a redoubt at the base of the Hill. Then, without waiting for orders, "our own men being impatient to advance,"[43] he skirted the heights of Chapultepec and pursued the retreating enemy northeastward toward the city.

"What Colonel Watson's orders were," he said later, "whether to enter the gate of the Castle or not, I am ignorant, as I did not receive from him any order or direction, and in going forward, deemed I could not be wrong, so long as the Enemy in large numbers were ahead."[44]

Terrett and his Marines raced up the road and through the marshy fields to the enemy battery that had earlier pinned down the battalion. As the gunners prepared to fire, the Marines rushed them. The artillerymen fled. The Marines kept on. Joined now by more men, Terrett led them unknowingly beyond the Belen causeway, their official line of approach to the city. They advanced under heavy fire.

Twenty soldiers from Worth's division led by Lt. Ulysses S. Grant joined them. Together, Marines and soldiers fought their way up the San Cosme causeway. Each causeway consisted of twin roads on either side of a raised aqueduct supported by heavy masonry arches 10 feet high. The enemy defended every arch.

Terrett and his men advanced heedless of the Mexican fire. They were now in front of the entire army.

With the help of a light artillery battery, they scattered a large body of Mexican lancers sent out to intercept them. Grant set up a mountain howitzer in a square church tower and directed effective fire against the Mexicans defending the block-house at the end of the San Cosme causeway. Henderson was hit in the leg but stayed in the fight. Halfway up the causeway, where the enemy had built a second defensive line, they stormed and took another redoubt. They continued to advance one arch at a time.

Worth's bugles sounded recall. Terrett went back to report to the general. Simms and Henderson plunged ahead with 25 men to the very mouth of the San Cosme gate. Enemy fire concentrated on this single party assaulting the city. The breast-work at the gate was too heavily defended to take frontally, so Marine Lieutenants Simms and Jabez C. Rich led seven Marines around to attack the strongpoint from the left. Four were hit. At the same moment, Henderson attacked from the front. Two of his men went down. Together, the two units seized the San Cosme gate and held it.

For 15 minutes, these men stood against all the fire the Mexicans could mass against them. Then Worth again sounded recall, and the Marines and soldiers withdrew. Six Marines had been killed. Worth, who had held up the invasion at Vera Cruz so that he could be the first to step ashore, raged at being denied the honor of being the first in the gate of the city and vindictive-ly put Terrett and his men on outlying picket duty. They stayed there for the next three days. It took a direct order from Scott to return them to their battalion.

Meanwhile, once Chapultepec fell, Quitman moved his division toward the city. The Marine battalion reformed at the base of the Hill, received new ammunition and advanced under fire up the Belen causeway, just behind the South Carolina regiment that had been assigned the lead.

At the Belen gate they were stopped. Several hundred Americans fought there, under fire from hidden Mexican sharpshooters and from the defenders of the blockhouse. One contemporary called it "the hottest point of the whole war." Marine Pvt. Thomas Kelly was among those killed. Quitman was supposed to hold here; but he climbed on a captured battery, waving his sword with a handkerchief tied to its point, and urged his men on. The enemy counterattacked repeatedly. At 1:20 the Marines and soldiers carried the Belen gate by assault.

It was dark before Worth established a permanent foothold at the San Cosme gate.

That night, the American army faced the city. The Marine battalion waited in front of the Belen gate. Up and down the line, men went to work chopping holes through buildings they would have to fight past at daybreak. As Marine Captain Baker drank coffee with Quitman, a lieutenant brought congratulations from Maj. Gen. Scott and a request that Quitman withdraw his men from their exposed position. Quitman sent back a reply that he would not pull back without a direct order. He added a request for entrenching tools and ammunition. When the lieutenant left, Quitman said to the Marine captain, "Baker, the capital is mine; my brave fellows have conquered it, and, by God, they shall have it!"[45]

At dawn on September 14, Quitman and Worth prepared to assault the two entrances to the city; but the city council sent out a white flag and word that Santa Anna had abandoned the city and retreated northward. Worth advanced eastward to the Alameda, a park in the western end of the city, and Quitman's men raced through the thronged streets into the Grand Plaza. They took possession of the National Palace, a huge complex of government buildings, offices and courts. Here, in ancient days, had stood the Halls of Montezuma.

At 7 A.M., a bullet-torn American flag was raised and Scott rode up. A company of battle-worn Marines was lined up to receive him. In recognition of the work of his soldiers and Marines, Quitman was named governor of the City of Mexico; and the Marines were stationed to guard the Palace.

Before he fled, Santa Anna had released the prisoners in the city's jails. They and disorganized bands of citizens now opened a guerrilla war in the streets and from the windows and the flat rooftops. Using their bayonets, the Marine battalion routed the Palace's defenders—and looters. It would take 36 more hours of street fighting to clean up the last resistance. Then, the climactic battle of this "unholy" war (as Grant later called it[46]) was over.

After the Mexican War, the expansion of the continental United States, except for the Gadsden Purchase and the purchase of Alaska, was completed.

The Marines settled down in the ancient city, met the native wine and women, and before long the bluenoses were referring to the "Hells of Montezuma." Mexicans say that some of the Irish and English names in Mexico City date from those days.

Colonel Watson turned over command of the Marines to newly brevetted Lt. Col. William W. Dulany and remained as commander of the first brigade of the army's second division. Watson fell ill and died in Vera Cruz on November 16. (The Army paymaster refused to pay for a lead coffin for his body.) The battalion moved down to Vera Cruz and in the spring was sent to Alvarado, where the veterans joined a newly organized Second Battalion of 367 men commanded by Maj. John Harris, leader of the Florida "Horse Marines." By the summer of 1848, both battalions were home again.

In the early 1840s, Marine officers and noncoms began wearing scarlet stripes on their dress trousers—to commemorate, tradition came to say, the Marine blood shed at Chapultepec and the Halls of Montezuma.

Americans learned in Mexico that war is pain and death as well as glory.

Bernard De Voto, a strong-minded Westerner who wrote a book about the Mexican War, expressed his feeling for the volunteers who went to fight that war:

> He was a good boy. You remembered how he had laughed and chattered. You remembered being harsh to him, in the unforgiveable stupidity of parenthood. One day he was playing with a tin sword or, with a wooden gun, shooting imaginary Indians round a corner of the barn. A day or two later his voice was not treble any more and it was not a wooden gun that was on his shoulder when the fifes shrilled and he marched off behind the silk banner which the ladies of the church had made. You saw his face when he waved to you at the curve in the road,

and you wouldn't see it again. He had died of fever at
Matamoros or of thirst on the way to Monclova, or a
Mexican lance had done for him at Buena Vista or he had
got halfway up the slope at Chapultepec. No children
would spring from his loins as he had sprung from yours.
So in Georgia you watched the upland where he had
hunted squirrels turn brown with autumn, or in Ohio you
saw the cows come in at milking time in still evening
with someone else whistling to his dog.[47]

This officer and five stalwart Marines fought for the
Union in the Civil War.
Marine Corps Photo, National Archives

SEMPER FIDELIS

V
THE
CIVIL
WAR
1857-1865

1
The End
of the Old Man

The old man still stood ramrod stiff. He had been a Marine for 50 years, Commandant for 36. His hair and beard were now white, but the courage he had displayed on the bloody deck of *Constitution* back in 1815 had not faded. Col. Archibald Henderson, at seventy-four, was about to face gunfire for the last time.

It was the morning of June 1, 1857. The nation was boiling with tensions that would rapidly build up to the Civil War. A host of secret political societies had found a home in the American Party, the "Know-Nothings," a compost heap of all who hated foreigners and Catholics and who campaigned to elect to public office only native-born Protestants. A year earlier, they had grown strong enough to put up former President Millard Fillmore of New York for the Presidency.

On this June day, the city of Washington was holding a municipal election; and bully boys known as Plug-Uglies were moving in. These were hired roughnecks imported from Baltimore to help local hoodlums make a political weapon of violence.

Washington's small police force was trying to keep the gangs of toughs away from the citizens lined up to vote. In the fourth ward, the police fought a street battle with the ruffians, who were armed with knives, iron bars, sacks filled with stones, hammers, revolvers. The police were overwhelmed by these Plug-Uglies, and in desperation Mayor William Magruder closed the polls and asked President Buchanan for Marines—the only Federal force in the city—to restore order in the streets.

At midmorning, an aide handed Colonel Henderson a message from the Navy Department ordering out the Marines.

[For the location of places in the Civil War see map No. 3 in the map section.]

Henderson, dressed in civilian clothes, grabbed his hat and umbrella and had the Marines fall out—cartridge boxes filled with ball.

By noon, two companies set out under the command of Capt. Henry B. Tyler, adjutant of the Corps. Lt. Charles A. Henderson, the Commandant's son and a veteran of the fighting for Mexico City, served as adjutant of the battalion. Brevet Maj. Jacob Zeilin commanded the first company; Brevet Capt. William A. T. Maddox and 2d Lt. George P. Turner led the second. Both Zeilin and Maddox had served in the conquest of California. Sixty of the men were brand-new recruits, in service less than a week. Still in mufti, Commandant Henderson followed the detachment.

The Marines marched to the stucco City Hall in Judiciary Square through streets swarming with hooting, jeering mobs yelling that the Marines would never get back to the navy yard alive. Captain Tyler calmly reported his men to the mayor.

Henderson received word that a gang had dragged a small brass cannon up cobblestoned Pennsylvania Avenue to a jumble of sheds and shacks at 7th and K Streets. He persuaded Mayor Magruder that the Marines should be sent to take the gun. Disregarding the danger, Henderson went ahead to make certain the mob did not turn the cannon against the advancing column of Marines.

He went alone, armed only with his umbrella, into the noisy crowd spoiling for trouble and found the cannon pointed down the street. He walked directly up to the muzzle and, as he later recalled, "placed myself between the gun & the street along which the troops were advancing, with my knee against the gun near its mouth and kept it there, until the right of the advancing line had passed it."

Tyler lined up his men in the street at shoulder arms. The toughs with the cannon prepared to fire. Henderson spoke up: "Men, you had best think twice before you fire this piece at the Marines."[1] The white-haired old gentleman with the umbrella ordered the mob to disperse and warned that the Marines' weapons were loaded with ball. Then, he stepped across the street and urged Captain Tyler to seize the cannon. As the officers talked, revolvers were fired at them from the mob. Major Zeilin sent a platoon rushing forward. The rioters fell back, firing pistols and throwing rocks at the advancing Marines.

The Marines grabbed the gun and started to haul it away. The mob surged up again. Lt. Charles Henderson dashed in and directed that the cannon be brought around behind the Marines' line. The rioters were firing wildly at the Marines. One Marine was shot in the face; others were hit by stones. The Marines no longer waited for an order. They fired into the crowd, which fled out of range. The officers dashed among their men, shouting at them to cease fire.

As Colonel Henderson moved through the ranks to stop the shooting, he put his umbrella under the musket of a tall sergeant to force him to aim into the air. A man ran out of the Market House to within two feet of the colonel and fired his pistol. His shot missed. The sergeant shot the man in the left arm. Henderson collared the wounded man and dragged him to the mayor.

Later, Captain Maddox excused the breakdown in discipline. He said that when the Marine was shot in the face, the mayor had shouted: "Why don't you fire?" Some of the Marines, hearing only the mayor's last word, opened fire.

Henderson went back and examined the cannon; it was heavily charged. From a distance, members of the mob continued to fire at the Marines, still standing in the street. One Marine was hit in the shoulder. Tyler ordered the Marines to prepare to fire, and the rioters scattered.

With the mob dispersed, the battalion was withdrawn to the City Hall and remained on duty there. Part of the unit went to the railroad station to intercept any more Plug-Uglies.

The old colonel had acted beyond the call of any duty. It was his last courageous act. On January 6, 1859, the butler went to the library of Henderson's home to call him for dinner. He found the Commandant slumped in his favorite chair, dead.

Archibald Henderson was buried in the Congressional Cemetery east of the Navy Yard on January 10. President Buchanan attended the services in the Marine Barracks. Henderson left a wife, who died nine days after his funeral, and six children. Marine Lt. Charles Henderson was serving in Paraguay when his father died.

Colonel Henderson, whose tour as Commandant had begun in controversy 38 years before, was one of the Corps' greatest leaders. No other man has served in the post as long. During the earlier years of his regime, the Corps became a respected, disciplined arm that served its country well in the Indian wars, the War with Mexico and a host of lesser conflicts around the globe.

The day after the Old Man died, another graybeard was appointed Colonel Commandant of the Corps. Lt. Col. John Harris was an unfortunate choice. He could boast a long and distinguished record. But now, sixty-eight years old, with 44 years in uniform, he could no longer muster the energy and vision that would be required to lead the Marine Corps through the great civil war that was about to rip the nation apart.

Harris' age was not the only forewarning that he would make a passive Commandant. Back when the Corps was sending the battalion to Maj. Gen. Scott in Mexico, Harris had written Commandant Henderson a letter in which he expressed, with unconscious candor, his lack of drive for either glory or duty. He wrote: "If you could not give the Command of a Battalion to me, then I would rather stay at home than go second to an Officer of my own Grade. . . . If Major Dulany's going will do equally well, I will relinquish to him. . . . I have no desire to go, but if you think the good of the service requires it, I shall not hesitate to do so."[2] The fire had already gone out of John Harris.

It had not always been so. Coming to the Corps from Chester County, Pennsylvania, he had been commissioned in 1814. He served with Decatur against the Barbary pirates and was brevetted a captain. Ten years later, he commanded a mounted company of Marines in Florida—the Horse Marines— and performed gallantly at the Hatchee-Lustee. He reached Mexico, as commanding officer of the Second Battalion, after the armistice had been signed. Early portraits give the impression of an aggressive man with a firm mouth, but by the time he had become Commandant, the aggressiveness had visibly given way to pomposity.

Actually, Harris was representative of what the Corps had become. The dozen years after the Mexican War marked a pause of peace for the nation, and under Henderson the Corps had aged. By 1860, the average Marine captain had served for 25 years, the average first lieutenant 13 years. Both battle experience and promotions had been scarce.

As frequently happens when a long reign ends, Henderson's death and Harris' appointment unlocked a flood of jealousy and hatred among the Corps' senior officers. Harris had enemies, and the bickering rose to such intensity that Lincoln's Secretary of the Navy Gideon Welles finally ordered him to "exhort the older members of the Corps to consider whether . . . they have anything to gain by a persistence to malevolent feelings to each other . . . [You should] require from the senior officers of the Corps . . . an example which the many young officers recently appointed can safely imitate."[3] The Corps was not ready to meet the challenge of the times.

2
"They Came Rushing in Like Tigers"

Like many Marines, Irish-born Pvt. Luke Quinn was a little man—five feet six and a half. He had enlisted in Brooklyn; and by 1859, with four years of service behind him, he was stationed at the Marine Barracks at the Washington Navy Yard, a respected Marine on whom an officer would call for a dangerous job.

Although the Civil War was less than two years away, duty in the nation's capital was easy—standing guard and participating in official ceremonies. The Barracks and Navy Yard were isolated in the southeast corner of town. Between them and the scattered marble palaces of government stretched open fields and muddy bogs. Washington was an unfinished, sprawling city. One could still shoot bird within sight of the White House.

Early on Monday afternoon, October 17, 1859, the Marines at the Navy Yard received urgent word from Commandant Colonel Harris to fall out—they were needed. The men formed in their bright blue dress uniforms with fancy blue frock coats, white belts and French fatigue caps. First Lt. Israel Greene, commanding the detachment, wore his light ceremonial sword. (The fact that he did not put on his heavy-duty saber would have its effect on history.) The black-mustached lieutenant, a native of Plattsburgh, New York, was thirty-five; he had joined the Corps during the Mexican War.

That October afternoon, Washington was fearful. Rumors flew: The slaves in Virginia had risen. One report said that 700 of them had seized the federal arsenal and gun factory at Harpers Ferry, where the Potomac and the Shenandoah meet— 55 miles northwest of the capital. Bumbling Secretary of War John Buchanan Floyd scrambled for troops. Washington's mayor hastily called out all the city's police and ordered mounted men to guard the roads leading into the capital.

Secretary Floyd sent cavalry Lt. J. E. B. Stuart galloping to bring back Lt. Col. Robert E. Lee, hero of the Mexican War, from his home just over the Potomac River in Arlington. Then, Floyd and Lee hurried to meet with President Buchanan, who ordered out the Marines—one more occasion for the Corps' proud boast: First to Fight.

Fear of a slave uprising perpetually haunted white Southerners. Their alarm was heightened by the increasingly militant activities of the Northern abolitionists, who would use force to abolish human slavery. Threats of a slave revolt had been simmering ever since the summer's night in 1831 when the Negro preacher Nat Turner had roused the slaves in Southampton County, Virginia, to butcher 55 white men, women, and children before dawn. Soldiers from Fortress Monroe and Marines from *USS Warren* and *Natchez* in Hampton Roads had marched to put down Turner's Rebellion. Even after Nat Turner was captured and hung, the terror remained in the air. It was still there in 1859.

Pvt. Luke Quinn and his 85 fellow Marines boarded a northbound Baltimore and Ohio train, taking with them two 12-pound howitzers. By now they knew this was no ceremonial assignment. The Marines transferred to the main east-west line at the Relay House eight miles outside Baltimore. Lt. Col. Lee had been given command of all forces at Harpers Ferry, and "Jeb" Stuart had volunteered to go along as his aide.

Lieutenant Greene, and Marine Maj. William W. Russell reconnoitered the area at Harpers Ferry before Lee's arrival. Russell, the paymaster of the Corps, had joined the expedition to help Greene, although as a staff officer he was not eligible to command. Greene and Russell learned that a group of white men and Negroes had invaded Harpers Ferry on Sunday night, cut the telegraph wires and seized the arsenal and armory. Militia and townspeople from nearby villages had battled them almost all day Monday. Several of the raiders and a number of local people, including the mayor, had been killed. Now, the invaders were barricaded on the armory grounds in a small brick building that housed two fire engines. The men held 13 hostages, both whites and Negroes. One was "Colonel" Lewis W. Washington, the great-grandnephew of the first President of the United States and the owner of an estate in the area. Everyone feared for the prisoners' lives. No one knew who led the raiders.

By ten o'clock, Lee had joined Greene and the Marines. Leaving the howitzers on the train, Lee marched the men across the bridge into Harpers Ferry. He had Greene post the Marines inside the Federal armory grounds around the engine house and stationed the militia outside the grounds. Luke Quinn spent the rest of that long night standing guard. The rain came down steadily.

Although rumors continued to buzz of slaves marching on Harpers Ferry, there had been no uprising—just an unknown number of grim men in a single building, ready to kill but hopelessly trapped. Lee sent off a message to Washington: He did not need the troops from Fortress Monroe; the Marines could handle the situation.

Lee's main worry was for the hostages. He reported later: "I made preparations to attack the insurgents at day-light. But for the fear of sacrificing the lives of some of the gentlemen held by them as prisoners in a midnight assault, I should have ordered the attack at once."[4]

Around midnight, they finally learned who commanded the raiders: John Brown of Kansas. Brown had made a religious crusade of opposing slavery. Human bondage was a moral evil; should it not be wiped out from the sight of God? Brown had been born in Connecticut on May 9, 1800 (the same year Nat Turner was born), and had farmed in the Adirondack wilderness at North Elba, New York. When Kansas became a bloody battleground between settlers from the slave South and the free North, Brown had gone there, killed pro-slavery settlers and led slaves out to safety and freedom. He was the hero of the radical abolitionists.

That summer Brown had assembled 21 young men in Virginia and hidden out in a rented farm five miles from Harpers Ferry. He saw this as another border area, like Kansas, which he could inflame over slavery. He planned to seize the federal arsenal and arm slaves who would rally to him and lead them to freedom. His men, armed with Sharps carbines, were deadly shots—truly sharpshooters. But the slaves did not rise; and now Brown was cornered, all but four of his men killed or wounded. Escape was impossible through the cordon of Marines and the militiamen from all over Virginia who were swarming into Harpers Ferry.

While the rainy night passed quietly, Lee judged that his best chance to capture Brown and save the hostages lay in striking swiftly. And don't risk a stray bullet killing a prisoner; use the bayonet.

First, Lee would give Brown an opportunity to surrender. The colonel wrote out a note and at 2 A.M. handed it to "Jeb" Stuart to deliver to the raiders' leader when ordered to. The message told Brown that escape was cut off and that if he would surrender Lee would guarantee his safety. If Brown refused—and Lee expected him to refuse—Stuart was to give a signal and the engine house would be stormed.

Lee offered the militia the honor of taking Brown; his raid was as much a violation of state soil as of Federal property. But the militia colonel turned the offer down. This was no job for civilians; use your "mercenaries," the militia colonel said. So Lee gave Lieutenant Greene the job of "taking those men out."

"At half past six in the morning," Greene wrote later, "Colonel Lee gave me orders to select a detail of 12 men for a storming party and place them near the engine house in which Brown and his men had entrenched themselves. I selected 12 of my best men and a second 12 to be employed as a reserve."[5] One of the first men Greene chose was the private from Brooklyn—Luke Quinn.

The storming party moved in close to the engine house, keeping out of Brown's line of fire. Three Marines carried sledgehammers to knock down the building's heavy twin doors. Lee ordered that there be no shooting. The Marines fixed their bayonets.

By now, it seemed, every living soul in Harpers Ferry was out to see the climax. They jammed the streets, hung from windows and sat on the roofs. Lee stood calmly, unarmed, on a slight rise about 40 feet from the engine house. He ordered Stuart to deliver the note to Brown.

Stuart approached the engine house with a white flag. The door opened a crack and a tall, gaunt man with a white beard stood there. Stuart recognized Brown; they had met in 1856 when the 1st Cavalry had restored order in Kansas after Brown's Pottawatomie massacre. Stuart handed Lee's message to Brown; he read it and started to argue. He wanted to be allowed to cross the bridge, where he would release his prisoners and then be on his own. His talk went on and on. Stuart could hear the prisoners shouting, pleading that he bring Lee to talk with Brown. But Stuart knew the colonel would not give an inch. At last, he cut off the palaver, stepped back from the door a pace, took off his plumed hat and waved it—the signal he had set with Greene for the Marines to attack. Later, Greene recalled:

> Suddenly Lieutenant Stewart [sic] waved his hat and I gave the order to my men to batter in the door. Those inside fired rapidly at the point where the blows were given upon the door. Very little impression was made with the hammers, as the doors were tied on the inside with ropes and braced by the hand brakes of the fire engines, and in a few minutes I gave orders to desist.
>
> Just then my eye caught sight of a ladder lying a few feet from the engine house, in the yard, and I ordered my men to catch it up and use it as a battering ram. . . . The men took hold bravely and made a tremendous assault upon the door. The second blow broke it in. This entrance was a ragged hole low down in the right hand door, the door being splintered and cracked some distance upward.

Greene, armed only with his light dress sword, was the first man through the hole. The men inside had been firing while the Marines rammed the door with the ladder; they were reloading when Greene squeezed through the opening. Major Russell, unarmed, plunged in after him. By now the raiders had reloaded. The next man in was shot through the abdomen, mortally wounded. He was Pvt. Luke Quinn. The fourth man in, Pvt. Mathew Ruppert, was shot in the face.

Greene did not hesitate.

> Getting to my feet I ran to the right of the engine, which stood behind the door, passed quickly to the rear of the

house, and came up between the two engines. The first person I saw was Colonel Lewis Washington, who was standing near the hose cart at the front of the engine house. On one knee, a few feet to the left, knelt a man with a carbine in his hand, just pulling the lever to reload.

"Hello, Greene," said Colonel Washington, and he reached out his hand to me. I grasped it with my left hand, having my saber uplifted in my right, and he said, pointing to the kneeling figure, "This is Ossawatomie."

As he said this, Brown turned his head to see who it was to whom Colonel Washington was speaking. Quicker than thought I brought my saber down with all my strength upon his head. He was moving as the blow fell, and I suppose I did not strike him where I intended, for he received a deep saber cut in the back of his neck. He fell senseless on his side, then rolled over on his back. He had in his hand a short *Sharps* cavalry carbine. I think he had just fired as I reached Colonel Washington, for the marine [Quinn] who followed me into the aperture made by the ladder received a bullet in the abdomen from which he died in a few minutes. The shot might have been fired by some one else in the insurgent party, but I think it was from Brown. Instinctively, as Brown fell I gave him a saber thrust in the left breast. The sword I carried was a light uniform weapon and, either not having a point or striking something in Brown's accoutrements, did not penetrate. The blade bent double.

By[that] time three or four of my men were inside. They came rushing in like tigers, as a storming assault is not a play-day sport. They bayoneted one man [Dauphin Thompson] skulking under the engine and pinned another fellow [Brown's lieutenant, Jeremiah Anderson] up against the rear wall, both being instantly killed. I ordered the men to spill no more blood. The other insurgents were at once taken under arrest, and the contest ended. The whole fight had not lasted over three minutes.[6]

The Marines brought out the four dead and two wounded

raiders and Quinn and Ruppert and laid them on the grass in the armory yard. Then, they brought out the two uninjured raiders, a Quaker and a former slave. Finally, the hostages emerged, Colonel Washington pausing to draw on his white gloves so the crowd would not see his soiled hands. The Marines kept away the curious and the vengeful. They buried Luke Quinn.

Greene and Stuart led a detachment to the rented farm across the Potomac in Maryland to collect the guns and pikes Brown had stored there for the slaves he expected to rise and join him. Brown and those of his men still alive were sent by train to the jail in nearby Charles Town. The Marines had to hold off the people who wanted to lynch Brown on the spot.

Because John Brown survived Greene's light sword, he was able to dramatize his martyrdom. With moving statements in the courtroom and in letters to his wife and friends, he rallied those who hated slavery. But after a seven-day trial, he was hanged in Charles Town. Among the troops massed around the scaffold were a civilian agitator named Edmund Ruffin, who, many say, fired the first shot on Fort Sumter only 16 months later; Maj. Thomas J. Jackson, who would be known as "Stonewall"; and a volunteer militia private from Richmond named John Wilkes Booth.

The Marines' engagement at Harpers Ferry marked the beginning. Before it was over, 600,000 Americans in uniforms of blue and of gray would be killed. Luke Quinn was the first.

3
"Under the Banner of Treason"

Abraham Lincoln believed that the Union was inviolable and human slavery evil, and his election made civil war virtually inevitable.

But for many citizens, ties of state and region proved stronger than loyalty to country. As the war approached, the Marine Corps, like the other services, was crippled by resignations. Very few enlisted men quit, but the Corps lost 32 percent of its 63 officers. Among the 20 who "went South" were some of the Corps' finest: two majors, Henry B. Tyler, the Adjutant of the Corps, and Brevet Maj. George H. Terrett; four captains, Jabez C. Rich, John D. Simms, Robert Tansill and Algernon S. Taylor; 11 first lieutenants, including Israel Greene of Harpers Ferry, and three second lieutenants, including Major Tyler's son, Henry, Junior. Terrett, Rich and Simms had all been heroes of the assault on the gates of Mexico City—the kind of men the Corps could not afford to lose.

Three sons of the late Commandant Henderson were sympathetic to the Rebellion. Charles A. Henderson, who had been a United States Marine lieutenant for 14 years and fought bravely at Mexico City, resigned in May 1861 and was later dismissed from the Corps, although he apparently did not serve in the armed forces of the Confederacy. Richard H. Henderson, who never was a U.S. Marine, joined the Confederate Marine Corps in 1861 and surrendered at Appomattox Courthouse. Another son, Octavius, served as a captain in the Confederate Army.

Resignations from the Corps were accepted until May 1, 1861; after that, any man who attempted to join the Confederacy was summarily dismissed. Fourteen of the 20 Marine officers who left the Corps were so dismissed. Commandant Harris referred to officers who resigned as "those who abandoned the service in its hour of need."[7]

Men were torn between conflicting loyalties. Those who chose the South did not simply seek to preserve slavery. Most were convinced that the United States was a compact of sovereign states and that a state could properly leave the Union. While most Northerners saw the conflict in terms of insurrection and rebellion, Southerners saw it in terms of political self-determination. This was to be a struggle over the nature of the United States—a struggle deeply influenced by the economic rivalry between North and South and by the Western expansion that the Marine Corps had helped to achieve. Men were forced to make terrible choices. Lincoln himself went to war, not to destroy slavery by force, but to save the Union.

Most of the men in uniform who did resign were Southerners, but place of birth did not always determine a man's decision. Among the Marine officers who joined the Confederacy, Jabez Rich and George Holmes were from Maine, Julius E. Meiere was from Connecticut, Israel Greene from New York and Adam Baker from Pennsylvania. Among those who stood with country and Corps were William Dulany, David M. Cohen, Addison Garland and Clement D. Hebb—all from Virginia.

Of those who "went South," Capt. Robert Tansill of Virginia, a veteran of 28 years in the Corps and the hero of the defense of Guaymas in the Mexican War, expressed his reason best. In his letter of resignation, he wrote:

> In entering the public service I took an oath to support the Constitution, which necessarily gives me a right to interpret it. Our institutions, according to my understanding, are founded upon the principles and right of self-government. The States forming the Confederacy did not relinquish that right, and I believe each State has a clear and unquestionable right to secede whenever the people thereof think proper, and the Federal government has no legal or moral authority to use force to keep them in the Union. . . . No personal consideration or advantage, however great, can induce me to aid in a cause which my heart tells me is wrong, and I prefer to endure the most terrible hardships rather than to prosper in the destruction of the freedom of my country.[8]

(Secretary of the Navy Gideon Welles had Tansill arrested in New York on his return from a cruise on August 23, 1861, when the war was already bloody. He was imprisoned in Fort Lafayette without hearing or trial until he was formally exchanged on January 10, 1862. Then he went South and 12 days later joined the Confederate Marine Corps as a captain. But he resigned shortly to accept a colonel's commission in the Confederate artillery.)

The right and wrong of the decision of men such as Tansill are still debated. After World War II, defeated German and Japanese officers were imprisoned and executed because their only defense was that they were loyally carrying out orders of their superiors—a kind of "blind loyalty" Tansill was not willing to live by.

At the same time Tansill was resigning, Ulysses S. Grant put his own feelings clearly:

> When I read of officers of the army and navy, educated by the government at West Point and Annapolis, and under a solemn vow to be defenders of the flag against all foes whatsoever, domestic or foreign, throwing up their commissions, going South and taking service under the banner of treason, it fills me with indignation.[9]

Grant did not believe that Tansill's oath allowed him to interpret the Constitution for himself. He called it treason.

Nineteen of the U.S. Marine Corps officers who went South joined the Confederate States Marine Corps. The CSMC was created in March 1861, even before the surrender of Fort Sumter, and in May was enlarged to a 10-company regiment of 46 officers and 944 men. It never reached full strength; and in October, 1864, it still mustered only 571 officers and men. An estimated 56 officers and 1,200 enlisted men served with the CSMC during the war.

Although many of the CSMC's officers had served in the USMC, Col. Lloyd J. Beall, the commandant of the CSMC, had never been a U.S. Marine. A West Point friend of Jefferson Davis, he had served for 30 years in the U.S. Army. The lieutenant colonel of the CSMC was Henry B. Tyler, formerly major and adjutant-inspector of the USMC, who had led the detachment in the Washington riot in 1857. The third highest Confederate marine was Major Terrett.

The gray-clad Confederate marines fought in 11 sizable actions during the war. The Confederate Congress voted them special thanks on four occasions: for service on *Merrimack* in its battle with *Monitor*; for the defense of Drewry's Bluff after *Merrimack* was finally destroyed in May, 1862; for service with Capt. Raphael Semmes on *Sumter* in 1862, and for cutting out *USS Underwriter* in the Neuse River, North Carolina, on February 1, 1864.

They fought to the very end. As Lee retreated westward from Richmond before Grant's attack, 200 Confederate marines led by Col. George H. Terrett and Capt. John D. Simms marched with Ewell's Corps in the rear guard. Three days before Lee surrendered at Appomattox Courthouse, Sheridan surrounded the Rebel rear guard at Sayler's Creek. Fighting bitterly, it repulsed three Union attacks before being forced to surrender.

Confederate marines and sailors from the James River Squadron came upriver to Richmond in a last-minute effort to join Lee. They arrived just after the last train had left. A locomotive was found in a railway workshop, and sailors and marines repaired the engine and put together a train. The marines tore down fences for fuel, and the unit chugged off to Danville, Virginia, where it manned trenches until stragglers came in with the news of the surrender at Appomattox. The leader of this brigade was Confederate Rear Adm. Raphael Semmes; and among its marine officers was Israel Greene, who had been in on the beginning at Harpers Ferry.

4
The Holocaust Begins

The Civil War revolutionized the Navy. Sail gave way to steam power—which increased a ship's speed and maneuverability but tied it to a coal supply. Rifled cannon replaced smoothbore guns, and the Navy experimented with mines, turrets, submarines and graduated gunsights. Explosive shells were introduced; the Russians had used them against the Turks in the Crimean War in 1853. Because the new shells shattered wooden hulls into deadly splinters, they hastened the changeover to steel ships.

The U.S. Marine Corps was not prepared for great and rapid change. Under Harris' tired leadership, it was satisfied to continue its traditional functions of guarding shore installations and policing the larger vessels. Occasionally, Marines would attempt courageous amphibious landings; but, on the whole, the Civil War was not to be a time of distinction for the Corps.

Between Lincoln's election and his inauguration on March 4, 1861, the nation slipped and slid, virtually without a helmsman, into the awful conflict, the scars of which could still be painful more than a century later.

In November 1860 the Corps had 63 officers and 1,712 enlisted men. Its first jobs were defensive. On January 5, 1861, Colonel Harris was ordered to send 40 men to occupy Fort Washington, a rotting, useless installation opposite Mount Vernon on the Maryland side of the Potomac. The Marine detachment was commanded by Capt. Algernon S. Taylor, who four months later would join the Rebellion. Thirty Marines were also sent to Fort McHenry at Baltimore; they were led by 1st Lt. Andrew J. Hays, who would also "go South."

Two days later, a secret expedition set out from New York to

207

reinforce Fort Sumter, the unfinished, five-sided works controlling the entrance to Charleston, South Carolina. The state had seceded, and Sumter's small Army garrison was threatened by Southern sympathizers. The unarmed, chartered *Star of the West* was loaded with 250 recruits; they were carried in tugs to the steamer waiting unseen outside New York harbor. As the ship headed south, it was joined by the sloop of war *Brooklyn*. But word of the expedition leaded out; and as *Star of the West* tried to enter Charleston harbor at dawn on January 9, it was fired on. Its United States flag made no difference. After a few near misses, *Star of the West* turned around, mission unaccomplished, and headed back to New York.

Florida seceded on January 10; and two days later the Warrington Navy Yard at Pensacola, the only major naval base on the Gulf of Mexico, surrendered. Early that rainy morning, the 39 Marines at the yard under Capt. Josiah Watson were ordered to fall out with their arms. The decision to surrender the yard was announced, and the Marines were told to stack arms. Their sergeant described the scene: "It was an order that all of the men seemed very reluctant to obey. They were very much affected, some of them to tears, and said they would not obey; they would not suffer the humiliation; they would sooner be shot."[10] Some of the Marines held onto their unloaded muskets for an hour after the order was given. Captain Watson signed a pledge not to bear arms against Florida; and, as "paroled prisoners of war," most of the Marines finally sailed north.

Before the surrender of the yard, Army Maj. Adam J. Slemmer took 49 soldiers and 30 sailors out to untenanted Fort Pickens on the western tip of Santa Rosa Island in Pensacola Harbor. By holding this key fort, they could neutralize the entire navy yard.

In April, 200 soldiers and 118 Marines under the command of 1st Lt. John C. Cash landed and reinforced Slemmer's detachment. The Union held Fort Pickens throughout the war.

A lack of leadership and a mixture of apathy and divided loyalties permitted the seizure of Federal military installations and arms to go unpunished. Washington at that moment was truly "a town of sedition and dismay."[11]

On February 4, representatives of six states met at Montgomery, Alabama, and created the Confederacy. Two weeks later, Jefferson Davis was inaugurated as its president.

When Abraham Lincoln took office on March 4, a raw, windy Monday, the Rebellion was already under way. The Marine Corps Band played in the line of march of the inauguration parade. And fearing Lincoln would be assassinated, Marines guarded the high board fence that framed the passage by which the official party entered the unfinished Capitol, its dome open to the sky and the statue of Armed Freedom standing awkwardly in the grass amidst piles of marble.

That night, the Marine Band played again at the Union Ball in the temporary building erected for the occasion behind the City Hall. But the mood in the divided city was one of tension, not festivity.

At 4:30 A.M., Friday, April 12, Brig. Gen. Pierre Gustave Toutant Beauregard (recently Captain, USA) ordered South Carolina troops to fire on the Federal garrison bottled up in Fort Sumter. President Lincoln had decided to supply Sumter, and the Confederacy sought to act before he could. A mortar shell burst over the fort. The war began.

The garrison in the fort surrendered on Saturday afternoon, after a 34-hour bombardment, and marched out on Sunday. The next day, Lincoln called up 75,000 men for three months' military duty to enlarge the 16,000-man Regular Army. North Carolina seceded; and on Wednesday, Virginia—the home of Washington and Jefferson and the site of Jamestown, Williamsburg and Yorktown—declared that it was leaving the Union.

One of Virginia's first military objectives was to seize the great navy yard along the Elizabeth River at Norfolk. This vast station contained supply depots, dry dock, machine shops and guns of all types. At the yard was a small squadron of naval ships in various stages of completion or repair, including the sloop of war *Cumberland* and the most desirable prize, the five-year-old sail and steam sloop *Merrimack*, 3,200 tons.

To guard the yard's 90 sprawling acres, sixty-eight-year-old Commodore Charles S. McCauley had only two dozen watchmen and 60 Marines commanded by Lt. Col. James Edelin, a round-faced veteran of 46 years in the Corps. McCauley wavered feebly between evacuating the yard and inaction. By

Wednesday afternoon, April 17, the day Virginia seceded, *Merrimack*, which was in for major repairs, was ready to get under way. But the Rebels had partially blocked the channel, and McCauley refused to permit *Merrimack's* boilers to be fired until Thursday morning.

Brevet Lt. Gen. Winfield Scott, now seventy-four and again commanding the U.S. Army, finally lent the Navy a battalion of 350 raw, undrilled militiamen of the 3rd Massachusetts Infantry. The Navy moved as fast as it could. Friday night—a week after the firing on Sumter—Commodore Hiram Paulding sailed from Washington aboard the eight-gun steamer *Pawnee* with 100 Marines, commanded by 1st Lt. Augustus S. Nicholson, who had stormed Chapultepec, and a group of demolition experts. Saturday afternoon, they loaded the militiamen, armed with old-fashioned muskets, at Fortress Monroe. At 6:45 P.M., *Pawnee* set out on the last 18-mile lap across Hampton Roads, around the blockade of sunken boats and up the Elizabeth River.

Meanwhile, back at the yard, Lt. Col. Edelin had hired a spy to watch Southern troop movements; and on Friday, his Marines foiled an attempt by 50 armed secessionists to seize a Federal tug. That night, Rebels captured the yard's powder magazine and 2,800 barrels of powder. On Saturday afternoon, McCauley ordered the ships at the yard scuttled and the guns spiked. At 8 P.M., *Pawnee* reached the navy yard wharf. Resignedly, McCauley turned over command of the yard to Paulding, who sent Nicholson's Marines to hold the gates and rushed men to stop the scuttling of *Merrimack*. He was too late.

Disturbed by an exaggerated report from Edelin's spy that 5,000 Rebel troops had gathered in the vicinity, Paulding decided to complete the destruction. The yard's Marines, the Marine guards of *Cumberland* and the ancient station ship *Pennsylvania*, and those who had arrived on *Pawnee* went to work. Thousands of muskets and carbines were smashed and thrown into the river; hundreds of guns were spiked (ineffectively); ammunition, shot and shell were dumped into the water; machine shops, depots, the Marine barracks and the dry dock were prepared for destruction. Gold and other valuables were put aboard *Cumberland* in trust of 2d Lt. Charles Heywood and his Marines. Said the correspondent for the *New York Times*,

"The crackling flames and the glare of light inspired with new energies the destroying Marines."[12]

At 2 A.M., the Marine barracks burst prematurely into flames, causing some of the wreckers to flee without destroying several important machine shops. Troops and Marines were reembarked. *Pawnee* and the tug that the Marines had saved on Friday towed *Cumberland* out of danger. At 4 A.M., the explosive charges were detonated; and within a half hour, the yard was an inferno.

The Rebels stormed into the burning yard and saved the dry dock and a thousand cannon that could be repaired. *Merrimack's* upper decks had burned, but her sunken hull and water-soaked machinery were whole. The South would raise and rebuild her as the mighty ironclad *Virginia*—for a brief moment, the world's most powerful warship.

5
"Their Backs to the Enemy"

When the war started, the U.S. Marine Corps was a small service of less than 1,800 officers and men. On July 25, 1861, four days after the disaster at Bull Run, Congress authorized the Corps' strength increased to 3,167; and by October the Marines numbered 2,964. This was the only expansion granted by Congress during the entire war. The President, acting under earlier legislation, approved two later increases of 500 men each. The Corps never exceeded 3,900 men at any time during the war.

Young Northern patriots rallied to home-grown Army units; and as in the past, recruiting was difficult for the Marine Corps. Starting in June, 1862, Colonel Harris offered recruits a $100 bounty. But he had no authority to do so, and 13 months later the Secretary of the Navy discovered and cancelled the Marines' bounty system. By then more than 1,100 men had been enlisted with promises of bounties, and President Lincoln himself decided to pay the unauthorized bounty rather than discharge the men.

Before the long war was over, 148 U.S. Marines would be killed in battle, 131 would be wounded and 312 would die of disease and other causes. More than 2,000 would desert—mostly during the final stages of the war, when all the services suffered such disloyalty.

As the nation prepared for battle, its war machine, which had lain idle and rusting so long, had to be rebuilt suddenly. Most Marines served on the swelling fleet of warships; eventually the Corps had more than 100 detachments at sea.

The Civil War also sparked a revolution in small arms. It progressed in three steps: from smoothbore to rifled barrel, from muzzle-loader to breechloader and from single shot to repeater.

212

At the war's outbreak, Federal arsenals bulged with 200,000 old-fashioned smoothbore, muzzle-loading muskets. The musket's range was so short that the bayonet charge was still an important tactic. Troops advancing in great enough mass could attack successfully through the musket's 100-yard range.

The Civil War's greatest change in small arms was from smoothbore to rifled barrel. Rifling increased both range and accuracy; a rifle could kill a man at 500 yards. The bayonet became less useful. A man could not hope to close with the enemy across a 500-yard field of fire and live. Defenders dug in, and trench warfare evolved into an elaborate science. The rifle shoved armies apart.

The rifle that slowly became standard was still a muzzle-loader. To use this weapon with which most men fought throughout the Civil War, a man had to reach into his pouch, take out a .58-caliber paper cartridge, open it with his teeth, pour the powder into the barrel, insert a bullet, drive it home with his ramrod and remove the ramrod. Then he had to prime the piece, cock it, aim and—finally—fire. A cool veteran might fire as many as three well-aimed rounds per minute.

In 1859, Christian Sharps had invented a single-shot breechloading rifle that fired eight to ten .54-caliber rounds per minute. With its greater muzzle velocity, Sharps' rifle could hit a man at 700 yards. It also permitted men to load and fire rapidly while lying prone. The Sharps rifle went into battle in 1862, and, although there were less than 2,000 of them, that was "enough to transform warfare on land as the *Monitor* had done on the sea."[13] Before the war was won, some Marines were using the 1863 model of the Sharps rifle.

The final development after rifling and breechloading was the repeating rifle. The one invented by Christopher Spencer in 1860 held seven metallic cartridges end to end in the stock, and a man advanced them into the chamber by working a lever. Its tested rate of fire was 14 rounds per minute. The Navy ordered 700 Spencers, and the Army used them effectively at Chicka-mauga in September 1863. By the end of the war, Sheridan's cavalrymen were carrying seven-shot Spencer repeating car-bines, the war's best small-arms weapon.

The war also brought new leadership in naval administration. The Marines' new boss, Navy Secretary Gideon Welles, was a tall, gray-bearded newspaperman from Hartford, Connecticut, who knew little about the Navy but proved to be an excellent administrator. He appointed Gustavus Vasa Fox to the newly created post of Assistant Secretary of the Navy. The forty-year-old Fox, born in Saugus, Massachusetts, had served in the Navy for 15 years and held the confidence of the professional Navy officers. He and Welles made a good team.

As the spring of 1861 wore on, Lincoln's Administration came under increasing pressure to get the war over. One swift, decisive stroke, it was said, would capture Richmond and crush the Rebellion before the Army's three-month volunteers went home. (In the south, some demanded an immediate invasion of the North.) But General in Chief Winfield Scott, who was old enough to remember something of war and high command, knew better. He wanted time to mold the new recruits into battalions and regiments that could march to battle and, once there, fight and win. But he failed to silence the quick-war boys who orated about celebrating victory on the Glorious Fourth of July.

Command of the 28,000 raw, undisciplined Union troops who had crossed the Potomac and encamped in Virginia was given to Brig. Gen. Irvin McDowell, a forty-three-year-old student of tactics who was unpopular with his men and at odds with Scott. Some 30 miles from Washington sat the Confederates' army of 23,000 equally green troops under the command of Beauregard, McDowell's West Point classmate and the victor of Fort Sumter. Across the Blue Ridge Mountains in the Shenandoah Valley waited the capable Brig. Gen. Joseph E. Johnston, former Quartermaster-General of the U.S. Army, with nearly 15,000 Confederates.

The Washington politicians and amateur strategists pressed Lincoln to attack. Lincoln pressed Scott; and late in June, McDowell came up with a plan. He would attack the rail junction at Manassas, Virginia, 25 miles southwest of Washington. At that point, the main north-south railroad, which connected Richmond and Washington, met the east-west branch coming out of the Shenandoah Valley. If McDowell could seize the railroad junction and cork Manassas Gap, the break in the mountains through which the east-west line emerged, he could keep Beauregard and Johnston separated and force open the road to Richmond—only 100 miles from Washington. It seemed logical.

The Union's first move was its worst. Brig. Gen. Robert Patterson, a decrepit veteran of the War of 1812, was sent into the Shenandoah Valley with 18,000 Pennsylvania militiamen to prevent Joe Johnston from joining Beauregard. This was the key to victory, but Patterson was no man for the job.

As McDowell got ready to march, the Marine Corps hastily threw together a battalion of 12 officers and 353 enlisted men and detailed it to cooperate with the Army. Brevet Maj. John G. Reynolds, in command of the battalion, had won his brevet leading a storming party at Chapultepec. Now sixty years old, he was a seasoned and trusted officer. But almost all of his Marines were recruits with less than three weeks in uniform and without training of any kind.

On Tuesday, July 16, McDowell moved out; and at 3 P.M., Major Reynolds led his Marine battalion onto Virginia soil and marched up the Warrenton turnpike. Brig. Gen. David Hunter, the West Pointer who had headed Lincoln's bodyguard before the war, commanded the division with which the Marines would fight. The Marines were assigned a place in the line of march directly behind and supporting Army Capt. Charles Griffin's six-gun "West Point Battery" of artillery. The Marines' march was at double time much of the way; the horse-drawn battery set a killing pace.

The enemy waited north of the railroad junction, across a little stream called Bull Run. Their army extended for more than eight miles behind the creek, which flowed southeast and was protected by banks so steep that it could be crossed only at a series of fords or at the arched Stone Bridge. Beauregard organized the army into six brigades. Because he had few general officers, one brigade of three Virginia regiments was commanded before the battle by Col. George H. Terrett, late of the U.S. Marine Corps.

As McDowell tarried, Beauregard was heavily reinforced by Johnston, who had completely fooled old Brig. Gen. Patterson. Not waiting passively for a Union attack. Beauregard prepared his own assault and dreamt of victory in front of Manassas and the swift seizure of Washington.

But McDowell was confident. Reconnaissance had shown

him that Beauregard had overshifted his army to the right, ready to cross Bull Run and attack east of the Stone Bridge. In response, McDowell planned to feint with half his force against Beauregard's front and swing his main body far to the west, beyond the Stone Bridge; cross Bull Run at unmapped Sudley Springs Ford, which his engineers found late on Saturday, and roll up the enemy's weakened left flank. Hunter's and Samuel P. Heintzelman's divisions would lead this looping Union assault.

The battle finally began early on Sunday morning, July 21. It was to be a beautiful summer day. The Union army stretched over the wooded countryside with its neat green fields. A host of civilian sightseers, including assorted Congressmen and ladies in carriages, rode out from Washington to witness the Sunday spectacle and the great Union victory.

Both generals prepared to attack; McDowell got the jump. The Marines were up and on the march by 2 A.M. Most had slept little; many not at all. The movement in the moonlight was confused and delayed. The Marines advanced with Griffin's battery, in the van of the main body, to encircle the enemy's left flank. They marched at double time, following a dirt road, and again found themselves unable to keep up with the artillery-men's horses. Separated from the battery, Reynolds reported to his brigade commander, Col. Andrew Porter, who ordered him to move up and support Griffin. It was 9:30, two hours behind schedule, before the army's lead elements encountered the first two regiments of the enemy.

Beauregard was already moving across the creek far over on his right front. He met the leading elements of the Federal feint; and when the Rebels spotted the main sweep around their left, they began shifting units to meet the threat. Having forded the stream two miles west of the Stone Bridge, the Union soldiers and the Marines, already tired, came under heavy fire.

Griffin's battery moved to within 1,000 yards of Confederate units strung out in a long line along the Warrenton turnpike. His guns dueled with the enemy batteries and forced the Rebel artillery to retreat. The Marines advanced on the right of Porter's brigade and helped push the enemy back.

Before long, the reinforced Confederate left flank stiffened; and the Union attack ground to a halt. The enemy counterat-tacked. The 8th New York Infantry and the 14th New York

Infantry, both militia regiments, broke. The inexperienced Union leaders failed to send in their reserves. Hunter was severely wounded, and Porter took command of the division. Griffin's battery again moved forward; the 14th New York Infantry rallied behind it. Under Griffin's aggressive fire, the Rebel artillery retreated behind a hill. Following Griffin through the timber into the fields beyond, the Marines moved up "in fine style in the rear of the Fourteenth."[14] They now stood where the enemy's left wing had been. Opposition melted and the Union divisions shoved the enemy back nearly a mile.

By 11 A.M., the two Northern assault divisions, supported by other units, had shattered the outnumbered and now disorganized defenders. The Rebel remnants fell back on Henry House Hill to try to form a new line. The Confederates held the interior positions on the field and could reinforce their broken left wing. The First Virginia Brigade, which had come from the Valley and was commanded by Brig. Gen. Thomas J. Jackson, now held "like a stone wall" behind the crest of Henry House Hill. The retreating Rebel units began to form on Jackson's bridge. It was 11:30. Johnston and Beauregard rode up to rally their men.

One final Union charge would break the enemy, open the road to Richmond and crush the Rebellion. At 1 P.M., Griffin's battery and a battery led by Capt. J. B. Ricketts charged up the flank of Henry House Hill to close with the enemy. But they were badly exposed, and their infantry support—the colorful New York Fire Zouaves and the Marines—came up slowly. Here was the vortex of the battle; here the Rebellion would live or die.

Then came two incredible accidents. Confederate Col. J. E. B. Stuart, mistaking the New York Zouaves for Alabama troops retreating, rode up with 500 men of his First Cavalry to rally them. Stuart quickly discovered his error; and before the surprised New Yorkers could react, his cavalrymen rode them down. The Zouaves fired a few dozen shots and fled. The 14th Infantry broke again. And, as Colonel Porter later reported, "The marines also, in spite of the exertions of their gallant officers, gave way in disorder."[15]

Griffin now saw a gray-clad regiment advancing on his right. It looked like a Wisconsin regiment that was uniformed in gray. He ordered his gunners to hold their fire until he could determine who was approaching. The advancing troops moved into musket range and at 70 yards opened fire. They were the 33rd Virginia Regiment. The Virginians swept over the gunners' position. The guns of the two Union batteries were captured, cannoneers hit, horses slaughtered. Ricketts was badly wounded and taken prisoner. The Union spearhead had been wiped out; the Rebellion was still alive.

At 2 P.M., the Rebel army opened a general offensive; but the Union regiments held fast and threw the enemy back. The Zouaves retook Henry House Hill. In 15 minutes, the Union recaptured the ground that had been lost. Northern reinforcements reached further and further to the southwest in a persistent effort to turn the Rebel flank. But Johnston, bringing up Rebel units from other parts of the field, matched the Northern sidestepping and kept the battle at a bruising, slam-bang standstill. Losses on both sides were enormous. Then, at the climactic moment, Jubal Early's brigade arrived in the Rebel line; and the whole Confederate force swept forward, bayonets gleaming, the Rebel yell piercing the air. At 4:40, the Union front collapsed; the rout began.

During the final struggle, the Marines broke three times. They were repeatedly urged back into position; but despite the shouts and cries of their officers, they finally fled as the rout became universal. Later, Commandant Harris would write to Secretary Welles, "It is the first instance recorded in its history where any portion of its [the Corps'] members turned their backs to the enemy."[16]

The entire Union army—now a disorganized mass of men, horses and wagons and preceded by the mob of hysterical sightseers—fled over the choked, dusty roads. Reynolds finally collected some 70 Marines at the Long Bridge over the Potomac at 14th Street—26 miles from the battlefield—and led them back to the barracks.

The Marine battalion had 44 casualties at Bull Run, including 16 men listed as missing. Nineteen were wounded, including Brevet Major Zeilin, who had fought so well in California during the Mexican War and at Bull Run commanded A Company. Ten Marines were killed in the action. Young 2d Lt. Robert E. Hitchcock, USMC, of C Company, who had been commissioned less than seven weeks before, was the only officer killed in Porter's entire brigade. The other dead Marines were nine privates who had never had a chance to learn to fight and live.

In his report to Commandant Harris, Major Reynolds noted that only 16 men in the whole battalion had had any length of service and said:

> The remainder were, of course, raw recruits, which being considered, I am happy to report the good conduct of officers and men. The officers, although but little experienced, were zealous in their effort to carry out my orders. . . . The abrupt hasty retreat from the field of battle presents a deplorable deficiency in both arms and equipment.[17]

It was an honest explanation, but hardly good enough; few men on either side had been long in uniform. Many of the Marines had fought courageously and fled only when there was no longer any hope. But it had been a day the Corps would long be ashamed of.

Back in Washington, an angry, frustrated crowd, enraged by rumors of atrocities against Union wounded, tried to attack Confederate prisoners in front of the Treasury building. An escort of Marines had to force back the mob at bayonet point.

Five days later, Reynolds was promoted to lieutenant colonel. There were no Marine Corps brevets won on the field at Bull Run.

The battle had two important effects: The quick-war boys were silenced at last, and the Rebels proved they could stand up to Federal power on the battlefield. It was going to be a long and bloody war, and trained fighters would have to win it.

6
Reynolds' Amphibious
Battalion

The Civil War event with the greatest significance for the U.S. Marine Corps' future was the creation of a special amphibious Marine battalion in the autumn of 1861. Commanded by Lt. Col. Reynolds, who had led the Marines at Bull Run, the battalion never made a combat landing and survived for only six months; but it participated in the most vital naval undertaking of the war—the great blockade of the Southern coast.

From the beginning, grim old Virginia-born General-in-Chief Scott respected the Southern fighting man and warned that the Confederacy would not be beaten with one punch. He developed a long-range war plan; and after the frightening jolt of Bull Run, people began to listen.

Scott said the Confederacy must be cut off from the manufactured goods it needed to survive and fight. He said the Navy must blockade the Southern ports and the Army must slice the Confederacy in two down the line of the Mississippi. Then the Rebellion, isolated, could be destroyed in detail. This "Anaconda Plan" became the keystone of the United States' war effort; it would squeeze the life out of the Confederacy.

Lincoln declared a blockade from the Rio Grande to Chesapeake Bay. At first, it was strictly a paper blockade; the Navy lacked ships to cover even a fraction of the 3,000 miles of enemy coastline and its 180 harbors and inlets. The British, threatened with the loss of Southern cotton for their mills, condemned the clearly unenforceable blockade as illegal. It was, in fact, a sieve; the vast majority of Confederate and British ships that dared make the attempt pierced it successfully.

Still, over time, this would grow to be one of the great naval blockades in history, "a really effective if not indeed a decisive weapon."[18] It was a deterrent. Shipowners, fearing capture of their ships and property, avoided the Southern ports entirely; and the blockade slowly pressed the fat and then the muscle out of the Confederacy. Luxuries—butter and tea—disappeared, and necessities—salt and soap—became rarities. Cotton, the South's chief export, piled up. Eventually, even the vitals of war, for which men would take great risks until the end, grew scarce. Northern productive capacity began to tell; and the defeat of the Rebellion became inevitable. Grant's pounding campaign to Richmond and Appomattox and Sherman's slashing drive through the South's heartland were in good part made possible and climactic by General Scott's Anaconda Plan of strangling encirclement.

Closing a ring of steel around the Confederacy was chiefly the Navy's job; and here the Marines saw most of their wartime action with amphibious landings, blockade duty and the garrisoning of shore positions. Marines led the way ashore and manned guns on the larger warships. The war at sea became a story of isolated engagements, duels of ships against forts and occasional amphibious operations. With a few dramatic exceptions, there was no Confederate Navy to fight.

The first serious enforcement of the blockade was attempted at Hatteras Inlet, a gap in the chain of sea islands that protrude like a giant arrowhead into the Atlantic off the North Carolina coast and form stormy Cape Hatteras. Important quantities of contraband were reaching the Confederacy through this break in the island chain. On August 28, 1861, 250 Army troops, reinforced by Marines from the squadron, made a small-boat landing and, supported by naval gunfire, seized the two Rebel forts on the eastern side of Hatteras Inlet. The Marines ashore were commanded by Capt. William L. Shuttleworth of *Minnesota*, Capt. Isaac T. Doughty of *Wabash* and young 1st Lt. Charles Heywood of *Cumberland*. The forts were won without a single Union casualty. Six hundred Rebel prisoners were stuffed aboard *Minnesota* for her Marines to guard. This small triumph erased some of the shame of Bull Run and compensated for the embarrassing inactivity of Maj. Gen. George B. McClellan's Army of the Potomac. The North held the Hatteras forts and kept that hole plugged for the rest of the war.

On the night of September 13, the Union blockaders attacked the Rebel schooner *Judah* at a wharf of the Rebel-held Pensacola navy yard. Seventy seamen and 20 Marines led by Capt. Edward McD. Reynolds and Orderly Sgt. Patrick Fitzsimmons rowed silently across the bay from the frigate *Colorado*. They boarded *Judah* under heavy fire. Pennsylvania-born Marine Pvt. John Smith was the first man to board; but "by a sad mistake"[19]—his distinguishing badge had disappeared—he was bayoneted and killed by one of his comrades. The Rebel ship burned to the waterline and sank in the bay.

By late October, the Federal government was ready to launch a major effort against the Southern coast. Its objective: to capture Hilton Head Island on the southern side of Port Royal Sound, South Carolina (near the Marine Corps' present-day Recruit Depot on Parris Island), and to establish there a major base for the Union blockade. Hilton Head was strategically located between Savannah and Charleston and about halfway between Key West and Norfolk.

This would be the largest American amphibious expedition yet attempted. In command were Flag Officer Samuel F. DuPont, commander of the South Atlantic Blockading Squadron, and Brig. Gen. Thomas W. Sherman, later to be known as "the other General Sherman." The New Jersey-born DuPont was an aristocratic officer—a member of one of the nation's great industrial families; he was intelligent, expert and liked by his men. He had worked with Marines on the Pacific coast during the Mexican War and commanded the ship that carried Frémont and Gillespie and their men from Monterey to San Diego. He had been a longtime friend of Archibald Henderson. He respected what Marines could do, and it was at his request that the Corps supplied the expedition with the amphibious battalion under Lt. Col. Reynolds. Reynolds was apparently the one field-grade officer who had the complete confidence of the Marines' disputatious Commandant. Colonel Harris lauded Reynolds as "an officer of skill and experience."[20]

The mighty expedition was delayed for weeks because, in the nervous aftermath of Bull Run, there was intense pressure to keep all possible Union troops between the enemy and Washington. But finally, on October 29, a month behind schedule, 70 ships, including 25 transports with more than 15,000 soldiers, sailed from Hampton Roads. Aboard the 17-year-old coastal sidewheeler *Governor,* chartered in Boston, sailed Reynolds' battalion of 350 Marines. The men were armed with .58 caliber rifled muskets.

On Friday, November 1, off Cape Hatteras, a vicious hurricane scattered the fleet. Two vessels were smashed against the rugged coast, and one supply ship broke up at sea. The Marines' transport, separated from the fleet, battled the storm for hours. Her smokestack went overboard and the steampipe burst. Finally, the rudder chain snapped, and the old *Governor* wallowed all night in the storm, practically out of control. Before dawn, the engine stopped completely. As a distress signal, the flag was flown at half mast, Union down.

Frantic efforts were made to keep the foundering ship afloat. The Marines strengthened bulkheads, hung onto ropes for hours and passed out buckets of water from flooded compartments. Noncoms brought the men food at their posts. Four overzealous Marines, hearing the order to lighten ship, dashed into the assistant surgeon's cabin and threw overboard his marble-top table.

On Saturday afternoon, the sailing frigate *Sabine,* out on blockade duty, drew alongside despite the gale and high seas and managed to pass over a line. The Marines quickly formed on deck and 30 made the dangerous transfer before the line parted. That night, *Sabine* put a chain tow aboard *Governor* and came alongside again to let the Marines try to leap across. Before the chain broke, seven men—one corporal and six privates—tried it without permission; all seven drowned or were crushed to death between the rolling hulls.

The next morning, a hazardous attempt was made to carry the Marines to safety in *Sabine's* boats. The effort failed. The Marines finally had to jump into the high-running sea and were picked up by the boats. All the Marines reached *Sabine* except for the seven who had been killed the night before. Reynolds, who argued with *Governor's* skipper over who should be the last man to leave the ship, later reported angrily: "Those drowned were lost through their disobedience of orders in leaving the ranks or abandoning their posts."[21]

Forty-eight hours later, *Governor* sank. Reynolds wrote: "It is impossible for troops to have conducted themselves better under such trying circumstances."[22]

The Marines were lucky to be alive, but their amphibious battalion had missed its chance. DuPont's remaining ships rendezvoused and on November 5 stood off Port Royal Sound. Their entrance was barred by Fort Walker, with 16 guns, at the tip of Hilton Head Island and by Fort Beauregard, with 19 guns, across the passage to the east at Bay Point on St. Helena Island. DuPont had given up all idea of landing because so many of his boats had been smashed in the storm. Instead, he would bombard the forts. On the sunny morning of November 7, he went in.

DuPont kept his ships moving, offering the forts difficult targets while pounding them with steady broadsides. DuPont's five runs past the forts proved that steam-maneuvered ships could fight land batteries successfully. It would be an important lesson to a future admiral named Farragut.

In his report to DuPont, the captain of *Wabash* wrote of his Marine detachment: "The marines were used as a reserve, and whenever called upon rendered prompt assistance at the guns, with the good conduct which has always characterized their corps."[23]

By early afternoon, the Rebels abandoned both forts. The Marine detachment and a company of seamen from *Wabash* went ashore and occupied Fort Walker; a force from the gunboat *Seneca* occupied Fort Beauregard. For the first time since Sumter fell, the Stars and Stripes flew over South Carolina.

Residents of the fertile coastal islands burned their cotton and fled to the mainland. Fear spread to the now-vulnerable port cities of Savannah and Charleston, and Robert E. Lee was summoned to defend them. But Sherman and DuPont failed to move. They secured their toehold on the Rebel shore and occupied nearby Beaufort, South Carolina, but did not strike home.

Still, the Union and the Navy now possessed an excellent base deep down on the Confederate coast. DuPont became the nation's hero, and Port Royal became the Navy's advance blockading base and a liberty port where a man could get drunk and tattooed.

Lt. Col. Reynolds and the Marine battalion finally arrived at Port Royal aboard *Sabine* after the forts had fallen. The Marines were assigned to garrison the fort on Bay Point, and on March 25, 1862, DuPont ordered them back to Washington.

Reynolds' amphibious Marine battalion had been ahead of its time. Even though it never made a landing in anger, an amphibious organization of Marines had been created in advance of a campaign specifically to serve with the fleet and to assault the enemy from the sea. Here was the seed of the modern Marine Corps.

7

A Barn, a Cheesebox and a Medal

The North needed time to marshal its strength before crushing the enemy in its embrace. It had to assemble men and ships, test leaders and draw plans before it dared attack the larger Southern ports of Norfolk, Charleston, Mobile and New Orleans. The spring of 1862 would see two of these four Rebel bastions fall.

First, the Marines on duty with the Atlantic blockading squadrons joined a series of minor landings. Lincoln called the targets of these operations "pet rabbits," and impatiently demanded that the Navy start going after "polecats." None of these early landings could win the war—even collectively they would not make the blockade impervious—but they contributed to the overall strategy of wearing the South down.

Before 1861 ended, Marine detachments on the ships of the South Atlantic Squadron, now based at Port Royal, helped raid the Rebel coast at Tybee Island, Georgia, south of Port Royal, and up the Ashepo and South Edisto Rivers, which flow into St. Helena Sound north of Port Royal. The Navy's new base was already valuable.

Further north, early in February 1862, an Army-Navy expedition squeezed through Hatteras Inlet and captured Roanoke Island at the north end of Pamlico Sound. Possession of Roanoke Island, the onetime site of the Lost Colony, opened access to Albemarle Sound above it and threatened the Confederate defense system behind Norfolk. The Army also seized the North Carolina coastal towns of Elizabeth City and New Bern (northwest of the present-day Cherry Point air station of the Marine Corps). Once again, the Federal commanders failed to strike inland. But the network of North Carolina sounds was lost to the Confederacy.

These small engagements on the fringe of the war were preliminary bouts to decisive battle—the kind of skirmishes that are soon forgotten. But to any man, the little-known place where he fights, and perhaps dies, is at the center of the maelstrom.

March 8, 1862, was another kind of day: a day of battle that closed one era of warfare and began a new.

On that Saturday morning, five handsome American frigates rode on the calm, broad waters of Hampton Roads where the James River, after flowing past Richmond, empties into lower Chesapeake Bay. On the south shore of the Roads, the Confederates held Norfolk and the great captured navy yard. To the west, the Union sailing frigates *Cumberland* and *Congress* lay at anchor off Newport News, blockading the mouth of the James. To the east, the frigates *Minnesota, Roanoke* and *St. Lawrence* guarded the seaward entrance to Hampton Roads from stations under Fortress Monroe. The wooden ships of the Union blockade controlled these waters.

In Washington, McClellan was mounting a new assault on Richmond. The thirty-five-year-old general was not going to repeat the mistake of Bull Run; rather than a frontal attack southward from Washington, he planned a flanking movement. He proposed to transport his army down Chesapeake Bay to Fortress Monroe, cross to the historic peninsula between the York and James Rivers and assault Richmond from the east. The Navy would protect his flanks and provide him with mobility southward across the James.

But on March 8, there appeared a strange obstacle to the Navy's performance of this role—in fact, a threat to the Union blockade and a danger to the entire Union cause.

The morning, warm and sunny, seemed peaceful enough for wartime. On the old sail-powered *Cumberland*, at the mouth of the James, Capt. Charles Heywood's Marines worked at their routine chores. Wash hung out on the rigging and the men lolled on deck.

Captain Heywood was only twenty-two, but he had already proved himself. A native of Waterville, Maine, commissioned on April 5, 1858, he had helped burn the Norfolk Navy Yard, been promoted to first lieutenant in May 1861 and landed with the Marines at Hatteras Inlet. Promoted again in November, he participated in small-boat raids up the James River that winter. Thirty years later, as Commandant, he would lead the Corps in another war.

The Union lookouts in Hampton Roads sounded the alarm shortly after noon. A monster was steaming slowly up from the south, out of the Elizabeth River and past Craney Island. Its high walls made it resemble "a derelict barn adrift on the tide."[24] Aboard the Union ships, the men were called to quarters. Here was an enemy such as no warship had ever met before.

After capturing the Norfolk Navy Yard nearly 11 months before, the Rebels had raised *Merrimack* and rebuilt her in the undamaged dry dock. Confederate Secretary of the Navy Stephen R. Mallory understood his problem: he could not build a wooden fleet to equal the North's; perhaps a smaller number of armored ships firing explosive shells held the answer for the South. As early as June 1861, he had ordered *Merrimack* converted into a radical vessel, which, he hoped, could defend the South's harbors and wreck the Union's wooden blockade.

This revolutionary warship, now named *CSS Virginia*, was a long time building. Confederate marines commanded by Capt. Reuben T. Thom guarded her. Escaped slaves and Union spies brought out word of her progress, but the naval command in Washington confidently assured everyone that their frigates would surround the strange machine and pound it to death.

Virginia was clad in iron. Above the waterline, four-inch-thick iron plating covered slanting 24-inch-thick oaken walls. She had ports for 10 rifled guns and a four-foot iron beak for ramming. She steered awkwardly, required 22 feet of water and made only five knots; but she would end forever the age of the wooden warship.

Excitement spread through the Union ships as *Virginia*, escorted by several small gunboats, steamed into Hampton Roads. Men dashed to their stations, unlimbered guns, hoisted sail. They watched *Virginia* come on slowly while her captain, Franklin Buchanan, a respected officer who had commanded the Washington Navy Yard when the war began, tested what his ship could do.

Cumberland's sailors and Marines watched *Virginia* turn

toward Newport News and their frigate. Buchanan believed *Cumberland* carried rifled guns, and he boldly set out to dispatch his most dangerous enemy.

To get at *Cumberland*, Buchanan had to pass *Congress*. The two ships traded broadsides. Some of the 61 Marines aboard *Congress*, commanded by 1st Lt. Joseph F. Baker, fired the midship guns on the spar deck. Then, *Virginia* steamed on for *Cumberland*.

To avoid the frigate's broadside, Buchanan approached straight at *Cumberland's* bow. His first shot—an explosive shell—killed and wounded nine of Heywood's Marines lined up in formation, foolishly exposed, on the foredeck. *Cumberland's* first reply zipped through one of *Virginia's* open gunports, but most of her fire bounced harmlessly off *Virginia's* greased, iron-sheathed sides. The two ships' guns dueled fiercely for ten minutes. Then Buchanan rammed. At full steam, *Virginia's* beak stabbed into *Cumberland's* starboard bow, ripping a hole below the waterline. As *Virginia* pulled free, her ram snapped and remained stuck in the frigate's hull. Now the ships had turned, and *Cumberland's* gunners poured three broadsides at the ironclad, damaging her ports and guns. Marines on *Cumberland's* upper deck sent accurate rifle fire at the enemy's ports; and aboard *Virginia*, 55 Confederate marines worked guns under the command of Captain Thom.

Cumberland refused to surrender. Buchanan, after raking again from the bow, rammed a second time. This attack was fatal; *Cumberland* began to sink. On the afterdeck, the Marines fired the last gun and those who could leaped overboard. Captain Heywood jumped and was carried to safety by a small boat. Heywood and Buchanan would meet again in this war—the next time face to face.

Cumberland went down with her flag still flying. A third of the 376-man crew was lost; 14 of the 46 Marines on board were killed. Heywood was later brevetted a major for gallantry.

Continuing the attack, *Virginia* blazed away at Federal shore batteries and sank two transports tied to a wharf. Buchanan moved to finish off *Congress*, which had sought refuge under the shore batteries and had run aground. *Congress* was now a stationary target, and *Virginia* bombarded her mercilessly at close range. Smaller Rebel ships of the James River flotilla, no longer afraid of the big wooden Union blockaders, also attacked the defenseless frigate; and by 4 P.M., she surrendered to *CSS Beaufort. Congress'* 434-man crew suffered 136 casualties. Many of the survivors swam to shore. Marine Pvt. Thomas Moore was killed and eight other privates were wounded or missing.

A mile away, the frigates *Minnesota, Roanoke* and *St. Lawrence* were struggling to join the battle. The winds, which had whipped up, now suddenly shifted; the channels became shallow, and all three warships grounded.

During the action with *Congress*, Buchanan was wounded. Lt. Catesby ap Roger Jones, *Virginia's* executive officer and a nephew of the late naval hero of the Battle of New Orleans, took command and tried to get at the stranded *Minnesota*. But the tide was ebbing, and he steered *Virginia* back toward Sewell's Point. It was 6:30 P.M.

The scene that the crippled American fleet presented in Hampton Roads that evening might be compared to the destruction at Pearl Harbor 80 years later. *Cumberland* was sunk; her flag still flew from the mast tip above the waters. *Congress* was burning. Three other frigates were aground, among them *Minnesota* out of reach of shore support and helpless. The overconfident Union commanders had been as unprepared to meet a radical new engine of war as the American commanders at Pearl Harbor would be to deal with a massive air attack from an unseen fleet.

But in Hampton Roads there was a difference: By one of the strangest coincidences in American naval history, salvation was on the way.

While *Congress* was striking its colors, a tiny "cheesebox on a raft," towed by a tug, passed Cape Henry and entered Hampton Roads virtually unnoticed. The little Union gunboat rode just above the surface of the water; she showed only a pilot house and an armored turret containing two 11-inch Dahlgren guns and protected by eight layers of inch-thick iron plates.

The previous July, Navy Secretary Welles had finally called for the establishment of a special board to study ironclads; and in August, Congress had appropriated $1.5 million to build one or more such ships. *Monitor's* keel had been laid on October 25; and on March 6, she had been towed out of New York, headed south.

On entering Hampton Roads, *Monitor's* commander, Lt. John L. Worden, reported to Capt. John Marston aboard *Roanoke*, who ordered him to aid the stranded *Minnesota*. In the dark, the gunboat slid next to *Minnesota* and tied up alongside at 11:30 P.M.

When the telegraph brought to Washington the news of Saturday's disaster, even Lincoln was shaken. Secretary of War Stanton feared that *Virginia* would steam up Chesapeake Bay and attack the capital. Only Welles remained calm; he pointed out that *Virginia's* draft was too deep to permit such an attack and expressed confidence in *Monitor's* ability to battle the Confederate ironclad. No one believed him. *Virginia* seemed an ultimate weapon that could ravage the Northern ports at will.

At dawn Sunday, *Virginia*, now commanded by Lieutenant Jones, emerged from the Elizabeth River to destroy *Minnesota*. As *Virginia* approached, *Minnesota* opened fire with her stern guns; and *Monitor* moved out from her shadow—a David against a Goliath.

The battle—the first between armored ships—was slugged out at close range for four hours. The two ironclads touched five times. *Monitor*, which could get off only one shot every seven or eight minutes, fired 43 rounds. *Minnesota's* Marines under Capt. William L. Shuttleworth, who had served with Perry on the Tabasco River in the Mexican War, fought energetically but with little success. Shuttleworth reported that at least 50 solid shots from *Minnesota* struck *Virginia* without effect. *Monitor* took 21 hits. *Virginia* set *Minnesota* afire.

Finally, *Virginia's* gunners scored a direct hit on *Monitor's* tiny pilot house and blinded Lieutenant Worden. His executive officer took charge and temporarily disengaged. Lieutenant Jones, his ship leaking from an earlier attempt to ram the more agile *Monitor* and from a momentary grounding, thought the fight was over and headed back to the navy yard for repairs. *Monitor's* commander saw his mission as staying and protecting *Minnesota*.

The battle was a tactical stalemate: *Monitor* had saved *Minnesota* and proved a match for the larger ironclad. *Virginia's* brief invincibility was finished. The age of iron ships had begun. The wooden navies of the world were suddenly obsolete.

Three times after that historic Sunday morning, *Virginia*

ventured into Hampton Roads; but the two ironclads never locked horns again. In April, *Monitor* was joined by the ironclad *Galena*, with a sergeant's guard of Marines, and the lightly armored floating battery *Naugatuck*. They kept watch to prevent *Virginia* from getting at McClellan's troop transports now anchored in the lower bay, ready for the drive on Richmond.

Navy Flag Officer Louis M. Goldsborough, the blustering veteran commanding the North Atlantic Blockading Squadron, refused to carry McClellan's troops across the James to outflank the Confederates as long as *Virginia* remained such a terrifying threat to his wooden ships. The Peninsula campaign stalled until President Lincoln himself ordered a landing at Willoughby's Point to flank Norfolk.

On May 9, the Confederate army suddenly pulled out from its defensive positions around Norfolk. *Virginia* was trapped in the James River. She was too unseaworthy to run the Union blockade and escape to sea and too heavy to steam up the shallow river to Richmond. Before dawn on May 11, the Rebels beached and set fire to their historic ship at Craney Island; two hours later, she blew up.

Capt. Charles G. McCawley, who had won a brevet at Mexico City, brought 200 Marines to regarrison the Norfolk Navy Yard. And Lincoln ordered the Federal gunboats to move up the James, destroy the enemy's works and, if possible, shell Richmond itself. *Galena* led the way upstream, *Monitor* following with *Naugatuck* and other gunboats. At 6 A.M. on May 15, they reached Drewry's Bluff, a high cliff eight miles below Richmond. There they found the channel blocked by sunken hulks and cribs of stones. In rifle pits on the shore and at guns atop the bluff waited Rebel militia, *Virginia's* crew and a two-company battalion of Confederate marines commanded by Capt. John D. Simms (of Mexico City and the Barrier Forts). The marines on the riverbank served as sharpshooters when the Rebel defenders opened fire.

The battle was a catastrophe for the U.S. Navy. *Galena* was riddled by 18 shots; Simms' marines killed three of her crew, including Marine Pvt. Joseph Johnson. *Naugatuck's* Parrott gun burst. At close range, *Monitor's* guns could not be elevated enough to reach the cliff-top batteries. As the ironclad dropped downstream to a better firing position, she was hit three times. But the Union ships fought back.

Aboard *Galena*, Marine Cpl. John F. Mackie fired on the enemy from the exposed deck and rallied the ironclad's crew. The bravery of the twenty-five-year-old Marine from New York City was described in his citation: "As enemy shell fire raked the deck of his ship, Corporal Mackie fearlessly maintained his musket fire against the rifle pits along the shore and, when ordered to fill vacancies at guns caused by men wounded and killed in action, manned the weapon with skill and courage."[25] Corporal Mackie's valor that morning earned him the Medal of Honor—the first ever received by a United States Marine.

At 11 A.M. *Galena* caught fire. The Union ships could not pass the barrier. They retreated, beaten.

On land, McClellan slowly pushed toward Richmond. After Robert E. Lee took command of the army facing McClellan and battled him to a standstill, McClellan withdrew from the Peninsula, his campaign a discouraging failure. But one more link had been forged in the ring around the Confederacy: Norfolk and its great navy yard were back in U.S. hands. And the dread *Virginia* was no more.

8
"We Onward Went" — New Orleans

The truth is that during the Civil War Marines had no consistent function in battle. They had not yet found a substitute for their traditional battle jobs: firing from the tops and boarding and repelling boarders. Naval commanders still saw the Marines on their ships primarily as policemen, not fighters. Farragut said, "I have always deemed the Marine Guard one of the great essentials of a man-of-war, for the preservation and maintenance of discipline. They work and fight their guns well. It is next to impossible to maintain the efficiency of the ship and proper discipline without the restraints of the soldiers [sic] over the sailors."[26]

During this war many Marines fought as shipboard gun crews and sharpshooters. Some were hastily thrown together as landing battalions, but they had neither the doctrine nor the training for amphibious assaults under fire. Working the guns was a make-do use of Marines who had, at this moment in their history, no essential role once the shooting began. When this war ended, their failure to evolve a vital wartime function would threaten the Corps' life.

Because the Confederacy had little naval strength, the Marines' main chance to fight came not on the high seas but in the nation's rivers and bays. Here the opposition was not a hostile navy but the forts with which the Confederates tried to control the waterways. The U.S. Navy attacked the forts aggressively, and a classic contest developed between a mobile offense and a static defense.

On the Union's second front in the West, the "Anaconda" strategy had two objectives: to close the Gulf ports and to gain control of the Mississippi, thus isolating the eastern half of the

Confederacy from its granaries in Texas, Louisiana and Arkansas. As the historian Bruce Catton wrote: "The outcome of the war would depend on what happened along the Mississippi."[27]

In the spring of 1862, Maj. Gen. U. S. Grant was pushing south from Cairo, Illinois; and a great naval force was preparing to pry open the mouth of the Mississippi River. On April 6–7, Grant was caught in the bloodbath at Shiloh Church on the Tennessee River. Afterwards, Grant's war shifted west to its main objective—the Mississippi. On June 6, the gunboat flotilla conquered Memphis and gave Grant his base for the climactic descent on Vicksburg.

Simultaneously, action was building far to the south on the Mississippi. At sundown on March 7 (the day before *Virginia* destroyed *Cumberland* and *Congress* in Hampton Roads), a powerful 24-gun steam sloop of war and a doughty, leathery Navy captain arrived at the river's mouth. The ship was the three-year-old *USS Hartford*; the man was sixty-year-old Capt. David G. Farragut—the same Farragut who had sailed as a boy with Porter and Gamble on the cruise of *Essex* back in 1813. Now, nearly half a century later, he commanded the expedition sent to take New Orleans and open the Mississippi.

Farragut's West Gulf Blockading Squadron included 17 warships of various classes plus a fleet of 21 mortar schooners commanded by David Dixon Porter, his able, vain foster brother. (Farragut's strongest ship, the 50-gun *Colorado*, drew too much water to pass over the river's bar.) The Army contributed 16,000 recruits and Maj. Gen. Benjamin F. Butler—a general the Army seemed most willing to give up for naval operations. Porter's schooners each carried a giant 13-inch mortar; Porter would, before this campaign was over, drop nearly 17,000 huge shells from these "chowder pots" into Fort Jackson and Fort St. Philip, which guarded the Mississippi some 90 miles below New Orleans. The two forts were the key to the Crescent City: If they were passed, New Orleans was doomed. Farragut's plan to drive past them was realistic; DuPont had shown at Port Royal that wooden ships under steam could fight shore batteries. Above the forts the Confederates had little strength, particularly since two of their ironclads, *Mississippi* and *Louisiana*, were not yet completed.

A total of 333 Marines served on 12 of Farragut's largest

ships. On some, they worked as gun crews; and on all, as sharpshooters. In command of the Marine detachments destined to see the most action were Capt. John L. Broome and 2d Lt. George Heisler on the flagship *Hartford*, 1st Lt. James Forney on *Brooklyn*, Capt. Alan Ramsay on *Richmond*, Capt. P. H. W. Fontané on *Mississippi* and 2d Lt. John C. Harris (the Commandant's twenty-one-year old nephew) on *Pensacola.*

Captain Broome was the squadron's senior Marine officer. Although born in New York City, Broome belonged to the prominent upstate New York family from which Broome County takes its name. His grandfather had fought in the Revolution and served as the state's lieutenant governor. Broome was commissioned in the Marine Corps in 1848 at twenty-four. He missed the Mexican War, but he reached Mexico with the Second Battalion after the armistice and was commended for gallantry in a minor fray at Laguna de Terminos. He would finally retire in 1888 after 40 years as a Marine and die in Binghamton, New York, ten years later.

In Captain Broome's detachment aboard *Hartford*, an observant eighteen-year-old Marine private named Oscar Smith kept a diary of his Marine Corps adventures.[28] Smith had left his home in tiny Finesville, New Jersey, and enlisted in the Corps on May 21, 1861. He served in Philadelphia on routine guard duty under the command of Brevet Major Zeilin, and toward the end of the year returned home briefly without permission. His family explained later that he had gone AWOL because he wanted a fighting assignment and had observed that men with exemplary records were kept on navy yard duty. In any case, on Saturday, January 18, Oscar Smith was made a member of *Hartford's* Marine guard.

Broome kept the guard on its toes; and by Thursday, Smith was already in trouble. He recorded in his diary: "On account of my firing my musket at the first roll at reveille, was given four hours extra duty by Captian Broom[e]."

Hartford's Marines learned to handle the guns, working with them almost daily. Smith wrote:

> February 28. Commenced practising at target firing at eleven o'clock. After dinner continued practising at all distances. I hit the barrel once at 150 yards and made all line shots. We afterwards drilled a short time. Sailors

drilled with small arms. A sailor was put in double irons for striking the Boatswain. Fire quarters at sundown.

Arriving at the mouth of the Mississippi, they crossed the bar on March 13 and anchored at Pilot Town. "We received 16 rounds of cartridges this evening," Smith wrote. The war was drawing near.

Smith was up at 4 A.M. the next morning and at daylight went ashore in a party of 27 Marines to take possession of a spot called Belize and raise the flag. He was one of nine Marines who stayed ashore overnight.

As the days passed, the ship was painted and cleared of unnecessary rigging. The men continued their gunnery drill for the dangerous run past Fort Jackson and Fort St. Philip. By the last week in March, the sailors began hanging chains on the sides of the ships to protect engines and boilers from enemy shot.

They had not long to wait. From Private Smith's diary:

> April 17. Part of the [mortar] schooner fleet is here. They are trimming their sails with branches. At six o'clock this evening the rebels sent a fire boat down, but it did no damage. Two boats towed it ashore. A large fire boat was sent down by the rebels at eight o'clock this evening. It neared us, but drifted to our right. Fire quarters. An ironclad ran into her afterwards and two gunboats played water on it with their hoses. . . . This afternoon a few shots were exchanged between the rebel forts and gunboats and our gunboats. I climbed the rigging to see the firing.

The next morning—Good Friday, April 18, 1862— Farragut's mortars opened on the two strong masonry forts. The bombardment continued for a week, but it could not reduce the forts. They had to be passed.

Farragut prepared with the greatest care for this perilous night operation. The sides of the ships were camouflaged with mud and the decks whitewashed to give the crews light to work by. Boilers were protected. Grappling irons were readied to push away fire rafts. Tubs of water were placed to fight fires.

Late on Easter night, April 20, a bold gunboat raid under

fire cut a hole in the barrier that the Confederates had built across the river with hulks and large cypress logs tied together by chain cables.

At 1 A.M. on April 24, the men in the Union fleet breakfasted on hardtack and coffee. An hour later, two red lanterns glowed on *Hartford's* mizzenmast—the signal to get under way. A division of gunboats led the fleet on the dark, calm waters, followed by Farragut and his heavier sloops of war. The fleet moved quietly along the north side of the river, nearest Fort St. Philip, which stood 700 yards upstream and opposite Fort Jackson. The enemy was alert.

This is how the dash past the forts appeared to a young Marine:

> . . . all the vessels weighed anchor and proceeded up the river. At the same time the mortars threw shell at a furious rate. All hands were called to quarters and lay down at the guns. While we lay thus the fort opened upon us, and shot whistled around us furiously. As soon as our guns could be brought to bear on the fort we opened fire. Then ensued a scene I cannot describe. Both sides fired incessantly and shot and shell flew around like hail. Hotly contested by forts and gunboats, we onward went. While the battle was raging fiercest a ram forced a fire raft against us, setting the ship on fire, while the heat drove us from our guns. The scene at this time was terrible. Our ship was aground and wrapped in flames. By what seemed a miracle we got off the ground, cleared the raft, and put out the fire. We ran down their boats wherever we came across them. The shore seemed lined with burning rafts and steamers. During the hottest part of the engagement a rebel gunboat came within pistol shot. Our Captain haled her and asked the Captain if he wished to surrender. He answered, "No, never." "Then fire upon her," said our Captain. A shower of grape from the top and a broadside dealt death among them.

Marine Lieutenant Heisler and two privates were wounded; Heisler would die of his wounds three months later.

On the other ships, the battle was equally fierce. Gunboat *Cayuga*, the first through the hole in the barrier, was hit 42 times. Gunners in the forts, unable to see Farragut's mud-coated ships, fired at their gun flashes. Pandemonium raged on the river. *Varuna's* Marines fought desperately before their speedy sloop was sunk. *Pensacola* lost her bearings in the dark, steamed too close to Fort St. Philip and took a battering; Marine Lieutenant Harris and six enlisted men were hit. The Confederate ironclad ram *Manassas* swept by *Pensacola*, almost scraping, and then tried to strike the port paddle wheel of the old sidewheeler *Mississippi*. Marine Corporals George Sanderson and William H. Woods on *Mississippi* were killed. The Navy lieutenant conning *Mississippi* maneuvered skillfully out of the way—his name: George Dewey.

Brooklyn, having missed the opening and hit the barrier, stood by bravely to cover *Hartford* and engaged Fort Jackson's guns. *Brooklyn* took a severe beating and then was struck midships by *Manassas*. Lieutenant Forney's Marines fought gallantly; Privates William Lenahan and Henry H. Roff were killed and three others were wounded.

In all, seven Marines died and 19 were wounded before Farragut's ships were past the forts. His fleet suffered 201 casualties in the hour-long battle.

At dawn, the fleet anchored beyond the forts for a time and then continued upriver seven miles to the Quarantine Station. Captain Broome took ashore a detachment of Marines, including Private Smith, to raise the United States flag and guard the station. Wrote Smith:

> They flew white flags and surrendered immediately. Two hundred men were in the encampment. Their officers were brought aboard and made to take the oath of allegiance. Some of the men appeared glad, others sulky. Part of the marines went ashore and took possession of the barracks. I was on post all the time ashore.

That night the Marines lay at their guns. Private Smith wrote:

> To look back upon the scene of action when daylight came and think of danger passed, was enough to make us feel proud, as we certainly were.
> April 25. Friday. Weighed anchor at two bells (5

o'clock) and started up the river. There are some splendid plantations along here. The negroes leave their work, run to the levee, and welcome us, waving their hats and handkerchiefs. When near the batteries a venerable old darkey gave his hat a great flourish and called for "Three cheers for Abraham," which set the ship in a roar of laughter.

Shortly after noon, in a drizzling rain, the fleet rounded Slaughterhouse Bend and steamed into sight of New Orleans. To Private Smith's eyes, "The scene was grand. The most splendid ships and passenger boats were set on fire by the rebels and sent down the river. The flames leaping up the masts burned them off, and they came down with a crash." The city was swathed in smoke; the citizens were burning their cotton, rice and ships. Hundreds of cotton bales floated in the river. From the levee a screaming, cursing mob greeted the invaders.

Two Navy officers were sent ashore under a flag of truce to demand the city's surrender. Mayor John Monroe refused.

At 10 A.M. Saturday morning, Farragut sent young Navy Lt. Albert Kautz to demand the surrender again. With him Kautz took Midshipman John H. Read and 20 Marines from *Hartford.* "We landed on the levee in front of a howling mob, which thronged the river-front as far as eye could reach," Kautz later wrote.[29] If the crowd fired a single shot, Farragut said, the ships would level the town.

Private Smith was a member of the landing party and described the scene: "The mob on the wharf hurrahed for [Jefferson] Davis and threatened to kill us if we came ashore, but unheeding them, we jumped on shore and fell in line. They crowded the wharf and gave us no room."

Standing in front of the drawn-up Marines, Kautz tried to reason with the crowd. It was fruitless. He ordered the Marines to take aim, hoping the crowd would open a path to the City Hall. Instead, women and children were shoved to the front, and the Marines were taunted to fire at them. Finally, to avoid bloodshed, Kautz decided to leave the Marines behind, except for one noncom. As Private Smith reported:

After a short consultation between Captain Broom[e] and Lieutenant Kortz [sic], they concluded to hoist a white handkerchief and go to the mayor. Accordingly a handkerchief was stuck on the point of Sergeant Knox's bayonet and the three [Kautz, Read and Knox] marched to the mayor, while we remained on the wharf. We were insulted and called all kinds of names by the filthy mob.

Lieutenant Harris and 30 Marines from *Pensacola* came ashore, on Farragut's order, to raise the flag over the U.S. Mint. The mob threatened them with pistols and knives. At the mint, the Marines removed the Confederate flag and raised the Stars and Stripes. A daring Rebel (who was later hung by Maj. Gen. Butler) tore down the U.S. flag. It was ripped to shreds and the pieces were thrown through a window into the City Hall room where Lieutenant Kautz was at that moment delivering Farragut's repeated demand for "unqualified surrender." The city fathers rejected the demand, and Kautz, Read and Knox had to be sneaked out into a carriage. They dashed to the levee. The mob chased them until they reached the safety of the Marines' muskets on the wharf.

Farragut now ordered Captain Broome to form a battalion from all the Marines in the fleet and, with two brass howitzers manned by seamen, to occupy the city's former Federal buildings. The Marines, 250 strong, landed at the foot of Canal Street and marched to the Customs House. Broome raised the U.S. flag and left a guard of 20 Marines under Capt. Alan Ramsay, a twenty-four-year-old veteran of Bull Run. The rest of the battalion marched to City Hall and formed in Lafayette Square, with the two howitzers commanding St. Charles Street. Through a crowd of thousands, Lieutenant Harris led a file of Marines into the building; and *Hartford's* boatswain's mate climbed up and took down the Louisiana state flag. By sundown, all the Marines had returned to their ships. The next morning Marines from *Brooklyn* went ashore and raised the flag again. Although on May 1 the Army occupied New Orleans, the South's richest city never actually surrendered.

Broome, Forney and Harris received brevet promotions for their part in the victory; and on May 9, the same day the Confederate army marched out of Norfolk, the Marines from *Brooklyn* raised a small U.S. flag over the Federal arsenal at Baton Rouge.

The effect of Farragut's triumph was international: Great

Britain and France postponed—forever—supporting the Confederacy. The war was barely a year old, and both Norfolk and New Orleans were back in Union hands. The noose of the Anaconda Plan was being drawn tight. Farragut prepared to head upriver to join Grant.

9
The Mississippi
and Mobile

With New Orleans subdued, Farragut now wanted to close the Confederacy's last major Gulf port, Mobile. But the Army needed help to come down the Mississippi; the Rebel fortress of Vicksburg, on bluffs commanding the river 400 miles above New Orleans, blocked the way. Farragut sent Porter and his mortar schooners over to Mobile and Farragut himself took *Hartford, Brooklyn, Richmond* and eight gunboats up the Mississippi to Vickburg.

On May 24, when the fleet arrived below Vicksburg, Farragut's officers quickly discovered that their guns could not be elevated enough to reach the bluff-top batteries. And their small Army force could not attack the city with any hope of success. So, leaving his gunboats to harass the enemy, Farragut on the 26th headed back to New Orleans. Without an adequate landing force, nothing had been won.

Lincoln ordered Farragut back up the river. Starting again on June 8, Farragut was fearful of the falling level of the river and troubled by the problem of securing coal for his ships. The steam Navy was finding itself tied to sources of coal, but the need to secure advanced bases had not yet become clear.

This time, Farragut took along Porter and his high-lobbing mortars. The old captain was determined to pass Vicksburg's batteries. At 2 A.M. on June 28, 1862, he finally made his run. Aboard *Hartford*, Pvt. Oscar Smith wrote:

> All hands were called at 1:45 o'clock this morning and breakfasted at two. Weighed anchor and started to attack the Vicksburg batteries, the *Richmond* and *Oneida* leading. As we approached the city the mortars fired briskly.

243

Many of their shot passed through the rigging and into the bulwarks of our ship. One shot cut the main topsail yard in two.

The flotilla moved up in two columns, with the heavier ships nearer the town: *Richmond, Hartford,* and then *Brooklyn. Richmond* plowed past. *Hartford,* a mile back, took a drubbing; the Marines manned two guns in the exchange. *Brooklyn* never made it; her captain misunderstood Farragut's orders. In the passage, 14 were killed; and Broome and two Marine privates on *Richmond* were among the 40 wounded. Farragut had passed the batteries, but again he did not have the troops to fight on land. Naval attack could not conquer Vicksburg. He pleaded with the Army for manpower, but received no reply.

Now, Farragut faced a new threat. The Rebels had just completed the ironclad ram *Arkansas* on the Yazoo River, which enters the Mississippi 12 miles above Vicksburg. On July 15, *Arkansas* steamed into the Mississippi, turned downstream, and headed straight for the Federal fleet sitting there with fires banked, unready.

Seemingly invulnerable, *Arkansas* steamed through the fleet's shellfire and found a safe berth under Vicksburg's guns. Humiliated, Farragut gave chase that very night and passed Vicksburg again, but failed to knock out the ram. Wrote Oscar Smith in his diary:

> At seven o'clock the fleet weighed anchor and started down the river. [Captain Charles Henry] Davis' fleet [of Union ironclads] engaged the upper batteries while Farragut's passed down engaging the lower batteries, and also with the intention of destroying the ram. This we found it too dark to do. We did not see her. The *Sumpter* [sic] came down with us. The *Winona* was sunk. Our men succeeded in running her ashore on the island below Vicksburg. Had three killed and six wounded on the *Hartford.* [One of the wounded was Broome, this time severely.] Received three shots. The engagement lasted about three-quarters of an hour.
>
> July 16. The whole fleet was on the lookout for the ram last night and was very cautious. We kept at our

guns. We can see the ram laying under the Vicksburg batteries getting up steam. . . . July 18. . . . The ram is still under the Vicksburg batteries. A strict watch is kept on her. Half of the marine guard is on the medical list. Fifty odd are on the list. Captain Broom[e] left the ship this morning, being unfit for duty since receiving his wound. Fisk died on the 16th. . . . July 20. Sunday. Divine service this morning. Everything prepared for attacking the ram tomorrow. In the afternoon we mustered around the capstan and our flag officer made a brief speech, in these words: "Men! The rebel ram lies at Vicksburg. She must be destroyed. To destroy her I want you to go to work heart and hand. As soon as she is destroyed we will go out of the river into salt water." We gave three hearty cheers as he retired. The weather is very warm.

July 21. This morning we were roused at three o'clock and got ready for action. About daylight firing commenced between the upper fleet and the rebels. The *Essex* came down and engaged the *Arkansas Traveler* [sic] under their batteries. The ram would not venture out in the river. . . .

The Navy Department now let Farragut withdraw to the Gulf. Captain Broome rejoined his ship, and on the 24th the fleet headed down the river. Passing Grand Gulf, which had been destroyed by Farragut's repeated attacks, Private Smith described the effect of war on the Mississippi: "Grand Gulf is in ashes, nothing remaining but chimneys excepting a school house and a single dwelling. The place looks like a cemetery, the chimneys answering for monuments."

Eventually, *Arkansas* was caught above Baton Rouge with her engines broken down; under Union attack, her crew destroyed the ram. That was the end of the Confederate Navy on the Mississippi.

In Washington, the stalemate on the river provoked a demand for drastic action. Rebel shore batteries still controlled the central portion of the river; and beef and grain poured across it to the Confederacy's armies. Navy Secretary Welles, over fierce Army objections, finally managed to have the Army's river gunboat fleet transferred to the Navy on October 1. Its command was given to David Porter, now an acting rear admiral. With the transfer of authority, the Army soldiers in the river fleet were given the grand title of "the Marine Brigade." They were not members of the Marine Corps but Army infantry, artillery and even cavalrymen. Although they grumbled under Navy command, they fought well against minor Rebel concentrations.

In mid-December the Union moved. Maj. Gen. William Tecumseh Sherman came down on Vicksburg from the north, supported by Porter. Grant tried to lead another force down behind Vicksburg to insure Sherman's success. Sherman and Porter, harried by the Rebels, bogged down in the bayous and swamps of the Yazoo Delta above Vicksburg. Porter's Marines fired as sharpshooters from the gunboats' pilot houses at enemy riflemen concealed behind trees and stumps. The Confederate cavalry prevented Grant from executing his part in the campaign. At the year's end, Sherman's attack at Chickasaw Bluffs, five miles north of the city, was stopped with heavy losses. Sherman reported candidly: "I reached Vicksburg at the time appointed, landed, assaulted and failed."

Grant now decided to attack Vicksburg from the river. He would open what Bruce Catton has called "the decisive campaign of the Civil War."[30]

By this time, the Rebels had built a stronghold downriver, high on the bluffs above the east side of the river at Port Hudson, to keep open their supply link to the western states. The Port Hudson bastion was cleverly situated on a right-angle turn of the river; its batteries had clear aim at Union ships working slowly upstream. At 9:30 P.M. on the muggy, misty night of March 14, 1863, Farragut made his bid to pass these Rebel guns.

On *Hartford*, Broome's Marines manned two of the nine-inch broadside guns. Marine Pvt. Thomas F. Butler was swept overboard and no one could stop to save him. *Richmond* took a crippling hit in her engine room and drifted downstream, but not before a single Rebel cannon shot wiped out nearly all of one of Captain Ramsay's Marine gun crews, killing two and wounding eight.

In the battle-smoke and fog, the veteran sidewheeler *Mississippi* grounded on the west bank and took a severe thumping during a half-hour of torment. The ship's commander ordered the crew to abandon ship and the executive officer, Lt. George Dewey, USN, to destroy her. One Marine was killed and seven were missing. Dewey courageously rallied men in the boats to row back and save the last men aboard. Marine Sgt. Pinkerton R. Vaughn of Downingtown, Pennsylvania, stayed aboard until all the crew had been taken off and the ship set afire to prevent her fall into Rebel hands. The twenty-four-old Marine earned the Medal of Honor that night. "Persistent until the last, and conspicuously cool under the heavy shellfire," his citation read, "Sergeant Vaughn was finally ordered to save himself as he saw fit." *Mississippi* drifted off and blew up.

Broome won a brevet promotion to lieutenant colonel at Port Hudson and wrote Commandant Harris that his men fought their guns in the battle "with their usual ability, and marked success, so much so to receive the praise of that distinguished Naval Commander Admiral Farragut."[31]

Only *Hartford*, with the little gunboat *Albatross* lashed to her port side, had gotten through. This time Farragut had failed. He took *Hartford* up to blockade the mouth of the Red River, conferred with Grant and returned downriver.

In April, Grant marched down the west bank of the Mississippi, crossed below Vicksburg and attacked it from the south. On April 30, he laid siege to the city. On July 4, 1863, while Lee was retreating from Gettysburg in the East, the great Southern fortress on the Mississippi finally surrendered. Four days later, Port Hudson fell. Now the South was split, and Lincoln announced, "The Father of Waters goes unvexed to the sea." The Confederacy tottered.

The Navy and Marines still had one final door on the Gulf to slam shut: Mobile. While Farragut had been battling on the Mississippi, the Rebels at Mobile had been building ironclads to destroy the Union's wooden ships and break the blockade. Farragut had to wait months for monitors that could fight the Rebel ironclads.

There were three keys to the defense of Mobile at the head of Mobile Bay, 30 miles above the Gulf. Guarding the bay's entrance were two solid masonry forts: Fort Gaines on Dauphin Island to the west and Fort Morgan on Mobile Point opposite. The third key was the new giant ram *Tennessee*, 209 feet long, covered with iron plate six inches thick and armed with six Brooke rifled guns throwing 110-pound and 90-pound solid shot. Admiral Franklin Buchanan commanded *Tennessee*, then probably the most powerful warship afloat.

The Rebels had also blocked the three-mile-wide entrance to the bay with embedded obstructions and 180 "torpedoes" or floating mines. For their own blockade runners, they had left open only a narrow passage covered by the guns of Fort Morgan. Through this gap Farragut intended to attack.

Marines were now serving on all of Farragut's ships but the four newly arrived monitors. These detachments were sergeant's guards except those on the flagship *Hartford*, now led by Brevet Maj. Charles Heywood; on *Brooklyn*, led by Capt. George P. Houston; and on *Richmond*, commanded by 2d Lt. C. L. Sherman. Heywood, the senior Marine officer, was twenty-four years old.

At 5:54 A.M. on August 5, 1864, Farragut gave the signal to begin the battle. The unwieldy, tough-skinned monitors went in first, followed by the wooden ships lashed together two by two. At 6:47, the monitor *Tecumseh* opened the attempt to invade the bay by firing twice on Fort Morgan. Then she headed straight for *Tennessee*, struck a mine and went down instantly with 93 men—the worst calamity suffered by the Navy down to World War II. Farragut, directing the action tied to *Hartford's* rigging, now ordered full speed ahead, "Damn the torpedoes."

Hartford steamed directly through the mine field. She brushed one torpedo, which failed to explode. *Brooklyn* followed. The fort and ships hammered at each other. On *Hartford*, Heywood's Marines worked the two after guns, pounding away at the enemy. Badly punished, the fleet entered the bay.

Tennessee and three paddle-wheel gunboats advanced at right angles to Farragut's fleet. *Tennessee* tried to ram *Hartford* and missed. The Rebel gunboats crossed the T, which enabled them to fire their broadsides while avoiding Farragut's. They hit his ships repeatedly, killing many. The Union fleet captured one gunboat, another was destroyed and the third finally fled up the bay toward the city. But the battle was not yet won.

The Union fleet anchored several miles above the fort, and the men breakfasted. Suddenly, *Tennessee* came at them from under Fort Morgan's guns. Farragut scurried back into the rigging and ordered the whole fleet to attack the ram. *Mononga-hela*, her prow reinforced with boiler iron, rammed *Tennessee* twice but could do no damage. The wooden *Lackawanna* rammed her at right angles and, as the two ships recoiled, *Lackawanna's* Marines, who had been keeping the ram's crew from their guns with small-arms fire, drove the Rebels inside with a rain of holystones and spittoons.

The surrounded *Tennessee* was taking heavy fire from Farragut's wooden ships and monitors. At 9:42, the ram raised a white flag. Her armor had been pierced, her exposed rudder chains had been shot away and she had lost her stacks and steering power.

Brevet Major Heywood was detailed to take a Marine guard aboard *Tennessee*. There, he met Buchanan, whose leg had been broken in the battle. Farragut wrote Navy Secretary Welles of this meeting:

> It is worth mentioning that the officer sent in command of the guard for the capture of the *Tennessee* was Capt. Charles Heywood, of the Marine Corps, who was one of the survivors of the *Cumberland*, sunk by Buchanan in Hampton Roads. Although a modest gentlemen, Captain Heywood could not resist the opportunity of informing the rebel Admiral that they had met before, and that he at least was exceedingly glad of the second meeting.[32]

The three Marine officers with the fleet received brevet promotions. Young Heywood was now a brevet lieutenant colonel and became known as "the boy colonel." Eight enlisted Marines earned the Medal of Honor at Mobile Bay: on *Brooklyn*, Sgt. J. Henry Denig of York, Pennsylvania; Sgt. Michael Hudson, born in County Sligo, Ireland; Cpl. Miles M. Oviatt of Cattaraugus County, New York, and Cpl. Willard M. Smith of Alleghany, New York. On *Richmond*, Sgt. James Martin, born in Derry, Ireland; Sgt. Andrew Miller, born in Germany, and Orderly Sgt. David Sprowle of Lisbon, New York. On *Oneida*, Sgt. James S. Roantree, who was born in Dublin. Of the Marines in the battle, two privates, Peter Murphy and William H. Smith, both on *Brooklyn*, were killed, and six others were wounded.

The Army went ashore and took Fort Gaines and Fort Morgan by the end of August. But Farragut did not have the amphibious strength necessary to capture Mobile and had to be satisfied with sealing off the great port.

The naval victory at Mobile Bay and Sherman's conquest of Atlanta on September 2 cheered the Union, which had grown discouraged as the war dragged on and Grant hammered his way toward Richmond with dreadful losses. These twin triumphs made possible Lincoln's reelection and sent the war hurtling toward its climax.

10
Sometimes, a Few Marines

Because the Marine Corps lacked a coordinated battle function during the Civil War, small detachments of Marines were frequently called on to perform special missions on the fringes of the war. These disparate incidents reflected the Corps' history in this war as much as did the larger encounters with the enemy. Here, then, are five brief stories of the most dramatic of these missions:

On November 8, 1861, in the Old Bahama Channel some 240 miles east of Havana, eight U.S. Marines clambered into a cutter at the side of the steam sloop *San Jacinto*. The sailors at the oars pulled to a British ship that had been forced to stop by the American warship's guns. These Marines were to be principals in the most spectacular international incident of the Civil War.

San Jacinto had been homeward bound when her commander, Capt. Charles Wilkes, famous for his exploration of the Pacific, heard in Cuba that Confederate emissaries to England and France were aboard the Royal Mail steam packet *Trent*, headed for St. Thomas, Virgin Islands. Although the unarmed *Trent* was a neutral ship steaming between two neutral ports, Wilkes waylaid her. He was determined to capture the Confederate commissioners—two former United States senators, James M. Mason of Virginia and John Slidell of Louisiana. In Wilkes' view, they were "live dispatches,"[33] and therefore contraband under international law.

Trent hove to after *San Jacinto* fired two shots across her bow. When Wilkes sent over his executive officer, Lt. Donald M. Fairfax, USN, Mason and Slidell declared they would be taken only by force. So Wilkes sent Lt. James A. Greer, USN, in a second cutter with eight Marines selected by their commanding officer, Marine Lt. John Schermerhorn.

The sight of armed American Marines aboard the British packet brought cries of "piracy" from her passengers. The Marines and seamen formed on deck, and Fairfax had his officers apply symbolic pressure on Mason's shoulders and escort him to the gangway. When Fairfax attempted to take Slidell prisoner, *Trent's* passengers protested noisily. Fearing Fairfax was in danger, Greer ordered the Marines, their bayonets fixed, into Slidell's cabin. Greer and the Marines took the prisoners to *San Jacinto.*

The Confederate commissioners were imprisoned at Boston, and the North applauded. But Great Britain was infuriated, and United States officials feared that the incident would encourage England to recognize the Confederacy. It hardly seemed worth the risk. To avoid a public protest, Mason and Slidell were released on January 1 and secretly put aboard a British ship for England.

Heavy fighting on the bloody road to Gettysburg and Vicksburg deterred Army recruiting in the North; and in March 1863, the U.S. Congress passed a draft law, the first compulsory service law in United States history.

The new law left two loopholes for the unwilling. A drafted man could escape service either by paying the government $300 or by hiring a substitute. These provisions enraged the mass of workingmen, for whom $300 was a half-year's pay. When the draft lottery was held in New York City, with its 400,000 foreign born, riots broke out. On Monday, July 13, began the bloodiest days in the city's history when an angry mob gathered near Central Park and burned the draft office.

The authorities sent out desperate calls for help. Among the first to respond was a naval brigade of sailors and Marines quickly formed at the Brooklyn Navy Yard. Veteran Marine Capt. John C. Grayson commanded a battalion of 180 Marines. That midnight, when the Marines arrived at City Hall, they were assigned to guard trouble spots and to protect vital property. On Tuesday, men of the brigade fought a pitched battle with a mob in Grand Street.

For three days, the rioters murdered, pillaged, burned, and

hung any Negroes they could catch. They set fire to police stations, hotels, stores and an orphanage for black children. Finally, on Thursday, the Seventh Regiment from the Army of the Potomac and two National Guard regiments arrived in the city, met the mobs with gunfire, killed a dozen men and brought the draft riot under control. By now, 400 people were dead or wounded. The Marine battalion stayed on duty in Manhattan until the following Monday.

The Marine Corps station at Mare Island, California, was first established by Marines under parole. In December 1862, some 150 Marines commanded by Maj. Addison Garland were passengers aboard the unarmed mail steamer *Ariel* en route to man the new navy yard being constructed on San Francisco Bay. Off the eastern end of Cuba, *Ariel* was captured by the British-built Confederate raider *Alabama* commanded by Capt. Raphael Semmes. Semmes was prowling for gold on ships returning from California. He ordered the Marines disarmed and paroled them—accepting their "pledge of honor," as was the courteous custom, that they would not fight the Confederacy until they had been exchanged for prisoners of war. Semmes then released *Ariel* under $261,000 ransom, and the Marines reached Mare Island two days after Christmas.

The next time U.S. Marines met Raphael Semmes it was a different story. The Navy had been hunting the raider captain, and the steam sloop *Kearsarge* cornered him and his now-legendary *Alabama* at Cherbourg, France. Over two years, *Alabama* had taken 63 American merchantmen and sunk one U.S. warship.

On Sunday, June 19, 1864, *Alabama* steamed out of Cherbourg and her guns opened the battle. When the ships had closed to 900 yards, *Kearsarge's* 12 Marines, manning the rifled gun on the forecastle, fired the first shot—an 80-pound shell—at the Rebel raider. The Marines worked that gun under Orderly Sgt. Charles T. Young as the two ships swung in seven great circles and hurled smashing broadsides at each other. *Kearsarge's* gunners, firing more carefully and slowly, hulled *Alabama* repeatedly at the waterline and finally shot away her rudder. In an hour, Semmes had lost his battle.

Alabama sank stern first. The British yacht *Deerhound*

saved Semmes and 41 others and took them to England. Semmes escaped to fight again. When he finally surrendered at the war's end, he was a rear admiral commanding a naval brigade with the Confederate army. He was paroled and returned to his home in Mobile.

But Navy Secretary Welles could not forget that Semmes had robbed unarmed ships and had fought the Union after surrendering *Alabama.* Welles called him a "pirate." With President Andrew Johnson's agreement, he ordered Semmes arrested despite his parole. Young Marine 1st Lt. Lyman P. French was sent to bring in Semmes. Taking with him two Marine sergeants, French traveled to Louisville, Memphis, Vicksburg and New Orleans searching for his quarry. In New Orleans, he heard that Semmes had left that city a few weeks earlier for his home.

In Mobile, French assembled 30 men and with his two Marine sergeants set out at night to capture Semmes at his home in the countryside. French was admitted by Semmes' young daughter and handed Semmes the order for his arrest. Semmes called it "an outrage." French posted guards inside and around the house all night to prevent any attempt to escape. The next day, they set out for Washington, where French delivered Semmes to the commandant of the navy yard. Semmes was imprisoned for three months and finally freed.

A New Orleans adventurer named Thomas E. Hogg devised a devious scheme to seize American merchant ships. Holding the rank of master's mate in the Confederate Navy and with the Rebel government's approval, Hogg would go aboard Northern ships with a gang of men as passengers. Once at sea, they would take over the ships and their cargoes for the Rebellion.

In November 1863, Hogg and his men seized the schooner *Joseph L. Gerrity,* sold her cargo of cotton and turned the ship into a blockade runner. U.S. agents pursued Hogg through Central America, but he escaped.

Next, Hogg planned to capture the American packet steamer *Salvador.* He collected men in Havana, but the U.S. consul there heard of the plot and warned officials in San Francisco. On November 10, 1864, Marines and sailors from *USS Lancaster* went aboard *Salvador.* Capt. David M. Cohen commanded the

Marines in the party. Hogg showed up with six companions. After *Salvador* sailed, the Marines searched their baggage and found pistols, cutlasses, knives, handcuffs, documents, gold and a Confederate flag. As soon as the ship was in international waters, Captain Cohen and his Marines arrested the conspirators. They were jailed in San Francisco. For taking the gang without bloodshed, Cohen received a special commendation from the admiral commanding the Pacific Squadron.

11
Amphibious
Disaster

In the Civil War, the Marines' most ambitious attempt to land from the sea directly in the face of enemy fire ended in disaster. This was a tragic episode in the long campaign to recapture the port of Charleston, the symbol of the war's beginning.

Rear Adm. Samuel F. DuPont tried for months to take the city, and failed. During one battle with Confederate ironclads, on January 31, 1863, eight Marines lost their lives. In DuPont's major effort, on April 7, his ships were severely battered by the Rebel forts guarding the harbor. The defeat produced one side effect: None of his monitors could be spared for the Gulf Squadron, and Farragut's attack at Mobile Bay was delayed.

The government in Washington demanded more aggressive action against Charleston. Rear Adm. John A. Dahlgren, the brilliant ordnance expert whom Lincoln so highly respected, received the assignment. Unfortunately, Dahlgren was also ambitious, conniving and inexperienced in battle command.

The second phase of the campaign opened on July 10 when the Union forces seized most of Morris Island, guarding the south side of Charleston harbor. At daybreak the next day, the attack advanced on Battery Wagner, a 15-gun earthworks on Morris Island. The squadron's Marines, pulled together as an improvised battalion, joined 3,000 sailors in an unsuccessful assault. A week later, the Army hit Battery Wagner again; this time it was repulsed with 1,515 casualties.

On August 10, Maj. Jacob Zeilin arrived from New York with Marine reinforcements, mostly recruits. He promptly organized all the Marines into a single unit and attempted to give them some landing-force training on Morris Island. He was clearly dissatisfied with their performance. Soon forced to return north by illness, Zeilin was eventually succeeded by Lt. Col. John G. Reynolds, the taut disciplinarian and veteran of the Mexican War who had commanded the Marines at Bull Run and the Marine battalion on *Governor* in 1861. Since then, Reynolds had feuded with Commandant Harris and been courtmartialed, but apparently he had regained his position of favor at head-quarters. This would be his last active command; he was retired the following year, after 40 years in the Corps, and died in 1865.

The Army laid siege to Battery Wagner and bombarded Fort Sumter, the island fortress in the center of Charleston harbor. In mid-August, the soldiers assaulted Wagner again with more slaughter. By the time the enemy finally evacuated Wagner on September 7, 2,318 men had been lost attacking the battery. But the harbor was now closed to blockade runners.

Army artillery and naval guns bombarded the still-defiant Fort Sumter, and by the end of August it was in ruins.

The night of September 8 was black and silent. Small boats shoved off from the ships of the Union fleet and started for Fort Sumter. They carried four 100-man volunteer divisions of both sailors and Marines and a fifth division of 125 Marines commanded by Capt. Charles G. McCawley, a veteran of Chapultepec. Their objective: to crack the nut that prevented Charleston's capture.

The Union commanders' plan called for one boat division to create a diversion on the fort's northwest front and then for three divisions to make the main assault. McCawley's three companies of Marines would cover the attackers with musket fire at a range of 150 yards and follow them ashore with the bayonet.

At 9:30, the thumping engines of the tug *Daffodil* broke the silence as she began towing the boats toward Sumter. Ironclad monitors escorted them. Near the point of departure, 800 yards from the fort, the tug became lost in the darkness and veered off. As soon as the boats cast free, the strong tide scattered them.

The Confederates had been alerted to the supposedly surprise attack by a demand to surrender the fort on the previous day, and they had heavily reinforced Sumter. The main assault force failed to wait until the diversion could be mounted. The defenders spotted the advancing boats and opened with musket fire.

The Marines in the boats replied vigorously. But in the chaos, one group, under 2d Lt. John C. Harris, thinking the attack called off, reported to a nearby Navy ship and missed the action. Two boatloads of Marines commanded by 1st Lt. Percival C. Pope, also by error, went forward and landed with the first wave of sailors and suffered 11 casualties before escaping.

The men started to scale the walls. But they had no ladders; and the defenders' rain of musketry, grenades, grape, bricks and chunks of masonry shattered their attack. One officer reached the parapet and was captured. In vast confusion, boats milled around the base of the fort; several were sunk; two were swamped.

Captain McCawley found himself in a four-oared boat in the middle of a swarm of crowded boats fleeing back to the ships. He tried to rally the boats; but finally, with those Marines who were still obeying his commands, he joined the retreat. The battle was over in 20 minutes.

The price of this lesson in amphibious assault was 127 men killed, wounded, missing or captured—mostly captured. They included 31 Marines. Two Marine officers were among the prisoners. One of them, 1st Lt. C. H. Bradford, was mortally wounded, and, although he was humanely cared for by a doctor who had known his father, he died the following February. Young 2d Lt. Robert L. Meade and the enlisted Marines spent a year in the Confederate prisons at Columbia, South Carolina, and Andersonville, Georgia, before being exchanged. Meade, who had helped to suppress the New York draft riots less than two months earlier, lived to fight in another rebellion on the other side of the globe 37 years later. Six Marine officers received brevet promotions for that night's unsuccessful work: McCawley, Pope, Meade, Louis E. Fagan, H. B. Lowry and William Wallace.

The assault on Sumter failed for many reasons: The men were not trained to perform a night amphibious assault against enemy-held positions. Unlike New Orleans and Mobile Bay, this harbor was defended in depth. No provision had been made for scaling the fort's ruined walls. The hoped-for surprise had washed out. The defenders had been ordered to fight to the death and they were ready. The later boats failed to put their men ashore and stiffen the attack. And, most damaging of all, there was a shocking lack of coordination between the Union's naval and army commanders. The result demonstrated all the horrors of interservice rivalry and a selfish grab for glory.

Later, the Marines were moved back from Morris Island to a new position farther south on Folly Island. Transfers and illness ate away the battalion's strength, and early in 1864 it was disbanded.

12
"A Duty to Perform"

On May 12, 1864, Commandant Harris, after a brief illness, died in Washington. He was eight days shy of his seventy-fourth birthday and had served in uniform for half a century. On Saturday the 14th, he was buried in Oak Hill Cemetery in Old Georgetown. That night, Secretary Welles wrote worriedly in his diary:

> Attended the funeral of Colonel Harris. His death gives embarrassment as to a successor. The higher class of marine officers are not the men who can elevate or give efficiency to the corps. To supersede them will cause much dissatisfaction. Every man who is overslaughed and all his friends will be offended with me for what will be deemed an insult. But there is a duty to perform.[34]

Welles was right; he knew headquarters politics. The choice of a Commandant had traditionally been a matter of seniority throughout the 88-year history of the Corps; and the senior officers, the men Welles disparaged, wanted the job. At the top of the list were Col. William Dulany, Lt. Col. Ward Marston, Lt. Col. John G. Reynolds and Maj. Isaac T. Doughty. Of the four, only Doughty had less than 40 years' service.

Marston approached Assistant Navy Secretary Fox to plead for Colonel Dulany's candidacy (and his own advance up the ladder). Fox blistered the room, denouncing Dulany and referring to his "reputation for women." Marston was shocked. But with Dulany out of the running, he went to work in his own behalf, as next in line. He tried to interest Senator Charles Sumner and Lincoln himself. But neither Welles nor Fox wanted any part of him. Perhaps they were right. In December, 1865, a court-martial, presided over by Admiral Farragut, found Marston, by then retired, guilty of failing to account for $8,000 in government funds and sentenced him to be dismissed from the service with loss of all pay and allowances. Later, the sentence was reduced to suspension for three years and the deduction of one-half of his retired pay until the deficiency was made up.[35] Such a finding against the Commandant, at that moment, might have destroyed the Corps.

Throughout much of the war, Welles had been disillusioned with the Corps' top officers. Back in the summer of 1862, the messy court-martial of John G. Reynolds, the most likely candidate to succeed Harris, had brought Welles' disdain to a boil. Reynolds had written the Commandant a disrespectful letter, and Harris ordered him brought up on charges. When the court acquitted Reynolds, Welles refused to approve the decision, explaining in his diary:

> Almost all the elder officers are at loggerheads and ought to be retired. Reynolds has been tried by court martial on charges preferred by Harris, and acquitted, though by confessions made to me personally guilty. But a majority of the anti-Harris faction constituted the court, and partisanship, not merit, governed the decision. I refused to approve the finding.[36]

Reynolds then applied for a command; and when Harris denied it, Reynolds preferred charges himself and attacked his chief with a diatribe of accumulated emotion. Welles, angry and disgusted, refused to try Reynolds' charges and threatened to fire all the officers involved if the feud continued. The Secretary wrote Harris a formal letter condemning the "state of things in the Corps which in the view of the Department demands a reform."[37]

Not until four weeks after Harris' death did Welles choose a new Commandant. On June 9, taking advantage of an 1862 retirement law, he shattered the tradition of seniority and ordered Dulany, Marston, Reynolds and Doughty all retired in grade. Welles note in his diary: "Concluded to retire the marine officers who are past the legal age, and to bring in Zeilin as

Commandant of the Corps. There seems no alternative. . . ."[38] The next day Welles named Major Zeilin Commandant.

Jacob Zeilin, Jr., had been born in Philadelphia in 1806, the son of a widely respected tavern keeper, and had been admitted to West Point before he was sixteen. After three years at the Military Academy, he was flunked out for deficiencies in philosophy and chemistry. He was commissioned in the Marine Corps in 1831; during the Mexican War, he won a major's brevet in the battles of San Gabriel and La Mesa and helped rescue Brig. Gen. Kearny at San Bernardo. He was the senior Marine officer on Commodore Perry's expedition to Japan and was wounded at Bull Run. Just three years before his selection as Commandant, he held only a regular commission as captain and his major's brevet. He was now a heavy-set, bearded man of fifty-seven with a distinguished record. When this war was over, he would be the first Marine ever to attain regular general officer rank.

Jacob Zeilin's years in command would be difficult ones for the Corps. He faced the immediate and impossible task of supplying the Navy's ships with adequate Marine detachments. He simply did not have men enough to fill the billets at sea, much less to form separate units for amphibious operations. And, as the war dragged to its end, desertions—which weakened all the services—thinned the Corps' rolls even further. After the war, he would have to wage a bitter battle against those who wanted to abolish the Marine Corps entirely.

13
The Last Chance

The Marines had one last chance to pull off a successful amphibious assault before the war's end. With the year 1864 nearing its close, the last-act curtain was rising.

Grant was battering Lee before Petersburg and·Sherman was marching toward Savannah to slice the Confederacy in two—horizontally, as Grant and Farragut had split it vertically along the Mississippi. The Navy had strangled Norfolk, New Orleans, Charleston and Mobile, its prime targets from the beginning. The war had started when the Rebels seized the Federal ocean forts; its end was made possible when the Union won them back. Only Wilmington, North Carolina, on the Cape Fear River, remained open to blockade-runners still squeezing arms and ammunition into the South. If Wilmington could be choked off, the Anaconda Plan would at last be fulfilled and the Confederacy isolated.

For two years, the North Atlantic Blockading Squadron had tried to plug the Cape Fear River and failed. Two thirds of the blockade-runners who made the dash reached Wilmington. Rear Adm. Sam Phillips Lee complained that he could not seize Smith's Island in the river's mouth without Army cooperation, but the Army would not help. The Navy itself had no modern Marine Corps concept.

When Grant took charge in the East in the spring of 1864, he agreed to help the Navy close the Cape Fear River on two conditions: that he would not have to interrupt his hammering toward Richmond and that the Navy would get rid of Rear Adm. Lee. In October, Secretary Welles replaced Lee with Rear Adm. David D. Porter. Grant was pleased; he knew Porter from Vicksburg and admired him as a fighter. But Grant, with his eye on his own main chance, contributed bumbling Benjamin Butler to the campaign.

At this time Sherman was ripping a path of hell eastward from Atlanta. A naval brigade was hastily formed at Port Royal, South Carolina, to aid him. The brigade included 182 Marines from 12 ships organized into an undersized battalion commanded by young 1st Lt. George G. Stoddard—a veteran of but two years' service and the sole Marine officer present. Noncoms led the companies. The men had only two days to train together before setting off on the evening of November 28, 1864, in seven small vessels up the Broad River behind Port Royal. Their goal: to cut the Savannah-Charleston railroad.

Twenty miles upstream, at Boyd's Neck, the Marines led the brigade ashore and covered the landing of the sailors and soldiers. On the 30th, the Rebels stopped the Marine point. The Army took over the lead. The next day, the Army pushed on to Honey Hill, where the enemy was entrenched. The naval brigade attacked, the Marines advancing on the extreme right flank. The Rebels counterattacked and drove the brigade back.

On December 6, it tried all over again. The Confederates stopped the brigade at Tullifinney Crossroads, less than a mile short of the railroad. This time, the Marines, in the lead, drove the Rebels back far enough to give the brigade's howitzers a clear shot at the railroad tracks. But Stoddard and the Marines were cut off and had to leave their wounded and escape through a waist-deep swamp. The guns bombarded the railroad and the brigade stayed there until December 26. The Marine battalion suffered 23 casualties, including four killed. Stoddard won a captain's brevet. But the Rebels still held the railroad.

Meanwhile, by December 10, Sherman had reached the coast. Before Savannah fell to his army on the 21st, Bragg pulled out of Wilmington to oppose Sherman's advance. Bragg's move left Wilmington's defenses weakened and Grant saw his opportunity. He ordered an attack to shut the Cape Fear River and seal off Wilmington.

Two Confederate fortifications guarded the river's entrance, 28 miles south of Wilmington: Fort Caswell to the west on the mainland, and Fort Fisher on Federal Point, a skinny peninsula separating river and sea. Because the main channel cut between Smith's Island and Federal Point, Fort Fisher became the Union's target.

On December 24, the Navy bombarded the fort to soften it for the Army's landing. On *Ticonderoga*, Sgt. Richard Binder, captain of a gun manned by Marines, earned the Medal of Honor. On Christmas Day, Butler sent ashore a third of his 6,500 troops; but finding the fort undamaged by the Navy's bombardment, he refused to attack. After some minor skirmishing, he reembarked his men, ignoring Grant's order to hold.

This fiasco created a storm back in Washington. Each service blamed the other. As the year closed, Grant added 1,500 more soldiers to the campaign and replaced Butler with Brevet Maj. Gen. Alfred H. Terry, a tough-minded thirty-seven-year-old Yale graduate, who 12 years later would be Custer's superior when the Sioux wiped him out on the Little Big Horn.

In January, 1865, while Grant still pounded away at Richmond and Sherman prepared to swing north from Savannah, the mightiest joint force of the war assembled off Cape Fear: 8,800 soldiers and 72 ships. Maj. Gen. Terry and Rear Adm. Porter planned a combined assault on Fort Fisher. This time, the Army and Navy would work together—at least in the planning stage.

Fort Fisher, a well-built log-and-sand works, was anchored at the tip of Federal Point by the Mound Battery, two cannon atop a man-made pile of sand 65 feet high. The battery commanded the inlet and kept Union warships away from the scurrying blockade-runners. Along the ocean front, 100 yards back from the beach, defense works constructed of palmetto logs and sand ran northward up the peninsula for a mile from the Mound Battery. Then they made a right-angle turn and cut westward across the peninsula. The northern face was 682 yards long, with earth 20 feet high and 25 feet thick and mounted with 21 guns; before it, the Rebels had planted minefields and constructed a log palisade to shield sharpshooters.

Terry and Porter's joint plan sounded simple: The Army would assault the fort's northern face near the river. The Navy would bombard the fort, and a diversionary Naval Landing Force of sailors and Marines would attack the fort's sea side.

Porter assembled a Marine battalion of 400 men from the ships. In command was Marine Capt. Lucian L. Dawson from *USS Colorado*, a Kentuckian who would mark his sixth anniversary in the Corps on January 13, the day the Union army hit the beach. The Marines were the fourth and final battalion of the naval regiment of 1,600 sailors and the Marines commanded by

Capt. K. Randolph Breese, USN. When Porter called for volunteers for the Naval Landing Force, almost every man in the fleet responded; quotas had to be set for each ship—somebody had to stay behind. The men had plenty of courage, but the sailors and Marines from the ships had never trained to fight together ashore. This would prove fatal.

The then-current naval concept of how a fort should be assaulted did not help. "The sailors," Porter's order said, "will be armed with cutlasses, well sharpened, and with revolvers"[39] in the traditional manner of naval boarding parties. The Marines carried muskets and 40 rounds each and would cover the sailors' attack from rifle pits. In his Landing Order on the day of the attack, Porter described the job of the Naval Landing Force: " . . . no move is to be made forward until the Army charges, when the Navy is to assault the sea or southeast face of the work, going over with cutlasses drawn and revolvers in hand. The Marines will follow after, and when they gain the edge of the parapet they will lie flat and pick off the enemy in the works." Rear Adm. Porter was to learn that you cannot "board" a fort.

Captain Dawson divided the Marine battalion of 365 men into four companies. He also had a detached company of 43 sharpshooters under 1st Lt. Louis E. Fagan of *Wabash* and a skirmish line of 25 men with Sharps rifles under 1st Lt. Charles F. Williams of *Ticonderoga*. Fagan and his sharpshooters were destined to be in the cockpit of the battle. Fagan was only 22, but he had already seen a lot of the war. A slim, handsome Philadelphian, he served as an Army private with Brig. Gen. Patterson in the Valley at Bull Run and fought at Shiloh before being discharged to accept a Marine Corps commission. He was brevetted a first lieutenant for his work during the night boat attack on Fort Sumter.

On January 13, Maj. Gen. Terry led the soldiers ashore five miles north of Fort Fisher, and Porter began shelling the Rebel works. "This time," wrote one Navy officer, "we came to stay."[40]

All the next day, the powerful battle fleet bombarded Fort Fisher. Ironclads dashed in to 1,000 yards from shore and splintered the northern face of the fort. The assault was scheduled for 3 P.M. on the 15th. The 1,600 sailors and 400 Marines would hit the fort's sea face as the Army struck the north face toward the river. Timing was all-important; if it was right, the enemy would be overwhelmed.

On the morning of the 15th, a warm, clear day, gunboats went in close to cover the landing, two miles above the fort. At the signal "Land Naval Brigade," 200 boats carried in the first wave. Most of the men were soaked in the high surf.

Fagan's sharpshooters were the first Marines ashore at 10:30 A.M. Landing north of the fort, the young lieutenant formed the Marines as they came ashore from the various ships, until Marine Capt. George Butler arrived from *Minnesota* and took command.

At 11, the fleet opened fire. Orderly Sgt. Isaac N. Fry, a Marine gun captain, earned the Medal of Honor for bravery aboard *Ticonderoga* during the bombardment.

Butler ordered Fagan to take 60 men and cover the sailors who were constructing a breastwork 600 yards from the fort and a series of rifle pits to within 200 yards of the palisade.

Fagan led his Marines through the loose sand. Enemy fire grew heavier, and Fagan spread his men as skirmishers. Reaching the entrenchments near the Army's sector, the Marines began digging in. They threw up piles of sand with their bayonets and bare hands to hide from the shower of grape and canister. Two of Fagan's men were seriously wounded and carried to the rear.

Fagan directed several of his best shots to knock out a field piece inside the palisade. Soldiers of the 147th New York Volunteers began flooding into his position, so Fagan led his men eastward to join the naval brigade.

As soon as he landed, Captain Dawson organized his four Marine companies and ordered 1st Lt. Williams' skirmishers to cover them. Fagan's unit had already moved up to the rifle pits. Dawson had no time to equalize his companies, to select sergeants to fill in for officers or to post guides. The order to advance came almost immediately.

The naval brigade, with the Marines leading, moved to within 1,200 yards of the northern face of the fort and waited there for the steam whistle on Porter's flagship *Malvern* to signal the attack. Captain Breese was having difficulty determining precisely when the Army would strike. Enemy shells came zipping out at the Marines, fell short and then bounded at them "jumping along for all the world like rabbits."[41] At three o'clock, the flagship's whistle blew and the three divisions advanced abreast. When the naval brigade closed to within 600 yards, the fleet lifted its bombardment. Now the Rebels reappeared on the parapet, and hundreds of rifles and muskets fired down on the sailors and Marines. The sailors' pistols and cutlasses were useless, and the withering Rebel fire stopped the brigade in its tracks. The men fell on their bellies. Their officers rallied them. They rose and advanced another 200 yards across the open beach. They were hit by everything the enemy had. The virtually unorganized men rallied again and moved up the exposed beach against fire they could not answer. The parapet looked like a solid flashing blue line. The toll was fearful.

The naval brigade's fate now rested with the better-armed Marines. Captain Breese ordered Dawson to move the Marines out of the half-finished entrenchments and 150 yards to the left, nearer the sea. There, Breese thought, they would find more concealment and they could cover the sailors' assault near the fort's sea face. Dawson, surprised at the order, questioned the messenger, but obeyed promptly and moved over on the double, skirmishers out.

Breese then ordered Fagan to the most advanced parallel of trenches nearest the beach. His Marines moved up in short dashes under fire, Fagan reported later, "marching to the front across a plain swept by the enemies [sic] fire, with alacrity and spirit."[42]

Near the sea, Fagan joined a column of sailors and Marines advancing under heavy musket fire that poured down from the corner of the fort. Fagan and his men inched their way steadily toward the corner. When the column halted some 40 yards from it, Fagan ordered his men prone to pick off the Rebels on the parapet.

Before most of Dawson's battalion was in position to cover the sailors, the sudden cry of "Charge! Charge!" was heard. Sailors and Marines, swept up in the excitement, plunged forward, cheering and yelling. The Army had not yet begun to attack, and the Confederates thought this the main assault. They concentrated all their fire against the lightly armed naval force. Some 350 Union muskets fought 2,000 in the fort.

The Marines charged abreast of the second division of sailors. Dawson remembered:

I could gain nothing on the first division until they got

under the heavy fire of the fort, when the first company of Marines got abreast with the centre of the first division of sailors. I had just reached the head of my men, after a hard run, when I saw the head of the line of sailors, who had reached the end of the stockade, begun to falter and turn back, and was myself about forty or fifty yards from the end of the stockade on the beach. I saw some six or eight men go around the end of the stockade, but immediately return; and it was at this instant that the whole line commenced doubling up and flying, everybody for themselves, except some thirty officers and men at the head of the line, who took cover under an angle of the stockade.[43]

The Marines hit near the sea end of the eight-foot-high stockade. A few, including Captain Butler, Cpl. John Rannahan and Pvt. James Shivers, raced around it. Pvt. Henry A. Thompson of *Minnesota* advanced the farthest. They planted the Stars and Stripes, but, faced by a superior force secure atop the sand fort, they had to come back.

It was over quickly. Sailors and Marines broke and started flooding to the rear. Dawson tried to halt his Marines' flight; he ordered them to lie down and fire at the parapet to reduce the Rebel fire. Nearly all the Marines in the forward two companies obeyed. The rear companies retreated without ever firing a shot. Fagan and his men held their positions until a Navy officer released them. Twenty-year-old Cpl. Andrew J. Tomlin of Goshen, New Jersey, a member of Fagan's command, raced across the fire-swept open beach, brought back a wounded Marine and was awarded the Medal of Honor.

The naval force had been repulsed; the attack shattered beyond recovery. As the panic subsided, Dawson ordered the Marines still with him to retreat by squads; he feared the fleet would reopen its bombardment. He stayed behind a slope of beach, 50 yards from the fort, with 30 Marines, for two hours, until sunset.

Other men remained on the beach—some pinned down by enemy fire and by fear, others wounded and unable to move. One of the wounded was eighteen-year-old Acting Ensign Robley D. Evans, who in later years would become famous as

Admiral "Fighting Bob" Evans. He had been hit twice but managed to get past the stockade with a small party. He was hit twice more and, although unable to stand, shot the sharpshooter who had been firing at him so accurately. Then occurred an act of heroism which is best told in Evans' own words:

> One of the Marines from the *Powhatan* [Evans' ship], a splendid fellow named Wasmouth [Pvt. Henry Wasmuth], came through the stockade, quickly gathered me up under one arm, and before the sharpshooters could hit him laid me down in a place of comparative safety; but a moment afterward the fleet opened fire again, and the shells from the New Ironsides and the monitors began falling dangerously near us. Occasionally one would strike short and, exploding, send great chunks of mud and pieces of log flying in all directions. Wasmouth again picked me up, and, after carrying me about fifty yards, dropped me into a pit made by a large shell. Here I was entirely protected from rebel fire, and several times called to him to take cover, but he said each time, "The bullet has not been made that will kill me." I was very drowsy and almost asleep when I heard a peculiar thud of a bullet, and looking up, found poor Wasmouth with his hand to his neck, turning round and round, and the blood spurting out in a steady stream. The bullet had gone through his neck, cutting the jugular, and in a few minutes he dropped in the edge of the surf and bled to death. He certainly was an honour to his uniform.[44]

This heroic Marine, a large robust man, had been born in Germany and become a naturalized U.S. citizen. A cabinet maker by trade in Philadelphia, Henry Wasmuth had enlisted in the Marine Corps on June 11, 1861, when he was twenty-five. He fought at Bull Run and was promoted to corporal. But a year later, he was reduced to private; and late in 1863, he served 15 days in solitary confinement on bread and water for falling asleep on post at the Marine Barracks in Boston. He was not the first—nor would he be the last—Marine to serve better in battle than in garrison.

Wasmuth did not die on the beach as Evans thought. He

was taken aboard *USS Fort Jackson* and lived until the 17th. On July 17, 1919, the Navy named Destroyer 489 after Pvt. Henry Wasmuth; she survived the Japanese attack on Pearl Harbor and later in World War II was lost at sea.

On the beach, Robley Evans awoke to find his shellhole nearly filled with water. He was surrounded by dead and wounded. Fearing drowning, he tried to climb out but found his legs useless. He pulled himself up. Then he had another sort of experience with a Marine:

> When I got out I saw a marine a short distance away, nicely covered by a pile of sand, and firing very deliberately at the fort. I called to him to pull me in behind his pile of sand, but he declined, on the ground that the rebel fire was too sharp for him to expose himself. I persuaded him with my revolver to change his mind, and in two seconds he had me in a place of safety—this is to say, safe by a small margin, for when he fired, the rebel bullets would snip the sand within a few inches of our heads. If the marine had known that my revolver was soaking wet, and could not possibly be fired, I suppose I should have been buried the next morning, as many other poor fellows were.[45]

Across the narrow peninsula, the battle for Fort Fisher was still underway. While the Naval Landing Force was being destroyed, Maj. Gen. Terry finally began his attack at the western end of the fort's northern face, toward the river. A sergeant and six Marines from Fagan's unit, who had been separated from their command, charged the fort along with the soldiers.

Captain Dawson, when he made his way to the rear, was ordered to gather all the sailors and Marines he could find with arms and report to Terry's headquarters. He assembled a force that included 180 Marines and led them to the breastworks behind Terry's station. They were instructed to cover the Army's left flank, freeing more soldiers for the continuing attack. The Marines remained there through the night. In the morning, they were relieved and returned to their ships.

The earlier naval attack had given the Army a momentary

advantage; but Confederate Col. William Lamb rapidly reorganized his defenders and fought the Army for seven hours. The battle was hand-to-hand on the ramparts. A detachment of 50 Confederate marines under young Capt. Alfred C. Van Benthuysen, who had been a soldier of fortune in Europe, fought in the battle's final stages. After resisting desperately, all of the Confederate marines were killed or captured; Van Benthuysen himself was severely wounded.

Shortly after 9 P.M., the Confederates fled to the tip of the peninsula for a last-ditch stand. Terry's soldiers mopped up until they had taken 2,083 prisoners. At 10 P.M., a victory signal went up from the fort. The men on the beach and the ships cheered, rockets sprayed the sky and the guns roared a salute. The greatest amphibious battle of the Civil War had been won.

The Army lost 540 men and the Navy suffered 274 casualties at Fort Fisher. Eleven Marine privates were killed in the assault; another three died in a magazine explosion the next day. Forty-one Marines were wounded and five listed as missing in action. Lt. William Wallace was badly wounded, the Corps' only officer casualty. Eight Marine officers were brevetted, including Dawson, Butler, Fagan and Wallace, and six Marines received the Medal of Honor. Three of them had gotten inside the palisade: Irish-born Cpl. John Rannahan, Canadian-born Pvt. John Shivers and English-born Pvt. Henry A. Thompson. (Of the 17 Marines who received the Medal of Honor in the Civil War, eight were foreign-born.) Carlile P. Porter, the admiral's son, who was a civilian serving as Breese's aide on the beach, won a special honor for bravery—a Marine Corps commission.

The fall of Fort Fisher denied Wilmington to the Confederacy. The Anaconda noose was now closed; the Rebellion was at last encircled.

For the Marines, the operation brought a large measure of criticism. Porter and Breese blamed the Marines for the failure of the naval attack. The admiral wrote to "My dear Fox" on the 21st from his flagship to defend his plan for the suicidal dash over the open beach:

> I expect you were disappointed at our sailors not carrying
> the works, they ought to have done it, and would but for
> the infernal marines who were running away when the

sailors were mounting the parapets, and every man fighting like a lion poor fellows. . . . The grape and canister and minnie balls never stopped them until they reached the top of the parapet, and found themselves deserted by the marines.[46]

Captain Breese was equally critical of the Marines, but his battle report was much fairer:

I can but attribute the failure of the assault to the absence of the marines from their position, as their fire would have enabled our boarders [sic] to use their cutlasses and pistols most effectively. By this I would imply the lack of proper organization, it being impossible in the short space of time, on account of throwing so many small squads of men from the different vessels together in one mass, lacking proper company formations, and wholly unacquainted with each other, to secure such organization.

This led to the confusion exhibited, for it was not due to any want of personal valor on the part of the officers or men.[47]

Captain Dawson, in his report, defended the Marines:

At the moment when the head of the line gave way, the Marines were not near enough to open fire effectually, and were on the double-quick, and quite exhausted; nor was there the slightest cover this side of the stockade, except a few sand-hills very near the stockade. I saw that the men were hopelessly repulsed . . . though a portion of the marines retreated with the sailors, it is but just to the rest to say that they remained and performed the duty of good soldiers until I passed the order to retreat.[48]

And he wrote quite accurately to Commandant Zeilin: "I do not think that the Marines (with all the light we now have on the subject) should alone be blamed, because the Admiral expected from them impossibilities."[49]

The accusations flew back and forth. The fact was that the

Marines had not done their job. But the whole naval plan was doomed to fail, and the attack was chaotic—badly organized, badly timed, badly executed. The attackers had few weapons that could hurt the enemy. The Navy was learning it could not take a fort with pistols and cutlasses. And just as the naval assault began, the Marines were ordered to shift their position to the beach. They were caught up in the attack; and when the sailors fled, many Marines broke too.

The war's big lesson for the Corps was: If Marines were to attack shore fortifications, pulling them together into makeshift battalions was simply not good enough. Fort Fisher was a beginning, but the development of a real Marine amphibious capability was still in the future.

14
"Struck Down in His Might"

In the end there was Lincoln. Weary, saddened, his eyes sunken now, he was inaugurated for his second term on March 4, 1865, in a drizzling rain and spoke without malice and of charity for all. He spoke of binding the nation's wounds, and many wept. In the crowd, not far from the speaker, John Wilkes Booth stood and listened. That night, hundreds forced their way inside the White House for the public reception, and Lincoln shook hands for hours. The Marine Band off to the side played sweetly.

On March 23, Maj. Gen. Terry and his army that had taken Fort Fisher joined up with Sherman at Goldsboro, North Carolina. On that same day, Lincoln, his wife and their young son Tad left Washington on *River Queen* and arrived the following evening at City Point, Virginia, the great Army base at the meeting of the James and Appomattox Rivers. General Grant came aboard and made them welcome.

By now, the North's purpose was no longer to occupy real estate but to destroy the Southern armies. The Union Navy had isolated the Confederacy and cut down its fighting and staying power: The Rebels were short of shells, short of shoes, short of food—above all, short of men. Lincoln met with Grant, Porter and Sherman and awaited the finish.

April came. On the first, Sherman crushed Lee's right flank; and on the second, a Sunday, Lee moved out of Petersburg, leaving Richmond exposed. On the third, the Confederate capital fell. The news thrilled the North. Washington was festive at last; the Marine Barracks sparkled with a display of candles and gaslight.

Lincoln wanted to go and see Richmond. At midmorning on

Tuesday (it was Tad's birthday), Admiral Porter's flagship *Malvern* and *River Queen*, the President and Tad aboard, steamed toward the city, escorted by the tug *Glance* with 24 Marines. A few miles short of the capital, *Malvern* grounded; and the President and Tad joined Porter in his barge, towed by *Glance*. A mile below the city, a grounded ship with Admiral Farragut aboard signaled for help. Porter sent *Glance* to assist, and the tug too became grounded. Lincoln proceeded to the city in the barge, now being rowed, without his Marine escort. Porter feared for his safety.

The small party went ashore at Rocketts Landing, escorted only by 12 sailors, armed with carbines and bayonets, and a handful of officers. A crowd of Negroes pressed around them, shouting with joy. Lincoln shook their hands. A cavalryman was found and sent galloping for a proper escort; the President and his party were vulnerable to any vengeful attack. They walked two miles to the center of the city. Lincoln saw Libby Prison; and Porter, as he would later write, "determined that the President should go nowhere again, while under his charge, without a guard of marines."[50]

Finally, the cavalry escort dashed up and conducted them more securely to the Confederate Executive Mansion. At evening, they rode in an ambulance back to Rocketts Landing and the safety of *Malvern*. After dark, someone hailed the ship from the shore. An officer was sent over in a boat for dispatches the caller was supposed to have. The officer returned empty-handed and reported that he had seen a black-mustached, villainous-looking stranger. Admiral Porter, his fear for the President increasing, stationed a Marine outside Lincoln's cabin.

On Saturday, April 8, the President sailed north to Washington on *River Queen*. He had six days to live.

The Confederacy died the next day, Palm Sunday, at Appomattox village in northern Virginia.

Good Friday night came, April 14; and in the darkened theater, Abraham Lincoln was shot in the brain by a man bursting with hate. The nation, still scarred and mourning its dead, wept. He died early Saturday morning, the day before Easter, and the nation put on crepe and gave its sprig of lilac. Said the Secretary of War, "Now he belongs to the ages."

He lay in the East Room of the White House and throngs

passed his open coffin. On Wednesday, the services were held there and his body was carried to the Capitol. Colonel Zeilin was among the honorary pallbearers, and in the cortege marched a battalion of Marines and the officers of the Corps. Then the casket began its long, final journey to Illinois.

When the procession stopped in Philadelphia, young Marine Captain Forney stood in the State House. Years later he wrote sadly: "The next time I saw the President he lay dead, and I, on duty, was standing at the head of his coffin in the corridor of the old State House in Philadelphia, looking down on his dear homely face, struck down in his might by a foul assassin. I was one of the Guard of Honor of officers, selected for that service. . . ."[51]

The war was over. The nation was stitched back together with bayonets and bullets. But it was changed forever. The South stood in ruins. Nearly four million slaves were now free men and women. More than half a million young Americans lay in their graves. At least that battered generation of Americans now realized that war was pain and filth, endless weariness and hunger, fire-gutted homes and squalid prison camps. More than ever before, war was madness.

For the Marine Corps, the Civil War raised the most basic question. Ships no longer fought in close-locked combat. Marines were not really needed to work the great guns. They were not trained to land on a beach or attack a fort. Some began to ask again: Do we need a Marine Corps at all?

To see the answer would take awhile. But the seed of that answer, amphibious warfare, had been carried ashore and planted at Hatteras Inlet, Port Royal, New Orleans, Tullifinney Crossroads, Fort Sumter and Fort Fisher. And those who believed in the Corps would struggle desperately to keep it alive until the answer could be seen by all. In time, it would be.

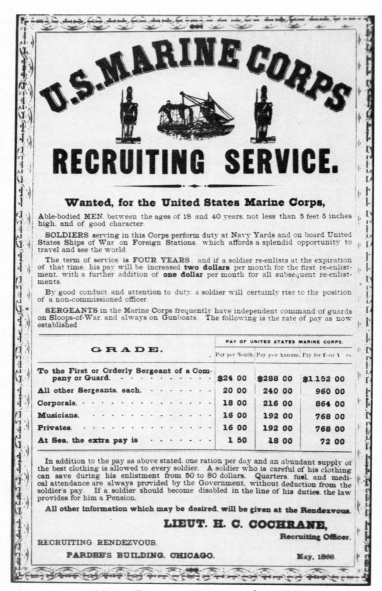

U.S. MARINE CORPS

RECRUITING SERVICE.

Wanted, for the United States Marine Corps,

Able-bodied MEN, between the ages of 18 and 40 years, not less than 5 feet 5 inches high, and of good character.

SOLDIERS serving in this Corps perform duty at Navy Yards and on board United States Ships of War on Foreign Stations, which affords a splendid opportunity to travel and see the world.

The term of service is FOUR YEARS, and if a soldier re-enlists at the expiration of that time, his pay will be increased **two dollars** per month for the first re-enlistment, with a further addition of **one dollar** per month for all subsequent re-enlistments.

By good conduct and attention to duty, a soldier will certainly rise to the position of a non-commissioned officer.

SERGEANTS in the Marine Corps frequently have independent command of guards on Sloops-of-War, and always on Gunboats. The following is the rate of pay as now established:

GRADE.	PAY OF UNITED STATES MARINE CORPS.		
	Pay per Month.	Pay per Annum.	Pay for Four Yrs.
To the First or Orderly Sergeant of a Company or Guard.	$24 00	$288 00	$1,152 00
All other Sergeants, each.	20 00	240 00	960 00
Corporals.	18 00	216 00	864 00
Musicians.	16 00	192 00	768 00
Privates.	16 00	192 00	768 00
At Sea, the extra pay is	1 50	18 00	72 00

In addition to the pay as above stated, one ration per day and an abundant supply of the best clothing is allowed to every soldier. A soldier who is careful of his clothing can save during his enlistment from 50 to 80 dollars. Quarters, fuel, and medical attendance are always provided by the Government, without deduction from the soldier's pay. If a soldier should become disabled in the line of his duties, the law provides for him a Pension.

All other information which may be desired, will be given at the Rendezvous.

LIEUT. H. C. COCHRANE,

Recruiting Officer.

RECRUITING RENDEZVOUS,

PARDEE'S BUILDING, CHICAGO.

May, 1866.

A Marine Corps recruiting poster from 1866.
Museums Branch, USMC

SEMPER FIDELIS

VI
SWEEP
TOWARD
EMPIRE
1848-1894

1
Marines Range the Globe

Throughout the half century between the Mexican War and the War with Spain, the Navy and Marine Corps kept open the sea lanes for the produce of a bountiful land and a booming industry. Marines ranged the globe, guarding the nation's interests and commerce. Although interrupted by the violence of the Civil War, the Marine Corps' story during this burgeoning imperialistic era can be seen best as one continuity of 50 expansive years.

After the Mexican War, the nation stretched from sea to sea. Texas, New Mexico, California and most of Oregon had been brought under the flag. The gold rush sucked a vigorous, adventurous population across the continent. Clipper ships raced around the Horn. And when the Compromise of 1850 promised to calm the rising anger over slavery, Americans' thoughts and dreams leaped across the Pacific. It was a time of production, expansion and confidence.

In the years before the Civil War, the Marine Corps protected American interests and citizens around the world: Buenos Aires (1852); Nicaragua (1853); Montevideo, Uruguay (1855); Paraguay (1855); the Fiji Islands (1855 and 1858); Puget Sound (1856), and the Isthmus of Panama (1856). Most significantly, the Corps joined in two dramatic ventures in East Asia: the opening of Japan and the attack on the forts protecting Canton, China.

2
Tokyo Bay

On the morning of July 8, 1853, the American frigates *Susquehanna* and *Mississippi* and sloops of war *Saratoga* and *Plymouth* steamed in a single column up mist-shrouded Tokyo Bay. The ships were cleared for action, their guns shotted, their crews at battle stations.

As the morning haze dissolved, the men could see Mount Fuji in the distance. The ships anchored on the west side of the outer bay. Although the Japanese were expecting the expedition, dignified, portly Commodore Matthew Calbraith Perry knew that he was going where he was not wanted.

For more than 200 years, the Japanese had held themselves aloff from the "barbaric" West. They had achieved stability by slamming the door on foreign influences, trade and Christianity and denying entry to the industrialized nations with manufactured goods to sell.

Now, Japan was about to be opened to the West—the most portentous event in which American Marines would participate between the Mexican and Civil Wars.

In March 1852, President Millard Fillmore had agreed to support a major expedition to begin relations with Japan. The previous attempt in 1846 had failed. Although the United States had gained access to the markets of China with Caleb Cushing's treaty in 1844, it could not yet trade with Japan; and the crews of American vessels wrecked on the Japanese coast still received harsh treatment. The Dutch managed a trading post on an island off Nagasaki under restricted and humiliating conditions, but they were the only Europeans permitted even a toehold in feudal Japan.

Now, the American eagerness for trade, especially markets

for cotton textiles; the need for coaling stations; the zeal of Protestant missionaries, and the booming whaling industry all made the time ripe for another effort. Commodore Perry reluctantly accepted the command of the East India Squadron to head the expedition. With him on his first voyage into the Pacific went six Marine officers and some 200 men under the command of Maj. Jacob Zeilin.

The squadron proceeded from its base at Hong Kong to the peaceful Ryukyu (Loo Choo) Islands, where the Americans marveled at Okinawa's pine forests and limestone tombs and the Marines drilled ashore. Perry, escorted by 200 sailors and Marines, paid a formal visit to the royal palace at Shuri. If the Japanese proved intractable, Perry decided, he would establish a coaling station on Okinawa.

When the American warships steamed up Tokyo Bay at eight knots against the wind and tide, the Japanese were awed. But they demanded that Perry withdraw and deal through the Dutch at Nagasaki. He refused and insisted on delivering the letter he carried from President Fillmore to a suitably high official at Tokyo (then called Yedo) with proper ceremony. After prolonged discussions, the Japanese compromised and permitted a meeting on July 14.

Perry's ships moved in closer, prepared to cover the landing with gunfire if necessary. The commodore was escorted ashore by a heavily armed honor guard of 300 that debarked from 15 launches and cutters. Cmdr. Franklin Buchanan of *Susquehanna* was the first and Major Zeilin the second American to step on shore. A hundred Marines lined the route to the flag-decorated pine building that had been erected overnight for the reception. The Japanese had 5,000 troops present with muskets, bows and pikes. Perry was accompanied by two bands and his staff. The Marines—in blue jackets with white crossed belts, white trousers and plumed shakos—presented arms as the commodore and his entourage came ashore and then marched at the head of the American procession. In the reception house, Perry delivered the President's letter; and the Japanese handed him a scroll ending, "Therefore, as the letter has been received you can depart."[1] The ceremonies took only half an hour. And the Americans departed, Perry announcing he would return the next spring to receive the Japanese answer and to negotiate a treaty.

Of this brief meeting on the side of Tokyo Bay, historian Samuel Eliot Morison has written, "It was unprecedented, unpredictable, and, in view of the consequences, one of the most important events of modern history."[2]

Learning that the Russians were sending their own expedition to Japan, Perry advanced his second visit and came back to Tokyo Bay on February 13, 1854. Again, the Japanese tried to persuade him to negotiate at Nagasaki. When that failed, they demanded he take his ships further out to sea. Instead, on February 24, Perry moved his squadron up the bay within sight of Tokyo; and the Japanese finally agreed to meet with him at Yokohama, then only a small village.

On Wednesday, March 8, Perry brought ashore 500 men, including every possible Marine. This time, the ceremonies and pageantry were even more grandiose. The Marines drew up in a hollow square and presented arms as Perry landed from his white-painted barge. Said the official narrative of the expedition:

> The Commodore, on landing, was received by the group of officers, who, falling into line, followed him. The bands now struck up a lively tune, and the Marines, whose orderly ranks in complete military appointment, with their blue and white uniforms, and glistening bayonets, made quite a martial and effective show, presented arms as the Commodore, followed in procession by his immediate staff, his guard of fine looking sailors and a number of his subordinate officers, proceeded up the shore.[3]

In the specially built Treaty House facing the harbor, the Japanese Commissioners presented an official reply to the President's letter that Perry had presented on his previous visit. While their document was being translated, the Commodore asked permission to buy a piece of land on an island in the bay for the burial of Marine Pvt. Robert Williams who had died two days earlier on *Mississippi*. The Commissioners refused the purchase but allowed the Marine to be buried at Yokohama, near one of the temples and in view of the squadron.

At 5 P.M. the next day, as the American ships lowered their flags to half-mast and a large crowd of Japanese watched silently, the chaplain and a party of Marines with reversed arms escorted the body to the temple grounds, marching slowly to a muffled drum. After the service, the Marines fired three volleys over the grave, and a Buddhist priest offered incense and prayers. Later, Williams' body was moved to Shimoda and buried beside a temple there.

During the three weeks of conferences, the Marines impressed the Japanese with the precision of their exhibition drilling. On March 14, Zeilin came down with hepatitis; Brevet Capt. William B. Slack took his place.

Perry and the Japanese signed the Treaty of Kanagawa on March 31. It opened the ports of Shimoda and Hakodate to American ships for coal and provisions, provided for the safety of shipwrecked American sailors, promised that any privileges granted another country would extend to the United States, allowed an American consul at Shimoda and provided for "perfect, permanent and universal peace" between the two nations. (Eighty-six years later that peace would be broken at Pearl Harbor.)

Perry had not obtained an agreement on trade, but the door was now ajar; and in four more years, the American consul Townsend Harris would negotiate a commercial treaty. On June 23, 1854, Perry left Japan for the last time. At Okinawa, he signed the Treaty of Naha establishing a coaling station and before returning home arranged to buy coal, cheaper than Japanese coal, on Formosa.

Perry's Treaty of Kanagawa had a monumental effect on Japan. It exposed Japanese minds to Western thought. It helped crush the already weakening power of feudalism in Japan and begin the Meiji modernization, which in great part was based on what the Japanese eagerly learned from the West.

In 1856 at Columbia University in New York, a paper by Commodore Perry was read that said ". . . to me it seems that the people of America will, in some form or other, extend their dominion and their power, until they shall have brought within their mighty embrace the islands of the great Pacific, and placed the Saxon race upon the eastern shores of Asia."[4] Prophetic words that would lead the Marine Corps to Chosin Reservoir and Da Nang a century later.

3
The Forts at Canton

During his second visit to Japan, Commodore Perry had left the sloop of war *Plymouth* at Shanghai. China was then enflamed by the T'ai P'ing Rebellion against the Manchu emperor, and Shanghai's foreign trading settlements were nervous about their safety.

On the evening of April 4, 1854, the foreign missions and the Shanghai racetrack were invaded by the Imperial Chinese army. A detachment of 60 sailors and Marines from *Plymouth* landed and was reinforced later that night. The men joined a similar force of 150 sailors and Marines from two British warships, plus 37 British and American volunteers. They attacked the Chinese soldiers and cleared the foreign settlements and the racetrack. Part of *Plymouth's* force remained ashore until June 15.

Danger to American commercial interests in China persisted, and trouble erupted at Canton in the fall of 1856. Marine detachments were repeatedly sent to Canton from U.S. warships lying off Whampoa in the Pearl River eight miles below the city. Early on November 16, an unarmed American boat sent upriver to find a channel was fired on from one of the four barrier forts protecting the river approach to Canton, and the American coxswain was killed. To retaliate and teach the Chinese to respect the Americans, Commodore James Armstrong sent the sloop *Portsmouth* to bombard the forts, which had seven-foot-thick walls designed by European military engineers. *Portsmouth* fired more than 230 shells and took several hits in reply.

After that indecisive encounter, Armstrong returned to his flagship in ill health and tried to negotiate an apology from the Chinese. He left Commander Andrew H. Foote of *Portsmouth* in charge and, when negotiations broke down, gave Foote authority to act.

Early on November 20, the aggressive Foote laid down a bombardment and put ashore a landing force of 287 men, including Brevet Capt. John D. Simms and the squadron's 50 Marines. The forts returned the ships' fire but were soon silenced. Led by the Marines, the landing force squelched resistance in a village behind the nearest fort and opened fire on the fort itself. The Chinese tried to flee, some swimming the river. The Marines picked off more than 40, seized the fort and raised the Stars and Stripes. Simms took his men back into the village, found that the enemy had reinforced it from Canton, and cleared it again. A thousand Chinese soldiers counterattacked. Simms had his men hold their musket fire until the Chinese were within 200 yards; then the Marines decimated them. The Chinese attacked twice more before retreating.

Early the next morning, Simms led an attack on the next fort, called "Fiddlers Fort." The Americans advanced through waist-deep ditches against heavy but inaccurate fire and stormed the fort. In the face of a horde of Chinese soldiers, Cpl. William McDougal, the Marines' standard bearer, placed the American flag on the fort's wall. Simms turned the fort's guns on the next objective, Center Fort on Napier Island in midstream, and dueled its guns. As Simms' Marines advanced on the island fort, the Chinese swarmed forward. The Marines threw them back. Again, McDougal planted the American flag over the fort as the landing force assaulted its walls. At dawn the next day, the landing force waded in to seize the fourth fort. The enemy fled at their approach and the final fort was taken.

In the entire operation, American casualties totaled seven dead and 22 wounded in action. No Marines were killed but six were wounded. In three days, the Americans had destroyed four Chinese forts and 168 cannon. They got their apology.

4
Struggle for Survival

The Marine Corps barely survived the three decades following the Civil War. Its strength atrophied; its officers aged; promotions almost disappeared; at times less than 2,000 men remained in uniform. And there was pressure to abolish it altogether.

As early as 1866, the House of Representatives instructed the Committee on Naval Affairs "to consider the expediency of abolishing the Marine Corps, and transferring it to the Army, and of making provision for supplying such military force as may at any time be needed in the Navy, by detail from the Army."[5] The Committee unanimously rejected the idea, but the Corps had to fight for its life.

From Appomattox to the sinking of the *Maine*, the nation was at peace for 33 years; and American factories and farms were producing more than the people at home could consume. The nation became an industrial beehive. The push to find new markets overseas intensified and irrevocably enmeshed the United States in the world's economic conflicts and wars. In time, the Marine Corps would become the spearhead of this reaching out.

The quick, easy war with Spain would make the United States an empire, the possessor of colonies and ruler of subject peoples. The nation had stretched its political, economic and even religious interests further and further beyond its shores, and over and over again called on its Navy and Marine Corps when the going got tough. On September 5, 1901, at the Pan-American Exposition in Buffalo, New York, just before he was struck by an assassin's bullet, President William McKinley, an exponent of industrialism and expansion, summed up the change: "Isolation is no longer possible or desirable. . . . God and man have linked the nations together. . . . The period of exclusiveness is past."[6]

When the Civil War ended, the American Navy was the largest in the world, though not the most proficient. During the following years of relative quiet, the fleet became obsolete, its commanders old and reactionary. Not until 1883 did the public begin to support a rebuilding program. Then, over the rest of that decade, it authorized 16 new cruisers and one battleship, *Texas.* In 1890, the largest naval building program up to that time added three larger battleships, *Indiana, Massachusetts* and *Oregon*—the first American warships of more than 10,000 tons. And in the next six years, six more battleships were approved. By 1896, the United States ranked again as a naval power—if not first class, substantial enough to make possible victory at Santiago and Manila Bay.

During these same tranquil years, the Marine Corps languished while the men who loved it despaired and yearned to see its élan and effectiveness restored. In 1874, the Congress again threatened to remove the Marines from sea duty. And as the Corps approached its hundredth anniversary, the *Washington Chronicle* on August 25, 1875, published a letter from Capt. Louis E. Fagan, who had been brevetted at Fort Fisher and who was now stationed at the Marine Barracks in Brooklyn, New York:

> Dear Sir:
>
> I have not read the articles in your paper concerning the Marine Corps, but if they are intended to reform matters in our organization, you will have the sympathy of many officers of the corps who wish a thorough examination to take place; it is *what we want*, what we have prayed for this ten years past, and we thank God that the opportunity is offered for the Marine Corps to stand or fall on its merits. If the Marine Corps is to be a place for self-seekers, drunkards and timeservers, for men who seek their own pleasure and convenience, rather than the country's good, I say the sooner it is wiped out the better; but you will find that there are those in the Corps who

have borne the "brunt of the fight," who have served faithfully, and who are not afraid to have their lives examined. I have . . . often prayed . . . that the Corps refreshed and strengthened, would take its place, where it rightfully belongs, at the very head of the military organizations of the country.[7]

Fagan's earnest letter was reprinted in the *Army and Navy Journal*, which commented on September 11:

The letter of Brevet Captain L. E. Fagan, U.S.M.C., which was republished in our last issue, has created considerable discussion in the Marine Corps, particularly among those of the Corps who have long been conscious of its many and very perceptible shortcomings, and anxious to do something to remedy them, and place the Corps upon a healthier and more reputable basis. Fortunately this class is by no means a small one, or a new one, but being almost entirely without the cooperation of the older officers, from whom better things should be expected, it has made but little headway. . . . A natural and becoming delicacy deters [the dissatisfied officers] from lodging the blame for the decadence of the Corps exactly where it belongs, but the time must come when endurance will cease to be a virtue, and the entire truth must be told.[8]

An emotional pamphlet proposing a reorganization of the Corps was published by 1st Lt. Henry Clay Cochrane, who was widely known for having accompanied President Lincoln to Gettysburg and had been commended for singlehandedly pursuing and recapturing 14 Rebel prisoners who had escaped from the Navy at Mound City, Illinois. Cochrane complained of "a deep seated and wide spread antipathy toward the Marine Corps" and even suggested to "sink forever the despised name, and rebaptize the corps the United States Naval Artillery."[9] He was one of a group of younger Marine officers who met in Norfolk and drew up a recommendation to the Congress "to reduce, reorganize and increase the efficiency of the Marine Corps."[10]

Brig. Gen. Jacob Zeilin retired as Commandant in November 1876, after 45 years of service. He was now 70, and it was more than time to go. President Grant appointed as his successor Col. Charles G. McCawley, the large domed, white-mustached veteran who had been brevetted at Chapultepec and again in the boat attack on Fort Sumter during the Civil War. His father, Capt. James McCawley, had commanded a Marine company in the Florida Indian wars.

During McCawley's 15 years as Commandant, the Corps was limited to some 2,000 officers and men; and he struggled constantly against public disinterest in the military. In its first hundred years, the Marine Corps had never exceeded 3,000 men; now, it drifted through the post-Civil War doldrums. It was plagued with desertions: in 1882, 500 out of the total strength of 1,861 enlisted men; in 1890, 520 out of 1,950 enlisted men. In 1882, McCawley wrote: "I am of the opinion that the principal cause of desertion is the fact that there are not enough men to do the duty required anywhere, and that the constant guard duty, without cessation, becomes onerous and leads to dissatisfaction."[11]

McCawley concentrated on recruiting, improving the training of the enlisted men and commissioning and promoting officers on their professional qualifications. From 1883 until 1897, all 50 new Marine officers were graduates of the Naval Academy. Before 1882 only one graduate, Charles H. Humphrey, had become a Marine; and he had resigned after a year. But of the "Famous Fifty," five became Commandants, 13 more became generals and 15 others made colonel. They dominated the Corps in its most germinal period from 1917 to 1936.

In 1880, McCawley appointed John Philip Sousa as the fourteenth leader of the Marine Band. Sousa's father had been a trombonist with the band and signed on his thirteen-year-old son as an apprentice. The teen-aged violinist and trombonist played in the band for five years; when McCawley called him back as leader, he was twenty-five and a conductor of light opera companies that performed mostly Gilbert and Sullivan works. Sousa led the Marine Band for a dozen years and wrote more than a hundred marches, which sounded the affirmative spirit of the age. One, *Semper Fidelis*, became the official Marine Corps march. He started the nationwide tours that made the band popular and world-famous.

Sousa resigned on July 30, 1892, to organize his own band. He concluded his Marine Corps career with a Saturday night concert on the White House grounds. President Benjamin Harrison attended. It rained that evening, but the people put up their umbrellas and stayed. The *Washington Post* reported, "Meanwhile, the bandsmen, being marines and consequently more or less waterproof, played away in spite of the rain and every selection evoked a round of applause."[12] Halfway through the concert, the rain became a deluge, and Sousa and the band finished up under the White House portico.

The Marine Band had had one well-known director before Sousa. In 1841, the cruiser *Brandywine* stopped at Naples and, needing musicians, signed on twenty-one-year-old Francis M. Scala at $8 a month. Although he spoke no English, by the time the ship reached Norfolk, Scala was the ship's bandleader. The short, stocky clarinetist had been so seasick on the voyage that he left the warship, went to Washington, joined the Marine Band and in less than a year was its leader.

During President John Tyler's Administration, Scala started the White House concerts that became traditional. During President Buchanan's regime, the band doubled in size and played for social functions at the urging of the President's niece and official hostess, Harriet Lane. Of President Lincoln, Scala said, "He was fond of music and was a great friend of the band."[13] Scala finally retired in December 1871, having served as the band's leader for 25 years.

During Scala's leadership, *The Marine's Hymn* came into use. Its origins are murky. There is a tradition that a Marine on duty in Mexico in 1847 wrote the original words to go with an old French melody. Many years later, Sousa wrote that the melody came from the gendarme's song in the opera *Geneviève de Brabant* by Jacques Offenbach.

On his sixty-fourth birthday in January 1891, Commandant McCawley retired in bad health; two months later, he suffered a stroke and died on October 13. After McCawley had been granted sick leave, Col. Clement D. Hebb served as acting commandant from September 4, 1890. When signing documents, he struck out the word "Commandant" and wrote in

"Colonel, Commanding U.S. Marine Corps." Hebb was relieved on February 10, 1891, by Col. Charles Heywood, who was to become one of the Corps' most able Commandants.

Born in Waterville, Maine, Heywood was a large man with sweeping white mustachio. He had been a Marine since 1858, when he was nineteen; he was now fifty-two—the first Commandant from the post-Mexican War generation. He had seen action aboard *Cumberland* during the battle with *Virginia* and aboard *Hartford* at Mobile Bay, and become widely known as "the Boy Colonel." During the violent railroad strike in the depression summer of 1877, he commanded a battalion of Marines that helped preserve order; and in 1885, he led 800 Marines to keep open the railroad across the Isthmus of Panama.

As its Commandant, Heywood worked hard to bring the Corps to a new level of efficiency and public respect. He modernized the training of Marines and established the School of Application. Officer schools and regular examinations for officer promotions were introduced. After the 1870 breechloading, rifled musket was replaced by the Springfield rifle, model 1884, caliber .45, rifle marksmanship was emphasized and systematized under the direction of Maj. Charles H. Lauchheimer. The Corps adopted the rapid-firing, multi-barreled Gatling gun and the Hotchkiss revolving cannon.

Heywood was to lead the Corps through the war with Spain and the Philippine Insurrection. When he took office, the Corps had 75 officers and 2,100 enlisted men; when he retired on October 3, 1903, it had grown to 278 officers and 7,532 men, and Marine Corps posts had been increased from 12 to 21. Heywood was promoted to brigadier general (1899) and major general (1902) by special acts of Congress. He died in Washington in 1915 and is buried in Arlington Cemetery.

Heywood had to continue the battle against those who would eliminate the Corps as outmoded and useless. *Harper's Magazine* (August 1891) reported:

> The new commandant . . . comes to his duties at a critical period in the history of the Marine service. A movement has been started to have the Marines withdrawn from the war vessels, and confined to shore duties at the yards and stations. It is urged that in these days of sailors who have no sails to handle, of seamen who must

primarily be gunners, Jack Tar should become a sea soldier, and stand guard himself, instead of having a Marine stand guard over him. . . . But the Marine Corps, pointing to the majority of aliens in the naval service, declares that this would be an unwise experiment. . . . The better plan, it says, is to augment the Marine Corps, to give it adequate training schools for recruits, perhaps even to enlarge its uses on shipboard, putting it in charge of the secondary batteries—the machine and rapid-fire guns and the torpedoes.[14]

In his first annual report that October, Heywood asked for increased sea duty for the Marines: "While the Marines are very useful in protecting Government property at our different Navy Yards, still, it is as Artillery-men aboard our new floating batteries, that their importance must be felt and acknowledged in the future." He asked that Marines be required to man ships' secondary batteries; thus far, they had been given these battle assignments only at a Navy captain's option.

The struggle for survival never ceased—largely against some younger Navy officers led by Capt. William F. Fullam, USN, who wanted Marines removed from their role as seagoing policemen. Fullam even inspired Navy seamen to petition the Congress to remove Marines from the warships. Many younger Navy officers believed that Marines had no place aboard modern naval ships. It was an emotional battle, and the acrimony was heightened in 1897 when President McKinley selected Capt. Charles L. McCawley, the late Commandant's son, as his naval aide. In his last year as Commandant, Heywood was still fighting off a Navy attempt to replace shipboard Marines with seamen.

This long-running battle over the Marine Corps' role resulted from the revolutionary changeover from sail to steam. Engines increased ships' speed and mobility but cut their range and endurance. They were now chained to stockpiles of coal. To control the seas, warships required bases where they could take on coal. Decades of debate within the armed services were needed to decide who should seize and hold such advanced bases—the Army, the Navy or the Marines.

Steam and new, complex weapons also brought more skilled

seamen onto warships; and the need for Marines to control the crews diminished. And since ships fought at greater distances, Marines had long ago become useless as sharpshooters in the tops or to repel boarders. The Marine Corps had to find new purposes to stay afloat.

This search for a new mission dominated the Corps' history throughout this post-Civil War era. From 1889 to 1894, Congress debated confining the Marines to shore duty and finally rejected the idea. Someone would be needed to land and hold advanced naval bases. Navy Capt. Henry Clay Taylor, then president of the Naval War College, said in 1894 that if seamen were given the landing mission, "I do not doubt that those seamen, and the officers [who] command them, would evolve . . . into a new corps, identical with . . . the present Marines."[15] The life-and-death test for the Marine Corps would come in 1898 at Guantanamo Bay, Cuba.

5
Crises at Home and Abroad

Despite its obscurity and small size in the years after the Civil War, the Corps was repeatedly called upon to maintain law and order at home and to protect Americans abroad.

When a Fourth of July fire destroyed much of Portland, Maine, in 1866, two companies of 117 Marines left the navy yard at Kittery, on an hour's notice, to help the victims and restore order. Massive fires in Boston in 1872 and 1873 brought out Marines stationed there to prevent looting. A number of times, Marines at the Brooklyn Navy Yard led by Lt. Col. John L. Broome helped revenue officers close illegal stills in the section of Brooklyn known as Irishtown; in March 1870, the Marines were stoned in Plymouth Street by disapproving mobs. During the bitter summer of 1877, Heywood and Capt. James Forney took Marine battalions from Washington and Norfolk to put down labor riots along the East Coast and to guard federal arsenals from which, it was feared, the railroad strikers might attempt to arm themselves.

Although this has been called the least active period in the Corps' history, Marines in surprising numbers were summoned to defend the American flag and citizens overseas. In one of many such instances, a force of 138 sailors and 43 Marines from *Hartford* and *Wyoming* under Captain Forney landed in June 1867 on the southern end of Formosa to punish tribesmen who had massacred the shipwrecked crew of the American bark *Rover*. All day, the party pursued the natives through the brush; the enemy fought the Americans guerrilla-style, firing and then retreating into the countryside. Suffering from wounds and sunstroke, the Americans finally returned to their ships. Forney received a major's brevet for gallantry.

296

The next year, small units of Marines landed at Osaka and Yokohama to protect foreigners against hostile Japanese. In July 1882, 70 Marines under Captain Cochrane and young Lt. Littleton W. T. Waller landed at Alexandria, Egypt, to help the British restore order. In 1884, a small Marine detachment participated in the rescue of the Greeley Arctic Expedition lost off Greenland. Another detachment, again under Captain Cochrane, helped try to stop the slaughter of seals in the Bering Sea.

Marines landed in Latin America repeatedly during these years. They joined an international landing force under an Italian admiral at Montevideo, Uruguay, in 1868, to help suppress a revolution. They fought pirates on the Mexican shore, guarded the American consulate at Buenos Aires, and made several landings in Nicaragua to guard American interests. In April 1873 and again that September, a detachment of Marines and sailors went ashore at the city of Panama to protect the trans-isthmus railroad, the open transit of which had been a U.S. responsibility by treaty since 1848.

A major expedition to the isthmus was undertaken in 1885. While the French Canal Company was digging the Panama Canal, the government of Colombia, which ruled the isthmus, collapsed; and Marines went ashore to guard the railroad. Rebels seized the cities of Panama and Colon and the entire rail line. When they burned Colon, 2d Lt. Charles A. Doyen led a Marine detachment ashore from *Galena* to protect the consulate.

Lt. Col. Heywood assembled a battalion of 10 officers and 212 men in New York and sailed for Panama on April 3—within 24 hours after he received his orders from Commandant McCawley. The battalion landed April 12, occupied the railroad buildings and reopened the transit by putting an armed guard of Marines on every train. Under Heywood's command, the Marines, reinforced by a second battalion, guarded the towns along the railroad and the trains themselves. They patrolled the city of Panama. But actual violence was minimal; and in a short time, Colombian troops were able to reoccupy the city. By the end of May, the danger was over. President Grover Cleveland ordered the Marines withdrawn.

6
Weekend War in Korea

On the other side of the globe, Marines saw action in Korea in 1871. French missionaries had been murdered and the French had failed in their attempt at retaliation. On May 19, the United States sent a flotilla of five warships from Nagasaki to the mouth of the Han River, where the crew of an American freighter had been massacred. On June 1, a surveying party on the river in two gunboats was fired upon from a large Korean fort. Two men were wounded. The American ships returned the fire and drove out the fort's defenders.

After waiting 10 days for an apology, Rear Adm. John Rodgers, the commander of the U.S. Asiatic Fleet, prepared a punitive expedition against the Han River forts. Early on Saturday, June 10, a force of 651 men, with 109 Marines commanded by Capt. McLane W. Tilton of the flagship *Colorado,* landed on the river bank near the first fort (a few miles from where Marines would land again in 1950). The men, each carrying 100 rounds and two days' rations, struggled under fire through knee-deep mud to dry ground. Advancing as shock troops, the Marines took the fort, a semicircular redoubt with 54 guns.

On Sunday morning, they occupied the second fort, three miles away, without opposition. Then, the Marines were fired on from a high ridge and stormed it; the Koreans fell back to the next ridge line, and a howitzer was hauled up to disperse them. With the Marines still in the fore, the expedition moved on the final and main fort, which the men called the Citadel.

The Marines worked their way to within 150 yards of the horseshoe-shaped fort before being stopped. When the rest of the landing force came up, Tilton's men charged through heavy fire to a ridge within 120 yards of the fort. Pvt. Dennis Hemahan was killed.

From the ridge, the Marines poured in effective rifle fire, killing more than 40 of the enemy in four minutes. Then, the Marines and sailors made their final assault in small units under covering fire. Close-in fighting broke out all along the line; the Koreans fought to the death. Marines and sailors climbed the walls and stormed the Citadel. Marine Pvt. Hugh Purvis, twenty-five, of *Alaska* was the first to scale the wall and with Cpl. Charles Brown of the flagship tore down the enemy's huge 12-foot-square yellow and black flag in the center of the fort. Irish-born Pvt. James Dougherty killed the Korean commander. They were among five Marines who won the Congressional Medal of Honor in hand-to-hand combat that day. The Americans spiked 182 cannon and threw them into the river. They had three dead and 10 wounded and counted 243 enemy dead.

Back on the flagship after the weekend war, Tilton wrote his wife, Nan: "I am glad to say I am alive still and kicking, although at one time I never expected to see my wife and baby any more, and if it hadn't been that the Coreans [sic] can't shoot true, I never should."[16]

The Americans had hoped to win a treaty that would open Korea as Perry had opened Japan. But the fighting hardly encouraged the Koreans to make such an agreement, and the squadron sailed off on July 3 empty-handed. It would be another decade before a treaty was signed.

A generation later, on July 24, 1894, during the Sino-Japanese War, 22 Marines and 28 sailors from *Baltimore* under Marine Capt. George F. Elliott, an Alabama-born West Pointer, hiked 31 miles from Chemulpo in an 11-hour forced night march to guard the American legation at Seoul. They slogged through submerged rice fields, detouring to avoid a Japanese division, and stayed in the capital a month.

Shortly thereafter, the American minister at Peking asked for a Marine guard to protect the legation there. Elliott and his Marines rushed by steamer and railroad to Tientsin, where Elliott was told that the emperor of China had forbidden foreign troops to enter his capital. Reporting his men to an American warship off Taku, Elliott was ordered to proceed to Peking alone. Because the Chinese army had stopped all trains, Elliott went by horseback, reaching Peking, 80 miles away, in two days. When peace came with a crushing defeat for China, Elliott returned to the coast and took his men back to their ship, now at Nagasaki. They had been ashore nearly six months. Six years later, Marines would fight their way into Peking.

*Marine commanders who landed at Guantanamo Bay,
Cuba, on June 10, 1898: Lt. Col. Robert W. Huntington,
commander of the First Marine Battalion, flanked by 1st
Lt. Herbert L. Draper and Capt. Charles L. McCawley.
Marine Corps Photo, National Archives*

SEMPER FIDELIS

VII
THE
FOUR-MONTH
WAR
WITH SPAIN
1898

The Spanish-American War climaxed the Marines' nineteenth-century adventures. In this brief war, they proved they could seize and hold advanced bases for the coal-powered Navy. The Marines finished the war a giant step closer to their modern amphibious role.

The crucial event began on June 10, 1898, when the First Marine Battalion landed on the eastern side of Guantanamo Bay, Cuba.

The war had started in April. By June, the Navy under Rear Adm. William T. Sampson had bottled up the Spanish Atlantic fleet in Santiago's narrow-necked harbor on Cuba's southeast coast. Guantanamo Bay, 40 miles east of Santiago, was chosen as the Navy's advanced base, and the Marines were ordered to seize and secure it.

On June 5, three warships under Cmdr. Bowman H. McCalla entered the bay and destroyed a blockhouse above Fisherman's Point. On the tenth, 40 Marines from *Oregon* and 20 from *Marblehead* scouted the proposed base and made contact with Cuban insurgents. That afternoon, the Marine battalion arrived from Key West aboard the auxiliary cruiser *Panther* and immediately went ashore in whaleboats and cutters towed by steam launches. Meeting no opposition, four companies of Marines, sweating under a blazing sun, pitched their camp of white tents among the palms on top of the small hill where the blockhouse had stood. They dragged up two three-inch field guns. Their commander, Lt. Col. Robert W. Huntington, an erect, bearded veteran of Reynolds' battalion at Bull Run, named the site above the bay Camp McCalla. Color Sgt. Richard Silvery of C Company raised the American flag for the first time in this war over Cuban soil.

[For the location of places in the Spanish-American war see map No. 5 in the map section.—*Au*.]

The Marines had 24 hours of peace; then, late on the afternoon of the eleventh, the enemy struck, killing Privates William Dumphy and James McColgan, who had been on picket duty. From the dense brush, the Spaniards peppered the Marine camp with Mauser rifle fire. The Marines had been busy housekeeping; some were bathing in the bay below the camp. As the *New York Journal* correspondent described the scene: "Up from the sea came a line of naked men, grabbing their carbines and falling into place as Lt. Col. R. W. Huntington issued his orders, getting a formation in semi-circle behind the brow of the hill, and waiting to see how much force would develop against him."[1] When the Marines opened fire with their new straight-pull Lee rifles, there was no answer; Huntington ordered a charge down the hill. "There was no fun in this for naked men, but they held their places and charged with the others." The Spaniards had fled.

Huntington sent Capt. George F. Elliott and his C Company to find them. Huntington, accompanied by Capt. Charles L. McCawley, the late commandant's son, and Sgt. Maj. Henry Good, also took out a unit. When Huntington's men joined up with Elliott's, the hidden enemy fired on the Marines at short range. They returned the fire but could not pursue the Spaniards through the thick undergrowth.

After midnight, the enemy attacked Camp McCalla from three sides. A wild battle raged in the darkness. One Marine and the battalion's Navy surgeon were killed; two Marines were wounded. When light came, the Marines dug in and cleared fields of fire through the brush. The camp had proved so vulnerable to attack that Huntington moved it to lower ground nearer the bay and made the hill his chief line of defense.

After dark, the battle started again. Sergeant-Major Good was killed. Stephen Crane, whose novel *The Red Badge of Courage* had already brought him fame, accompanied the battalion as a correspondent for *McClure's Magazine* and described this as a night that "strained courage so near the panic point."[2]

To secure their beachhead against the hundreds of Spanish and Cuban troops in the area, the Marines set out to destroy the enemy's source of water, the well at Cuzco, a village by the sea six miles to the east. At 9 A.M. on June 14, C Company, led by Captain Elliott, and D Company, commanded by Capt. William F. Spicer—150 Marines—accompanied by some 50 insurgent

Marines from the North Atlantic Squadron relax in camp at Pensacola, Florida, in 1888. Spicer Street was named for Capt. William F. Spicer, who during the War with Spain landed with the Marines at Guantanamo Bay, Cuba. U.S. Navy Historical Center

Marine Guard aboard the screw steamer Pensacola,
which participated in Farragut's capture of New Orleans.
This photograph was taken some time after the Civil War.
Official U.S. Navy Photo

*Sgt. John H. Quick earned the
Medal of Honor at Guantanamo
Bay, marched with Waller on
Samar and won the Navy Cross for
bringing ammunition to Bouresches
in World War I.*
*Marine Corps Photo, National
Archives*

*Marines of Huntington's battalion
training in Florida before the
invasion of Guantanamo Bay, Cuba,
in the War with Spain.
Museums Branch, USMC*

*Marine Guard of Philadelphia at the American
consulate, Apia, Samoa, in April 1899. The Marines
commanded by 1st Lt. Constantine M. Perkins (white
uniform) fought in a joint American-British landing
force that was repulsed by hostile Samoans.
Museums Branch, USMC*

Marines fighting Filipino insurgents.
Marine Corps Photo, National Archives

Littleton Waller Tazewell Waller
fought in the Boxer Rebellion, led the
disastrous march on Samar, and
battled the Cacos in Haiti. This
full-dress portrait was made during
World War I.
Museums Branch, USMC

U.S. Marines climb the wall of
Peking to help rescue the besieged
legations during the Boxer Rebellion
in 1900.
Brown Brothers

Marines at Vera Cruz, Mexico. Left to
right are Capt. Frederick H. Delano,
Sgt. Maj. John H. Quick, Lt. Col.
Wendell C. Neville, Col. John A.
Lejeune and Maj. Smedley D.
Butler. Quick and Neville won the
Medal of Honor; Butler earned two.
Both Neville and Lejeune were to
become Commandant of the Corps.
Marine Corps Photo, National
Archives

Marines in Nicaragua in 1932 display captured rebels'
skull and crossbones flag.
Marine Corps Photo, National Archives

Capt. Christian F. Schilt earned the
Medal of Honor for making ten
daring flights into Quilali, Nicaragua,
in January 1928 to bring in medicines
and supplies and fly out eighteen
wounded when the Marines were
besieged there.
Museums Branch, USMC

After the death of rebel leader Charlemagne Peralte in October 1919, President Philippe Sudre Dartiguenave of Haiti decorated four Marines: Maj. James J. Meade, Sgt. Herman H. Hanneken, Cpl. William R. Button and H. R. Woods. Museums Branch, USMC

Marines guard forced-labor road gang under the infamous corvee system during the occupation of Haiti. Marine Corps Photo, National Archives

Marines in the Dominican Republic in 1916 fire a 3-inch field piece. Museums Branch, USMC

Capt. Roy S. Geiger, a pioneer
Marine aviator, won the Navy Cross
in France in 1918 and again on
Guadalcanal. As a lieutenant general,
he commanded the Tenth Army on
Okinawa in World War II.
Museums Branch, USMC

Lt. Alfred A. Cunningham was the
first Marine to report for naval flying
training on May 22, 1912, which is
considered the birth date of Marine
Corps aviation. Cunningham led the
1st Marine Aviation Force to France
in 1918 and was the officer in charge
of the Marine Corps' aviation until
December 1920.
Museums Branch, USMC

Cubans under a Colonel Tomas, headed for Cuzco.

Crane described the Marines at that moment in a dispatch published in the *New York World* on June 30:

> Their linen suits and black corded accoutrements made their strong faces very businesslike and soldiery. Contrary to the Cubans, the bronze faces of the Americans were not stolid at all. One could note the prevalence of a curious expression—something dreamy, the symbol of minds striving to tear aside the screen of the future and perhaps expose the ambush of death. It was not fear in the least. It was simply a moment in the lives of the men who have staked themselves and have come to wonder which wins—red or black.[3]

Crane called the Cubans, dressed in white duck given them by the Navy, a "hard-bitten, undersized lot . . . hardy, tireless, uncomplaining peasants."[4] They moved out along a path through the bush and the Marines followed.

The expedition marched silently up a chalky cliff and across tall ridges under a fierce tropic sun for more than an hour. Colonel Tomas was up front, a revolver in one hand, a machete in the other. The main party stayed at the bottom of the ridges, while one C Company platoon moved along the ridge tops. The heat felled several Marines, including Captain Spicer.

Firing broke out as the main body of Marines advanced toward the village. Cuzco, nestled in a horseshoe of hills, was defended by six companies of the Sixth Barcelona Regiment and Cubans, based in a blockhouse.

The Marines scrambled up a razor-backed hill, cutting themselves on bushes and cactus. Marines in brown and Cubans in white intermingled on the hillside. They could not see the enemy. In three minutes, they were at the crest and targets of a hail of Mauser bullets, which, Crane wrote, "sang in the air until one thought that a good hand with a lacrosse stick could have bagged many."[5]

Second Lt. Louis J. Magill took 50 men of C Company to bypass the enemy's position and cut off their escape. The Marines climbed a hill overlooking the well. The Spaniards shot at them from the green underbrush in the valley.

At that moment, the cruiser *Dolphin*, which had accompanied the Marines just offshore, began firing. The ship's officers had misunderstood Elliott's signal, and Magill's Marines were directly in the line of *Dolphin's* shells. The men were forced to dive for cover. Sgt. John H. Quick, a tall, silent native of Charleston, West Virginia, improvised a signal flag from his blue polka-dot handkerchief and a stick, and, with his back to the Spanish fire, coolly wigwagged *Dolphin* to cease firing. Enemy bullets whipped about him, as he stood erect on the ridge-top waving his flag. The enemy concentrated their fire on his lone figure in relief against the sky. To Stephen Crane he seemed nerveless. Crane wrote, "As he swung his clumsy flag to and fro, an end of it once caught on a cactus pillar, and he looked over his shoulder to see what had it. He gave the flag an impatient jerk. He looked annoyed."[6]

Dolphin stopped its shelling, and Quick picked up his rifle. The enemy began to retreat. By 3 P.M., the Marines had destroyed Cuzco's well and a signal station. The Cubans with the Marines chased the Spaniards for a mile and captured 18 prisoners.

The enemy lost 60 dead; only one Marine had been wounded. "The Marines had done their work most admirably," wrote Henry Cabot Lodge in his history of the war; they fought "with the steadiness and marksmanship of experienced bushfighters."[7] Sergeant Quick received the Medal of Honor and became a national hero.

Once Cuzco Well was destroyed, the Marines were no longer harassed. They stayed until after Santiago fell in July and were pulled out of Guantanamo on August 5.

Today on McCalla Hill stands a plaque that reads:

Commemorative
of a
Battalion of United States Marines
Under the command of Lieutenant Colonel
Robert W. Huntington
Which disembarked at this point June 10, 1898:
the first United States armed forces landed
on Cuban soil
and of
Acting Asst. Surgeon John Blair Gibbs, U.S. Navy

Private William Dumphy USMC
Acting Sergeant-Major Henry Good USMC
Private James McColgan USMC
Sergeant Charles H. Smith USMC
Private Goode Tourman USMC
Here killed in action with Spanish troops.

Those weeks at Guantanamo are usually cited as the first appearance of the kind of amphibious landing forces that would dominate the Corps' second century. This landing heralded a new purpose for the Marines evolving out of the nation's need—which supporters called "manifest destiny" and critics labeled "imperialism."

The debate over "American imperialism" was not invented in the middle of the twentieth century. Even before the war with Spain, powerful voices protested against a nation half republic, half empire. This opposition's strength rose and dipped over the years, when the American people were asked, repeatedly, to pay in treasure and blood for the material profits of expansion.

The Spanish-American War, short and one-sided, was rooted in nationalistic muscle-flexing, in commercial expansion as foreign trade grew increasingly important, in a moralistic desire to see the Cuban people freed from Spain, in an interest in a canal to connect the Atlantic and Pacific, and in a deep-grained passion to spread American dreams of freedom and democratic government around the globe. When the war was virtually over, John Hay, then the U.S. ambassador to Great Britain, wrote Theodore Roosevelt that "It has been a splendid little war." In fact, it was bloody, mismanaged, disease-haunted. Only flag-waving euphoria made it seem "splendid."

The trigger for the war was the blowing up of the cruiser *Maine* in Havana harbor. But the sparks were there long before. After 1895, the bitter struggle between the Cubans and their Spanish rulers, led by Governor General Valeriano "Butcher" Weyler, aroused righteous anger in the States. Cuban propaganda was spread and magnified in the sensational, jingoistic American press. American volunteer "filibusters" sailed to fight in the Cuban cause.

And far away, the Filipinos were also rebeling against their Spanish conquerors. Few Americans had their eye on the

Philippines or even knew just where Manila was. But both native revolts on opposite sides of the world made clear to all the vulnerability of the aging Spanish empire.

The pressure for intervention in Cuba seemed to subside after a new government in Madrid replaced Weyler with Gen. Ramon Blanco y Arenas and ordered him to conduct the war on the island more humanely, to aid the virtually starving rural population and to release imprisoned American citizens. But in mid-January 1898, violence broke out in Havana. The U.S. consul, Fitzhugh Lee, an ex-Confederate cavalry commander who had a sympathy for rebellion, asked that the Navy be alerted. The white-painted two-stack armored cruiser *Maine* was sent to Havana on a courtesy call. Its crew was received cordially. A case of sherry was sent to the officers' mess, and the officers were entertained at a bullfight. Everything appeared peaceful.

February 15 was the second night of the carnival season, and Havana's streets were filling with fun-seeking masked celebrants. Out in the harbor, *Maine's* commander, Capt. Charles D. Sigsbee, sat in his cabin writing a letter home. He later remembered:

> At taps, ten minutes after nine o'clock, I laid down my pen to listen to the notes of the bugle, which were singularly beautiful in the oppressive stillness of the night. The marine bugler, Newton, who was rather given to fanciful effects, was evidently doing his best. During his pauses the echoes floated back to the ship with singular distinctness, repeating the strains of the bugle fully and exactly. . . .[8]

Half an hour later, 1st Lt. Albertus W. Catlin, commanding *Maine's* Marine detachment, was looking for a pen among his papers, when suddenly, at 9:40, the ship was rocked by two explosions, the first a crack like a pistol shot and the second a roar that engulfed the cruiser's entire forward section. All the lights went out. First Lt. Catlin groped his way to the deck.

Marine Pvt. William F. Anthony, Captain Sigsbee's orderly and a veteran of 14 years in the Corps, made his way below deck despite the havoc and the danger, met the captain in the smoke-filled companionway and reported that the ship was sinking. When the Navy captain and the Marine private stepped on the deck, *Maine* was already settling in the harbor's mud. One of its stacks lay in the water; the entire bow was gone; water rushed into the hole where the bow had been. Ammunition was exploding overhead. Wounded men littered the black waters. The forward magazines near the crew's quarters had blown up.[9] Among the nearly 250 men killed were 28 Marines, including Bugler C. H. Newton.

Back home, Pvt. Bill Anthony was suddenly a national hero. For his courageous act of plunging into the flaming, explosion-wracked ship to warn his captain, he was promoted to sergeant. But he was a tragic figure with a serious drinking problem. He was retired the following year as a sergeant major and went home to Albany, New York. Quickly forgotten, he was out of work, despondent and drinking. On November 25, 1899, at the age of 46, he committed suicide in New York City's Central Park by taking an overdose of cocaine.

When *Maine* was sunk, the press screamed for vengeance. The Navy appointed a Board of Inquiry, and President McKinley pleaded for patience and calm. The argument seesawed between those who wanted war and those who clung to a hope for peace. Said Speaker of the House Thomas B. Reed, "A war will make a large market for gravestones."[10]

Secretary of the Navy John D. Long left Washington briefly late in February, after *Maine* had been destroyed; and Assistant Secretary Theodore Roosevelt, eager for a fight, cabled Commodore George Dewey, commanding the American squadron at Hong Kong, to get ready to tackle the Spanish fleet. Secretary Long rushed back to town the next morning to bank the fire.

On Monday, March 28, an Associated Press report on the findings of the Board of Inquiry hit the headlines. The Board found that the *Maine* explosion had been caused by a submarine mine. The country was shaken; war was now inevitable. The slogan: "Remember the Maine!"

As war fever climbed, Spain tried futilely to conciliate. But in the United States, the war hawks had the momentum. On April 19, the Congress recognized Cuba's independence from Spain, although promising not to annex the island. On April 20, McKinley sent an ultimatum to Spain and two days later proclaimed a blockade of Cuban ports. On the twenty-third, he called for 125,000 volunteers. Dewey was ordered to proceed with his four gray-painted cruisers and two gunboats to the Philippines and attack the Spanish fleet there. On Monday, April 25, war was formally declared as existing from the twenty-first.

The United States was not ready for war. With *Maine* gone, it possessed only five battleships and two armored cruisers. Five more battleships were under construction, but at least another year would be needed to complete even the first two of these. In a dramatic 68-day dash, *Oregon*, the best of the American fleet, raced 11,000 miles from Puget Sound, through the Strait of Magellan, to Key West. The entire nation cheered its swift progress, but *Oregon's* long passage was a powerful reminder of the need for an isthmian canal.

The Army was in worse shape than the Navy. It was small—28,000 men—although experienced fighting the Indians on the plains. But decades of peace and slow promotions had diluted its best officer talent and entangled the War Department in bureaucratic red tape. With the war, the Regular Army was abruptly enlarged to 61,000, plus the volunteers. It had neither stockpiles of supplies nor trained reserves.

In June 1896, the Marine Corps' authorized strength had been increased by 500 men, to a total of 93 officers and 3,574 enlisted men. But at the war's start, only 77 officers and 2,900 men were in uniform, scattered over 40 ships and 15 shore stations on both coasts. The senior officers were Civil War veterans no longer fit for arduous field duty. Fortunately, an increasing number of the younger officers were graduates of the Naval Academy. Once war was declared, Congress enlarged the Corps on May 4 by another 24 officers and 1,640 enlisted men.

Even before that, Commandant Heywood had given orders on April 16 to assemble men from all East Coast stations as a Marine Battalion to fight in Cuba. A force of 23 officers and 623 enlisted men, chiefly recruits, gathered at the Brooklyn Navy Yard. Lt. Col. Huntington organized them into five companies and an artillery battery with four 3-inch rapid-fire guns. On April 22, Huntington paraded his battalion through Brooklyn and boarded *USS Panther.* A Navy band played *The Girl I Left Behind Me.*

The battalion encamped at Key West, which had quickly become a lawless war boom town jammed with sailors, Marines, civilians. The Marines were kept busy at drill and target practice. Key West was a hellhole of flies and mosquitoes and endless dust; fresh drinking water had to be distilled on the naval ships that filled the harbor. It was a totally inadequate base.

Soon, even Key West was not near enough to the action at Santiago, and the Marine battalion sailed to establish a forward base at Guantanamo Bay to coal and repair the fleet. The Marines spent the summer there (June 10 to August 5) and then stood off Manzanilla while the Navy demanded the Spaniards surrender that port. The Marines actually started into the boats on the morning of August 13 before the Spaniards caved in. The battalion was at Portsmouth, New Hampshire, by August 26. The local citizens gave them a clambake and the YMCA presented each man with a Bible. The First Marine Battalion was the only Marine expeditionary force to serve in the war.

Meanwhile, around the globe, Commodore Dewey had sailed from Hong Kong on April 24 with his squadron. He was 7,000 miles from a source of supplies or ammunition and facilities for ship repairs. At 11:30 P.M. on April 30, the darkened flotilla entered Manila Bay. At daybreak it passed Manila and closed on the enemy fleet at anchor near Cavite. At 5:42, Dewey on the forward bridge of *Olympia* gave his famous order to his executive officer: "You may fire when you are ready, Gridley."

The Americans made five runs past the stationary Spaniards, wreaking havoc and taking hits in return. Fearing his ammunition was running low, at 7:35 Dewey pulled off to count his casualties (none) and let his men breakfast. Then he returned to destroy the rest of the Spanish ships. It was only five days since war had been declared. When word of his victory reached home, Dewey became the nation's idol.

Dewey's ships carried Marines who fought at the guns during the "turkey shoot." On the morning of May 3, 1st Lt. Dion Williams took a detachment from *Baltimore* and occupied the arsenal and dockyards of the Cavite Naval Station, which had been manned by 800 Spanish marines. The Spaniards also surrendered Corregidor Island in the harbor; and the governor of Manila, fearing the destruction of the city, agreed not to fire on the American ships. Although it would be June 30 before the Army began to arrive to occupy the city, Dewey's boldness had made the United States a power in the western Pacific. The cost: seven Americans slightly wounded.

Immediately after his victory, Dewey's position was precarious. His ammunition was depleted; resupply was weeks away. Even communication was difficult; it took a cutter six days to make the round trip to the cable head at Hong Kong. And, most serious of all, there were no troops anywhere around to seize and hold the ground. Dewey cabled Washington: "I control bay completely and can take the city any time, but I have not sufficient men to hold."[11]

As part of Dewey's conquest, on May 19, the exiled Filipino insurgent leader Emilio Aguinaldo was brought back to the islands from Hong Kong to rally the people against the Spaniards. Dewey soon learned the Aguinaldo would not be used by the Americans; he pressed the commodore for a declaration of Philippine independence that was not in Dewey's power to make. On July 2, Aguinaldo declared himself president of a revolutionary republic. Within 17 months, Marines would be fighting the Filipino nationalists.

One other incident that would be meaningful to the Marines in the future: On June 20, the cruiser *Charleston*, escorting troop ships to the Philippines, stopped at Spanish-held Guam with orders to seize the island. *Charleston* fired at ruined Fort Santa Cruz in Apra Harbor, and two Spanish officers came out by boat to apologize for not being able to return the salute. (Perhaps the Americans' aim was not too good.) The Spaniards had not even heard of the war. A force of 16 sailors and 30 Marines under Lt. John Twiggs Myers went ashore to accept the Spanish surrender. The following year, a battalion of Marines garrisoned a naval station there; and Marines stayed on Guam until World War II.

While Dewey waited for troops to occupy Manila, the Army in Cuba landed at Daiquiri, 20 miles east of Santiago, on June 22 and moved on the city. On July 1, the Spaniards fought bravely at El Caney; and the army, including Theodore Roosevelt's well-publicized Rough Riders, made its costly frontal assault (on foot) up San Juan Hill. With its land defenses crumbling, the Spanish fleet on Sunday morning, July 3, dashed out of Santiago harbor. The Spaniards almost made it to the open sea. But the

Navy rallied and in a four-hour running battle destroyed all four Spanish warships. Maj. Robert L. Meade, a nephew of Gen. George Meade, who had commanded the Union Army at Gettysburg, was the senior Marine officer with the squadron. Only one American was killed. Marine Capt. Littleton W. T. Waller was decorated for rescuing survivors from the burning Spanish ships. Santiago surrendered on July 17. Spain was finished as a world power.

Late in July, the Army attacked the south coast of Spanish-held Puerto Rico. On July 27, the Navy anchored off Playa del Ponce, and the next morning 1st Lt. Henry C. Haines and nine Marines came ashore from *Dixie*, raised the Stars and Stripes and mounted at Colt automatic gun atop the customs house. When the Army arrived two hours later, Haines and Naval Cadet G. C. Lodge, the son of powerful Senator Henry Cabot Lodge, went into Ponce itself and released prisoners held at the city hall by the Spaniards. The Puerto Ricans gaily welcomed the Americans. Haines directed Lodge to raise the flag over the city hall, and the mayor turned the city over to the naval cadet.[12]

On Friday, August 12, the United States and Spain suspended hostilities. The little war had lasted less than four months—but it had transformed the United States into a power on the world stage.

On January 1, 1899, a battalion of Marines and detachments from the ships gathered off Havana participated in the official transfer of Cuba to United States control. A party of sailors raised an American flag over the hulk of the sunken *Maine*. And on March 3 the Congress passed the Navy and Marine Corps Personnel Bill, which doubled the size of the Corps to 225 officers and 6,000 enlisted men.

Although its numbers were pitifully small, the Marine Corps proved itself a force in readiness during the Spanish-American War. Huntington's battalion was formed and moved out in quick order. The landing at Guantanamo strengthened the idea of using the Marines to seize and hold advanced bases for the Navy. And the Corps gained a new sense of pride and mission with men such as Anthony and Quick and Elliott. The war made the Corps heroic in the public's eye and pushed it on to a vastly larger role in the great war less than 20 years in the future.

*Company H, First Marine Battalion, on hike from
Olongapo, Philippine Islands, in 1901.
Marine Corps Photo, National Archives*

SEMPER FIDELIS

VIII
ON
IMPERIAL
DUTY
1899-1902

1
The First Colonial War

The road from the Spanish-American War to World War I was amazingly short. The United States had jumped into the competition for empire among the great powers hungrily eyeing the Philippines, China and Latin America. The rivals would soon brutalize each other around the globe.

In the Pacific, control of the Philippine Islands, with their 6.7 million people, was America's most violent problem. The Filipinos wanted independence, and the Philippine Insurrection became the United States' first colonial war overseas.

In 1888, the islands' people had revolted against the power of the Spanish friars who controlled large landholdings and ruled life in the villages. The Filipinos' leader, the highly educated Dr. José Rizal, was arrested by the Spaniards in 1892 and executed at the end of 1896. He became the people's hero and martyr.

After Rizal's arrest, the secret Katipunan movement was organized; and when the Spaniards brutally suppressed it in 1896, its leaders fled to the hills and made war. One of these was Emilio Aguinaldo, whose resistance centered in Cavite Province. Exiled to Hong Kong in December 1897, he was brought back the following May by the Americans to fight the Spaniards. But Aguinaldo refused to accept the replacement of Spanish rule with American.

When President McKinley decided to annex the Philippines, the United States Senate engaged in a historic constitutional debate over whether the federal government had the power to acquire territories and govern them as colonies. Should the United States become an imperial power? Should it rule people not as citizens but as subjects?

[For the location of places in the Philippine Insurrection see map No. 8 in the map section.—*Au.*]

The country was vigorously divided. On February 6, 1899, the Senate ratified by a margin of two votes the Treaty of Paris ending the war with Spain and annexing the Philippines. The decisive fact ensuring the treaty's acceptance was that two days earlier fighting had broken out between Aguinaldo's insurgents and the U.S. Army, and there had been American casualties.

Germany, Japan and Russia had been pressuring the United States for footholds and naval stations in the Philippines. McKinley's decision in favor of annexation was a response to those foreign pressures, as well as to domestic pressures—for a political role on the global stage and for an economic share in Asia's markets. There was even religious pressure behind the decision: to civilize and Christianize the heathen Filipino tribes. Annexation extended American power to the China Sea.

The Filipino establishment welcomed American protection against both Aguinaldo's revolutionists and the foreign powers. The United States proclaimed "benevolent assimilation," but as the Army's numbers grew, racial antagonism made tensions between the Filipinos and the American troops.

Although the U.S. Army held Manila and Cavite, the insurgents controlled most of Luzon. The Army's commander in the islands, Maj. Gen. Elwell S. Otis, stayed at his desk and left the fighting to his divisional commanders, Major Generals Arthur MacArthur and Henry W. Lawton. They had a difficult time against the insurgents and blamed the antiexpansionists and the Democratic press back home for encouraging and prolonging the rebels' resistance. But as one historian has written, in a passage that could almost as well describe a later Asian war:

> The fleet and self-reliant Filipino warrior had only his arms for equipment, and his commissary was a bag of rice. The American expeditions, loaded with impedimenta and tied to a railroad line on a plodding mule train, could repel but never grasp the mobile forces that dissolved like mist in the jungles and steep defiles.[1]

Maj. Gen. Lawton understood the flexibility needed to fight this kind of warfare. He was a daring, energetic officer, a reformed alcoholic, a veteran of the wars against the Apaches on the plains. He had received Geronimo's surrender and now he wanted Aguinaldo's. He was not to get it.

On Washington's Birthday, 1899, with annexation already a fact, the Filipinos in Manila rose against the Americans. The U.S. Army, holding the city and a line around it, numbered 14,000, against an estimated 40,000 insurgents. The Filipinos were better armed with Mauser rifles and smokeless powder captured from the Spaniards. The U.S. soldiers still used black powder ammunition. But they pushed the insurgents northward; and on June 13, the Army also fought a major battle against 3,000 insurgents at the Zapote River south of Manila. The insurgents were defeated with heavy losses; the Americans took 40 casualties.

As the hot summer rainy season began, roads turned into quagmires, rivers rose and plains became swamps. The soldiers suffered from exposure and exhaustion; their clothes and shoes rotted; they were felled by malaria and lived on buffalo meat and rice. But they took control of important towns in central and northern Luzon and pursued Aguinaldo, now the president of the revolutionary republic. The rebels retreated and fought in hit-and-run guerrilla style.

Once the Army volunteers started returning home, the Marine Corps began to arrive in strength. Col. Percival C. Pope, an eccentric, completely bald veteran of the Civil War, arrived at the Cavite Naval Base with the First Battalion on May 23, 1899. And Lt. Col. George F. Elliott brought the Second Battalion of 364 men on September 21. The blue-shirted Marines at Cavite, now numbering 30 officers and 916 men, took charge of the base and the surrounding area and joined in operations with the Army and manned outlying posts.

On Saturday morning, September 23, 250 Marines commanded by Capt. John Twiggs Myers and sailors from the fleet landed at the town of Olongapo on Subic Bay north of Manila to destroy a large rifled Krupp gun. They met heavy Mauser fire from the dug-in enemy but destroyed the gun.

The Marines' most important engagement in this part of the insurrection came when, in early October, with the return of the dry weather, they joined the Army's effort to clear out the rebels from around Cavite. Elliott, as commander of the First Marine Brigade, led 375 Marines organized in six companies against the enemy at Novaleta, a village one and a half miles south of the base of the Cavite Peninsula. The Marines planned to coordinate their attack with two Army columns, one of which would outflank the enemy defenses at Novaleta as the other simultaneously attacked Cavite Viejo. Because the terrain was so difficult, Elliott divided his Marines into two columns, one under big, rugged Capt. Henry C. Haines and the other under Capt. Ben H. Fuller, an Annapolis graduate from Big Rapids, Michigan.

At 10:15 Sunday morning, October 8, the Marines moved out from the outpost at Caridad near the middle of the peninsula. They advanced up a single six-foot-wide road, flanked by impassable flooded rice paddies and bamboo thickets which could conceal a hidden enemy. The gunboat *USS Petrel* supported the Marines by laying down an advance barrage. Soon, the Marines were under fire from the front and both flanks. At Novaleta, the enemy was entrenched in a position from which the Spaniards had earlier been unable to dislodge them. Within 250 yards of the enemy trenches, the Marines caught their breath in old rifle pits behind a small dike. They had already lost 50 men to the heat.

As the Marine buglers sounded the charge, the men broke from the dike in silence. They crossed a stream over a ruined bridge in the face of heavy fire, pushing the enemy back. Elliott went in with "young [Smedley] Butler's company and the first two men were wounded in his command. He did well."[2] The Marines hit the enemy line; it gave way. The wounded Marines in the rear were attacked; 20 men were sent back to save them. Then, the Army struck the enemy flank. The insurgents fled—or hid their arms and pretended to be friendly peasants.

First Lt. David D. Porter, the tall, headstrong son of Commodore David Porter, had been the first into the enemy's position, followed by 1st Lt. George C. Thorpe. Elliott later criticized the two young officers' "bravado" for standing on the parapets exposed to fire, but he cited them for "personal bravery shown after the charge was sounded."[3]

Pvt. B. O'Shea was killed and two of the 11 wounded Marines later died. It was the Corps' first real fight in the insurrection.

In mid-December, Maj. Gen. Lawton was killed on a river bank north of Manila. It had been hoped that he would pacify the islands with a policy of conciliation. But with Lawton dead, Maj. Gen. Otis' command was given the following May, as one historian wrote, to "Arthur MacArthur, the precise, arrogant, dandified general who would finally tranquilize the islands by a policy of relentless subjugation."[4] The war went on.

A third battalion of 340 Marines arrived at Cavite on December 15, led by Maj. Littleton W. T. "Tony" Waller, a small, dashing, egocentric 19-year veteran from Virginia with a fiery mustache. (Years later, Smedley Butler would call Waller "the greatest soldier I have ever known."[5])

As the Army pressed the insurgents northward, more Marines were needed to protect the Cavite naval station and man the outposts surrounding it. In addition, plans were made for a naval base at Subic Bay; and in December, 117 Marines led by Capt. Herbert L. Draper occupied Olongapo there. Over the next months, Draper held elections for local officials, started a school, built roads and issued rations. He led frequent week-long patrols against the insurgents in the interior, burning their villages, especially after they attacked a small water party and killed two Marines. By spring, the Marines had wiped out the rebel force around Subic.

The Marines at Cavite were given increasing responsibilities early in 1900. A thousand .30 caliber Krag-Jörgensen bolt-action rifles arrived as the first replacements for the Lee 6mm. rifles. Two more companies were sent to Subic Bay and a post was established at Port Isabela nearby. The Marines based at Cavite and Olongapo manned 12 detachments and guarded five lighthouses.

But many of their outposts had to be pulled back when half the Marines in the Philippines were suddenly transferred to China that summer. The Boxer Rebellion threatened the foreign legations and settlements at Peking and Tientsin, and the Marines and soldiers in the islands were the most readily available manpower to protect Americans in North China.

To replace them, the Navy asked that another battalion of Marines be sent to Cavite. Maj. William P. Biddle, who had commanded the Marines on *Olympia* in the Battle of Manila Bay, organized a small battalion in Washington, but in the end it was shipped directly to China as the crisis there grew more dangerous. A fifth battalion was organized; it too was sent to China. A sixth battalion was raised, but only two of its companies ever reached the Philippines. China had become the most urgent problem.

2
The Boxers

Late on the evening of May 31, 1900, Capt. John Twiggs Myers, 49 Marines with fixed bayonets and three sailors with a Colt automatic gun led a force of 337 men from six nations up Legation Street in Peking. They had rushed to the Chinese capital to guard their countries' legations.

The city was boiling with the ferment and dangers of the Boxer Rebellion, an uprising based on a fanatical hatred of foreigners and Christians. The Boxers were rampaging violently through the countryside, and the 500 foreigners in Peking were tense and anxious. In response to the diplomats' call for armed help—over the protests of the Empress Dowager Tzü Hsi and her government—the men were assembled from 17 warships gathered off the Taku bar, ferried to the small port of Tangku and sent on by boat and railroad. They detrained at the terminal outside Peking's walls amid a vast and ominous throng of Chinese and marched to their posts, a tiny force to face a mass upheaval.

The Boxer Movement had flared up two years earlier among the peasants of North China. It sought to restore the potency of the Peking regime and to exterminate the foreigners. The feeble Imperial authorities were unable to control the Boxers' violence and in the end openly supported their murdering sweep across the land.

The foreigners had long been asking for trouble. The decaying and corrupt Manchu Dynasty had tried futilely to keep them out of China and had permitted foreign merchants to do business only six months a year in a precisely limited area on the Canton waterfront. The arrangement was unrealistic, given the pressures of Western industrialization. The Opium War between Britain and China and the resulting Treaty of Nanking in 1842

[For the location of places in the Boxer Rebellion see map No. 6 in the map section.—Au.]

had forced China to permit trade at four additional ports and to cede the island of Hong Kong.

This started an avalanche. In the decades that followed, France, Russia, Portugal, Italy, Japan and Germany all occupied, annexed, controlled, grabbed chunks of China. And China's defeat in the Sino-Japanese War of 1894–1895 spurred their greed. Germany seized the port of Kiaochow; Russia demanded and received leases to Port Arthur and Dairen, and France grabbed a naval base and a huge sphere of influence in southern China. By the end of the century, the foreign powers had carved most of China into areas of economic domination. And the avaricious rivalry continued. The Chinese did not have the strength to resist.

The United States was not much involved in this rush to the trough. It had signed the Treaty of Wanghia in 1844, demonstrated its muscle in the battles at the Canton forts in 1856 and established a legation in Peking. But before the annexation of the Philippines planted the American flag across the Pacific, the United States had claimed no sphere of influence; and U.S. national policy, when it was finally crystallized in March 1900, called for an "Open Door" that would increase the potential of American trade with China.

Meanwhile, in September 1898, the Empress Dowager deposed her reform-minded nephew; and her new reactionary leadership decided to stop appeasing the powerful foreigners. As one response, Marine detachments were stationed briefly at Peking and Tientsin.

By the beginning of 1900, the Imperial leaders were prepared to modernize the Chinese army and even to accept the Boxers' support. The anti-foreign spirit had spread. The xenophobic Boxers butchered Christian missionaries and converts, the symbols of the Western presence in the countryside. Claiming magical powers that made them invulnerable in battle, the Boxers fanned the peasants' superstitiousness and aroused hopes that partially offset their despair over the famines of the previous two years. Racing across North China, the Boxers neared Peking in May 1900, terrifying the foreigners there.

The arrival of the legation guards eased their fears. On June 3, German and Austrian sailors strengthened their defenses. But the Boxers continued to burn and kill near the city. Imperial troops fraternized with them. After Boxers cut the railroad, Captain Myers suggested that the legations organize a common defense. On June 8, the Boxers severed the telegraph line, isolating Peking; and on June 9, they destroyed the racetrack three miles outside the city and burned a Christian Chinese in the flames. Myers sent Capt. Newt H. Hall and 20 Marines to protect the people in the Methodist Mission, three-quarters of a mile from the legations. Hall's men dispersed a threatening crowd with bayonets.

Rear Adm. Louis Kempff, who had arrived at Taku in the cruiser *Newark* on May 27, cabled the Navy Department for a battalion of Marines from the Philippines. The diplomats in Peking now called for a relief force; and on June 10, the first of five trains with 2,129 armed men from eight countries left Tientsin by the railroad for Peking. They never got through.

The relief expedition was led by British Vice Adm. Sir Edward Seymour. The first train carried half the British contingent of 915 men and all 112 American sailors and Marines. The Americans were led by Capt. Bowman H. McCalla, USN, the captain of *Newark*, who had put the Marines ashore at Guantanamo exactly two years earlier. At Langfang, halfway to Peking, on the evening of the second day, the expedition found the rails torn up and the station and water tanks wrecked. The weather was intensely hot and drinking water scarce. On the afternoon of the third day at a place called An Ping, Boxers attacked the trains. They were thrown back, leaving some 60 dead; but they attacked again and again, recklessly. The Boxers destroyed the tracks behind the expedition; the fifth train could not shuttle back to Tientsin as planned. The expedition was trapped. Seymour decided to fall back to Yangtsun; and by June 19, burdened with 264 wounded, he gave up any idea of going on to Peking and started down the river to Tientsin, with three Marine sharpshooters at the point. The expedition had failed because Seymour insisted, with a don't-give-up-the-ship stubbornness, on sticking to the railroad.

Meanwhile, on June 13, 1,600 Russian troops arrived at the foreign settlements outside the walls of Tientsin. This was the second most important city in North China, with a million inhabitants, located 30 miles from the coast and 80 miles from Peking. The foreign settlements there were now defended by a force of 2,400. On the night of the fifteenth, much of the French settlement was burned by the Boxers.

The foreign navies off Taku attacked the four forts at the mouth of the Pei Ho River on June 17. Only the Americans stayed out of the battle. Rear Adm. Kempff felt he was not authorized to participate; Washington was suspicious of the other powers' motives. Also, it was a Presidential election year and "imperialism" was an issue of intense controversy.

Nine hundred assault troops captured the Taku forts in heavy fighting. Their victory kept open the route to Vice Adm. Seymour, to Tientsin, and, it was hoped, to Peking. It also brought the Chinese armies into battle against the foreigners. The Chinese bombarded and attacked the Tientsin settlements in strength. The defenders fought from behind barricades of bales of cotton, wool and rice improvised by a twenty-five-year-old American mining engineer named Herbert Hoover.

By the night of June 20, the Tientsin garrison was low on ammunition; and a young British civilian, James Watts, and three Cossacks made a heroic 12-hour ride to Taku for help. A relief column set out. A force of 140 U.S. Marines, the first to arrive from Cavite and led by Major Waller, left Taku in a commandeered railroad train for Tientsin. They were joined by 440 Russian infantrymen and camped 12 miles from the city. Stopped by a blown-out bridge, the column detrained and marched toward Tientsin, fighting from village to village. In one two-hour battle, four Marines were killed and nine wounded; the Marines had to retreat and leave their dead behind. While the Marines and Russians were forced back to their camp of the previous night, the Marines served as rear guard. Lieutenants Smedley D. Butler and A. E. Harding and four enlisted men carried a badly wounded Marine private for six miles. The enlisted men received the Medal of Honor; the two lieutenants were breveted.

Bolstered by a British naval detachment and additional Russian troops, some 2,000 men started out again for Tientsin. With the Marines in the van, they battled their way to the foreign settlements.

After resting 12 hours, the relief force next went to the rescue of Seymour's missing expedition, which had fought down the Pei Ho River and was now holed up eight miles from

Tientsin in the German-built Hsiku Arsenal. "We are going to the relief of our comrades or die trying to reach them," Marine Pvt. James J. Sullivan wrote in his diary.[6] From the arsenal, a squad of British Marines had tried to reach Tientsin; all of them were captured and decapitated. The relief force reached Seymour at noon on June 26, blew up the arsenal and escorted the battered expedition into Tientsin. Private Sullivan wrote, "We were not attacked on our way back having an army of 4,000 men, and we could lick 5 times that number of Chinamen."[7] (Sullivan was to die on the march to Peking.)

Seymour's men carried out 232 wounded, including 28 Americans. They had 62 dead, among them four Americans. The fresh relief force guarded the long, slow-moving column on the retreat. Seymour's decimated expedition was finished as a fighting force. Captain McCalla, who had been wounded three times, turned his men over to Major Waller and returned to his ship.

The Russians at Tientsin now attacked the Chinese and were thrown back. A British naval detachment and 42 U.S. Marines led by 2d Lt. Wade L. Jolly then reinforced them, and together they drove the Chinese from their fortified positions. The tireless Waller wrote of his Marines:

> Our men have marched 97 miles in the five days, fighting all the way. They have lived on about one meal a day for about six days, but have been cheerful and willing always. They have gained the highest praise of all present, and have earned my love and confidence. They are like Falstaff's army in appearance, but with brave hearts and bright weapons. [8]

Five had been killed and eleven wounded.

(On the outside of the envelope of his report which he sent through Cmdr. Frederic M. Wise of *Monocacy,* Waller penned this note: "Captain Wise: Please open and read and add Russian casualties, 2 killed, 9 wounded. I need whisky."[9])

In Peking, back on the morning of June 11, the foreigners had waited at the railroad station for Seymour's expedition, which did not come. That afternoon, the chancellor of the Japanese legation returned to the station alone and was murdered by Chinese troops, who cut out his heart and sent it to their general.

Two days later, the Boxers ranged the city in force, killing Chinese Christian converts and burning and looting foreign stores and churches. Marines went out to the rescue, shooting any Boxers they saw. Captain Myers later wrote:

> It was realized at the time that these rescuing parties served to inflame the Boxer element more deeply against the foreigners, but it was more than flesh and blood could stand to see the terribly burned and lacerated bodies of those who escaped to our lines, and refuse to send aid to their comrades known to be still within the power of the fiendish Boxer hordes.[10]

After the foreign navies seized the Taku forts, the Chinese attacked the Peking legations. On the twentieth, the 55-day siege of Peking began with an assault on the Austrian mission. The German minister, Baron Klemens von Ketteler, was killed. Captain Myers, with 15 Marines and 20 British and Russians, ventured out and escorted in Captain Hall and his Marines, as well as 26 American missionaries, their families and a horde of converts who had taken refuge in the Methodist Mission. By 6 P.M., the isolated Legation Quarter, an area three-quarters of a mile square and now jammed with more than 3,000 people, was under constant attack.

The Marines and the Germans, whose legations were the southernmost, manned a section of the Tartar City Wall, which formed the southern side of the Quarter. It was imperative to prevent the Chinese from dominating the legations from the top of the 45-foot-high wall. On the twenty-fourth, the American Marines and the Germans pushed out from their back-to-back positions atop the wall. They took casualties but secured a section of the wall overseeing the Quarter and built barricades of bricks, stones and beams to hold it. The Chinese put up barricades facing them.

The Marines kept a guard of 15 men on the 40-foot-wide top of the wall, relieving them at night. A half-dozen Marines manned a trench leading to the legation and another seven or eight held a barricade at Legation Street.

The Chinese made their only assault on the wall on the twenty-seventh. They crept out from their barricade, 400 yards from the Marines, and tried to catch them napping in the heat of the afternoon. The Marines waited until the Chinese got within 200 yards and then mowed them down. The survivors fled.

The intensity of the Chinese attacks on the legations increased. On June 28, Captain Hall, under intense fire, temporarily abandoned the position on the wall. By July 3, a quarter of all the foreign military professionals had been killed or wounded. As is so often the case, many of the best men were among the first to fall.

At 3 A.M. that morning, Captain Myers led 14 Marines, 16 Russians and 25 British Marines over the barricade in the most important counteroffensive of the siege. Attacking through the darkness and rain, they shoved back the Chinese and killed many of them in hand-to-hand fighting. Myers was badly wounded in the right leg by a Chinese spear. Two Marines, Privates Albert Turner and Robert E. Thomas (Myers called them "two of the best men in the guard"[11]), and one Russian were killed.

Myers was breveted a major for his heroism; and when a monument to the British Marines was erected outside the Admiralty in London, one bas-relief depicted the American Marine captain leading his men on the Peking wall. Myers, who came from a distinguished military family, was a great-nephew of Maj. Levi Twiggs, USMC, killed at Chapultepec. His father was the quartermaster general of the Confederate Army and after the Civil War had moved to Wiesbaden, Germany, where the future Marine was born. The family came back when the boy was five years old. He graduated from the U.S. Naval Academy and joined the Marine Corps in 1895.

Inside the Legation Quarter, conditions worsened. Sanitation was impossible and the stench was foul. Rice and pony meat were the best of the diet. The trapped foreigners were tortured by torrential rains and heat up to 110 degrees in the shade. The Chinese bombarded the Quarter with cannon and steadily inched their barricades closer and closer. The defenders found an ancient bronze gun, and Gunner's Mate Joseph Mitchell of the U.S. Navy adapted it to fire ammunition made for a Russian 9-pounder that had been left behind at Tientsin. Although it had no sights, "Betsey," as the gun was called, was used effectively at short range.

July 13 was a terrible day. The Japanese, who won unanimous praise for their effective fighting throughout the siege, were pushed back in the northern section. The Germans saved their area with a bayonet charge. The British were severely pressed, and the Americans fought fiercely on the wall. At dusk, two mines exploded under the French Legation; and the Chinese swept in. The French shoved them back out. Five defenders were killed that day and twice that number wounded.

Two nights later, Captain Hall, now in command, and Pvt. Daniel J. Daly of Glen Cove, New York, went to the top of the wall at 9 P.M. to determine where to build a new barricade nearer the Chinese position. When the coolies failed to show up with the necessary sandbags, Hall went down to find them. Daly volunteered to stay. He held the top of the wall alone with his bayoneted rifle all that night.

On the thirteenth, the situation in Tientsin also came to a crisis. The Chinese had been shelling the foreign settlements continually. The old walled Chinese city, now garrisoned by 12,000 Imperial troops and 10,000 Boxers, was shaped like a square; the middle of each side was pierced by a fortified gate, which could be approached only by a causeway. Each causeway was bordered by open field, canals and marshes.

The allies had assembled about 14,000 men, many of them colonial troops from Indochina and India, to attack the walled city. The Japanese would lead the main assault against the South Gate, supported by the Americans, British and French. The Russians were to threaten the city from the rear.

Col. Robert L. Meade, USMC, had arrived at Taku on June 25 from Cavite. A tall, slim, peppery veteran of the Civil War and the war against Spain, he was now fifty-eight. Meade commanded the First Marine Regiment, 451 officers and men, and the United States Ninth Infantry—a total of 1,021 men— brought from the Philippines. They were brigaded with the Second Battalion of the Royal Welch Fusiliers and a British naval force, all led by Brig. Gen. A. R. F. Dorward of the British Army. The general inspired no one's confidence. His attack was badly planned, and by nightfall he would run up 700 casualties.

The causeway was the only way to reach the South Gate, but Dorward extended his men the length of the wall, exposing them to enemy fire they could not return. They were slaughtered. The Japanese came straight up the causeway and took the most casualties. The Americans led by Colonel Meade advanced on the Japanese right across a marshy plain. The Marines, armed with Krag-Jörgensen rifles, struggled through the flooded rice paddies, moving up in rushes of 50 to 75 yards. Chinese batteries and snipers enfiladed the Americans' line and forced them over toward the center of the attack, where they came under heavy fire and suffered severe casualties.

The Marines were in the heart of the action throughout the day-long battle. At the city wall the enemy fire was fierce. The sun was cruel. Cartridges ran low; water became scarce. A bullet struck Capt. Austin R. Davis in the chest, killing him. Capt. Ben H. Fuller, who had arrived at Tientsin only the night before, commanded F Company, an artillery unit that silenced a Chinese gun with its three rapid-fire guns and three Colt automatic guns. (These latter were early machine guns that fired 6mm ammunition.) A Mauser bullet went right through Fuller's hat. Eighteen-year-old 1st Lt. Butler, who had had a huge Marine Corps emblem tattooed on his chest at Cavite, was hit in the right thigh while carrying mortally wounded Private Partridge from the field—the young lieutenant, who had been commissioned at sixteen after lying about his age, would be promoted to captain before his nineteenth birthday. First Lt. Henry Leonard brought Butler to safety. Leonard and Sgt. Clarence E. Sutton also saved 1st Lt. S. D. Hiller, who was badly wounded. Leonard himself was later wounded in the left arm and was rescued by Sgt. J. M. Adams and Cpl. H. C. Adriance. Leonard's arm had to be amputated. (Many years later, when Butler was court-martialed at the end of his career, after earning two Medals of Honor, Henry Leonard, then a civilian lawyer, would defend him.) The Americans, with five Marines dead and 11 wounded, were finally pinned down and withdrew after dark.

At 3 A.M. on July 14, the Japanese blew up the South Gate; and there was a rush through the hole. By sunup, Tientsin was taken. Foreign flags flew from its walls and foreign soldiers looted the city. Meade was breveted a brigadier general.

The allies built up their forces at Tientsin to fight through to Peking. But their international army was wracked by imperialistic rivalries that delayed their setting out.

The Americans were reinforced by another Marine battalion, the Fourteenth Infantry and a battery of light artillery.

Their force, now totaling more than 2,000 men, was commanded by Maj. Gen. Adna R. Chaffee, USA, a veteran of the Indian fighting.

Maj. William P. Biddle took over from Meade, who was invalided home. The Marine regiment now had 29 officers and 453 enlisted men. Waller commanded the first battalion of Marines; Capt. Franklin J. Moses, the second battalion, and Fuller, F Company of artillery.

At dawn on August 4, the first units of the International Relief Force, about 17,000 strong (figures disagree), marched out of Tientsin for Peking. Lt. Wirt McCreary, USMC, was put in charge of 30 junks carrying the Americans' supplies. Out of an old blue flannel shirt he created an admiral's flag. which gave him the right of way on the river. The Marines hiked in the rear of the column, missing most of the action and excitement, trudging on hour after hour in the heat and dust. The men cursed.

They followed the river, fought a couple of skirmishes and reached Yangtsun, 25 miles on their way, in 36 hours. There, the Americans and British led the attack.

First Lt. Frederic M. Wise (Navy Commander Wise's son) in Dunlap's company wrote years later:

> Word came back that we were to drive a heavy force of Chinese out of some earthworks far over to our right.
>
> We stood there with mouths and throats gritty with dust; without a drop of water in our canteens and no chance to get any. Then when it seemed we had stood there for hours that afternoon, the orders came to deploy to our right and attack.
>
> The plain in front of us was a furnace. Dust rose in thick clouds. There was no air to breathe. That heavy heat and dust left us choking.
>
> As we started forward there was a crash of sound at our rear. Our own artillery, firing over our heads, was covering our advance.
>
> We advanced a thousand yards. Down on us, every step of the way, beat the blazing sun, heavier every second.
>
> Another thousand yards. My men began to stagger

again. They were taut and game, but all in. Here one turned ghastly white. There one dropped dead from heat. More and more men were staggering. . . .

Another man dropped dead from heat. Chinese bullets were whizzing over our heads. They were shooting high, as usual. . . . We stopped, fired, advanced, again and again.

Now we were close to it. Behind the earthworks the Chinese were milling. We went on. We could see them begin to break. . . .

Then we were on the earthworks. Over them. Behind them.

They were empty. The Chinese, every man for himself, were vanishing rapidly amid the tombs in the dust of that endless plain.

Men and officers collapsed in the shadow of those earthworks. We couldn't have made another hundred yards to save our lives.[12]

The battle and the intense heat cost the Marines two wounded in action and two dead of heat prostration.

After resting at Yangtsun, the American, British, Japanese and Russian detachments, some 14,000 men, set out again at dawn on the 8th. The march was grueling in the heat of the treeless plain. For days, they plowed through steaming fields of ten-foot-high grain. Smedley Butler wrote: "Nearly fifty per cent of our men fell behind during the way, overcome by the sun.—In the cool of the night they would catch up with us and start on again next morning."[13]

The bond of friendship between the American Marines and the Royal Welch Fusiliers—begun at the walls of Tientsin—was welded during the ordeal of the march. Years later, the First Marine Battalion asked John Philip Sousa to write a march to honor its British comrades in China. *The Royal Welch Fusiliers* was first played at the Gridiron Club dinner in Washington on April 26, 1930; present was President Hoover, who had been at Tientsin.

The situation in Peking had grown more and more desperate. The legations were under perpetual attack. The last of the ponies had been eaten; trees were stripped of bark and stray dogs killed for food. The small children of the Chinese converts were dying. (Ironically, there was a superabundance of champagne, which had been stocked by two stores in the enclave.)

The Chinese armies were now in disarray, fleeing before the invading relief force. Several Chinese commanders committed suicide. On August 12, the allies took Tungchow, a rich, walled city 14 miles from Peking, and looted it. When reconnaissance found no resistance between Tungchow and Peking, the Russians' general suggested that the expedition rest three miles from the capital and then launch a coordinated attack at dawn on the fifteenth.

As the relief force approached, the Chinese in Peking tried to overwhelm the legations' defenders. The fighting reached a climax. The Chinese brought up a new 2-inch Krupp gun that did great damage before it was put out of action by the defenders' two machine guns.

The relief force planned to advance in four parallel columns against Peking's eastern wall. But the Russians jumped off at midnight on the thirteenth and captured the Tung Pien gate (the Americans' designated objective) before sunrise. The other nations' forces moved up. The Americans, including two companies of Marines, scaled the wall south of the Tung Pien to stop sniping and relieve the pressure on the Russians, who could not advance beyond the gate. First Lt. Butler was wounded in the chest but saved by a button on his blouse; and two privates were hit. Pvt. Dan Daly earned his first Medal of Honor.

The British Indian troops advanced most quickly without opposition and were signaled by semaphore to enter the Legation Quarter through the Water Gate, a giant seven-foot sewer tunnel. Inside the enclave, Myers' Marines cleared obstructions for them. American Marines and Russian sailors on the wall above rushed the Chinese, routed them and raised the flag over the city gate. The British emerged into Canal Street at 2:30 P.M.; the thirsty soldiers were greeted with bottles of champagne. Maj. Gen. Chaffee reached the legations two hours later. The siege was over. In the Quarter, 66 foreigners were dead, 150 wounded.

At 7 A.M. the next day, Chaffee ordered an assault on the Imperial City in the center of the Tartar City. Marines led one of the attacking columns. But Chaffee called off the attack just short of the inner city at the insistence of the Russians and the

French. Fifteen men died in this meaningless fight. The Empress Dowager and her court had fled; the allies drove out the Chinese troops and plundered the city.

In August, the British landed at Shanghai; the Russians extended their hold on Manchuria, and Japanese marines landed at Amoy opposite Formosa. The intense competition for the potentially rich Chinese market went on. The Anglo-Japanese Alliance and the Russo-Japanese War of 1904 brought Japan to new and fateful power in East Asia. But the United States returned its attention and manpower to its most festering problem: the Philippine Insurrection.

The Marines remained in Peking until September 28; on October 11, they sailed back to the Philippines. An unusually large number of enlisted Marines—33—was awarded the Medal of Honor for bravery in China. Captain Hall had a less happy fate; it took a Court of Inquiry to clear his name of charges of cowardice for abandoning the barricades on June 28. The Court at Cavite declared it "an error of judgment."[14]

Of the small detachment in Peking, seven Marines had been killed (six of them on the wall) and ten wounded. The seven were buried near the chapel of the Russian Legation; later, their bodies were sent home.

And the United States was now entangled in Asian rivalries that would enmesh all Americans in the generations ahead.

Far to the south, the Marine detachment from *Philadelphia* fought in the Samoa Islands. The cruiser's landing party of Marines and sailors went ashore near Apia on April 1, 1899, with a British force to intervene in a tribal war. The 20 U.S. Marines were commanded by 1st Lt. Constantine M. Perkins. As the 62 British Marines and sailors and 56 Americans moved inland, natives attacked their flank and rear. Four U.S. Marines made a stand when the party began to retreat. Four Americans were killed and five, including Marine Pvt. Henry L. Hulbert, were wounded. English-born Hulbert, Sgt. Bruno A. Forsterer and Sgt. Michael J. McNally received the Medal of Honor for covering the retreat. During World War I, Hulbert would earn the Navy Cross at Belleau Wood and die in action at Blanc Mont at the age of fifty one.

3
Samar

By the time the First Marine Regiment returned from China in October 1900, the situation in the Philippines had hardened. In June, Maj. Gen. MacArthur had instituted a six-month amnesty in an effort to defuse the insurrection; if it failed, he was prepared to get tough. The insurgents rejected the amnesty, in part hoping that the Democrats, who opposed annexation, would be victorious in the American elections that November. But McKinley won and MacArthur got tough.

On September 1, the Taft Commission had taken over the legislative power in the islands and was trying to incorporate Filipinos into government on the local and regional levels. Judge William Howard Taft regarded the rebels as outlaws and their cause "a conspiracy of murder and assassination."[15]

The return of the men from China lifted Marine Corps strength in the islands to 1,678. The Marines were organized as a brigade, with two regiments of two battalions each, plus a battalion with the fleet and two companies of artillery. The First Regiment went to Olongapo on Subic Bay and the Second and brigade headquarters were at Cavite. The Marines' prime assignments were to guard naval bases and administer local military government.

After Aguinaldo was captured in March 1901 and took an oath of allegiance to the United States, the spirit quickly went out of the insurgency. Military government ended on July 4, 1901; and Judge Taft became the Philippines' Civil Governor. But the fighting continued; and in the following year of guerrilla war, the Marine Corps met victory and disaster.

On September 28, 1901—just two weeks after Theodore

[For the location of places in the Philippine Insurrection see map No. 8 in the map section.—Au.]

Roosevelt succeeded the assassinated McKinley in the Presidency—at 6:45 in the morning at Balangiga on the southern end of the island of Samar, 450 bolo-wielding Filipinos attacked the garrison of the U.S. Ninth Infantry's C Company while the men were breakfasting in the mess tents. Forty-eight soldiers were killed; of the 28 survivors, 13 were wounded. The rebels got away with most of the company's rifles and 28,000 rounds of ammunition.

The Americans wanted revenge. Hardbitten, stubby Major "Tony" Waller was sent to Samar with a Marine battalion of 14 officers and 300 enlisted men. The Marines had fought alongside the Ninth Infantry at Tientsin and Peking. On October 24, Waller disembarked his headquarters and two companies at Basey on the west coast of Samar. Capt. David D. Porter took the rest of the men south to Balangiga. Waller's battalion came under the command of Brig. Gen. Jacob ("Hellroaring Jake") Smith, USA, headquartered across the straits at Tacloban, Leyte.

Brig. Gen. Smith instructed Waller and Porter to send out punitive expeditions. Waller later said that Smith ordered him to take no prisoners over the age of 10 and make the interior of Samar "a howling wilderness." The Marines conducted daily combat patrols and made a number of landings from the sea. They tracked down rebel bands and recovered equipment that had belonged to the massacred C Company. They burned a village that had supplied the rebels with rice. Marine patrols were fired on, but the enemy always faded into the jungle.

Under persistent pressure from the Marines, the rebels concentrated their forces upriver from Basey at the Sohoton Cliffs, volcanic formations rising 200 feet almost straight up from the river. There, they had prepared fortresslike caves and stored supplies. Waller went after them. On November 15, he took out a force in two columns, one led by Captain Porter, twenty-four, and the other by Capt. Hiram I. Bearss, a fearless, energetic twenty-six-year-old Hoosier. Waller wrote: ". . . the second column, fifty men under Captain Bearss, in accordance with my orders, destroyed all villages and houses, burning in all, one hundred and sixty five."[16] Waller followed the two columns by boat. On the night of the sixteenth, the two columns met on the river's left bank below the cliffs.

The men breakfasted on black coffee, hardtack "and plenty

of beans" and then found a trail and followed it. It was booby-trapped with pits and poisoned spears and several guns made of bamboo. Acting Cpl. Harry Glenn of H Company was on point when he came upon a bamboo gun that commanded the trail, its fuse burning. He rushed forward and pulled out the fuse. Coming over the crest of the cliff, the Marines found the enemy gone; but fires were still smoldering and food cooking. Across the river on the opposite cliffs 150 yards away, they saw two camps where Filipinos were busy cooking and cutting bamboo. Quietly, Porter brought up his men and a Colt automatic gun. On a signal, they opened fire with every weapon, scattering the enemy and killing about 30.

Without waiting for Waller's detachment to come up the river, the Marines scrambled down the cliff, crossed in two dugout canoes and scaled the cliffs on rickety bamboo ladders. The enemy fired two volleys at them and vanished. The Marines destroyed the rebel camp. They found tons of rocks on platforms suspended over the river, ready to be dropped on any approaching boats. It would have been impossible for Waller to advance up the river before the cliffs were taken.

Waller commended Porter and Bearss and, among others, Gunnery Sgt. Quick and Corporal Glenn for conspicuous conduct. He wrote: "Glenn risked his life to pull out the fuse of the bamboo gun. Sergeant Quick now holds the medal of honor for Guantanamo. I do not believe there is anything too good for him."[17] Years later, Porter and Bearss were awarded the Medal of Honor for this action.

On December 8, Waller set out on an expedition that became one of the most terrible and dramatic disasters in Marine Corps history. It was an ordeal not against the insurgents but against the jungle.

The Army wanted to map routes to string telegraph wire between the strongpoints in Southern Samar: from Basey west coast to Balangiga on the south coast, and from Basey across the island to Lanang on the east coast. And Waller himself had his own ambitions. As he wrote to the Commandant after the affair was over:

> Remembering the general's [Brig. Gen. Smith] several talks on the subject and his evident desire to know the

terrain and run wires across, coupled with my own desire for some further knowledge of the people and the nature of this heretofore impenetrable country, I decided to make the trial with 50 men and the necessary carriers.[18]

With Waller went Captains Porter and Bearss, 1st Lt. Alexander S. Williams and 2d Lt. Frank Halford, 50 Marines, 2d Lt. C. DeW. Lyles and a few soldiers of the Seventh Infantry, two native scouts and 33 native carriers. Capt. Robert H. Dunlap, twenty-one years of age, was left in charge at Basey with instructions to prepare a supply camp and to meet Waller's expedition.

The first leg of the journey, from Basey to Balangiga, took four days. Waller led a column along the coast; Bearss headed a second one that followed a parallel route two miles inland. Waller's men had to wade rivers up to their necks; Bearss' captured a few rebels. On the third day, the reunited columns were fired on. When they reached Balangiga, Waller sent a detachment back to that spot; and 15 natives were killed and two tons of rice destroyed.

After going around to Lanang by boat, Waller and his force started up the Lanang River on December 28. He intended to cross the island westward, directly to Basey. By the second day, rapids forced them to abandon the boats, which the soldiers took back to Lanang.

The Marines started climbing into the jungle-covered mountains. They had to cross and recross the meandering river; for every 12 miles hiked, they figured they advanced only 4 or 5 toward their objective. The going was incredibly difficult; the men crawled over huge logs, cut through vines and undergrowth. The rain was incessant, the mountain nights, cold. The men broke out with fever and sores from the wetness, leeches and thorns. Finding little to eat along the way, they cut their rations in half. Then the trail disappeared, and the river suddenly turned and flowed back to the east. By now, the men were down to one piece of raw bacon each. Everything was too wet to make fires. The party came to an exhausted halt.

Recognizing the dangers if they stalled in the rain-drenched jungle, Waller decided to press ahead with 2d Lt. Halford, a former college athlete, and the 13 strongest men; meet Dunlap as planned; and send back help for the rest. Waller's account says this was January 3; Porter's says January 1. One day probably seemed like another in their agony. Porter, Bearss and Williams stayed with the main party, which was to rest and follow as rapidly as it could the trail Waller would mark.

Struggling forward, Waller's detachment found a clearing with bananas, young coconut palms and sweet potatoes. The men ate and regained some strength. Waller sent back a message telling Porter that he had decided he could not go on and would return to the main party. He instructed Porter to build rafts so that the entire force could float down the river back to Lanang.

Porter, who had been following Waller's trail, now halted and started building rafts. The men could not find any wood strong enough to float with a full load. Bearss wanted to report this to Waller; and with Porter's agreement, he set off with Corporal Murphy and a Filipino guide. They found Waller at the clearing and told him the raft idea would not work. Waller decided to leave a note for Porter on a pole in the trail and to plunge on westward. Communication between the two groups was never closed; that gap would be fatal.

When Porter had not heard from Bearss by midafternoon, he sent out a native bearer, who returned without having found Waller or Bearss. Porter and Williams tried to figure out what Waller was doing. Their men, now feverish and crippled, were down to a few cans of bacon and one ration of coffee. The officers decided that the only thing to do was to try to get back to Lanang.

At 8:30 A.M. on January 3, Porter took Gunnery Sgt. Quick, six Marines and six Filipinos and started for Lanang. Williams was to stay with the rest of the men, wait for Waller a reasonable time and then follow Porter. Porter left Waller a note in a tin can on a tree and blazed the tree to attract his attention.

Meanwhile, Waller was trudging westward through the perpetual rain. He found another clearing where his men could bathe and eat. They climbed into the mountains, crossing several rivers. And then near a large river, they luckily came upon five Filipinos. Waller explained to them that he needed a guide to Basey. A man and a twelve-year-old boy knew the way. On the fifth, they started out over trails and across two rivers; and then, with another stroke of good luck, they found Captain

Dunlap coming up to establish his supply camp. The exhausted men were put in a cutter and arrived at Basey on the 6th.

Waller wrote:

> My heart bled for these men when I looked at them. Most of them had no shoes, cut, torn, bruised and dilapidated they had marched without murmur for twenty-nine days, and having accomplished what no white troops had done before, they thought not of it but of each other. They spoke of me, my age [forty-five], and to them well known injury to my foot and they wondered how I had stood it.[19]

Waller went back and for nine days searched the jungle for signs of Porter. Finally, on the seventeenth, sick with fever, Waller returned to Basey.

Porter had been struggling back to Lanang. The return trip was worse than the march out. The men were without food. Porter later reported: "Words are inadequate to describe the sufferings and hardships endured, resulting from the lack of food, constant downpour of rain, floods and sore feet. The men's feet were like pieces of raw beef and their bodies covered with sores caused by being constantly wet and the chafing of belts and clothes."[20] The rains raised the rivers, by 15 feet at one point, making crossing impossible. At a potato patch a mile from where they had abandoned their boats at the beginning of the journey, they left four men who were too weak to go on.

Porter finally reached Lanang on the evening of the eleventh. Five days later, an Army relief party found the four men Porter had left behind.

Williams, with the 31 weakest Marines and 30 Filipinos, was having the toughest time. He knew that if he stayed still the men would starve. The twenty-four-year-old lieutenant slowly followed Porter's path. The men were sick, many unable to move on their own. One by one, those had to be left along the trail to die.

It had rained steadily for 18 days. They had no food except roots and a few sweet potatoes. The Filipinos, in better shape, carried the rifles and built shelters and found food for themselves. At one point, three native bearers tried to kill Williams with his own pistol but could not make it work. One native struck Williams repeatedly with a bolo; Marines protected him with sticks. The other bearers and a trusted scout named Slim stood by and watched the struggle.

By the time an Army relief party found them on the seventeenth, 18 of the Marines had to be carried out on stretchers. Nine were missing; they had gone insane or had died in the jungle.

The starving survivors were strung out along the trail for more than a mile. They were taken directly to Tacloban for medical care. Waller estimated that the men had hiked 190 torturous miles.

Events now moved swiftly to another tragic climax. Waller was ill with a fever at Basey. On January 10, he ordered 1st Lt. John H. A. Day to have a Filipino, confessed to have come into town as a rebel spy, shot.

On the twentieth, Gunnery Sgt. Quick arrived from Tacloban with a message from Porter to Waller recommending that the natives who had been mutinous on the march be executed for attacking Williams and refusing to help the desperate Marines. Porter later reported: "From my conversation with Lt. Williams U.S.M.C. and most of the men . . . these natives should have been shot at the time to insure safety, but the men were so weak that they could hardly handle their rifles."[21]

When Quick reported to Waller in his sickbed, Waller asked the sergeant-hero what he thought about Porter's recommendation. Quick is said to have replied, "I would shoot them all down like mad dogs."[22] Waller called in Dunlap and Day; they concurred in the execution plan, so Waller ordered Day to organize a firing squad.

Waller also accused a native runner, Victor, then in the guardhouse, of having tried to steal his bolo while he slept on the march. The Filipino stood before the major in silence. Waller ordered Day to have him shot.

Twenty minutes later, Victor was executed in the middle of the street, and his body was left lying there as a warning. Then, Day ordered nine other Filipinos who had been on the march executed. Day refused to order Slim shot; he had been a policeman for Day in Basey before the march. On Waller's order, Slim was killed by two Marines.

On the twenty-second, Waller notified Brig. Gen. Smith: "It

became necessary to expend eleven prisoners. Ten who were implemented [sic] in the attack on Lt. Williams and one who plotted against me."[23]

On February 29, Waller returned to Cavite and learned that Maj. Gen. Chaffee had charged him with the murder of the 11 Filipinos. The newspapers in the United States were calling Waller "The Butcher of Samar"; and Secretary of War Elihu Root and Gen. Nelson A. Miles, the commanding general of the Army, had ordered a general court-martial. It was an election year, and American harshness in suppressing the Philippine Insurrection was an important campaign issue.

The military court convened in Manila on March 17 to try Waller and Day for murder in violation of the 58th Article of War. On the court were seven Army officers and six Marine officers, including Col. James Forney and Maj. William Biddle. Because Waller was already being mentioned as a possible successor to Heywood as Commandant, he expressed concern about Marine officer rivalry on the court. His defense lawyer was Maj. Edwin F. Glenn, USA, who himself was charged with using the "water cure" for interrogations, torturing the town president of Ibarras, Panay, and burning the town.

The trial brought out that on October 23, Waller had issued an order, saying "Place no confidence in the natives and punish treachery with death. . . . We have also to avenge our late comrades in North China, the murdered men of the Ninth U.S. Infantry."[24]

Waller asserted that Brig. Gen. Smith had sent him a handwritten note saying: "The interior of Samar must be made a howling wilderness." On the stand, Smith denied that he had told Waller to kill and burn and take no prisoners.

Some saw racial implications in the way the Filipinos had been so summarily disposed of. Many Americans in the Philippines were accustomed to calling the natives "Googoos" or "niggers." And back home, political leaders repeatedly spoke of the Filipinos as "an inferior race"; Governor Taft himself referred to them as "little brown brothers."

On the next to the last day of his 18-day trial, Waller gave the court a statement in his own defense, saying: "As the representative officer responsible for the safety and welfare of my men, after investigation and from the investigation I had, considering the situation from all points, I ordered the eleven men shot. I honestly thought I was right then, I believe now that I was right."[25]

The court by a vote of 11 to 2 swiftly acquitted Waller. Chaffee disapproved the acquittal but let the verdict stand. First Lt. Day was also tried and acquitted. Brig. Gen. Smith was later tried and convicted and was retired by President Theodore Roosevelt. Later still, the Judge Advocate General of the War Department decided that the Army-run court in Manila had not had jurisdiction to try Waller and declared its verdict null and void.

The ugly affair damaged Waller's career. Both in 1910 and 1914, he was a candidate for Commandant but was never selected. He went on to serve in Panama, Cuba and Haiti and retired in 1920 as a major general. His was a distinguished Marine Corps family; two sons served as Marines in both World Wars, Littleton, Jr., winning the Navy Cross in France, and a grandson was twice wounded with the 1st Marine Division in Korea.

Waller's battalion returned to Cavite from Samar on March 2, 1902. The following year, most of the Marines in the Philippines were shifted to Olongapo. Over the years, their number was reduced; and the brigade was finally disbanded in 1914. But for years afterward, it was a tradition in the Corps to greet any Marine who had shared the hardships of the march on Samar with the command: "Stand, gentlemen! He served on Samar."

At Ocotal, Nicaragua, in 1928, a company of mounted Marines form in front of the house where rebels led by Augusto Sandino surrounded the Marine garrison in July 1927. Museums Branch, USMC

IX
IMPERIALISM
IN THE
CARIBBEAN
1901-1934

SEMPER FIDELIS

1
The Caribbean Interventions

The Marines were the cutting edge of American imperialism in the Caribbean. U.S. intervention there climaxed between the War with Spain and the beginning of the Good Neighbor Policy in the 1930s. During these three decades much of the Marine Corps served in the Caribbean as an essential weapon of American foreign policy.

This policy had four goals: (1) to control the sea-lanes between the United States and the Panama Canal; (2) to keep other foreign powers—especially the newly muscular Germany—out of the Caribbean; (3) to support American investors in these underdeveloped agricultural countries—what came to be called "Dollar Diplomacy"; and (4) to establish and maintain the local political stability that these strategic and economic purposes required.

The Marines enforced United States policy in a series of "Banana Wars." They extended American power southward, licensed by President Theodore Roosevelt's 1904 corollary to the Monroe Doctrine, in which he proclaimed the United States' unilateral right to intervene in the Western Hemisphere. The Marines kept law and order, suppressed revolts against governments that accepted American aims and prevented the coming to power of independent-minded leaders. The Marines protected American lives, interests and property. They developed public works, education and medical care to help create social stability and economic viability. When ordered to, the Marines went in and supported "our people" and squashed anti-U.S. nationalists. As Maj. Gen. Smedley Butler put it, "Marines are given orders, and they go."[1]

Many who have written about this high-handed chapter in

[For the location of places in the Caribbean see map No. 5 in the map section.—*Au.*]

347

American history have called the Marines' opponents "bandits." Certainly, many of the thousands killed by the Marines were truly bandits; but often they were peasants fighting to overthrow their governments, whether good or bad, or throw out the American occupiers. In general, they can most fairly be called "rebels," because they opposed the forces in power—both their own countrymen and United States Marines.

During the first three decades of the twentieth century, the United States became a capital-exporting nation to the Caribbean. American financiers built railroads; the United Fruit Company grew to gigantic proportions; mining interests and banks moved in; and sugar plantations were concentrated under American control.

This powerful economic presence spurred the development of some of these small nations; it tended to raise wages; it generated taxes, and it improved communications. But all too frequently, it corrupted public officials, dominated governments for its own benefit, increased dependence on single-crop agriculture and suppressed social reforms.

There was hardly a moment in the first third of this century when U.S. Marines were not ashore on some other nation's territory in the Caribbean. They landed in Panama, Cuba and Mexico; and they made three major interventions: Nicaragua (1912–1913 and 1926–1933); Haiti (1915–1934); and the Dominican Republic (1916–1924). Said one respected historian, "In all three interventions, [the United States] called the tune, and in in all three cases it maintained its troops on foreign soil against the will of the inhabitants of the countries concerned."[2]

If the United States had not used its Marines to ensure law and order and exclude other powers, the Caribbean might have become studded with European naval bases and economic rivalries. But the price the United States paid for its interventions was heavy; they brewed hatreds and nationalist movements that at best insisted on American hands-off and at worst turned eventually to the United States' modern-day rivals for world power.

Sumner Welles, an exceptionally astute American diplomat in Latin America, said of the "constant interference and even . . . armed intervention" in the Caribbean: "No aspect of our earlier inter-American policy has done more harm than this to the welfare of the entire hemisphere."[3]

2
Securing the Canal—Panama

The Marine Corps played a critical role in the complex maneuvering by which the United States built and dominated the Panama Canal.

Marines went ashore on the Isthmus of Panama—then part of Colombia—late in 1901, when Colombian officials refused to run the trains across the isthmus without American protection. Marines had landed there to protect American interests repeatedly since 1860. This time, 245 Marines landed at Panama City on the Pacific coast; and a smaller force landed at Colon on the Caribbean. They served as train guards while Colombian troops and Panamanian Liberals skirmished.

On September 22, 1902, Lt. Col. Benjamin R. Russell arrived at Colon with a Marine battalion of 342 men. While one company stayed in Colon, the remainder went to Panama City, the center of the disturbance. They guarded the trains and managed to keep the peace; and after the Liberals laid down their arms and the Colombians took over the trains, they reembarked on November 17.

Meanwhile, in Washington, the government was encouraging—and New York business interests were financing—the Panamanians to revolt against Colombia. The government of Colombia refused to ratify the treaty that would turn over the French canal-building concession to the Americans. With "remarkable split-second timing,"[4] the cruiser *Nashville* arrived at Colon on November 2, 1903, and a Panamanian revolution started in Panama City. The next morning, 4,000 Colombian troops arrived at Colon by sea. *Nashville's* captain, Cmdr. John Hubbard, refused to let them ride the trains to put down the revolution in Panama City. Hubbard twice sent ashore a landing force and finally persuaded the Colombians to return to their ships.

With the revolution in full swing and the Republic of Panama proclaimed, a Marine battalion arrived in the transport *Dixie* on the evening of the fifth. Maj. John A. Lejeune immediately landed two of his companies at Colon and relieved *Nashville's* landing force. Although the Marines left again in 24 hours, they and the Navy, acting on orders from Washington, had given the revolution enough weight to succeed. The United States instantly recognized the new republic and procured a treaty gaining the rights to the isthmus canal. Years later, the United States paid Colombia $25 million for this imperious interference.

During those unsettled days in 1903, the Navy sent an expeditionary force to Real de Santa Maria and Yaviza, two strategic border points through which Colombia could attack Panama. In mid-December, the sailors were joined by Capt. Smedley D. Butler and a company of Marines. They were reinforced by the Marine detachment from *Boston.*

Lejeune's Marines established a camp ashore and were joined by a battalion under Maj. Louis C. Lucas. On January 3, 1904, the Commandant, Brig. Gen. Elliott, arrived with two more battalions, totaling 635 men, and assumed command of all the Marines in Panama. It was the first time a Commandant had taken charge of troops in the field since Henderson had done so in the Florida Indian war. Organized into a provisional brigade of two regiments commanded by Lt. Cols. Biddle and Waller, the Marines spent their time scouting, mapping the country and studying the defenses of the canal and Panama City. In mid-February, Colombia agreed not to invade Panama; and the brigade began withdrawing to Guantanamo. By the end of March, only Lejeune's 1st Battalion of the 1st Regiment remained in the Canal Zone. He was kept busy protecting his men from tropical and venereal diseases.

The next fall came trouble: the Panamanian army ungratefully threatened to take over the country. The Marine battalion's A Company moved into the hospital on Ancon Hill in the Canal Zone, and the rest of the battalion was held in readiness. Under the threat of action by the Marines, the Panamanian general agreed to retire and his army was disbanded. In 1911, the U.S. Army began to take over the defense of the Canal Zone.

Smedley Butler was present for the dedication of the Canal in 1913, when

> . . . a group of important and pompous army officials boarded a tug to make the first trip. None of the Marines had been invited to join them. I walked down to the Canal to watch the festivities.
> By golly! A dugout shot around the bank. It was proudly flying a little Marine flag, and two Marines were paddling like the devil. They went through first, cheered and applauded by the crowd.[5]

The Canal opened for business in August 1914. A couple of hundred Marines stayed in Panama until early that year, with a side trip on expeditionary duty to Nicaragua in 1912. The Marines had served as a force in readiness that helped President Roosevelt make the Panama Canal American.

3
Pacifying Cuba

In Cuba, the Marines made three significant landings but did no actual fighting. The Corps primarily guarded American sugar and mining properties and railroads and freed the Cuban army to fight the opposition.

The United States Army had occupied Cuba at the beginning of 1899 and turned it free three years later. But the Platt Amendment, shoehorned into the new Cuban constitution, reserved for the United States the right to intervene to protect Cuban independence as well as life, individual liberty and property. The provision was broad enough to cover a variety of self-serving American actions.

By the summer of 1906, Cuba was torn by strife between two political factions. Insurrection spread swiftly across the island. American sugar property was destroyed. The "ins" wanted American intervention to protect them against the stronger "outs." The "outs" wanted intervention because they were confident they would win any free elections.

A battalion of Marines, under Maj. Albertus W. Catlin, who had commanded the Marines on *Maine* when she was sunk, was sent to Cuban waters. On September 13, 130 Marines and sailors from the cruiser *Denver* landed at Havana and camped in front of the president's palace. The next morning, the U.S. State Department ordered them back to their ship. During the next few days, elements of Major Catlin's battalion went ashore specifically to protect threatened sugar plantations and to guard the railroads.

President Roosevelt rushed Secretary of War William Howard Taft to Cuba. He arranged a truce, but the turmoil continued, and Taft recommended mobilizing for intervention. An expeditionary force of 5,400 men sailed for Cuba, including a Marine battalion in the transport *Dixie.* The Marine Corps was prepared to contribute two more battalions from its shore stations. Organized as the 1st Marine Regiment under Lt. Col. George Barnett, they were ready to sail in 36 hours but were delayed by the lack of sea transportation.

After the Cuban government of Estrada Palma resigned on September 28, the 2,800-man Provisional Marine Brigade, including 500 men of the 1st Regiment, landed at Havana. During October, the Marines, now commanded by Colonel Waller, patrolled towns and plantations, keeping the peace. By November 1, Army troops had relieved many Marine detachments, and the Corps' strength in Cuba was down to one thousand organized as the 1st Provisional Regiment.

Pacification took longer than expected; but a general election made José Miguel Gomez, leader of the Liberal Party "outs," president on February 1, 1909. Nine days earlier, the last of the Marine regiment left Cuba.

In the following years, Cuban politics sank into inefficiency, graft and corruption. In 1912, a revolt mounted in Oriente Province by Evaristo Estenoz took a strident racial form. It was feared that Estenoz wanted to create a black republic on the eastern end of Cuba, an area spotted with American-owned copper mines, sugar holdings and railroads. The American government started mobilizing again.

The 1st Provisional Marine Regiment of 800 men, now commanded by Col. Lincoln Karmany, quickly arrived at Guantanamo Bay on May 28 and guarded American property and railroads. The Marines freed the Cuban army to fight the rebels, who were burning sugar plantations and railroad property. One American-owned railroad had the gall to send the Marine Corps a bill for tickets for the Marines who had ridden its trains as guards. It was not paid.

On the night of June 9, a detachment of Marines was attacked at El Cuero; but the rebels were repulsed without casualties on either side. In late June, Estenoz was killed in a skirmish; and within another month, the rebellion had been crushed. The Marines began withdrawing to Guantanamo.

The Cubans continued to settle their political differences with guns. Gomez and the Liberals lost power and marched on

353

Havana. Although many Cuban army garrisons went over to the Liberals, the government mustered enough strength to invade Santa Clara province and captured Gomez on March 7, 1917.

The United States was fast approaching war against Germany, and rebels now rampaging through eastern Cuba threatened to endanger the Allies' sugar supply. The American sugar companies pressed for intervention; and on March 4, a six-company battalion of Marines was carved out of the 1st Brigade in Haiti and shipped to Cuba. Two hundred and twenty Marines occupied Guantanamo City to protect American property and the naval station's water supply. Units from the brigade and from a division of battleships briefly occupied threatened plantations. Several ships' Marine detachments plus the 43rd and 51st Companies from Haiti patrolled Santiago. Later, the 43rd Company was sent to guard the iron mines and ore docks at Daiquiri; and the 55th Company occupied posts at Nipe Bay on the north coast. Under pressure of the war in Europe, the last of the Marines were withdrawn from the Guantanamo district by May 23 and returned to the United States.

Bands of rebels continued to roam the countryside; and, to protect the sugar-producing areas, the 7th Marine Regiment, under Lt. Col. Melville J. Shaw, went to Cuba in August. The 9th Regiment joined it in December, and they were formed into a brigade commanded by Col. James E. Mahoney. By August 1919, only a two-company battalion remained in Cuba. On February 6, 1922, it sailed for Guantanamo Bay.

Two years later, Gerardo Machado became president. He developed into a vicious dictator and in 1933 was ousted by a leftist junta. With United States encouragement, the Cuban army responded by putting into power Fulgencio Batista. He also ruled tyrannically and dominated Cuban political life until Fidel Castro's revolution overthrew him in 1959.

4
Back to Vera Cruz

The Marine Corps' invasion of Mexico in 1914 was triggered by an incident reminiscent of an earlier day—an insult to the American flag.

At the time, Mexico was ripped apart by a violent social revolution and savaged by revolutionary generals determined to overthrow a government dominated by business interests and the Catholic Church. Americans had more than $2 billion invested in Mexico; 70,000 Americans lived and worked there. In February, 1913, tough, hard-drinking Gen. Victoriano Huerta deposed the reformer President Francisco Madero and his vice president; and one of Huerta's generals murdered them both. The United States moved Army troops to Galveston and naval ships to ports on both Mexican coasts. The Marine Corps assembled some 2,170 men under Colonel Lincoln Karmany and shipped them to Guantanamo to stand by. But President Taft refused to intervene.

President Woodrow Wilson, who took office the following month, came up with a new principle: the United States would recognize only those Latin American governments that had come to power by constitutional means. Deeply sympathetic to the hopes of the Mexican people, Wilson refused to recognize Huerta's reactionary government, which was fighting a Constitutionalist army led by stubborn, cautious Venustiano Carranza and his regional chiefs Pancho Villa, Emiliano Zapata and Alvaro Obregón, names that were to become part of the folklore. Wilson called Huerta's regime "a government of butchers."[6]

In this atmosphere of tension, on April 6, 1914, a whaleboat from *USS Dolphin* was loading supplies at a dock in the oil refinery port of Tampico, which was then threatened by the revolutionary army. Huerta's men arrested seven sailors and *Dolphin's* paymaster and threw them into jail. They were released in less than an hour, but Rear Adm. Henry T. Mayo demanded that the Mexicans apologize by firing a 21-gun salute to the American flag. Huerta waffled and offered substitute apologies that were deemed unacceptable.

On Monday, April 20, President Wilson asked Congressional approval to use armed force to win respect for the flag. He had already sent a fleet, including seven battleships, to intercept supplies Huerta was receiving from Germany.

The Americans planned a naval demonstration off Tampico. This was changed to a landing at Vera Cruz, Mexico's principal port, when the German ship *Ypiranga* was reported bringing 200 machine guns and large amounts of ammunition there for Huerta. The United States wanted to seize these arms—but to avoid an incident with Germany, it had to be done after they had left the German ship and before they reached Huerta's hands.

Elements of the Marine Corps' 1st Advanced Base Brigade, commanded by Colonel Lejeune, were already in Mexican waters. The 1st Regiment was at New Orleans and the 2d Regiment was at Pensacola. Four rifle companies of the 2d were rushed to Mexico. At the same time, the 4th Regiment of Marines was organized on the West Coast under Col. Joseph H. Pendleton and sent down the west coast of Mexico.

Ypiranga was due at Vera Cruz at 10:30 Tuesday morning, April 21. Rear Adm. Frank F. Fletcher was ordered to land a force of sailors and Marines at 8:30 A.M., take the Customs House and prevent the delivery of the German arms. First ashore were the Marines of the 2d Regiment led by Lt. Col. Wendell C. Neville and Major Butler's battalion that had come up from Panama. Five hundred Marines of the 2d Regiment seized a main pier and the cable station and an electric power plant nearby. When Neville moved his main body a half mile toward the railroad station, the Marines were fired on. They had to fight to take the roundhouse just west of the city. By dark, the Americans controlled the section of the city around the rail yards and the Customs House. During the night, more Marines and sailors landed; and these Marines formed a provisional 3rd Regiment led by Major Catlin, the Fleet Marine Officer.

The next morning, the two Marine regiments advanced

house-to-house to clear the city against a determined sniper defense from rooftops and windows. That afternoon, Lt. Col. Charles C. Long's 1st Regiment landed; and Lejeune took command of all the Marines ashore as the 1st Marine Brigade. By the end of the second day, the Americans had been able to clear only half the city; the heavy Spanish-style construction enabled the Mexican defenders to slow their progress.

On the third day, the Marines searched each building for hidden snipers, and the center of the city was occupied. By the fourth day, 7,000 armed Americans were ashore, including 2,469 in the Marine Brigade. Another regiment of 894 men joined the brigade on April 29, and Colonel Waller, as the senior officer, took over command from Lejeune on May 1. In a flurry of governmental generosity, nine Marines, all officers with the rank of captain or above, received the Medal of Honor.

Ypiranga lay passively at Vera Cruz for several weeks and later unloaded its arms at another Mexican port. Major Butler, in civilian clothes, went on a secret spying mission to Mexico City at Rear Adm. Fletcher's request to check on military strengths and defenses—in case the Mexican refusal to apologize inspired further military action. After the U.S. Army arrived, the Marines manned two-thirds of the American outpost line through a row of hot, mosquito-infested sand hills to the beach northwest of the city.

Both factions in the Mexican fighting condemned the American invasion, while in the United States volunteers flooded into recruiting stations. No one knew whether the United States was at war or not.

On July 15, Huerta left Mexico in *Ypiranga.* The demanded apology to the flag was never made, but Huerta had been overthrown. The cost: 19 Americans dead, 71 wounded—and more than 300 Mexicans dead.

Pancho Villa continued to make trouble on the northern border. His March 9, 1916, shooting-up of Columbus, New Mexico, sent Brig. Gen. John J. Pershing and 6,000 Regulars chasing after him into Mexico. By 1917, Carranza had held an election and become Mexico's legitimate President; the last of the American punitive expeditionary force had withdrawn, and Mexico had a new and lasting constitution—the acme of its revolution.

5
Nicaragua

The Marine Corps' first major Caribbean intervention began in Nicaragua on the Central American mainland in 1912. This biggest of the "Banana Wars" ranged over 20 years and reached two climaxes separated by World War I.

The original decision to send in the Marines had two causes: fear of European meddling in a country so close to the Panama Canal; and the desire to protect the American investments that the U.S. government had encouraged in Nicaragua, which was increasingly dominated by the great fruit companies.

As early as 1853, United States Marines had landed in Nicaragua to protect American interests and property, including Cornelius Vanderbilt's railroad between the two oceans. Marines landed again in 1857 and several times in the 1890s. By the time of President Taft's Administration, the brutal dictator José Santos Zelaya was leading Nicaragua into bankruptcy. Conditions grew so bad that the local Conservative party joined with the foreign investors and bankers to oust the dictator. Taft was reluctant to intervene; but when Zelaya shot two American citizens, Secretary of State Philander Knox protested. Not wanting to take on both the Conservatives and the United States, Zelaya resigned.

On May 19, 1910, Marines and sailors landed near Bluefields on the Atlantic coast to guard American property. They were joined by a two-company battalion of Marines from Panama commanded by Major Butler. Now, the Liberal government started to fall apart; the Conservatives marched into Managua, the capital, and two American banks, which had loaned Nicaragua $14 million, set up a national bank and took control of the country's customs.

In 1912, the Conservative president, Adolfo Diaz, faced with strong Liberal opposition, told the Americans that he could not guarantee the protection of American citizens and property and asked the United States to intervene. He figured that an American presence might help his unpopular regime hold power. He was right. The first phase of the Marine intervention in Nicaragua would keep in power the Conservatives, who accepted American economic domination of their country.

Early in August, a small force of U.S. sailors arrived in Managua; and a detachment of Marines and sailors entered Bluefields. On the fourteenth, Butler's battalion of 13 officers and 341 enlisted men landed at Corinto on the Pacific coast and moved into the capital. The Marines' Nicaraguan intervention had begun.

Reinforcements were arriving at Corinto; and Butler, in Managua, had to communicate with them. He sent a detachment of 10 Marines and 40 sailors on a commandeered train. At the town of Leon, armed rebels seized the train and sent the humiliated Americans back to Managua on foot.

Butler angrily set out with 190 officers and men to open the railroad between Managua and Corinto. With him went Marine Lieutenants Alexander A. Vandegrift, Edward A. Ostermann and Richard Tebbs. Near Leon, a rebel leader threatened Butler in a long tirade and drew his pistol. Butler grabbed the gun and with a flourish unloaded it. The watching rebels roared with laughter, and Butler took their leader along as his hostage. At Leon, a hostile mob gathered; a huge woman brandishing a machete approached Butler, screaming at him. Instead of shooting her and starting a battle, Butler chucked her under the chin; she fled. Butler went on to Corinto, conferred with the American naval officers there and returned to Managua.

On September 4, Colonel Pendleton arrived at Corinto with the 1st and 2d Battalions of the 1st Provisional Regiment, a total of 753 Marines. He left one battalion at Corinto and took the other directly to Managua.

Pendleton assigned Butler the job of clearing the railroad from Managua southward through Masaya to Granada. Armed with machine guns and three-inch field pieces, Butler entrained three companies and ran into a pitched battle between government troops and Gen. Benjamin Zeledon's Liberal army near

Masaya. Butler arranged meetings between Zeledon and U.S. Rear Adm. William H. H. Southerland and was finally permitted to pass through the rebel lines. In Masaya, rebel snipers opened up on the train. The Marines returned the fire, some jumping off the train to take cover. Butler raced his train ahead, leaving some Marines behind. Capt. Nelson P. Vulte rounded up most of the men, grabbed a handcar and overtook the train when Butler halted to reorganize his forces. Butler was fit to be tied until Zeledon sent him a note of apology and returned three Marines who had been abandoned in the skirmish. It was here that Marines began calling the sharp-tempered Butler, his eyes bloodshot and sunken from malaria, "Old Gimlet Eye."

Approaching Granada, Butler faced a faction of rebels under Gen. Luis Mena. He ordered Mena to surrender or he would attack Granada; at the last minute, Mena's letter of surrender arrived. He was allowed to go into exile. Pendleton, having heard a rumor that Butler was besieged, rushed to Granada with reinforcements and a load of rations and Red Cross supplies for the inhabitants, who had been starved by the Liberals. "The gratitude of the inhabitants, who had been at the mercy of their vindictive enemies for several weeks, was unbounded and freely and frankly expressed—especially by the women of that city."[7]

Zeledon's army still controlled the 500-foot hill of Coyotepe that dominated both the railroad and Masaya. On the night of October 2, the U.S. Marines and sailors and government troops moved into position to assault the hill. Pendleton had the artillery bombard it throughout the next day. At 5:15 on the morning of October 4, the Americans attacked. Maj. William N. McKelvy's 1st Battalion was in the center and bore the brunt of the fighting; Butler's, consisting of two companies of Marines and one of sailors, was on the left, and a battalion of sailors from *California,* on the right. The Marines and sailors charged up the hill through ineffective rebel fire, and in 40 minutes the battle was over. Most of the rebels fled. Zeledon was killed by his own men while attempting to get away. Seven Marines and sailors were killed.

Masaya fell, and later Leon surrendered to Lt. Col. Long and a force of 1,200 Marines and sailors. The revolution was finished. The bulk of the Marines withdrew from Nicaragua in

January 1913, leaving a strong guard of 105 men at the legation in Managua. The Marines had been the key to keeping Diaz and his unpopular Conservatives in power.

During World War I, the Marine Legation Guard stayed in Managua and became a resented symbol of American imperialism. Nicaraguans recognized that the Marines were there to prevent an anti-American from coming to power. The embarrassing problem was that the anti-American Liberals would win any fair election. Finally, by 1924, a relatively honest election was held, and a coalition government was inaugurated. The Marines were withdrawn on August 4, 1925—but not for long.

By the end of October, both the Conservative president and the Liberal vice president had fled the country, and right-wing General Emiliano Chamorro took over. The United States refused to recognize him.

When rioting broke out, Marines landed again at Bluefields. This time, they guarded a "neutral zone" to keep the warring factions away from American property. In 1926, Chamorro resigned; Adolfo Diaz returned to power, and the United States recognized his government.

Diaz, unable to end the Liberal rebellion, called on the United States for help; but President Calvin Coolidge chose to stay out of the mess. Then the rebels started raiding American fruit, lumber and mining companies, and a U.S. citizen was killed; Americans began talking about the danger of Bolshevism. Coolidge announced that he would protect American lives and property and authorized the sale to President Diaz of 3,000 Krag rifles, 200 Browning machine guns and three million rounds of ammunition.

Marines went ashore at three points on the east coast; and on January 6, 1927, Marines and sailors landed at Corinto and rushed to guard foreigners in the capital. The 2d Battalion, 5th Regiment landed at Bluefields, established a neutral zone there, and, leaving the 51st Company behind, sailed through the Panama Canal for Corinto. On February 1, the Marines led by Lt. Col. James J. Meade took over the defense of Managua. The rest of the 5th Regiment arrived; and on March 7, Brig. Gen. Logan Feland, a veteran of World War I, took command of the 2,000 Marines now in Nicaragua. They garrisoned 14 towns along the railroad. The Marines' second Nicaraguan intervention was in full bloom.

In February, Marine Observation Squadron One, VO-1M, commanded by Maj. Ross E. Rowell, a forty-two-year-old Iowan, arrived with eight officers, 81 enlisted men and six DeHavilland aircraft. During their service in Nicaragua, the Marines would be among the first fliers to dive-bomb an organized enemy, to use air-to-ground communication during combat and to move troops and supplies by air.

The renewed Marine intervention started out hopefully. President Coolidge sent Henry L. Stimson as his personal envoy to work out a peaceful solution. Stimson arranged a fragile truce that would keep Diaz in office until the 1928 elections. Both sides asked for more Marines to keep order. The 11th Regiment led by Col. Randolph C. Berkeley and another Marine air squadron, VO-4M, arrived before Stimson left on May 22. The Marines, now numbering 3,300 men, were organized as the 2d Marine Brigade.

Both Nicaraguan parties turned in large quantities of arms and ammunition, but about 150 Liberals led by Augusto C. Sandino refused to disarm and fled to Nueva Segovia province in the north. They became the core of the guerrillas who would fight the Marines for the next five years, and Sandino became the Marines' ablest opponent. This most renowned and charismatic of the rebel leaders was a slender, frail-looking man, an energetic Liberal partisan and a nationalist. He had worked in the Mexican oil fields and marched with Pancho Villa.

Clashes between Marines and rebel bands continued sporadically. At 2 A.M. on May 16, one large mounted group raided the town of La Paz Centro, and Capt. Richard B. Buchanan and the Marine garrison charged at them down the main street. Buchanan and Pvt. Marvin A. Jackson were killed.

After Stimson's truce went into effect, the Marine brigade was cut back to about a thousand men. The Marines set about creating the Guardia Nacional de Nicaragua, manned by Nicaraguans and with American Marine Col. Robert Y. Rhea and shortly afterward Col. Elias R. Beadle in charge. Recruiting for the Guardia proved extremely difficult.

As Sandino and other rebel leaders began operating near the Honduran border, the Marines worked their way north into rebel territory. In this wild, thinly populated country of coffee plantations and mines, the law was seldom enforced. Capt. Gilbert D. Hatfield and a Marine patrol probed Nueva Segovia and established a base at Ocotal, the province's capital. In July, they were joined by the First Company of the Guardia. The garrison had three Marine officers, two Guardia officers, 38 Marines and 48 Nicaraguan guardsmen. The townspeople, most of them friendly to Sandino, expected trouble.

On the night of July 15, it came. Hatfield, anticipating an attack, had doubled the guard. In small groups, Sandino's men slipped into the town. At 1:15 A.M., a Marine sentry at the walled Spanish house where the Marines were billeted spotted someone moving in the street and fired the first shot. The rebels attacked immediately and surrounded the house. The Guardia in another building could support the Marines only with rifle fire. Three charges were turned back by the Marines. After two hours of fighting, there was a lull; at dawn, the battle started again. The rebels demanded that Hatfield surrender; he replied that Marines did not know how to surrender.

At mid-morning, two Marine DeHavillands arrived overhead and strafed the enemy. Lt. Hayne D. Boyden landed near Ocotal and from a peasant discovered the seriousness of the situation. He raced back to Managua for help. In the second plane, Chief Marine Gunner Michael Wodarczyk, the Polish-born flier known as the "Polish Warhorse," strafed the rebels until his ammunition was gone.

In mid-afternoon, five DeHavillands led by Major Rowell appeared just as the Sandinistas were about to attack again. The planes dive-bombed the town, dropping their 17-pound bombs from heights of 600 and 300 feet, and then strafed for 45 minutes. The rebels fired back. "The ground was strewn with the dead and dying. Houses, in which they had taken refuge, were demolished. Groups were in stampede."[8] This was the Marines' first use of dive-bombing and low-altitude support of ground troops, which would become so basic to Marine Corps aviation in the future. On their way back, the planes bucked a thunderstorm and, out of gas, were forced down at Leon. For this day's work, Rowell won the first Distinguished Flying Cross awarded to a Marine.

Hatfield's men cleaned up the few rebels who stayed to

fight. Fifty-six enemy bodies were recovered; the Marines had one dead and five wounded.

Meanwhile, Brig. Gen. Feland had ordered Maj. Oliver Floyd to take a strong mounted patrol of 225 Marines and Guardias and go after Sandino. But the rebel leader escaped to his mountain fortress called El Chipote; and, with the start of the rainy season, Floyd left a garrison at Jicaro and returned to Managua.

The Marine brigade was further reduced. The Americans were underestimating Sandino; he was crafty, popular, effective. At 1 A.M. on September 19, he struck the Marine detachment in the village of Telpaneca, east of Ocotal, and left two Marines dead.

In those rugged northern mountains, Marine aviation linked together and supplied the scattered garrisons and patrols. Because the DeHavillands were too small for the job, five trimotor Fokker transports, part of the Marines' aviation modernization, were brought in to haul everything from ammunitions to mules.

On October 8, 1927, rebel rifle fire shot down one of two Marine planes patrolling near Quilali. Gunner Wodarczyk piloting the second plane saw the plane crash and burst into flames; he raced off to notify the garrisons at Ocotal and Jicaro. The two downed fliers, 2d Lt. Earl A. Thomas and Sgt. Frank E. Dowdell, forced natives to lead them toward Jicaro and were hiding in a cave when Sandino's men found them.

Within an hour of the crash, 1st Lt. George J. O'Shea at Jicaro rode to the rescue with a detachment of Marines and Guardias. The next morning, a reconnaissance plane dropped a message telling O'Shea that the remains of the downed plane was three miles away on Sapotillal Ridge. It took the men three hours to reach the base of the ridge; as they advanced up the hill, the enemy opened fire. They were caught between two rebel groups and fought their way out of the trap and back to Jicaro. Marines did not reach the crash site for another ten days. Thomas and Dowdell were never seen again.

Meanwhile, on Nicaragua's east coast, the Marines supervised local elections. Because they helped keep the voting honest, the Liberals won easily and became more amenable toward the Marines' presence. In fact, early in 1928, the newly elected Liberals petitioned President Diaz to place a Marine officer in command of the Bluefields police department.

The pursuit of Sandino went on vigorously in the north, with numerous clashes between the Marines and rebel detachments. To finish the affair, Sandino would have to be driven from his fortress on El Chipote. The attempt ended in disaster. First, patrols scouted the area, and planes bombed and strafed El Chipote. Then, on December 19, 1927, one patrol of 140 Marines under Capt. Richard Livingston left Jinotega and 60 men under Guardia 1st Lt. Merton A. Richal left Telpaneca to converge on Sandino's hideout.

On December 30, Livingston's column was ambushed a mile south of Quilali. In 80 minutes, five Marines and two members of the Guardia were dead and 23 Marines including Livingston and two Nicaraguans wounded. On New Year's Day 1928, Richal's patrol, which was approaching Quilali from the north, was hit by dynamite bombs and machine-gun fire. First Sgt. Thomas G. Bruce, a first lieutenant in the Guardia who had won the Navy Cross at Ocotal, was killed instantly. A Guardia sergeant, Policarpo Gutierrez, lost his left arm recovering Bruce's body. Then the enemy charged, and the patrol's point fell back. The Marines' machine gun jammed; a mortar and a 37mm gun went into action. Richal was shot in the face and lost his left eye. Gunnery Sgt. Edward G. Brown organized an attack up Las Cruces Hill and took the crest. There, the Marines dug in to wait for help.

In a few minutes, Marine planes strafed the enemy; and a reinforced rifle platoon, coming out of Quilali to meet Richal, heard of the battle and pushed ahead to the Marines on the hill. The combined force spent the night on Las Cruces, and, after an early-morning air drop of water and nails for stretchers, headed into Quilali.

Sandino took the offensive and laid siege to Quilali. There were some 30 wounded in the town. Despite the absence of an airfield, 1st Lt. Christian F. Schilt, a tall thirty-two-year-old airplane racer from Olney, Illinois, volunteered to fly in medicines and bring out the wounded. The Marines on the ground leveled walls to convert the main street into a landing strip. It was perilously short and ended at the top of a steep cliff. Schilt's Vought O2U-1 Corsair biplane had no brakes, so when it landed, Marines had to act as "wing runners" and grab hold of the wings to slow the rolling plane. Schilt disarmed his plane and left his parachute behind to eliminate all possible weight. On take-offs, the enemy fired their rifles at the unarmed plane. On landings, Schilt had to stall his engines and drop the plane the last ten feet; the lurching aircraft made three great bounces, and, with Marines clinging to its wings, finally rolled to a stop 200 feet from the precipice.

During January 6–8, Schilt made 10 daring flights into Quilali, bringing in 1,400 pounds of medicines and supplies and flying out 18 of the most seriously wounded to Ocotal. On the eighth landing, Schilt's tail-skid assembly was wrecked; and on the ninth, the center section struts bent under the strain. But both times he took off again with two wounded men. For at least three of the wounded, Schilt's courage meant they would live. President Coolidge awarded 1st Lt. Schilt the Medal of Honor on the White House lawn. (The following year, Schilt and Charles A. Lindbergh worked out air routes over Nicaragua for Pan American Airways.)

El Chipote was still the Marines' target. Ground patrols pressed the rebels back into their redoubt, where the Marines' planes could bomb and destroy them. Several hundred rebels were now gathered on the mountain top; and Major Rowell led a four-plane attack there on February 1. Sandino met the low-flying Vought Corsairs with a barrage of rifle and machine-gun fire. After Rowell had dropped his two bombs and fired 200 machine-gun rounds, engine trouble forced him to break off. The other planes continued the attack, dropping four 50-pound and eighteen 17-pound bombs and firing 2,800 machine-gun rounds. When a strong patrol led by Maj. Archibald Young cautiously probed the top of El Chipote, they found that Sandino and most of his men had fled.

The rebels continued to ambush Marine patrols. On February 27, they attacked a 35-man patrol led by 1st Lt. Edward F. O'Day, killing five and wounding seven.

Recognizing the difficulty of suppressing Sandino's rebellion, the Marine Corps was now rebuilding its strength in Nicaragua. In January 1928, the 11th Regiment, commanded by Col. Robert H. Dunlap, a veteran of Samar and France, returned; and Brig. Gen. Feland resumed command of the enlarged brigade. The Marines in the north were heavily reinforced and organized as a special military zone under Dunlap's command. They destroyed rebel camps and supplies. The effect of this buildup was that the rebels avoided tackling the strong patrols and backed further into the eastern interior.

On the east coast, newly arrived Maj. Harold H. Utley listened as a new strategy against Sandino was proposed by Capt. Merritt A. Edson, the commander of the Marine detachment on *USS Denver.* The thirty-year-old, red-headed Vermonter and several other junior officers had worked out a plan using the Coco River, which rose in the mountains near El Chipote and wandered many miles to the Atlantic. Their idea was to throw a defensive screen across the lower section of the river, at the same time send a strong unit upstream into the bowels of Sandino's territory and then crush the rebels between the two forces of Marines. Sandino would either have to sideslip into Honduras or surrender.

Since the Coco basin was unmapped, Edson was instructed, as a first move, to take five Marines from *Denver* and scout as far upriver as possible. The patrol set out on March 8 in a 16-foot flat-bottomed launch powered by a motor salvaged from a Model T Ford. They returned 20 days later with information that Sandino was recruiting men as far east as Bocay, 350 miles upriver from the Atlantic coast, and that a strong force of Marines based in Huaspac, at the junction of the Coco and Huaspac rivers, could block the rebels from getting into the lower stretches of the Coco. Edson went on the sick list with malaria; but by April 14, he, 2d Lt. Jesse S. Cook, Jr., and 37 Marines from *Denver* established a base camp at Huaspac.

The rebels were raiding the gold mines in the area south of Edson's position. Major Utley sent combat patrols after them and gave Edson the job of preventing their escape northward into Honduras. Edson took 32 men in three boats and lay his ambush at Great Falls up the Huaspac River, but the rebels did not appear. So he pushed his men on a hard march through the rain-swept jungle toward Bocay, living on bananas, beans, beef and monkey meat—"the sweetest and most tender of any meat I have ever eaten," said Edson.[9] They reached Bocay, a settlement of 50 thatched huts, on June 2—only to learn that a small group of rebels had passed through the town the previous day. Edson's first Coco River patrol returned to the coast.

After conferring with Feland, Utley sent Edson upriver again on a second Coco River patrol. His goal was to reach

Poteca, where Sandino's forces were reportedly concentrated. Edson started out from Bocay on July 26 with 21 Marines. It rained steadily for five days; the river rose 20 feet and became a raging terror. The Marines lived off the land and fought skirmishes with rebel bands. On August 6, when they were still a day's hike from Poteca, two OL-8 amphibians airdropped rations and mail. One pilot spotted an enemy camp 2 miles upriver, bombed and strafed it and notified Edson. The Marines, advancing in boats and through the jungle, caught the rebel party by surprise. The Marines opened a fire fight on both sides of the river; the rebels, armed with Russian-made rifles and two machine guns, gave them a tough battle. Pvt. Myer Stengel was killed (and later was awarded the Navy Cross) and four Marines were wounded; the rebels had at least 10 dead. Edson won his first Navy Cross that day.

When the Marines finally reached Poteca on August 17, Edson learned that Sandino himself had been with the rebel party the Marines had attacked and had fled after the initial bombing. But Sandino was now locked between Edson in the Coco Valley and the Marines in Nueva Segovia province to the west.

There, a 37-man Marine-Guardia patrol under Capt. Robert S. Hunter, an experienced 15-year veteran, ran into a sizable rebel band near the Bocaycito River. One Marine on point, Private Honyust, was a full-blooded American Indian—a rarity in the pre-World War II Marine Corps. The patrol drove off the enemy's advance elements but then was ambushed along a narrow jungle trail. A corporal was killed, and Hunter was mortally wounded, shot in the chest and shoulder. A young Naval Academy graduate, 2d Lt. Earl S. Piper, took command and organized a perimeter defense on Casa Hill for the night. In the morning, the Marines had to fight a 45-minute battle to break out. Captain Hunter struggled up from his stretcher to join the fight. The next day, Piper's men reached the La Flor coffee plantation and set up a strong defensive position. Hunter died there. It took a week for reinforcements led by Maj. Keller E. Rockey to reach the patrol.

There was a lull in the fighting during the Nicaraguan elections in November 1928. Some 900 Marines and sailors helped the Guardia to limit corruption and intimidation. The

Sandinistas tried to disrupt the voting; but, for the first time, the Liberals won a national election; and Gen. Jose Maria Moncada became president.

The Americans were convinced that Nicaragua could not be left on its own until a trained constabulary was established to enforce the laws. In March 1929, Col. Douglas C. McDougal took command of the Guardia and changed his predecessor's policy. He organized a Guardia battalion and put it in the field against the rebels.

The Marines assigned to train the Guardia had their hands full. There were nine mutinies in the Guardia between 1928 and 1932. On October 5, 1929, at Telpaneca, the Guardias killed their commanding officer, Marine Sgt. Lewis H. Trogler. Marine Sgt. Charles J. Levonski, a second lieutenant in the Guardia, was sent in with additional men. The garrison mutinied again and seized two Americans—Levonski and 2d Lt. James C. Rimes—and fled toward Honduras. Some of the newly arrived Guardias remained loyal and helped the two Americans escape to safety.

Early in 1929, the fighting picked up again. Patrols were ambushed and Marines killed. First Lt. Herman H. Hanneken, who had killed the rebel leader Charlemagne Peralte in Haiti 10 years earlier, captured another guerrilla chief. Hanneken's Marines had pitched camp near a small stream, and the lieutenant sent eight of his men to bathe in the creek. Wary of an ambush, Hanneken told Cpl. Roy Waddle to have four of the men stand guard while the others took their turn in the water. Suddenly, Pvt. Merle W. Rittenour, guarding the trail, saw a man approaching on a mule. The Marines leaped from the water, grabbed Springfield rifles and waited. Half asleep, his head on his chest, the rebel leader Manuel Jiron was surrounded by the Marines and taken prisoner. Since Sandino had gone to Mexico to raise money for his forces, Jiron's capture was a heavy blow to the rebels. But the guerrilla fighting went on.

As the Guardia was able to carry more of the burden, Marines were shipped out of Nicaragua. The last of the 11th Regiment left for the States on August 20, 1929. With only 2,000 Marines left in the country, the anti-guerrilla campaign became less effective than ever. The Marines' thinly spread, heavily equipped patrols did not have mobility enough to catch up with the lightly loaded, elusive rebels. In the spring of 1930, the

Marines tried to deprive them of food by dragging the local population off their farms and into concentration areas. After a couple of months, this unpopular scheme was allowed to die.

Meanwhile, Sandino had returned. Reportedly, he had found financial help in New York. On June 19, Marine planes spotted his camp with about 150 men on top of a fortified hill. The fliers blasted them. A bomb fragment wounded Sandino in the leg, and he retreated into the Coco basin's wilderness to recuperate.

The Marines followed and mounted three expeditions between August 1930 and February 1931 into the jungle area between the Coco and Bocay rivers in far northern Nicaragua. Among the most effective patrol leaders was 1st Lt. Lewis B. Puller, who had won his commission as a jungle fighter in Haiti and was now a captain in the Guardia. Puller—a native of West Point, Virginia; grandson of a Confederate cavalry officer; and cousin of George S. Patton—had attended Virginia Military Institute, and quit to enlist in the Corps in 1918. As a Gendarmerie officer in Haiti, he had led many patrols and survived many ambushes. In Nicaragua, his aggressiveness won him the label "The Tiger of the Mountains." He received his first two Navy Crosses for his fighting there. He would win three more.

Increasingly, the Americans depended on the Guardia to eliminate the rebels. In the beginning of 1931, an effort was made to enlarge the Guardia and use it entirely in the field. Realizing that the Americans, overwhelmed by the Depression at home, were tiring of the occupation, President Moncada agreed, and Marine strength was severely reduced. By June, only one battalion and the aviation units remained.

Then, in three minutes in mid-morning of March 31, an earthquake destroyed most of the city of Managua and killed an estimated 2,000 inhabitants. Two Guardia officers were among the dead. The Marines immediately went to work rescuing the injured, battling fires and taking care of the homeless. First Lt. Evans F. Carlson won the first of his three Navy Crosses for his work in the emergency as Department Commander of Managua. A stream of American aircraft brought in medicine and supplies; Marines flew the first 92 missions.

The rebels continued the sporadic guerrilla war in the northeast. Coming down the Coco River, 150 rebels led by

Pedro Blandon ambushed a Marine-Guardia patrol and killed Capt. Harlan Pefley. Two days later, Marine aircraft spotted the rebel column; and a patrol attacked and killed Blandon and eight of his men. Responding to this new rebel activity, the garrisons at Bluefields and Puerto Cabezas were increased.

In April 1932, there was a Guardia mutiny at Kisalaya; and the commanding officer, Lt. Charles J. Levonski—who had been taken prisoner by mutineers in 1929—was shot to death.

The Guardia's worst disaster came on April 21, 1932, when the rebels ambushed a Guardia patrol led by 1st Lt. Laurin T. Covington and killed four men. First Lt. Laurence C. Brunton brought a relief column to the rescue. The rebels laid another trap; Covington and Brunton were both killed and the combined patrols, routed. Ten Guardia were killed that day.

On September 20, Lieutenant Puller set out from Jinotega with Company M, his special mobile patrol of about 40 men. While crossing a mountain stream on the twenty-sixth, they were ambushed by rebels firing machine guns and Browning automatic rifles from cover. Guardia Lt. William A. Lee, Puller's second in command, was wounded in the head and right arm. A Marine gunnery sergeant, Lee was an expert shot. While Puller directed the attack, Lee was able to pin down the enemy with a light shoulder-fired Lewis machine gun until the Guardia had climbed the ridges above the trail and could fire on the rebels. The patrol killed 16 guerrillas and suffered two dead and three wounded. To save his wounded, Puller headed back to Jinotega, some 75 miles away. Company M fought through two ambushes and arrived at base safely on the thirtieth. For this patrol, "Chesty" Puller received his second Navy Cross and "Iron Man" Lee, his third.

The Liberals won the election on November 6, 1932, and Juan B. Sacasa became president. Retiring President Moncada planned to drive the final spike in a new railroad line he had built inland 80 miles from Leon to El Sauce. It was heard that Sandino would try to destroy the line and kill Moncada; Puller volunteered to protect him. On December 26, Puller took seven Marines including Lee and 64 Guardias and entrained for El Sauce. At 4:30 P.M., they approached a construction camp a few miles short of El Sauce just as 100 guerrillas were sacking the camp. Machine-gun fire sprayed the boxcar. Mounted rebels

371

encircled the train, firing rifles and throwing dynamite bombs. Puller's men jumped from the train with their guns blazing. Lt. Bennie M. Bunn tossed his pistol to a Guardia and took the man's BAR. He walked directly at the enemy, firing short bursts from the hip. The rebels broke. Bunn later was given the Navy Cross. Now, each force tried to flank the other, and the Guardias decimated the rebels. In 70 minutes, 32 guerrillas were killed. Three days later, Moncada formally opened the line. He promoted Puller to major and Bill Lee to captain in the Guardia on the spot.

On the evening of January 2, 1933, the day after Sacasa was inaugurated, the last elements of the 5th Regiment sailed from Corinto. The second Nicaraguan intervention was over.

The first intervention had brought Nicaragua momentary stability and discouraged European intervention, but the second was less successful. When it ended, Sandino remained at large; and the U.S. occupation had aroused many Latin Americans to a deep fury.

Before the Marines left Nicaragua, a Marine officer, writing about the Guardia, made a dire and accurate prediction: "At best, there is sure to be a shake-up in the Guardia; it will soon become a partisan force, used to further the party in power."[10] In 1934, President Sacasa granted Sandino amnesty, and the Guardia murdered him. Two years later, the Guardia's leader, Anastasio Somoza, backed by his Marine-created force, made himself president and then dictator of Nicaragua. By building native constabularies, the Marines gave strong men a strong weapon.

For the Marine Corps itself, the long, nasty, tough second Nicaraguan campaign taught ground troops and fliers to operate together and introduced such World War II leaders as Edson, Puller, Carlson, Rowell and Schilt to jungle fighting. In another decade, that introduction would pay off.

6
Haiti

The intervention in Haiti was the Marines' longest and perhaps least effective. Certainly, it was one of the most severely criticized. It began at 5:50 P.M. on July 28, 1915, when two companies of Marines and three of sailors landed at the navy yard at Bizoton, three miles from Port-au-Prince, the Haitian capital. It ended 19 years later on August 15, 1934, with the withdrawal of the 1st Marine Brigade.

When the Marines arrived at Bizoton, they marched into chaos. The day before, 162 of 167 political prisoners in the National Penitentiary had been slaughtered on the order of President Vilbrun Gjuillaume Sam. The next morning, an aroused mob stormed the French Legation where President Sam had taken refuge and hacked his body to pieces. Another crowd entered the Dominican Legation and shot to death the prison's commanding officer. That evening, the Marines, led by Capt. George O. Van Orden, landed, marched on the capital, suffered some casualties, placed guards at various foreign legations and took charge of the city.

Haiti, which lies 48 miles east of Cuba and occupies the western third of the island of Hispaniola, had been a French colony. The French had imported more than a million African slaves to work the sugar plantations; the slaves drove out the whites and created the second independent nation in the Western Hemisphere, ruled by a succession of cruel and corrupt military dictators, each in turn replaced in a bloody revolt.

By 1910, the country was heavily indebted to American, French and German bankers. The creditors formed the Banque Nationale, a private bank, to act as the government treasury. By the end of 1914, the government was broke and revenues had shrunk. President Woodrow Wilson wanted a stable government in Haiti and proposed steps to ensure financial recovery. The Haitian Senate laughed.

There were rumors that the Haitian government would seize the Banque Nationale's gold reserve. Such reports were surely believable. Nervously, the National City Bank of New York, which was backing the Haitian bank at the urging of the U.S. Department of State, arranged with the government in Washington to have the gold secretly transferred to New York. Sixty-five Marines under Maj. Charles B. Hatch snatched it. They arrived aboard *USS Machias* on December 17, brought $500,000 in gold on board and left immediately for New York. The 5th Marine Regiment was aboard *USS Hancock* in Haitian waters, standing by in case of trouble.

By March 4, 1915, General Sam had led a "caco" army to Port-au-Prince and had himself named President. "Caco" is an ambiguous term. What it means depends on the eye of the beholder: revolutionary, mercenary, bandit. A caco, usually a poor peasant, was a member of an organized group that, either out of loyalty or for pay, supported a Haitian political or military leader. The cacos were the Marines' enemy in Haiti, and Marine officers like Smedley Butler used the word interchangeably with "bandit." In any case, the cacos were the men who fought the American occupation for two decades.

President Sam brought a brief interlude of quiet to Haiti; but in less than four months, another wave of revolution inundated the country. This one was led by red-headed Dr. Rosalvo Bobo, who typically went to northern Haiti near the Dominican border and gathered caco support. On June 19, the French landed men at Cap Haitien, the nation's second largest city, to protect their citizens; and Rear Adm. William B. Caperton, USN, arrived on July 1 and took charge of the port. President Wilson did not want Germany or anyone else to move in and exploit Haiti's weakness. Europe was already at war, and Germany had repeatedly demonstrated its interest in a foothold in Haiti.

Meanwhile, Bobo's revolution had broken out in Port-au-Prince, and Caperton rushed over on July 28 to try to put out the fire. There, he learned of the massacre in the prison the day before and the mob violence sweeping the capital. He received orders to land troops and promptly did so. It was the beginning of a long stay for the Marines.

Caperton also put out a call for Marines from Guantanamo; and by the next afternoon, the 24th Company arrived and went ashore. Americans and Haitians clashed on July 30, and two sailors were killed. Within 24 hours, five companies of the 2d Marine Regiment left Philadelphia, led by Col. Eli K. Cole, and arrived on August 4. They eased the tension in the capital. Marines landed at Cap Haitien; and in Port-au-Prince, Caperton occupied Fort Nationale and ordered all Haitian soldiers out of the city. Some resisted, and two Haitians were killed.

A struggle for power now raged between Bobo and Philippe Sudre Dartiguenave, the presiding officer of the Haitian Senate who was willing to accept U.S. domination. Bobo's forces, anticipating that the Haitian Congress would elect his opponent, threatened to use guns to prevent that body from meeting. Marines were sent in; they stood by while the legislature elected Dartiguenave as president.

The price for American armed support was a ten-year treaty that put Haiti's customs under U.S. control and provided for a constabulary to be led by American officers. The treaty was renewable for another ten years on demand by either side. It gave the intervention the smell of legitimacy.

Marines kept arriving; by the end of August, the 1st Brigade of Marines had 88 officers and 1,941 men garrisoning ten towns. Colonel Waller now commanded all American forces ashore.

But the cacos in the north, opposing the government shored up by Americans, were far from finished. They skirmished with the Americans at the port of Gonaives early in September. Learning that the Gonaives Marine garrison was besieged, Maj. Smedley D. Butler and Lt. Alexander A. Vandegrift sped there in a small boat; and Butler led the local Marine detachment, the 7th Company, in pushing the cacos out of town. That evening, Butler heard the rebels were burning the railroad, and he turned out the men, still in their underwear. They raced down the street to the railroad and lit into the rebels. "It was the funniest fight I ever saw," Butler reported later.[11] Butler took 50 mounted men and pursued the enemy. He caught up with the rebel general and, as Butler told the story, pulled him off his horse and forced him to surrender.

Butler pushed an aggressive campaign to snuff out the cacos opposition. He wrote much later, "A lot of north Haiti was burned before we got through."[12]

At Cap Haitien, where Colonel Cole commanded the 1st Battalion, 1st Marines,* the cacos began cutting off the food supply and practically encircled the city. Cole tried to persuade their chiefs to put down their weapons but had little success. As a show of force, he sent out strong patrols of Marines. A five-squad patrol commanded by Capt. F. A. Barker was fired on. When two other Marine patrols fought their way through to support Barker, the cacos surrounded the combined Marine force. Cole brought in sailors from *Connecticut* to take over guarding the city while he led out the rest of the Marines to join the fight. The cacos fought well enough to win the Marines' respect but were finally driven off, leaving 40 dead on the field. Ten Marines were wounded.

A disturbance was reported at Petite Riviere de l'Artibonite further south, and half a company of mounted Marines was sent out from St. Marc. In a fight with the cacos on September 26, Sgt. John Platt of the 24th Company was killed—the first Marine to die in action in Haiti. (In front of the Marine barracks at Guantanamo, there is a plaque honoring Sergeant Platt.)

Now, Waller came north with the 11th Company, landed at Fort Liberte and marched to Ouanaminthe near the Dominican border. This area had been the seedbed of many Haitian revolutions, and Waller stationed Marine garrisons at the frontier town and at Fort Liberte.

More Marines were poured into the northern areas that the cacos dominated. Cole and Butler moved their headquarters inland to the town of Grande Riviere du Nord and sent out strong patrols. Butler took a mounted detachment of 40 veteran Marines on a deep reconnaissance into the mountains. After dark on October 24, while his command was leading its horses across a river in a deep ravine near little Fort Dipite, it was ambushed from three sides. Twelve horses were killed. The Marines fought their way to a defensible position a mile away.

---

*U.S. Marine regiments are referred to as 1st Marines, 4th Marines, etc.; Army regiments are referred to as 1st Infantry, etc. Although this form did not come into common use until the 1930s, it is used consistently in this book after World War I. The first permanent Marine Corps regiments were organized in 1913.

Their only machine gun had been lost in the river. Gunnery Sgt. Daniel J. "Fighting Dan" Daly stole back on his own and, under fire, recovered the gun from the back of a dead horse. All night, the cacos kept up a poorly aimed fire; the Marines returned it only when the enemy closed in. At daybreak, squads led by Capt. William P. Upshur, 1st Lt. Edward A. Ostermann and Gunnery Sgt. Daly moved out in three directions and chased off the cacos. Upshur and Ostermann with 13 Marines then took Fort Dipite, and burned it and the houses nearby. Upshur, Ostermann and Daly received the Medal of Honor. It was the hard-boiled sergeant's second; his first had been earned at Peking as a private 15 years before. He would be decorated again in France.

Throughout the next weeks, the Marines pressed after the Haitians; the enemy repeatedly fought and fled. The cacos were driven back into their final retreat, an "impregnable" old French masonry fort called Fort Riviere, on a mountain top south of Grande Riviere du Nord.

During the night of November 17, a strong force of Marines and sailors surrounded the fort. At 7:30 A.M., Major Butler blew a whistle and all units attacked. They took the cacos totally by surprise. Some of the rebels tried to leap the walls and were mowed down by the Marines' automatic Benet rifles. The Marines of the 15th Company, led by Capt. W. W. Low and accompanied by Butler, made their final rush across rocky bare ground and reached the opening in the fort's wall. They found the tunnel was four feet high and three wide; only one man could enter at a time. The Marines flattened themselves against the wall. Sgt. Ross L. Iams said, "Oh, hell, I'm going through," and was the first man in, followed quickly by Butler's diminutive orderly, Pvt. Samuel Gross (real name: Samuel Marguiles). Butler was the third man in. More Marines crawled through; and a wild, hand-to-hand struggle was underway with rifles, bayonets, machetes, clubs and rocks. In 15 minutes, more than 50 cacos were killed. Butler blew up the fort. Iams, Gross and Butler received the Medal of Honor. It was Butler's second; he had earned his first at Vera Cruz the year before. Daly and Butler are the only Marines ever to receive the Medal of Honor for two separate actions.

The ferocity of Waller's campaign in the north was condemned in Washington, and the Marines were ordered to limit their activities to protecting peaceful inhabitants and themselves. Fewer encounters followed, and two years of relative peace began. Still, on January 5, 1916, 75 cacos attacked the Marine provost marshal's building at Port-au-Prince. Seven armed Marines and ten gendarmes armed only with clubs chased off the attackers.

On February 1, Rear Adm. Caperton issued a proclamation that the Gendarmerie d'Haiti would assume all military and police duties and the Marine brigade would be held in support. By autumn, most of the Marines had been withdrawn. Just before the United States entered World War I, three more companies were pulled out to help form the 5th Marines for duty in France. About 600 Marines were left in Haiti.

By the time the Marines had finished this first phase of their Haitian intervention, public opinion in the black republic was vigorously anti-American. The occupation could not be expected to "win the hearts and minds" of the Haitians; and there were enough cases of American incompetence, insensitivity and even brutality to enflame opposition.

To supplant Haiti's inefficient and corrupt political leaders, Americans took over the main executive posts of the government: customs, public works, public sanitation, agriculture and the Gendarmerie d'Haiti. Friction was constant and exacerbated by the division of American rule between civilian appointees of the President of the United States and the Marines.

In the meanwhile, the Marine-officered Gendarmerie was taking over much of the job of keeping the peace. From the beginning, recruitment for the Gendarmerie was difficult because the Haitian police were universally hated. Training was complicated by the language gap: none of the recruits knew English and the Marines knew no Creole and little French.

Smedley Butler had been put in charge of organizing the Gendarmerie on December 3, 1915, with "the imposing rank of major general."[13] A total of 120 Marines served as officers—captains as colonels in the Gendarmerie, first lieutenants as majors, second lieutenants as captains and noncoms as first lieutenants. By the time Washington ratified the treaty with Haiti early in 1916, Butler had in being a constabulary with 1,500 enlisted men garrisoning 117 posts.

The gendarmes' first test came in March, when the cacos made a number of attacks on their new posts in the north. Before dawn on March 3, at Cerca-la-Source near the Dominican border, a Gendarmerie detachment was routed in a surprise attack and abandoned its arms and equipment to the cacos. When Krag-Jörgensen carbines started arriving for the gendarmes, they gave a better account of themselves. And their numbers increased, so that a year later they totaled 2,533 Haitians and 115 Americans.

Tests of 1,200 gendarmes revealed that 95 percent had syphilis, and many had hookworm and other diseases. Partly for this reason, in the early days gendarmes on guard or sentry duty almost invariably fell asleep at their posts. Medical treatment greatly alleviated the problem.

The Gendarmerie worked, under Butler's direction, at cleaning up the cities, overseeing the repair of telegraph lines, improving irrigation projects and taking charge of road building with forced labor. The so-called "corvee system" of forced labor quickly became a source of bitterness. Local officials used the system to get rich, and some gendarmes accepted bribes to excuse men from the road-gang lists. When the Marines had arrived, Haiti had been virtually roadless. Using forced labor, they built and repaired 630 miles of road; and by the end of 1917, an automobile could travel the 180 miles from the capital to Cap Haitien in 14 hours, a trip that had taken three days on horseback.

An effort was made to recruit and train Haitians as officers for the Gendarmerie, but the program failed because all young Haitians of "good families" who signed up found the instruction and duty onerous and unpopular and soon resigned.

When the United States entered World War I, Brig. Gen. Eli K. Cole, who had replaced Waller as Marine brigade commander, faced a new National Assembly extremely hostile to American domination. The legislature refused to accept American proposals for revising the Haitian constitution in order to give renewed legality to the occupation. (Later, it developed that the American version of the new constitution had been drafted by Assistant Secretary of the Navy Franklin D. Roosevelt. This became a political issue; and in the 1920 U.S. election campaign, the Republican Presidential candidate, Warren G. Harding, declared: "If I am elected I will not empower any Assistant Secretary of Navy to draft a constitution for helpless neighbors and jam it down their throats at the point of bayonets borne by United States Marines."[14])

The conflict with the Haitian legislature reached a climax on June 19, 1917, when the National Assembly was pushing through a constitution unacceptable to Washington. Cole instructed Butler, in his capacity as "a Haitian officer," to stop it. Butler rushed to President Dartiguenave and insisted he send his chauffeur to round up two cabinet members. They reluctantly signed a decree dissolving the legislature.

No Haitian would dare take the President's decree to the legislature, so Butler went himself. He was greeted with loud hissing. The gendarmes on duty cocked their rifles. Butler ordered them to put down their weapons. He handed the decree to the presiding officer, who, instead of reading it to the delegates, began a tirade against it. The hall was in an uproar. Tables and chairs were thrown over, deputies shouted and surged forward. The gendarmes again prepared to shoot. Finally, the presiding officer rang a bell for order and read the decree, declared the Assembly dissolved and directed the hall cleared. The gendarmes locked the doors. Butler grabbed the decree and stuffed it in his pocket. He would use it later in a U.S. Senate hearing when his opponents charged that the president's decree had never existed.

The constitution in the form desired by the United States was presented to a plebiscite without public discussion and under Gendarmerie supervision. The Gendarmerie had orders to turn out a large vote in favor of the constitution, but less than 100,000 votes were cast. Only 769 were negative, and even some of those were dubious. The whole procedure was "in essence farcical."[15]

A new era of guerrilla warfare began on October 11, 1917, when the cacos were rising against the corvee or forced-labor system. They attacked the home of Capt. John L. Doxey, commanding the Gendarmerie district of Hinche in the heart of the mountains of central Haiti. The gendarmes easily beat off the attack, killed the cacos' leader and captured their second in command. He implicated three Peralte brothers, who lived near Hinche. Two brothers were arrested and tried by Marine Corps provost courts. One was acquitted; but Charlemagne Peralte was sentenced to five years of hard labor and put to work sweeping the streets of Cap Haitien. This humiliation enflamed European-educated Charlemagne Peralte's hatred of the Gendarmerie and its Marine leaders—a hatred that would last until his death.

On September 3, 1918, Peralte escaped to the hills. Although Col. Alexander S. Williams, now chief of the Gendarmerie, ordered the corvee abolished the following month, Peralte soon gathered several thousand followers and became the most effective caco leader to fight the Marines. Peralte commanded in the north; his assistant, Benoit Batraville, directed the cacos in the center of the country. They operated in scattered groups and attacked Gendarmerie detachments to seize rifles and ammunition. A hundred cacos struck Hinche on October 17, and the gendarmes led by Gendarmerie Lt. Patrick F. Kelly, a courageous Marine first sergeant, killed 35 in an hour's battle. On November 10, the Marine Corps' 143rd birthday, Peralte and some 60 cacos raided the town of Maissade, northwest of Hinche. They burned the Gendarmerie barracks and other buildings, and robbed the city hall.

The fighting went on sporadically; and after the end of the war in Europe, Marine Corps morale in Haiti dropped. Many officers in the wartime-expanded Corps were inexperienced, and enlisted men assigned to the Caribbean felt that they had missed the big show and resented having to stay in service after the Armistice in Europe. Enemy activity increased, and the Marines in Haiti came in for severe criticism.

Cacos ambushed gendarme patrols, killed gendarmes repairing telephone lines, and made a major attack on Cerca-la-Source. There, now-Captain Kelly, the gendarme commander, escaped death when one of his men shielded him from enemy fire. The Haitian who saved him lost an arm and a leg.

Marine Sgt. Nicholas B. Moskoff, a lieutenant in the Gendarmerie, and five of his men were ambushed at Dufailly by a large force of cacos on March 21, 1919. Moskoff was mortally wounded in the spine by the first volley. Taking the wounded Marine with them, his gendarmes fought a two-hour retreating battle. Moskoff's Haitian second-in-command was killed, and the men saw the cacos chop off his head with a machete. Moskoff was the first Gendarmerie officer killed.

The cacos became too strong for the Gendarmerie to handle

alone. In March, 1919, the Marine Brigade, now commanded by Brig. Gen. Albertus W. Catlin, who had been wounded at Belleau Wood, was reinforced from Guantanamo; and the 4th Marine Air Squadron (VO-9M) brought in the first 13 planes. Lt. Lawson H. M. Sanderson was one of the earliest pilots to experiment with low-level glide bombing. Combined Marine-Gendarmerie patrols were constantly in the field. In July, Col. Frederic M. Wise, another Belleau Wood veteran, became the third chief of the Gendarmerie, commanding 2,500 Haitians and 112 Marines serving as officers.

Peralte was getting supplies from Port-au-Prince; and, as his weapons improved, his attacks became more effective and more vicious. On October 7, he and 300 men dared invade the capital itself. Alerted by a warning of the cacos' approach, the Marines and gendarmes drove them from the city. The next day, the gendarmes assaulted Peralte's camp 15 miles from Port-au-Prince and scattered his men.

Twenty-six-year-old Marine Sgt. Herman H. Hanneken, a captain in the Gendarmerie, plotted to capture or kill Peralte. The tall blond Marine had started to become a priest, wandered West, worked as a cowpuncher and finally joined the Corps. He now arranged for two loyal Haitian civilians and a gendarme to denounce the American occupation and establish themselves as caco chiefs at Fort Capois, five hours into the interior from Grande Riviere du Nord. Hanneken's three "secret agents" attracted a large number of followers and were visited by emissaries from Peralte. The leader of the three, a well-to-do Haitian named Jean B. Conze, risked his life repeatedly by coming into town to report to Hanneken. The Marine faked several attacks on Fort Capois and once returned to Grande Riviere du Nord with his arm in a sling, pretending to have been wounded in battle. He then sent off part of his detachment to Cap Haitien and let it be known that his weakened force feared a cacos attack on Grande Riviere du Nord.

Conze urged Peralte to attack the town. Peralte agreed and with a thousand men arrived at Fort Capois on Sunday, October 26, 1919, to plan the assault. They decided to strike on Friday night, October 31. Peralte himself would wait at Mazare a half hour away and, after the expected victory, would enter the town triumphantly.

Marines led by Maj. James J. Meade secretly strengthened the garrison at Grande Riviere de Nord with men and a machine gun during the night before the attack. Hanneken and twenty-three-year-old Marine Cpl. William R. Button, a first lieutenant in the Gendarmerie, their faces blackened and with 20 well-armed gendarmes in dirty, old civilian clothes, went to Mazare.

Peralte did not show up. About 10 P.M., Hanneken's gendarme "deserter," Pvt. Jean Edmond Francois, appeared and reported that Peralte had changed his mind; he would await the outcome of the battle on top of a hill between Fort Capois and Grande Riviere. When the town was taken, Conze, who was leading the attack, would send back to Peralte the code message "General Jean."

Hanneken decided that he, Button and their men would bring Peralte the "good news." Led by Francois, they hiked for three hours and passed Peralte's first outpost with the countersign. Francois, who was well known to the cacos, went ahead to Peralte and was instructed to bring the news-bearing detachment to him. Hanneken's group had to pass six more outposts. Francois led the way, followed by Hanneken armed with two revolvers and Button carrying a Browning automatic rifle. The disguised gendarmes were armed with carbines and carried their ammunition in straw sacks.

They passed the first four outposts successfully but were stopped at the fifth. Hanneken, pretending exhaustion, stepped by the sentry; but the commander of the outpost questioned Button about his BAR, until Button pulled away, saying he had to keep up with his leader.

At the final guardpost, Peralte stood over a fire talking with a woman. Francois dropped back, and Hanneken and Button moved within 15 feet of Peralte. Hanneken said, "All right!" and, as Peralte tried to get away, shot him twice in the chest with his .45. Button cleared the camp with his Browning.

The gendarmes took positions to ward off counterattacks and remained on the hilltop until daybreak. Then they slung Peralte's body on a mule, and, fighting off caco attacks, returned to Grande Riviere du Nord.

Meanwhile, Major Meade and his men had thrown back the caco assault on the town. The next day, the Marines and Hanneken went to Fort Capois to destroy the cacos there.

Hanneken's gendarmes were to hit the fort at daybreak, while the Marines struck from the other side. But long after the appointed hour, the Marines still had not attacked; and caco guards spotted Hanneken's force. His men came under heavy rifle and cannon fire. They crawled on their stomachs without concealment toward the fort. The cacos finally fled before the Marine detachment arrived to prevent their escape. During the next week, more than 300 cacos surrendered to Hanneken.

The two St. Louis-born Marines, Hanneken and Button, were awarded the Medal of Honor for "extraordinary heroism." Young Button died at Cap Haitien of malaria. Hanneken killed another rebel leader the next April, for which he received the Navy Cross; was commissioned in 1920; fought in Nicaragua and World War II, and retired as a brigadier general. A silent, cold-eyed Marine, he was widely known as "Hard Head" and "Haiti" Hanneken.

Peralte's death ended the caco uprising in the north; but his assistant, Benoit Batraville, continued the cacos movement in the mountains of central Haiti. He gathered some 2,500 men, and part of his force raided the town of La Chapelle. With the new year, Col. John H. Russell, now the Marine brigade commander, opened a campaign against him. The Marine brigade numbered 1,344 men and the aviation squadron, and the Gendarmerie, 2,700. Russell and hard-driving Lt. Col. Louis McC. Little, who had fought Aguinaldo and the Boxers, instituted a system of rotating patrols, so that, as one tired, the next would take over and keep constant pressure on the rebels. On the night of January 14, 1920, Batraville boldly sent 300 men to attack Port-au-Prince. Although the assault was especially well executed, half the cacos were killed, wounded or captured.

On April 4, a patrol of Marines and gendarmes led by Marine Sgt. Lawrence Muth, a lieutenant in the Gendarmerie who had come to Haiti with his friend "Chesty" Puller, was ambushed while climbing a narrow trail near Las Cahobas. Muth and Marine Private Stone were hit immediately. The patrol retreated, leaving Muth, whom the men erroneously thought dead, lying at the ambush.

A Marine patrol led by Lt. Col. Little recovered Muth's body. His heart had been cut out and his head severed. The

384

Marines learned that Batraville had been at the scene of the ambush and had used his machete on Muth.

On May 18, a patrol of 29 Marines led by Capt. Jesse L. Perkins and Sgt. William F. Passmore attacked Batraville's camp. Passmore, with an automatic rifle, was the first man into the camp, followed by Perkins and two other Marines. There stood Batraville. He fired at the sergeant and Passmore shot him. The main body of the patrol, led by 2d Lt. Edgar G. Kirkpatrick, dispersed the remaining enemy. Sgt. Albert A. Taubert saw Batraville trying to get up and killed him with his revolver. Batraville's rifle had belonged to Gunnery Sgt. Dan Daly; it had been taken in the cacos' last attack on Port-au-Prince; Batraville's pistol had been issued to Sergeant Muth. With Batraville's death, the caco movement was destroyed.

The end of World War I had already eliminated the rationale that the Marine occupation was needed to counter the threat of a German invasion of the Caribbean. And with the end of the caco resistance, there was peace in Haiti. But the Marines stayed.

The Marine Corps occupation was severely criticized. The Marines were accused of trying civilians over whom they had no jurisdiction, even under martial law. They were attacked for being unwilling to turn over control of public works in their charge. In some cases, individual Marines dealt with Haitians corruptly and handled them brutally. The prejudice of some against blacks also damaged relations between the Corps and the Haitians. Over the long occupation, there were individual cases of drunkenness, rape, torture to get information and the shooting of escaping prisoners.

A first-hand study by Dr. Carl Kelsey, Professor of Sociology at the University of Pennsylvania, while acknowledging that such criticisms were well-founded, went on to say:

> On the whole I feel that the men of the Marine Corps deserve our respect. . . . there were many more acts of kindness than of cruelty. The good things have not been advertised to the world. Day after day I have talked with officers and men who are bending all their energies towards helping the Haitians. I have seen peasants going

out of their way to call on and bring presents to men who have been stationed in their communities.[16]

But Dr. Kelsey was highly critical of the corvee, saying, "In my opinion this was the greatest mistake made by the Marine Corps in Haiti."[17]

In 1921–1922, two investigations were made into the conduct of the Marines in Haiti. A naval court of inquiry, consisting of Marine Maj. Gen. Wendell C. Neville and two admirals, visited the island and concluded that there had been a "small number of isolated crimes or offenses that have been committed by a few individuals." In one terrible and explosive case, a Marine private, a lieutenant in the Gendarmerie, and two other Marines got drunk, made two Haitians dig their own graves and shot them. But the court said that charges of practically indiscriminate killing of natives were not warranted. This finding was attacked as a whitewash, and Haiti was visited by a Select Committee of the U.S. Senate. The Committee took months of testimony and reported that most of the incidents that could be confirmed apparently resulted from the failure of superior officers to keep full control of subordinates, especially when they were patrolling or stationed in remote areas. The Committee felt that there was an important lesson to be learned from the charges of misconduct in the "bandit campaign": "The lesson is the extreme importance in a campaign of this kind for higher command to require daily operations reports to be prepared by patrol leaders. In the early days of the outbreak such reports were not systematically required."[18]

The Senate Committee also condemned the lack of coordination among the various elements of the occupation administration that reported to different departments in Washington. The Committee recommended that one man be given overall responsibility for the entire occupation. As a result, early in 1922, Brig. Gen. John H. Russell, commander of the 1st Marine Brigade, was appointed United States High Commissioner to Haiti with the rank of ambassador. But by then authority would have been better placed in the hands of a civilian administrator.

The Gendarmerie was beginning to overcome its failure to handle the caco revolt and its reputation for exacting tribute from the people. It was able to improve its arms and equipment:

the Marine Corps lent it 4,000 Springfield rifles. And over the next few years, the better Haitian families' opposition to their sons entering the service relaxed. Suitable officer recruits underwent a two-year course of training; and by 1926, 53 Haitian officers were on duty. The Marines instilled in the Gendarmerie their own pride in rifle marksmanship; and in the 1924 Olympic Games, Haiti tied France for second place, outshot only by the United States team.

Most of the 1920s were years of peace in Haiti. The brigade was reduced to little more than 500, and it was used to back up the Gendarmerie.

It was also the era of a romantic Marine Corps story. The Gendarmerie had taken charge of the island of La Gonave in the bay of Port-au-Prince. In 1925, Marine Sgt. Faustin E. Wirkus, a young ex-miner from Pittston, Pa., was made commander of the gendarmes on the island. He was well known for having killed the caco leaders Estraville and Olivier while leading patrols in the Haitian mountains. As the man responsible for the island's 12,000 impoverished inhabitants, Wirkus took a deep interest in their well-being and ruled for almost four years with nearly absolute power. He was widely written about as the "White King of La Gonave."

In 1928, the Gendarmerie's name was changed to the Garde d'Haiti to reflect its military as well as police duties. By then, it had about 200 officers and 2,600 enlisted men, and 46 percent of its officers in the grade of captain and below were Haitian.

The following year, the Marines had to deal with the last major crisis of the Haitian intervention. By now, Louis Borno had been president of Haiti since 1922, and there was a spreading demand for popular elections. But Borno announced that there would be no election in 1930 and that the president would again be chosen by the appointed Council of State, which had replaced the legislature dissolved in 1917 with Smedley Butler's help.

In this atmosphere of political tension, on October 31, 1929, 200 students from the agricultural college outside Port-au-Prince marched on the capital to protest the reduction of the allowance paid them for attending school. The strike spread; and in mid-December, protesting students, now 20,000 strong, were joined by government employees. There were violent clashes with the authorities and arrests. At Cayes, 20 Marines commanded by Capt. Roy C. Swink routed with machine-gun fire 1,500 peasants armed with machetes and clubs. The Marines fired over their heads. The crowd advanced again. The Marines killed six and wounded 28. In other towns, mobs were handled without gunfire. Martial law was invoked and the crisis finally quieted down.

President Herbert Hoover appointed a commission of prominent citizens to examine the United States' Haitian policy. After 17 days in Haiti, the Forbes Commission reported to the President on March 26, 1930. It praised Brig. Gen. Russell's efforts and the material progress that had been achieved. It recommended that the Marine brigade be gradually phased out of Haiti and that all the government services be rapidly turned over to Haitians. Hoover adopted the commission's recommendations. They were popular in both the United States and in Haiti, although many Haitians would have preferred the immediate removal of the Marines.

In May, Borno resigned and left Haiti. In November, elections were held, and the new National Assembly named Stenio Vincent as president. Russell was replaced by a civilian American minister. The Garde d'Haiti's American officers were withdrawn on August 1, 1934; and on the fifteenth, the 1st Marine Brigade departed from Haiti. The long occupation was over. In 1958, a Marine Corps mission came back to Haiti for five years to help the dictator François "Papa Doc" Duvalier strengthen his army.

7
The Dominican Republic

The third major Marine intervention in the Caribbean began in the spring of 1916 while Europe was aflame. President Wilson feared for American security in the area; the government of the Dominican Republic had quit and left the little country, sharing the island of Hispaniola with Haiti, awash with trouble.

The Dominican Republic, known earlier as Santo Domingo, had been torn apart by political fighting for more than 70 years. In 1904, with the country virtually bankrupt, Theodore Roosevelt had forced the Dominicans to allow the United States to collect their customs duties and pay off their creditors. His aggressive action became the model for U.S. imperialism in the Caribbean. In 1911, 750 Marines of the 2d Provisional Regiment sat in their ships off the Dominican coast for two months, while American commissioners tried to arrange political stability and peace.

On May 5, 1916, when political factions were battling in the capital, Santo Domingo city, 150 men of the 6th and 9th Companies of Marines under Capt. Frederic M. "Fritz" Wise came over from Haiti to guard the American and Haitian legations. The next day, the Dominican president resigned. By May 15, a battalion of Marines under Maj. Newt H. Hall (who had been at Peking) and a battalion of sailors entered the city and manned the key points of the capital. There was no resistance, but the Dominicans were angry and sullen.

Marines kept pouring in. Col. Theodore P. Kane arrived with three more companies and took command. By the end of May, 750 Marines were ashore. On the north coast at Puerto Plata, where anti-government rebels ruled, Marine guards of several ships and a naval detachment, all under Maj. Charles B.

389

Hatch, landed in the face of heavy rifle fire on June 1. Naval gunfire drove the Dominicans from their positions; and, with the sailors leading, the Americans took one of the two forts defending the city. Marine Capt. Herbert J. Hirshinger was mortally wounded. The rebels retreated southward. Further west along the northern coast, Marines and sailors led by Captain Wise landed on the morning of May 26 and took Monte Cristi; a counterattack was repulsed later with devastating machine-gun fire.

Col. Joseph H. Pendleton arrived with the 4th Marines from San Diego and took command of all U.S. forces ashore. He landed the regiment at Monte Cristi and prepared to advance up the Zaza River valley 75 miles to Santiago, where the rebels had set up a government. On June 26, leaving 235 Marines at Monte Cristi, he led 837 men toward Santiago. At the same time, the 4th and 9th companies left Puerto Plata to meet Pendleton inland at Navarette and jointly attack Santiago. The United States government was prepared to fight to suppress anti-American power in the Dominican Republic.

Pendleton pushed ahead for 24 miles and early on the second morning faced two fortified ridges called Las Trencheras, a position the Dominicans had long regarded as invulnerable. It was now held by a strong rebel force in two lines across the Marines' route of march. At 8 A.M., the regiment attacked. A battery of artillery bombarded the enemy; a machine-gun company protected the artillery's flank. Under covering fire, the regiment moved up. It was stopped. The two Marine battalions were not working well together. But Maj. Robert H. Dunlap, Pendleton's chief of staff, took command of some of the front-line units and led a bayonet charge which drove the rebels from their first line of trenches. Accurate Marine rifle fire dislodged them from the second trenches near the crest of the second ridge. The 45-minute battle cost the Marines one dead and four wounded. It was the first fight in which the Marines had attacked with modern artillery and machine-gun support.

After Las Trencheras, the going continued to be heavy. Roads were virtually impassable; bridges had to be repaired. Pendleton advanced 10 miles, and that night the rebels attacked the Marine camp and were driven off. On July 3, the Marines charged a large entrenched force of rebels blocking the road at

Guayacanas; one corporal was killed and ten privates were wounded. First Sgt. Roswell Winans and Cpl. Joseph A. Glowin won the Medal of Honor. Glowin kept firing his Colt gun even after he was wounded, and Winans cleared a jammed gun while exposed to enemy fire. Capt. Julian C. Smith led the 6th Company to fight off a rebel attack on the supply train. Pendleton reached Navarette the next day.

Meanwhile, the two companies from Puerto Plata headed for Navarette by railroad. They skirmished with the enemy. Lt. Col. Hiram I. Bearss, the veteran of Samar, brought up the Marine detachment from *New Jersey* and took command of the "railroad battalion."

At Alta Mira, the rebels held a ridge pierced by a railroad tunnel. On a handcar, Bearss led 60 men through the tunnel to cut the enemy's escape; but the rebels fled and avoided the trap. There is a Marine Corps story of Bearss standing atop a trench in a hail of bullets, yelling at a private who stuck up his head: "Get down, you damn fool! You'll get shot."[19]

Bearss joined Pendleton at Navarette on July 4. The next day, a peace delegation came out from Santiago and met with Pendleton. The following afternoon, the Marines peacefully marched into the city. They occupied towns around Santiago and rounded up rebel leaders.

By fall, 47 Marine officers and 1,738 enlisted men were in the Dominican Republic; they were organized as the 2d Brigade. The country's temporary president insisted on holding general elections in November. The Americans opposed the idea because they feared the chief rebel leader, Desiderio Arias, would win and damage American interests.

There were violent clashes between Marines and Dominicans around the capital. The result was that the State Department, with President Wilson's approval, imposed a military government on November 29. The United States would take over the country's entire administration—a step more radical than those taken elsewhere in the Caribbean. The military governor, Capt. Harry S. Knapp, USN, established strict censorship and forbade the traditional carrying of firearms. In protest, Dominican cabinet members and officials refused to serve in the military government. Knapp had to appoint Americans to all the important administrative posts. Pendleton headed the Departments of War, Navy, Interior and Police, and Col. Rufus H. Lane, USMC, ran the Departments of Foreign Relations, Justice and Public Administration.

In the north, east of Santiago, Governor Juan Perez refused to submit to the American occupiers. At San Francisco de Macoris, twenty-nine-year-old 1st Lt. Ernest C. Williams from Broadwell, Illinois, commanded 125 Marines. He feared that the local Dominican garrison would release the hundred prisoners held in the Fortaleza. As soon as he learned of the establishment of military government, Williams decided to seize the fort. Immediately taking with him the dozen Marines available, he rushed its open gate. Before they could reach it, eight of his men were cut down by rifle fire. Williams threw himself against the gate, just as it was being closed, and forced his way in. His pistol jammed. Drummer Schovan jumped in front of him and grabbed the rifle of a Dominican about to fire at the lieutenant point-blank. Williams and his four Marines killed two guards and quickly took control of the prison and prisoners. Williams received the Medal of Honor for his daring.

With many well-armed followers, Governor Perez fled south by train. Several Marine detachments were sent after them; they fought a few skirmishes but could never close with the rebels.

Brig. Gen. Pendleton's 2d Marine Brigade provided muscle for the American military government. The Marines fought a guerrilla war against organized rebel groups and tried to disarm the populace. Disarming proved difficult and unpopular; the Marines made house-to-house searches and used strong-arm methods, trying to neutralize the opposition to their occupation.

During the first half of 1917, a hundred patrols went out after the rebels. "Hiking Hiram" Bearss made a colorful reputation pursuing (with shirttail flying) and fighting a rebel leader known as Chacha. Chacha and three of his men surrendered, but the rest continued the war under Vincentico Evangelista. Late in March, a patrol led by Capt. R. S. Kingsbury was attacked by the rebels; it killed 15 and wounded a number of them, including Evangelista. In June, Evangelista was persuaded by First Sgt. William West to surrender with 200 of his men to Lt. Col. George Thorpe. (Thorpe had been a hero of Novaleta in the Philippines and in 1903 had led 19 Marines on a daring 500-mile trek into Abyssinia to escort the first U.S. diplomatic mission to Addis Ababa.) Shortly after Evangelista surrendered, he was killed "while attempting to escape."[20] With his death, the rebels' strength was broken and the fighting subsided.

But occasional clashes continued, and it was believed that German agents were arming the rebels and fanning the Dominican people's hatred of the American occupation. Once the United States entered World War I, most of the best officers left for France. Many of the Marines who remained were poorly trained and disgruntled with their assignment. At times, Dominican civilians were collected into the towns while the rebels lay waste the countryside. Frequently, the rebels ambushed Marine patrols. Marines succumbed to malaria and dengue fever and sometimes to corruption and misuse of their power. It was hard, boring and often dangerous duty.

One fight in particular became famous in the Marine Corps. Near the town of Manchado, a mounted patrol of four Marines led by Cpl. Bascome Breedon was ambushed while crossing a stream on August 13, 1918. The Marines killed a number of the enemy; but one by one, they were cut down. The last Marine alive, Pvt. Thomas J. Rushforth, had bullet and machete wounds in his body and left hand. A rebel tried to decapitate him, missed and partly severed his right hand. Rushforth escaped in a shower of bullets; one went through his saddle and hip; another pierced his horse's neck. The Marine reached camp covered with blood. He was commended by the Secretary of the Navy but was denied the Medal of Honor because no witnesses to the action were left alive.

At the direction of the Secretary of the Navy, the military government in 1917 had disbanded the Dominican army and organized a native constabulary, the Guardia Nacional Dominicana. The Guardia was regarded as a tool of the oppressors, and no respectable Dominican would serve in it. During the early years, almost all of its officers were Marine Corps officers or noncoms. Training centers were set up at Haina and Santiago. At first, the Guardia guarded the border with Haiti and garrisoned towns; but after the United States entered World War I and Marines were withdrawn to France, the Guardia was sent into the field to help the remaining Marines fight the rebels.

Once the war in Europe was won, the 15th Regiment and the 1st Air Squadron brought the 2d Marine Brigade's strength up to 3,000 men. By the middle of 1919, the 15th and half of the 3rd Regiment began vigorous patrolling in Seibo and Macoris provinces. The Marines' new aggressiveness raised the level of combat. And the guerrilla war entered a new dimension with the addition of primitive Marine air power to the struggle. The aviation squadron's six biplanes dive-bombed and machine-gunned enemy concentrations and became the eyes of the men on the ground seeking to root out the rebels in the jungles and mountains.

The military government achieved many social improvements in the Dominican Republic. Roads were built, public health measures were introduced and education was made available to more children. At first, the high wartime price of sugar provided funds, but the collapse of sugar prices in 1920 brought much of these good works to an end.

By the close of that year, President Wilson had decided to discontinue the American occupation. The size of the brigade was progressively reduced as wartime enlistments ran out and many Marines, resentful that they had not served in France and had been kept in uniform after the Armistice, left for home.

The reduction of Marine strength—as well as the postwar depression and unemployment—encouraged the Dominican opposition to the occupation. As a result, the brigade commander, Brig. Gen. Logan Feland, stepped up patrolling in the fall of 1920. In October 1921, a cordon system was put into operation in the eastern part of the country. Under Col. William C. Harllee, a renowned marksman, Marines surrounded and cordoned off large areas and rounded up every suspicious-seeming adult male. Round-ups were often conducted in the middle of the night and many civilians were pulled in on very little evidence. At the subsequent trials, more than 500 convictions were obtained. But these ruthless tactics aroused such anger among the people that cordoning had to be discontinued.

As the Dominican occupation slipped into its final years, the Marine Brigade commander, Brig. Gen. Harry Lee, also a veteran of the fighting in France, was directed to win the people's friendship and insist that the Marines deal with the Dominicans fairly and sympathetically. Amnesty was offered to anyone who had not committed a serious crime; and by the time the offer of amnesty expired on May 31, 1922, armed opposition was practically eliminated. A number of rebel leaders who surrendered were given suspended sentences on good behavior. Obviously, the Dominicans welcomed peace.

By October 21, 1922, a provisional government had assumed control of the country; and on July 12, 1924, a constitutional government was installed. The 2d Marine Brigade began leaving the Dominican Republic. The final large contingent shipped to San Diego, was reorganized into the 4th Marines and in March 1927 transferred to Shanghai, China. The last Marine company left the Dominican Republic in September 1924.

The Marines left behind a stable and solvent government. But it did not last long; and in 1930, the Guardia, renamed the Policia Nacional Dominicana—which the Marines had helped create—took over the Dominican government. General Rafael Trujillo, who had started his rise in 1919 as a lieutenant in the Guardia, became dictator. He maintained his contacts with Marine Corps officers,[21] especially Col. Richard M. Cutts,[22] the last commandant of the Policia, a U.S. national rifle champion and a White House aide to President Franklin D. Roosevelt. Trujillo became a bestial tyrant; and by 1960, the United States government was encouraging his enemies. He was assassinated on May 30, 1961. Four years later, the Marines landed again.

The eight-year Dominican occupation did its share to build throughout Latin America a heritage of hatred against United States imperialism.

The Marine interventions in the Caribbean never had the full support of the American people. These military actions were always controversial and debated, and opposition increased whenever there were reports of American atrocities and when Latin American resentment reached a fever pitch.

After World War I, the rationalization that the interventions were necessary to protect the Panama Canal and keep European powers away from American shores did not attract much support. In 1929, the United States Senate disavowed Theodore Roosevelt's corollary to the Monroe Doctrine that had assumed a unilaterally declared U.S. right to intervene.

In 1933, President Franklin Roosevelt, using the term "good neighbor" in his inaugural address, moved toward a new hemispheric relationship that emphasized non-intervention, freer trade relations and aid for economic development. The United States agreed at Montevideo that "No state has a right to intervene in the internal or external affairs of another."[23] The next year, the United States deserted the Platt Amendment, which had permitted it to interfere in Cuban affairs; withdrew from Haiti, and began negotiating a treaty with Panama. The era of prolonged interventions was over.

This is not to say that military interference was finished in the Caribbean. The Bay of Pigs disaster in 1961, the Cuban missile crisis in 1962 and the Dominican invasion in 1965 were all danger-filled reminders that the United States still regarded the Caribbean as vital to its national interest. And the Marines continued ready to perform whatever duty their government ordered to protect that vital interest.

8
"An Efficient and Very Mobile Force"

As the nation tiptoed into the world's troubles between the Spanish-American War and World War I, the Marine Corps changed enormously. In those two decades, the Corps swelled from 3,800 men to 13,600 in 1916. Even more important, its mission was transformed from the pre-1898 duty of supplying gunners and guards aboard warships to the embryo of a permanent expeditionary force that could go ashore and seize and hold advanced bases.

Such a metamorphosis had started with the advent of coal-driven ships but it was not made without opposition. Some planners wanted the Corps taken out of the Navy entirely and integrated into the Army; others wanted the Corps removed from naval ships and concentrated exclusively for expeditionary work. The Corps itself fought for both roles: to stay afloat and to defend the newly needed advanced bases.

During this same period, the Corps had three Commandants—and recurring controversy over the post. When Maj. Gen. Commandant Charles Heywood retired on October 3, 1903, President Theodore Roosevelt selected Brig. Gen. George F. Elliott to succeed him. The fifty-six-year-old native of Green County, Alabama, had studied at West Point for two years and was discharged for deficiencies in mathematics and French. Strangely, Jacob Zeilin and Elliott, the only two Commandants to attend the U.S. Military Academy, both flunked out.

Right after leaving West Point in 1870, Elliott was commissioned as a Marine officer and had a long and active career: the railroad strike of 1877, Korea and Peking in 1894, Guantanamo in 1898, the battle of Novaleta in 1899. During his seven years as Commandant, Marines landed throughout the Caribbean as well as in China, Korea and North Africa, and established posts at Hawaii and Midway.

Elliott was party to a nasty feud with Col. Charles H. Lauchheimer, the Adjutant and Inspector of the Corps. As a result, in 1910, President Taft banished Lauchheimer from Washington to the Philippines. The fight was rooted in a tangle of the Corps' high-pressured campaign to keep Marines on battleships, the rivalry between line and staff officers, Elliott's heavy drinking and Lauchheimer's alleged efforts to have him dismissed. Lauchheimer's exile aroused accusations of partisan politics and anti-Semitism. Jewish leaders charged discrimination; the affair grew into a scandal. It was called a second Dreyfus Affair. Lauchheimer, a member of a prominent Jewish family in Baltimore, was an Annapolis graduate and had many political connections in Washington. After Elliott retired in 1911, political pressure brought Lauchheimer back to Washington just before the 1912 election. By 1916, he was a brigadier general. When he died in 1920, while still on active duty after 36 years, his family contributed the Lauchheimer Trophy for marksmanship to the Corps.[24]

Long after Elliott's retirement on his sixty-fourth birthday, the former Commandant—on Thanksgiving Day 1922—sent an inspirational message to the Corps: "I can tell you a text in the Bible that points directly to our Marine Corps—it is in Revelations: 'Be ye faithful unto death. . . .' That is our motto, isn't it? 'Faithful unto death.' "[25]

Picking a successor to Elliott brought more bitterness. The obvious candidate was "Tony" Waller, who had a spectacular record as a fighting Marine. But the uproar over the killing of the Filipinos on Samar and his courtmartial had scarred his reputation. Waller mustered substantial support in Congress, especially among the representatives from his native Virginia; and it was not until February 3, 1911, that President Taft finally appointed Col. William P. Biddle. It was a highly political appointment pressed by Senator Bois Penrose of Pennsylvania.

A member of the notable Philadelphia family, Biddle had served on *Olympia* in the Battle of Manila Bay and in the Philippines and in China during the Boxer Rebellion. While he was Commandant, advanced base forces were organized and the first Marine fliers were trained; but relations between the Navy and the Marine Corps were strained. By the end of 1913, President Wilson's Secretary of the Navy, Josephus Daniels, was determined to alter the Marines' function, concentrate them in fewer stations, relieve them of guard and police duty and give them expeditionary-service training.

When the heavy-set Biddle retired early in 1914, after 30 years' service, Waller again was the center of controversy and again was passed over. Col. George Barnett, the first Naval Academy graduate to become Commandant and a veteran of the Spanish-American War and the Cuban intervention, was appointed Major General Commandant for a four-year term and led the Corps into World War I.

All three of these Commandants shared in the Corps' transformation. As soon as the General Board of the Navy was created in 1900 to advise the Secretary of the Navy, the Marine Corps was designated the best possible force to defend advanced naval bases. And the following year, the Board recommended that the Commandant organize four 104-man companies, each "ready for instant use"[26] on expeditionary service. A battalion was created and trained. In 1908 and 1909, the Congress increased the strength of the Corps to provide men for such assignments. And in 1910, Elliott established an Advanced Base School, first at New London, Connecticut, and later at Philadelphia.

President Roosevelt removed the Marines from shipboard duty with Executive Order No. 969 on November 12, 1908. This was a victory—for the moment—for Navy Capt. William F. Fullam and his adherents, who wanted the Marines taken off American warships. Roosevelt reportedly intended to transfer the Marine Corps to the Army. The Corps fought back; Waller, Neville, Lauchheimer, Butler and Frank L. Denny organized to defend it. And Admiral Dewey, president of the Navy's General Board, led the fight to keep the Marines in the Navy. Dewey was willing to remove them from the policeman's job afloat but he wanted the Navy to retain control over the Corps.

Roosevelt's vision of the Corps' new mission—"To furnish the first line of the mobile defense of naval bases and naval stations beyond the continental limits of the United States"[27]—was ahead of its time. His Executive Order created a great fight in the Congress. Commandant Elliott reacted to the Secretary of the Navy's order that the Marines be removed immediately from 13 ships by demanding that if they were taken off any Navy ships, they be removed from all. As a result, more than 2,000 Marines were transferred ashore and their shipboard places were filled by sailors. The Marine Corps lobbied vigorously and effectively against the change, and public opinion was marshalled in the Corps' support. Representative Thomas Butler, chairman of the House Naval Affairs Committee and Smedley Butler's father, held hearings. The issue was resolved the following March, when Senator Eugene C. Hale, chairman of the Senate Committee on Naval Affairs, amended the Naval Appropriations Bill to provide that eight percent of the enlisted men on board battleships and armored cruisers must be Marines. The Senate passed the amendment, 51 to 12. Just before he left office, Roosevelt restored the Marines to the warships but left their duty assignments up to the ships' captains. Three weeks after President Taft was inaugurated, he gave the Marines back their previously assigned duties aboard ship. Sensing a continuing danger to the Corps, a group of officers formed the Marine Corps Association to support it.

Meanwhile, the struggle to use the Marines in expeditionary roles went ahead. Among early Marine Corps studies that developed advanced-base doctrine were those by Maj. Henry C. Haines, Maj. Dion Williams, Maj. John H. Russell and Lt. Col. Eli K. Cole. Williams, then a captain in the naval intelligence service, wrote the first report in 1902. He advocated that the Marine Corps should garrison naval stations and should be kept under Navy control. He wrote: "Long experience has shown that the so-called cooperation of the Navy and the Army in a campaign is a myth and that neither will subordinate itself to the other, each having its own work to do in its own way."[28] He urged that the Corps be enlarged to 15,000 men and that all its officers be trained at the Naval Academy. Williams predicted that it would be necessary to establish temporary bases in a naval campaign; and, he said, "The Navy has in the Marine Corps an efficient and very mobile force, ever kept at a high state of discipline. . . ."[29]

Much of Williams' thinking was eventually adopted. By 1914, the Corps had organized two "fixed defense" regiments of 1,250 men, at Philadelphia and Mare Island, California, and had plans to form two "mobile defense" regiments in case of war. The mobile regiments would oppose enemy landings that were beyond the range of the guns of a fixed defense unit guarding an advanced base.

During January 1914, the Marines' Advanced Base Force trained with the Atlantic Fleet at Culebra Island off the east coast of Puerto Rico to test both men and equipment. The Fixed Defense Regiment was commanded by Col. Charles G. Long and the Mobile Regiment by Lt. Col. John A. Lejeune. They worked together as the First Advanced Base Brigade under Colonel Barnett. When Barnett was named Commandant, he turned over the brigade to Lejeune, who took it to the invasion of Vera Cruz.

In the long run, these Culebra exercises were crucial to the future of the Marine Corps. The previous May, Captain Fullam, as inspector for the Navy, had reported that the Marines advanced base force was a failure. He again recommended that the Marine Corps be organized into battalions and removed from naval vessels. Admiral Dewey and the General Board rejected Fullam's recommendations, fearing that if they were followed the Marine Corps would eventually be absorbed by the Army.

The Marines wanted to keep both their shipboard and new advanced base defense missions. To many, the very existence of the Corps seemed threatened by Fullam's ideas. Only much later, with the wisdom of hindsight, did the Corps come to recognize that Captain Fullam was pointing the way to the future.

But first there was a war to fight. With World War I, the Naval Appropriations Bill of August 1916 enlarged the Navy, and, largely as a result of Barnett's, Lejeune's and Lauchheimer's efforts, increased the Marine Corps from about 8,000 to more than 13,000 enlisted men, and from 343 and 600 officers. A Marine Corps Reserve was established, and eight brigadier generals were authorized. Waller, Pendleton, Cole and Lejeune were among those promoted. Jauntily attired in their four-dent "Montana peak" campaign hats, the Marines began getting ready for action in France.

*World War I Marine Corps recruiting poster by artist
James Montgomery Flagg.
Museums Branch, USMC*

SEMPER FIDELIS

X
WORLD
WAR
I
1914-1919

1
Belleau Wood—5 p.m., June 6, 1918

Lines of steel-helmeted Marines with bayonets fixed moved forward toward the mile-square French hunting preserve. Its dense underbrush, trees and great boulders made superb cover for doves or the machine-gun nests of the gray-uniformed Germans threatening Paris only 40 miles away. This was Belleau Wood, and the Marine Corps was entering its greatest battle so far.

At 5 P.M. on that sunny spring afternoon—June 6, 1918—three companies of the 3rd Battalion, 5th Marines, led by tall, slim Maj. Benjamin S. Berry, approached the wood from the west, advancing through a quarter-mile-long field of green wheat splashed with red poppies. There had been no pre-assault artillery fire; this was supposed to be a surprise attack. But the Germans in the wood were expecting them. Their massed Maxim machine guns rippled the waist-high grain and chopped gaps in the Marine line.

As the attack started, forty-four-year-old veteran Marine First Sgt. Dan Daly, winner of two Medals of Honor and hero of Peking and Haiti, crouched with his men of the 73rd Machine Gun Company in a grove on the edge of the wheat field. Floyd Gibbons, a war correspondent for the *Chicago Tribune,* described the scene he saw:

> The bullets nipped the tops of the young wheat and ripped the bark from the trees three feet from the ground on which the Marines lay. The minute for the Marine advance was approaching. An old gunnery sergeant commanded the platoon in the absence of the lieutenant, who had been shot and was out of the fight. This old sergeant

[For the location of places in the Western Front in World War I see map No. 7 in the map section.—*Au.*]

405

was a Marine veteran. His cheeks were bronzed with the wind and sun of the seven seas. The service bar across his left breast showed that he had fought in the Philippines, in Santo Domingo, at the walls of Pekin, and in the streets of Vera Cruz. . . .

As the minute for the advance arrived, he arose from the trees first and jumped out onto the exposed edge of that field that ran with lead, across which he and his men were to charge. Then he turned to give the charge order to the men of his platoon—his mates—the men he loved. He said: "Come on, you sons-o'-bitches! Do you want to live forever?"[1]

The first waves—advancing in well-disciplined but obsolete lines—were slaughtered. The German gunners took a dreadful toll. Many of the men who survived were pinned down in that wheat field; a few struggled to the edge of the wood but could not hold. After dark, they crawled back.

Said the Marines' general, "It was a costly failure bravely attempted."[2]

In the advance, Major Berry was severely wounded in the left forearm. Floyd Gibbons, trying to help him, took three bullets; the third destroyed his left eye. Berry, despite his wounds, rose and rushed forward to his men.

(Before the battle, Gibbons had sent to Paris a dispatch reporting that the Marines were entering combat. Hearing that he had been wounded and apparently killed in action, the censor passed the story unchanged. It was against the rules to identify units in combat, but the censor's sentimentality let the world know that the Marine Corps was in action. By such a fluke came glory.)

On Berry's right, the 3rd Battalion, 6th Marines moved out under Maj. Berton W. Sibley, a short, swarthy forty-one-year-old Vermonter. The young lieutenants shouted, "Follow me!" And the men swept silently across the fields of grass in four waves at right dress into the southern end of Belleau Wood. Men fell. The Germans were aiming low, shooting the Marines in the legs.

On a rise of ground, watching them proudly and trying to keep one eye on Berry's fate was the 6th Regiment's commander, Col. Albertus W. Catlin. A Marine for a quarter of a century, Catlin, from Gowanda, New York, now forty-nine, had commanded the Marines aboard *Maine* when she was sunk and received the Medal of Honor at Vera Cruz in 1914. Suddenly, he went down; a sniper's bullet had pierced his right lung and paralyzed his right side. Still conscious, he ordered a runner to have Lt. Col. Harry Lee come forward and take charge of the attack. Catlin survived an eight-hour ambulance ride to a Paris hospital and was shipped home.

Sibley's battalion reached the wood and entered a roaring hell. German machine guns were placed so that when one was assaulted, the next gun mowed down the attackers. The wood crawled with sharpshooters and was strung with elaborate tangles of barbed wire. With Sibley leading them, the Marines stayed low, hurled their grenades and went forward in rushes, using rifle and bayonet. The fighting was hand-to-hand, wild as a riot. Marines shot the enemy sharpshooters out of the trees. It was a jumbled melee won by sergeants and privates.

Sibley's 82d Company under Capt. Dwight Smith fought its way several hundred yards into the wood. As the Marines advanced, machine guns ripped their forward lines mercilessly. The 83rd Company led by 1st Lt. Alfred H. Noble of Federalsburg, Maryland, also met the German fire. Both companies were forced to swerve from their eastern course to the north. Sibley's two other companies were pinned down by the entrenched machine guns. Second Lt. Louis F. Timmerman, Jr., led his platoon of the 83rd straight through the mile-wide wood; beyond it, they were the target of fire from every side. They dashed back into the wood and captured two machine guns. The platoon charged out again and was decimated; Timmerman was shot in the face. The enemy fire was so intense that he had to pull his six surviving men back into the shelter of the wood. Another small group of Marines joined them, and together they manned the two captured machine guns. Others strengthened the isolated group. One arriving Marine had had his wounds treated by a German medic. Soon, Timmerman had 40 Marines with him; and they fought to hold the ground they had taken. Timmerman won the Distinguished Service Cross.

To Sibley's right, Capt. Randolph T. Zane and his 79th Company of Maj. Thomas Holcomb's 2d Battalion, 6th Marines met murderous enemy fire. In 40 minutes, Lt. Graves B. Erskine's platoon of 58 was reduced to 5. Erskine sent a wounded Marine to find Captain Zane and tell him they could not move forward. An hour later, the wounded man crawled back to report that the captain had said: "Goddammit, continue the advance." They did.[3]

Holcomb's 96th Company stormed the village of Bouresches at the southeast corner of the wood. The company commander, thirty-five-year-old Capt. Donald F. Duncan from Kansas, advanced calmly smoking his pipe; he took a Maxim bullet through the stomach, and then a shell killed him. A bullet momentarily knocked out tall, thin 2d Lt. Clifton B. Cates, the 4th Platoon commander. He recovered, found an abandoned French rifle and with 1st Lt. James F. Robertson led some 30 men into the town. They fought in the streets. Twenty-three Marines held the town for half an hour until others began arriving. The isolated Marines drove off a counterattack.

Word reached the 6th Marines' command post that the men in Bouresches were low on ammunition. By now it was dark, the sky ominous with heavy rain clouds. Two Marines volunteered to take a truck loaded with ammunition through to Bouresches. They raced down the shell-pocked road. Every time a German flare brightened the sky, they stopped the truck and froze. German artillery and machine guns had the road zeroed in. They kept slipping off the road; a wheel broke. Finally, they reached the edge of Bouresches and delivered the ammunition. The two volunteers were 2d Lt. William B. Moore, a young Princeton track and football star, and Regimental Sergeant Major John H. Quick, then almost forty-eight, the tall, silent veteran of Guantanamo, Samar and Vera Cruz. Both men were awarded the Distinguished Service Cross and the Navy Cross.

The night was a torment of confusion. Units were disorganized, their officers unable to form them in the darkness. German shells killed many; and several times, Marines fired on their comrades. Inside Belleau Wood, Sibley's Marines lay on their stomachs, the flank of their line entirely unprotected. But Sibley had no intention of withdrawing. The men dug in for the night, and two companies of the 2d Engineers crept up to reinforce them.

Through that long night, many of the wounded lay where they had fallen. On June 6, 31 officers and 1,056 men of the Marine Brigade were casualties. But the Marines had a foothold in Belleau Wood.

2
The Marine Brigade

When World War I began, nearly four years earlier, the Marines had been busy with brush wars in Haiti, the Dominican Republic and Mexico. But this was to be a totally new dimension of warfare: world-wide, wholesale slaughter. When it was finished, 8.6 million men in uniform would be dead; 21 million, wounded. Of these, 116,000 dead and 243,000 wounded would be Americans.

In the summer of 1914, the pressure cooker of European hostilities had exploded; and when Germany invaded Belgium on August 4, Europe was in flames.

The Germans swept through Belgium, outflanked the French fortifications and plunged down on Paris. But in the desperate Battle of the Marne, the French stopped the Germans outside Paris. The invaders pulled back and dug in behind the Aisne River. They had missed their chance. The Western Front settled into brutal, immobilized trench warfare. The machine gun was lord of the battlefield.

By 1917, four million Allied soldiers faced 2.5 million Germans on the Western Front in an unending war of attrition, devouring hundreds of thousands of lives. The Allies began to falter. The French army, torn with horrendous casualties, mutinied; and revolution in Russia freed more German divisions for the Western Front.

The United States had tried to stay out of it. In 1916, President Woodrow Wilson was reelected on the slogan: "He kept us out of war." But when the crunch came, the United States would not let England and France go under. Five months after his reelection, Wilson asked for a declaration of war.

On April 6, 1917, the United States finally entered the war. Its armed strength was puny compared with that of the grappling giants overseas. The U.S. Regular Army plus the Federalized National Guard on the Mexican border totaled only 208,-000 men. The Navy numbered 73,000. American air power consisted of a section of the Army Signal Corps with 130 pilots and 55 planes. Before peace came, four million Americans would enlist or be drafted into the Army and 800,000 would join the Navy. The Marine Corps started with 511 officers and 13,214 enlisted men. By war's end, the Corps, under the slogan "First to Fight," had grown to 2,462 officers and 72,639 enlisted men.

In that April of 1917, the Germans were confident that any American contribution would be too little and too late to make a difference. But the Allies urged the United States to send at least a token force as quickly as possible, more to shore up the morale of their own bone-weary, discouraged armies than to help defeat the Germans in the trenches.

First to go was Maj. Gen. John J. Pershing, commander of the American Expeditionary Force (AEF). In his small staff that landed at Liverpool on June 8 were two Marine officers: Lt. Col. Robert H. Dunlap and Maj. Logan Feland.

On June 14, the first echelon of the AEF sailed for France. One-fifth of its strength was in the 2,759 men of the 5th Marine Regiment. They were commanded by Col. Charles A. Doyen, 34 years a Marine.

As most Marines saw it, their main responsibility in the war was to support the Navy of which they were part. But Commandant George Barnett insisted that the Marine Corps was a force-in-readiness, able to share with the Army the first call on the Western Front. A week after *Lusitania* was sunk by a German submarine in May 1915, Col. John A. Lejeune, then Assistant to the Commandant, had said that if the United States were to fight a naval power, the Marine Corps would defend advanced naval bases; but if it faced a non-naval power, the Corps would be "the Advance Guard of the Army . . . first to set foot on hostile soil in order to seize, fortify, and hold a port from which as a base, the Army would prosecute its campaign."[4]

Once the United States declared war, Commandant Barnett pushed for a Marine combat role with the Army and told the Congress, "I do not want the Marine Corps to be considered a police force."[5] On May 22, 1917, the Corps' authorized enlisted strength was increased to 30,000; and three days later, despite Army objections, President Wilson signed an executive order attaching the 5th Marine Regiment to the Army for service in France. The Marines landed at St. Nazaire with the first expeditionary force on June 26; by the evening of July 3, the entire regiment had unloaded its ships and was ashore under canvas.

Then, two disputes raged simultaneously. The first was between Pershing and the European Allies. The AEF commander stubbornly insisted that the Americans fight as a separate army; the Allies wanted to feed them into their own forces in smaller units. The second argument was between Pershing and the Marines. He used the Marines along the line-of-communication as guards and military police; they had to fight for combat assignments.

The 5th Regiment had three commanding officers before it got into action: Col. Charles A. Doyen, Lt. Col. Hiram I. Bearss and Col. Wendell C. Neville. The 6th Regiment of Marines was organized at Quantico, Virginia, and arrived in France between October 5, 1917, and February 6, 1918. Colonel Catlin commanded. He and Neville had been Annapolis classmates.

On October 23, 1917, the two regiments—later joined by the 6th Machine Gun Battalion of Marines—were formed into the 4th Brigade of Marines. Doyen, now a brigadier general, was in command; and the Kentuckian Lt. Col. Feland was his chief of staff. At the outset, the 4th Brigade numbered 258 officers and 8,211 enlisted men; in eight battles it was to suffer 11,968 casualties, of whom 2,461 were killed.

The Marine Brigade and the Army's 3rd Infantry Brigade (the 9th and 23rd Infantry Regiments) plus an artillery brigade were joined together as the 2d U.S. Division—a total of 28,059 men. The Marine and infantry brigades each consisted of two regiments of three rifle battalions and a machine-gun battalion. Doyen, a native of Concord, New Hampshire, commanded the division for its initial two weeks, in October–November, the first Marine ever to lead an Army division. Then he was superseded by Maj. Gen. Omar Bundy, USA.

Pershing insisted that his troops learn to fight in the open, not only in static, defensive trench warfare. His men would move forward.

Most of the men in the ranks were recruits. According to Colonel Catlin, 60 percent of the 6th Marines were college men, many of them athletes. They had a lot to learn: trench digging, conducting and repelling trench raids, hand-grenade throwing, rifle-grenade firing, bayonet skills, the use of the gas mask, how to make barbed wire entanglements. And there was constant marching with a 45-pound pack and marksmanship practice with the Springfield '03. The Marines grew wiser and tougher and meaner.

More Americans were being rushed "over there"; by the end of the year, 50,000 were arriving each month. The 1st Division went into action on October 23, long before the 2d. In mid-March 1918, the Marines went into the line in a "quiet" sector near Verdun; for most, it was their first experience under fire. On April 12, the 74th Company of Marines was severely gassed and had to be evacuated. The 74th, 45th and 84th Companies all had chances to repel German raids on their positions.

The Germans decided to launch a major attack in the West before American weight could be brought to bear. It was now or never. In March, the United States still had only six complete divisions in France, less than 300,000 men. The Germans calculated that the war could be over by midsummer. But they did not give full credit to the willingness of U.S. soldiers and Marines to take punishment in battle and stand firm.

On March 21, the Germans struck their first blow against the British armies in the north. In four days, the Germans advanced 14 miles, the greatest movement on the Western Front since 1914. In this Second Battle of the Somme, the British Fifth Army was practically destroyed before the Germans were stopped. On April 9, they struck a second blow, but in 20 days of vicious fighting they failed to break the British. By April's end, the Allies had suffered 350,000 casualties; the Germans, at least 200,000.

The third German attack hit the French to the south, between Soissons and Reims, on May 27. The Germans took Soissons and reached the north bank of the Marne River at Château-Thierry, 40 miles from Paris. This Third Battle of the Aisne brought the Americans into action.

In this crisis, General Ferdinand Foch was named commander-in-chief of all the allied armies in France. He wanted to fight; and Pershing, putting aside his dream of an American army, threw his 2d and 3rd Divisions into the all-out effort to stop the Germans. On May 31, the 3rd U.S. Division held them at Château-Thierry. Newspapers back home headlined that the Marines had won that battle. But the fact is: no Marine ever claimed he fought in Château-Thierry.

Stopped there at the river, the Germans twisted right toward Vaux and Belleau Wood, still on the north side of the Marne. On May 31, the American 2d Division was brought up the Paris–Metz highway, through crowds of defeated French soldiers and frightened civilians, all pouring rearward, convinced that the war was lost. In Paris, under long-range bombardment for two months, the French government was preparing to evacuate; hundreds of thousands were fleeing. It seemed to the eager young soldiers and Marines of the 2d Division that only they were marching toward the war.

On June 1, Château-Thierry finally fell. The Germans took Vaux and moved into Belleau Wood. The French general commanding the sector placed the 9th U.S. Infantry between the Paris–Metz highway and the Marne, facing Vaux, and urgently called for another regiment. Maj. Gen. Bundy, commanding the 2d Division, ordered Brig. Gen. James G. Harbord, USA, who had taken command of the Marine Brigade when the ill Doyen went home to die, to put in one of his regiments.

Thus did the 6th Marines move up to the left of the 9th Infantry and deploy north from Le Thiolet on the Paris–Metz highway. Major Holcomb's 2d Battalion was on the Marine right, Maj. Maurice E. Shearer's 1st Battalion on the left to the north. The 5th Marines and the 23rd Infantry took positions in support. Bundy and Harbord agreed that the Marine Brigade would fight as a unit north of the highway and the 3rd Infantry Brigade to the south of it, "and on that spur of the moment decision came the alignment and the tremendous consequence, to the glory of the United States Marines, to the fortunes of the two brigades, and to the future of the world."[6]

That evening, the Germans knocked a hole in the French line to the front and left of the Marines. The 23rd Infantry, Maj. Julius S. Turrill's 1st Battalion of the 5th Marines, a part of the 6th Machine Gun Battalion and a company of Engineers rushed over in a forced march of 10 kilometers to plug the wound before it became fatal. By dawn, they were in place; and Harbord put in Maj. Frederic M. Wise's 2d Battalion, 5th Marines to strengthen the defense between Turrill on the left and Shearer on the right. Wise's men were stretched over more than two miles of the line. (Later, Turrill was pulled back in reserve, and the 23rd Infantry filled in.) Now, from the 9th Infantry south of the highway, through the Marines, to the 23rd Infantry, this section of the front—12 miles long—was American.

The Marine line, holding a landscape of grain fields dotted with clumps of woods, was terribly thin. The men were short of ammunition, hot food and water. German shells peppered their positions, taking a toll. The Marines dug in.

By the night of June 2, the Germans held a line from Vaux to Bouresches to Belleau and occupied Belleau Wood. The Americans faced them across rolling farmland from Triangle Farm to Lucy to Hill 142. The Marines' job was, simply stated, "Hold the line at all hazards."[7] Harbord countermanded a French order to dig trenches several hundred yards to the rear; he said, "The Marines will hold where they stand."[8] With bayonets and mess kits, the men dug shallow foxholes, in which a rifleman could lie prone and do his job. There would be no falling back; the Germans were not to pass.

The Germans ordered an advance on Marigny and Lucy and through the wood. Further south, other German divisions were ordered to cross the Marne.

That afternoon of June 3, the German infantry, in extended lines, bayonets fixed, attacked the Marine positions through the wheat fields. Marines were hit; Lt. Lemuel C. Shepherd, Jr., took a bullet in the neck. They waited, watched the Germans come on in waves—and then, when they were only 100 yards away, the Marines opened with a deadly rifle fire. They mowed the enemy down and finally forced the survivors to stop and break through the grain fields for the trees behind them. That charge was the peak of the German drive; the Marines had held.

Wise later wrote:

> If ever there was a miracle in the war, that was it. With a wide front, much of it open, to pick and choose, the German attack had smashed squarely into the center of

those lone two and a half miles we held. Had the same force hit either of our flanks, they could have crumpled us and cleaned us up.

I was in no position to exploit our success. The only thing in the world we could do was stick in our fox holes and hold that line. Out in front of us were Germans in unknown force. Both of our flanks remained unprotected. God alone knew how far back of us any support might be. But the Germans never attacked us again.[9]

The German offensive was finished for the moment, unable to pierce the defense and extended to its utmost in men and supplies. German casualties were enormous. Paris was now out of reach. The German commanders gave the order to dig in on a defensive line including Torcy, Belleau Wood, Le Thiolet and Hill 204 just west of Château-Thierry.

But the French were exhausted; all that night they made their way back through the American lines. One French major ordered Capt. Lloyd Williams, commanding Wise's right-hand company, to withdraw his men. As legend has it, Williams retorted: "Retreat, hell. We just got here." (Wise later claimed he had said the famous words.[10])

By 8 A.M. on June 4, Maj. Gen. Bundy took command of that piece of the Western Front. Now, the 23rd Infantry held the line from the Paris–Metz road north to Triangle Farm; then Holcomb's battalion to Lucy, and Berry's to Hill 142. Artillery, communications and supply were moving up.

The next two days were a standoff; the Germans continued to make local assaults and were thrown back by the Marines' expert fire. Between the two forces fell a rain of rifle and machine-gun fire and shrapnel. The Marines recognized the bravery of the worn-out German troops advancing in close formation to certain death. And shot them down.

The 167th French Division arrived to help out, and Bundy could consolidate. His 3rd Brigade was now on the south; the Marine Brigade to the north. They touched at the Triangle Farm. Each of Bundy's four infantry and Marine regiments held some 2,000 yards of the line, with two battalions up front and one in reserve. Catlin later wrote: "We now stood facing the dark, sullen mystery of Belleau Wood, Berry on the west and Holcomb on the south."[11] It was time for the Americans to attack.

Again, the Germans coiled to strike; but at 3:45 A.M. on June 6, the Americans and French jumped off first. The plan: On the 2d Division's left, the 167th French Division was to attack, while the Marines took Hill 142 to eliminate its flanking fire against the 167th. Then, in the climactic second phase at 5 P.M., the 2d Division was to seize the ridge overlooking the towns of Torcy and Belleau and occupy Belleau Wood and the town of Bouresches at the southeast corner beyond the wood.

But the battle would not go that way.

The Marines had made an important mistake. When the French had pulled back on June 4, they had told the Marines that Belleau Wood was empty of Germans; and the Marines had failed to send out scouting patrols to check for themselves. The French were wrong. The Germans were there—a regiment of German infantry with an interlocking network of machine-gun nests and covered by artillery—the hard-nosed tip of their push toward Paris.

Before dawn, the 1st Battalion, 5th Marines (Turrill) was supposed to hit Hill 142 with the 8th and 23rd Machine Gun Companies and D Company of the 2d Engineers. The 3rd Battalion, 5th Marines (Berry) would move up on Turrill's right. But most of Turrill's command was still scattered on previous assignments. By H-Hour, only Capt. Orlando C. Crowther's 67th Company and Capt. George W. Hamilton's 49th Company were on the mark. In the dark, they went over the top in four waves, and, with bayonets fixed, advanced in ranks into the wheat fields. After 50 yards, the machine guns destroyed them. Hamilton forced his men to their feet and to rush into a small woods. There, they fought the entrenched Germans with steel. Crowther and 1st Sgt. Daniel A. "Beau" Hunter were both killed almost immediately. Hamilton urged his men through the woods and into another field of wheat, where again they came under heavy fire until they could reach the next little woods. Hamilton's men overran their objective by 600 yards. Three Marines actually got into Torcy, where the Germans were concentrated. One of the three, wounded, was sent back for reinforcements. The two others found a hole and continued to fight from it. Two Germans attacked them. All four men died in that hole.

Hamilton had lost all five junior officers, and the 67th Company had only one of its five officers still alive. Hamilton tried to reorganize the two Marine companies; he established strong points and set up a defensive line. Suddenly, the Germans counterattacked, hurling grenades at the few Marines.

Gunnery Sgt. Ernest A. Janson of the 49th Company spotted 12 Germans with automatic rifles crawling toward the Marines. He yelled a warning and killed the first two Germans with his bayonet. The others fled. For his swift stroke that saved his company, the thirty-nine-year-old sergeant from New York City (who served under the name of Charles Hoffman) was the first Marine in World War I to win the Medal of Honor.

The rest of Turrill's units began showing up and went into action. Capt. Lloyd Williams' 51st Company of Wise's battalion was thrown in on Turrill's left. But both Turrill's flanks hung unprotected, and his men were exhausting their ammunition. His battalion lost nine officers and most of 325 men and by afternoon won Hill 142.

At 5 P.M., with a good three hours of daylight left, the second part of the American offensive began. Berry's and Sibley's battalions went over the top and into a hail of German bullets. They moved forward and entered Belleau Wood.

3
Bois de la Brigade de Marine

As June 7 began, the battlefield was littered with the dead and wounded. The Marine Brigade held a line more or less from Triangle Farm to Bouresches (the Germans still held the railroad station there), through the bottom of Belleau Wood and then north toward Hill 142.

The shelling and firing went on all day. After midnight, the Germans attacked and were stopped cold. At 4 A.M. on June 8, Sibley's battalion attacked and by ten o'clock had been halted with heavy losses. The German defense was too strong.

The battle was deadlocked. And that night south of Belleau Wood, the 1st Battalion, 6th Marines, now led by Maj. John A. "Johnny the Hard" Hughes, moved up to replace Sibley's weary battalion. Sibley had lost 400 men, killed, wounded and missing. Second Lt. Timmerman's platoon, for example, had 19 men left. Every officer of the 82d Company was out of action.

Major Shearer, for the wounded Berry, took over the 3rd Battalion, 5th Marines and replaced Holcomb's men on the right and in Bouresches.

Throughout June 9, an enormous, thundering American and French artillery barrage devastated Belleau Wood. The attractive hunting preserve became a jungle of shattered trees filled with the smell of death.

The Germans counterfired, shelling Lucy and Bouresches and the ground between, and reorganized their defense inside the wood.

At 4:30 A.M. on June 10, Hughes' battalion and some of Maj. Edward B. Cole's 6th Machine Gun Battalion attacked Belleau Wood. At first, the attack went easily; but by 7 A.M., the 75th Company had been stopped by enemy machine guns, and Major

Cole was mortally wounded. Brig. Gen. Harbord had seriously underestimated the German strength in the wood.

Next, Harbord ordered Wise's 2d Battalion, 5th Marines to attack the middle of the wood from the west, while Hughes advanced from the south. Wise's units were understrength and tired from days and nights of fighting and shelling. The thirty-nine-year-old New Yorker—a veteran of China, the Philippines and the Caribbean—had lost 25 percent of his men. Wise later insisted Harbord had ordered him to attack the *southern* edge of the wood.[12]

Before dawn on June 11, Wise's battalion moved through the freshly plowed wheat fields and into a thick protective morning mist. As they advanced on Belleau Wood, the men began to fall under heavy fire. The lead companies were shot to pieces. Lloyd Williams was wounded early and died that night. In the wood, it was small-unit, close-range warfare in the underbrush, with isolated platoons against the terror of the interlocking machine-gun fire. Wise wrote later, "Nothing in all our training had foreseen fighting like this. If there was any strategy in it, it was the strategy of the Red Indian. The only thing that drove those Marines through those woods in the face of such resistance as they met was their individual, elemental guts, plus the hardening of the training through which they had gone."[13]

There were no landmarks in the wood; and, unfortunately, these determined Marines were off-target. Rather than heading northeast as expected, they moved directly across the wood's narrow waist. Wise's left-hand companies (Capt. Charles Dunbeck's 43rd and Capt. Lester Wass' 18th) ended up where his right should have been.

At 7 A.M., Brig. Gen. Harbord announced: "The northern end of the Bois de Belleau belongs to the 5th Marines."[14] He was wrong. The Marines had not reached the northern part of the wood. Wise's company commanders were further south than they thought they were—a massive and costly error.

Where they did hit, the Marines smashed the German defenders momentarily and destroyed their southern defense line. One German private, whose company had 30 men left out of 120, wrote in a letter, "We have Americans [Marines] opposite us who are terribly reckless fellows."[15] The Germans began calling them a name in which the Marines took pride: *Teufelhunde*—Devil Dogs.

North of Wise, the Germans established a new defensive line in the wood and poured in reinforcements. They were in front of Wise and on his left flank. And half of Wise's battalion was wiped out. That night, engineers and Marine replacements came up and went directly into the line.

Pershing's headquarters had already announced to the world that the Americans had taken Belleau Wood. So, on June 12, the local commanders needed to make good the news. That afternoon, still believing there would be light resistance, Harbord ordered Wise to make another attack at 5 P.M. This time, the assault was led by the 55th Company of Lt. E. D. Cooke, USA; Dunbeck's 43rd; and Wass' 18th. Again, Hughes' battalion was to hit from the south, as Wise attacked from the west.

Because of the misinformation about the Marines' location, the artillery barrage struck 1,000 yards too far in advance, leaving the German defenders nearest the Marines unharmed. The Germans met the attack with everything they had, including mustard gas. The remaining Marines charged forward yelling. It was brutal no-quarter-given combat with rifle, pistol, bayonet. Pvt. Aloysius Leitner, though mortally wounded, continued fighting and helped capture six Germans operating a machine gun. He won the Army Distinguished Service Cross and the Navy Cross posthumously.

Wise later told this story:

> One squad of his company, Wass told me, had taken a German machine gun camouflaged behind a brush pile in the middle of the woods, that day. The minute they got among the Germans with bayonets, the Germans, who had worked the gun up to that minute and had cut up the Marines pretty badly, surrendered. The Marines took them all prisoners. Not one was killed. And that minute another German machine gun opened up on their flank. They left their prisoners, charged the second gun, and captured it. The minute they got among those Germans with bayonets, every one of them surrendered. And that minute the captured gun crew they had left behind them opened fire on them again. They couldn't play back and forth like this all day. They bayoneted every man of that

Daniel J. "Fighting Dan" Daly was the only enlisted Marine ever to win the Medal of Honor for two separate actions—at Peking and Haiti. He also earned the Navy Cross and Army Distinguished Service Cross at Belleau Wood. Commandant Lejeune called Sergeant Daly "the outstanding Marine of all time." Museums Branch, USMC

Leaders of the Marine Brigade in France in World War I: Maj. Gen. John A. Lejeune and Brig. Gen. Wendell C. Neville. *Museums Branch, USMC*

U.S. Marine in France, sketched by Capt. John W. Thomason, Jr., who in his writing and illustrations captured the flavor of the Corps of that era. *Collection of Mrs. John W. Thomason, Jr.*

Marine Corps women reservists put up recruiting posters in New York City during World War I. *Marine Corps Photo, National Archives*

*French army officers teach newly arrived Marines how
to wear gas masks.
U.S. Signal Corps Photo, National Archives*

*U.S. Marines on their way to the front in France in 1918.
Museums Branch, USMC*

U.S. Marines on review just before the fighting at
Belleau Wood.
Brown Brothers

Marines firing .30-caliber Browning machine gun in the
Meuse-Argonne offensive.
Marine Corps Photo, National Archives.

Wounded Marines of the Fourth Brigade
being trucked to a hospital in France.
U.S. Signal Corps Photo, National
Archives

Marines march in the giant parade in
Paris on July 4, 1918, after the victory
in Belleau Wood.
Brown Brothers

Marine on watch on the Rhine River Patrol during the occupation of Germany following the 1918 Armistice.
U.S. Signal Corps Photo, National Archives

Brig. Gen. Smedley D. Butler and mascot "Sergeant Jiggs" were symbols of the post–World War I Marine Corps.
Marine Corps Photo, National Archives.

"Horse Marines" of the Legation Guard in Peking mounted on Mongolian ponies.
Marine Corps Photo, National Archives

"China Marines" watch Chinese refugees streaming to safety across the bridge over Soochow Creek, Shanghai, in 1932.
Marine Corps Photo, National Archives

Capt. Earl H. Ellis was a brilliant planner who helped revolutionize Marine Corps thinking and point the way to the amphibious strategy of World War II in the Pacific. Ellis died mysteriously in the Japanese-held Palau Islands in 1923. Harris and Ewing; photo courtesy Museums Branch, USMC

In early amphibious experiment, Marines unload a 75mm gun from a "Beetle boat" at Culebra, Puerto Rico, in 1923. Museums Branch, USMC

Formation of new F4B-4 fighters fly in echelon over San Diego in 1934. Museums Branch, USMC

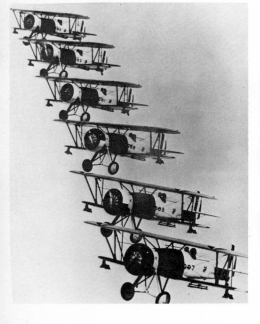

Twentieth century Marine Corps rifles: top to bottom, .30-caliber Krag-Jorgensen adopted in 1900; bolt-action Springfield M1903; and Garand M-1 of World War II. National Rifle Association; photo courtesy Museums Branch, USMC

second German gun crew, went back and captured the first gun all over again, and bayoneted every man of that crew before they went on.[16]

Now, the Marines pushed the Germans northward among the rocks and ravines of Belleau Wood. On the right, they pushed the Germans out of the wood; but other elements were still fighting inside. The entire Marine line was bombarded by high-explosive and mustard-gas shells. In the wood, young Capt. Edward C. Fuller, the commander of the 75th Company and the son of the future Commandant, was mortally wounded. At 3 A.M. on June 13, the Germans struck at the wood's eastern side and at Bouresches, where Shearer's sharpshooting battalion stopped them cold.

Early that morning, Turrill's 1st Battalion, 5th Marines was sent in but found that Wise was not where he was supposed to be; the western part of the wood was unexpectedly full of Germans.

Holcomb was ordered to relieve Wise's chewed-up battalion. But before he could move up, the Germans opened a vicious mustard-gas attack. Holcomb's battalion suffered 160 gas casualties; Hughes' and Wise's battalions were also gassed. The 74th, 96th and 78th companies had to be evacuated because of the gas that choked men to death. Gunnery Sgt. Fred W. Stockham of Detroit and the 96th Company gave his gas mask to a wounded Marine whose mask had been shot away. Stockham was overcome by the poison gas and died several days later. He was awarded the Medal of Honor posthumously.

Finally, on the morning of the 15th, the 17th Company of Capt. Roswell Winans, the young Hoosier who had won the Medal of Honor as an enlisted man in the Dominican Republic, gained a foothold on the western side of the wood. Later that day and into the night, the Marine Brigade was relieved by the 7th Infantry and the French. The front remained under Colonel Neville's command, with Lt. Col. Feland in charge in Belleau Wood.

The bearded, exhausted Marines went to the rear; the Germans in their official reports called them vigorous, self-confident and remarkable marksmen. Two thousand eight hundred replacements filled the holes in their ranks.

In two weeks of battle, the Marine Brigade had taken more

than 50 percent casualties. Holcomb lost 21 officers and 836 men; Sibley, 14 officers and 400 men; Turrill, 16 officers and 544 men; Wise, 19 officers and 615 men.

As the Marines went to the rear to recuperate, a new German battalion came into Belleau Wood, with a second on its right and a third in reserve. They held the northern end of the wood in strength.

The 7th Infantry, untried in battle, was unable to budge the Germans from the wood. Shearer's 3rd Battalion, 5th Marines was brought back to clean out the German resistance, which Harbord continued to underestimate. Shearer attacked at 7 P.M. on June 23, quickly took 130 casualties and bogged down before the German machine guns. It was a badly mangled operation.

Now, the Marine Brigade took over the front again. Shearer's battalion was in the middle of the deadly wood; Ralph S. Keyser, relieving Wise (who had been severely criticized by Harbord and had blown up angrily at the general), was on his left, and Sibley's battalion extended the line to Bouresches on the right. Holcomb, Turrill and Hughes were in reserve.

At 5 P.M. on June 25, following a massive all-day barrage— all too long delayed—Shearer's battalion began to move through the wood. The artillery had knocked out the enemy machine-gun nests. The Marines took heavy casualties, but the Germans were running out of reinforcements and began pulling back to the Belleau–Torcy road north of the wood. One Marine runner, Pvt. Henry P. Lenert, stumbled into a German position and was asked by its captain in English whether there were more troops behind Shearer. The quick-thinking private assured him that the 6th Marines were ready to pass through and attack at dawn. The captain conferred with his officers and then told the young Marine to lead the 82 Germans back to brigade headquarters as his prisoners.

At 7 A.M. on June 26, Capt. Robert Yowell's 16th Company of Shearer's battalion reached the north edge of Belleau Wood; and the battalion commander sent Harbord the message: "Woods now U.S. Marine Corps entirely."[17]

Shearer's men had suffered 250 casualties, killed 150 Germans, taken some 300 prisoners and captured 30 machine guns. That night, they were relieved by Holcomb's battalion. The fighting and the dying were not finished, but Belleau Wood was taken.

The French parliament declared July 4 a national holiday in honor of the Americans fighting on French soil. A gigantic parade was set in Paris, and the 2d Division sent a battalion made up of one company organized out of each regiment. The officers picked the old hands to go to the rose-strewn welcome awaiting them in the capital. There, the Marine Corps flag was hailed with enormous cheers and the cry of *"Vive les Marines!"* But after a night of celebration, the men headed back to the front again. The French premier, Georges Clemenceau, had offered to open his nation's brothels to the Americans; but Pershing turned him down.

The French general commanding the Sixth Army gave the Marines the ultimate compliment and ordered that henceforth the Bois de Belleau would be called the "Bois de la Brigade de Marine." Years later, speaking at the cemetery there, Marshal Foch called it "the cradle of Victory." [18]

The price had been shockingly high: 126 officers and 5,057 enlisted men of the Marine Brigade dead and wounded. During the bloody month of June, the 2d Division had 1,811 battle deaths, of which 1,062 were Marines.

The survivors would never forget. Twenty-two-year-old Gunnery Sgt. Don V. Paradis of the 80th Company, 6th Marines, wrote his family in Detroit, after censorship was lifted:

> I was knocked down by shell concussion and caught in machine gunfire several times but managed to pull through safely. We were in the front lines for sixteen days without any relief and when we did go back it was only into reserve for six days when we came back to the lines again. . . . I am the only sergeant left in our first Platoon that is of the old bunch of course we have all new ones now. . . . We . . . are getting a little real rest and a chance to clean up, which sure means a whole lot as all of us had cooties and had not had a chance to get a real bath. For a month and four days we did not have our clothes off, not even our shoes, only to rub our feet and perhaps wash them with a canteen of water.[19]

General Pershing wrote the 2d Division: "You stood like a wall against the enemy advance on Paris."[20]

The battle had another unhappy aftermath. An envious

rivalry broke out between the Marines and the soldiers of the division. The Army chafed under the glory—and publicity—won by the Marine Brigade. Even the 3rd Brigade's successful July 1 attack on Hill 192 and Vaux, between Bouresches and Château-Thierry, did not compensate. When Clemenceau visited division headquarters, neither Brig. Gen. Harbord nor any of the top Marine officers was invited to meet him. The bitterness simmered for a generation among many of the Army's highest leaders and even helped keep the Marine Corps out of Europe in World War II. But the fortunes of war had shoved the Marines into the battle, and they had stopped the enemy and then driven them out of Belleau Wood.

4
Soissons—Two Days in Hell

On July 15, the Germans—49 divisions strong—lunged again toward Paris, crossed the Marne River between Château-Thierry and Reims and seized a bridgehead four miles deep.

But the military balance had changed. Germany was being drained of fighting men, while the Allies were receiving constant transfusions from America. A million Yanks had reached France, and great numbers of them fought alongside the French to contain the July 15 attack. In 48 hours, the Germans were thrown back across the Marne with dreadful losses to both armies. That was the Germans' last offensive on the Western Front; it would be 22 more years before they marched into Paris.

With this German failure on the south side of their Château-Thierry pocket, General Foch aimed a counterblow at its northern side. His first objective: to cut the Mauberge highway between Château-Thierry and Soissons, over which the Germans were supporting their 40 divisions in the pocket.

Now commanded by Colonel Neville, who had just returned from the hospital, the Marine Brigade moved up as part of the 2d Division to join the counteroffensive. Harbord, promoted to major general, commanded the division; on its left was the First Moroccan Division—a unit of crack assault troops including the tough French Foreign Legion. Further to the left was the U.S. 1st Division. All were part of the French Tenth Army and the spearhead of the Allied counterattack. The Aisne-Marne Offensive now starting would continue till the war was won.

The troops were dumped into the great Retz Forest south of Soissons. The Marines made a silent, confused forced night march to reach the jumpoff point. The forest roads were jammed with men, trucks and guns. Stumbling forward through the rain

425

and moonless black, each man clung the pack of the man in front. Just as the five-minute preparatory barrage began, the last units came up at double time.

At 4:35 A.M. on July 18, the men fixed bayonets; and the three divisions moved forward. In the 2d Division's sector, the 5th Marines, led by Colonel Feland, held the left. The dog-tired Marines met the Germans in the oak forest and advanced northeast for three kilometers against their machine guns. They fought the Germans Indian-style, moving from tree to tree and shooting snipers out of the limbs.

Two sergeants in the 66th Company of the 5th Marines received the Medal of Honor for bravery during this advance. When the company was stopped by a German strongpoint, Serbia-born Sgt. Louis Cukela crawled out on the flank, circled behind the German position, rushed the machine gun and killed or drove off its crew with his bayonet. Picking up German hand grenades, he blasted out the remainder of the strongpoint, destroyed two machine guns and brought in four prisoners. Austrian-born Sgt. Matej Kocak went forward alone, unprotected by covering fire, to wipe out a hidden machine-gun nest. In the face of heavy fire, he attacked the position and scattered the crew with his bayonet. Then he rallied a group of Moroccans who had become separated from their company and led them in destroying another machine-gun nest.

The Moroccan division crushed heavy resistance with bayonets and knives but was delayed enough to expose the Marines' left flank to raking German machine-gun fire. The 17th Marine Company was pressed too far north and with some Moroccans took the town of Chaudun.

As the Marines emerged from the forest, the July morning was hot; and soon the men were racked with thirst. Led now by French tanks, they charged through steaming waist-high wheat fields ablaze with blooming red poppies. At Beaurepaire Farm, the division swung to the southeast. The 3rd Infantry Brigade on the Marines' right was held up until 6 P.M. by a stubborn defense at Vauxcastille, where the fighting was hand-to-hand.

By mid-afternoon, the 2d Division's units were jumbled. Turrill pulled together parts of his 1st Battalion, with some elements of Shearer's 3rd Battalion and the 8th Marine Machine Gun Company, and joined the 23rd Infantry to clean out the village of Vierzy, where the Germans were making a stand.

Marines and infantrymen assaulted the town from different sides, meeting triumphantly in its streets.

At 7 P.M., the 9th Infantry, reinforced by both Turrill's 1st and Keyser's 2d Battalions, pressed forward again. Stopped by German machine guns, Keyser's Marines took a pounding from enemy artillery and suffered heavy casualties. By dark, the Marines and the 3rd Brigade were exhausted, used up.

On the morning of the 19th, Lt. Col. Harry Lee's 6th Marines, most of which had been in reserve, took over the lead. German divisions had been rushed up to halt the offensive at all costs. They would cut up the 6th Marines cruelly.

The Marines moved out, with Hughes' 1st Battalion on the right and Holcomb's 2d Battalion on the left and Sibley's 3rd Battalion in support. Crossing flat, open country, the lead battalions were slaughtered by German artillery, guided by air spotting. The guns knocked out the French tanks. In half an hour, so many Marines had been hit that two of Sibley's companies were sent to fill in.

Sgt. Don V. Paradis remembered:

> What few of us were left fell into these foxholes. We even piled on top of each other to seek cover from that murderous shellfire. I laid there with every muscle in my body twitching, hardly knowing what I was doing. We could hear the wounded calling for help, but very little could be done for them until after dark came.[21]

Of the 196 men in his company, 54 were left.

The Germans finally stopped the Marine advance six miles from its starting point and less than a mile short of its objective, the Mauberge highway. It was hopeless to go on; the lead battalions had lost more than 50 percent of their men. The survivors dug in. French units replaced them during the night; and then, the Marines carried out their wounded.

In two days, the Marine Brigade had lost 2,015 men killed and wounded; the 6th Marines took two-thirds of the losses. But Foch's attack had pushed the Germans back from the Marne to the Vesle River and triggered the general retreat of the German army. It had turned the war around. As the German chancellor said, "The history of the world played out in three days."[22]

The Marines and the rest of the 2d Division moved to the

rear, some companies with only 25 or 30 men left. Maj. Gen. Harbord called them "a victorious remnant."[23]

On July 26, Brig. Gen. John A. Lejeune took over the Brigade. The Louisiana-born Annapolis graduate brought with him as the Brigade's adjutant Lt. Col. Earl H. Ellis, a brilliant officer destined for a strange fate. A few days later, Lejeune, now a major general, assumed command of the 2d Division. Newly promoted Brig. Gen. Neville resumed command of the Marine Brigade for the rest of the war.

The day Lejeune took over the Brigade, he told the men: "I have this day assumed command of the Fourth Brigade, U.S. Marines. To command this brigade is the highest honor that could come to any man. Its renown is imperishable and the skill, endurance and valor of the officers and men have immortalized its name and that of the Marine Corps."[24]

5
St. Mihiel and Blanc Mont Ridge

Between July 25 and September 12, the Marine Brigade had only 15 casualties. The men spent ten days in a quiet sector of the front around Marbache in the Moselle valley and trained for the next round.

The Allies gathered strength. Foch became a Marshal of France and planned a massive offensive along the entire Western Front. Pershing finally got his American army—the U.S. First Army—and, preliminary to Foch's offensive, prepared to wipe out the four-year-old bulge in the line at St. Mihiel, where the Germans had pushed out from the fortress city of Metz on the Moselle River. For two years, there had been little fighting there.

Meanwhile, to the northwest, French and American divisions kept pounding away until, by August 6, exactly two months after the earlier offensive began at Belleau Wood, the line between Reims and Soissons had been hammered straight. The American soldiers carried the heaviest load and took 50,000 casualties.

Still further north, two days later, the British tore open the enemy line. The stricken German High Command called it a "Black Day" for Germany. Germany's leaders decided the war must be ended, and the Kaiser ordered the politicians to sue for peace. Later, some Germans might rant that they had been "stabbed in the back," but in fact they had been broken on the battlefield.

To clip off the St. Mihiel salient between the Meuse and Moselle rivers—the last salient in the Western Front—Pershing had 19 divisions of his own army and six French divisions. Col. William "Billy" Mitchell, USA, commanded 1,400 supporting airplanes.

When the Germans realized that the salient in front of Metz was going to be hit hard, they began pulling back to their Hindenburg Line positions. They had barely started retreating when, at 1 A.M. on September 12, the roaring bombardment of 3,000 guns began; and after four hours, behind a rolling barrage, came the troops.

In the sector of the 2d Division, again at full strength, the 3rd Infantry Brigade led the attack, with the 5th Marines supporting the 9th Infantry on the right and the 6th Marines following the 23rd Infantry on the left. Resistance was slight. At the end of the second day, the Marine Brigade took over the line, fought forward and stood off counterattacks from the Hindenburg Line. Casualties were comparatively light because of the heavy artillery barrage and because the enemy was already falling back when the Marines advanced; the Brigade had 132 dead and 574 wounded. And the persistent St. Mihiel salient had disappeared.

The Germans expected Pershing to go on to Metz; but even before the St. Mihiel attack was finished, reserve troops were moving north to the area between the Meuse River and the Argonne Forest, where Foch wanted to deliver his hardest blow.

The American First Army stood from the Meuse west to the Argonne; the French Fourth Army was west of the forest. Facing the Americans, the Germans had built elaborate defensive positions in great depth; and they controlled the heights on both flanks, the bluffs east of the Meuse and the tree-covered hills of the Argonne on the left. This American sector was at the southern end of the great offensive that Foch opened on September 26 against the main German defensive system from the Meuse all the way to the North Sea.

Although the American First Army outnumbered its opponents eight to one, the enemy's stubborn, shrewd defense and the difficult terrain that Foch had chosen made the Meuse-Argonne battle an epic slugging match. The Germans stayed to fight, and the American soldiers knocked their heads against the enemy's wall in the most bullheaded fashion—at the cost of thousands of lives. Not until the U.S. 2d Division finally took Blanc Mont Ridge to the south on October 5 did the Germans start withdrawing.

Meanwhile, back of the German lines, the generals and

politicians were groping for a way out of the war; and on October 4 they sent President Wilson a cable asking for an armistice. But the young men on both sides continued to die.

At the beginning of the great offensive, the 2d and the 36th U.S. Divisions were turned over to the French Fourth Army, commanded by the distinguished General Henri Gouraud, a French "marine" who had lost an arm at Gallipoli. Pershing was still fighting with Foch to keep the American Army intact, and the release of these two divisions to the French was a compromise.

Lejeune also had to battle French pressure to break up his brigades to support the French divisions. He insisted that the 2d Division fight as a unit and told Gouraud if his division were not divided, it would take Blanc Mont Ridge, which dominated the Arnes Valley in Champagne and was the key to the French Fourth Army's front. Winning the ridge would free the city of Reims. The 2d Division was assigned to take the ridge.

On the cold, starlit night of October 1–2, the Marine Brigade occupied a 2-mile section of the front just north of Somme-Py. The desolate, white-chalk, war-gutted land was ripped by trenches, shellholes, concrete fortifications and tangled wire. In the far distance the towers of Reims were barely visible. The next night, the Marines occupied the so-called Essen Trench, as the Germans withdrew.

At 5:50 A.M., on the gray, misty morning of October 3, the French and Americans attacked. With the Marines on the left and the 3rd Brigade on the right, the two 2d Division brigades were to converge on the pine-covered Blanc Mont Ridge, commanding the scene. The 2d Battalion, 6th Marines led the 4th Brigade's attack, accompanied by a battalion of French tanks. By 8:30, the 2d Battalion captured the German main line of resistance, except for the western slope of Blanc Mont Ridge.

In the assault, two Marines of the 78th Company performed acts of bravery that earned them the Medal of Honor. Chicago-born Pvt. John J. Kelly, running through the American artillery barrage, attacked a machine-gun nest, killed the gunner with a grenade, shot another German with his pistol and brought eight members of the crew back as his prisoners. Cpl. John H. Pruitt, a native of Fayetteville, Arkansas, saw his fellow Marines falling before the fire of two German machine guns, attacked the two guns, destroyed them and killed the two gunners. Then, he

431

captured 40 Germans in a nearby dugout. Shortly afterward, while sniping at the enemy, Pruitt was mortally wounded by shellfire. He died the next day, his twenty-second birthday. Kelly and Pruitt were the last of only six men of the Marine Brigade to win the Medal of Honor in World War I.

Because the French had been unable to move up on the Marines' left, the 1st Battalion, 6th Marines, and the 2d and 3rd Battalions of the 5th Marines had to extend to the left and the 1st Battalion, 5th Marines was ordered to help the French eliminate the machine-gun complex called the "Essen Hook." Capt. LeRoy P. Hunt's 17th Company finally killed and captured the Hook's detachment of 100 Germans. Hunt received the Navy Cross.

The Germans doggedly held the western tip of Blanc Mont Ridge; and later in the afternoon, the French commanders ordered the 2d Division to attack again. The 23rd Infantry advanced another two kilometers; but the 5th Marines, who had been designated to lead the Marine Brigade's attack, received the order too late, and Lejeune postponed their attack until morning. The delay was costly. The Germans heavily reinforced Blanc Mont Ridge during the night.

October 4 was the bloodiest day of the war for the Marines. The 5th Marines led the way and took a beating. Young Maj. Henry L. Larsen of Denver led his 3rd Battalion forward some two kilometers before it was enfiladed from both sides by machine-gun fire and had to retreat. All three battalions of the 5th Marines now came under heavy fire from virtually every side. They hung on, struggling forward, their ranks cut up by shrapnel and machine-gun bullets. Maj. George Hamilton's 1st Battalion fought with bayonets and clubbed rifles. The hardest hit companies were down to two dozen men; the 1st Battalion to hardly more than a hundred. In the day's fighting 1,100 Marines were killed and wounded, most of them from the 5th Marines. The Germans still held part of Blanc Mont Ridge.

At 6 A.M. the next day, Maj. George Shuler's 3rd Battalion, 6th Marines assaulted the German strongpoint on Blanc Mont Ridge and captured 205 of the enemy and 65 machine guns. Catching the Germans in their dugouts, where they had fled from the pre-attack artillery barrage, the battalion suffered no casualties.

That afternoon, the 6th Marines, with the 2d Battalion

leading, tried to°move toward St. Etienne-à-Arnes beyond the ridge, but the battalion had only 300 men left, and a strong machine-gun defense stopped them at the edge of the woods southeast of the town.

October 6 saw more heavy fighting, and the 2d Division's depleted frontline units were relieved during that night. Early on the eighth, army units attacked; and the 6th Marines' 76th Company, commanded by Capt. Macon C. Overton, occupied St. Etienne. On Overton's right, the 75th Company was reduced to a handful of enlisted men led by Sgt. Aralzaman C. Marsh. Marsh held his ground against a German counterattack that evening. The last Marine unit, the 3rd Battalion, 6th Marines, with less than 300 men now left, was relieved on October 10. The German armies east of Reims were in retreat to the Aisne River.

The men of the two Marine regiments and the 6th Machine Gun Battalion received their third citation for gallantry from the French, entitling them to wear the green and scarlet cord of the *fourragère* on their left shoulders. In a week of continuous combat, the Marine Brigade had lost 494 dead and 1,864 wounded.

One of the wounded was 1st Sgt. Daly. Lejeune called the wiry little sergeant "the outstanding Marine of all time."[25] Born on November 11, 1873, Daly had been a newsboy in New York City's Park Row and enlisted for the Spanish-American War but saw no action then. The only enlisted Marine ever to win the Medal of Honor for two separate actions—at Peking and Haiti—he was awarded the Navy Cross and Army Distinguished Service Cross for heroism at Belleau Wood, where he put out an ammunition dump fire and singlehandedly captured a machine-gun nest with grenades and an automatic pistol. When Daly arrived home after the Armistice, reporters asked him how he had won his DSC. Daly explained, "I was out there pickin' pansies for my gal in Brooklyn one day," when a car loaded with "brass hats" drove up and they pinned a medal on him. He was the sergeant who had asked his Marines if they wanted to live forever; he died in his bed in Glendale, New York, at age sixty-three.

Now, in France, the 2d Division was ordered to rejoin the American First Army in the Argonne Forest and the final battle of the war.

6
Meuse-Argonne: The Last Battle

The weather turned bitter cold; the rain became sleet. And Germany started to fall apart in the face of irreversible pressure.

In mid-October, the Kaiser fired Gen. Erich Ludendorff, his field commander. In quick order, Bulgaria, Turkey and Austria quit the war. The British broke the German lines near Valenciennes; the German Navy mutinied, and the Germans asked for an armistice. But terms had to be argued out, and the end had to wait for the dramatic 11th hour of the 11th day of the 11th month—at the cost of still more lives. On Sunday morning, November 10, the Kaiser fled to Holland. The next morning, the Western Front fell silent. The carnage stopped. Those still alive now would live—even though the world was safe for absolutely nothing.

But in those final weeks of battle, the Allies kept turning the screw, to make it clear there was no alternative to surrender. On November 1, while the politicians wrangled, the Marine Brigade entered its last battle. During the final 11 days before the Armistice, the brigade would suffer 277 killed and missing and a total of 1,263 casualties.

The vast battle the Marines now joined was already under way between the Argonne Forest and the Meuse River. Across this 15- to 25-mile-wide defile, the Germans manned intricate defenses in depth; above it, they commanded the high ground on both sides and on the watershed spine running up its center. Here, while the Marine Brigade was fighting on Blanc Mont Ridge, half a million Americans and Frenchmen had attacked; and, by October 11, 75,000 men were dead and wounded and thousands more downed by influenza. The need for replacements became urgent.

The 2d Division, rested and retrained and with recruits filling in for the fallen, now was brought to battle with the American First Army's V Corps commanded by Maj. Gen. Charles P. Summerall. V Corps had been fighting up the central spine; and the division was placed in the center of the American drive, as its spearhead.

"The Army that went into action on November 1, 1918, was the greatest America has ever sent to war,"[26] wrote Maj. Gen. Harbord. The 2d Division faced a 2-kilometer-wide sector of the Hindenburg Line called the Kriemhilde Stellung. The division's attack was preceded by explosive and gas shells that ripped the enemy defenses for two hours. The Marines jumped off at 5:30 A.M., "leaning on" a rolling barrage. Overhead, squadrons of planes covered the assault. The day, for a brief change, turned warm and sunny. In the lead were the 1st Battalion, 5th Marines on the right and the 1st Battalion, 6th Marines on the left. The other battalions followed in a column of battalions. Beyond the Marines' right were the 3rd Brigade and then the 89th Division; on their left, the 80th Division. After reaching their first objective, the Marines were to take over the entire division front and advance to the crucial heights of Barricourt.

The Marines fought through a war-pocked landscape, ruined villages, barbed wire mazes and the Germans' protective barrage. On the right, heavy machine-gun fire killed Captain Overton of the 76th Company and Capt. Kirt Green of the 80th. The Marines plunged through the German lines. The divisions on both sides of the 2d were held up, and a specially prepared Marine-infantry battalion under Marine Maj. George A. Stowell came up to protect the Marines' left flank and took the village of Imécourt.

By 8 A.M., as planned, the 2d Battalion of the 5th Marines and the 3rd Battalion of the 6th Marines took over the lead. The former seized Landreville. The latter ran into heavy going at Bayonville, where the Germans, resisting stubbornly, had a second defensive line called the Freya Stellung. Tanks helped the Marines take this position. About noon, the final Marine battalions leapfrogged into the lead and reached Barricourt Heights, their day's objective, by mid-afternoon. That night, the Germans pulled out.

The Marines' progress had been spectacular and decisive,

although against admittedly fall-away defenses. The Germans had been forced to retreat behind the Meuse and to fight only a delaying action in front of the river.

November 2 was a day of rest and probing patrol actions, and then the 3rd Infantry Brigade took over the division lead and advanced 6 miles through heavy rain during that night and the next day and night. The Germans were demoralized by the novel night attacks. The Americans were now racing after the withdrawing enemy. American divisions on the far right crossed the Meuse.

By November 6, the Marine Brigade had its front line along the Meuse. The retreating Germans had destroyed all the bridges, and the 2d Division's crossing was repeatedly postponed. By November 10, the Germans were fleeing with little pretense of trying to stop the Allies; but, to keep open a retreat route, several enemy divisions were holding at the river and on the ridge two to four miles behind it.

The 2d and 89th Divisons were ordered to cross the river and assault the ridge. Enemy artillery and machine guns prevented the Engineers from floating foot bridges across the river at the Marines' main crossing point, a mile northwest of Mouzon. But at a second crossing point, a bit to the south near Letanne, the 2d Engineers, under fire, managed to put one bridge in place. By 11:30 P.M., November 10, the Corps' birthday, the 1st and 2d Battalions of the 5th Marines, under Maj. George W. Hamilton, were over. They took heavy casualties.

After driving the enemy from their immediate front, the Marines waited until a battalion of the 89th Division joined them; and then all three battalions advanced eastward toward Moulins until they learned of the Armistice. Some units did not get the word until 11:45 A.M. By then, the 18th Company was a mile beyond the river.

The two Marine battalions that crossed the Meuse lost 31 killed and 148 wounded—as it proved, unnecessarily.

Gunnery Sgt. Paradis, who fought the entire war without a scratch, figured that of the original 300 men in his 80th Company, only 44 were still there at the Armistice. Of these, 36 had been wounded once or more and returned to the company; 12 had survived every battle.[27]

This climactic six-week battle, which Americans call

Meuse–Argonne, was enormous. Nearly a million Americans were engaged. It was fought by 26 American divisions and seven French divisions. The U.S. First Army suffered 117,000 casualties. The Germans, who used 470,000 men in strongly fortified positions, had 100,000 casualties. Only the arrival of fresh American riflemen in overwhelming numbers had insured the final victory.

Maj. Gen. Lejeune described the final moments of the war for the Marines: "During the last two hours before the Armistice, the enemy's artillery fire was intensified and our artillery sent as good as it received. A few minutes before eleven o'clock, there were tremendous bursts of fire from the two antagonists and then—suddenly—there was complete silence."[28]

That night, the men in the field warmed themselves and dried their clothes over small bonfires and fired rockets and flares into the air all along the front. The lights went on again. Slowly, the earth was covered green once more, marked with the red poppies and the new white gravestones.

7
On Other Wartime Duties

The 4th Brigade was at the heart of the Marine Corps story in World War I, but it was not the entire story by far.

During the war, 78,839 Marines served in the Corps. Of these, 31,871, less than half, served in Europe with the American Expeditionary Force or on shore duty with the Navy. Between May and November, 1918, the Marines suffered 12,179 casualties, including 3,284 deaths, in France.

Every Marine was a volunteer, except for 7,088 who were drafted in the war's last weeks. The Corps' enormous expansion caused the creation of a wartime Marine Corps Reserve with 496 officers and 6,760 enlisted personnel by the war's end. On August 12, 1918, the Secretary of the Navy authorized the Commandant to enroll women as reservists; and the next day, Mrs. Opha M. Johnson became the first woman Marine. In all, 277 women served as enlisted Marines up to the rank of sergeant during the war.

The huge increases in personnel required new facilities. More than 46,000 Marines were trained at the newly developed base at Parris Island, South Carolina, and others, at Mare Island, California. Advanced unit training was provided at the new base at Quantico, Virginia.

Throughout the war, the Corps, led by its energetic Commandant, battled strenuously to expand the 4th Brigade to a division and to send its own artillery units to France. But, in the face of Army opposition and the shortage of guns, it failed. An Advanced Base Force of 7,958 men was kept in readiness but never saw active service. And the Corps did send to France the 5th Brigade commanded by Brig. Gen. Eli K. Cole. Composed of the 11th and 13th Regiments and the 5th Brigade Machine Gun

Battalion, it arrived at Brest on September 24, 1918. It never fought as a brigade, but supplied replacements to the 4th Brigade and performed a variety of other support duties. (One enlisted man in the 11th Regiment, James J. "Gene" Tunney, was assigned to athletic duties and became the AEF's heavy-weight boxing champion. He won the world championship in 1926.) Many men of the 5th Brigade reacted to the fragmentation of their unit with an intense and lasting sense of resentment.

Marine officers also led Army units on the Western Front. Colonel Wise commanded the 59th Infantry at St. Mihiel and in the Meuse–Argonne campaign. Lt. Col. Dunlap, who had come to France with Pershing, won the Navy Cross leading the Army's 17th Field Artillery Regiment in the Meuse–Argonne. Colonel Bearss commanded the 102d Regiment of the 26th Division at St. Mihiel. One of the most colorful officers in the Corps, "Hiking Hiram" took his most famous "hike" on the rain-swept night of September 12, 1918, when he led his regiment of New Englanders for 9 kilometers through the fortified forest of Montagne to clip off the salient at Vigneulles.

Exactly two weeks later, Bearss led the 1st Battalion of the 102d 2 kilometers inside the Hindenburg Line in a diversionary attack on the east side of the Meuse River. After desperate hand-to-hand fighting, they took the town of Macheville. The Germans counterattacked and drove them out. Four times the town changed hands; each time Bearss was the first man in and the last out. At dark, he was ordered to withdraw, the feint a success. For this action, he won the Distinguished Service Cross.

In October, while fighting in the Argonne, a shell burst permanently injured Bearss' spine. The short, stocky Hoosier— who had won the Medal of Honor at the Sohoton Cliffs on Samar and served in the Boxer Rebellion, at Vera Cruz and in the Dominican Republic—was retired after 21 years as a fighting Marine with 11 decorations for bravery.

The war also spurred the infant growth of Marine Corps aviation, which had been born on May 22, 1912, when Lt. Alfred A. Cunningham, a thirty-year-old Georgian, was assigned to the Navy's aviation camp at Annapolis. He became Naval Aviator No. 5 and the first Marine to win his wings.

When the United States entered World War I, Marine

aviation consisted of only 39 men. In January 1918, the 1st Marine Aeronautic Company, led by Maj. Francis T. Evans, the fourth Marine flier, started flying antisubmarine patrols in the Azores. And in July, 753 men of the 1st Marine Aviation Force arrived at Brest. Soon, four squadrons (200 officers and 1,000 enlisted men) were serving under the Navy as the Day Wing of the Northern Bombing Group in the area around Dunkirk and Calais. But, until late September, the Marines in France had not a single plane of their own and did most of their flying with British and French squadrons. They participated in 43 joint combat raids and 14 raids that were completely Marine. Marine fliers were also credited with downing 12 enemy planes (although some authorities regard the figure as a high estimate).[29] Major Cunningham commanded the 1st Marine Aviation Force, with Maj. Roy S. Geiger, the fifth Marine aviator, as second in command.

Two Marines earned the Medal of Honor in the air on October 14, 1918: 2d Lt. Ralph Talbot of South Weymouth, Massachusetts, and Gunnery Sgt. Robert G. Robinson of Wayne, Michigan. On a raid over Belgium, motor trouble separated their plane and one other from their formation, which was bombing the Thielt railway junction. Twelve enemy planes attacked them. Robinson shot down one. A bullet shattered his left elbow. His gun jammed; he cleared it with one hand and kept firing. Bullets hit him in the stomach and hip and he collapsed. Talbot then shot down another plane with his front guns. With Robinson unconscious and the motor failing, Talbot dived to escape the enemy planes, crossed the German trenches at a height of 50 feet, landed at the nearest hospital to get help for Robinson and returned to his airdrome. Eleven days later, Talbot, who had just finished his freshman year at Yale University before joining up, crashed on take off and was killed. His observer, 2d Lt. Colgate W. Darden, Jr., was thrown clear and severely hurt; but he survived to become the governor of Virginia.

Marine aviation forces had 47 casualties during the war. Three Marines were killed in action or died of wounds; three were wounded, and 16 died of influenza. By the Armistice, there were 2,462 officers and men in Marine aviation.

The Corps took pride in the fact that, despite its eagerness to fight with the Army in France, it met every call from the Navy for additional men. Marines served on American battleships overseas and on many cruisers. They maintained sizable forces in Cuba, the Dominican Republic and Haiti and manned a variety of ships' detachments and shore stations from Guantanamo to Peking. They took over the Virgin Islands, which were acquired from Denmark just before the declaration of war. And they guarded 75 naval shore establishments in the United States.

Strangely, the Marines' first wartime encounter with the Germans had come not in France but on the Pacific island of Guam. The German cruiser *Cormoran* had been chased into Guam's harbor by the Japanese in 1914 and was interned. On April 7, 1917, the U.S. governor demanded the cruiser's surrender. A cutter racing to warn the Germans on the ship was fired on by U.S. Marines commanded by 1st Lt. Ethelbert Tabot. The Germans blew up their ship and jumped into the bay. Seven were killed; the rest were rescued and escorted by a detachment of Marines to an Army prison camp in Utah.

In June 1918, the Marines participated in another curious adventure. The flagship of the U.S. Asiatic Fleet, *Brooklyn,* was docked at Vladivostok on Russia's Siberian coast. Aboard was a detachment of 75 Marines augmented by 50 Marines from Cavite. On June 29, troops of the Czechoslovak Legion seized control of Vladivostok from the Bolshevik-led Russians. The Legion, made up of 40,000 prisoners and deserters from Austro-Hungary, opposed the Bolsheviks and had made an incredible trek across Russia to Vladivostok—the long way around—hoping to fight with the Allies on the Western Front.

Thirty Marines from *Brooklyn* under Capt. Archie F. Howard, a young Annapolis graduate from Clay Center, Kansas, were sent ashore to protect the American consulate and to join an Allied force of British, Japanese, Chinese and Czechs patrolling the city. Marines also guarded German and Austrian prisoners of war on Russian Island, 5 miles from Vladivostok, and helped patrol the Vladivostok Navy Yard.

The Bolsheviks in Vladivostok constantly expected a revolt among the crew of *Brooklyn* because three times each day a red flag was raised on the warship. It was, in fact, the Navy meal pennant.

441

8
Watch on the Rhine

Six days after the Armistice, the tired 4th Marine Brigade began its long march into Germany with the U.S. Third Army, the American share of the Army of Occupation. The footsore Marines hiked all the way, some 200 miles, 10 hours a day, 50 minutes to the hour. They trudged through the devastated war area, across the Belgian frontier and through Luxembourg. In every Belgian town, the people turned out to cheer their passage. They followed behind the retreating German army. It was a time of armistice, not peace.

The Marines reached the German border at Diekirch on the Sauer River on November 23 and stopped there. Some received fresh uniforms at last. And on December 1, six months to the day after the old-timers had gone into the line at Belleau Wood, they marched peacefully into Germany and down the Ahr Valley. "During each halt the troops were scattered for billeting in the towns and farmhouses. The Germans were reserved but showed no hostility; many of the Americans felt more at home with them than they had with the French."[30] Gunnery Sgt. Paradis felt differently: "I've seen all of this country and people that I want and sure hope they get us out soon. The more I see of them and their pussyfoot ways the worse I dislike them. They try to treat us nice and when I think of the misery and suffering they have caused us I feel like shooting up the whole town."[31]

The Marines led the 2d Division down the Ahr and on December 9 approached the Rhine River, as agreed to by the Armistice. "The men walked silent, remembering the old dead."[32] Some of the men felt the war should have been pushed into the Fatherland; others thanked God it had not.

On Friday the thirteenth, they crossed the Rhine in a driving rain.

The battalion came into a town with paved streets and trolley-cars and tall factory chimneys that did not smoke. Platoon commanders said it was Remagen; those towers to the right would be the bridge. There was a bridge, a great steel structure of high black arches. The battalion filed upon it.[33]

The Marines moved upriver into their sector of the bridgehead east of the Rhine at Koblenz. The bridgehead had a radius of 30 kilometers from the city. The 5th Marines settled in the Wied Valley and the 6th Marines along the Rhine. A few manned the Rhine River Patrol in the American sector; but most were kept occupied drilling, shooting on the rifle ranges, and on maneuvers. They began to eat better. They stayed there for the next seven months, impatient, bored, eager to go home.

In July 1919, the Marines finally began moving out through the French port of Brest, where Brig. Gen. Smedley Butler, who had finally gotten over as commander of the 13th Marines, was running the huge, teeming military Camp Pontanezen. On August 9, the Marine Brigade paraded in the thick summer heat of New York City; with the rest of the 25,000 men of the 2d Division, it marched up Fifth Avenue from Washington Arch to the north end of Central Park. Then, it entrained to Quantico and was formally returned to the naval service. On August 12, it was reviewed by President Wilson in Washington. After that, at last, demobilization. The great crusade was over—for now.

World War I was the Marine Corps' first Big Show. It changed the Corps for all time—in size, in capability and in ambition.

The Marines' leadership had by no means been ready for the vast expansion the war made possible. Before the war, the Marines had seen their role as supporting the Navy, manning ships and shore stations and defending advanced bases. Then, suddenly, large numbers of Marines were shipped to France, at the Commandant's insistence, to perform a function identical to the Army's. Their organization, staff system, weapons, uniforms, supply and even drill had to conform with and duplicate the Army's. That was the price of admission the Corps had to pay to the fight in France.

443

Until August 1916, the Corps had an authorized strength of 10,265. On December 11, 1918, it reached 75,101. This explosive growth—700 percent—forced the Corps to think on a large scale and taught its officers to manage large units of troops. Marine participation with the Army at battalion, regimental and brigade strength related to the future, not the past.

The war also gave the Corps, and especially its junior officers who would be around awhile, experience fighting a powerful foe. Massive warfare with modern weapons provided new and awful lessons that would prove invaluable after Pearl Harbor, only 23 years in the future.

And, finally, the public attention that the Corps received gave it a new certainty. The doubts articulated by Teddy Roosevelt and Captain Fullam were gone. Although by mid-1919 its enlisted strength was reduced to 27,400 and the postwar revulsion against war and killing affected the Corps as much as the other services, the Marine Corps had made a crucial transition to modern warfare and toward a new vision of its function as a major force-in-readiness for the nation.

*U.S. Marines guard the border of the International
Settlement in Shanghai in 1937.
Museums Branch, USMC*

SEMPER FIDELIS

XI
GETTING
READY
1919-1941

1
The Lean Years

After World War I, the Marine Corps prepared to fight the next war rather than to re-fight the last one.

This did not happen suddenly. At first, Marines gloried in the Big Show in France. But some of their more prescient leaders began to see who the next enemy would be and what kind of war the Marines would have to fight. Men like Lejeune, Russell and Ellis started to get the Corps ready.

At home, the Corps stumbled into two roadblocks: postwar civilian revulsion against everything military and the Great Depression, which squeezed both fat and muscle from all military budgets. In July 1919, Congress slashed the Marine Corps to 1,093 officers and 27,400 enlisted men; but it was unable to enlist even that number. By 1933, authorized strength had dropped to 15,000 enlisted men. Not until World War II began in 1939 was it raised again to 25,000.

During these lean years, the Marines survived on public relations. The Corps crowed about its heroism in France; and, led by Smedley D. Butler's frenetic enthusiasm, it sent rifle and athletic teams around that nation; staged full-dress recreations of Civil War battles, and started building at Quantico, Virginia, the world's largest football stadium. In both 1921 and 1926, the Corps took on the highly visible job of protecting the U.S. mails against robberies.

Fortunately, the Corps had, for eight years of this period, the leadership of one of the most attractive Commandants in its history: John A. Lejeune, a battle-decorated, popular, forward-looking, publicity-aware general. He wanted the Corps to be known and respected throughout the country, and he fought its battles in the Congressional cloakrooms and the White House.

He understood the uses of political power and laid the foundation for the Corps' amphibious revolution.

Lejeune became Commandant on July 1, 1920, when George Barnett was retired prematurely and abruptly. He had alienated Navy Secretary Josephus Daniels and Congressman Thomas Butler, father of Smedley Butler and senior member of the House Naval Affairs Committee. Smedley Butler thought Barnett had conspired to keep him from leading a regiment into combat in France. His father called Barnett "a rocking chair warrior."[1] During the Lejeune years, Congressman Butler was the Marines' good and powerful friend and until his death in 1928 supplied important help with appropriations.

The congressman's son, a round-shouldered, beak-nosed 130-pounder, was one of the Corps' best-known characters, outspoken, colorful, full of drive and ambition. He wore two Medals of Honor. When Lejeune retired in 1929 to become Superintendent of the Virginia Military Institute, Butler expected to be named Commandant. Although he had helped make Lejeune Commandant, Lejeune strongly recommended as his successor Wendell C. "Buck" Neville, who had led the 5th Marines and the 4th Brigade in France. Neville won the job but died on July 8, 1930. Again, Butler's hopes rose. He was now a major general, the youngest Marine until then to hold that rank and the Corps' ranking general. However, President Herbert Hoover passed over both Butler and Maj. Gen. Logan Feland and chose Brig. Gen. Ben H. Fuller—quiet, sixty-year-old "Uncle Ben," a Marine for 39 years.

Butler was furious, but he had made too many enemies. One incident that had not helped his cause occurred in 1926, during Prohibition days, when Butler preferred charges in San Diego against Col. Alexander S. Williams for turning up at a hotel dance "very drunk."[2] Williams, who as a young lieutenant had been with Waller on the tragic march on Samar, was relieved of his command. Six months later, his car plunged into San Francisco Bay and he drowned. His death was declared accidental, but many people called it suicide blamed Butler.

After Fuller was named Commandant, Butler made some imprudent public remarks against the Italian Fascist leader, Benito Mussolini. The Italian government protested, and a court-martial was ordered. As his defense lawyer, Butler engaged Henry Leonard, who had saved his life in China. The case was settled with a reprimand before the trial started; but Butler retired in 1931, a very angry man.

Two more Marines became Commandant before Pearl Harbor. John H. Russell, who had won fame in Haiti, took over after Fuller retired for age early in 1934. Although Russell was from the older generation, he played a major part in preparing the Corps for World War II. When he too retired for age at the end of 1936, President Franklin D. Roosevelt reached down and picked a junior man, much as Navy Secretary Welles had done during the Civil War. Roosevelt selected Brig. Gen. Thomas Holcomb, fifty-seven, a descendant of Commodore Joshua Barney, an expert shot and a veteran of the fighting in France. Holcomb was a stern silent man with steel-rimmed glasses and known as a planner and administrator. This time, there were no dramatic resignations; and Holcomb, now a major general, led the Corps into its biggest war.

2
China Marines

In these years of apparent peace, the Marine Corps was surprisingly busy overseas. Marines "intervened" in the Dominican Republic until 1924; in Haiti until 1934, and in Nicaragua, for the second time, from 1927 until 1933, as described in Part IX. In addition, a few Marines landed again at Vladivostok in 1919 and in Honduras in 1924 and 1925.*

The second world-wide war boiled up earliest on the far side of the Pacific, where China, chaotic and crippled, was squeezed between Soviet communism and Japanese imperialism. China became the main stage outside the Caribbean for the Marine Corps: first, in the 1920s when Chiang Kai-shek's Nationalists fought the warlords and Communists for control of the country, and again in the 1930s when the Japanese invaded China. In 1928, more than 5,000 U.S. Marines (a fourth of the Corps)—and in 1937, 2,536 Marines—were stationed in China.

Marine ships' detachments had gone ashore at Hankow and Shanghai in the fall of 1911, and a battalion of 375 men under Maj. Philip M. Bannon went to Peking. China's Manchu Dynasty—shaken by the foreign invasion against the Boxer Rebellion and destroyed by the Revolution of 1911—finally abdicated on February 12, 1912. The Marine legation guard at Peking was kept at more than 500 men until May, when the situation seemed to quiet down.

During China's turmoil, Japan moved in on the wounded giant. Japan had already annexed Korea in 1910; and while

*On December 5, 1929, Marine Capt. Alton N. Parker was the first pilot to fly over large parts of the Antarctic continent. He and three Marine sergeants were members of the Byrd Antarctic Expedition. Master Tech. Sgt. Victor H. Czegka went back with Rear Adm. Richard E. Byrd's second expedition in 1933–1935.

European powers were massacring each other in World War I, Japan scooped up Germany's islands in the Central Pacific, grabbed the German economic monopoly in China's Shantung Province and pressed demands that "effectively envisaged China's subordination to Japan's will."[3] None of the Western powers was prepared to slap down the Japanese. When China bowed to Japan's Twenty-one Demands in 1915, a new era opened in Asia. Japan was hungry for a mainland empire, and its appetite would not be suppressed until after Hiroshima—30 years later.

Inside China, the nationalist leader Sun Yat-sen had himself named the "Provisional President of China" in Canton on May 5, 1921. Less than two months later, the Chinese Communist Party was born at Shanghai—with Moscow's midwifery. But the Peking government and the provincial warlords still dominated most of the vast country. When Sun Yat-sen asked the United States for help and was rejected, he sent a mission headed by Chiang Kai-shek to Moscow.

After Sun Yat-sen died of cancer in 1925, Chiang Kai-shek made himself commander-in-chief of the National Revolutionary Army. In March 1927, aided by an uprising of Communist-organized workers, he captured the great port city of Shanghai and then seized Nanking.

Leading the right wing of Sun Yat-sen's Kuomintang Party, Chiang on April 12 turned on the Shanghai workers' organizations and killed some 300 Communist and labor leaders. Six days later, he organized his own Nationalist government in Nanking. His armies defeated the Communist-led troops, and soon Chiang controlled a one-party dictatorship.

This was a time of riots, panic, disruption of trade. There was fighting between the northern warlords and the southern revolutionaries, between the Kuomintang and the Communists, and between the left and right wings of the Nationalist movement itself. Anti-foreign disorders spread. Foreign warships gathered at Shanghai.

Into this danger-fraught situation came the Marines. Small Marine detachments had gone to Tungchow, Peking, Tientsin, Chinwangtao, Canton and especially Shanghai from 1920 to 1926. (One private first class in the Peking detachment was future U.S. Senator "Mike" Mansfield.) But the major intervention began early in 1927 when the International Settlement at

Shanghai, the great trading center between China and the industrial world, was threatened by civil war and anti-imperialist violence.

On February 9, 1927, four companies of 341 Marines from Guam landed at Shanghai; and a few weeks later arrived 1,228 Marines of the 4th Regiment, commanded by Col. Charles S. "Jumbo" Hill. They stayed aboard ship at the Standard Oil compound five miles below the city.

The 4th was the only Marine regiment on duty continuously between the two world wars. Activated on April 16, 1914, it had fought in the Dominican Republic from 1916 to 1924. It would stay in Shanghai for the next 15 years without ever firing a shot and become famous as the "China Marines." Seven of its China-duty members eventually became Commandants of the Corps: Alexander A. Vandegrift (who commanded the 3rd Battalion in 1927); Clifton B. Cates; Lemuel C. Shepherd, Jr.; Randolph McC. Pate; David M. Shoup; Wallace M. Greene, Jr.; and Robert E. Cushman, Jr. China was a nursery for the Marine Corps leadership of World War II.

When the steel-helmeted 4th Marines marched ashore in 1927, their job was not to solve China's problems but to help the British and the six other foreign powers present keep the Chinese out of the International Settlement. This area of the city, completely controlled by foreigners, was dotted with white buildings and hotels and clubs for Occidentals only. It was the target of Chinese anti-foreign resentment.

To reinforce the 4th Marines with men and artillery and aviation elements, Brig. Gen. Smedley Butler arrived on May 2 with most of the 6th Regiment, commanded by Col. Harold C. Snyder. Butler took charge of all the Marines in China as the 3rd Marine Brigade. When two additional battalions joined it, the 3rd Brigade numbered 238 officers, 18 warrant officers and 4,179 enlisted men.

Although the crisis had passed by the time Butler got to Shanghai, he placed the Marines on perimeter defense alongside the British at Soochow Creek that bordered the Settlement and sent machine-gun-armed truck patrols through the city.

In June, with Chiang in control at Shanghai, Butler left the 4th Regiment there and took most of the other Marines north to Tientsin, where he had fought 27 years before. From Tientsin,

Marine pilots flew Jennys on regular reconnaisance patrols over Chiang's army. In a year and a half, three Marine fighter squadrons marked up 3,818 sorties.[4]

The U.S. Army already had 1,800 soldiers at Tientsin and along the railroad to Peking. The Legation Guard in Peking now totaled 516 Marines, including a detachment of 22 men mounted on Mongolian ponies. These "Horse Marines" were trained and equipped like cavalry to protect Americans. In truth, they were used mostly to climax Marine parades with a galloping dash, their sabers flashing.

The Marines, both in Shanghai and up north, were ordered to avoid conflicts with the Chinese. They filled their days with drilling, athletics and parades. The energetic Butler kept his Marines at Tientsin ready to leave instantly for Peking if trouble should start. Trucks with machine guns, ammunition and rations stood by like fire engines to evacuate Americans from Peking.

The day before Christmas, 1927, a tremendous fire broke out in the Standard Oil Plant on the Hai Ho River at Tientsin. A million pounds of candle grease ignited in two huge warehouses. Within minutes, the Marines were on the spot. To prevent a massive explosion, they formed human chains and passed gasoline tins out of an adjoining warehouse. By mid-afternoon, 2,000 Marines were fighting the flames. It took four days to put the fire out.

On July 25, 1928, the United States became the first of the powers to sign a tariff treaty with Chiang Kai-shek's government in Nanking. After Chiang became president of China, the 3rd Marine Brigade was withdrawn in January 1929, leaving 500 Marines in Peking and 1,150 of the 4th Regiment at Shanghai.

Life in Shanghai was comfortable and exotic. Chinese "roomboys" and White Russian girlfriends helped do the chores and counteract the boredom—even on a Marine's pay of $21 a month. He could buy a steak for 30 cents, Scotch for less than a dollar, beer for two cents a quart. It was very good duty.

In September 1931, the Japanese struck. Their army invaded Manchuria and seized most of China's iron ore and much of its coal, electric power and cement. Japan was out to grab land and resources, to erect a buffer state between itself and the Soviet Union and to forestall American economic expansion in

Asia. War with flabby, apparently defenseless China seemed a small price to pay for those goals. But the road led elsewhere.

Although the League of Nations objected to Japan's aggression, no one came to China's aid; and Japan ignored the League's protests. The United States declined to join any collective effort to stop Japan, which set up in Manchuria the puppet state of Manchukuo. Chiang Kai-shek, unable to contain Japan, re-opened diplomatic relations with the Soviet Union after a five-year break. In March 1933, Japan walked out of the League of Nations. It was the first step toward world war.

Anti-Japanese tension mounted in Shanghai. In January 1932, the Japanese army attacked Chinese soldiers in the Chapei district of Shanghai across narrow Soochow Creek from the International Settlement. The fighting spread, and the 4th Marines again took to the barricades facing the creek. To help keep the conflict out of the Settlement, they were soon reinforced by 334 Marines from the Philippines; the Marine detachment from the ill-fated *USS Houston,* and the U.S. Army's 31st Infantry. Stray shells fell into the American sector, and the Marines were exposed to fire from both warring sides.

The battle ended when the Chinese pulled out of Chapei on March 3; and by June, the emergency was officially over. The Marines returned to garrison and shipboard duty, and the 31st Infantry, to the Philippines.

But the early 1930s were terrible years for China. Not only did the world-wide Depression wreck its export trade, but drought and famine swept the land. The peasants were milked for taxes to support the vast military establishments, and the countryside was ripe for revolution. In response, Chiang Kai-shek raised a series of military campaigns against the Communists. In October 1934, the Red Army broke through Chiang's lines and began its historic Long March of 6,000 miles to Shensi Province in China's far northwest.

In January 1936, Japan walked out of the Second London Conference on naval strength and in November signed a treaty with Nazi Germany. The following month, some of Chiang's own military colleagues kidnapped and held him until he agreed to end the civil war against the Communists and fight the Japanese. Ironically, the man who saved him from assassination and negotiated for a common front against the Japanese was his Communist enemy, Chou En-lai.

At the Marco Polo Bridge outside Peking on the balmy summer night of July 7, 1937, Japanese and Chinese troops clashed; and the Second Sino-Japanese War began. The Chinese Twenty-ninth Army manned positions in Peking against possible Japanese attacks. A cavalry squad approached; the Chinese at the barricades opened fire. The mounted men were not Japanese but U.S. Marines—the Horse Marines. One Marine was wounded, and the rest ducked into a side street until the mix-up was untangled. That was the only fighting in Peking itself.[5]

After the Japanese marched into Peking on August 8, Chiang Kai-shek and Chou En-lai finally agreed on a united front. The Red Army became the Eighth Route Army of the National Revolutionary Army.

The Japanese fired on American hospitals, churches and schools across China. They sank the gunboat *USS Panay,* patrolling the Yangtze River, and killed three Americans and seriously wounded 11. President Roosevelt had urged a "quarantine" against aggressors, but Americans still sold shiploads of scrap steel to Japan. The Russians were supplying China with war supplies, planes and pilots.

For the China Marines in that summer of '37, training was stepped up: conditioning hikes with heavy packs, rifle practice and weapons drill and parades out to the Race Course. On August 12, when fighting between the Japanese and Chinese approached Shanghai, Col. Charles F. B. Price sent his two battalions of the 4th Marines to the south bank of Soochow Creek. Lt. Col. William H. Rupertus' 1st Battalion and Lt. Col. Roswell Winans' 2d Battalion sandbagged 58 strongpoint and positioned automatic weapons to provide interlocking fields of fire. Capt. Wallace M. Greene, Jr.'s, E Company was formed into a special "riot company" to deal with disorders and looting. Most of its 90 Marines were organized into four-man "fighting teams"—the forerunners of the Marines' four-man fire teams of World War II.

By the fourteenth, "Bloody Saturday," the fighting grew intense. Thousands of Chinese refugees crowded across the creek into the Settlement. Chinese bombs, aimed at the Japanese ships in the Whangpo River, killed some 500 Chinese. Japanese antiaircraft fire sprinkled Marine positions. An antiaircraft shell killed one and wounded 18 aboard *USS Augusta.*

Two companies of Marines arrived from Cavite; and the 6th Marines and the headquarters of the 2d Marine Brigade, commanded by Brig. Gen. John C. Beaumont, arrived from San Diego. There were now 2,536 Marines in China. Col. Thomas S. Clarke's 6th Marines—Lt. Col. Alphonse de Carre's 1st Battalion and Lt. Col. Cates' 2d Battalion—rotated with the 4th Marines on the line.

On October 25, when the Japanese established an amphibious beachhead north of Shanghai, the massive battle reached a climax. The Chinese began an orderly retreat; and by the end of the month the fighting was over. In mid-February, the 2d Brigade and 6th Marines left; and once again the 4th Marines were alone on guard in Shanghai.

The Japanese conquered the capital in the infamous "rape of Nanking"; and the National government fled to Chungking, far up the Yangtze River. Within the year, the Japanese occupied Hankow and Canton. The Chinese armies were cut off, except for Russian supplies creeping in through Central Asia.

Duty in Shanghai during this emergency proved especially important to two Vermont-reared Marines who in World War II would command the Corps' first two Raider battalions. Maj. Merritt A. Edson, veteran of the Coco River patrols in Nicaragua, studied Japanese amphibious tactics at close range. And Capt. Evans F. Carlson came back to Shanghai for the third time, specifically to study the Chinese language. He learned a lot more. The American journalist Edgar Snow, whom Carlson had met in China in the 1920s, encouraged him to go and observe the Chinese Communist armies in Yenan. Getting permission from Chairman Mao Tse-tung on December 7, 1937, Carlson was the first foreign military officer to visit the Communist armies. In Shansi Province, he hiked with a small detachment 200 miles through bare, treeless mountains in freezing weather. He studied guerrilla warfare and how the Chinese Communists used surprise and feints, stayed constantly in motion and fought only when they felt strong enough to win. He became an ardent devotee of the smart, tough, spartan guerrillas. Of the Japanese army, he said, "Its effort to conquer Shansi was about as effective as an attempt to plow the ocean."[6] When he returned to Shanghai, Carlson reported what he had learned to Naval Intelligence and wrote to Franklin Roosevelt, as the President had asked him to. FDR had come to know Carlson when he commanded the Marine guard at the Little White House at Warm Springs, Georgia.

The skinny six-foot Marine had talked with Chou En-lai and Mao Tse-tung in Chinese, slept in a Yenan cave and in 1938 traveled for three months in the remote areas of China and Inner Mongolia where the Communists were fighting the Japanese. After that experience, he tried personally to convince Chiang Kai-shek to send more help to the under-equipped Communists; and he began to make public statements warning Americans of war with Japan and trying to rally American support for the hard-pressed Chinese. This intense son of a New England preacher was already widely regarded as a maverick. He returned to the United States, resigned and wrote and made speeches about what he had seen in China. He went back to China as a civilian in 1940, became convinced war with Japan was imminent and rejoined the Corps in April 1941. Sent to England, he studied the methods of the British Commandos, a mission that helped give birth to the Marine Raiders.

Once World War II began in 1939, the Marines in China were increasingly isolated. By the summer of 1940, the British, French and Italians in Shanghai were no longer effective partners there.

Maj. Lewis B. "Chesty" Puller had one potentially dangerous brush with the Japanese in Shanghai. In 1933, he had commanded the 50-man Horse Marines in Peking. One night in 1940 when he was back in China, 80 Japanese soldiers invaded Shanghai's International Settlement and rounded up 200 Chinese. Puller took 22 Marines, hurried to the spot where the Chinese were being held, ordered his men to set up two heavy machine guns and drew his pistol on the Japanese officer. The Japanese left without their prisoners.

In January 1940, the United States finally restricted the shipment of war supplies to Japan. In September, after France fell to Hitler, Japan seized northern Indochina; when Germany attacked the Soviet Union in 1941, Japan took the rest. The United States froze Japanese assets in the States, embargoed petroleum exports to Japan and on November 26 told Japan to get out of China and Indochina. These measures were intended to drain Japan of oil and to halt her conquest of the Asian mainland. In fact, they turned Japan's aggressiveness southward and led directly to the attacks on American, British and Dutch holdings in the Pacific—and the raid on Pearl Harbor.

As the Japanese tightened their hold over China and formally joined the Axis Powers, war between Japan and the United States appeared increasingly likely. Adm. Thomas C. Hart, commander of the American Asiatic Fleet, urged that the 4th Marines be pulled out of China. Finally, on November 10, 1941, orders arrived from Washington to evacuate the regiment. The 1st Battalion sailed for Subic Bay on *President Madison* on November 27, and the rest of the regiment rushed to sail the next day aboard *President Harrison.* The Japanese tried to block the evacuation. But the Marines loaded *President Harrison* by lighter; and at 9 A.M. on the twenty-eighth, the remainder of the regiment formed behind its band and marched down Bubbling Well and Nanking roads to the dock on the Bund. A cheering crowd lined the route. A lighter took the Marines downstream to the ship. At 2 P.M., *Harrison* weighed anchor. It was the end of the pre-war China Marines.

3
Toward a New Mission

While Marines were guarding Soochow Creek and chasing Sandino in Nicaragua, back home something even more important—and more revolutionary—was developing in the Corps.

The story starts with the cloak-and-dagger mystery of Earl H. "Pete" Ellis. Born in the prairie village of Iuka, Kansas, on December 19, 1880, Ellis enlisted as a Marine private in 1900 and became the Corps' most prophetic thinker and planner of his time. He was a lieutenant colonel when he died, May 12, 1923, on Koror in Japan's newly acquired Palau Islands.

After Ellis' death, Commandant Lejeune acknowledged that Ellis had been on a secret military intelligence mission when he disappeared.[7] He was trying to find out whether the Japanese were fortifying their mandated Pacific islands, where no foreigner was welcome.

Even before World War I, during which he won the Navy Cross in France, the young, slim Marine officer had been fascinated with the problems of advanced base defense. He learned Japanese while on two tours of duty in the Philippines and became convinced that the United States would have to fight the next war in Japanese waters. In 1921, he predicted in detail how the Marine Corps would, in the war he saw coming, capture western Pacific bases from Japan. Ellis revolutionized Marine Corps thinking. His brilliant paper, "Advanced Base Operations in Micronesia, 1921," was accepted in toto by the Commandant and became the famous Operations Plan 712. Much of what he foresaw is now history.

In death, Ellis became a legend. To this day, what happened to him is unknown. The official story was that he took a leave of absence from the Corps and went traveling. The Japanese said he became ill in the Palaus and died. It is believed that they murdered him.

What is known for sure is that in 1922 Ellis was hospitalized in Japan for acute alcoholic poisoning. Although ordered home, he decided to complete his mission to penetrate the Japanese-held islands. He walked out of the Yokohama Naval Hospital on the night of October 6 and disappeared. Later, it was learned that he had gone, disguised as a commercial traveler, to the Marshall Islands and after several months made his way on a Japanese ship to the Palaus.

In 1950, Marine Lt. Col. Waite W. Worden unearthed some facts about Ellis' last days on Koror. He had lived with a native girl named Metauie, drank heavily and spent much of his time prowling around Japanese installations. Japanese police in civilian clothes, presuming or knowing Ellis was a spy, shadowed him closely. One morning, according to a native woman who had known him on Koror, he went "crazy drunk," and by 5 P.M. he was dead. Worden commented, "With his apparent unquenchable thirst, and his frantic searches, at times, for something to drink, it would not have been too difficult to poison him."[8]

Gen. Holland M. Smith, who called Ellis "one of our most brilliant strategists," added a haunting footnote:

> The mystery of Ellis' death deepened when a young [sic] chief pharmacist's mate [Lawrence Zembsch, a wartime Navy lieutenant] from the U.S. Naval Hospital in Yokohama volunteered to go to Palau and recovered his body. He cremated the body but returned to Yokohama a mental case, unable to give a coherent story of his trip or any intelligent information about Ellis. His condition improved, and it seemed possible he would regain enough mental equilibrium to tell his story, but both he and his wife died in the ruins when the 1923 Japanese earthquake demolished the hospital.[9]

A Marine Corps historian who probed the Ellis case wrote that Zembsch had reported "that Ellis had been known for what he actually was while he was staying in the Marshalls."[10]

460

What involved Ellis so passionately that it lured him to his death was no less than a vision, still invisible to most everyone, of how the Marine Corps could most effectively meet the new danger to the United States in the Pacific. He was by no means alone in recognizing that the balance of power in the Pacific had shifted and that Japan's new position astride America's sealanes conflicted with U.S. economic and political interests. Ellis' unique contribution was that he knew what the Marine Corps should do about the threat.

He urged that the Corps get ready to assault heavily defended Japanese islands and capture the bases necessary to project American power across the Pacific. He wrote:

> To effect such a landing under the sea and shore conditions obtaining and in the face of enemy resistance required careful training and preparation, to say the least; and this along Marine Corps lines. It is not enough that the troops be skilled infantry men or artillery men of high morale; they must be skilled water men and jungle men who know it can be done—Marines with Marine training.[11]

The Marine Corps was ripe for a new vision of the future. Its leaders were increasingly aware that the Corps' existence could not long hang on—and was, in fact, even endangered by—its heroic performance in World War I. Not only had the Marines' well publicized feats attracted powerful and jealous enemies, but the Corps was vulnerable because its World War I mission and organization had been so totally imitative of the Army. If the Corps existed only to do what the Army could do (even though better perhaps), very soon the powers-that-be might be convinced that the Marine Corps was an unnecessary carbon copy.

Lejeune understood the danger. He knew that the Corps could not survive on memories of Belleau Wood and re-enactments of Civil War battles. In a memorandum to the General Board of the Navy on February 11, 1922, Lejeune declared that it was vital to have "a mobile Marine Corps force adequate to conduct offensive land operations against hostile Naval bases . . ."[12]

This was revolutionary. Previously, it had been accepted that Marines would be used to *defend* advanced bases for the Navy. Marine advanced base units were essentially coast artillery. But, with Guantanamo and Manila in memory, Lejeune was carrying this mission a giant step forward. He wrote, "The primary war mission of the Marine Corps is to supply a mobile force to accompany the Fleet for operations on shore in support of the fleet. . . ." He added that the Corps should be used "in conjunction with Army operations on shore, when the active naval operations reach such a stage as to permit its temporary detachment from the Navy."[13]

Lejeune's memorandum was a direct reaction to the Washington Disarmament Conference that had ended only five days earlier. At that conference, the world's naval powers set the rules by which they hoped to prevent a naval arms race. They established ratios of capital ships among the big powers, and they froze the status quo of naval bases in the western Pacific. The Americans, Japanese and British were neither to strengthen nor construct naval bases there for 10 years.

Lejeune pointed out to the General Board that, while navies were now limited by agreement, the mobile forces assigned to them were not restricted. He also emphasized the importance of the American island of Guam because the United States had no naval bases between Honolulu and Manila. He saw a future job for the Marine Corps—the one Ellis had predicted.

In 1927, the Joint Board of the Army and Navy gave the Corps the responsibility to "provide and maintain forces for the initial seizure of advanced bases and for such limited auxiliary land operations as are essential to the prosecution of the naval campaign."[14]

Under the pressure of severe Depression austerity, the role of the Marine Corps was reexamined again in 1931–1932. One result was Navy Department General Order No. 241 on December 7, 1933, based on a suggestion from Maj. Gen. John H. Russell, Assistant to the Commandant. The General Order established the Fleet Marine Force—a permanent Marine strike force to be kept in a state of readiness for operations with the fleet. The FMF's mission would be to execute landing operations. By the time the Corps was withdrawn from its Caribbean interventions, the theoretical revolution was complete.

Simultaneously, the Corps had begun primitive training in advanced base assault. In early 1922, a Marine force led by Lt. Col. Richard M. Cutts joined naval exercises in the Caribbean. Marine officers discovered that they had to learn how to attack a base as well as to defend one. At the end of 1923, a Marine expeditionary force led by Brig. Gen. Eli K. Cole tried to land against a defending force commanded by Col. Dion Williams. Some 3,000 men participated and it was a fiasco. Boats landed on the wrong beach, naval bombardment was inadequate, transports were badly loaded. But the fact that exercises were held and errors were spotted marked progress. After 1,500 Marines joined in joint Army–Navy exercises at Oahu, Hawaii, in 1925, the Marines were too busy in Nicaragua, Haiti and China to participate in fleet exercises again until 1932.

In the meanwhile, work on a viable amphibious assault doctrine had begun in 1931 under Brig. Gen. Randolph C. Berkeley, the first general officer to head the Marine Corps Schools. In January 1933, the Joint Board issued a general doctrine for joint overseas expeditions. The Marine Corps Schools' curriculum was radically revised to eliminate its Army orientation and teach how to defend and seize advanced bases. Specific Pacific islands were used as models. On November 14, 1933, all classes at Quantico were suspended; and staff and students, some 70 officers, devoted all their time to producing a landing operations manual. They worked on the frontier of military knowledge. By the following July, the Navy Department was able to publish a manual. In July, 1935, a board headed by Lt. Col. Charles D. Barrett finished the first edition to be widely distributed. Titled *Tentative Landing Operations Manual,* it became the Bible of amphibious warfare. Eventually adopted by both the Navy and the Army, it underwent repeated revisions, based on new experience, well into World War II.

The manual dealt with all the basic elements of amphibious operations: the nature of the landing force, the allocation of command responsibilities, ship-to-shore movements, survival on the beachhead, fitting naval gunfire support to the need of the landing force, the coordination of close air support, logistics, the combat-loading of transports, the use of landing craft. In all this, the Marine Corps was exploring new ground. Ever since the World War I defeat at Gallipoli, the presumption had been that

463

the defense had all the advantages against amphibious landings. The Marine Corps aggressively set out to prove that conclusion was wrong. By December 1941, it had a workable doctrine ready to go.

After World War II, Gen. Alexander A. Vandegrift summed up the importance of what the Marine Corps had achieved:

> Despite its outstanding record as a combat force in the past war, the Marine Corps' far greater contribution to victory was doctrinal: that is, the fact that the basic amphibious doctrines which carried Allied troops over every beachhead of World War II had been largely shaped—often in the face of uninterested and doubting military orthodoxy—by U.S. Marines, and mainly between 1922 and 1935.[15]

During this same period, the Corps focussed its attention on still another field of special knowledge—its experience fighting "small wars." In 1922, Maj. Samuel M. Harrington pulled together the Marines' expertise, and his paper was incorporated in the Marine Corps Schools' curriculum. By 1940, the Corps had developed a unique *Small Wars Manual* that was still in use when the Corps planned its pacification program in Vietnam 25 years later.

To prove out their doctrine, strategy and tactics of amphibious landing operations and "small wars," the Marines pressed hard against a scarcity of funds and frustrating bureaucratic opposition. Nothing could be accomplished alone. Marines could never make it ashore without the Navy and naval air. In amphibious assault, the Navy and Marine Corps were extensions of each other. As Adm. Richmond Kelly Turner, who commanded Marine landings throughout World War II, said, "No one service invented amphibious warfare. The Marines contributed much (patterned on Japanese methods) to its development in recent years. But so also did the Navy, including Naval Aviation. Furthermore, beginning in 1940, the Army contributed a great deal."[16]

The first real chance to test the landing operations manual's theories came in 1935. By then, enough Marines were available to make up an expeditionary force. Fleet landing exercises, which took place each winter until Pearl Harbor, attacked the problems and tested the equipment for amphibious assault. Marines practiced daylight and night landings. Naval gunfire support was improved; for example, surface-bursting shells replaced the armor-piercing shells that warships normally carried. Close air support was added. Landing craft were tried out.

The last fleet landing exercise (Flex-7) was held in the Caribbean in February 1941 and included the 1st Marine Division and the 1st Marine Aircraft Group—a larger amphibious force than had been previously assembled. But there were still defects: landing craft were still inadequate; naval gunfire lacked fire control equipment, proper guns and projectiles; and communication between ships and shore was faulty.

Because of the need for a larger base, the Marine Corps obtained a new site for amphibious exercises at New River, North Carolina—the future Camp Lejeune. In June and July 1941, exercises were held there, climaxed with a two-division landing. By now, amphibious training was under hard-driving Maj. Gen. Holland M. Smith.

As the Corps learned the ropes, it also trained Army divisions in amphibious tactics. The 1st Infantry Division later participated in the invasions of Sicily and Omaha Beach; the 3rd Infantry Division landed at Casablanca, Sicily and Anzio; the 7th landed at Attu, Kiska, Kwajalein, Leyte and Okinawa; the 9th Division landed at Algiers, Palermo and Normandy. And the two original Marine divisions fed men trained in amphibious assault into newer Marine divisions. "Officers and men of the Navy, Army and Marine Corps, trained in these exercises, ultimately found their way into every theater of war where amphibious operations were conducted."[17]

Since existing Navy equipment proved unsuitable for lifting men and weapons ashore against hostile fire, efficient landing craft were badly needed.

In the early 1920s, the Marines experimented with a British-designed "Beetle boat" and a Christie amphibian tractor. Both were useless. In 1936, the Marines tried out five different commercial boats as possible landing craft. They even tested fishing boats and boats seized from rum runners; but all had exposed rudders and propellers, and men had to drop as far as 10 feet into the water.

The answers started to take shape when Andrew J. Higgins, a New Orleans boat builder, working with the Marine Corps and Navy, modified the shallow-water Eureka boat that he had designed for trappers and oil drillers on the Gulf Coast. In April 1941, Maj. Ernest E. Linsert showed Higgins pictures that Capt. Victor H. Krulak had taken of landing boats the Japanese used at Shanghai in 1937. One type had a ramp in its bow. At his own expense, Higgins put a retractable bow ramp on his 36-foot Eureka boat; this became the precursor of the LCVP of World War II.

At the same time, a lighter to get tanks ashore was developed with similar experiments and failures. Higgins again solved the problem. He designed a 50-foot boat, originally designed in a smaller version for use in South America, to carry a 30-ton tank and land it over a bow ramp. Senator Harry S. Truman's War Investigating Committee had to intercede with the Navy before Higgins' model became the standard LCM.

The crucial amphibian tractor was developed after Maj. Gen. Louis McCarty Little, then commanding the FMF, was shown a picture in a 1937 issue of *Life* magazine of the Alligator created by Donald Roebling, Jr., grandson of the builder of the Brooklyn Bridge. By 1940, Roebling's tractor had been improved to travel 29 mph on land and 9.7 mph in the water. In February 1941, Krulak persuaded Adm. Ernest J. King, commander of the Atlantic Fleet, to ride in an aluminum Alligator at Culebra, Puerto Rico. The vehicle broke a track on a reef and the impatient admiral waded ashore. But in July, Roebling had the first steel-welded Alligator ready; and by the end of World War II, 15,654 LVTs had been built and had become the key to successful amphibious assault.

Simultaneously, Marine aviation learned to provide close air support for amphibious landings. The Marines had practiced air support techniques in the mountains of Nicaragua; but faster planes brought more complex problems and required more reliable communication between air and ground. The toughest problem was to hit the enemy and not friendly troops nearby.

In January 1939, the Navy's General Board declared that Marine aviation's prime mission was the support of the FMF in landing operations and in the field. Marine aviation was still a small organization; when World War II began, the Corps had only 251 planes of all types. At that time, Marine aviation's director was Col. Ralph J. Mitchell, who had won the Distinguished Flying Cross in Nicaragua. Brig. Gen. Roy S. Geiger commanded that 1st Marine Aircraft Wing (MAW) at Quantico, and Brig. Gen. Ross E. Rowell, the 2d MAW, which was based at San Diego and had most of its air group on Hawaii.

When summoned to war, the Marine Corps had certainly not ironed out all the problems of amphibious assault. That would require the test of combat. But the Corps had a mission, a doctrine, a knowledge of tactics, officers and men trained in landing operations and the most essential equipment to get them ashore. The Marines had worked for some 20 years to get ready. They would lead the way across the Pacific.

*Marines fighting on Eniwetok Atoll in the
Marshall Islands in February 1944.
U.S. Coast Guard Photo, National Archives*

SEMPER FIDELIS

XII
WORLD
WAR II
1941-1949

1
December 7, 1941

Sunday morning started sunny and bright. After breakfast, Marine Capt. Leonard Ashwell, the officer of the day, strolled out of the mess hall. He heard the roar of aircraft engines and looked up to the northern sky. He recognized two formations of Japanese torpedo bombers flying eastward from the direction of nearby Barber's Point. Then, down over the mountains came 21 Zero fighters. Ashwell raced to the guardhouse to sound the alarm. The Zeros hit. It was 7:55 A.M. War had come to Ewa Mooring Mast Field, the Marines' airfield four miles west of Pearl Harbor.

The Zeros drove in low, some of them 20 feet above the ground. They strafed the 47 planes of Marine Aircraft Group 21, parked wing tip to wing tip against sabotage, and in repeated passes destroyed or damaged every one.

Marines dashed to their stations and organized a makeshift defense. They tried futilely to get planes into the air. They broke out spare machine guns and wrenched others from wrecked planes. They fought back with rifles and pistols. There were no antiaircraft guns. Lt. Col. Claude A. "Sheriff" Larkin, the group commander and senior Marine aviator in the Pacific, was wounded while driving to the field but took command of his men by 8:05.

Half an hour later, the Japanese swept back from the direction of Pearl Harbor. They concentrated on strafing buildings and hospital tents and men. Master Technical Sgt. Emil S. Peters and Pvt. William C. Turner shot down a Val bomber with the machine gun in the rear cockpit of a parked dive bomber. Turner was mortally wounded. The Zeros attacked a third time, but now the Marine gunners were able to deflect the blow.

[For the location of places in the Pacific in World War II see map No. 8 in the map section.—*Au.*]

Walter Lord in *Day of Infamy* tells: "Up above, Lieutenant Yoshio Shiga raked Ewa with his Zero fighter. He noticed a Marine standing beside a disabled plane and charged down, all guns blazing. The man refused to budge . . . kept firing with a pistol. Shiga still considers him the bravest American he ever met."[1]

Dive bombers came from the direction of Pearl Harbor and bombed and strafed Ewa. They were followed by fighters, which, two and three at a time, strafed the field, protecting the Japanese raiders as they assembled to return to their carriers. The last of the enemy planes headed out to sea at 9:45 A.M. It was all over in less than two hours. At Ewa, four enlisted Marines were dead or fatally wounded, 13 wounded. The field was a junkyard of burning planes.

The Japanese struck Pearl Harbor two minutes after they hit Ewa. The guard bugler turned out the Marines at the Navy Yard. The men of the Marine Barracks and the 1st and 3rd Defense Battalions raced for the armories and gun sheds and fired their rifles at the planes, as warships began exploding. At the Naval Air Station on Ford Island, the Japanese destroyed the seaplanes before the sailors and the 102 Marines there could react. "There was no ready ammunition at any aircraft gun position on the island."[2]

Within six minutes after the attack started, Col. Harry K. Pickett, commander of the 485-man Marine Barracks at the Navy Yard, ordered out his Marines. They had already set up eight machine guns and were getting ammunition. Hundreds of Marines on the barracks' parade ground were issued rifle ammunition. They got 38 machine guns into action and shot down three dive bombers. Nine Marines were wounded. Colonel Pickett ordered 3-inch antiaircraft guns dragged from storage to the parade ground. But all their ammunition was at the Lualualei depot, 27 miles back in the hills. The last Japanese planes had left long before the shells reached Pearl Harbor. The Marines were no more prepared for undeclared war than any other Americans.

The targets of the Japanese were the warships of the United States Pacific Fleet, berthed in Pearl Harbor. The Japanese sank four battleships and damaged four more and three cruisers. Marines helped defend the stricken ships; the cruiser *Helena's*

Marine gunners shot down a plane. When *USS Arizona* blew up, Maj. Alan Shapley of Detroit, a former Annapolis quarterback, was hurled into the water, regained consciousness and saved a Marine from drowning. Among 877 Marines in the ships' detachments, 108 were killed and 49 wounded. In all, 2,280 Americans were killed and 1,109 wounded. The Japanese lost 29 planes, five midget submarines and fewer than 100 men.

The militarists in Tokyo planned to wipe the European powers and the United States out of the western and southern Pacific. In Europe, France had already fallen to the Nazis; the British had their backs against the wall. Japan was poised to conquer Thailand, the Philippines, Borneo, Singapore and, the richest prize of all, Dutch-ruled Java.

The Japanese knew the U.S. Pacific Fleet spent each weekend in Pearl Harbor. They had sent six carriers far north of normal shipping lanes, and, 275 miles north of Pearl Harbor, launched 360 warplanes at the unsuspecting Americans. At that very moment, Japan's envoys in Washington were waiting to confer again with Secretary of State Cordell Hull. By the time they met, Hull already had in hand the first message sent from Ford Island at 7:58: "AIR RAID PEARL HARBOR—THIS IS NO DRILL!!"

The Americans were vulnerable to a sneak attack because their military leaders had stupidly underestimated the Japanese—and defensive preparations were criminally sloppy. Naval historian Samuel Eliot Morison was also critical of the Japanese planners: "On the tactical level, the Pearl Harbor attack was wrongly concentrated on ships rather than permanent installations and oil tanks. On the strategic level it was idiotic. On the high political level it was disastrous."[3] The Japanese neutralized the American fleet for the moment, but they brought down on themselves all the power of the United States.

The Japanese also had one important bit of bad luck. The two U.S. aircraft carriers in the Pacific, *Enterprise* and *Lexington*, were not in Pearl Harbor that Sunday morning. *Enterprise* steamed some 200 miles west of Hawaii, having ferried Marine Fighter Squadron 211's planes to Wake Island. *Lexington* was on her way to Midway Island to deliver Marine Scout Bomber Squadron 231's planes; she turned back to Pearl when she heard of the attack. Ten days later, those 17 Marine planes flew directly from Oahu to Midway, 1,137 miles distant, the longest single-engine landplane massed flight then recorded.

The effect of the hit-and-run Pearl Harbor raid was bad enough, but the disaster was not total. A number of heavy cruisers were also at sea, the carrier *Saratoga* was at San Diego and the battleship *Colorado*, at Bremerton, Washington. The carrier *Yorktown* and three battleships, plus planes and destroyers, were promptly shifted from the Atlantic into the Pacific.

Immediately after the attack, all the Marines in the Pearl Harbor Navy Yard area were pooled to strengthen its defenses and provide an infantry reserve in case of an amphibious landing. By the end of the month, Marines of the defense battalions were being shipped out to reinforce the tiny garrisons at Midway, Johnston Island and Palmyra. The job of reorganizing began at once.

2
"Marines Surrender Hard"

Despite American fears, the Japanese had no intention of landing on Hawaii. They had gobbled up enough of the Pacific and Southeast Asia to choke a python and would need months to digest their kill.

U.S. Marines met the Japanese face to face on the ground only in four places: China, Guam, Wake and the Philippines. The encounters in China and on Guam were quickly finished; Wake and the Philippines took longer.

That morning (December 8 in China), 2d Lt. Richard M. Huizenga was supervising the loading of Marine Corps supplies aboard *President Harrison* on the docks at Chinwangtao, northeast of Tientsin. The raid on Pearl Harbor was already over when a truck driver brought him word of the attack. The lieutenant rushed back to his men at the railhead. He found the 21 Marines surrounded by Japanese soldiers. Chief Marine Gunner William A. Lee, who had won three Navy Crosses in Nicaragua, was organizing a strongpoint and had broken out two machine guns and Thompson submachine guns and BARs. Their situation was hopeless but they were ready to fight. The Japanese captain allowed 2d Lt. Huizenga to communicate with Maj. Luther A. Brown at Tientsin, who ordered him not to resist.

In both Tientsin and Peking, the Japanese surrounded the Marine Barracks and demanded that the Marines surrender. Col. William W. Ashurst, the senior Marine officer at the U.S. Embassy, was given until noon to decide whether to fight or surrender. After communicating with the commander of the U.S. Asiatic Fleet in Manila and with Major Brown at Tientsin, Colonel Ashurst ordered his men, fewer than 200 Marines, to lay down their arms. He hoped that as embassy guards they would

475

be repatriated with the diplomatic personnel. But it was not to be. The Marines were imprisoned in Shanghai.

On the island of Guam, the garrison of 153 Marines was as helpless as the handful of Marines in China. The island lay among the Japanese-held Mariana Islands and had been neutralized by the 1922 disarmament treaty. The 1941 American war plan, Rainbow 5, conceded Guam's capture.

In addition to the Marines, Guam had 271 Navy personnel and a native force of 326 armed with obsolete rifles. Lt. Col. William K. McNulty commanded the Marines; 122 of them were at Sumay barracks on the south side of Apra harbor; the rest were stationed in villages around the island.

At 5:45 A.M. December 8, Guam time, the garrison commander and island governor, Capt. George J. McMillin, USN, was informed of the attack on Pearl Harbor. At 8:27, Japanese bombers from Saipan hit. They immediately sank the minesweeper *Penguin* in Apra harbor. Her guns were Guam's only weapons larger than .30 caliber machine guns. Planes bombed and strafed the island the rest of that day and the next. There was no effective defense.

At 4 A.M. on December 10, 400 Japanese sailors landed at Dungcas Beach, just north of the town of Agaña on Guam's west coast. And 5,500 soldiers landed at Tumon Bay north of the beach and on the southwest coast. When the first enemy sailors reached Agaña, a detachment of native troops commanded by Marine 1st Lt. Charles S. Todd met them in the plaza with rifle and machine-gun fire. They pushed the invaders back twice and lost 17 men, but they could not hold out long.

Captain McMillin saw that the situation was futile. Shortly after 6 A.M., he surrendered to the Japanese naval commander. He sent orders to the Marines at Sumay not to resist, but scattered fighting continued the rest of the day as the Japanese spread out over the island. Nineteen of the garrison were killed and 42 wounded, including four Marines killed and 12 wounded. The surviving Americans were shipped to prison camps in Japan. It would be two and a half years before Marines returned to Guam.

The day after Guam fell, the defenders of Wake Island scored the first American victory of the war. It was heartening but temporary.

At 5 A.M. on December 11, Japanese cruisers, escorting transports loaded with 450 Special Naval Landing Troops, opened fire on Wake. Marine lookouts had spotted the flotilla in the light of the half moon; but Maj. James P. S. Devereux, commanding the Marine defense battalion detachment, held his fire to prevent the enemy from locating his guns prematurely. At 6:15, the new light cruiser *Yubari* and three destroyers closed to 4,500 yards. Now, the Marines opened up. The 5-inch guns of Battery A at Peacock Point, commanded by 1st Lt. Clarence A. Barninger, hit *Yubari* three times; the cruiser turned tail and fled, trailing smoke. On Wilkes Island, Battery L's 5-inch guns, commanded by 2d Lt. John A. McAlister, sank the lead destroyer *Hayate*; she was the first Japanese surface craft sunk by U.S. naval forces in the war. The Marine gun crews were so excited they stopped firing and started cheering. Platoon Sgt. Henry A. Bedell, an old China hand, brought them back to business, bellowing: "Knock it off, you bastards, you get back on the guns. What d'ya think this is, a ball game?"[4]

The keyed-up Marine gunners promptly hit a second destroyer and the lead transport and sent off the other two transports. Their accurate firing then found a light cruiser, and she also turned away. First Lt. Woodrow W. Kessler's Marines at Battery B on Peale Island scored on a destroyer.

The Marine gunners had driven off the invasion force. Four Marine Grumman F4F Wildcats, led by Maj. Paul A. Putnam, of Washington, Iowa, chased the retreating ships, strafed them, dropped 100-pound bombs and scooted home to re-arm. The planes shuttled out; damaged two warships and a transport, and Capt. Henry T. Elrod of Thomasville, Georgia, sank the destroyer *Kisaragi*. There were no survivors.

The battle was an unqualified victory for the Marines. They had sunk two destroyers, damaged a cruiser and several other ships, shot down three Japanese bombers and damaged four more. The enemy lost some 500 men; on Wake, there were no casualties. Historian Morison wrote: "The eleventh day of December 1941 should always be a proud day in the history of the Corps. Never again, in this Pacific War, did coast defense guns beat off an amphibious landing."[5] But the Marines' superb shooting could not save Wake.

The Japanese were determined to take the atoll. A lonely

477

speck 450 miles from the nearest land, it was made up of three islands in the shape of a wishbone open to the northwest. The main island was Wake; Wilkes was at the tip of the southern branch of the wishbone, and Peale at the tip of the northern. The atoll, which had been visited by the Wilkes Exploring Expedition in 1841 and annexed by the United States in 1899, sat astride the Pacific lines of communication of both the United States and Japan—a strategically placed coral aircraft carrier.

When war came, there were on Wake only 388 Marines of the 1st Defense Battalion commanded by small, wiry Major Devereux, who had been an enlisted Marine in Nicaragua and China; Major Putnam's Marine Fighter Squadron 211 of 61 men and 12 blue and gray Wildcats (flown off *Enterprise* on December 4); 68 Navy personnel; five Army communications men; 70 Pan American civilians, and 1,146 civilian contract employees who had been trying to pound Wake's coral boulders into a naval air base. Navy Commander Winfield Scott Cunningham, a lanky aviator, was the atoll commander.

Only the understrength Marines were armed. A total of six 5-inch and a dozen 3-inch guns were emplaced on Peale and Wilkes islands and on Peacock Point at the base of Wake. There were Marines enough to man but six of the 3-inch antiaircraft guns.

After sunrise on Monday (Sunday, December 7 in Hawaii), Pan American's *Philippine Clipper* took off and headed west toward Guam. The Marines were finishing breakfast. Major Devereux was shaving. At 6:50, Army Capt. Henry S. Wilson dashed into the major's tent with an uncoded message that Hawaii was under attack. Devereux told the bugler to sound Call to Arms. Marines grabbed their Springfield '03 rifles and ammunition and World War I-style helmets, piled into trucks and rushed to their batteries. By 7:35, all positions were manned. Aviators had their planes warmed up and dispersed as much as possible; civilians started digging foxholes. The Clipper was recalled and returned. A four-plane patrol went up and swung to the north to scout for enemy planes.

Just before noon, 36 twin-engine bombers, approaching from the south, swooped down out of a rain cloud. The island had no radar; and with the constantly roaring surf, nobody heard or saw the bombers until 15 seconds before the first bombs fell.

In ten furious minutes, the Japanese destroyed seven of the eight Wildcats on the ground; wrecked the Pan Am Station, riddled the Clipper; killed 10 civilians; and killed 23 aviation Marines and wounded 11 more. The enemy fliers flew off intact, waggling their wings to celebrate their success.

An hour later, the Clipper managed to take off for Midway to the northeast. The Marines and some volunteers from Dan Teters' civilian construction crew cared for the wounded, repaired damage, salvaged planes and mined the runway to prevent an airborne landing. The Marines could not get permission to use the contractor's ditchdiggers to bury their communications wires.

For the next two days, Wake was pounded. Only three Wildcats were operational. Lt. David D. Kliewer and Tech. Sgt. William J. Hamilton flew in on the flanks of one enemy raid and shot down a straggling bomber. Captain Elrod shot down two more. The bombers hit guns, ammunition, barracks, radio station and machine shops. They burned the hospital to the ground, killing four Marines, 55 civilians and several corpsmen.

On the third night, December 11, the Japanese made their first attempt to land and were thrown back by the Marine gunners.

At Pearl Harbor, the American naval commanders organized a relief expedition built around three fast-carrier task forces with *Lexington*, *Enterprise* and *Saratoga*. But the relief expedition was crippled by indecisiveness and excessive caution. Naval officers feared risking their then-irreplaceable carriers.

Bombers clobbered the island almost daily; there was no hiding from the hell they dropped. By December 14, two planes had been wrecked; and VMF-211 was down to one again. Cannibalizing planes, the Marines on the seventeenth had four Wildcats that could do battle.

On Saturday, December 20, a Navy PBY arrived: Wake's first physical contact with the outside world since the island was attacked. The plane brought the plans of the relief expedition, cheering all hands, and took off again early the next morning. Two hours later, the first Japanese carrier dive bombers and fighters appeared. They promised that the Japanese were preparing another landing attempt.

The twenty-first was a bitter day; Battery D on Peale was

virtually destroyed. On the twenty-second, only two Wildcats could fly. Capt. Herbert C. Freuler and 2d Lt. Carl R. Davidson took them up and attacked 33 carrier dive bombers and six Zeros. Davidson dived at one of the bombers; a Zero shot him down. Freuler exploded another Zero. A Zero tailed him and wounded him twice. He escaped and crash-landed his plane on Wake. That wiped out the Marine airpower for good. What was left of VMF-211, less than 20 able-bodied men, joined the Defense Battalion as infantry.

It was now a race between the American relief expedition and the enemy landing force. The Japanese won. *Saratoga* was still 600 miles from Wake; but Rear Adm. Frank Jack Fletcher spent December 22 refueling. Then it was too late.

The Marines spotted the Japanese amphibious force at 2:15 A.M. on December 23, an intensely dark, moonless night. This time, the Japanese came to stay. They brought six heavy cruisers, six destroyers and two carriers. In the landing force were an estimated 1,500 men.

At 2:35, the enemy landed simultaneously on Wilkes and the southern shore of Wake. About 100 men hit Wilkes. There, big, tough Marine Gunner Clarence B. McKinstry, commanding Battery F, began the battle by firing a .50 caliber machine gun at the landing barges. On Wake Island, 1,000 Japanese landed against some 85 Marines on the beach. An unmanned 3-inch gun on a slight rise was the only large weapon that could bear on the two destroyer-transports disembarking their men. Second Lt. Robert M. Hanna quickly gathered a scratch crew, raced to this gun and threw 15 shells into the grounded landing craft. But the enemy scrambled ashore. Devereux sent Major Putnam, Captain Elrod and the VMF-211 Marines between the enemy and Hanna's gun. They fought off several hundred Japanese for six hours, until all but one of the defenders, Marines and civilians, were killed or wounded. Among the dead was Hank Elrod. The thirty-six-year-old flier was the first Marine aviator in World War II to earn the Medal of Honor—awarded for his courage in the air and on the ground.

The Marine Defense Battalion had no infantry component; small detachments, bolstered by a few civilian workers, met repeated enemy attacks and shouting bayonet charges. They fought the enemy with machine guns, rifles and grenades. The

Japanese captured the hospital and tied up the wounded Marines with telephone wire. Maj. George H. Potter, Jr., Devereux's executive officer, and 40 men fought from a defense line that crossed the airstrip. At 5 A.M., a half hour before dawn, Commander Cunningham sent a message to Pearl Harbor: "ENEMY ON ISLAND ISSUE IN DOUBT." The Japanese were firmly established on the atoll. The Marines' thin line was just too thin.

At Pearl, Vice Adm. William S. Pye, temporarily commander of the Pacific Fleet, fearful of losing *Saratoga*, ordered the mismanaged relief expedition back to Hawaii. On *Saratoga*, sailors and Marines were furious; Marine aviators cursed and wept. Wake's last hope was snuffed out.

At 7:30, Cunningham and Devereux, knowing now that no relief could be expected, decided to surrender. Devereux, with Sgt. Donald Malleck carrying a white rag on a mop handle, walked south to meet the nearest Japanese commander. But the fighting continued for hours, and Devereux had to go to each Marine position to bring the battle to a halt. As Morison wrote, "Marines surrender hard."[6]

The final battle was fought on little Wilkes Island, where there were 70 Marines and a number of sailors and civilians. Gunner McKinstry's Marines were forced back to join men from Battery L commanded by 2d Lt. McAlister. From this position, they were able to block the way to the main island.

Capt. Wesley McC. Platt's command post on Wilkes was on the far side of the Japanese landing force. Down near the beach, on that side, the Marine machine gun nearest the landing was able to repel attacks until dawn.

As day broke, Captain Platt led Platoon Sgt. Raymond L. Coulson and eight Marine riflemen against nearly 100 Japanese. They drove the surprised Japanese back toward the McAlister–McKinstry line. McAlister gathered 24 Marines and counterattacked from his side. Platt and McAlister joined forces and together wiped out the rest of the Japanese landing force on Wilkes.

But Platt was now out of communication with Devereux's command post. Under dive bomber attack, he and his Marines marched east toward Wake Island. At 1:30 P.M., Platt saw three men approaching: two Marines and a Japanese officer with a large sword. The Marines were Devereux and Malleck; the major told Platt that the atoll had been surrendered. The battle for Wake was over.

The Japanese made prisoners of 470 officers and men and 1,146 civilians. The American dead were 49 Marines, three sailors and about 70 civilians. Enemy casualties in taking Wake were estimated to total 820 killed and 333 wounded.

The prisoners kept hoping for an American counterattack until they sailed on January 12 for Shanghai. En route, they were half-starved and repeatedly beaten. Two Marine sergeants from VMF-211 and three sailors were beheaded. In Woosung prison camp near Shanghai, the Wake Marines joined Colonel Ashurst and the Marines from North China. They would be there a very long time.

3

Bataan and Corregidor—
"An Example of Courage"

Marine Capt. Francis H. "Joe" Williams and a demolition team spent Christmas Day erasing the Olongapo Naval Station on Subic Bay, the Philippines, from the face of the earth. They blew up and burned everything except the Marine Barracks, which stood too close to the civilian town. Then, the last elements of the 4th Marine Regiment left for the naval base at Mariveles on the tip of the Bataan Peninsula, on their way to Corregidor, "The Rock."

Gen. Douglas MacArthur, commanding the defense of the Philippines, had not asked for the 4th Marines to be assigned to his command until December 20. By then, the Japanese were already advancing on Manila.

The war had come to the Philippines at 3 A.M. December 8 (local time). Marine Lt. Col. William T. Clement, the duty officer at Navy headquarters on the Manila waterfront, brought the message to Adm. Thomas C. Hart, commander of the U.S. Asiatic Fleet, at the Manila Hotel. Clement's radio operator had intercepted the message that told the world of the attack on Pearl Harbor.

The Japanese bombed the Philippines that first day of the war. They caught American air power on the ground at Clark Field, knocked out one third of the fighters and half the bombers. By December 12, they had won control of the air, destroyed the Navy Yard at Cavite and landed on both ends of Luzon, the main Philippine island. The day after Christmas, MacArthur declared Manila an open city, not to be defended, and brought the U.S. forces to the Bataan Peninsula on the northern side of Manila Bay.

The defense of the Philippines was heroic, but the Americans' resistance there did not affect the enemy's grand strategy. All the Americans and Filipinos had the strength to do, in the end, was to deny the use of Manila Bay to the Japanese Navy for a time. Holding out beyond any realistic hope of relief, their courage and suffering on Bataan and Corregidor became important symbols back home in those defeat-strewn early days of the war.

The 4th Marines had arrived at Olongapo at the end of November with only 44 officers and 728 enlisted men. Since the regiment had been allowed to dwindle by attrition in China, Col. Samuel L. Howard had only two battalions, each short one company and each company short one rifle platoon. The 1st Battalion, soon after arriving in the Philippines, went to Mariveles on the tip of Bataan.

Across Manila Bay, at Cavite, the 1st Separate Marine Battalion, commanded by Lt. Col. John P. Adams, provided antiaircraft defense for the naval base there. After the battalion's 3-inch guns shot down one dive bomber, enemy planes stayed above the guns' range and bombed the base at will. By December 10, it was in flames.

On Christmas Day, while Captain Williams was wrecking the Olongapo Naval Station, Adams' battalion completed the destruction of Cavite. The next night, 411 men from Adams' command were the first Marines to make the seven-and-a-half-mile voyage from Mariveles to Corregidor to man the beach defenses of that island fortress. Most of the 4th Marines joined them during the next two nights; and on New Year's Day, the Separate Battalion became the 3rd Battalion, 4th Marines.

Remaining on Bataan were Batteries A and C and the radar detachment of Adams' battalion. Battery A, commanded by 1st Lt. William F. Hogaboom, and Battery C, commanded by 1st Lt. Willard C. Holdredge, were incorporated into a naval battalion organized to protect Mariveles. The 120 Marines in the two antiaircraft batteries were an infinitesimal part of the 80,000 American and Filipinos bottled up on the 30-mile-long jungle-covered peninsula. In mid-January, 49 Marines were brought back from Corregidor to guard MacArthur's advance headquarters on Bataan.

On the night of January 22–23, a 900-man Japanese amphibious force landed behind the American-Filipino front across

Bataan. This brought the Marines into action. Hogaboom and Holdredge were ordered to take out patrols made up mostly of sailors, with Marines as squad and platoon leaders. They set up blocking positions on a hill above the landing site at Quinauan Point. The next day, Hogaboom—a young Annapolis graduate from Vicksburg who was to die as a POW—led a patrol down. The Americans got a taste of jungle warfare, fighting an enemy they could not see. The Japanese added firepower and Hogaboom retreated to the high ground. Meanwhile, a patrol led by Holdredge surprised the Japanese on Longoskawayan Point and killed a number of them before they pushed Holdredge's men back onto the ridges.

The patrols were reinforced by a machine-gun platoon and an 81mm mortar platoon from the 4th Marines on Corregidor. Holdredge ran into a superior force and was among the many wounded before the Americans could fall back to the ridges.

On the twenty-seventh, a skirmish line of some 200 men, including 60 to 75 Marines, attacked. The fighting was fierce, but they could not dislodge the Japanese. Two days later, a battalion of Philippine Scouts, supported by the Marines' mortars and machine guns, smashed the enemy and wiped out the landing force. That threat to Mariveles was finally eliminated.

Most of the naval battalion joined the 4th Marines on Corregidor in mid-February. On March 12, MacArthur left the Philippines; and on April 3, the Japanese, now greatly strengthened, reopened their offensive on Bataan. The defenders, dazed by the incessant bombardment, suffering from disease and short rations, were driven back. In a week, it was all over. Munitions and fuel dumps at Mariveles were blown up. Small craft took all possible men over to The Rock. And on April 9, 75,000 Americans and Filipinos, including 105 Marines, went on the infamous Death March and into captivity.

The very next day, the siege of Corregidor began. The 4th Marines, armed with Springfields and wearing their World War I-style helmets, dug into their beach-defense positions, strung barbed wire, laid mine fields and placed their guns and communications to meet the inevitable attack.

Overall, Corregidor was three and a half miles long. The western end was a broad area a mile and a half wide, and to the east ran a long, narrow tail. In the middle was the extensively tunneled Malinta Hill, which contained the headquarters for the defenders. The Marines' 1st Battalion guarded Malinta Hill and the island's eastern tail. West of the 1st Battalion was Lt. Col. Adams' 3rd Battalion, and the 2d Battalion covered the rest of the shoreline. About 100 Marines were sent over to bolster the defenses on nearby Caballo Island and tiny El Fraile Island.

The men on the exposed beaches took a beating. The Japanese pounded them from the air and with 105mm guns on Cavite Province. The enemy could spot any movement in daylight. The beach defenders received food after dark and before dawn, mostly rice and a little canned salmon. Water was scarce. The 11,000 men isolated on Corregidor held out for 27 brutal days.

The 4th Marines were joined by personnel from the naval battalion and the sunken ships and by more than 700 Philippine Air Cadets. The regiment, which had started with less than 800 Marines, had, in the end, nearly 4,000 men from all the services, including 72 Marine officers and 1,368 enlisted Marines. Most of the newcomers were in terrible physical shape, gaunt, emaciated. The 275-man naval battalion of sailors from Mariveles and the scuttled submarine tender *Canopus* became the 4th Battalion, 4th Marines. It had only six Marines: now-Major Williams, their commanding officer, and five noncoms. Williams' battalion joined the regimental reserve commanded by Maj. Max W. Schaeffer.

Williams has gone down in Marine Corps history as a special hero. During the bombardment he was "a giant among men at a time when courage was commonplace."[7] "Wherever the bombardment was heaviest, he showed up to see how his men weathered the storm . . . he led rescue parties from 4/4 into the . . . holocausts of flame, choking smoke and exploding ammunition to rescue the wounded."[8]

The 4th Marines were determined to get back at the enemy they had been unable to hit. Their morale was high; almost until the end, they hoped for rescue. As Morison described the scene:

> . . . the toll of casualties rose, and the nervous strain was almost unbearable. A certain number of officers and men gave in under the tension. Some saw hallucinations, others became completely ineffectual and could not per-

form their duties. But the tough and the strongminded held the team together and inspired the rest. Colonel Howard's 4th Marine Regiment . . . lived up to the great traditions of the Corps in the last bitter days. The backbone of Corregidor's beach defense, it set an example of courage for those who began to give under the strain.[9]

The Japanese set their D-Day for the night of May 5. On April 29, the Emperor's birthday, they celebrated by beginning a bombardment that never let up day or night. The water supply in the East Sector was knocked out; wire communications were ruined; casualties mounted. The defensive installations of the 1st Battalion, defending the island's eastern tail, were virtually destroyed. On the night of May 3, the submarine *Spearfish* made the last evacuation from The Rock, taking a few officers and 14 nurses who had been ordered out.

Starting at 10:45 P.M. on May 5, the Japanese poured in the most intensive bombardment yet on the strip of beach between Cavalry and Infantry Points, east of Malinta Hill, where they planned to land. But their barges, carried by a strong incoming tide, actually headed for North Point, almost at the island's tail.

As the first enemy battalion came ashore, the whole area erupted with gunfire. Japanese casualties were high. On the beach, Platoon Sgt. William "Tex" Haynes emptied two pistols at the advancing enemy, then fired a .30 caliber machine gun cradled in his arms until a grenade wounded him severely. A Company's 2d Platoon, commanded by Master Gunnery Sgt. John Mercurio, defended the beach between Cavalry Point and North Point and was overwhelmed.

By midnight, a second battalion landed in the light of the newly risen full moon. Enough Japanese made it ashore to drive onto the hogback that ran down the middle of the island's tail. They seized Denver Battery on high ground behind Cavalry Point and forced a hole in the center of the defenders' line. Marine Gunner Harold M. Ferrell organized a new line on the hogback to protect the rear of the defenders on the beach. Lt. Col. Curtis T. Beecher sent squads one at a time to build up the line Ferrell had begun. These men took severe casualties; the 1,000 yards to the Denver Battery was a deathtrap.

By 1:30 A.M., the surviving defenders on the eastern end of the island were isolated. Colonel Howard ordered up Major Schaeffer's two reserve companies. Two platoons of Lieutenant Hogaboom's company got into position; but the third platoon was chopped to pieces. Capt. Robert Chambers, Jr.,'s company was shelled by the guns on Bataan, and only the equivalent of one platoon ran the gauntlet.

Major Schaeffer ordered three counterattacks against the dug-in Japanese, who had set up machine guns at the base of a stone water tower. Schaeffer's reserves drove up the slope and were repeatedly shoved back. Sgt. Major Thomas F. Sweeney and Quartermaster Sgt. John E. Haskin, two oldtimers and close friends, personally attacked the machine gunners. Haskin was killed bringing more grenades up to Sweeney on top of the water tower. Sweeney destroyed one of the guns before he too died.

At 4:30, Colonel Howard ordered up his last reserves, Major Williams' 4th Battalion, which had been waiting in the hot confusion of the Malinta Tunnel. When Williams' men reached the "line," Schaeffer's command had been almost wiped out. Williams took charge. Opposing units slugged it out 30 yards apart. "It was a barroom brawl."[10]

At dawn, Williams moved along the line, telling his Army and Navy officers to be ready to attack at 6:15. Every man was in the line. There were no reserves. The companies on the left pushed the enemy back some 200 yards; but on the right, the men could make no progress. The fighting was at grenade range.

At 9:30, Japanese tanks were unloaded off barges at Cavalry Point; by 10, they were in position, and enemy artillery pounded the area in front of the Japanese line. The Americans began falling back in disorder. At 10:30, Williams ordered the units on the left back to the ruins of a concrete trench in front of the Malinta Tunnel. Casualties were severe. "It was each man for himself."[11] Only Williams, now wounded, and about 150 men made it to the trench. The Japanese were less than 300 yards away, and their tanks were moving to outflank them. At 11:30, Williams was told the decision had been made to surrender at noon.

The order went out to destroy all weapons larger than .45 caliber. The Marines of the 2d and 4rd Battalions, who had never been brought to battle, smashed their rifles on the rocks.

Some veterans were crying openly. Colonel Howard ordered the regimental colors burned. He wept, "My God, and I had to be the first Marine officer ever to surrender a regiment."[12]

Two Marines, Capt. Golland L. Clark, Jr., (who later died aboard a prison ship at Formosa) and 1st Lt. Alan S. Manning, took Lt. Gen. Jonathan M. Wainwright's truce flag to the enemy. At midnight, Wainwright broadcast a surrender message to all the forces in the Philippines.

The total losses of the 4th Marines in the Philippines were 330 killed and 357 wounded. Most of them fell on Corregidor, where 1,283 Marines were taken prisoner. For thousands of Americans and Filipinos, the next three years brought death and brutal mistreatment in Japanese prison camps. Of the 4th Marines, 239 officers and men died in Japanese hands.

4
Going On the Offensive

The final battle for Corregidor was, in reality, a mopping-up operation. The Japanese had already swept on to grab the riches of Southeast Asia, from Java (March 9) to Rangoon, Burma (March 8). They could have left Corregidor's holed-up defenders to starve.

By the time Corregidor surrendered, the Japanese tide had crested. Two great sea battles stopped them. On May 4–8, American and Japanese aircraft carriers fought the Battle of the Coral Sea at the southern end of the Japanese offensive. *Lexington* was lost and *Yorktown* damaged, but the Americans drove off the enemy force advancing against Port Moresby on the southern coast of New Guinea, opposite northern Australia.

Far to the north, the Battle of Midway, June 3–5, finished the last Japanese offensive in the Pacific. The Japanese lost four big carriers; and with its air cover destroyed, the enemy amphibious force heading for Midway turned back. After that victory, the U.S. Navy was ready to go on the attack.

By Pearl Harbor Day, the Marine Corps had grown to two divisions and 65,000 men. It had 13 aviation squadrons and 251 aircraft of all types. Just six days earlier, Admiral Harold R. Stark, the Chief of Naval Operations, had opposed the formation of a third Marine division and the use of dive bombers by the Marines.

In the forefront of the Corps were its static Defense Battalions, each organized on the average with 952 Marines but tailored for the job assigned. The 5th Defense Battalion was on Iceland, where it had arrived with the 1st Provisional Marine Brigade (6th Marines reinforced) in July. The 3rd, 4th and part of the 1st Defense Battalions were in Hawaii. The rest of the 1st

490

was divided over tiny Wake, Johnston and Palmyra islands. The 7th Defense Battalion guarded Samoa far to the south and the 6th, Midway in the north. These islands west of Hawaii now formed America's Pacific frontline.

On January 23, 1942, the 2d Marine Brigade (4,798 Marines) arrived to build Samoa into the main Marine base in the Pacific. With the coming of the 3rd Marine Brigade and MAG-13, 10,000 Marine ground troops were in the Samoan area by the end of May. It became a combat training center and a staging base for future amphibious operations in the Solomon Islands.

At the northern end of the line, Midway, by the end of 1941, was Hawaii's strongest outpost. The isolated two-island atoll, 1,135 miles northwest of Pearl Harbor, had been an American coaling station since 1867.

On the night of December 7, 1941, two Japanese destroyers had shelled Midway's air base to cover their carriers' withdrawal from Hawaii. One round zipped into the Sand Island power plant's air vent and exploded inside the concrete building. First Lt. George H. Cannon, the St. Louis-born commander of Battery H, 6th Defense Battalion, was severely wounded; but he refused to be evacuated until the other wounded had been cared for and Cpl. Harold R. Hazelwood had the switchboard operating again. Cannon died from loss of blood a few minutes after reaching the aid station and was the first Marine in World War II to be awarded the Medal of Honor. Hazelwood was awarded the Navy Cross. In the 23-minute attack, four men were killed and 19 wounded.

In the next three weeks, Midway was reinforced by VMSB-231, which made its historic flight directly from Oahu; by VMF-221, which flew off the deck of *Saratoga* after she had been pulled back from Wake, and by elements of the 4th Defense Battalion.

In May 1942, Adm. Chester W. Nimitz, commander of the U.S. Pacific Fleet expected—because the U.S. had broken the Japanese code—a Japanese attempt to capture Midway and destroy the American fleet. The atoll was sent most of the 3rd Defense Battalion, two rifle companies of the 2d Marine Raider Battalion, five light tanks and vital search radars. The newly organized MAG-22 received dive bombers and fighters, which were soon to prove obsolete for this war; and by the month's end, Midway was jammed with more than 100 Marine, Army and Navy planes.

At 6:16 A.M. on Thursday, June 4, the Midway Marines began their part in the decisive Battle of Midway, which was to become chiefly a struggle between the aircraft of opposing carrier forces. The Japanese fleet sent 108 planes against Midway; and 25 Marine fighter pilots led by Maj. Floyd B. Parks and Capt. John F. Carey tackled the incoming dive bombers. In the opening encounter, the faster, more maneuverable Zeros shot down nine of 12 Marine pilots. A second group of 13 Marine fighters led by Capt. Kirk Armistead followed up the attack. Both groups made their kills; but, in all, 15 of the 25 Marine pilots, including Major Parks, were killed. At 6:30, the enemy carrier planes struck the atoll through heavy antiaircraft fire and did widespread damage in a violent half hour.

Marine dive bombers attacked the Japanese carriers far north of the island after an unsuccessful attempt by Army and Navy planes from Midway. The first Marine striking unit, led by Maj. Lofton R. Henderson, scored no hits; and only half its 16 planes got back to Midway. (Henderson was shot down, and the airfield on Guadalcanal was named in his honor two months later.) Then, 15 B-17s took a crack at the enemy fleet, and failed. A second wave of 11 Marine bombers, led by Maj. Benjamin W. Norris, also missed and lost three aircraft. (Norris did not return from a mission to find the already burning carrier *Hiryu* that evening.) Half of Midway's aircraft were now gone.

But two hours later, carrier planes attacked the four Japanese carriers just as their planes, returned from Midway, were being refueled and rearmed for a second strike. The planes from *Enterprise* and *Yorktown*, taking full advantage of this phenomenal break, knocked out three of the enemy carriers loaded with aircraft. That evening, dive bombers from *Enterprise* mortally wounded the remaining *Hiryu*.

The next morning, 12 Marine bombers from Midway, led by Capt. Marshall A. Tyler, attacked two damaged enemy cruisers. Capt. Richard E. Fleming of St. Paul, Minnesota, his plane in flames, slammed into an after turret of the cruiser *Mikuma*. He was awarded the Medal of Honor.

In the Battle of Midway, the United States lost *Yorktown* and 98 carrier planes. Marine Corps casualties were 49 killed and 53 wounded. Expressing the survivors' bitterness, Lt. Col. Larkin at Ewa protested to President Roosevelt through his son, Maj. James Roosevelt, USMCR, of the fatal inadequacy of the Marines' antiquated aircraft.

The Japanese lost four carriers, some 322 planes and a great portion of their experienced naval pilots. They never recovered. And the United States went on the offensive.

The preliminary steps had already been taken. On March 12, the U.S. Army had landed at Nouméa, New Caledonia, where nickel mines might attract the enemy. Two weeks later, 500 soldiers, the Marines' 4th Defense Battalion and VMF-212 moved up to Efate in the New Hebrides. (At noon on April 18, 16 B-25s led by Lt. Col. James H. Doolittle, USA, bombed Toyko.) And on June 14, the 1st Marine Division reached Wellington, New Zealand.

At the end of May, Admiral Nimitz proposed sending the 1st Marine Raider Battalion to raid and destroy the seaplane base that the Japanese were building at Tulagi in the Solomons. But the tide turned faster than that. The Battle of Midway set the stage for a bigger operation. From now on, the rest of the Marine Corps story in this war would be of attack.

5
First, Carlson's Raiders

Evans Carlson, still the idealist, more than ever the believer in *Gung Ho*, was now 46 years old, gaunt, his face deeply lined, hair grayed. His 2d Raider Battalion was just nine months old. The Raiders were a controversial pet idea of President Roosevelt and Secretary of the Navy Frank Knox. Before the United States entered the war, two young captains, Samuel B. Griffith, II, and Wallace M. Greene, Jr., had been sent to England and Scotland to observe the British Commandos; and on their recommendation, Commandant Holcomb had authorized two raider battalions. Lt. Col. Merritt A. Edson formed one on the East Coast; Lt. Col. Carlson, the other on the West Coast.[13] They were organized to make hit-and-run raids, spearhead amphibious landings and fight as guerrillas behind enemy lines.

The Raiders were all picked men, all hardened to hike 50 miles a day without food and then to fight a battle with automatic weapons and knives. They were tough, with great confidence in themselves and a pride in being Raiders.

Although half of Carlson's battalion had been diverted to Midway, the rest was about to launch the first truly Raider operation. This raid on Makin Atoll in the Gilbert Islands, was planned, allegedly, to distract the enemy from the Guadalcanal landings, although the value and purpose of this bit of bravado are certainly not clear today.

Two big submarines, *Nautilus* and *Argonaut*, slipped out of Pearl Harbor on August 9, 1942, two days after the Marines had landed on Guadalcanal. Crowded in these boats were 222 Marines of A and B Companies, 2d Raider Battalion. It was thought that on Makin the Japanese had only some 43 defenders, but the Marine raid would still have very mixed results.

On the moonless night of August 17, the men, faces blackened, poured into rubber boats. The high seas flooded their outboard motors. Helped by the tide, the Marines paddled for an hour toward the east side of Butaritari, Makin's largest island. As dawn broke, 15 of the boats grounded on the designated beach across the island from Government Wharf; three other boats landed slightly to the north, and one boat, a mile south—as it turned out, behind the enemy. The men in the main element hid their boats, posted guards, made contact with the subs by radio and oiled their soaked weapons. Suddenly, the great advantage of surprise was lost when a Raider accidentally fired his BAR.

The small Japanese garrison quickly manned its machine-gun posts, and its snipers climbed to the bushy tops of the coconut palms. Lt. Merwyn C. Plumley and his A Company crossed the island to the lagoon side, and headed toward the enemy strongpoint two miles south. Carlson had *Nautilus* shell both it and two ships in the lagoon. Machine gunners and snipers worked over the Raiders. Second Lt. Wilfred S. LeFrancois and his men turned back a *banzai* charge. The former enlisted man from Watertown, New York, was hit in the right shoulder by five machine-gun bullets. Constantly in the van, with a shotgun for close-in fighting, Sgt. Clyde Thomason, a reservist from Atlanta, wiped out a Japanese attack before a sniper killed him. He was the only man in this operation to receive the Medal of Honor.

Carlson was everywhere, encouraging his men, coolly smoking his pipe. Machine guns, a flamethrower, snipers slowed the Marine advance; and Carlson had to send in B Company. Just before noon, Japanese planes bombed and strafed the invaders; and two flying boats put ashore 35 more Japanese. The Marines destroyed the planes. Frustrated by the snipers in the coconut groves, Carlson retreated northward to draw the Japanese into more open ground. It worked. The enemy pursued, and the next enemy bombing raid clobbered them—in the Marines' former positions.

Lt. Oscar F. Peatross and 11 Marines in the boat that had landed far to the south wrecked the Japanese strongpoint and radio station and killed a number of the enemy. After dark, Peatross' eight surviving Raiders returned to their submarine.

Carlson also tried to slip off the island, as the plan required;

but less than half of the men made it. The rest paddled and bailed, boats capsized, men lost their weapons, giant waves threw the exhausted men back onto the beach. Among the 120 Marines now on the atoll, more than a half dozen were wounded. During the rainy night, red-headed Pfc. Jesse Hawkins of Paragould, Arkansas, took two bullets in the chest but drove off an enemy patrol.

In the morning, Maj. James Roosevelt, Carlson's executive officer, plowed through the surf with four boats. Five Marines on *Nautilus* volunteered to bring ashore weapons, ammunition and a line. They were strafed by seaplanes, and only one man reached the beach. There were now 70 Americans left on Makin.

There is a story that a Raider officer set out to surrender the unit but could find no Japanese left on Butaritari to surrender to. The Raiders discovered that the enemy were either dead or had fled to smaller islands. The Raiders armed themselves with Japanese weapons, destroyed arms and installations and counted 86 enemy dead. That second night, with natives' help, the Raiders put their last four boats and a native canoe into the water on the lagoon side and struggled back to the submarines. This time they made it.

In addition to Thomason's Medal of Honor, the Raiders' bravery was recognized when Carlson, LeFrancois, Peatross, Plumley, Roosevelt and 13 others received the Navy Cross.

But 21 Marines were dead, and nine Raiders, still alive, had been left behind. They were captured and moved to Kwajalein. Vice Adm. Koso Abe ordered them executed; and on October 16, they were beheaded. After the war, Abe was hanged on Guam for this atrocity.

Although the Makin raid heartened the folks back home and Carlson's Raiders were widely publicized, the action had another disastrous aftermath. In good part as a result of it, the Japanese recognized their vulnerability and fortified the Gilberts intensely. The Marines found nearly 5,000 dug-in Japanese waiting for them on Tarawa.

6
The Canal

Eight months after Pearl Harbor and two months after the Battle of Midway, the United States began its first amphibious attack in the Pacific. The idea: Adm. Ernest J. King, commander-in-chief, United States Fleet, figured that the Japanese were overextended. The target: Guadalcanal and Tulagi in the enemy-occupied Solomon Islands, less than 600 miles southeast of the huge Japanese base at Rabaul. The instrument: the 1st Marine Division.

This was to be the germinal battle of the Pacific war. Men of all services learned to fight and defeat the Japanese. It was the first advance toward Tokyo and the Marines' longest engagement in World War II.

First, important decisions had to be made. General MacArthur wanted to strike directly at Rabaul, not at the out-islands; but the Navy refused to risk its scarce aircraft carriers. Gen. George C. Marshall, the U.S. Army Chief of Staff, wanted MacArthur in charge of the operation; the Solomons were in his theater. But King insisted on Admiral Nimitz because the Navy would provide the men and ships and planes. The newly organized Joint Chiefs of Staff had to resolve that one and, to give the job to the Navy, shifted the boundary line between the general's and the admiral's theaters of responsibility.

Then, Rear Adm. Richmond Kelly Turner, a tall, able naval aviator with no amphibious experience, was given command of the amphibious force, Task Force 62; the Marines were irritated by that. Finally, the Marine Corps wanted clear-cut command of operations ashore; but the Navy regarded the Marines as a subordinate extension of the fleet. This dispute was not resolved in time for this landing.

The Navy assembled a mass of power: three carriers (*Saratoga, Enterprise* and *Wasp*), two new battleships, heavy and light cruisers, 250 carrier aircraft. The 19,000-man Marine landing force was built on the 1st Marine Division. This was the first time a Marine division had sailed from the United States. It had the 1st and 5th Marines, but its 7th Marines, on duty at Samoa, was replaced by the 2d Marines from the 2d Division at San Diego. Added to the 1st Division were the 1st Raider Battalion, the 1st Parachute Battalion and the 3rd Defense Battalion. In command of the Marines was a veteran of Nicaragua, Vera Cruz, Haiti and China, quiet, persistent Maj. Gen. Alexander A. Vandegrift.

Vandegrift had expected to train his division in New Zealand until early 1943. When he got the word on June 26, he was shocked: Less than five weeks to get ready and he did not even know where Guadalcanal was. He managed to have the landing delayed a week, until August 7. But the Japanese were building an airfield on Guadalcanal, and the landing had to be made before planes from there could attack the invading armada.

When the division's rear echelon, the 1st Marines, arrived at Wellington, New Zealand, on July 11, it had only 11 days to empty and reload its ships for combat. Because of labor problems, the Marines had to do the whole job themselves, round the clock, working through day after day of heavy rains. But under the direction of Lt. Col. Randolph McC. Pate, the division's logistics officer, it was done.

On July 17, Lt. Col. Merrill B. Twining and Maj. William B. McKean flew up to Guadalcanal in an Army B-17 and inspected the landing beaches. No accurate maps existed; the Army took aerial photographs; but, through a succession of foul-ups, they never reached the Marines. The division intelligence officer, Lt. Col. Frank B. Goettge, flew to Australia and hunted down colonial officials, traders, planters, missionaries, shipmasters—anyone who knew Guadalcanal or Tulagi.

The Marines were headed for one of the wettest places on earth: rain-heavy, volcanic islands, jagged, jungle-covered and steaming with tropical heat, stinking with jungle decay. Guadalcanal itself was 90 miles long and 25 wide. North of it, across the 20-mile-wide Sealark Channel, lay Florida Island. Snuggled up against the southern shore of Florida were Tulagi Island with an excellent harbor and the small twin islets of Gavutu-Tanambogo. From coastwatchers' reports, especially those of a lanky British captain, W. F. Martin Clemens, on Guadalcanal, the Marines expected to find only 1,500 Japanese on Tulagi, both troops and laborers, and 2,300 (600 soldiers and 1,700 laborers) on Guadalcanal.

There would be five simultaneous landings. Group X-Ray, led by the 1st and 5th Marines and Vandegrift himself, would land on Guadalcanal's northern coastal plain about three miles east of Lunga Point, where on July 4 a reconnaissance plane had first seen Japanese working on the airstrip. The Marines' prime mission was to seize and hold that airfield.

Brig. Gen. William H. Rupertus, the assistant division commander, would take Group Yoke to the north side of Sealark Channel. Lt. Col. Merritt A. Edson, "Red Mike," would lead his 1st Raider Battalion and other detachments ashore on Tulagi's south coast. Maj. Robert H. Williams would land his 1st Parachute Battalion on Gavutu-Tanambogo; and the 1st Battalion, 2d Marines would sweep the coast of Florida Island behind the off-islands.

Many new recruits filled out the ranks of the division, but the old timers were the reinforcing steel. Samuel B. Griffith, II, who would lead some of them ashore on Tulagi, later described them this way:

> They were a motley bunch. Hundreds were young recruits only recently out of boot training at Parris Island. Others were older; first sergeants yanked off "planks" in Navy yards, sergeants from recruiting duty, gunnery sergeants who had fought in France, perennial privates with disciplinary records a yard long. These were the professionals, the "Old Breed" of United States Marines. Many had fought "Cacos" in Haiti, "bandidos" in Nicaragua, and French, English, Italian and American soldiers and sailors in every bar in Shanghai, Manila, Tsingtao, Tientsin, and Peking.
>
> They were inveterate gamblers and accomplished scroungers, who drank hair tonic in preference to post exchange beer ("horse piss"), cursed with wonderful fluency, and never went to chapel ("the God-box") unless

forced to. Many dipped snuff, smoked rank cigars or chewed tobacco (cigarettes were for women and children). . . . They knew their weapons and they knew their tactics. They knew they were tough and they knew they were good. There were enough of them to leaven the Division and to impart to the thousands of younger men a share both of the unique spirit which they animated and the skills they possessed.[14]

A rehearsal of the hastily assembled force was held in the Fijis from July 28 to 31. Because the site had been badly chosen, only one-third of the Marines participated in the amphibious practice. After the war, Vandegrift called the rehearsal "a complete bust," though in later years he somewhat softened that judgment.[15]

Another nervous note: It would take five days to unload the landing force and its equipment; but Vice Adm. Fletcher, the always cautious commander of the Expeditionary Force, warned that he would permit his big carriers to stay and risk air attack for only two days. In a heated meeting, Vandegrift objected vigorously.

The task forces left the Fijis at dusk on July 31. Bad weather kept the enemy planes at Rabaul grounded, and the 82 ships were not spotted. By the night of August 6, the entire group was west of Guadalcanal. The Marines slept in their green utilities, packs ready, weapons oiled. They had beans for breakfast. At 6:13 A.M., the heavy cruiser *Quincy* opened fire. Ships and carrier dive bombers began pounding the shorelines and quickly silenced the enemy's few guns.

At 6:50, as the sun rose on that overcast Friday morning, the Marines scrambled down the cargo nets and into 475 36-foot Higgins boats (only 116 had ramps). At 9:13, after a four and a half mile trip, the first units of the 1st and 3rd Battalions, 5th Marines came ashore at Red Beach, a 1,600-yard strip of black sand just east of the Tenaru River. The landing went smoothly. The Marines were met only by midday air attacks; and at dark, 11,000 Marines were on Guadalcanal.

On the beach, supplies piled up in a chaos of confusion and congestion. Sweating Marines and sailors stripped to the waist manhandled the crates. Vandegrift felt he could not spare men from the line to clear the beach. The Marines managed the unloading badly, and they would pay later for this failure.

The 1st Battalion, 5th Marines, under the regimental command of Col. LeRoy P. Hunt, who had led the company that took the Essen Hook at Blanc Mont in World War I, moved west and crossed the shallow Lunga River with a tank company at noon Saturday. They squelched some minor opposition and by 3 P.M. were at the enemy's strongpoint at Kukum on Lunga Point. The enemy had fled abruptly. Within the next hour, the 1st Battalion, 1st Marines, whose regimental commander was Col. Clifton B. Cates, another decorated veteran of the fighting in France, occupied the airstrip that was soon named Henderson Field.

Across the Skylark Channel, H-hour was even earlier: 8 A.M. The 1st Battalion, 2d Marines made two landings on Florida Island at H minus 20 minutes to protect the Tulagi force's flank. The Marines on Florida did not have to fire a shot. Edson's Raiders, led at first by Major Griffith, waded through waist-deep water to Tulagi's 600-yard-wide Blue Beach. Many were cut bloody on the coral. They entered the jungle, crossed the island's central ridge and moved south along the far shore. The second wave of Raiders, with A Company led by Capt. Lewis W. Walt, a Colorado State University athlete and student-body president, and C Company led by Maj. Kenneth D. Bailey—followed by the 2d Battalion, 5th Marines—covered the near coast. Bailey, a rugged six-foot-three former University of Illinois football end, roused a machine-gun nest in a cave, went in and cleaned it out with a BAR.

Walt and Bailey met the toughest resistance at a deep ravine in front of Hill 281. The Japanese were dug into coral caves and snipers were tied into the coconut palms. That night, they made four *banzai* counterattacks, one even reaching to battalion headquarters. When it was over, one BAR man, Pfc. Edward H. Ahrens, lay in his foxhole shot twice in the chest, bayoneted three times. Around him sprawled 13 enemy bodies. Walt carried him back for help. The dying Marine said, "Captain, they tried to come over me last night, but I don't think they made it." Walt replied, "They didn't, Johnny, they didn't."[16]

At dawn, two battalions of the 2d Marines came ashore and blasted the caves with dynamite attached to long poles. Saturday

501

afternoon, Hill 281 and Tulagi were finally secured with 200 Japanese dead. Edson earned his second Navy Cross, exactly 14 years after his first on the Coco River.

On Gavutu and Tanambogo, the fight was even meaner. Here was the Marines' first true amphibious assault—an attack from the sea against defended beaches. Fletcher's carrier planes destroyed the enemy's seaplane base and its 23 aircraft; and the warships pounded the islands, where the Japanese were hidden in coral caves and dugouts. At noon, the 1st Parachute Battalion, 395 drenched men, landed on Gavutu in three waves—after a seven-mile ride in choppy seas—and met a hail of rifle and machine-gun fire. The first boatloads were decimated on the beach. In two hours, one in 10 Marines was a casualty and most of the rest were pinned down. A squad did overrun Hill 148 and raised a small American flag, which Pfc. Edward Cooke pulled out of his pack.

Enemy automatic fire covered the causeway between the two little islands. After dark, the first landing attempt on Tanambogo was repulsed. Although 30 Marines got ashore, Japanese resistance was so overwhelming that they had to withdraw with heavy losses. On Saturday, the 3rd Battalion, 2d Marines landed on Gavutu but could not force the causeway. At 4:20 PM, I Company and two tanks assaulted Tanambogo. The Japanese destroyed the first tank, jamming its track with an iron bar, and killed all but one of its crew with hand grenades and knives. The second tank, accompanied by 60 Marines, blasted the enemy dugouts until K Company moved up the causeway from Gavutu and met the defenders with bayonets.

That night was filled with close-in fighting; and by late Sunday, the Marines secured the twin islets. On the three smaller islands were 1,500 dead Japanese; Marine casualties were 108 dead and 140 wounded.

From the first afternoon, the Japanese had sent air attacks against the collected American warships. Antiaircraft gunners and carrier pilots, alerted by the intrepid coastwatchers, shot down at least 30 bombers; but they managed to damage a destroyer and set fire to a transport.

Saturday evening, Vice Adm. Fletcher withdrew his three carriers and started south—even earlier than he had warned he would. Vice Adm. Robert L. Ghormley, commander of South

Pacific Forces, approved the move. Turner protested. Vandegrift was alarmed. Nimitz called Fletcher's decision "most unfortunate."[17] Vandegrift later wrote, "Fletcher was running away twelve hours earlier than he had already threatened during our unpleasant meeting."[18]

As the carriers moved off to the southeast, leaving Turner's ships between Guadalcanal and Tulagi without air protection, the Japanese Eighth Fleet was charging, unrecognized, down the wide channel called "The Slot" between the two strings of Solomon Islands. At 1:30 A.M. Sunday, the Japanese struck. "The resulting melee was one of the worst defeats ever suffered by the U.S. Navy."[19] In the brief Battle of Savo Island, three U.S. cruisers and the Australian cruiser *Canberra* were sunk, and the cruiser *Chicago* lost part of its bow. In those dark, shark-infested waters, 1,023 Americans died. No enemy ship was sunk. Much later, Turner wrote, "We took a hell of a beating."[20]

The Japanese failed to go after the sitting-duck transports, which continued to unload frantically off Lunga Point until they left for Nouméa that afternoon. Now, some 16,000 Marines were abandoned in the Solomons with 37 days' supply of food and four days' of ammunition. The rest, including 1,400 of the 2d Marines in the division reserve, had not been unloaded. The Marines ashore felt angry, depressed, cut off, but determined to hold.

The survival of the five battalions on Guadalcanal depended on the airfield. Holding it became Vandegrift's foremost concern—a defensive stance. Because the transports had carried away the bulldozers and other construction equipment, the airstrip had to be made operational as fast as possible with captured equipment and by hand. Col. Pedro A. del Valle's 11th Marines and the 3rd Defense Battalion pulled their guns tight around the strip, and the infantry-trained artillerymen and engineers patrolled the jungle to the south.

The Japanese controlled the air and sea but had little strength on the island. Vandegrift expected them to make amphibious landings of their own. He had the Marines build a defensive front facing the sea from Kukum eastward around Lunga Point to the mouth of the Ilu River. Enemy destroyers and submarines shelled the area at will and high-flying bombers attacked the airfield. Single bombers nicknamed "Washing

Machine Charlie" harassed the Marines all night. Their weapons could not reach the enemy planes.

Obviously, there were questions to ask about the planning of the Guadalcanal operation, so swiftly thrown together and called "Operation Shoestring" by the participants. Although they had met only meager opposition in landing on Guadalcanal, the Marines were left to their own devices, cut to two meals a day, short of all kinds of equipment and dependent on abandoned Japanese rice, trucks, fuel, even cigarettes. After Midway, the strategic opportunity had presented itself before American strength was ready. Between planning and reality was a gap that would take many lives to fill.

Fortunately, the enemy committed his forces to the Solomons piecemeal and chose to bomb and shell the airfield rather than destroy the irreplaceable supplies jammed up on the beachhead.

Henderson Field was declared ready on August 12, but no planes were available. On the night of August 15, four destroyer-transports scooted in with aviation gasoline, ammunition, bombs, ground crews and a Navy Seabee unit (including Ensign George W. Polk, who was killed while a CBS correspondent in Greece in 1948). On the twentieth, 31 planes finally arrived rived from the escort carrier *Long Island*, standing 200 miles off Guadalcanal. These were the forward echelon of Marine Aircraft Group 23, and the Marines cheered their coming.

The next day, Maj. John L. Smith, commander of VMF-223, scored Henderson Field's first kill—he would finish with 19 planes shot down. Army and Navy planes also began to show up. On September 3, Brig. Gen. Roy S. Geiger, a cold, tough bear of a man who had been one of the earliest Marine fliers, took command of all planes flying out of Henderson. The Seabees and the Marines' 1st Engineer Battalion kept the field operating, mastering the mud and repairing hundreds of bomb and shell craters—a never-ending job.

Meanwhile, the bulk of the Japanese were located beyond the brown-flowing Matanikau River, seven miles west of Lunga Point. A prisoner said they were ready to surrender. Lt. Col. Goettge, the division intelligence officer, took out a 25-man reconnaissance patrol in two lighters. In the moonless dark, on August 12, they waded ashore west of the Matanikau. The

Japanese attacked them on the beach, and only three enlisted Marines escaped. During the next week, three companies of the 5th Marines fought through the stifling jungle in that area, but the enemy did not stay to fight. The three companies killed 65 Japanese and lost four Marines killed and 11 wounded

The first crucial contest for Guadalcanal—the Battle of the Tenaru River—began on the night of August 18, when nearly 1,000 Japanese soldiers landed 22 air miles east of the Lunga River and 500 Special Landing Force troops landed west of the Marines' perimeter. The next day, a Marine combat patrol ran into part of the former unit and in an hour-long fight killed 31 of the 35 men. Now discovered, the Japanese commander decided to attack toward the airfield at once.

At 3:10 A.M., on August 21, after an exchange of rifle fire with the 2d Battalion, 1st Marines, commanded by Lt. Col Edwin A. Pollock, 200 screaming Japanese, bayonets fixed, rushed from the east at the sandbar across the mouth of the slow, scum-green Ilu River, which the Marines' maps mistakenly identified as the Tenaru River. The enemy ran into a single strand of barbed wire and a storm of bullets. Many were killed in the bright moonlight; but, fighting with knives, bayonets and rifle butts, some broke into the battalion's position west of the river before the battalion reserve, G Company, could counterattack and drive them back across the creek. The crocodiles fed on many bodies. The Japanese then waded beyond the breakers and plunged through the surf west of the Ilu's mouth. They came up against the Marines' strength: machine guns and artillery placed to repel an attack from the sea. By dawn, the sandy battlefield was littered with enemy bodies.

At 7 A.M., the 1st Battalion of Cates' 1st Marines crossed the Ilu upstream and in a well-coordinated attack squeezed the Japanese, now concentrated in a coconut grove, onto the point of land on the Ilu's east bank. The Japanese attacked with bayonets, trying to escape toward the east through the surf, along the beach and overland. Fighter pilots from VMF-223 strafed them. At 3 P.M., Vandegrift ordered five light tanks to attack across the sandspit. The tanks pivoted through the coconut grove, chasing the enemy, grinding over their bodies. It was, said Vandegrift, "war without quarter."[21] In two more hours, the Battle of the Tenaru was over. Nearly 800 Japanese were dead, piled up in the grove and on the sandspit; 15 were taken prisoner, and a few escaped into the jungle. Their commander, Col. Kiyono Ichiki, committed suicide. The Marines, with 34 dead and 75 wounded, had won their first big battle on Guadalcanal. "From that time on, United States Marines were invincible."[22]

The Japanese next sent toward Guadalcanal a fleet of three aircraft carriers, eight battleships, six cruisers, 22 destroyers and five transports loaded with troops. On August 24, the "Cactus Air Force" pilots of Henderson Field scored their first major success by shooting down six presumably unbeatable Zeros and 10 bombers. American carrier planes sank a light carrier, a cruiser and a destroyer and shot down 90 planes. The next morning, bombers from Henderson Field sank a transport and a destroyer. The Japanese ships turned back to Rabaul.

On the last day of August, the Japanese high command made a decision to delay their offensive in New Guinea and clean up Guadalcanal first. For the Americans on Guadalcanal, the situation was already desperate, even without the pressure this decision promised. Their needs had to compete against both the North African invasion and MacArthur's campaign in the Southwest Pacific.

To strengthen the perimeter, the 2d Battalion, 5th Marines; the 1st Raider Battalion, and the 1st Parachute Battalion moved over from the north side of Sealark Channel. Before dawn on September 8, 700 men of Edson's Raiders and the Parachute Battalion made an amphibious raid near Tasimboko, 18 miles east of Lunga Point. MAG-23 planes and two destroyer-transports supported their attack. With the paratroopers protecting their flank and rear, the Raiders stormed the village. The Japanese fled into the jungle. Edson destroyed their supply dump and threw their guns into the sea. He brought back in triumph a Japanese general's white dress uniform.

Edson estimated that 4,000 Japanese had been in the area—part of the Kawaguchi Force that had landed during the last two nights of August via the so-called "Tokyo Express." They planned to attack Henderson Field in what would be the second major contest for Guadalcanal—the Battle of Edson's Ridge.

The 1st Marines guarded the east side of the Marine perimeter, the 5th Marines the west side. In between, facing southward for a stretch of four miles, the defensive line was covered only by strongpoints and outposts. Eight hundred Raiders and Paramarines, weakened by battle and malaria, held the center of that thin line. Their positions keyed on a long, kunai grass-covered ridge that ran south from Henderson Field and offered the Japanese the best high-ground approach to the airstrip. Captured enemy documents convinced Edson that they would attack here. On Saturday, September 12, Edson, always meticulous, walked the ground and organized a "cushion defense" in depth. He ordered his men to dig in on the southernmost tip of what was about to become known as Bloody Ridge or Edson's Ridge.

In the dim moonlight that night, the enemy probed the Raider-paratrooper positions. Fighting broke out all along the southern front, and Edson's right flank was pushed back. Early Sunday morning, Edson counterattacked but could not uproot the enemy. His now-exhausted men established a new line on higher ground further back on the ridge.

In the meanwhile, Henderson Field was attracting an extra helping of Japanese air raids; and over the weekend, Navy pilots flew in 60 planes to bolster the plane-short, fuel-short Cactus fliers.

At 9 P.M. Sunday, "Washing Machine Charlie" dropped a green flare; Japanese destroyers in the channel opened up; south of Edson a red rocket rose, and two battalions—screaming "Gas! Gas!"—hit Edson's precarious line.

In the center, Capt. John B. Sweeney's Raider B Company withstood the heaviest assault. But on the west or right flank, the enemy drove a hole between A and B Companies. B Company's right platoon was surrounded and fought its way back 250 yards to join C Company, which was in reserve. Up on the ridge, the rest of B Company held; and Edson called in 105mm howitzer fire to within 200 yards of his men. The Japanese came on, took over some of B Company's foxholes, cut communication lines, threw in a heavy mortar barrage and then attacked the two paratroop companies to the east or left of the Raiders. The paratroopers, fighting hard, were driven back along the ridge, leaving B Company's left flank exposed. B Company, down to 60 men, was now being hit on three sides. Edson had them fall back to make a last-ditch stand with C Company, only 1,500 yards from the airfield. Edson moved among his men, rallying them. C Company exhausted its grenade supply; Major Bailey brought up more and crawled from foxhole to foxhole, handing them out. Despite a severe head wound, he led his men in hand-to-hand combat and in covering B Company's retreat.

Fighting off repeated attacks in the dark, the Marines finally stood on the last spur of the ridge. If the enemy broke through here, Henderson Field would be doomed.

The Japanese attacked again and again and were stopped again and again. The Parachute Battalion counterattacked and took 40 percent casualties. About 30 Japanese sneaked through Edson's line and seized two machine-gun positions from the 1st Engineers just east of the division CP. Three Japanese were killed right in front of Vandegrift. Headquarters troops and artillerymen rushed to plug the gap.

At 4 A.M., the 2d Battalion, 5th Marines strengthened Edson's battered left flank. And with dawn, the corpse-covered ridge was silent. The Marines still held, and the Cactus Air Force rose to bomb and strafe the retreating enemy. On Edson's Ridge, 40 Marines had been killed and 103 wounded—one in every five Marines who fought there. Edson and Bailey received the Medal of Honor.

While Edson was under attack, other Japanese units struck the 3rd Battalion, 1st Marines to the east, near the Ilu River. Six Marine tanks lunged forward without infantry support and only one survived. But by Sunday night, about half the original Japanese force was hacking its way through the jungle, fleeing toward the Matanikau. Henderson Field had been saved.

The 3rd Battalion, 2d Marines was brought over from Tulagi to reinforce the perimeter; and after a long argument between Vandegrift and Turner, 4,262 fresh men of the 7th Marines arrived on September 18 with tanks, ammunition, gasoline and rations. Of the 7th Marines' arrival, Vandegrift wrote, "I knew from previous experience that Turner held certain strategic and tactical ideas which so long as they pertained to naval operations were valid enough. When he got into the work of the generals, however, he should have saved his time. In this instance he favored the quaint notion of sprinkling little groups of the 7th Marines all over Guadalcanal."[23]

Bringing the 7th Marines to Guadalcanal was expensive:

Wasp was sunk; the battleship *North Carolina* was damaged, and the destroyer *O'Brien* was hit and later broke in two. The transports that brought in the 7th Marines took out the 1st Parachute Battalion (which had suffered all told 50 percent casualties), 162 other American wounded and eight Japanese prisoners.

Vandegrift now had 19,200 men. He could build up the southern rim of his perimeter and switch to an "active defense." First, he wanted to destroy a growing Japanese force on the far bank of the Matanikau River to the west.

The newly arrived 1st Battalion, 7th Marines, commanded by jungle-wise, barrel-chested Lt. Col. Lewis B. Puller, now forty-four and still loving a fight, passed through the perimeter on September 23. Puller followed a rugged jungle trail, and late the next day, with B Company in the van, fought a Japanese unit on the slopes of Mount Austen, which dominated the scene south of the Marine beachhead. Puller, the only officer in the battalion to have experienced combat, baptized his men new to battle. When Capt. Chester Cockrell was killed and his B Company was mauled, Capt. Zach D. Cox led a charge and drove off the enemy. The Marines suffered seven killed and 25 wounded.

The 2d Battalion, 5th Marines came out in the morning to reinforce Puller; and most of the combined force pressed westward to the Matanikau. On the afternoon of the twenty-sixth, near the river's mouth, Puller's force was stopped by heavy mortar and machine-gun fire; Marine casualties were high.

Vandegrift ordered out the depleted Raider Battalion, now commanded by Lt. Col. Griffith, and sent Colonel Edson up front to take command, with Puller as his executive officer. Edson planned an aggressive two-pronged attack for the next day; but during the night, the Japanese crossed the river and set up on high ground. When the Raiders climbed toward them on Sunday morning, the twenty-seventh, the enemy's fire wounded Griffth in the shoulder, and a machine-gun burst killed Medal of Honor winner Kenneth Bailey.

The message informing Edson that the Raiders had been stopped was garbled; he thought they had crossed the river and closed with the enemy's main body. He ordered the attacks forward at 1:30 P.M. A and B Companies of Puller's battalion, led by Maj. Otho L. Rogers, circled the Japanese position by sea. They landed and advanced to a high ridge 500 yards inland. A mortar round killed Rogers, and the enemy cut off the Marines from the beach. They were trapped.

Overhead, 2d Lt. Dale M. Leslie flying a dive bomber spotted the word "HELP" spelled out with white undershirts. He radioed to Edson; and Puller, his men in danger, collected the available landing craft, boarded the destroyer *Ballard* offshore and rushed to the rescue.

From the ridge, Sgt. Robert D. Raysbrook semaphored to the destroyer that the Marines were cut off. *Ballard* blasted out a path, and the Marines fought their way to the sea. Platoon Sgt. Anthony P. Malanowski, Jr., from Baltimore, covered A Company's withdrawal with a BAR until he was killed.

The Marines set up a perimeter on the beach, and Higgins boats moved in to take them off. The Japanese drove the boats away. Second Lt. Leslie strafed the enemy and herded the landing craft back toward the beach. The Marines flocked on board. Coast Guardsman Douglas Munro placed his boat between the Japanese and the Marines and was killed. The cost of the "active defense" operation: 60 Marines dead and 100 wounded. It had been a costly failure.

The "Tokyo Express" kept landing troops nearly every night and brought in 150mm howitzers, which threatened Henderson Field from a range the Marines' guns could not reach. Vandegrift had to try again to dislodge the enemy at the Matanikau, but this time the Marines would go in five-battalion strength.

On October 7, Marines led by Col. William J. Whaling, a jungle warfare expert and Olympic marksman, skirmished with an enemy force that had crossed the river inland; and Edson's 5th Marines ran into another Japanese bridgehead near the coast. A mortar section run by the spectacular mortarman, goateed Master Gunnery Sgt. Leland "Lou" Diamond, now fifty-two years old and known throughout the Corps, shared in pounding the enemy. After two days of heavy fighting, the enemy bridgehead was wiped out in hand-to-hand combat. (John Hersey accompanied a Marine patrol during this action and afterwards wrote *Into the Valley*, one of the great books about men in combat.)

The Marines upriver could finally advance on October 9;

they crossed the river and wheeled northward toward the coast in three columns. Whaling led the column on the right; Lt. Col. Herman H. Hanneken, who had killed Charlemagne Peralte in Haiti in 1919, commanded the center column, and Puller led the left-hand column. Whaling and Hanneken reached the coast easily; but Puller ran into a strong enemy force at a deep circular ravine. He called in artillery and mortar fire, and the Marines' machine guns picked off the survivors as they tried to climb out of the ravine to escape. Then, the Marines re-crossed the Matanikau. The cost of the three-day operation: 65 Marines dead and 125 wounded.

By mid-October, both sides were pouring men and arms onto this godforsaken jungle island. The Japanese had put on Guadalcanal about 20,000 men, including the Sendai Division. Vandegrift's force, which had evacuated 800 battle casualties and had 1,960 hospitalized malaria patients, was at just about the same strength. The Marines—and their enemies—were tired, filthy, on short rations, riddled with disease.

On the night of October 11 off Guadalcanal's northwest tip, the U.S. Navy sank one Japanese cruiser and severely damaged another. Two American cruisers were damaged and the destroyer *Duncan* sunk; but this Battle of Cape Esperance was the first tactical victory for the United States in Iron Bottom Sound, as the Sealark Channel was now being called.

Early on October 13, the transports *McCawley* and *Zeilin* brought Vandegrift reinforcements: 2,850 soldiers of the 164th Infantry of the Americal Division and 295 Marines. But otherwise, it was a bad day. Air raids, the 150mm howitzers and a ferocious nighttime naval bombardment chewed up Henderson Field and the new Fighter 1 strip nearby. By the next dawn, most of the gasoline supplies had gone up in flames; 41 more men were dead, and only 42 of the 90 planes could still fly. Air bombing and howitzer shelling continued all day; by mid-afternoon, Henderson Field was useless. The following day, despite all efforts by the Marine fliers, enemy transports put 3,000 soldiers ashore in broad daylight. At night, naval shelling again pounded the Americans. Japan's all-out effort was finally having its effect. The situation ashore had become ominous. Vandegrift demanded that the Navy take control of the sea around Guadalcanal.

Late on the afternoon of the sixteenth, 26 planes of VMF-212 arrived, led by Lt. Col. Harold W. Bauer, Annapolis quarterback in 1930, who had already downed five enemy planes on "visits" to Guadalcanal. The Marine planes came in during an attack by nine Japanese dive bombers. With his fuel tanks almost empty, Bauer went right after the enemy alone and in a virtuoso performance shot down four of the bombers before running out of fuel. Bauer won the Medal of Honor for his spectacular feat; on November 14, he was shot down into the sea and killed. He then had 11 enemy planes to his credit.

The Japanese bombardments heralded a major coordinated attempt to retake Henderson Field. One enemy force of 2,900 men would cross the mouth of the Matanikau. The main body with 5,600 troops set out October 16 on an eight-day, single-file trek through the rugged rain forest south of the airfield. This force was completely unknown to the Marines. Vandegrift only expected the attack from the west; and on the evening of the twenty-third, nine 18-ton tanks tried to penetrate the Marine line there. The Marines destroyed all nine, plus three others before they could attack, and killed hundreds of infantrymen assembled to follow the tanks. The premature western assault failed.

Vandegrift and Commandant Holcomb, who had spent three days on Guadalcanal, flew to conferences at Nouméa with Vice Adm. William F. Halsey, Jr. The aggressive Halsey had replaced Ghormley as commander of the South Pacific Area. (Vandegrift was delighted.) And Brig. Gen. Rupertus became acting commander of the 1st Marine Division.

Late on Saturday, October 24, Puller's understrength 1st Battalion, 7th Marines, guarding the perimeter's southern face east of the Lunga River, began detecting signs of the Japanese main body. It had abandoned its artillery and mortars on the punishing hike through the jungle.

At 9:30 P.M. in a lashing rain, the Japanese swept past a 46-man outpost far in front of Puller's barbed wire. Sgt. Ralph Briggs telephoned a whispered warning to Puller. The Japanese, screaming and throwing grenades, attacked at a spot the Marines named Coffin Corner. With supporting fire from the 2d Battalion, 164th Infantry on the left, Puller's men stopped them. When A Company on the left fired all its ammunition, Puller told Capt. Regan Fuller to hold with the bayonet. The enemy regrouped and came on again, a half dozen times. Twenty-five-year-old Sgt. "Manila John" Basilone mowed them down with his machine guns. He had to send out men to push aside the piled-up bodies to free their field of fire. One Japanese element penetrated the Marine line, seized a mortar position and nearly wiped out a C Company machine-gun nest until Basilone, moving silently, lugged up another gun on his back and fired on the enemy. When ammunition ran low and the re-supply route was cut off, Basilone fought through the Japanese to bring up more.

The big machine-gunner was the first enlisted Marine in World War II to earn the Medal of Honor. One of ten children of an Italian-born tailor, young Basilone had driven a laundry truck in Raritan, New Jersey, and then served as an Army private in the Philippines before joining the Marines. In recommending him for the Medal of Honor, Puller said he had "contributed materially to the defeat and virtually the annihilation of a Japanese regiment."[24]

The 3rd Battalion, 164th Infantry came through the rain and mud and was scattered among Puller's Marines to stand against the fury of the repeated assaults. The soldiers' new M-1 rifles added much-needed firepower to the Marines' older Springfield '03s. As the American fire took its toll, fewer and fewer of the enemy came forward. At dawn, the Japanese pulled back. The perimeter and airfield had again been saved. Puller won his third Navy Cross.

The defenders spent the day, the first fair weather in three days, absorbing blows from Japanese aircraft, destroyers and howitzers. Capt. Joseph J. Foss of VMF-121 shot down four fighters—for the second time in three days.

The Japanese launched a new night attack, throwing themselves at the Americans over and over again, but could not penetrate. To the west, between the perimeter and the Matanikau, another enemy force attacked Hanneken's 2d Battalion, 7th Marines on a ridge parallel to the coast—now called Hanneken's Ridge. F Company was overrun, and the Japanese fired two of its machine guns until they were driven off.

That night, twenty-four-year-old Platoon Sgt. Mitchell Paige from Charleroi, Pennsylvania, won a battlefield commission and became the second enlisted Marine to win the Medal of Honor in World War II. Paige commanded a machine-gun section in a saddle between E and F Companies. In the darkness and pelting rain, the Japanese stormed the Marines' position; and they battled hand-to-hand until all Paige's men were killed or wounded. Alone, the sergeant fought the gun, killed the oncoming soldiers; and when the gun was destroyed, he moved to his right and brought back another gun and a few riflemen. They opened fire. As dawn came, Paige saw Japanese crawling to an unattended gun; he raced them to it, while the enemy concentrated their fire on him. He won. Three Marines started to bring him belts of ammunition; each in turn was hit. Paige would fire a burst and then move; grenades would hit where he had been. He would fire again. He threw two ammo belts around his shoulders, picked up the hot machine gun and led the riflemen he had collected down the ridge, their bayonets fixed, whooping like Indians. The enemy melted away. And then all was quiet. The battle was over. Paige's arms were blistered from fingertips to elbows. There were more than 100 Japanese bodies in front of his sector. That was the end of the enemy's strongest effort to recapture Henderson Field. Bulldozers shoved 2,000 Japanese corpses into mass graves.

Elsewhere, events had their impact on the grimy Marines hanging on to Guadalcanal. Commandant Holcomb, following his visit to the battlefield, won endorsements from Halsey, Nimitz and King for the Marines' principle that the landing force commander, once ashore, should be on the same command level as the naval task force commander and free to make his own decisions. This not only ended the dispute between Vandegrift and Turner, but shaped lines of command for future Pacific amphibious operations. And most crucial of all, on October 24, President Roosevelt settled a hot-and-heavy controversy within the Joint Chiefs of Staff and sent each member of the Joint Chiefs a strong message demanding that "every possible weapon"[25] be sent to Guadalcanal. This was not a decision lightly made. German submarines were taking a dreadful toll in the Atlantic, sinking 88 ships in October alone; and the Allied North African invasion was already underway.

As a result of FDR's decision, Guadalcanal began to receive meaningful numbers of new men: the 147th Infantry, the 8th Marines, C and E Companies of Carlson's 2d Raider Battalion and additional Marine and Army artillery, including two batteries of 155mm guns that could finally answer the Japanese 150mms. Air power was bolstered by Marine Aircraft Group 11.

Rear Adm. Turner used the infusion of manpower to start his long-desired second front—a plan Vandegrift continued to oppose. All the ground reinforcements except the 8th Marines were directed to Aola Bay, 40 miles east of the Lunga River.

Vandegrift, his numbers increased, mounted another campaign to the west. The 1st Engineer Battalion bridged the Matanikau on the night of October 31, and Edson's 5th Marines crossed over. The 1st Battalion ran into the main enemy resistance at the base of Point Cruz. The 3rd Battalion was brought up; and the next morning, the 2d Battalion, now led by Maj. Lewis W. Walt, who had been a notable Raider, covered the western side of the enemy pocket. The Marines attacked; and by November 3, the Japanese were wiped out. Second Lt. Paul Moore, Jr. (later to become the Episcopal Bishop of New York), won the Navy Cross and was shot through the chest leading his F Company platoon in driving the enemy into the sea.

The Japanese, whipsawing the Americans, landed troops near Koli Point to the east of the Lunga perimeter. Adm. Isoroku Yamamoto wanted to keep the Americans' attention and forces divided. But other Japanese commanders, worrying about the price of this battle, were suggesting that Guadalcanal be left to wither and Japanese defenses be concentrated closer to Rabaul.

While Edson fought west of the Matanikau, Hanneken took the 2d Battalion, 7th Marines on a forced march 13 miles east of the perimeter. On November 3, the enemy hit his flank and forced the battalion to retreat some five miles to Koli Point. Hanneken called in air strikes, but the first "friendly" planes bombed and strafed the Marines. Vandegrift rushed Puller's 1st Battalion, 7th Marines to the scene by boat and two 164th Infantry battalions overland to envelop Koli Point from the south. And Carlson's Raiders hiked from Aola Bay through the jungle to block any Japanese retreat eastward.

On the 8th, the 7th Marines and 164th Infantry advanced and located the enemy at swampy Gavaga Creek 2,000 yards east of the Metapona River. Puller's battalion met heavy resistance; Puller was wounded. Maj. John Weber took over the battalion, which by now had 25 percent casualties, including half its officers. Hanneken's 2d Battalion circled around to the east side of the Japanese and the 2d Battalion, 164th Infantry faced them on the south. (Across the world, Eisenhower's troops were going ashore in North Africa.)

The battle went on for two days before most of the enemy were able to escape south along Gavaga Creek through a gap in the 164th.

Carlson's Raiders pursued the retreating Japanese. The heroic native scout, Vouza, who wore the Silver Star that Vandegrift had awarded him, led the way through the jungle. Lt. Col. Carlson put his main party on a parallel trail and then had a smaller group strike the Japanese in the rear. When they whirled to meet their attackers, the larger Raider force would hit their flank. The 400 Raiders hiked 150 miles and fought a dozen guerrilla skirmishes in the jungle. By December 4, they had lost 16 killed and 18 wounded and figured they had killed 488 Japanese. It was a historic patrol. Carlson won his third Navy Cross.

The Raiders stayed in the vortex of controversy. Some admirals were eager to create more Raider battalions and to use Marines only in small units. The Corps wanted to keep its divisions. An independent-minded maverick, *Gung Ho* Evans Carlson never again commanded troops directly in combat. After Guadalcanal was over, he was made executive officer of the new 1st Raider Regiment commanded by Col. Harry B. Liversedge, who had led the 3rd Raider Battalion. Lt. Col. Alan Shapley took over Carlson's old 2d Battalion and later the 2d Raider Regiment. Early in 1944, all the Raider battalions were converted into the new 4th Marines.

When the Japanese landed nearly 2,000 more troops west of the perimeter, the Marines and soldiers in the Point Cruz area went after them. On one patrol, Cpl. Barney D. Ross, the former boxing champion, won the Silver Star; he killed 22 Japanese and stood guard over three wounded Marines through the night after his unit withdrew.

The Japanese were preparing still another counteroffensive and a showdown. They intended to land their veteran, battle-tried 38th Division, 10,000 men, far west of the Marine perimeter. On Friday, November 13, an enemy naval force came into Iron Bottom Sound to knock out Henderson Field before the troop transports showed up. During that star-filled night, they sank the cruisers *Atlanta* and *Juneau* and four destroyers, killing

Rear Admirals Daniel J. Callaghan and Norman Scott. But the enemy naval bombardment force never reached the airfield. A wild, running sea battle raged for three nights; and American fliers sank seven of the 11 troop transports coming down The Slot.

This hard-fought and crucial Naval Battle of Guadalcanal prevented the enemy from landing their troops under cover of darkness. At first light on the fifteenth, the four surviving transports were run aground at the landing beaches. American guns, planes and ships attacked the 2,000 soldiers and reduced the transports to hulks.

This was the climax of the struggle for Guadalcanal. The Japanese could no longer significantly reinforce their troops. "The Japanese never again advanced and the Allies never stopped."[26] FDR called it "the turning point in this war."[27]

Now, the 1st Marine Division could be relieved from its over-long stint on the island. It had done its job. Doing it, the division had lost 650 dead, 31 missing and 1,278 wounded. Thousands of men had been stricken by malaria and other jungle diseases. The Marines were exhausted. On December 9, they started shipping out to Australia. Many were too weak to climb the transports' cargo nets.

On that same day, Vandegrift passed the command of the troops on Guadalcanal to Maj. Gen. Alexander M. Patch, USA. More Army units landed, including two regiments of the Americal Division and Maj. Gen. J. Lawton Collins' 25th Division. In the first week of January, the 6th Marines arrived to complete, with the 2d and 8th Marines, the 2d Marine Division. Brig. Gen. Alphonse De Carre served as division commander; Maj. Gen. John Marston, who was senior to Patch, remained in New Zealand.

By January 7, 1943, Guadalcanal held about 50,000 Americans, including the 2d Marine Division's 14,733. The Japanese had there an estimated 25,000 weary men, and the U.S. fliers were making it extremely difficult for them to add fresh soldiers. Henderson's air strength was built up to a level unimaginable in the early Operation Shoestring days. On January 15, Major Foss bagged three more Zeros, bringing his total of kills to 26, one more than Eddie Rickenbacker's World War I score. By the end of the month, VMF-121 had downed 164 planes at a cost of 20 pilots, including ace Lt. William P. Marontate (13 kills).

Maj. Gen. Patch began his campaign to push the enemy off Guadalcanal by assaulting their positions on and around Mount Austen, three miles south of Henderson Field. In an intense jungle battle, the enemy strongpoint was isolated and its defenders reduced to starvation. After a final convulsive Japanese counterattack on January 21, it was destroyed.

Patch ordered an advance in the greatest strength yet against the enemy to the west. His command was now designated the XIV Corps. The Army units moved out on January 10; and the 2d Marine Division's 2d and 8th Regiments attacked three days later on the right flank, between the 25th Infantry Division and the sea. The enemy, shrewdly dug in, met the Marines with crossfire down the long axis of successive valleys and ravines. On January 15, the fresh 6th Marines took over for the 2d, which was long overdue to leave Guadalcanal for New Zealand. In five days, the 6th and the 8th Marines, with gunfire support from naval ships offshore, advanced 1,500 yards and killed more than 600 Japanese. They took two prisoners.

The Americans pressed westward. The 6th Marines along the coast had heavy going; but the Japanese, though still full of fight, were falling back now. Pursuing the enemy toward Cape Esperance, the Americans reached the Poha River on January 25. Then, aerial reconnaissance warned of a large naval concentration at Rabaul; and Patch and Halsey feared the Japanese would attempt again to retake the island. Patch pulled back troops and left the 147th Infantry to continue the pressure, with the 6th Marines in support.

But, unknown to the American commanders, Japan's Imperial War Council had on January 4 decided to evacuate Guadalcanal. The Japanese would keep the island under air attack from a new airfield being built at Munda Point on New Georgia Island, 175 miles northwest of Henderson Field. Munda became the new focal point for both the Tokyo Express and the Guadalcanal fliers.

On Guadalcanal, the Japanese put up a determined rearguard stand at the Bonegi River from January 30 to February 2, And 12,000 soldiers, most of them wounded and weakened by disease, were evacuated by the night of February 7. They escaped completely undetected by the American generals—an incredible performance.

After precisely six months of battle, the Guadalcanal campaign was over. President Roosevelt draped the Medal of Honor around Vandegrift's neck.

The tenacious Japanese had lost some 23,000 dead in battle and from disease, including 600 of their best naval pilots. Total American ground forces lost in combat were 1,598 killed and 4,709 wounded, of which 1,152 dead and 2,799 wounded were Marines. In addition, Marine aviation units had 55 dead, 85 missing and 127 wounded.

The contribution of Marine fliers to the defense of Guadalcanal was incalculable. The pilots and their gunners climbed from a primitive, often shell-pocked field day after day to do combat in all kinds of weather and against all odds. Before the island was secured, four fliers besides Lt. Col. Bauer had earned the Medal of Honor: 1st Lt. Jefferson J. DeBlanc, Capt. Joseph J. Foss, Maj. Robert E. Galer and Maj. John L. Smith. Foss had shot down 26 planes, Smith 19, Marion E. Carl 18½, Galer 13, Marontate 13, Bauer 11, DeBlanc 9. The battle for Guadalcanal was truly three dimensional.

Rear Adm. Raizo Tanaka, a most able opponent, wrote later, "There is no question that Japan's doom was Guadalcanal."[28] Other Japanese commanders would have cause to speak similarly of other battles in the months to come—Tanaka was only the first.

The island was an unattractive piece of geography— malarial, harborless, soon to be left behind. Some disputed the value of the sacrifice it cost. But the United States had to start attacking somewhere, and the Japanese decision to resist so insistently made the price almost inevitable.

Guadalcanal had been a brutal experience; it would be the Marines' longest battle of the war. Some of the higher commanders believed the Marines should have been relieved much sooner, but there had been no one to replace them. The Guadalcanal Marines became battle-hardened veterans of jungle warfare and aerial combat, and they spread their knowledge through the rapidly expanding Corps.

Strategically, the battle for Guadalcanal diverted Japanese strength; saved New Guinea from being overrun; sped up MacArthur's advance through New Guinea and the Philippines, and gave the United States a springboard from which to go after the enemy through the Central Pacific.

7
Isolating Rabaul

Now, the objective was Rabaul, the massive base on the eastern end of New Britain Island. As long as the enemy there could send out planes and ships to smash Allied landing operations, MacArthur could not advance along the northern coast of New Guinea and Nimitz could not pierce the Bismarck Archipelago and break out into the Central Pacific.

MacArthur wanted to conquer Rabaul, but the Allies at the Quebec Conference in August 1943 accepted the Joint Chiefs of Staff's recommendation to neutralize it. The Conference also fixed the grand Pacific strategy that would attack Japan both over the New Guinea–Philippine route (MacArthur) and through the Central Pacific islands (Nimitz).

To pulverize Rabaul, rather than to occupy it, required a series of landings and an enormous amount of bombing; but it cost much less in lives and materiel than a frontal assault. In the 10-month campaign to neutralize Rabaul, Marines participated in the air and on the ground. Three amphibious operations were particularly important: New Georgia, Bougainville and Cape Gloucester.

But first, the Japanese air war against Guadalcanal had to be controlled. The job was made easier when in February 1943 Marines began to switch to the gull-winged F4U Vought Corsairs, which could fly faster than any Japanese plane. On the afternoon of April 7, 76 fighters from Henderson Field shot down 39 of 160 attacking planes. First Lt. James E. Swett, a lanky twenty-two-year-old from San Mateo, California, earned the Medal of Honor and became an instant hero when he knocked off seven dive bombers in 15 minutes on his virgin combat flight. Swett, flying a Wildcat, shot down the first three

520

over The Canal; then, he was hit by an American antiaircraft shell. He flew over Florida Island and shot down four more bombers before a Japanese rear gunner winged him. Swett killed the gunner and then ran out of ammunition. He crash-landed in the water, breaking his nose.

On June 30, Swett, now a captain, shot down three planes and on July 11 over Rendova added two more. That day, his wingman, 1st Lt. Harold E. Segal of New York City, scored three kills—the first when he shot a Zero off Swett's tail. Segal finished the war with 12 planes to his credit; but on July 11, both Swett and he ended in the drink. Segal was picked up by a destroyer; Swett spent 12 hours in the ocean off Japanese-held New Georgia before he was rescued by natives in a canoe and taken to a Navy patrol boat.

In the meanwhile, on April 18, in a carefully planned coup of inestimable value, Army P-38s shot down over Bougainville a twin-engine bomber carrying Fleet Adm. Isoroku Yamamoto, Commander in Chief, Combined Fleet, and erased Japan's most formidable naval mind.

The air assault on Guadalcanal climaxed in June, when the enemy took unacceptable losses—107 of 120 planes on June 16, for example—and gave up their daylight raids. The air action began to shift to the skies over Rabaul.

The first significant amphibious advance up the Solomons was to seize the Japanese air base at Munda Point on the northern end of New Georgia Island. The New Georgia operation was badly planned. It required five amphibious landings, 30,000 soldiers and Marines and more than a month of treacherous fighting. It wasted American lives.

The campaign started prematurely. On June 21, O and P Companies of the 4th Raider Battalion landed at Segi Point, at the southern end of New Georgia, and rescued Coastwatcher Donald G. Kennedy, whom the Japanese were hunting down. The Raiders then set out to destroy a 3-inch coastal gun at Viru Harbor before an Army force tried to land there. Led by Lt. Col. Michael S. Currin, the Raiders paddled eight miles through the moonless night and then plunged into the jungle. After four days struggling through mangrove swamps and across rivers, they overwhelmed the Japanese encampment on both sides of Viru Harbor. Eight Marines were killed in the final assault.

521

At the northern end of New Georgia, Army troops and the 9th Marine Defense Battalion landed on Rendova Island, across the lagoon from Munda Point, on June 30. Of the planes that rose to oppose the landing, 101 were shot down. On July 5, Army troops crossed over to Zanana Beach on New Georgia proper; and Marine Col. Harry B. Liversedge took two battalions of the 37th Infantry Division plus Lt. Col. Griffith's 1st Raider Battalion ashore as a blocking force at Rice Anchorage behind Munda Point. That night, in the naval Battle of Kula Gulf, the cruiser *Helena* and two Japanese destroyers were sunk.

Colonel Liversedge, a veteran of France and an Olympic shot-putter, known as "Harry the Horse" because of his 6′4″ height, led his 2,600 men southwest toward Bairoko Harbor to cut off Munda's defenders from both reinforcement and escape. Soldiers and Marines fought through the thick rain-sodden jungle along a route scouted by a daring Raider patrol led by Capt. Clay A. Boyd. Liversedge's men ferried their equipment across the flooded Tamakau River on rafts made of ponchos and branches. After a brief fire fight with a Japanese patrol, Griffith's Raiders swept forward as swiftly as possible. On July 8, they killed 50 Japanese; but 400 Japanese attacked Liversedge's perimeter at Triri and pushed back its defenders until the Raiders hit the enemy rear.

The next day, the Raiders attacked again and were beaten back. On the morning of the tenth, the Raiders, without food for 24 hours, dispersed the enemy at the village of Enogai and seized their 140mm coastal guns. Late that afternoon, an Army company brought up food that had been airdropped at Triri. The hungry and angry Marines dined on K-rations and Japanese canned fish, rice and sake. Japanese casualties were estimated at 350; since advancing from Triri, the Marines had lost 51 dead and 74 wounded.

When Currin's 4th Raider Battalion (short 200 men) arrived on July 18, Liversedge set out to attack Bairoko Harbor, the next Japanese-held indentation on the coast toward Munda. On the twentieth, he sent the Marines along the coast and the soldiers straight across the intervening Dragons Peninsula.

An air strike Liversedge had requested never came, and the Marines were met by well-placed automatic weapons hidden in log and coral bunkers and by snipers in trees with light Nambu machine guns. After 20 minutes of furious combat, Griffith threw in his only reserve platoon and took pillbox after pillbox with heavy casualties. Griffith messaged Liversedge: "I have committed the works."[29] Liversedge sent up Currin's battalion, and the Marines inched forward a yard at a time. The Japanese began bombarding them with 90mm shells. The Raiders, always without artillery, had no weapons to reply. A screaming attack pushed the Marines back; D Company, 1st Battalion counterattacked and sent the enemy reeling. Q Company, 4th Battalion followed with a direct assault but was butchered and forced to retreat. Liversedge desperately needed help, but the Army battalion that was supposed to attack the enemy's flank had been held up in the jungle by strong resistance. By now, the Raiders had suffered 30 percent casualties; and, after reconnoitering the front lines, Griffith recommended that Liversedge withdraw. The Marines, only 300 yards from Bairoko, their objective, were exhausted from seven hours of battle, low on ammunition, out of water and burdened by 200 wounded. The next day, they struggled back to Enogai, carrying their dead and wounded. When the 25th Division finally entered Bairoko, it had been evacuated. The Raider battalions were returned to Guadalcanal; less than half of their 933 survivors were judged still effective for combat.

The whole operation had been mismanaged. The Japanese simply reinforced Munda over another route; Liversedge's trail block had not even cut the main Munda–Bairoko trail. The Americans' courageous fighting hardly justified the effort and the cost: 128 Marines dead and 307 wounded.

After a long, botched campaign, the Army, helped by Marine tanks, seized the Munda airfield on August 5. Historian Morison wrote, "We certainly took it the hard way."[30] But the Japanese had lost 358 planes trying to hold Munda; and VMF-123 and -124 were soon flying from the field.

The next move in the Solomons, 10 days later, was a bit smarter: Halsey leapfrogged heavily defended Kolombangara Island just north of New Georgia and took lightly defended Vella Lavella instead. The Allies should have learned a crucial lesson from this: Bypass enemy strongpoints and hit them where they ain't.

American air power continued drumming away at Rabaul.

The most spectacular Marine flier that fall was Maj. Gregory Boyington, who shot down five planes on his first mission on September 16. He was called "Pappy" because he was all of thirty-one years old. He designed and led fighter-sweeps, daring the Japanese pilots to come up and fight. His Black Sheep Squadron, VMF-214, downed 57 enemy planes in its first month of combat. Boyington earned the Medal of Honor and became the Marine Corps' top ace with 28 kills—counting the six planes he had destroyed earlier with the Flying Tigers in China. When he was shot down, badly wounded, over Rabaul on January 3, 1944, he parachuted into the sea, was picked up by a Japanese submarine and imprisoned until the end of the war.

These months also saw command changes important to the Marines. In July 1943, Turner was succeeded by Rear Adm. Theodore S. Wilkinson as commander of Amphibious Forces, South Pacific Area. Turner moved over to the Fifth Fleet in the Central Pacific. And now-Lieutenant General Vandegrift took command of the I Marine Amphibious Corps, responsible for all Marine amphibious units in the South Pacific. Vandegrift had a hand in planning the next operation before turning over the job on September 15 to Maj. Gen. Charles D. Barrett, an expert Marine planner. But when Barrett was killed in a fall at Nouméa, Vandegrift was recalled and completed the planning. On November 9, Maj. Gen. Roy S. Geiger took over I MAC; Vandegrift finally headed home to become Commandant of the Corps.

By the fall of 1943, three Marine divisions were in the Pacific. The 1st was preparing for Cape Gloucester on New Britain; the 2d for Tarawa in the Gilbert Islands, and the 3rd for Bougainville.

Bougainville was the final giant step up the Solomons to acquire an airfield that would bring the Allies within land-based fighter range of Rabaul. To deceive the Japanese, feints were sent against the Treasury Islands by the 8th New Zealand Brigade Group and against Choiseul Island by the Marines. Thirty-year-old Lt. Col. Victor H. Krulak took 656 men of the 2d Parachute Battalion ashore on Choiseul just after midnight on October 28. Krulak—a small, wiry man and like all Annapolis coxswains nicknamed "Brute"—had the unusual assignment of raising a rumpus so that the Japanese would think his landing was the beginning of the next big operation. In truth, the main American landing was to strike north of Bougainville's Empress Augusta Bay. Krulak's "Paramarines" landed on Choiseul and hiked south toward the enemy's barge base at Sangigai. They killed only seven of a 10-man Japanese unit so that the survivors could carry word of the landing back to the enemy commanders. Then, the Marines hit Sangigai from two sides. When E Company attacked along the coast, the Japanese fled into the hills and ran right into the rest of Krulak's force. In an hour-long hand-to-hand fight, four Marines were killed and 12 wounded; Krulak was wounded in the arm and face.

Maj. Warner T. Bigger led an 87-man patrol north to the Warrior River and bombarded an enemy supply base with mortar fire. The Japanese landed from barges to cut off Bigger's return and fought the patrol on the river bank. It was rescued by landing craft under cover of two PT boats, one commanded by Lt. John F. Kennedy, USNR, who had previously had his *PT 109* rammed by a Japanese destroyer. When one of the landing craft began to sink, Kennedy's boat, *PT 59*, took aboard some of the Marines, including three seriously wounded. Cpl. Edward J. Schnell of Wilmette, Illinois, critically wounded with a bullet in his chest, died in Kennedy's bunk. The next night, the rest of Krulak's parachutists were withdrawn from Choiseul.

The site of the main landing midway up Bougainville's west coast—210 miles from Rabaul—was the most uninviting on the 125-mile-long island. The narrow beaches were backed by brackish lagoons and swamps; and further inland, the Marines faced dense jungle more impenetrable than Guadalcanal's. Intelligence estimated that 17,000 Japanese were at the southern end of the island; 5,000 at the northern tip, but only 300 at Cape Torokina, where the "hit-'em-where-they-ain't" landing was contemplated.

The 3rd Marine Division was commanded by Maj. Gen. Allen H. Turnage, a veteran of France, Haiti and China, and composed of the 3rd, 9th and 21st Marines, with the artillery of the 12th Marines, the engineers of the 19th Marines and Seabees. To it were added the 2d and 3rd Raider Battalions and the 3rd Defense Battalion. The division had not been in combat, but many of its men were experienced and most had had jungle warfare training at Samoa and Guadalcanal. The assault would be made by two landing teams: the 3rd Marines plus the 2d Raider Battalion and the 9th Marines plus the 3rd Raider Battalion. When the division was entirely ashore, the 37th Infantry Division would land.

On the bright morning of November 1, the Marines landed on 12 beaches from Cape Torokina northward. The rough surf wrecked 86 of the 9th Marines' landing craft. On the extreme right, the 1st Battalion, 3rd Marines, met the strongest resistance; its boats were caught in a crossfire from Cape Torokina and Puruata Island just offshore. The enemy's single 75mm gun sank four of the landing craft.

As the Marines reached the beach, machine guns, mortars and rifle fire opened up from solid log and sand bunkers. The gunfire of four destroyers had accomplished little. The landing became a shambles. One of the first men ashore, Sgt. Robert A. Owens, twenty-three years old from Greenville, South Carolina, alone charged the fire port of the destructive 75mm gun, which had by now hit 14 boats. Owens drove the crew out through the rear of the bunker and silenced the gun before he was killed. His Medal of Honor citation recognized his act as "indomitable and aggressive in the face of almost certain death."

Working expertly, the Marines knocked out Cape Torokina's 25 bunkers. Enemy air attacks strafed the narrow beaches; cargo piled up. There were now 14,000 men ashore. The Marines spent the rain-filled night huddled three to a foxhole, one man always awake. Infiltrators were disposed of with bayonets and knives.

That night, in the naval battle of Empress Augusta Bay, U.S. Navy Task Force 29 successfully protected the beachhead and sank a cruiser and a destroyer.

The Marines had two jobs ashore: to build an airfield and to expand and strengthen the perimeter. The 2d Raiders, aided by 29 dogs of the 1st Marine War Dog Platoon, pushed inland up the Mission Trail. In the muck of the swampland, the amphibian tractor (LVT) proved invaluable. By November 5, the perimeter was 10,000 yards along the beach and 5,000 yards deep.

Two days later, the northern flank of the beachhead was attacked by a counterlanding of 475 men. One enemy detachment met a patrol led by Lt. Orville Freeman and wounded the

526

future Secretary of Agriculture. By the next day, the Japanese force had been eliminated in close-range fighting.

On the seventh and eighth, a strong enemy force hit a trail block the Raiders had set up inland west of the junction of the Piva and Numa Numa trails; the seesaw battle ended shortly after noon on the ninth when the superior firepower of four Raider companies finally prevailed. The Raiders occupied the Piva–Numa Numa junction and dug in. They had lost 12 killed and 30 wounded. Two battalions of the 9th Marines now moved through the Raider positions and occupied Piva Village. And the Army's 148th Regimental Combat Team arrived and took over the northern half of the beachhead perimeter. By November 13, there were 33,861 soldiers and Marines ashore.

An airfield site was selected 1,500 yards inland beyond the Marine perimeter; and the 2d Battalion, 21st Marines was sent forward to hold the area. But the enemy got there first and ambushed E Company in a coconut grove.

The Japanese set up strong blocks on both the Numa Numa and the East-West trails in front of the Marines. The 2d and 3rd Battalions, 3rd Marines moved up the trails until Lt. William Kay, an expert scout known as "The Fox," found a 400-foot jungle hill from which the entire area could be dominated. First Lt. Steve J. Cibik and his platoon occupied the height late on November 20 and the next morning hurled back three enemy attacks.

When the Marines moved forward again, they ran into heavy going. This became known as the Battle of Piva Forks. On Wednesday, November 24, Thanksgiving Day back home, the two battalions of the 3rd Marines attacked across the east branch of the Piva River. After a 20-minute artillery barrage, the 2d Battalion advanced only 250 yards through the jungle before it took 70 casualties. Flamethrowers destroyed the enemy bunkers. The 3rd Battalion on the left side of the trail stopped a flank attack in hand-to-hand fighting. By the time the Marines reached their objectives, they counted 1,071 enemy bodies and had 115 casualties themselves. Back at the beachhead, a shipment of Thanksgiving turkeys arrived; the cooks roasted them and sent a share to the units up front.

The 1st Battalion, 9th Marines attacked down Cibik Ridge

and tried to capture a small 20-foot-high knoll where about 70 Japanese were dug in with an ample supply of grenades. The Marines never did take the crest of "Grenade Hill" until the enemy withdrew. Then, the Marines held the high ground from which the enemy could threaten the beachhead.

Under command of Maj. Richard Fagan, the newly arrived 1st Parachute Battalion and M Company of the 3rd Raider Battalion were sent to raid Koiari, 10 miles down the coast from Cape Torokina, in the early hours of November 29. They landed in the middle of a Japanese supply dump. An officer, expecting Japanese boats and carrying only a sword, greeted them at the beach. Surprise was mutual; the officer was killed. When the enemy recovered, they hit the beachhead with mortar shells, grenades and machine-gun fire and rushed the Marines. Casualties mounted. Fagan radioed a request that his outnumbered unit be pulled out. Enemy artillery repulsed two rescue attempts by landing craft. Three U.S. destroyers were rushed to the scene, and the ships and 155mm guns at Cape Torokina lay a box of fire around the beleaguered Marines. Behind that shield, the landing craft raced to the beach and took off the men. The detachment, which totaled 614 men, had 15 killed, 99 wounded and seven missing. The raid had been a bloody failure.

The final move to anchor the perimeter required the seizure of a large hill mass where the enemy made a strong stand on a spur of Hill 1000 that the Marines came to call Hellzapoppin Ridge. It took until December 18 before the Japanese were finally dislodged by the 21st Marines, working with effective Marine close air support.

By the end of January 1944, the Marines were withdrawn; they had lost 423 killed and 1,418 wounded on Bougainville. For this price an air base had been bought 210 miles from Rabaul. The high-risk venture had paid off. From the strip at Torokina, VMF-216 had flown close support missions at Hellzapoppin Ridge; and by the end of the year, the Piva bomber field was functioning. Now, fighter aircraft could escort bombers all the way to Rabaul.

On March 9, a force of some 12,000 Japanese soldiers came over the mountains and attacked the Torokina perimeter, determined to push the American XIV Corps' two Army divisions and the 3rd Marine Defense Battalion into the sea. The enemy made six major assaults in the next two weeks and 6,843 Japanese died in the futile attempt. The enemy, having lost control of sea and air, never tried again.

American air power continued to wallop Rabaul; and by February, mastery of the sky had been won over that hard-hit base. Marine 1st Lt. Robert M. Hanson, the Corps' third leading ace in the war with 25 kills, was shot down. The Japanese lost nearly 400 planes defending Rabaul; and on February 20, they pulled back the remainder to Truk. That altered the strategic situation critically. Although planes from Bougainville kept bombing Rabaul, the great Japanese base was already impotent.

MacArthur wanted to occupy Cape Gloucester on the western end of New Britain Island, 350 jungle miles from Rabaul, to protect his flank as he moved up along New Guinea's coast. After the war, Historian Morison judged: "General MacArthur believed that Cape Gloucester must be taken . . . . The wisdom of hindsight makes it seem superfluous."[31] For the 1st Marine Division alone, this "waste of time and effort"[32] would cost 310 killed and 1,083 wounded, plus weeks of battling jungle, rain and disease.

After the Army landed in Marine amphibian tractors at the Aware Peninsula on the southern New Britain coast, the 1st Marine Division assaulted Cape Gloucester the day after Christmas 1943. The now hard-nosed division was commanded by Maj. Gen. Rupertus and refreshed from its Melbourne fling. The Marines were armed with the semiautomatic M-1 rifle, which had replaced the bolt-action Springfield '03; and most of the officers and noncoms were Guadalcanal veterans. To the frustration of Intelligence, these experienced Marines were loath to take prisoners.

The 1st and 3rd Battalions of Col. Julian N. Frisbie's 7th Marines went in east of the cape, followed by the 3rd Battalion, 1st Marines. On the other side of the cape, Lt. Col. James M. Masters, Sr.,'s 2d Battalion, 1st Marines (Masters' Bastards) landed on a black volcanic beach near Tauali to set up a jungle trail block.

The main landing on the east side went easily, although the Japanese resisted the lead company's advance toward the airfield. By that night, 11,000 men were ashore; and the immediate beachhead was secure. Once again, 1st Division Marines lay in the moonless jungle dark and monsoon rains, waiting for the Japanese to attack.

They hit the center of the perimeter, and a disorganized battle raged in the rain-soaked pitch-black darkness. The Marines were attacked again and again over the next few days, but the strength of the assaults steadily diminished.

Meanwhile, Col. William J. Whaling's 1st Marines moved cautiously toward the cape's airfields. Men and tanks had to eliminate the Japanese from solid beach defenses at Hell's Point. By the evening of December 29, the 1st Battalion, 1st Marines reached the airfield; and three battalions looped a perimeter around the strips. The Japanese waited in the hills south of the airfield and the next day fought Lt. Col. Lewis W. Walt's 2d Battalion, 5th Marines on Razorback Hill, which dominated the field. Finally, the 3rd Battalion, 1st Marines, took the summit. At noon on the last day of 1943, Maj. Gen. Rupertus formally raised the American flag on Cape Gloucester. MacArthur sent his congratulations: "Your gallant division has maintained the immortal record of the Marine Corps and covered itself with glory."[33]

On the other side of the peninsula, the Tauali trail block was hit four times; and on January 5, 1944, the battalion there started moving over to join the main force.

On January 2, the 3rd Battalion, 7th Marines started south of Target Hill through the wet, stinking jungle eastward toward Borgen Bay. At a 20-foot-wide sluggish jungle stream, the Marines met enemy fire; and the 3rd Battalion, 5th Marines joined on their right. The Marines could not see the enemy hidden across the stream in foxholes and log bunkers. Each Marine who tried to cross was picked off. The stream became a deathtrap known as Suicide Creek.

Before dawn the next morning, the Japanese attacked the eastern end of the perimeter at Target Hill. They took 102 casualties beating their heads against the Marine line there.

As the battle of Suicide Creek continued, the Marines finally crossed on the enemy's flanks but could not dislodge them. First Lt. Elisha Atkins, a Harvard Phi Beta Kappa student and football player known to the men as "Tommy Harvard," led his machine-gun platoon across. The men were hit by automatic fire and forced back into the creek. Atkins, hit three times, ordered his men to leave him there. On the Marines' side of the creek, Pfc. Luther J. Raschke of Harvard, Illinois, crept to the edge of the stream, while three Marines covered him, and called to Atkins: "Tommy Harvard, Tommy Harvard." They finally found the lieutenant, weak from the loss of blood, and carried him to safety. Raschke was awarded a Silver Star.[34] Atkins survived to become a doctor and professor of medicine at Yale.

Maj. Gen. Rupertus sent Lt. Col. Puller, the 7th Marines' executive officer, to get the 3rd Battalion moving. Engineers of the 17th Marines rushed a corduroy road across the coastal swamp and late that afternoon three Sherman tanks lumbered up. The Engineers cut down Suicide Creek's 12-foot-high bank with an unprotected bulldozer. Snipers shot two drivers, Cpl. John E. Capito and Staff Sgt. Keary Lane, before Pfc. Randall Johnson, crouching out of the line of fire and moving the controls with a shovel and an axe handle, opened the way for the tanks and half-tracks. Then, the tank-infantry teams went about the business of eradicating the Japanese. And the assault battalions broke through and pushed forward a thousand yards. At Suicide Creek and Target Hill, 41 Marines were killed and 218 wounded. Still ahead were an estimated 1,300 Japanese.

The Marines set out to find Aogiri Ridge, hidden in the jungle, where Intelligence knew the Japanese were entrenched. As the three assault battalions approached, enemy fire stopped them. The commander and executive officer of the 3rd Battalion, 5th Marines, were both wounded; and Puller took over that battalion also until Lt. Col. Walt could come up and take command. (It was Navy Cross No. 4 for "Chesty" Puller.)

The enemy did not waste manpower this time but waited for Walt's Marines to penetrate the thick jungle. In 24 hours, 15 Marines were killed and 161 wounded as the Japanese beat back repeated Marine attacks. By January 9, the attackers were running out of strength. A 37mm gun was dragged up. Walt called for volunteers, and he and his runner put their shoulders to one wheel and helped push the gun up Aogiri Ridge, stopping every few feet to fire. As more Marines joined them and were hit, others took their places and the line surged forward.

Walt's men clung to the forward slope and crest of the ridge, ten yards from the enemy. At 1:15 A.M. on the tenth, they were hit by four screaming bayonet attacks through a driving rain. Walt called in artillery within 50 yards of his own lines. Finally, a fifth charge was beaten down; and with first light, the fight was over. Aogiri Ridge would be known as Walt's Ridge.

Lt. Col. Henry W. Buse, Jr., now commanding the 3rd Battalion, 7th Marines, was assigned the job of taking the final Marine objective—Hill 660. Capt. Joseph W. Buckley, a Marine since 1915, led a detachment with two tanks and two half tracks to block the coastal trail behind the hill. Buse's Marines had to sling their rifles and pull themselves up Hill 660's steep muddy face. It took them two days to seize the hill; and when they did, Buckley's gunners picked off the fleeing enemy soldiers on the beach and in the surf.

On January 16, a last counterattack was destroyed; and the battle for Cape Gloucester was finally won. The remaining Japanese, starving and sick, started pulling out of western New Britain on the long, killing march to the east. The Marines pursued them with a number of overland expeditions and a shore-to-shore landing by the 5th Marines, now commanded by Col. Oliver P. Smith, on the Willaumez Peninsula on March 6. The Marines lost 17 killed and 114 wounded there. On April 24, the exhausted 1st Marine Division began to be relieved by the 40th Infantry Division.

The 1st Division convinced itself it was going back to the interrupted pleasures of Melbourne but was shipped instead to Pavuvu, the largest of the Russell Islands—a haven of rotten coconuts, coral, rats, land crabs and rain, rain, rain. Pavuvu was a hell of mud and boredom and loneliness. The only U.S.O. show to reach the Marines there arrived because Bob Hope insisted on squeezing in a morning performance for them. Maj. Gen. Rupertus, in Washington for conferences, finally won agreement that 4,860 of his men with 24 months overseas would be rotated home. Those who stayed behind, after six months or so, began to get ready for Peleliu.

The ring around Rabaul was already closed by the time the 1st Division left New Britain. The 3rd New Zealand Division landed on the Green Islands on February 15. Elements of the 1st Cavalry Division hit Los Negros Island two weeks later and ran into tough opposition before securing the Admiralty Islands and magnificent Seeadler Harbor. And on March 20, Emirau was occupied without resistance by the newly reformed 4th Marines, made up of former Raider units. At Rabaul, planes no longer rose to fight; in the harbor rested only the hulks of sunken ships.

In April, MacArthur's troops leapfrogged ahead to Hollandia, New Guinea. Marine ground forces in the South Pacific were returned to Admiral Nimitz's command for the drive up the Central Pacific. Most Marine air units went into MacArthur's Southwest Pacific command. No longer would Marines ashore have their own close air support—except briefly at Peleliu and Iwo Jima—until both drives toward Japan met again on Okinawa. In the meantime, Marine fliers did a close-support job for the Army in the Philippines.

But the fighting in the Central Pacific islands had already begun.

8
Tarawa

"Hawk" was a lean, six-foot Texan from El Paso, the twenty-nine-year-old commander of the Scout-Sniper Platoon of the 2d Marines. "The bravest man I have ever known," wrote Robert Sherrod, a *Time* correspondent who landed with the Marines at Tarawa. First Lt. William Deane Hawkins was a natural leader. He had worked his way through the Texas College of Mines as a ranch hand and bellhop and was rejected for Army and Navy flight training because he had been badly scarred by scalding water as an infant. Enlisting in the Marine Corps, he had shipped overseas as a private first class, landed on Tulagi as a sergeant and been commissioned a month later. After he was dead, Tarawa's assault commander said quietly, "It's not often that you can credit a first lieutenant with winning a battle, but Hawkins came as near to it as any man could."[35]

At 8:55 A.M. on Saturday, November 20, 1943—15 minutes ahead of the first assault wave—Hawkins led five men up the seaplane ramp at the tip of the 550-yard-long pier jutting out from Tarawa. They raced along the pier, and Hawkins signaled the rest of the men in the LCVP to follow. The Japanese began firing at them, hitting the gasoline drums stored on the pier. Hawkins waved the men back, and with his four scouts and 2d Lt. Alan G. Leslie, Jr., began fighting down the length of the pier. Leslie's flamethrower burned two shacks in which machine gunners waited to enfilade the approaching landing craft. The scouts cleared the pier.

Then, Hawkins' platoon of 34 expert fighters moved toward shore in three amtracs (LVTs); and behind them roared the assault waves of the 2d Marine Division, hardened veterans of Guadalcanal, into one of the most desperate battles in Marine Corps history.

The assault on Tarawa launched the advance onto the Central Pacific island stepping-stones toward Japan. The landing—three weeks after the 3rd Marine Division assaulted Bougainville—was part of a three-pronged invasion of the Japanese-held Gilbert Islands. The 165th Regimental Combat Team of the Army's 27th Infantry Division, a New York National Guard unit, was sent north to take Makin, which Carlson had raided earlier. The V Marine Amphibious Corps Reconnaissance Company occupied Apamama south of Tarawa Atoll—and the 2d Marine Division attacked Tarawa. The Army's 6,470 soldiers needed three days to defeat the 300 Japanese troops on Makin and lost only 66 dead, but Tarawa was a 76-hour slaughterhouse.

The American commanders knew it would be tough. Tarawa was a triangular coral atoll of islands and reefs, 12 miles across and 18 miles long. On the island of Betio, at the southwest corner of the atoll, the Japanese had built a small airfield. Betio was three miles long and 600 yards across at its widest point. Since Carlson's Raiders had struck Makin, the Japanese had made Betio a fortress they considered impregnable, fringed with a forest of 200 guns and manned with 2,600 first-class troops and 2,200 laborers. "Corregidor was an open town by comparison."[36] The Japanese boasted that a million Americans could not take Betio in a hundred years.

The Americans insisted on assaulting Betio because they wanted its airfield from which to step up the island chain into the Marshall Islands. At Tarawa, 1,113 Marines and attached Navy personnel were killed and 2,290 wounded. The battle teetered on the beaches; only the determination of individual Marines pushed it forward.

The price for Tarawa was so high because the planners (1) assigned too few Marines to take it; (2) vetoed the proposal to land artillery on the adjoining island to bombard Betio before the invasion; (3) gambled on the long shot that the water over the coral reef surrounding Betio would be at least 3.5 feet deep, enough to float the LCVPs; and (4) had too few amphibian tractors in case the water was shallower—as it proved to be.

Before the landing craft started for the three beaches on the northern or lagoon side of Betio, warships and carrier planes laid down the greatest naval barrage ever to pound so small a target. Shells and bombs knocked out enemy guns and communications, but it was not enough. And when the landing was delayed by 40 minutes, the naval gunfire was lifted because smoke concealed the landing craft. The defenders were handed a precious half hour to shift men to the lagoon side.

Then, three waves of the 2d and 3rd Battalions, 2d Marines and the 2d Battalion, 8th Marines, mostly battle dressed in mottled green dungarees and helmet covers, headed for the beaches in 93 amtracs able to crawl over the coral reef. On the east (Beach Red 3)—toward the middle of the island—Maj. Henry P. "Jim" Crowe's 3d Battalion, 8th Marines touched shore at 9:10 A.M. On the west (Red 1), elements of Maj. John F. Schoettel's 3rd Battalion, 2d Marines made it seven minutes later, despite heavy casualties. Schoettel himself could not get ashore; at 9:59, he radioed that the issue was in doubt. Told to land his reserve, he replied, "We have nothing left to land."[37]

In the center of the assault at Red 2, resistance was toughest and initial losses were heaviest. The 2d Battalion, 2d Marines reached the beach at 9:22. A machine gun killed its tall, popular commander, Lt. Col. Herbert R. Amey, Jr., when his LVT was stopped by barbed wire and he started to wade in the last 50 yards. Lt. Col. Walter I. Jordan, an observer from the 4th Marine Division, took over Amey's badly shot up battalion.

The Marines found the narrow beaches backed by a coconut log seawall about four feet high. Starting within 15 feet of the wall, the Japanese commander, Rear Adm. Keiji Shibasaki, had cleverly sited machine guns and artillery to throw back any assault. The first three waves of Marines were pinned to the beaches between the water and the log wall. If a Marine raised himself to fire his weapon, he risked immediate death. Two amtracs of Crowe's battalion found a breach in the wall near the base of the long pier, dashed through and unloaded their Marines near the airstrip. But the flanking fire was unbearable and they had to reboard and scoot back to the beach.

In another amtrac, all but five Marines were killed on the reef. One survivor, Staff Sgt. William J. Bordelon, Jr., of the division engineers, the 18th Marines, scrambled to the beach with Sgt. Elden H. Beers of Deer Park, Washington, and Pvt. Jack G. Ashworth, Jr., of Los Angeles. They hurriedly made up demolition charges, and the wiry Bordelon went over the sea wall and destroyed two pillboxes. He was shot in the left arm. As he went out alone again and attacked a third pillbox, he was hit by machine-gun fire. Severely wounded, he picked up a rifle and covered Marines scaling the seawall. An enemy grenade ripped Beers' stomach. Bordelon heard cries for help from the blood-stained water, went back and dragged ashore one of his demolition men and another Marine who had been hit while trying to rescue the wounded engineer. Repeatedly refusing medical aid, Bordelon destroyed a fourth pillbox with a rifle grenade and then was killed instantly. Twenty-two-year-old Bordelon, who had enlisted at San Antonio, Texas, right after Pearl Harbor, was awarded the Medal of Honor posthumously.

After the third wave, the Marines were forced to use LCVPs because of the shortage of amtracs; and the landing craft grounded at the outer edge of the coral reef. The men had to wade in. They were destroyed in the water. Junior officers and noncoms kept the survivors going.

Ten Sherman medium tanks and a number of light tanks got ashore in the fifth wave. The 2d Tank Battalion commander, Lt. Col. Alexander B. Swenceski, badly wounded, dragged himself up on a pile of bodies to keep from drowning and lay there until the next day.

Col. David M. Shoup, thirty-nine years old from Battle Ground, Indiana, commanded the assault. When the commander of the 2d Marines had fallen ill just before the invasion, tough, able Dave Shoup had been spot-promoted to colonel and replaced him. By 11 A.M., Shoup, along with Maj. Thomas A. Culhane, Jr.; Lt. Col. Presley M. Rixey, commander of the 1st Battalion, 10th Marines of the division artillery, and a sergeant with a radio on his back, waded to the side of the pier. Although wounded in the leg, Shoup directed the battle from there, under fire in waist-deep water.

He had the warships bombard the eastern end of the island and brought Maj. Wood B. Kyle's 1st Battalion, 2d Marines toward the center beach with orders to move westward and help the men on Red 1. He sent half of Maj. Robert H. Ruud's 3rd Battalion, 8th Marines to support Crowe on Red 3. Rudd's men waded in, under fire, for 700 yards—an incredible ordeal; some drowned in water over their heads; others were killed by the enemy. Only 100 of Ruud's first wave, 30 percent, reached Betio. Signaling frantically, Shoup drew the second wave toward the pier; but they found little shelter there and casualties mounted.

The third wave was practically wiped out. Few of the fourth wave landed; the rest were held off under heavy fire.

By noon, the assault had stalled; masses of sweating Marines hugged the 20-foot-wide beaches, unable to advance or retreat. Rifles and grenades were of little use against the dug-in enemy, and flamethrowers were scarce. Reinforcements could not get in. Landing craft were stuck on the reef full of dead and wounded. Small groups of Marines charged over the log wall and tried to move forward to kill the enemy and destroy his bunkers and machine guns. Half of the bravest were shot down.

On Red 1, at the western end of Betio, a 500-yard cove exposed the Marines to a murderous crossfire. I and K Companies of 3rd Battalion, 2d Marines charged over the barricade and lost half their men in two hours. L Company was grounded 500 yards offshore, and 35 percent of its men were hit in the water. L Company's commander, Maj. Michael P. Ryan, and assorted survivors formed a small separate beachhead at the island's western tip, 600 yards from the main landing.

Six Sherman tanks were led in over the reef by Marines walking ahead of them with flags. The tanks' commander found so many dead and wounded Marines on the beach that he could not maneuver. He took the tanks back into the water, and they rumbled toward the western end of the island. Four tanks drowned in potholes; the two surviving tanks were hit but reached Ryan's beachhead and helped protect his flank. Ryan's force managed to advance 500 yards but had to pull back to a tighter perimeter when dark came.

On Red 2, in the center, Jordan used flamethrowers and TNT charges; and one company crawled about 100 yards inland. East of the long pier, large, red-mustached Crowe, of Boston, Kentucky, who had been an enlisted Marine for 14 years and won a Silver Star on Guadalcanal, also pushed ahead about 100 yards. Of four tanks that tried to support Crowe's Marines, three were destroyed, one by a friendly dive bomber. Some of Crowe's men reached the triangle between the airfield's runway and taxistrips; but on their left flank near the water, they were stopped by a strongpoint near the base of the short Burns-Philp Wharf.

Hawkins' Scout-Sniper Platoon was up over the seawall all day, destroying bunkers. His 34 men killed ten times their number of Japanese. Hawkins himself rode an amtrac and personally cleaned out six machine-gun nests. He took two bullets in his shoulders but kept fighting.

About noon, Shoup came ashore and set up a command post 15 feet inland, in the shadow of a huge coconut log bunker still crowded with scores of Japanese. Marines covered the entrances to contain them. Shoup sent Col. Evans Carlson, the former Raider who was with him as a 4th Division observer, out to the command ship, the battleship *Maryland*, to hurry more men, water, ammunition and guns to the pier. Destroyers and planes gave close support all day long.

At 1:31, Maj. Gen. Julian C. Smith, commander of the 2d Division, radioed Maj. Gen. Holland M. Smith, commander of the V Marine Amphibious Corps, who was on Rear Adm. Richmond K. Turner's flagship at Makin. He asked for the release of the corps reserve, the 6th Marines, who were standing by off Tarawa to support either invasion. When Turner swiftly approved the request, Julian Smith ordered the 1st Battalion, 8th Marines, his own last division reserve, to land; but communications failed, and the battalion was still waiting in its boats after midnight.

By nightfall, some 5,000 Marines were ashore on the edge of Betio; 1,500 had been killed or wounded. The survivors were struggling for a toehold, refusing to be pushed back into the sea.

That night, the smell of death pervaded the beachheads. The Marines, expecting the customary Japanese night attacks, prepared for the worst. They dug foxholes in the sand and over the seawall. Reinforcements were boated to the far end of the long pier and then worked their way under and alongside the log cribwork to the beach. The artillerymen of the 10th Marines lugged pieces of their 75mm pack howitzers ashore on their backs. Brig. Gen. Leo D. Hermle, the assistant division commander, organized carrying parties on the pier to bring ammunition and water through the enemy fire.

On Betio, unlike the defense of Edson's Ridge on Guadalcanal, there was no room to fall back and regroup, no possibility of a defense in depth—nothing but a very thin line of Marines.

Miraculously, the Japanese did not attack. The pre-invasion bombardment had shredded their wire communications; Rear Adm. Shibasaki could not pull together his scattered and hard-hit forces. Had he attacked that first night, he might have driven the Marines off Betio. Because he did not, he lost the battle.

At dawn, Hawkins and his scouts resumed their deadly work clearing out enemy bunkers. Hawkins led his men against a strongpoint covered by five machine guns. He crawled forward under heavy fire, shot point-blank into the bunker's ports and hurled in grenades. Wounded in the chest and hand, he, again, stayed in the fight and destroyed three more pillboxes before an explosive machine-gun bullet severed an artery in his shoulder. He was dying when his scouts carried him to the rear.

His Medal of Honor citation said, "His relentless fighting spirit in the face of formidable opposition and his exceptionally daring tactics served as an inspiration to his comrades during the most crucial phase of the battle." Betio's airfield was later named Hawkins Field.

Shoup's plan for the second day was for the 1st Battalion, 8th Marines to land and fight westward to strengthen the Red 1 beachhead. Then, Ryan would clean up the western end of the island. In the center, Kyle and Jordan would drive straight across and cut the island in two. And east on Red 3, Crowe would smash the strongpoint at the Burns-Philp Wharf.

At 6:15 A.M., the first waves of Maj. Lawrence C. Hays, Jr.'s 1st Battalion, 8th Marines finally began wading the 500 yards to shore. They were hit by flanking machine-gun fire and decimated. The carnage in the water was worse than on the first day. Weary, bearded Marines ashore attacked to suppress the enemy fire, which came from bunkers, trees, privies the Japanese had built over the water and the hulk of a Japanese freighter. By 8 A.M., half the men of Hays' battalion had reached the beach and struggled westward to help Ryan. But they had lost most of their flamethrowers and demolitions and without them could make little progress against the bunkers.

In the center, A and B Companies of Kyle's battalion fought to the south coast and took the Japanese entrenchments, which had been set up to repel an attack from the sea. Lt. Col. Jordan with these men and some from the 2d Battalion, 2d Marines—a total of no more than 135 Marines—formed a precarious perimeter there. The enemy counterattacked, and the Marines took heavy casualties. Kyle's C Company fought off a Japanese attack and joined them. Kyle assumed command of this isolated band,

and Jordan reverted to his "observer status" with high praise from Shoup.

At the eastern end of the main perimeter on the lagoon, Crowe's battalion could not advance against the enemy pillboxes but at dusk managed to take the wharf and extend a line to the middle of the airfield triangle.

By late afternoon, Ryan's Marines had overrun three 80mm coastal guns and established a line across the island, 200 yards in from Betio's western beaches. Their advance cheered the Marines' commanders and allowed Col. Maurice G. Holmes to land his 6th Marines. Holmes sent his 2d Battalion around to Bairiki, the island just east of Betio, where it landed without resistance. By 6:35 P.M., Maj. William K. Jones brought the 1st Battalion, 6th Marines ashore on Betio's western beaches in rubber boats towed by LCVPs.

Everywhere, small groups of Marines inched forward from shell craters, ruined buildings, from behind fallen trees and piles of battle debris. In the blazing heat, they hurled grenades and blocks of TNT into bunkers; and flamethrower operators dashed forward and sprayed the interiors with liquid fire.

Shortly after noon, momentum had been created. The fighting was intense, but the hope of victory seemed real for the first time. The water over the reef deepened and some LCVPs could get to the beach. At 5:06 P.M., Shoup radioed: "Casualties many. Percentage dead not known. Combat efficiency—we are winning."[38] Three hours later, the veteran Col. Merritt A. Edson, now the 2d Division's chief of staff, arrived and took overall command ashore. Shoup concentrated his attention on his own combat team trying to join the northern and western beachheads.

By the end of the second day, the main perimeter stretched about 400 yards on either side of the long pier in the middle of the landing areas. Kyle's force held on the south coast, and the entire western side of Betio was in Marine hands.

On the third morning, Jones' battalion led by three light tanks, pushed along the south shore to link up with Kyle's men. On Betio's north side, Crowe and Ruud attacked the strongpoint east of the wharf with tanks, flamethrowers and mortars. Marines climbed its sandpiled sides. The Japanese charged them to protect this key position. One man broke their attack: 1st Lt.

Alexander Bonnyman, Jr., of Atlanta, executive officer of the 8th Marines' 2d Battalion Shore Party. The previous days, Bonnyman had fought heroically on the long pier and ashore. He had crawled 40 yards in front of the Marine position to place charges in the entrance of a bombproof. Now, he stormed the bastion, directed the placement of demolition charges and seized the top of the bunker. As the enemy poured out, he turned his flamethrower on them. Then, standing on the bunker, he fought off their counterattack and led his men down before he was mortally wounded. Bulldozers sealed up the bunker, and the Marines burst forward 400 yards without further casualties. Bonnyman's was the third and last posthumous Medal of Honor earned on Tarawa, where only Colonel Shoup was awarded the highest medal and lived to wear it.

At 11 A.M., Lt. Col. Kenneth F. McLeod's 3rd Battalion, 6th Marines landed on the western beaches and followed Jones' battalion along the south coast. Julian Smith came ashore; on the way in, his LVT driver was hit, and the general had to transfer to another amtrac. By afternoon, Jones' battalion and elements of 2d and 3rd Battalions, 8th Marines had formed a line across the island near the eastern end of the airfield. At 7:30 P.M., the Japanese counterattacked and briefly drove a hole between Jones' A and B Companies. The enemy threw themselves against the Marine line again and again into the night. The Marines fought them off with grenades and rifle fire; artillery shelled as close as 75 yards in front of the Marines' positions, and destroyers fired from the lagoon. By 5 A.M. of the fourth day, the enemy's spasmodic attacks had been shattered; within 50 yards of the Marines lay 200 Japanese bodies.

Now, on D-Day plus three, two jobs remained: to wipe out the western strongpoint between Red 1 and 2 and to sweep the island's eastern tail. The 3rd Battalion, 2d Marines and the 1st Battalion, 8th Marines with a new supply of flamethrowers eliminated the pocket to the west by 1:15 P.M. The 6th Marines, with tanks and flamethrowers, reached the eastern tip by 1:10. Betio was secured. Marines and Seabees were already repairing the airstrip for which so many had died.

Of the 4,836 Japanese soldiers and Korean laborers on Betio, only 146 were taken prisoner; of those, 17 were Japanese. The rest were killed. The mopping up continued for two days. The stench of rotting bodies was terrible.

Lt. Col. Raymond L. Murray's 2d Battalion, 6th Marines was sent up the atoll's other islands. The Marines found no resistance until they reached Buariki, the northern-most large island, on November 26. There, 175 Japanese made a last-ditch stand. The next morning, the Marines killed all but two whom they took prisoner. The battalion had 32 killed and 59 wounded in this last round.

The bloodiness of the battle for Tarawa shocked the nation. Some protested the judgment of frontally assaulting so strongly defended an island and questioned whether Tarawa should have been bypassed, as were Rabaul and Truk, infinitely bigger enemy bases. Others felt the amphibious lessons learned were worth the price; they would save lives later in this island war.[39] There is no way to settle that argument. It is only possible to quote Maj. Gen. Holland M. Smith, true believer in amphibious assault and commander of all the Marines in the Gilberts invasions:

> Was Tarawa worth it? My answer is unqualified: No. From the very beginning the decision of the Joint Chiefs to seize Tarawa was a mistake and from their initial mistake grew the terrible drama of errors, errors of omission rather than commission, resulting in these needless casualties. . . . Tarawa should have been bypassed. Its capture—a mission executed by Marines under direct orders from the high command—was a terrible waste of life and effort . . . . The futile sacrifice of Marines on that strategically useless coral strand makes me sad today as it did then . . . . In the strategical scheme of the Central Pacific offensive, it taught me that the instrument of high policy known as the Joint Chiefs of Staff was not infallible. Tarawa was a mistake.[40]

Whatever the strategical correctness of this battle, anyone reading the story of Tarawa must wonder what drove individual Marines forward against such a fierce and concentrated defense. Every man was scared, and many did cower in the meager shelter of seawall or shell holes; but as Colonel Shoup wrote after the battle, "A surprising number . . . displayed a fearless eagerness to go to the extreme for their country and fellow men."[41]

Robert Sherrod explained best the mystery of courage: "The Marines fought almost solely on *esprit de corps*, I was certain. It was inconceivable to most Marines that they should let another Marine down, or that they could be responsible for dimming the bright reputation of their corps. The Marines simply assumed that they were the world's best fighting men."[42]

9
The Marshalls: Swift Victory

Tarawa, in Holland Smith's acerbic view, again offered the decision makers a lesson they should have learned at Munda Point: Leapfrog the enemy's strongpoints. Leave his island garrisons to rot. And no more cruel primitivism of Marines walking helplessly through the sea into the face of unanswerable gunfire.

It was now 1944, two years after Pearl Harbor; and new American fleets and forces had been built. The nation's bull-like strength was beginning to press against Japan. Nazi Germany was still Enemy Number One, and the invasion of Normandy was being mounted; but since the Battle of Midway, it had been only a matter of time—and mass (and good men dead)—before the attackers of Pearl Harbor were driven to their knees.

The question was "How?" The Allies planned to approach Japan from three directions: the China–Burma–India push to open the Burma Road and the two fists of the American cross-Pacific offensive—MacArthur's the left and Nimitz's the right. The long-range plan was to bomb Japan itself from the mainland of China. MacArthur, the Supreme Commander of Allied Forces in the Southwest Pacific Area, took the southern route: over the land masses of New Guinea and the Philippines. He was determined to keep his pledge to return to the Philippines. Nimitz ran the direct line over the Central Pacific islands. MacArthur used land-based air power; Nimitz depended on carrier-based air, the powerful new weapon that gave the Navy enormous mobility in choosing its amphibious targets.

In a raging interservice squabble, Army and Navy wrestled for priorities over manpower and equipment. Slowly, despite MacArthur's most vigorous and reasoned objections, the Navy's

Pacific strategy won the support of the Army Air Forces, which hungered for bomber attacks directly from the Marianas against Japan. The new B-29 Superfortress could dump 10,000 pounds of bombs on a target 1,500 miles away.

In the end, Japan would be crushed from the air. The men on the ground and in the ships made that possible; and for them, it was a brutal war. With Japan's soldiers trained to die (even at their own hands) rather than surrender, there could be no cheap victory.

On January 1, 1944, Vandegrift of Guadalcanal succeeded Holcomb of Belleau Wood as Commandant of the Marine Corps. Now, the Corps had 390,000 men and women, five divisions and four air wings. The Women's Reserve was activated in February 1943 and by June 1944 had enrolled its full strength of 1,000 officers and 18,000 enlisted women. They were led by Col. Ruth C. Streeter.

Rupertus' 1st Division was fighting at Cape Gloucester; Julian Smith's 2d Division was in Hawaii licking its Tarawan wounds; Turnage's 3rd Division was shipping out from Bougainville; Harry Schmidt's 4th Division was moving from San Diego to Kwajalein, and Keller E. Rockey's 5th Division was shaping up at Camp Pendleton, California. The Marine Corps had grown big—too big, some complained. Vandegrift said candidly, "I know that General Holcomb had won permission to establish the 5th Division practically over General Marshall's dead body."[43]

Army, Navy and Marines teamed up to cross the Central Pacific quickly. By Washington's Birthday, they would control the vast Marshall Island chain. The first major target in the Marshalls was Kwajalein Atoll, the world's largest atoll with 93 islands and a lagoon 60 by 30 miles. Seven hundred miles northwest of Tarawa, it lay in the very heart of the Marshalls; and Nimitz chose it boldly.

The Japanese had held the Marshalls for a quarter of a century; Kwajalein was their administrative and communications center, and they were completing a bomber strip there. The American commanders expected Kwajalein's defenses to be even more impenetrable than Tarawa's. But the American (including Marine) planners were wrong. "Contrary to American fears, the enemy had not, before the outbreak of World War II, been building up his Pacific military bases as mighty fortresses."[44] Instead, Japan had been spending its resources on an aggressive battle fleet. And that fleet did not intend to defend the Marshalls. As soon as U.S. fliers won mastery over the skies, Kwajalein was isolated and could be freely and massively bombed.

At the northern end of the atoll were the twin islands of Roi and Namur, linked by both a sandspit and a man-made causeway. Holland Smith planned that the 4th Marine Division would grab the twins and the Army's 7th Division would capture Kwajalein Island at the atoll's southern end, 44 miles away. The brand-new 4th Marine Division, although it had not yet been in combat together, was spiced with combat veterans and former Raiders.

The American expeditionary force used the costly know-how from Tarawa: Naval gunfire would be vastly increased and improved. Before the main amphibious assault, lesser islands nearby would be seized so that artillery could be emplaced on them. (Julian Smith had wanted to do that at Betio.) For the first time, Naval Underwater Demolition Teams would swim in and check out the beach defenses in advance. Finally, the troop-carrying LVTs would be escorted by heavily armed armored amtracs.

As Kwajalein was attacked, Capt. James L. Jones' V Amphibious Corps Reconnaissance Company, which had taken Apamama in the Gilberts, and an Army battalion easily seized Majuro Atoll, 265 miles to the southeast. On January 31, 1944, they raised the American flag for the first time over territory that had been Japan's before Pearl Harbor.

That same morning, the 25th Marines landed on five small islands near Kwajalein Atoll's Roi and Namur islands. Controlling both sea and air, Rear Adm. Richard L. Conolly moved his battleships in close and won from the Marines the appreciative nickname "Close-in Conolly." The seas were rough and the landings sloppy; but by the end of the day, the 14th Marines' howitzers were registered to add their 5,000 rounds to the bombardment of Roi-Namur. The landings cost the 25th Marines 24 dead and 40 wounded.

The next morning, February 1, the 23rd Marines struck Roi and the 24th Marines, Namur. Because it had been difficult to reassemble the LVTs, these main assaults were a shambles.

Fortunately, when the 23rd landed on Roi at 11:33 A.M., resistance was light; and by 6 P.M., organized opposition in the rubble was finished. Col. Louis R. Jones, the 23rd's commander, called Roi a "pip." Namur was not.

There, anti-tank ditches prevented the 24th Marines' amtracs from moving inland; and resistance stiffened. Riflemen and demolition teams destroyed the enemy pillboxes. At about one o'clock, Namur was rocked by three tremendous explosions. A pilot overhead thought the entire island had blown up. A Marine demolition team had exploded an enemy storehouse of heavy munitions and torpedo warheads. Twenty Marines were killed and 100 wounded.

When the 2d and 3rd Battalions re-opened the offensive, five light tanks led the way. Japanese swarmed over them and were shot down. As fierce fighting continued, Maj. Gen. Schmidt, the 4th Division's commander, who had served in China and Nicaragua, took command ashore. He ordered the 23rd's 3rd Battalion over to support the 24th Marines and brought Sherman tanks from Roi across the sandspit. The tanks cleared Namur's most northerly point, but the day ended with the Marines still embattled.

During the night, Japanese popped out of their holes to harass the Marines; and at dawn, the Japanese counterattacked. Fighting raged for 25 minutes before the attack was eradicated. All morning, Lt. Col. Aquilla J. Dyess of the 24th's 1st Battalion led his men forward. Standing on the parapet of an antitank ditch, directing a flanking attack against the last enemy position, he was killed by machine-gun fire. The Marine officer from Augusta, Georgia, was awarded the Medal of Honor. Shortly after noon, the assault battalions met at Namur's northern point; and at 2:18 P.M., the island was declared secured.

At the southern end of the atoll, the 32d and 184th Regiments of the Army's 7th Division also landed on February 1. Their amphibious assault was superbly executed, but it took the soldiers four days to secure crescent-shaped Kwajalein Island. Holland Smith was impatient. The Army fought in a different, slower style than did the Marines. The Marines plunged ahead, leaving by-passed strongpoints to be stamped out by following units. "In contrast to the Marines, the Army was taught not to advance until all possible fire had been brought to bear on the path ahead of the troops. This took time."[45] Which technique cost fewer American lives was continually debated.

The 25th Marines and the Army's 17th Infantry cleaned up the atoll's lesser islets; they made 30 landings and had to fight on ten of the islands. By February 7, the entire atoll was in American hands. The 4th Marine Division figured it had defeated 3,563 of the enemy; its own losses were 313 killed and 502 wounded.

The victory at Kwajalein had been so surprisingly swift that the next offensive, against Eniwetok Atoll, 326 miles northwest of Roi, was moved up from its planned date of May 1 to February 17.

At dawn that day, the aircraft carriers of Vice Adm. Raymond A. Spruance's Fifth Fleet hurled a swarm of warplanes against the great Japanese base of Truk—the so-called Gibralter of the Pacific. In two days, the Navy pilots shot up more than 200 of 365 planes, destroyed some 40 naval and merchant ships and almost killed "Pappy" Boyington and six other American pilot-prisoners who were being transferred to Japan through Truk at that moment. The dramatically successful carrier raid neutralized Truk, demoralized the government in Tokyo and left the Japanese unable to offer significant air opposition in the Central Pacific.

Eniwetok was another vast atoll, 40 islands with a lagoon 21 by 17 miles. The 10,000 troops for this Army-Marine expedition were commanded by Marine Brig. Gen. Thomas E. Watson. Although the reinforced 22d Marines, led by Col. John T. Walker, had come from 18 months of garrison duty on Samoa, this orphan regiment was well trained; and its rifle squads were effectively organized into fire teams of three or four men to give them greater flexibility in combat.

Walker's Marines would tackle Engebi, a triangular island where the Japanese had built an airfield at the north end of the atoll. The Army, with some help from the Marines, would assault Eniwetok Island and Parry Island, which were believed to be lightly held. Intelligence discovered that the Japanese had brought in 2,586 troops from Manchuria in great secrecy; their presence encouraged the Americans to strike as soon as possible.

Paralleling the tactics so effective at Kwajalein, the battleships closed in tight; and the Marines seized five islets near

Engebi on windy, overcast February 17. Not a single enemy ship or plane challenged the invasion.

The next morning, the 22d Marines assaulted Engebi's lagoon-side beaches. Most of the island's 1,200 defenders concentrated in a large coconut grove. At some points, they were dug into defensive "spider webs." Each of these was centered on a camouflaged underground core from which radiated tunnels usually lined with oil drums laid end to end. The Japanese hid in these webs and jumped up to shoot the advancing Marines from behind. The Marines quickly learned to toss in smoke grenades; and, as the smoke revealed the outline of the spider web, they destroyed it with demolitions.

The fighting was fierce; but by 3 P.M., Engebi was declared secured. A thousand of the enemy were dead; only 19 surrendered. The 22d Marines had lost 64 killed, 81 missing and 158 wounded.

On February 19, the 106th Infantry of the 27th Infantry Division stormed Eniwetok Island. Maj. Clair W. Shisler's 3rd Battalion, 22d Marines, in reserve aboard ship, came ashore by 3:15 P.M., and began attacking side by side with the 1st Battalion of the 106th. Flamethrowers seared the log emplacements in the dense underbrush. After dark, the 106th continued its attack; but the Marines, following their doctrine, dug in for the night. "On the Marines' 400-yard front, there was no shooting, but on the adjoining front GIs shot at anything that moved, including Marines. . . . Fortunately, God loves the Marines, and apart from a few wounds the main results were unpleasantness and foul language."[46] The next day, Eniwetok Island was secured.

Heavy bombardment softened up Parry Island, just northeast of Eniwetok Island. For three days, ships and planes and howitzers on the nearby islands all hurled shells onto this island of no more than 200 acres. At 9 A.M. on February 22, the 22d Marines' 1st and 2d Battalions landed with the 3rd Battalion again in reserve. Parry was bitterly defended. The 2d Battalion needed help from tanks and bulldozers before it secured the northern end at 2 P.M. The 1st Battalion was met at the shoreline by machine guns and mortars and hand-to-hand fighting. The Japanese had three light tanks, and Shermans had to wipe them out. The 3rd Battalion came ashore under fire; and at 1:30, it and the 1st Battalion started moving south. They secured Parry the next morning after overcoming determined resistance from the dug-in enemy.

The Japanese had planned their Marshalls defense as a delaying action, but the Americans had not been delayed. Eniwetok Atoll was conquered three months ahead of the original plan. The Marines there lost 254 killed and 555 wounded; the 106th Infantry had 94 killed and 311 wounded. Only 66 of the enemy surrendered.

During the following weeks, the 22d Marines made 29 additional landings among the Marshall Islands, sweeping out enemy pockets. They killed 2,564 Japanese of a total garrison estimated at 13,000 men; the rest were left to starve, and the enemy-held islands were kept neutralized by the 4th Marine Base Defense Aircraft Wing for the remainder of the war.

In March, the Joint Chiefs of Staff took a fresh look at the Pacific war and decided on new priorities and a new timetable. They pretty much gave up on bombing Japan from China because air base defense would depend on Chiang Kai-shek's dubious capabilities. MacArthur was ordered to invade the Philippines by mid-November. Nimitz was ordered to bypass Truk, invade the Marianas on June 15 and then take the Palaus to protect MacArthur's flank into the Philippines. By February 15, 1945, attacks were to be launched against both Formosa and Luzon.

The Joint Chiefs at the same time divided up the military strength left behind in the backwash of the South Pacific area. MacArthur's force was increased from six to 12 Army divisions and Nimitz now had four Marine and six Army divisions.

These were major decisions. With the help of Nimitz's fleet and using Army Engineer Amphibian Brigades, MacArthur landed at Hollandia, New Guinea, on April 22 and captured three airfields at Lake Sentani. By the end of July, he would reach the western tip of New Guinea, with the Philippines ahead. In the Central Pacific, the swift seizure of the Marshalls and the decision to bypass Truk freed great striking power for the Marianas.

Both MacArthur's and Nimitz's drives were galloping ahead. The nervousness of the Guadalcanal days was gone; the nation had confidence in victory. American power now being assembled against Japan was invincible.

10
The Marianas: Decisive Battle

June 1944 was a momentous month. Eisenhower's army stormed across the English Channel; in the Pacific, the U.S. Navy fought the war's greatest carrier battle, and Marines and soldiers leapt forward a thousand miles to a new kind of target. The Marines landed this time not primarily to seize advanced naval bases or air bases to support the fleet—but to capture something significantly different: bases for strategic airpower. From the Marianas, B-29s could reach Japan itself.

These 15 volcanic islands were larger than coral atolls and provided plenty of room for artillery sites and a cave-buried defense-in-depth. Only the four largest and southernmost islands—Guam, Rota, Tinian and Saipan—were of military importance. All but Guam had been Japanese since World War I. The Marines' first objective would be Saipan. It was 13 miles long; and Garapan, a town of 10,000 people on its west coast, was Japan's Central Pacific capital. On Saipan's southern end was Aslito Airfield, 1,200 miles from Tokyo. Three miles to the south lay Tinian with three new airfields.

The U.S. Joint Expeditionary Force steaming toward the Marianas compared to the North African landing force in size: 535 ships and 127,571 troops. They were commanded by Vice Adm. Turner, his fifth big amphibious operation. "He had learned more about this specialized brand of warfare than anyone else ever had, or probably ever would."[47] The troops were commanded by the sixty-two-year-old Alabamian, Lt. Gen. Holland M. Smith. "Howlin' Mad," a veteran of 38 years in the Corps with duty in France and the Caribbean, was the hard-driving, bad-tempered father of modern amphibious warfare. He directly commanded the Northern Landing Force (the V

Amphibious Corps) of the 2d and the 4th Marine Divisions, headed for Saipan and Tinian. Maj. Gen. Roy S. Geiger led the Southern Landing Force (the III Amphibious Corps), targeted for Guam and consisting of the 3rd Marine Division and the 1st Provisional Marine Brigade. Said Lt. Gen. Smith, "The Marine Corps had come of age."[48]

In reserve were two Army divisions, the 27th and 77th, although Smith, dissatisfied with the performance of elements of the 27th on Makin and Eniwetok, accepted that division reluctantly.

The enemy intended to defend. U.S. submarines had prevented the Japanese garrison, reinforced out of Manchuria, from being fully manned or equipped; but on Saipan alone, Lt. Gen. Yoshitsugu Saito commanded nearly 32,000 men, far more than U.S. Intelligence expected to find there. And the Japanese were eager to challenge the American armada itself; their Mobile Fleet was hurrying up to save Saipan. The U.S. naval commanders welcomed this threat; they hoped for a second Battle of Midway.

Vice Adm. Marc A. Mitscher's fast carriers bombed enemy airfields from the Bonins to the Marshalls and wiped out all the planes they could find in the Marianas themselves. Battleships bombarded Saipan and Tinian; and Navy underwater demolition teams daringly cleared paths for the Marines' amtracs and tanks.

The Marine divisions that would assault the Marianas had been changed considerably since the Marshalls operation. The old 12-man rifle squad, on the recommendation of a board headed by Lt. Col. Samuel B. Griffith II, was now enlarged by one man and divided into three four-man fire teams—each team consisting of one BAR-man and three riflemen—plus the squad leader. The fire-team leaders were trained for independent command in combat. The division's BARs had been increased from 558 to 853. Flamethrowers had been increased from 24 to 243 portable ones plus 24 long-range Ronsons that could be mounted on light Satan tanks. The tank battalion now had 46 medium Sherman tanks instead of 54 light tanks. The number of pack howitzers had been reduced and mortars increased. And for an amphibious operation, a 535-man amphibian tractor battalion was added. Although the basic division had been tightened from 19,965 to 17,465 men, its firepower had been greatly strengthened.[49]

D-Day at Saipan, June 15, was cool and clear. On a two-division front almost four miles long, eight veteran battalions of Marines headed for the beaches on the southern half of Saipan's west coast. Naval gunfire blasted the beaches, and carrier planes strafed to within 100 yards ahead of the landing craft. First in went 24 LCI-G gunboats firing rockets and 40mm guns. Then came the lead wave of 96 amtracs—LVTs—loaded with Marines and escorted by 68 armored amtracs—LVT(A)s—, each with a howitzer and a machine gun. The amtracs took severe losses crossing the reef and lagoon and on the beaches. The first Marines landed at 8:43 A.M. and at once came under intense fire. In 20 minutes, 8,000 Marines were ashore. They were fighting from the moment they jumped out of their amtracs.

On the left flank, the 6th and 8th Marines landed 900 yards too far north and suffered heavy casualties. All four assault battalion commanders, including Tarawa veterans Lt. Cols. Henry P. Crowe and Raymond L. Murray, were wounded early in the fighting. Japanese long-range artillery and mortars and machine guns behind the beach were deadly. The 6th Marines were stopped 400 yards beyond the beach; by midday 35 percent of the regiment had been killed or wounded.

Both assault battalions of the 8th Marines landed on one beach, and the confusion delayed the seizure of Afetna Point in the center of the beachhead. They needed help from the regiment's reserve battalion and even the division reserve, the 1st Battalion, 29th Marines. The enemy artillery was ferocious; more than a third of the 8th Regiment were casualties.

Further south, a few men of the 23rd Marines powered ahead to the ridge line a mile behind the beach; but others were stopped almost at the water's edge. By the day's end, the regiment had cleared the shattered village of Charan Kanoa, where the bougainvillea were blazing red, and clung to a beachhead some 800 yards deep.

To the south on the far right flank, the 25th Marines, heavy with former Raiders, received brutal enfilading fire from Agingan Point south of the beachhead. The 1st Battalion was held within a dozen yards of the beach. At 9:30 A.M., the Japanese hit the battalion's open flank; naval gunfire and air strikes broke up the attacks. When the enemy tried a second time, the 4th Tank Battalion's Shermans wiped out two Japanese companies. The 25th Marines made it to the ridge line, but an enemy force isolated on the tip of Agingan Point continued to fight.

Sunset found 20,000 Marines holding only half the planned beachhead. An estimated 2,000 men had been killed or wounded by the well-hidden enemy; preinvasion air and naval gunfire support had once again proven inadequate. The Japanese still held Afetna Point in the middle of the beachhead and shelled the Marines from the ridge above the coastal plain. Because of the unexpectedly strong resistance and the submarine-sighted approach of the Japanese fleet, the landing on Guam, set for June 18, was postponed.

The first night ashore was filled with enemy counterattacks; and at dawn, the 2d Division protected against attacks from the north while the 4th Division fought its way across to Magic-ienne Bay on Saipan's east coast to split the island. Early on the second day, June 16, the 2d Battalion, 8th Marines mopped up Afetna Point. But a lone enemy soldier, spotting the Marines from the smokestack of the ruined Charan Kanoa sugar refinery, enabled the Japanese artillery to work over the beachhead with devastating accuracy.

The 4th Division's first attempt to bisect the island failed. The 25th Marines, plus the 3rd Battalion, 24th Marines, led by Lt. Col. Alexander A. Vandegrift, Jr., inched to within half a mile of Aslito Airfield. In those first two days, the 4th Division took 2,200 casualties. Holland Smith decided to land the 27th Infantry Division, starting with the 165th Infantry.

At 3:30 A.M. on June 17, 500 of Lt. Gen. Saito's troops roared down the coastal plain and hit the 2d Marine Division hard. The attack, headed by 44 tanks, erupted into a vicious battle against the 1st Battalion, 6th Marines commanded by twenty-seven-year-old Lt. Col. William K. Jones, who had led it at Tarawa. The Marines fought back with all the firepower they had; mostly infantrymen fought tanks. Pvt. Robert S. Reed of Cabot, Arkansas, hit four tanks with his bazooka and then climbed on a fifth and dropped in a grenade. Sgt. Alex B. Smith of Lake Providence, Louisiana, knocked out three tanks. Pfc. Charlie D. Merritt of Greenville, South Carolina, and Pfc. Herbert J.

Hodges of Anchorage, Kentucky, hit seven tanks with their bazooka. Only a dozen of the Japanese tanks survived; more than 300 enemy soldiers were killed; and by 7 A.M., the assault was squashed.

Despite its losses, the 2d Division attacked to the north and east. On the eighteenth, the 24th and 25th Marines fought through to Magicienne Bay on the east coast; and the 165th Infantry occupied Aslito Airfield, which was renamed Isely Field. The enemy still held the hilly jungle southeast of Aslito, and his main force was concentrated in the north behind a line that ran from south of Garapan across to Magicienne Bay, which the Marines called Magazine Bay. The Japanese understood their problem perfectly; the Emperor sent a message: "Although the frontline officers and troops are fighting splendidly, if Saipan is lost, air raids on Tokyo will take place often; therefore you will hold Saipan."[50]

This was the battle situation for the 78,000 Americans ashore when the U.S. Navy entered "the greatest carrier action of all time"[51]: The Battle of the Philippine Sea. Mitscher's 98,618-man Task Force 58 destroyed the enemy planes on Guam early on June 19, just before Japanese carriers hurled four massive air attacks against the American fleet west of the Marianas. The young American fliers triumphed. In two days, they shot down 476 Japanese planes in "the Great Marianas Turkey Shoot"; only 50 U.S. planes were lost in combat. Submarines sank two large Japanese carriers and U.S. carrier pilots destroyed a third. The Japanese were left with 35 carrier planes operational. But the second-day strike required a perilous night recovery, and Mitscher won every pilot's everlasting love; he ignored the menace from enemy submarines and planes and ordered all the lights of the task force turned on. Although 80 planes were lost, most of their crews were saved. The final toll over the two days was 76 American fliers dead.

Task Force 58 failed to destroy the Japanese fleet, but it had won mastery of both the sea and air and made possible the conquest of the Marianas. "And victory in the Marianas made an American victory over Japan inevitable."[52]

The Japanese in the Marianas were now sealed off without hope, but they fought on. Holland Smith and Maj. Gen. Ralph C. Smith, USA, commander of the 27th Division, got into a

Marines charge ashore on Guadalcanal in the first offensive action of the Pacific war. Wide World Photos

Guadalcanal was a tropical hell of rain and malaria. After winning their longest battle of World War II, Marines camped in coconut groves like this. Sgt. Mundell, USMC Photo

Lt. Col. Evans F. Carlson learned guerrilla tactics observing the Chinese Communists in Yenan. He led the 2d Raider Battalion in the Makin raid and on Guadalcanal. U.S. Navy Photo

Maj. Gregory "Pappy" Boyington, the leading Marine Corps ace of World War II with twenty-eight kills, briefs the fliers of his Black Sheep Squadron for an attack against Rabaul. Shortly after this picture was taken, Boyington was shot down over Rabaul and imprisoned by the Japanese for the rest of the war. USMC Photo

Capt. Joseph J. Foss was the Marine Corps' No. 2 ace with twenty-six kills. After the war, he was elected governor of South Dakota. Official U.S. Navy Photo

These weary 1st Division Marines are coming out of twenty-three days in the front lines on Cape Gloucester. *Brenner, USMC Photo*

At Tarawa in November 1943, 2d Division Marines who survived the deadly waters off Betio Island crouch on the narrow beach behind the seawall and begin to attack inland against heavy Japanese resistance. *USMC Photo*

Marine reinforcements wade ashore beneath Betio's long pier which the "Hawk" and his men cleared in the initial assault on Tarawa Atoll. *USMC Photo*

Marines destroy a Japanese
strongpoint on Betio.
USMC Photo

The wounded from Tarawa are towed
on a rubber boat to landing craft by
their buddies.
USMC Photo

24th Marines attacking on Namur
Island of Kwajalein Atoll.
Zurick, USMC Photo

A Marine lies dead on the beach of
Parry Island, Eniwetok Atoll, and a
rifle marks another Marine who was
killed near the water's edge.
Navy Dept. Photo, National Archives

Lt. Gen. Holland M. Smith led the
Marine drive across the Central
Pacific. When the Army's 27th
Division bogged down on Saipan,
where this picture was taken,
"Howlin' Mad" relieved its
commander and started a violent
interservice feud.
Navy Dept. Photo, National Archives

2d Division Marines crawl under
enemy fire to their positions on the
beach at Saipan. The landing craft of
the soaking wet Marine was hit by
Japanese mortar fire.
Sgt. James Burns, USMC Photo

*First Marines to reach the beach on
Saipan take cover behind a sand dune
and wait for next waves to join them.
Sgt. James Burns, USMC Photo*

*1st Division Marines fight in the crazy-quilt Umurbrogol
ridges on Peleliu in September 1944.
Pfc. John Smith, USMC Photo*

First waves of the Marines' 4th and 5th Divisions assault
Iwo Jima at 9 A.M. on February 19, 1945. In the
background looms Mount Suribachi.
Navy Dept. Photo, National Archives

Men of the 28th Marines, whose job
it was to take Suribachi, disgorge
from landing craft onto Iwo Jima.
Photo by George Burns

Marines under fire from Suribachi
cling to the black volanic ash of Iwo
Jima's beach on D-Day.
Louis Lowery, Leatherneck Magazine

Badly shocked by a Japanese mortar shell, a Marine is helped to an aid station on Iwo Jima.
Staff Sgt. Cornelius, USMC Photo.

The first flag raising on Iwo Jima by men of E Company, 28th Marines on the rim of Mount Suribachi's crater on February 23, 1945.
Louis Lowery, Leatherneck Magazine

The most famous war photograph ever taken:
AP Photographer Joe Rosenthal's picture of the raising
atop Suribachi of the larger flag from LST 779. This
photograph became the model of the giant U.S. Marine
Corps Memorial at Arlington National Cemetery.
Wide World Photos

Two Marines attack Japanese caves
on Iwo Jima with flamethrowers.
Navy Dept. Photo, National Archives

Marines manhandle crates of supplies
out of landing craft and up Iwo's beach.
U.S. Coast Guard Photo

A chaplain celebrates Mass for Marines on Iwo Jima while the fighting continues.
U.S. Office of War Information Photo, National Archives

Marines killed in the first wave lie in the sands of Iwo Jima.
Joe Rosenthal, Wide World Photos

1st Division Marines and flamethrowing tank advance on Okinawa.
USMC Photo

dispute over orders to the 105th Infantry, which was assigned to clean up the enemy dug in on Nafutan Point at the island's southeast corner. Both Smiths had issued orders; therefore, Holland Smith charged, Ralph Smith had contravened an order from his Marine superior.

Opening the second phase of the Saipan invasion, the two Marine divisions pivoted in a great turning movement northward against the enemy defense line across the island's waist. Their full-scale attack began at 6 A.M. on June 22. By now, the Landing Force had taken 6,165 casualties—2,514 in the 2d Marine Division, 3,628 in the 4th Division and 320 in the 27th Infantry Division. But the two Marine divisions were still powerful offensive weapons.

On the far left, the 6th Marines took the summit of 1,133-foot-high Mount Tipo Pale. The 8th Marines tackled Mount Tapotchau, the extinct volcano that dominated the center of the island. To the 2d Division's right, the 4th Division's 24th Marines fought along Magicienne Bay; and the 25th Marines' 3rd Battalion led the advance nearly 2,000 yards, until it was stopped by the Japanese entrenched in caves. The battalion's commander, Lt. Col. Justice M. Chambers of Huntington, West Virginia, a former Edson Raider who wore pistols on his hip and in his armpit, and Lt. Col. Evans Carlson, now on the 4th Division staff, tried to carry to safety Pfc. Vito Cassaro, Chambers' radioman, who had been hit by machine-gun fire. Carlson took a burst in his right arm and left thigh. The great Raider leader had seen his last combat.

Holland Smith kept the pressure on. The Americans now faced Lt. Gen. Saito's main line of resistance where he had 15,000 men. That evening, Holland Smith ordered the 27th Division to pass through the 25th Marines and all three divisions to attack the next morning. He also brought north two battalions from the 105th Infantry as a reserve for the 27th. Ralph Smith ordered the remaining 2d Battalion, 105th Infantry to mop up at Nafutan Point, where 1,000 Japanese soldiers and civilians still held out. But that battalion was in corps reserve. And Holland Smith later objected that Ralph Smith had again issued an order to a unit not under his tactical control. The dispute between the Marine and Army Smiths was heating up.

On June 23, the 106th Infantry arrived late at the line-of-departure. The Army attack was delayed and exposed the flanks of the Marine divisions on either side. The 106th and 165th were unable to advance in the center of the line, where the steep ridges were honeycombed with strongly defended caves. The front looked like a sagging "U" with the 27th Division in the bottom.

In the south, the 2d Battalion, 105th Infantry was hours late in launching its attack at Nafutan Point and then made no progress.

That night, the 27th Division was hit by two tank-led counterattacks. On the rugged slopes of Mount Tapotchau, Pfc. Harold G. Epperson of Akron, Ohio, a machine gunner with the 1st Battalion, 6th Marines, helped break up an enemy counterattack and killed several Japanese. Suddenly, a Japanese soldier, assumed to be dead, hurled a grenade into Epperson's position. He dived on the grenade and died to save his fellow Marines. He was awarded the Medal of Honor.

Holland Smith was angered at the 27th Division's failure to move swiftly enough; and Ralph Smith agreed with him. Early on the twenty-fourth, Holland Smith sent Ralph Smith a message beginning "Commanding General is highly displeased with the failure of the 27th Division . . . "[53] and demanding that the Army move forward. The 27th Division was faced with advancing up heavily fortified "Death Valley" exposed to fire from the sheer sides of Mount Tapotchau on its left and from heavily wooded "Purple Heart Ridge" on its right. The 106th and 165th could make virtually no progress and took casualties. That evening, Ralph Smith was replaced by Maj. Gen. Sanderford Jarman, USA.

Holland Smith called the relief of Ralph Smith "one of the most disagreeable tasks I have ever been forced to perform."[54] When Holland Smith posed the problem to Admirals Turner and Spruance aboard *Indianapolis*, they both agreed to, and Spruance, the overall commander, directed Ralph Smith's replacement by Jarman. In making his case against Ralph Smith, Holland Smith cited the two earlier conflicts over orders but stressed the Army division's "defective performance."[55]

Historians of the incident have said: "The corps commander [Holland] Smith had reason to be dissatisfied . . . The 27th

Division had been slow to take Nafutan Point and had retarded the advance of the two marine divisions. A far more patient corps commander than Holland M. Smith might reasonably have concluded that a command shake up within the division was necessary. Holland Smith was not a patient man."[56]

The relief exploded into bitter controversy. Lt. Gen. Robert C. Richardson, Jr., top Army officer in the Central Pacific, was furious and convened a board of Army officers to investigate what was regarded as an insult to the Army. The board, headed by Lt. Gen. Simon B. Buckner, Jr., decided that Holland Smith had overreacted, although he had had the legal authority to relieve Ralph Smith. In Washington, General Marshall's advisors concurred that the 27th Division's performance had been deficient but felt that its commander's relief had been an act of bad judgment. Lt. Gen. Richardson came to Saipan and held a heated argument with Holland Smith. To cool things off, the War Department transferred Ralph Smith to Europe. After the Saipan operation, Holland Smith assumed command of the Fleet Marine Force, Pacific, which had no control over Army divisions.

Meanwhile, the battle of the Smiths broke out in the press and created a prolonged public ruckus. In Marines' eyes, Ralph Smith had failed either to force his division's advance or to replace his subordinate commanders. So the general responsible for the success of the Saipan operation replaced him, despite the storm he well knew would follow.[57] But the interservice bitterness aroused by the incident would fester for a very long time.

The battle for Saipan could not wait. On June 25, the 8th Marines; the 1st Battalion, 29th Marines, and the Division Scout Company captured the summit of rugged Mount Tapotchau. On the right, the 4th Division easily overran Kagman Peninsula north of Magicienne Bay. And after Maj. Gen. Jarman replaced the commander of his 106th Regiment, it seized all but the northern tip of Purple Heart Ridge. On the twenty-sixth, the 2d Battation, 105th Infantry secured Nafutan Point in the south. But there, 500 enemy soldiers and sailors, some in American uniforms, crashed through the Army's trap and stormed across Aslito Airfield, until the survivors were wiped out by the 25th and 14th Marines.

In the north, the American attack pressed inexorably forward against dogged opposition. Holland Smith described the fighting:

> Although they resisted from caves and hideouts in the ridges, and tried to harass us at night from by-passed pockets, we dug them out and smoked them out in hand-to-hand combat. With flame throwers and hand grenades, the Marines ferreted the Japanese out of their holes and killed them. Patrols covered the terrain yard by yard, combing thick vegetation and rocky fastnesses for snipers. It was war such as nobody had fought before: a subterranean campaign in which men climbed, crawled, clubbed, shot, burned and bayonetted each other to death.[58]

By June 30, central Saipan was under U.S. control. The 2d Marine Division had taken 4,488 casualties since the landing; the 4th Division, 4,454, and the 27th Division, 1,836. The Japanese withdrew to their final defensive line across the northern part of the island.

The three American divisions began their climactic offensive on July 2. The 2d Marines went into the ruins of Garapan and had a taste of street fighting. On the Fourth of July, they cleaned up Mutcho Point above Garapan; and the 6th and 8th Marines reached the coast at Tanapag Harbor. Then, the 2d Division was squeezed out of the front to rest up for the coming invasion of Tinian. The 27th and 4th Divisions charged up the narrower end of Saipan. Holland Smith assigned the 27th, now commanded by Maj. Gen. George W. Griner, USA, to tackle the west coast, centered on the village of Makunsha, and aimed the 4th Division at Marpi Point, Saipan's northern tip. When the 27th Division ran into a heavily defended area called Paradise Valley, inland from Makunsha, the 2d Marines had to be fitted back into the line. Lt. Gen. Saito, wounded and headquartered in a cave in a Paradise Valley hillside, ordered a final *banzai* attack and committed *hara-kiri*. In a nearby cave, Vice Adm. Chuichi Nagumo, who had led the raid on Pearl Harbor and was now commander of the no longer existing Central Pacific Area Fleet, shot himself in the head.

At 4 A.M. on July 7, Saito's survivors carried out his last order and made a desperate, savage attack that had no possible purpose but to kill Americans. An estimated 3,000 screaming Japanese came stampeding down the west coast plain against the 105th Infantry and shattered both the 1st and 2d Battalions. The attack plunged on to hit the 3rd Battalion, 10th Marines. The foremost battery, Battery H, cut its fuses so that its shells exploded 50 yards from the muzzles of its 105mm howitzers. The battery's survivors finally pulled back into an abandoned Japanese machinery dump. The enemy killed the artillery battalion's commander, Maj. William L. Crouch. The battalion's other batteries also formed a defense, aided by elements of the 1st Battalion, 106th Infantry, and a few men from the 4th Battalion, 10th Marines. One of them, Pfc. Harold C. Agerholm of Racine, Wisconsin, grabbed an abandoned ambulance Jeep and under heavy fire singlehandedly loaded and evacuated 45 wounded Marines over three hours before he was mortally wounded by a Japanese sniper. He was awarded the Medal of Honor.

When the attack lost enough steam to be stopped, the 106th Infantry counterattacked and retook the Marine positions. By 6 P.M., most of the ground lost, and now covered with Japanese dead, had been regained. The two crushed battalions of the 105th had suffered 406 killed and 512 wounded; the 3rd Battalion, 10th Marines lost 45 killed and 82 wounded.

Holland Smith brought the 2d Division back into the line, and the American attack was resumed against tough pockets of resistance. By 4:15 P.M. on July 9, the 4th Division reached the northern coast; and Vice Adm. Turner declared Saipan secured.

There was one final tragedy. Hundreds of frightened Japanese civilians committed suicide by leaping from the cliffs above Marpi Point. Some were forced to their deaths by Japanese soldiers. Nine thousand Japanese civilians and 3,000 native Chamorros were interned.

The bloody three and a half week battle for Saipan had cost 3,426 American dead and 13,099 wounded. Enemy dead were estimated at more than 32,800. It was a costly struggle, but as a Japanese admiral said after the war was over, "Our war was lost with the loss of Saipan."[59] Holland Smith agreed; he termed it "the decisive battle of the Pacific offensive."[60]

On July 18, the day the fall of Saipan was announced to the

Japanese people, Premier Gen. Hideki Tojo and his cabinet resigned; and Gen. Kuniaki Koiso formed a new government. But no Japanese political leader dared to propose peace. On November 24, 100 Army B-29s rose from Saipan to strike Tokyo for the first time since Doolittle's raid in 1942.

Even before Saipan was secured, Tinian was bombarded across the three-mile channel to the south. This handsome island, checkerboarded with sugar cane fields, was 12 miles long by 5 wide at its center and protected by steep coral cliffs and 9,000 Japanese soldiers and sailors. To assault it would require not a ship-to-shore but a more unusual shore-to-shore movement. Despite that difference, Holland Smith would call the Tinian invasion "the perfect amphibious operation in the Pacific war."[61]

Tinian was superbly suited for major airfields. The Japanese had a large field with two airstrips on Ushi Point at the northern end of the island and one at Gurguan Point on the west side and were finishing still another behind Tinian Town on the southwest coast. From the Ushi field on August 6, 1945, the B-29 "Enola Gay" would carry the atomic bomb to Hiroshima.

The Japanese had to expect an invasion of Tinian; so, to gain tactical surprise, the American commanders decided to gamble and land on two narrow beaches, one only 60 yards wide and the other 160 yards, on the northwest coast below Ushi Point. These obscure beaches were within range of Saipan's artillery and appeared too small for a big assault force. Evans Carlson called them "the enemy's back door."[62]

By mid-July 1944, 13 battalions of Marine and Army artillery were pounding Tinian. Naval gunfire, carrier planes and P-47s from Isely Field also hit airfields, roads and Tinian Town itself. A new weapon joined the air bombardment: napalm powder was added to aircraft fuel and the inflammable mixture dropped in fuel tanks on woods and cane fields. As Holland Smith wrote later: "We were resolved that there would be no repetition of our Tarawa and Saipan experiences, where we suffered from lack of preliminary preparation and lost heavily in consequence."[63]

When Smith assumed command of the Fleet Marine Force, Pacific on July 12, Maj. Gen. Harry Schmidt, who had led the

4th Division on Saipan, took over the V Amphibious Corps and Maj. Gen. Clifton B. Cates headed Schmidt's division. Maj. Gen. Thomas E. Watson continued in command of the 2d Division. Smith retained overall command of the Expeditionary Troops; but on July 20, he sailed to oversee the invasion of Guam.

On the two nights before the Tinian invasion, men of the V Corps Amphibious Reconnaissance Battalion under Capt. James L. Jones, Lt. Col. William K. Jones' brother, went in with naval UDT "frogmen" to scout the beaches' approaches and exits. Swimming in from their rubber boats, they found the larger beach (White 2) framed by coral barriers, leaving merely a 70-yard-wide passage free for 16 LVTs. The smaller beach (White 1) could accommodate only eight LVTs at a time. Beyond the beaches were cliffs six to ten feet high. To widen the access for vehicles, the Seabees devised an ingenious portable ramp that would carry the weight of a 30-ton medium tank.

Because of the tight landing conditions, the individual Marine went ashore without a pack. He stuffed his pockets with emergency rations, a spoon, an extra pair of socks and a bottle of insect repellant. Over his cartridge belt he folded his poncho.

The landing force had 533 amtracs, including 68 armored amphibians and 10 amtracs with the special portable ramps, and 130 DUKWs, plus a variety of other landing craft. The plan was for the 4th Division to assault the narrow White beaches directly from Saipan. The 2d Division would feint in front of Tinian Town and then follow the 4th Division ashore over the White beaches. The 27th Infantry Division would stay in reserve on Saipan, ready to go on four hours' notice.

The 2d Division's realistic demonstration sent empty landing craft within 400 yards of the shore and held in place the Japanese troops defending Tinian Town. But hidden 6-inch guns smashed the battleship *Colorado*, killing 43 and wounding 176, including 41 Marine casualties.

At 7:47 A.M. on July 24, eight amtracs landed Company E, 24th Marines on narrow White Beach 1. The Marines destroyed a small beach defense detachment and moved rapidly inland to make room for the rest of the 2d Battalion. By 8:46, both the 2d and 1st Battalions, 24th Marines were ashore.

White Beach 2 was more heavily defended. Until antiboat mines could be cleared, the first Marines had to avoid the beach and climb the nearby rocky ledges. The 25th Marines were ashore at 9:30; and by dark, both regiments held a beachhead 4,000 yards wide and 1,500 deep. Four artillery battalions of the 10th and 14th Marines were also landed. Ashore then were 15,600 Marines with 48 medium tanks and 15 light tanks armed with Ronson flamethrowers. Marine casualties on J-Day numbered only 15 killed and 225 wounded. There were 438 Japanese dead. The Marines had achieved tactical surprise over beaches the Japanese had regarded as impassable.

Maj. Gen. Cates expected a counterattack to throw the Marines back into the sea as soon as the enemy could readjust to the shock of the landing's location. He brought ashore his division reserve, the 23rd Marines, and ordered the men to dig in and string barbed wire along the entire perimeter. They placed machine guns to provide interlocking fire and bazookas to cover possible tank approaches.

Cates' preparations were well taken. The Marines faced a night of hard fighting. At 2 A.M., 600 Japanese naval troops counterattacked on the left flank; in three hours of fierce battle in the moonless dark, the 24th Marines slaughtered 476. Japanese soldiers broke through between the 24th and 25th Marines, and the 14th Marines wiped them out. On the right or south, the Japanese attacked at 3:30. Six light tanks in the lead were met by a wall of fire; five were swiftly destroyed. But the enemy infantrymen kept coming, until by dawn 267 Japanese bodies lay among the 23rd Marines' foxholes. The night's battle had killed 1,241 of the enemy and, as Cates said, "broke the Jap's back."[64]

The second day, the 8th Marines came ashore and with the 24th Marines occupied part of Ushi Airfield. The 23rd Marines pushed southward. In the center, the 25th Marines took 290-foot Mt. Maga in a double envelopment. The entire second-day operation went well with light American casualties.

On July 26, the 8th Marines cleared the rest of Ushi Airfield, and P-47s were flying from it two days later. By the end of the twenty-sixth, the two Marine divisions now ashore were stretched across the width of Tinian. They rolled steadily southward over the gentle landscape against minor resistance and overran the airstrip at Gurguan Point.

The Marines pushed through stifling cane fields that hid

nests of Japanese. As the 24th Marines approached Tinian Town on July 30, enemy machine gunners and riflemen concealed in coastal caves north of the town stopped them. The Marines called up tanks and armored amtracs offshore; flamethrowers seared the caves, and combat engineers then sealed them with demolition charges. The now-classic Marine tank-infantry team worked well.

The Marines found Tinian Town flattened and deserted. They encountered only one Japanese soldier. The town's defenses had been laid out to meet an assault from the sea, and the enemy commanders recognized that they could not deal with a tank-reinforced land attack.

On July 31, the Marines assaulted the southern end of the island preceded by a mighty bombardment from artillery, warships and 126 aircraft. The Japanese waited for the Marines there on a high plateau fronted with cliffs and jungle.

On the east coast, the cliff before the plateau rose almost vertically, and the 2d and 6th Marines halted at its base. Further inland, the 8th Marines, now opposed at every step, grabbed a foothold on the plateau. To the west, the 23rd Marines met heavy mortar and machine-gun fire but fought to the plateau's top. On the western end of the line, the 24th Marines found the road to the high ground heavily mined.

That night, the enemy tried to throw the 8th Marines back off the plateau; but Col. Clarence R. Wallace was determined his regiment would hold. The Japanese hit the 2d Battalion again and again. Maj. William C. Chamberlain, the 2d Battalion's executive officer, called simply "Let's go!" and led the Marines to wipe out the Japanese. The two battalions of the 8th Marines held.

At 5:15 A.M. on August 1, 1,600 well-armed soldiers and sailors charged the Marines atop the plateau. This was the major effort for the Japanese. In one hour, the Marines suffered 74 casualties, killed 200 Japanese and stopped the attack. The enemy made an orderly retreat into the cliffs and woods to the southeast.

That morning, after the 3rd Battalion, 6th Marines replaced the battered 2d Battalion, 8th Marines on the plateau, the advance was held up by crowds of civilians who approached waving white cloths. Nearly 8,500 civilians, Japanese and Korean, emerged from their caves and surrendered during the next five days.

At 6:55 P.M., Maj. Gen. Schmidt declared the island secured. Organized resistance was over, but many die-hard Japanese were still prepared to kill Marines. Just before dawn on August 2, hundreds of the enemy attacked the 6th Marines; Lt. Col. John W. Easley, the 3rd Battalion's commander, was killed. More assaults followed for the next three days as the enemy tried to take Marines with them into death. The final mopping up was given over to the 8th Marines under the command of Brig. Gen. Edson, the 2d Division's assistant commander.

Overall, the conquest of Tinian cost the 2d Marine Division 105 killed and 653 wounded and the 4th Division 212 killed and 897 wounded. About 5,000 Japanese troops were killed.

Success on Tinian was the result of boldness fortified by luck. The overwhelming preinvasion bombardment and the decision to land on unexpected beaches cut down casualties and knocked the island's defenders off balance. They never recovered enough to stand effectively against the Marines' superior manpower and firepower.

The third phase of the Marianas campaign was the recapture of Guam, the American possession that the Japanese had scooped up so easily at the very beginning of the war. They made Guam a much tougher nut to crack than Tinian. In 21 days of fighting, Guam cost 1,744 Americans dead and 6,540 wounded.

Lying about 100 miles south of Saipan, Guam was shaped like a sock hanging on a line. The heel on the west coast contained the island's main treasure: Apra Harbor, a large anchorage. The Marines planned to land north and south of the heel, double-envelop Apra Harbor and grab the airfield on Orote Peninsula, which forms the harbor's south side.

There were twice as many Japanese troops on Guam as on Tinian, and their leaders figured pretty well where the Marines would land. Being much larger (30 miles long and 4 to 8 miles wide) and more rugged than both Saipan and Tinian, Guam gave the defenders more room to maneuver and made it difficult to root them out of the densely covered volcanic hills. Finally, the Japanese gained extra time to dig in by forcing a month's delay of the invasion—from June 18 to July 21—first by sending their battle fleet at the Marianas and then by defending Saipan so doggedly.

But the Japanese could not take all the credit. The American commanders landed on obvious and strongly defended beaches, and the northern landing site was backed by a palisade of coral ridges from which the enemy could pepper the Marines on the beaches and contest every step taken inland. And once the Japanese fled to the north, the Americans pursued them into the jungle.

The Marines of Maj. Gen. Geiger's III Amphibious Corps sweated out the delayed invasion for an average of 50 days on crowded transports under the broiling sun. Geiger had 20,328 men of the 3rd Marine Division—the 3rd, 9th and 21st Marines, veterans of Bougainville—and 9,886 men of the new 1st Provisional Marine Brigade made up of the reactivated 4th and the 22d Marines, which had fought at Eniwetok. Maj. Gen. Turnage still commanded the division; and Brig. Gen. Lemuel C. Shepherd, Jr., led the brigade. In charge of the corps artillery was Brig. Gen. Pedro A. del Valle. It was an experienced team.

The invasion delay was used to pound Guam with weeks of intense naval and air bombardment on "a scale and length of time never before seen in World War II."[65] But, as always, many enemy installations escaped destruction. Starting on July 14, UDTs swam in to clear the approaches to the invasion beaches; they destroyed 900 log cribs and wire cages filled with coral. On the reef, they left a sign: "Welcome Marines!"[66]

Also waiting for the Marines were 18,500 Japanese soldiers and sailors under the operational command of Lt. Gen. Takeshi Takashina. They were concentrated around Apra Harbor and the island's airfields, including the strip built on the former Marine Barracks' golf course on Orote Peninsula. During the time gained by the delay in W-Day, the Japanese had energetically strengthened their beach defenses and dug a system of trenches and foxholes across the neck of Orote Peninsula. Many of the island's 21,500 native civilians were put to work as forced labor.

The preinvasion bombing told the Japanese where to expect the landing. The 3rd Division would assault a 2,500-yard front between Adelup Point and Asan Point, north of Apra Harbor and south of Agaña, the island's capital. Simultaneously, the 1st

Provisional Marine Brigade would land five miles further south, below Orote Peninsula. The brigade's job was to capture the peninsula—fast.

Early on July 21, the transports' loudspeakers blared out *The Marine's Hymn* as the men climbed into their amtracs. Leading the assault were LCI(G) rocket-armed gunboats followed by LVT(A)s firing 37mm guns and then 360 troop-carrying LVTs. When the first Marines were within 100 yards of the beaches, they were hit by artillery and mortars. Naval gunfire and planes roared in and squelched this damaging fire. By 8:33 A.M., Marines were ashore on all the beaches—back on Guam after two and a half years.

The ring of ridges behind the northern beaches was strongly defended. On the far left, Japanese manned guns and mortars above the beach and caused heavy casualties among the 3rd Marines on the beach and the reef. They could advance neither up nor around sheer, 300-foot-high Chonito Cliff that came right down to the sea, until tanks and flamethrowers fired squarely into the enemy's caves. By afternoon, Chonito Cliff and Adelup Point had been cleared. Then, the 3rd Marines faced a ridge, 400 feet high, jungle covered and protected by mortars and machine guns. The assault by Capt. Geary R. Bundschu's A Company finally reached the crest, but the captain was among those killed, and the company could not hold Bundschu Ridge.

In the center, the 21st Marines' 2d and 3rd Battalions fought up two defiles through which flowed branches of the Asan River. The 2d struggled through a series of ridges in what became known as the battle for Banzai Ridge. F Company's Marines assaulted a 100-foot cliff frontally, pulling themselves up, clinging to bushes in the tropical heat. The right-hand platoon was nearly decimated. E Company also climbed up; but the long confinement on shipboard had weakened the men. The few who made it dug in under machine-gun fire from the next ridge less than 50 yards away.

On the right flank of the northern beaches, the 9th Marines took 231 casualties and secured a beachhead 1,500 yards deep. There were many gaps in the division's 400-yard perimeter; the enemy still held most of the high ground. In all, W-Day cost the 3rd Division 105 men killed, 526 wounded and 56 missing in action.

On the southern beaches, the 1st Brigade ran a gauntlet of fire registered on the beach; and the 22d Marines on the left took severe losses. Once through that, the 22d advanced into the ruins of Agat village and to high ground 1,000 yards inland. On the right, the 4th Marines seized Bangi Point; fought up Hill 40, and reached the foot of Mount Alifan. Brig. Gen. Shepherd now had a beachhead 4,500 yards long and 2,000 yards deep, at the cost of 350 casualties. He brought the 305th Infantry wading in from his reserve.

That first night, the Japanese counterattacked the brigade in force. All along the southern beachhead, brilliant star shells exposed the enemy to the dug-in Marines. Japanese carrying demolition charges infiltrated the perimeter and were killed. Light tanks probed the Marine lines; four were swiftly knocked out. The Japanese attacks reduced one A Company rifle platoon to four men. At dawn, the infiltrators were mopped up. The counterattack cost the enemy 600 dead; the brigade suffered some 50 killed and twice that number wounded.

On the northern front that same night, the Japanese tried to push the Marines off the high ground. The 21st Marines had heavy casualties but clung to the edge of its cliff. The Japanese attempted to take back Chonito Cliff and Adelup Point from the 3rd Marines. Pfc. Luther Skaggs, Jr., of Henderson, Kentucky, his leg shattered by a Japanese grenade, improvised a tourniquet and fired his rifle and hurled grenades at the enemy for eight more hours. Then, Skaggs, the first Marine to earn the Medal of Honor on Guam, coolly crawled out of his foxhole and continued to battle until the enemy were exterminated.

On the second day, the 9th Marines occupied the ruins of the former U.S. Navy Yard at Piti; that made the unloading of supplies easier. The 3rd Battalion assaulted the mine-littered offshore islet of Cabras. And the 3rd Marines fought desperately to reach the top of Bundschu Ridge, a natural fortress for the enemy; but mortar and machine-gun fire drove them back again. In this battle, Pfc. Leonard F. Mason of Middlesboro, Kentucky, alone attacked two machine guns. Japanese riflemen on higher ground shot him repeatedly; but Mason moved around the machine-gun position, and, although mortally wounded, killed five Japanese with his BAR and wiped out the position.[67]

The second night, the enemy again charged the 21st Marines and were slaughtered. These aggressive night attacks were devouring the best of the enemy's troops, and Lt. Gen. Takashina began planning an all-out counterattack while he still had the strength. On July 23, the 3rd Marines found that the Japanese had withdrawn from Bundschu Ridge, leaving behind deadly nests of riflemen and machine gunners. The Marines worked steadily forward on the high ground.

On the southern front, the 4th Marines fought up the slopes of Mount Alifan and took Magpo Point on the right end of the beachhead. On the left, the 22d Marines tried to pry open the base of Orote Peninsula and ran into trouble. Enemy artillery was registered on the ground over which the Marines had to advance, and the regiment suffered more than 100 casualties.

On July 24, the day Tinian was invaded, the 22d Marines advanced between the sea and the rice paddies at the peninsula's base and then spread out on a two-battalion front. Shermans destroyed five tanks and pounded concrete and coconut log bunkers. Enemy guns hidden in Orote's cliffs also joined the battle until two LCI(G)s closed in offshore and stifled their fire. Meanwhile, the 2d Battalion crossed the peninsula and advanced along its northern coast.

The 22d Marines spent July 25 trying to seal off the peninsula, and the 4th Marines came into line on the 22d's left. The 77th Infantry Division, Geiger's reserve, probed the foothills of the mass called Mt. Tenjo. And patrols of the 9th Marines and the 22d Marines linked the two beachheads along Apra Harbor's shore.

That night, Lt. Gen. Takashina launched the most massive counterattack of the war to date. The Marines were overextended; "their front line resembled a sieve."[68] All along the five-mile front on the northern beachhead, vulnerable gaps separated the Marine units. The enemy pounded the entire perimeter. In the sector of the 1st Battalion, 21st Marines, the Japanese annihilated 50 men of B Company and dashed through that hole. Many of the attackers were loaded down with explosives and land mines that blew up with roar after roar. The Japanese hit Marine tanks in the rear and the battalion's mortar platoon, 200 yards behind the front line.

The sake-flushed Japanese struck hardest against Lt. Col. Robert E. Cushman's 2d Battalion, 9th Marines, which was attached to the 3rd Marines on Fonte Hill. The battalion withstood seven major attacks, climaxed before dawn on July 26 by waves of Japanese charging, screaming, into close-quarter combat. Half of Cushman's men were killed or wounded. With first light, Shermans got into the fight and smashed the final attack; the battalion was barely able to hold on.

Capt. Louis H. Wilson, Jr., of Brandon, Mississippi, the twenty-four-year-old commander of the battalion's F Company, had been wounded three times the previous day. When the Japanese counterattacked, he left the medical aid station and rejoined his men. At one point in the battle, he dashed 50 yards in front of his line to rescue a wounded Marine. All night, he led his men in hand-to-hand fighting. Then, he took a 17-man patrol up a critical nearby slope against intense fire that cut down 13 of the men. He and the four surviving Marines seized the critical high ground. Wilson received the Medal of Honor.

Twenty-five men of the division's Reconnaissance Company tried futilely to cover the 800-yard gap between the 21st and 9th Marines. Many infiltrators flooded through, and some reached the command post of the 3rd Battalion, 21st Marines at Hill 460. Headquarters troops fought them off until L Company, 9th Marines sneaked up, hurling grenades, and wiped them out.

More than 50 Japanese attacked the division hospital 200 yards from the beach. Patients were hastily evacuated, and hospital personnel and 41 walking wounded formed a defense. Two Pioneer companies and a motley of rear-echelon men rushed over; and by noon, the hospital was back in operation. During the mopping up, Lt. Col. Hector de Zayas, commander of the 2d Battalion, 3rd Marines, was killed.

On Orote Peninsula, 500 drunken Japanese soldiers joined in the general counterattack. They charged the 22d Marines, screaming. Most of them were blown up by artillery and the rest were killed in hand-to-hand fighting.

The Japanese lost an estimated 3,200 men in the night's counterattack; the Marines had a total of 600 killed and wounded. Lt. Gen. Takashina had shot his bolt and failed. From now on, he could only wage a battle of attrition.

At 7 A.M. on July 26, the 4th and 22d Marines jumped off to assault Orote. Both regiments advanced to the main enemy defense line, where they were stopped cold and had to pull back to safety and dig in for the night.

The next morning, the 4th Marines, supported by tanks,

again battered the Japanese defenses. A sniper killed the 4th Marines' executive officer, Lt. Col. Samuel D. Puller ("Chesty" Puller's younger brother). The 22d Marines advanced against vicious automatic weapons fire. Tank-infantry teams kept pressing forward; by dark, the 22d Marines were on the high ground overlooking the former Marine Barracks.

On July 28, the 22d Marines took the town of Sumay, the barracks ruins and the cliffs along the harbor. But the 4th Marines ran into a defense-in-depth of pillboxes and minefields. There was no way around them. E and I Companies led a frontal assault, smashed through with help from Marine and Army tanks and reached positions just shy of the former Marine rifle range. The next morning, the Marines swept on to the tip of the peninsula. Retaking Orote Peninsula had cost 115 Marines killed, 38 missing and 721 wounded.

At 3:30 P.M. on July 29 at the charred ruins of the Marine Barracks, "To the Colors" was blown on a captured Japanese bugle; and the American flag was officially raised on Guam for the first time since December 10, 1941.

Meanwhile, the 77th Infantry Division was patrolling all of southern Guam; and the 3rd Division after a deadly contest had occupied the Fonte Plateau. On July 28, units from the separate beachheads met at Mt. Tenjo. But the main body of Japanese survivors was already filtering up to the northern jungles. In the flight, Lt. Gen. Takashina was killed by a Marine tank's machine gun. By now, an estimated 9,000 Japanese had been killed; only 50 prisoners had been taken. There were still plenty of the enemy alive on Guam.

On July 31, the 3rd Division, with the 77th Division on its right, drove into the rain-soaked hill country of northern Guam. The 3rd Marines entered the rubble of the capital of Agaña. The 9th Marines took Tiyan airfield. At the edge of the northern plateau, the 77th Division secured the village of Barrigada and 640-foot Mt. Barrigada.

The enemy fought with well-laid ambushes, mines and roadblocks. The thick northern jungle hid the Japanese and kept the American units out of touch with each other. As a result, one tank-led Army patrol powered through two roadblocks and attacked a third, which, unfortunately, was held by the 2d Battalion, 9th Marines. Seven Marines were wounded before the tanks' guns could be stopped.

With the 1st Battalion, 9th Marines on August 3, Pfc. Frank P. Witek of Derby, Connecticut, was caught in an ambush, stood up and killed eight Japanese at point-blank range with his BAR to enable his platoon to take cover. As the men pulled back, Witek stayed with a badly wounded Marine until stretcher bearers arrived and then covered their retreat. After that, Witek raced ahead again, throwing grenades and firing at the enemy. He destroyed a machine-gun emplacement and killed eight more Japanese before he was killed. He was awarded the Medal of Honor.

Throughout the fighting on Guam, the Marines experimented with the use of several platoons of war dogs. These were mostly Doberman pinschers, trained to kill on command, dig Japanese out of their caves, spot snipers, carry messages under fire and provide night security. Four of the dogs and two of the handlers were killed in action.

The 77th Division was now prepared to attack 840-foot Mt. Santa Rosa, near the east coast, where the Japanese had constructed their last-stand positions. The Marine division drove directly north in the center of the island and the 1st Marine Brigade came up on the western side.

At noon on August 7, the Army opened its final offensive. Tanks and riflemen were quickly enveloped in a raging battle. The Marines found less resistance in their zones. VMF-225 flew combat air patrols from Orote airfield. The next day, the 77th Division found Mt. Santa Rosa undefended. In the jungle fighting, there was a discouraging number of incidents of Americans firing on Americans. And Marine patrols found groups of Guamanians whom the Japanese had used as laborers and then beheaded.

The 1st Brigade reached the northwestern coast, and the 9th Marines advanced to Pati Point at the northeastern corner of the island. On August 10, Maj. Gen Geiger announced that all organized resistance had ended. Guam was American once more.

Although the island was officially secured and the enemy was unable to fight effectively, thousands of Japanese were still alive on Guam. Many died of starvation; the rest were eliminated over months of guerrilla warfare. Guam was rapidly converted into a major naval and training base, and two great B-29 airfields were carved out of the northern jungle.

The Marianas campaign had brought American air power within striking distance of the Japanese homeland. It had also drawn out the enemy fleet and destroyed its naval aviation. The enemy made the Americans pay dearly for their achievements. For the Marine Corps alone, casualties in the Central Pacific campaign from Tarawa through the Marianas had totalled 6,902 dead and 19,471 wounded—the equivalent of much more than an entire Marine division.

11
Peleliu and the Philippines

Peleliu was another bad mistake. Out in the middle of nowhere—one of the Palau Islands some 500 miles east of the Philippines—it cost the United States 1,794 dead and 7,800 wounded. It was not worth it. Adm. William F. Halsey, Jr., had recommended a last-minute cancellation of the invasion. When his carrier sweeps discovered that Japanese air power in the central Philippines was "a hollow shell,"[69] he judged the Peleliu operation unnecessary. He recalled, "I feared another Tarawa—and I was right."[70]

After the war, historian Samuel Eliot Morison said of the Palaus: "Admiral Halsey had the right idea; they should have been bypassed."[71] They were not isolated and neutralized because Admiral Nimitz was committed to protect the flank of General MacArthur's move into the Philippines and Nimitz saw the Palaus* as a staging point for the invasion of Leyte. As a result, the Marines assaulted Peleliu. But it was of little purpose. Eight days later, the Army landed on Ulithi Atoll and won a real anchorage—with no lives lost.

The 28,484 men of the 1st Marine Division (reinforced) fought on Peleliu—"one of the bloodiest battles of the war"[72]— because MacArthur had won his fight to return to the Philippines. He had consistently opposed the Central Pacific campaign. He even took his case to the public and was quoted on page one of *The New York Times*: "Island hopping . . . is not my idea of how to end the war as soon and as cheaply as possible."[73] Admiral King called MacArthur's strategy "absurd."[74]

---

*Lt. Col. Earl H. Ellis had died on Koror Island in the Palaus in 1923. See page 459.

On March 12, 1944, the Joint Chiefs of Staff finally reached a compromise: MacArthur would head for the Philippines and Nimitz into the Marianas. And in July at Honolulu, MacArthur convinced President Roosevelt and Admiral Nimitz that unless he returned to the Philippines all Asia would "lose faith in American honor."[75] The decision intensified Army-Navy rivalry and therefore increased the pressure for speed on the Marines' offensive timetable and consequently the number of their casualties. It also permitted MacArthur to engage in massive battles throughout the Philippines, which he insisted on liberating island after island.

The Japanese helped the general win support for his return to the Philippines. That summer, their armies struck southward in China, pushed the 14th U.S. Army Air Force back from its airfields nearest Japan and cut off Chiang Kai-shek from the Chinese coast, where the Allies might have landed without fighting.

So, Peleliu. Maj. Gen. William H. Rupertus, the 1st Marine Division's commander, predicted that, although this would be a hard fight, it would take only two or three days. His misjudgment would make the Marines bitter.

Of course, Rupertus and the other planners for Peleliu did not know that the Japanese would change their style of defense so radically and successfully. But the enemy had learned an important lesson from the prolonged fighting on Saipan and from a defensive experiment they had made on Biak Island. On Peleliu, instead of trying to shove the Marines off the beaches, the Japanese burrowed into caves in the Umurbrogol ridges, the central spine of the island; and the Americans felt compelled to dig them out. This cost time and lives, which was exactly what the enemy wanted—they would do it again on Iwo Jima and Okinawa. The days of the wasteful beach-and-*banzai* defense were over.

Peleliu, shaped like a horse's skull facing northeast, was only six miles long and two across at its widest; but it was known to hold 10,200 first-class Japanese troops, some of them proud veterans of Manchuria. They constructed a tough defense-in-depth. They mined the beaches, sank underwater obstacles and dug huge antitank ditches, all covered by interlocking fields of fire. And in the central mess of coral ridges and boulders, they created an elaborate network of caves and tunnels, well armed and stocked. There, they were prepared to fight to the death. And they did.

At 8:32 on Friday morning, September 15, 1944, the 1st Marine Division, straight from its miserable rest area on Pavuvu, assaulted Peleliu's western beaches. At the same time, in Europe, the Americans took Aachen, the first major German city to fall, and paratroopers dropped on Arnhem; and in the Southwest Pacific, MacArthur's soldiers landed at Morotai. Back home, for once, the Marines were virtually forgotten.

Col. Lewis B. "Chesty" Puller landed his 1st Marines on the left flank to attack the Umurbrogol ridges just north of Peleliu's airfield.

Col. Harold D. "Bucky" Harris landed his 5th Marines in the center to plunge straight across the island and capture the airfield.

Col. Herman H. "Haiti" Hanneken took his 7th Marines into the beaches on the right to clean up the island's wide southern end.

The only division reserve was the 2d Battalion of the 7th Marines—with the Army's 81st Infantry Division a floating reserve on eight hours' call. The odds did not favor the Marines—9,000 infantrymen (plus a lot of firepower, of course) against 10,000 heavily fortified Japanese.

Colonel Puller did not like the smell of the whole operation—knocking heads with a well-prepared enemy and too few men in back-up. But the commanders in charge pointed reassuringly to the three days of preliminary bombardment. And Maj. Gen. Rupertus did not want Army troops on Peleliu if he could help it.

Enemy guns and mortars on the high ground were zeroed in on Peleliu's broad reef and white coral sand beaches. At both ends of the proposed beachhead, the Japanese had enfilading fire. A chaplain who went in with the assault wrote: "How we got through the murderous mortar fire which the Japs were laying down on the reef we'll never know. The bursts were everywhere and our men were being hit, left and right."[76] The Japanese destroyed 26 LVTs, disabled many more and hit every one of the 30 tanks unloaded with the fourth wave.

Puller's K Company, commanded by Capt. George P. Hunt,

landed on the extreme left flank against vicious raking fire. K Company "was destined to execute a classic example of a small-unit attack on a fortified position."[77] That is official language to describe one hell of a fight.

Hunt wrote much later:

> Among the 235 of Company K were every type, tall and short, stocky and thin, fair and dark, but unifying them into one driving spirit was an unshakable loyalty to each other, a unity far deeper than mere comradeship, and governed by a stern, silent code of mutual respect which could not be broken by a man in battle without his incurring the humiliating contempt of former friends. This was a force that would never allow them to let each other down and that would impel them to perform acts of bravery which, in the normal circumstances of peace, would seem incredible.[78]

(Of the eight Medals of Honor earned by Marines on Peleliu, six were awarded to men who covered grenades with their bodies to save their comrades.)

K Company's objective was a point of coral 30 feet high, jutting out into the sea at the north end of the entire beachhead and infested with Japanese machine guns and antitank guns. The 3rd Platoon on the left landed 100 yards south of The Point and fought northward to within 50 yards of it. The 2d Platoon made about 75 yards straight ahead westward, ran into a 10-foot-deep tank trap and took heavy fire from an unexpected ridge 40 feet high on its right front; the ridge was honeycombed with Japanese caves. The 2d Platoon was surrounded in the tank trap; the machine-gun section kept off the Japanese. Each platoon was quickly shaved down to squad strength. To close the gap between them, Captain Hunt sent in his reserve 1st Platoon, which had to fight through five concrete pillboxes to reach The Point.

Since the enemy guns were oriented to the beach, Hunt's Marines hit The Point from the rear and by 10:15 seized the crest. An enemy 47mm gun was still firing below them. The 1st Platoon leader, 2d Lt. William A. Willis, a New Yorker, eased himself down the cliff and lobbed in a smoke grenade. Then, a

Corporal Anderson fired in a rifle grenade that ignited the gun's ammunition. As the Japanese raced out in flames, the bullets in their belts popping, the Marines killed them.

Hunt could locate only 32 survivors from his 1st and 3rd Platoons to form an isolated perimeter defense atop The Point. They set up a captured machine gun. When evening finally came after a long day of battle, Willis said to the captain, "Anyway, there's one thing to be said for our situation. We'll be able to kill some more of the bastards."[79]

South of the ridge that had stopped Hunt's 2d Platoon, the rest of Puller's 3rd Battalion ran into trouble. A Company of the 1st Battalion hurried up to help, took heavy casualties and stormed the ridge's southern slopes. On Puller's right, Harris' 5th Marines quickly moved to the near side of the airfield and set up a defensive line, expecting a tank attack. For 15 minutes, K Company of the 5th Marines was the exposed right flank of the entire invasion because Hanneken's 7th Marines had hit underwater obstacles and mines and fierce fire from the promontory south of the beach and from a nameless islet nearby. Many Marines had to wade in.

There was an exceptional amount of confusion between the 5th and 7th Marines, although this was an experienced division with many veterans of Guadalcanal and Cape Gloucester. Part of the 3rd Battalion, 7th Marines landed on the beach of the 3rd Battalion, 5th Marines. Sherman tanks sent to help I Company of the 7th Marines destroy a large blockhouse attached themselves to I Company, 5th Marines by mistake. And the 3rd Battalion, 5th Marines pushed dangerously far forward because it thought the 3rd Battalion, 7th Marines was ahead of it, when actually that unit was 200 yards to the rear. Headquarters personnel had to plug the hole. Partly because of such foul-ups, L Company, 5th Marines was the only element to cross the whole island on D-Day.

When, at 5 P.M., the commander of the 3rd Battalion, 5th Marines was wounded and his executive officer killed, Lt. Col. Lewis W. Walt, the 5th Marines' executive officer, took command. He made a personal reconnaissance accompanied only by his runner, located his scattered companies and built a perimeter near the airfield.

Late that afternoon, the Japanese counterattacked. They did

not rush out in a wild *banzai* charge but advanced carefully, taking advantage of cover. A dozen enemy tanks clanged across the airfield and struck the junction of the 1st and 5th Marines in the woods southwest of the field. Having anticipated exactly this, Colonel Harris had heavy machine guns, 37mm antitank guns and three tanks in place. The Shermans' first armor-piercing shells tore right through the light Japanese tanks and exploded harmlessly; but when the tankers switched to high explosive ammunition and four more Shermans joined in, most of the Japanese tanks were destroyed.

The amphibious assault failed to meet its D-Day objectives. The Marines managed only to advance about 300 yards in the confused fighting on the northern beaches and to shove a narrow wedge across the island. For this, they suffered 210 dead and 910 wounded, not counting the many cases of heat prostration and combat fatigue.

During the night, small units of Japanese attacked the Marines isolated on The Point. Hunt's men used grenades to avoid revealing their positions. Mortars pounded the Marines; then came furious fire fights. The Marines' ranks thinned. By morning, Hunt had 18 men and one machine gun left. Because the division command post ashore could not communicate with the 1st Marines, Brig. Gen. Oliver P. Smith, the assistant division commander, did not know how precarious their situation was.

On the second day, the Marines fought the dogged enemy and a torturous shortage of water. Drinking water had been floated ashore in oil drums that had not been properly cleaned; the men retched. Their tongues grew too swollen to talk or swallow.

On the right, the 7th Marines with flamethrowers and bazookas pulverized pillboxes and concrete gun emplacements. Nineteen-year-old Cleveland-born Pfc. Arthur J. Jackson charged a large pillbox, poured in automatic fire, hurled grenades and explosives and killed all 35 Japanese soldiers inside. Under heavy fire, Jackson stormed one gun position after the other. His one-man assault wiped out 12 pillboxes and 50 Japanese. He received the Medal of Honor and a battlefield commission.

Slowed down by the lack of water, the 7th Marines did not clear the strongly-defended twin bulges at the southern end of the island until D plus three; they counted 2,609 enemy dead but took not a single prisoner. They lost 47 killed, 414 wounded and 36 missing.

In the center, the 5th Marines were bedeviled by American planes and artillery; the 2d Battalion alone had 34 casualties from "friendlies." The regiment went on to secure the swampy eastern peninsula of the island by D plus six.

On D plus one, the 1st Marines captured the stubborn ridge; and B Company linked up with Hunt's isolated survivors on The Point. That night 500 Japanese tried to retake The Point. The outnumbered Marines fought them off for four hours with automatic weapons, mortars and grenades. Their firepower decided the issue. When K Company was relieved by I Company the next morning, Hunt (who won the Navy Cross, as did Willis) had only 78 of the 235 men he had led ashore.

Now, most of the enemy were holed up in the crumbled mass of coral, rubble, crags and gulches known as the Umurbrogol ridges. These stark, crazy hills, none more than a few hundred feet high, were porous with hundreds of connected caves, some of which held two men, others large enough for artillery and 150mm mortars and even a battalion of men. The Japanese commander, Col. Kunio Nakagawa, was tied by telephone and suboceanic cable with higher headquarters on Babelthaup Island to the north, a fact not discovered until the battle was over.

The 1st and 5th Marines assaulted Umurbrogol's slopes. They could not dig in to escape the Japanese mortars. There was no front line, just small groups of Marines fighting and attacking in every direction. The heat was scorching, 110 degrees; the coral ridges were shadeless. In the first three days, Puller's regiment had 1,236 casualties—nearly half its strength.

On Monday, September 18, the 2d Battalion, 7th Marines had to relieve the depleted, exhausted 1st Battalion, 1st Marines. The 2d Battalions of the 1st and 7th Marines fought up Hill 210 in the blazing heat and took the crest. Not many made it to the top.

Pvt. Russell Davis, a scout with the 1st Marines, later described it:

> As the riflemen climbed higher they grew fewer, until only a handful of men still climbed in the lead squads.

These were the pick of the bunch—the few men who would go forward, no matter what was ahead. There were only a few. Of the thousands who land with a division and the hundreds who go up with a company of the line, there are only a few who manage to live and have enough courage to go through anything. They are the bone structure of a fighting outfit. All the rest is so much weight and sometimes merely flab. There aren't more than a few dozen in every thousand men, even in the Marines. They clawed and clubbed and stabbed their way up. The rest of us watched.

Watching them go up, Buck, the old rifleman, said, "Take a look at that sight and remember it. Those are riflemen, boy, and there ain't many like them. I was one once."[80]

The rugged fighting, terrible heat and lack of water all took their toll. Casualties were shockingly high, corpsmen and stretcher bearers gave out and rear echelon troops had to help. The Negro Marines of the 16th Field Depot won particular praise in this dangerous service.

September 19, the fighting was intense. The 1st Marines' 2d Battalion assaulted the Five Sisters, five ridges separated by steep cliffs, while C Company attacked the rear of Hill 100, later called Walt Ridge. F and G Companies' survivors had to be consolidated into one understrength company. Fighting upward in fast squad rushes, C Company surprised the enemy, but then was hit by fire from the next ridge 50 yards away. The men stayed, isolated, calling for help, and fought on the crest all night. The company commander, Capt. Everett P. Pope of Milton, Massachusetts, had only 15 men left. By dawn, they had exhausted their ammunition and were using bayonets, chunks of coral, broken ammunition boxes and their fists to fight off the counterattacks. When the enemy brought up machine guns, the Marines finally had to retreat.[81]

Puller sent both his 1st and 2d Battalions against Hill 100, throwing cooks, wiremen and supply handlers into the line. The attackers fell back with severe losses. The 7th Marines' 1st and 3rd Battalions had to relieve them. For two days, they flung themselves at the hill, gaining a few yards and being forced to retreat, each assault costing lives. These "fruitless frontal assaults"[82] were draining the division. Experienced platoon leaders and sergeants were virtually gone. The men attacked again and again, but there were not enough of them to hold. One sergeant, trying to rally his exhausted remnant, said, "Let's get killed up on that high ground there. It ain't good to get it down here."[83] The men went.

In that first week, while the 1st Marines were attacking the ridges, the 5th Marines had taken the airfield; and the 7th Marines had painfully seized all the island to the south. But the Japanese still held the ridges overlooking the airfield. The cost to date: 3,946 Marine casualties. The 1st Marines had 56 percent casualties; in the nine rifle platoons of Maj. Raymond G. Davis' 1st Battalion, not one original platoon leader and only 74 of the original nearly 500 riflemen were left. Puller's regiment had 1,672 casualties—"the highest regimental losses in the history of the Corps."[84] Said a sergeant, "This ain't a regiment. We're just survivors."[85]

That first week raised serious questions about the Marine doctrine that pounding straight ahead as fast as possible conserved American lives. Marines advanced with infinite courage when ordered to, but these bullheaded tactics against a skillful enemy who could not retreat and would not surrender simply did not work. Finally, somebody had to call a halt to the slaughter and start looking for a smarter way to invade the Umurbrogol ridges.

On September 21, Maj. Gen. Roy S. Geiger, commander of the III Amphibious Corps, ordered the 1st Marines replaced immediately by the 321st Infantry of the 81st Infantry Division. Rupertus stubbornly protested that the 1st Marines could finish the job; but the enlisted Marines welcomed the soldiers.

A tactical change was needed; and at 7 A.M. on September 24, the second phase of the battle opened. The 321st Infantry drove up the narrow west coast plain to isolate the Umurbrogol hill mass from the north while the 7th Marines continued the pressure on the central ridges. The 321st found a trail to the east coast just north of the enemy bastion and seized strongly-defended Hill 100, which dominated the trail.

The 5th Marines dashed up to the northern end of the island and in tough, yard-by-yard, cave-by-cave fighting with flamethrowers and tanks cleared the Amiangal ridges there. On September 28, its 3rd Battalion took Ngesebus Island just north of Peleliu in a shore-to-shore landing well supported by naval gunfire, artillery and Corsairs of Maj. Robert F. "Cowboy" Stout's newly arrived VMF-114. The rest of the 5th Marines cleaned up most of the resistance on northern Peleliu by September 29. The 1st Division had a total of 5,044 casualties.

Now, the Marines had to concentrate on the Umurbrogol. The 7th Marines attacking those central ridges were hampered by typhoon rains, dysentery and a shortage of rations. But by the end of October 3, despite heavy casualties, they captured two important hills, Walt and Boyd Ridges. Col. Joseph F. Hankins, the division Provost Marshal, was killed by a sniper in a cave above Dead Man's Curve on the west road; he was the highest ranking officer killed on Peleliu.

The next afternoon, Marines of L Company, 7th Marines climbing Hill 120 were caught in a crossfire. A platoon led by 2d Lt. James E. Dunn of Duluth, Minnesota, was wiped out. Bullets broke Dunn's hold on the cliffside, and he fell to his death. Capt. James V. "Jamo" Shanley tried to rescue the wounded; a mortar shell wounded him mortally. Second Lt. Harold J. Collis rushed out to aid him and was killed at his side. (Shanley, who had earned a Navy Cross on Cape Gloucester, was awarded his second posthumously.) Three hours after the 48 Marines had started to climb that ridge, 11 were left.

By the end of October 5, the 7th Marines were finished; the 1st Battalion had 100 men still able to fight and the 2d Battalion was down to 30 percent effective. The 5th Marines, descendants of the Marines of Belleau Wood, came down from the north to replace them.

Colonel Harris finally changed the Marines' style of assaulting the Umurbrogol. Although division headquarters objected and called for faster results, Harris insisted that his men advance deliberately, trying to save lives. It worked. Attacking the north side of the pocket, Harris' tired, under-strength 5th Regiment seized Wattie Ridge, Baldy Ridge, Hill 120 and finally Hill 140, which dominated the area. By October 11, the Marines held the high ground on the northern side of the Umurbrogol.

When the 5th Marines were relieved by the 321st Infantry

on the morning of October 15—one month after D-Day—1,150 Japanese still held an area of 400 yards by 500 yards. Except for some heavy fighting by the 5th Marines south of the pocket, where the enemy had reoccupied caves, the 1st Marine Division's offensive action on Peleliu was over. The Marines returned to Pavuvu. It looked a lot better now.

The 1st Division had 1,124 killed, 5,024 wounded and 117 missing—a total of 6,265 casualties. The 81st Infantry Division had 277 killed and 1,008 wounded on Peleliu. The Japanese had an estimated 10,200 killed and 302 taken prisoner. The Army took over the battle, supported by VMF-114 and VMF(N)-541, and methodically squeezed the pocket until organized resistance ceased on November 27. Peleliu had been a brutal and unnecessary battle. The Marines had led the way to a pointless victory at a dreadful cost.

Although Marines fought and died on Peleliu in support of the Philippine invasion, the only Marines to fight in the Philippines themselves were 1,500 men of the V Amphibious Corps Artillery commanded by Brig. Gen. Thomas E. Bourke and the fliers of the 1st Marine Aircraft Wing.

The artillerymen went to Leyte by a fluke. Back during the Marianas operation, they had exchanged places with Army artillery units; and the mix-up had never been straightened out. The Marine gunners landed north of Dulag on Leyte on October 23 (A-Day plus three) and supported the Army's advance. On December 6, when Japanese paratroopers jumped onto Buri airfield, Capt. Eugene S. Roane, Jr., organized the Marine defense there in a battle that lasted for five days. On December 13, the Marine artillerymen were pulled out of Leyte.

The arrival of the Marine fliers in the Philippines was the result of a frightening new development in the war: the kamikaze. The truth is that Marine aviation had been unable to perform its primary role: supporting the Marine Corps' amphibious assaults. There were two reasons for this: First, as the Central Pacific campaign advanced in giant steps beyond the range of land-based fighter planes, the Navy was reluctant to turn over escort aircraft carriers to the Marines. Secondly, the Marines failed to make a determined fight to get onto carriers for close support missions. The leaders of Marine aviation were more attracted to the glories of aerial combat than to the mundane work of supplying close air support to Marines on the ground. Said a respected historian of Marine aviation, "High-ranking Marine officers—aviators and nonaviators alike—showed a remarkable lack of foresight in failing to insist that their flyers be put on escort carriers at this time [1943]. . . . [T]he top Marine aviators . . . were too deeply interested in shooting enemy planes out of the wild blue yonder, so they lost sight of their primary mission."[86] In fact, in June 1943, the requirement that Marine pilots meet carrier qualifications was actually dropped—with Marine Corps agreement. No pilot could become an ace in close support, and no Marine won the Medal of Honor in the air after January 1944. Once in the vast Central Pacific where air support had to be carrier-based, the war left the Marine fliers behind.

One rear-area unit, VMF-422, met tragedy. Led by Maj. John S. MacLaughlin, Jr., 23 Corsairs left Tarawa on January 25, 1944, on a 700-mile flight to Funafuti. Only one pilot, Lt. John E. Hansen, made it. The rest hit bad weather and ran out of fuel. Twelve pilots landed in the sea and got into one-man life rafts surrounded by sharks. After two days, a destroyer picked them up. The flight lost 22 aircraft and six pilots.

By mid-1944, the Marine Corps had five air wings and 112,626 aviation personnel, including 10,457 pilots. Admiral King thought the whole program too large; in view of how Marine air was used, he was right. Commandant Vandegrift proposed a deal: one wing be dropped but Marine pilots be put onto escort carriers. King agreed if Admiral Nimitz concurred. So Vandegrift went out to sell Nimitz.

But it was the unexpected and terrifying appearance of the desperate Japanese kamikaze suicide planes at Leyte that brought Marine aviation back into the war. The kamikazes threatened the American aircraft carriers and applied enormous pressure on the Army's land-based fighters. Admiral Halsey suggested to General MacArthur that he bring up MAG-12 from the Solomons. As a result, Marines provided air support to Army ground troops, not to Marines.

For the most part, Army divisional and regimental commanders were exceedingly dubious about the value and safety of close air support. And they were especially wary of the Marine system, unlike Army and Navy doctrine, of managing close air support by direct radio communication between the attacking aircraft and ground liaison parties with the frontline troops.

On October 20, 1944, the first Marine flier in the Philippines was Maj. Gen. Ralph J. Mitchell, commanding general of the 1st Marine Aircraft Wing. When the Japanese Navy was destroyed as an offensive force in the great naval Battle of Leyte Gulf on October 23–26, planes from lost and damaged American carriers tried to land at the primitive Tacloban, Leyte, airfield. Mitchell, a pilot since 1921, grabbed a pair of signal flags and brought in the Navy planes himself.

On December 3, 66 Corsairs of MAG-12 and 12 Hellcats of VMF(N)-541 arrived at Tacloban to help stop the kamikazes and the flow of Japanese reinforcements into western Leyte. The Marines destroyed at least 22 Japanese ships and 67 aircraft, but they never flew the close-support missions they had trained for.

MacArthur next sailed to the Lingayen Gulf north of Manila; and on January 6 alone, kamikazes hit 16 ships of his invasion fleet. The Army landed unopposed on January 9; and two days later, Col. Clayton C. Jerome, commander of MAG-32, and two other Marines went ashore and laid out an airfield on a rice paddy near Mangaldan. It became headquarters for MAG-24 and -32; and by the end of January, 3,472 Marines and 174 Douglas Dauntless dive bombers were operating there.

The Marine fliers experienced their most dramatic Philippine adventure when MacArthur ordered the 1st Cavalry Division to dash down to Manila, free the American prisoners interned in the Santo Tomás University and seize the Malacanan Palace. Marine Capt. Francis R. B. "Frisco" Godolphin visited 1st Cavalry headquarters and found the division G-2, Lt. Col. Robert F. Goheen, who had been a student of his at Princeton University. With a bit of old-school-tie cooperation, they arranged for MAG-24 and -32 to support the race to Manila. Starting at dawn on February 1, Marine air liaison parties accompanied the soldiers; and Marines flew a nine-plane dawn to dusk screen for the division. Marine dive bombers scouted and bombed ahead of the column, helped it skirt delaying battles, bombed roadblocks and rode shotgun on its exposed left flank. The 1st Cavalry sped into Manila on the evening of February 3 and freed 3,700 Santo Tomás internees. It was a daring feat, and the division's commanding general praised the Marine fliers close support; as he said, "They will try anything once."[87]

Marines also flew close support missions for guerrilla forces in the Philippines. Late in February, for example, six Marines were put ashore 50 miles behind enemy lines in northwestern Luzon. They called in Marine planes to support the attack of Col. Russell W. Volckmann's guerrillas on the port of San Fernando. They used Nicaragua-style cloth panels to mark the friendly front lines. Army P-51 Mustangs and Marine Corsairs dropped fragmentation bombs 200 yards in front of the guerrillas. When the enemy rallied, five Marine dive bombers strafed and bombed the Japanese and drove them from the ridge above the city.

Having won the enthusiastic support of the 1st Cavalry Division, the Marines convinced the commander of the 6th Infantry Division to use them to dive-bomb the heavily defended Japanese Shimbu line in the mountains northeast of Manila. They also blasted Nichols Field, Corregidor and the hulks of ships that provided the enemy cover in Manila harbor. In April, when heavy rains washed out the rice paddy field at Mangaldan, MAG-24 and -32 moved south to Clark Field. On Luzon, the two air groups flew 8,842 combat missions.

Not satisfied with having gained a strategic base on Leyte and Luzon, MacArthur insisted on freeing all the bypassed Philippine Islands. MAG-12, -14 and -32 gave direct support to the 41st Infantry Division taking the Zamboanga Peninsula on the large southern island of Mindanao. Even before the invasion, 16 Marine Corsairs flew from a guerrilla-controlled grass airstrip on the enemy-held island. Later, the Marines established a field at San Roque, naming it for Lt. Col. Paul Moret. From Moret Field, Marines flew direct support missions for approximately 50 landings on Panay, Cebu, Negros, Mindanao and the islands of the Sulu Archipelago. In April, MAG-24 established a field at Malabang and named it for Capt. John A. Titcomb, who had been killed on Luzon.

In the Philippines, Marine aviation lost 100 men killed in action, 127 wounded and 50 dead from accidents and other causes. Marine fliers got their chance at last to prove the value of their concept of close air support. But to fly support missions for Marines, they would still have to win a place on carriers.

This began to happen when at Pearl Harbor in August 1944 Commandant Vandegrift and Admiral Nimitz agreed that Marine squadrons would be assigned to escort carriers for close support missions, and Aircraft, FMF Pacific was established with 1,620 Marine planes of all types. The following month, the process accelerated when Vandegrift exiled the old-timer Maj. Gen. Ross E. Rowell to Lima, Peru, to help train the Peruvian air force and gave Maj. Gen. Francis P. Mulcahy the top Marine aviation job in the Pacific.

On October 21, 1944, the day after MacArthur landed on Leyte, Marine Carrier Groups, Aircraft, FMF Pacific became a tactical command under Col. Albert D. Cooley. By May 1945, Marines were aboard four escort carriers, each with 18 fighter planes and 12 torpedo bombers. The long-range plan was for Marines to have eight escort carriers in time for the invasion of Japan. But in the meanwhile, the invasion of Iwo Jima was covered almost entirely by Navy pilots.

Before the Marines got their own escort carriers, eight Marine fighter squadrons flew from four large attack carriers during the first six months of 1945. Fifty-four Marine pilots of VMF-124 and -213 went aboard *Essex* and flew combat strikes against Okinawa, Tokyo and Southeast Asian airfields at Cam Ranh Bay and Bien Hoa and Tan Son Nhut at Saigon. On January 12, 500 American carrier planes, including a few Marines, shot up Saigon and sunk 14 warships and 33 merchant ships. Marine Lt. Joseph O. Lynch was one of four pilots shot down and saved by the French; pilots captured by the Japanese were shot.

At Iwo Jima, the Navy's attack carriers launched prelanding strikes by 600 planes. Among them were 24 Marine Corsairs commanded by Lt. Col. William A. Millington of VMF-124. Marines flew some close support missions there from the large carriers until February 22, when the job was turned over to the Navy's escort carrier planes and Army P-51s. Marine close air support for Marines had not yet come into its own.

12
Iwo Jima—"The Toughest Yet"

Lt. Gen. Tadamichi Kuribayashi was fifty-four years old, five feet nine, over 200 pounds and had a pot belly. As a young man, he had been for two years a military attaché in the United States and he respected American power. This smart, tough cavalryman, former commander of the Emperor's Imperial Guards, would transform the invasion of Iwo Jima into the costliest battle in Marine Corps history.

The Americans decided to assault Iwo Jima because it was halfway between the Marianas and Tokyo—about 670 miles from each. It could provide an emergency landing field for B-29s fire-bombing Tokyo and a base for shorter-range fighters escorting the giant Superfortresses. Iwo Jima was a sulfurous flyspeck (its name means Sulfur Island), volcanic, ugly, waterless, stinking—but strategic.

Three divisions of Marines (controversially minus one regiment) would try to seize it. This time, there would be more Marine casualties than Japanese. Of the 80 Marines who received the Medal of Honor in World War II, 22 earned it here.

Lt. Gen. Kuribayashi appreciated Iwo Jima's strategic value. The island was actually part of the Prefecture of Tokyo; and he wrote his son, "this island is the gateway to Japan."[88] He had 23,000 well-armed troops, 361 artillery pieces and 22 tanks. (The tanks were commanded by Lt. Col. Takeichi Nishi, who had won an equestrian jumping gold medal riding Uranus in the 1932 Olympic Games at Los Angeles.) Kuribayashi shipped out the traditionalist officers who insisted on meeting the Americans flamboyantly on the beaches. He went underground and "fortified Iwo to near perfection."[89] He would make the American Marines come to him and buy every rocky inch with blood. "Iwo was in effect all beachhead. It was an amphibious assault that lasted for thirty-six days."[90]

Kuribayashi knew that he was doomed. The Japanese Navy had been shattered; its air power crushed. Japan was cut off from the raw materials and oil of Southeast Asia (which had been the original reason for the war). American fleets and planes roamed almost at will; Tokyo itself was being bombed; the war was rushing to its climax. Kuribayashi would have to fight without hope of reinforcement or salvation.

Coming against him from Saipan was a tremendous force of Americans: 800 ships and 220,000 men. B-24s out of the Marianas struck Iwo Jima for 74 consecutive days before the invasion. But Intelligence saw that the Japanese defense lines, blockhouses and pillboxes were growing stronger. Lt. Gen. Holland Smith, present rather superfluously in his last combat assignment as Commanding General, Expeditionary Troops, expected that one in four of the 60,000 assault troops would be killed or wounded.

In a brutal, deadly way, Iwo Jima was what the Marine Corps was all about: young men—Tony Stein, John Basilone, Doug Jacobson, Jack Lummus—assaulting a defended objective from the sea and then advancing in the face of death and disfigurement, exhausted beyond reason, seeing their leaders and buddies dying around them, but moving forward. Like it or not, a lot of American history converged on this desolate little island.

Iwo Jima was only five miles long, porkchop-shaped with the thick end, two and a half miles wide, toward the north. It smelled like rotten eggs. Nothing lived there but wading birds and the waiting Japanese. At the southern end was the steep cone of the extinct 550-foot volcano, Mount Suribachi. In the center was a flat area where the Japanese had two airfields. Toward the north the land rose to the Motoyama Plateau, level enough in the middle, but cut hideously by gorges and ravines plunging down to both coasts. At the very north was a morass of cliffs and ridges that the defenders had perforated with caves, beautifully camouflaged gun emplacements and 11 miles of tunnels. Japanese like Kuribayashi had learned.

The invasion started with arguments and bitterness. The Marines wanted the Navy to produce ten days of pre-invasion bombardment; they got three. The Navy said it had to conserve ammunition for the forthcoming invasion of Okinawa. The Marines accused the Navy of sending carrier Task Force 58 scooting off to bomb Japan on February 16–17, 1945, because of all the attention the Army's B-29s were winning, when it should have stayed and saved Marine lives at Iwo Jima. (TF 58 now included eight Marine air squadrons—144 Corsairs and 216 Marine pilots.) Admiral Spruance insisted the carrier attacks would prevent Japan-based aircraft from interfering with the Iwo Jima landing. The arguments were complex; the fact was simple: The Marines assaulted Iwo Jima with less than optimal gunfire preparation.

On D-Day minus two, the Japanese made a mistake. Contrary to orders, artillery opened up on 12 LCI gunboats covering the UDT reconnaissance of Iwo Jima, hitting all the boats but exposing the hidden batteries to naval gunfire. The Navy took full advantage of this expensive break.

Monday morning, February 19, was lovely: cool, clear, calm. The Marines ate the now traditional D-Day steak-and-eggs breakfast and went to work. In 482 amtracs, behind a heavy naval bombardment and a final rolling barrage, they roared toward Iwo Jima's ugly southeastern beaches to meet a determined, highly disciplined enemy. They landed on loose black gravel-like volcanic ash in which men sank to their ankles and vehicles were immobilized.

The 4th and 5th Marine Divisions made the initial assault with four regiments; the two from the 5th Division on the left (south); the 4th Division's two on the right. At the extreme south, ex-Raider Col. Harry B. "The Horse" Liversedge's 28th Marines were to take Suribachi and cross the island's narrow neck. On Liversedge's right, Col. Thomas A. Wornham's 27th Marines headed for Airfield No. 1. Maj. Gen. Keller E. Rockey's 5th Division had not yet been in battle as a unit, but its ranks included many combat veterans. Rockey himself had won the Navy Cross at Belleau Wood.

The experienced 4th Division was commanded by Maj. Gen. Clifton B. Cates, who had commanded the 1st Marines on Guadalcanal. Its two assault regiments were Col. Walter W. Wensinger's 23rd and Col. John R. Lanigan's 25th. Lanigan's Marines had to seize the quarry at the far right or north end of the invasion beaches.

In reserve were Col. Walter I. Jordan's 24th Marines and Col. Chester B. Graham's 26th Marines, plus the veteran 3rd Marine Division commanded by Maj. Gen. Graves B. Erskine. At forty-seven, Erskine was one of the youngest generals in the Corps and one of the toughest. His 3rd Division would not fight on D-Day but would make up for it later.

The plan of Maj. Gen. Harry Schmidt, in command of the V Amphibious Corps, was simple. Take the airfields as fast as possible; grab Suribachi to the south, and then combine all forces and drive north. The operation was scheduled for 14 days. But it would consume a month of fighting and 5,931 Marines killed and 17,372 wounded—one Marine casualty for each Japanese on the island. Kuribayashi knew his business.

When the amtracs were 400 yards from the beaches, 24 Marine Corsairs and 24 Navy Hellcats led by Lt. Col. William A. Millington of VMF-124, flying off *Essex*, strafed the beaches. But the enemy waited below ground.

The first Marines hit the beach at 8:59 A.M. and faced a sloping terrace pushed eight to 15 feet high by the sea and wind. The rise blocked their fields of fire. Men and vehicles floundered in the volcanic ash. Foxholes filled up as soon as they were dug. Within 15 minutes, the Marines started receiving heavy mortar fire, then machine-gun and rifle fire from an invisible enemy. Now, the landing beaches were ablaze. Unlike Tarawa (or Omaha Beach), there was not even a seawall to hide behind.

All eight assault battalions were ashore in 90 minutes. At 10 A.M., the first 16 tanks landed; three immediately struck mines. The beaches were littered with the mangled and the dead. "They had died as amphibious creatures die: not far inland, not far from the sea."[91]

Cpl. Tony Stein of Dayton, Ohio, and A Company, 28th Marines, had improvised a hand-held machine gun from a wrecked Navy fighter's gun and in those early moments attacked pillbox after pillbox, killing 20 Japanese. Eight times under intense fire, he struggled barefoot to the beach for more ammunition. Each time, he dragged back a wounded Marine. The twenty-four-year-old veteran of Guadalcanal and Bougainville received the Medal of Honor.

The commander of B Company, 28th Marines, Capt. Dwayne E. Mears, armed only with a pistol, attacked pillboxes until he was killed; and by 10:35, Lt. Frank J. Wright and four men of B Company's 1st Platoon had crossed the 700 yards of the island's narrow southern neck. Half an hour later, Lt. Wesley C. Bates and six men of the 2d Platoon joined them. The 28th's 1st Battalion took heavy casualties, and Colonel Liversedge brought up his 3rd Battalion from reserve. At 3:45, the 2d and 3rd Battalions tried futilely to attack Mount Suribachi against gun fire pouring down from the "Hot Rock." They needed armor, but most of the tanks could not get off the beach. At 5 P.M., the 2d Battalion attacked the mountain alone, advanced 150 yards and then had to fall back.

To the right of the hard-hit 28th, the 27th Marines reached the southern end of Airfield No. 1. Gunnery Sgt. John Basilone, who had been the first enlisted Marine to earn the Medal of Honor on Guadalcanal and had turned down a commission, led his machine-gun platoon past the end of the airfield and raced toward the island's west coast. He climbed a blockhouse and destroyed it with grenades and demolitions and then under fire guided a tank through a minefield. About 10:30, a mortar shell mortally wounded Basilone and four of his men. This time, they gave "Manila John" a Navy Cross posthumously.

By mid-afternoon, the 27th had seized the cliffs overlooking the west coast; and the 26th Marines landed to reinforce them. The Negro drivers of the Army's 471st Amphibian Truck Company brought the 13th Marines' guns ashore, and they started adding artillery support.

Further north, the 23rd Marines were stopped within 250 yards of the water with many casualties on the congested beach. Capt. John J. Kalen, commander of A Company, bled to death there. First Lt. William E. Worsham took command, tried to lead an end run around a strongpoint and was killed. The mortar platoon leader, 1st Lt. Frank S. Doyoe, Jr., took over and was hit in the left shoulder. First Lt. Arthur W. Zimmerman now led the men toward the airfield and brought up a tank that smashed a huge blockhouse. He was A Company's fourth commander.

In the first wave, Sgt. Darrell S. Cole of Flat River, Missouri, led his machine-gun section of B Company up the sloping beach toward Airfield No. 1 and, under fire, destroyed two positions with grenades and a third with his machine gun. His unit was pinned down by grenades and knee mortars. Cole

594

advanced, hurled his last grenade at a pillbox, went back for more and wiped out the strongpoint before a grenade killed him. He was awarded the Medal of Honor.

The situation on the beach became desperate as the surf rose and the wounded began piling up. By nightfall, the 23rd had fought to the edge of the airfield. Two battalions of the 24th Marines were landed to stiffen the center of the beachhead.

At the extreme north, Colonel Lanigan's 25th Marines landed below a strongly fortified cliff. The right flank battalion, the 3rd, led by Lt. Col. Justice M. Chambers, veteran of Tulagi and Saipan, took a terrible beating and lost many of its officers trying to capture Quarry Ridge. The 2d Battalion headed for the high ground above the quarry, from which the Japanese were firing on the beaches. After an eight-hour battle, the two battalions captured the heights; but the 3rd Battalion had only about 150 men left. The 1st Battalion, 24th Marines had to replace them.

D-Day was bloody and frustrating. Few Marines ever saw a live Japanese; not a single prisoner was taken. By the day's end, 30,000 Marines were ashore and Suribachi was isolated; but the first-day objectives had nowhere been reached. Although the confusion on the beachhead made exact casualty figures impossible to calculate, an estimated 548 Marines had been killed and 1,775 wounded.

The Marines dug in expecting the customary *banzai* counterattack. But if they had not absorbed the significance of the defense of Saipan, Biak and Peleliu, Kuribayashi had. All night, the Japanese rained artillery and mortar shells on the crowded, chaotic beachhead, content to kill more Marines at little cost to themselves.

On the second day, the enemy continued to blast the beachhead from the high ground to the north. Pfc. Jacklyn H. Lucas of Plymouth, North Carolina, and three other Marines of C Company, 26th Marines were ambushed in a ravine. Two grenades landed among them. Lucas, hurling himself over the other men, fell on one grenade and pulled the second under him. He absorbed the explosions with his body. Only seventeen years and six days old, Lucas was the youngest Marine ever awarded the Medal of Honor.

To the south, the gray sides of Suribachi held 1,600 Japanese, dug into well-concealed pillboxes, bunkers, caves and spider holes. That morning in a light rain, the 2d and 3rd Battalions of the 28th Marines again plunged toward the base of the volcano. Each strongpoint had to be attacked with flame-throwers followed by Marines with grenades and demolitions. At nightfall, they had advanced some 200 yards and closed off 40 caves.

By noon on Wednesday, the 1st and 3rd Battalions reached the base of Suribachi. Tony Stein was wounded in the shoulder by shrapnel and sent to the beach; he would be back. Along the east coast, the 2d Battalion ran into fierce mortar fire; but the survivors kept moving into the face of death. Pfc. Donald J. Ruhl, twenty-one, of Columbus, Montana, fought aggressively for two days and then smothered a grenade with his body to save the life of Sgt. Henry O. Hansen of Somerville, Massachusetts. By evening, the 28th Marines formed a semicircle around Suribachi. A cold rain began to fall. Fifty kamikazes hit the American invasion fleet, badly damaged the carrier *Saratoga* and sank the escort carrier *Bismarck Sea.*

On Thursday, Suribachi was surrounded. The rain turned the ground into mush and clogged the Marines' weapons. Hundreds of Japanese still hid in the caves on the mountain-sides. On Friday, February 23, a four-man patrol led by Sgt. Sherman B. Watson of the 2d Battalion scaled the volcano; they found machine guns but no Japanese. Two other patrols scouted the slopes, but none drew enemy fire.

First Lt. Harold G. Schrier, a tall, slim, ex-Raider, was sent with 40 men from E Company to secure the crest. The battalion commander, Lt. Col. Chandler W. Johnson, gave Schrier a small American flag that the battalion adjutant, 2d Lt. G. Greeley Wells, had brought ashore in his map case. The route was steep, and sometimes the men had to climb on their hands and knees. In half an hour, they reached the crater's rim; the caves inside were silent. The Marines found a 20-foot piece of pipe, lashed the flag to it and thrust the end of the pipe into the soft ground near the north rim. It was 10:20 A.M. As the flag went up, Marines below shouted and the bells and whistles of the ships of the fleet sounded out. At the base of Suribachi, Secretary of the Navy James V. Forrestal watched the flag go up and said to Lt. Gen. Smith: "Holland, the raising of that flag on Suribachi means a Marine Corps for the next 500 years."[92]

Sgt. Louis R. Lowery photographed the flag-raising for *Leatherneck* magazine. Two Japanese charged out of a cave, and BAR-man Pfc. James A. Robeson shot one. Before the other was killed, he threw a grenade. Lowery leapt over the crater's rim and slid 50 feet down the mountain; his camera was smashed but his negatives were safe.

Six men raised that first flag: 1st Lt. Schrier; Platoon Sgt. Ernest I. Thomas, Jr.; Sergeant Hansen (whose life Pfc. Ruhl had saved); Cpl. Charles W. Lindberg; Pfc. James R. Michels, and Pvt. Louis Charlo, a Crow Indian. Of these six, Hansen, Thomas and Charlo would be killed on Iwo Jima—Thomas on March 3, his twentieth birthday—and Lindberg and Michels would be wounded. Only Schrier got through Iwo Jima safely.

Lt. Col. Johnson figured someone would grab that historic flag; he wanted it saved. So he had 2d Lt. Wells get a larger one from *LST 779*. As it was raised on top of Suribachi, Associated Press photographer Joe Rosenthal, who was on his fourth invasion with the Marines, made the picture that became the most famous war photograph ever taken and was later reproduced as a postage stamp and as a giant statue at Arlington National Cemetery.

The men in Rosenthal's photograph were by happenstance a cross section of the nation: left to right, Pfc. Ira H. Hayes of Bapchule, Arizona; Pfc. Franklin R. Sousely of Flemingsburg, Kentucky; Sgt. Michael Strank of Conemaugh, Pennsylvania; Pharmacist's Mate Second Class John H. Bradley of Appleton, Wisconsin; Pfc. Rene A. Gagnon of Manchester, New Hampshire, and Cpl. Harlon H. Block of Weslaco, Texas. (Sousely, Strank and Block were all to die in action on Iwo Jima.)

On Suribachi, the 28th Marines and the 5th Engineer Battalion set about destroying 165 concrete pillboxes and sealing 200 caves. The 28th Marines had 115 killed and 375 wounded, in addition to the 385 casualties it suffered on D-Day itself.

Meanwhile, seven badly hurt battalions were moving north against Lt. Gen. Kuribayashi's main force. Guns on the high ground dominated the Marines, who fought through the rough crazy-quilt terrain taking heavy casualties. By the end of Tuesday, the Marines controlled Airfield No. 1 and nearly one third of the island.

On Wednesday, the 3rd Division's 21st Marines, veterans of

Bougainville and Guam, came ashore to help take Airfield No. 2. In the first 58 hours, the landing force had 4,500 casualties. There were uncountable acts of individual heroism. Northeast of Airfield No. 1, Sgt. Ross F. Gray of A Company, 25th Marines crawled forward alone with a satchel charge. Three riflemen covered him. He hurled the explosives, ran back, got another charge and blasted another emplacement. The Marine from Marvel Valley, Alabama, singlehandedly killed more than 25 Japanese, destroyed six positions and opened the path for his men. Nearby, the commander of G Company, 24th Marines, Capt. Joseph J. McCarthy, a big ex-Chicago fireman and Silver Star winner on Saipan, led a squad across open ground under fire, blasted a pillbox with grenades, killed two Japanese, charged and destroyed another pillbox and then called to his company which swarmed over the ridge in front of the airfield. Both Gray and McCarthy received the Medal of Honor.

The nights were filled with mortar and artillery fire, local counterattacks and repeated attempts to infiltrate the the Marine lines. By Thursday, the sleepless Marines were exhausted, living on K rations and water in the cold, heavy rain. The 26th Marines were severely mauled and had to pull back. The 21st Marines took a pounding. A machine-gun bullet entered Lt. Col. Chambers' collarbone and lung; awarded the Medal of Honor, he was the third battalion commander of the 25th Marines to fall in three days.

Friday and Saturday, the Marines could make little progress. Although 2,000 Seabees started repairing Airfield No. 1, the second field further north was ringed with hundreds of pillboxes; and enemy artillery was sited to fire straight down the open ground of the runways. Here was the Japanese main defense line. Cpl. Hershel W. Williams of Quiet Dell, West Virginia, received the Medal of Honor for destroying a series of pillboxes with his flamethrower in four hours of intense battle. But there were always more strongpoints. The Americans massed all possible artillery, tanks and naval gunfire on the Japanese positions. It did not seem to make a dent.

Eventually, a dozen tanks reached the fringes of Airfield No. 2; and in the center, Col. Hartnoll J. Withers' 21st Marines attacked the field. K Company's commander, Capt. Rodney L. Heinze, was killed on the edge of the runway. On his right, I

Company's commander, Capt. Clayton S. Rockmore, took a bullet in the throat and was killed. Quickly, lieutenants were hit and sergeants took over the companies. Then, 1st Lt. Raoul J. Archambault, who had been decorated on both Bougainville and Guam, rallied the remaining men of the two companies. They knew the tall, lean Archambault and followed him in a wild charge across the runways. The first dozen Marines onto the ridge beyond the airfield were thrown back; Lt. Dominick J. Grossi led them right back up again and this time they held. They fought the Japanese in ankle-deep sand with rifle butts, bayonets, knives. The survivors opened a gap in the main enemy line.

On the right of the 21st Marines, the 24th had an equally tough fight. They ran into a major Japanese defense point on a ridge called Charlie-Dog. The Japanese opened a mortar barrage and drove them off the ridge. Lt. Col. Alexander A. Vandegrift, Jr., the commander of the 3rd Battalion, was wounded in both legs. By now, after six days of battle, the Marines had 7,758 casualties.

As the second phase of the battle for Iwo Jima opened against the main Japanese defenses on the northern Motoyama Plateau, the Marine commanders were under pressure to finish the struggle quickly. The Pacific Fleet had to be freed for the invasion of Okinawa only five weeks in the future.

On Saturday, the 9th Marines came ashore; only the 3rd Marines remained in reserve. Maj. Gen. Schmidt organized a three-division front. In the center, the 9th and 21st Marines of Erskine's 3rd Division entered an inferno of bunkers and caves and fissures of evil-smelling sulfur fumes. The 5th Division advanced along the west coast on the left, fighting over one ridge after another. On the right, the 4th Division faced "the most extensive and powerful defenses on the island"[93]: Hill 382, the highest point on northern Iwo Jima and bristling with artillery, antitank guns and machine guns; Turkey Knob, a small knoll that contained a vast Japanese communications center of reinforced concrete; and a depression known as the Amphitheater. The Marines called the complex the Meat Grinder.

The main effort had to be right up the middle. Col. Howard N. Kenyon's fresh 9th Marines pounded away at the Japanese center. In the first two days, 20 of the tanks supporting them were knocked out. Against heavy enemy fire, the 9th Marines slowly overwhelmed Hills Peter and Oboe. Pvt. Wilson D. Watson, twenty-four, of Tuscumbia, Alabama, led his squad forward with a BAR and grenades. On Tuesday morning, February 27, he held the crest of a hill alone for 15 minutes and, firing from the hip, killed 60 Japanese. He was not scratched.[94]

By the end of that day (D plus eight), the 3rd Division had massed more artillery, broken out on the Motoyama Plateau and cut through the main line of resistance. But at 3 A.M. on March 4, Lt. Gen. Kuribayashi counterattacked; and the 9th Marines took severe casualties. The 21st Marines relieved the 9th and reached the high ground overlooking unfinished Airfield No. 3.

Killed with the 21st was Sgt. Reid Carlos Chamberlain who had fought with the old 4th Marines on Bataan and Corregidor and, although wounded, had escaped and joined the guerrillas on Mindanao. Commissioned in the U.S. Army, he eventually returned to the States by submarine and plane and received the Distinguished Service Cross. But he resigned his Army commission and rejoined the Marines as a corporal. While running messages to the front lines north of Iwo Jima's Airfield No. 2, Chamberlain was shot in the head.

After blasting through the center of the main Japanese line with flamethrowers and bazookas, the 3rd Division had to wait for the divisions on both sides to catch up. The 5th Division pushing up the west coast ran into some of the heaviest fighting on Iwo Jima. On February 28, the 27th Marines assaulted Hill 362A in hand-to-hand fighting. The next day, the 28th Marines, the men who had conquered Suribachi, took over the attack. A Company went around the right side of the hill and came under heavy fire. Cpl. Tony Stein, back in action, led 20 men to clear the ridge. Only seven returned; Stein was among the dead. On this day Sergeant Hansen, Sergeant Strank and Corporal Block were all killed in front of Hill 362A. But by the day's end, the 28th Marines had occupied the deadly height. Liversedge was awarded his second Navy Cross.

Now the regiment attacked Nishi Ridge, which extended from the plateau almost to the sea. It took until March 3 to capture the ridge, and for the 26th Marines, fighting through deep gorges, to battle to the top of Hill 362B. On March 3 alone, the 26th Marines took 281 casualties. Five Marines of the 5th

Division won the Medal of Honor that day. One of them was Sgt. William G. Harrell of Rio Grande City, Texas, and A Company, 28th Marines. He battled a night attack until a grenade tore off his left hand. He continued to fight and pushed away another grenade, which exploded, killing his attacker and severing Harrell's right hand. As the 5th Division grew depleted by the fierce struggle, headquarters and weapons company men had to fill in on the line.

On the east side of the American offensive north of Quarry Ridge, the 4th Division ground into the Meat Grinder. Progress was terribly slow. On February 26 and 27, the 23rd Marines battled up Hill 382. The 1st Battalion hit the reverse slope; and Sgt. Fritz G. Truan, a famous rodeo cowboy leading A Company's assault platoon, was killed. The 3rd Battalion was reduced to company strength. Nineteen-year-old Pfc. Douglas T. Jacobson of Port Washington, New York, with the 3rd Battalion, grabbed a bazooka and killed the crew of a 20mm gun; then he destroyed two machine-gun positions, a tank, two pillboxes and a blockhouse. Jacobson kept going on his one-man attack and killed 75 Japanese and captured 16 positions on Hill 382. Marines compared him to Sergeant York in World War I. He was awarded the Medal of Honor. (After the war, Doug Jacobson accompanied Tony Stein's body home to Dayton, Ohio, for burial. Jacobson stayed in the Corps, served in North China and retired as a major.)

The 3rd Battalion fought at the hilltop hand-to-hand and was beaten off. The 25th Marines tried to envelop Turkey Knob and failed. By March 1, the 24th Marines had to replace the remnant of the 23rd, and Schmidt and Erskine asked for the 3rd Marines, who were still in transports off Iwo Jima, to be brought to battle. Vice Adm. Turner turned them down on the grounds that there were enough Marines ashore. The argument over that decision grew long and heated. The V Amphibious Corps operations officer (who was to command the Marine Brigade in Korea) said the decision was wrong and increased casualties.

March 2 was a day of desperate fighting. E Company of the 24th Marines tried to outflank Hill 382 from the right; all its officers except 2d Lt. Richard Reich were killed or seriously wounded; but joined by F Company, it finally took the hill. The Japanese still fought from pillboxes and caves.

601

There was no letup. The 24th Marines drove ahead north and east of Hill 382; and the 25th Marines kept beating against Turkey Knob, where the Japanese destroyed them with mortar and rocket fire. Exhausted squads and fire teams attacked enemy strongpoints. Most of the Marines' experienced leaders had been wiped out; less well trained individual replacements were filling the assault ranks and morale was plummeting. On March 3, the 23rd Marines relieved the 25th Marines and attacked the blockhouse on Turkey Knob with flamethrowers and demolition teams. But at day's end the enemy still held it. The 4th Division was now down to 50 percent of combat strength.

The toll had been so gruesomely severe that Maj. Gen. Schmidt had to declare Monday, March 5—two weeks after D-Day—a day of rest, regroupment and replacement. There would be no attacks.

On the next day, the whole brutal process started again with a tremendous artillery barrage that had little effect. Maj. Gen. Erskine tried a new tactic to take Hill 362C. At 5 A.M. on March 7, the 21st Marines and the 3rd Battalion, 9th Marines, jumped off in the dark to surprise the enemy. (In Europe on this day, American GIs seized the Remagen bridge over the Rhine River.) Moving silently through a light rain, the Marines caught the Japanese asleep. But with daylight, they discovered that they had captured the wrong hill. Their real objective was still 250 yards in front of them, and surprise had been lost. Now, in vicious battle, trapped in a labyrinth of crags, E and F Companies were all but annihilated; of E Company seven men survived, of F Company, five. The 3rd Battalion, 9th Marines finally took Hill 362C, and the Marines at last held much of the high ground on the Motoyama Plateau.

Trying to link up with the 3rd Battalion that afternoon, B Company, 9th Marines was cut off. Second Lt. John H. Leims of Chicago crawled out 400 yards across fire-swept terrain and brought his men back. After dark, he crawled out alone twice more under machine-gun fire and carried in wounded Marines.[95]

The 9th and 21st Regiments split Iwo Jima and reached the northeastern coast on March 9. But Lt. Gen. Kuribayashi still held a square mile of the island; he would defend it to the death.

The 5th Division on the right also had trouble making forward progress when the attack began again on March 6. The next day, H Company of the 26th Marines took a 30-foot knoll just north of Nishi Village. Suddenly, the entire hill exploded. The Japanese had blown up their own command post and caused 43 Marine casualties.

As the 27th Marines approached the sea, the Japanese defended every crevice. On March 8, tall, slim 1st Lt. Jack Lummus, of Ennis, Texas, an All-America football end from Baylor University who had signed with the New York Giants, led E Company's assault on a final jumble of rocks. Knocked down by a grenade explosion, he rose and under fire rushed a gun emplacement. A second grenade shattered his shoulder; he attacked a second pillbox and killed all its occupants. Lummus called to his platoon to follow him, and he wiped out a third position. A land mine blew off both his legs, but he still yelled to his men to attack, and they plunged in a wild charge to the ridge above the sea. Lummus died later that day and was awarded the Medal of Honor.

Lt. Gen. Kuribayashi was now holed up in a pocket on a long ridgeline above a deep gorge near Kitano Point, the island's northern tip. By March 9, the 5th Division was battling in sight of the sea toward that ridge over some of the worst ground on Iwo Jima. Progress was measured in feet, not yards. That day, the commander of the 1st Battalion, 27th Marines, Lt. Col. Justin G. Duryea, and the commander of the 2d Battalion, Maj. John W. A. Antonelli, were both wounded when Duryea's runner stepped on the detonater of a 6-inch naval shell buried in the ground. The explosion tore off Duryea's left arm at the elbow and smashed his left knee. Antonelli's eyes were damaged and his eardrum broken, but he walked out of the division hospital and returned to his battalion.

On the eastern side of the renewed offensive, the 4th Division bypassed Turkey Knob and the Amphitheater and worked an anvil-and-hammer tactic with the enemy in between; the 23rd and 24th Marines were the hammer while the tank-supported 25th Marines to the south served as the defensive anvil. By dark on March 8, the division was down to 40 percent combat efficiency and had lost many experienced officers and noncoms. Then at 11 P.M., some thousand Japanese Navy personnel, cut off from Kuribayashi's control, counterattacked the junction of the 23rd and 24th Marines in Iwo Jima's only

603

banzai attack. The fighting went on all night; at daybreak, 800 Japanese bodies were found. The night's attack cost the Marines 90 killed and 257 wounded, but it eliminated most of the enemy force holding the eastern part of the island.

On March 9, more than 300 B-29s from the Marianas dumped 1,665 tons of fire bombs on wind-swept Tokyo. This most destructive bombing mission of the war destroyed 16 square miles of the Japanese capital and killed nearly 84,000 people.

On March 10, the 23rd Marines gained 700 yards, "an enormous amount of ground . . . by Iwo standards";[96] and patrols reached the east coast near Tachiiwa Point. The 25th Marines completely surrounded Turkey Knob. Japanese resistance on eastern Iwo Jima was virtually finished.

Now, the job was to clean up fiercely defended pockets that no longer had any central command direction. The Japanese stayed in their pillboxes and caves and made the Marines pay. There were few Marines left who had landed on D-Day; and the replacements, although willing, were new to battle and often felt they were working and fighting with strangers. By March 16, the 3rd Division at terrific cost cleaned up the strongpoint known as Cushman's Pocket and reached Kitano Point.

The 5th Division still faced Lt. Gen. Kuribayashi's final stronghold in the gorge at the northwestern end of the island. Here, artillery was useless. Each Japanese had to be killed at close range by flamethrowing tanks and riflemen. Pvt. Franklin E. Sigler of Glen Ridge, New Jersey, took over his rifle squad and led it against a gun position that had held up his company for days. He wiped out the gun's crew with grenades and in a one-man assault continued the attack. Although severely wounded, he directed fire on the Japanese caves and carried three wounded squad members to safety. He received the Medal of Honor.

Although Iwo Jima was officially declared secured at 6 P.M. on March 16, the next day (D plus 26) the Marines fought in the 700-yard-long gorge that had many rock outcroppings and all its approaches covered by well-hidden machine-gun and rifle fire. On March 21, the Marines in the gorge finally destroyed the enemy command post with four tons of explosives. But Lt. Gen. Kuribayashi had already moved out to another cave nearer the sea. By March 24, the enemy pocket was squeezed into an area

50 by 50 yards. Then, the exhausted Marines sealed the remaining caves. The general's body was never found.

Still, on March 26, some 200 Japanese on the western coast attacked Marine and Army units and an Army field hospital. Seabees, Army Air Corps and medical personnel and the Negro troops of the Corps Shore Party, who "conducted themselves with marked coolness and courage,"[97] broke the enemy attack. But it had killed 53 Americans and wounded 119. Pvt. James M. Whitlock and Pvt. James Davis of the all-Negro 26th Depot Company won the Bronze Star. And 1st Lt. Harry L. Martin of Bucyrus, Ohio, who rallied his men of the 5th Pioneer Battalion and killed four Japanese before he died, was the last Marine to earn the Medal of Honor on Iwo Jima.

As Admiral Nimitz said after the battle was won, "Among the Americans who served on Iwo Island uncommon valor was a common virtue."[98]

In April and May, 1,600 more Japanese were killed on the island.

The total of Marine casualties on Iwo Jima was 25,851. (Navy doctors and corpsmen suffered 738 dead and wounded with the Marines.) The enormous number of casualties was severely criticized back home.

Iwo Jima swiftly began serving the purpose for which so many had been sacrificed. The Seabees changed the face of the island; and before the end of the war, 2,500 Superfortresses made emergency landings on Iwo Jima. Army fighter planes started arriving on March 6, and VMTB-242 arrived from Tinian on March 9. By that summer, Japanese air power was so reduced that B-29s did not need fighter escorts; but still, 1,191 escort sorties and 3,081 strikes against targets in Japan were flown from Iwo Jima.

While the battle for Iwo Jima was still going on, Secretary Forrestal spoke of his "tremendous admiration and reverence for the guy who walks up the beaches and takes enemy positions with a rifle and grenades or his bare hands."[99] As other analysts put it: "to a greater degree than was necessary, taking Iwo Jima was like throwing human flesh against reinforced concrete."[100]

Said Holland Smith, "Iwo Jima was the most savage and the most costly battle in the history of the Marine Corps. Indeed, it has few parallels in military annals."[101]

13
The Last Battle: Okinawa

On the ships of the armada steaming north from Ulithi, the Marines lightened the pre-invasion tension with songs built on bad puns: "After Rabaul Is Over," "Tarawa Boom-de-ay" and "Goodbye, Mama, I'm Off to Okinawa."

Easter Sunday 1945 promised to be one more bloody island steppingstone to Japan. The Marines could not know that Okinawa would be their last big battle in World War II. They only knew they were going to hit a beach within 350 miles of the enemy's homeland; it had to be rough.

The war seemed endless. Many of the Marines had already made one amphibious assault; some had made three. The war in Europe was being fought inside Hitler's Germany; the atomic bomb was still an untested secret; the Russians were not yet ready to attack the Japanese. Most military planners were convinced that the Allies would have to invade Japan itself and that the Japanese would fight to the last man.

The battle for Okinawa—rejoining MacArthur's and Nimitz's campaigns—would be the Pacific's biggest: 548,000 Americans of all the services taking part before it was over. Initially, the United States Tenth Army would land with a front of four divisions—two Army and two Marine—led by ill-starred Lt. Gen. Simon Bolivar Buckner, Jr., a Confederate general's son who had just spent four years in Alaska and was destined to die on Okinawa watching the Marines advance.

The Americans were headed for a number of surprises. Most astonishingly, the Japanese would not defend the invasion beaches at all—or the two airfields immediately behind them. Secondly, the invaders would fight for 82 days and suffer 75,000 casualties to secure the island; Lt. Gen. Mitsuru Ushijima's

Thirty-second Army would do its job superbly, eating up the clock of war. And, finally, more U.S. Navy men would die in battle than either soldiers or Marines, because bombers and some 1,900 kamikaze suicide planes would clobber the fleet offshore, sinking 36 ships (including 12 destroyers) and damaging 368 more—"The greatest material and personnel damage in the history of the United States Navy."[102] And in the air, 763 U.S. aircraft would be lost. If the Americans had not been able to mass overwhelming power—in the tradition of Grant and Sherman—this would have been a disaster at the very gates of Japan.

But Okinawa was a climactic victory. The Japanese were already tightly squeezed. The Battle of Leyte Gulf the previous October had given the United States control of the western Pacific. American submarines were sinking most of Japan's merchant shipping and cutting off its essential supplies. American bombers had been pounding Japan's great cities since November. And Japan's air power was stomped on so heavily that it did not effectively contest the Okinawa landing.

Before the invasion, the Navy's fast carriers went in close and bombed Japan's airfields. Marine squadrons were on board. From *Bennington*, Maj. Herman Hansen led Corsairs of VMF-112 against Kyushu's airfields; and Maj. Thomas E. Mobley, Jr., took VMF-123 over Hiroshima and Kure. From *Bunker Hill*, Maj. Herbert H. Long's Corsairs of VMF-451 helped punish the enemy carrier *Ryuho*. When *Franklin* was hit by two bombs 55 miles off Japan's coast on March 19—causing the worst naval inferno of the carrier war—among *Franklin's* 772 dead were 65 Marines of VMF-452 and VMF-214 ("Pappy" Boyington's old squadron). In the same fight, *Wasp* was also knocked out of the war with 302 casualties. Although the price was horrendously high, the U.S. carrier offensive cut down mass kamikaze attacks against the fleet off Okinawa until the troops were well ashore.

To meet the American juggernaut, the Japanese on Okinawa itself did the only thing they could. They dug into the rocky southern end of the island and waited. Lt. Gen. Ushijima commanded some 100,000 men, one-fifth of them Okinawans drafted into service. He dragged out the battle, hoping the kamikazes could destroy the U.S. fleet, isolate the Tenth Army and disrupt the invasion of Japan. The Japanese even threw in their last naval trump, the giant battleship *Yamato*, with fuel enough for only a one-way voyage, in the attempt to sink American ships.

Skinny and 60 miles long, Okinawa, the largest of the Ryukyu Islands, was to be the main advance base for the invasion of Japan. After the smothering heat of the South Pacific, the Americans at first would find it cool and climatically comfortable. The small neat farms, villages with red-tiled roofs, rolling countryside and umbrella-topped pines were attractive. The hills were dappled with large womb-shaped family tombs, many of which the Japanese converted into machine-gun strongpoints.

Most of Okinawa's 500,000 peaceful people, ruled by Japan since 1875, lived on the southern third of the island. North of the two-mile-wide Ishikawa Isthmus bottleneck, the island was barren, wild and mountainous. The stubby northern Motobu Peninsula gave Okinawa its greatest width of 18 miles and pointed toward the island of Ie Shima, three and a half miles to the west.

South of the narrow isthmus rose a series of cross-island ridges, ideal for defense. The Japanese, using them effectively, dug caves and tunnels and entrenched mortars in the reverse slopes. To the south were the main towns: Naha, the capital and port on the west, and Shuri, the ancient citadel in the center. The Japanese had built three airfields on the west coast. The east coast offered two vast bays. The U.S. Navy wanted to assault the east coast and grab these inviting anchorages, but the Army and Marines argued for the rapid capture of the airfields. Winds and tides gave the final decision to the western Hagushi beaches north of Naha.

Heading into this final battle, the Marine Corps had 421,600 men and women in uniform. (By comparison, the Corps had started World War I with less than 14,000 Marines and at its end had 75,101.) There were now six Marine divisions organized equally into two corps. Each division's table of organization called for 856 officers and 16,069 enlisted men, plus assorted support and artillery units. Marine aviation in the Pacific had four wings, containing 16 air groups and 70 tactical squadrons. In addition, 44 squadrons were preparing to go overseas on new escort carriers. Women Reservists numbered 18,365— proudly freeing the equivalent of one division of men for combat. And 16,000 Navy doctors and corpsmen were assigned to the Marines. Much of this power would be brought to bear on Okinawa.

Before L-Day (the invasion of Iwo Jima, being planned at the same time, was designated D-Day), Maj. James L. Jones' Amphibious Reconnaissance Battalion invaded Keise Shima, five miles off Naha, on the night of March 27. They found no Japanese, and the Army set up 24 155mm guns to fire on southern Okinawa. The Army's 77th Division seized nine islands of Kerama Retto, killing 975 Japanese and giving the Navy an anchorage 15 miles west of Naha.

Starting on the twenty-sixth, kamikazes hit the invasion fleet. Coming in underneath the radar at dawn and dusk, they crashed six ships before L-Day, including Adm. Raymond A. Spruance's flagship *Indianapolis*; and near misses damaged 10 more.

The Navy blasted Okinawa with 27,226 rounds, 5-inch and larger, before the main landing. For the most part, this was wasted; the naval gunfire could have been better used on Iwo Jima. Minesweepers destroyed 257 mines; UDT swimmers blew up 2,700 posts embedded in the reef off the west coast landing area. Carrier aircraft flew 3,095 sorties against the island; and by March 29, Okinawa's air strength had been eliminated.

Sunday, April 1—Easter and April Fool's Day—dawned clear and calm and a pleasant 75 degrees. Five hundred carrier planes, including four Marine squadrons from *Bennington* and *Bunker Hill*, strafed and napalmed the landing beaches. Ten battleships, 9 cruisers, 23 destroyers and 177 gunboats pounded the beaches with 3,800 tons of shells. The 96th Infantry Division landed at the southern end of the beachhead, with the 7th Infantry Division on its left. They were the assault element of the Army's XXIV Corps commanded by the veteran Maj. Gen. John R. Hodge, USA.

Two Marine divisions landed to the Army's left, north of the Bishi River. They were organized into the III Amphibious Corps under Maj. Gen. Roy S. Geiger. The 5th and 7th Marines of the oldest Marine division, the 1st, landed on the right, with the 1st Marines in reserve. The 1st Division was led by Maj. Gen. Pedro A. del Valle, the Puerto Rico-born Naval Academy graduate who had commanded the artillery on Guadalcanal and Guam.

The Marines' newest division, the 6th, attacked on the far

northern end of the front, with the 22d and 4th Marines in assault and the 29th Marines (the last regiment formed in the war) in reserve. Some of the 6th Division were veterans starting their second Pacific tour. The division was commanded by Maj. Gen. Lemuel C. Shepherd, Jr., the VMI graduate who had been wounded three times in France and served on Cape Gloucester and Guam.

The 2d Marine Division, the III Corps' floating reserve, made a diversionary feint at the southeastern side of the island to immobilize the defenders. Ironically, the 2d Division, which never landed, suffered the most casualties on L-Day when kamikazes hit two transports and killed 16 and wounded 37 Marines.

The assault troops stormed the western beaches and climbed the seawall that they had feared would be worse than Tarawa's. Several Marine units landed on the wrong beaches; but the first wave was ashore by 8:32 A.M., and all eight Marine battalions, by 9 A.M. There were few casualties. By 1 P.M., the 4th Marines had secured Yontan Airfield and were plunging ahead with their tanks against light opposition. The 1st Marine Division also met only minor resistance from Japanese service troops and Okinawan home guards and advanced swiftly. The Army captured Kadena Airfield. By the end of L-Day, the Americans had carved out a beachhead four miles wide and two miles deep. The absence of opposition amazed and relieved everyone from generals to privates. In less than eight hours, 50,000 men had been landed with only 28 killed, 27 missing and 104 wounded in the four assault divisions. It looked deceptively easy.

On Monday, the 4th Marines, running into heavier resistance, killed 250 Japanese and advanced another 1,000 yards. The 1st Division still met only light opposition. The Marines' 6th Engineer Battalion repaired enough of Yontan Airfield so that afternoon the first artillery spotter plane landed, and by April 8, four-engine transports were evacuating the wounded to Guam.

While the 1st Marine Division cleaned up, the 6th Marine Division wheeled north toward the Ishikawa Isthmus; and the Army divisions swung south. On L-Day plus two, they bisected the island. No one yet knew where the main body of Japanese was holed up.

It was not all a cakewalk. The terrain grew more rugged toward the north. On the second day, L Company, 22d Marines, ran into trouble. As it entered a deep ravine, the whole hillside blazed with enemy fire. The company commander, Capt. Nelson C. Dale, was severely wounded; six Marines fell, and a machine-gun team was destroyed before it could fire a shot. Lt. Daniel B. Brewster's 2d Platoon was isolated. Six Marines were killed trying to reach it before Sgt. Otis Thorpe got through. Pfc. Anthony Caso crawled back to report the location of the enemy guns. Several corpsmen were killed trying to help the wounded. Lt. Marvin D. Perskie now led the company to save the men up front. The Marines dashed forward, blasting caves and killing the enemy. Only ten of Brewster's platoon walked out.

Tuesday night, the 6th Division was anchored at the base of the isthmus—12 days ahead of schedule—and by Thursday, held a line across the northern end of the isthmus. Ishikawa had a magnificent beach; the Marines swam, roasted pigs and chickens and "liberated" horses to carry their mortars and ammunition. The 1st Division occupied the Katchin Peninsula on the east coast. But the Army to the south started to encounter strong enemy outposts and massed artillery fire and had to throw back a counterattack. By the end of the first week, the XXIV Corps had been stopped.

On April 10, the Army's 27th Division landed; and there were 160,000 American troops on Okinawa. But the 2d Marine Division, veterans of Guadalcanal and Tarawa, was shipped back to Saipan, "a move which turned out to be unwise."[103] American Intelligence was seriously underestimating the enemy's strength.

Off the east coast, Major Jones' reconnaissance battalion scouted six islands guarding Nagagusuku Wan (later to be called Buckner Bay). Elements of the 27th Division wiped out the defenders on Tsugen Shima there and opened up the east coast for the unloading of supplies. By April 11, a half million tons of cargo had been put ashore on Okinawa.

On L-Day plus one, Maj. Gen. Francis P. Mulcahy, USMC, set up the command post for the Tenth Army's land-based Tactical Air Force. MAG-31 began operating from Yontan; and MAG-33, from Kadena. Marine aviators got back into the Marine war at Okinawa. They flew some close support for the ground forces—their prime intended mission—but mostly they battled

611

the intense and continuous air counteroffensive that the Japanese hurled against the American and British warships.

The first major kamikaze raid—the war's largest—struck on April 6 and 7 with 699 planes, of which 355 were suiciders. They sank six ships and seriously damaged 10. On April 7, VMF-311—flying Corsairs with the new 20mm cannon instead of .50 caliber machine guns—scored the Marines' first kamikaze kill.

That same day, the battleship *Yamato*, venturing toward Okinawa without air cover, was sunk by the carrier fliers. It was a Navy show; but one Marine, Lt. Kenneth E. Huntington, raced through antiaircraft fire and stuck his bomb on *Yamato's* forward turret.

In Tokyo on that same April 7, Gen. Kuniaki Koiso resigned as prime minister and the aged Adm. Kantaro Suzuki was chosen to replace him and find a way out of the war. Wrote historian Samuel Eliot Morison: "It is a sad reflection that this costly operation [Okinawa], and everything that followed until 16 August, was unnecessary from any point of view but that of keeping 'face' for the military leaders who had started the war."[104]

The next major kamikaze raid came on April 12 and 13 with 185 suicide planes. Major Hansen shot down three kamikazes to become an ace and win the Navy Cross. Lt. John M. Callahan destroyed three enemy fighters in five minutes. And Maj. Archie G. Donahue got five kills to bring his total for the war to 14.

In the big raid of April 15 and 16 with 165 enemy planes, Lt. William E. Eldridge shot down four suiciders and Capt. Floyd C. Kirkpatrick and Lt. Selva E. McGinty, three each. At dusk on April 22, 80 Japanese planes attacked the ships on the radar picket line; and Navy and Marine pilots shot down 54. Maj. Jefferson D. Dorroh destroyed six planes and Maj. George C. Axtell, Jr., and Lt. Jeremiah J. O'Keefe got five each.

Meanwhile, on the ground the 6th Marine Division discovered that the enemy force in the north had chosen to make its stand in the mountains of the Motobu Peninsula up the west coast. On April 8, the 29th Marines attacked the peninsula and found the enemy concentrated in a complex cave system centered around 1,200-foot Mount Yaetake. The terrain was so rugged and mines and roadblocks so numerous that tanks were useless. The 4th Marines joined the 29th in the most strenuous kind of mountain fighting.

Battling at short range and blowing up caves and pillboxes, the 4th Marines attacked the Yaetake hill mass early on April 14. To the Marines the enemy seemed like phantoms; hidden from sight, they picked off the officers and anyone with a map or a pistol. The next day, small, tough Col. William J. Whaling, the expert jungle fighter from Guadalcanal and Cape Gloucester, took over the 29th Marines from Col. Victor F. Bleasdale, a highly-decorated veteran who had received the Navy Cross and a battlefield commission long ago in France.

The Marines attacked Mount Yaetake from three sides. The 1st Battalion, 22d Marines filled the gap between the 4th and 29th Marines and reached Yaetake's western slopes. A twenty-year-old squad leader in the 4th Marines, Cpl. Richard E. Bush of Glasgow, Kentucky, led his men through artillery fire to seize a crucial ridge. Seriously wounded, Bush was dragged behind rocks with other wounded men. A grenade landed among them. Bush pulled it to him as it exploded. Amazingly, he lived; he was the only Marine to win the Medal of Honor on Motobu.

On the 16th, the 4th Marines' A and C Companies reached Yaetake's crest; and the Japanese threw them back. The Marines took the crest again. Fighting at close quarters, neither side could hold the summit. Finally, supporting fire enabled the Marines to stay. All available men, including Lt. Col. Fred D. Beans, the ex-Raider commanding the 1st Battalion, carried ammunition and water up to the assault troops just in time to meet a *banzai* attack. Seventy-five Japanese were annihilated; and by dark, the Marines held the mountain permanently.

When the 29th and 4th Marines reached the north coast on April 20, organized resistance on the peninsula was finished. The battle had cost the Marines 213 dead and 757 wounded.

On April 16, the 77th Infantry Division had assaulted Ie Shima, where the Japanese had three runways, and for six days fought 7,000 troops concealed in caves and bunkers. Ernie Pyle, the widely loved Hoosier war correspondent, was killed there on April 18 by a machine-gun burst. Pyle had gone ashore with the Marines on L-Day and had written this impression of the Marines on Okinawa:

> In peacetime, when the Marine Corps was a small outfit, with its campaigns high-lighted, everybody was a volunteer and you could understand why they felt so superior. But with the war the Marine Corps had grown by

hundreds of thousands of men. It became an outfit of ordinary people—some big, some little, some even draftees. It had changed, in fact, until marines looked to me exactly like a company of soldiers in Europe. Yet that Marine Corps spirit still remained. I never did find out what perpetuated it. The men were not necessarily better trained, nor were they any better equipped; often they were not so well supplied as other troops. But a marine still considered himself a better soldier than anybody else, even though nine-tenths of them didn't want to be soldiers at all. . . . No, marines don't thirst for battles. I've read and heard enough about them to have no doubts whatever about the things they can do when they have to. They are o.k. for my money, in battle or out.[105]

On April 21, the 77th Division captured the dead-volcano peak of Ie Shima; and the 22d Marines reached the northern tip of Okinawa.

In the meanwhile, on Friday, April 13, the men were told of the death of President Roosevelt. Many were deeply shaken. On Sunday, services were held throughout the vast invasion force. One young lieutenant, who had gone ashore with the 1st Marines on L-Day, wrote home to Doylestown, Pennsylvania: "By far the most serious event of the two weeks was the news of the death of President Roosevelt. The shock threw us all off balance and we spent all day yesterday in argument and meditation over the possible and probable future. We feel, quite naturally, more isolated than usual."[106]

On April 19, after days of preparatory bombardment, the three divisions of the XXIV Army Corps attacked down the width of the island, four miles north of Naha. The infantry-tank advance was supported by 324 pieces of artillery and 650 Navy and Marine planes with rockets, bombs, napalm and strafing. The Japanese defense was keyed on Shuri Ridge and dug into underground caves connected by elaborate tunnels. The attack failed to break through.

The Army fought for five days, measuring its progress in yards. Lt. Gen. Ushijima, under enormous pressure, pulled back to his inner ring of defenses around Shuri. He had anticipated such a move and built his defenses in concentric rings bristling with interlocking automatic weapons and artillery.

The failure of the April 19 attack and the heavy casualties in the following days raised doubts about Buckner's bulldog straight-ahead tactics. Commandant Vandegrift—who had recently been made the first four-star general on active duty in the Marine Corps—visited Okinawa on April 21; and he and Maj. Gen. Geiger tried to convince Buckner to bring back the 2d Marine Division and land it behind the enemy. Vandegrift promised to have it underway from Saipan in six hours. Vice Adm. Richmond K. Turner and Maj. Gen. Hodge supported his idea. But Buckner and the Tenth Army staff argued that a landing on the southeast coast might be another Anzio.

The American press became critical. Homer Bigart on Okinawa wrote, "Our tactics were ultraconservative. Instead of an end run, we persisted in frontal attacks."[107] And David Lawrence called it "a worse example of military incompetence than Pearl Harbor."[108] But the generals and admirals, fearing another Smith versus Smith scandal, did not oppose Buckner openly.

So the "slugging match" continued. And on May 1, the 1st Marine Division replaced the unfortunate 27th Infantry Division, which went north and released the 6th Marine Division for battle.

One sidelight: As they had previously in this war, the Marines had in their ranks Navajo Indians and used them to talk over the telephone in their own language so messages could not be intercepted by the enemy. They made possible swift, secret communication.

The arrival of the 1st Division before the Shuri defenses opened the second phase of the campaign for the Marines. With the Army, they now faced the main body of Japanese. Shuri was the core of the Japanese defenses, which were anchored at Naha on the west and Yonabaru on the east. Shuri itself was protected on three sides by cave-riddled ridges.

The 1st Division went into action on the west coast near the Machinato Airfield. In a driving rain, the Marines fought toward the Asa River but repeatedly had to pull back under heavy fire. In this battle, nineteen-year-old Corpsman Robert E. Bush of South Bend, Washington, with the 5th Marines, was giving plasma to a wounded Marine officer on a ridge crest when the enemy counterattacked. Holding the plasma bottle high with one hand, Bush fired his pistol at the oncoming enemy until his ammunition ran out. He was seriously wounded and lost his right eye, but he picked up a discarded carbine and shot six more Japanese charging over the hill.[109]

The enemy planned a major counterattack for the night of May 3–4, coordinated with a 159-plane kamikaze raid. The kamikazes did severe damage. In fighting them off, Lt. Thomas A. Gribbin II and Lt. Melvin S. Jarvis each received the Navy Cross for chasing suiciders through antiaircraft fire and shooting them down before they could reach their destroyer targets.

The enemy counterattack started when the Japanese stole up both coasts by barge to get in behind the American lines. Seven hundred men skirting the west coast landed by mistake too close to the 1st Marines and were destroyed. Those who landed elsewhere on the west coast were hunted down by the 1st Reconnaissance Company and war dog platoons. The east coast counterlanding penetrated the Army's lines but finally was smashed with 400 enemy killed. On May 5, the 1st Marines were dug in on commanding ground above the Asa River. All across the front, the Japanese had at least 6,200 dead. They had also lost 59 artillery pieces. The defeat of the counterattack had been "decisive."[110]

With the 1st Marines on May 7, Pvt. Dale M. Hansen of Wisner, Nebraska, coolly destroyed a pillbox with his bazooka; and when enemy fire wrecked his weapon, he grabbed a rifle, leaped across the crest of a ridge, shot four Japanese to death and beat off two others with the rifle butt. Then, he rampaged on to wipe out a mortar position and kill eight more Japanese. With the 5th Marines that same day, Pfc. Albert E. Schwab, a husky flamethrower operator from Tulsa, Oklahoma, advanced straight up a ridge under fire and burned out a machine-gun position that had his company pinned down. When a second machine gun opened fire, Schwab continued his attack and, although mortally wounded by the machine-gun's fire, destroyed the gun before he died.[111]

May 8 was V-E Day in Europe. But for the men on Okinawa, it was another day of fighting in a cold rain. As the only celebration of the war's end in Europe, at noon all the artillery and ships fired at the enemy.

The 6th Division moved in on the right of the 1st, and the 22d Marines replaced the 7th Marines on the high bluff overlooking the Asa River. On May 9, the 1st Marines started to clear the enemy off Hill 60; and the 5th Marines attacked the stubborn Awacha Pocket. In this fight, Maj. Paul H. Douglas, the future United States Senator from Illinois, was seriously wounded in the arm when serving as a stretcher bearer. The fifty-three-year-old economics professor had enlisted as a private and won the Bronze Star on Peleliu.

Late that night, the 6th Engineer Battalion threw a footbridge over the Asa River; and four companies of the 22d Marines scurried across the bridge and waded the river under fire. Then a two-man Japanese suicide team with satchel charges rushed the bridge and destroyed it and themselves. The Marines tried to enlarge their bridgehead south of the Asa but in six hours of fighting could advance only 150 yards. Although more companies waded the river, the Marines were unable to crack the enemy line. Badly needed tanks could not cross the muddy stream.

Teamwork of tanks and infantry was indispensible throughout the struggle for Okinawa. The Tenth Army lost 153 tanks during the campaign. It has been judged that "the tank-infantry team on Okinawa reached the apex of its development for the entire Pacific War."[112] Tanks and flamethrower tanks (nicknamed Zippos after the cigarette lighter) destroyed caves and bunkers at short range, while infantrymen and engineers removed mines and prevented the enemy from laying satchel charges on the tanks. When the tanks crushed a target, the riflemen cleaned it out and held the ground. Lt. Gen. Buckner called this technique of attacking fortified caves the "blowtorch and corkscrew" method: flamethrowers were the blowtorch and demolitions were the corkscrew.

South of the Asa River, C Company, 22d Marines was devastated in a two-day effort to take a small fortified coral hill called Charlie. After a brutal fight starting on May 10, one platoon was cut off. The company commander, Capt. Warren F. Lloyd, took Sgt. Joe Passanante's squad and rushed a machine-gun-armed tomb; in five minutes, half the squad was down. But the survivors seized the top of the little hill; it cost C Company's 256 men, 35 killed and 68 wounded. (Captain Lloyd, twenty-four years old, came from a Marine family; his father, three brothers and brother-in-law were all Marines.)

May 10 also saw one of the war's most spectacular Marine air feats. Capt. Kenneth L. Reusser and his wingman, 1st Lt. Robert R. Klingman, of VMF-312, were flying on combat air patrol over Ie Shima when they intercepted a Nick fighter at 38,000 feet. Using the last of his ammunition, Reusser shot up the enemy's left wing and tail. Klingman's guns froze at the high altitude, but he made three attacks at the enemy plane. On the first, his Corsair's propeller almost cut off the Nick's rudder and sawed into the rear gunner's cockpit. The second pass severed the rudder and ripped the right stabilizers; the final approach cut off the stabilizer. The Nick went into a spin and lost both its wings. Klingman landed his plane at Kadena out of gas and on its belly.

On May 10 and 11, the Japanese attacked the American fleet with 217 planes, including 104 kamikazes. They knocked the carrier *Bunker Hill* out of the war; among the 389 men killed were 29 Marines. In this fight, Marine pilots shot down four enemy planes; one went to Capt. James E. Swett, who ended the war with 15½ kills. Now, the only Marine fast carrier pilots left were on *Bennington*. When she sailed for Leyte Gulf in June, that ended World War II for the Marine squadrons on the fast carriers.

The Marines finally went into action from the escort carriers (CVEs) that Commandant Vandegrift had won for them. On the morning of May 10, 30 Marine planes flew the first strike, a close support mission, off *Block Island*. The second Marine CVE, *Gilbert Islands*, arrived on May 21. *Cape Gloucester* and *Vella Gulf* reached the Pacific war zone after the long battle for Okinawa was finished. "The CVEs were badly used during their brief taste of the Pacific war. . . . The boss of all the escort carriers at Okinawa, Rear Admiral Calvin T. Durgin, frowned upon the idea of the Marine specialization which had been agreed upon."[113] He would rarely assign the Marine squadrons to close combat support, for which these pilots had been specially trained.

The general American offensive that opened on May 11 began two weeks of bloody fighting. East to west across the island, the 96th Division fought for the hill mass called Conical

Hill; the 77th Division pounded at the Shuri heights in the center; the 1st Marine Division attacked toward Shuri up the crucial Wana Draw, and the 6th Marine Division faced its greatest test against Sugar Loaf Hill. The goal of the entire effort was to smash the enemy's Shuri defense line.

Under fire in the dark, the 6th Engineers assembled a Bailey bridge over the Asa River. At 11 A.M., Lt. Col. Robert L. Denig, Jr.,'s Marine tanks rumbled across and helped the 22d Marines leap ahead, take the high ground overlooking Naha and send patrols through the capital's suburbs to the banks of the Asato River. Inland, the 1st Division seized vital Dakeshi Ridge and finally cleaned up the Awacha Pocket.

By May 14, the Tenth Army reached the enemy's main line of resistance. The Marines could not break through the defenses west of Wana and northeast of Naha. Eighteen Marine tanks were knocked out and the infantry units took heavy losses.

The 22d Marines had come up against a steep, rectangular mound 300 yards long and 50 feet high; someone named it Sugar Loaf Hill. In front of it was open ground, murderous to cross. Sugar Loaf was actually the spearhead of a triangular group of three hills that formed the western anchor of the Shuri defense line. Sugar Loaf was backed on the southeast by Half Moon Hill, which rose to Shuri, and on the southwest by The Horseshoe. The complex blocked the way both left to Shuri and right to Naha. All three hills were laced with caves and tunnels and covered by interlocking fire. Any troops attempting to flank Sugar Loaf would be met by mortars hidden on the other two hills and by fire from Shuri heights.

When the 22d Marines reached Sugar Loaf on May 12, they had no clue to its importance. G Company led the first attack. Two platoons were pinned down; and Capt. Owen T. Stebbins, the company commander, and Lt. Dale W. Bair led the 40 men of the remaining platoon charging to the hill. One hundred yards later, only 12 men were still on their feet; both Stebbins' legs were chopped up by machine-gun bullets. Bair was hit in the left arm; but he rallied 25 Marines; and, led by tanks, they reached Sugar Loaf's top. While the men gathered up their wounded, Bair, six feet two and 225 pounds, stood on the crest with a light machine gun in his good arm, blasting any Japanese who fired on his men.

For two days, the 22d Marines repeatedly took Sugar Loaf and repeatedly were driven off. On May 14, the 22d was down to 62 percent of combat efficiency. But the division had been brought to a complete halt, and the regiment was ordered to take Sugar Loaf that day at any cost. F and G Companies tried and failed. At 5 P.M., they were sent forward again, supported by E Company's fire. By 7:30, three of their four tanks had been destroyed; of the 150 men who had started the assault, only 44 could still fight. They clung to the base of the hill under mortar fire; grenades rolled down on them. Maj. Henry A. Courtney, Jr., the 2d Battalion's twenty-eight-year-old executive officer from Duluth, Minnesota, led the men around the hill under heavy fire. He blasted out caves as he went; and, at 11 P.M., reinforced by 26 men and an LVT load of grenades, they stormed the crest, hurling their grenades. At midnight, Courtney saw the enemy gathering for a *banzai* attack less than 100 yards away. He instantly led an attack, killed many of the enemy and forced the rest back into their caves. While organizing the crest's defense and helping his wounded, Courtney was killed by an enemy mortar burst. He was awarded the Medal of Honor for "great personal valor."

At 2:30 A.M., K Company went up to support Courtney's 25 remaining men. Near the top, Cpl. Donald Golar, a red-headed former San Francisco longshoreman, fired his light machine gun until his ammunition was gone. Of the dozen Marines near him, only he and two riflemen were left. Golar emptied his pistol at the Japanese and then flung it at them. He hurled grenades taken from fallen Marines and fired a dead Marine's BAR until it jammed. He and Pvt. Donald Kelly started carrying wounded Marines to safety, when Golar was killed.

By 8 A.M., Courtney's last eight men were ordered off the hill. First Lt. George E. Murphy, who had played end for Notre Dame, led a platoon from D Company up Sugar Loaf. The platoon was decimated when the enemy charged the crest. Murphy was hit in the back by a mortar fragment. He turned around and emptied his pistol at the Japanese before he fell dead. By noon, the few survivors of K Company and the 11 left from Murphy's platoon were taken off Sugar Loaf.

For two days, the 29th Marines, on the 22d's left, hurled themselves at Half Moon Hill under fire from Shuri's heights. Japanese howitzers knocked out several tanks. Lt. Col. Jean W.

Moreau, commander of the 1st Battalion, was severely wounded by an artillery shell. Cpl. John A. Spazzaferro was hit by six bullets before he withdrew with the last two men of his 14-man squad. His platoon leader, Lt. Edgar C. Greene, who called Spazzaferro "the toughest guy I ever saw,"[114] was shot in the side and fell by the railroad track that ran between Half Moon and Sugar Loaf. Greene saw the corporal still firing his Tommy gun despite his wounds. Then Spazzaferro collapsed 10 feet from Greene. Four Japanese approached; Greene played dead. One Japanese took Greene's wristwatch but withdrew his hand from Greene's pocket covered with blood. After the Japanese had moved on, Greene called "Spazz!" and was relieved to see the tough corporal grin. The two men lay there until tanks rescued them the next day.

By the end of May 16, I Company, 22d Marines, reached the top of Sugar Loaf with the help of tanks; but when counterattacks forced the 29th Marines off the north slope of Half Moon, I Company, depleted by casualties, was in danger and had to come back from Sugar Loaf. The 6th Marine Division regarded May 16 as its bitterest day on Okinawa; casualties were high. The 22d Marines was down to 40 percent combat efficiency, and the 29th Marines took over the attack on Sugar Loaf. By now the entire Tenth Army had 3,963 killed, 18,258 wounded and 302 missing. Okinawa, which had seemed so easy at first, had changed into a brutal battle.

A young lieutenant in a 1st Marines' rifle company, which had four of its seven officers out of action since coming south, wrote home: "You can be as reckless as possible and never get hit—or be too careful and get blown to bits. I take the middle way—going in the open when I have to and staying in my holes the rest of the time."[115]

On May 17, Maj. Gen. Shepherd organized an attack by Colonel Whaling's 29th Marines on all three hills at once. E Company reached Sugar Loaf's crest four times and each time was driven off. The company had 160 men killed and wounded. But by now the enemy had also been badly hurt. Lt. Col. William G. Robb's 2d Battalion attacked Sugar Loaf again the next morning. Capt. Howard L. Mabie of D Company designed a skillful, tank-led double envelopment; and although six tanks were disabled, the battalion secured Sugar Loaf at last.

The Marines had turned the corner; but in nine days, the 6th

Division had a total of 2,662 battle casualties and 1,289 "non-battle" casualties from combat fatigue and exhaustion. The cost had been "tremendous."[116]

On May 19, Col. Alan Shapley's 4th Marines replaced the 29th. Bringing the rested 4th Marines out of reserve was crucial. G Company seized the western end of Half Moon; E Company enveloped its eastern flank. And before the day was out, the 3rd Battalion had taken the north slope of The Horseshoe and that night held it against a fierce counterattack.

While the 6th Division had been battling into the Sugar Loaf complex, the 1st Division on its left was fighting forward under the guns on the Shuri hill mass. The 1st Division and the 77th Infantry Division came up against the Wana defenses just northwest of Shuri. Behind Wana Ridge was a steep gorge, the Wana Draw, through which flowed the southern branch of the Asa River. Heavily fortified Hill 55 guarded the western entrance to the draw. Eastward toward Shuri, Wana Draw narrowed under steep dominating cliffs, 200 to 300 feet high.

For days, the 5th Marines tried to penetrate Wana Draw. The 7th Marines fought up the western nose of Wana Ridge. Tanks and howitzers pounded the high ground. The 1st Battalion was reduced to a single company, and the 3rd Battalion lost 12 officers in its rifle companies. In five days before Wana Ridge, the 7th Marines suffered 51 killed and missing, 387 wounded and 91 "non-battle" casualties. On May 19, the 1st Marines replaced that battered regiment.

The 1st Marines attacked the northern slope of Wana Ridge and after a tough grenade battle seized the ridge top, except for the summit of 110 Meter Hill at the ridge's eastern end. By May 20, the 5th Marines had taken Hill 55 at the western end of Wana Draw and were striking into the draw. But as long as the enemy held 110 Meter Hill, it was impossible to stay in Wana Draw or approach Shuri itself.

On the night of May 21, the rains began; and the battle became deadlocked in an oozing sea of mud. The mud clogged weapons, immobilized vehicles, infected wounds and fouled food and clothes.

Up to this time, the XXIV Corps to the east of the Marines had hammered at Shuri's defenses. The 77th Division in the center, measuring its gains in yards, finally pushed into the

622

outskirts of Shuri. On the far left, the 96th Division took Conical Hill and turned the enemy's eastern flank. On May 22, Maj. Gen. Hodge put in the 7th Division, which seized the high ground south of the east coast port of Yonabaru in a surprise night attack. But then the rains made the roads impassable; and the Army, like the Marines, bogged down. The rain continued for nine days; the whole front became a swamp—stalemated.

Two battalions of the 4th Marines waded the ankle-deep Asato River on May 23; but the next day, the rains had made the Asato a chest-high torrent. Finally, the 4th and 22d Marines crossed over and burst into the ruins of Naha, fighting Japanese holed up in shells of buildings and in the tombs on the ridges.

Under the full moon on the night of May 24, as part of a mass air attack, the Japanese sent a suicide force to cripple Yontan and Kadena Airfields. One enemy plane got through and made a wheels-up landing on the Yontan runway. Some 10 soldiers poured out, threw grenades and explosives and sprayed the area with small arms fire. Two Marines were killed and 18 wounded, probably mostly by wild friendly fire. The raiders destroyed eight planes, damaged 26 others and blew up 70,000 gallons of gasoline before they were killed. It was a flamboyant gesture.

By May 28, the rains finally stopped; and slowly the Americans began to close in on Shuri. On Tuesday, May 29, at 7:30 A.M., the 5th Marines assaulted Shuri Ridge despite heavy mortar fire and took the crest. Lt. Col. Charles W. Shelburne of the 1st Battalion asked permission to attack Shuri Castle, which was 800 yards to the east in the 77th Infantry Division's zone. Maj. Gen. del Valle approved the move at once, estimating that the 77th Division would need two more days of hard fighting to reach the castle. Capt. Julian D. Dusenbury led his A Company through the mud into the ruins of the castle at 10:15. Dusenbury, who came from Claussen, South Carolina, hoisted over the parapet the Confederate flag he carried in his helmet. Buckner must have smiled, but del Valle promptly sent over the 1st Division flag that had flown on Guadalcanal, New Britain and Peleliu. The Army was more than annoyed at the Marines. But the deadly Wana Draw had been bypassed, and the ancient Okinawan citadel was now in American hands.

In the end, the castle had fallen so swiftly because Lt. Gen.

Ushijima, with his flanks crushed, had started pulling his main force out of the Shuri defense line to the far southern tip of the island. He left behind a tough rear guard that delayed the Americans. Artillery and naval gunfire pounded the retreating Japanese. Ushijima set up his headquarters inside Hill 89, 11 miles south of Shuri. It would take three more weeks of fighting to secure Okinawa.

The rains began again, and the Tenth Army's pursuit bogged down in the mud until, on the last day of May, the weather broke out into welcomed sunshine; and Marines and soldiers occupied the city of Shuri. By now, the Tenth Army had captured all but a few square miles of Okinawa and killed an estimated 62,500 Japanese. Lt. Gen. Buckner's army had lost 5,655 killed and missing and 23,909 wounded. The Marines' ranks were filled with individual replacements; and the inexperienced men seriously diluted the level of combat effectiveness and the sense of teamwork. The replacement system was simply not effective when casualties were as heavy as they were in this prolonged battle.

While the Army and the 1st Marine Division pushed southward after Ushijima, the 6th Marine Division attacked the Oroku Peninsula across the Kokuba estuary south of Naha. The peninsula was the site of Naha's airfield, and its high ground dominated Naha harbor. The 4th Marines led the shore-to-shore amphibious assault early on June 4.

Fortunately, the Japanese had decided to defend the center of the peninsula, not the beaches. The 4th Marines encountered only mud, mines and scattered machine-gun fire as they raced from their LVTs 300 yards to high ground. The 29th Marines followed them ashore. The 6th Reconnaissance Company landed on Ono Yama, the island in the middle of the estuary, and protected the engineers while they built a 340-foot Bailey bridge from Naha to the island and then to the peninsula.

On June 5, Okinawa was whipped by a severe typhoon that damaged more American ships than any kamikaze attack. By the next day, the Marines on Oroku Peninsula began running into defenses supported by machine guns and 20mm cannon. The Japanese, led by Rear Adm. Minoru Ota, who had fought the Marine Raiders on New Georgia, were dug into the hills. The Marines slowly encircled them and then closed in on their caves.

To prevent the Japanese from escaping, the 22d Marines blocked the base of the peninsula.

The fight in the center of the peninsula was vicious, and the 4th Marines' casualties mounted. The 29th Marines could make little progress in hard fighting. Pvt. Robert M. McTureous, Jr., of Altoona, Florida, a replacement who had been with H Company only seven days, saw stretcher bearers hit by machine-gun fire while they carried out the wounded. Filling his shirt with grenades, the 138-pound McTureous charged in a furious one-man attack and smashed grenades into the cave entrances from which came the heaviest fire. He returned for another supply of grenades and went out again and silenced "a large number of hostile guns." He was seriously wounded in the stomach but crawled back 200 yards to the Marines' lines before calling for help. He died four days later and was awarded the Medal of Honor posthumously.

By June 9, the Japanese were pressed into a small pocket; and the next night, the survivors tried to break out of the trap. Tanks and eight battalions of Marines pounded them; and by June 12, the last enemy strongpoint was taken. The survivors began fleeing. First Lt. Spencer V. Silverthorne, a Williams College graduate who had served as a language officer since Bougainville, working under fire, persuaded 56 Japanese to surrender. Pfc. Harry M. Tuttle, an interpreter, found as he said, "Their greatest fear was of maltreatment at the hands of their captors."[117] Fear rather than dishonor was clearly the reason that many Japanese fought to the death or committed suicide when cornered.

By the fourteenth, organized resistance on Oroku Peninsula was declared at an end. More than 4,000 Japanese had been killed in the 10-day battle. The Marines had 1,608 casualties and 30 tanks disabled.

Meanwhile, the XXIV Corps and the 1st Marine Division were slogging southward from the Naha-Yonabaru Valley toward the island's highest hill mass. Tanks and trucks were mired in the rain and mud until the skies cleared on June 7. Toward the south, resistance stiffened. On June 10, the 7th Marines waded 400 yards across the mouth of the muddy Mukue River, scaled a seawall and stormed through the heavily mined ruins of the town of Itoman. Directly to the east, the 1st Battalion, 1st

Marines had to take Yuza Hill. C Company attacked in the face of machine-gun and artillery fire and lost 70 of its 175 men; all of the company's officers were killed or wounded. The battalion took the hill by noon; but there were so many replacements that, as one Marine said, "nobody knew anybody else."[118]

A small-plane strip was leveled north of Itoman; and in the next dozen days, VMO-3 and VMO-7 flew out 641 wounded. The eight-minute flight to the hospital replaced the long rough ride in an ambulance Jeep and saved lives.

Now the 7th Marines faced the defenders of Kunishi Ridge, "the most frantic, bewildering and costly close-in battle on the southern tip of Okinawa."[119] This coral ridge ran northwest to southwest for 1,500 yards and formed the western anchor of the enemy's last heavily defended line. Both slopes of Kunishi Ridge were full of caves, fortified tombs and weapon emplacements. Between the 7th Marines and the ridge lay a broad valley of grasslands and rice paddies, giving the defenders unobstructed lanes of fire and the attackers little cover.

Col. Edward W. Snedeker proposed a night attack; and at 3:30 A.M. on June 12, his 7th Marines tried to cross the valley. C and F Companies, leading the assault, achieved complete surprise and seized a piece of the ridge's crest. B and G Companies, sent to reinforce them in daylight, were stopped. The lead companies were isolated and badly in need of ammunition, rations and medical supplies.

Darkness allowed the rest of the attackers to reach the height. By the next dawn, the 7th Marines were on the ridge and the Japanese were in it. Enemy snipers were deadly. One marksman killed or wounded 22 Marines before he was located and dispatched. The isolated Marines had to be supplied by tanks and air drops. Sherman tanks shuttled back and forth, carrying up supplies and reinforcements and taking down the badly wounded. Some of the wounded had to be strapped to the tanks' sides, with sandbags protecting them against enemy fire. Twenty-one tanks were destroyed or damaged; the Marines fought from cave to cave for four days.

The 2d Battalion, 1st Marines assaulted Kunishi Ridge at 3 A.M. on June 14. Flares, shot up by mistake, exposed the men to the enemy. Two platoons from E Company and one from G Company made the crest but were cut off by heavy enemy fire.

Casualties mounted rapidly and tanks came up to support the men. Even water had to be carried up by the tanks.

First Lt. Marcus H. Jaffe, who had recently taken over command of G Company, wrote home:

> I have taken the company up against two objectives. The first we cracked with only light casualties. The second was a bitch all the way around. The attack was planned badly from above, supply and evacuation was almost an impossibility, and we had some damn bad luck when a f——d up Army M7 began firing its 105 into the troops. . . . The two assault platoons did a great job in working up to and securing their objective—then the tide turned and not a thing seemed to go right. I know now that in the prosecution of war on this scale—with the terrible potential to kill possessed by our weapons—the inadequacies of the human mind and body cannot prevent needless slaughter. Fortunately for my peace of mind (though the sorrow will exist for others) the personnel of this company and battalion has changed so much in the past month that very few of the dead are good friends of mine.[120]

Three days later, he wrote that of the 21 officers who had started out in his battalion's line companies, only six were left.

After dark on June 15, the 2d Battalion, 5th Marines relieved the shot-up 1st Marines; and the 7th Marines were also thrown into the battle. By the end of June 16, Kunishi Ridge was painstakingly cleaned out; it cost the Marines 1,150 casualties.

The 6th Marine Division, freed from the Oroku Peninsula, now joined the battle in the south. The 22d Marines promptly attacked and seized Mezado Ridge beyond Kunishi Ridge near the west coast. There was no reserve division to relieve the exhausted Marines. Later, Maj. Gen. Geiger recommended that a Marine corps be built of three divisions so one could always be rested.

Some worn-out Marines finally received relief when Col. Clarence R. Wallace's 8th Marines of the 2d Division entered the lines. The regiment had been brought back from Saipan at the end of May and had occupied two islands north of Okinawa without opposition. On June 18, as the Tenth Army was facing a weakening defense, the 8th Marines demonstrated the value of fresh troops and advanced 1,400 yards. Early that morning, Lt. Gen. Buckner came forward to watch the 8th Marines go into action. At the 3rd Battalion's observation post, a Japanese shell drove a piece of coral into Buckner's chest, wounding him mortally.

Admiral Nimitz immediately gave Maj. Gen. Geiger command of the Tenth Army. The veteran Marine aviator became for a few days the first Marine officer ever to command a field army. He was promoted to lieutenant general and led the Tenth Army in the final days of the battle for Okinawa. On June 23, Gen. Joseph W. Stilwell, USA, who had commanded U.S. forces in the China–Burma–India Theater, took over from Geiger, who was named commanding general, Fleet Marine Force, Pacific.

Before Stilwell arrived, the Tenth Army pressed the remaining Japanese into three small pockets. On the west, the 5th and 8th Marines reached the sea at the bottom of the island on June 19. While the 22d Marines were eliminating resistance at Mezado Ridge, its commander, Col. Harold C. Roberts, was killed by a sniper. Pfc. Nicholas Woloshuk, Jr., picked off off the man who shot him. Roberts was awarded his third Navy Cross. The big native New Yorker had earned his first at Belleau Wood, where he served as a Navy corpsman with the Marines, and after being commissioned in the Marine Corps, had won his second in 1928 on Nicaragua's Coco River.

The 29th Marines on the extreme western flank reached the tip of Okinawa on June 20, but the 4th Marines still had to battle the enemy in the Kiyamu hill mass. June 21 was the final day of the organized campaign, and the Marines spent it in heavy fighting. In the rifle platoons, there were few Marines left who had landed on Easter Sunday.

At 1:05 P.M. on June 21, Lt. Gen. Geiger declared Okinawa secured, although the Army was still crushing a Japanese last-ditch stand. At noon on June 22, Lt. Gen. Ushijima committed *hara-kiri* on a cliff overlooking the sea.

Even on that day, the kamikazes struck Okinawa again. Capt. Robert Baird of VMF(N)-533 downed two and became the first Marine night fighter ace of the war. A suicider was also shot down by Capt. Kenneth A. Walsh, who had won the Medal of Honor in the Solomons and had not had a kill since 1943. This raised Walsh's wartime total to 21 and placed him fourth among the Marine Corps' 120 aces after Boyington, Foss and the late Robert M. Hanson.

By the end of the campaign, a fourth Marine Aircraft Group, MAG-14, had been brought up to Okinawa. And early in June, Maj. Gen. Louis E. Woods had taken over as commander of the 2d MAW from Maj. Gen. Mulcahy. In all of the Okinawa battle, 700 Marine planes had participated. Eighty-six pilots and 11 crewmen were killed in combat flights; 24 aviation Marines were killed on the ground, and 156 were wounded.

After organized resistance ended, General Stilwell ordered southern Okinawa mopped up. The Americans finally counted 107,539 enemy dead on Okinawa. Intelligence judged that total enemy casualties numbered 142,000, of which 42,000 were Okinawan civilians; but all such figures were only guesses.

American casualties could be counted more accurately. The Tenth Army had 7,613 killed and missing and 31,807 wounded or injured in action. In addition, it had 26,221 "non-battle" casualties. This latter category consisted chiefly of neuropsychiatric cases. Said the official Army history of the campaign, "The most important cause of this was unquestionably the great amount of enemy artillery and mortar fire, the heaviest concentrations experienced in the Pacific war. Another cause of men's nerves giving way was the unending close-in battle with a fanatical foe. The rate of psychiatric cases was probably higher on Okinawa than in any previous operation in the Pacific."[121] This was stark commentary on the failure to provide for the relief of combat troops during the long Okinawan battle.

The Marine Corps (and its attached Naval medical personnel) had a total of 20,020 casualties at Okinawa, of which 3,561 were battle deaths. The Navy had 4,907 killed in action, more than either of the other services.

The invasion of Japan itself was still ahead. The 6th Marine Division shipped out of Naha for Guam to get ready for this next fearsome operation. And rumors swept the 1st Division that it was going to Hawaii. As the division historian recorded:

> It had been nearly two years [from the time the Division left Melbourne] since some of the men had tasted a civilian environment. For a great majority it had been

something over a year. There was the desire to tie up, if possible, alongside a woman. But there were other desires, too—to flick a light switch, to see road signs and civilian cars, to watch children at play, to be able to spend money, to drink a *cold* beer, or "a good glass of milk."[122]

But to everyone's horror the division was sent up to make camp on Okinawa's Motobu Peninsula. The division had been fighting the Japanese longer than any other American division. Now, it expected to fight in the streets of Tokyo.

14
The End of the War

The Pacific war pounded to a finish. Japan's naval power had been smashed; but its armies of 4.7 million men had not been conquered, and 1.5 million soldiers waited to defend Japan itself. American Intelligence figured that to invade Japan would cost a very minimum of 100,000 Americans killed and wounded.

Two invasions were planned against Japan. The first, named Olympic, would attack the southern home island of Kyushu on November 1, 1945. The second, called Coronet, would land on Honshu's Tokyo Plain in March 1946. The great offensive was approaching its climax.

All six Marine divisions were to penetrate Japan. Maj. Gen. Harry Schmidt's V Amphibious Corps, with the 2d, 3rd and 5th Marine Divisions and three air wings, would join ten Army divisions attacking the southern end of Kyushu. A grand total of 815,548 troops would participate in the operation. The Japanese were estimated to have 450,000 troops on the island; and they had still hoarded 11,000 planes, including 5,000 kamikazes. The later assault on Honshu would be made by 11 Army divisions and the III Marine Amphibious Corps, now led by Maj. Gen Keller E. Rockey. The commander of the entire invasion would be General of the Army MacArthur.

Not all American military leaders were convinced that these invasions of Japan were necessary. In the main, the U.S. Army's generals believed that the Japanese army must be defeated and the home islands occupied. The naval members of the Joint Chiefs of Staff predicted that sea and air power would strangle Japan. Said Fleet Admiral William D. Leahy, Chief of Staff to Presidents Roosevelt and Truman, "I believed that a completely blockaded Japan would then fall by its own weight."[123]

That July, American air and sea power, striking day and night, lay siege to Japan. B-29s averaged 1,200 sorties a week. B-24s escorted by Marine Corsairs attacked from Okinawa.

But the political front outraced the military. On July 15, President Truman met with Stalin and Churchill at Potsdam, outside Berlin. And on the twenty-fourth he ordered the Army Air Forces to drop an atomic bomb on Japan on the first day after August 3 that weather conditions permitted.

The next step was to offer the Japanese the chance to surrender unconditionally without either invasion or atomic destruction. On July 26, the United States, the United Kingdom and the Republic of China issued the Potsdam Declaration. It promised that the Japanese people would not be enslaved, but it insisted that Japan be disarmed and occupied and its war-making power be destroyed. Two days later, Prime Minister Suzuki announced that Japan would continue to fight.

Events rushed ahead. On August 6, the B-29 "Enola Gay" rose from North Field, Tinian, and at 8:15 A.M. exploded its single atomic bomb over the city of Hiroshima. Bombing attacks against Japan by 550 B-29s and carrier aircraft followed. On August 8, the Soviet Union declared war on Japan and started to roll into Manchuria, Sakhalin Island and Korea. On August 9, a second atomic bomb swallowed Nagasaki in a mushroom-shaped cloud. On August 10, Japan asked for peace on the terms of the Potsdam Declaration, with the sole condition that the Emperor retain his throne. Three days of discussion followed; and then, Truman announced that the Emperor could stay, subject to the Supreme Commander of the Allied Powers. On August 14, Emperor Hirohito made the decision to surrender. At 6:15 A.M. on August 15, Fleet Admiral Nimitz ordered all offensive operations against Japan stopped at once. His message concluded with the warning: "Beware of Treachery." The war was done.

The cavalcade that had started for the Marines at Ewa and Pearl Harbor, at Wake and Corregidor was over. The hatred and the gut-churning fear could now subside. The dead would be remembered and then in time forgotten. The maimed would try to splice their lives together. Those who had fought and survived, the heroes and the cowards, would lie awake with their memories. The captains would savour their good fortune and

632

regret their mistakes. And hundreds of thousands of men would feel only joy that the killing was finished, that they lived and could go home.

On the day that Emperor Hirohito surrendered, the 5,400 men of the 4th Marines loaded into transports at Guam and sailed the next evening for Japan. The Marines prepared their weapons, just in case; but Lt. Col. Fred D. Beans, now the regiment's commander, ordered them to lock their weapons, not to put a bullet in the chamber and not to fire unless fired upon.

The reborn 4th Marines, the regiment that had been forced to surrender at the war's beginning, was chosen to lead the Navy into Japan. Reinforced, it became the keystone of the Fleet Landing Force, which also included a provisional regiment of 2,000 Marines from 33 ships of the Third Fleet, a naval regiment of 956 sailors and a British battalion of 450 Royal Marines and sailors. The Fleet Landing Force was commanded by Marine Brig. Gen. William T. Clement, who had served in Shanghai with the old 4th Marines and under orders had escaped from Corregidor by submarine. Later, he had fought on Guam and Okinawa.

Clement's job was to occupy the Yokosuka naval base and airfield on the west side of the mouth of Tokyo Bay, while the Army's 11th Airborne Division landed at Atsugi Airdrome 14 miles southwest of Tokyo. Maj. Frank Carney led the 2d Battalion, 4th Marines ashore across the bay on Futtsu Cape at 5:58 A.M. on August 30 and claimed to be "the first American combat troops to set foot in Japan."[124]

There was no opposition; the Japanese cooperated completely. The 4th Marines moved inland from Yokosuka to establish a perimeter, and its patrols linked up with the 11th Airborne Division. By mid-afternoon, MacArthur, Nimitz and Halsey were all ashore.

The formal surrender ceremonies were held on Sunday, September 2, aboard the battleship *Missouri* in Tokyo Bay—in front of the 31-starred flag that Commodore Perry had carried into Tokyo Bay in 1853. From *Missouri's* flagstaff flew the flag that had flown over The Capitol in Washington on Sunday, December 7, 1941.

Lt. Gen. Geiger represented the Corps at the surrender; but

if any Marines expected to be the first to march in the streets of Tokyo, they were disappointed. That honor went to the 1st Cavalry Division, which had been the first into Manila.

MAG-31 commanded by Col. John C. Munn arrived from Okinawa at Yokosuka on September 7. Before Lt. Col. Beans relieved Brig. Gen. Clement, he witnessed a ceremony in which 120 released prisoners of war from the old 4th Marines received the colors of the new 4th Marines. Clement shook hands with Marines he had last seen on Corregidor.

By January 1946, the 1st and 2d Battalions, 4th Marines sailed for the United States and the headquarters detachment joined the 6th Marine Division at Tsingtao, China. The 3rd Battalion remained at Yokosuka as a guard battalion.

In the meanwhile, Maj. Gen. Schmidt's V Amphibious Corps occupied Kyushu with the 2d and 5th Marine Divisions. The 32d Infantry Division substituted for the 3rd Marine Division in order to leave one full Marine division in the Marianas. The 5th Marine Division began arriving at Sasebo on September 22. The next day, the 2d Marine Division landed at Nagasaki and curtained off the city's atom bomb–devastated section.

In December, the 5th Marine Division returned to the United States. By July 1946, the 2d Division turned over its responsibilities to the 24th Infantry Division and ended its involvement with Japan that had begun on Guadalcanal.

On September 4, Marines returned to Wake Island, scene of their heroic defense at the war's beginning. The first man ashore was Col. Walter L. J. Bayler, who had become known as "the last man off Wake Island." Brig. Gen. Lawson H. M. Sanderson, commanding general of the 4th Marine Aircraft Wing, received the surrender of 1,262 Japanese military and naval personnel. Another 1,288 had died of starvation, and 600 had been killed by American bombs. An unknown number of Americans were found buried in two common graves.

Other bypassed Japanese islands were also occupied. At Truk, 38,355 Japanese surrendered to Marine Brig. Gen. Robert Blake; and in the Ryukyus, 105,000 surrendered to General Stilwell.

The day before the 4th Marines landed at Yokosuka, special

naval rescue teams, with medical personnel and Marine security detachments, raced ahead to reach the prisoners of war in the many large camps in the Tokyo-Yokohama area. On August 29, the first 739 POWs, including those from the Shinagawa hospital camp, were taken on board the hospital ship *Benevolence*.

Weeks more were required before all the prisoners could be rescued from Manchuria, Korea, China, Formosa and other parts of Japan. Among thousands of Allies, 2,270 Marines had been captured by the Japanese. They were held in 33 camps throughout East Asia. Only 1,756 ever returned to the United States. The rest died or were killed in captivity.

In addition, the Germans captured four Marines in Europe, where they were working with the French underground for the Office of Strategic Services. Maj. Peter J. Ortiz (two Navy Crosses), Sgt. John P. Bodnar and Sgt. Jack R. Risler surrendered to the Gestapo just south of Lake Geneva rather than get into a fire fight for which the local populace would suffer reprisals. Another member of the unit, Sgt. Frederick J. Brunner, swam a river and escaped to a Resistance group. The Germans' fourth Marine prisoner, 2d Lt. Walter W. Taylor, was captured near Nice after he was knocked out by a grenade explosion.

Few Marines served in Europe. Three hundred and six Marines participated in D-Day at Normandy, including four officers on Eisenhower's staff and enlisted men who acted as riflemen on shipboard and exploded floating mines in their ships' paths. Others worked 5-inch batteries during the North African and Normandy landings. And there was a Marine Barracks at Londonderry, Northern Ireland. On August 29, 1944, Marine detachments from *Augusta* and *Philadelphia* landed on the islands of Ratonneau and If near Marseilles and disarmed 700 Germans.

Among the Marines who served with the OSS, Capt. John Hamilton, who was actually the movie actor Sterling Hayden, jumped into Yugoslavia with Gunnery Sgt. John Harnicker and a Navy radio operator. Working with partisans, they provided for the rescue of Allied pilots downed in enemy-held territory. And Capt. Walter R. Mansfield, a demolitions expert, parachuted into Yugoslavia to help Tito's partisans blow up rails and bridges. Late in 1944, Mansfield dropped into China with Cpls. John Owens and Cedric Poland and ambushed Japanese truck convoys and troop detachments with Chinese guerrillas. Another Marine who worked with the Chinese guerrillas was Lt. Robert H. Barrow, who later played a dramatic part in the Korean war.

Most of the Marines imprisoned by the Japanese were captured early in the war; the rest were chiefly fliers who were shot down. Best known of this latter group, "Pappy" Boyington, the war's leading Marine ace, was downed over Rabaul and imprisoned near Tokyo. He was repeatedly beaten, and the Japanese never reported his existence. Marine Lt. Donald Carlson, who was shot down over Tokyo, was kept in solitary confinement for 40 days and had all his teeth knocked out. Both men were liberated at the end of the war.

The first Marines captured at Peking and Tientsin were put in Woosung Prison near Shanghai, where Col. William W. Ashurst, commander of the Peking Embassy Guard, became the senior officer prisoner. The Marines captured on Guam were eventually taken to Osaka. Eighty Marines and sailors regarded as "uncooperative" were made to shovel coal and iron ore in a steel mill. These men lost an average of 45 pounds apiece. Others worked in rice paddies and as stevedores on the docks.

When the Marines captured on Wake were removed to Japanese camps and Woosung Prison, they had to leave behind 300 civilian construction workers and 100 servicemen and civilians too ill to be moved. On the night of October 7, 1943, nearly 100 American civilians on Wake were lined up on the beach and executed by a machine-gun firing squad. After the war, Rear Adm. Shigematsu Sakaibara and several of his officers were hung for this crime.

A few Marines managed to escape their captors. In March 1942, four enlisted Marines escaped from Woosung, but they were recaptured a month later. In October 1944, Marine Cpl. Jerold Story, one of the four, and a British and an American naval officer escaped from Shanghai's Ward Road Gaol and made their way to Chungking and freedom.

While 901 prisoners were being moved by train from Shanghai to Peking on the night of May 9, 1945, two Wake Marines, 1st Lt. John F. Kinney and 1st Lt. John A. McAlister, and two North China Marines, 1st Lt. Richard M. Huizenga and 1st Lt. James D. McBrayer—and Lewis S. Bishop, a former Flying Tiger pilot—jumped out of a window. Chinese guerrillas found them and turned them over to Nationalist troops. The group participated in many local patriotic rallies and, when asked to sing the American national anthem, obliged by singing *The Marines' Hymn*. In time, all five returned safely to the United States.

When the cruiser *Houston* was sunk off Java on March 1, 1942, only 368 men of 1,064 men aboard—and 24 of 74 Marines—survived. The Japanese put them to work unloading transports; and they were eventually taken to Burma, where they were forced to work building a railroad. Some ended up as stevedores in Saigon.

The largest group of Marine prisoners was captured in the Philippines: 105 Marines on Bataan and 1,283 on Corregidor. Of these, 490 men never survived their wounds, malnutrition, beatings and disease or were executed, killed by American bombs or massacred at the Puerto Princesa prison camp.

In April 1942, thousands of Americans and Filipinos made the 85-mile Bataan Death March to Camp O'Donnell. When Corregidor fell on May 6, the prisoners organized themselves; and nearly half the men who made up a military police company to keep order with moral and physical persuasion were Marines.

Of the prisoners from the Philippines, 40 to 50 men of all services died daily in prison camps near Cabanatuan, 75 miles north of Manila. A thousand of the prisoners were shipped to the Davao Penal Colony, a huge plantation on Mindanao. There, a dozen men, including Capt. Austin C. Shofner and 1st Lts. Jack Hawkins and Michiel Dobervich of the 4th Marines, escaped in April 1943 and reached the guerrilla forces of Col. Wendell W. Fertig, USA. They served with the guerrillas for six months, raiding Japanese garrisons, and then were taken to Australia by submarine.

One hundred and forty American prisoners, including 23 Marines, were murdered at the Puerto Princesa prison camp on Palawan Island in the Philippines on December 14, 1944. The Japanese killed them with burning gasoline and machine-gun fire; those who tried to flee were picked off in the water by rifle fire. One Marine and four other men escaped.

One day earlier, 1,619 prisoners in Manila were herded into the hold of a Japanese ship. They were jammed in so tightly that some went berserk and killed one another. Others died of suffocation, including Lt. Col. John P. Adams, commander of the 3rd Battalion, 4th Marines. Fifteen prisoners died that first night. The next morning, U.S. Navy planes bombed the convoy; and a number of prisoners were killed and wounded. The ship limped into Subic Bay; and the following day, planes attacked again, killing many prisoners. Japanese guards shot prisoners who tried to climb out of the hold. Many drowned swimming to shore. In all, 419 were killed, including 21 Marines. Ashore at Olongapo, the 15 prisoners in the worst condition were beheaded. They included Lt. Col. Samuel W. Freeny, executive officer of the 1st Battalion, 4th Marines.

The remaining POWs were taken to Formosa, where 400 were killed when their unmarked ship was bombed. The survivors were moved to Moji on Kyushu; en route, 30 to 40 prisoners died each day. Only 470 reached Moji and 300 of them died in the next month. The rest were sent to prison camps in Korea where they were liberated at the end of the war.

It is estimated that in all 184 men of the 4th Marines were killed by American fliers and submariners who had no idea that they were attacking ships carrying American prisoners. Some unmarked prison camps in Japan were also bombed by American planes.

Most of the prisoners of the Japanese endured inhumane treatment and unbelievable brutality. They were underfed, overworked, humiliated, denied medical care, beaten, tortured, killed. When they could, many Marines and other POWs tried to sabotage the Japanese war effort by wrecking machines and tools, adding water to oil drums and slowing their work to a snail's pace. Frequently, they were painfully punished for their efforts. A few Japanese guards gave prisoners extra food and medicine, but they were the exception. The POWs survived on hope and group discipline and faith in an ultimate American victory.

15
North China: Bitter Taste of the Future

Fifty-three thousand Marines went into North China in the autumn of 1945 to ensure the surrender of the Japanese armies—and stayed to wrestle the Chinese Communists.

In Europe at the end of World War II, a reasonably clear line was drawn between Communist and non-Communist blocs; but no such line could be fixed in Asia. Generalissimo Chiang Kai-shek's Nationalist government, which the United States recognized and supported, and the armies of the Chinese Communist revolutionary movement battled for four more years. The Marines, as the amphibious tip of American sea power, remained in China until practically the end of that struggle. At the same time in southeast Asia, nationalist and communist factions were fighting against the resurrection of Western colonialism. The turmoil there would go on for decades, its outcome shaping the westward expansion of United States power.

The Joint Chiefs of Staff wanted to see Chiang's armies established throughout China and particularly in industrial Manchuria, which the Russians had already overrun. The Marines were sent to disarm and replace the Japanese garrisons in North China's ports and communications centers, to begin repatriating the Japanese and to prevent great quantities of Japanese arms from falling into Communist hands. On V-J Day, the Nationalists controlled only southeast China; and until they could be brought north, the Marines would attempt to fill the strategic vacuum in North China. The Communists, who had 170,000 regular troops there, were prepared to take over all North China if they could; but, as one Marine officer later wrote candidly, "the presence of the Marines frustrated this."[125]

The civil war that the Marines encountered in China was massive. Nationalist armies numbered three million men and the Communists', one million. Naively, the Marines were charged with both supporting the Nationalists and retaining their own neutrality. As a result, they became the first Americans to do battle with Chairman Mao Tse-tung's forces.

Maj. Gen. Keller E. Rockey's III Amphibious Corps was assigned to China. Many of its officers and senior noncoms had served in China between World Wars I and II. On September 30, the 1st Marine Division landed at Tangku and moved to the Tientsin–Peking region. And on October 11, the 6th Marine Division landed at Tsingtao on the Shantung Peninsula. They all came under the command of Lt. Gen. Albert C. Wedemeyer, USA, commander of United States forces in China.

Before either landing, the pattern was already stenciled. On September 20, an advance party led by Brig. Gen. William A. Worton, Rockey's chief of staff, and Col. Charles C. Brown, the corps G-2, arrived at Shanghai. Both Worton and Brown had served in China. When the party flew up to Tientsin, no one knew what opposition might be offered by the Japanese—or by the Chinese Communists.

Worton conferred with the Japanese commanders in Tientsin and Peking. And he was visited by Gen. Chou En-lai, the leading Communist representative in wartime negotiations between the Communists and Nationalists. In a stormy meeting, Chou warned Worton that the Communists would fight the Marines if they moved to Peking. Although Peking was not named in Worton's directives, he was determined that the Marines would occupy the city. He told Chou that the III Amphibious Corps was combat-experienced and that the Marines would drive through any force that tried to stop them. The gauntlet was down.

Worton's insistence on establishing a Marine presence in Peking had two purposes: to make sure the Nationalists, rather than the Communists, gained control of the ancient city that was a potent symbol of national power and to use Peking's two first-class military airfields to bring in the Nationalist troops who would relieve the Marines—especially since Worton had found Tientsin's airfield inadequate. The meeting between Worton and Chou pointed to the coming clashes between the Marines and Chinese Communists.

Although the 1st Division expected to occupy its assigned places in North China peacefully, Maj. Gen. DeWitt Peck brought it in from Okinawa ready for trouble. The 7th Marines, designated the division's assault troops, landed at Tangku on September 30. While the 2d Battalion stayed in the port, the 3rd Battalion went by train directly to Tientsin, where it was met by a noisy, cheering throng of thousands and was billeted in the buildings of the race track west of the city. On the first day, 5,400 Marines were ashore.

That evening, Lt. Col. John J. Gormley took his 1st Battalion, 7th Marines to Chinwangtao, an ice-free port 150 miles north of Tangku. The British had developed Chinwangtao as the port for their Kailin coal mines. The situation was tense; troops of the Communist Eighth Route Army were in the area and small-arms fire was frequently heard. Gormley disarmed the Japanese troops at Chinwangtao and Peitaiho, and the Communist leaders in the area sent word that they would cooperate with the Marines—an attitude that did not last long.

The 1st Marines were posted at Tientsin, where, on October 6, 50,000 Japanese troops surrendered to Rockey, acting in the name of Chiang Kai-shek. They were allowed to keep one rifle and five rounds of ammunition for every ten men to protect themselves and their supplies. The Marines found the teeming city exciting. "Although the billets were 'musty, damp and dirty (the Japanese had ripped out plumbing, sabotaged heating and water supplies), wine, women and steaks were cheap.'" The Marines hired "roomboys" to do onerous housekeeping chores and quickly discovered the British concession where "bad vodka, poor wine and poisonous Chinese whiskies and Russian women were the main attractions" and the French concession where there was "a large five-story bazaar and a larger house of ill-repute."[126] As in pre-war days, the younger officers were especially attracted to the White Russian girls. The Marines soon whipped up an inflation that slowed down the most extravagant living.

On October 6, the Marines had their first fire fight with the Chinese Communists, pretty much as Chou En-lai had promised. In preparation for the movement of the 2d and 3rd Battalions of the 5th Marines to Peking, Engineers guarded by a rifle platoon of the 1st Marines tried to remove a series of roadblocks 22 miles northwest of Tientsin and were fired on by

40 to 50 Communist soldiers. Three Marines were wounded. The detachment returned to Tientsin. On the seventh, a 1st Marines rifle company and a platoon of tanks, covered by carrier planes, removed the roadblocks; and the 5th Marines went into Peking. Later on, a Communist general in civilian clothes appeared at III Corps headquarters in Tientsin and apologized for the attack on the road.

The Communists beat Maj. Gen. Lemuel C. Shepherd, Jr.,'s 6th Marine Division to Chefoo, on the north coast of the Shantung Peninsula. The Marines' landing was cancelled; and the 29th Marines, who had been assigned to Chefoo, were switched to the port of Tsingtao on the south side of the Shantung Peninsula. Tsingtao, 475 miles southeast of Peking, was an important industrial city with the best harbor and airfield north of Shanghai.

The 6th Marine Division landed on October 11 under a show-of-force umbrella of carrier air power. Soon enough, Maj. Gen. Shepherd received a message from the area's Communist commander warning that the arrival of Nationalist troops at Tsingtao would bring civil war. Shepherd replied that he had no control over the movement of Nationalist troops to Tsingtao and pointedly added that in case disorders broke out "my Division of well-trained combat veterans will be entirely capable of coping with the situation."[127]

By now, the Communists were attacking Marine units guarding communications routes in the 1st Division's zone. On October 18, six Communist soldiers were killed while firing on a Marine-guarded train between Peking and Langfang. Jeep patrols were also fired on, and three Marines were wounded in October. In the 6th Division's area, the Communists harassed low-flying Marine reconnaissance planes with small-arms fire. The Marine pilots were ordered not to reply, and MAG-32 arrived on October 21 and began flying patrols over the Shantung Peninsula.

Life was not all tension for the Marines in Tsingtao. There were many pleasures. For 25 cents a Marine could have a hot bath, manicure, pedicure and brisk massage. Chinese sold everything from watches to freshly made "Scotch." Inflation soon took hold; Japanese beer increased six times in price, and speculators had a heyday trading for American dollars. On

Thanksgiving Day, the 22d Marines' football team beat the 29th Marines, 25-14, in the Rice Bowl in Tsingtao Stadium.

Meanwhile, Maj. Gen. Claude A. "Sheriff" Larkin, who had commanded MAG-21 at Ewa on Pearl Harbor Day, brought the 1st Marine Aircraft Wing to Tientsin. At the end of October, Maj. Gen. Louis E. Woods relieved him. MAG-12 and MAG-24 were based at Peking and MAG-25 and MAG-32 at Tsingtao.

In both Tientsin and Tsingtao, Chinese mobs attacked and robbed Japanese and German civilians. At Tientsin, the 1st Marines waded into the fighting and stopped the rioting; and in Tsingtao, squad-sized street patrols of the 22d and 29th Marines kept the peace. Meanwhile, the repatriation of 326,375 Japanese military personnel and 312,774 civilians began on October 22. It was a huge job.

Japanese troops continued to guard outlying bridges and stretches of railroad track between Peking and Chinwangtao because Maj. Gen. Peck did not want to expose small units of Marines to Communist attacks. Two Nationalist armies totaling 56,000 men were airlifted to Peking and Tientsin and garrisoned the cities. But their commanders were in no hurry to replace the Japanese on the roads and rail lines.

The Marines were caught in a fluid and dangerous situation. Pressure grew to start withdrawing them and avoid involvement in a civil war once Nationalist troops were present in North China.

Chiang Kai-shek was eager to recover the industrial complex and rich agricultural resources of Soviet-occupied Manchuria. But the Soviet commanders refused to let Nationalist troops land there and turned over some ports to the Communists under Gen. Lin Piao. This meant Chiang Kai-shek would have to enter Manchuria overland through the Chinwangtao region and increased the danger that the Marines would become involved.

On November 14, Chiang's American-trained divisions attacked north into Manchuria. Lt. Gen. Wedemeyer reported, "He visualizes utilizing the Marines as a base of maneuver."[128] The Marines were in an impossible position. Wedemeyer and senior Marine officers felt that the directives under which they operated were "ill-considered and ambiguous."[129] Back home in November, seven joint resolutions were introduced in the Congress calling for the withdrawal of the Marines from China.

When Ambassador Patrick J. Hurley resigned suddenly on November 27, President Truman instantly appointed General of the Army George C. Marshall to be his special representative to China. Truman called for a ceasefire in China, a unified government and army and an end of the civil war "particularly in North China."[130] Marshall suspended the movement of Nationalist troops to North China. That meant the Marines would stay.

They were ordered to protect the ports and the rail traffic bringing out the coal urgently needed in Shanghai, Peking and Tientsin. The 7th Marines provided most of the rail and bridge guard detachments between Chinwangtao and Tangku. It was lonely dangerous duty in the cold of the Chinese winter.

On the morning of November 14, the Communists, firing from a village, stopped a train carrying Maj. Gen. Peck to Chinwangtao. The next day, Peck started out again and found several hundred yards of tracks torn up. A Chinese track gang made repairs while the Marines answered sniper fire. A mine exploded killing several of the work gang, and Peck finally had to fly to Chinwangtao.

On December 4, two members of the 1st Battalion, 29th Marines were shot by two Chinese. One Marine was killed; the other survived by pretending to be dead and watched the Chinese disappear into a nearby village. The battalion executive officer set up a 60mm mortar and gave the village head man a half hour to surrender the two killers or he would shell the village. When the deadline expired, 24 rounds of white phosphorus were fired outside the village walls. Nobody was hurt, but word got back to the United States that the Marines had fired into an unarmed village, and criticisms appeared in the press.

Increasingly, the Marines aided the Nationalist armies that were fighting Communists. The Marines provided the Nationalists with arms, ammunition and replacement parts. When the Eighth Chinese Nationalist Army fought the Communists near Tsangkou, Maj. Gen. Shepherd turned over to the Nationalists one unit of fire for the infantry weapons of a Marine division.

A disaster occurred on December 8 when planes from MAG-32 flew back to Tsingtao after a Pearl Harbor anniversary air show-of-strength at Tientsin. VMSB-343's scout-bombers tried to fly through a snow storm, and six pilots crashed into the

644

mountains of the Shantung Peninsula. Communist villagers rescued the only two survivors. The Communists treated the Marine fliers well and later released them and several other fliers who had also crashlanded.

Clashes between the Marines and the Communists subsided once General Marshall arrived in Chungking and organized a cessation of hostilities. The fighting practically stopped; there was hope for peace in China.

On January 11, 1946, 45,981 Marines (of the Corps' declining strength of 301,700) were in North China. General Marshall's January order for a 20 percent reduction of all Marine units in China was welcomed by Marine Corps Headquarters; available manpower was being stretched thin. By now, the Marines in China were chiefly repatriating Japanese and Koreans and making certain that the coal essential to the cities was brought safely from the mines. Marshall also directed the Marines to supply men for the new truce teams until Army replacements arrived. In mid-March, the Marines created six six-man liaison teams, including a Nationalist and Communist officer and headed by a colonel or lieutenant colonel. Two teams were assigned to the railroad lines and the others to troubled areas. The situation of those teams in the depths of China was frequently tense; sometimes, their members were shot at.

Marshall regarded the Marines' presence in North China as an embarrassment to his peace negotiations. He and Wedemeyer became convinced that the Nationalists would provide adequate security forces only when they were persuaded that the Marines were leaving. Instead, the Nationalists increased their activities in Manchuria and occupied Mukden. By mid-April, Nationalists and Communists were battling in Manchuria. Chiang was now less willing than ever to divert troops to relieve the Marines from rail and mine security details.

Economies and demobilization forced the reduction of the 6th Marine Division to the 3rd Marine Brigade, built chiefly around the 4th Marines, and required the 1st Division to disband the third infantry battalion of each regiment and one battery of each battalion of the 11th Marines. By the end of April, III Corps strength was down to 30,379.

In succeeding months, despite a substantial reduction of Marine forces in China and a complicated shifting of commands, the Marines continued to support the truce teams, protect coal production, keep open communications between Tientsin and Chinwangtao and maintain garrisons at Peking, Tientsin, Tangku, Peitaiho, Chinwangtao and Tsingtao. During those early months of 1946, the situation quieted in North China. Only one Marine was killed in combat there in the first half of the year. But by the end of June, political negotiations between the Nationalists and Communists broke down completely. General Marshall's mission for unification and peace had failed.

In July, the Communists began their "Third Revolutionary Civil War." They reorganized their forces, greatly expanded now, as the People's Liberation Army and demanded that all American military forces be withdrawn from China immediately. The Communists began to make their objections perfectly clear.

The Marines promptly were caught in two serious incidents. In the heat of Saturday, July 13, eight Marines from the Bridge 109 Detachment at Lin-Shou-Ying, 15 miles from Peitaiho, went into a nearby village to get ice for their beer cooler. This violated a directive that the men stay within their barbed wire defensives. As they left the icehouse, 80 blue-uniformed Communists surprised and surrounded the Marines. One man escaped in the gathering dusk. In response to a radio call, all available men of the 1st Battalion, 7th Marines boarded a special train to Lin-Shou-Ying and pursued the Communists and their captives through a rainy night and into the next day. On the sixteenth, a 200-man combat patrol from the 2d Battalion continued the chase. The patrol returned on the eighteenth without having found the missing Marines.

Once the Marines obeyed a Communist demand that all Marine units return to their positions of July 13, the men were finally returned on July 24, after each had written a letter attesting to his good treatment. Throughout the long negotiations, the Communists hammered at the point that the Marines were supporting the Chinese Nationalist Army.

Five days later occurred an even more violent encounter. A Marine supply convoy left Tientsin at 9:15 that morning for Peking. The escort, commanded by 2d Lt. Douglas A. Cowin of Ann Arbor, Michigan, consisted of 31 men from the 1st Battalion, 11th Marines and a 10-man 60mm mortar section of the 1st Marines. The escort rode at both ends of the 15-vehicle convoy.

Two of its Jeeps had TCS radios; but when the convoy was ambushed, the radios were out of range of the Marines at either Tientsin or Peking. The Communists had planned their attack well.

Shortly after 11 A.M., 44 miles from Tientsin, the point of the convoy had to thread its way through rocks spread across the road. Ahead was a roadblock of oxcarts. The Marines dismounted cautiously. Immediately, a dozen grenades were thrown from a clump of trees 15 yards to the left of the road. As he jumped from his Jeep, 2d Lt. Cowin was killed; and most of the men with him were killed or wounded. The survivors took cover and returned the Communist fire. The main body of the convoy was hit by steady rifle fire from trees 100 yards to the right of the road. Few men in the trucks or passenger vehicles were armed; they took cover in a ditch. The rear guard was attacked by fire from both sides. Platoon Sgt. Cecil J. Flanagan took command of the escort and went up and down the long line of vehicles directing fire. The machine gun and mortar in the rear guard prevented the Chinese from rushing the convoy. At 1:15, when there was a lull in the firing, three Marines turned a Jeep around and dashed for help.

At 3:30, the Communists, estimated at 300, started withdrawing to the sound of bugles. Gathering up the wounded and covered by a rear guard of Flanagan's men, the convoy headed for Peking, leaving behind three damaged trucks. The Marines had three killed, one man who died of his wounds and 10 others wounded.

Meanwhile, the Jeep racing back to Tientsin overturned on the outskirts of the city, injuring two of the three Marines. They commandeered a passing vehicle and brought word of the ambush to Col. Wilburt S. Brown, commanding the 11th Marines. A heavily armed combat patrol of 400 Marines rushed out; but when it arrived at the scene at 8:45, the enemy dead and wounded had been removed. All the Marines could do was tow in the shot-up trucks.

General Marshall recognized that the incident represented a toughening of the Communists' attitude. As a result, patrols were strengthened, more powerful field radios were used and many Marine bridge and rail detachments were withdrawn. But there were no more attacks.

By the summer of 1946, the combat efficiency of the

Marines in China had dropped drastically because of the turn-over of experienced personnel. MAG-24 was operating with only 20 percent of its aircraft available because of a shortage of qualified mechanics. And 1st Division units were rated at 25 and 35 percent of combat efficiency.

The Marines at Tsingtao were reduced to the reinforced 3rd Battalion, 4th Marines under Col. Samuel B. Griffith, II, the former Raider and Chinese-language student. On September 3, the rest of the 4th Marines sailed for Camp Lejeune. The regiment was finally home after nearly 20 years overseas. In September 1948, the 4th Marines joined the Sixth Fleet in the Mediterranean; and after the American Consul General was killed by a sniper during the Arab-Israeli war, 62 Marines from the regiment were at Haifa and 41 were in Jerusalem to guard the American consulate. Two Marines were wounded on duty in Jerusalem.

In August 1946, 4,700 Marines of the 1st Marine Division were stationed from Tangku to Chinwangtao. Within 15 miles on both sides of the railroad were 25,000 Communist soldiers. On August 4, a coal train heading for Tientsin was derailed. Four Marines in the caboose and Chinese railroad police fought off the ambushers until a relief train rescued them. Frequently, snipers shot at bridge and station outposts. This harassment worked. By September 30, Marine rail guards were replaced by Nationalist troops at all the most exposed outposts. The Marines ended their responsibility for guarding the delivery of coal to Chinwangtao.

On September 18, Maj. Gen. Samuel L. Howard, who had commanded the 4th Marines in Shanghai in 1941, replaced Rockey as commander of the 1st Division. Maj. Gen. Howard addressed a statement to the people of North China that said in part: "The U.S. Marines have no part in the establishment of our nation's policy. We are an organization whose traditional duty is to support and uphold that policy and to protect American lives and property in any part of the globe. We are in China to carry out the directives of our State Department or those of General Marshall. This we propose to do."[131]

The division's ammunition supply point at Hsin Ho, six miles northwest of Tangku, was an oval two miles across and one wide, ringed with barbed wire fence and spotted with eight sentry towers. On October 3, at about 10 P.M., the sentry at Post 3 was fired on by a large group of Chinese. They cut the wire fence and began carrying off ammunition boxes. The remainder of the guard—52 Marines in all—dashed up and took firing positions. At 11 P.M., when 100 men from the 1st Battalion, 5th Marines at Tangku arrived, the Chinese had disappeared, leaving behind one dead and one wounded Communist soldier. Thirty-two cases of ammunition were missing in the well-executed raid by the 53rd Communist Regiment.

On January 7, 1947, General Marshall left China, his peace mission washed out; and Truman nominated him as Secretary of State. At the end of January, mediation officially ended.

Plans were already underway to bring the rest of the Marines home from China. The 7th Marines embarked for the United States; and the 11th Marines headed for Guam. The air units started leaving. The 1st Marines stayed in Tientsin, with one battalion ready to fly to Shanghai on six hours' notice; and the 5th Marines remained in Peking and Tangku. Their prime responsibility now was to evacuate Americans and support the U.S. Army detachment in Peking.

While the 1st Division was pulling out of China, "the Communists made their most punishing attack against the Marines."[132] The target again was the ammunition at Hsin Ho, which the Communists wanted to seize before it was turned over to the Nationalists. The enclosure was now triangular with two long sides about two miles in length and the short side a mile long. At 1:15 A.M. on April 5, 1947, a bugle sounded, followed by rifle and machine-gun fire. The two sentries at the most distant northern post returned the fire for about 10 minutes until they were killed. The Communists killed three Marines in a patrol Jeep and drove back the main guard. Eight Marines were wounded. The raiders took all the ammunition they could carry.

C Company, 5th Marines came out from Tangku; but the Communists were ready for them. When the self-propelled 105mm howitzer in front of the column reached a narrow place in the road near Hsin Ho, it struck a land mine and blocked the road. Marines were hit by intense fire from an irrigation ditch 40 yards east of the road. They took cover behind their trucks and fired back. Two waves of Communist soldiers, 35 or 40 men, rushed forward throwing grenades and then continued the fire fight for 15 minutes before they were driven off. Eight more Marines were wounded in the ambush.

By the end of the month, the Hsin Ho ammunition dump was handed over to the Nationalist army. At Hsin Ho and Tsingtao, the Marines turned over to the Nationalists 6,500 tons of ammunition.

In May, Lin Piao's People's Liberation Army command, equipped with Japanese weapons, attacked in Manchuria and defeated the Nationalist armies. The Communists had the initiative, and they never again lost it.

By the end of August, the 1st Marine Division had pulled out of China. All that remained was the Fleet Marine Force, Western Pacific at Tsingtao under Brig. Gen. Omar T. Pfeiffer. He had 4,026 men, including the 3rd Battalion, 4th Marines and the 2d Battalion, 1st Marines, and VMF-211 and VMR-153. Their job was to guard American naval installations and by airlift to provide emergency protection for the 7,500 Americans still in China.

By this summer of 1947, the Communists—supplied with Japanese and captured American arms—were clearly winning the civil war. Lt. Gen. Wedemeyer visited China as the head of a special commission and warned that the Communists, by furthering the aims of the Soviet Union, were a danger to America's strategic security. He recommended, as the only alternative, giving military assistance to the Nationalists, whom he described as "the presently corrupt, reactionary and inefficient Chinese National Government."[133]

That fall, the 2d Battalion, 1st Marines was designated the 1st Marines; and the 3rd Battalion, 4th Marines became the 3rd Marines. Cordoned behind Nationalist defenses at Tsingtao, they had little contact with the Communists. But on Christmas Day, 1947, Communists killed one Marine and seized four more in a hunting party and did not release them until April 1, 1948. Four days later, the four-man crew of a Marine plane that crashlanded near Tsingtao was captured by the Communists and not returned until July 1.

In the summer of 1948, while the Russians began their blockade of West Berlin, the Chinese Communists advanced into northern and central China. In Manchuria by November 1948, the Nationalists lost 400,000 troops "and mountains of

American military supplies."[134] The senior American Army general in Nanking blamed the disaster on "the world's worst leadership."[135]

The Marines, now under Brig. Gen. Gerald C. Thomas, were given the job of evacuating Americans from North China and Manchuria, while the Army brought them out through Nanking and Shanghai. The 9th Marines from Guam arrived at Tsingtao.

In January 1949, the Communists won the massive 65-day battle of the Hwai-Hai and swept through Peking and Tientsin. The complete defeat of the Nationalists was now inevitable. The 9th Marines moved to the Whangpoo River at Shanghai to protect American lives. Tsingtao was doomed; and by February 3, all the Marines there were on board ships except for C Company, 3rd Marines, which served as a shore patrol. In March, the bulk of the 3rd Marines relieved the 9th Marines at Shanghai. On April 20, the Communists shelled and machine-gunned British warships in the Yangtze, killing 40 men and wounding 73. Corpsmen and stretcher bearers from the 3rd Marines took the wounded aboard the American hospital ship *Repose*.

With the last 119 American civilians evacuated, the 3rd Marines sailed from Shanghai on April 29 for the United States. It left behind only its C Company at Tsingtao, the remnant of the task force that had once numbered more than 50,000. C Company stayed aboard a cruiser and sent patrols ashore. In mid-May, it was relieved by C Company, 7th Marines, which had come out from Camp Pendleton. By May 26, when Shanghai had fallen to the Communists and Tsingtao was about to be taken, the last Marines left China. They had had 10 killed and 33 wounded there since the end of World War II. It was the close of the long and colorful era of the China Marines.

By using the Japanese and helping the Nationalists to oppose the Communists' takeover of China, the Marines "ensured the enduring enmity of the Communists."[136] In essence, the Marines had provided a base for the Nationalists to recover North China and Manchuria, much as the Marines had been used earlier to support governments favored by American policy in the Caribbean. The Marines had begun to confront the Communists in Asia—a confrontation that in the years ahead would be played out in Korea and Vietnam.

16
Summing Up the War

The Marine Corps had grown to maturity in World War II. It had done its job, proved itself.

By V-J Day, the Corps had ballooned to an all-time peak of 485,833 men and women, of whom 242,043 were overseas. Of the overall total, 116,628 were in Marine aviation. The Corps' readiness and the amphibious nature of the Pacific war had stimulated this vast expansion.

Approximately 450,000 new Marines had been trained at the Recruit Depots at Parris Island and San Diego. Not all those who joined the Marines in World War II were volunteers; 70,729 were draftees and 5,241 were Selective Service volunteers inducted into the Marine Corps Reserve. In legalistic terms, the Corps could not accept volunteers ages 18 to 36 after December 5, 1942; so 224,875 World War II Marines came in through the Selective Service System—though most of them volunteered to become Marines.

The war saw the first black Americans in the Corps since 1798. This was the result of President Franklin D. Roosevelt's Executive Order 8802. A recent Marine Corps study concluded, "There is no question but that the order was unpopular at Headquarters Marine Corps."[137] The month after Pearl Harbor, Commandant Holcomb said, ". . . the Negro race has every opportunity now to satisfy its aspirations for combat, in the Army—a very much larger organization than the Navy or Marine Corps—and their desire to enter the naval service is largely, I think, to break into a club that doesn't want them."[138] Many Marines felt theirs was a small "elite" service, and there was a strong Southern tradition among the commissioned officers. But

Secretary of the Navy Frank Knox insisted that the Marine Corps start recruiting a thousand blacks per month.

The first black Marines to enlist on June 1, 1942, were Alfred Masters and George O. Thompson. One of the earliest recruits was Edgar R. Huff of Gadsden, Alabama, who was to become the senior sergeant major in the Corps. Huff, who served 30 years, said, "I wanted to be a Marine because I had always heard that the Marine Corps was the toughest outfit going and I felt that I was the toughest going."[139]

The first black unit, the 51st Composite Defense Battalion, was activated in August 1942 at the new camp built near Camp Lejeune at Montford Point, North Carolina. The battalion was to consist of 1,085 Marines commanded by white officers headed by Col. Samuel A. Woods, Jr., a native of South Carolina and a Marine for 25 years. Among the recruits were college graduates and veterans. Charles W. Simmons, who became sergeant major of the 51st, had a masters degree from the University of Illinois. George A. Jackson had been an Army lieutenant and Gilbert H. "Hashmark" Johnson had served in both the Army and the Navy. By May 1943, the last white Drill Instructor had left Montford Point; and from then on, all recruit training was done by black DIs led by Sgt. Major "Hashmark" Johnson.

During World War II, 19,168 blacks enlisted in the Corps. They served in two defense battalions, the 51st and 52d; 51 depot companies, and 12 ammunition companies. Segregated units with 12,738 blacks served overseas in all major campaigns from Saipan on.

After they participated in their first amphibious assault at Saipan, Commandant Vandegrift said, "The Negro Marines are no longer on trial. They are Marines, period."[140] Pvt. Kenneth J. Tibbs of Columbus, Ohio, and Pfc. Leroy Seals of Brooklyn, New York, were fatally wounded on Saipan on D-Day—the first black Marines to die in combat. Pfc. Luther Woodward, a former Memphis truck driver, tracked and killed Japanese on Guam and received the Silver Star, the highest decoration won by a black Marine in World War II.

Nine black Marines were killed in action or died of wounds in World War II and 78 others were wounded in action. They were almost all in "labor troop" units. The 3rd Ammunition

Company received the Presidential Unit Citation for its role with the 4th Marine Division on D-Day at Saipan; and the 6th Ammunition Company and the 33rd, 34th and 36th Depot Companies were awarded the Navy Unit Commendation in the Iwo Jima campaign.

In March 1945, three black Marines were sent to Platoon Commanders class at Quantico. None of the three was commissioned although they became a lawyer, a doctor and a college professor after returning to civilian life. The next three black officer candidates also washed out. At last, on the Corps' 170th birthday, Frederick C. Branch of Hamlet, North Carolina, who had served in the 51st Defense Battalion, became the Marines' first black officer. Lieutenant Branch returned to active service in the Korean war. In 1946, three black Marines were commissioned from the V-12 program; one of them, Lt. Herbert E. Brewer of San Antonio, served in the Korean war and by 1973 was a colonel, the highest ranking black in the Marine Corps Reserve. By June 1949, blacks were fully integrated into the Corps.

Because of Commandant Holcomb's initial resistance, the Marines were the last of the services to form a Women's Reserve. Holcomb liked to tell the story that, when he finally approved the idea, Archibald Henderson's picture fell off the wall of the Commandant's House in Washington. The program was announced on February 13, 1943; and Mrs. Ruth Cheney Streeter of Morristown, New Jersey, was chosen to lead the women. Major Streeter, who had been the president of her class at Bryn Mawr College, was the mother of three grown children and held a pilot's license.

"Free a Marine to Fight" was the slogan designed to attract women recruits, and Commandant Vandegrift told them that they were responsible for putting the 6th Marine Division into the field. By the end of the war, 18,460 women were on duty from Washington to Pearl Harbor, filling jobs from clerks to control tower operators. Eighty-five percent of the personnel at Marine Corps Headquarters were women. Mrs. Streeter was a full colonel when she was succeeded after the war by Col. Katherine A. Towle. It was decided to keep a nucleus of trained women in the postwar Corps. In 1948, women Marines were totally integrated into the Regular Corps, as were women in all the services.

The rapid demobilization of all the armed services deflated the Corps by July 1946 to 156,000 and by the following July to the low point of 92,000. After that, the Corps rebuilt to its assigned postwar level of 108,200. This was only one-fifth of its wartime high, but still four times what its strength had been in 1939 when World War II began. The Fleet Marine Force was down from six to two divisions, one at Camp Lejeune and one at Camp Pendleton, and a reinforced brigade on Guam.

The Marines' wartime performance had been monumental. They had suffered 91,718 casualties, of whom 19,733 were killed in action, died of wounds or missing, presumed dead. In addition, 67,207 Marines were wounded and 4,778 were "non-battle" casualties in combat zones. Eighty Marines received the Medal of Honor, 48 of them posthumously; and Marines earned 957 Navy Crosses for heroism. Seven Navy corpsmen serving with the Marines were awarded the Medal of Honor, and corpsmen and other naval medical personnel received 69 Navy Crosses.

Of course, the Marine Corps' role in the Pacific war was part of a larger whole involving all the services. The purpose of amphibious assault was not to capture Japanese islands for themselves but to make possible an attack on the enemy's homeland. Wartime leaders argued over the best routes to approach Japan and which islands should be assaulted and which neutralized or bypassed. But the United States did not have the long-range power to reach Japan directly. There was no shortcut. It could be done only by men seizing advanced naval and air bases from which land-based and carrier-based aircraft could bomb Japan intensively and from which the final invasion could be mounted. The Marine Corps had prepared itself to do precisely that job.

Along the way, the complexities of amphibious assault had to be conquered. Command of the sea and air around the target had to be mastered. The Marine landing force commander had to win from the Navy the responsibility for the conduct of operations ashore. Logistics, combat loading and beach control had to be perfected. All kinds of technical advances had to be created and absorbed: communications, air support control, radar, landing craft, underwater demolition teams, escort carriers, flamethrowers, demolitions and the essential amphibian tractor. The Navy had to learn to deliver ships' gunfire effectively against an entrenched enemy. Ashore, infantry fire teams increased small-unit flexibility and infantry-tank teams provided riflemen with artillery. Rifle companies grew from 183 men to 242, chiefly by the addition of a machine-gun platoon. Some problems were not solved satisfactorily, especially the actual use of close air support and the feeding of replacements into battle.

The most significant fact was that the Marines were ready for the mission the war thrust upon them. Years before, their best minds had seen the future and the Marines' role in it. They had developed the doctrine of offensive amphibious warfare and started to build the means to fight it. They stumbled often; they did things wrong as well as right; but through trial and error, they learned from their successes and their mistakes. They won some of the toughest fighting in all man's history of killing other men.

That spirit that Ernie Pyle wrote about on Okinawa was crucial to the Marines' triumph. They had a belief in themselves, the conviction every winner needs that he is the best. Certainly, there were a few "supermen": Basilone, Boyington, Edson, Hawkins, Shoup and others, both celebrated and unnoted; they were precious models. But more important still was the ingrained faith that a Marine does not let another Marine down, in a bar or on a beachhead. It was the spirit that Carlson dramatized with the phrase "Gung Ho"; it was the spirit that drove Marines forward in the face of danger and almost certain death.

Now, the Marines' biggest war was over. The early defeats and the later victories were memories. Unforgettable names had been added to the Marine Corps' story: Wake, Corregidor, Guadalcanal, Tarawa, Iwo Jima, Okinawa.

In the beginning, the United States had been thrown out of the Western Pacific; but it had fought back and returned in even greater strength. Americans were willing to die because they believed they had a right to be there; and they would not permit another power to deny them that right. They defeated Japan neither to preserve Western colonialism in Asia nor to free

Asians from Japanese domination. They fought from the defense of Pearl Harbor to the surrender in Tokyo Bay for their own national purpose. It had not been easy; it had been a long and bloody war in which more than 400,000 Americans had died around the world. It had taught Americans the extent of their strength. They had still to learn its limits.

In his 1946 Commandant's report, General Vandegrift summarized the Marines Corps' postwar mission: "To provide a balanced Fleet Marine Force, including its air support component, for service with the Fleet in the seizure or defense of advanced Naval Bases or for the conduct of such limited land operations as are essential to the prosecution of a Naval campaign."[141] And the Marines would continue to develop amphibious operations, serve on armed naval vessels and protect naval property.

An analysis of the Marines' performance in World War II concluded, "It is imperative that the United States have a branch of the service which devotes full time to devising ways of projecting land power overseas against targets held by hostile forces."[142]

All too soon, the need for this capability would be brutally evident. The Marines' experience in North China was a clear signal of this. World War II had made the United States a Pacific power—the only Pacific power. The western frontier of that power now stood on the far side of the Pacific—5,000 miles west of San Francisco. There, it would come up against new forces; and the nation would call on the Marine Corps once again.

Marines of the 1st Division return from a sniper patrol in the Punchbowl area of eastern Korea in December 1951. Front to back, they are Sgt. Albert L. Ireland, Pfc. Linden L. Brown, and Pfc. Robert D. Glover, Jr. Master Sgt. R. Olund, USMC Photo

SEMPER FIDELIS

XIII
THE
KOREAN
WAR
1946-1953

1
Changes between the Wars

Following its great triumphs of World War II, the Marine Corps should have been riding high. But during the brief interlude—less than five years—between the surrender in Tokyo Bay and the North Korean attack across the 38th Parallel, the Corps wrestled with four critical problems at home: the pressure to demobilize, the effect of the atomic bomb on the battlefield, the integration of blacks into the armed forces and the unification of the military services. The solutions to these problems changed the Corps significantly.

It was a time when the United States and the Soviet Union were becoming locked in an ideological and power struggle. In Europe, the "Iron Curtain" dropped between the communist and western armies—except for the aberration of West Berlin 100 miles east of the Curtain. The Truman Doctrine and the Marshall Plan held that line in 1947. The Soviet bloc swallowed Czechoslovakia in 1948, but the Soviet attempt to dislodge the Western Powers from West Berlin in 1948–49 was defeated. The Soviet Union was not prepared to start World War III for West Berlin.

On the other side of the globe, the United States refused to allow the Soviet Union to participate in the occupation of Japan, but otherwise no sharp "line" was drawn. As a result, the Soviet-supported North Koreans tried to reunite the Korean peninsula by force in 1950 and started a major war. When United States soldiers and Marines counterattacked and approached the border of the year-old People's Republic of China, the Chinese shoved them back to the 38th Parallel. Some Americans would have "unleashed" Chiang Kai-shek's forces on Taiwan and extended the war into China. But the United States

661

refused to pay the price to conquer North Korea, and both sides settled for a divided Korea.

In Southeast Asia, American power first supported and then supplanted French colonialism. In less than a generation, nationalist movements, heavily supported by Communist China and the Soviet Union, threw the United States out of South Vietnam, Cambodia and Laos. American leaders were forced to learn something about the limitations of American power.

For the first half of this short period, Marine Corps problems had to be solved by Commandant Alexander A. Vandegrift, the hero of Guadalcanal who in April 1945 had become the first four-star general on active duty in the history of the Corps.

Demobilization was the immediate headache. Pressure to get the men home after V-J Day was, in Vandegrift's word, "torrential."[1] In all the services, demonstrations erupted among civilians-in-uniform demanding to go home. On January 10, 1946, a delegation of Marine noncoms delivered a petition to Lt. Gen. Roy S. Geiger in Hawaii; he broke all of them to privates and had his sergeant major rip off their chevrons. Vandegrift wrote Geiger that a demonstration "to an old-line Marine . . . still borders on near mutiny."[2]

By early 1946, the 3rd, 4th and 5th Marine Divisions had been disbanded and the 6th Division reduced to the 3rd Marine Brigade. By the end of that year, the Corps was out of Japan and its forces in China had been cut severely. One year after World War II ended, the Marine Corps has shrunk from a wartime peak of 485,000 men and women to 156,000—and by February 1948, it was down to an actual strength of 92,000.

The Corps' postwar leaders had not only to absorb the lessons of World War II but to prepare for atomic war. Official Marine Corps historians later wrote: "the atomic bomb of Hiroshima rendered obsolescent in 10 seconds a system of amphibious assault tactics that had been 10 years in the making. Obviously, the concentrations of transports, warships, and aircraft carriers that had made possible the Saipan and Iwo Jima landings would be sitting ducks for an enemy armed with atomic weapons."[3]

Lt. Gen. Geiger, as commanding general of Fleet Marine

Force, Pacific, observed the test atomic explosions at Bikini Atoll in July 1946 and urged a complete review of amphibious concepts. A special board of Maj. Gen. Lemuel C. Shepherd, Jr., Maj. Gen. Field Harris and Brig. Gen. Oliver P. Smith studied the mysteries conjured up by atomic weapons. The crucial question: How can Marines achieve the surprise, speed and dispersion need to survive on a potentially atomic battlefield?

The answer: "vertical envelopment." Instead of assaulting a beachhead frontally in concentrated, slow-moving waves of landing craft, Marines would leapfrog it with carrier-based helicopters.

In 1948, Marine Helicopter Experimental Squadron I (HMX-1) commanded by Col. Edward C. Dyer began training at Quantico with a few small helicopters. Colonels Merrill B. Twining and Victor H. Krulak led the creation of the first manual of helicopter amphibious doctrine, known as *Phib-31*. At the time, Sikorsky helicopters could lift only two combat-equipped Marines. The choppers brought ashore their first Marines from the escort carrier *Palau* in an amphibious exercise on May 23, 1948, at New River, North Carolina. In August, the squadron received its first Piasecki HRP-1 helicopter. Six combat-ready Marines could be lifted in this to-be-famous "Flying Banana."

As soon as Marines landed in Korea, in August 1950, their commander, Brig. Gen. Edward A. Craig, started using a Sikorsky HO2S-1 helicopter for reconnaissance and to reach his forward units. A year later, transport helicopter squadron HMR-161 arrived in Korea with larger Sikorsky HRS-1s and began troop- and supply-carrying operations. In theory at least, Marine assaults were freed from both landing beaches and airfields.

During the next two years in Korea, the HRS-1s of HMR-161 and the smaller HO2S-1s of VMO-6 airlifted more than 60,000 men and 7.5 million pounds of cargo and evacuated 9,815 wounded. The HRS-1s carried companies and battalions into combat. By the war's end, the helicopter was firmly established as the vehicle of vertical envelopment.

None of these revolutionary developments signaled the end of waterborne amphibious assault. The landing at Inchon, Korea, proved that. The Corps continued to perfect its skill at conventional warfare and amphibious operations. The combining of Marine ground and air elements under a single command became the keystone of the Marine Corps' image of itself as a balanced ground-air amphibious force-in-readiness.

On July 26, 1948, President Truman signed Executive Order No. 9981 ending segregation in the armed services. Commandant Clifton B. Cates protested that segregation was not a problem to be solved by the armed forces but by American society.

Although there were only 2,200 blacks among a total of 93,000 Marines in mid-1947, the change wrought by integration was fundamental. The process began slowly. Athletic teams were integrated. And at Parris Island, by the spring of 1949, Maj. Gen. Alfred H. Noble, Navy Cross winner at Belleau Wood, integrated recruit platoons and NCO clubs. The deactivization of the camp at Montford Point in September 1949 marked the end of the seven-year segregated era for blacks in the Marine Corps. Black women had not been enlisted when the Corps was segregated; the first two, Annie E. Graham of Detroit and Ann E. Lamb of New York, became Marines in September 1949. Finally, on November 18, 1949, the Corps issued instructions that all individual black Marines be assigned to vacancies in any unit where they could be used effectively.

The Korean war buildup hastened integration. When the war began, the Corps' overall strength of 74,279 included 1,502 black Marines on active duty; of those, 427 were stewards. Three years later, the Corps' strength was at 249,219 and included 14,731 blacks on active duty (of whom 538 were stewards). The percentage of blacks in the Corps had risen from two to six. After the war, Maj. Gen. Oliver P. Smith said that he had had a thousand black Marines in Korea and that two had won the Navy Cross and many, the Silver Star and Bronze Star. He added, "They did everything, and they did a good job because they were integrated, and they were with good people."[4] The day of black labor and stevedore units was over.

After each war the Marine Corps has had to scramble for its life. One would think that its unchallengeable record in World War II would have finally made the Corps invulnerable. Not so.

World War II was not yet won before the pressure was intensified to unify the armed services. This was an old idea given new strength by the enormous wartime growth of the military, by the development of air power and by the abject failure of coordination at Pearl Harbor. For the most part, the Army leadership wanted unification; the Navy did not. An acrimonious debate began in Congress as early as 1943; and once the war was over, President Truman pressed to modernize "the antiquated defense setup."[5]

The Marine Corps opposed unification, and Commandant Vandegrift was the spokesman of that opposition. Marines feared that under a single Department of Defense they would be devoured by the Army and at the very least they would lose their air arm to the Air Force. Vandegrift wrote former Commandant Holcomb, "The Army is back on the job in full force trying to absorb the Navy and with it the Marine Corps."[6]

In May 1946 at hearings before the Senate Naval Affairs Committee, Vandegrift charged that the Army was trying to limit the Corps to ceremonial functions and small ineffective units on landing beaches. Declaring that he placed the Corps' fate in the hands of the Congress and ultimately the American people, he made an emotional statement:

> We have pride in ourselves and in our past but we do not rest our case on any presumed ground of gratitude owing us from the nation. The bended knee is not a tradition of our Corps. If the Marine as a fighting man has not made a case for himself after 170 years of service, he must go. But I think you will agree with me that he has earned the right to depart with dignity and honor, not by subjugation to the status of uselessness and servility planned for him by the War Department.[7]

Vandegrift testified that in the years since 1829 the Congress had five times rejected proposals to destroy or severely damage the Corps. He felt that he was fighting for the Corps' survival and that if the Army had its way it would take "the first step in the total abolition of the Corps."[8] Marines saw themselves as members of an organizational David among Goliaths.

When HR 2319 was introduced in February 1947, it did not

mention the Marine Corps. Vandegrift wanted its roles and missions defined by law; he feared that otherwise the Corps would be exposed to any future president's wish to reduce or eliminate it. He pointed out forcefully that Andrew Jackson and Theodore Roosevelt had attempted to curtail the Corps and that President Truman "unfortunately held no particular love for the Marines."[9]

To plan the Corps' defense through this struggle, Vandegrift created a team headed by Brig. Gen. Gerald C. Thomas and Brig. Gen. Merritt A. Edson. Vandegrift and Navy Secretary James V. Forrestal went to see Truman personally and argued for a Congressional charter for the Corps. Gen. Dwight D. Eisenhower, now the Army's Chief of Staff, opposed having "two land armies"[10] and recommended that the Marines be limited to units of regimental size. He told Vandegrift that the Army dreaded the Corps' expansiveness ever since the publicity over Belleau Wood. Vandegrift assured him that the Marine Corps had no ambition to become a second army; it wanted to remain the amphibious partner of the Navy and not to build up for protracted campaigns on large land masses.

On July 26, 1947, while flying to his mother's deathbed in Missouri, President Truman signed the National Security Act organizing the military under a single Secretary of Defense and establishing the Air Force as a separate arm.

The Marines won their basic point: The act formalized in law for the first time the Corps' special amphibious function. The Corps was assigned the mission of seizing and defending advanced bases and engaging in land operations related to a naval campaign; it retained the Fleet Marine Force and was given responsibility for amphibious doctrines and representation on the Joint Staff.

Because the new law created a host of problems, Forrestal, as the first Secretary of Defense, called a conference at Key West in March 1948 (the Commandant was not invited) and began to hammer out the services' roles and missions. The Corps did, in fact, remain virtually a "second army" with a manpower ceiling of 400,000. In 1949, despite the opposition of the second Secretary of Defense, Louis A. Johnson, the Commandant sought a place on the Joint Chiefs of Staff for discussion of matters affecting the Marine Corps.

Finally, during the Korean war, the Corps won its long and intense political struggle. Public Law 416 of the 82nd Congress, enacted on June 28, 1952, guaranteed that the Corps would consist of at least three combat divisions and three air wings and that the Commandant would have co-equal status with members of the Joint Chiefs in matters of direct concern to the Marine Corps. The new law, said Commandant Shepherd, affirmed "that the Marine Corps shall be maintained as a ready fighting force prepared to move promptly in time of peace or war to areas of trouble."[11]

The Congressional hearings on the bill, sponsored by former Marines Senator Paul Douglas and Congressman Mike Mansfield, showed that all the members of the Joint Chiefs opposed the concept that the Marine Corps should come directly under the Secretary of the Navy rather than the Chief of Naval Operations. That battle was not won until 1954, when Secretary of the Navy Robert B. Anderson issued orders putting the Commandant on a level with the Chief of Naval Operations rather than subordinate to him. The Corps saw itself as a partner—not a part—of the Navy.

Vandegrift was not around for these later battles. Some Marines were convinced that he was not re-appointed because of the bitter unification fight. He was succeeded at the end of 1947 by Maj. Gen. Clifton B. Cates, the decorated veteran of World War I who had led a regiment on Guadalcanal and a division at Tinian and Iwo Jima.

The interservice in-fighting more clearly cost the Corps "Red Mike" Edson, holder of the Medal of Honor and two Navy Crosses. The great Raider leader, who had served longer overseas in World War II than any other Marine officer and was a leading candidate to become Commandant, opposed unification with vigor. Some ardent Marines credit him with saving the Corps. When he was ordered not to oppose unification in public, Edson retired to rouse support for the Marine position. In an article entitled "Power-Hungry Men in Uniform," he wrote that he disliked "an American replica of the Prussian general staff system."[12] Immediately after he retired, he said:

I am a military man and proud of it. But when we reach the point where the military are directing, rather than supporting, our country's policies, we are far along the road to losing what this country has always stood for. It was because of this trend of events that I finally reached the very difficult decision to resign from the Marines and return to Vermont.[13]

Edson was recalled to active duty briefly in the Korean war and on August 14, 1955, at the age of fifty-eight, was found dead in his garage of carbon monoxide poisoning.

1st Lt. Baldomero Lopez leads the men of the 3rd
Platoon, A Company, 5th Marines over the stone seawall
at Red Beach, Inchon, Korea, on September 15, 1950.
Within minutes, Lopez was shot while throwing a
grenade. He smothered the explosion with his body and
earned the Medal of Honor posthumously.
Sgt. W. W. Frank, USMC Photo

Under fire, Cpl. Reule Fake leads a
Navy corpsman and another Marine
up Siberia Hill, Korea, to rescue a
wounded Marine.
USMC Photo from United Press
International

Marine sniper Lt. Fred J. Fees fires at enemy troops across the Han River near the Seoul railroad bridge.
U.S. Army Photo

Supported by tanks, Marines fight their way into the center of Seoul.
Wide World Photos

Hunched in their parkas against the shrieking wind, the column of Marines moves torturously back from the Chosin Reservoir after being hard hit by the Chinese Communists at the end of November 1950.
David Douglas Duncan; courtesy, Museums Branch, USMC

Cold, exhausted Marines take a brief break on the march south from Yudam-ni. The Chinese repeatedly severed the escape route of the 5th and 7th Marines as they fought to link up with other Marine units at Hagaru. USMC Photo

The long line of Marines moves again down the winding road among the frozen North Korean hills. David Douglas Duncan; courtesy, Museums Branch, USMC

Only the dead and wounded ride. The rest walk out.
David Douglas Duncan; courtesy, Museums Branch,
USMC

Bone-weary, hungry, unceasingly
cold, they endured.
David Douglas Duncan; courtesy,
Museums Branch, USMC

The breakout from the Chosin
Reservoir was one of the great
fighting retreats of military history.
David Douglas Duncan; courtesy
Museums Branch, USMC

The Marines trudge southward from Koto-ri through the snow-covered, wind-swept Korean hills. Sgt. F. C. Kerr, USMC Photo

Col. Lewis B. "Chesty" Puller earned his fifth Navy Cross commanding the Marines' rear guard out of Koto-ri. USMC Photo

Marines rush a wounded comrade on a stretcher down a Korean hillside to a waiting HRS-1 helicopter for a life-saving flight to a hospital. Staff Sgt. M. McMahon, USMC Photo

Marine F4U supplies accurate close air support for Marines fighting on the ground in Korea. Staff Sgt. Ed Barnum, USMC Photo

Panther jet of the 1st Marine Aircraft Wing makes a napalm run against an enemy troop area in Korea as part of a ninety-two-plane attack, June 10, 1953. USMC Photo

After the tragic 1956 Ribbon Creek "death march," Marine Corps drill instructors came in for public attention. Tech. Sgt. John H. Groves, one of the best DIs at Parris Island, bawls out a recruit for not knowing the name of a pack buckle. Bob Lerner, Look Collection, the Library of Congress. Copyright © Cowles Communications, Inc., 1957

Groves drills his recruit platoon in the manual of arms. Bob Lerner, Look Collection, the Library of Congress. Copyright © Cowles Communications, Inc., 1957

2
The Pusan Perimeter

When the Korean war exploded in June 1950, the first combat troops to ship out from the United States mainland were Marines. General of the Army Douglas MacArthur was threatened with a Dunkirk-like disaster; but he was even then concocting a daring amphibious assault behind the invading North Korean army. And he wanted Marines to make his gamble work.

The war they went to fight resulted from mammoth postwar changes in Asia. With Japan's defeat, United States power, ideology and self-interest clashed with Soviet (and then Chinese) power, ideology and self-interest along the ill-defined border on the Pacific edge of Asia.

During World War II, the United States had proposed the 38th Parallel as the temporary line for dividing the bleak, mountainous Korean peninsula into sectors in which the Russian and American armies would accept the surrender of Japanese forces. That seemed a practical arrangement in 1945. The Russians were already in Korea, and a line even that far north stretched American capabilities to their utmost. It also kept 21 million of the 30 million Koreans—and the capital city of Seoul and its port of Inchon—under American control. But after the Soviet Union refused to let a United Nations commission hold elections in its half of Korea in 1948, the 38th Parallel hardened into a rigid frontier. The United States and the Soviet Union each created a satellite state in its own zone.

The United States grew ambivalent about Korea and the "harsh and fumbling" American occupation.[14] After the Joint Chiefs of Staff decided they had little strategic interest in keeping 45,000 American military personnel in South Korea, the United States withdrew the last of its forces in June 1949. It left

[For the location of places in the Korean war see map No. 9 in the map section.—*Au.*]

500 military advisors to the government of President Syngman Rhee, the autocratic nationalist leader who had returned from long exile to head the Republic of Korea. President Truman was wary of the men "of extreme right-wing attitudes" surrounding Rhee; Truman said, "I did not care for the methods used by Rhee's police to break up political meetings and control political enemies."[15] Because Rhee threatened to attempt to reunite the Korean peninsula by force, the United States gave the South Koreans no tanks, fighter planes or heavy weapons.

On January 12, 1950, Secretary of State Dean Acheson, speaking before the National Press Club in Washington, defined the United States' strategic frontier in Asia. He said, "The defensive perimeter runs along the Aleutians to Japan and then goes to the Ryukyus . . . to the Philippine Islands."[16] He excluded Korea and Formosa. The Communists took him at his word.

On Saturday evening, June 24, 1950, Secretary Acheson on his Maryland farm telephoned President Truman at home in Independence, Missouri. He told the President that some eight hours earlier—before dawn on June 25 Korean time—eight North Korean divisions led by Russian-made T-34 tanks had invaded South Korea.

The United States government was totally surprised—even though this was a period of Communist pressure around the globe: Berlin, Czechoslovakia, China, Indochina.

The United Nations' Security Council convened in New York on Sunday afternoon. That evening, Truman decided to send the Republic of Korea ammunition and military supplies and to evacuate American citizens; and on Monday, he authorized MacArthur to use his air and naval forces south of the 38th Parallel. Although the Republic of Korea (ROK) army was disintegrating, Truman did not commit U.S. ground forces because he feared other Communist strikes elsewhere. But he enlarged the arena of concern by ordering the U.S. Seventh Fleet into the Formosa Strait to protect the Nationalist Chinese from attack and prevent Chiang Kai-shek from attacking mainland China. (This intervention between the Chinese political foes would have enormous political effects later on.)

With the Soviet Union absent and unable to use its veto power (it had been boycotting the Security Council for six months over the presence of Nationalist China), the United Nations on Tuesday night called on its members to help repel the armed attack on South Korea and to restore peace. The UN and U.S. decisions to intervene caught the American commanders in Tokyo off guard. Vice Adm. C. Turner Joy, MacArthur's naval commander, said later, "As a consequence, we had no plans for this type of war."[17]

Events moved swiftly. On Wednesday in Washington, Commandant Cates proposed to the Chief of Naval Operations that the Fleet Marine Force be used in Korea. On Wednesday in Korea, American fighter planes, covering the evacuation of Americans and other foreign nationals, shot down seven North Korean aircraft. That same day, Seoul fell; most of the ROK army was trapped north of the Han River. On Thursday, the U.S. Navy began bombarding the Korean coast and made its first kill: a South Korean minecraft.

MacArthur visited the Korean front on Friday and found that of the 98,000-man ROK army only 25,000 troops could be accounted for. He urged President Truman to use United States combat troops. Truman immediately approved sending an Army regimental combat team from MacArthur's four understrength divisions on occupation duty in Japan. By Friday night (Washington time), the United States was fully committed to the defense of the Republic of Korea.

Unlike both World Wars I and II, this was America's war from the beginning. But, as in both those earlier wars, the United States military was not ready. On July 1, Lt. Col. Charles B. Smith and 406 soldiers from the 1st Battalion, 21st Infantry flew to Korea. In the rain on July 5, Task Force Smith, now 540 strong, went into battle above Osan near the west coast and was overwhelmed by two North Korean regiments with 33 tanks. The next day, the enemy scattered two battalions of the U.S. 34th Infantry, which had moved in behind Smith's original positions. The United States had to throw in its forces piecemeal, and they were getting beaten.

During the night of July 11–12, a demolition party including a Marine officer and four enlisted Marines from the cruiser *Juneau* were the first Americans to land in North Korea. In a whale boat from the destroyer *Mansfield*, they went ashore south of Songjin on the east coast and rigged two 60-pound charges in a railroad tunnel. Later, broadcasts by the North Korean radio indicated that the next train had detonated the charges.

The rapid American buildup was chaotic and expensive. On July 8, Truman named General MacArthur head of the United Nations Command in Korea. On July 13, Lt. Gen. Walton H. Walker took charge of the U.S. Eighth Army's 18,000 soldiers then in Korea. On July 20, Maj. Gen. William F. Dean's 24th Infantry Division defending Taejon was shattered and lost nearly 30 percent of its 12,200 men. Dean, after wandering in the mountains for 36 days, was captured and held prisoner for more than three years. By the third week of July, the decimated 24th and the understrength 25th Infantry Division and 1st Cavalry Division from Japan with 39,000 men—many of them neither physically nor psychologically ready for combat—were being squeezed into the southeastern corner of Korea around the port of Pusan, a pocket 100 miles north to south and 50 miles wide.

It was now a race between the North Korean advance and the arrival of reinforcements from the United States. American pilots and soldiers helped slow down the North Koreans. Some ROK divisions fought valiantly. On July 29, Lt. Gen. Walker called a halt to the Eighth Army's retreat and ordered his forces to stand or die. He said, "A Marine unit and two regiments are expected in the next few days to reinforce us. . . . There is no line behind us to which we can retreat. . . . There will be no Dunkirk, there will be no Bataan. . . . We must fight until the end. . . . We are going to hold this line. We are going to win."[18]

By the end of July, the U.S. Army had taken 6,003 casualties and the ROK army about 70,000; but the North Koreans were losing the race for Pusan. Their enveloping drive from the west was held at the Naktong River and outside the town of Masan. By August 5, 47,000 U.S. ground combat troops were in Korea, and U.S. and ROK forces had numerical superiority. Some 500 American planes were destroying bridges and railroads vital to the North Koreans' long supply lines. Then, the United Nations Command took its first offensive action. Maj. Gen. William B. Kean led the 35th Infantry, the 5th Regimental Combat Team from Hawaii and the 1st Provisional Marine Brigade to meet the North Korean 6th Division southwest of Masan.

MacArthur had requested a Marine regimental combat team

672

on July 2, and the Marines landed at Pusan's docks on the night of August 2. They were the first troops to leave the continental United States. (The 9th Infantry—which had fought with the Marines before—left Tacoma, Washington, three days later and, because of the shorter voyage, reached Pusan two days ahead of the Marines.)

When the war began, the Marine Corps had 74,279 men and women on active duty. On July 7, it created the provisional brigade built around the 5th Marines at Camp Pendleton and Marine Aircraft Group 33 at El Toro, California. An integrated air-ground Marine team was going into combat under a single commander. This example of the Marine Corps ideal would not last long.

The Brigade was commanded by Brig. Gen. Edward A. Craig, a slim, white-haired Connecticut Yankee who had fought on Bougainville, Guam (where he won the Navy Cross) and Iwo Jima. Brig. Gen. Thomas J. Cushman led MAG-33. Their command totaled 6,534 men. Lt. Col. Raymond L. Murray commanded the major ground element, the 5th Marines. This was the regiment of Belleau Wood, Nicaragua, Guadalcanal, New Britain, Peleliu and Okinawa. Commissioned out of Texas A&M in 1935, Murray had fought at Guadalcanal (Silver Star), Tarawa (Silver Star) and Saipan (Navy Cross). The 1st Battalion, 11th Marines, commanded by Lt. Col. Ransom H. Wood, was the Brigade's artillery.

Lt. Gen. Shepherd, the new commanding general of Fleet Marine Force, Pacific, and his G-3, Col. Victor H. Krulak, flew ahead to Tokyo to confer with MacArthur. There, on July 10, they learned that MacArthur wanted to land an entire Marine division far behind the enemy lines and cut off the North Koreans from their base. It was a bold plan. Shepherd told MacArthur that the 1st Marine Division could be ready to land on September 15. On the spot, Shepherd drafted a message for MacArthur's signature requesting that the Joint Chiefs send a Marine division.[19]

It was D-Day minus 67 for the Inchon landing.

Commandant Cates saw the Brigade off from San Diego on July 14, just seven days after it had been activated and 12 days after MacArthur had requested it. Most of its officers and noncoms were combat veterans of World War II. Its equipment

673

had been retrieved from mothball in the California desert. But its three rifle battalions had only two companies apiece.

Craig and Cushman flew to Tokyo. MacArthur told them of his plan for an amphibious landing at Inchon and agreed that the Marine air-ground team would be kept intact.

On July 19, President Truman, on the Joint Chiefs' recommendation, called up 33,000 Marines in the Organized Marine Corps Reserve to active duty. Within 12 days, reserve units began arriving at Camp Pendleton; and by September 11, all organized ground reserve units had reported for duty. On August 7, 50,000 Marines of the Volunteer Reserve were notified that they too would be called to active duty.

The Marine Brigade sailed for Japan to prepare for MacArthur's amphibious counterattack. But suddenly on July 25, plans changed. The North Koreans, on an "end run," were closing on Pusan from the west as well as from the north. The Eighth Army, too short of troops to cover the whole 120-mile front, was falling back to contract its lines. While still at sea, the Brigade's ground elements were diverted directly to Korea. Amphibious assault had to wait.

The next day, Craig flew to Taegu, Korea; reported to Walker; flew over the combat area, and scouted the southwest side of the folding Pusan Perimeter in a Jeep. When the Marines docked at Pusan on the evening of August 2, Craig still did not know where they would be sent the next morning. They would be a fire brigade. They unloaded all night under searchlights and, after a final hot meal back on their ships, boarded trains and Army trucks and headed west 40 miles to the area around Changwon. Each Marine carried only his pack, weapon, ammunition and rations.

The ROKs guarded the shorter northern face of the Pusan Perimeter. On the longer western side, the 1st Cavalry and 24th Infantry Divisions stood behind the Naktong River, with the 25th Division, reinforced by the Army's 5th Regimental Combat Team and the Marine Brigade, to the south of them. Opposing them at this southern end of the line was the veteran North Korean 6th Division reinforced by the 83rd Motorcycle Regiment with machine guns on Russian "jeeps" and motorcycle sidecars.

On August 3, in the Marine Brigade's first action, Corsairs of Lt. Col. Walter E. Lischeid's VMF-214 (the Black Sheep squadron of World War II) flew off the escort carrier *Sicily*. During the following days, the planes struck Seoul and Inchon and on August 6 were joined by Maj. Arnold A. Lund's VMF-323 off *Badoeng Strait*. The night fighters of VMF(N)-513 operated out of Japan. On August 5, Maj. Kenneth L. Reusser, now executive officer of VMF-214, won a second Navy Cross; flying at daringly low altitudes, he shot up enemy tanks, a tanker, trucks and soldiers near Inchon.

On the ground, the Marine Brigade took its first casualties on the night of August 3–4, when trigger-happy novices wounded three Marines. Brig. Gen. Craig was furious.

Task Force Kean was now ordered to launch the Americans' first counterattack of the war—from Chindong-ni to Chinji. The 35th Infantry would strike from the northeast; the 5th Regimental Combat Team would take the direct road westward through the center, and the Marines would loop to the southwest along a road 17 miles longer through Kosong and Changchon. The attack would begin on August 7, coincidentally the eighth anniversary of the Marines' landing on Guadalcanal.

On the night of August 6, the 3rd Battalion, 5th Marines dug in on Hill 255. Its commander, Lt. Col. Robert D. Taplett, a rangy thirty-one-year-old native of Tyndall, South Dakota, was ordered to rush reinforcements forward to help beleaguered F Company of the 5th Infantry hold Hill 342. Taplett sent 2d Lt. John H. Cahill with 52 men from G Company. After they had advanced three miles through artillery fire, two Marines were wounded by rifle fire from U.S. soldiers who had not gotten the word that the Marines were in the area.

The sun rose and the heat became stifling. Cahill led his platoon up the steep hill, and men fell out. Cahill and Sgt. Lee Buettner went ahead to locate the Army unit on the summit and were fired on by the enemy—the first North Korean action against the Marine Brigade on the ground. Only 37 of the 52 Marines reached the crest; by then, three Marines were dead and eight wounded.

The North Koreans surrounded the hill. An airdrop of water and ammunition fell into enemy territory. The Marines' 2d Battalion was sent forward; but D and E Companies, stopped by the 112-degree heat and some enemy fire, did not reach the perimeter until the following day.

Just before dawn on August 8, the enemy attacked in

hand-to-hand fighting. When D Company arrived, the Army company and Cahill's platoon pulled out. Cahill had six Marines killed and 12 wounded. D Company came under heavy fire. While trying to bring in the body of 2d Lt. Wallace J. Reid, Capt. John Finn, Jr., the company commander, was hit in the head and shoulders and crawled back to the lines. His executive officer, 1st Lt. Robert T. Hanifin, Jr., took command. The enemy attacked again. Hanifin collapsed from heat exhaustion, and veteran Master Sgt. Harold Reeves and 2d Lt. Leroy K. Wirth of the 11th Marines took over. On August 9, D Company, with eight dead and 28 wounded, turned the crest of Hill 342 over to the all-black 24th Infantry.

Other Marine elements were also receiving their baptism of fire. On August 8, the enemy seized the peak north of the Marines' Hill 255 and opened fire on the 5th Marines. From their new position, the enemy could cut the Masan–Chindong-ni supply road. H Company's commander, Capt. Joseph C. Fegan, Jr., ordered 2d Lt. John O. Williams and his 1st Platoon to attack. Grenades and machine-gun fire pinned them down 30 yards from the enemy. Fegan told Williams to fall back and ordered up the 3rd Platoon. There was no response. The men were shaken by the 1st Platoon's defeat; Fegan himself had to take over the assault. Then, Cpl. Melvin James led the assault squad into the enemy's left flank and hit them with BAR fire. James pulled six wounded Marines to safety. Tech. Sgt. Ray Morgan and Pfc. Donald Terrio attacked the enemy's right flank and destroyed two machine guns. Captain Fegan carried out Sgt. Edward F. Barnett, who had been shot in the elbow and hip. The 3d Platoon wiped out the enemy position at a cost of six Marines killed and 32 wounded. The next morning, H Company crossed a saddle and shoved the enemy from the heights.

The Marines now headed south. The 1st Battalion led by Lt. Col. George R. Newton seized Hill 308 and cleared the vital Tosan road junction. Then, the 2d Battalion, commanded by Lt. Col. Harold S. Roise of Moscow, Idaho, assumed the lead and at the narrow Taedabok Pass, nine miles short of Kosong, ran into an ambush of automatic fire from the high ground. Taplett's 3rd Battalion took an alternate route to leapfrog ahead. Maj. Morgan J. McNeely sped ahead with a patrol to scout the road. His Jeep disappeared around a bend. G Company found the bullet-riddled Jeep and McNeely and his five men lying on the ground. Three had been killed and three, severely wounded. First Lt. Jack Westerman dashed to the Jeep and brought back McNeely, mortally wounded. Westerman, wounded himself, was awarded the Navy Cross. The rest of the patrol had to be left there until the next morning.

On August 11, with Taedabok Pass cleared, the Marines pushed aggressively toward Kosong at the bottom of the Marines' road loop and started for Sachon. H Company led the way into Kosong behind two M-26 Pershing tanks. Marine air and ground worked well together. The 11th Marines and VMF-323 flushed out and destroyed an estimated hundred troop-laden vehicles of the enemy's 83rd Motorcycle Regiment. The North Koreans shot down two of the first four attacking Corsairs. Lt. Doyle Cole was pulled from the bay by Brig. Gen. Craig in his helicopter. But Capt. Vivian Moses drowned in a rice paddy after he crashlanded and was knocked unconscious. Only the day before, Moses had been shot down in enemy territory and been rescued by helicopter. His was MAG-33's first combat death in Korea.

August 12 was a fighting afternoon. At the village of Changchon, the enemy grabbed the hills on both sides of the road and tried to ambush the approaching Marine column. About 1 P.M., the Marine point—a 15-man Jeep-borne detachment of Capt. Kenneth J. Houghton's Reconnaissance Company—moving a mile ahead of B Company, sprang the trap prematurely. B Company was also taken under fire from both flanks. Pershing tanks moved up. Capt. John L. Tobin, B Company commander, sent the 1st Platoon to help the Recon Company and the 3rd Platoon to attack the hill on the right front from which the Recon Company had been fired on. The 3rd Platoon took the hill easily; but the enemy waited on the reverse slope, counterattacked and drove the Marines halfway back down. A Company attacked a hill on the right and took the crest by 5 P.M. Corsairs hit the enemy machine-gun positions and picked over a column of vehicles hightailing it back to Sachon, four miles up the road. B Company attacked on the left side of the road and seized Hill 202 by 8 P.M. The Marines had suffered three killed and 13 wounded. The men were dog-tired and

677

without water or rations. In four days, they had driven the enemy back 22 miles.

The Marines expected to reach Sachon the next day. But that afternoon, the 3rd Battalion had been hurried all the way back to Chindong-ni to help stem an attack that had overrun two Army artillery battalions. Taplett's Marines arrived at dusk and immediately took the first ridge north of the road. By 10 A.M. the next morning, they commanded two ridgelines without a single casualty.

The Brigade was now engaged on two fronts 25 miles apart. Craig commanded both of them by helicopter. At midnight, Lt. Col. Newton received orders to return to Chindong-ni. But before the 1st and 2d Battalions could withdraw from Chang-chon, B Company had to fight off a furious night attack. At 4:45 A.M., North Korean veterans of the Chinese civil war struck the company's front and flank. The 3rd Platoon on the left flank was surprised and overrun. The enemy captured two machine guns and turned them on the Marines, until, at dawn, 3.5-inch rocket launchers destroyed the guns. Captain Tobin ordered the 3rd Platoon's survivors to hold, and artillery supported them with pinpoint shooting. The enemy kept coming. Tobin consolidated the 1st and 2d Platoons in a single perimeter. After an hour's slugging match, the enemy fell back to the lower slopes of Hill 202. Ordered to return to the road in order to move out, B Company disengaged a squad at a time. The company had 12 killed, 18 wounded and eight missing. Captain Tobin asked permission to recover the eight missing Marines on the left flank. Lt. Col. Newton denied his request because the battalion was late in obeying Brigade orders to withdraw. The 1st and 2d Battalions left for Chindong-ni with Engineers and tanks covering their rear. The men were bitter that the eight Marines—whether dead or alive—had been left behind.

The Eighth Army's first offensive had stopped the North Korean 6th Division's sweep against the southern end of the Pusan Perimeter. But further north another crisis had already erupted.

On August 15, the Brigade moved by railroad 75 miles north to Miryang. There, the Marines ate their first hot meal in 13 days, bathed in the muddy Miryang River and replaced their rotted uniforms. They came under control of the 24th Infantry Division, Brig. Gen. John H. Church commanding. They were going into the Battle of the Naktong.

The Marines were hardening now, more confident. They had marched in Korea's heat and hills. Young men had been tried in battle. A British military observer saw them pass through Miryang and reported:

> If Miryang is lost Taegu becomes untenable and we will be faced with a withdrawal from Korea. I am heartened that the Marine Brigade will move against the Naktong salient tomorrow. . . . these Marines have the swagger, confidence and hardness that must have been in Stonewall Jackson's Army of the Shenandoah. They remind me of the Coldstreams at Dunkerque. Upon this thin line of reasoning, I cling to the hope of victory.[20]

The Naktong River was the last natural barrier on the western side of the Pusan Perimeter, and its valley offered the enemy a lowland corridor to Pusan. The North Koreans had started crossing the river at a number of points on August 6. Their offensive endangered the lifeline from Taegu, the provisional capital, all the way to Pusan. They came over most threateningly at the Naktong Bulge, an area four miles by five, east of the river and west of Miryang and Yongsan. At the bulge, the river bends sharply westward around a hill mass dominated by Hill 311. Blocking the east side of this oxbow were two hills: Cloverleaf Hill north of the Yongsan–Naktong road and mile-and-a-half-long Obong-ni Ridge south of the road. By August 10, most of the North Korean 4th Division had crossed the Naktong, overrun the bulge area and begun driving eastward. On August 18, Taegu was evacuated and the South Korean government fled to Pusan.

Task Force Hill—about three Army infantry regiments under Col. John G. Hill, USA, who had brought the 9th Infantry to Korea—tried futilely to contain and counterattack the enemy. The official Army history of the war reports: "When the attack of 15 August failed, General Walker knew he must commit more strength into the bulge if he was to drive out the enemy. Impatient and angry, he came to Church's command post during the morning and said, 'I am going to give you the Marine brigade. I want this situation cleaned up, and quick.' "[21]

The all-out counterattack began at 8 A.M. on August 17. While the 19th and 34th Infantry Regiments hit from the northeast and part of the 21st Infantry blocked on the south, the Army's depleted 9th Regimental Combat Team and the Marine Brigade struck westward in the center along the Yongsan–Naktong road. On the left, south of the road, the Marines attacked Obong-ni Ridge—which was being called No Name Ridge—under cover of the 9th RCT; and then north of the road, the soldiers were to attack Cloverleaf Hill while the Marines covered them. The attack was less than expertly managed.

> Shortage of transport had delayed the arrival of the brigade and had adversely affected the artillery preparation; a misunderstanding with the Army unit on the right led to a lack of flank support; the air strike from the escort carriers was 15 minutes late, so that the 18 Corsairs had only half their intended time to work over enemy positions. The advance uphill, against a numerically superior and entrenched enemy, was carried out with great bravery but at heavy cost; of the 240 men of the 2d Battalion [5th Marines] which led the attack, 142 had become casualties by mid-day.[22]

When Roise's 2d Battalion made the Marine attack, Capt. Andrew M. Zimmer, now in command of D Company, moved up with 2d Lt. Michael J. Shinka leading the 3rd Platoon. On its right was Staff Sgt. T. Albert Crowson's 1st Platoon and on its left, the 2d Platoon of E Company. The understrength rifle platoons crossed a rice paddy in eerie silence. When they were halfway up the steep, bare slope, dozens of machine guns opened up on them, inflicting heavy casualties. With the artillery ineffectual and the Corsairs late, Crowson's platoon was stopped. Captain Zimmer sent in Tech. Sgt. Sidney S. Dickerson's 2d Platoon, which had been covering the assault. The Marines came under automatic weapons fire from both flanks.

By mid-morning, Mike Shinka had only 15 men left. When they reached the crest of Hill 109, one peak of Obong-ni Ridge, his nine remaining Marines came under intense fire. Running short of ammunition, they withdrew partway down the slope. By then, Shinka had six men able to fight. He went back up to the crest of Hill 109 looking for his wounded. He pulled Pfc. George J. Hric, who had been shot in the stomach, out of his foxhole. A bullet shattered Shinka's chin. He tossed a grenade at a North Korean who was crawling up the hill and continued to drag out the wounded man. A bullet hit Shinka's right arm and sent him spinning down the hill.

On D Company's left, 1st Lt. William E. Sweeney took E Company against Obong-ni Ridge. Second Lt. Nickolas A. Arkadis' 1st Platoon neared the crest and was hit by flanking enemy fire and short "friendly" artillery shells. At 11:30, E Company was ordered back to leave room for an air strike; but some Marines within 25 yards of the summit were caught in the strafing. Enemy machine gunners enfiladed E Company and its attack crumbled.

By noon, the 2d Battalion had 23 dead and 119 wounded— nearly 60 percent of the 240 riflemen in the attack. "2/5 took a terrible beating as platoons and squads, decimated by the heavy fighting, advanced and fell back."[23] Arkadis, Dickerson and Wirth were among the wounded. With the battalion short a third rifle company, "the ridge could not be taken."[24] The Marines had been stopped.

At 1 P.M., Brig. Gen. Craig ordered Newton's 1st Battalion to pass through the shot-up 2d Battalion and seize the ridge. Starting at 4 P.M., the 9th Infantry successfully attacked Cloverleaf Hill. When Captain Tobin was seriously wounded in the chest and arm, Capt. Francis I. "Ike" Fenton, Jr., took command of B Company. Under flanking enemy fire from the 9th RCT zone, B Company stalled. Pershing tanks and 81mm mortars blasted the enemy gunners; and by evening, the company held the crest of the two northern most hills of Obong-ni Ridge in the rain.

Meanwhile, to the south, A Company passed through E Company at 3 P.M. and halfway up Obong-ni Ridge came under severe machine-gun fire. First Lt. Robert C. Sebilian, leading the 1st Platoon, was hit, and Tech. Sgt. Orval F. McMullen pressed the attack. The 1st Platoon advanced to the saddle between Hills 109 and 117 and then was pinned down. On his left, 2d Lt. Thomas H. Johnston's 2d Platoon was cut in half and finally stopped. The diminutive Johnston rose and charged in a one-man assault, hurling grenades at the enemy machine gun. He reached the saddle south of Hill 117 before he was killed. Tech. Sgt. Frank J. Lawson took command of what was left of the platoon, now no more than a squad. Capt. John R. Stevens, a World War II signal officer, sent A Company's 3rd Platoon to join Lawson, and it too was stopped by machine-gun fire and grenades.

Four Pershing M-26 tanks of the 3rd Platoon, A Company Tanks had supported the Marines' attack all day and were back refueling and re-arming when word was received at 8 P.M. that four enemy T-34s were approaching the Marine lines. Second Lt. Granville G. Sweet ordered his 1st Section to load with 90mm armor-piercing shells. Corsairs destroyed the enemy's rear tank and dispersed its accompanying riflemen. The front T-34 was demolished by 75mm recoilless rifles and Tech. Sgt. Cecil R. Fullerton's lead Pershing. The second enemy tank was knocked out by 3.5-inch rockets, the recoilless rifles and the two lead Marine tanks. The Pershings' fire exploded the final enemy tank behind the two blazing T-34 hulks. In five minutes, the Marines had shattered the myth of T-34 invincibility.

By dark, the Marines held the northern end of Obong-ni Ridge. B Company was on the crest of Hills 102 and 109, and Stevens tied in his A Company on B's left to prepare for the expected enemy counterattack. On A Company's far left flank, 1st Lt. George C. Fox's 3rd Platoon dangled unprotected.

At 10 P.M., mortar shells began falling among A Company's foxholes; and white phosphorus shells wiped out the company's mortar section. Starting at 2:30 A.M. with a green flare signal, the North Koreans smashed down on A Company; and B Company was hit three times by soldiers covered by automatic fire from Hill 117. A Company's 2d Platoon fought vastly superior numbers of enemy for a half hour; Tech. Sgt. Lawson was wounded three times. The platoon was finally overrun and the Marines' line penetrated. The two companies were split. The enemy reached A Company's command post behind the 2d Platoon and pushed it back down the draw. Stevens' executive officer, 1st Lt. Fred F. Eubanks, Jr., attacked singlehandedly up the gully; he was joined by 2d Lt. Francis W. Muetzel, who had been left for dead in his foxhole when the 2d Platoon retreated.

He had regained consciousness and fought through the enemy to the Marine lines. Marine artillery helped A Company's hard-pressed riflemen; and by dawn, the enemy attack was spent. B Company still held its two hilltops.

A Company counterattacked at 7 A.M. BARman Pfc. Harold Twedt knocked out two machine guns before he was killed. Finally, the remnant of A Company, aided by a precise air strike, seized Hill 117. Major Lund ordered Capt. John P. Kelley to destroy a nest of four machine guns 50 yards in front of the Marines. Dive-bombing his Corsair with exquisite accuracy, Kelley put his 500-pound bomb right on the target. The Marines on the ground were knocked off their feet; one BARman was killed. But the strike was totally effective, and the Marine advance gained overwhelming momentum. Twenty men pushed south to take Hill 147, the next peak, and continued on to wipe the enemy from Hill 153, Obong-ni's highest crest. By mid-afternoon, the Marines held all of Obong-ni Ridge.

The next objective was Hill 207, west of Obong-ni Ridge. Taplett's 3rd Battalion climbed it from the north on the morning of August 18, with G Company on the right spur and H Company on the left. By 12:37, the two companies had taken the crest against light opposition. Now the entire Naktong Bulge was swarming with North Korean troops scurrying for the river in panicked retreat. Artillery, aircraft and mortars plastered the fleeing targets. "Victory turned into slaughter when the Brigade supporting arms concentrated on the masses of Communists plunging into the river."[25] "The enemy was killed in such numbers that the river was definitely discolored by blood."[26]

The 3rd Battalion attacked Hill 311, the final ridge in the bulge itself. When Captain Fegan was wounded and evacuated, H Company's attack bogged down. G Company circled the hill from the south, and 1st Lt. Robert D. Bohn sent Cahill's 1st Platoon around to the west. It overran the northern half of the summit until it was thrown back by the defenders facing H Company. Cahill was among the platoon's ten casualties. G and H Companies spent a quiet night and early in the morning of August 19 occupied the hilltop without opposition. The Naktong Bulge had been cleaned out at a cost to the Marines of 66 dead, one missing and 278 wounded. The North Korean 4th Division had been decisively defeated.

683

The Marine Brigade was shipped back to a bivouac area near Masan that became known as the Bean Patch. The men ate hot meals again, checked their weapons, received mail and beer. On August 29, Brig. Gen. Craig awarded 87 Purple Hearts at a ceremony attended by President Rhee. The 1st Battalion, 11th Marines went over to Chindong-ni to assist the 25th Division. Eight hundred replacements joined the Brigade, and volunteers were recruited out of supporting units for the rifle companies. In the ranks, there were rumors of a coming amphibious operation.

On August 29, Col. "Chesty" Puller's 1st Marines and the headquarters of the 1st Marine Division began landing at Kobe, Japan. Puller, now fifty-two, had scrambled to get this command and had reported to Camp Pendleton only 25 days before. The 1st Division was being pieced together with Murray's 5th Marines and Puller's 1st. The newly activated 7th Marines was to be the division's third rifle regiment; and the 3rd Battalion, 6th Marines, with the Sixth Fleet in the Mediterranean was shipped from Crete through the Suez Canal to complete the 7th Marines. The division's commander, Maj. Gen. Graves B. Erskine, had been sent on a secret State Department mission to Southeast Asia in July. He had been succeeded by Maj. Gen. Oliver P. Smith, a lanky native of Menard, Texas. A scholarly, meticulous and abstentious officer, Smith had been a Marine since 1917. He commanded the 5th Marines at Cape Gloucester and served on Peleliu and Okinawa. Arriving in Tokyo on August 22, he struggled to extract the 5th Marines from the Pusan Perimeter, since the 7th Marines could not arrive in time for D-Day on September 15 at Inchon. Without the 5th Marines, Smith would have only one Marine regiment for the invasion. MacArthur ordered the 5th Marines returned to the division.

But again the enemy upset the Marines' plans. On September 1, the North Koreans launched an offensive with 98,000 men and penetrated the UN lines all around the perimeter. MacArthur rescinded his order releasing the 5th Marines. Smith was offered the Army's 32d Infantry but declined because the regiment had not been trained for amphibious assault. Finally, a compromise was worked out by which the 5th Marines would join the 1st Marine Division after September 5—but first they would return to the Naktong.

684

On the afternoon of September 1, the well-rested Brigade was trucked back to Miryang.

> There the North Koreans threatened Miryang and with it the lifeline of the entire Eighth Army position. There, for the moment at least, was the most critical spot of the far-flung battlefield. An hour before noon General Walker ordered General Craig to prepare the marines to move at once. Just after noon the action order came and the marines made ready to depart at 1330. They were going back to the bulge area.[27]

The enemy had already reoccupied the Naktong Bulge; driven a hole eight miles deep and six miles wide into the 2d Infantry Division, which had replaced the 24th Division along the Naktong, and had briefly seized Yongsan. It was the North Koreans' final lunge to reach Pusan before the United Nations' forces could gather unbeatable strength.

Lt. Gen. Walker put the Brigade under operational control of Maj. Gen. Lawrence B. Keiser, USA, commanding the 2d Infantry Division. He was ordered to restore the river line.

The Marines were to jump off on September 3 four miles east of their earlier battleground near the Naktong. Newton's 1st Battalion was to advance south of the Yongsan-Naktong road and Roise's 2d Battalion north of it. But on the night of September 2, the enemy smashed the 9th Infantry, through which Roise was to pass.

At 7:15 A.M., D and E Companies moved forward. With tanks and artillery, the Marines' firepower stopped the North Korean 9th Division cold. At 8:55 A.M., A and B Companies attacked from below Chukchon-ni, but they were out of position and had to wade through hundreds of yards of knee-deep rice paddies under small-arms fire. At 11 A.M. they launched their attack from the edge of the paddy, making so frightful a noise that a company of North Koreans jumped from their foxholes on the forward slope of the ridge ahead and fled. Marine BAR and riflemen killed most of them. And A Company took the ridgetop.

Corsairs routed the enemy in front of the 1st Battalion and sent them fleeing north across the road to Hill 117 in front of the 2d Battalion. D Company, now commanded by 1st Lt. H. J.

Smith, raced to cut off their retreat, was isolated and took heavy casualties. Along the road, Marine tanks battled enemy antitank guns and put five North Korean tanks out of action. That night, the 2d Battalion was two miles west of Yongsan.

On the high ground south of the road, B Company, with help from A Company Engineers, continued to press the enemy into the 2d Battalion's zone. A Company enveloped Hill 91 and seized it in heavy fighting.

This had been another rough day for Roise's 2d Battalion with 18 Marines killed and 77 wounded, most of them in D Company. Therefore, on September 4, the 3rd Battalion passed through the 2d; and the 1st and 3rd pushed quickly forward past abandoned North Korean vehicles and hundreds of enemy dead. The Marines gained 4,000 yards before setting up defenses for the night.

As the Marines advanced in rain and fog on September 5, North Korean artillery and mortars greeted them from Obong-ni Ridge, their old battleground. Lt. Col. Murray planned to retake the ridge with the 1st and 3rd Battalions, while the 9th Infantry attacked toward Cloverleaf Hill. But shortly after noon, the situation changed; and Murray had to shift his attention from Obong-ni to the road. Suddenly, taking advantage of the lack of air support in the heavy weather, the enemy mounted a daytime counterattack. In a driving rain, North Korean soldiers and tanks attacked B Company, which had dug in on Hill 125. The enemy armor came up the road; and at the same curve that had been the site of the tank battle of August 17, the leading North Korean T-34 surprised and destroyed the Marines' first two M-26s. B Company's 3.5-inch rockets came to the rescue and wiped out two T-34s and an armored personnel carrier. Eight wrecked steel monsters now lay at that road bend.

Meanwhile, B Company on Hill 125 above the bend was hard pressed until the 9th Infantry threw in its artillery firepower and Marine reinforcements from A Company were shifted over. Artillery and mortar fire finally finished off the enemy attack. For the day, the Marine Brigade had 35 killed and 91 wounded. The counteroffensive had neutralized two enemy divisions.

That night, the 2d Infantry Division took over the Marine positions; and Craig ordered the Brigade back to Pusan "for further operations against the enemy."[28] At dawn on September 6, the Marines returned to Pusan by truck through an icy rain.

That same day, another kind of battle broke out in Washington when a newspaper reported that a congressman had asked President Truman to give the Commandant a voice on the Joint Chiefs of Staff. The President had exploded and written the congressman: "For your information the Marine Corps is the Navy's police force and as long as I am President that is what it will remain. They have a propaganda machine that is almost equal to Stalin's." After the story hit the headlines, Truman gave the Marine Corps a public apology for his "unfortunate choice of language" and praised the "immediate response of the Marine Corps to a call for duty in Korea." But he did not back down from his view of the Corps.[29]

In three air-ground operations in exactly one month, the Marine Brigade had had 172 killed and 730 wounded. MAG-33 had flown 995 close-support missions, 80 percent of them directed by Tactical Air Control Parties on the ground. The Brigade's initial operation as part of Task Force Kean had been the first sustained Eighth Army counterattack of the war. "The next Brigade operation, the first battle of the Naktong, ranks with the hardest fights of Marine Corps history."[30] It drove the enemy back across the river with heavy losses. But ten days later, the Marines had to push them back again—although this time the Brigade was withdrawn before it could complete the job. The Marines had helped stop the North Korean invasion and save the Pusan Perimeter.

At Pusan for the next six days, the men slept in the open on the docks where they had landed a month before and ate their meals on the transports that would carry them around the Korean peninsula. The rifle battalions received their third rifle companies. And Marine officers gave weapons training to 3,000 men of the 1st Korean Marine Corps Regiment, which was to become the 1st Marine Division's fourth rifle regiment.

On September 13, after 67 days of existence, the 1st Provisional Marine Brigade was deactivated and its units joined the 1st Marine Division and sailed for Inchon.

3
"We Shall Land at Inchon"

General MacArthur possessed the vision and the unshakable faith that, even while his army was pinned into the southeastern corner of Korea, he could build a second assault force and strike a killing blow at the enemy's spine. He insisted that X Corps, this second force, land from the sea at the west coast port of Inchon; drive inland to the capital city of Seoul, the nexus of South Korea's communications, and sever the North Koreans' lifeline. He would reverse roles: He would invade; he would attack.

The experts—Army, Navy and Marines—tried to dissuade him. The risks were dangerous. The amphibious force would have to approach Inchon through a long, narrow channel at the one three-day period of the month when the tides were high enough (at least 29 feet) to carry the landing craft over the harbor's vast protective mud flats. His force would have to assault the urban waterfront of a large Oriental city in which determined defenders could hole up and work havoc against American ships, landing craft and Marines.

MacArthur was adamant. He rejected all the alternative landing sites proposed to him. He refused to delay the attack a month to permit time for buildup, training and rehearsals. The Army's Chief of Staff, the Chief of Naval Operations, the Commanding General of the Fleet Marine Force, Pacific, all came out to Tokyo. On August 23, the generals and admirals (but not the Marines) gathered in MacArthur's mahogany-paneled conference room in the Dai Ichi Building. They spoke of the tactical hazards: the natural obstacles, the shortage of time, the unlikelihood of surprise, the expectation of enemy mines, the advent of the typhoon season. The seventy-year-old general listened to their presentations and then, calmly smoking his pipe, talked to them for 45 minutes. He stressed his belief in the overwhelming psychological advantages of the bold strategic stroke. In a dramatic near-whisper, he finished: "We shall land at Inchon, and I shall crush them!"[31]

The 1st Marine Division would deliver his amphibious blow. The 5th Marines would be shipped around from Pusan, and the newly arrived 1st Marines, from Japan. The division's third regiment, the 7th Marines, could not reach Korea until a week after the September 15 D-Day.

Fortunately, the post-World War II Marine officers and noncoms—and the Navy's leaders—were veterans of amphibious assault. And fortunately, also, the enemy—as long as the Chinese and Russians stayed out of the fight—had no aircraft, no submarines, no navy to oppose the American assault.

The landing would be conducted by the two-division X Corps, activated especially for this operation. The 7th Infantry Division would come in behind the 1st Marine Division. Overall command was given to MacArthur's chief of staff, Maj. Gen. Edward M. Almond, USA. The Marines had hoped that command of X Corps would go to Lt. Gen. Shepherd. But MacArthur decided otherwise—whether because, with Saipan in memory, the Army did not want Marines to command Army units or whether Almond wangled the job was long debated among Marines.

Time was the dragon. Inchon's extraordinary tides—among the most extreme in the world—flooded high enough for only three hours. The landing would have to be made in two parts. First, the Marines insisted, they had to capture the fortified island of Wolmi-do, which dominated the inner harbor. The 3rd Battalion, 5th Marines, would assault the island on the morning tide. The rest of the 5th Marines and the 1st Marines would land in the city itself on the evening tide. In between, the Marines on Wolmi-do would be exposed to hours of danger. And after the main landing, only two hours would remain before dark to get men and equipment ashore. "The planning was necessarily carried out in violation of all the rules and in record time."[32] It was the best that could be done.

Marine Corsairs led by Maj. Donald Bush flew photo-reconnaissance missions. And two weeks before D-Day, Navy

Lt. Eugene F. Clark, an old Asia hand, stole in with two South Koreans and scouted Inchon's mud flats and seawalls and radioed back his findings. He sent friendly Koreans to Seoul and Kimpo Airfield to check on enemy strengths. He even managed to relight the beacon of the harbor lighthouse on Palmi-do island to guide the amphibious task force.

Wolmi-do was blasted from sea and air for five days. Marine fliers of VMF-214 and -323 started napalm attacks on September 10 to burn off trees screening the North Korean guns. Navy planes followed up. On D minus two, five destroyers closed on Wolmi-do in broad daylight to entice the North Koreans into exposing their gun positions. The precarious tactic worked, the enemy batteries on the island and in the city revealed themselves—damaging three destroyers—and Wolmi-do rocked with naval and air bombardment.

Amphibious expert Rear Adm. James H. Doyle ordered the invasion force, Task Force 90, to sea a day early to avoid the 125-miles-per-hour winds of Typhoon Kezia. But still the armada had heavy going on the typhoon's edge. On September 12, the flagship *Mount McKinley* docked at Sasebo, Japan, to pick up MacArthur and his entourage. Lt. Gen. Shepherd came along as MacArthur's amphibious advisor. In addition to the 1st Division's Marines, the landing force of 25,040 men included nearly 3,000 men of the 1st Korean Marine Corps Regiment and about 2,750 specialized U.S. Army soldiers. The Secretary of the Navy required that all U.S. Marines who were not yet eighteen years old be removed from the operation, which subtracted some 500 young men from the landing force.

The column of 19 ships led by the destroyer *Mansfield* snaked through the dark passage toward Inchon, aided by the light on Palmi-do. D-Day on Friday, September 15, a warm, pleasant day, started with Marine and Navy carrier planes bombing and strafing through the early overcast. At 6:33 A.M., one platoon of Lt. Col. Taplett's G Company and three platoons of his H Company hit the northwest end of Wolmi-do. The rest of the assault companies landed two minutes later. They were greeted by only a few scattered shots.

Landing in water over his head, 1st Lt. Robert D. Bohn recovered and wheeled G Company to the right and up the northern slope of Radio Hill. Most of the North Koreans there surrendered. Capt. Patrick E. Wildman sent a detachment from H Company to hold the North Point of Wolmi-do and to block the long causeway leading to Inchon. The rest of H Company raced to the Standard Oil tanks in the industrial area of Wolmi-do facing Inchon. Ten tanks landed from A Company of the 1st Tank Battalion. At 6:55, Sgt. Alvin E. Smith, the guide of G Company's 3rd Platoon, raised the flag on the shell-torn crest of Radio Hill. On *Mount McKinley's* flag bridge, MacArthur rose from his swivel chair and said, "That's it. Let's get a cup of coffee."[33] And he sent a message to the fleet: "The Navy and Marines have never shone more brightly than this morning."[34]

It wasn't quite over. Capt. Robert A. McMullen's I Company, the battalion's new third rifle company, landed in the fourth wave and was met by a flurry of grenades from a bypassed enemy platoon at North Point. The North Koreans refused to surrender and a dozer tank sealed them in their holes. Another tank flushed out 30 North Koreans from a cave and they did surrender.

In less than an hour, the Marines held half of Wolmi-do. Engineers blocked the causeway to Inchon with mines to keep out enemy tanks. H Company moved slowly through the industrial area, and G Company cleared the rest of Radio Hill. By 8 A.M., the island and the harbor were under control. The Marines used the swimming pool at North Point, a pre-war resort, as a POW stockade. Total American casualties so far were 14 wounded. The initial phase had gone well.

At 10 A.M., Taplett ordered G Company to seize tiny Sowolmi-do, which was linked to Wolmi-do by a narrow 750-yard causeway. At the far end of the causeway waited an enemy platoon, cornered and ready to fight it out with machine guns and rifles. VMF-214 made a close support napalm attack. And a Marine mine-clearing team led over tanks followed by riflemen. At the end of the causeway, a fire fight erupted. In half an hour, it was over with 17 North Koreans dead and 19 prisoners; eight others later escaped to the mainland. On Sowolmi-do, three Marines were wounded. No Marines had yet been killed.

By 1 P.M., the tide had rolled back, leaving more than a thousand Marines stranded on their captured islands in a sea of mud. These were tense, silent hours. While Corsairs searched inland for enemy reinforcements (and found none), Lt. Col.

Taplett organized a defense against counterattack from Inchon. He proposed sending a tank-infantry force into the seemingly empty city but was denied permission.

For the main landing, Newton's 1st and Roise's 2d Battalion, 5th Marines, would land in the very heart of Inchon, on Red Beach, actually a strip of stone seawall, north of Wolmi-do. They would seize a 3,000-yard arc, with Cemetery Hill on the left and Observatory Hill in the center, and press through the city's streets and already burning buildings to the inner tidal basin on the right. Puller's 1st Marines would land three miles to the southeast on Blue Beach in a suburban industrial area at the base of the promontory on which Inchon sat. The 5th Marines would attack directly through the city; the 1st Marines would envelop it from the rear.

The final bombardment started at 2:30. Four cruisers and six destroyers and Navy Skyraiders and Marine Corsairs set the whole waterfront aflame. As the waters in front of Inchon rose again, the barrage climaxed with 6,000 rockets.

At Red Beach, two assault platoons of Capt. John R. Stevens' A Company landed on the left at 5:33 P.M., climbing their ladders up the seawall as though attacking from a trench. They met heavy fire from the northern or left flank and from bunkers directly in front. Several Marines were hit immediately; the others could advance only a few yards. With the 1st Platoon pinned down on the left, 1st Lt. Baldomero Lopez, a twenty-five-year-old Annapolis graduate from Tampa, Florida, brought in the 3rd Platoon. Casualties mounted. As Lopez tried to hurl a grenade against a machine-gun bunker, he was hit in the right shoulder and arm. Unable to throw his grenade, he swept it under him and smothered its explosion with his body.[35] Two Marines attacked the bunker with flamethrowers and were shot down.

The second wave was late; so without waiting, 2d Lt. Francis W. Muetzel took his 2d Platoon south of Cemetery Hill and up a street toward the Asahi Brewery. When the Marines reached the brewery, they were ordered back to the beach to help out. But Muetzel found the south side of Cemetery Hill a good approach and assaulted it. In ten minutes, his platoon took the summit and captured the dazed members of a North Korean mortar company. That was the key to Red Beach. At 5:55,

Captain Stevens fired an amber star cluster as a victory signal. A Company had 8 killed and 28 wounded.

On the right, Capt. Samuel Jaskilka's E Company landed at 5:31. The seawall rose four feet higher than the landing crafts' ramps; the Marines put up wooden ladders and hurled grenades over the wall. Quickly, 2d Lt. Edwin A. Deptula's 1st Platoon was on shore without casualties. It pushed inland and reached the British Consulate at 8:45. Another platoon seized the lower slopes of Observatory Hill. Together, they secured the right flank for the next 22 waves of landing craft.

From Wolmi-do, the 3rd Battalion added its firepower and removed the mines from the causeway so its tanks could move to the mainland.

C and D Companies were assigned to capture 200-foot-high Observatory Hill behind the center of Red Beach. But elements of the two companies landed on the wrong beaches, and Capt. Poul E. Pedersen, commander of C Company, was delayed when his boat took a stalled LCVP in tow. The confusion gave the enemy on Observatory Hill time to recover from the pre-assault bombardment and set up their machine guns.

Now, eight supply-laden LSTs approached the seawall against enemy mortar and machine-gun fire. LST crews fired their 40mm and 20mm cannon wildly at the beach and drove Muetzel's platoon from the crest of Cemetery Hill and down the reverse slope. Muetzel's platoon still had not had a single casualty, but the LSTs killed one 2d Battalion Marine and wounded 23. As soon as the ships came close enough, angry Marines stormed aboard and demanded that the sailors stop shooting.

As the uncontrolled firing finally stopped, 2d Lt. Byron L. Magness led the 2d Platoon of C Company against Observatory Hill. Second Lt. Max A. Merritt's 60mm mortar section followed the riflemen, and Tech. Sgt. Max Stein was wounded knocking out a machine gun with grenades. Magness' group seized the saddle between the two peaks of Observatory Hill as darkness took over.

Capt. Francis I. Fenton, Jr., brought B Company ashore in the 2d Battalion zone to avoid small-arms fire; and Lt. Col. Newton radioed him to assume C Company's mission and assault the northern half of Observatory Hill. In the darkness, B

Company fought up the hill; six Marines were wounded on the way up. Fenton gained the crest at 8 P.M. and made contact with Magness' force in the saddle on his right.

Further right, 1st Lt. H. J. Smith's D Company attacked the southern half of Observatory Hill. Smith thought Jaskilka's E Company had already taken the southern peak; and D Company, with 2d Lt. Ray Heck's 1st Platoon in the lead, marched up the street toward the top of the hill. They were greeted by machine guns on their right; and in a 15-minute fire fight, one Marine was killed and three Marines and the Navy corpsman wounded. F Company covered the extreme right flank of Red Beach.

Meanwhile, around on the southern side of the Inchon promontory, Puller's 1st Marines were assaulting Blue Beach through thick black smoke and the brown haze of wind-whipped rain. This landing—unrehearsed and conducted by a regiment which, unlike the 5th Marines, had not fought together—was chaotic.

On the left, Blue Beach One, Lt. Col. Allan Sutter's 2d Battalion started landing on schedule at 5:30. It met no opposition, but the naval bombardment had caused a landslide that blocked the only exit road. The amphibious vehicles came to a halt. F Company grounded in the mud 300 yards offshore, and the Marines had to wade in. Six-hundred Marines of the two companies finally plunged ahead on foot to the high ground toward the northeast, leaving the LVT crews to dig out the road with picks and shovels.

To the right on Blue Beach Two, the 3rd Battalion ran into some scattered fire. On the left side of this area, some of I Company's aluminum ladders buckled; but the Marines had anticipated that and Engineers anchored cargo nets to the top of the 15-foot seawall. When G Company's lead LVT got stuck in the mud, it stopped the others. Capt. George C. Westover dismounted his men, and they fanned out to block the lowland corridor leading to the beach.

Lt. Col. Thomas L. Ridge found a cove and ramp on the right of the beach usable and shifted many of the LVTs there. And, having expected confusion on the beach, Puller came ashore at H-plus 30 minutes to take charge.

As G and I Companies rapidly cleared the beach, they took casualties from a machine gun in a tower 500 yards inland. The gun was silenced by fire from the LVTs. The Marines advanced through smoke-filled streets and past blazing buildings. While G Company pushed into the lowland area, I Company veered right to the tip of Hill 233 on the southern end of the beachhead. The 2d Battalion had one killed and 19 wounded.

The 1st Battalion in reserve was supposed to land behind the 2d Battalion on Blue Two, but by mistake wound up two miles to the left of the beachhead at the inner tidal basin. Lt. Col. Jack Hawkins, who had made a spectacular escape from a Japanese POW camp in World War II, rounded up most of his men and sent them in the correct direction. But the boats for one platoon of B Company had already pulled away and left the platoon at the tidal basin all night. In the morning, it hiked over to rejoin its company, rounding up prisoners on the way. Because of the heads-up work of a smart coxswain, C Company landed at the right place. And eventually most of the 1st Battalion moved forward to its assembly area half a mile inland.

Blue Beach was a dreadful example of a landing attempted without adequate time for training or rehearsal. There was a serious shortage of Navy guide boats. Groups of landing craft and entire assault waves landed in the wrong places. But despite the confusion, assault-wise Marine officers kept the attack going. Fortunately, there was no significant opposition.

By night, the 2d Battalion had secured enough of Hill 117 directly ahead to cover the Inchon–Seoul highway with fire. G and I Companies blocked the center. And H Company's 1st Platoon circled to the extreme right and attacked a North Korean company on the small cape topped by Hill 94. The enemy fled, leaving 30 casualties.

The buildup on the beaches went on all night. The 1st Shore Party Battalion, under Tarawa veteran Lt. Col. Henry P. Crowe, worked by floodlight to unload the LSTs' ammunition, rations, water, fuel, engineer supplies and combat vehicles. The ships had to be ready to pull out on the morning tide. Bulldozers moved along the seawall under some enemy fire, pushing down masonry that blocked the unloading. The Engineers managed to get a switch engine and six cars running in the Inchon railroad yards.

By 10 P.M., the 1st and 2d Battalions of the 11th Marines, delayed by the confusion in the inner harbor, were ready to deliver artillery fire. Tanks crossed the causeway, which the enemy had failed to destroy, and joined tanks landed from the LSTs at Red Beach. There were 13,000 Americans ashore. Marine casualties for D-Day had been 22 killed, 174 wounded in action and 14 non-battle casualties.

On Saturday morning, the 1st and 5th Marines attacked at dawn. Murray's 5th Marines moved through the southern part of Inchon, leaving the seaport to be cleared by the extremely zealous Korean Marines. The 5th advanced three miles and linked up with Puller's 1st Marines. That closed off Inchon. Together, the two regiments moved through the sprawling, dead seaport until they held a line about three miles long with its flanks on the water.

Five miles away, eight planes of VMF-214 intercepted six T-34 tanks heading toward Inchon in broad daylight with no infantry support. The fliers thought they knocked out all the enemy tanks, but this proved to be incorrect. Capt. William F. Simpson's Corsair was hit and failed to pull out of its dive; Simpson was killed.

At 10:45 A.M., Maj. Gen. Smith ordered Murray and Puller to advance to the Force Beachhead Line, a right-angled front pointing like an arrowhead toward Kimpo Airfield. The Inchon–Seoul highway was the boundary between the regiments with the 5th Marines north of it and the 1st Marines to the south. Where the road bent left to skirt hills and Ascom City, two of 2d Lt. Granville G. Sweet's M-26 tanks spotted three intact T-34s—survivors of the air strike—and swiftly exploded all three. The Marine tankers also found two wrecked T-34s. The last of the original six attacked by the planes must have escaped. By evening, the 5th Marines were on commanding high ground but still some 3,000 yards short of the FBHL. The division had met little opposition; casualties for the day were four killed and 21 wounded.

On this same Saturday, 180 air miles to the south at its nearest point, the Eighth Army attacked the Pusan Perimeter and engaged North Korean units that might have reinforced the defenders of Kimpo and Seoul. Raids and bombardments along both coasts sought to keep the enemy commanders off balance.

The 5th Marines now looped left to Kimpo Airfield, 16 miles

away; and the 1st Marines drove straight ahead to Yongdungpo, 20 miles up the highway.

At dawn on Sunday, 2d Lt. Lee R. Howard's 2d Platoon of the 5th Marines' D Company was dug in on a knoll west of the Inchon–Seoul highway and short of Ascom City, a large village that after World War II had ballooned into a huge United States service command base. Howard watched a column of six T-34s approach from the direction of Seoul. There were at least 200 enemy infantrymen riding on them and marching alongside. He notified 1st Lt. Smith waiting on a hill to the rear with tanks, recoilless rifles and 3.5-inch bazookas. Howard let the tanks pass, and then his platoon opened up with machine guns, rifles and BARs. Cpl. Okey J. Douglas knocked out the lead tank with his 2.36-inch bazooka and singlehandedly went on to damage the second enemy tank. The heavier weapons at Smith's position began firing. The T-34s tried to deploy into the rice paddies. First Lt. William D. Pomeroy's M-26 tanks attacked. F Company, 11th Marines on the other side of the road joined the firing. Bazookaman Pfc. Walter C. Monegan, Jr., raced down and at point-blank range wrecked two tanks in succession. All six T-34s were destroyed and almost all the enemy infantrymen were killed. One Marine was slightly wounded.

Just then, a column of Jeeps came speeding up the road from the rear. They carried Generals MacArthur, Almond, Shepherd and Smith and a host of officers and press correspondents and photographers. The officers inspected the brand-new carnage of dead bodies and blazing tanks amid a flurry of picture taking. Afterward, seven armed North Koreans were flushed out of a culvert over which MacArthur's Jeep had been parked.

The 2d Battalion, 5th Marines, advancing toward Kimpo, fought through Ascom City's sprawling maze of buildings, warehouses, streets and caves. West of the town, the 3rd Battalion and the Korean Marines skirmished with enemy detachments. By 6 P.M., Smith's D Company and a platoon of tanks swept onto the southern tip of Kimpo Airfield's main runway. The three 2d Battalion rifle companies set up independent perimeters, and Lieutenant Deptula's 1st Platoon of E Company outposted the village of Soryu-li several hundred yards northeast of E Company.

Squeezed between the advancing 5th Marines and the Han

697

River beyond the airfield, the North Koreans counterattacked at 3 A.M. Deptula's separated platoon held its fire until the enemy were in its midst. Then Sgt. Richard L. Marston leaped up, shouting "United States Marines!"[36] and firing his carbine on full automatic. Rifles and BARs joined in. A dozen North Koreans went down and the rest fled, only to rally and hit back three more times. Finally, a T-34 came up; and Deptula was forced to withdraw to E Company's main position. One Marine had been killed and one wounded.

At 5 A.M., E Company was hit by small-arms fire. Captain Jaskilka thought the shots came from D Company and stood up and shouted for it to stop. He discovered his mistake just as the enemy attacked from two sides. Cpl. Russell House rushed forward hurling grenades and was killed; he won the Navy Cross posthumously.

At F Company's perimeter, a six-man demolition team tried to blow up a bridge; Sgt. Ray D. Kearl killed four of the infiltrators. When the North Koreans launched their main attack at dawn, B Company's fire dispersed most of them before they could reach the 2d Battalion.

The 1st Battalion seized Hills 118, 80 and 85 between Kimpo and Yongdungpo. Near Ascom City, Muetzel was seriously wounded and lost his right leg. Sgt. Joseph M. Ward grabbed an enemy grenade; it exploded as he threw it back. He lived to receive the Navy Cross.

By 10 A.M. on Monday, September 18, Kimpo and its 6,000-foot-long runway were secured; and D Company occupied Hill 131 overlooking the Han River north of the airfield. The 2d Battalion had four killed and 19 wounded taking Korea's largest airfield. A helicopter with Lt. Gen. Shepherd aboard was the first American aircraft to land at Kimpo; and the next day, Maj. Gen. Field Harris deployed VMF-212, VMF-312 and VMF(N)-542 to the field. VMF-214 and VMF-323 on the carriers and VMF(N)-513 at Itazuke in Japan started flying close support for the 1st Marines.

In the south on September 18 and 19, the Eighth Army, which was finding it difficult to switch over to the offensive, finally crossed the Naktong against strong opposition. By the nineteenth, the North Korean High Command began moving its main forces northward. The Inchon strategy was working. But the slowness of the Eighth Army seemed inexcusable. It had 140,000 men in combat units—including 60,000 U.S. soldiers—against an estimated 70,000 enemy soldiers, more than half of whom were reluctant South Korean conscripts.

While the 5th Marines moved on Kimpo, the 1st Marines advanced up the Inchon–Seoul highway, punched its way through the village of Mahang-ri and ran into an enemy strongpoint in a defile halfway to Sosa. There, the enemy hit 2d Lt. Bryan J. Cummings' lead tank and threw back the accompanying riflemen. Although his engine went dead, Cummings opened his hatch and dragged in the lone Marine still clinging to his tank, as the enemy scrambled down the hill. Inside, the rescued Marine went berserk and had to be knocked out. Choking from his gun's fumes, Cummings opened a port; a grenade flew in and exploded, wounding Cummings and two Marines. At that moment, Sgt. Marion C. Altaire brought up his M-26 and swept the back of Cummings' tank with machine-gun fire, killing the swarming North Koreans. Corsairs poured bombs and rockets on the ridges, G Company fought for the hills above the pass and more tanks added their fire. Finally, the 2d Battalion drove the enemy from the high ground on the left of the road and sent the survivors fleeing toward Sosa. Behind, they left 250 dead and wounded and 70 prisoners. It had been the Marines' stiffest fight so far.

By noon the next day, the 3rd Battalion took Sosa against light opposition. The 1st Marines' three battalions occupied a line of hills beyond Sosa. Enemy guns and mortars hammered them there as the North Koreans prepared to hold Yongdungpo, Seoul's ugly industrial suburb on the near side of the Han River.

The capital was now the Marines' target. And the enemy was gathering to defend it. The 5th Marines was ordered to cross the Han and hit Seoul from the mountainous northwest, and the 1st Marines was to fight straight up the highway and through Yongdungpo. The Korean Marines would protect the division's left flank and the 32d Infantry, its right.

The 5th Marines faced the difficult task of crossing the 400-yard-wide river without bridging materials. Why such materials were not at hand is unclear. The LVTs of the Marines' 1st Amphibian Tractor Battalion were collected; and Lt. Col. John H. Partridge, commander of the Marines' 1st Engineer Battalion, provided two 50-ton "rafts" to lift across tanks, vehicles and equipment. The place chosen for the crossing was a former ferry site between the village of Haengjiu and steep Hill 125, both on the far side of the river. Seoul was four ridge-broken miles away.

On the moonless night of September 19, a swimming team from the Reconnaissance Company led the way across the Han. It consisted of Capt. Kenneth J. Houghton, 2d Lt. Dana M. Cashion, ten enlisted men and two Navy officers serving as interpreter and public relations officer (with a tape recorder). At 8 P.M., the swimmers stripped to their skivvies and swam the dark river with a silent breast stroke. They towed two rubber boats loaded with arms, equipment and clothes. In 40 minutes, Houghton's team was across and had overpowered two stray Koreans. The team failed to check the crest of Hill 125 and all too quickly gave the signal that it was safe for the LVTs on the south bank to cross. Nine roaring amtracs started to bring the rest of the Recon Company led by 1st Lt. Ralph B. Crossman. Suddenly, the enemy hidden on Hill 125 opened fire; bullets and mortar shells pummeled the water and shore. The two Korean prisoners tried to escape and the Marines killed them. One of the swimmers, Pfc. Alphonse O. Ledet, Jr., was missing. Four of the LVTs grounded in the mud near the north bank. The last Recon platoon was ordered to stay on the south bank and cover them with fire. The swimming team tried to return across the river now pockmarked by Marine mortar shells. Captain Houghton was knocked out by a concussion and dragged aboard a grounded LVT. Two other swimmers were slightly wounded. Gunnery Sgt. Ernest L. DeFazio led the rest of the swimmers back to the south bank. The free LVTs also raced back to the south bank, and most of the men in the grounded vehicles swam or waded to safety. No one knew who, if anyone, had given the order for the amtracs to retreat in the face of the surprisingly strong resistance.

DeFazio with eight men went back and searched for Captain Houghton, located him in the LVT and returned with two amtracs that were finally freed from the mud.

Embarrassed by this repulse, the Marine commanders ordered Taplett's 3rd Battalion to cross the Han in strength at 6:30 A.M. The enemy was ready for them. The first assault wave of six LVTs took 200 hits, but the amtracs' armor limited casualties to four crewmen wounded. Captain McMullen's leading I Company landed under intense fire. His company, which had been the reserve force on Wolmi-do, was made up of newcomers to combat who had formed the Brigade's third rifle companies at Pusan. Their only support crossing the Han was the machine-gun fire from their own LVTs and four Corsairs of VMF-214, which clobbered Hill 125. The company landed and attacked the hill. Halfway up, the 3rd Platoon's mortar section was cut down by machine-gun fire; 1st Lt. William F. Sparks was wounded and the men fell back. Casualties were heavy. The 2d Platoon rode its amtracs a few hundred yards inland and attacked. McMullen sent the 1st Platoon through the 3rd, and all three platoons assaulted the hill. McMullen was hit but stayed in command to lead the final assault. With close support from VMF-214, the Marines took the crest. I Company had 43 dead and wounded.

By 9:40, I, G and H Companies had all taken their assigned high ground north of the river. The Marines recovered the two grounded LVTs. And Pfc. Ledet showed up after spending the night alone on the enemy side of the river and was able to report on enemy strength and movements. The 1st and 2d Battalions came across to bolster the Marine beachhead. The Marines had crossed the Han—the hard way. MacArthur pinned a Silver Star on Maj. Gen. Smith.

On September 21, Navy Lt. Thomas Coleman was shot down in North Korean territory; and Marine Lt. Arthur R. Bancroft of VMO-6 flew a helicopter to rescue him. The chopper was destroyed on the ground, and 1st Lt. Robert A. Longstaff in a second helicopter made a daring landing under fire and picked up the stranded airmen. (Bancroft was killed eight days later by antiaircraft fire while trying to rescue the crew of an OY that had been shot down. The airplane's observer, Capt. Edwin E. Rives, was killed; and the pilot, Lt. Thomas D. Odenbaugh, was captured.)

The 7th Marines and the 3rd Battalion, 11th Marines landed at Inchon on the twenty-first and began moving up to the Kimpo area. It was only 35 days since the regiment had been activated. The plan now was for the 7th Marines to swing to the division's left flank and cut off any enemy escape to the north. The 1st and 5th Marines would advance on Seoul astride the Han River. The

5th Marines would clear the north bank and open crossing sites for the 1st Marines in the Yongdungpo area. But the North Koreans' stubborn and skillful defense forced another change in plans.

South of the Han River, the 1st Marines closed on Yong-dungpo from the south and southwest. The 3rd Battalion took the ridges of Lookout Hill. And the 2d Battalion fought up the highway and took Hill 72, after the Engineers cleared a mine-field that had destroyed the lead M-26. A mile further at Hill 146, the North Koreans blocked the highway. A dozer tank smashed into a roadblock of trees and earth-filled rice bags and exploded in a second minefield. The Engineers led by 1st Lt. George A. Babe again went about their dangerous mine-clearing work. Sutter's 2d Battalion finally took Hill 146.

On September 19, before it crossed the river, the 1st Battalion, 5th Marines had seized the three hills between the airfield and Yungdungpo. At noon, the 32d Infantry began freeing the 1st Battalion, 1st Marines on the far right to be trucked north to relieve the 1st Battalion, 5th Marines, for its river crossing the next day. Since it was already dark when the 1st Marines arrived, Lt. Col. Hawkins did not take possession of the two forward hills (Hills 80 and 85) of the three that the 5th Marines had held. Before dawn, the enemy reoccupied them. To capture them again would take many Marine lives.

Early that same morning, September 20, a strong enemy force led by five T-34s came down the Inchon-Seoul highway. D and F Companies of the 1st Marines stood on a ridge south of the road three miles short of Yongdungpo. Further back, E Company was dug in at right angles across the highway. The Marines held their fire and let the enemy column come through until it reached E Company. Then, all three companies opened up and slaughtered the panicked enemy. An ammunition truck that had strangely been leading the column blew up with a spectacular display. In the light of the explosion, nineteen-year-old Pfc. Walter C. Monegan, Jr., of Melrose, Massachusetts, who had knocked out two tanks on September 17, charged down the hillside from F Company. The Marines shifted their fire to protect him. Monegan and Cpl. William Cheek closed within a hundred yards of the lead tank. Monegan wrecked it with one 3.5-inch projectile and then blew up a second tank. Pfc. Robert

Perkins reloaded the bazooka; and as Monegan took aim at a third tank, machine-gun fire found him and "Monegan—killer of tanks" was dead.[37] He was awarded the Medal of Honor.

The 11th Marines closed the highway behind the attacking enemy with a curtain of artillery fire. The Marines counted 300 North Korean bodies and four destroyed tanks.

Puller's regiment prepared to attack Yongdungpo. First, the city was smashed and burned with shells, rockets, incendiary shells and napalm. The 2d Battalion advanced up the highway to the first of two bridges over branches of the Kalchon River, a tributary that flowed north into the Han before Yongdungpo. The 1st Battalion attacked Hills 80 and 85, which the enemy had reoccupied. C Company recaptured Hill 80 easily, but the enemy was entrenched on Hill 85 and the battle there was vicious.

The North Koreans met Capt. Robert P. Wray's double envelopment by bending their flanks into a horseshoe and battling C Company's platoons head on. On the left, 2d Lt. John N. Guild led the attack and was badly wounded in the chest by machine-gun fire. He refused medical aid and pressed his 2d Platoon forward until he died. On the right, 2d Lt. Henry A. Commiskey raced ahead of his 3rd Platoon and charged up the steep slope under heavy fire. First onto the crest, he jumped into a machine-gun emplacement and killed four North Koreans. With his .45 empty, he grappled with a fifth enemy and killed him. Commiskey pushed forward alone and cleaned out a second position, killing two more of the enemy. Then, the North Koreans broke and ran. The twenty-three-year-old Marine from Hattiesburg, Mississippi, was awarded the Medal of Honor. John Guild was given a posthumous Navy Cross.

At dawn on September 21, B Company crossed the wreckage of the Kalchon River bridge north of Yongdungpo under cover of fire from the Marines on Hill 85. Taking heavy casualties, Capt. Richard F. Bland's company pushed ahead 2,000 yards between a dike and the Han River until it entered a fire fight with the enemy on a second dike. Artillery was slow to support B Company because it was advancing southward against the grain of the battle. Its platoon leaders were wounded, and Staff Sgt. Frank Quadros took command of the survivors of the 1st and 3rd Platoons.

Pfc. Albert H. Collins of Tulsa, Oklahoma, ducked across a fire-swept area to get a supply of belted ammunition for his machine gun. Returning, he was struck by enemy fire and crawled the last 40 yards. He found the other Marines of his machine-gun crew dead or wounded. Although he was bleeding badly, Collins loaded the gun and opened fire. As his ammunition ran out, he died. He was awarded the Navy Cross. Bland's company, with 40 wounded, held the dike and was reinforced by C Company. They could not advance into the city.

Meanwhile south of Yongdungpo, the 2d Battalion fought its way toward the burning city. By noon, D Company was slugging it out at 100 yards with the enemy entrenched behind a dike on the battalion's left front. E and F Companies assaulted a ridge on the right of the highway, took heavy casualties and had to withdraw at dusk. VMF-214 skillfully covered their withdrawal, but the enemy still controlled the high ground. The day's fighting had cost the 2d Battalion 11 dead and 74 wounded. As it had lost 28 killed and 226 wounded since D-Day, Puller put in his 3rd Battalion. After Maj. Edwin H. Simmons' Browning heavy machine guns dueled the enemy's Russian Maxims in World War I style, Ridge's 3rd Battalion waded the Kalchon against strong resistance.

The enemy had contained the 1st Marines' two main drives slanting in from the northwest and the southwest. But in the center, 200 Marines of A Company daringly penetrated the very heart of Yongdungpo. They were led by six-foot-four Capt. Robert H. Barrow, a native of St. Francisville, Louisiana, who had fought as a Marine with the Chinese guerrillas behind the Japanese lines during World War II.

After hiking through a mile of open rice paddies in grain as high as their heads, Barrow's Marines waded the Kalchon without a shot being fired and dripping with mud climbed the dike on the far side. By noon, they had advanced several hundred yards up the broad main street of the dead-seeming city. "It was an eerie kind of experience," Barrow said later.[38] Knowing he was far ahead of the other attacking columns, he radioed for instructions. Lt. Col. Hawkins told him to keep going.

As Barrow's Marines closed on the Inchon-Seoul highway coming along on their right, they ran into an enemy force.

Second Lt. John J. Swords' 3rd Platoon cut it to ribbons. Swords led his men to the top of a dike topped by a macadam road. There, on the far side of the city, their fire could cover Seoul's dirt airstrip and the approaches to Seoul itself. To the north they directed telling machine-gun fire on the enemy troops pushed back by B Company's attack. The rest of A Company quickly occupied more of the dike top and formed a "sausage-shaped" defense. They covered the junction with the highway, the location of a crucial enemy supply center in a five-story building. A Marine's grenade blew up a camouflaged mountain of ammunition, and the entire countryside shook with the explosion. The "mushroom-shaped cloud" from the exploding ammunition dump marked their position; their radio was unable to reach the battalion command post. They took plasma from the enemy supplies for their dozen wounded. They threw back small enemy attacks and hoped their ammunition would hold out. To defend the hundred-yard section of the dike reaching to the road intersection, they dug foxholes along the gently sloping incline of the 25-foot-high dike and placed machine guns and BARs on top of the dike to fire in all directions. For some unexplained reason, Lt. Col. Hawkins sent no reinforcements to support the isolated company deep behind enemy lines or to exploit its achievement.

At dusk, five T-34s rumbled down the dirt road paralleling the dike and opened fire at 30 yards with 85mm shells and machine guns. They were the first tanks that the Marines of A Company had ever fought. "They stood cool and tall and let them have it," Barrow remembered. The bazooka men let fly, and Cpl. Francis Devine exploded one tank. Like battleships, the remaining tanks cruised down the road in column, reversed course and paraded back—and then repeated the entire maneuver again, firing all the time. Bazookas damaged two more tanks. The remaining pair made a fifth pass and then rolled off. In this hour of bombardment at close range, A Company had suffered exactly one casualty, and that from concussion. Foxholes had protected the Marines against the machine guns, and the enemy's armor-piercing shells smashed deep into the dike before exploding.

At 9 P.M., a large enemy force hit the 3rd Platoon on the north end of the dike nearest the road junction. Conserving their ammunition carefully, Barrow's Marines threw the North Koreans back in a 15-minute fire fight. Half an hour later, they returned and were repelled again. By midnight, the 3rd Platoon had dispatched five such attacks. Just before the last, Cpl. Billy D. Webb from Tulsa, Oklahoma, went out into the streets among the burning buildings with his M1 and with one shot killed the enemy commander who had been exhorting his men to attack. Webb's shot finished it. Dawn found 310 dead around A Company's perimeter. At 8 A.M., the 1st and 3rd Battalions attacked and swiftly reached the isolated company. A Company's dramatic stand had won the battle for Yongdungpo.

Still ahead lay Seoul; and enemy forces, including the 78th Independent Regiment and the 25th Brigade, prepared to fight to hold it.

The 5th Marines attacked the capital in earnest from the northwest early on September 22. It was one week since D-Day and the beginning of a very bloody battle. The North Koreans, 10,000 strong and well armed, had organized a Main Line of Resistance on a formidable hill complex across the Marines' front. The 25th Brigade defended these hills; it was led by men who fought with the Communist army in China. They would not panic and run. They had to be dug out and killed.

The 5th Marines attacked with the 3rd Battalion on the left, the 1st Koreans Marines in the center and the 1st Battalion on the right. The fighting was intense, and the regiment made little progress. The 1st Battalion, in an all-day fight, did take Hill 105-S.

On the morning of September 23, the 7th Marines' headquarters and 3rd Battalion crossed the Han; and the rest of the regiment came over the following day. Its initial mission was to protect the northern flank and rear of the 5th Marines.

The Korean Marines, who had been beaten back the previous day tried unsuccessfully to straighten the line. The enemy mortars were deadly. That afternoon, the 2d Battalion, 5th Marines passed through the Korean Marines and attacked Hill 56, where enemy resistance was strongest. At the time the Marine officers did not realize this hill was a crucial part of the enemy's MLR.

F Company took heavy casualties crossing a thousand yards of paddies and hit Hill 56 directly from the east. The 1st Platoon fought furiously at close range until only seven able-bodied Marines were left. D Company attacked the adjoining ridge saddle from the north. Its 1st Platoon was caught in the open by intense fire; half its men were struck down in five minutes. The platoon leader, 2d Lt. Ray Heck, was mortally wounded, and his senior noncom, Staff Sgt. T. Albert Crowson, who had commanded the platoon at the Naktong, had his leg shattered. First Lt. Smith, the company commander, personally retrieved the battered platoon. That night, D and F Companies, isolated, clung to the slopes of Hill 56, waiting for the expected counterattack. In one of the mysteries of the war, it never came.

On September 24, the 1st Marines crossed the Han unopposed after the Engineers cleared the crossing site of mines. Puller ordered Hawkins and his 1st Battalion to pass through Sutter's 2d and drive eastward. Since Sutter was already in motion, the order was received with skepticism. But Puller was firm; he said, "You'll just have to advance a little faster."[39] The men moved out at double time.

Maj. Gen. Almond was "dissatisfied with the marines' progress,"[40] and impatiently told Maj. Gen. Smith that Seoul was to be captured by September 25. MacArthur wanted to proclaim the capital's liberation exactly three months after the North Korean invasion. It was neat public relations, but the enemy would not cooperate.

Almond changed X Corps' attack. He ordered the 32d Infantry (40 percent of its men were Koreans) and the ROK 17th Regiment to cross the Han and attack Seoul from the southeast. The 5th and 1st Marines would advance jointly from the west and southwest. The 7th Marines would still protect the left flank. Almond visited Murray's and Puller's command posts and told them what he wanted done, bypassing and infuriating the usually patient Maj. Gen. Smith.[41]

The 5th Marines went to work on the heights just west of Seoul. The 3rd Battalion attacked from the northwest. The 1st Battalion secured the north bank of the Han for Puller's crossing and then relieved the 3rd Battalion. The 2d Battalion attacked the enemy's MLR, which was now called Smith's Ridge after D Company's commander.

What was left of D Company had the job of clearing the enemy from the wooded spine of Smith's Ridge. As the company approached in the morning mist, the defenders on the ridge opened up and pinned down the Marines for two hours. Two Marine tanks were disabled. First Lt. Smith ordered every man into the line and kept two machine guns firing. First Lt. Karle Seydel made five trips under fire to bring up ammunition. The two opposing forces were now in grenade-throwing range, a competition at which the baseball-conditioned Marines excelled. Both sides tried to flank their opponents. In one attempt, Sgt. Robert Smith's squad was wiped out, with eight men killed. Corpsman James Egresitz went to help the wounded and was killed. Only three wounded Marines ever got back.

About 10:30, the mist and smoke lifted; and artillery and VMF-323 could help out. The fliers destroyed four tanks, but five of their planes were damaged by flak.

First Lt. Smith had 40 men and four officers left when he launched the final assault. As the Marines pressed forward, Smith was killed at the head of his men. At the finish, 26 Marines remained. By then, there were more dead than living North Koreans on Smith's Ridge. The surviving enemy fled toward Seoul, and the Marines shot down as many as they could. At 1:30, their objective was secured. First Lt. Seydel was the only D Company officer unwounded. Of 206 men, the company had 36 killed, 116 wounded and evacuated and 26 who were wounded and stayed—178 casualties. Marines referred to this day's fight as "the epic of Dog Company."[42]

On the east side of Smith's Ridge, Capt. Uel D. Peters' F Company—which now had less than 90 men left, counting the wounded who refused evacuation—had two prolonged fire fights and took its objectives. Cpl. Welden D. Harris, who had killed three North Koreans in hand-to-hand combat the day before and been wounded twice, received a third and mortal wound. He was awarded the Navy Cross posthumously.

At 3 P.M., Jaskilka's E Company moved up from reserve to take Hill 105-N beyond Smith's Ridge. Two tanks were destroyed. The remaining three could advance only after Staff Sgt. Stanley B. McPherson of A Company, 1st Engineer Battalion went ahead under fire and cleared a path through the enemy minefield. By then, not enough daylight remained to take the hill. But the day's battle on Smith's Ridge had been crucial— "the western defenses of Seoul had fallen."[43] Lt. Col. Roise estimated that 1,500 North Koreans were dead on Hill 56 and

Smith's Ridge. Since landing at Pusan, the 5th Marines had had 17 of its 18 original platoon leaders and five of its six company commanders killed or wounded.

While the 5th Marines were assaulting the MLR so painfully, the 1st Marines had crossed the Han. For the first time, all three Marine regiments were in position to attack on a single front.

And at last, after overcoming fierce rearguard resistance, the Eighth Army broke out of the Pusan Perimeter on September 23. In three days, it gained 35 miles. The 31st Infantry of X Corps' 7th Infantry Division pushed south from Inchon to meet the 1st Cavalry Division, which was spearheading the Eighth Army advance.

At 7 A.M. on September 25, X Corps attacked Seoul itself. The 5th Marines smashed through the MLR ridge line, and the 1st Marines swept forward in tough street fighting. South of the city, the 32d Infantry and the 17th ROK Regiment crossed the Han and occupied South Mountain, Seoul's highest point. As programmed, Almond and MacArthur announced the city's capture. It wasn't true.

The fliers found Seoul "a flak trap." Close air support was energetic and effective, but antiaircraft fire gave Maj. Gen. Harris' 1st MAW a hellish day. Lt. Col. Walter E. Lischeid of VMF-214 was shot down in flames over the western edge of the city. In the next two hours, Lt. Col. Richard W. Wyczawski of VMF-212 and Lt. Col. Max J. Volcansek, Jr., of VMF(N)-542 were both shot down and injured. Lischeid's death started a legend. He was killed flying Corsair No. 17. On D plus two, Captain Simpson had been killed flying plane No. 17; and two days later on *Sicily*, Tech. Sgt. George C. Underwood was killed when the new No. 17 accidentally discharged its guns. On September 23, Maj. Robert Floeck was killed in this same plane, but the aircraft was saved. Now, when Lischeid was killed in No. 17, Capt. John S. Thach, USN, of *Sicily* banned that number plane from the carrier.[44]

In the northwest part of the city, the 2d Battalion, 5th Marines ran into tough fighting. E Company grabbed Hill 72 ("Nellie's Tit") and Hill 105-C. To the left, the 3rd Battalion met even stronger resistance; and H and I Companies took Hill 105-N with heavy casualties.

The 1st Marines made a 90-degree turn to the northeast and

slashed toward the heart of the city. As always, "liberation" was expensive. Watching the artillery destroy Korean homes, Puller said, "They'll remember us for a thousand years for this, and hate our guts."[45]

A small force of tanks and 50 Engineers ran into an ambush at the base of Hill 105-S, which had supposedly been secured. First Lt. Babe was shot in the arm. The detachment was in trouble until a flame tank flanked and seared the enemy emplacements with short bursts of flaming napalm. Tech. Sgt. Pasquale Paolino of the Engineers discovered a cave dug into Hill 105-S, banged on Second Lt. Cummings' tank and directed its fire into huts at the cave's mouth. A few North Koreans emerged with their arms over their heads; and when they were allowed to surrender, some 120 more followed, including two women. The women later claimed to have been stripped and mistreated by the Marines, causing a brief uproar in some newspapers back in the United States.

The tanks then took the lead in front of the 3rd Battalion, 1st Marines and fought up broad Ma-Po Boulevard through successive roadblocks and against automatic-weapons and mortar fire from the rooftops and buildings. The 1st and 3rd Battalions gained 2,000 yards by nightfall. The enemy was defending the city savagely.

The pressure continued to take Seoul fast enough to meet MacArthur's political objectives. Shortly after 8 P.M., Maj. Gen. Smith received an urgent message from X Corps saying that aviators had reported the enemy fleeing Seoul to the north. The message ordered an immediate attack. Smith was certain the fliers had spotted fleeing refugees; his Marines were still under fire. Smith and his operations officer called Corps headquarters to argue against a night assault into the city. They were told that Maj. Gen. Almond wanted the attack to begin at once. Smith obeyed orders; and the attack was directed to begin—with caution—at 1:45 A.M., following a 15-minute artillery barrage. At 1:38, Puller decided the preparation was inadequate and ordered the barrage repeated. The attack was delayed until 2 A.M. At 1:53, Puller received a flash message from Lt. Col. Ridge, commander of his 3rd Battalion, that a strong enemy force supported by tanks and self-propelled guns was moving down Ma-Po Boulevard from the center of the city toward the 1st Marines. Almond's attack was postponed.

Fortunately, these North Koreans of the 25th Brigade had run into an 11-man 3rd Battalion patrol led by Cpl. Charles E. Collins, which was out among the streets in front, seeking to make contact with a patrol from the 5th Marines. A fire fight began at 1:30. While Collins covered his men with his M-1, members of the patrol raced back to warn Maj. Edwin H. Simmons, who was coordinating the battalion's frontline defenses. Tanks attacked G Company's roadblock. Simmons called in artillery. The first enemy tank killed Pfc. Varga, his radioman. Marines destroyed that tank and forced the second to retreat. Machine gunners, riflemen and artillery blasted the enemy column out of existence with an enormous concentration of firepower. By 6:30, the last of seven tanks was destroyed, more than 475 of the enemy were killed and 83 prisoners taken. Simmons earned the Silver Star; and Corporal Collins, who had covered his patrol's retreat, "miraculously"[46] returned safely, disguised in white civilian Korean clothes.

Another enemy force hit the 32d Infantry at 5 A.M. and overran a portion of its front until a counterattack could restore the line. The Army regiment reported killing 394 of the enemy and taking 174 prisoners. X Corps' insistence that the enemy was fleeing and its announcement that the city had been captured were surely "a bit premature."[47]

Once these enemy attacks were annihilated, the two climactic days of the battle for Seoul actually began. The 7th Marines drove southeast to pinch out the 5th Marines while the 1st Marines fought northeast through the center of the city.

Col. Homer L. Litzenberg, commander of the 7th Marines, sent D Company down the Kaesong–Seoul highway at 6:30 A.M. on September 26 to meet the 5th Marines. First Lt. William F. Groggin, the company machine-gun officer, led the column through hundreds of cheering Koreans. The Marines moved through a narrow valley between Hills 296 and 838 toward Sodaemun Prison at the northwest corner of Seoul. Suddenly, machine guns opened up from a tower and the high ground. Since the welcoming throngs had prevented the use of flankers, D Company was caught on the low ground. Its counterattacks were thrown back. Groggin and Capt. Richard R. Breen, the company commander, were among the wounded. The enemy closed in behind D Company and repulsed a small tank-infantry relief force. By 4 P.M., the now-surrounded company withdrew a thousand yards to the cut between the two hills and prepared a tight perimeter for an all-night defense. Breen had 40 casualties. In the morning, a second relief column escorted D Company back to the regimental CP.

Taplett's 3rd Battalion, 5th Marines spent September 26 clearing the last resistance from the Hill 296 complex. Captain McMullen's I Company led the attack, but McMullen underestimated the enemy's strength and called off his artillery support. The North Koreans tore huge holes in the Marines' line. McMullen led the company into close-in fighting and drove the enemy to lower ground. The North Koreans counterattacked uphill; and a wild melee began. Before the enemy finally gave way, I Company was badly battered. McMullen was carried off with his seventh battle wound in two wars.

On I Company's right, G Company inched forward against stubborn resistance. When Cpl. Bert Johnson was hit while setting up his machine gun, Pfc. Eugene A. Obregon, his ammunition carrier, dashed up and, firing his pistol, dragged Johnson to the side of the road. Under fire, Obregon started to bandage Johnson's wound. A platoon of enemy charged them. Obregon grabbed Johnson's carbine, covered him with his own body and fired coolly at the enemy. The nineteen-year-old Marine from Los Angeles was killed by a machine-gun burst and was awarded the Medal of Honor. The enemy attack was repelled and Johnson was rescued.

In the 1st Marines' zone, the 1st Battalion on the right cleaned up strong resistance around Seoul's red brick main railroad station at the base of 900-foot-high South Mountain, which was in peacetime a pleasant city park. Fighting was intense among the terminal buildings and railroad cars. C Company finally cleared the station, and A Company secured the northwest tip of South Mountain. The 32d Infantry attacked from the south side of South Mountain, killing 500 North Koreans and destroying five tanks.

On the 1st Marines' left, Sutter's 2d Battalion passed through the 3rd and attacked along Ma-Po Boulevard's street car line into the center of Seoul. Every few yards, determined detachments defended rice-bag barricades eight feet high and five feet thick across the width of the avenue. Engineers, protected by riflemen, cleared mines in front of the barriers and then the M-26s smashed them. The teamwork was effective, but the Marines had to fight a battle of 360 degrees as North Koreans fired from roofs, windows and side streets. Suicide squads tried to destroy the Marine tanks and managed to blow up a flame-thrower tank. It was slow, brutal street fighting.

Advancing up the broad boulevard littered with abandoned enemy gear, Capt. Goodwin C. Groff's F Company was stopped a hundred yards short of Kung Hua Noon Circle. The company was supposed to advance up the left street from the circle; and E Company, which was following, was to take the right fork. Then, the two companies were to converge again and assault the Duksoo Palace at the head of the boulevard. Lt. Col. Sutter had told them, "Move out fast and keep going."[48]

With F Company pinned down, Capt. Norman R. Stanford, the new commander of E Company, and his runner, Pfc. Edward Cavanaugh, worked up to the intersection. Stanford, an Annapolis graduate from Cohasset, Massachusetts, had won the Navy Cross on Okinawa. He and Cavanaugh kept close to the buildings. The circle was a mess of dead bodies, debris and abandoned guns; the buildings were on fire. Stanford found F Company stopped by a barricade with an antitank battery. Waving up his four tanks, he sent them against the barrier. The fighting was severe; in the last 250 yards, E Company had 20 casualties, including Stanford. Once his company destroyed the barrier, it led the way up the avenue toward the palace.

On September 27, Litzenberg's 7th Marines fought in the immense ridges just north of the city. Murray's 5th Marines battled through the streets, barricades and minefields in western Seoul; its 3rd Battalion took the Middle School and attacked toward the Capitol building.

On the right of the Marines' front, Puller's 1st Marines raised the American flag above the French Embassy at mid-morning and got into a furious fight at the city's main intersection. Second Lt. Cummings' tank knocked out two 76mm self-propelled guns in the middle of the intersection, and then his tank was destroyed by mines. The North Koreans were fighting stubbornly. Sutter's 2d Battalion battled through a maze of streets and in the afternoon raised the flag over the Russian and United States Embassies.

Shortly after 3 P.M., Taplett's 3rd Battalion, 5th Marines, burst into the Government House compound; struck the North Korean flags, and raised the American. By the day's end, Tech.

Sgt. George W. Bolkow's 3rd Platoon of A Company captured the crest of rocky Hill 338 northwest of Government House.

As dusk fell, resistance in front of the Marines collapsed; and except for mopping up enemy pockets and snipers, the battle of Seoul was over. The next day, the 1st Marines advanced and dug in on the northeastern part of the city. The North Koreans were retreating north to Uijongbu. The 7th Marines seized the high ground north of Seoul on both sides of the main highway leading to Uijongbu.

September 29 was a day of fighting and ceremonies. The 7th Marines had a full day of battle. The 1st Marines repulsed two counterattacks before dawn. Its E Company on Hill 132 held positions 300 yards in front of the battalion. At 4 A.M., Pfc. Alfred Walsh and Pfc. Stanley R. Christianson, manning a listening post protecting the company, heard a large enemy force approaching. Christianson sent Walsh back to warn the others and opened fire. He killed seven of the enemy before their automatic weapons overwhelmed him. His one-man defense allowed his platoon to beat off the enemy attack and kill 41 North Koreans. The Marine from Mindoro, Wisconsin, was awarded the Medal of Honor posthumously.

At midmorning, General MacArthur and President Rhee arrived separately at Kimpo Airfield and drove to the Government Palace along a route guarded chiefly by the Marines. During the liberation ceremonies, Puller's Marines protected the distinguished audience. Artillery could be heard in the distance and shook glass loose from the broken skylights. At noon, MacArthur opened the proceedings restoring the capital to the Republic of Korea; his five-minute speech ended with the Lord's Prayer.

By now, the North Korean invaders had been routed throughout South Korea. On September 26, the Eighth Army had advanced a hundred miles; and the following morning, the 7th Cavalry linked up with the 31st Infantry above Osan—near where, at the war's beginning, Task Force Smith had met defeat. The North Koreans were throwing away their weapons, putting on civilian clothes and trying to escape to the north. By the last day of the month, the ROK 3rd Division was five miles below the 38th Parallel. The North Korean army had been virtually destroyed.

The three Marine regiments took blocking positions in a

semi-circle north of Seoul. There were occasional fire fights. Early on October 1, the 7th Marines drove north toward Uijong-bu, with VMF-312 flying close support. First Lt. Robert O. Crocker was shot down by small-arms fire and then killed on the ground. The enemy rear guard fought tenaciously. By the evening of October 3, the 7th Marines entered the ruins of Uijong-bu. The three-day advance had cost 13 killed and 111 wounded.

On October 5, the Marines received orders to return to Inchon where a Marine cemetery was dedicated on the 6th. The amphibious operation ended on October 7, and the Marines headed for Wonsan on the east coast—and a new war.

The entire Inchon–Seoul campaign had been executed with daring and speed. Seoul was taken in less than two weeks. The enemy lost an estimated 13,666 casualties, 4,692 prisoners and 44 tanks. Total casualties to the 1st Marine Division were 421 dead and 2,029 wounded in action, nearly half of them during the fight around and inside Seoul. Eleven 1st MAW planes were shot down. Care for the wounded was remarkable. During the entire Inchon–Seoul offensive, Navy surgical teams operated on 2,484 patients; only nine of them died after reaching an aid station. Chances that a wounded Marine would live were figured to be 199 to 1.

In his report to the United Nations' Security Council, MacArthur called the campaign "decisive." He said "the enemy is thoroughly shattered." And he added, "A successful frontal attack and envelopment has [sic] completely changed the tide of battle in South Korea. The backbone of the North Korean army has been broken and their scattered forces are being liquidated or driven north with material losses in equipment and men captured."[49] Naval historians have written: "History records no more striking example of the effectiveness of an amphibious operation."[50]

The old general's self-assurance had been responsible for this bold campaign. The desperate days of retreat and defense had been converted into victory. The North Korean aggressors had been driven from the Republic of Korea. American, South Korean and United Nations fighting men had turned back Communist expansion by force in Asia. But suddenly, somehow, this did not seem enough. Self-assurance led to arrogance and to disaster.

4
The Reservoir

The American decision to cross the 38th Parallel was a watershed of history. Not because American forces invaded a small hostile country; there was nothing unique about that. But because the decision led to a massive defeat of American arms; it brought the United States to battle with the People's Republic of China; it encouraged Asian nationalist and Communist movements to oppose the Western powers; it heated up a period of McCarthyite frustration and fear in the United States; it stimulated the concept of basing America's defenses on nuclear weapons; it convinced many Americans that they had to confront Communism and nationalism elsewhere in Asia, and it marked the first significant rollback of the long American thrust westward across the Pacific.

Secretary of State Acheson called what happened after the United States crossed the Parallel, "the greatest defeat suffered by American arms since the Battle of Manassas and an international disaster of the first water."[51]

The decision was a split one. According to Acheson, Dean Rusk and John Allison in the State Department's Far Eastern Division urged that a crossing of the Parallel "should not be precluded";[52] Paul Nitze and George Kennan opposed it. Pentagon planners favored crossing the Parallel and "uniting" Korea. The buck stopped on President Truman's desk.

On September 27, even before the liberation ceremonies in Seoul, the Joint Chiefs of Staff, with the President's approval, gave MacArthur his orders:

> Your military objective is the destruction of the North Korean Armed Forces. In attaining this objective you are

716

authorized to conduct military operations, including amphibious and airborne landings or ground operations
north of the 38th Parallel in Korea, provided that at the
time of such operations there has been no entry into
North Korea by major Soviet or Chinese Communist
Forces, no announcement of intended entry, nor a threat
to counter our operations militarily in North Korea. . . .
under no circumstances, however, will your forces cross
the Manchurian or USSR borders of Korea and, as a
matter of policy, no non-Korean Ground Forces will be
used in the northeast provinces bordering the Soviet
Union or in the area along the Manchurian border.
Furthermore, support of your operations north or south
of the 38th Parallel will not include Air or Naval action
against Manchuria or against USSR territory. . . .[53]

MacArthur's staff developed a plan for the Eighth Army to
drive north as far as Pyongyang, the capital of the People's
Democratic Republic of Korea, and for X Corps to land at
Wonsan on the east coast and cut westward to trap the North
Korean forces retreating from the south. After linking up, both
commands would advance north to points 50 to 100 miles below
the Manchurian border. Only ROK units would proceed beyond
that restraining line.

On October 1, the ROK army started crossing the 38th
Parallel; President Rhee was still determined to unite Korea.
Two days later, China's Prime Minister Chou En-lai warned the
Indian ambassador in Peking that if American troops crossed the
Parallel, China would enter the war. In Washington, some read
his statement not as a realistic "announcement of intended
entry" but as political blackmail. The swift momentum of the
UN offensive that had begun on September 15 was not to be
stopped.

On October 7, the United Nations supported the idea of a
unified, democratic Korea.[54] Acheson said it encouraged "General MacArthur's adventurism."[55] Two days later, the 1st Cavalry Division attacked across the Parallel. The Eighth Army
smashed the North Koreans' defenses above the Parallel. And on
Sunday, October 15, President Truman met with General Mac-
Arthur on Wake Island. In reply to the President's question,

MacArthur said he saw "very little"[56] chance that the Chinese would intervene; the war would be over by Thanksgiving.

Possibly as early as October 12—three days after U.S. forces crossed the Parallel and three days before the Wake Island conference—and certainly no later than October 16, "volunteers" of the Chinese People's Liberation Army secretly entered Korea from the north. On October 26, General Lin Piao's experienced Chinese Fourth Field Army attacked ROK units at the Yalu River and 50 miles below the border. The two leading ROK regiments were destroyed. The II ROK Corps on the Eighth Army's right was driven back. On Sunday, November 1, the Chinese attacked the 1st Cavalry Division and the next day hit the 7th Marines.

Still, the initial Chinese intervention proved limited. When the Eighth Army had been forced back to the Chongchon River after 12 days of fighting, the Chinese broke off battle action on November 6. There were no further Chinese attacks for two weeks. It appeared that full-scale war with China could still be avoided.

On November 6, MacArthur asserted that the North Korean armies had been destroyed; but on November 24, the very day representatives from Peking arrived at UN headquarters at Lake Success, New York, he launched a general "end the war" offensive and sent United States troops all the way to the Yalu—despite his orders. With the North Korean army "shattered," the North Korean capital occupied and Chinese armies lurking in the distance, the reasons for MacArthur's action were at best murky.

As soon as the UN offensive began, the Chinese counterattacked again all along the front. Said one analyst, "While China crossed the Yalu on October 15th, she did not cross the Rubicon until November 26th."[57] MacArthur started blaming the political leaders in Washington for his miscalculation and failure. The world tiptoed to the brink of World War III.

Why did the Communist Chinese tackle the massed armed forces of the United States and the United Nations? In retrospect, it seemed that the Chinese wanted to preserve a buffer between themselves and American power based in Japan. Before the North Koreans invaded South Korea in June, this buffer had consisted of the two Korean states. American reoccupation of

South Korea had still left North Korea as a buffer; the October–November offensive threatened to wipe out that shield entirely. But whatever the motivation, the effect of the Chinese invasion of North Korea was that China prevented the unification of Korea by force and gained enormous prestige in Asia.

There were other factors in the Chinese decision: MacArthur, as early as August 26, had spoken out so strongly in support of the Nationalist regime on Formosa that President Truman forced him to retract his statement and considered replacing him with General Omar Bradley. The People's Republic of China started an anti-American propaganda campaign condemning the United States for preventing the "liberation" of Formosa, rearming Japan and keeping Peking out of the United Nations. The Communist Chinese invaded Tibet and helped their ideological comrades in Indochina.

And the United States made a major mistake in analyzing military intelligence, insisting, right up to the fatal November 24 offensive, that the Chinese armies were not in North Korea in strength. Said the official U.S. Army history of the war:

> . . . apparently the Central Intelligence Agency and the administration generally did not evaluate the available intelligence so as to reach a conviction on the question of whether the Chinese intended to intervene in the Korean War different from that held by General MacArthur. It must be inferred that either Washington was undecided or that its view coincided with that of the Commander in Chief, Far East, since it did not issue directives to him stating a different estimate.[58]

MacArthur refused to believe that the Chinese would intervene in full force and proclaimed that, if they did enter the war, American air power would interdict and destroy them. He and his intelligence officers were wrong. When his "end the war" offensive began, 180,000 Chinese soldiers were waiting in front of the Eighth Army and 120,000 in front of X Corps—a total of 300,000 men.

Early in November, Marine fliers of VMF(N)-542, attacking Sinuiju at the mouth of the Yalu River, had reported hordes of trucks moving from Manchuria into northwest Korea. President

Truman, after first refusing permission, finally acceded to Mac-Arthur's insistence on bombing the bridges across the Yalu, as long as dams and power plants were not hit and Manchurian territory and air space were not violated. Truman also denied MacArthur permission for "hot pursuit" across the border against MIG-15 jets, which had by now joined the war. Mac-Arthur warned that the restrictions provided enemy aircraft "a complete sanctuary."[59]

Air Force and Navy bombers attacked the 12 bridges across the Yalu and Tumen Rivers. On November 8 occurred the first all-jet air battle in history. U.S. fliers knocked out four bridges and damaged most of the others during November, but the results were disappointing and the bombings stopped on December 6 when the Yalu froze over. By then, the Chinese had already invaded North Korea.

Clearly, the interlocking invasions of North Korea by the forces of both the United Nations and Communist Chinese represented a confrontation of significance in the world's history. The armed forces of two of the world's major nations would meet in battle.

As the Eighth Army moved into North Korea in early October, the 1st Marine Division was ordered to load out of Inchon and seize Wonsan on Korea's east coast, 110 air miles above the 38th Parallel. Wonsan was Korea's petroleum refining center and one of the best natural harbors on the peninsula. But on October 10, the I ROK Corps occupied Wonsan and its deserted airfield. Five days later, the Marine transports sailed from Inchon with 30,184 troops, including 21,176 Marines. The remainder were U.S. Army and Navy personnel and members of the Korean Marine Corps.

The Navy found Wonsan harbor and beaches blocked by more than 2,000 Soviet-made mines that had been assembled and laid under Russian supervision. Attempting to clear a channel, four minesweepers were blown up by mines, and survivors rescued under fire from enemy shore batteries. Because many were magnetic mines that let 12 ships pass before they exploded, the sweeping was slow and dangerous. The crowded transports sailed endlessly back and forth for a week that the bored troops dubbed Operation Yo-Yo. Dysentery swept the men. While the Marines still fumed in their ships, Marine Air Group 12 began arriving at Wonsan; and on the evening of October 24, Bob Hope and Marilyn Maxwell put on a USO show there.

In the west, Pyongyang was captured on the twentieth; and 4,000 men of the 187th Airborne Regiment parachuted 30 miles north of the capital, trying unsuccessfully to cut the North Korean escape routes. In the center of the peninsula, ROK forces drove north. MacArthur predicted the war was almost over.

When he returned from Wake Island, MacArthur moved his restraining line north to a point 30 to 40 miles below the Manchurian border. And on October 24, he took it upon himself to eliminate the restraining line completely and instructed Lt. Gen. Walker and Maj. Gen. Almond to occupy all of North Korea with all their forces. The next day, the Joint Chiefs of Staff asked MacArthur why he had issued this "radically different" order.[60] He replied that the ROK Army was not strong enough to secure North Korea and declared that he had the authority to make this vital change. Apparently, no one had the courage to countermand his order.

As a result of MacArthur's new instructions, Almond on October 25 sent Maj. Gen. Smith the decisive order for the Marines to relieve I ROK Corps troops at the Chosin and Fusen Reservoirs, a hundred air miles north of Wonsan. After many chaotic changes of plans, Almond assigned the Marine division a zone of action 300 road miles north to south and 50 road miles wide, reaching all the way to the Manchurian border.

On that same day, the Marines finally began to land over Yellow and Blue Beaches at Wonsan in "as anticlimactic a landing as Marines have ever made."[61]

While the 5th and 7th Marines headed north, the 1st Marines went to work in the Wonsan area. The 1st Battalion, 1st Marines immediately entrained in gondola cars for the small lovely seaport of Kojo, 39 miles south of Wonsan, to protect a supply dump and relieve a ROK battalion. The 3rd Battalion stayed at Wonsan. Maj. Gen. Smith began to worry about the dispersion of his division; the Marines were being used like Army troops in a land campaign.

At Kojo, Lt. Col. Hawkins, the 1st Battalion commander, deployed Capt. Wesley B. Noren's B Company on three high points of ground two miles south of Kojo; Capt. Robert P. Wray's C Company on a line of hills a mile and a half to the north, and Capt. Robert H. Barrow's A Company between C Company and Kojo. Everything seemed quiet. But more than a thousand soldiers of the veteran North Korean 5th Division were based in the village of Tongchon, two miles south of B Company's outposts.

At 10 P.M. on October 27, B and C Companies were attacked. The North Koreans crept up silently, hurled grenades and surprised and overran B Company's 1st Platoon. They killed 15 Marines, seven in their sleeping bags. The 3rd Platoon repulsed an attack. C Company was hard hit; 20 Marines were cut off until morning; but Wray's Company threw back the assaults while losing six killed and 16 wounded.

B Company was struck repeatedly, and the 1st Platoon withdrew with 30 men missing. Sgt. Clayton L. Roberts covered the platoon with a machine gun until he was killed. Captain Noren organized a 360-degree defense. F Battery, 11th Marines added mortar and artillery fire. Noren brought out his wounded in ponchos through the knee-deep mud of the rice paddies. The enemy moved into Kojo and attacked 2d Lt. John J. Swords' A Company platoon. When it was already light, 200 North Koreans dashed out of Kojo for the hills; nearly half were killed. The final count of Marine casualties in the all-night battle was 23 killed, 47 wounded and four missing.

The next afternoon, in response to Hawkins' urgent calls for help, Lt. Col. Sutter's 2d Battalion and Colonel Puller's Regimental Command Group joined the 1st Battalion. Marine fliers destroyed Tongchon, and two U.S. destroyers bombarded Kojo. On the afternoon of October 31, Hawkins' battalion was relieved by Korean Marines and returned to Wonsan by LST. A week later, Hawkins was replaced. Sutter's battalion hiked back to Wonsan on November 3.

On October 28, Lt. Col. Ridge's 3rd Battalion, 1st Marines was trucked 28 miles west from Wonsan to the Taebaek mountain village of Majon-ni to relieve the 26th ROK Regiment and to control the major road net that intersected there. One road led to Pyongyang and another to Seoul. The road from Wonsan twisted through a 3,000-foot mountain pass of deep gorges and hairpin turns—soon to be known as Ambush Alley.

Ridge's Marines were to keep the enemy away fron Wonsan and block their escape route to the north. Each rifle company was assigned one of the three roads to patrol, and Major Simmons' Weapons Company set up roadblocks where the battalion perimeter crossed each road. First Lt. Leroy M. Duffy's Engineers dug out an OY strip on the edge of the mountain-ringed valley, through which ran the Imjin River. The Marines screened all Koreans who entered the perimeter. If they showed signs of having served in the North Korean army—head close-cropped, neck with a tanned line left by a uniform or feet with callouses from military shoes—they were put into the prison stockade; in 17 days, the Marines assembled 1,395 prisoners, most of them voluntary ones.

From the POW interrogations and from civilians, the Marines learned that the North Korean 15th Division was in the vicinity, intending to use the upper Imjin as a base for guerrilla operations.

On November 2, an H Company platoon was ambushed in a deep gorge five miles south of Majon-ni. The Marines managed to get off the message, "We've been hit, send help, send help,"[62] before their radio failed. Capt. Clarence E. Corley, Jr., the company commander, rushed out with his other two rifle platoons, heavy machine guns and 81mm mortars. The mortars pounded the enemy positions on the cliffs. Pfc. Jack Golden lugged a 94-pound machine gun up to a height from which he fired down on the enemy. Corsairs appeared, and the North Koreans vanished into the hills. The battalion medical officer, Lt. Robert J. Fleischaker, USN, and his team treated the wounded, most of whom were evacuated by helicopter the next day.

The same morning that H Company's patrol was attacked, a supply convoy escorted by a G Company rifle platoon was ambushed seven miles west of Wonsan and forced to turn back. Nine men were killed and 15 wounded. Ridge's Marines had to be supplied by an Army air drop.

Colonel Puller was determined to push a truck convoy through to Majon-ni. On the afternoon of November 4, Barrow's A Company started out with a convoy of 24 supply trucks. Barrow put his Engineer platoon in front, and they filled in four cratered roadblocks. At the fifth roadblock, the Engineers got into a fire fight with North Koreans hidden on the heights above the narrow road. Barrow had to turn back. It was now dark, and the trucks began the eight-mile trip to Wonsan with their lights out. One truck with 21 Marines missed a hairpin turn and plunged over the edge. A human chain brought the injured men 60 feet up to the road, and the convoy got back with eight men wounded, 16 injured and five vehicles destroyed.

The convoy started out again the next morning. Barrow, figuring that the enemy in Ambush Alley waited for the sound of approaching trucks, placed an infantry platoon a thousand yards ahead of the vehicles. At the scene of the previous day's ambush, the platoon surprised 70 guerrillas and killed most of them. This time, the convoy reached Majon-ni without casualties.

A Company joined the perimeter defense; and at 1:30 A.M. that night, the North Koreans attacked. After a long fire fight, the enemy overran the battalion OP when the five Marines there ran out of ammunition. The position was recaptured quickly once the early morning fog lifted. And A Company escorted 619 prisoners back to Wonsan.

On November 6, Puller sent Sutter's 2d Battalion to the hamlet of Muchon-ni near the highest pass along Ambush Alley on the road to Majon-ni. At a horseshoe bend, the convoy was stopped by a landslide roadblock and then attacked by enemy concealed on the high ground. E Company counterattacked and suffered eight killed and 38 wounded before the North Koreans were chased off.

At Majon-ni, 250 of the enemy attacked an H Company observation post on November 8; one Marine was killed and 10 wounded. On November 10, the 3rd Korean Marine Corps Battalion arrived to reinforce the perimeter. The U.S. Marines at Majon-ni celebrated the Corps' 175th birthday with a traditional cake their cooks managed to bake. On November 13, the American and Korean Marines were relieved by the 1st Battalion of the 15th Infantry, which continued the fighting there. The U.S. Marines had lost 20 dead and 45 wounded at Majon-ni and in Ambush Alley. The 1st Marines moved north.

By now, the Army's 7th Infantry Division had landed at Iwon, 60 air miles northeast of the port of Hungnam; and most of the 3rd Infantry Division had landed at Wonsan.

While the 1st Marines were busy at Kojo, Majon-ni and Muchon-ni, the 7th and 5th Marines prepared to advance to the Manchurian border. The 7th Marines, issued parkas and some other cold weather gear, moved 50 air miles north to Hamhung by road and rail during the last three days of October. North Korean forces repeatedly attacked Army and Marine convoys out of Wonsan. On one supply train, they killed six Marines and wounded eight in hand-to-hand fighting.

The 7th Marines was to relieve the 26th ROK Regiment, which already on October 29 had taken 16 Chinese prisoners north of Hamhung near Sudong. Over in northwest Korea, the 8th U.S. Cavalry Regiment and the 6th ROK Division were surprised and badly hurt by the Chinese, who had penetrated between MacArthur's two major forces.

MacArthur had divided his army. The Eighth Army and X Corps, under separate commands, were split by the Taebaek mountains, running north and south in the center of the Korean peninsula. There were no good east–west roads through the mountains north of Pyongyang and Wonsan. Most of MacArthur's top commanders later said they disagreed with his strategy. MacArthur said they never told him so to his face. Courage was also needed at headquarters.

The Marines' new arena of action stretched northward from the estuary of the Songchon River, a spacious flatland containing the port of Hungnam and the industrial city of Hamhung eight miles upriver. The Marines would follow a road and narrow-gauge railroad north from Hungnam through Hamhung into the Taebaek mountains. From the port, the dirt and gravel road ran 78 miles to the little village of Yudam-ni at the western end of the Chosin Reservoir. For the first 43 of those miles, the road rose gently through fairly level terrain. But at Chinhung-ni, a one-lane road suddenly started climbing among mile-high peaks. It first rose 2,500 feet through narrow, twisting Funchilin Pass, with a cliff on one side and an abyss on the other. Two miles before the village of Koto-ri, the road entered a rugged plateau and followed the Changjin River, which flows north into the reservoir. At the larger town of Hagaru, the road divided around both sides of the reservoir's southern tip. The western branch climbed through the 4,000-foot Toktong Pass and then descended through gorges into the broad valley leading to Yudam-ni. This primitive road zigzagging through wild mountain country would become the Marines' Main Supply Route (MSR)—the focus of the attention of the world.

Although there were Chinese soldiers ahead and the Eighth

Army was some 60 air miles away across the Taebaek range from the Marines' left flank, Colonel Litzenberg's orders remained to lead the Marine division north to the Manchurian border by this route. The 7th Infantry Division, also part of X Corps, would drive northward on the Marines' right toward Hyesanjin on the Yalu River. The I ROK Corps would advance up the coastal road to the northeast.

On October 30, VMF-312 attacked 500 enemy troops at Hagaru; they were believed to be Chinese. Litzenberg gathered his officers and noncoms at the regimental command post. "We can expect to meet Chinese Communist troops," he said, "and it is important that we win the first battle. The results of that action will reverberate around the world, and we want to make sure that the outcome has an adverse effect in Moscow as well as Peiping."[63] He told his men they might soon be taking part in the first battle of World War III.

On November 2, the 7th Marines relieved the 26th ROK Regiment 37 miles north of Hungnam at Majon-dong on the MSR. As A Company moved forward carefully, it came under long-range Chinese fire and took a few casualties. The 3rd Battalion, 11th Marines fired 26 artillery missions in response.

The Marines entered a long narrow valley—Hill 698 on the left and Hill 727 on the right. D Company replaced a ROK unit on the exposed slopes of Hill 698. As the Marines climbed higher, they came under scattered fire. Hurling grenades, the two assault platoons reached the crest but took severe casualties and had to be recalled under fire. E Company passed through D Company and occupied a plateau 150 yards below the crest.

In the valley, the 7th Marines' "walking perimeter," protected on all sides, advanced under cover of close support from VMF-312 and VMF(N)-513, which blasted the ridgelines on both sides. The Chinese replied with mortar fire, and one 120mm round wounded three men in the 1st Battalion command post.

At dusk, the Marines dug in at a bridge a mile south of Sudong. Litzenberg placed the 1st Battalion's rifle companies on the high ground up front and the 2d Battalion on the slopes along the center of his position. The 3rd Battalion protected the regiment's rear. All three battalion command posts and mortars were situated in the valley along the road. The Marines did not know that the Chinese had their 371st Regiment to the north and west, the 370th Regiment to the east and the 372d Regiment hidden several miles ahead. Many of these troops had formerly been in the Chinese Nationalist Army and were armed with Japanese rifles confiscated in Manchuria and American-made machine guns and mortars captured from the Nationalists.

Two Chinese battalions began to attack at 11 P.M. in a well-coordinated double envelopment. By 1 A.M. on November 3, the Marines' 1st and 2d Battalions were under full-scale attack on both flanks. The Chinese had avoided the obvious approach down the valley from Sudong and attacked from the ridgelines. Coming swiftly and silently, they struck A and F Companies on the right and B Company on the left. They burst on the Marines with grenades and submachine guns; and where they found room between defensive positions, they flooded into the low ground.

Suddenly, a North Korean tank supporting the Chinese lumbered through A Company's roadblock and into the 1st Battalion command post, firing ineffectively. Bazookas and recoilless rifles opened up, and the tank swung around and headed north. One of its shells all but wiped out the antitank crew at the roadblock before the tank disappeared around a bend in the road.

In the hill-fighting east of the MSR, A Company's 1st and 2d Platoons and elements of B Company were forced back. Sgt. James I. Poynter of Bloomington, Illinois, was critically wounded when the Chinese surrounded his A Company squad. Poynter bayoneted several of the enemy. Then he rushed at three Chinese machine guns setting up 25 yards ahead. He grabbed grenades from fallen Marines, charged the machine-gun emplacements in succession, killed the crews of two and put the last out of action before he was mortally wounded. His swift daring disorganized the enemy and gave his squad time to defend itself.[64]

Across the road, the rest of B Company was attacked. Staff Sgt. Archie Van Winkle, a reservist from Seattle, led his platoon through withering fire. He and every man who charged with him was hit. Van Winkle's one arm hung uselessly, but the Alaska-born sergeant dashed 40 yards through enemy fire to reach his isolated left-flank squad and reunite his men. Hit in the chest by a grenade burst, he refused evacuation until he was carried off unconscious.[65] Both Poynter and Van Winkle were awarded the Medal of Honor. And 1st Lt. Chew Een Lee of Sacramento, California, commander of B Company's machine-gun platoon, received the Navy Cross for exploring the slope above his position and drawing fire to expose the enemy positions to his gunners. Although Lee was seriously wounded in the right arm, he led a counterattack that drove back the enemy.

The Chinese swarmed into the valley from both sides, overran the 7th Marines' 4.2-inch Mortar Company and seized a sharp curve in the road between the 2d and 3rd Battalions. By dawn, they had cut the MSR and controlled the terrain between the Marine rifle companies on the hillsides and the 2d Battalion command post. Litzenberg had to call in supporting arms to avoid destruction. Mortars, howitzers and aircraft went to work raking the enemy. Scores of Chinese on the hillsides and along the valley floor were eradicated. Marines learned that if they could hold their positions against a Chinese night attack, once day came, Marine firepower would crush the enemy.

By midmorning, the 1st Battalion had cleared the valley. Its heavy machine guns took a fearsome toll; 662 enemy dead were later counted in the battalion's zone. The 2d Battalion fought in two directions. E Company attacked Hill 698 against a concentrated grenade barrage. The squad led by Cpl. Lee H. Phillips of Stockbridge, Georgia, had five men left when it gained the crest. The defenders counterattacked. Phillips took three men against the final rocky point. They pulled themselves over the rocks with one hand and hurled grenades with the other. He and his last two men fought off a final counterattack. And the Marines held Hill 698. (Twenty-year-old Phillips was killed in action on November 27.)[66]

D Company tried to cross the valley and attack a Chinese roadblock on a spur of Hill 727. It took until evening before the riflemen, artillery and aircraft forced the Chinese to retreat from the roadblock and freed the MSR. A hundred Marine casualties were evacuated, but accurate casualty figures were destroyed when the 7th Marines withdrew from Yudam-ni in December.

The Chinese regiments, badly hurt, pulled back three miles from Sudong to a line established by the 372d Regiment. And Marine air reported 300 enemy trucks on the move south of the Chosin Reservoir.

On November 4, while Maj. Gen. Smith brought the division command post north to Hungnam, Litzenberg continued his advance. The Reconnaissance Company took the lead in Jeeps and in the middle of Sudong surprised a group of Chinese soldiers. The Marines killed three and captured 20 in a half-hour fight. Then they climbed toward Chinhung-ni six miles up the road, while C Company followed the railroad tracks on the other side of the river.

The lead Recon platoon spotted Chinese soldiers at the Samgo Station just north of Chinhung-ni and killed most of them. Nearby, the Marines found a North Korean T-34 camouflaged under a pile of brush on the right side of the road. Second Lt. Donald W. Sharon, Staff Sgt. Richard B. Twohey and Cpl. Joseph E. McDermott climbed on the tank. When the periscope began to revolve, McDermott smashed its glass and Twohey dropped in a grenade. The three Marines jumped off, and the tank came after them. Twohey jumped back on it and dropped another grenade down the periscope. As it exploded, the tank stopped and began smoking. A second tank hidden in a hut emerged; a Corsair destroyed it with rockets. Almost instantly, two more tanks were discovered and, under fire, their crews surrendered. The 7th Marines settled into a perimeter around Chinhung-ni.

Up ahead, the Chinese held Funchilin Pass. Litzenberg sent the Recon Company to outpost the southern tip of Hill 891, east of the road some 2,000 yards into the pass. This spur, to be known as How Hill, commanded the road; it turned out to be part of the enemy's forward line. As they approached the main hairpin turn at 4:30 P.M., the Recon Company's two lead Jeeps were destroyed. The 3rd Platoon was pinned to the road for 45 minutes, until darkness and an air strike permitted it to retreat with two killed and five wounded.

The next morning, the 3rd Battalion took the lead. The Chinese on How Hill hit the Recon Company's 1st Platoon at the same hairpin; it withdrew with four wounded. I Company tried to advance on Hill 897 on the left and G Company toward How Hill on the right, but machine-gun fire stopped them. Capt. Thomas E. Cooney, commanding G Company, was wounded twice. An artillery duel went on the rest of the day, and further ahead Marine fliers destroyed 21 trucks. They reported the ridges between Chinhung-ni and the Chosin Reservoir were alive with enemy troops. The planes blasted all the enemy positions they could find in the 11 miles between Koto-ri at the top of the pass and Hagaru at the reservoir. But the 7th Marines were stopped at the pass.

Early on November 6, 1st Lt. Howard H. Harris led H Company around the ridgeline to envelop the strongpoint on the tip of How Hill. It took the Marines until midafternoon to cover the rugged ground and get in position for the assault. Two Corsairs bombed the mountain top. The Marines climbed the steep slope of a nose extending from the summit; they were met by machine-gun fire and grenades. As the assault platoons prepared to attack, 2d Lt. Robert D. Reem of Lancaster, Pennsylvania, collected his squad leaders for instructions. A grenade fell in their midst; Reem smothered it with his body and was killed.[67]

The Marines charged the hilltop three times and were stopped each time. On the fourth attempt, Sgt. Charlie Foster reached the top and was killed, but the Marines finally took the nose. The enemy still held How Hill's crest, and the Marines' ammunition was running low. Litzenberg ordered H Company to disengage and withdraw. The Marines fought their way back with two dead and six wounded. Artillery and mortars pounded the hill all night.

The next morning, the Chinese were gone. The 3rd Battalion occupied Hills 891 and 987 without opposition. The 7th Marines had 46 killed, 262 wounded and six missing.

Meanwhile, 1st Lt. William F. Goggin had led a fast-moving patrol of 15 Marine volunteers and Corpsman James Walsh through the mountains to the west and radioed that Koto-ri was clear of enemy. As they had in western Korea, the Chinese had pulled back in front of the Marines. On November 10, the Marine Corps' 175th birthday, the 1st Battalion occupied Koto-ri.

That day on the high plateau, winter struck. The sub-zero cold and severe wind put hundreds of Marines into shock. They were getting their first taste of the ordeal to come. The cold became a vicious enemy. To survive, men had to live with great care; the penalty was frostbite, frozen feet, hands and faces. They piled on layers of clothing. They carried their canteens inside their clothes, extra socks next to their bodies. Only the dry portions of rations could be eaten safely. Entrenching tools would not break up the frozen earth. Oil froze weapons. They had to be wiped almost dry; when possible, lubricated with light hair oil. Artillery fire was slowed and ranges shortened. The cold-weather Shoe Pac made feet sweat when marching and freeze when standing still. A new vapor-barrier boot was rushed out from the United States. Vehicle engines had to be warmed up every few hours; mechanics could not expose their hands while making repairs. Jeep ambulances were useless; the wounded would freeze to death.

The Marines did extensive patrolling as combat stopped. The 2d Battalion, 5th Marines was sent northeast up toward the Fusen Reservoir. Lt. Col. Roise's Marines set up positions blocking the Sinhung corridor and patrolled the routes to the north. They were in touch with 7th Infantry Division patrols coming down the highway but did not try to penetrate the enemy defenses near the Fusen Reservoir. After November 9, Roise was ordered back to the MSR leading to the Chosin Reservoir. The 2d Battalion came around on November 13 and 14 and relieved the 7th Marines at Koto-ri to advance toward Hagaru.

On November 11, X Corps ordered an advance to the border: I ROK Corps on the right, the 7th Infantry Division in the center and the 1st Marine Division on the left. But within the next week, these orders were changed; and the direction of the Marines' attack was shifted. Instead of heading straight north, the Marines were to go north to Yudam-ni and then west, to reduce the enormous gap between X Corps and the Eighth Army and to cut the main Chinese supply routes. Only then would the Marine division head north to the border.

X Corps' three separate columns advancing through rugged country could not support each other. "Its headlong rush to the border"[68] paid no heed to the Chinese that MacArthur knew were there. Although these were days without important contacts with Chinese forces, Maj. Gen. Smith was worried. He anticipated attacks on the MSR. His units were spread out over a single mountain road.

Smith feared his Marines were out on a limb. With the Eighth Army already thrown back in the west, his left flank was wide open. On November 15, he wrote the Commandant: "I believe a winter campaign in the mountains of North Korea is too much to ask of the American soldier or marine, and I doubt the feasibility of supplying troops in this area during the winter or providing for the evacuation of sick and wounded."[69]

Smith garrisoned the key points on the MSR and set his 1st Engineer Battalion to strengthen the Hamhung–Hagaru road for tanks and heavy vehicles. He and Maj. Gen. Harris planned an airstrip capable of taking C-47 cargo planes near the burned-out town of Hagaru, which the 7th Marines had occupied on November 15. The temperature was four degrees below zero. Three days later, enough work had been done on the road for heavy equipment to get through and begin work on the Hagaru airstrip. Maj. Gen. Smith "deliberately slowed" the Marine advance at Hagaru; his caution would "prove the division's salvation in the weeks ahead."[70]

On November 17, the 5th Marines was ordered to move up the east side of the Chosin Reservoir and seize Sinhung-ni, seven miles northeast of Hagaru. And on the twenty-first, the 1st Marines, relieved of earlier assignments around Wonsan, was free to protect the MSR behind the two forward Marine regiments. The Marines also received help from the 41st Independent Commando, Royal Marines—235 reconnaissance specialists led by Lt. Col. Douglas B. Drysdale. The unit had requested service with the American Marines and was assigned to work with the Recon Company to protect the division's endangered left flank. The two Marine forces would together fight the Chinese as they had 50 years before.

On November 21, the 17th Infantry of the 7th Infantry Division reached the Yalu without opposition at snow-covered Hyesanjin. This would be the only American unit to push through to the border (except for a small task force from the 32d Infantry, which reached the Yalu a week later).

On November 24, the day after Thanksgiving, the Eighth Army jumped off on MacArthur's "end the war" offensive. And the next day, X Corps issued new orders for the Marine division to move out from Yudam-ni on November 27, head west 55 miles, seize Mupyong-ni and then advance north to the Yalu. The 7th Division would approach the Yalu on the east side of the Chosin Reservoir. Until now, the Marines' left flank had been exposed; this plan would lay open both flanks.

The Chinese reacted swiftly to the new offensive. On November 25, they hurled back the II ROK Corps, the right wing of the Eighth Army, near Tokchon, about 70 air miles southwest of Yudam-ni.

The 7th Marines seized Yudam-ni west of the Chosin Reservoir against light resistance on November 25. On the previous day en route, the Marines were fed a belated hot turkey Thanksgiving dinner—it would be their last full meal for 17 days. The 5th Marines followed the 7th, intending to pass through it at Yudam-ni and lead the attack westward to Mupyong-ni on the twenty-seventh.

On November 26, the 7th Marines captured three soldiers of the 60th Chinese Division. They said that three divisions were now in the hills around Yudam-ni and planned to move southeast and cut the MSR below Yudam-ni after the two Marine regiments had passed.

That same day, the II ROK Corps on the Eighth Army's right flank was torn to shreds under a second day of Chinese attacks. The Eighth Army's offensive was stopped and rolled back even before the Marines could jump off. The dangerous gap between the Eighth Army and X Corps widened.

Long-range Marine patrols probed outward from Yudam-ni. One patrol of A Company, 7th Marines, with 1st Lt. Frank N. Mitchell's platoon at the point, moved southwest along a snow-covered ridgeline and when it approached the village of Hansan-ni was hit by enemy fire at pointblank range. As the Marines took many casualties immediately, Mitchell dashed forward, grabbed a BAR from a wounded Marine and fired it until his ammunition was exhausted. The enemy struck the patrol's front and left flank; and Mitchell, although wounded, led the hand-to-hand struggle that repulsed the attack. As darkness gathered, the lieutenant from Indian Gap, Texas, led a party of litter bearers through the enemy lines to search for the wounded. Alone, he covered his men's withdrawal until he was killed.[71] The company hiked back to Yudam-ni. B Company, sent out to the same area, had ten Marines wounded.

It was cold at Yudam-ni. The Manchurian wind screamed in from the north over the bare hills and down the arm of the Chosin Reservoir that approached the village from the northeast. Yudam-ni, 3,500 feet above sea level, lay in a valley surrounded by five great ridges on which waited the frozen riflemen of the 7th Marines. They were guarding the dirt roads running west and north and the vital MSR leading south to Hagaru. On the night of November 26, when Lt. Col. Roise's 2d Battalion, 5th Marines arrived, the temperature stood at zero.

The next morning, the 2d Battalion, 5th Marines and the 3rd Battalion, 7th Marines, supported by three battalions of the 11th Marines, started west. The 5th Marines advanced along the road between the steep heights of the Northwest and Southwest Ridges and the 7th Marines along the slopes of both the ridges. The Chinese were there. Within the hour, both Marine battalions came under heavy fire. Covered by mortars, artillery and air strikes, Capt. Uel D. Peters' F Company, 5th Marines, attacked the enemy's northern flank and pushed the Chinese off a spur of Northwest Ridge. D Company, now led by Capt. Samuel S. Smith, spearheaded the main move west along the road. The Chinese were dug into the massive height of Sakkat Mountain straight ahead. They stopped D Company. Roise discontinued the attack. G Company, 7th Marines fought along the peaks of Southwest Ridge until the defenses on Sakkat Mountain drove it back. G Company's commander, Captain Cooney, was mortally wounded. B, C and I Companies of the 7th Marines came forward as reinforcements. But the Marine attack, having gained 1,500 yards, was finished. If the Chinese had permitted Roise's battalion to advance three more miles to its next objective, it would have been isolated and trapped. Here in front of Sakkat Mountain was the high-water mark of the Marines' advance toward the Yalu.

By 6:30 P.M. on November 27, Yudam-ni was pitch black; the temperature plunged to 20 degrees below zero. Squads took turns in the warming tents. On Northwest Ridge, the Marines were immobilized in their foxholes by the painful cold. Flesh froze; carbines and BARs froze. And silently through the night came hordes of Chinese soldiers over mountain trails leading to North and Northwest Ridges. Gen. Lin Piao was sending the 9th Army Group led by Gen. Sung Shin-lun, one of China's best field commanders, to drive X Corps into the sea and wipe out the 1st Marine Division. The 79th and 89th Divisions were to strike the knockout blow against the northwest side of the Marine perimeter, and the 59th Division would swing around to the south to hit South Ridge and Toktong Pass and cut the MSR between Yudam-ni and Hagaru. Three divisions skilled at night attack would fall on two regiments of Marines. If General Sung succeeded, the Marines at Yudam-ni would be completely encircled.

By 9 P.M., the Chinese were in position a few hundred yards from the Marines, who waited unknowingly on the Northwest Ridge. Suddenly, an enemy patrol jabbed at the 5th Marines' roadblock just south of the ridge and was dispersed. The Chinese probed Peters' F Company on the western end of Northwest Ridge, and Chinese mortar shells rained down on the Marine front line. Then came the first assault wave. It hit the junction of E and F Companies on the ridge. The Marines piled up dead Chinese in front of them; but the attackers kept coming, broke the link between the two companies and poured through the gap. Staff Sgt. Robert S. Kennemore of Greenville, South Carolina, a veteran of Guadalcanal, rallied his leaderless E Company platoon. A grenade landed in the midst of a machine-gun squad; Kennemore placed his foot on it to absorb the explosion and lost both legs. They gave him the Medal of Honor.

Capt. Samuel Jaskilka rushed in reinforcements to contain the penetration on E Company's side of the break. The Chinese tried to envelop F Company's rear but were cut down by the Marines' firepower. By midnight, the main enemy force here had been virtually annihilated.

At the same time just to the north, another enemy force assaulted H Company, 7th Marines on Northwest Ridge's Hill 1403. Capt. Leroy M. Cooke's right flank collapsed under the weight of the enemy's numbers. Cooke called in supporting mortar fire, stopped the onslaught and led a counterattack. Chinese grenades and machine guns smashed this assault and killed Cooke. First Lt. Howard H. Harris, returned to duty after illness, went forward to take command and found all but one of Cooke's officers wounded.

For two hours, the Chinese were silent while they brought up reserve battalions. At 3 A.M., they began a second major assault against the entire two-mile Northwest Ridge front. In the broad draw at the center, machine-gun fire from Jaskilka's E Company mowed down the first waves; the Chinese following them took cover. Pfc. R. A. Jackson destroyed an enemy machine gun with a grenade just as the gun's fire killed him. On the left, some 200 Chinese hit Peters' F Company and overran two machine-gun positions. Second Lt. Bernard W. Christofferson led a counterattack, killed 20 Chinese with his submachine gun and recaptured the machine guns. On the right, the Chinese attacked Harris' H Company for an hour and finally drove the Marines back fighting. Their surrender of Hill 1403 was dangerous, making it possible for the enemy to cut off the 2d Battalion, 5th Marines and fire down on the 2,000 Marines in the valley.

East of the MSR, another Chinese division crossed the spine of North Ridge where D and E Companies, 7th Marines were isolated on Hills 1282 and 1240. At 10 P.M., Capt. Walter D. Phillips' E Company on Hill 1282 drove off a harassing force. The Chinese struck in strength at midnight and were thrown back in savage fighting. They charged repeatedly for two hours accompanied by whistles, bugles and chants. Each wave was mowed down by machine guns, grenades and mortars. The Marines took heavy casualties but held Hill 1282.

Shortly after 10 P.M., the enemy swept down the ridge at Hill 1384, north of 1282; overran an outposted platoon of I Company, 5th Marines, and forced a platoon of South Korean police, just above Taplett's 3rd Battalion command post, to retreat. H&S Company also had to withdraw across the MSR. Taplett's command post at the bottom of North Ridge was left in a no-man's-land. The battalion commander stayed in his blacked-out tent issuing orders to his rifle companies over his field telephone. At about 3 A.M., his executive officer, Maj. John J. Canney, left the CP to retrieve the H&S Company; he was killed. With Taplett remained his S-3, Maj. Thomas A. Durham, with pistol drawn; Pfc. Louis W. Swinson was outside covering the approaches with his rifle.

Lt. Col. Murray sent two A Company platoons to support Phillips' E Company on the spurs of Hill 1282 just above the village. They arrived at the climax of the Chinese attack. E Company was dwindling to a handful of men. The enemy finally forced a wedge between the two small groups of Marines making a last-ditch stand. Captain Phillips, throwing grenades in the melee, was killed. His executive officer, 1st Lt. Raymond O. Ball, immobilized by two wounds, fired his rifle and shouted encouragement until he was hit several more times and mortally wounded. First Lt. John Yancy and Staff Sgt. Daniel M. Murphy tried desperately to hold the line. (Yancy, a former Raider, won his second Navy Cross. He had earned his first on Guadalcanal eight years before, almost to the day.) E Company was reduced to a platoon, and the two A Company platoons had 40 killed and wounded. The Chinese now held the commanding ground of Hill 1282.

Meanwhile, at 1:05 A.M., the Chinese assaulted D Company, 7th Marines on Hill 1240, just southeast of 1282. By 2:30, Sgt. Othmar J. Reller's platoon had fought off three attacks and was overrun. The rest of the company came under attack, and Capt. Milton A. Hull's command post fell a half hour later. With D Company down to a few squads of effectives, Captain Hull— wounded in the forehead, his face covered with blood—led a counterattack against the crest. The Chinese retreated and then fought forward again. Hull was hit in the shoulder. By dawn, he had 16 men who could fight. The enemy had them surrounded until reinforcements cut their way through.

While the two Chinese divisions attacked Yudam-ni, the 59th Division had swept around far to the southeast. C Company, 7th Marines, less one platoon, was on Hill 1419 east of the MSR, five miles south of the village. At 2:30 A.M., the Chinese struck and inflicted heavy casualties. The seesaw battle raged until dawn. Then, artillery fire from Yudam-ni helped force the Chinese back into the hills. But they had C Company surrounded and outnumbered.

Two miles further south, the 240 Marines of the reinforced F Company, 7th Marines held an isolated hill in the middle of Toktong Pass. Capt. William E. Barber, its Kentucky-born commander, had won the Silver Star on Iwo Jima. At 2:30, the Chinese struck "Fox Hill" and began a siege of five nights and days that is one of the epic stories of the Marine Corps.

The enemy quickly overwhelmed the two forward squads of 1st Lt. Robert C. McCarthy's 3rd Platoon; of 35 Marines, 15 were killed and nine wounded. Repeated Chinese attacks seized the hill's peak and tried to drive between the 2d and 3rd Platoons. There, Pfc. Robert F. Benson, Pvt. Hector A. Cafferata, Jr., and Pfc. Gerald J. Smith and his fire team wiped out two enemy platoons and prevented a breakthrough. When the Chinese attacked, New York City-born Cafferata had jumped from his sleeping bag; he never had time to put on his boots. Every member of his fire team was hit, and the Chinese threatened to pierce the Marine line. The big Marine fought alone, a target for concentrated fire. His rifle quit, and he took another from a wounded Marine. With rifle and grenades, he killed 15, wounded many more, forced the others to withdraw. Reinforcements moved up. The Chinese attacked again. A grenade landed in a shallow entrenchment where wounded Marines lay. Cafferata, still bootless in the fierce cold, grabbed the grenade and threw it back. It exploded, severing one finger and seriously injuring his right hand. Despite the pain, he continued to fight until hit in the arm by a sniper's bullet.[72]

Another unit of Chinese, approaching along the MSR, attacked F Company's rear and was annihilated. By daybreak, F Company had 20 dead and 54 wounded; but the Chinese attack, after suffering an estimated 450 casualties, petered out.

It had been a dreadful night. From Yudam-ni south, the Marines had hundreds dead and wounded. The Chinese had cut the Marines' link with the sea repeatedly from Yudam-ni to Koto-ri. Along the MSR, the Marines held strongpoints, like covered-wagon circles—isolated and embattled.

At Yudam-ni, the Marines started counterattacking just before dawn on November 28. Two platoons of G Company, 5th Marines, led by 2d Lts. John J. Cahill and Dana B. Cashion, drove north across the MSR and reached Taplett's command post. H&S Company reoccupied its former positions. Cahill and Cashion daringly plunged ahead up Hill 1384 and nearly reached the peak before Taplett ordered them to withdraw and form a defense line overlooking Yudam-ni. Their attack had relieved some of the pressure on the Marines in the valley.

Two platoons of Capt. Jack R. Jones' C Company, 5th Marines, led by 2d Lts. Byron L. Magness and Max A. Merritt, attacked up Hill 1282 shortly after daybreak. They overran 50 Chinese in hand-to-hand combat and reached the summit in time to destroy an entire Chinese company attacking up the opposite slope. The Chinese unit lost 94 of its 116 men. Marine losses on Hill 1282 totaled 15 killed and 67 wounded in A and C Companies, 5th Marines, and an estimated 120 killed and wounded in E Company, 7th Marines. But the Marines had retaken Hill 1282.

A thousand yards to the southeast, the remnant of Hull's D Company, 7th Marines, clung to Hill 1240, surrounded by Chinese troops. The 3rd Platoon of C Company, 5th Marines fought up the hill. They could see the Chinese massing to attack but could not call in supporting fire because communications were broken. Two battalions struck the Marines at 11 A.M.; but the depleted C Company platoon and the 16 remaining D Company Marines held out under heavy mortar fire until relieved by B Company, 5th Marines, at 5 P.M. The Marines lost half of the 3rd Platoon and practically all of D Company.

West of the MSR on Northwest Ridge, the Chinese on Hill 1403's peak could enfilade the entire valley. Further west on the same ridge, E and F Companies, 5th Marines, still held out; 500 Chinese dead were piled up in front of their positions. At 5:45 A.M. on the twenty-eighth, Murray alerted Roise to the probability of withdrawing his battalion to Southwest Ridge.

At dawn, Murray and Litzenberg conferred. They canceled the Marines' scheduled westward attack; and at 11 A.M., Murray ordered Roise to pull back to Southwest Ridge. Shortly after 4 P.M., Maj. Gen. Smith ordered the Marines to head south and reopen the road to Hagaru. The drive to the Yalu was dead. Murray brought his command post to the center of Yudam-ni, where Litzenberg's was located; and the two regimental commanders together planned the defense of Yudam-ni and the breakout to Hagaru.

The first job was to rescue C and F Companies, 7th Marines, embattled on the hills down the MSR. Two futile attempts to reach F Company on Fox Hill were made from Hagaru, seven miles to the southeast. On the twenty-eighth, Litzenberg's 1st Battalion, out of Yudam-ni, tried to get through. A Company fought, marched and climbed for five hours and then was stopped a mile short of C Company on Hill 1419. Lt. Col. Raymond G. Davis sent B Company, which was following A Company, on a flanking movement west of the road. Called in by forward air controller 1st Lt. Dan C. Holland, VMF-212 flew daringly close to the ridges. The air strikes and mortar fire routed the Chinese. The two rescue companies formed a protective shield around C Company's perimeter. It was now dark. F Company was supposed to fight its way north from Toktong Pass, but its casualties and the surrounding Chinese made this impossible. Litzenberg

739

ordered Davis to return to Yudam-ni. He reached there at 9 P.M., bringing out C Company and its 46 wounded.

At the pass, F Company had spent the day caring for its 54 wounded, collecting weapons and ammunition from Marine and Chinese dead and recovering an airdrop of ammunition and medical kits. The Navy corpsmen had a terrible time. They had to melt the morphine Syrettes in their mouths before giving injections. Because the blood plasma was frozen, Marines died. Relief columns from both Yudam-ni and Hagaru had failed to break through, but the Marines on Fox Hill felt sure they could hold.

Starting at 2:15 A.M. on November 29, the Chinese attacked F Company again. At dawn, the Marines recovered the few yards they had given up during the night. Five more Marines had been killed and 29 more wounded, including both Captain Barber, severely hit in the left leg, and 1st Lt. Robert C. McCarthy, the leader of the 3rd Platoon. Nearly half of Barber's men were now casualties. Marine planes dropped ammunition and supplies right on the target marked with the previous day's colored parachutes. And 1st Lt. Floyd J. Englehardt flew in his Sikorsky helicopter with batteries for the company radios. The helicopter was damaged by Chinese fire, but he managed to take off again.

That day, another attempt was made to rescue the Marines on Fox Hill. Maj. Warren Morris, executive officer of 3rd Battalion, 7th Marines, led a composite battalion out of Yudam-ni at 8 A.M. It was engaged by large numbers of Chinese; and at 1:15, when air observers warned Litzenberg that the battalion was about to be surrounded, he ordered Morris to return to Yudam-ni immediately.

The Marines at Yudam-ni and Fox Hill spent a third night without much sleep or a hot meal. At 2 A.M. on November 30, the Chinese hit Fox Hill again. (It was Captain Barber's thirty-first birthday.) The air drops had now brought his Marines ample mortar ammunition and grenades; in a heavy snowstorm, they destroyed three Chinese companies at a cost of one Marine wounded. Barber's men felt that the Chinese, who had been unable to take Fox Hill in three nights, now never would. And the Marines at Yudam-ni were heartened to hear that the Marines at Hagaru had successfully repulsed a large Chinese force in an all-night battle.

The Chinese had repeatedly severed X Corps' vital artery with roadblocks that isolated Yudam-ni, Fox Hill, Hagaru and Koto-ri. Then they prepared to attack the division's center at Hagaru.

Fourteen miles southeast of Yudam-ni, Hagaru sat on a frozen plain crossed by the frozen Changjin River at the bottom tip of the frozen Chosin Reservoir. Low hills rose on the west and steep ridges on the east. Here the Marines had division headquarters, supply dumps, hospital facilities and the partly finished C-47 airstrip. Lt. Col. Thomas L. Ridge, commanding the 3rd Battalion, 1st Marines, estimated that at least a regiment would be needed to defend the place adequately. He had only his battalion, two artillery batteries and service troops. His G Company and a platoon of the Weapons Company had not yet arrived. But Ridge had to hold Hagaru at all costs.

Even with the cautionary restraints of the Marine commanders, MacArthur's headlong dash for the Manchurian border had left the UN forces inexcusably exposed.

Ridge's S-2, 2d Lt. Richard F. Carey, had sent two Korean scouts to investigate the Chinese beyond the Hagaru perimeter, mingle with them, determine their concentrations and if possible their plans. In two dangerous sorties, the agents located the Chinese units south and west of Hagaru and, by talking with Chinese troops and even officers, learned that they would attack Hagaru on the night of November 28. With this information, Ridge placed H and I Companies on the southern and southwestern sides of the perimeter. They would also protect the men building the airstrip. He hoped to put G Company, scheduled to arrive late on the twenty-eighth, on East Hill just east of the MSR. Major Simmons' Weapons Company manned a roadblock where the perimeter crossed the MSR to Koto-ri and defended the southern nose of East Hill.

Ridge knew he was cut off when his attempts to reach F Company on Fox Hill to the northwest failed, and a platoon and three tanks trying to patrol south to Koto-ri were stopped within sight of the Hagaru perimeter, with one killed and five wounded. The road was cut both above and below the town.

At 11 A.M. on November 28, Maj. Gen. Smith arrived at Hagaru by helicopter and opened the division command post. A half hour later, Maj. Gen. Almond flew in, conferred with Smith and left to visit the 31st Infantry, which had been badly hurt east of the Reservoir. Then, Almond was ordered back to Tokyo, where he learned that the entire Eighth Army was in full retreat.

When G Company could not come north to Hagaru, Ridge placed detachments from the Army's 10th Engineer Battalion and X Corps' headquarters on East Hill. The 7th Marines' Antitank Company defended the area north of the hill. Other units were spread between these elements. The perimeter was very weak.

The men were ready in their foxholes, and it had begun to snow when the Chinese attacked H and I Companies at 10:30 P.M. The enemy took frightful losses smashing against the Marines, who were supported by artillery and mortars. Six-foot-two 1st Lt. Joseph R. Fisher, I Company's commander, seemed invulnerable as he dashed from foxhole to foxhole encouraging his men. Second Lt. Wayne L. Hall, commanding the 3rd Platoon, was jumped by three Chinese and killed all three with his .45. Machine-gun bullets plowed through the wooden walls of the medical clearing station behind the company, and one bullet penetrated Maj. Gen. Smith's quarters. I Company managed to hold on.

H Company was hard hit. The 3rd Platoon leader, 1d Lt. Wendell C. Endsley, was killed. By 12:30, the Chinese fought through this platoon and reached H Company's command post. But they failed to exploit the penetration. Instead, cold and hungry, they looted the provision tent and galley. First Lt. Harrison F. Betts gathered 30 Marines and counterattacked; every one of the 30 was wounded. One wounded Marine saved his life by pretending to be dead while enemy soldiers stripped off his parka. A few Chinese got close enough to fire on the men operating the bulldozers under floodlights on the airstrip. A group of Engineers counterattacked and cleared the airstrip. The men went back to work. Ridge sent a pick-up platoon of signalmen and engineers to support H Company.

On the other side of the perimeter, the Chinese overran East Hill. The service troops defending there included a large portion of newly recruited ROK troops; the Army engineer company had 77 American enlisted men and 90 ROKs. These platoons fell back; Capt. John C. Shelnutt, the Marine officer attached, was killed. His Marine radio operator, Pfc. Bruno Podolak, voluntarily remained at his post now behind enemy lines and radioed back reports. He was the only American alive up on East Hill. By 4 A.M., the defenders barely clung to the reverse slopes, and East Hill was ripe for a disastrous breakthrough. But the Chinese were satisfied to hold the high ground and did not attack the command posts and supply dumps below. Marine gunners quickly pivoted around and plugged the hole with howitzer fire.

The main Chinese assault had spent itself. A counterattack cleaned out the Chinese who had penetrated H Company and restored the southern perimeter. New snow covered the bodies of hundreds of Chinese dead.

After daylight on the twenty-ninth, 250 Marine, Army and ROK service troops led by Maj. Reginald R. Myers, the 3rd Battalion's executive officer, counterattacked East Hill against an estimated 4,000 Chinese. Myers repeatedly exposed himself to intense fire to direct the men new to combat. At 9:30, VMF-312 planes hit the hill with napalm and bombs. Myers kept his force struggling up over treacherous ground under fire, skillfully calling in mortar and artillery fire. By noon, 170 of his men had disappeared, casualties or exhausted in the subzero cold. Pfc. Podolak, wounded in the back, joined the attacking force. Some of the men led by Marine 1st Lt. Robert E. Jochums pushed onto an outlying spur, the furthest point of the advance. Stopped by enemy fire, Myers' men set up a defensive line until the Marines' A Company, 1st Engineer Battalion, came up. They could not dislodge the enemy on the hilltop. That would have to wait for G Company's arrival from Koto-ri. But the counterattack had killed an estimated 600 of the enemy and wounded 500. Ridge's defenders had more than 500 casualties. The need for reinforcements from further south was urgent.[73]

The Chinese had already struck at Koto-ri and Chinhung-ni. At the latter point, where the 1st Battalion, 1st Marines protected the division's rear, the enemy had probed the perimeter starting on the night of November 26. By November 30, Lt. Col. Donald M. Schmuck, who had replaced Hawkins, took out A Company and part of B Company and in a narrow mountain valley to the west killed 56 and with close air support routed the rest of a battalion of Chinese, many of them mounted on Mongolian ponies.

At Koto-ri, Sutter's 2d Battalion, 1st Marines first ran into fire fights with Chinese detachments on November 27. The next day, Colonel Puller ordered D Company north to clear the MSR. Less than a mile north of the perimeter, it ran into the enemy entrenched on the high ground. F Company was sent out to help. By the end of the day, both companies were forced to return to Koto-ri. They had four dead and 34 wounded.

That evening, G Company, 1st Marines; the 41st Commando, Royal Marines, and B Company, 31st Infantry arrived at Koto-ri on their way to Hagaru. Puller organized them into a task force under Lt. Col. Drysdale, the Royal Marines' commander, to fight through the 11 miles to Hagaru, where they were desperately needed. Describing the Chinese positions to Drysdale, Puller said, "They've got us surrounded. The bastards won't get away this time."[74]

Task Force Drysdale started out at 9:45 A.M. on November 29, followed by a convoy of 1st Marine Division headquarters troops under Maj. Henry J. Seeley. The British Marines seized the first hill up the road. But when Capt. Carl J. Sitter's G Company passed through them to attack Hill 1236, a mile and a half north of Koto-ri, it had to uproot entrenched Chinese. And another mile further north, at Hill 1182, G Company ran into mortar and machine-gun fire. Drysdale decided to wait there for tanks that were scheduled to join his column. When he started out again at 4 P.M., the task force was led by 17 tanks; and 12 more were coming up in the rear. In between, the column consisted of approximately 922 men in 141 vehicles. They moved slowly as the lead tanks blasted enemy pockets, climbed roadblocks and bypassed craters. VMF-212 Corsairs covered them. A Chinese mortar round wounded every man in one truck. The riflemen repeatedly had to leap from the trucks and engage in fire fights. Maj. Gen. Smith radioed for the tanks in front of the column to press on to Hagaru, even if the trucks could not get through.

In a mile-long valley nearly halfway to Hagaru, enemy fire forced Task Force Drysdale to halt just before dark. On its right rose a steep hill where the enemy had mortars and machine guns; on the left, a frozen creek wound through a flatland several hundred yards wide, with the Changjin River and wooded hills beyond. Drysdale was to call the site of this ambush Hell Fire Valley. It would be the scene of one of the ugliest defeats in Marine Corps history.

Again, the men piled out of the trucks to return the enemy fire. Pfc. William B. Baugh threw himself on a grenade that landed in his truck and was mortally wounded.[75] A mortar shell set an ammunition truck on fire, creating a roadblock that split the column. Enemy fire prevented the truck's removal. During this action, the front section of the column, including the lead tanks, G Company, three-fourths of the British Marines and a few Army infantrymen—some 400 men—fought forward, with Drysdale in command, to reach Hagaru. Remaining in Hell Fire Valley were 61 Commandos; most of B Company, 31st Infantry, and nearly all the Marine headquarters and service troops. Marine Lt. Col. Arthur A. Chidester took charge and ordered the vehicles turned around for a dash back to Koto-ri.

The Chinese would not let them escape. One attack severed the column 200 yards north of Chidester and another cut the road south of the stalled convoy. Chidester and Maj. James K. Eagan were wounded and captured. (They were never seen again.) When darkness stopped the Marine air strikes, the enemy approached. The men in the valley were now divided into four perimeters. The largest was the most northern group led by Marine Maj. John N. McLaughlin. He had about 130 men including soldiers, Marines, Commandos and Associated Press photographer Frank Noel. Three hundred yards south of Mc-Laughlin was the remnant of two Army platoons in a drainage ditch. Thirty yards further south were about 18 headquarters troops led by Capt. Michael J. Capraro and another hundred yards south a few more Marines with Major Seeley.

The men caught in the valley hoped that the following tanks would come to their rescue. But some of the tanks were stopped by heavy resistance a mile from Major Seeley, and the rest of their convoy scurried back to Koto-ri with heavy truck losses.

Until midnight, the Chinese in Hell Fire Valley were content to keep the little perimeters pinned down and to loot trucks. Then, the enemy began probing. The headquarters and service troops, including many veterans of World War II, fought well with the combat-trained Commandos. By 2 A.M., McLaughlin's men were out of grenades. Many men had exhausted their ammunition. Some of the Commandos slipped away to reach Koto-ri for help. Noel and two men tried to escape in a Jeep and were captured. By 4:30, the Chinese demanded that the trapped men surrender. McLaughlin and a Commando went out to parley, hoping to stall until air support could return at dawn. The Chinese gave him ten minutes to decide. McLaughlin talked with his 40 remaining able-bodied men. None had more than eight rounds of rifle ammunition. He agreed to surrender if the Chinese would allow the evacuation of the seriously wounded to Koto-ri. The Chinese agreed, and the battle of Hell Fire Valley was over.

McLaughlin had delayed enough so that a sizable group led by Major Seeley escaped over the mountains to Koto-ri. The Chinese did not send back the wounded but permitted the most critically wounded to be put in a Korean hut, where they were later recovered and taken to Koto-ri.

Task Force Drysdale had approximately 162 killed or missing and 159 wounded, a total of 321 casualties. Of B Company's 190 soldiers, 119 were killed, wounded or missing. Forty-four Marines were listed as missing; of these, 25 eventually escaped or were released from prison camps.

Drysdale and his half of the column fought through successive roadblocks into Hagaru, losing one tank and several vehicles. Drysdale was wounded. Sixty-one of 235 Royal Marines and 48 of 205 G Company Marines were casualties. Those who got through reported to Lt. Col. Ridge at 7:15 P.M. More than 300 men and a dozen tanks had arrived to help defend Hagaru.

The next morning, November 30, G Company repeated Myers' effort to retake Hagaru's steep, snow-covered East Hill. Captain Sitter's Marines attacked from two sides; but the difficult terrain and long-range enemy fire defeated the attempt. The Marine units along the MSR received air drops of supplies and ammunition. Among those dropped at Koto-ri was a recreation package including contraceptives. When some were taken to Chesty Puller, he said, "What the hell do they think we're doing to these Chinese?"[76]

That night at Hagaru, large numbers of Chinese poured down East Hill and wiped out half of one G Company platoon. Captain Sitter moved from foxhole to foxhole encouraging his men and deployed service troops as they came up to reinforce. The enemy repeatedly penetrated the lines and were met with hand-to-hand combat. Sitter, fighting with his men, was painfully wounded in the face, chest and arms by grenade bursts but refused to be evacuated.[77] Marine howitzers, tanks, a group of headquarters personnel under 2d Lt. Carey and the 41st Commando helped repulse the attack and restore the lines before G Company was safe.

Meanwhile, on the thirtieth, a conference was held in Hagaru with Almond, Smith and the commanders of the 7th Infantry Division. Almond wanted to fall back toward Hamhung; Smith insisted that he would evacuate his wounded and fight his way out.

Most pressing was the fate of two infantry battalions and one artillery battalion of the 7th Infantry Division east of the Chosin Reservoir. They were trying to reach Hagaru and had taken 400 casualties. They were unable to fight their way out. By the night of December 1, the first Army survivors, mostly walking wounded, reached the Marine lines at Hagaru. The three Army battalions had now suffered casualties estimated as high as 75 percent. They were fighting toward Hagaru under constant attack. Losses of officers and noncoms left units leaderless. Many of the troops were ROKs who understood no English. At dark on December 1, the column was within four and a half miles of Hagaru and safety. But Lt. Col. Don C. Faith, who had assumed command, was mortally wounded; the column disintegrated. Small demoralized bands of men, wounded and frostbitten, tried to cross the ice of the reservoir; before dawn, 670 survivors of Task Force Faith had reached Hagaru.

The next morning, Marine Lt. Col. Olin L. Beall and three enlisted men searched at the reservoir for survivors. They drove onto the ice and saved a few wounded men under Chinese fire. Beall then organized a task force of trucks, Jeeps and sleds to bring back more soldiers. The Chinese sniped at the rescuers crawling out on the ice but did not hinder the escape of the Army wounded; they actually helped in some cases. Beall rescued 319 soldiers that day, most of them wounded or frostbitten. In all, 1,050 of the original 2,500 soldiers were saved. A Marine patrol counted more than 300 dead in the abandoned trucks of Task Force Faith. The 385 able-bodied soldiers who reached Hagaru were organized into a provisional battalion.

Casualties were now an overwhelming problem. One hundred and fifty-two were flown out by VMO-6, most of them from Yudam-ni. Although the Hagaru airstrip was less than half completed, a trial landing was attempted on the afternoon of

December 1. An Air Force C-47 bounced down and took off half an hour later with 24 casualties. Three more planes made it that afternoon and carried out 60 more. In 12 days and nights, D Company, 1st Engineer Battalion had hacked out of the frozen earth enough of an airstrip to fly out the wounded, bring in supplies and reinforcements and make a breakout possible.

5
The Breakout

The Marines began to change direction late on November 29. The evening before, MacArthur had summoned his field commanders, Walker and Almond, to Tokyo and authorized them to retreat. He reported to Washington that he had gone on the defensive against "overwhelming force." He said, "We face an entirely new war."[78] He had gambled and lost. His army was divided and overextended. Washington turned down his request that Chiang Kai-shek's Nationalist army be brought into the war.

On the bitter cold Korean peninsula, weary soldiers and Marines, huddled in their parkas, fought for their lives. The 1st Marine Aircraft Wing gathered five squadrons at Yonpo Airfield below Hungnam to cover them. Navy ships, which had scattered in the euphoric expectation of the war's end, hurried back to lift them from North Korea.

On the twenty-ninth, Maj. Gen. Smith ordered the 7th Marines to turn south and open the MSR to Hagaru, where Ridge defended. Puller commanded at Koto-ri and Schmuck at Chinhung-ni at the base of the mountains. The next day, at the Hagaru conference, Maj. Gen. Almond ordered the total withdrawal of the Marines—from Yudam-ni 78 miles all the way to the sea.

Litzenberg and Murray, issuing orders jointly, established a new defensive line south of Yudam-ni, where the ground was better suited for a holding action. Maj. Maurice E. Roach took a jury-rigged battalion to hold the high ground above Yudam-ni. He had his men wear green neckerchiefs ripped from parachutes and called his unit the Damnation Battalion.

As the first tricky step, the 5th Marines pulled out of their positions north and west of Yudam-ni, freeing the 7th Marines to

749

drop back further south. These dangerous disengagements were made in daylight when the Marines could count on air cover and artillery. Roise's 2d Battalion, 5th Marines withdrew from the west for a mile and gave up Hill 1426 to the enemy. This released Harris' 3rd Battalion, 7th Marines to take new positions astride the road 4,000 yards south of Yudam-ni.

The breakout began at 8 A.M. on December 1. While Taplett's 3rd Battalion, 5th Marines led the main force down the road, Davis' 1st Battalion, 7th Marines was to dash eight miles across the ridgetops that night to rescue Barber's beleaguered company still holding open Toktong Pass. Taplett and Davis would join up in the area of Fox Hill. Despite six inches of snow on the Yonpo runway, the Corsairs were overhead.

The one tank that had made it through to Yudam-ni before the Chinese cut the MSR took the point on the road. Because of the shortage of space, only drivers and the seriously wounded were allowed to ride the trucks. Even Litzenberg and Murray walked. Before the Marines set out, 85 officers and men were buried at Yudam-ni (their bodies were transferred to the United States after the war). There was no room for the dead.

Only the 1st and 3rd Battalions, 5th Marines remained north of Yudam-ni. "Pulling them out was to prove equivalent of letting loose of the tiger's tail."[79] G Company, the last 3rd Battalion company in place, was within grenade-throwing distance of the Chinese. To prevent them from swarming over the company as it came down off the top of Hill 1282, VMF-214 Corsairs kept down the Chinese with dummy runs. It worked. Once G Company was far enough away, planes and artillery clobbered the enemy. G Company had left behind ammunition with time charges. Hill 1282 erupted with explosives. G Company managed the difficult disengaging maneuver without a casualty and escaped across the bridge south of Yudam-ni. The Engineers blew up the bridge. The rear guard, B Company, 5th Marines, stole away from nearby Hill 1240 without supporting fire, using its own machine guns to cover its withdrawal. The Marines now held a line below Yudam-ni along a row of hills from west of the MSR eastward to the tip of the Reservoir's arm.

The Marines were now "attacking in another direction" as Smith was to call it. Below Yudam-ni, Harris' battalion attacked Hill 1542 west of the MSR and Hill 1419 (C Company's old battle site) to the east. Harris' battalion had its hands full. The Corsairs could not uproot the dug-in enemy, and G and I Companies could not hold the crest of Hill 1542. With H Company unable to take Hill 1419 by itself, Davis had to send up his A and B Companies to help. By 7:30 P.M., they finally secured Hill 1419 and cleared the way for Davis to break off and head over the ridgetops. He quickly sent his dead and wounded to the main force on the road and replaced his casualties with Harris, H Company. Each man carried an extra bandolier of ammunition and a sleeping bag. They took only six machine guns and two 81mm mortars. Mortar and machine-gun ammunition was initially carried on litters. As the ammunition was expended and casualties mounted, the litters would be put to other use.

At 9 P.M., they plunged ahead. It was 16 degrees below zero; and Davis feared that if he allowed his men to stop, their own sweat would freeze and kill them. The front men had to struggle through snow often knee-deep. Behind them, the path was pounded into ice; men slipped and fell and climbed back up the ridges on hands and knees. In the darkness, all the snow-covered peaks began to look alike. On the ridges, they guided by the stars; but in the deep valleys, the stars were blotted out. Compass orientations did not check.

On the point, 1st Lt. Chew Een Lee, his right arm still in a sling, led 1st Lt. Joseph R. Kurcaba's B Company. By mistake, they veered to the southwest and headed toward the enemy on the eastern slopes of Hill 1520. Davis tried to warn Kurcaba of the danger ahead, but the radio failed. With his radio operator, Cpl. LeRoy Pearl, and his runner, Pfc. Vincent C. Michaels, Davis struggled forward through the snow in the darkness. They overtook the point as the men were stumbling up the ridge into enemy territory. The Chinese opened fire. B and C Companies attacked and wiped out an enemy platoon.

When Davis allowed a break, the men began collapsing in the snow, despite the cold and enemy bullets. Officers and noncoms had to shake and cuff them awake. They pushed on. At 3 A.M., Davis called a halt and organized a perimeter. The men took turns sleeping in the empty silence of the bleak, icy wasteland.

At daybreak, the battalion swerved left and attacked Hill

1653, a mile and a half north of Fox Hill. Unable to communicate either with Marine planes above him or with Fox Hill, Davis worried about entering the range of friendly mortar fire. The head of the battalion met little opposition; but H Company, bringing up the rear with the wounded, had to fight off the enemy's wolflike harassment.

As Davis' riflemen advanced toward Hill 1653, Fox Hill finally came through on Corporal Pearl's radio. Captain Barber, now commanding from a stretcher, wanted to send out a patrol to guide Davis in; the offer was declined. Barber covered Kurcaba's final attack with a VMF-312 strike. At 11:25 A.M. on December 2, B Company entered F Company's lines.

From Fox Hill, the men of Davis' forward companies went back to help with the 22 litter cases. Supervising this, Lt. Peter A. Arioli, USN, the regimental surgeon who had volunteered to accompany the battalion, was killed by a Chinese sniper. His was Davis' only battle death, although two Marines cracked under the night's strain, had to be tied down and died before they could be evacuated.

Davis' battalion, to be known as the Ridgerunners of Toktong Pass, dug in on the high ground around Fox Hill. Barber's Marines stayed in their foxholes. Over five nights and days of fighting, they had 26 killed, three missing and 89 wounded—50 percent casualties. Six of Barber's seven officers were wounded, and most of the unwounded men suffered frostbite. Only 82 of his original 240 men could walk. Theirs was a stand that Marines compared to those of Wake Island and Edson's Ridge.[80] Both Barber and Davis were awarded the Medal of Honor.

At the same time Davis had left Yudam-ni, Taplett's battalion—with the radio call sign Darkhorse—had started leading the main body down the MSR. Taplett passed through Harris' battalion and had advanced only 1,400 yards when Chinese fire from both sides stopped it. H and I Companies fanned out but needed until 7:30 P.M. to clear the enemy. Pressing on, I Company east of the road was halted again by Chinese dug in on the western side of Hill 1520. Taplett and Davis were fighting on opposite sides of the same mile-high land mass, but they did not know it. The enemy and terrain made mutual support impossible. Taplett's Marines spent the night fighting. The Chinese attacked and cut off Capt. Harold G. Schrier's I Company. Staff Sgt. William G. Windrich of Hammond, Indiana, organized a squad and held an overwhelming enemy force at bay while the other Marines withdrew. Seven of his men were hit, and he was wounded in the head by a grenade burst. Returning to the company, Windrich gathered volunteers and rescued the wounded. Hit in the leg and unable to stand, he rallied his men to drive off another attack before he bled to death.[81]

All but 20 of Schrier's men were casualties; I Company now existed only on paper. Both G and H Companies were reduced to two-platoon strength. Taplett called for reinforcements and was sent the remnants of D and E Companies of the 7th Marines from the green-scarfed Damnation Battalion.

Tough fighting on the ground and daring flying among the ridges were needed before Taplett could resume the advance. The Engineers built a bypass around a bridge the Chinese had blown. G and H Companies attacked along either side of the MSR, and the composite D-E Company moved down the road behind the Engineers and Staff Sgt. Russell A. Munsell's lone tank.

While the spearhead battalions moved south, the three battalions holding the rear line below Yudam-ni were under tremendous pressure. Five VMF(N)-542 planes helped Roise's rearguard battalion during the early hours of December 2. F Company was forced off the left flank of Hill 1276, and Roise ordered it retaken. Two attempts in the darkness were repulsed by enemy machine guns. After dawn, planes strafed and rocketed the Chinese. F Company took the crest; the machine guns on the reverse slope drove them off again. Corsairs blasted the Chinese at midmorning; but by then, it was time for Roise to pull out; and the futile, costly counterattack was dropped.

Simultaneous Chinese night attacks all along the rear line were driven off, except on the extreme left where the Chinese shoved Lt. Col. Harris' G and I Companies off Hill 1542. Although reinforced by about a hundred artillerymen and headquarters troops thrown together as J Company, Harris had to give ground under persistent attack until he had less than 200 men left. When J Company was routed, artillery Sgt. James E. Johnson of Pocatello, Idaho, took charge of his leaderless platoon and covered its withdrawal. He was last seen, wounded, struggling hand-to-hand with the enemy.[82] Harris' Marines were finally able to hold enough of Hill 1542's slopes to keep Chinese small-arms fire off the MSR.

As the vehicle train started creeping south on the morning of December 2, there were not enough riflemen to protect the high ground. Air cover kept major Chinese elements away, but infiltrators were able to knock off a number of Marine drivers.

Leading the breakout, Taplett's Darkhorse battalion had to fight for nearly every foot of the road. What was left of his G Company took Hill 1520 on the left by noon. H Company on the right fought through a Chinese strongpoint. D-E Company was stopped 300 yards further on, where a bridge over a rock ravine had been blown out. Twelve Corsairs drove the enemy out of the ravine; but by 2 A.M. on December 3, D-E Company was exhausted and ineffective with heavy losses, particularly among its noncoms. The battalion had to halt 1,000 yards short of Fox Hill.

At dawn on December 3, the ground was covered with six inches of new snow. Tech. Sgt. Edwin L. Knox's Engineer platoon held the point behind the tank. G Company came down to the road to take over from D-E Company, the remnant of which was now commanded by 2d Lt. John J. Cahill, the same officer who had led the first Marines into action four months before—when the temperature had been more than 100 degrees higher.

During the night of December 2, Davis' men around Fox Hill counterattacked to clear Toktong Pass and dislodge the battalion of Chinese barring the way to Hagaru. The Marines drove the enemy right into the path of Taplett's H Company. Pvt. James T. Beard, firing his BAR from the hip, crushed a series of enemy positions. He killed a machine-gun crew with a grenade, turned the gun on the retreating enemy and killed 17 before he ran out of ammunition. Helicopter pilot 1st Lt. Robert A. Longstaff was shot down and killed while trying to rescue a badly wounded Marine. By 10:30 A.M., the enemy battalion had been slaughtered by mortars, machine guns, rockets and napalm. At 1 P.M., Munsell's tank came into the pass and Davis' and Taplett's battalions met.

Davis', Taplett's and Barber's wounded were put aboard

trucks. Taplett's rifle companies had been reduced in three days from 437 men to 194. To make room, the walking wounded had to get off and struggle painfully toward Hagaru on foot. Litzenberg walked alongside his Jeep filled with wounded.

Munsell's tank led off again, followed by Davis' Ridgerunners and Lt. Col. Stevens' 1st Battalion, 5th Marines. Marine Corsairs blasted the enemy in front and on the flanks. Planes from six Marine squadrons flew 145 sorties, mostly in close support. Taplett's Marines provided security for the artillery, followed by Roise and finally Harris as the rear guard. And up from Hagaru moved the Royal Marine Commandos with a platoon of tanks to clear the road. As the point from Yudam-ni came within a few hundred yards of Hagaru that evening, the men in the front closed ranks—the wounded who were able climbed down off the trucks—and they marched silently into the perimeter.

As the rest of the column moved toward Hagaru, at 2 A.M. on December 4, the prime movers for eight 155mm howitzers ran dry of diesel fuel. Unaware of this break in the line behind them, the troops in front pushed ahead. But Chinese hit the cannoneers and drivers of the 4th Battalion, 11th Marines. Two drivers were killed, and a few others panicked and tried to bypass a blown-out bridge by crossing the ice of a small stream. Chief Warrant Officer Allen Carlson of the 11th Marines dashed after one of the fleeing trucks, cursing loudly, and brought back a howitzer. He rounded up a crew and started firing point-blank at the enemy. E Company, 5th Marines circled around; by 8:30, the enemy strongpoint had been eliminated. The stalled howitzers were abandoned; and at 2 P.M., the last elements of Harris' rear guard entered the Hagaru perimeter.

The head of the column had needed 59 hours to cover the 14 miles to Hagaru, the rear units, 79 hours. Some 1,500 casualties had been brought out, a third of them suffering from frostbitten feet, hands and faces.

While the Marines rested, regrouped and prepared to fight their way to the sea, the Chinese were strangely absent. Two B-26s mistakenly bombed and strafed the perimeter on the evening of December 5. The evacuation of the wounded was the most urgent problem. The division surgeon, Capt. Eugene R.

Hering, USN, set the standard: To be approved for evacuation, a man had to be in worse condition than Lt. Cmdr. Chester M. Lessenden, USN, the 5th Marines' surgeon, who had both feet painfully frozen and refused to be flown out. By nightfall of the fifth, 4,312 men—3,150 Marines, 1,137 soldiers and 25 Royal Marines—had been flown out of Hagaru by Marine and Air Force aircraft.

Five hundred and thirty-seven replacements were flown into Hagaru. Many of them were Marines wounded in the Inchon-Seoul campaign. The Air Force offered to evacuate the troops at Hagaru, but Maj. Gen. Smith refused. He wanted all able-bodied men to come out with all possible equipment.

The press met with Smith at Hagaru, and a British correspondent asked if this were a "retreat" or "retirement." Smith replied quietly that since the Marines were surrounded, there was no rear and therefore there could be no "retreat." So much for rhetoric.

To prepare the next stage of the breakout, more than 370 tons of supplies were flown into or air-dropped on Hagaru: ammunition, hand grenades, gasoline and diesel oil, rations and communication wire. The air-drop damage rate was especially high among the artillery and mortar ammunition, but Smith said that the amount received gave the division a vital margin.

Even though delay would allow the Chinese time to get in position in the hills down along the MSR, the need for recuperation was so compelling at Hagaru that the move to Koto-ri was postponed until December 6. The plan was for the 7th Marines to lead the way while the 5th Marines and Ridge's 3rd Battalion, 1st Marines protected the rear. After Koto-ri, the remaining elements of the 1st Marines would take over the rear guard. Everyone except drivers, relief drivers, radio operators and casualties would walk out.

MAW-1 would cover the column with 24 planes, while Marine, Navy and Air Force search and attack planes scouted ahead and among the ridges on the flanks. Four hundred and ninety soldiers including 385 survivors of Task Force Faith were organized into a provisional battalion ("the 31/7") and attached to the 7th Marines. Maj. Gen. Smith flew ahead to Koto-ri by helicopter to organize the next step southward. By air, the trip took only ten minutes.

Although the Chinese had not attacked at Hagaru, Intelligence reported masses of enemy troops were assembling both at Hagaru and above the road to Koto-ri. Seven Chinese divisions were identified in the area.

On the morning of December 6, Murray sent Roise's 2d Battalion against East Hill where the Chinese still threatened Hagaru itself and dominated the road south to Koto-ri. Capt. Samuel S. Smith's D Company led the assault. After two hours of fighting, Chinese resistance collapsed; and the hill was taken with one Marine killed and three wounded.

D Company was unable to secure the next ridge of the same land mass until 2:30 P.M. F Company occupied the first hill, and both companies hit the Chinese assembling at the saddle between the two hills. First Lt. George C. McNaughton led a patrol onto the saddle and captured 220 Chinese. The saddle was then turned over to a small force from the Antitank Company and the Army's 4th Signal Battalion.

This became the fiercest battle of the entire breakout. From dusk until 2 A.M., the Chinese attacked there again and again, taking frightful losses. Mortars and machine guns on both sides took their toll. D Company, which had been virtually wiped out on Smith Hill northwest of Seoul, was hard hit again. First Lt. Seydel, the company's only officer not wounded in the earlier battle, killed seven Chinese and was himself killed. D Company had 13 dead and 50 wounded and was forced to fall back and tie in with F Company. Next, the Chinese attacked A, C and E Companies of the 5th Marines on the perimeter to the northwest of East Hill. The Marines' firepower was devastating. Estimates of Chinese dead in the 22-hour battle ran as high as 800. The enemy had made a major effort to destroy the Marines and been crushed.

The 7th Marines were already following the route of Task Force Drysdale—in the opposite direction. Three hundred artillerymen filled the regiment's ranks, giving Litzenberg about 2,200 men. The 1st Battalion moved out on the east of the road; the 2d Battalion supported by tanks, along the MSR; the Provisional Battalion ("31/7"), in the valley along the west side of the road, and the 3rd Battalion behind the regimental train.

They started leaving the perimeter at 6:30 A.M. on December 6 in a silvery fog. The survivors of F Company of Fox Hill had the point. Barber had been flown out, and 1st Lt. Welton R. Abell commanded the reinforced company. Almost immediately, the lead dozer tank was hit by three rounds from a 3.5-inch bazooka; and then after allowing F Company to pass, the Chinese opened up on the column. Not until two companies and tanks attacked the hill could the advance start again at noon. F Company's last remaining officer of the Fox Hill battle, 1st Lt. John M. Dunne, was killed. Four thousand yards out of Hagaru, another strongpoint stopped the column until 3 P.M. The flank battalions ran into continual opposition. Along the ridgeline to the east, long columns of Chinese reinforcements were sighted moving toward the MSR. Air attacks could not stop them.

The Marines fought past a succession of strongpoints, roadblocks and blown bridges. In Hell Fire Valley, a Chinese machine gun held up the 2d Battalion; it was midnight before Army tank fire destroyed the gun. Another 1,200 yards and everything stopped while the Engineers repaired one blown-out bridge, and soon afterwards, a second. Fearing the arrival of the Chinese reinforcements, the column kept going all night long.

The 2d Battalion covered the last few miles into Koto-ri without trouble. But at 2 A.M., the regimental train was hit by enemy fire; three officers in the regiment's command group were killed and wounded. When Chaplain Cornelius J. Griffin entered an ambulance to console a dying Marine, machine-gun bullets shattered his jaw and killed Sgt. Matthew Caruso by his side. Lt. Col. Harris and Major Roach directed H Company in beating off the attack. At 5:30, Harris disappeared and was never seen again; presumably the son of Maj. Gen. Field Harris had been killed. The 2d and 3rd Battalions were sent back up the MSR again from Koto-ri to keep the road open for the other units. The 2d Battalion also helped rescue 22 British Marines who had been stranded ever since Drysdale's fight a week earlier. They had survived for five days on food and medical supplies airdropped after an OY pilot had spotted the letters HELP stamped in the snow.

With the 7th Marines safe at Koto-ri, the Chinese moved in and attacked the flanks of the Division Train No. 1, which had been delayed starting out from Hagaru. After dark on December 6, the 3rd Battalion, 11th Marines had to repulse an enemy attack. Further on, Chinese mortar shells set several trucks on fire and blocked the convoy again. And at dawn, the enemy attacked in force. They almost overran the artillerymen before they were stopped; several hundred of the enemy were killed.

The Chinese also attacked the Division Headquarters Company and burned several trucks. Bandsmen set up two machine guns and kept the Chinese at a distance. Six-foot-four, 240-pound 1st Lt. Charles H. Sullivan emptied his carbine, then hurled it like a javelin and drove the bayonet through a Chinese chest at 15 yards. By daylight, a company-strength group of the enemy closed to within 30 yards before strafing runs by VMF(N)-513 helped stop them. Four planes of VMF-312 dropped four tons of explosives and napalm, and the Chinese broke and ran.

During this ambush, the Military Police Company was guarding 160 Chinese prisoners, lying in the middle of the road. When the Chinese fired on them, the prisoners tried to break. Both Chinese and Marines fired into them and killed 137.

Division Train No. 2; Steven's 1st Battalion, 5th Marines; Ridge's 3rd Battalion, 1st Marines, and the 41st Commando moved out of Hagaru. Drysdale held an inspection of his Royal Marines before setting out.

By 10 A.M. on December 7 only Roise's battalion; 1st Lt. Vaughan R. Stuart's tank platoon, and Capt. William R. Gould's A Company, 1st Engineer Battalion were left in Hagaru. Five demolition teams prepared piles of equipment and clothing for burning, placed charges in the ammunition dumps and bull-dozed the mountain of surplus rations and saturated them with fuel oil. While Roise's Marines were still pulling off the southern tip of East Hill, explosions shook the earth. Roise was furious; rockets, shell fragments and all kinds of debris rained down but fortunately did not injure any of the Marines. And finally, the Engineers blew the bridge, leaving Hagaru to small groups of Chinese who dared the flames and explosions to pick over the ruins of the Marines' former forward base. The name of Hagaru had joined Belleau Wood, Guadalcanal and Iwo Jima in Marine Corps history.

As the final units moved on Koto-ri, the Engineers blew all the bridges along the route. Pathetic hordes of Korean refugees scurried after the troops in blind panic. Many were killed in the fighting. By midnight, the last of the 1st Marine Division reached Koto-ri. In the two frantic days of December 6 and 7, the division had suffered 103 killed, 7 missing and 506 wounded—616 casualties. But it had brought to Koto-ri 10,000 troops and a thousand vehicles. The perimeter was bursting to its seams. The "advance" southward would continue as soon as it became light.

In the Koto-ri perimeter were approximately 2,300 U.S. Army soldiers, 40 ROK police, 150 Royal Marines and more than 11,600 United States Marines. With OYs spotting from the Koto-ri strip, tanks, mortars, artillery and planes kept the Chinese at bay. Colonel Puller had the strip lengthened so that larger aircraft could evacuate casualties.

The mountainous ten miles from Koto-ri to Chinhung-ni were expected to be especially dangerous. It was decided to have Schmuck's 1st Battalion, 1st Marines strike northward from Chinhung-ni. Task Force Dog from the 3rd Infantry Division was rushed up from Hamhung to relieve Schmuck. On December 2, Schmuck himself had led a squad-sized patrol north and located a large body of Chinese. He called in artillery fire from Koto-ri and slaughtered them.

Before the force at Koto-ri could get out, a critical problem had to be solved. The Chinese had blown a bridge three and a half miles south of Koto-ri. There, water from the Chosin Reservoir flowed out of a tunnel and into four large steel pipes to run the turbines of a power plant in the valley below. Where the pipes crossed under the road, they had been covered by the destroyed one-way bridge. On the uphill side was a concrete gatehouse and on the other, a sheer drop. There was no possibility to construct a bypass. The gap of 16 feet (24 feet with the abutments) had to be spanned if the division would bring out its vehicles, guns, tanks and the wounded.

Lt. Col. Partridge studied the break from the air and figured it required four 2,500-pound sections of an M-2 steel Treadway bridge. He ordered eight sections air dropped in case any were damaged. A hundred-man detail worked all night at Hungnam's Yonpo Airfield, and eight Air Force C-119s parachuted the sections inside the Koto-ri perimeter on December 7. One section was damaged and one fell into Chinese hands. Plywood panels were also dropped. Tanks could cross on the metal spans alone, but the narrower vehicles had to keep one wheel on the metal span and the other on the plywood center. Two Army Brockway trucks would carry the bridge sections to the site.

On December 8, in a heavy snowstorm, and with the temperature at 14 degrees below zero, the 7th Marines moved out from Koto-ri. Puller held the perimeter there and formed the rear guard. Visibility was 50 feet; air cover was absent. Schmuck's battalion hiked up from Chinhung-ni. Its mission was to seize Hill 1081, which controlled the narrow, tortuous Funchilin Pass three miles above Chinhung-ni—and the vital bridge site. Schmuck's Marines took only a radio Jeep and two ambulances. Captain Wray's C Company seized the southwestern nose of the hill. Captain Noren's B Company attacked its western slope, while Captain Barrow's A Company assaulted the steep ridge leading to the summit. The snowstorm hid them from the Chinese 6th Division, which was dug in to meet an attack from the north. Said Robert Barrow much later, "They were clearly in a position to control, dominate and absolutely stop the 1st Marine Division from moving south. They had to be dislodged."[83]

Two machine guns stopped Noren's company until a patrol worked around and routed the gunners. Struggling through the deep snow, the company took an enemy bunker complex by surprise in a brief savage fight. Barrow led his three platoons up the ice-covered "almost sheer cliff" in the wind-lashed blizzard. As the storm lifted momentarily, they deployed slightly, attacked the razor-backed ridge and enveloped the Chinese strongpoint on one crest of Hill 1081. So complete was the surprise that only one enemy machine gun offered effective resistance; and it was knocked out by Cpl. Joseph R. Leeds and his fire team, who had crawled up to it on hands and knees. Leeds went in first and killed nine Chinese in the bunker; he was mortally wounded. Marine losses were 13 killed and 17 wounded who had to be taken down. About midnight, when it was 25 below zero, the Chinese counterattacked along the ridgeline; and Barrow's men drove them off.

For the troops trying to come down from Koto-ri, December 8 was a frustrating, snow-blinded day. After 117 Marines, soldiers and Royal Marines were buried in a common grave at Koto-ri, the 3rd Battalion, 7th Marines moved out and met fire from automatic weapons west of the road. Litzenberg urged

Major Morris, who had replaced Lt. Col. Harris, to commit his reserve company. Morris replied, "All three companies are up there—50 men from George, 50 men from How, 30 men from Item. That's it!"[84] Lt. Col. Randolph S. D. Lockwood's 2d Battalion moved from the road to get behind the enemy position. By then it was dark, and the attack had to be postponed.

Litzenberg's Army Provisional Battalion found less opposition east of the road. The Ridgerunner battalion, commanded by Maj. Webb D. Sawyer since Davis had become regimental executive officer, pushed down the road itself and ran into heavy Chinese fire. First Lt. Kurcaba was killed and Lieutenants Chew Een Lee and Joseph R. Owen were wounded. Stevens' 1st Battalion, 5th Marines moved east of the road and took Hill 1457. Because the advance had fallen short, the trucks following the 7th Marines had to back up and the Brockway trucks returned closer to Koto-ri. All told, casualties were light on December 8; weather and terrain had prevented the division from securing its objectives.

When December 9 broke cold and clear, American planes went to work; and Schmuck's Marines discovered that they had not occupied the final slopes of Hill 1081. In hard fighting, A Company took the crest. The entrenched Chinese doggedly defended the last 200 yards. Staff Sgt. Ernest J. Umbaugh led a grenade attack and was killed in the final assault. By 3 P.M., with help from mortars and four Corsairs, the Marines seized Hill 1081 just as the point of the 7th Marines' column appeared on the snaking road far below. Barrow had only 111 able-bodied men left of the 223 he had brought to battle. He, Umbaugh and Leeds were awarded the Navy Cross. The Marines counted 530 enemy dead for the crucial, desperately defended ridge. No Chinese surrendered; none escaped. It was the last Chinese large-scale effort to stop the Marines.

The clear weather made air and artillery support possible, and the 7th Marines could advance more easily. C Company came upon 50 Chinese so badly frozen in their foxholes that the Marines simply lifted them up and sat them on the road under guard. Frequently now, Chinese who were freezing to death, whose fingers had to be broken from their rifles, were surrendering to the Marines.

About noon, the bridge sections arrived at the pass, and

even Chinese prisoners were put to work constructing the abutments and laying the Treadways and plywood panels. By 3:30, the job was done; and by 6 P.M., the first vehicles began to inch across.

Suddenly, an accident crushed every hope. A tractor towing an earth-moving pan broke through the plywood center panel. The bridge became impassable for wheeled vehicles. An expert tractor driver, Tech. Sgt. Wilfred H. Prosser, carefully backed the tractor off the wrecked bridge. Lt. Col. Partridge calculated that if the Treadways were placed as far apart as possible, M-26 tanks could pass with two inches to spare and Jeeps with barely half an inch on the 45-inch interval between the inboard edges of the Treadways. Bulldozers skillfully positioned the Tread- ways while Sawyer's battalion kept the Chinese away from the bridge site. When the repairs were made, the vehicles started across. Engineers guided them over with flashlights. The col- umn crossed the bridge all night long. Marines, Korean refugees and even cattle crunched southward on the crisp snow.

At 2:45 A.M. on December 10, the first elements of Sawyer's battalion began arriving at Chinhung-ni. (It was Robert Tap- lett's thirty-second birthday.) For the rest of the column, it was a march of stops and starts. The Chinese were sighted east of the road and kept moving south despite artillery and air attacks that cut up their ranks. There were occasional fire fights along the twisted mountain road to Chinhung-ni. By mid-afternoon, the last elements left Koto-ri; the tanks brought up the rear. Chesty Puller stayed until they started. His Jeep carried out several wounded and three dead Marines. Puller walked to the pass.

The forward units were already aboard trucks heading for Hungnam. But there was a severe shortage of vehicles, and most of the men had to continue to walk out. Shortly after midnight, the Chinese struck at Sudong, south of Chinhung-ni. Armed with grenades and burp guns, they killed several drivers and set their vehicles on fire. The whole column came to a halt. A confused fight erupted until Lt. Col. John U. D. Page, USA, and Marine Pfc. Marvin L. Wasson teamed up and routed 20 Chinese at the head of the vehicle column. A grenade killed Page and wounded Wasson. After getting first aid, the Marine went back into the fight with Lt. Col. Waldron C. Winston, USA, who directed a counterattack by Marine and Army service troops. UPI correspondent Harry Smith also fought in the ambush. Wasson, calling for machine guns to cover him, fired three white phosphorus rounds from a 75mm recoilless rifle and destroyed a house serving as a Chinese strongpoint. Then, he helped push trucks of exploding ammunition off the road. It was daybreak before the road was cleared. Eight men had been killed and 21 wounded; and nine trucks and an armored personnel carrier, lost. Wasson received the Navy Cross.

At the rear of the division came 40 tanks, guarded only by the Recon Company. The Recon Marines also had to keep back the thousands of refugees, infiltrated by Chinese soldiers, who followed the Marine column. Because of a mix-up in orders, Schmuck had not received Maj. Gen. Smith's instructions that the 1st Marines were to protect the tanks.

The brakes of the ninth tank from the rear froze. The tanks in front moved ahead, but the tail of the column stalled 2,000 yards from the Treadway bridge. Five Chinese soldiers emerged from among the refugees, and one called in English that they wanted to surrender. First Lt. Ernest C. Hargett, leader of the Recon platoon guarding the last tanks, went out cautiously to meet them. Cpl. George A. J. Amyotte covered him with a BAR. Suddenly, the leading Chinese stepped aside and the others opened up with burp guns and grenades. Hargett's carbine failed to fire in the sub-zero cold. The former Marine football star hurled himself at the Chinese, swinging his carbine. He crushed one skull. A grenade explosion wounded him. Amyotte shot down the other four Chinese one by one. As Chinese attacked from the high ground on the flanks, Hargett's platoon fell back fighting. The enemy overran the last tank and killed its crew. Half of Hargett's men were wounded. Amyotte, wearing fiberglass body armor and firing from prone, covered the platoon. A grenade exploded squarely on his back, but he coolly continued to pick off the enemy.

A Chinese explosive charge blew Pfc. Robert D. DeMott over the cliff. He was thought dead. But he landed unconscious on a ledge and later managed to climb up to the road and walk among the Korean refugees to Chinhung-ni. He was the last Marine out from the Reservoir.

Hargett and his remaining 24 men fought their way through. His platoon had two killed and 12 wounded. Tank crewmen finally freed the frozen brake. Cpl. C. P. Lett, who had never driven a tank before, took over a second tank, which had been deserted by its crew, and maneuvered it to safety.

After the freed tank and Letts' tank crossed the Treadway bridge with Hargett's men, Chief Warrant Officer Willie S. Harrison of the Engineers blew up the bridge. By midnight on December 11, the division's last elements arrived at the staging area at Hungnam. From Koto-ri south, the division had suffered 75 more dead, 16 missing and 256 wounded. But the breakout was complete.

The 1st Marine Division had beaten off at least seven Chinese divisions and left the 9th Army Group impotent to prevent the Hungnam evacuation or to march westward and reinforce the attack on the Eighth Army.

The issue had, in fact, been decided by the failure of the enemy's initial attacks at Yudam-ni. Marine firepower had inflicted heavy casualties on the Chinese and enabled the Marines to consolidate at Hagaru and avoid destruction in detail. The Chinese had also suffered from the Korean cold and from shortages of transport, supplies, food and communications. They could not save their wounded. Their problems became progressively more difficult the longer the Marines were able to hold out.

No one knew better than the Marines on the ground that the breakout could hardly have been succeeded without the air support of Marine, Navy and Air Force pilots. Crash landings threatened death in the frozen hills, and a pilot could not survive 20 minutes in the frigid waters off the coast. To make air support possible, runways had to be cleared of snow and carrier decks scraped free of ice inches thick. One time, VMF-214 had to cancel all flights because of 68-knot winds and the coating of ice on *Sicily's* flight deck.

Despite all the hazards, Marine aviators flew hundreds of close-support and search-and-attack missions for Marine, Army and ROK ground units. The Marine Corps system of a forward air controller on the ground talking directly to the pilot overhead proved itself invaluable. And from November 1 until Christmas, the transports of VMR-152 lifted five million pounds of supplies to the troops and evacuated more than 4,000 casualties. VMO-6's OYs and helicopters performed unending rescue and evacuation

765

missions and were often the only physical contact between ground units separated by the enemy.

On December 10, VMF-311, the first Marine jet squadron to fly in combat, arrived at Yonpo. Its fliers covered both X Corps and, with Fifth Air Force jets, the Eighth Army.

As Maj. Gen. Smith wrote Maj. Gen. Harris, "During the long reaches of the night and in the snow storms many a Marine prayed for the coming of day or clearing weather when he knew he would again hear the welcome roar of your planes as they dealt out destruction to the enemy."[85]

Even before the last elements of the 1st Marine Division arrived at Hungnam, the first were loading out. X Corps organized a defensive line around the port. Lt. Gen. Shepherd was on the scene to help with the evacuation of the Marines. The job was enormous. More than 105,000 troops, 91,000 Korean refugees, 17,500 vehicles and mountains of supplies had to be sea-lifted out.

Col. Edward H. Forney, deputy chief of staff of X Corps, was the Corps evacuation officer. By December 14, 22,215 Marines were on board ships; they headed for Pusan the next day. On the eighteenth, MAG-12's command post flew to Itami, Japan. The disastrous Chosin Reservoir campaign was over.

A Marine Shore Party Company, an Air and Naval Gunfire Liaison Company and part of the 1st Amphibian Tractor Battalion helped finish the cleanup at Hungnam. Among the last troops off the beaches on Sunday afternoon, the day before Christmas, were A and B Companies of the Marine Amtrac Battalion, covering the flanks of the final withdrawal. Then, the remaining ammunition and supplies were blown up in one volcanic eruption that seemed to destroy the entire Hungnam waterfront.

Time magazine summed up the feat that had been accomplished:

> The running fight of the Marines and two battalions of the Army's 7th Infantry Division from Hagaru to Hamhung—40 miles by air but 60 miles over the icy, twisting mountainous road—was a battle unparalleled in U.S. military history. It had some aspects of Bataan, some of Anzio, some of Dunkirk, some of Valley Forge, some

of the "Retreat of the 10,000" (401–400 B.C.) as described in Xenophon's *Anabasis*.[86]

Newsweek called the overall debacle "America's worst military licking since Pearl Harbor,"[87] and *Time*, "the worst defeat the United States ever suffered."[88] MacArthur later decried these assessments as "the emotional reaction of irresponsible writers."[89]

But no one could point to a worse American defeat. Blunt-spoken Chesty Puller, who was to receive his fifth Navy Cross—the only Marine ever awarded five—for "superb courage" commanding the division's rear guard out of Koto-ri, wrote his wife: "The leadership, especially that of the higher command during this operation, has not been of top grade, especially in determining an estimate of the situation and the capabilities of the enemy."[90]

The only saving grace was the truly heroic effort of disciplined, determined American Marines and soldiers against an able enemy and sub-zero cold. Puller wrote his wife, "We were ordered to retreat and did so."[91] They saved themselves and restored some share of the nation's pride despite the arrogant hubris of the politicians and the generals.

General MacArthur painted the picture rose: "This was undoubtedly one of the most successful strategic retreats in history, comparable with and markedly similar to Wellington's great Peninsula withdrawal. Had the initiative action not been taken and an inert position of adequate defense assumed, I have no slightest doubt that the Eighth Army and the X Corps would have been annihilated." He called the action "the most successful and satisfying I have ever commanded."[92].

The 1st Marine Division alone from November 30 until December 11 had 2,103 battle casualties—342 dead, 78 missing and 1,683 wounded. And the United Nations forces had been ignominiously thrown out of North Korea.

6
Fighting Back

After its trial in the north, the 1st Marine Division recuperated in the 5th Marines' old Bean Patch at Masan. Strengthened by nearly 3,000 replacements, as well as new weapons and equipment, the Marines ate fresh food and played touch football and got ready again for battle.

On December 23, the Eighth Army's doughty commander, Lt. Gen. Walton H. Walker, was killed when a ROK truck crashed into his Jeep head on. Lt. Gen. Matthew B. Ridgway, the paratroop leader, came out and took command the day after Christmas. He found his army nervous, apprehensive, uncertain. He set out to rebuild its self-confidence. The Marines liked his style.

On New Year's Eve, the Chinese attacked. They drove the United Nations' front back from approximately the 38th Parallel and reconquered Seoul, Inchon and Wonju. The U.S. 2d and the ROK 8th Divisions were badly mauled.

Four Marine air squadrons supported the retreating UN ground forces, but the 1st Marine Division was out of action this time. On January 9, 1951, Ridgway assigned the division a blocking and anti-guerrilla mission, still far behind the front, in the Pohang area on the east coast. Another 1,800 Marine replacements were rushed out. The next month was devoted to sending out "rice paddy patrols" and hunting elusive North Korean guerrillas, who were more eager to escape than fight. At least the exercise served to restore morale and combat-readiness and introduce the division's replacements to the Korean winter. The month's work cost the division 26 dead, 10 missing and 148 wounded in action.

On February 10, the 27th Infantry Division recaptured

Inchon and Kimpo Airfield. The Chinese reacted immediately; they attacked at midnight of the eleventh. Although Maj. Gen. Smith wanted his division kept on the UN flank near the sea, the Marines were shifted to Chungju in the middle of the peninsula. There, they served under Maj. Gen. Bryant E. Moore, commanding general of IX Corps, who had fought with the Marines for Henderson Field. And the 1st Marine Aircraft Wing came over from Japan to Airfield K-3 near Pohang.

As the Chinese offensive died out, Ridgway started Operation Killer, a limited counter-offensive along the entire Eighth Army front. He wanted the pressure kept on. At 8 A.M. on February 21, the Marine division advanced north from Wonju, with the 5th Marines on the right and the 1st Marines on the left. They moved against negligible resistance through an area of rocky heights and narrow valleys; mud and poor roads snarled traffic. They reached their first objective, a ridgeline about three and a half miles south of the high ground dominating Hoengsong, by dusk on February 24.

For the most part, Fifth Air Force planes supported the Marines while Marine aircraft flew for U.S. Army units. The Marine air wing was no longer directly under division control, and the Marine commanders protested the breakup of their ground-air team and the frequent delays in receiving close air support through the Joint Operations Center. But their complaints went unanswered.

On February 24, Maj. Gen. Moore's helicopter crashed into the Han River; and he died of a heart attack a half hour later. Maj. Gen. Smith commanded IX Corps for nine days. As the commander of a major U.S. Army unit, he followed in the footsteps of Lejeune, who had led the 2d Infantry Division in World War I, and Geiger, who had commanded the Tenth Army on Okinawa after Buckner was killed. Chesty Puller, who had been promoted to brigadier general and replaced Maj. Gen. Craig as assistant division commander, took over the division while Smith had the corps.

Puller moved the 1st Marines straight ahead toward Hoengsong with the 7th Marines on its left. The 3rd Battalion, 1st Marines, now commanded by Lt. Col. Virgil W. Banning in place of Ridge, had to cross the 200-foot-wide, chest-deep Som River. The Engineer Company was unable to help; and Major

769

Simmons, commanding the Weapons Company, proposed a field-manual designed "Swiss bent bridge" of A-shaped trusses of timbers tied together with telephone wire. This solution enabled the battalion to cross on March 1.

The Marines found the second half of Operation Killer tougher; but by the end of March 4, they occupied the line of hills north of Hoengsong. In eight days, the division had 48 killed, 2 missing and 345 wounded. Since the Chinese still proved more willing to retreat than to fight, Ridgway had been unable to achieve his objective of killing many enemy troops.

Dissatisfied, he continued the northward pressure under the name of Operation Ripper. The Marine division moved out on the morning of March 7. This time, MAG-33 was able to send 11 flights of four planes each to support the Marine regiments. For the next week, individual platoons fought rearguard defenders screening the Chinese withdrawal. On March 15, the 1st ROK Division found Seoul deserted by the enemy. The capital, in changing hands four times in nine months, had been pounded into rubble.

At this time, the 1st Marine Division had 25,642 men and the 1st MAW 4,645. All told, there were 277,119 Americans serving in Korea, 21,184 men from 10 other nations and 249,815 members of the ROK army. That made a total of 493,503. The enemy was estimated to have 504,000 Chinese and North Korean soldiers in Korea.

The second phase of Operation Ripper began on March 14. Mud, flooded streams and inadequate roads continued to hamper progress more than the enemy. The next afternoon, Major Sawyer's 1st Battalion, 7th Marines, on the extreme left of the Marines' zone, took the town of Hongchon without a fight. But the units toward the right began to meet more determined opposition in the hills east and north of Hongchon. The 1st Marines' 2d and 3rd Battalions ran into a fire fight around Hills 246 and 428 in the middle of the division's sector and suffered seven killed and 87 wounded without taking the hills. In the morning, the enemy had vanished. Sawyer's battalion captured Hill 399, just east of Hongchon, by attacking its bunkers with grenades. On March 20, the Marines easily reached Phase Line Buffalo.

The 1st Korean Marine Corps Regiment rejoined the division on the twentieth and advanced through a trackless wilderness between the 5th Marines on its left and the 1st Marines on the right. In a tough three-day fight, the Korean Marines seized Hill 975. Once that strongpoint fell, the objectives of Operation Ripper had been reached. The Eighth Army had returned nearly to the 38th Parallel.

Ridgway, wanting to maintain the momentum, set a new objective: Phase Line Kansas, partially north of the 38th. The 7th Marines was chipped off from the Marine division and attached to the 1st Cavalry Division. The 1st Marines was sent to division reserve, and the 5th Marines and 1st KMC Regiment continued to drive northward. On April 2, the 5th Marines had to ford the deep Soyang River. After Lt. Col. Joseph L. Stewart, the regimental executive officer, planned the crossing, he found a Jeep waiting to start him on his journey home. He was the last man to leave Korea from the 1st Provisional Marine Brigade, which had landed at Pusan exactly eight months before.

The 5th Marines and the KMC Regiment were pulled out of the line. On April 4, the 7th Marines was among the first Eighth Army units to recross the 38th Parallel. Ridgway's purpose now was to break up the spring offensive that the Chinese were known to be mounting in the Iron Triangle area in the center of Korea. On April 8, the 1st Marine Division was ordered to relieve the 1st Cavalry Division and prepare to press the attack.

Then, on April 11, President Truman announced that he had fired General MacArthur. Trouble between the general and the President had been long simmering. At the heart of the dispute was a difference of views over the Constitutional arrangement that the civilian leadership determines foreign policy and the military carries it out. Back in August, the President had forced MacArthur to withdraw a public statement to the Veterans of Foreign Wars recommending that Chiang Kai-shek be brought into the war. MacArthur believed that opening a second front in China would compel the Communist Chinese to reduce their effort in Korea. Truman believed it would bring in the Soviet Union and start World War III.

On March 24, while Washington was working toward a Korean ceasefire, MacArthur issued a statement demanding that the Chinese surrender and announcing that he was ready to meet the enemy commander in the field. "By this act MacArthur left me no choice—I could no longer tolerate his insubordination," Truman said afterwards, "General MacArthur had openly defied the policy of his Commander in Chief, the President of the United States."[93] When a letter from MacArthur, again advocating the use of Chinese Nationalist troops, was read in the House of Representatives on April 5, the die was cast. Four days later, the President relieved him on the recommendation of the Joint Chiefs of Staff. Truman explained, "General MacArthur was ready to risk general war. I was not."[94]

MacArthur had miscalculated. Based on his conviction that Communist China would not enter the war, he had sent American troops to the Yalu, despite his orders, and advanced his army into North Korea on widely separated fronts. It had been beaten. The Administration in Washington, for failing to control his activities, had to share the blame for the resulting "shattering defeat."[95]

MacArthur asserted that the war's goal was an open-ended "victory." Both the Joint Chiefs and America's allies feared a widening of the war. MacArthur's civilian superiors tried to make him understand that this was not World War II but a war of limited aims. The general was still fighting the last war. His dismissal insured that this war would be confined to the Korean peninsula.

During these events, the fighting paused. Ridgway, replacing MacArthur, took over the United Nations command; and on April 14, Lt. Gen. James A. Van Fleet assumed command of the Eighth Army.

In the first three weeks of April, enemy antiaircraft fire shot down 16 Marine planes; nine pilots were killed, one captured. Capt. Valdemar Schmidt and Cpl. Robert Sarvia flew their helicopter 20 miles behind enemy lines to rescue an Air Force pilot. The chopper was shot down, crashlanded and rolled over. While Marine fighter pilots covered him, Capt. Frank E. Wilson in another helicopter picked up the two Marines and the Air Force flier and brought back his chopper to a field lit by headlights and flares.

The Eighth Army was moving forward again toward the vital Iron Triangle when, on the night of April 22, the Chinese opened their massive Fifth Phase Offensive. They hit the 6th ROK Division on the Marines' left. The entire ROK division collapsed before midnight and opened a vast gap, ten miles deep and ten miles wide, on the Marines' flank. The 1st Marines rushed up from reserve by truck through thousands of retreating ROKs. About midnight, the KMC on the right and the 5th Marines in the division's center came under attack. The KMC struck back and drove the Chinese from Hill 509. Capt. James T. Cronin, commander of the 5th Marines' B Company, sent 2d Lt. Harvey W. Nolan's platoon racing the enemy for possession of Hill 313 just north of Hwachon. Nolan's Marines climbed the last 200 yards on hands and knees. Machine-gun fire stopped them, killing seven and wounding 17. In the morning, the enemy had abandoned the hill.

The heaviest fighting came on the extreme left where Major Sawyer's 1st Battalion, 7th Marines stood off nearly 2,000 Chinese. During three hours of furious fighting, the Marine line bent but did not break. Lt. Col. Robley E. West's 1st Battalion, 1st Marines came up and extended Sawyer's left to prevent the enemy from widening the penetration.

With dawn's light, VMF-232 and VMF-214 went into action supporting the Marine regiments. Marine aircraft flew 205 sorties that embattled day. The division was ordered to fall back to Line Pendleton centered on the town of Hwachon. The 1st and 3rd Battalions, 1st Marines faced west to contain the breakthrough and permit Sawyer's battalion to disengage and fall back. Banning's 3rd Battalion, 1st Marines seized Hill 902, a 3,000-foot mass dominating the area. By the day's end, the division formed a front that bent around like a fishhook on its exposed left end.

At 8 P.M., the Chinese attacked Captain Wray's C Company, 1st Marines on Horseshoe Ridge. The assault continued for four hours; if it succeeded, the entire battalion would be endangered. Ammunition ran short until Cpl. Leo Marquez started lugging ammunition and grenades to the men in the firing line. He escaped unwounded although bullets holed his helmet, cartridge belt and shoe. C Company held.

At midnight, Capt. Horace J. Johnson's G Company, on the center of Hill 902, was almost overrun. Tech. Sgt. Harold E. Wilson of Birmingham, Alabama, was repeatedly wounded leading his platoon to hold off the attackers. Unable to fire his weapon, he resupplied his men with rifles and ammunition taken from the wounded. He brought up and placed reinforcements. A mortar round blew him off his feet. Although dazed by the concussion, he refused medical aid and moved from foxhole to foxhole directing fire. At dawn, with help from the 11th Marines, the Army's 987th Armored Field Artillery Battalion and Marine aircraft, the final attack was repulsed. Wilson accounted for every man in his platoon and finally walked a half mile to the aid station. In addition to the concussion, he had been wounded in the head, shoulder, right arm and left leg. He received the Medal of Honor.

On the division's center and right, the 5th Marines and the KMC Regiment continued to withdraw. The division's line contracted enough so that the 7th Marines could drop into reserve.

On the afternoon of April 25, a mortar round scored a direct hit on the 3rd Battalion, 1st Marines' command post and wounded Col. Francis M. McAlister, the regimental commander; Lt. Col. Banning, the battalion commander; Maj. Reginald R. Myers, the executive officer, and Maj. Joseph D. Trompeter, the battalion S-3. Banning and Myers had to be evacuated; Trompeter took over the battalion and Major Simmons replaced Myers. In 48 hours, the 1st Marines had had nearly 300 casualties.

With the crisis under control, Maj. Gen. Smith, who had led the division at Inchon, Seoul and the Chosin Reservoir, was relieved by Maj. Gen. Gerald C. Thomas. A native of Missouri and graduate of Illinois Wesleyan University, Thomas had enlisted in May 1917; won the Silver Star at Belleau Wood and Soissons, and been wounded in the Meuse-Argonne. He had served in Haiti and China and during World War II had served on Guadalcanal and Bougainville. He had been a longtime associate of General Vandegrift.

The Marines pulled back east of the Pukhan River and then continued to withdraw south of the Soyang River and past Chunchon to form a new line northeast of Hongchon. There the retreat stopped.

Van Fleet shuffled units, and the Marine division again came under Almond's X Corps. Action diminished to patrolling and artillery firing, until the Chinese attacked en masse again on May 16. This time, they struck the eastern side of the front, broke through the 5th and 7th ROK Divisions and made a 30-mile penetration.

Although the Marines were not in the path of this attack, an enemy force in regimental strength slashed in behind the 7th Marines and tried to cut the MSR. Two Marine tanks were disabled, but Capt. Victor Stoyanow's I Company held and the company commander led a counterattack. Tanks and riflemen sealed off the Chinese escape route and slaughtered most of the attacking force.

Air Force, Navy and MAW planes, controlled chiefly by VMO-6, hurled air strikes at the enemy's main offensive. On May 18, the Marines extended their lines eastward to ease the pressure on the 2d Infantry Division, enabling that division to face east against the hole in the Eighth Army line. All four Marine regiments (including the KMC) were in action. The Chinese swiftly ran out of steam and supplies and paid for their aggressiveness with enormous losses. They began to retreat, often out of control. Remnants of units surrendered. The fleeing enemy left behind a screen of North Korean troops as their rear guard. The North Koreans were told that if they did not stand and die they would be executed.

The United Nations army pursued through mountainous terrain that gave every advantage to its defenders. The Marine division jumped off on May 23 and at first made progress easily. But resistance soon stiffened. Marine aircraft shot up the Chinese escaping westward along the southern side of the Hwachon Reservoir. By the last day of May, the 7th Marines broke through the pass leading into Yanggu at the eastern end of the reservoir; and the 5th Marines advanced to a ridgeline 6,000 yards northeast of the burnt-out town. The division's losses for May totaled 83 killed and 731 wounded.

Marine officers, having lost control of the air wing, were increasingly displeased with their close air support. During the Inchon–Seoul campaign, the average delay in receiving requested air support had been 15 minutes. In May–June 1951, with air support under Air Force control, the delay was 80 minutes—35 minutes of which was taken up clearing the request through the Joint Operations Center. And only 65 to 70 percent of the sorties called for were ever received. Maj. Gen. Thomas complained to

Maj. Gen. Almond that on May 29, when the 5th and 7th Marines were under heavy enemy fire, they had requested 92 sorties and received 55—of which 20 were Marine Corps planes. And practically all of those delivered were two to four hours late.

Starting on June 1, the 5th and 7th Marines pushed up from Yanggu and as far east as the Soyang River valley. The enemy stood in a maze of nameless ridges and well-placed positions. The Marines fought over ridge after endless ridge. The ground in the middle was dominated by a large land mass that rose toward the peak of Hill 1316 on the southern rim of a valley to be called the Punchbowl.

On the morning of June 2, the 3rd Battalion, 1st Marines' command group was again the victim of an enemy mortar barrage. It killed one officer and wounded 40 Marines, including four company commanders, and prevented the battalion from attacking.

By June 4, three Marine regiments were in line—the 1st on the left, the KMC in the center and the 5th on the right. The Korean Marines fought a furious five-day battle over the rugged terrain leading up to Hill 1316. At 8 P.M. on June 10, the 1st Marines, briefly led by Col. Wilburt S. "Bigfoot" Brown, a colorful veteran of both World Wars, Nicaragua and China, ran into expertly defended enemy bunkers that had to be wiped out with grenade and bayonet attacks. Despite strong support from the 11th Marines, Maj. Clarence J. Mabry's 2d Battalion engaged in what Colonel Brown called "the hardest fighting I have ever seen"[96] and suffered 14 killed and 114 wounded. On Mabry's left, Lt. Col. West's 1st Battalion had nine killed and 97 wounded against determined North Korean resistance. Nineteen-year-old Cpl. Charles G. Abrell of Terre Haute, Indiana, three times wounded, attacked a bunker; he clutched an armed grenade that killed the enemy gun crew and himself.[97]

Because of the heavy casualties, Maj. Gen. Thomas brought the 7th Marines, now commanded by Col. Herman Nickerson, Jr., onto the line to advance up the So-chon valley. In the next week, 10 Marine tanks were lost to mines.

During the last days of June, two months of hard fighting came to an end. The Marine division started digging in on the heights above the Punchbowl. And the Eighth Army occupied the lower half of the strategic Iron Triangle, which had been the enemy's main assembly and supply area.

The war was one year old on June 25. An estimated 1,250,000 men had been killed, wounded or captured in battle. Two million civilians were dead and three million homeless. The border between the Communist and free worlds was virtually back at the 38th Parallel where the war had started.

At last, the United States was prepared to accept the *status quo ante*, make peace along the 38th Parallel and leave the unification of Korea to be achieved by peaceful means. On June 23, following informal meetings with George Kennan, the Soviet delegate to the United Nations, Jacob Malik, suggested truce talks. And on June 25, this idea was supported by the rulers in Peking. The talks began at Kaesong on July 10. Action on the battlefront slowed down; and in mid-July, the 2d Infantry Division relieved the Marines.

On August 22, the Communist delegates walked out of the truce talks. The war heated up again, and the Marine division went back into action. What followed was the division's final month-long explosion of mobile warfare in the Korean war. The objectives were two complex, strongly defended ridges just north of the Punchbowl depression: Yoke Ridge immediately to the north and Kanmubong Ridge further north across a narrow valley. Here, the North Korean defenders fought with tenacity and strong artillery support.

On August 27, when the division was ordered back into action, it had few veterans left from the Chosin Reservoir campaign. The 7th Marines and the KMC Regiment moved up through a quagmire created by torrential rains. On August 31, the 7th Marines attacked the section of Yoke Ridge east of Hill 924 and the KMC attacked on its left against Hills 924 and 1026. By the end of September 1, the KMC's 3rd Battalion had taken Hill 924 despite enemy mines, mortars and automatic-weapons fire. The Korean Marines were driven from Hill 924's crest by a surprise midnight counterattack and retook it the following morning. The 3rd Battalion, 7th Marines needed until the afternoon of September 2 to take its objective, Hill 602. The following day, the KMC Regiment broke up a North Korean

777

counterattack in a three-and-a-half-hour battle and finally seized Hill 1026. By that evening, the Marine division held the northern rim of the Punchbowl.

The cost of the four-day battle had been 109 dead and 494 wounded, including the losses in the KMC Regiment. Despite the Air Force's interdiction campaign, the North Koreans' strength in artillery, mortars and machine guns was estimated to have equaled that of the Marines and their attached Army units.

The effort to take Yoke Ridge forced a six-day halt to bring up a new reserve of artillery and mortar ammunition over the almost impassable supply routes. And as the Marines moved deeper into the rugged highlands, the logistic problem became ever more difficult.

On September 11, the 7th Marines resumed the offensive to seize Hills 673 and 749, the first objectives on Kanmubong Ridge. Mortar and machine-gun fire stopped H and I Companies halfway up the steep southeast spur of Hill 680, an intermediate objective. The battered companies were twice driven back. Although most of his men were hit, 2d Lt. George H. Ramer of Meyersdale, Pennsylvania, led I Company's 3rd Platoon to the top and wiped out a bunker. He was wounded twice. The enemy counterattacked and forced the Marines off the peak. Twenty-four-year-old Ramer covered their retreat until the enemy killed him.[98]

Across a valley to the east, the 1st Battalion could make no more progress against Hill 673. Sgt. Frederick W. Mausert III of Cambridge, New York, rescued two wounded Marines under fire. He was wounded in the head but led his men in a bayonet charge against a bunker and silenced its machine gun. As his unit approached the ridgeline, twenty-one-year-old Mausert made a target of himself to draw enemy fire and allow his men to attack. Wounded again, he stormed the topmost bunkers and destroyed another machine gun before he was killed.[99]

In the darkness, Colonel Nickerson sent the 2d Battalion into the valley between the assault battalions in order to trap the North Koreans on Hill 673. At dawn, the 2d Battalion swept upward, surprised the defenders, grabbed the crest of 673 and moved on against Hill 749. Across the valley, G Company attacked; and all three 3rd Battalion companies met on the summit of Hill 680. The two-day fight cost the Marines 22 killed and 245 wounded.

Part of the reason for the heavy casualties was the scarcity of close air support. The Fifth Air Force was giving first priority to interdicting the enemy's buildup. The entire Eighth Army was assigned only 96 close support sorties a day. To cripple the enemy's concentration of artillery dug into rock emplacements much more was needed. "As a consequence, General Thomas reported, many of the 1,621 casualties suffered by the 1st Marine Division during the hard fighting in September were due to inadequate close air support."[100] The men on the ground paid with their lives.

One air development, on the other hand, was saving lives: the helicopter. On September 13, the Marine Transport Helicopter Squadron 161, which had arrived in Korea on the last day of August with 15 HRS-1 Sikorsky helicopters, lifted a day's supplies to the 2d Battalion, 1st Marines. The choppers brought in 18,848 pounds of cargo and evacuated 74 casualties. Lt. Col. George W. Herring's squadron performed a similar feat on the 19th and two days later brought the first combat troops into action by helicopter. "A new era of military transport had dawned."[101]

On the thirteenth, Col. Thomas A. Wornham's 1st Marines relieved the 7th Marines attacking Hill 749. Lt. Col. Franklin B. Nihart's 2d Battalion drove to the summit at 3 P.M., after a battle of small arms, automatic weapons and hand grenades. The 3rd Battalion finally took Hill 751 on the left by the end of September 14. The next day was comparatively quiet, but after midnight a North Korean regiment counterattacked to drive the 2d Battalion off Hill 749. The depleted Marine companies stopped wave after wave of enemy attackers. As casualties mounted, Cpl. Joseph Vittori of F Company led a three-man counterattack. On the extreme flank, he leaped from foxhole to foxhole to fire on the enemy and manned a machine gun when its gunner was struck down. The young BARman from Beverly, Massachusetts, made repeated trips through heavy shell fire to bring up ammunition before he was mortally wounded.[102] The next day, the 1st Battalion passed through the 2d and finished the job of occupying Hill 749. During the four-day battle for

Hill 749, the division had 90 killed, one missing and 714 wounded.

The 5th Marines then attacked Hill 812, a bare hill mass 1,000 yards ahead, and, after two days of hard fighting, seized the hill on the eighteenth. The enemy counterattacked twice; and by day's end, Lt. Col. Houston Stiff's 2d Battalion had 16 killed and 98 wounded. The enemy still occupied Hills 980 and 1052 looming above the battalion.

On the nineteenth, the 2d Battalion battled the enemy for control of The Rock, a huge granite knob on the ridgeline 700 yards west of Hill 812. The Marines held the top and eastern side of The Rock, the North Koreans the western side. At 3:15 A.M. on the twentieth, the enemy tried to retake Hill 812. They pushed back E Company's left platoon, but the company counterattacked and the 2d Platoon struck the enemy flank and sent them scurrying to their own side of The Rock, leaving 60 dead.

On September 20, 1951, Lt. Gen. Van Fleet called off the X Corps offensive because of the high casualty rate and because "it was unprofitable to continue the bitter operation."[103] As it turned out, that was the end of the war of movement in Korea.

7
The Long Outpost War

The war settled down into a static conflict with sudden bursts of vicious local battle for the next 22 months. Changes in the ground held by both sides were minute, but the piling up of casualties was horrendous. The Marines suffered about 40 percent of their total dead and wounded in Korea during those long, disheartening months.

With the end of the war of movement, the Marine division held a 13-mile section of the 125-mile front. It stretched from the Punchbowl eastward to the I ROK Corps, which guarded the coastal end of the line.

To relieve a ROK regiment on remote Hill 884 near the eastern end of the Marine sector, Maj. Gen. Thomas tried an experiment. He ordered HMR-161 to airlift the Division Reconnaissance Company to the hill by helicopter. Such a sizable troop lift had never before been attempted. On September 21, each helicopter brought five fully equipped Marines, who descended from the hovering craft by knotted 30-foot ropes. A total of 224 men, including a heavy machine-gun platoon, was landed in four hours. On foot, it would have taken the Marines 15 hours just to climb the hill.

Another helicopter experiment was less successful. E Company, 1st Marines was moved from reserve at night to meet a threat against the front line. Although 223 Marines were lifted on the evening of September 27, the operation was not attempted again; and it was decided that night lifts should be confined to movements within friendly territory.

On October 11, the entire 3rd Battalion, 7th Marines was flown close to the front by 12 helicopters in 156 flights. The lift carried 958 combat-equipped Marines in five hours and 50 minutes. Four days later, six HMR-161 helicopters brought 19,000 rounds of ammunition to help a surrounded ROK unit and evacuated 24 wounded. On the Marine Corps Birthday, the 5th Marines relieved the 1st Marines in the line. Nearly 2,000 combat-equipped men were transported by helicopter—the largest helicopter lift so far—952 men were carried in and the same number taken out, all in 10 hours.

During this period, the ground troops confined their activities to extensive patrolling in order to take prisoners, plant mines and fight guerrillas behind the lines. One Marine, Sgt. Albert Ireland, earned his ninth Purple Heart, five in World War II and four in Korea. Both sides spent a lot of time and energy building complicated and formidable defenses in depth.

On October 25, the truce talks were resumed at Panmunjom, just south of the 38th Parallel. And by November 27, a cease-fire was agreed upon based on a line of demarcation. A lull set in all along the front. On December 18, lists of prisoners of war were exchanged. The Communist list named 3,198 American POWs of whom 61 were Marines, including two naval corpsmen. By the end of the year, there were 24,535 Marines in Korea; none of them had arrived prior to January 1, 1951.

On January 1, 1952, Lt. Gen. Franklin H. Hart relieved Lt. Gen. Shepherd as commander of FMFPac, and Shepherd became the Commandant of the Corps.

Maj. Gen. John T. Selden replaced Maj. Gen. Thomas as commander of the 1st Marine Division on the eleventh. Selden had served two years in Haiti before being commissioned during World War I. He had commanded the 5th Marines at New Britain and served as chief of staff of the 1st Marine Division on Peleliu. Brig. Gen. William J. Whaling continued as assistant division commander.

By this time, the division was occupied by the routine of trench warfare, sniping by day and patrols and raids at night. Action was so light that Camp Tripoli was set up near Wontong-ni for training in small unit leadership and offensive tactics. The arrival of new thermal boots and lightweight armored vests helped keep down casualties from frostbite and shell fragments. And Col. Keith B. McCutcheon, the innovative helicopter pioneer who had taken over HMR-161, continued to experiment with troop and supply lifts that made movement easier in the Korean hills.

Starting on March 17, the Marine division was shifted to the extreme western side of Korea as part of a realignment of divisions along the entire front. The Marines replaced the 1st ROK Division just above the Imjin River to strengthen the protection of the ancient invasion route to Seoul. Here, the division took responsibility for 32 miles of the Jamestown Line, and here it would remain for the rest of the war.

This was an area of coastal lowlands, climbing into steep hills and narrow valleys toward the northeast. The Marine sector started on the Kimpo Peninsula in the west, crossed the Han River and ran along the southern side of the Imjin. Crossing that river, it continued northeast along the key terrain until it crossed the 38th Parallel and, two and a half miles further on, met the 1st Commonwealth Division at the Samichon River. Instead of North Koreans, the Marines now faced the 65th and 63rd Chinese armies.

By the end of April, MAG-12 also moved to the west side of Korea. VMO-6 and HMR-161, of course, had come up behind the Marine division even more promptly. The 1st Marine Aircraft Wing headquarters and MAG-33 remained in the Pohang area. The wing, continuing to operate under the Fifth Air Force, was commanded by Maj. Gen. Christian F. Schilt, who had won the Medal of Honor at Quilali in 1928. On April 11, he was relieved by Brig. Gen. Clayton C. Jerome, a veteran of five campaigns in World War II and most recently Assistant Commandant for Air.

Through the spring of 1952, the Marine division and the enemy opposite pounded each other with artillery barrages and probed with patrolling jabs. At first, the Marines established an outpost line in front of the Main Line of Resistance. Occasionally, patrols suffered casualties in hand-to-hand fighting. On the night of April 15, the Chinese twice attacked a platoon of E Company, 5th Marines positioned on a 400-foot hill known as Outpost 3. Machine gunner Cpl. Duane E. Dewey of Grand Rapids, Michigan, smothered a grenade that landed in his position while he and his assistant gunner were having their wounds treated by a corpsman. Miraculously, Dewey survived and a year later received the Medal of Honor at the White House from the new President, Dwight D. Eisenhower.[104] In the struggle at Outpost 3, the Marines had 6 killed, 5 missing and 25 wounded.

Late in April, the Marine front was extended another 6,800 yards to the west; and the outpost lines were withdrawn and replaced with forward outposts and listening posts. The 5th Marines created an infantry-tank Everready Rescue Force to dash in and rescue the United Nations Truce Team at Panmunjom in case that became necessary.

On May 12, Gen. Mark W. Clark relieved Ridgway as United Nations commander in Korea. To increase the pressure on the enemy, Clark assigned UN aircraft to knock out major industrial targets, including hydroelectric plants, in North Korea. Prime target was the Suiho plant at the Yalu, which supplied a quarter of northeast China's electrical power. Strikes flown between June 23 and 27 by Marine, Navy and Air Force planes virtually blacked out North Korea for two weeks. Col. Robert E. Galer led MAG-12's planes and Col. John P. Condon led MAG-33 in these strikes. All 150 Marine aircraft returned safely.

On August 5, Galer, a Medal of Honor winner in World War II, was leading a flight of 31 aircraft when his engine was hit. He had trouble breaking loose from his cockpit; and as he dropped spreadeagled before his parachute opened, his plane nicked his shoulder. He recovered in time to pull the ripcord and landed safely deep in enemy territory. After eluding enemy soldiers, he guided a rescue helicopter to him with a small survivor radio and was hoisted aboard. On the return flight, the helicopter was hit by enemy aircraft fire but landed safely on a rescue ship at Wonsan.

The Marines sent out repeated patrols between the two dug-in armies. On May 8, the 1st Battalion, 5th Marines launched a raid to dislodge the Chinese from former Outpost 3. While C Company feinted against a nearby hill, 1st Lt. Ernest S. Lee's A Company assaulted the 450-foot hill on which Outpost 3 marked the forward point. The Marines ousted a reinforced enemy platoon but came under artillery and mortar fire. As they approached the peak, the 1st Platoon threw back a counterattack but had to withdraw when it received a barrage of more than 400 rounds in five minutes. A Company was unable to reach its final objective and suffered 7 killed and 66 wounded.

After the 7th Marines replaced the 5th Marines in the line, the 1st Battalion went out early on May 28 to seize Hill 104 and Tumae-ri Ridge. C Company made a feint to the left and got into hand-to-hand fighting. Second Lt. John J. Donahue and his platoon of Capt. Earl W. Thompson's A Company took Hill 104 with bayonets fixed. But the company was unable to take Tumae-ri Ridge and returned to the MLR with 9 killed and 107 wounded.

Two Marines were awarded posthumous Medals of Honor in this costly miscarriage. Nineteen-year-old Cpl. David B. Champagne of Wakefield, Rhode Island, saved three members of his A Company fire team when he threw back an enemy grenade, which exploded and blew off his hand. Pfc. John D. Kelly of Homestead, Pennsylvania, a radio operator with C Company, turned his radio over to another man and joined the assault. Kelly personally wiped out one position, killing two of the enemy, and then singlehandedly attacked a machine-gun bunker. He was painfully wounded but destroyed the bunker and killed three Chinese. As he tried to reach a third bunker, he was mortally wounded.[105]

The Chinese celebrated the end of the war's second year by attacking the 2d Battalion, 5th Marines late on June 24. They overran Outpost Yoke, killing nine and wounding 23 of its 34 Marines. Artillery fire finally drove off the attackers.

The Marines celebrated the Fourth of July by having all their front-line battalions attack the enemy's forward positions. One 2d Battalion, 5th Marines patrol got into an hour-long fire fight, losing one Marine killed and 11 wounded. On the night of July 2, G Company, 7th Marines met a battalion-sized Chinese force on Outpost Yoke. Many Marines were hit immediately. Staff Sgt. William E. Shuck, Jr., led his machine-gun squad and a rifle squad up the hill and was wounded. Ordered to pull back, he made sure all the dead and wounded were evacuated. He was killed by a sniper's bullet.[106] Four Marines were killed and 40 wounded in this action. In further celebration, the division fired 3,202 artillery rounds at the enemy on the Fourth. And on July 6–7, the 1st Battalion, 7th Marines climaxed the festivities by an abortive two-company raid in the Outpost Yoke area. C Company took Yoke but Chinese artillery drove it off again with heavy casualties. The official history of the war concluded baldly: "Marine casualties from the operation were out of proportion to the results achieved—12 dead, 85 wounded, and 5 missing. It had been a high price to pay for a venture of this type, particularly when the primary objectives went unaccomplished. During the entire 4–7 July period, 22 Marines had lost their lives in combat operations. Division reported that 268 Marines had been wounded during the long Fourth of July."[107] Maj. Gen. Selden had objected to the attack order, but "Corps turned a deaf ear."[108]

The next battle was big and long. At 1 A.M. on August 9, the Battle of Bunker Hill (Hill 122) opened when a Chinese raiding party forced a squad of Marines from E Company, 1st Marines to evacuate Hill 58A, which was a quarter mile in front of the MLR and halfway to the Chinese outpost line. It had been held by the Marines since June.

To recapture the lost hill, a reinforced E Company platoon set out at 4 A.M.; but enemy fire sent it back to the MLR. After daybreak, Marine and Air Force jets poured bombs and napalm onto Hill 58A. Artillery pounded it. At midmorning, an A Company platoon reoccupied the hill, and an E Company platoon quickly reinforced it. But a few minutes later, the Chinese drove the Marines down the southern slope. By midafternoon, the Marines had taken 75 casualties and given up Hill 58A again.

That night, the embattled hill changed hands twice more. C Company forced the Chinese off the crest, but they stormed back and retook it. Concentrated shelling caused most of the 1st Marines' 17 killed and 243 wounded.

At this point, Col. Walter F. Layer, who had recently taken command of the 1st Marines from Col. Walter N. Flournoy, changed the objective from Hill 58A to Hill 122—Bunker Hill. This hill had a 350-yard-long crest about 700 yards in front of the MLR and across a long draw southeast of Hill 58A. Hill 122 ran south to Hill 124; Hill 122-124 was known as Bunker Ridge. Much of the enemy fire on the Marines had been directed from an observation post on Hill 122. By moving the attack to Hill 122, Colonel Layer hoped to surprise the enemy and neutralize the capture of Hill 58A.

A diversionary attack was launched against Hill 58A on the night of August 11 by a reinforced rifle platoon and eight gun and flame tanks. The flame tanks climbed the hill firing their machine guns and then reversed course and ran over the hill again before retiring. The gun tanks remained east of the hill to support the 3rd Platoon of D Company, which assaulted and took the hill. The Chinese counterattacked, and then both infantry elements withdrew.

Meanwhile, B Company, led by Capt. Sereno S. Scranton, Jr., made the main assault on Bunker Hill. As the Marines swept forward, the Chinese answered with small-arms fire and hand grenades and then gave ground in close-in fighting. By 3 A.M. on August 12, the Marines had a precarious foothold on Bunker Hill and quickly began digging in.

At 3 P.M., the Chinese opened an intense artillery and mortar barrage. The resulting casualties forced a decision for B Company to pull back from the ridgetop and take positions on the reverse or eastern slope. An hour later, 350 Chinese attacked from the west. B Company, now reinforced by Capt. Howard J. Connolly's I Company, fought them off; and the Chinese withdrew to the northern slope of Bunker Ridge. At the same time, the 3rd Battalion's reconnaissance platoon occupied Hill 124. Marine mortars and artillery supported the defenders, and gun and flame tanks covered the steep draw on Bunker Hill's right flank. B and I Companies dug into Bunker Hill's reverse slope.

The Chinese tried some diversionary tactics of their own. They attacked Hill 48A, Stromboli, a Marine outpost far to the east of Hill 122, and hit the 1st Marines' main line shortly after midnight on August 13. Although they did not penetrate the 2d Battalion, they turned back a reinforcing squad sent out to Hill 48A and repeatedly struck at the isolated defenders there. When a second reinforcing unit finally crashed through, the Chinese broke off the action.

At 1 A.M., the Chinese stepped up their fire at the Marines on Hill 122. The 11th Marines boxed the area with defensive fire. Half an hour later, the Chinese attacked; and a four-hour battle raged on Hill 122 until they were repulsed by the Marines' artillery, tanks, rockets and mortars.

Capt. William M. Vanzuyen's G Company, 7th Marines came out from reserve to reinforce Captain Connolly's positions on Bunker Hill just before dawn. And at mid-day, Capt. John G. Demas' H Company, 7th Marines relieved the other Marines on the hill. During August 12 and 13 at Bunker Hill, the 1st

Marines reported 24 killed and 214 wounded. An additional 40 Marines had been casualties in the Stromboli area.

At 9 P.M., an enemy battalion hit Bunker Hill again. The few Chinese who penetrated Captain Demas' positions were killed. Enemy mortar and artillery fire had killed seven H Company Marines and wounded 21. One of the dead was Corpsman John E. Kilmer of Highland Park, Illinois, who was wounded while aiding the casualties. As enemy mortar fire increased, Kilmer shielded a wounded Marine with his body and was mortally wounded.[109]

Bunker Hill was reinforced by a platoon of A Company, 1st Marines late on August 14; and that night, the whole Bunker Ridge complex erupted in a fire fight. Marine artillery protectively boxed in the hill and held the attackers in check. By 4 A.M. the battle was over. Captain Demas' Marines suffered 7 killed and 28 wounded before being relieved by B Company, 1st Marines. The enemy attacked the hill again on the sixteenth in their persistent effort to destroy the Marines; and the next morning, C Company relieved B Company. The Chinese continued sporadically to attack the hills—on the night of August 25 alone, F Company had 65 casualties there—and on September 4, E Company had 12 killed and 40 wounded. But the issue was no longer in doubt.

Throughout the August struggle for Bunker Hill, the Marines on the ground had received full close air support. And in a 24-hour period starting 6 P.M. on August 12, Marine artillery fired a record 10,652 rounds in support.

The Bunker Hill battle became a subject of debate. Since the Marines proved unable to neutralize Hill 58A from Bunker Hill, the value of the entire bloody operation was questioned. And the decisions to feed in companies piecemeal and to fight a reverse-slope defense were severely criticized.

Marine casualties had been 48 killed and 313 listed as seriously wounded and "several hundred additional wounded were treated at 1st Marines medical facilities and returned to duty shortly thereafter."[110] Rear area units had to be culled for 200 replacements, and Commandant Shepherd authorized an airlift of 500 enlisted Marines to the division. He also increased the next two monthly replacement drafts by 500 men, and emergency replacements came out from Camp Pendleton. The first major Marine action in west Korea's war of position and attrition had been costly.

By now the Marine division was being used as one more infantry division holding the transpeninsula front. In this positional war, there was no rationale for having a Marine division in the line rather than an Army division. This assignment did not diminish the Corps' eagerness to do its share, but it increased the Corps' need to justify its existence as a specialized elite organization. And, incidentally, it weakened the Corps' argument that it required its own aviation element for close support.

In the two months following the dubious Battle of Bunker Hill, the Marines did not especially distinguish themselves. During August, three daylight-manned outposts in front of the 5th Marines, at the right of the division's line, were lost to the enemy. The last of the three was Outpost Irene. When the 2d Battalion outpost detail went out to man it at dawn on August 17, the Marines found it already occupied. The Chinese forced the Marines and two reinforcement parties to withdraw. During this clash, Pfc. Robert E. Simanek of Detroit, Michigan, threw himself on a grenade and was gravely wounded but survived to receive the Medal of Honor from President Eisenhower.[111]

Early on September 5, the enemy made a coordinated attack against Bunker Hill, Stromboli and four outposts in front of the 5th Marines on the east end of the Marine sector. A reinforced company attacked Outpost Bruce, on Hill 148, a mile in front of the line, and caused 32 Marine casualties. Two Marines and a Navy Corpsman won the Medal of Honor in this fight. Pfc. Fernando L. Garcia of San Juan, Puerto Rico, threw himself on a grenade to save his platoon sergeant's life and was killed. Corpsman Edward C. Benfold moved forward to check on two Marines in a large crater. Two enemy grenades dropped into the crater. Benfold picked them up in both hands, leaped from the hole and hurled himself at two charging Chinese. He pushed the grenades against their chests, killing them, and was himself mortally wounded. Pfc. Alford L. McLaughlin, a machine gunner from Leeds, Alabama, was painfully wounded but fired two machine guns alternately from the hip until his hands were blistered. Then, standing up in full view, he defended his position with a carbine and grenades and killed an estimated 150 Chinese and wounded 50 more. He was the only one of the three who survived that night's battle.

The Chinese continued to assault Outpost Bruce the next two nights. Although every defender was either killed or wounded, the Marines held the hill. In the 51-hour siege there, 19 Marines were killed and 38 wounded. At the other outposts, five more were killed and 32 wounded.

Starting on September 5, the enemy also began attacking three outposts in front of the Korean Marine Corps Regiment at the western end of the division line on the mainland. Maj. Gen. Edwin A. Pollock, who had relieved Maj. Gen. Selden as the division's commander on August 29, emphasized the need for holding ten of the key outposts along the division front. (Pollock had earned the Navy Cross on Guadalcanal and fought at Iwo Jima.) On September 19 and 20, the Chinese twice gained control of Outpost 36 in fierce fighting. With air support from three Marine attack squadrons, the Korean Marines regained the hill and held it. Early in October, Outpost 37, nearby, changed hands four times before the Korean Marines were forced to give it up on the afternoon of October 5. In the same battle, Outpost 36 was lost again. And Outpost 86, at the southwestern end of the Korean Marine front, changed hands four times before it was given up.

On the eastern end of the division line, the 7th Marines, which had replaced the 5th Marines, tried to defend nine permanent outposts. Beginning on the night of October 2, the Chinese assaulted Outposts Seattle and Warsaw and overran them in less than an hour. At Warsaw, Pvt. Jack W. Kelso picked up a grenade that landed in his bunker, rushed outside and hurled it back at the enemy. He was wounded as it left his hand. Then the eighteen-year-old from Madera, California, covered four Marines escaping from the bunker and was mortally wounded.[112] A platoon from his I Company counterattacked and recaptured Outpost Warsaw. But three counterattacks to recover Outpost Seattle failed. At the two outposts, 13 Marines were killed and 88 wounded. A fourth attempt to retake Outpost Seattle on October 6 failed after five hours of heavy fighting with 12 Marines dead and 44 wounded. That night, the Chinese made determined attacks against five outposts and two MLR positions. A company overran the two squads holding Outpost Detroit;

only two wounded Marines escaped. To the east, a company also attacked Outpost Frisco and overwhelmed its defenders. A platoon from I Company came out from the MLR and restored control. Staff Sgt. Lewis G. Watkins of Seneca, South Carolina, a guide of this platoon, led the assault up the hill. He was hit but took an automatic rifle from another wounded Marine and stopped the fire of a machine gun holding up the attack. A grenade came near him and several Marines; he picked it up and was about to throw it away when it exploded, killing him.[113] Later in the day, the decision was made to abandon Outpost Frisco. In the outpost fighting of October 6–7, 10 Marines were killed, 22 missing and 128 wounded. By the end of the first week of October, the Marine division had surrendered to the Chinese six outposts on commanding ground in front of its sector.

During the attacks on the Marine outposts in September and October, air strikes received by the Marine division increased. Marine fliers also participated in two massive air raids against Pyongyang, the North Korean capital, on July 11 and August 29. And 1st Lt. John W. Andre of VMF(N)-513 shot down a Yak fighter, which added to his four kills in World War II, made him the first Marine nightfighter ace in Korea. Late in September, Maj. Alexander J. Gillis of VMF-311, flying with an Air Force squadron, became the first naval aviator to destroy three enemy aircraft in Korea. All three of his kills were MIG-15s. The third plane disabled Gillis' F-86, and he spent four hours in the Yellow Sea before a helicopter picked him up. On September 10, 22 jet fighters from VMF-115 attacked troop concentrations 35 miles south of Pyongyang. On the return flight, six of the pilots flew in formation into a 3,000-foot mountain, failing to clear the peak by 600 feet.

The enemy's next significant move was to mount a major attack at the most vulnerable point on the Marine division's Main Line of Resistance. This was the Hook, a deep salient pointing north near the western end of the division's sector. It was protected by two outposts: Warsaw, 600 yards to the northeast, and Ronson, 275 yards west of the Hook, replacing the enemy-seized Seattle. The Hook was important because it overlooked the Samichon valley, a major corridor to Seoul, and dominated the Imjin River behind the MLR.

Col. Thomas C. Moore's 7th Marines defended this western

end of the Marines' sector. All three battalions were on line to protect an overextended six-mile front. Only one company was in reserve. Col. Moore had 3,844 Marines, 144 medical officers and corpsmen, 3 Army communicators and 774 Korean service troops and interpreters. Opposite them were two Chinese regiments and 120 artillery pieces. The Chinese had closed in on the MLR for months by digging intricate trench systems.

The attack on the Hook was preceded by 48 hours of intense enemy artillery fire, directed mostly against the Hook, Ronson and Warsaw. About 2,850 artillery and mortar rounds devastated bunkers, trenches and communications lines in the 1st Battalion's area. The destruction exceeded the Marines' ability to repair the damage. The coming attack was well advertised.

The MLR sector that included the Hook was defended by Capt. Paul B. Byrum's C Company. One squad was outposted on Ronson and a reinforced platoon on Warsaw. On the right flank was Capt. Dexter E. Evans' B Company. The enemy advanced its 3rd Battalion, 357th Regiment for the attack.

At 6:10 P.M. on October 26, Outpost Ronson was hit and in half an hour was overrun. No one escaped. By 7 P.M., Warsaw's defenders were locked in hand-to-hand fighting and trying to keep their attackers from their bunkers. Artillery and mortar fire smothered the Hook. Lt. Col. Leo J. Dulacki, the 1st Battalion commander, ordered Capt. Frederick C. McLaughlin's A Company forward to support C Company on the MLR.

The enemy struck in battalion strength and by 7:38 had reached the main trenches 400 yards southwest of the Hook. A few minutes later, the Chinese hit both east of the salient and directly against the nose of the Hook. The enemy, under artillery support, overran the trenches and advanced along the crest and on both sides of the ridge. The Marines pulled back covered by a small rear guard. To the southwest, the attack penetrated C Company's line; the 1st Platoon formed a perimeter defense. At 11:30 P.M., Colonel Moore reported Warsaw in enemy hands.

Colonel Moore sent up his reserve, H Company from Lt. Col. Charles D. Barrett, Jr.'s, 3rd Battalion. And Maj. Gen. Pollock ordered Lt. Col. Sidney J. Altman's 3rd Battalion, 1st Marines out of reserve to support the hard pressed 7th Marines. The 2d Battalion, 11th Marines pounded Warsaw and the enemy formations.

At 12:30 A.M., the Chinese launched a diversionary attack against Outpost Reno, two miles west of the Hook. An ambush patrol hidden behind Reno surprised and dispersed the first enemy attack. At 4 A.M., another Chinese company hit Reno for 40 minutes before withdrawing. Nine Marines were killed and 49 wounded there.

At the Hook, Captain McLaughlin's A Company passed through C Company and counterattacked until heavy fire stopped its advance. Then, Capt. Bernard B. Belant's H Company moved up to continue the counterattack. By this time, the Chinese controlled more than a mile of the MLR. At 8 A.M., Captain Belant started his attack and was met by a barrage of enemy fire. Immediately, 2d Lt. George H. O'Brien, Jr., leaped from his trench and, shouting for his platoon to follow, zigzagged across an exposed saddle and up the enemy-held hill through a hail of fire. He was shot through the arm and thrown to the ground; getting up, he urged his men onward, stopped to assist a wounded Marine and raced for the trenchline. He killed at least three Chinese with his carbine and grenades. He was knocked down three more times by grenade concussions but continued to lead his men for four more hours. As enemy fire stopped the Marine advance. O'Brien organized his remaining men's defense; and when they were relieved, he covered their withdrawal. The Marine from Fort Worth, Texas, received the Medal of Honor.

A second Marine, 2d Lt. Sherrod E. Skinner, Jr. (whose twin brother was also a Marine officer), won the Medal of Honor posthumously that night. Skinner was an artillery forward observer; and when the enemy hit the MLR, he organized the surviving Marines at the observation post, fought off the attackers and called in artillery fire. He twice left his bunker to direct machine-gun fire and bring up ammunition. He was wounded both times. When the position was overrun, he directed his men to feign death. They were searched several times by enemy groups. When an enemy soldier tossed a grenade into the bunker, Skinner rolled on top of it to shield two other Marines and was killed.[114]

H Company had driven a wedge into the enemy position and regained the initiative. Planes from three Marine squadrons dumped bombs and napalm on the enemy. That day, 72 planes, including 67 Marine aircraft, flew close support missions. The 11th Marines and A Company, 1st Tank Battalion also support-ed the frontline troops.

Capt. Murray V. Harlan, Jr.'s, I Company moved up to recapture the Hook. The 1st Platoon crept forward under fire at 1:50 P.M., taking severe casualties. By 5 P.M., a few Marines reached the trenches; but a heavier barrage sent them back to the reverse slope. By midnight, B Company, 1st Marines joined the attack on I Company's left. The Chinese met them with small-arms fire and grenades, and for an hour and a half the battle was a stand-off. B Company pulled back to leave space for an artillery and mortar barrage. At 3:40 A.M., on October 28, B Company made the final charge; and by 6 A.M., the Marines again held the Hook. In the next two hours, the 7th Marines also reoccupied Ronson and Warsaw. The battle for the Hook was finished. Marine losses were 70 killed, 386 wounded and 39 missing of whom 27 turned up as prisoners. It was calculated that Chinese supporting fire had laid at least 15,500 artillery and mortar rounds on the Marines. They had withstood a heavy blow and come back to win.

The fall's upsurge of fighting ended with a Chinese attack against four Korean Marine outposts just before midnight on the last day of October. After some sharp fighting that cost the Korean Marines 154 casualties, the attacks were thrown back.

Winter crept in. Van Fleet strengthened his line by inserting another ROK division; and by year's end on line were 11 Korean divisions, three U.S. Army, 1 Marine and 1 British Common-wealth. In reserve were one Korean division and three U.S. Army divisions.

In its third winter, the war was a dragged-out conflict that was unpopular both at home and in the battle theater. In the 1952 Presidential campaign, Dwight D. Eisenhower had prom-ised he would go to Korea if elected; and he began a four-day visit to the battlefront on December 2. Maj. Gen. Pollock briefed the President-elect at his command post. But the peace negotia-tions were stalled on the issue of the exchange of war prisoners. The Communists demanded the repatriation of all North Korean and Chinese prisoners; the United Nations refused to force the return of 60,000 men who did not want to return to their homelands. On October 8, the senior UN delegate had recessed the talks hoping to force the Communists' hand. In December, the United Nations voted an Indian compromise based on the concept of voluntary repatriation run by a repatriation commission. The change of Administrations in Washington in January 1953 and the death on March 5 of the Soviet premier, Joseph Stalin, which changed the Communist world, apparently made negotiations on the prisoner issue possible. By the war's end, 7,190 Americans had been captured and an estimated 2,730 had died in enemy hands. Of the survivors, 21 U.S. Army soldiers (plus one British Marine) chose to go to China rather than return home.[115]

The winter was relatively quiet. Both sides eased their offensive activity if not their vigilance. Lt. Gen. Maxwell D. Taylor replaced Van Fleet as Eighth Army commander. Every Marine regiment and air group changed commanders. Maj. Gen. Jerome turned over the 1st MAW to Maj. Gen. Vernon E. Megee, who had enlisted in the Corps in 1919, earned his wings in 1932 and served at Iwo Jima and Okinawa.

The Marine aviators in Korea ran into a maelstrom of controversy when a broadcaster in the United States charged that Marine planes were the most careless about bombing and strafing friendly troops. The Marine Corps replied that of the 63 incidents between January and October 1952 in which UN casualties resulted from Fifth Air Force flights, 1st MAW pilots were responsible for 28.5 percent. Although Marine aircraft accounted for only 14.5 percent of the FEAF planes, Marine fliers were performing 30 to 40 percent of the close support missions and virtually all of the very close support.*

In February 1953, the fighting on the ground started to pick up again with small-unit efforts against enemy strongpoints in no-man's-land. On the division's right, the 5th Marines was particularly aggressive. The regiment was now commanded by Col. Lewis W. Walt, who had won two Navy Crosses in World War II. Early on February 3, Colonel Walt sent A Company against Hills 31 and 31A and a tank-artillery feint against three hills west of the target area. With A Company, young 2d Lt.

---

*On February 16, 1953, Capt. Ted Williams, the baseball star, crashlanded his burning Panther jet at a forward base while returning from his first mission, a large-scale raid in North Korea. Williams, who had also flown in World War II, flew 37 combat missions in Korea.

Raymond G. Murphy of Pueblo, Colorado, although wounded himself, made several trips up and down the fire-swept hill carrying wounded Marines to safety. Then, he covered the Marines' retreat and killed two of the enemy. At the base of the hill, he organized a party and led it back up to search for missing men.[116] The main purpose of the raid was not achieved: no prisoners were taken. But enemy casualties were estimated at 390. The Marines had 14 killed and 91 wounded.

On February 25, Walt sent a two-platoon assault against Hill 15, the site of former Outpost Detroit two miles east of Hills 31 and 31A. This time, bad weather wiped out almost all the planned air strikes, and the raid was unsuccessful. B Company made another attack against Hill 31A on March 19 but withdrew with heavy casualties.

One week later, the 5th Marines became involved in the bloodiest fighting yet in western Korea. This four-day battle for Outposts Carson, Reno and Vegas (previously called Allen, Bruce and Clarence) would cost the Marines 1,015 casualties.

The fight was part of a Chinese attack against Eighth Army outposts across the front. On March 23, the enemy had overrun the Army position called Old Baldy, 25 miles northeast of the "Nevada Cities" outposts. The Chinese hoped to shortcircuit an unexpected UN spring offensive and seize dominant ground that could remain in their hands when a truce went into effect.

The three Nevada Cities outposts stood on high ground in front of the 5th Marines' 1st Battalion and about 10 miles northeast of Panmunjom. Reno, the middle outpost, was the nearest to the Chinese line and 1,600 yards from the Marine line. Vegas to the east was the highest and 1,310 yards from the MLR. Carson was furthest west and 820 yards from the MLR. Each was manned by about 40 Marines (a rifle platoon) two corpsmen and weapons company personnel. A reinforced squad held a blocking position called Reno Block on a small hill between and slightly to the rear of Reno and Vegas.

At 7 P.M. on March 26, 1953, the Chinese on the hills facing the Nevada Cities outposts opened up with a barrage. In 20 minutes, 1,200 mortar rounds hit Carson. Coordinated fire struck outposts and the MLR all along the Marine division front. Small-unit attacks felt out several outposts.

At 7:10, 3,500 Chinese converged on the Nevada Cities outposts from three directions. Another company made diversionary probes at Outposts Berlin and East Berlin in the 3rd Battalion's sector and were driven off. Marine artillery replied in force. But the sheer weight of numbers, 20 to 1, proved decisive. In an hour, the 54 Marines on Carson were fighting with bayonets, knives, rifles and bare fists. They stopped the Chinese. But the 40 Marines at Reno were pushed back into their cave defense, and the Chinese were sealing the entrances. Within two hours, only seven of the Marines on Reno were still able to fight. On Vegas, the Chinese in overwhelming numbers swarmed over the Marines.

Reinforcements were rushed out from the MLR. An advance platoon from F Company was ambushed but fought its way to Reno Block. Two squads from C Company came under fire all the way out; 10 Marines were wounded. Both those units were trying to reach the defenders on Reno. A D Company platoon heading for Vegas had to fight hand-to-hand near the Block. Two F Company platoons then struggled to the Block through a storm of shells; one platoon took 70 percent casualties in minutes. But slowly the Marines were building up strength at the Reno Block.

A final message from Reno received at 11 P.M. could not be understood. Three minutes before midnight contact with Vegas was lost. A platoon from E Company was on its way to Vegas, but both outposts had fallen. The Marines at the Block, now at company strength, fought off three Chinese attacks. At 1:44 A.M. on the twenty-seventh, Capt. Ralph L. Walz, the commander of F Company, reported that he had one platoon left at the Block. His remaining Marines stood off three more attacks in the next hour. By 3 A.M., the relief forces from F and C Company were ordered to return to the MLR. They had 35 percent casualties. When they withdrew, Corpsman Francis C. Hammond of Alexandria, Virginia, remained behind with C Company's wounded and was killed by a mortar shell.[117]

Trying to reinforce Vegas, two platoons from D and C Company got within 400 yards of the outpost; and F Company, 7th Marines joined them. By 3 A.M., they were within 200 yards of Vegas, but the position was in Chinese hands and the relief elements were ordered to return. It was later learned that 1st Lt.

Kenneth E. Taft, Jr., in charge at Vegas, had been killed and some of his H Company Marines captured. At Reno, 2d Lt. Rufus A. Seymour, the officer in charge, was captured with several of his men. All of the original Marines on Reno except five had been killed. The 1st Battalion had 5 killed, 51 wounded and 39 missing (at Reno) for a total of 95 casualties; the 3rd Battalion had one killed, eight wounded and 40 missing (at Vegas) for a total of 49. The 1st Marines had 4 killed and 16 wounded.

During the morning of the twenty-seventh, planes from three Marine squadrons, Air Force jets and artillery pounded the enemy-held area. The Marine commanders made a decision to try and recapture Vegas but let Reno, further away, go. At 11:20 A.M., D Company, 5th Marines set out for Vegas but took such a beating from Chinese artillery and mortars that in 50 minutes only nine men in the 1st Platoon were still able to carry on. D Company crawled up the muddy slope to within 200 yards of Vegas. The 2d Battalion's Provisional Company joined the counterattack. E Company, 5th Marines and F Company, 7th Marines were thrown into the fight and replaced D Company in the van on Vegas' slopes. Three platoons of Marines seized part of the hill in a 90-minute hand-to-hand fight. Two F Company platoons made it to within 50 yards of the peak before being repulsed by machine-gun and mortar fire. Corpsmen William R. Charette of Ludington, Michigan, with F Company moved about helping the wounded under intense fire. When a grenade landed near a Marine he was aiding, he threw himself over the wounded man. The blast wounded Charette in the face and tore off his helmet and medical kit. He ripped part of his uniform to make emergency bandages. Finding a Marine whose armored vest had been blown off by an exploding shell, he put his own battle vest on the wounded man. He saved many lives that night and was the only corpsman in the Korean war to receive the Medal of Honor and live to wear it.[118]

Before midnight, Capt. Ralph F. Estey's F Company, 7th Marines withstood three enemy attacks and set up a perimeter defense at the base of Vegas. In the early morning hours of the twenty-eighth, it made three assaults on the summit but was repulsed every time, despite repeated Marine air strikes. F Company reached to within 15 yards of the trenchline on the left side of Vegas and battled the Chinese in a 22-minute fire fight. Squad leader Sgt. Daniel P. Matthews of Van Nuys, California, saw a corpsman trying to remove a wounded Marine exposed to fire from a machine gun on the peak. He worked his way to the gun emplacement and leaped onto the rock fortification surrounding the gun. Although severely wounded, Matthews shot two Chinese, routed a third and silenced the machine gun before he was killed. The wounded man was carried to safety.[119]

By noon, Estey's F Company had 43 effectives left after six assaults on Vegas and was relieved by Capt. Herbert M. Lorence's E Company, 5th Marines. MAG-12 flew seven four-plane strikes against the outpost and nearby enemy-held hills. E Company attacked the crest at 1 P.M., digging the Chinese out of their holes. The final assault was made by the 1st Platoon led by Staff Sgt. John J. Williams, who had taken charge after 2d Lt. Edgar R. Franz had been wounded and evacuated. In six minutes, the Marines held Vegas again.

Fifteen minutes later, the Chinese counterattacked. Enemy artillery and mortar shells hit the Marines on the crest at the rate of one round every second. Marine tanks and artillery placed a protective curtain of fire around the outpost. And gradually the Chinese opposition began to slacken. By 2 P.M., the enemy held only the topographical crest at the northernmost point of the ridge. Maj. Benjamin G. Lee, operations officer of the 2d Battalion, 5th Marines who had won the Silver Star as an enlisted man on Guadalcanal, directed the buildup of the Vegas defense. After 10 hours of fighting, there were only 58 Marines from E and F Company on the hill. During the afternoon, 150 men from F Company, 5th Marines strengthened the rear trenches. Panther jets of MAG-33 joined the MAG-12 planes in bombing enemy postitions.

That night, the Chinese attacked both Carson and Vegas and were beaten off. In a second assault, they managed to drive the Marines from the high ground; but it was swiftly retaken. Just before midnight, at least 200 of the enemy made a third attempt to recapture Vegas. The 11th Marines' fire and the defenders, bolstered by E company, 7th Marines, threw them back and seized the critical northern segment of the outpost. Virtually at the end of the battle, Major Lee and Captain Walz were killed instantly by a 120mm enemy mortar round. Maj.

Joseph S. Buntin, executive officer of the 3rd Battalion, 5th Marines, took charge as outpost commander.

After a day of furious digging-in in the rain, the Marines on Vegas met another attack at 6:50 P.M. on the twenty-ninth. Three companies approached both flanks. Marine artillery fired 6,404 rounds and sent the Chinese battalion reeling. The enemy came back twice more before midnight and still again in battalion strength in the early hours of the thirtieth. By 2:15 A.M., they gave up their persistent efforts to take Vegas.

Marine casualties in the battle totaled 1,015: 116 killed, 801 wounded and 98 missing, of whom 19 were taken prisoner. The Marines figured they had caused 2,221 enemy casualties and destroyed the Chinese 358th Regiment as a fighting unit.

The 1st Marine Aircraft Wing had flown 218 close support missions against the Nevada Cities hills. The enemy fired 45,000 rounds of artillery and mortar fire at the Marines, and Marine and Army artillery units replied in kind. In addition to the Medal of Honors cited, 10 Marines won the Navy Cross in the battle.

In view of the loss of Reno, a new Outpost Elko was established on Hill 47, southeast of Carson and 765 yards in front of the MLR; and Vegas was strengthened with a detachment of 135 men. The 7th Marines replaced the 5th Marines after 68 days on the line. Some Marine dubbed Vegas "the highest damn beachhead in Korea."[120]

On March 28, in the midst of the Vegas battle and three weeks after Stalin's death, the Communists notified the United Nations that they were prepared to discuss the return of sick and wounded prisoners. After six months of stalemate, the two sides sat down again at Panmunjom on April 6. A provisional command was established at Munsan-ni to process the prisoners of both sides. Marine Col. Wallace M. Nelson commanded the United Nations Personnel and Medical Processing Unit. Marines swiftly built the Freedom Village POW recovery station. Operation Little Switch began on Monday, April 20; and in the next week, 6,670 North Korean and Chinese prisoners were returned and 684 were received from the enemy. Among the 684 were 149 Americans, including 15 Marines and three Navy corpsmen who had been attached to the 1st Marine Division. All the Marines had been wounded before they were captured. The first Marine freed was Pvt. Alberto Pizzaro-Baez of Puerto Rico and H Company, 7th Marines, who had been captured in October 1952.

On April 26, the plenary truce talks resumed at Panmunjom; and by June 4, the final agreement on the repatriation of prisoners had been hammered out. But President Rhee denounced the armistice plan and boycotted the Panmunjom meetings. The South Korean National Assembly unanimously rejected the truce terms. On June 17, the details of the truce line were settled; but the next day, ROK guards released 27,000 North Korean POWs who did not want to be repatriated. They quickly disappeared into the South Korean populace. At the end of the month, General Clark was authorized by Washington to sign the armistice without the South Koreans if necessary.

Meanwhile, back at the front, the Chinese attacked Outposts Carson and Elko on April 9. In the resulting fire fights, 14 Marines were killed, 4 missing and 66 wounded. A few smaller skirmishes followed before the Marines were relieved on May 5, after 13 months in line, by the 25th U.S. Infantry Division and its attached Turkish Brigade. News reports said the Marine commanders protested, wanting the division to remain on the line. The 11th Marines artillery units and the 1st Tank Battalion did remain up front.

In reserve, the division served as a counterattack force and pursued a training program that included two regimental amphibious exercises. A third was cancelled because of the impending POW repatriation. On June 1, Maj. Gen. Pollock gave over command of the division to Maj. Gen. Randolph McC. Pate, a veteran of the Dominican Republic, China and World War II and an experienced staff officer who had most recently commanded the 2d Marine Division at Camp Lejeune.

During the last days of May, the Chinese conquered Outposts Carson, Vegas and Elko and in the middle of June drove ROK units back more than 4,000 yards in the center of the UN front. In the former action, the 25th Division was supported by Marine artillery, tanks and planes.

While the division was in reserve, the 1st Marine Aircraft Wing continued to fly as part of the Fifth Air Force. Pilots had to fly a hundred combat missions before being rotated. In April, the wing flew 3,850 combat sorties, including 1,319 in close support. On April 17, VMF-115 set a record with 262 sorties in a single day. In one series of three interdiction strikes that day, Lt. Col. Joe L. Warren; Maj. Samuel J. Mantel, Jr., and Maj. John F. Bolt, Jr., led 23 Panther jets in firing 4,630 rounds of 20mm ammunition and dropping 22 tons of bombs on an enemy supply concentration point on the east coast. In May and June, flying was restricted by seasonal bad weather; but the wing still flew 3,359 and 3,276 sorties. By July 11, Major Bolt, who had shot down six planes in World War II, became the first Marine jet ace, with six MIG-15s downed. Between February 27, 1951, and June 11, 1953, Marine fliers had executed more than 80,000 combat sorties for the UN divisions.

The 1st Marine Division went back into the line on July 7 and 8 and immediately entered heavy fighting. Since Outposts Carson, Vegas and Elko had all been lost in the meantime, the eastern sector of the division front was now considerably weakened; and Outposts Berlin and East Berlin were more vulnerable to enemy attack. On the night of July 7, the Chinese attacked those two outposts, only 325 yards from the MLR. Berlin, manned by both 7th Marines and Turkish troops, re-pulsed the onslaught; but East Berlin, 500 yards to the east, fell in close-in fighting. Two relief platoons were forced to return to the MLR. At dawn, only 18 men were still holding out at Berlin. A two-platoon unit tried to retake East Berlin at mid-morning. Chinese shells reduced the first platoon to 20 men; the second platoon fought at the outpost's main trenchline and by 12:33 P.M. recaptured East Berlin. There were only 20 able-bodied Marines left after an hour of hand-to-hand fighting in which Marines literally threw Chinese down the reverse slope. That night, the Chinese attacked both outposts again; and the rein-forced Marines pushed them back. In the two-night battle, the 7th Marines had 19 killed, 2 captured and 140 wounded.

It was a period of monsoon rains and for the next ten days there was little action. Patrols occasionally ran into ambushes and fire fights.

On July 19, the truce negotiators at Panmunjom reached final agreement on all the remaining points in dispute. But that night, a Chinese battalion again struck at the Berlin complex. Thirty-seven Marines were then on East Berlin and 44 on Berlin. In a fierce two-hour battle, both outposts were overrun. A decision was made not to try to recapture them; and finally, a defense-in-depth replaced the outpost system. Artillery tanks and air blasted the now-enemy-held positions. Fifty Marines had been killed, 12 captured and 118 wounded.

The 1st Marines replaced the 7th Marines in the line on July 26; but during the transfer period, the Chinese attacked late on the twenty-fourth. This time their targets were Hills 111 and 119 on the MLR itself. Hill 119, called Boulder City, was directly behind the former Berlin outposts, and Hill 111, to the far right at the eastern end of the division's line. The attack on Hill 111 was a diversion but it temporarily penetrated the Marine lines. The main enemy force hit Boulder City, and hand-to-hand combat developed along 700 yards of frontline trenches. G Company, 1st Marines was cut to half strength. I Company came up in relief, but the Chinese intercepted a coded message and their artillery created 35 more casualties as G Company moved to the rear.

In the 5th Marines' sector, the Chinese struck at Outposts Esther and Dagmar. They seized part of the forward trenches at Esther. The H Company defenders led by 2d Lt. William E. Bates hung onto the rear trenches. Flamethrowers and supporting fire finally broke up the attack by 6:40 A.M. Twelve Marines were killed and 98 wounded in the battle.

The fighting at Hill 119 continued into the early morning hours. The enemy held most of the forward trenches and briefly occupied the rocky crest itself. Capt. Louis J. Sartor of I Company, 1st Marines led a counterattack at 1:30 A.M. Two hours later, the MLR had been restored; and by 5:30, additional Marines had secured Hill 119. The fighting there went on through the morning of the 25th before the last of the enemy were driven off the forward slope of Boulder City. That night, the Chinese attacked again and reached the trenchline. They killed 19 Marines and wounded 125 before being driven off. Since July 24, Marine casualties totaled 43 killed and 316 wounded. One of the dead was Staff Sgt. Ambrosio Guillen of El Paso, Texas, the last Marine to earn the Medal of Honor in Korea. Though critically wounded in hand-to-hand fighting, he rallied his men, refused medical attention and saw that the wounded were evacuated before he succumbed.

On the night of July 26, with the armistice approaching, the

Chinese made two final lunges at the 1st Marines on Hill 119. This was to be the last ground action for the 1st Marine Division in Korea. Had the Chinese succeeded in winning Boulder City, they would have forced the Eighth Army to withdraw, under the terms of the armistice, so that it no longer controlled all of the Imjin River. But the Marines held.

It had been a costly finale for both sides. Eighth Army officers estimated that the Chinese suffered 72,000 casualties in July. The Marines alone had 1,611. During those last weeks, the enemy had made substantial local gains at key points along the UN front.

On Monday morning, July 27, 1953, the armistice agreement was signed at Panmunjom. Marine Col. James C. Murray, who had been involved in the truce talks for two years, was in charge of the UN Command staff group that worked out the final line of demarcation.

The war was finished after three years, one month and two days of battle. The Marines had 4,262 killed in battle and 20,038 wounded. Forty-two Marines had been awarded the Medal of Honor for valor—26 of them posthumously. When the armistice became effective at 10 P.M., thousands of white star cluster shells illuminated the sky all along the 155-mile front.

8
The Marine POWs

Two hundred and twenty-one U.S. Marines had been captured by the enemy. Forty-nine were officers and 172 enlisted men; 190 were ground troopers and 31 aviators. All but one of the aviators were officers. By one estimate, one in every 570 of the Marines who served in Korea was taken prisoner in contrast with the U.S. Army's one in 150.[121]

Of the 221 Marines captured, 194 (43 officers and 151 enlisted men) returned. The Marine POW survival rate was 87 percent. The survival rate of all U.S. POWs was only 62 percent.

Of the 194 Marines who made it back, 172 returned in the two prisoner exchanges, 18 escaped in May 1951; two enlisted men escaped within a week after being taken, and two others were released by the enemy after a brief captivity.

Fifteen wounded Marines had been returned in April's Operation Little Switch, and 157 were repatriated after the armistice in Operation Big Switch. Six corpsmen who had served with the 1st Marine Division were also returned then.

During Operation Big Switch, Marine Col. Albert F. Metze, who had been a POW himself in World War II, was the Processing Unit Commander. On August 5, the first day of the exchange, Marine Pfc. Alfred P. Graham, Jr., was the fifth man to be processed. Sgt. Robert J. Coffee and Pfc. Pedron E. Aviles were the only other Marines returned the first day.

It took a month before all 3,597 U.S. servicemen were returned during Big Switch. The Marine who had been a POW longest was Capt. Jesse V. Booker, who had been shot down on August 7, 1950. Col. Frank H. Schwable, the senior Marine captured, and Maj. Walter R. Harris were released on September 6, 1953, the last day of the switch.

Two of the most renowned Marine POWs were Lt. Col. William G. Thrash, a VMA-121 pilot, and Maj. John N. Mc-Laughlin, who had been taken prisoner in the November 1950 ambush of Task Force Drysdale. Both had defied their captors throughout their long imprisonment and provided strong leadership for their fellow captives.

Of the 190 ground Marines captured, 42 were taken prisoner in the Task Force Drysdale debacle, 40 in the outpost fighting in October 1952 and 39 in the final outpost battles in March and July 1953. Those groups totaled 121 and left only 69 ground Marines captured during the rest of the war.

Three Marines captured with Task Force Drysdale had been POWs in World War II: Staff Sgt. Charles L. Harrison, who had been captured on Wake Island; Warrant Officer Felix J. McCool, captured on Corregidor; and Master Sgt. Frederick J. Stumpges, a survivor of the Bataan Death March.

In general, the Marine POWs who returned felt that they had been given much harsher physical treatment by the North Koreans than by the Chinese. The Chinese used mental pressure rather than physical brutality and made great efforts to indoctrinate them politically. The Chinese attempted to separate "progressive" or cooperative prisoners from "reactionary" or resistant ones. Major McLaughlin in particular was subjected to intimidation and maltreatment because he was a leader among the officer-prisoners and persistently non-cooperative toward his captors.

Among the worst punishment, in addition to beatings and near-starvation, was solitary confinement in a vermin-infested "hole" in a crouched position for 56 hours or more. Second Lt. Roland L. McDaniel was confined to the hole for ten days and emerged with pneumonia and tuberculosis. Second Lt. Richard L. Still was sentenced to the hole for three months for trying to escape. First Lt. Felix F. Ferranto spent more than two years of his 33 months as a prisoner in solitary confinement or isolated with small units of "non-cooperative" POWs. And two aviators, Capt. Gerald Fink and Capt. Arthur Wagner, received especially severe treatment for their resistance.

In January 1952, six ranking officers, including Major McLaughlin, were sentenced to solitary confinement for periods of three to six months. After that, tension among the prisoners in

Camp 2 was highly charged with suspicion of informers and opportunists until Lt. Col. Thrash arrived in June and restored discipline. As a result, in September, Thrash was confined to solitary for eight months. On one occasion, he was beaten and thrown outside half naked in sub-zero weather and nearly died.

On November 10, 1952, Marines at Camp 2 managed defiantly to observe the traditional Marine Corps Birthday by making a cake with stolen eggs, sugar and flour and celebrating with stolen rice wine.

During the last months of the war, with the approach of the truce agreement, the treatment of prisoners improved. They received warmer clothing and better medical care. Clearly, the Communists wanted to repatriate the prisoners in as good condition as possible for propaganda purposes.

In the summer of 1952, the Chinese gained a propaganda weapon that had a world-wide effect. They extracted false confessions from two U.S. Air Force fliers that the United States had used germ warfare by dropping bacteriological bombs on North Korean towns. After that, all captured fliers were subjected to severe stress, beatings and torture to confess to such war crimes. Marine Master Sgt. John T. Cain, an enlisted pilot with VMO-6, refused to make such a confession even though he was confined to the hole and actually taken before a firing squad. Capt. John P. Flynn of VMF(N)-513, who had been shot down over Japan in World War II, also withstood brutal interrogation and refused to "confess."

Thirty-nine Air Force men and one Marine did succumb to intense pressure and torture and made confessions. The Marine was Colonel Schwable, the 1st MAW Chief of Staff, who had been shot down on a reconnaissance flight on July 8, 1952. Schwable was held in solitary confinement until December, interrogated incessantly, kept near starvation and refused medical attention. He finally signed a false statement. The forty-five-year old Annapolis graduate and veteran of 20 years' service had been a pioneer night-fighter pilot who had shot down four planes as commander of VMF(N)-531 in World War II. A Court of Inquiry in 1954 decided that he had resisted "to the limit of his ability before giving in." The Court recommended that Schwable should not be disciplined but judged that his usefulness as a Marine officer had been "seriously impaired."[122]

One enlisted Marine POW was disciplined for cooperating with the enemy by writing a pro-Communist magazine article. Fourteen Marines admitted signing peace appeals or petitions but were judged not to have acted dishonorably.[123]

Despite published reports that no American POWs attempted to escape from captivity in this war, Marine Corps records show that 18 Marines and a U.S. Army interpreter attached to the 1st Marine Division escaped in May 1951 after several months as prisoners. The Marines were 1st Lt. Frank E. Cold and 17 enlisted men (including Staff Sgt. Harrison, the Wake Island survivor). They had been brought south to perform work details behind the enemy lines. When an artillery barrage dispersed their guards, they fled in the opposite direction. They made their position known to an Army observation pilot with panels of wallpaper stripped from a Korean house and were rescued by three Army tanks.

In addition, two enlisted Marines escaped after a few weeks' captivity and two were released after four days in enemy hands. Although no Americans escaped from a permanent enemy prison camp and reached friendly lines, the Corps credits Marines with seven unsuccessful escape attempts, for which they were severely punished by their captors. First Lt. Robert J. Gillette managed to evade his captors for several weeks and Capt. Paul L. Martelli, for 10 days.

Five Marines later received awards for their conduct while prisoners of war: Lt. Col. Thrash, Major McLaughlin, Major Harris, Captain Flynn and Master Sgt. Cain.

But the nation was distressed by the behavior of many American POWs in Korea. Said one investigator, "Almost one of every three American prisoners in Korea was guilty of some sort of collaboration with the enemy. . . . some of them had behaved brutally to their fellow-prisoners."[124] As a result, in 1955, Secretary of Defense Charles E. Wilson appointed an Advisory Committee on Prisoners of War, headed by Assistant Secretary of Defense Carter L. Burgess and including among its ten members retired Marine Maj. Gen. Merritt A. Edson. The committee recommended and President Eisenhower put into effect a new Code of Conduct, which said clearly that a prisoner of war should give only his name, rank, service number and date of birth. It said he will not surrender willingly. If captured, he will resist and try to escape. He will do nothing that might be harmful to his fellow prisoners or disloyal to his country and its allies. After the record of the Korean war, such a Code of Conduct appeared necessary.

The Marine POW record had been clearly superior. When the United States Congress investigated the issue of prisoner-of-war conduct in Korea, the Senate report summarized: "The United States Marine Corps, the Turkish troops, and the Colombians as groups, did not succumb to the pressures exerted upon them by the Communists and did not co-operate or collaborate with the enemy. For this they deserve greatest admiration and credit."[125]

9
The Korean Experience

The 1st Marine Division remained in Korea for more than a year and a half after the armistice was signed. One regiment, initially the 5th Marines, defended the division's sector north of the Imjin River, while the other two stood guard behind the river. The forward regiment was also responsible for security in the UN's half of the division's 28-mile-long slice of the 4,000-yard-wide demilitarized zone.

In August 1954, the 3rd Marine Division under Maj. Gen. Robert H. Pepper, and MAG-11 and MAG-16 came out and took up stations in Japan to provide an amphibious capability there. The 1st Marine Division was relieved in March 1955 by the U.S. 24th Infantry Division and returned to Camp Pendleton after an absence of nearly five years. In mid-1956, the 1st Marine Aircraft Wing transferred from Korea to the Naval Air Station at Iwakuni, Japan.

This had been a major war in the number of men involved, the duration of the fighting, the number of casualties and the significance of the conflict to the world. It ended pretty much where it began—at the 38th Parallel. North Korea gained 850 square miles and South Korea gained 2,350 square miles north of the 1950 boundary. But the results could not be measured on the ground. Whether the war had been a defeat for the United States and its allies, a stalemate or a defeat for the Communist powers depended entirely on the perception of the viewer. Both sides had tried to reunite Korea by force and failed. But the Communist world had been shown that its armies could not overrun a non-communist neighbor, and the United States had been shown that even its enormous power had limits.

The price paid for these lessons was tremendous. Communist military casualties were estimated at 1.4 million. The United Nations had 996,937 killed, wounded and missing. Of this total, the Republic of Korea's casualties were 850,000. United States casualties were 136,937: 33,629 were battle deaths and 103,308 wounded in action. The U.S. Marine Corps had 30,544 casualties; 4,262 killed, 244 non-battle deaths and 26,038 wounded. For the Corps, these were more casualties than in any conflict until that date except World War II.

There had been 74,279 men and women on active duty in the Corps when the war began. An estimated 424,000 Marines served during the hostilities; the peak was September 30,1953, when 261,343 were in uniform. The greatest strength in Korea was in April 1953, when 35,306 ground and air Marines were there.

The war created several fundamental problems for the Corps. Perhaps the most important was the use of the 1st Marine Division, after Inchon, as one more infantry division engaged in a major land war. Although the division (with the Korean Marines attached) was the largest in the Eighth Army and was respected as a crack outfit, Marine analysts recognized that its role during most of the war "could be considered an inefficient, though not ineffective use of Marines."[126] As a military organization specialized in amphibious warfare, the Corps was being misused. Essentially, this occurred because of the Marines' own desire to be a fighting force-in-readiness. They were ready and able and were used as needed.

Utilization of the Marine division as part of a large land army also led to the loss of integration with its own air arm. The 1st Marine Aircraft Wing flew 127,496 combat sorties in Korea, far more than the 80,000 sorties flown by all Marine aviation in World War II. But less than a third of the Korean sorties, about 39,500, were flown in the Corps' aviation specialty: close support of ground troops. And after October 1950, when the 1st MAW was put under operational control of the Fifth Air Force for the rest of the war, it primarily flew interdiction and bombing raids deep into enemy territory. The 1st MAW's commanding general had "virtually no tactical control over his own units."[127]

The issue was doubly frustrating because the interdiction program failed to prevent the enemy from building up its troop and artillery strength. The Commander of the Seventh Fleet said after the war, "The interdiction program was a failure."[128] And General Ridgway wrote years later, "In Korea, where we had air mastery over practically the whole peninsula, MacArthur himself acknowledged our inability to isolate the battle area by air bombardment or to choke off the flow of reinforcements and supply."[129]

Not only did the Air Force give close support a low priority, but differences in close support doctrines and tactics were never resolved. Where Marine procedures filled close support requests in five to 15 minutes, Air Force procedures, Marines said, resulted in delays from 30 minutes to nearly four hours. Toward the war's end, some of the conflicts were eased by informal understandings, increased cooperation and greater decentralization of control among Air Force, Army and Marine commanders.

Marine pilots saw a lot of action. They downed 35 enemy planes. In addition to Major Bolt's six kills, Maj. Alexander J. Gillis and Maj. John H. Glenn destroyed three MIGs each and Maj. Roy L. Reed, two. By late 1952, the F9F Panther jet had pretty much replaced the venerable Corsair. Marine aviators suffered 258 killed and 174 wounded in action. A total of 436 planes were lost in combat or operational accidents.

At the same time, the war enabled the Corps to make enormous progress in the use of the helicopter and the evolution of vertical envelopment. In September 1951, the Marines had executed "the first helicopter lift of a combat unit in history."[130] The helicopter also cut to minutes the time needed to carry wounded to hospitals; it saved lives. And it swiftly laid miles of communications wire that would have taken weeks by men on the ground. HMR-161 lifted 60,046 men and 7.5 million pounds of cargo during the war. It evacuated 2,748 wounded, and VMO-6 flew out 7,067 wounded.

Another major change in the Corps during this war was the integration of black Americans into Marine units. At the war's beginning, there were 1,965 black enlisted men on active duty; by 1943, there were 19 officers and 14,468 men. The first black officer to lead Marines in combat was Lt. William K. Jenkins of Elizabeth, New Jersey, who served with B Company, 7th Marines. The Marines in Korea had only one black pilot, 2d Lt. Frank E. Petersen, Jr., of Topeka, Kansas, who flew 64 combat missions with VMF-212 and earned the Distinguished Flying Cross. Petersen was the fourth black to become a naval aviator. The first, Navy Ensign Jesse L. Brown, was killed on December 4, 1950, flying close support for the Marines breaking out of the Chosin Reservoir.

One black enlisted man who made an outstanding record in combat was Pfc. A. C. Clark of Minden, Louisiana. An automatic rifleman with H Company, 5th Marines, Clark earned the Bronze Star in August 1952 for rescuing his platoon leader, who had been wounded on a combat patrol. He earned the Silver Star the following December 13 when, although wounded, he covered the evacuation of two wounded Marines, killed three of the enemy and silenced a machine gun.

In tactical terms, the static warfare that dominated most of the war reduced the 1st Marine Division's combat and amphibious efficiency. Amphibious assault was an offensive capability that received no call in Korea after 1950. Individual unit amphibious readiness was rated in mid-1953 at between 25 and 60 percent.

In western Korea, the division tried to solve the problem of being spread over so wide a front by setting up a long, thin MLR with outposts. These vulnerable outposts were manned by too few Marines to stand off determined enemy attacks. The outpost system of defense was expensive in lives. Ultimately, as vital outposts were lost to the enemy, the division switched to the defense-in-depth posture used by its neighbor, the British 1st Commonwealth Division, and by the Chinese, who built entrenched defenses to a depth of four to 14 miles behind their own MLR.

During the long period of static warfare, Marine leaders felt that some UN policies hampered combat aggressiveness and counter-defense measures. One example cited was the restriction late in 1952 on previously encouraged large-scale raids to capture prisoners. Plans for raids of company size or larger thereafter required the approval of higher headquarters. The purpose was to minimize casualties in forays initiated by lower-echelon commanders. But regimental and battalion commanders felt such limitations prevented them from capitalizing on local targets of opportunity. In a war that had settled into an essentially political and propaganda confrontation, the cost of such "aggressive" operations was often unjustifiable. The offensive-minded tradition and training of Marine professionals made this dispute particularly acute, while higher headquarters worried about overall casualty rates and the fragility of the truce negotiations.

The Chinese, on the other hand, appeared more willing to take large numbers of casualties to achieve local gains. They became expert in limited-objective warfare. They developed adroit "creeping tactics," digging trenches toward UN positions, and built up artillery strength to hammer UN troops. They would invariably smother an advanced outpost with artillery fire, make an initial frontal attack that was actually a feint and envelop the outpost from the rear. At the same time, they would set up an ambush behind the outpost to prevent its defenders from escaping and reinforcements from reaching them.

The prolonged outpost warfare was predominantly night fighting, and the Chinese "had a marked superiority in night operations."[131] They were also skilled in the construction and camouflage of bunkers, trenches and tunnels and artillery and mortar emplacements. Their well-prepared reverse slope fortifications were often impervious to anything less than 1,000-pound bombs.

The Marines gained a high respect for Chinese combat effectiveness, the leadership of their officers and the patience and tenacity of their soldiers. The Chinese soldier traveled light and, armed with a submachine "burp" gun, achieved great mobility over the traditionally more heavily burdened American fighting man.

This mobility gave the enemy the advantage of tactical surprise in the darkness. Often, American soldiers and Marines were unaware of the enemy's presence until he was suddenly within grenade-throwing range. The military historian S. L. A. Marshall wrote of the Chinese that by 1953, "They had become as tenacious and earth-seeking as ants, and in that lay a great part of their success. Two and one half years of war in Korea were a bonanza for Communist China. On that training ground her armies became as skilled as any in the world in the techniques of hitting, evading and surviving."[132] The Chinese were tough and able opponents, prepared to resist the extension of American power onto the Asian mainland.

In this war, the United States had proved that it would help defend a nation that was prepared to defend itself against aggression. But as the Vietnam war was to demonstrate, some in the United States had not yet recognized the fact that it could not effectively project its power into Asia at will.

As for the Marine Corps, in the Korean war's first months, it had fulfilled its modern roles as a force-in-readiness and as experts in amphibious assault; and throughout the long conflict, it had proved itself again an elite fighting Corps that would do the job assigned with professionalism and courage.

A Marine sergeant is dwarfed beside the thirty-two-foot high figures of the Marine Corps War Memorial. The statue, modeled on Joe Rosenthal's photograph of the Iwo Jima flag-raising, was sculpted by Felix de Weldon and dedicated at the Arlington National Cemetery on November 10, 1954.
Wide World Photos

SEMPER FIDELIS

XIV
TUMULTUOUS
TIMES
1953-1965

1
Around the World

Between the Korean armistice in July 1953 and the Marines' landing at Da Nang, South Vietnam, on March 8, 1965, Marines met a variety of crises abroad, as Marines have throughout the nation's history. The two most critical overseas ventures during this period were the landing in Lebanon in 1958 and the intervention in the Dominican Republic in 1965. The other major events can be summarized in a brief sampling that suggests the range of the Corps' modern responsibilities.

1953: In August, the 2d Battalion, 6th Marines rescued victims of an earthquake in Greece's Ionian Islands.

1954: During the United States-supported coup against the government of Col. Jacobo Arbenz Guzman of Guatemala, the 2d Battalion, 8th Marines stood by to protect American citizens and property. On the Marine Corps Birthday, the Marine Corps memorial statue of the Iwo Jima flag-raising was officially dedicated at Arlington National Cemetery.

1955: In January, a battalion of Marines helped evacuate 26,000 Chinese to Taiwan from the Tachen Islands off the Chinese mainland. In October, Marine pilots brought emergency supplies to flood-inundated Tampico, Mexico.

1956: Gen. Randolph McC. Pate succeeded General Shepherd as Commandant of the Corps. On January 7, Master Sgt. Bertrum E. Strickling and Cpl. Thomas E. Rhodes of the Marine Security Guard used small arms and tear gas to fight off a stone-throwing mob trying to break into the American Consulate General in Jerusalem. E Company, 2d Marines reinforced the U.S. Naval Air Station at Port Lyautey, Morocco, during fighting between the French and Moroccans. In November, during the Suez crisis, the 3rd Battalion, 2d Marines evacuated U.S. nationals from Alexandria, Egypt, and a UN truce team from Haifa, Israel.

1957: In February, the 3rd Marines stood by during an Indonesian revolt. Marine helicopters assisted flood victims in Ceylon and Spain. The Commandant restored the post of Sergeant Major of the Marine Corps, the first occupant being Sgt. Major William Bestwick.

1958: On May 13, when Vice President Richard M. Nixon's car was stoned by a mob in Caracas, Venezuela, the 1st Battalion, 6th Marines was flown to U.S. Caribbean bases. In June, sailors and Marines from the Guantanamo Naval Base in Cuba were kidnapped and later released by forces of Fidel Castro; and in July, Marines entered Cuban territory to protect the base's water supply during fighting between the Cuban army and Castro's forces. In mid-year, MAG-11 arrived in Taiwan to strengthen Nationalist Chinese air defenses after the People's Republic of China began bombarding the Kinmen Islands of Quemoy and Little Quemoy.

1960: Bypassing nine senior officers, Maj. Gen. David M. Shoup, Medal of Honor winner at Tarawa, succeeded Gen. Randolph McC. Pate as Commandant of the Corps. In March, Marines helped rescue earthquake victims at Agadir, Morocco. In June, when White House Press Secretary James C. Hagerty and Ambassador Douglas MacArthur II were besieged by a mob in Tokyo, a Marine helicopter rescued them from their car.

1961: In May, Marines from the 3rd Battalion, 6th Marines and HMR-262 helped with relief work after an earthquake in Turkey. In November, eight helicopters from HMR-264 aided hurricane victims in British Honduras.

1962: The M-14 rifle replaced the M-1 and the M-60 machine gun, the venerable Browning. On February 20, Marine Lt. Col. John H. Glenn, Jr., of New Concord, Ohio, orbited the earth three times in the first manned American space capsule.* In May, the 3rd Marine Expeditionary Brigade, commanded by Brig. Gen. Ormond R. Simpson, landed in Thailand. Before the

*In the next dozen years, eight more Marines and former Marines became astronauts. Among them, Lt. Col. R. Walter Cunningham flew in Apollo 7, the first manned Apollo mission. Fred Haise was on the aborted Apollo 13 mission. Lt. Col. Jack Lousma flew in the second Skylab mission in 1973. Lt. Col. Gerald P. Carr commanded Skylab 3, the record-setting 84-day earth-orbiting mission in 1973–74. Vance D. Brand flew with the Russians in the joint Apollo-Soyuz space mission in 1975.

last Marines left Thailand early in August, 5,000 Marines had been sent there. In October, the entire 189,000-man Marine Corps participated in the worldwide alert of U.S. military forces during the Cuban missile crisis. The 5th Marine Expeditionary Brigade of more than 11,000 men sailed from Camp Pendleton for the Caribbean, and the 2d Marine Division was deployed to Key West, Florida, and Caribbean waters.

1963: In January, Marines from the Eighth and Eye Barracks in Washington helped keep watch over the painting of the Mona Lisa while it was on display in the National Gallery of Art.

1964: Gen. Wallace M. Greene, Jr., an Annapolis graduate from Waterbury, Vermont, succeeded General Shoup as Commandant of the Corps.

Throughout the period, Marines engaged in amphibious exercises around the world as well as cold-weather training in California and jungle training in Panama.

2
Tragedy at Ribbon Creek—1956

The Corps' most traumatic experience during this period occurred at home. At Parris Island, South Carolina, on Sunday night, April 8, 1956, an angry drill instructor, Staff Sgt. Matthew C. McKeon, marched 74 Marine recruits into a tidal swamp called Ribbon Creek. Six young men were drowned.

The tragedy shocked the nation and tarnished public support of the Marine Corps. Calls were widespread to reform the Corps' recruit-training practices, which gave non-commissioned drill instructors (DIs) virtually absolute control over their "boot" charges. The newly installed Commandant, General Pate, relieved the general commanding the Recruit Depot and created a recruit training command to effect reforms. He explained, "In a very real sense the Marine Corps is on trial for the tragedy of Ribbon Creek just as surely as is Sergeant McKeon."[1]

After a 15-day-long public trial, Staff Sgt. McKeon was found guilty of negligent homicide and drinking on duty. He was acquitted of oppressing recruits and of manslaughter. He was sentenced to be confined at hard labor and forfeit some pay for nine months, to be reduced to the rank of private and to be given a bad conduct discharge. The Secretary of the Navy reduced the sentence to three months' confinement at hard labor and demotion to private. Following the trial, McKeon spent only 12 more nights in the Parris Island brig.

The high point of the trial was the appearance, at the request of the defense lawyers, of retired Lt. Gen. "Chesty" Puller. Puller defended the Corps. He said, "The definition of military training is success in battle. . . . I'll quote Napoleon. He stated that the most important thing in military training is discipline. Without discipline an army becomes a mob. . . . In my opinion

822

the reason American troops made out so poorly in the Korean war was mostly due to lack of night training. . . . I would say that this night march was and is a deplorable accident."[2]

In the year after the Parris Island "death march," 197 drill instructors were relieved for a variety of causes; and an emotional battle raged between Marine generals and many veteran officers and noncoms. Under public and Congressional pressure, the Corps ordered an end to "hazing and maltreatment" of recruits. But some young combat leaders argued that a civilian teenager had to be kicked around if he was to be hardened enough to obey a sergeant's order to crawl forward into enemy fire, even to his death. The DIs were warned that they could no longer order recruits to dry-shave while double-timing, "to march in swamps, marshes or streams," to scream obscene phrases about themselves. DIs were forbidden to bury recruits in dirt, lock them in wall lockers or scrub them with sand.

But the conversion of a civilian youngster into a battle-ready Marine continued to be a tough and toughening process. Brig. Gen. Wallace M. Greene, Jr., who was assigned to reform training at Parris Island, said, "A DI's real reward is being able to shape men into Marines." And Tech. Sgt. John H. Groves, a Korean veteran and one of the best of Parris Island's DIs at the time, added, "We have to train men so we can tell them to go forward and draw enemy fire—and we're not going to reward them with a 72-hour pass."[3]

3
Landing in Lebanon—1958

Bikini-clad sunbathers and soft drink vendors greeted F Company, 2d Marines when it "stormed" ashore on Red Beach four miles south of Beirut, Lebanon, on the afternoon of July 15, 1958. Four companies of Marines drove 700 yards inland and secured the Beirut International Airport. There was no opposition at all.

The Marines landed because Lebanon's President Camille Chamoun had asked for help to restore peace in his unstable, riot-torn little country on the eastern end of the Mediterranean. Lt. Col. Harry A. Hadd's 2d Battalion, 2d Marines was the United States Sixth Fleet landing force nearest Lebanon when President Eisenhower made the decision to intervene. Thirteen hours later, Hadd's Marines were ashore.

The landing followed in the long tradition of U.S. Marine interventions. The Middle East was torn by another outburst of the disruption that bubbled up repeatedly after the British and French presence had been diminished by World War II. The entire strategic, oil-rich area had become a hotbed of nationalism and a pressure point in the Cold War.

In 1954, Gamal Abdul Nasser had risen to power in Egypt and excited a militant pan-Arabism. After he made an arms deal with the Communists, the Arab world split, Jordan and Iraq siding with the Western powers and Egypt and Syria, with the Soviet Union. In July 1956, Nasser nationalized the Suez Canal. In response, the Israelis, British and French attacked Egypt until the United Nations and the United States forced them to stop.

Throughout this turmoil, Lebanon, smaller than Connecticut, tried to walk a tightrope. It chose that pose because of both its commercial interests and its conglomerate population—half

[For the location of places in the Mediterranean see map No. 2 in the map section.—*Au.*]

its people belonging to several Christian communities and most of the rest Moslem, with some Jews and Druzes. After nearly 80 years of French hegemony in 1943, the Lebanese had worked out a domestic political formula with a Christian president and a Moslem premier. The situation was highly explosive.

International events hammered at Lebanon's delicate internal compromises. When President Chamoun refused to break with Great Britain and France over the 1956 Suez crisis, his Moslem premier resigned. The following spring, Chamoun was the only Middle Eastern leader to accept the Eisenhower Doctrine, which promised military and economic assistance to any Middle Eastern nation threatened by Communist aggression. Then, in February 1958, Chamoun's antagonists, Egypt and Syria, merged into the United Arab Republic.

Tension inside Lebanon mounted that summer as Chamoun's six-year term approached its end. The constitution prohibited a president from succeeding himself; but Chamoun controlled a large majority in the parliament, where presidents were elected. Tension turned to violence on May 8; the anti-Chamoun editor of the Beirut newspaper *Telegraph* was murdered. Riots broke out in Tripoli, an oil port and Moslem center in northern Lebanon. Led by Rashid Karami, rebels burned the United States Information Agency building there. On May 12, leaders of the Basta, the Moslem quarter of Beirut, began a general strike led by Saeb Salam, a former premier. Rebel groups in various parts of the country rose to arms. Conditions in Lebanon became chaotic.

Gen. Fuad Chehab, the Christian commander of the Lebanese army, feared the army's disintegration into Moslem and Christian factions. He tried to stay neutral and contain the anti-government forces in their strongholds in Tripoli, the Basta and the central countryside.

President Chamoun asked the United States, Britain and France to intervene if the situation got out of hand. On June 6, Lebanon filed a complaint against the United Arab Republic with the United Nations' Security Council, which then sent observers to Lebanon.

Chamoun's internal troubles came to be seen as part of an international crisis on July 14, when military officers in Iraq deposed the pro-Western government and murdered the king and premier. King Hussein of Jordan feared he would be overthrown next. The Western position in the Middle East seemed threatened. Chamoun formally appealed for help, and President Eisenhower immediately ordered Gen. Nathan F. Twining, Chairman of the Joint Chiefs of Staff, to land the amphibious units of the U.S. Sixth Fleet.

The crisis caught the Sixth Fleet off balance. Its landing force had been built up to the 2d Provisional Marine Force led by Brig. Gen. Sidney S. Wade, who had commanded the 1st Marines in the latter days of the Korean war. But on July 14, Wade's force was divided: The 1st Battalion, 8th Marines was north of Malta on its way home. The 3rd Battalion, 6th Marines, which was relieving the homebound battalion, was enroute from Crete to Athens. Only Hadd's 2d Battalion, 2d Marines, off the southern coast of Cyprus, was in position to land in Lebanon on 24-hour notice. And even the Landing Ship, Dock carrying its artillery battery, shore party detachment, underwater demolition team, heavy equipment and two of its M-48 tanks, was steaming to Malta for repairs. Fortunately, the LSD *Fort Snelling* supporting the 3rd Battalion, 6th Marines, was near Rhodes and some 400 miles from Lebanon.

Earlier, Marine Maj. Victor Stoyanow, a Korean veteran, had traveled to Beirut incognito and inspected the possible landing beaches. The Marines' contingency plan called for one Battalion Landing Team to go ashore northeast of Beirut and a second one to land south of the city and seize the airport. When this second BLT was relieved, it would move into the city. The military objective was to guard the Lebanese government against an invasion by neighboring Syria's army of 40,000 men and 200 Russian T-34 tanks.

At 12:30 A.M. July 15 (Beirut time), Adm. Arleigh A. Burke, Chief of Naval Operations, notified Adm. James L. Holloway, Jr., in London and Vice Adm. Charles R. Brown, commanding the Sixth Fleet, of Eisenhower's decision to intervene. The Marines were ordered to land south of Beirut at 3 P.M. and grab the airport.

The chance that the Marines would face opposition was remote. It was possible that rebel groups would try to repulse the invasion, that factions of the Lebanese army might resist or that the Syrian army would counterattack. But none of these was a serious threat, and none happened.

President Chamoun welcomed the promptness of the intervention. But when U.S. Ambassador Robert McClintock informed General Chehab an hour and a half before the landing, he was "visibly upset."[4] He had not approved the invasion and feared that it would split his army and incite the rebels. The general asked the ambassador to have the Marines stay aboard their ships and come around to Beirut's harbor and unload only a few tanks. McClintock agreed and tried to radio the Sixth Fleet, but it was too late to stop the Marines. Their amphibian tractors reached Red Beach at 3:04 and rumbled onto the airfield. E Company cleared the civilians from the beach, G Company secured the airport terminal and F and H Companies set up defensive positions around the airfield. No shots were fired.

At 3:30, Ambassador McClintock's naval attache arrived at the beach and told Hadd that the ambassador and General Chehab wanted the Marine battalion to return to its ships and land only its tanks on the Beirut docks. Hadd and then Capt. Victor B. McCrea, USN, the amphibious force commander, both refused. Vice Adm. Brown approved McCrea's decision.

President Chamoun, who had by now received reports that he was to be assassinated, asked McClintock over secret voice radio to send a Marine company with tanks to guard the Presidential Palace in Beirut. McClintock rushed a military attache to Hadd, who, believing his battalion was "extended to the maximum," again refused the ambassador's request.[5] Shortly thereafter, Captain McCrea directed Hadd to supply a 100-man detail. But by then, General Chehab, under McClintock's pressure, had promised that the army would guarantee Chamoun's safety. Hadd said later that if the order had not been rescinded, he would have told McCrea that the Marines could not comply. They already held a long perimeter; they lacked shore party support, and the Palace was next to the rebel-held Basta. McClintock was critical of what he regarded as the Marines' lack of flexibility. The hurry-up invasion was not prepared for all contingencies.

In cooperation with the Lebanese army, the Marines kept the airport open for commercial air traffic. McClintock asked Hadd and McCrea to meet with him in the American Embassy. But none of the three Americans was willing to leave his post. When McClintock insisted, Hadd and McCrea finally called on the ambassador separately and tried to resolve the "bizarre disagreements"[6] between the American diplomatic and military leaders. McClintock later described the meeting with McCrea: "The captain did arrive, puffing, accepted a large bourbon and soda, and said, 'Ambassador, by our landing today we have prevented an economic depression in the United States!' "[7]

The combination of tension and farce continued as the amphibious force tried to unload its ships. On shore, wheeled vehicles could not negotiate the soft sand; and off shore, an overlooked sandbar prevented the LSTs from beaching. The Marines had to improvise until *Fort Snelling* showed up that evening. Even then, the landing craft carrying the shore party was caught on the sandbar and did not reach the beach until 2:30 A.M. And the tanks arrived ashore short of ammunition. As Lt. Col. Hadd commented later, "the delay in the beaching of the causeway and the unloading of the LSTs would have been disastrous if the landing had been opposed."[8]

Early the next morning, the 3rd Battalion, 6th Marines, commanded by Lt. Col. Robert M. Jenkins, landed over Red Beach. Brig. Gen. Wade ordered Hadd's battalion to prepare to advance into the capital. Wade drove ahead into the city and met with McClintock at the embassy. When Wade arrived, the ambassador was talking on the telephone with General Chehab, who was asking McClintock to halt the Marines' move into the city. Both McClintock and Chehab were concerned that Lebanese army units might try to stop the Marines.

McClintock asked Wade to hold up the Marines. The general said he had no authority to cancel the order but he would delay the move an hour. McClintock and Wade rushed to see President Chamoun, who agreed that the Marines should enter Beirut. Chehab asked for another 30-minute postponement, to which Wade agreed. He ordered Hadd to start out at 10:30.

By now, a detachment of Lebanese army tanks had set up a roadblock on the main road between the airport and the capital. Wade returned to the airport past the Lebanese tanks. Receiving another request from Chehab for a delay, Wade again postponed the Marine advance until 11 A.M.

At that hour, the Marines boarded their tanks, trucks and LVTPs and moved out. They halted in front of the Lebanese tanks, one mile from the airport. The Lebanese had their guns pointed at the Marines' lead vehicles. McClintock, Chehab, Admiral Holloway and Wade all met at the roadblock and retired to an army schoolhouse a short distance from the road to confer about the awkward situation: A United States Marine force invited ashore by the government of Lebanon was threatened by the guns of that government's army.

At the schoolhouse, General Chehab asked the Marines to take a different route into the city. Holloway and Wade refused. McClintock found a compromise: He, Chehab and Holloway would ride together at the head of the Marines into Beirut; and they would bypass the Basta. At 12:30, the column started with the ambassador's car leading the way into Beirut. The Marines took control of the port area, patrolled the bridges over the Beirut River on the road leading north to Tripoli and furnished guards for the embassy and the ambassador's residence.

During the night, a few rebels sniped at Marine positions south of the airfield; the Marines replied with rifle fire. There were no casualties on either side. The next day, two Marines in a Jeep made a wrong turn and entered the Basta. They were disarmed and taken to a rebel command post. After receiving a long lecture about American imperialism, they were released; their Jeep and weapons were later returned.

In the following days, cooperation increased between the Lebanese army and the Marines. And on the morning of July 18, the 1st Battalion, 8th Marines under Lt. Col. John H. Brickley landed at Yellow Beach four miles north of Beirut and formed a perimeter to guard the beachhead and the northern approaches to the city. They were met only by spectators, ice cream vendors and children swimming in the Mediterranean.

Not knowing what reaction the Lebanese intervention would arouse, the 2d Marine Division at Camp Lejeune and the 2d Marine Aircraft Wing at Cherry Point, North Carolina, were prepared to move to the Mediterranean; and the 3rd Battalion, 3rd Marines on Okinawa was ordered to sail for the Persian Gulf, to land in Iran or Saudi Arabia if needed. None of these units was brought to Lebanon.

On July 17, British paratroopers landed in Jordan at the request of King Hussein. On the eighteenth, the 2d Battalion, 8th Marines under Lt. Col. Alfred A. Tillman arrived at Beirut from Camp Lejeune by an airlift via Port Lyautey, Morocco. It took 34 hours in the air and 54 hours overall for 26 transport planes to bring the approximately 800 men.

The next day, the U.S. Army's 24th Airborne Brigade from Germany began arriving at the Beirut airport. This created the usual interservice problem over command of American forces ashore. Admiral Holloway asked the Joint Chiefs of Staff to name an officer to coordinate the units of the two services. The Marines wanted Lt. Gen. Edwin A. Pollock, now commanding general, Fleet Marine Force, Atlantic, to get the assignment. But the Joint Chiefs selected Maj. Gen. Paul D. Adams, USA, who took command from Brig. Gen. Wade on the twenty-sixth.

Meanwhile, the military scene was peaceful except for some harassment of the Marines' outlying positions. On July 19, a patrol from the 6th Marines went out to disperse rebels who were sniping at American planes as they landed at the airfield. The Marines got involved in a confused three-cornered fire fight with the rebels and Lebanese police in civilian clothes. A Lebanese army unit moved into the area to halt the rebel aggressiveness.

General Chehab placed Lebanese troops between the Americans and rebel positions in the Basta area. And the 1st Battalion, 8th Marines began sending out motorized platoon-strength patrols with helicopter cover. They reconnoitered as far as 20 miles east of the battalion's position north of the city. On the twenty-ninth, the Army relieved the Marines at the airport. All three Marine battalions took up positions in and northeast of the city. By the end of July, the Army and Marines had encircled Beirut with an armed perimeter. Some sniper activity continued, but the only two Marine deaths resulted from accidental shootings by other Marines. One Army sergeant was killed and another wounded by rebels.

Plans to end the intervention began as soon as it started. President Eisenhower called on the United Nations to safeguard Lebanese independence, but a Japanese resolution in the Security Council to have the UN protect Lebanon was vetoed by the Soviet Union.

Robert D. Murphy, Under Secretary of State for Political Affairs, arrived in Beirut as President Eisenhower's personal representative to speed a political solution for the internal

Lebanese problems that had instigated the intervention. Murphy and Admiral Holloway agreed that the causes of Lebanon's internal conflict were domestic and bore little relationship to international issues. Murphy worked toward getting the Lebanese to hold a presidential election.

Col. William A. Eddy, a Lebanon-born, Arabic-speaking retired Marine officer employed by the American Arabian Oil Company, arranged a meeting between Murphy and two of Saeb Salam's colleagues on July 24. Murphy assured the rebel leaders that the Americans had not landed to keep President Chamoun in office. After that, the rebel harassment of American troops lessened. In long discussions, Murphy also convinced the left-wing Druze chieftain Kamal Jumblat and the Tripoli Moslem leader Rashid Karami of the United States' intentions. These understandings led to an election on July 31. The parliament chose General Chehab as president.

The Americans began to withdraw their nearly 15,000 soldiers and Marines. On August 14, the 2d Battalion, 2d Marines re-embarked; and on September 15, the two 8th Marines' battalions sailed for the United States. The Army assumed responsibility for the Beirut dock area; and the 3rd Battalion, 6th Marines guarded the northeastern approaches to the city.

When Chehab took over the presidency on September 23, he named Rashid Karami as his prime minister with a cabinet composed chiefly of anti-Chamoun leaders. In reaction to this and to the torture and murder of a journalist of the militant Christian Phalange Party, Chamoun's supporters called a general strike of Christians. American forces stayed out of the conflict, but the Lebanese army had to break up a clash between the irregular forces of the two factions. Beirut continued to resemble an armed camp.

On September 29, the 3rd Battalion, 6th Marines left Lebanon; and the regiment's newly arrived 2d Battalion assumed the job of serving as a ready reserve for the Army troops ashore. On October 23, the Lebanese formed a more balanced government with representatives from each of the major parties. Two days later, the last U.S. Army troops left the country.

Although the intervention could not solve the bloody musical chairs of Lebanon's chronic political chaos, it helped maintain peace and demonstrated that the United States would support a small country that feared for its independence. Violence was minimized by well-disciplined American soldiers and Marines who did not permit harassment to escalate. The United States did not use its military power to sustain one partisan faction against the other, but its presence made a temporary political solution possible. And the landing force was pulled out again voluntarily as soon as possible.

4
Dominican Power Play—1965

The overthrow of two dictators—Cuba's Fulgencio Batista and the Dominican Republic's Rafael Trujillo—combined to bring the Marines back to battle in the Caribbean in 1965.

The drama began in Cuba on New Year's Day 1959 when Fidel Castro destroyed Batista's American-supported regime.* This led to the disastrous effort on April 17, 1961, to oust Castro with the Bay of Pigs invasion, planned by the Central Intelligence Agency and executed by Cuban refugees.** In October 1962 came the attempt by the Soviet Union to install nuclear weapons 90 miles off the United States coast and the nerve-wracking Cuban missile crisis. These events aroused fears in the United States over Communist exploitation of unrest elsewhere in Latin America.

Six weeks after the Bay of Pigs fiasco, Generalissimo Trujillo was shot to death. The CIA-assisted assassination generated exactly the kind of dangerous disquiet that Washington feared would lead to a Castro-oriented takeover.

In the prolonged disorder created by Trujillo's successors and rivals, the Marines landed in the Dominican Republic on April 28, 1965. "Armed and authorized to return fire, they were the first combat-ready U.S. forces to enter a Latin American country in almost forty years"[9]—ever since Franklin D. Roosevelt had apparently ended the era of unilateral military interven-

*A few weeks later, a Marine team led by Col. Robert D. Heinl, Jr., arrived in Haiti to strengthen the army of François "Papa Doc" Duvalier. The mission was withdrawn in 1963 after Duvalier declared Heinl *persona non grata.* In 1972, the State Department reported that former Marine noncoms were training Haitian militiamen through a private American corporation.

**Marine Col. Jack Hawkins played a significant role in the preparation of the Bay of Pigs invasion.

[For the location of places in the Caribbean see map No. 5 in the map section.—*Au.*]

833

tion. With Castro declaring his intention to spread his revolution, President Lyndon B. Johnson was determined to prevent a "second Cuba."

After the Marine occupation of the Dominican Republic from 1916 to 1924, Trujillo's 30-year-long tyranny had "presented the United States with no real difficulties";[10] he insured political and economic stability. And the dictator, who had been trained as a soldier by the Marines, continued his close ties to the Corps through Col. Richard M. Cutts. After Trujillo's death and with his "front man for many years" Joaquín Balaguer[11] still in the presidency, a U.S. Navy squadron with Marines aboard stayed off the Dominican coast for several months to discourage a pro-Castro revolution.

In November 1961, two of Trujillo's brothers returned to the country; and Secretary of State Dean Rusk warned them against seizing power. U.S. warships with 1,800 Marines again steamed off Santo Domingo (Ciudad Trujillo), the capital. The brothers left. In January, Balaguer was forced out of office.

The United States played an active hand in the fluid Dominican political scene and helped, through the Organization of American States, to encourage the elections that brought the popular Juan Bosch to the presidency in February 1963. The U.S. Military Assistance and Advisory Group at the time was headed by Marine Col. David C. Wolfe, who had commanded VMF(N)-513 in Korea. After Bosch was in office seven months, a military coup, supported by conservative business interests, sent him into exile in Puerto Rico. In December 1963, President Johnson finally recognized the military-imposed government on the understanding that elections would be held in 1965.

Bosch's overthrow was followed by a period of low sugar prices, unemployment, demonstrations, riots and finally civil war. The government, dominated now by Donald J. Reid Cabral, grew increasingly weak and unpopular. On Saturday, April 24, 1965, a faction in the Dominican army, seeking the return of Bosch and the 1963 constitution without elections, revolted against Reid Cabral's government. Overnight, pro-Bosch soldiers took up positions in Santo Domingo. Crowds rioted in the streets and demanded Bosch's return. The rebellious troops handed out thousands of guns to the crowd. Reid Cabral asked

Marine Lt. Col. Ralph Heywood, the U.S. naval attache, if the United States would intervene.

Sunday, the pro-Bosch rebels captured the National Palace and arrested Reid Cabral. He resigned and was allowed to go into hiding. At noon, the U.S. Navy's six-ship Caribbean Ready Group began moving from Puerto Rico toward the Dominican Republic, in case it became necessary to evacuate U.S. citizens. Aboard were the 3rd Battalion, 6th Marines and Marine Medium Helicopter Squadron 264—1,702 Marines in the 6th Marine Expeditionary Unit.

The government in Washington worried about a Communist takeover if Bosch and his supporters regained power. It hoped the anti-Bosch elements of the Dominican armed forces would form a junta and restore order. As Bosch seemed on the verge of returning to the island Sunday afternoon, the Dominican Air Force strafed the rebellious Army camps near Santo Domingo and with the Navy attacked the National Palace. The Navy fired a few shells into the city. Fighting in the capital spread swiftly.

On Monday morning, the U.S. Navy Ready Group stood 30 miles off the Dominican coast, out of sight. Gen. Elías Wessin y Wessin, leader of the anti-Bosch military, asked for United States troops to intervene. That would have been awkward. It would have put the United States in the posture of intervening to support an unpopular regime that had overthrown the constitutionally elected President Bosch. Washington instructed the embassy to stay neutral, obtain a ceasefire and begin evacuating U.S. citizens.

When efforts to negotiate a ceasefire failed on Tuesday, Wessin y Wessin led anti-Bosch military units into the capital. The Dominican Air Force rocketed and strafed the city. U.S. Ambassador W. Tapley Bennett, Jr., who had just returned to the island, refused to mediate and urged the pro-Bosch forces to surrender. He asked the U.S. Navy to make a show of force off Santo Domingo. A confused battle raged in the streets. Hundreds were killed and wounded in "the bloodiest single battle in Dominican history."[12]

Evacuation operations began Tuesday morning. American civilians and foreign nationals gathered at the large resort Hotel

El Embajador in the western suburbs near the sea and were moved by buses and trucks to Port Haina, six miles west of Santo Domingo. (In 1921, the Marines had established a camp at Haina to train officers for the Policia Nacional Dominicana. A graduate of its first class was Rafael Trujillo.)

Unarmed Marines were carried to Port Haina by helicopter to manage the evacuation when the high speed transport *Ruchamkin* and the tank landing ship *Wood County* reached the pier. The helicopter carrier *Boxer* and the amphibious transport dock ship *Raleigh* steamed off downtown Santo Domingo. Rapidly, 1,178 U.S. nationals were taken aboard the Navy ships.

By Tuesday night, it seemed that the crisis was over; and the anti-Bosch forces had won. But they failed to follow up their advantage against stubborn rebel resistance, and the tide turned. The pro-Bosch forces pushed back Wessin y Wessin's troops and tanks and consolidated their hold on most of downtown Santo Domingo. By Wednesday afternoon, the anti-Bosch forces clearly could not put down the revolt. Dominican Air Force Col. Pedro Benoit, who headed a new anti-Bosch junta, asked that U.S. Marines be landed.

Now, there was no concern about awkwardness. Asserting that the rebels were Communist-dominated, Ambassador Bennett supported Benoit's call and recommended that Marines be landed near the Hotel El Embajador, where more civilians had gathered. The Dominican police said they could not guarantee the evacuees' safety. Bennett asked the Navy to take them from the hotel by helicopter and to reinforce the Marine Guard of one noncom and six men at the embassy.

A Marine platoon promptly landed by helicopter on the embassy grounds and started shooting at pro-Bosch snipers. Unarmed Marine pathfinders, an unarmed rifle platoon and helicopter support teams landed on the polo field next to the Hotel El Embajador, followed by an armed platoon wearing body armor.

At 6 P.M., President Johnson authorized the landing of 500 Marines from *Boxer* to protect American lives. The Marines were not to fire unless fired upon. Although no Americans had been hurt, Johnson said, "Where American citizens go that flag goes with them to protect them."[13]

As soon as the order arrived from Washington at 6:53, Col.

George W. E. Daughtry, commanding the 6th Marine Expeditionary Unit, put ashore two rifle companies and his battalion headquarters by vertical envelopment. HMM-264 helicopters took in 536 fully armed Marines from *Boxer* and brought out 684 civilians from the hotel. By 11:30 P.M., the operation was completed without a casualty. *Raleigh,* which had rushed 200 evacuees to San Juan, Puerto Rico, was ordered back to Santo Domingo at best speed. She was prepared to land the remaining rifle company and supporting arms over the beach at Port Haina so that they could move down the main highway to join the Marines at the hotel.

On Thursday afternoon, Colonel Daughtry, who had commanded the 1st Battalion, 7th Marines in the fighting in west Korea, visited the embassy with Commodore James A. Dare, commander of the Ready Group. Sniper fire pinned them down in the building, and Marines returned the fire.

By now, President Johnson and his advisors were resolved to forestall the establishment of what they perceived as a pro-communist Bosch government. The Joint Chiefs of Staff ordered the rest of the Marines to land at Haina at 5:30 P.M. The LVTs, tanks and anti-tank Ontos joined the rest of the battalion an hour later. Fifteen hundred Marines were now ashore.

The 3rd Brigade of the U.S. Army's 82d Airborne Infantry Division began landing in C-130s at San Isidro Airfield, eight miles east of Santo Domingo, at 2:30 A.M. on Friday. Because the Dominicans did not man the control tower after dark, a naval aviator and two Marine officers rushed there by helicopter to turn on the lights and talk down the planes. The commanding general of the airborne division took charge of all U.S. ground forces ashore.

Lt. Col. Poul F. Pedersen, another Korean veteran, took the 3rd Battalion, 6th Marines eastward from the polo grounds into the city with its flank at an intersection designated Checkpoint Charlie. At 4 P.M. Friday, the left flank platoon advanced north along Avenida Presidente Rios to occupy Checkpoint Delta at the junction with Avenida San Martin. Several hundred yards up the street, the Marines were hit by small-arms and machine-gun fire from rebels holed up in a housing project west of Avenida Presidente Rios. In minutes, one Marine was killed and eight were wounded. Because the housing project was full of civilian families, the Marines could not use their recoilless rifle; but the riflemen swept through the area. Since darkness was approaching and the Marines were new to combat, the platoon was ordered to consolidate its position at Checkpoint Charlie and try to reach Checkpoint Delta at dawn.

Meanwhile, the paratroopers had advanced from the airfield on the eastern side of the city and fought the pro-Bosch rebels near the Duarte Bridge over the Ozama River. Four soldiers were wounded. The paratroopers established a bridgehead west of the river and occupied the electric power plant nearby, relieving the junta's soldiers there to move into the area between the two American forces according to plan. But the Dominican soldiers promptly left for the military base at the airfield, taking with them their tanks, half-tracks and artillery. "They made an impressive sight as they came into San Isidro. The only trouble was that they were headed in the wrong direction."[14] There were now no friendly troops between the Marines and U.S. Army soldiers. Both commanders called for more forces.

Fearing the spread of fighting between Americans and Dominicans, President Johnson ordered that a ceasefire be obtained through the OAS and the Papal Nuncio, even though the anti-junta forces still controlled downtown Santo Domingo. The Papal Nuncio arrived at the U.S. Embassy Friday afternoon when the building was under fire. He had to confer with Ambassador Bennett in the ambassador's bathroom. After a meeting at the junta's headquarters at San Isidro late that afternoon, a ceasefire was finally signed.

Early Saturday morning, May 1, the Marines tried to advance again from Checkpoint Charlie to link up with the Army. One Marine was killed and three were wounded by the rebels in the housing project. The Marines moved north up Avenida Presidente Rios and then east along Avenida San Martin. And a 200-man armored paratrooper force came westward, suffering two killed and two wounded. The two U.S. forces met at 12:45 on Avenida San Martin.

Ambassador Bennett, stressing that "Castro-like" elements had taken over the anti-junta movement,[15] urged that the American forces on both sides of the city be allowed to link up. But former Ambassador John Bartlow Martin, who had returned to the Dominican Republic as President Johnson's personal representative, met with the anti-junta forces and agreed that the U.S. Marines and soldiers would stay out of the city, except for an enlarged zone around the U.S. Embassy. Therefore, the anti-junta leaders protested against the meeting of the two forces on the Avenida San Martin; and at 3:45 P.M., they were ordered to return to their original positions.

The rebels also agreed to an International Safety Zone running west from Checkpoint Charlie around the polo grounds and to the sea. This arrangement left a gap between the U.S. Marines and soldiers.

Meanwhile, early Saturday morning, Lt. Gen. Bruce Palmer, Jr., USA, arrived from Washington to command the American forces. He had the stated mission to protect American lives and the unannounced mission to prevent a Communist takeover. He brought with him the 82d Airborne's 2d Brigade. That same day, the 1st Battalion, 6th Marines landed at the airport; and Brig. Gen. John G. Bouker arrived with the 4th Marine Expeditionary Brigade staff. There were now two Marine battalions and four Army battalions on hand.

On his arrival, Lt. Gen. Palmer told his military commanders that he did not recognize the ceasefire; and he warned Washington that, if American forces were not permitted to link up, there was a risk that the country would be taken over by the opposition. He wanted to establish an armed cordon through the center of the city to confine the pro-Bosch rebels and give the U.S. forces control of the city's key installations. Former Ambassador Martin strongly opposed moving American troops downtown, fearing that the killing of Dominicans by Americans would aid the Communists.

The link-up problem was solved on Sunday with the Washington decision to open a corridor connecting the American forces from the International Security Zone to the airport but detouring around the anti-junta stronghold in the center of Santo Domingo. A newly arrived OAS Special Committee approved the plan. It was executed right after midnight on Monday, May 3; and by 1:30 A.M., the link-up had been accomplished and the rebel forces were sealed off in the central city. Shortly afterwards, the Marine detachment from *Newport News* landed at Haina and occupied the University of Santo Domingo, where arms were reportedly hidden. The following day, the 1st

Battalions of both the 2d and 8th Marines and HMM-263 arrived. The buildup continued until 22,200 armed Americans were ashore and another 10,000 stood by off the coast. While the Dominicans continued to fight sporadically, the intervention settled into armed vigilance and political maneuvering. Sniping and brief skirmishes continued and caused American casualties. Four Marines were killed and one wounded in downtown Santo Domingo on May 6. Several Marines were hit at the embassy, but the two main objectives had been achieved: to "prevent a Communist takeover" and to avoid major fighting between Americans and Dominicans.

An Inter-American Peace Force was created with units from five Latin American countries; and on May 25, the first contingent of Brazilian troops arrived. President Johnson immediately ordered the withdrawal of 600 Marines; and by June 6, all the Marines at least had left. Among the approximately 6,000 who had served ashore, nine had been killed and 30 wounded.

On June 1, 1966, the Dominicans elected Balaguer president over Bosch. Johnson offered Balaguer his full support; and by the end of the summer, the international peace-keeping force, which consisted mainly of United States troops, was removed. Balaguer was re-elected four years later and again in 1974.

Fearing a "second Cuba," the United States had used its ready power to support a military faction opposed to the democratically elected Juan Bosch. But the time had passed when the United States could march into Latin America; the Marine-led intervention was widely condemned. Even America's friends called President Johnson's action imperialistic. What hope the United States had stirred in Latin America with the start in 1961 of the Alliance for Progress and what prestige it had gained in its handling of the 1962 Cuban missile crisis were converted, said a Council on Foreign Relations analyst, into "violent hostility. . . . The impetuosity of the original U.S. intervention had alienated practically the entire hemisphere but the studied moderation of subsequent U.S. policy had at least partially redeemed the initial adverse effects."[16] The most recent retired Marine Commandant, Gen. David M. Shoup, was highly critical of the size of the American reaction. He wrote, "Only a fraction of the force deployed was needed or justified. A small

1935-model Marine landing force could probably have handled the situation."[17]

But the fundamental objection was to the renewal of the American policy of intervention in a small nation's internal politics. Former Ambassador Martin called the intervention necessary but "illegal."[18] And Senator J. William Fulbright, chairman of the Senate Foreign Relations Committee, criticized it as "a unilateral military intervention in violation of inter-American law, the 'good neighbor' policy of thirty years' standing, and the spirit of the Charter of Punta del Este . . ."[19]

*Marines of E Company, 3rd Marines, hurl grenades as
they attack up a ridge near Vietnam's
demilitarized zone in 1968.
Staff Sgt. Shearer, USMC Photo*

SEMPER FIDELIS

XV
THE
VIETNAM
WAR
1954-1975

1
The 11 Years to Da Nang

When the first men of the 3rd Battalion, 9th Marines hit the beach north of Da Nang on the morning of March 8, 1965, they were greeted with even more festivity than the 2d Marines had encountered at Beirut. Giggling Vietnamese girls draped the Marines, including Brig. Gen. Frederick J. Karch, with garlands of red and yellow flowers.

But the welcome was deceptive; this was no Beirut. Before this was over, 14,691 Marines would die and 88,633 would be wounded in Indochina. This American attempt to gain a military foothold on the mainland of Asia would be the highwater mark of America's thrust across the Pacific.

The 9th Marines' Vietnam landing capped off a very long prologue. It had begun during World War II, when the U.S. Office of Special Services had helped Ho Chi Minh's guerrillas fight the Japanese; and Ho's Viet Minh had helped rescue downed American pilots and supply intelligence about Japanese military movements.

Ho Chi Minh's Indochinese Communist Party had formed the Viet Minh in 1941 as a national-front organization to fight both the Japanese and the French. The French had been the colonial power in Vietnam for most of a century, and Ho had joined the Communist Party in France in 1920 after failing to convince the post-World War I Versailles Conference to support self-determination for the peoples of Indochina.

During World War II, the Japanese let the pro-Vichy French manage rice-rich Vietnam for them. But by 1945, the French there had become increasingly pro-de Gaulle. The Japanese interned French civil servants and troops and governed Vietnam through Prince Bao Dai, who had been the front man for the French in central Vietnam before the war. After Japan surren-

[For the location of places in Indochina see map No. 10 in the map section.—*Au.*]

dered to the Allies, Bao Dai abdicated and Ho Chi Minh proclaimed Vietnam's independence as the Democratic Republic of Vietnam.

With the end of World War II, the British occupied southern Vietnam and Chiang Kai-shek's forces moved into the north. The British used Japanese soldiers to keep Saigon out of Viet Minh hands—as the Americans were doing against the Communists in North China—and rearmed 5,000 French troops. The French took over the Saigon government; and by the end of 1945, the British pulled out. In the north, the Chinese allowed Ho Chi Minh's government to remain in Hanoi; but early in 1946, Chiang Kai-shek agreed to withdraw in favor of the French. Ho made a deal with the French under which French troops would enter northern Vietnam and Paris would recognize Ho's regime as a free state within the French Union.

Ho had two goals: national liberation and the "modernization" of Vietnam. Tensions rose between the French and the Viet Minh. On November 23, 1946, a war began that climaxed with the defeat of the French at Dien Bien Phu in 1954.

United States interest in Vietnam started slowly and grew during the Cold War. The United States had repeatedly urged the French to move toward granting Vietnam its independence. But after the Communist victory in China in 1949 and Ho's recognition by Peking and Moscow, the United States recognized the regime of Bao Dai, whom the French had installed once again. With the outbreak of the Korean war in 1950, President Truman increased arms shipments to the French in Indochina. The containment of communism in Asia was American policy, and the French fight in Indochina was seen as a way to effect that policy. Vietnam became part of the Cold War. "Anticommunism preempted anticolonialism or pronationalism in importance."[1] By 1954, American aid was paying for 80 percent of the French war against the Viet Minh and running at more than $1 billion per year. In April, Lt. Col. Julius W. Ireland landed VMA-324 at Da Nang and turned over 25 dive bombers to the French.

That spring, the French lost most of the country to the Viet Minh and their Chinese instructors who had come south in greater numbers after the Korean armistice in 1953. Because the French did not send draftees overseas, they were short of

846

soldiers. Less than half of those who defended Dien Bien Phu were French. The French asked for American intervention; one suggestion was that President Eisenhower send a division of Marines. After a major debate in Washington over how far the United States should go to prevent a French defeat in Indochina, the Eisenhower Administration finally decided not to send American troops or air or naval manpower to battle in Vietnam. The French position deteriorated.

Partly as a result of these events, the major powers held the Geneva Conference from April 26 to July 21, 1954. On May 7, after an eight-week battle, Dien Bien Phu near the Laotian border fell, despite the infusion of $10 million worth of U.S. equipment. The French weakness in Indochina was obvious. (At least one non-active-duty Marine, John Verdi, flew "Boxcar" missions over Dien Bien Phu.)

At Geneva, the Viet Minh agreed to evacuate the forces it had south of the 17th Parallel in return for nationwide elections in July 1956. Civilians could cross the 17th Parallel for 300 days after the armistice went into effect. An International Control Commission with representatives from Canada, India and Poland would oversee the agreements. Dismayed by the results of the conference, the United States refused to sign the agreements and wanted to insure that the southern, French-occupied portion of Vietnam would not also be lost to Ho Chi Minh's Communists. Secretary of State John Foster Dulles led in the formation of the Southeast Asia Treaty Organization (SEATO) to prevent the further spread of communism and try to fill the power vacuum in Southeast Asia.

At the time of the Geneva Agreements, the U.S. Military Assistance Advisory Group, commanded by Lt. Gen. John W. O'Daniel, USA, and based in Saigon, already had 342 men. In June 1954, an anti-insurgency team headed by Col. Edward G. Lansdale, USAF, a Central Intelligence Agency specialist, also arrived; at least one Marine officer, Capt. Richard Smith, became a member of this team. The United States also started to help train and build up the Vietnamese armed forces. In August, Lt. Col. Victor J. Croizat became the first U.S. Marine assigned to the MAAG. He helped create refugee centers and later became the senior U.S. advisor to the small Vietnamese Marine Corps, which had been formally organized in October 1954 to serve with the budding Vietnamese Navy's river and coastal forces. In working with the Vietnamese Marine Corps, Croizat was joined by Capt. James T. Breckinridge. He and Tech. Sgt. Jackson E. Tracy worked at Nha Trang as small-unit tactics instructors. By the end of the year, the Vietnamese Marine Corps, now at two-battalion strength, was better disciplined than most Vietnamese units. Croizat left Vietnam in 1956 and was succeeded by Lt. Col. William N. Wilkes, Jr.

Prime Minister Ngo Dinh Diem, a nationalist and Roman Catholic Protégé of New York's Francis Cardinal Spellman, sought the departure of the French Expeditionary Corps from South Vietnam. And by 1955, Lt. Gen. O'Daniel had taken over the French responsibility for training and organizing the Vietnamese armed forces.

In October 1955, Diem held a referendum in the south, defeated Bao Dai and proclaimed the establishment of the Republic of Vietnam with himself as president. Diem refused to start the process toward the nationwide elections decreed by the Geneva Agreements. His power base was strengthened by large American military aid and the movement from the North of more than 800,000 Vietnamese, the great majority of them Catholics. Diem consolidated his rule by political arrests and "re-education," and South Vietnam became a repressive and corrupt police state.

Resistance mounted against Diem's rule and the American presence; and in late 1960, Hanoi's Communist government began to support the guerrillas in the south. At the year's end, the National Liberation Front of South Vietnam (loosely called the Viet Cong) was created to overthrow the Saigon government and get rid of the Americans. During the following year, the Viet Cong insurgency spread rapidly. The Viet Cong launched a campaign of terrorism, assassinating and kidnapping thousands of civilian leaders. President John F. Kennedy quietly sent 400 Special Forces soldiers and 100 more military advisors to South Vietnam.

The United States in 1962 built up the level of military aid and advisors and appointed Gen. Paul D. Harkins, USA, commander of the new U.S. Military Assistance Command, Vietnam (MACV). His chief of staff was Marine Maj. Gen. Richard G. Weede, who had commanded the 5th Marines in Korea. President Kennedy authorized U.S. advisors to return Viet Cong fire. Three U.S. Army transport helicopter companies arrived to give the Vietnamese army greater tactical mobility against the Viet Cong. The first Marines in the Vietnam buildup were 42 men of the 1st Radio Company, FMF, at Pleiku. In less than a year, U.S. helicopter crews were firing at insurgents and flying strafing missions. Vietnam was to be a helicopter war.

Among the early arrivals was a Marine helicopter squadron, which on Palm Sunday, April 15, 1962, set up near Soc Trang, an abandoned Japanese fighter airstrip in the Mekong Delta, 85 miles southwest of Saigon. This was Marine Medium Helicopter Squadron 362 (HMM-362) commanded by Lt. Col. Archie J. Clapp; it flew from *Princeton* into an area dominated by the Viet Cong. Vietnamese troops provided perimeter security. The Marine task unit, called "Shufly," consisted of about 450 Marines commanded by Col. John F. Carey. Its Sikorsky UH-34D helicopters carried supplies and troops to isolated or threatened Vietnamese villages and troop concentrations. Before being relieved by HMM-163 on August 1, HMM-362 flew 50 combat troop lifts involving 130 landings against Viet Cong opposition. On some missions as many as 24 helicopters participated. Seventeen of its choppers were damaged. On one such mission on May 9, eight of the 22 helicopters carrying Vietnamese soldiers were hit at least once. On July 18, the largest helicopter lift in Vietnam thus far took Vietnamese troops north of Saigon in 18 Marine helicopters, followed by 12 of the U.S. Army and 11 of the Vietnamese Air Force. Although HMM-362 suffered no Marine casualties during its tour, 109 Americans were killed or wounded in combat in Vietnam during 1962.

In September, HMM-163 moved to the air base at Da Nang, 380 miles north of Saigon. This was the Marines' operating area in contingency plans. On October 6, during a Vietnamese troop lift, five Marines and two Navy men from Marine Task Unit 79.5 were killed in a crash caused by mechanical failure. In April 1963, a 3rd Marine Division platoon was flown in from Okinawa to strengthen security at the Da Nang base. An air-ground team was formed. The addition of American helicopters to the guerrilla war substantially supported Diem and discouraged the Viet Cong—for the moment.

Meanwhile, the Soviet Union began aiding the Pathet Lao

army in Laos. In response, on May 17, 1962, the 3rd Marine Expeditionary Brigade began landing 3,000 men as part of Joint Task Force 116 at Bangkok, Thailand. They were flown 350 miles north to Udorn, which was 35 miles from Vientiane, Laos' political capital. The brigade was commanded by Brig. Gen. Ormond R. Simpson, assistant commander of the 3rd Marine Division, and included the 3rd Battalion, 9th Marines; HMR-261, and VMA-332. The Marines show-of-force was out of Thailand by August 7.

In Vietnam during the spring and summer of 1963, militant Buddhists rebelled against Diem's government. There were armed clashes, and seven Buddhist bonzes set themselves on fire to protest the regime's immorality. Mao Tse-tung announced his support of the Buddhists. As students rallied to the Buddhists' leadership, Diem's forces raided the pagodas and killed and jailed their bonzes; Diem closed the universities in Saigon and Hue and arrested thousands of students. The United States deplored Diem's actions and his failure to win popular support. On November 1, Vietnamese army officers, with American encouragement, executed a coup. They murdered Diem and his brutally powerful brother and set up a military junta headed by Gen. Duong Van Minh. Three weeks later, President Kennedy himself was assassinated (by a former Marine).

At this crucial juncture, the United States pledged support to General Minh and opposed efforts to neutralize South Vietnam. By now, the Viet Cong controlled much of the South Vietnamese countryside. The non-communist political forces in South Vietnam had been seriously weakened and fragmented by both the NLF and the Diem regime. When Minh was overthrown in a coup in January 1964, Gen. Nguyen Khanh, the commanding general of I Corps, took over the government in Saigon by force. The Vietnamese army held the capital but could make little progress against the Viet Cong. Saigon itself was political chaos. "Over the next months Saigon took on the pace and style of a Marx Brothers movie."[2]

In June, Lt. Gen. William C. Westmoreland replaced Harkins at MACV and Henry Cabot Lodge succeeded Gen. Maxwell Taylor as ambassador. And the United States announced it was sending 5,000 more men to South Vietnam.

On another level, during the first half of 1964, extensive

clandestine operations were carried out against North Vietnam. Marine Maj. Gen. Victor H. Krulak, the Pentagon's chief specialist on counterinsurgency warfare, played a leading role in planning these attacks. Air operations were also staged against North Vietnamese and Pathet Lao troops in Laos. And destroyer patrols were sent into the Gulf of Tonkin to collect intelligence information and exert pressure on North Vietnam.

The Republican Presidential nominee, Senator Barry Goldwater, and the Pentagon recommended greater U.S. involvement and carrying the war to North Vietnam. The Secretary General of the United Nations, French President Charles de Gaulle and the Soviet government all pressed for reconvening the Geneva Conference to find a neutralist non-military solution. In July, the United States announced that its military aid mission would be increased from 16,000 to 21,000 men. But President Lyndon B. Johnson promised American boys would not be sent to fight in Vietnam.

The issue was soon settled. North Vietnamese torpedo boats attacked the destroyer *Maddox* in the Gulf of Tonkin on the night of August 2, 1964. Two nights later, a second attack was reported against *Maddox* and *C. Turner Joy.* Hanoi denied the second attack had taken place. President Johnson ordered carrier air attacks against North Vietnamese torpedo boat bases, naval craft and a major oil storage depot. And at his instigation, the Congress passed overwhelmingly the Gulf of Tonkin Resolution authorizing the President to "take all necessary measures to repel any armed attack against the forces of the United States and to prevent further aggression." It allowed the President to use force to assist any SEATO country that asked for help.

The United States went into this war in force to stop Communism and to save the Vietnamese people. That was the rationale. As had Wilson, Roosevelt, Eisenhower and Kennedy before him, Lyndon Johnson "believed in the essential goodness of the United States and its almost infinite capacity for righting the wrongs of mankind."[3]

While American military intervention was vigorously debated in Washington, the political situation in Saigon grew more and more chaotic. Then, on February 7, 1965, the Viet Cong attacked the American compound at Pleiku, killing eight Americans and wounding at least 80. The United States retaliated by bombing North Vietnam—while Soviet Premier Alexei Kosygin was in Hanoi. And the Marines' 1st Light Anti-Aircraft Missile Battalion, equipped with Hawk surface-to-air missiles, began arriving at Da Nang.

Prolonged political infighting in Saigon resulted by mid-1965 in the coming to power of a group of younger officers led by Maj. Gen. Nguyen Van Thieu and Air Vice Marshal Nguyen Cao Ky (age thirty-four). But the NLF was steadily blanketing the countryside, and the South Vietnam Army (ARVN) was increasingly demoralized. On March 2, American bombers attacked North Vietnam "in the first nonretaliatory raid"[4] and began flying against North Vietnamese targets on a sustained basis. On March 8, the Marines landed to defend the American air base at Da Nang. The war on the Asian mainland was now openly American.

2
"The Dirty War"—1965-1967

The Marines were the first Americans to be committed to the Vietnam war overtly as combat troops. They landed at Red Beach just north of Da Nang an hour late because the sea was rough; but by 9:18 A.M., Lt. Col. Charles E McPartlin, Jr., had his battalion ashore. Lt. Col. Herbert J. Bain's 1st Battalion, 3rd Marines started to come in by air from Okinawa in Marine KC-130s; and by the end of March 12, all the Marines were on hand. The planes were attacked by Viet Cong small-arms fire.

Two Marine helicopter squadrons, HMM-162 and -163, were already operating out of Da Nang; and two Hawk batteries were also on the base. The newly arrived ground forces of Brig. Gen. Karch's 9th Marine Expeditionary Brigade were to provide close-in security for the airfield and defend the ridgeline west of the field. I Company, 9th Marines took over Hill 327, the dominant terrain feature, and K Company, Hill 268 to the north. The 3rd Marines stayed on the air base to protect against infiltrators and mortar attacks. Across the Cau Do River, a mile south of the field, the area was all Viet Cong territory, except for the thin ribbon along Highway One.

The Marines found themselves in the center of the I Corps Tactical Zone, the northernmost military region of South Vietnam. The I Corps Zone stretched from the North Vietnam border at the 17th Parallel, down a narrow strip of coast to a spur of the Annamite Mountains at Sa Huynh—north to south about 225 miles. The zone was only 30 to 70 miles wide. In it lived some 2.6 million people, most of them rice farmers or fishermen. Government troops held the sizable towns and the cities, of which Da Nang was the largest; but the Viet Cong controlled the countryside. To cope with them, the Zone contained some

25,000 regular ARVN soldiers plus assorted regional and militia forces.

The 5,000 Marines in the Da Nang area were strengthened on April 10 by Lt. Col. David A. Clement's 2d Battalion, 3rd Marines. One of its reinforced companies was sent by chopper 42 miles north to Phu Bai, eight miles below Hue, which was South Vietnam's ancient capital and third largest city. The company was relieved four days later by Lt. Col. Donald R. Jones' 3rd Battalion, 4th Marines from Hawaii.

The first Marine fixed-wing tactical aircraft, the F4B Phantom II jets of VMFA-531, arrived at Da Nang on April 10. Maj. Gen. William R. Collins, commanding general of the 3rd Marine Division, arrived in Da Nang in May. Maj. Gen. Paul J. Fontana established the 1st Marine Aircraft Wing's advanced headquarters at Da Nang. The Marines were redesignated the III Marine Amphibious Force.

As the Marine buildup sped rapidly ahead, Brig. Gen. Marion E. Carl, a leading Marine World War II ace, brought in a 6,000-man brigade with the 4th Marines. On May 7, it started landing at Chu Lai, a difficult stretch of beach 57 miles south of Da Nang. Lt. Gen. Krulak, now commander of the Fleet Marine Force, Pacific, had long recommended building a second jet air base there. The field was a radically new expeditionary Short Airfield for Tactical Support (SATS) with aluminum runway matting, arresting gear and later a catapult. On June 1, Seabees and Marine Engineers had the airstrip ready for MAG-12's Douglas A-4 Skyhawks.

By early June, Maj. Gen. Lewis W. Walt, the junior major general in the Corps, had taken over III MAF and the 3rd Marine Division, while Brig. Gen. Keith B. McCutcheon replaced Fontana as commanding general of the 1st MAW.

The Viet Cong ambushed an ARVN battalion near Ba Gia on May 30; only three American advisors and 65 of 400 Vietnamese soldiers broke through. Marine helicopters and VMFA-531 went to their aid, but requests for support from a Marine battalion were not acted on in time.

The Viet Cong was displaying new strength; and by the first week in June, the Marines had suffered 208 casualties, with 29 killed in action. Clearly, the Marines—and the Army's 173rd Airborne Brigade at Bien Hoa near Saigon—were in the war to fight. The policy of simply "advising" the South Vietnamese army and securing coastal bases had failed. Commandant Wallace M. Greene, Jr., had visited Da Nang and told the press that the Marines were in Vietnam to "kill Viet Cong."[5]

There were now 51,000 U.S. servicemen in Vietnam, including 16,500 Marines. The Americans' job had been to secure the major bases and free the South Vietnamese to carry the fight to the enemy. But even with this help, the war was going badly. On June 26, General Westmoreland received authority to commit his American forces to battle when he decided they were needed.

At 1:30 A.M. on July 1, an 85-man enemy demolition force infiltrated the Da Nang airfield and destroyed three planes and damaged three more. The raiders killed one Air Force airman and wounded three Marines. As a result, the Marines extended their area of responsibility to the heavily populated areas south and east of the field; and the 2d Battalion, 9th Marines arrived to guard the area to the south.

On July 12, 1st Lt. Frank S. Reasoner of Kellogg, Idaho, and A Company of the 3rd Reconnaissance Battalion became the first Marine whose courage earned the Medal of Honor in Vietnam. His reconnaissance patrol was ambushed deep in Viet Cong territory. Enemy machine-gun and automatic weapons fire struck Reasoner and five men on the point and isolated them from the rest of the patrol. One of his men was hit; Reasoner killed two Viet Cong and silenced an automatic weapons position in an effort to evacuate the wounded Marine. He organized a base of fire. Casualties mounted. Reasoner's radio operator was hit and tried to reach a protected spot; he was hit again. Reasoner raced through machine-gun fire to help him and was mortally wounded.

The Marines established a fourth but temporary coastal enclave to the south in the II Corps Tactical Zone when a battalion of the 7th Marines went ashore at Qhi Nhon, 175 miles below Da Nang, to secure the beach for the 1st Cavalry Division and support the Pleiku–Kontum area inland to the northwest.

By the end of July, the decision was made in Washington to send the 1st Cavalry Division to Vietnam and to increase the U.S. military presence there from 75,000 to 125,000 men. The authorized strength of the Marine Corps was increased in August from 193,000 to 223,000 men. And a decision was made not to call up the American armed forces' reserves. Instead, voluntary enlistments were stepped up and the draft was doubled from 17,000 to 35,000 a month. That crucial decision would intensify opposition to the war in the United States during the years ahead.

By mid-August, the Marines had four regiments and four air groups in Vietnam.* The 3rd and 9th Marines were in the Da Nang area. The 3rd Battalion, 4th Marines was at Phu Bai. The rest of the 4th Marines; the 3rd Battalion, 3rd Marines, and 1st Battalion, 7th Marines were at Chu Lai. The 2d Battalion, 7th Marines was at Qui Nhon under Army control. Among Marine air units, MAG-16 and MAG-11 were at Da Nang, with one helicopter squadron at Phu Bai. MAG-12 was at Chu Lai and MAG-36 would arrive there on September 1. One MAG-36 helicopter squadron went to Qui Nhon.

On August 18, the Marines launched Operation Starlite, their first offensive operation. Col. Oscar F. Peatross led three battalions out of Chu Lai against the 1st Viet Cong Regiment on the Van Tuong Peninsula, 15 miles south of the Chu Lai airstrip. One company in LVTs crossed a river from the north; a battalion landed by helicopter on the west, and a battalion in amphibian tractors attacked the southeastern beach.

That day, two Marines earned the Medal of Honor. New York City-born Cpl. Robert E. O'Malley of I Company, 3rd Marines led his squad against the strongly entrenched enemy. He raced across a rice paddy, jumped into a trench and with his rifle and grenades killed eight Viet Cong. Then he led his squad to help a neighboring unit that was taking heavy casualties. Though wounded three times, he covered the evacuation of his squad's wounded by helicopter. Lance Cpl. Joe C. Paul, a native of Williamsburg, Kentucky, fought with H Company, 4th Marines near Nam Yen. When five of his platoon were wounded, Paul rushed forward, placed himself between them and the enemy and fired his automatic weapon to divert the enemy attack and allow the casualties to be evacuated. He was mortally wounded but continued firing until he collapsed.

*The Marines were involved in their first charges of atrocities in Vietnam on August 3 when men of the 1st Battalion, 9th Marines destroyed most of the houses in the village of Cam Ne, six miles southwest of Da Nang. CBS television pictures of a Marine burning one house with a cigarette lighter and Morley Safer's report horrified Americans back home. Keyes Beech of the *Chicago Daily News* reported that Marines "have killed or wounded Vietnamese civilians and burned dozens of homes in the dirtiest war Americans ever had to fight."

Marine patrol struggles through rice paddy near Gio Linh on March 25, 1967.
UPI Photo

Marine choppers airlift a Marine battalion from Valley Forge into Viet Cong territory in Quang Ngai province during Operation Double Eagle on February 4, 1966. Steve Van Meter, UPI Photo

Marines race into position against the enemy as their helicopters start to rise out of the line of fire. UPI Photo

CH-53 helicopter resupplies Marines on Hill 119 southwest of Da Nang. Cpl. W. P. Barger, USMC Photo

3rd Marine Division flamethrower tank burns out enemy position in Vietnam. USMC Photo

*In Hue, Marines battle North Vietnamese during the
1968 Tet offensive.
Kyoichi Sawada, UPI Photo*

*Marine carries wounded buddy to
evacuation helicopter near Khe Sanh.
Kyoichi Sawada, UPI Photo*

Exhausted Marines find momentary refuge in church at An Hoa during enemy mortar attack in 1967.
Frank Johnston, UPI Photo

Under intense enemy fire, Marines advance to recapture the Citadel in Hue after the North Vietnamese 1968 Tet offensive.
Kyoichi Sawada, UPI Photo

Tank brings out bodies of dead Marines killed in hand-to-hand combat with North Vietnamese north of Con Thien in July 1967.
Dana Stone, UPI Photo

Marines hurry refugees aboard helicopter on American Embassy parking lot just before the 1975 fall of Saigon. Nik Wheeler, Sipa-Liaison

On April 12, 1975, helicopters of HMH-463 come in to extract Marines and last U.S. civilians from soccer field near Phnom Penh's U.S. Embassy. Gunnery Sgt. Donnie Shearer, USMC Photo

Marines board the deserted container ship Mayaguez from the destroyer escort Harold E. Holt in futile attempt to rescue Americans captured by Cambodians on May 12, 1975. Official U.S. Navy Photo

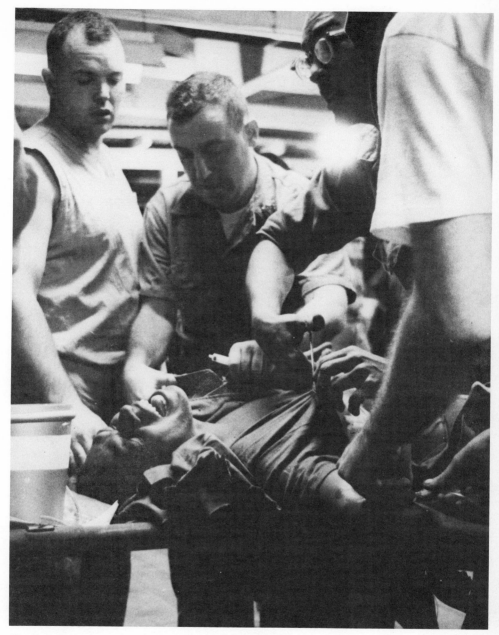

*Navy surgeons at Marine First Medical Battalion field
hospital near Da Nang start working to save the life of
Cpl. Andre A. Williams, who was shot in the chest by a
Viet Cong while on night patrol. The doctors' swift,
expert skill kept Corporal Williams off the list of 14,691
Marines killed in Indochina and among the 88,633
wounded Marines who survived.*
*James Hansen, Look Collection, the Library of
Congress. Copyright © Cowles Communications, Inc.,
1967. With permission of Andre A. Williams*

Body bags with fallen Marines are lifted aboard
a helicopter during the battle for Khe Sanh. Over 200
years, 41,411 Marines have been killed at action
in their nation's wars.
David Douglas Duncan; courtesy Museums Branch,
USMC

The Viet Cong had entrenched themselves with their backs to the sea and fought tenaciously in close combat. But the Marines' firepower was too strong. Despite the enemy's rocket launchers, mortars and automatic weapons, they were cornered; few surrendered. By August 24, 45 Marines and 614 Viet Cong were reported killed. The enemy fled inland from the coastal peninsula where they had until then found sanctuary.

This operation was followed on September 7 by Operation Piranha on the Batangan Peninsula, eight miles further south. This time, results by the 7th Marines "were not so spectacular."[6]

Meanwhile, on August 5, the Viet Cong attacked the Esso storage terminal on the Hai Van Peninsula across the bay from Da Nang. The peninsula was defended only by two under-strength Vietnamese Regional Force companies. The raiders destroyed nearly two million gallons of fuel.

Marines, Navy and Seabees built up China Beach on the South China Sea east of Da Nang. This eight-mile oceanfront was bounded by 2,000-foot-high Monkey Mountain to the north and Marble Mountain to the south. On October 27, 47 Viet Cong raiders attacked China Beach by boat. A handful got through and destroyed 19 helicopters and damaged 35 more and wrecked the nearly completed naval hospital across the road. Three Americans were killed and 91 wounded. At that same time, 20 Viet Cong attacked the airstrip at Chu Lai and destroyed two and damaged six of MAG-12's A-4s with satchel charges.*

On November 10, United States and Vietnamese Marine units for the first time participated in a combined amphibious operation. They landed at Tam Ky, between Chu Lai and Da Nang, and swept the area but met no opposition. Six days later, the 3rd Battalion, 3rd Marines, loaded out from Chu Lai and landed south of Hoi An, the capital of Quang Nam province. This area was controlled by Viet Cong, and the three-day operation killed 25 and captured 15. That same rain-swept night, the 1st Viet Cong Regiment, supposedly destroyed in Operation Starlite, overran the district capital of Hiep Duc, in the narrow Que Son valley 25 miles west of Tam Ky. MAG-16 and -36, airlifting in 788 ARVN troops, encountered heavy antiaircraft machine-gun fire; 21 of the 30 helicopters were hit. With air cover support by MAG-11 and -12, Hiep Duc was retaken; but because of the

---

*On November 4 near Chu Lai, correspondent Dickey Chapelle was killed by a booby trap while accompanying a Marine patrol.

frustrating shortage of ARVN troops was later abandoned. This was now the period of the northeast monsoon with rains averaging an inch per day; the Viet Cong attacked isolated garrisons and outposts and ambushed units coming to the rescue. It was classic guerrilla warfare, striking weak spots and keeping regular forces on the move. The Viet Cong would not risk a stand-up battle.

The enemy ran into trouble when they attacked Thach Tru on Highway One on November 22. They met a Vietnamese Ranger battalion supported by gunfire from two U.S. destroyers and by Marine aircraft. The 3rd Battalion, 7th Marines was brought in by helicopter and the next day attacked to the west. It was later determined that the enemy force was not Viet Cong but the 18th Regiment of the North Vietnamese army, the PAVN.

The 3rd Marines had already begun a "pacification" program intended to liberate hamlets and villages from Viet Cong domination, provide them with security and encourage the acceptance of government control. The first such Marine effort was at the hamlet of Le My, eight miles northwest of the Da Nang air base; it became a Marine civic action showplace. The program worked well enough in thinly populated areas but was less successful in the 9th Marines' densely populated zone south of the air base, where the Viet Cong were stronger.

The Marines also undertook small-unit patrolling and night ambushes to protect the rice harvest from the Viet Cong and tried to extend the pacification program to the south. Its success depended on the Popular Forces militia to provide the villages with security, but these troops proved inadequate to the job. As a result, the Marines called on their Caribbean experience and a bit of the British model in Malaya. Combined Action Companies were created with a Marine squad and a Navy corpsman assigned to work with each Popular Force platoon. The first of these units was established at Phu Bai by the 3rd Battalion, 4th Marines—partly as an expedient way to stretch the thinly spread battalion there. The Marines assigned received some training in counterinsurgency techniques as well as the Vietnamese language and history. By January 1966, a second Combined Action Company was formed at Da Nang under Lt. Col. William W. Taylor, who had organized the oroginal company at Phu Bai under 1st Lt. Paul R. Ek. The concept offered the possibility of effective civic action and eventually grew to a regiment-sized force.

Operation Harvest Moon, which began on December 8, was supposed to attack Viet Cong units that had moved into the Que Son valley and harassed government garrisons north of Hiep Duc. The enemy destroyed two ARVN battalions that came into the valley from Highway One. Two Marine battalions were "helilifted" into the battle area; and on December 10, a third battalion, flown in against heavy opposition, landed between the two Marine battalions. This Task Force Delta was first commanded by Brig. Gen. Melvin D. Henderson and later by Brig. Gen. Jonas M. Platt. B-52s made their first four strikes in support of Marine ground forces. By December 16, the Viet Cong had faded away. But Lt. Col. Leon N. Utter's 2d Battalion, 7th Marines was ambushed at Ky Phu and accounted for 105 enemy dead before it reached Highway One. Capt. Harvey C. Barnum, Jr., of Waterbury, Connecticut, won the Medal of Honor when, making a hazardous reconnaissance, he found the commander of H Company, 9th Marines mortally wounded and his radio operator dead. Barnum strapped on the radio, took charge of the decimated company under heavy fire and led it against the enemy. The Marines had 45 killed and 218 wounded. Since the Da Nang landing, U.S. Marine casualties totaled 454 dead and 2,093 wounded at year's end.

At the beginning of 1966, 180,000 American troops were in South Vietnam, including 38,000 Marines. There were brief periods of truce over Christmas and during the Vietnamese holiday of Tet in mid-January. President Johnson halted the bombing of North Vietnam from December 24 to January 31, 1966, and tried to begin peace talks. Early in February, he met in Honolulu with Thieu and Ky to restate their common war aims.

The rest of the 1st Marine Division was ordered to Vietnam to occupy the two southern provinces of I Corps. This actually meant that the remainder of the 1st Marines and all of the 5th Marines would join Maj. Gen. Walt's forces by the end of June.

Once the Tet holiday was over, a major offensive was planned against the 325A PAVN Division in the area between I Corps and II Corps at the southern end of the Marines' zone. The 3rd Battalion, 1st Marines and 2d Battalion, 4th Marines landed near Thach Tru on January 28 in the largest amphibious operation of the war until that time. And the next day, the 2d Battalion, 3rd Marines was flown in by helicopter five miles west of the landing beaches. On D plus 4, the 2d Battalion, 9th

Marines was brought into the mountains northwest of the beaches. But most of the North Vietnamese had moved south into Binh Dinh province, where they were attacked by the 1st Air Cavalry Division and II Corps troops. The operation went on until March 1 but resulted in little action for the Marines.

In an effort to make the civic action program work, Col. Edwin H. Simmons' 9th Marines tried out a new technique called County Fair south of Da Nang. Combined units of Vietnamese and Marines sealed off a hamlet, searched it and checked identity cards to try to spot the Viet Cong guerrilla cell left in the community. It was hoped that if the Viet Cong infrastructure were eliminated, pacification would succeed. The process was made more palatable by giving the villagers medical help, setting up a community kitchen and providing entertainment while the hamlet was searched. Arms caches, propaganda materials and Viet Cong themselves were uncovered.

February and March saw the Marines engaged in some hard fighting. On the night of February 27, the 2d Battalion, 1st Marines went to the rescue of an ARVN regiment northeast of Phu Bai in the north and attacked well-prepared Viet Cong positions. On March 4, Marine helicopters lifted an ARVN battalion to a battle near Quang Ngai city; and the 2d Battalion, 7th Marines followed it into the fight. Three more Marine battalions were thrown into the action by the next day. The Marines and ARVN reportedly destroyed a third of the 36th PAVN Regiment. On March 9, the Special Forces camp at A Shau near the Laotian border was wiped out in a vicious two-day fight. Marine and Air Force pilots flew close support, resupply and medical evacuation missions. The Marines lost three helicopters and one A-4C. "There was no saving the camp. On 11 March evacuation began. There was panic among the irregulars. Some tried to rush the helicopters, had to be cut down by U.S. Green Berets and Marine crewmen."[7] Twelve of the 17 Green Berets and 172 of the 400-man Vietnamese garrison were finally lifted out. On March 20, the 3rd Battalion, 7th Marines and 2d Battalion, 4th Marines were flown in to help an ARVN battalion under attack at An Hoa; and in four days of heavy fighting, 405 Viet Cong were killed. Before March was over, the 1st Battalion, 7th Marines had to help out an ARVN battalion northwest of Quang Ngai city. The war had heated up for the Marines.

By now the 1st Marine Division under Maj. Gen. Lewis J. Fields was based in Chu Lai. Walt, now a lieutenant general, retained command of III MAF and turned over the 3rd Marine Division at Da Nang to Maj. Gen. Wood B. Kyle.

Emboldened by President Johnson's support at Honolulu, Prime Minister Ky on March 10, 1966, fired his I Corps commander, Gen. Nguyen Chanh Thi, an able rival for power, and triggered a major crisis throughout South Vietnam. Buddhists, students and workers demonstrated against the Saigon junta. They called for national elections in the South and an end to the war. Da Nang, Hue and Hoi An were all rocked by riots and disruption. The port of Da Nang was closed down entirely. Thousands of Vietnamese vented their stifled anger against the military, the Americans and the suffering they were forced to endure. In Saigon, mobs burned American vehicles. In Hue, the Buddhist-student "struggle movement" seized the radio station and closed the university. The 1st ARVN Division demonstrated against the government. In Da Nang, a general strike was staged; and the mayor joined the opposition to the Saigon regime. Americans feared the downfall of South Vietnam's military government.

Ky declared Da Nang an enemy-held city; and to liberate it, on April 5, he brought 1,500 Vietnamese marines and two companies of National Police in American-piloted transport planes. The American commander closed the air base's gates to prevent bloodshed, and Ky flew back to Saigon weaker than ever. American noncombatants were evacuated from Da Nang and Hue by Marine helicopters. F Company, 9th Marines blocked an anti-Ky military force marching on Da Nang. The Buddhists controlled central Vietnam, and President Thieu agreed to hold elections for a constitutional assembly and to transfer power to the civilians. The American policy of supporting the stability of the military regime was for the moment totally undermined.

On May 15, Ky struck back. He airlifted a thousand Vietnamese marines into Da Nang and seized the city's key installations in a week of confused fighting. In Saigon, 50,000 workers struck in protest. Vietnamese troops fired shells at the Da Nang air base where Ky's marines were stationed.[8]

Lt. Gen. Walt himself had to go to the Tourane River bridge, east of Da Nang, where Vietnamese Army engineers had armed the bridge and an ammunition dump with high explosives. When Walt arrived with his G-3, Col. John R. Chaisson, a Marine platoon was facing the Vietnamese. While a very angry Walt met the Vietnamese warrant officer in the middle of the bridge, the U.S. Army advisor to the Vietnamese troops and a couple of Marines sneaked under the bridge to try to cut the wires between the detonator and the explosives. The Vietnamese officer refused to pull back his men and threatened to blow the bridge if the Marines advanced. When the Army advisor gave Walt a thumbs-up signal, the general warned the Vietnamese he had five minutes to remove his men and disconnect the detonator. He refused. Time ran out. Walt told the Marines—now built up to a company—to cross the bridge. The Vietnamese ordered the detonator's plunger pushed down. But nothing happened. Walt walked off the bridge and the Marines took over.[9]

Ky's troops invaded the Buddhist pagodas and created hundreds of casualties. Vietnamese aircraft rose to bomb Da Nang, and Walt sent up Marine jets to shoot them down if they attacked the city. The Vietnamese pilots backed down. Ky's forces than lay siege to Hue, where, on May 26, workers and students destroyed the USIS library. Nine Buddhist bonzes and nuns burned themselves to death across the country. On May 31, the United States consulate at Hue was sacked and burned. The Americans deserted Hue. By mid-June, Hue surrendered to Ky's army. The Buddhist "struggle movement" was crushed. The Ky junta remained in power, as the Americans desired and made possible.

During this same period, the 3rd Marine Division pressed southward from Da Nang in a series of "search and clear" operations, cordoning off areas and attempting to eradicate the guerrillas. Five Marine battalions fought the Viet Cong's skillful Doc Lap Battalion. After three months, the Marines had opened Highway One as far south as An Hoa.

Deep in enemy territory, 25 miles west of Chu Lai, Staff Sgt. Jimmie E. Howard, a former Marine football player and coach at San Diego, commanded the 18-man 1st Platoon of C Company, 1st Reconnaissance Battalion. The tall, big sergeant from Burlington, Iowa, had earned the Silver Star and three Purple Hearts in Korea. His job now was to hold an observation post atop grass-covered Hill 488 and spot enemy troops trying to descend out of the hills to the coast.

At 10 P.M. on June 15, the platoon's third night on Hill 488, it was attacked by a North Vietnamese battalion. Lance Cpl. Ricardo Binns' four-man observation team out front was hit first. Binns shot the nearest enemy soldier; each Marine flung a grenade, and they scrambled to the crest. Lance Cpl. John T. Adams of Portland, Oregon, emptied his rifle at the enemy and using it as a club killed two more before he was shot to death. Cpl. Jerrald R. Thompson of Palmer, California, was wounded by a grenade; he killed two North Vietnamese with his knife before he died.

The 16 remaining Marines formed a tight perimeter and threw back assault after assault. Howard directed their defense. A grenade wounded him severely; he could no longer move his legs. He distributed his ammunition to the other men, maintained radio communication and called in artillery fire and air strikes. The enemy taunted them: "Marines, you die!" Flares lighting the bare mountainside revealed hordes of the enemy. The planes worked them over, bombing and strafing. The Marines used up their grenades. They squeezed off single shots and threw back rocks.

By dawn, five of Howard's men were dead and all the rest but one were wounded. Corpsman Billie D. Holmes, badly hurt himself, cared for the wounded. The Marines held.

When evacuation helicopters approached, Howard coolly waved them off and called for more air strikes to secure the landing zone.

Maj. William J. Goodsell brought his helicopter in 10 feet off the ground. It was hit, and Goodsell died of gunshot wounds. A second chopper was hit; its crew chief was killed. Helicopters finally brought in 1st Lt. Marshall Darling's C Company, 5th Marines onto the southern slope. The Marines climbed rapidly, wiping out enemy positions as they went. When they reached Howard's position, his men had eight rounds of ammunition left. The battle went on. Four more Marines were killed, including 2d Lt. Ronald Meyer, just a year out of Annapolis. Darling and Lance Cpl. James Brown crawled out and carried in Meyer's body under fire. By noon it was over. Binns and Holmes were recommended for the Navy Cross. Howard received the Medal of Honor for saving his platoon from annihilation.[10]

In June up north, North Vietnamese units crossed the Demilitarized Zone (DMZ) to support the Viet Cong. The

Marines responded by building up to five-battalion strength. Task Force Delta, commanded by Brig. Gen. Lowell E. English and including some 8,000 Marines and 3,000 South Vietnamese, did battle with the 324B North Vietnamese Division (while other enemy units attacked Pleiku and Saigon). Operation Hastings opened on July 15 in the vicinity of Cam Lo on the east-west Route 9 below the DMZ and at a 700-foot hill called the "Rock Pile." Three battalions attacked north of the enemy and the others hit them from the south.

On July 18, two Marines with K Company, 4th Marines earned the Medal of Honor. The company had been put down to block an enemy jungle trail network on July 15 and was immediately attacked. Capt. Robert J. Modrzejewski of Milwaukee led his men to capture an enemy strongpoint and then fought off a series of counterattacks over the next three days. The surrounded company was assaulted by a regiment-size enemy force on the eighteenth. Although wounded, Modrzejewski led the defense and brought in air and artillery strikes at close range. When the 3rd Battalion was ready to withdraw, rear security was assigned to a platoon of 32 Marines led by Staff Sgt. John J. McGinty III of Boston. They held off the enemy for four hours. When two squads were isolated, McGinty charged through heavy fire and found 20 men wounded and the corpsman killed. He reloaded weapons and magazines for the wounded and directed their fire. He was wounded but led his men in driving off their attackers. The enemy tried to flank the Marines, and McGinty killed five with his pistol and brought in supporting fire within 50 yards of his position, finally routing the enemy.

In another scrap on a narrow jungle trail near the DMZ on July 24, I Company, 5th Marines was ambushed and its lead platoon hard hit. Lance Cpl. Richard A. Pittman of San Joaquin, California, with the second platoon in line, heard the lead unit's cries for help, dropped his rifle, took a machine gun and several belts of ammunition and rushed forward. Coming under fire, Pittman silenced it with his gun. Two automatic weapons opened on him, and he destroyed them both. He kept going 50 yards further up the trail until he reached the spot where the leading Marines had fallen wounded. Attacked by 30 or 40 of the enemy, Pittman braced himself in the middle of the trail and raked them with machine-gun fire. When his gun jammed, he picked up an enemy submachine gun and then another Marine's pistol and forced the enemy to flee. Out of ammunition, he hurled a final grenade at them and rejoined his platoon. He was awarded the Medal of Honor.

When the enemy started pulling out and Operation Hastings ended on August 3, the Marines had killed 824 of the enemy. But the North Vietnamese had succeeded in pulling substantial numbers of Marines and ARVN soldiers to the north and away from protecting the population centers.

Four miles below the DMZ near Cam Lo on August 8, a reconnaissance patrol flushed a large enemy unit. A platoon of E Company, 4th Marines was flown in to go after it. But the search was futile. The enemy remained hidden until the helicopters returned just before dark to recover the platoon. When most of the Marines had been lifted out, the enemy opened fire. They damaged two choppers, stranding 21 Marines. Back at Dong Ha, E Company's commander, New York City-born Capt. Howard V. Lee heard the radio messages from his trapped men. He took seven Marines and all the ammunition they could manage in two light choppers and raced out to the encircled perimeter. Lee took command. The enemy attacked in full force. A grenade wounded Captain Lee in the body and eye, but he continued in command throughout the embattled night. Another chopper flew in with more ammunition. It was hit and its crew picked up rifles and joined the fight. The 20 remaining Marines fought on through the night against repeated attacks until they were rescued the next morning.[11]

Soon, the North Vietnamese 324B Division struck again in the same area between Route 9 and the DMZ. Three Marine battalions met them. Maj. Gen. Kyle moved his advance 3rd Division command post to Dong Ha, where Route 9 and Highway One intersect. Operation Prairie I continued until the end of January 1967 and involved seven Marine battalions and three ARVN battalions. The Marines had 225 killed and 1,159 wounded.

Down in Quang Tin province six miles west of Tam Ky, two days after Captain Lee's fight, the 1st Battalion, 5th Marines fought a tough battle against well-entrenched North Vietnamese. Lt. Col. Hal L. Coffman's battalion was sweeping the area as part of Operation Colorado. At about 3 P.M., it was ambushed by a large enemy force in the hamlet of Cam Khe. Capt. James Furleigh's A Company was met by heavy fire from a tree line and had to pull back through the fire-swept paddies. Five Marines were immediately killed. The enemy had fire superiority. Heavy rain made it impossible to call in supporting arms. Lance Cpl. R. P. Donathan tried to knock out the machine gun that had stopped the company, and was killed. Corpsman T. C. Long, who went to his rescue, was hit in the right knee and trapped under Donathan's body. The other Marines could not get to them. Coffman sent in 1st Lt. Darling's C Company on Furleigh's right flank. The enemy tried slipping around the Marines' left, and Furleigh had Staff Sgt. Albert J. Ellis bring up the 3rd Platoon there. The skill of the Marine riflemen was pitted against the enemy superiority in numbers and firepower. Pfc. George Fudge, a deadly sharpshooter, picked off at least ten North Vietnamese and knocked out a machine gun with a grenade. Lance Cpl. Robert Goodner destroyed two automatic weapons with his 66mm rocket launcher (LAAW). But Ellis' platoon needed help to prevent the enemy from turning the flank.

Coffman sent B Company there. It came under fire from the enemy holding a trench to its front. A 60mm mortar zeroed in on the company command post until Sgt. Peter Rowell's mortar silenced the enemy weapon. The rain continued, but the ceiling had risen enough to let four medical evacuation helicopters come in. Two of the H-34s were shot down. In the third, 1st Lt. Ellis Laitala made ten trips bringing in ammunition and medical supplies and taking out the wounded. Capt. Robert J. Sheehan flew the fourth chopper spectacularly; he made nine trips and his chopper was hit three times, while flying out 20 casualties. As the weather cleared, Marine A4D jets roared in with 2,000-pound bombs.

On the far right, Darling's C Company had the toughest part of the fight. It had to dig the enemy out of a long, deep trench near the road. Darling put his 2d and 3rd Platoons on a firing line and sent the 37 men of Lt. Arthur Blades' 1st Platoon to assault the enemy. In the 3rd Squad on the platoon's right nearest the trench line, all six of its men were hit, three of them killed. Responding to Blades' call for help, Darling sent forward a group of Marines and a machine-gun crew. His executive officer, 1st Lt. Ron Benigo, was hit in the back of the head while carrying a wounded Marine from the paddy but brought out two more men before he was forcibly evacuated.

Blades placed his reinforcements on his left flank and freed his remaining two squads to attack the trench line with automatic-weapons fire and grenades. Four of the six Marines in the 2d Squad were hit and a corpsman rushing up to help them was killed. Blades led his last squad forward. Its leader, Cpl. Christopher Cushman, stood up to spot a sniper. Lance Cpl. Walter McDonald, a combat photographer, shot the sniper and dropped a grenade on another enemy soldier in the trench.

The enemy now began to fall back before the Marines' onslaught. Three engineers with the platoon worked their way up the trench itself to press the enemy from the rear while Blades' Marines attacked their front. Blades kept his men moving forward, firing and hurling grenades. Finally, the enemy broke and ran; Cushman shot one and McDonald two more. The rest died in a blaze of grenades and automatic rifle fire. K Company, 5th Marines was flown in, but the main battle was over.

The next morning, Commandant Greene and Lt. Gen. Walt arrived in a chopper and walked the trench line. Greene asked 1st Lt. Darling what had happened. "Well, General, we got into a fight with the enemy," Darling said. The Commandant asked what he did. "General," he said, "we killed them."[12]

That night, enemy 82mm mortars bombarded the battalion command center; and the enemy assaulted the battalion perimeter. B Company threw them back with a wall of fire.

In fiscal 1966, the Marine Corps took in 80,000 volunteers and nearly 19,000 draftees. It was authorized to reach a strength of 278,184 by July 1, 1967; its peak during the Korean war had been 261,343. As a result of these increases, elements of the 5th Marine Division, which included the 26th, 27th and 28th Marines with the 13th Marines as artillery, began arriving in Vietnam. Its first commander was Maj. Gen. Robert E. Cushman, Jr. A native of St. Paul, Minnesota, and an Annapolis graduate, Cushman had won the Navy Cross on Guam and spent four years on the staff of Vice President Richard M. Nixon.

The South Vietnamese election for a constituent assembly to draft a new constitution was held on September 11, 1966. All communists and neutralists were barred from running; the Buddhists boycotted the elections. The following month in Australia, President Johnson declared, "I believe there is a light at the end of what has been a long and lonely tunnel."[13] He was using the same figure of speech as had French Lt. Gen. Henri Navarre before the battle of Dien Bien Phu.[14]

By now, there were 60,000 Marines in South Vietnam. They claimed 7,300 enemy killed. The Marines had suffered 1,700 dead and more than 9,000 wounded. The Marines' area of responsibility covered 1,800 square miles and nearly a million people. In contrast to the U.S. Army's primary policy of "search and destroy," the Marines were believers in "clear and hold" tactics that would pacify the hamlets and eradicate Viet Cong control. Said Lt. Gen. Walt, "It is slow because you are changing minds. That takes time."[15]

The war effort required enormous resources. There were now nearly 400,000 Americans in Vietnam, and the war was costing the American taxpayer $2 billion a month. American forces tackled the enemy's main forces and killed many of their troops, but the countryside seemed impenetrable. Most ARVN soldiers lacked the will or discipline to risk their lives either to defend the American shored-up government in Saigon or to oppose the Communists. The Saigon politicians went through the American-prodded motions of writing a constitution and holding national elections. When the presidential election was finally held in September 1967, the military ticket of Thieu and Ky predictably won. But it was surprisingly close. The runner-up was an unknown politician who declared he wanted to recognize the NLF and start peace negotiations. The election was "a fiasco of noble proportions."[16] President Thieu promptly put a number of the defeated candidates in jail, including the runner-up.

The war itself seemed to run on a treadmill. Soon there would be half a million American troops in Vietnam. Counting Vietnamese, Koreans and others, Thieu's side had 1.3 million men in uniform. They attacked enemy bases in the south and fought a series of battles with North Vietnamese troops in the Central Highlands and near the DMZ. Hundreds of Americans and thousands of Vietnamese died. It all seemed to make no progress, no difference—except that the fighting created uncounted hundreds of thousands of homeless refugees, whose villages had been destroyed and their crops killed with herbicides. The cities, bulging with American goods and dollars, were wracked by horrendous inflation and flagrant corruption—and hatred of the foreign invaders.

In mid-October 1966, Secretary of Defense Robert S. McNamara returned from Vietnam and gave President Johnson a highly pessimistic report. He said in part: "There is no sign of an impending break in enemy morale and it appears that he can more than replace his losses. . . . Pacification is a bad disappointment. . . . full security exists nowhere (not even behind the U.S. Marines' lines and in Saigon); in the countryside, the enemy almost completely controls the night."[17]

Lt. Gen. Walt began 1967 with 67,729 Marines and 2,649 Navy personnel in the III Marine Amphibious Force. The South Vietnamese had 75,000 troops in I Corps, counting all levels of soldiers and militia. The Marines had Maj. Gen. Kyle's 3rd Division in the two northern provinces. Maj. Gen. Herman Nickerson, Jr.'s, 1st Division covered Quang Nam province and had Task Force X-Ray, commanded by Brig. Gen. William A. Stiles, with two battalions in each of the two southern provinces. The Korean Marines' 2d Brigade was in Quang Ngai province. Maj. Gen. Louis B. Robertshaw commanded the 1st Marine Aircraft Wing.

Vietnam was unlike World War II or Korea. It reminded Marines like Walt and Krulak of the occupations of Nicaragua and Haiti. But Vietnam was on a vast and more deadly scale, and half of the country was in the hands of a hostile and dedicated government and army.

There were those who believed that the Marines were in the wrong place—that they should have been posted in the Mekong Delta, where they could have utilized their 30-year-old amphibious capability. The criticism made sense, but the Marines were not about to move under Army control. In the north, they were again in the ambiguous situation of serving quite like an army force. They were in Vietnam—and stayed in Vietnam—not because they were specialists but because they existed. They were needed and they wanted a piece of the action. But it was increasingly hard to justify "a second army" in Vietnam, even in

"Marineland," as I Corps was called back in Saigon. Once again, a separate Marine command with its own air force would, in time, become a source of trouble.

In early 1967, Lt. Gen. Walt was deeply concerned about the guerrilla war. As he expressed it, "This is first a political war, second a psychological war and third a military war." He said, "Fighting the guerrilla is not the easy part of the war. In 1966, half my casualties were from guerrillas, and these are the nasty kind of casualties—the dirty war." Walt wanted to reorient the ARVN from fighting the enemy's main force to fighting the guerrillas and from living off the villages to helping them. As he saw it, "The more troops I get in here, the larger my area of control. We're taking over hamlets every day. We're protecting more people every day." But he was not sanguine about the prospects: "Some of these areas have been VC-controlled for 20 years. The kids are hard-core communists today. Some people say it will start snowballing, but I don't see any sign so far."[18]

In the first weeks of 1967, the Marines performed assorted "clear-and-secure" operations to block infiltration routes leading down out of the hills toward Hue and to open sections of Highway One. Two battalions of the 26th Marines fought Operation Chinook; four Marines were killed and 73 wounded. The 1st Division had 17 killed and 52 wounded south of Da Nang. And further south, Task Force X-Ray had 10 killed and 50 wounded.

Down in the inhospitable Mekong Delta, the Marines had one chance to perform amphibiously. On January 5, the 1st Battalion, 9th Marines, as the Seventh Fleet's Special Landing Force, with HMM-362 landed 62 miles south of Saigon and worked with two Vietnamese marine battalions. This operation, called Deckhouse V, introduced U.S. combat troops to the Delta. "Intelligence proved bad and results were unimpressive: 21 enemy killed, 7 Marines were killed, and 35 Marines were wounded."[19] During the rest of 1967, Special Landing Force Marines made 22 more landings—but all of them were up north in the I Corps area.

The minute the 1967 Tet holiday truce ended at 7 A.M. on February 12, the 1st Marines began Operation Stone in the familiar area south of Da Nang. Typically, the Marines had to go back over previously "cleared" territory. In ten days, the Marines claimed 291 enemy dead and took 65 prisoners, while suffering nine killed and 77 wounded.

On February 25, the Marines were given permission to fire artillery into the DMZ and into North Vietnam itself. The reaction was quick. Early on February 27, the enemy hurled some 50 140mm Soviet rockets into and near the Da Nang airfield. Later, patrols found 134 firing points within five miles of the base. The attack damaged 17 aircraft and destroyed five communication vans. It killed 32 civilians and wounded 40, and killed 11 American servicemen (including one Marine) and wounded 26.

The Special Landing Force, now the 1st Battalion, 4th Marines and HMM-363, landed at the southern end of I Corps on February 16 and in 10 days accounted for 204 enemy dead; five Marines were killed and 55 wounded. Then, the Landing Force landed again near Thach Tru to support the 7th Marines and three ARVN battalions—fighting over an area that had been the battleground more than a year earlier. In the same period, a battalion of the 5th Marines supported an attack by ARVN and ROK Marines southwest of Chu Lai. Up north in Quang Tri province, five Marine battalions fought Prairie II near the DMZ, losing 93 killed and 483 wounded. As soon as that operation was over, Maj. Gen. Kyle returned to Camp Pendleton to take over the 5th Marine Division; and Maj. Gen. Bruno A. Hochmuth assumed command of the 3rd Division.

On March 20, the same Special Landing Force went ashore four miles south of the DMZ near Gio Linh to help with Prairie III and was greeted by a thousand rounds of mortar, rocket and artillery fire. An ammunition convoy was ambushed and badly cut up the next day. Sgt. Walter K. Singleton of Memphis and A Company, 9th Marines was killed on the twenty-fourth when he took a machine gun and singlehandedly entered the enemy strongpoint, killed eight of its defenders and scattered the rest to save his wounded.[20] Before the Landing Force re-embarked on April 1, it had had 29 killed and 230 wounded. By the time Prairie III was called off on April 19, the Marines had lost 55 killed and 529 wounded. Prairie IV started the next day in the same place. It would be the toughest yet.

In this period, the first Marine A-4 was shot down by a SAM missile from a site inside the DMZ. Electronic warfare-capable

EF-10B and EA-6A aircraft were used against the missiles. And the Marines' new A-6A Intruder aircraft were already hitting targets in North Vietnam.

In Quang Nam province in the center of I Corps, the 2d Battalion, 5th Marines had 5 killed and 55 wounded in three days of battle; and the Da Nang air base was hit by another rocket attack on March 15. At the southern end of the Marines' zone, Operation Desoto ended on April 7 with 76 Marines killed and 573 wounded. After that, two Army brigades came into the Chu Lai area under III MAF and allowed the 7th Marines to shift north to Da Nang. The war's leaders thought a greater concentration of troops up north might help. On April 12, Commandant Greene asked Congress for 40,000 more Marines for Vietnam. And shortly afterwards, General Westmoreland told the press: "We'll just go on bleeding them until Hanoi wakes up to the fact that they have bled the country to the point of national disaster for generations. Then they will have to reassess their position."[21]

Between Chu Lai and Da Nang, the Marines now focused their efforts in the Que Son valley. Again, this inland battleground had been fought over repeatedly; but the Viet Cong still dominated it. In an initial skirmish, eighteen-year-old Pfc. Gary W. Martini of Lexington, Virginia, won the Medal of Honor in death. He tried to save two Marines wounded when the enemy killed 14 and wounded 18 Marines in his platoon of F Company, 1st Marines. Two more Marine battalions were airlifted into the valley and coordinated their attack with ARVN Rangers in Operation Union. Before it was over in mid-May, more units had joined the fight and 110 Marines had been killed and 473 wounded. Enemy dead were figured at 865 dead and another 777 "probable."

In the north began the first bloody battle for the U.S.-built airstrip on the Khe Sanh plateau in the mountainous jungle of the northwest corner of South Vietnam. This had been Green Beret country since 1962—guarding the east-west invasion path along Route 9. On March 16, E Company, 9th Marines was ambushed and had seven killed and nine wounded near Hill 861, five miles northwest of the Khe Sanh Combat Base. On April 24, B Company, 9th Marines, working north of Hill 861, was attacked furiously and lost 14 killed and 17 wounded. The next day, the 3rd Battalion of Col. John P. Lanigan's 3rd Marines flew into Khe Sanh and fought the enemy entrenched on Hill 861. The 2d Battalion was also airlifted in and by the end of April 28, the two battalions had taken the hill.

Then, the 2d Battalion went further west after Hill 881 North and the 3rd Battalion after Hill 881 South. Marine casualties were heavy before the latter objective could be taken with the help of massive artillery support and more than 150 sorties by the 1st MAW. The 2d Battalion found itself up against a North Vietnamese regiment and finally captured Hill 881 North in heavy fighting. On May 9, the battalion again was engaged in a major fire fight and had 24 Marines and 19 wounded. That night, a seven-man reconnaissance team was ambushed and four were killed and the rest wounded; three CH-46 helicopters trying to rescue the team were hit. The 325C North Vietnamese Division pulled back, and the 26th Marines came in to relieve the 3rd Marines and protect the Khe Sanh airstrip. In that first battle, the Marines had had 155 killed and 425 wounded. It was only the beginning at Khe Sanh.

While the fighting was going on around Khe Sanh, to the east the enemy was attacking Marine bases and cutting Route 9 to prevent the reinforcement of the Khe Sanh area. At Con Thien on May 8, the 1st Battalion, 4th Marines was assaulted by two enemy battalions and had 44 killed and 100 wounded.

On May 18, the 9th Marines moved up into the southern half of the DMZ itself for the first time, with strong Marine-Air Force air support. The Seventh Fleet now had two special landing forces: Alpha and Bravo. Alpha made an amphibious assault with helicopters, landing craft and naval gunfire support in the northernmost corner of the DMZ. It ran into heavy resistance along the sandy bank of the Ben Hai River. Bravo joined the operation, and Vietnamese police removed 13,000 civilian refugees from the buffer zone. By landing behind the enemy battalions south of the DMZ, the Marines forced them to pull back into the hills. At the end of May, seven Marine battalions finished up Prairie IV with 489 of the enemy killed. Marine losses were 164 killed and 999 wounded. The whole series of Prairie operations to that date had cost the Marines 525 killed and 3,167 wounded.

On June 1, Lt. Gen. Walt, who had commanded III MAF for

two years, was relieved by Lt. Gen. Cushman, who had been his deputy. Maj. Gen. Nickerson replaced Cushman; and Maj. Gen. Donn J. Robertson, who had earned the Navy Cross on Iwo Jima, took over the 1st Marine Division. At the 1st Marine Aircraft Wing, Maj. Gen. Robertshaw was relieved by Maj. Gen. Norman J. Anderson.

In the south in Quang Tin province, Union II developed into a fierce 11-day battle in the Que Son valley with the 5th Marines fighting two North Vietnamese regiments. The enemy was strong and well dug in. After much artillery and air pounding, the fighting became bunker-to-bunker. Capt. James A. Graham of Wilkinsburg, Pennsylvania, earned the Medal of Honor posthumously on June 2. He led his F Company across a wide rice paddy in the face of mortar and small-arms fire. When his 2d Platoon was pinned down by two machine guns, Graham charged with his company headquarters men through the 2d Platoon and forced the enemy to abandon one machine gun. Graham himself killed 15 of the enemy. As his men and the 2d Platoon withdrew, Graham stayed with one Marine too seriously wounded to be moved. His last radio message reported that he was being attacked by 25 of the enemy.

Together, Union I and II took a toll of 1,566 enemy dead. The Marines lost 220 killed and 714 wounded. Ten days later, the fighting was resumed with a new name: Operation Adair, and continued through the end of June.

At the northern end of the zone, June and July saw a series of hard-fought operations. The enemy continued to build up around Khe Sanh and sporadic fighting went on through June. Between May 13 and July 16, the Marines there had 52 killed and 555 wounded. Operations Crockett, Ardmore, Cimarron, Buffalo and Hickory II cost hundreds of Marine casualties. The 11th Engineer Battalion cut a "firebreak" 600 meters wide and nine miles long between Con Thien and Gio Linh, stripped it of vegetation and filled it with barbed wire, minefields, sensors, watchtowers and strongpoints. On July 2, B and C Companies, 9th Marines were heavily attacked and took severe casualties. The 3rd Battalion helicoptered in to join the rest of the 1st Battalion and hit the enemy's left flank. That first day, 84 Marines were killed and 190 wounded. Two battalions of the 3rd Marines were flown into the battle area, and the fighting continued until July 14 with 159 Marines dead and 45 wounded. The enemy reportedly lost 1,301 dead—and two prisoners.

The Da Nang air base was hit by 122mm rockets shortly after midnight on July 15 from launchers in a village six miles southwest of the city. The results of the attack were serious. Eight airmen were killed and 138 wounded and 37 Marines were wounded. Ten planes were totally wrecked and a number severely damaged.

On August 19, Capt. Stephen W. Pless of Atlanta, Georgia, was piloting a small helicopter gunship near Quang Ngai when he heard on his radio that a U.S. Army helicopter was down on a remote beach and under attack. On the beach, Pless saw four Americans being bayoneted and beaten by more than 30 Viet Cong. Diving low, he scared off the enemy. As they raced to the trees, Pless fired his machine guns and rockets at them. One of the Americans on the ground waved, and Pless landed under fire to rescue the downed men. The wounded man stumbled toward the helicopter. Gunnery Sgt. Leroy N. Poulson ran out and found two others still alive. The copilot, Capt. Rupert E. Fairfield, jumped out to help. Lance Cpl. John G. Phelps fired his machine gun at the Viet Cong, who rushed Pless' craft repeatedly. With the three wounded men aboard, Pless took off. A U.S. Army gunship arrived and attacked the enemy. Pless' overloaded helicopter struck the water four times before it was able to rise and carry out the three wounded soldiers.[22]

The enemy stepped up their artillery and rocket attack on major Marine bases during late August and early September. The attacks killed men and destroyed aircraft and ammunition dumps at Dong Ha, Marble Mountain, Phu Bai and Da Nang.

Since the bombing of North Vietnam had failed to suppress North Vietnam's support of the Viet Cong, a barrier of barbed wire and "highly sophisticated devices," mines and sensors was begun across the northern border of South Vietnam. The plan met serious doubts in the Pentagon. Commandant Greene candidly opposed the project, and Marines on the scene felt the enemy would simply circumvent the barrier and continue to walk in through Laos. It was predicted that "McNamara's Wall" would be no more effective than the Maginot Line.

Navy Chaplain Vincent R. Capodanno of Staten Island, New York, earned the Medal of Honor in death on September 4 when he went into a large-scale battle with the 2d Platoon, M Company, 5th Marines south in Quang Tin province. Disregarding intense enemy fire, Lieutenant Capodanno moved unarmed around the battlefield giving medical aid to the wounded and administering last rites to the dying. A mortar round tore off part of his right hand and wounded him in the arms and legs. He refused medical attention. He raced over to help a wounded corpsman under fire from a machine gun 15 yards away and was killed by a burst from the enemy gun.

In this action, Sgt. Lawrence D. Peters of Johnson City, New York, was killed leading his squad in the same 2d Platoon. Although seriously wounded four times, Peters stood in full view of the enemy to force them to expose their positions, until he died. He too was awarded the Medal of Honor posthumously.

As more Army troops of the Americal Division moved into the southern part of I Corps, the 5th Marines shifted north to Da Nang and the 1st Marines were sent still further north to join the 3rd Marine Division. That division focused its attention on the defense of Con Thien, a red clay hill 500 feed high just south of the DMZ and west of Highway One. It was held by one battalion; and in early September, the enemy tried to attack the Marine strongpoint. Heavy fighting went on repeatedly into early October against various elements of the 4th, 9th and 26th Marines. When the pressure against Con Thien lessened, MACV in Saigon declared the battle a substantial victory.

Two pieces of Marine equipment came under debate during this period. The Colt-manufactured high-velocity M-16 rifle, which had replaced the M-14, was accused of jamming and causing American deaths. This new 5.56mm rifle had been chosen as the successor to the controversial M-14 and filled the need for a lightweight weapon with a high rate of fire. Admittedly, the new weapon still had "bugs" in it and failed under combat conditions. Modifications reduced its rate of fire, improved extraction and brought down the malfunction rate. During the same period, the CH-46 helicopter was found to have structural faults that caused a number of accidents.

In October, the 1st Marines, newly moved north, went to work in the Hai Lang National Forest, an enemy base area. Special Landing Force Alpha (1st Battalion, 3rd Marines) and two ARVN battalions joined them. By the end of the month, the

3rd Division's Operation Kingfisher was closed down. Since July 16, it had cost 340 Marines killed and 3,086 wounded; III MAF claimed 1,117 enemy dead and five captured. In the Hue area, the 3rd Division screened the western approaches to the populated coastal area, killed 123 enemy and suffered 17 dead and 260 wounded.

On November 1, Vice President Hubert H. Humphrey visited the Marines and at Da Nang presented the 3rd Division with the Presidential Unit Citation for more than two years of fighting in the five northern provinces. Clearly, this had become a long and costly war. The list of American casualties seemed endless. And, although "body counts" of enemy dead were notoriously unreliable, the North Vietnamese and Viet Cong were also paying a heavy price for trying to wage war in South Vietnam.

Twice, early in November, the Viet Cong hit district headquarters and refugee settlements 15 miles southwest of Da Nang; they killed civilians and destroyed 559 houses. Two Marine battalions retaliated and by the month's end had killed 125 of the enemy, losing 21 Marines dead and 137 wounded. On November 14, Maj. Gen. Hochmuth was killed when his UH-1E helicopter exploded and crashed near Hue. Maj. Gen. Rathvon McC. Tompkins, winner of the Navy Cross on Saipan, took over the 3rd Division.

During the last weeks of 1967, Marine operations, although expensive in casualties, harvested less results in hurting the enemy. And as more Army units moved into the southern area of I Corps, the Korean Marine Brigade moved north to Da Nang.

"The year ended almost exactly as it had begun."[23] The Marines had been in the midst of some of the heaviest fighting and so far had been able to keep some semblance of control over the northern boundary of South Vietnam. At year's end, 77,679 Marines were in III MAF. There were 21 Marine battalions, 31 ARVN battalions, 15 U.S. Army battalions and 4 Korean Marine battalions in I Corps. The Marines were now concentrated in the three northern provinces with four of their seven infantry regiments along Route 9 south of the DMZ. Commandant Leonard F. Chapman, Jr., of Key West, Florida, who succeeded Greene on January 1, 1968, reported that the Marines had killed 17,876 enemy soldiers during the past year. The toll had been high: 3,452 Marines killed and 25,994 wounded. Marine casualties since 1962 now totaled 5,479 dead and 37,784 wounded. Only in World War II had the Corps suffered more.

The Marines took particular pride in their pacification efforts, but admittedly these had been a mixture of success and failure. The heavy influx of North Vietnamese troops had succeeded in drawing American forces from the populated coastal areas and reduced the effectiveness of the pacification program. The ARVN proved incapable of "pacifying" areas cleared by the United States Army and Marines, and Ky's 1966 offensive against the civilian supporters of Gen. Nguyen Chanh Thi and the Buddhists had destroyed much of the non-communist infrastructure in I Corps. In addition, the year of heavy fighting and the spread of "free-fire zones," from which civilian population was banned, had doubled the number of refugees. There were now an acknowledged 530,000 refugees in I Corps. Although the American commanders were highly optimistic, the light at the end of the lonely tunnel still seemed a long way off.

3
Tet and Khe Sanh — 1968

The Americans later insisted that they had known the Tet Offensive was coming; they said that the North Vietnamese buildup had been no secret. But at the time, few believed Intelligence reports that the enemy intended to attack South Vietnam's cities and towns. General Westmoreland, expecting battle at Khe Sanh, started shifting forces northward. Afterwards, some would say that he did exactly what North Vietnam's Gen. Vo Nguyen Giap wanted him to do—pull American strength away from the cities.

Along the six-mile-deep DMZ stood the North Vietnamese 324B and 325C Divisions. In mid-January 1968, the 304th Division came in from Laos and joined the 325C near Khe Sanh. Soon, elements of three more North Vietnamese divisions were identified south of the DMZ.

The 3rd Marine Division was strung out along the northern face of South Vietnam. Units of the 1st Marine Division were moved north, and Westmoreland sent the 1st Air Cavalry Division and the 2d Brigade of the 101st Airborne Division into the two northern provinces. As 1968 began, there were a quarter of a million allied soldiers in I Corps.

By now, the Marine Corps had 21 of its 36 ground battalions, 14 of its 33 fixed-wing squadrons and 13 of its 24 helicopter squadrons in Vietnam. Of the Corps' total strength—298,498 Marines—81,249 were in Vietnam.

Westmoreland keyed his northern defense on holding the Khe Sanh Combat Base on the plateau in the coffee-growing hills near Route 9. He saw Khe Sanh as the plug at the western end of the DMZ and believed that, if the base fell, the North Vietnamese would flank the Marine defenses along the DMZ.

He strengthened Khe Sanh; he did not want it to become an American Dien Bien Phu.

The decision to defend Khe Sanh was certainly controversial. President Johnson involved himself intimately. The Joint Chiefs of Staff supported the decision in writing. Their former chairman—and former ambassador in Saigon—General Taylor disagreed. Critics said the enemy was luring American strength into the remote hills. As one official Marine historian has written, "In the last analysis, Khe Sanh was defended because it was the only logical thing to do. We were there, in a prepared position and in considerable strength. A well-fought battle would do the enemy a lot more damage than he could hope to inflict on us."[24] And an Air Force historian added, "The base had become a symbol of U.S. determination to see the war through."[25]

Khe Sanh itself was the responsibility of Col. David E. Lownds' 26th Marines. When four enemy regiments were reported within 20 kilometers of its airstrip, Lownds' 2d and 3rd Battalions were moved over from the coast to help the 1st Battalion defend the base.

After some small-scale contact, the second battle of Khe Sanh opened on January 20. Two 3rd Battalion companies attacked a North Vietnamese battalion entrenched between Hills 881 North and 881 South. The next day, the enemy bombarded the Khe Sanh base, destroying 1,500 tons of ammunition, and captured the village of Khe Sanh on the highway. The Marines had to replenish the ammunition by air.

Lt. Col. John F. Mitchell's 1st Battalion, 9th Marines was rushed into the area; and more than a thousand civilians were airlifted out. The 37th ARVN Ranger Battalion of 318 men and two additional Marine 105mm howitzer batteries joined the garrison. More guns could have been added, but the limiting factor was the number of artillery shells that could be flown in. The monsoon rains—and the enemy—had closed Route 9.

Despite the American planning and buildup, when the Tet Offensive began the enemy simply bypassed Khe Sanh and attacked the population centers. General Giap's strategy worked.

In an enormous, surprise, coordinated offensive, more than 60,000 of the enemy—starting early on Tuesday, January 30—attacked every important American base and most of the cities and provincial and district capitals throughout South Vietnam. A great portion of the ARVN troops charged with defending the cities was absent for the Tet holiday.

At 2:47 A.M. Wednesday, a team of Viet Cong commandos armed with antitank rockets and explosive charges blasted their way into the walled compound of the United States Embassy in Saigon. They killed four U.S. Army MPs and wounded Cpl. George B. Zahuranic; he, Sgt. Ronald W. Harper and Sgt. Rudy A. Soto, Jr., were the only Marines on guard in the building. The commandos drove off a helicopter-borne paratrooper assault force. Marine Cpl. James C. Marshall was killed on a compound rooftop. The invaders held the embassy compound for six and a half hours before 12 were killed and two wounded men were captured. Pictures of the bloody raid against the center of the American presence in Vietnam shocked Americans back home.

Viet Cong battalions penetrated Saigon; a commando unit attacked the Presidential Palace, and two battalions blew up aircraft and fought American troops at Tan Son Nhut airfield. The enemy hit the Bien Hoa Air Base and the Long Binh military headquarters. They holed up in Cholon, Saigon's Chinese section, for two weeks and kept the city in chaos. Destruction was widespread; tanks and helicopter gunships demolished buildings, and fire swept through entire areas of huts.

In the north, the enemy overran all five provincial capitals. They opened the jails and released thousands of prisoners. Their troops had infiltrated in advance, hidden among the holiday traffic and an apathetic—or sympathetic—people. They attacked Tam Ky and Quang Ngai city and in heavy fighting were thrown back. They attacked Quang Tri city, where the 1st ARVN Division and the 1st Air Cavalry Division stopped them.

Further northwest at Cam Lo, the North Vietnamese smashed the defenses of the District Headquarters. There, young Cpl. Larry L. Maxam of Glendale, California, a fire team leader with D Company, 4th Marines spotted the enemy massing to assault the remaining defensive wire. Repeatedly wounded by grenade fragments, Maxam grabbed an abandoned machine gun and fired on the advancing enemy. A grenade struck him in the face; he was hit by rifle fire. But continuing to fire his machine gun, he forced the enemy to retreat. Despite further wounds, he defended half the perimeter singlehandedly for an hour and a half, until he was finally overwhelmed by the enemy fire.[26]

One objective of the enemy's Tet Offensive was to crush the Americans' air mobility and close support capability. On January 29 and 30, rockets and mortars hammered MAG-11 at Da Nang and MAG-16 at Marble Mountain; and rockets crashed into MAG-12 and -13 at Chu Lai.

At Da Nang, mortar shells and rockets hit U.S. and ARVN positions in the early hours of January 30. The enemy attacked I Corps headquarters; the duty section and a Combined Action Platoon stopped the first assault. Marine and Vietnamese MPs and Vietnamese Rangers rushed up; and in a formless battle, the attackers were killed or expelled. The North Vietnamese 2d Division approached the city from the south and west and was intercepted by reconnaissance elements of the 1st Marine Division. Overhead in his command helicopter, Lt. Gen. Cushman spotted 200 of the enemy across the river south of the air base. He radioed Maj. Gen. Robertson, who sent the 3rd Battalion, 5th Marines, followed by the 2d Battalion, 3rd Marines, to stop them.

Further south at Hoi An, the enemy invaded the city until ARVN troops counterattacked. On February 5, the enemy again fought into Hoi An and again were thrown back.

At the ancient imperial capital of Hue, enemy battalions infiltrated the city. Some of their soldiers waited in the tea rooms and bars until the pre-arranged time to change into uniform. They swiftly and easily took the center of the city on January 31. South of the Perfume River, they captured the provincial headquarters and the university and to the north, most of the imperial Citadel, except for the corner occupied by the 1st ARVN Division headquarters. They seized all the key installations but the high-walled MACV compound and some isolated pockets of resistance. They murdered hundreds of selected Vietnamese and foreigners.

The North Vietnamese forced the Americans and ARVN to fight in the cities. In most places, Americans and ARVN troops dislodged the enemy in a few days; but in Hue, the battle would go on for a month.

Early on the morning of January 31, A Company, 1st Marines rushed to Hue by truck to reinforce the MACV compound. A Company was followed by the command group, 1st Battalion, 1st Marines; G Company, 5th Marines, and a tank platoon. They fought through to the compound by mid-afternoon, and then two Marine platoons crossed the Perfume River bridge with heavy casualties. But they could not breach the Citadel wall and at dusk withdrew across the river.

F and H Companies, 5th Marines joined the Marines at Hue. At first, there was reluctance to use American firepower to retake the revered city. But when the ARVN counterattack slowed down and its commander asked for Marine help south of the river, the Marines went to work under the command of Col. Stanley S. Hughes of the 1st Marines. Fighting was house-to-house, reminiscent of the battle for Seoul. The Marines used recoilless rifles, tank guns, rockets and tear gas.

In this battle, Sgt. Alfredo Gonzalez of Edinberg, Texas, commanded the 3rd Platoon of A Company, 1st Marines. On the way into Hue, he led his platoon to clear out snipers. One Marine on top of a tank was hit and fell exposed to enemy fire; and Gonzalez, although wounded himself, carried him to safety. Then, he and his men destroyed the enemy strongpoint. When his company was pinned down on February 4, Gonzalez moved from position to position firing antitank weapons at the enemy's fortified emplacements until he was mortally wounded. He was awarded the Medal of Honor posthumously.

Not until February 6 did five companies of Marines recapture Hue's hospital, jail and provincial headquarters. Resistance south of the river was wiped out by February 9, with an estimated 1,053 enemy dead. Then, the Marines crossed the river and joined the ARVN in the final assault on the old city.

On February 12, Lt. Col. Robert H. Thompson's 1st Battalion, 5th Marines moved into the city from the north by helicopter and landing craft. The monsoon rains washed out most tactical air support. The Marines advanced on the left flank, with the 3rd ARVN Regiment in the center and the Vietnamese marines on the right. It took until February 22 for them to seize the southeast wall of the Citadel and drive the North Vietnamese from the city. The U.S. Marines stayed out of the struggle for the Imperial Palace; and on the twenty-fourth, the South Vietnamese flag finally flew over the Citadel. On March 2, the battle was declared finished. After more than a month of fighting, in which

142 Marines died and 857 were seriously wounded, the ancient city on the Perfume River lay in ruins.

The Marines' 27th Regimental Landing Team, commanded by Col. Adolph G. Schwenk, and the 3rd Brigade of the 82d Airborne Division were rushed to Vietnam. Schwenk's 27th Marines began arriving in Da Nang by air from Camp Pendleton by February 17 and took over the troublesome area between Marble Mountain and Hoi An. Schwenk's third battalion, which had been based in Hawaii, arrived directly from an amphibious exercise at sea. By the end of February, there were 24 Marine and 28 U.S. Army battalions operating in I Corps. Lt. Gen. Cushman headed the largest combat command ever held by a Marine, excepting Lt. Gen. Roy S. Geiger's brief command of the Tenth Army on Okinawa.

But command changes began to recognize the new Army–Marine mix in I Corps and also suggested wider concern over the way the war was going. Westmoreland established a MACV forward command post at Phu Bai on February 9 under Gen. Creighton W. Abrams, Jr., USA, the former Vice Chief of Staff of the Army. And Westmoreland asked for 206,000 more men, in addition to the 535,000 already in Vietnam.

On March 10, Westmoreland made two moves that seriously affected the Marines. First, he organized the Provisional Corps under Lt. Gen. William D. Rosson, USA, with Marine Maj. Gen. Raymond G. Davis, who had earned the Medal of Honor at the Chosin Reservoir, as his deputy. Prov Corps took operational control of the 3rd Marine Division, the 1st Air Cavalry Division and the 101st Airborne Division. And, secondly, the 1st MAW's fixed-wing aircraft were finally, after much debate and compromise, turned over to the "mission direction" of the Commanding General, Seventh Air Force. This change had been fiercely opposed by the Marine leaders; to a significant degree, it broke up the Marine air-ground team again.

The creation of Abrams' and Rosson's commands and the "single manager" for tactical air resulted from the Army, and Westmoreland especially, being dissatisfied with the Marines' leadership in Vietnam. "Disclaimers by both Army and Marine Corps spokesmen did not completely still the clamor."[27] The old interservice wounds from Bellau Wood, Saipan, Okinawa and Korea ached once more.

The most important question was: What had the enemy accomplished with his Tet Offensive? American military leaders insisted that the enemy had gained no new territory, rallied no general popular support and been badly hurt as a fighting force. That was all true. U.S. estimates were that the enemy had lost more than 15,000 soldiers. The enemy had caused tremendous destruction and chaos and killed an estimated 165,000 civilians. But if their goal had been to occupy most of the two northern provinces, as Westmoreland said, they had failed. U.S. military spokesmen called Tet a victory—as they had once heralded the raising of the Berlin Wall as a triumph for the West.

The true effect of Tet was much more devastating. The enemy had demonstrated that, despite the enormous American military buildup and the best available American military brains, they were able to mount a powerful invasion of South Vietnam. The massive bombing of North Vietnam had weakened neither their will nor their capability. The government in Saigon was rocked; the sense of hopelessness spread among the people of South Vietnam. And above all, the North Vietnamese dramatically undermined support for the war back in the United States. All the optimistic statements of progress and victory were no longer—and never again—credible.

On March 1, Clark Clifford replaced McNamara, who had become disillusioned with the war, as Secretary of Defense. On March 22, President Johnson suddenly recalled General Westmoreland, who had commanded MACV since 1964, and announced that General Abrams would succeed him. And on March 31, Johnson halted the bombing of North Vietnam except near the DMZ, urged the start of peace talks and took himself out of the 1968 election campaign. Preliminary talks started in Paris on May 13, but the war went on—for a very long time.[*]

First, the four Marine battalions and the ARVN Rangers at the remote Khe Sanh Combat Base fortified the perimeter around the airstrip and the chain of hills to the north and west. During the last weeks of January, the North Vietnamese had probed and bombarded the Marine positions. Early on February 5, while the Tet Offensive was still alive, electronic sensor

---

[*]March 16, 1968, was the date of the massacre of several hundred South Vietnam civilians by U.S. Army troops in the village of My Lai in Quang Ngai, the southernmost province under III MAF command.

devices warned the two companies of the 3rd Battalion, 26th Marines on crucial Hill 881 South that the enemy were approaching through the 20-foot-high elephant grass. Artillery and air hit them hard. A battalion attacked the north slope of Hill 861A; and Capt. Earle G. Breeding, Jr.'s, E Company, 26th Marines stopped them in a hand-to-hand brawl, leaving 109 enemy bodies hanging on the barbed wire. The Marines had seven dead and 35 wounded.

During the night of February 6, the 66th North Vietnamese Regiment accompanied by nine Russian-made tanks captured the relocated Special Forces camp near Lang Vei on Route 9 six miles southwest of the airstrip. The Marines at Khe Sanh could not send a rescue force, but Marine helicopters pulled out 14 of the 24 Green Berets and most of the Montagnards. Air and artillery pounded the abandoned base and destroyed three enemy tanks. The next day, the enemy attacked the Marine defenses around Khe Sanh and penetrated Capt. Henry J. M. Radcliffe's A Company, 9th Marines until a counterattack drove them out. Twenty-one Marines were killed and 26 wounded. The enemy kept up their bombardment; and on February 23 alone, 1,307 mortar and artillery rounds smashed into the Khe Sanh base. On the twenty-fifth, a patrol from B Company, 26th Marines was ambushed south of the base. A platoon sent out to help the trapped patrol was also hit by the enemy. In all, 26 Marines were killed and 21 wounded.

The North Vietnamese lay siege to Khe Sanh, digging their trenches ever closer. Round-the-clock bombing, including B-52 strikes, and heavy artillery fire tried to halt them. The base was supplied and 852 wounded were removed by air, despite fire from concentrations of enemy antiaircraft weapons. On February 29 and March 1, the enemy made their last major effort to breach the perimeter and were repulsed by the ARVN Rangers. The shelling and bombing continued, but the worst of the battle was over. Between November 1967 and the end of March, the Marines at Khe Sanh had had 205 killed and 1,668 wounded. The Marines figured that two North Vietnamese divisions had been destroyed.

As the monsoon season ended, Lt. Gen. Cushman planned a triple spring offensive: the relief of Khe Sanh, a raid into the A Shau valley in Thua Thien province and an attack into the DMZ.

To relieve Khe Sanh, the 1st Air Cavalry Division with an ARVN battalion approached Khe Sanh from the east and south, while the 1st Marines and three ARVN battalions moved westward to open Route 9. The cavalrymen established a base and airstrip at Ca Lu, five miles east of Khe Sanh; by April 6, they linked up with the 9th Marines south of the airstrip. By the twelfth, Route 9 was open to traffic again. The Lang Vei camp was reoccupied. When the 3rd Battalion, 26th Marines took Hill 881 North on Easter Sunday, April 14, the 77-day battle for Khe Sanh was declared over. It had been a tremendous effort of artillery fire, air supply and bombing. The Americans had poured on the enemy 100,000 tons of bombs and 150,000 artillery rounds. There had been 679 air drops; and while 455 aircraft had actually landed at Khe Sanh, the enemy had destroyed only four fixed-wing aircraft and 17 helicopters.

On May 23 at the White House, President Johnson presented the Presidential Unit Citation to the 26th Marines. Colonel Lownds, who had shaved off his handlebar mustache for the occasion, and Sgt. Major Agrippa W. Smith, the senior enlisted man at Khe Sanh, received the award for the regiment.

The A Shau valley operation was carried out by elements of the 1st Air Cavalry and 101st Airborne Divisions and a number of ARVN battalions. Between April 19 and May 16, they had many small unit actions, counted 735 enemy dead and captured large quantities of enemy weapons and trucks.

But the III MAF's attack into the DMZ was frustrated when the enemy in force attacked Dong Ha, at the intersection of Highway One and Route 9, in an effort to reach the 3rd Marine Division command post. On April 29, the 2d ARVN Regiment tackled a North Vietnamese regiment four miles north of the base; and then the 2d Battalion, 4th Marines engaged the enemy's main body in a tough three-day battle a mile and a half northeast of Dong Ha. On May 1, three companies attacked the fortified village of Dai Do. G Company led by Capt. M. Sando Vargas, Jr., of Winslow, Arizona, was pinned down by enemy fire and isolated from the rest of the battalion. Although wounded, Vargas set up a defense perimeter at the edge of the village, and G Company fought off counterattacks throughout the night. The next morning, Capt. James E. Livingston of Telfair, Georgia, led his E Company through several hundred yards of intense fire to reinforce Vargas' men. They destroyed more than 100 bunkers and drove out the enemy. Although he was twice wounded, Livingston consolidated his remaining men and Vargas' company and tried to attack the next village. They were stopped by a counterattacking enemy battalion. Wounded a third time and now unable to walk, Livingston stayed on the field, deploying his men and getting the wounded evacuated. Vargas was also hit a third time; but when he saw the battalion commander, Lt. Col. William Weise, seriously wounded, Vargas crossed the fire-swept field and carried Weise to a protected position. Then, he helped organize the battalion's defense. Both Vargas and Livingston received the Medal of Honor.

The 3rd Battalion, 9th Marines plus U.S. Army and ARVN elements tried to trap the enemy; and heavy fighting continued until May 16. The North Vietnamese 320th Division attacked again at the end of the month and was battered by units of the 4th, 9th and 3rd Marines.

The enemy's aggressiveness had been weakened but not rubbed out by the losses of the Tet Offensive. On May 5—in what was called Mini Tet—they launched 119 rocket and mortar attacks throughout South Vietnam. In I Corps, they hit III MAF headquarters at Da Nang, the MACV compound at Hue and the 101st Airborne Division headquarters, as well as airfields at Da Nang, Marble Mountain, Quang Tri and Chu Lai. More such attacks took place on May 11 and 13; and on the nineteenth, rockets blew up an ammunition dump, destroying 80,000 gallons of fuel and several helicopters. The rocket and mortar attacks went on throughout the month. And on May 27, enemy forces assaulted Tam Ky, destroying 300 houses and killing 50 civilians.

The rocket and mortar attacks called for a change in tactics, and the 1st Marine Division started more mobile operations to push the North Vietnamese further away from Da Nang. As a result, the 2d Battalion, 7th Marines on May 9 got into a fight with a large enemy force near the ruined railroad bridge over the Ky Lam River; and four days later, the 3rd Battalion met the well dug-in enemy two miles further west. The enemy was in the area in strength. The 27th Marines took over the fight and pressed the battle toward the west, while the 7th Marines screened the corridors leading from the mountains toward Da

Nang. The Marines' "Sting Ray" technique of sending six-man recon teams to spot the enemy for air and artillery fire was used effectively.

Further south in Quang Tin province's western reaches, the North Vietnamese on May 10 hit the Special Forces camp at Kham Duc, which was supported by a section of Marine 105mm howitzers. Lt. Gen. Cushman sent in U.S. Army reinforcements; but when the enemy attacked in regimental strength, the camp was abandoned. While 1,400 persons were being flown out, one C-130 with 150 Vietnamese aboard was shot down and everyone was killed. Large quantities of equipment had to be destroyed or abandoned.

In May, action also heightened around Khe Sanh where six Marine and two Army battalions had been posted the previous month. The enemy's 304th Division ambushed convoys and engaged the 3rd Battalion, 4th Marines in a two-day battle west of Khe Sanh. Other fights broke out east and south of the base. When the fresh 308th North Vietnamese Division replaced the battered 304th, Task Force Hotel, led by Brig Gen. Carl W. Hoffman, staged a counteraction from two large fire support bases, Loon and Robin, which were blasted out of the rain forest five miles south of Route 9 near the Laotian border. By early June, Marine companies there were heavily engaged; and on June 16 and 18, the enemy attacked the 3rd Battalion, 4th Marines and were repulsed. The fighting cost the enemy 725 killed and captured and forced the 308th to withdraw after two weeks of battle.

Westmoreland left Saigon on June 11, and Lt. Gen. Cushman's proposal that Khe Sanh be abandoned was finally acted on. Everything possible was removed and the rest burned, blown up or buried. Working east along Route 9, the 1st Marines and the 11th Engineer Battalion dismantled six tactical bridges behind them. By July 5, the base at Khe Sanh had been razed and was replaced by Landing Zone Stud at Ca Lu further east. The North Vietnamese proclaimed the "fall" of Khe Sanh a victory; in Washington, the White House spokesman insisted it was a military decision. In Paris, the North Vietnamese spokesman called the American explanation that the base was no longer essential "sour grapes." MACV said that the new mobile tactics in Quang Tri province made the base unnecessary. Maj. Gen.

Davis, now commanding the 3rd Marine Division, announced that combat bases and strongpoints would either be closed down or made defendable by a single reinforced company. The new emphasis would be on mobility. Clearly, if the defense of Khe Sanh had served any purpose, it had been outlived.

Throughout June, enemy artillery damaged 3rd Marine Division bases. At Dong Ha on June 20, an ammunition dump exploded, destroying a quarter of a million artillery and mortar rounds. But by the end of the month, enemy offensive activity decreased noticeably in conjunction with North Vietnamese professions in Paris of a desire to negotiate a settlement.

For seven days beginning on July 1, the American Operation Thor blasted an area 10 miles by 16 miles, north from the southern edge of the DMZ. It was bombarded by Marine, Navy and Air Force planes, Strategic Air Command B-52s, two cruisers and six destroyers and 118 pieces of artillery. After that paroxysm of fire, the 3rd and 9th Marines and the 2d ARVN Regiment swept the area from Route 9 to the DMZ.

In Quang Nam province, the 27th and 5th Marines tried to keep the enemy off balance. But on August 18, the enemy hit a number of targets and especially Da Nang again with rockets and mortars. And on August 22, they shelled Saigon for the first time in two months. ARVN Rangers intercepted the 38th North Vietnamese Regiment south of Da Nang; but before dawn on August 23, the Viet Cong routed a Popular Force detachment south of the air base and seized the southern end of the Cam Le Bridge that carried Highway One northward into Da Nang. The Marines' C Company, 1st Military Police Battalion stopped the Viet Cong at the northern end of the bridge; and at dawn, A Company, 27th Marines struck the Viet Cong rear and broke their hold on the bridge. ARVN Rangers came to the rescue of the Popular Force men under attack. The enemy continued the pressure south of Da Nang and by the end of August had lost some 1,072 dead there.

Highway One and the railroad had been opened again from Da Nang north to Hue. And the 27th Marines on September 10 began to leave Vietnam for California and Hawaii. Its place south of Da Nang was taken by the 1st Marines, which was relieved up north by U.S. Army troops. Further south and west, elements of the 7th and 5th Marines fought occasional sharp actions. The 9th and 3rd Marines operating near the DMZ, thwarted an attack across the line by the rejuvenated North Vietnamese 320th Division. On September 30, the 16-inch rifles of *New Jersey* added gunfire support ranging 24 miles inland. If not spectacularly effective, it was a dramatic gesture.

In the fall, with the DMZ seemingly more secure, the 1st Cavalry Division (Air Mobile) was pulled back from I Corps, leaving the northern front to the 3rd Marine Division and the 101st Airborne Division (Air Mobile). As the monsoon rains returned, the enemy made an attack on the Thuong Duc Special Forces camp in central Quang Nam province between Da Nang and Laos; it was broken up by Marine artillery and bombing. The 2d Battalion, 5th Marines counterattacked up Route 4, while the 7th Marines and other units of the 5th attempted to land behind the enemy. The fighting went on in the area around Hill 163 until October 19.

Just before the American elections, President Johnson announced the cessation of all air, naval and artillery bombardment of North Vietnam starting on November 1. Two days later, North Vietnamese in Paris announced they were ready to participate in peace talks and began withdrawing most of their regiments out of South Vietnam. But on November 5, they charged that the United States was continuing reconnaissance flights over North Vietnam. The United States replied that those flights revealed increased North Vietnamese efforts to resupply their forces in the south through Laos.

November 1 marked the beginning of two programs. The first was Le Loi, a stepped-up pacification campaign to return control of the rural population to pre-Tet levels and restore the damage done by the enemy's 1968 offensives. The second was the Phoenix program aimed at eradicating the Viet Cong infrastructure in the villages and hamlets.

In an area 10 miles south of Da Nang called "Dodge City," the 1st Marine Division staged an intensive "cordon and search" operation. Six Marine battalions were used to cordon off the area five miles wide and three miles deep. Three-man fire teams were positioned every 50 feet around the perimeter. As the cordon tightened in the first week of December, the fighting grew heavier until, by December 9, 1,210 of the enemy had been killed and 182 captured. Throughout the Marine Corps zone of responsibility, aggressive operations killed hundreds more of the enemy as the year wound down.

More than 62,000 enemy were claimed killed in the Marine zone during the year, while Marine casualties totaled 4,618 killed and 29,320 wounded.* Marine Corps strength peaked in September with 85,520 Marines in Vietnam. After the tremendous exertions at Tet and in the fighting at Hue and around Da Nang and Khe Sanh, the quality of enemy forces was judged to have declined. North Vietnamese increasingly filled in for the worn-thin Viet Cong units. But 1968 had by no means been a vintage year for the American war in Vietnam.

*Just before Christmas, two Marines, Staff Sgt. Robert J. Hammond and Sgt. Robert J. Chicca, were among the members of the crew of *Pueblo* who were released by North Korea after 11 months of captivity.

4
Getting Out 1969-1973

As 1969 began, Richard M. Nixon entered the White House. During the election campaign he had suggested to the American people that he had a plan for getting the United States out of Vietnam. He had said, "Vietnam has been a profoundly sobering lesson in the limits of U.S. power. . . . What we must do is to work . . . toward ensuring that we have no more Vietnams."[28] Staying there had suddenly become no longer "vital" to America's national interest.

After months of resistance and haggling, the Saigon government agreed to join in four-party negotiations that included the National Liberation Front. On Januray 24, all four delegations sat down in Paris at one round table.

In Vietnam, American forces kept up the military pressure. The enemy launched a late February burst of rapid jabs and rocket attacks against American military installations. President Thieu pressed a repressive heel down harder on critics of his regime. By May, the NLF began calling for new elections in the South to establish a coalition government.

The Nixon Administration spoke of a "Vietnamization" of the war—strengthening the ARVN to take over more of the fighting and release American forces from actual combat. This would "change the color of the dead," said the critics. On May 14, the President proposed a "mutual withdrawal" of American and North Vietnamese forces and leaving a final political solution to all factions in South Vietnam that renounced the use of force. On June 8 at Midway, Nixon announced that the first 25,000 of the 540,000 United States troops in Vietnam would be pulled out by the end of August. Troop withdrawals quieted the American "doves" while Vietnamization reassured the "hawks."

Despite these hopes and expectations—and the angry peace movement in the United States—the fighting went on. During the next three years, 15,000 more Americans and hundreds of thousands of Vietnamese were killed; the ARVN suffered more casualties than it had in the previous three years, and the ground war spread beyond Vietnam into Laos and Cambodia.

The enemy was now less active, apparently hurt by the fighting of the previous year. General Abrams reduced the big-unit, search-and-destroy operations and concentrated on attacking their base areas and interdicting their supply lines. Pacification, which had once meant "winning hearts and minds," continued to mean bombing villages, defoliating crops and jungle and removing peasants from the land to clean out Viet Cong-dominated areas.

In April 1970, after the overthrow of Prince Norodom Sihanouk, 74,000 American and ARVN troops invaded Cambodia. There were demonstrations of protest in Saigon. In the United States, the reaction was vigorous and led, most dramatically and tragically, to the killing of four students at Kent State University by Ohio National Guard troops. The Cambodian invasion itself destroyed North Vietnamese equipment, and the Cambodian army stopped the Viet Cong from receiving military supplies through the port of Sihanoukville. When American forces pulled back from Cambodia at the end of June, the North Vietnamese occupied the country's northern provinces and organized new supply routes through the Mekong valley.

In February 1971, 21,000 ARVN troops, supported by American air power, crossed into Laos to cut the Ho Chi Minh trail. Planning by both the ARVN and the Americans was weak. And not even American advisors were supposed to accompany the ARVN into Laos. The North Vietnamese counterattacked in strength. American aircraft reportedly killed thousands of North Vietnamese. Marine planes and helicopters participated in this action. Eighty-nine American helicopters were destroyed. Although some ARVN units fought well, the South Vietnamese were no match for the enemy; after 45 days, their units had suffered nearly 50 percent casualties. Marine helicopters helped get the ARVN out again. The traffic continued down the Ho Chi Minh trail. This late in the day, it was a pretty poor show.

During this entire period, the air war against both halves of

Vietnam, Laos and Cambodia was stepped up. "After two years and a few months of his [Nixon's] administration the United States had dropped more bombs on Indochina than it had in both the European and the Pacific theatres during World War II."[29] Anger and resentment rose against the American strategy.

This was the environment in which the Marine Corps fought the final years of the Vietnam War. As 1969 began, the 3rd Marine Division, commanded by Maj. Gen. Raymond G. Davis, was screening the DMZ. The division was under the operational control of the U.S. Army's XXIV Corps, which also contained the 1st Brigade of the 5th Mechanized Infantry Division and the 101st Airborne Division. The 1st Marine Division under Maj. Gen. Ormond R. Simpson guarded the approaches to Da Nang. Maj. Gen. Charles J. Quilter commanded the 1st Marine Aircraft Wing.

On January 13, in the largest Special Landing Force operation of the war, the 2d and 3rd Battalions of the 26th Marines landed at Batangan Peninsula, south of Chu Lai. This had been the battlefield of the first regiment-sized combat action of the war back in August 1965. Resistance now was minimal; and by February 9, both battalions were back on board the ships of the Seventh Fleet. The Marines were keeping alive their amphibious expertise and image.

Col. Robert H. Barrow's 9th Marines went aggressively into the mountains in the southwestern corner of Quang Tri province on January 22 in Operation Dewey Canyon. The enemy had built up a well-stocked jungle base area with a number of artillery pieces near the Laotian border. Despite the unpredictable monsoon weather, Barrow's regiment had to be supported entirely by helicopters. The Marine air groups flew 1,617 sorties in support. For one ten-day period no resupply at all was possible. By February 18, fighting was heavy; the 1st Battalion in the center of the line found strong resistance. In one action on Washington's Birthday, 1st Lt. Wesley L. Fox of Herndon, Virginia, was serving as commander of A Company when it was ambushed in the norther A Shau valley. The enemy charged, and Fox and all but one of his command group were wounded. Advancing into heavy fire, Fox knocked out one enemy position and led his men to drive the enemy into retreat. He was wounded again in the final assault but stayed in command, established his company's defense and saw that his casualties were evacuated. Three days later, Cpl. William D. Morgan of Pittsburgh, a squad leader with H Company, charged an enemy bunker to draw its fire and let his squad rescue two wounded Marines. Morgan was killed but enabled his men to save the two casualties and overrun the North Vietnamese position. Lance Cpl. Thomas F. Noonan, Jr., of Brooklyn, New York, a fire team leader in G Company, also lost his life trying to save a wounded Marine under fire.[30] In Dewey Canyon, 130 Americans were killed and 932 were wounded.

During Tet 1969, which began on February 16, the enemy again infiltrated into Da Nang and the surrounding countryside. They followed their earlier patterns of attack, hitting particularly through the Viet Cong-dominated hamlets south of the Cau Do River. They were quickly routed. Both the 1st and 7th Marines participated in the counteractions. Lance Cpl. Lester W. Weber of Aurora, Illinois, a machine-gun squad leader with M Company, 7th Marines was sent with his 2d Platoon to help a squad under heavy attack near Bo Ban. When his platoon was attacked, Weber plunged into the tall grass of the rice paddy, killed one enemy soldier and forced 11 others to retreat. He fought a second North Vietnamese hand-to-hand and killed him. Seeing two enemy soldiers firing from behind a dike, Weber dived into their position and wrestled their weapons from their hands and killed them. As he dashed forward to attack a fifth enemy soldier, he was mortally wounded. He was awarded the Medal of Honor posthumously.

On March 19, when an enemy battalion penetrated the perimeter of D Battery, 11th Marines near An Hoa, Corpsman David R. Ray of Nashville, Tennessee, went to the aid of the wounded. He was hit, killed one enemy soldier and wounded a second who attacked him. Ray continued to treat the wounded until he was fatally wounded. As his last act, he threw himself over a wounded Marine when an enemy grenade exploded nearby.[31]

On March 26, Lt. Gen. Nickerson succeeded Lt. Gen. Cushman as commanding general of III Marine Amphibious Force. Nickerson had commanded the 1st Marine Division and subsequently been deputy commander of III MAF. Lt. Gen. Cushman returned to Washington to become deputy director of the Central Intelligence Agency; at the beginning of 1972, he would succeed General Chapman as the Commandant of the Marine Corps.

Marine fighting during the first half of 1969 was less intense than it had been in 1968. When the first 25,000 American troops left Vietnam by the end of August, among them went 8,388 Marines, including the 9th Marines and part of the 1st MAW.

In Quang Nam province, Pipestone Canyon was the most significant 1st Division operation of the year. Four Marine battalions and ARVN units went after the 36th North Vietnamese Regiment south of Da Nang. It was a "clearing" operation typical of many in the later years of the war. Behind the Marines came a U.S. Army engineer company with giant Rome plows that dug up the land at the rate of 200 acres a day. When the operation was finished in early November, 54 Marines had been killed and 540 wounded. In August, the 7th Marines moved into the Que Son valley and joined the U.S. Army in battling the 2d North Vietnamese Division outside Hiep Duc. On the twenty-eighth, Mexican-born Lance Cpl. Jose F. Jimenez, a fire team leader with K Company, led a charge against well-camouflaged North Vietnamese. He killed several and destroyed two enemy positions in the face of concentrated automatic weapons fire before he was mortally wounded.[32] By the end of the month, more than a thousand of the enemy had been killed.

Through the fall, the 3rd Marines fought a number of engagements along the DMZ. The 3rd and 4th Marines and MAG-36 left Vietnam by mid-December, as 45,000 more Americans were withdrawn, including 18,483 Marines. The 3rd Marine Division finished its Vietnam service after 40 months of combat and moved to Okinawa. More and more, the U.S. Army was taking over the Marines' responsibilities in the northern provinces. The enemy had reduced their activity mostly to guerrilla and terrorist activity.

The seventy-second and last Special Landing Force operation of the war began on September 7 when the 1st Battalion, 26th Marines landed south of Hoi An. While a Korean Marine battalion held a blocking position, the Marines attacked by helicopter and landing craft. A second Korean Marine battalion landed to the north and swept south against the combined U.S.-Korean block.

The first serious action of 1970 was a North Vietnamese

attack on Fire Support Base Ross in the Que Son valley. On the dark, rainy night of January 6, three enemy sapper teams penetrated the perimeter behind an enemy barrage. Although 38 of the sappers were killed and three captured, the Marines lost 13 killed and 40 wounded.

The war seemed to be slowing down for the Marines, but men were still being killed and wounded and performing exceptional feats of courage. Early on May 8, Lance Cpl. Miguel Keith, an eighteen-year-old native of San Antonio, Texas, was serving as a machine gunner with Combined Action Platoon 1-3-2 in Quang Ngai province when his platoon was attacked by a larger enemy force. Keith was seriously wounded but moved across a fire-swept field, firing his gun at the enemy. He charged five enemy soldiers, firing as he advanced, killing three and dispersing the others. A grenade knocked him to the ground. Bleeding severely, he charged 25 enemy soldiers massing to attack, killed four and drove off the rest before he was mortally wounded. His daring helped his platoon rout the attackers. He was the last Marine in Vietnam to be awarded the Medal of Honor.

By April 15, another 12,900 Marines left the country, including the 26th Marines, MAG-12 and the 1st Antitank Battalion and most of the 1st Tank Battalion, the 3rd Amphibian Tractor Battalion and the 1st Shore Party Battalion. Four tactical air squadrons departed.

During the Vietnam war, 730,000 men and women served in the Marine Corps compared to some 600,000 in World War II. At its peak in 1968, the 85,755-man Marine force in Vietnam included two divisions, two regimental landing teams and the aircraft wing. (The first woman Marine to be ordered to a combat zone was Master Sgt. Barbara J. Dulinsky, who arrived at MACV in Saigon in March 1968.)

By 1970, Marine redeployment had left the Army outnumbering the Marines in I Corps. As a result on March 9, XXIV Corps became the senior U.S. command in the zone. Lt. Gen. Keith B. McCutcheon became the new commanding general of III MAF, which was now a division-wing team under operational control of Army headquarters. III MAF's area of responsibility was limited to Quang Nam province and small pieces of the neighboring provinces. It was headquartered at Da Nang's Red

Beach, near where the 9th Marines had first landed five years earlier. The 1st Marine Division consisted primarily of the 1st, 5th and 7th Marines and the artillery regiment, the 11th Marines. It totaled about 21,000 Marines and 1,200 Navy men. Their main job was to keep the enemy away from Da Nang.

On April 18, Maj. Gen. Edwin B. Wheeler, the 1st Marine Division commander, broke his leg in a helicopter crash and was succeeded by Maj. Gen. Charles F. Widdecke, Navy Cross winner on Guam.

In July and August, the 7th Marines supported ARVN troops attacking enemy bases and on August 31 made one last sortie into the Que Son area. Called Operation Imperial Lake, this was the final major Marine offensive effort of the war; and before the action was over, it also involved the 5th and 1st Marines, the Korean Marines and U.S. Army units patrolling the mountains closest to the Quang Nam lowlands.

Then, the 7th Marines left Vietnam and the 5th Marines took its place. Lt. Gen. McCutcheon went home terminally ill in December, and Lt. Gen. Donn Robertson took over command of III MAF. In all of 1970, the Marines had 403 killed and 3,625 wounded, compared to 1,051 killed and 9,286 wounded in 1969.

The 5th Marines started for home in February 1971, leaving only the 1st Marines outside Da Nang. Of the air groups, only the fixed-wing MAG-11 and the helicopters of MAG-16 were left. On April 14, III MAF removed to Okinawa; the 1st Marine Division to Camp Pendleton, and the 1st MAW headquarters left for Japan. The Marines were organized now as the 3rd Marine Amphibious Brigade with 13,600 men under Maj. Gen. Alan J. Armstrong. And as the Combined Action Program phased out, terrorist activity in Quang Nam province increased.

Marine ground and air operations in Vietnam stopped on May 7, the day VMA-311 flew its last air strike into Laos. On the air side, the Marines had lost 252 helicopters and 173 fixed-wing aircraft in combat and 172 helicopters and 81 aircraft operationally during the war. The last ground troops sailed on June 25.

As Commandant Cushman said in April 1972, "We are pulling out heads out of the jungle and getting back into the amphibious business."[33]

When the North Vietnamese opened a major Easter offensive on March 30, 1972, only about 500 Marines were in the country. MAG-12 and -15 moved into Vietnam with their Skyhawks and Phantoms. An air task force and MAG-15 set up at Nam Phong, Thailand. Intensive bombing of North Vietnam was resumed; and on May 8, President Nixon ordered Haiphong harbor mined.

Although there were still 70,000 U.S. soldiers in South Vietnam, the ground battle was left to the Vietnamese. Marine Capt. John W. Ripley, advisor to the 3rd Vietnamese Marine Battalion, won the Navy Cross for personally blowing up the bridge at Dong Ha. Marine helicopters from *Okinawa* carried South Vietnamese marines into battle; but by May 4, all Quang Tri province had been lost.

The last U.S. combat troops left Vietnam on August 11. In September, the ARVN stopped the enemy's drive north of Hue and recaptured Quang Tri province.

On December 18, after the Paris peace talks broke down again, President Nixon ordered the heaviest bombing of the war against North Vietnam. For the first time, B-52s bombed Hanoi; more than a dozen were shot down by North Vietnamese missiles.

At last, agreement was reached in Paris; and a ceasefire began in Vietnam on January 28, 1973. MAG-12's Skyhawks flew the final sorties of the American war over the Mekong Delta. By the end of March, the last American soldiers were out of the country. It had been the longest war in U.S. history.

Twenty-six Marine prisoners of war were repatriated; 12 other had returned earlier. The Marine Corps listed eight Marines as dead while captured; two were still counted as captured and 47 as missing in action.

On August 14, 1973, the American bombing of Cambodia finally stopped. It was more than four years since the decision had been made to get out of the war.

5
Black Americans—Green Marines

By the time of the Vietnam war, the Marine Corps was totally integrated. Marines leaders liked to say there were no white or black Marines—all were "green Marines" wearing combat green.

Of the 448,000 Marines who served in Vietnam from 1965 on, 41,000 were black. The stories of a few of them demonstrate their contribution to the Corps' share in this war.

Five black Marines earned the Medal of Honor in Vietnam. All five were killed shielding fellow Marines from exploding enemy grenades. For his heroism on February 28, 1967, Pfc. James Anderson, Jr., of Compton, California, was the first black Marine to earn the Medal. The others were Pfc. Oscar P. Austin of Phoenix, Arizona; Sgt. Rodney M. Davis of Macon, Georgia; Pfc. Robert H. Jenkins, Jr., of Interlachen, Florida, and Pfc. Ralph H. Johnson of Charleston, South Carolina.

The senior black officer in Vietnam was Lt. Col. Frank E. Petersen, Jr., of Topeka, Kansas. He had received the Distinguished Flying Cross in Korea and in May 1968 was named commanding officer of Fighter Attack Squadron 314, a Phantom jet unit at Chu Lai. He flew 280 combat missions, was shot down and rescued and awarded the Legion of Merit.

The first black to command a Marine infantry battalion was Lt. Col. Hurdle L. Maxwell who commanded the 1st Battalion, 6th Marines in 1969 and retired in 1971 with 20 years of service.

Sgt. Major Edgar R. Huff became the first black battalion sergeant major in an infantry battalion and senior sergeant major in point of service in the Corps. He served two tours in Vietnam and was severely wounded in January 1968 while rescuing a radioman trapped in an open field by enemy fire. Huff received

901

the Bronze Star and two Purple Hearts and later became sergeant major of the III MAF. When he retired in 1972, he was the first black Marine with 30 years' service.

Sgt. Major Agrippa W. Smith of the 1st Battalion, 9th Marines was the senior enlisted man in the battle for Khe Sanh. He had enlisted at Montford Point back in 1943 and eventually became sergeant major of the 26th Marines.

James E. Johnson, who had joined the segregated Corps in 1944 as a "steward duty only" private, rose to be a chief warrant officer. He retired in 1965 and later became Assistant Secretary of the Navy for Manpower and Reserve Affairs.

In 1968, Maj. Edward L. Green, a Vietnam veteran, became the first black officer on the faculty at the Naval Academy. In the Annapolis Class of 1972, eight of the 12 black midshipman joined the Marine Corps. In 1972, Green succeeded Lt. Col. Petersen as Special Assistant to the Commandant for Minority Affairs.

In 1964, the Marine Corps had only 48 black commissioned officers; by 1973, it had 282. But only 24 were majors or higher among a total of 5,300 Marine officers in those ranks. In 1964, the Corps had only 184 blacks in the top three enlisted ranks; by 1973, it had 1,394. Still, only two percent of Marine officers were black, and the 28,839 black enlisted men were disproportionately in the lower ranks.

Even this record was not achieved painlessly. There were ugly incidents and violent clashes during the 1960s in the United States; at Kaneohe, Hawaii; on Okinawa, and in Vietnam. Both the nation and the Corps were adjusting to the new battle for desegregation and racial equality that followed the Supreme Court's 1954 decision. Camp Lejeune reportedly had 160 incidents of assaults, muggings and robberies with racial overtones in 1969.[34] On the night of July 20, just before the 1st Battalion, 6th Marines, was to ship out for the Mediterranean, a big party was held and some white Marines were assaulted by groups of blacks. One white Marine, Cpl. Edward Blankston, died of head injuries and two other white Marines were stabbed. Forty-four men were charged and 13 convicted of riot, disobedience or assault. One black Marine was sentenced to nine years at hard labor for manslaughter. A special inquiry criticized leadership at Lejeune and young militant blacks. But the tension was widespread.

There were clashes and "fraggings" between the races on Okinawa and in the rear areas in Vietnam. In December 1969, Commandant Chapman said, "We've got a problem."[35] Time, concern and effort were needed to try to solve the problem. Major Green has written, "Although it is doubtful that the influence of racial prejudice will ever be completely eradicated . . . the military has made commendable progress in moving toward this objective. . . . When a commander makes his subordinates aware that discriminatory behavior will not be tolerated within his command, it will not exist."[36]

6
Defeat and Bravado

The end came one week shy of 21 years after the fall of Dien Bien Phu and nearly three years after the last combat Marine had been withdrawn from Vietnam. When the last GIs had marched to their ships in 1973, they had left behind $5 billion worth of military equipment, including hundreds of tanks, 500 fighter-bombers, 625 helicopters and enough arms to equip a 700,000-man South Vietnamese army. But it was not enough; nothing could have been.

In March 1975, the North Vietnamese army, well trained and well armed with Soviet weapons, drove down from the north and sliced into the central highlands from the west, chopped up South Vietnam and surrounded Saigon. Da Nang, the Marines' old base, fell on March 29 without a struggle. The ARVN dropped back and was squeezed into an ever-tightening circle around the capital. As the South Vietnam retreat turned into confusion and panic, ships of the U.S. Seventh Fleet began gathering in the South China Sea to support an evacuation from Saigon.

Meanwhile, Cambodia fell to communist-led Khmer Rouge troops. Marine Col. Sydney H. Batchelder, Jr., flew into Phnom Penh on April 3 to manage the evacuation of the Cambodian capital. On Saturday morning, April 12, 360 Marines and corpsmen of the 2d Battalion, 4th Marines took off in CH-53 helicopters of HMH-462 from the amphibious assault ship *Okinawa* in the Gulf of Siam and landed in Phnom Penh. Lt. Col. George P. Slade's Marines swiftly formed a perimeter around a soccer field 1,000 yards from the United States Embassy while the last Americans and 159 Cambodians were evacuated. Then, under rocket and mortar fire, the Marines were flown out by HMH-463;

and their command group was lifted out by two Air Force helicopters. The entire operation took two hours and 23 minutes.

Off the coast of South Vietnam, the Seventh Fleet flotilla carried the 6,800-man 9th Marine Amphibious Brigade commanded by Brig. Gen. Richard E. Carey. The Marines and their 68 transport helicopters were embarked in 16 Navy amphibious ships and eight American merchant ships of the Military Sealift Command. There were also 10 U.S. Air Force helicopters in the carrier *Midway*. All stood in readiness to pluck out the last Americans from Saigon.

The evacuation was delayed because Ambassador Graham A. Martin did not want to alarm the already desperate South Vietnamese. Finally, U.S. Air Force jet transports began frantically carrying out the last thousand Americans and tens of thousands of Vietnamese from Saigon's Tan Son Nhut airfield. Many pro-American Vietnamese were unable to escape, and some Americans were forced to pay Vietnamese officials large bribes to obtain exit visas for their Vietnamese wives and children. Ambassador Martin's aloofness and stubbornness were blamed by many, and the ambassador's management of the evacuation was widely and bitterly criticized.[37]

Once the process did begin, Marines in Jeeps escorted buses filled with refugees to the U.S. Defense Attaché Office compound next to Tan Son Nhut. There, 18 Marines of the Embassy Security Guard under Gunnery Sgt. Vasco D. Martin, Jr., held a perimeter with M-16s and machine guns. On April 25, 40 men of 1st Lt. Bruce P. Thompson-Bowers' 3rd Platoon of C Company, 9th Marines were quietly flown in from *Hancock* to help them. President Thieu fled to Taiwan, blaming the Americans for not coming to his aid. Former Vice President Ky was taken to Camp Pendleton.

Communist bombs, shells and rockets rained down on Tan Son Nhut on Monday evening, April 28, and early Tuesday, killing two Marine security guards. The airfield could no longer be used. At Ambassador Martin's urgent telephone call, President Gerald R. Ford set in motion Operation Frequent Wind, the final evacuation of Saigon by helicopter.

On Tuesday afternoon and evening, HMH-462 and -463 flew in elements of Col. Albert Gray's Regimental Landing Team-4, principally units of the 2d Battalion, 4th Marines, to the

DAO compound at Tan Son Nhut and brought out, under fire, 395 Americans and 4,475 Vietnamese and others. By midnight, the Marines set fire to the buildings and were flown out. Tens of thousands of South Vietnamese tried to reach the American fleet in barges, fishing boats, sampans and rafts. Fourteen 54-man detachments from the 3rd Marine Division under Maj. David A. Quinlan helped evacuate 67,437 Vietnamese on American ships.

Unexpectedly, the Marines were called on to evacuate more than 2,000 people from the American Embassy itself, instead of 100 as originally planned. There was room for only one CH-46 at a time on the embassy roof and one heavier CH-53 at a time on the parking lot. But starting at 5 P.M. Tuesday, two strings of helicopters put down at the embassy.

Late Tuesday, 130 Marines were flown over from Tan Son Nhut to beef up the 41-man embassy security guard led by Master Sgt. Juan J. Valdez. The Marines manned the gates with bayonets, and some used rifle butts to knock off Vietnamese trying to climb the barbed-wire-topped wall.

The last night was pandemonium. After dark, the rooftop landing zone was marked only with a barrel of burning oil and rubbish; from 2:15 A.M. on, a chopper was sent into each landing zone every ten minutes. Ambassador Martin went home to get his poodle and boarded a HMM-165 helicopter piloted by Capt. Gerald Berry on the roof at 5 A.M. In all, 978 Americans and 1,120 Vietnamese and others were lifted out of the embassy.

Eleven Marines with M-16s crouched on the roof. Maj. James Kean and Master Sgt. Valdez had pulled their men into the main building and barricaded the doors. Then, they moved up through the building until they held only the top floor and the roof. Vietnamese raced through the building's six floors and tried to reach the roof through the tear-gas smoke. The Marines, now under small-arms fire on the roof, marked their position with a red-smoke grenade. The last CH-46 landed; and just before 8 A.M., the Marines piled on board. The last man brought out the embassy's flag in a brown paper bag.

A total of 1,373 Americans and 5,595 Vietnamese and others had been evacuated from Saigon by helicopter. It required 530 evacuation sorties to get them out.

Four Marines were killed in those final days. Lance Cpl. Darwin J. Judge, a nineteen-year-old Eagle Scout from Marshalltown, Iowa, and Cpl. Charles McMahon, Jr., twenty-two, of Woburn, Massachusetts, both members of the Embassy Security Guard, were killed early Tuesday in a rocket attack on Tan Son Nhut. Capt. William C. Nystul of Coronado, California, and 1st Lt. Michael J. Shea of El Paso, Texas, were also killed Tuesday when their CH-46 helicopter crashed into the South China Sea near the carrier *Hancock.*

Left behind in the confusion at the embassy was the plaque commemorating the five Americans who had been killed defending the embassy during the Tet attack in 1968. Also left behind were the bodies of Corporal McMahon and Lance Cpl. Judge. The Provisional Revolutionary Goverment that took over Saigon returned them later; and they were buried on March 4, 1976, in their hometowns.

Judge and McMahon—and James C. Marshall, who had been killed at the U.S. Embassy in Saigon during the 1968 Tet attack—were members of a Marine Corps unit that had been created following the end of World War II: the Marine Security Guard Battalion.

Since 1949, Marines have served as security guards at U.S. Foreign Service posts under agreements between the Corps and the Department of State. This responsibility had grown by 1967 to require the formation of the battalion. By mid-1976, 1,100 Marines were serving in 114 embassies, consulate general offices and missions in 97 countries, as well as with American delegations to international conferences. The Marine Security Guard Battalion had company headquarters in Frankfurt, West Germany; Karachi, Pakistan; Hong Kong; Panama City, and Nairobi, Kenya. The Marines protected classified materials, official personnel and government property.

At least one other member of the battalion was killed in action: Staff Sgt. Charles W. Turberville, who died during a September 26, 1971, terrorist attack on the U.S. Embassy in Phnom Penh, Cambodia.

When Greeks overthrew the government on Cyprus and Turkish forces armed with American weapons invaded the island in the summer of 1974, Marines of the 16-man Security Guard Detachment under Gunnery Sgt. Robert L. Boyd defended the U.S. Embassy in downtown Nicosia. They were armed with .38 caliber pistols. Just after noon on August 19, only five Marines of the detachment were in the embassy when hundreds of well-organized, rock-throwing Greek Cypriotes attacked. They entered the grounds, broke windows and burned automobiles and an effigy of Secretary of State Henry A. Kissinger. Two Marine sergeants were sent to the embassy roof and tried to disperse the mob with tear-gas grenades. Armor-piercing bullets from an AK-47 killed a woman secretary and mortally wounded Ambassador Rodger P. Davies, who was standing in a hallway near his office behind closed and shuttered windows. The ambassador died on the way to the hospital. The following January, a crowd broke into the embassy building and was routed by Marine tear gas. No Marines were killed or wounded in either incident.

In Southeast Asia, Marines were involved in one more convulsion of violence. On Monday, May 12, 1975, two weeks after the evacuation of Saigon, a Cambodian gunboat stopped and seized the old, unarmed American container ship *Mayaguez* steaming from Hong Kong to Sattahip, Thailand. In Washington, America's leaders decided to use the merchant ship's capture to prove to the world that, despite the loss of the Indochina war, the United States had not become a "paper tiger."

President Ford put on alert a 1,100-man battalion landing team of the 3rd Marine Division on Okinawa and rushed ships and planes to the scene. By Tuesday noon, the Cambodians had taken *Mayaguez* to three-mile-long Koh Tang (Tang Island), 34 miles from the mainland. On Wednesday, Capt. Charles T. Miller and his 39-man crew were transferred by fishing boat to an island—ironically named Koh Rong—at the harbor of Kompong Som, formerly Sihanoukville. (The ship's third mate, David C. English of Seattle, was a former Marine who had fought in Vietnam.) U.S. Air Force jets sank three Cambodian gunboats. Trying to turn back the fishing boat, the planes strafed it, reportedly hitting several of the Americans, and dropped tear gas that left everyone retching.

The alerted 2d Battalion, 9th Marines, commanded by Lt. Col. Randall W. Austin, sped from Okinawa to U Tapao Air Force Base in Thailand despite the usual official Thai protests.

Before dawn on Thursday, 227 Marines flew the 195 miles from U Tapao in 11 Air Force helicopters to recapture the ship and attack Koh Tang.

Forty-eight Marines of D Company, 4th Marines, and 12 sailors, commanded by Maj. Raymond E. Porter, climbed down by rope from three Air Force HH-53s to the deck of the destroyer escort *Harold E. Holt,* which then went alongside *Mayaguez.* At 7:25 A.M., led by Cpl. Carl R. Coker, the Marines boarded the ship—eighteenth-century-style. *Mayaguez* was empty.

Under fighter cover, 179 Marines from Capt. James H. Davis' G Company assaulted Koh Tang an hour before the Marines boarded *Mayaguez.* One platoon was to land on the western side of the island's narrow neck leading to its northern end. The remainder of the company and the battalion command group headed for a larger landing zone on the eastern side of the neck. A second wave of E Company under Capt. Mykle E. Stahl was prepared to follow G Company in.

The attack on Koh Tang was a mistaken effort to rescue *Mayaguez'* crew. They were not there. And Cambodian armed strength on the island was seriously underestimated.

The Cambodians shot down the first two helicopters approaching the island's eastern landing zone at 6:15 A.M. One crashed in flames; seven Marines, two Navy corpsmen and the Air Force co-pilot died in the chopper; three Marines were killed in the surf. The remaining 13 men swam out to sea. After more than three hours in the ocean, they were rescued by the guided-missile destroyer *Henry B. Wilson.* While in the water, 1st Lt. Terry Tonkin, using a survival radio, managed to direct Air Force planes in firing runs against enemy positions on the island. The other helicopter landed on the beach with its tail shot off, and the 3rd Platoon Marines and the helicopter crewmen formed a defensive perimeter in the trees at the water's edge. No more helicopters dared land on the eastern side. There, the 20 isolated Marines and four airmen, led by Marine 2d Lt. Michael A. Cicere, held out all day under intermittent enemy fire. One Marine and one airman were wounded.

On the western side of Koh Tang, one of the first two helicopters—with Captain Davis aboard—was shot up and limped back to the coast of Thailand. The second helicopter disembarked the 1st Platoon under 2d Lt. James McDaniel.

909

When the chopper took off again, it crashed into the sea; one of its four crewmen was killed.

The remaining four helicopters were diverted to the western landing zone, and three were finally able to land there. The fourth, containing Lt. Col. Austin's command group and an 81mm mortar section, landed on the shore 1,300 yards to the south to avoid enemy fire.

First Lt. James D. Keith, G Company's executive officer, took charge of the men on the western landing zone beach and set up a perimeter. The command group moved northward against resistance. Of the 179 Marines in the landing force, 131 made it ashore; and of those, 20 were isolated on the eastern shore and 29 were with the separated command group.

The main force of 82 men had landed at the western tip of a man-made cut across the heavily jungled island. On both sides of the cut, visibility was limited to 5 to 15 feet. The Marines were pinned down by fire from a wooded area 75 yards from the beach. The Cambodians fought hard.

Second Lt. McDaniel led a reinforced squad south against an enemy strongpoint. The patrol—all new to combat—was hit by fire on its flank. Lance Cpl. Ashton N. Loney of Albany, New York, was killed and five Marines, including McDaniel, were wounded. The fighting was sharp and at close range. Staff Sgt. Seferino Bernal, Jr., and Pfc. Jerome N. Wemitt rescued wounded men under fire. Keith, fearing the patrol would be encircled, ordered it back to the landing zone. The Cambodians followed the Marines, attacked the perimeter and were driven off. Keith called in Air Force strikes at the enemy's strongpoints. The fire fight and grenade duel continued all morning.

Meanwhile, the *Mayaguez'* crew had already been released two hours before the Marine attacks. But that was not known at the time. Planes from the carrier *Coral Sea* bombed Ream Airfield in Cambodia and an hour later bombed the Ream Naval Base and an inactive oil refinery near Kompong Som. At 10 A.M., the fishing boat bringing the *Mayaguez'* crew back to their ship approached the destroyer *Wilson*. The men were safe.

Since all but one of the eight helicopters bringing the first wave of Marines to Koh Tang had been destroyed or damaged, only five helicopters could be rounded up to fly in the second wave of 127 Marines. Before they reached Koh Tang, the crew of

Mayaguez was aboard *Wilson*; and the assault was briefly called off. The five helicopters headed back toward U Tapao but, at Lt. Col. Austin's insistence, reversed course again for Koh Tang.

After Air Force strikes and a mortar barrage, 2d Lt. Richard H. Zales led a platoon against the Cambodians between Keith's perimeter and the approaching battalion command group and scattered the enemy into the jungle. At 12:45 P.M., the two Marine elements linked up.

Four of the five helicopters carrying the second wave managed to land and discharge 100 Marines—19 of G Company and 81 of E Company—and pick up six wounded Marines. The fifth chopper, trying to land in the isolated eastern landing zone, was badly damaged by enemy fire and made an emergency landing on the coast of Thailand. There were now 225 Americans on Koh Tang.

The only remaining job was to get them out. After an attempt to rescue 2d Lt. Cicere and his men at 2:15 P.M. failed with damage to one helicopter, the men on the eastern side were finally evacuated by one helicopter at 6:10 P.M. under heavy fire from Cambodian automatic weapons. On the western side, a C-130 dropped a 15,000-pound bomb; and by 8:10, a helicopter hovering at the water's edge lifted out the last 29 men under automatic weapons fire in total darkness. The destroyer *Wilson* had an armed boat close to the shore covering the final departure. Three missing Marines were left on the western side of Koh Tang; nobody knew whether they were dead or alive. It had been a tough vertical assault.

All told, connected with the *Mayaguez* operation, 41 Americans had been killed (including 23 Air Force men killed in a Thailand helicopter crash) and 50 wounded. That made 56,869 Americans in uniform who had died and 303,704 who had been wounded in connection with the Vietnam war. The totals included 14,691 Marines killed and 88,633 wounded.[38]

In Washington, the political leaders felt the *Mayaguez* affair had made their point. It was, somehow, an appropriate finish to the United States Marines' longest and most disastrous overseas war.

On July 2, 1976, North and South Vietnam were officially declared reunited as the Socialist Republic of Vietnam with Hanoi as its capital.

7
"Men Stalking Each Other"

The Vietnam war had divided the American people as had no other overseas war. Many condemned it as immoral; others believed it vital to America's national interest. These views were irreconcilable. They tore the nation apart.

The United States had tried to move into the post-World War II power vacuum in Southeast Asia. This intervention climaxed a long tradition of sending American force to impose the American will across the seas. It was a process in which the Marines had repeatedly served as the spearhead: Tripoli, Mexico, Canton, the Philippines, Peking, the Caribbean, two World Wars and Korea. Over and over again, American power had thrust outward with the Marine Corps in the van.

In Vietnam again, the Marines, as a force-in-readiness, had been among the first to fight. The Marine Corps had not been responsible for the decisions that shipped hundreds of thousands of Americans into Vietnam, but its leaders were certainly eager to go. As former Commandant Shoup saw it, "In early 1965, there was a shooting war going on and the Marines were being left out of it, contrary to all their traditions."[39] Some Marines were already on the scene; but as in all the nation's wars, the Corps outspokenly sought a fighting role.

Not only ordinary Americans were divided over what Shoup called "our confident and aggressive actions."[40] Leaders in Washington also differed over whether it was essential to the United States that Southeast Asia not go communist. Shoup, who could never be faulted for either his courage or his candor, said:

> From the beginning of our growing involvement in the affairs of Vietnam, I had opposed the idea that such a

small country in that remote part of the world constituted either an economic interest or a strategic threat to the welfare of the United States. In the past I have frequently expressed concern about military policies or plans which would commit American troops to a land war against the oriental peoples of Southeast Asia.[41]

When Lyndon Johnson sent a largely drafted and draft-driven civilian army to fight an undeclared, ideological war on the mainland of Asia, many young Americans were not prepared to die to prevent Indochina from going communist. But some were—and more than 56,000—willing or not—were killed in the effort. In 1967, a Navy chaplain with the Marines in Vietnam said, "Most of these kids know why they are here. Today I talked with a kid with his third Purple Heart in three months here. I asked him if he wanted to go home. He said he wanted to go home and see his wife and new baby, but he'd be back."[42]

It was certainly the ugliest war in which the Marine Corps ever fought. It was a war against civilians as well as armies—a war of booby traps and assassinations, murder and terror. In February 1967, Lance Cpl. Ralph D. Mase of Little Rock, Arkansas, a fire team leader with I Company, 1st Marines, went on a patrol looking for Viet Cong only a mile south of Marble Mountain. He was the second man in the column. His foot touched a wire and tripped a booby trap. It was simply a grenade in a C ration can. Kicking the wire, Mase pulled the grenade out of the can. The grenade exploded, sending fragments into his right arm. It was that kind of war.

Late that same night, Cpl. Andre A. Williams of Springfield, Massachusetts, and his sentry dog, Rocky, served as the point of a patrol from Combined Action Company E-2 out of the village of Nam-O. Half an hour later, Rocky smelled danger. Instantly, a Viet Cong stepped from a doorway and shot Williams through the chest. His patrol leader killed the Viet Cong; and a Medevac helicopter rushed Williams to the Marine First Medical Battalion field hospital, where a swift operation saved his life. It was that kind of war.[43]

After the Marines had been fighting for four years, I visited Vietnam again in July 1969 and at Hoi An wrote in my notebook: "Here in the countryside, there is firing every night, assassina-

913

tions every month. The refugee camps are filled with wives and children of men still hiding out in the 10-foot-high grass with the Viet Cong. Twelve-year-old girls carry rifles and wear black pajamas. Marines must go armed and wear steel vests to walk in the road." It was still that kind of war.

Lt. Gen. Walt called it "the chevron war"—small unit actions and patrols in the hamlets and rice paddies led by noncoms in their teens and twenties. He compared it to fighting the Indians in the American West—"men stalking each other in the thick green gloom of deep forest."[44]

But in Vietnam, the guerrillas—"bandits," the Marines had called them in the Caribbean—had a real army of their own. The Marines had to fight two wars: the nasty guerrilla war in the populated areas—the villages and paddies, and the big-unit, artillery-supported conventional war against the North Vietnamese army up north in the jungle. American strength and technology fought a native nationalism dressed in communist ideology and supported by major powers. Each side had the capability of using and experimenting with modern weapons. Vietnam was both the most impersonal and the most personal of wars.

At its core, it was a matter of heart and spirit. The Americans, so far from home, were the foreigners; in a long Vietnamese tradition, they were the hated. Even those Vietnamese who huddled under the protection of American guns in fear of Viet Cong terror knew that they could buy only some small piece of time. In the end, the war was lost because the military dictatorship in Saigon failed to win the loyalty of its people and the American leaders failed to wage a guerrilla war successfully. As the Americans had taught the British 200 years before, it is difficult for soldiers and guns to suppress a revolution across the sea.

This war ripped at men's souls. In Vietnam, men bombed and were killed; men booby-trapped and were maimed. Marines did kill civilians and torture prisoners. They burned homes and they built schools and hospitals. They brought the Vietnamese guns and napalm, food and medicines. They created orphans and constructed orphanages. They both killed and cared for. It was an impossible assignment—a most terrible war.

The Marines
are looking for
a few good men
...who want to lead

Modern U.S. Marine Corps recruiting poster.
USMC Photo

SEMPER FIDELIS

XVI
"IN STEP
AND
SMARTLY"
1975-

In a cold, drizzling rain on the morning of November 10, 1975, several hundred green-raincoated Marines gathered silently before the Marine Corps War Memorial at Arlington National Cemetery. Standing in the sanctuary of America's heritage, they could see the Washington Monument and the Jefferson and Lincoln Memorials through the gray mist. It was the Corps' official two-hundredth birthday, and the Marines were assembled at the giant green-bronze statue of the Iwo Jima flag-raising to remember the three million Americans who have been United States Marines.

Two Marines who had raised that flag on Mount Suribachi 30 years before lay in nearby graves. The last former Marine alive of the six men portrayed in the famous statue, René A. Gagnon, attended the ceremonies. Former Navy corpsman John H. Bradley was the only other survivor. Leading the Marines at the memorial service was the new Commandant of the Corps, tall, lean Gen. Louis H. Wilson, who had won the Medal of Honor as a twenty-four-year-old captain on Guam in World War II.

The Marine Band played. Prayers were said. And the President of the United States spoke. Quoting the golden inscription on the gleaming black marble base of the statue— "Uncommon valor was a common virtue"—President Ford called the Marine Corps Birthday "the bicentennial of its uncommon valor." The President said, "The Corps has become a living monument to devotion and self-sacrifice . . . always faithful to the cause of freedom."

At the ceremony's end, a rifle salute cracked out, echoing among the hills. A Marine bugler sounded Taps.

That evening, some two thousand Marine officers and their

ladies attended a Birthday Ball in Washington, one of many held around the world. They watched a pageant review the Corps' "200 years proud." Their greatest applause resounded for the tableaux of a Navy corpsman and a Marine rifle squad. The Commandant spoke feelingly of "our Marine Corps and our heritage." The pageant swept over the American saga and brought back to mind Marines who had helped shape that story:

John Basilone, the kid who drove a laundry truck in New Jersey and wiped out a Japanese regiment on Guadalcanal. William Deane Hawkins, "The Hawk," the first man ashore at Tarawa. "Chesty" Puller and his five Navy Crosses. William Barber and Fox Company holding Toktong Pass. "Hiking Hiram" Bearss, with his shirttails flapping. Dan Daly, the New York City newsboy who fought around the globe. John Quick, under fire, signaling at Guantanamo and carrying ammunition through to Bouresches. James Swett, the youngster who shot down seven Japanese planes in his first 15 minutes of combat. The Raiders: Merritt Edson and Evans Carlson. John T. Myers and bantam Smedley Butler in China. Herman Hanneken and Christian Schilt. Littleton Waller Tazewell Waller. Earl Ellis. George Terrett. Archibald Gillespie. John Marshall Gamble. Archibald Henderson and John Lejeune. David Shoup and Lewis Walt. The long line from John Trevett to John Glenn.

As anyone who has gone to war knows, only a few heroes are remembered. Many Marines performed acts of courage and gave their lives, unwitnessed and unsung. They deserve commemoration as much as those whose moment of valor was recognized with the Medal of Honor or Navy Cross.

When the pageant had run its course and the Marine Corps story had been told again, the Commandant cut the traditional birthday cake with the sword that the state of Virginia had given Presley O'Bannon in 1807 on his return from "the shores of Tripoli." The first slice of cake, as custom dictated, was handed to the oldest Marine present, Gen. Gerald C. Thomas, the eighty-one-year-old retired veteran who had fought as a sergeant at Belleau Wood.

It had been a day for looking back over 200 years. The Commandant's birthday message also looked forward. It closed: "Marching shoulder to shoulder we shall gain in strength and readiness as we move ahead, in step and smartly."

The bicentennial came at a time when the Marines were once again under attack. The Vietnam war had disrupted the nation and the Corps, left them uncertain of both their responsibilities and their power.

The Corps was by then almost unique among the world's major nations. Its nearest competitor was the 17,000-man Soviet Naval Infantry. The British Royal Marines were down to 6,000 men. Of course, there were marine corps—usually created with the help of the U.S. Marine Corps—throughout East Asia and Latin America. But in big power terms, the question was raised: Were the American Marines after two centuries a vestige of a bygone imperial age?

The Senate Armed Services Committee told the Corps to re-evaluate its mission and clean house of substandard manpower. General Wilson took office as Commandant in July 1975, when General Cushman retired early.* Wilson immediately appointed the so-called Haynes Board, chaired by Maj. Gen. Fred E. Haynes, Jr., a veteran of three wars, to find answers to the questions being asked both inside and outside the military establishment:

Was there need for a 196,000-strong Marine Corps when the nation after the Vietnam war seemed no longer willing to intervene abroad?

As the Marines had not made a major amphibious assault since Okinawa (1945) and Inchon (1950), should the Corps' main mission still be to attack enemy shores from the sea?

What should be the Marines' role in the future?

Was the Marine Corps prepared to fight an enemy armed with sophisticated modern weapons?

Should the Marine Corps continue to possess its own air wings?

Why did this "elite" force have higher rates of desertion, absence-without-leave and drug abuse than the other services?

The Marine Corps has been challenged throughout its history—after the War of 1812, the Civil War, the Spanish-American War and both World Wars—after every major war the nation has fought. There was nothing new about that. These repeated attacks were not the work of some perennial cabal out to destroy the Corps. They resulted from the nature of the

---

*Gen. Earl E. Anderson, the Assistant Commandant, also retired early, in part because of an internal controversy over succession procedures.

Marine Corps itself—wedged awkwardly between the Army and the Navy on anybody's organization chart.

After Vietnam, nobody proposed mothballing the Corps. Not only would that have meant getting rid of some of the nation's best; but, said the authors of one critical study, "doing away with the Corps would be politically infeasible in any event."[1] That was true. In a political brawl, the Corps always managed to take care of itself.

The most serious post-Vietnam challenge questioned the Corps' future purpose. Its mission had evolved over the years; as Lt. Gen. Krulak put it, "The Marines don't have a role except to be malleable enough to do what comes on the horizon."[2]

The single thread running through the entire Marine Corps story was that the Corps is the armed force that can best project American power onto hostile shores. The early Marines, starting out as soldiers on American men-of-war, put armed force ashore with the Navy at Nassau, the Penobscot, Tripoli, Sumatra, Africa, California, Mexico and China.

With the coming of steam propulsion, steel ships and long-range naval guns in the mid-nineteenth century, naval warfare changed. And there was a greater urge to extend American power overseas. In 1898, half the Corps was on shipboard duty; but 20 years later, only two percent was afloat.[3] Down to World War I, the Corps fought small or decrepit nations (Mexico, China, Spain, the Philippines, Nicaragua, Haiti). It was "more closely associated than the other services with American intervention abroad,"[4] and became an expeditionary force that led the way as America expanded overseas.

The turning point, if there was any single moment, came in 1908 when President Theodore Roosevelt's Executive Order 969 removed Marines from warships and enlarged their duties to "furnish the first line of mobile defense of naval bases and naval stations beyond the continental limits of the United States."[5] The Marine Corps kicked like a mule, and sea duty was retained. But Roosevelt had pointed to the future.

The Corps went on from defending to seizing advanced naval bases and, in World War II, to capturing island air bases for the strategic bombing of Japan. Until the atomic bombs were dropped on Hiroshima and Nagasaki, the Marines were ready to join in the climactic attempt to assault the enemy's homeland itself.

With the end of World War II, the unification of the armed services and the opening of the Cold War, the Marine Corps emphasized that it was a force-in-readiness—in Commandant Cates' words "a ready striking force."[6] The idea and the slogan "First to Fight" had been there since World War I, and the Corps came to see its mission as stepping in swiftly to deter or contain aggression until the Army could mount the major land effort. "Our first and paramount characteristic is readiness," Commandant Wilson told the Senate Armed Services Committee in February 1976. "This mission is meant to provide the fleets with a ready capability to project combined arms combat power ashore. . . . we have extensive overseas interests that are vulnerable."[7]

The American experiences in Korea and Southeast Asia threw into doubt the Marine Corps' mission as a readiness force because they demonstrated limits of America's power and cooled American ardor for costly interventions overseas.

It finally became clear to all that the United States was not an Asian power but a Pacific power. Massive American military muscle had ruled the Pacific Ocean—43 percent of the earth's surface—since the Japanese surrender in 1945. No nation was able to challenge the United States there. The long westward thrust of American power had been stopped only when it tried to climb onto the mainland of Asia—threatening the Yalu River border in the north and injecting a half million men into Vietnam in the south. But it still dominated the high seas and the island chain skirting Asia's Pacific coast.

The United States had been pushing its power across the Pacific for a century and a half. It based an East India naval squadron at Hong Kong as early as 1835; and between then and 1900, American Marines fought at Quallah Battoo, Canton, Formosa, the Han River, Manila Bay and Tientsin. Americans have been fighting and dying on the rim of Asia for a very long time. Even after the defeat in Vietnam, American power still stood 5,000 miles west of San Francisco. The Far East was still the American Far West.[8]

But the frontiers of American power had been shoved back. In the Pacific, the line of the Philippines, Taiwan, Okinawa, South Korea and Japan was not secure. In Europe, where the United States still kept 300,000 men three decades after World War II, advanced Mediterranean bases were under threat. General Shoup wrote, "It is a grim revelation that there are limits of U.S. power and our capabilities to police the world."[9] These limits and the uncertain future of bases overseas promised a reduction of pre-positioned American forces abroad and increased the need for a mobile readiness force.

At the same time, Americans were determined to avoid "another Vietnam." Some analysts interpreted this as a lasting opposition to any military interventions. A Brookings Institution study of the Marine Corps said, "There is growing public disenchantment with military ventures overseas, particularly those involving the use of ground troops."[10]

Since the Corps is designed to project American power onto hostile shores, this post-Vietnam view implied that a neo-isolationist United States, pulling back into a "fortress America" stance, no longer needed the Marines' offensive capability. But the trauma of Vietnam did not insure a total or permanent reversal of past national behavior. To limit military capabilities to temporary political moods was always precarious.

As the story of the Marine Corps demonstrates, military interventions abroad have been a constant feature of American life. They have had a variety of purposes: show of force, evacuation of U.S. nationals, protection of U.S. interests, control of "choke points" to guard free transit of the seas and intervention on a lasting basis. Except for the brief preoccupation with the Civil War, there never was a period when American military and naval forces have not been engaged in "ventures overseas." The Marines' ventures ranged from New Providence (1776), Santo Domingo (1800) and Tripoli (1803) to Lebanon (1958), the Dominican Republic (1965), Vietnam (1965–1973) and Koh Tang (1975). The Marines calculate that they made 180 landings in the 134 years starting in 1800. There is little evidence that the American people have ever been disenchanted for long.

The widespread "disenchantment" over Vietnam was not with the original intervention. It was with the escalation of the immoral and frightful cost of that involvement to both Americans and Vietnamese and the refusal of the responsible American leaders to find and take an "exit." The Vietnam war, fought in good part by unwilling and draft-compelled young Americans, became unpopular as it was intensified and protracted.

In the future, the United States will pick its spots for

intervention more carefully and be more sensitive to the possibility that the price of intervention can rise out of line with the national interest involved. In a particular armed intervention, political leaders will need to make rational, hardheaded assessments of the relationship between the national interest and the cost in blood and money: to get in when a vital national interest warrants the cost and to get out if the cost exceeds the stake. There will be a continuing need for professional military forces capable of reacting swiftly and successfully when the American people's elected leaders deem intervention essential to the nation.

Commandant Wilson talked about the Marine Corps' future role this way:

> Everyone knows we need an Army, we need a Navy and we need an Air Force. It is very difficult to explain why we need a Marine Corps. [With] a country such as ours that has an $180 billion investment overseas and roughly overseas trade of some $74 or $80 billion a year, we need a force that can project power overseas. . . . I think it is inconceivable that we should not have this capability to project power ashore overseas. . . . [The Marine Corps] is not a defensive force but a means of projecting power ashore where we may be required. Of course, that's our mission. . . . I am not concerned about the future of the Marine Corps so long as we have ready forces such as we have today, because I am convinced that when the call comes, they have my telephone number—and I expect a call.[11]

The United States has always sought—and will presumbaly continue to seek—to project its power overseas when it feels its vital interests or the rights of its citizens are endangered. As a member of the Haynes Board wrote: "History has demonstrated again and again the cyclic nature of political affairs. It is dangerous to reduce the only viable forcible entry capacity the nation has as long as the U.S. continues to have overseas interests that are both vital and vulnerable."[12]

After the American pullback from Indochina and Thailand in the mid-1970s, military planners began to direct renewed attention to the United States' military interests in Europe. Although the U.S. maintained sizable deterrent forces in Europe, the possibility of a conventional war there raised serious questions: Must not a European war inevitably escalate to use tactical and strategic nuclear weapons? Can the pre-positioned Allied forces in Western Europe withstand a Soviet onslaught? Will it be possible to reinforce those Allied forces from the United States in the face of the large Soviet submarine fleet and Soviet antiaircraft missiles and long-range antiship cruise missiles? If an amphibious assault of Europe were required, would modern weaponry make such an assault impossible?

The answers to those questions affected the Marine Corps' future. Some planners believed the Corps should strengthen its firepower and help defend Europe. They said that a pre-positioned conventional deterrent remains credible only if it can be reinforced and that the Marine Corps' ready force serves this purpose. Others denied that the Corps should have a role in Europe and saw the Corps' future value not in supplementing U.S. Army forces in Europe but in intervening against non-superpowers, where American interests and citizens are endangered or where the superpowers' interests clash. After Vietnam, the entire concept of what battle the Marines should prepare to fight came under challenge.

The crux of the post-Vietnam attack on the Marine Corps was the charge that the Corps, in classic military habit, was preparing to fight World War II over again. Specifically, the Corps was criticized for continuing to emphasize amphibious assault—"this peculiar type of combat."[13] Critics warned that the multi-division World War II Marine Corps trained for amphibious assault would never be needed again.

No one advocated that the United States eliminate all amphibious-trained Marines. Even the Brookings Institution study acknowledged the value of one and a third divisions of amphibious Marines. The question became: What should the greater part of the Corps be prepared to do? If most of its amphibious mission were obsolete or if it were to supply just more "army," there could be no military justification for keeping a three-division Marine Corps.

The Brookings study proposed four options: that the rest of

the Corps be eliminated; that it beef up the Army defending Europe; that it replace the Army garrisoning the Pacific islands; or that it take over the airborne readiness assignment from the 82d Airborne Division, the Army's own elite competitor as a "quick insertion" force.

Among these options, the deactivization of the bulk of the Corps would be militarily foolish and politically impossible. The Pacific garrisoning option offered a rationale for maintaining a three-division Corps, but it would be a geographically limiting mission and obliterate the concept of a worldwide readiness force. To have the Corps serve as supplementary Army manpower could erase any Marine Corps uniqueness and open the way for eventual Army absorption.

"The Marine Corps wants to get off this European kick," said one general. The Corps already had a responsibility in the Joint Strategic Objectives Plan to provide two Marine Amphibious Forces—80,000 men and 1,000 planes—"ready to go" as a strategic reserve for NATO. Marine planners desperately wanted an assignment on Europe's flanks—not in the center. Said Lt. Gen. Leslie E. Brown, Chief of Staff of Headquarters, Marine Corps, "We are not desirous to have the central European commitment. We prefer to stay light and maneuverable."[14] Commandant Wilson pointed out that there are 8,000 miles of coastline between Europe's North Cape and Greece, and added, "We are the only ones who can project this power ashore."

But the prospect of simply reinforcing the Army was disconcerting to many Marines. In Vietnam, the Marines had to serve pretty much like Army troops in the Corps' longest war. There was no Inchon-type amphibious assault of North Vietnam. Commandant Wilson said candidly that the Marines could have been used better if they had exercised their amphibious expertise down in the Mekong Delta.

Finally, replacing the Army's airborne division would stir up violent political and interservice conflicts; but it would eliminate the duplication of readiness strike forces, whether air-delivered or sea-delivered. Rivalry between the Army Airborne and the Marines went back at least to the post-Korean war Strategic Army Corps and Strike Command. The 1965 Dominican Republic intervention ballooned beyond all need with the 82d Airborne Division and the Marine Corps competing to

925

prove their ability to get there fast. And shortly after the first Marine battalions landed at Da Nang, the 173rd Airborne Brigade reached Saigon. As General Shoup commented, "With these initial deployments the Army-Marine race to build forces in Vietnam began in earnest and did not slow down again until both became overextended, overcommitted, and depleted at home."[15]

The fact that none of these Brookings options precisely fit the need suggested the possibility that there was nothing sacred about a three division-air wing Marine Corps. To some serious degree, the Corps was once again a service in search of a mission that justified its size.

The Corps' mission always determined how it would be structured, trained and equipped. It has been said that amphibious warfare had "shaped the Corps into a distinctively tailored light infantry force" and left its ground units "short on firepower and cross-country mobility." Although others believed the Corps was already too heavily equipped, the question remained: Could the Marines, as then armed and equipped, survive in a European war or a conflict like the 1973 Middle East war, both of which would feature armor and precision-guided weapons?

When the post-Vietnam debate erupted, the Corps had an authorized strength of 196,300 men and women. Of these, 113,000 were in its combat forces: 51,000 in three divisions; 37,000 in three air wings, and 24,900 in "force troops"—tanks, amphibian tractors, support troops, etc. Elements of its three division-air wing Marine Amphibious Forces were deployed at sea in the Mediterranean and Western Pacific and intermittently in the Caribbean. Additionally, the Corps was authorized an organized reserve of 35,000 Marines, essentially a fourth division and air wing.

The Corps constructed its combat forces on "a building block principle" that gave it flexibility; "We can make units as heavy or as light as we choose," said General Wilson. Tank battalions and LVT battalions could be added to an expeditionary force as the situation required. Thus, a Marine Amphibious Force (a combined division and air wing) could be mounted out with the kind of mobility, firepower and air cover best suited to the fighting ahead.

By its own estimate, the Corps was short of everything from men (192,000 in 1976 instead of 212,000) to amphibious shipping and naval gunfire support. (There was virtually not a gun larger then 5 inches left in the entire U.S. Navy.) But the Corps was continually being modernized. In mid-1976, the first new super-sized *Tarawa*-class amphibious ship was commissioned. The Corps had three squadrons of VSTOL vertical-short-takeoff-landing AV-8A Harrier aircraft. The British-made Harriers' ability to operate from short runways, road and decks and their agility made them valuable for close support. The Corps also had precision-guided bombs, Hawk and Redeye antiaircraft missiles and Jeep-mounted TOW heavy antitank wire-guided missiles and one-man Dragon medium antitank guided missiles. The first TOW platoon was activated at Camp Lejeune in April 1976. The Corps' M-48 tanks with their 90mm guns were being replaced by the M-60 with a 105mm gun. And it was to get the latest heavy-lift helicopter, the CH-53E, which could lift 16 tons, and a new attack helicopter mounting TOW missiles.

Some Marine futurists saw the day when high-speed "surface effect" air cushion ships (hovercraft, etc.) would carry VSTOL aircraft and amphibious forces armed with electronic and laser-beam-aimed weapons swiftly in dispersed formations across future beach-heads.

Unlike the Brookings study, which examined alternative missions for the Corps, the Haynes Board analyzed structure. In March 1976, it recommended to the Senate Armed Services Committee that the Corps remain a global strategic force-in-readiness. It opposed organizing the Corps specifically for combat in one theater; Maj. Gen. Haynes said, "the Marine Corps has basically a global role. It has to be prepared to go anywhere. . . . If maintained as a combined arms air-ground team, we can go anywhere and fight and make a good account of ourselves."[16]

Focusing on "mid and high intensity wars," the Board urged that the Marines retain their three division-air wing strength and improve their firepower by adding antitank and antiaircraft missile and artillery punch. It proposed concentrating tank units in two of the three divisions and adding amphibian tractor units for battlefield mobility. It suggested that ground reconnaissance units be strengthened so that they could search and fight, rather than search and run. In the air, the Board recommended developing the VSTOL force and keeping the A-6 all-weather attack plane for close support. Said Haynes, "We reject out of hand any reduction in the close support attack role."[17]

The Corps' integrated air arm had long been its most controversial element. Over half a century, the Marines increased their firepower and mobility with aircraft and helicopters. At first, the Corps, because it was lightly armed with artillery and tanks, built up its own air force to reach beyond the range of naval gunfire for close support. Its aviation capability grew to include fighter and attack aircraft that could dogfight enemy planes and bomb deep inside enemy territory. The Corps accumulated 13 types and 22 models of combat aircraft and helicopters. The question was widely asked whether the Corps was justified in maintaining 12 F-4 fighter-attack squadrons primarily for air-to-air combat and interdiction, when the Air Force and Navy were equipped to perform these jobs.

The questioning also attacked the Corps' need for its own close air support if Marines were to be used in land campaigns with the Army rather than in amphibious assault. And the development of sophisticated surface-to-air missiles complicated the job of close air support. The debate over Marine Corps aviation was made more trenchant because by 1976 between 35 and 50 percent (depending on who was calculating) of the nearly $4 billion spent annually on the Corps went for its air arm. The private Center for Defense Information, which wanted military expenditures reduced, labeled the Corps' tactical air force "an expensive luxury."[18]

Marines argued persuasively that they have created highly effective air-ground close support coordination surpassing anything that the Air Force could provide. And they pointed out that all their fighter aircraft must have a close-support capability as well. Marine close air support for Marines on the ground has been superlative. Marines believed that in amphibious assault independent of the Army, the retention of the close support part of its ground-air team would be imperative.

The Haynes Board's most novel announced proposal was that the Corps form one or more experimental "mobile assault regiments," strong and nimble enough to tackle an armored enemy. Such a regiment would consist of two infantry battalions mounted in LVTs ("currently the only means we have of moving relatively in a protected sense across the battlefield"[19]) and supported by a battalion of tanks and self-propelled artillery.

Although the Board pressed to enlarge the Corps' firepower, Maj. Gen. Haynes said, "Its great utility is its mobility." To equip Marines with new weapons within assigned manpower and budget limits, the Corps, he said, would give up not air power but some peacetime troop strength, perhaps reducing battalions from four rifle companies to three. (The first battalions rushed to Korea had two rifle companies.)

Exploring how the Marines could fight a modern enemy better armed than the North Vietnamese, the Board used the 1973 Middle East war as a prime model. In such a war, the Marines would destroy the enemy's forward air defenses with laser-directed missiles so that VSTOL aircraft and ground forces could survive. Haynes admitted the Marines would need Air Force bombardment as a replacement for naval gunfire support in a "high-intensity" amphibious assault. But in the end, seizing or defending ground would still depend, Haynes asserted, on the Marine rifleman and "the kind of capacity that the Marine has been known for and that is to stick it out."[20]

For the next decade, the time frame of the Haynes Board study, the Corps would have to use landing craft and helicopters to get into combat and to supply battlefield mobility. Later, Haynes predicted, Marines would go into battle in VSTOL aircraft or in "an air cushion vehicle which will go 50 knots across the surface of the sea and which will go across the surf-line." Haynes added, "I would say that by 1988 or '89, we will not be jumping off landing barges."[21] Testing of Marine air cushion vehicles will begin about 1980. Said Lt. Gen. Lawrence F. Snowden, Deputy Chief of Staff for Plans and Operations, "The technology is essentially here. The job is to get it packaged and put to our application."[22]

Some analysts opposed loading down Marines with more armor, artillery and mechanized vehicles. They feared increasing a Marine task force's weight and slowing its strategic mobility and reaction time. They called this direction of thinking the "Fort Benning mentality" and blamed it for losing the Vietnam war against a lightweight, flexible enemy.

The critical military fact of the Vietnam war and the

enormous tank losses of the 1973 Middle East war may be that the day of Guderian's tank-fighter-bomber team is over. Although it is too early to predict accurately how the new weapons will change warfare, some Marines believe that tanks are on their way out—like the battleship—and that they can now be killed with inexpensive, lightweight weapons. The battlefield of the post-industrial future, in this view, will be dominated not by tanks and manned aircraft but by precision-guided antitank and antiaircraft missiles operated by small units of men skilled in camouflage and night operations.

The new military technology of electronics and lasers is revolutionizing warfare. Vietnam and the 1973 Middle East war may prove in perspective to have been laboratories for a historic evolution of warfare, pushing armies apart again as did the arrival of the rifle and the machine gun a century ago. The so-called "one-shot one-kill" weapons have made tanks, planes and helicopters exceedingly vulnerable. One observer said that the 1973 Sinai campaign proved the M-60 tank was easy game for the Soviet wire-guided, rocket-propelled antitank Sagger missile and ended the U.S. Army generals' Vietnam love affair with the helicopter as a weapons platform.[23]

The Marine Corps has participated fully in the technological revolution. At Twenty-nine Palms in the California desert, it experimented with laser bombs and hand-held designators that lock in on a target, and it worked on artillery that can ride the beam in for a "first kill." Commandant Wilson said of the future, "We are entering a new age of technology which has unlimited potential."

The "smart weapons" revolution required basic changes in Marine Corps thinking. Marines believe, paradoxically, that the Marine with his rifle will regain supremacy on an electronically dominated battlefield. Former Commandant Cushman wrote:

> In such an environment, the infantryman would be part of a search and attack system, designed to help him defeat an enemy from increasing standoff distances. However, he would remain an infantryman. The cold steel bayonet charge would remain in his repertoire, perhaps as an anachronism, yet available as an act of last resort. These new developments would tend merely to

correct an old imbalance, in which the infantry has done a small share of the killing but a large share of the dying.[24]

And Commandant Wilson added:

I have for years believed that we have a vast amount of firepower which is not used properly to help the infantry-man who finally is the one who must take the objective. We are working at the Marine Corps base at Twenty-nine Palms to develop this into a very sophisticated system where we ensure that commanders at every level are able to put the maximum amount of firepower—air, artillery, tanks and infantry—to help the rifleman, because I believe that finally it's the young infantryman, the eighteen-year-old high school graduate, who must shoulder his musket, button up his jacket and take the high ground.

Maj. Gen. Haynes predicted: "In ten years, the infantryman will return to a position of dominance on the battlefield because we will have shoulder-fired, fire-and-forget weapons which will be effective both against tanks and aircraft; and he will be protected by light armored vehicles."[25]

To fight and survive and win on a battlefield of the future, Marines will have to be more heavily armed and armored, possess the means for dispersal and rapid mobility and carry modern weapons that can destroy attacking tanks, aircraft and the enemy's new weapons at greater distances. To coordinate these heavyweight requirements with the mission of swift "forcible entry" by sea or air is the Corps' real challenge.

While the Marine Corps was rethinking its mission and structure, its quality as an "elite force" also came under attack. Could the Corps sustain its right to be regarded as an elite force at its three-MAF size? The end of the Vietnam war draft that had driven resentful young men to "volunteer" and the pressure to compete for recruits in a peacetime all-volunteer armed force saddled the Corps with serious problems of recruiting and discipline. The Marine Corps was ill-prepared for the all-volunteer era because it erroneously thought that virtually all its Vietnam recruits were "true volunteers." It found itself with the highest per capita rates of desertion, absence-without-leave and drug abuse in the armed forces.[26]

Several explanations were offered for this disturbing record of "troop quality": the large number of high school dropouts among recruits, the Corps' changed racial makeup and its insistence on severe standards of discipline. While the other services were selling the attractions of career-training and beer-in-the-barracks, the Corps was advertising its need for "a few good men" and warning young men it was not promising them a rose garden.

At the end of 1975, Commandant Wilson presented the Senate Armed Services Committee a report from the Haynes Board admitting that the Corps "has had a manpower quality problem" and stating that it had begun to take corrective measures. It got rid of 4,000 "unsuitable" Marines and raised to 75 percent the desired proportion of high school graduates among recruits. (Only 46 percent were high school graduates in 1973.) The increased requirement for high school graduates reduced the percentage of blacks being enlisted in the Corps from 19 to 15 percent. Commandant Wilson commented, "I think this is about right—15 percent black—because they constitute about 12 percent of the population. I think this would be a good mix."

Wilson also sought to raise the quality of leadership, improve living and working conditions, curtail excessive reassignment of individuals and units and revamp training techniques. Above all, he put the emphasis on the quality rather than the quantity of recruits.

The key problem remained to attract and keep intelligent and motivated young people. Because only 27 percent of recommended first-term enlistees—and 12 percent of all first-termers against an optimum of 20 percent—re-enlisted, the Marines had to recruit 50,000 young men and women a year. Clearly, the post-Vietnam Corps did not have an excess of well-qualified candidates. The Corps had to be able to fill these ranks with high-quality people against competition from the other services in an all-volunteer armed force if it were to justify maintaining its size and calling itself "elite."

Recruit training abuses further undermined the Corps'

reputation as an elite force. In 1974 and 1975, 178 Parris Island drill instructors and 182 San Diego DIs were punished for abusing recruits. After the senseless and fatal beating of Pvt. Lynn E. McClure of Lufkin, Texas, at the San Diego training center and the grotesque shooting of a recruit by a Parris Island DI, subcommittees of the House and Senate Armed Services Committees ordered investigations into Marine Corps recruiting and training practices. And a *New York Times* editorial referred to the Corps as "once the elite of the United States armed forces."

The *Times* commented that "not all Marines have yet learned to draw the line between toughness and sadism. . . . A few training officers seem to have difficulty in distinguishing between the tough but human disciplines that build men and a perverted sadism that degrades and destroys them."[27]

In the most shocking case, Private McClure, a "problem recruit" who had reportedly been emotionally disturbed and rejected by both the Army and Air Force, was beaten into unconsciousness with pugil sticks on December 6, 1975, by other recruits in training at San Diego and died three months later after surgeons had removed part of his skull. Training abuses reminded the public of the indefensible practices exposed after the Ribbon Creek "death march" 20 years earlier. The new incidents suggested either that the Corps silently condoned these practices, while publicly decrying them; or that, incredibly, it had been unable to control recruit training and prevent brutality by its own experienced and selected noncommissioned officers.

When the first DI courtmartialed in the McClure case was acquitted of all charges, the *New York Times* editorialized:

> The acquittal . . . leaves totally unresolved the serious issues of Marine recruiting policies and brutal boot camp training practices. . . . The combination of recruiting mentally unfit youths and subsequently exposing them to inhumane treatment is an affront to human decency and to the honor of the armed forces. An earlier response to such outrages by a mere reprimand and reassignment of several officers, including a colonel, suggests that the Marine Corps authorities themselves do not fully appreciate the gravity of these horrors.

The editorial said that the DIs may be "technically innocent of wrongdoing because they may be following procedures condoned if not authorized by their superiors."[28] In any case, no one was left responsible for the recruits death.

A former Marine and member of the editorial page staff of *The Wall Street Journal* wrote in that newspaper:

> . . . despite official disavowals, maltreatment and brutality in recruit training have not been isolated incidents, and it does little good for the Corps' many well-wishers to pretend otherwise. . . . a large and visible minority [of "sadists and martinets"] held sway [in the 1950s] at the recruit training depots because their activities were tacitly condoned at higher levels. . . . The gung-ho spirit is best inculcated through pride rather than fear. In its broadest sense, *Semper Fidelis* means loyalty not only to the Marine Corps but to the human traditions of society at large. It is clear from the congressional hearings that those traditions are often, perhaps routinely, violated and abused in Marine boot camp.[29]

Many Marines denied that training abuses were widespread. Commandant Wilson called them "infinitesimal" among all the recruits who go through boot camp. He said:

> Sadism has no part in Marine training. Punishment to where a man drops has no part in Marine training. But stress does have, to a certain point. . . . These days, there are regulations that are so specific that they leave little room for deviation on the part of the drill instructors. For those drill instructors who for their own reasons decide to make it more stressful, they are the ones who have to be checkreined.
>
> I am dedicated to the fact that we are going to have recruit training being done with firmness and fairness and dignity.We'll make whatever change is necessary, whatever supervision is necessary, to insure that this is done. . . . On the other hand, I am responsible for carrying out the mission of the Marine Corps—which we have long believed and continue to believe: that we'll be the

first to fight. . . . The ultimate is not to have abuses at the recruit depot. The ultimate is to train a man to be able to take care of himself and to live in the stressful situation of battle.

One Marine with an intimate grasp of the recruit training problem was Lt. Gen. Robert H. Barrow, then the Deputy Chief of Staff for Manpower. A DI himself long ago, Barrow became a noted combat commander in Korea and Vietnam and served as commanding general of the Parris Island recruit depot for nearly three years. He said:

> We had more abuse at Parris Island and San Diego than the Marine Corps is willing to admit or the public ever understood. . . . The odd thing about this [was] almost without exception the individual who experienced it believed it was good for him. . . . That is why it never comes out. . . . The Marine Corps has been unwilling to recognize that it is a problem because people believe it was good for them. . . . A lot of DIs don't raise their voice, they don't raise their hand, they don't engage in any form of hazing, and they get the same good results. But they are powerful people of strong character, who have great confidence in themselves and don't need to engage in this kind of nonsense. . . .
>
> I've gotten a lot of hate mail from Marines and former Marines saying you are ruining recruit training. . . . It is at once the most precious thing we have in the Marine Corps, and it's our most fragile thing. . . . We can't let the DIs screw it up and we can't let the policy makers screw it up. . . . This thing is the guts of the Marine Corps. . . . "readiness" comes from the boot camp experience because that's where discipline is taught. One of the training objectives at Parris Island is "to develop in the individual a sense of discipline and insure a respect for authority and an instant and willing obedience to orders." When you've said that, you've said everything.
>
> . . . The DI is a professional who knows right from wrong. He know the policy. There isn't a DI down there who doesn't know the moment he does something wrong

that it is wrong. . . . One reason we're sensitive to a DI who does something wrong is because he is being disobedient. He is being very un-Marine-like. It is the only place in the Marine Corps where we have NCOs who are willingly disobedient. My real expectation of him is that he be obedient of orders which say: Don't abuse a recruit.[30]

Barrow believed that the Ribbon Creek tragedy of 1956 "started all this nonsense." He explained:

Whatever the level of artificial stress, recruit abuse—and by abuse I mean language, hazing and out and out striking—at the time of Ribbon Creek, and there was some, after Ribbon Creek, the level of abuse went up a little, when all the officer structure was superimposed on the DIs and all the rules and regulations and public outcry and publicity, which pointed a finger at the DI, saying in effect, you immoral character, you abuse our sons. The DIs reacted just as most people do whose self-image is being threatened: By God, we'll show you.

Barrow found that the DI came to believe he was expected to be tough beyond the rules.

Pointing out that 55 percent of the Marine Corps is twenty-years of age and under, Barrow explained that young men become Marines mainly for two reasons:

First, many, if not most, want desperately to believe in something. Most of us want one or more strong personal commitments—religion, home, community, or some other institution which would extract from us involvement and strong beliefs. In today's world, the opportunity for such positive commitment has waned significantly and many young people look around them in vain for such opportunities. For many, the search ends with the Marine Corps. . . . Second, there is an inherent need in all males of the animal world to prove their masculinity or manliness. . . . In the past, it has accounted for such decisions as opening the new frontier, "going to sea" and other forms of adventure. . . . The opportunity for legitimate proving of one's manliness is shrinking. A notable exception is the Marine Corps. The Marine Corps' reputation, richly deserved, for physical toughness, courage and various demands on mind and body, attracts those who want to prove their manliness. Here too their search ends.

Perhaps unwittingly, the Marine Corps exploits and builds on these two basic desires, to believe in something and to prove one's manliness; and in the process, the Marine Corps gains from it two of its most important virtues—spirit and discipline—virtues which are the mark of excellence in any military organization and which are absolutely essential to success in combat.[31]

Congressman Paul N. McCloskey, Jr., a Korean war Marine officer, put it clearly when he said that he objected to physical abuse of recruits but that Marine Corps training should be "as tough as combat itself."

The Marine Corps has long experience with young men who end up in the brig while on garrison duty but prove valiant fighters in battle. No responsible Marine commander condoned abusing such men to make them cooperate or to turn them into effective Marines. The system broke down, as it repeatedly did, because noncoms and officers charged with training these men were inadequate to deal with them intelligently.

It is difficult to train and lead young men so that they will remain thinking human beings and still react instantly and unquestioningly to a sergeant's order that they advance into deadly enemy fire. The requirements of an "elite" killing force like the Marine Corps run opposite to all meaning of the term "elite" in a democratic society where the ideal is individuality, self-determination and the questioning of authority. But the preservation of a free society can depend on young men willing, trained and disciplined to fight and die on order.

The realities of power in today's world insure a place for the Marines of the future. As U.S. troops pre-positioned overseas are reduced and withdrawn, there will be a greater need for mobile strike forces ready to go anywhere in the world "in step and smartly." The Air Force–Army Airborne combination can perform one part of this mission, but it has earned no monopoly.

This job can be suitably assigned to the Navy's Marines, whether sealifted or airlifted into battle. It is a legitimate role for the Marines in modern three-dimensional warfare.

The world now lives with the threat that any major war will escalate to the use of tactical and strategic nuclear weapons. Mankind may never again see the kind of slugging match between the massed armies of the great powers that dominated warfare during the century and a half between Napoleon and Hiroshima. So far, the superpowers of the atomic era have repeatedly avoided direct confrontation. It is possible that their armed forces are already neutralized and confined to fighting client nations of their enemies, revolutions, terrorism and "wars of national liberation" and separating the armies of smaller states that lunge for each others' throats. This may be the unrecognized if optimistic lesson of Hiroshima.

Certainly, men have not outgrown the vicious insanity of war. But if, in fact, nuclear weapons have brought an end to the battlefield slaughter of Shiloh, Verdun and Stalingrad—until some Dr. Strangelove develops a scientific antidote to mutual nuclear devastation—the major powers may come to depend once again on the elite corps of an earlier day. In such a future, the United States Marine Corps would serve uniquely as a corps of expert, volunteer killers trained and insprited to give their lives to take their objective—members, to repeat Stephen Crane's words, of "a mysterious fraternity borne of smoke and danger of death." Then, a great nation's fate and freedom may again rest in the hands of such a band of brothers.

We few, we happy few, we band of brothers;

For he today that sheds his blood with me

Shall be my brother.[32]

APPENDICES

Appendix 1

Bibliography

This is a functional bibliography intended primarily for the reader who wishes to explore more extensively any part of the United States Marine Corps' story. Rather than a catalogue of every document or book examined in constructing this history, this bibliography presents the more useful sources with some evaluation. In all, the research for this book has included many interviews, documents and correspondence in the files of the Marine Corps' History and Museums Division, monographs, professional and popular periodical articles and more than 300 books. Whenever any source is quoted directly, the reference will be found cited in the Source Notes. A review of the overall Marine Corps histories will be found in the bibliography for Part XVI.

Part I
The Continental Marines 1775–1784

In its bicentennial year, the United States Marine Corps published a superbly detailed account of the Continental Marines: *Marines in the Revolution* by Charles R. Smith (1975). Until the appearance of this handsome volume, the telling of the story of the American Marines in the Revolution depended on the files in the Historical Branch at Marine Corps Headquarters and on many scattered sources.

The wealth of more general material on the Revolution contains little about the Marines. Four modern books give comprehensive accounts of the war that are both readable and authentic: Christopher Ward's two-volume *The War of the Revolution* (1952); Lynn Montross' *Rag, Tag and Bobtail: The Story of the Continental Army, 1775–1783* (1952); Willard M. Wallace's *Appeal to Arms: A Military History of the American Revolution* (1951), and John Richard Alden's *The American Revolution: 1775–1783* (1954). The latter two have especially useful bibliographies.

In the literature of the Navy in the Revolution, Gardner W. Allen's *A Naval History of the American Revolution* (1913) is a classic, with extensive quotations from contemporary accounts. Oscar Paullin's *The Navy of the American Revolution* (1906) is invaluable for its treatment of the administrative side of the naval war. Alfred T. Mahan's *The Major Operations of the*

941

Navies in the War of American Independence (1913) is primarily interested in the war between France and England. It includes a useful glossary of the naval terms of sailing days. Lionel Casson's *The Ancient Mariners* (1959) is excellent on ancient navies and marines.

Diaries, journals and local histories are numerous, and the interested reader will be led to them by his introductory reading. Those with areas of special interest might turn to Samuel Eliot Morison's *John Paul Jones* (1959); James A. James' *The Life of George Rogers Clark* (1928); Col. G. W. M. Grover's *Short History of the Royal Marines* (1948); William Stryker's *The Battles of Trenton and Princeton* (1898); and Alfred Hoyt Bill's *The Campaign of Princeton 1776–1777* (1948). Any serious investigator will want to look at *Naval Records of the American Revolution, 1775–1788*, edited by Charles Henry Lincoln, which is an annotated bibliography of the documents in the Library of Congress.

Part II
Establishing the Corps 1798–1815

For the naval war with France there is probably no better source than the precise and readable *Our Naval War with France* by Gardner W. Allen (1909). The role of the Marines in the incident at Curaçao is well described in the unpublished article "Setting the Pattern: The Navy and Marine Corps at Curaçao, 1800" by the late Michael O'Quinlivan of the Historical Branch, USMC Headquarters.

The war with Tripoli is interpreted thoroughly in *The First Americans in North Africa* by Louis B. Wright and Julia H. Macleod (1945). It deals with diplomatic events more extensively than with military actions. Fletcher Pratt's *Preble's Boys: Commodore Preble and the Birth of American Sea Power* (1950) offers vivid portraits of the naval captains of the period. William Ray's firsthand account, *Horrors of Slavery: or The American Tars in Tripolitan Slavery*, was published originally in Troy, New York, in 1808 and reprinted in 1911 in *The Magazine of History*, extra number 14.

Much has been written about the War of 1812. The classic work is Theodore Roosevelt's *The Naval War of 1812* (1882). Despite its opinionated, florid style, it offers a careful appraisal of the strengths of opposing ships and a detailed account of the Battle of New Orleans. C. S. Forester's *The Age of Fighting Sail: The Story of the Naval War of 1812* (1956), on the other hand, makes exciting reading and offers skillful interpretative writing. Forester takes a special interest in the naval captains' decisions and the alternatives they could have pursued. Glenn Tucker's *Poltroons and Patriots: A Popular Account of the War of 1812* (1954) is pleasant reading, but overlong. It is especially useful on the battles of Bladensburg and New Orleans.

To look further into special aspects of the war, one may find the following valuable:

BIBLIOGRAPHY

On the battle of Lake Champlain, the article "Commodore Macdonough at Plattsburg" by Rear Adm. A. T. Mahan in the *North American Review,* vol. 200, no. 705, August 1914. On the battle of Bladensburg, Edward D. Ingraham's brief, readable *A Sketch of the Events Which Preceded the Capture of Washington* (1849); and the issues of the *National Intelligencer* published in Washington from August 23 through December 20, 1814. *The Dawn's Early Light* by Walter Lord (1972) effectively tells the story of the actions at Washington, Baltimore and New Orleans. For the battle of New Orleans, in addition to the more general sources, the second volume of James Parton's *The Life of Andrew Jackson* (1860). For the cruise of *Essex,* the basic document is David Porter's fascinating *Journal of a Cruise Made to the Pacific Ocean* (1815). The second edition (1822) omits some of the more colorful events in the Marquesas Islands but has a new preface in which Porter answers his British critics and a lengthy account of the adventures of Captain Gamble after Porter left him in the islands. An interesting report of Gamble's experiences is to be found in an article by Marine Corps historian Edwin North McClellan entitled "John M. Gamble" and published in the *Thirty-fifth Annual Report of the Hawaiian Historical Society for the Year 1926.* Gamble's report to Porter was published in the *Niles Weekly Register* (Baltimore), vol. 9, December 23, 1815. An account of Gamble's funeral and an obituary appeared in the *Army and Navy Chronicle,* vol. III, no. 12, dated September 22, 1836. The story of *Essex* can be found in *The First Cruise of the United States Frigate Essex* by Capt. George Henry Preble (Salem, Mass., 1870).

Part III
Archibald Henderson and the Indian Wars 1817–1842

The files in Marine Corps Headquarters have been essential to this entire chapter. Very little has been written about the Second Seminole War. A useful source book on the war is *The Origin, Progress and Conclusion of the Florida War* by John T. Sprague (1847), which contains many official reports. Capts. Philip N. Pierce and Lewis Meyers published a brief summary of the Marines' part in the war in the *Marine Corps Gazette* in September 1948. Colonel Henderson's Florida journal has apparently been lost, but extracts are preserved in his biographical file at Marine Corps Headquarters.

Marine Lieutenant Sprague's dramatic journal of his assignment to remove the Creeks to the West can be found in *Indian Removal* by Grant Foreman (1932), by far the most readable volume on this whole disgraceful episode in American history. It is a superb book. Two other volumes in the long series on the American Indian published by the University of Oklahoma Press are useful here: *The Southern Indians* by Robert S. Cotterill (1954) deals bitingly with the years up to 1835; and *The Seminoles* by Edwin C. McReynolds (1957) is invaluable on that tribe, which taught the Marines so much about guerrilla warfare. A classic work on removal is Annie Heloise

943

Abel's "The History of Events Resulting in Indian Consolidation West of the Mississippi" in the annual report of the American Historical Association for 1906.

An eyewitness account of the Heath-Perry affair is in Alexander Slidell Mackenzie's *Life of Commodore Oliver Hazard Perry* (1840). The attack at Quallah Battoo is described in vivid detail in *Surgeon of the Seas—The Adventurous Life of Surgeon Jonathan M. Foltz* by Charles S. Foltz (1931).

Part IV
The Mexican War 1842–1847

There is no better account of the Wilkes expedition than Charles Wilkes' own monumental five-volume *Narrative of the United States Exploring Expedition* (1845). Volume five contains most of the material about the Marines with the expedition. Of more recent vintage is a delightful essay by Samuel Eliot Morison in his *By Land and By Sea* (1953), written from the perspective of World War II. *The Hidden Coasts* by Daniel Henderson (1953) is a breezy and rather gee-whiz biography of Wilkes with relatively little devoted to the great expedition.

The most comprehensive account of Catsby Jones' "invasion" of California at Monterey is in "The Conquest of California" by Maj. Edwin N. McClellan, which appeared in the September 1923 issue of the *Marine Corps Gazette*. K. K. Bechtel published a four-page pamphlet on the incident titled *Commodore Jones' War 1842* (1948); it includes an eyewitness report.

Commodore Perry's bout with King Ben Crack-O is related in the germinal biography of Perry, *Matthew Calbraith Perry, A Typical American Naval Officer* by William Eliot Griffis (1887)—but the book's tortuous style is as ridiculous as its title. Edward M. Barrow's biography of Perry, *The Great Commodore* (1935), is in good part based on Griffis and is much more readable. Samuel Eliot Morison's biography, *"Old Bruin,"* is, of course, the work of a great historian.

Claude M. Feuss' *The Life of Caleb Cushing* (1923) does not deal with the Marines directly but is interesting for its account of the politics and details of Cushing's mission to China. Much more informative are Cushing's reports and correspondence in Senate Document No. 67, 28th Congress, 2nd Session, pp. 44–69. An offbeat account of his mission is "The Treaty of Wangha 1844" by Ping Chai Kuo in *The Journal of Modern History* for March 1933.

The most respected general account of the Mexican War is *The War With Mexico* by Justin Harvey Smith (1919); even historians who argue with Smith's conclusions praise his factual accuracy. *Texas and the Mexican War* by Nathaniel W. Stephenson (1921) is excellent on the background of the war and the political struggles leading up to it. *Rehearsal for Conflict* by Alfred H. Bill (1947) and *The Story of the Mexican War* by Robert S. Henry (1950) are competent bird's-eye summaries but contain little about the Marines. The

944

most readable book is *The Year of Decision: 1846* by Bernard DeVoto (1943), a lively, opinionated, emotional report of the war and the America that fought it. Any investigator of the Marine Corps' role will have to go to the Corps' archives, and especially the biographical files of Gillespie and Terrett.

Much has been written about the conquest of California, but relatively little about Lieutenant Gillespie's part in it. That tale is usually told through Frémont's story. Frémont himself wrote prodigiously, though his *Memors of My Life* (1886) and other writings must be read with skepticism. Antagonistic to Frémont, DeVoto disagrees violently with *Frémont—The West's Greatest Adventurer* by Allan Nevins (1928), which is both calm and sympathetic. *Stephen Watts Kearny* by Dwight L. Clarke (1961) is a spirited, detailed pro-Kearny account.

There are several interesting Frémont and Gillespie items in *The Century* magazine for March and April 1891. "The proceedings of the court martial in the trial of Lt. Col. Frémont" (Senate Executive Document No. 33, 30th Congress, 1st Session) demonstrates the political machinations and Frémont's play to the press gallery. It includes testimony by and about Gillespie. Lorrin L. Morrison's monograph *Warner: The Man and the Ranch* (1962) touches on Kearny and Gillespie. For other Marine Corps activities with the Pacific Squadron in California, "The Marine Corps' Participation in the Liberation of California" by Lt. Norman Schachter, USMCR, is a useful manuscript; a copy is in the Corps' archives.

The best account of the early amphibious operations in the Gulf of Mexico is *The Home Squadron Under Commodore Conner in the War with Mexico* by Philip S. P. Conner (1898), the son of the commodore. It includes an account of the landing at Vera Cruz by William G. Temple, who was present. For the amphibious operations under Perry, see his various biographies.

For Scott's campaign and the Marine battalion's exploits leading to the Halls of Montezuma—in addition to the general histories of the Corps and of the war—the following are of special interest: *Captain Sam Grant* by Lloyd Lewis (1950) is by far the best-written book on the campaign. Grant's *Personal Memoirs* (1885) are modest and clear but give little credit to the Marines. Scott's *Memoirs* (1864) consist primarily of his reports. *Service Afloat and Ashore* by Lt. Raphael Semmes, USN, (1851) is an eyewitness account with a great deal of local color. *Life and Correspondence of John A. Quitman* by J. F. H. Claiborne (1860) is of great value in following the Marines once they went into battle. *Decisive Battles of the U.S.A.* by J. F. C. Fuller (1942) includes a professional report of the fight for Chapultepec. And the proceedings of the courtmartial of 1st Lt. John S. Devlin, USMC, entitled "The Marine Corps in Mexico," deals with the personal controversy that erupted between Lt. John G. Reynolds and Devlin over the events of September 13. Buried in it are many details of the Marines' climactic action.

In Mexico City, my research was greatly aided by Antonio Arriaga, Director of the National Museum of History, located in the castle on Chapultepec; by Manuel Oropeza, Museum Curator, who familiarized me with the battlefields, and by Master Gunnery Sgt. Sterling McGinnis, USMC, then commander of the Marine Guard at the U.S. Embassy.

Part V
The Civil War 1857–1865

Although the Civil War has been an American passion, few accounts treat the Marine Corps' role in this conflict. Biographical and subject files in the Marine Corps' Historical Branch are essential sources. Bernard C. Nalty's mimeographed monograph *The United States Marines in the Civil War* (1958) is a thorough official summary. Jane Blakeney's *Heroes: U.S. Marine Corps 1861–1955* (1957) is uniquely valuable for citations of honors and decorations and has been used in this chapter and those that follow.

The classic account of the prewar incident at Harpers Ferry is *John Brown* by Oswald Garrison Villard (1910, 1929). Another useful study is *Thunder at Harper's Ferry* by Allan Keller (1958). Lee's report can be found in the Corps' Harpers Ferry file, and Israel Greene's letter is reprinted in the *Marine Corps Gazette* for September 1929. The *New York Weekly Tribune*, October 22 to December 3, 1859, contains full contemporary articles and comment. Also of interest in setting the scene are *The Southampton Insurrection* by William S. Drewery (1900) and "American Slave Insurrections Before 1861" by Harvey Wish in the *Journal of Negro History*, July 1937.

Ralph W. Donnelly, a former reference historian with the U.S. Marine Corps, has made a twenty-year study of the Confederate Marine Corps and published *The History of the Confederate States Marine Corps* (1976), by far the most comprehensive work done on the subject. Other sources on the Confederate Marine Corps include particularly Donnelly's "The Confederate Marine Corps" in *The United Daughters of the Confederacy Magazine*, December 1970; "The Confederate Marine Corps" by Maj. G. W. Van House in the *Marine Corps Gazette*, September 1928; an unpublished thesis by Maj. James C. Gasser, Alabama Polytechnic Institute (1956), a copy of which is at Marine Corps Headquarters; and "Battle Honors and Services of Confederate Marines" by Donnelly in *Military Affairs*, Spring 1959. The Historical Branch also has a separate file on the Confederate marines.

There are no adequate accounts of the Marines' part in the first Battle of Bull Run. An important source is Official Records, Series 1, Vol. 2, Serial No. 2. Although they differ in details, three interesting secondary accounts are in *The Civil War* by Shelby Foote (1958); *Lee's Lieutenants* by Douglas Southall Freeman, volume one, (1942), and *The Coming Fury* by Bruce Catton (1961).

The following sources are useful for readers interested in specific actions during the war: *How the Merrimac Won* by R. W. Daly (1957) and Bruce Catton's article on this battle in the *New York Times Magazine*, March 4, 1962. For the battle of New Orleans, *The Night The War Was Lost* by Charles L. Dufour (1960), a thorough account oriented chiefly to the Confederate side of the story. Maj. Edwin North McClellan also wrote "The Capture of New Orleans" in the *Marine Corps Gazette* for December 1920. A firsthand account is the diary of an enlisted Marine, "Diary of Oscar Smith, U.S. Marine Corps, aboard Flagship *Hartford*, 1861–1862." A typescript, with a foreword dated

August 24, 1937, by the author's son Carl, is in the Library of Congress. The typescript covers the period from May 19, 1861, to December 24, 1862. Albert Kautz's account is in *Battles and Leaders of the Civil War*, vol. II (1887).

In 1975, the Marine Corps History and Museum Division published the diary of 2d Lt. Frank L. Church who commanded the Marine guard on Rear Adm. David D. Porter's flagship during the disastrous Red River Campaign in the spring of 1864. Entitled *Civil War Marine*, the monograph was edited and annotated by James P. Jones and Edward F. Keuchel.

For Mobile Bay, see Charles Heywood's biographical file at Marine Corps Headquarters and *Harper's Magazine*, August 1891. The New York City draft riots are described in Carl Sandburg's *Abraham Lincoln: The War Years* (1939) and in "New York's Bloodiest Week" by Lawrence Lader in *American Heritage*, June 1959. Accounts of the sinking of *Governor* with Reynolds' battalion and Wilkes' report on the *Trent* Affair can be found in Senate Executive Document No. 1, 37th Congress, 2nd Session (1861). There is an interesting chapter on the capture of Raphael Semmes in the *History of the United States Marine Corps* by M. Almy Aldrich (1875). For the seizure of the pirates on *Salvador*, see "The *Salvador* Pirates" by Benjamin Franklin Gilbert, in the *Civil War History Quarterly* for September 1959.

The battle for Fort Fisher is reported in "The Federals and Fort Fisher" by Edwin H. Simmons in the *Marine Corps Gazette*, January and February 1951; "The Capture of Fort Fisher" by McClellan, in the *Marine Corps Gazette*, March 1920; "Fort Fisher and Wilmington Campaign" by James M. Merrill, *North Carolina Historical Review*, October 1958, and *The Naval History of the Civil War* by David D. Porter (1886). The story of Henry Wasmuth's heroism is told in the very readable *A Sailor's Log* by Robley D. Evans (1901).

There is considerable detail about Lincoln's visit to Richmond in Sandburg's biography of Lincoln and in *An End To Valor* by Philip Van Doren Stern (1958).

Of the numerous general studies of the Civil War, the following are most readable and useful: the various histories by Bruce Catton; the three volumes by Carl Sandburg, and the Confederate-oriented work of Douglas Southall Freeman. A well-written recreation of Washington during the war is *Reveille in Washington 1860–1865* by Margaret Leech (1941). A study of the Civil War's revolution in weapons is *Lincoln and the Tools of War* by Robert V. Bruce (1956).

The best of the naval histories of the war include David D. Porter's book; the lively *Civil War on Western Waters* by Fletcher Pratt (1956); and *Mr. Lincoln's Navy* by Richard S. West, Jr., (1957). *Diary of Gideon Welles* is extremely valuable, especially for the appointment of Commandant Zeilin.

Several volumes of the *Campaigns of the Civil War* series, now back in print, offer details on naval actions and equipment: *The Blockade* by J. R. Soley, *The Atlantic Coast* by Daniel Ammen and *The Gulf and Inland Waters* by A. T. Mahan. In that series, *Outbreak of War* by John G. Nicolay covers many of the early incidents and the Battle of Bull Run.

Part VI
Sweep Toward Empire 1848–1894

Because this chapter concerns the role of the Marine Corps around the globe in the periods of relative peace before and after the Civil War, the events and developments that it reports are scattered in many sources.

Two general volumes are worth attention: *Old Bruin,* the biography of Commodore Matthew C. Perry by Samuel Eliot Morison (1967), is a superbly readable and thorough account that ranges over the whole era from the War of 1812 through the expedition to Japan in 1853–54, with an acute awareness of the significance of the Navy's changeover from sail to steam.

Margaret Leech's *In the Days of McKinley* (1959) offers an overview of the politics and economics of the later period described in this chapter. Although this book has no specific interest in the Marine Corps itself, it captures the commercial spirit of the time and deals extensively with the long and difficult conversion of the post–Civil War nation into an imperial power.

There is no better source for Perry's expedition to Japan than the report compiled from notes and journals and authenticated by Perry himself: *Narrative of the Expedition of an American Squadron to the China Seas and Japan performed in the years 1852, 1853 and 1854* by Francis L. Hawks (1856). A basic account of the 1856 attack on the forts below Canton is in *Marine Corps Historical Reference Series Number 6* (revised 1962) entitled "The Barrier Forts" by Bernard C. Nalty. The attack on the Korean forts in 1871 is reported in M. Almy Aldrich's history of the Corps (1875) and in "Our First Korean War" by Capt. J. F. terHorst in the *Marine Corps Gazette,* December 1953.

As always, the files at Marine Corps Headquarters, and especially the biographical files of the Marines themselves, are essential for the precise details of Marine actions and attitudes.

Part VII
The Four-Month War with Spain 1898

The most useful document about the Marine Corps' part in the Spanish-American War is the mimeographed monograph No. 3 in the Marine Corps Historical Reference Series: *The United States Marines in the War with Spain* by Bernard C. Nalty. A second printing (November 1959) is available at the Marine Corps Historical Branch. Its notes contain a valuable bibliography.

The Correspondents' War by Charles H. Brown (1967) includes vivid eyewitness accounts of the Marines' engagements at Guantanamo Bay. My understanding of the topography at Guantanamo was increased by a visit to the Marine Corps base there on assignment for *Look* magazine.

Clyde H. Metcalf's history of the Corps (1939) contains considerable detail about the War with Spain. Among more general volumes are: *The Splendid Little War* by Frank Freidel (1958), a well-edited compilation of participants' accounts of the battles; Margaret Leech's *In the Days of McKinley*

(1959), which places the war in the perspective of its time; *The War with Spain* by Henry Cabot Lodge (1899), and *Remember the Maine* by Gregory Mason (1939).

Two books from more individual points of view are *The Reminiscences of a Marine* by Maj. Gen. John A. Lejeune (1930) and *Admiral Richard Wainwright and the United States Fleet* by Capt. Damon E. Cummings, USN (1962).

Part VIII
On Imperial Duty 1899–1902

The Marine Corps' role in the Philippine Insurrection has not attracted much published attention. The battles of Novaleta and the Sohoton Cliffs and Waller's march across Samar are best sighted in the Marine Corps biographical and subject files. A thorough account of Waller's adventure and courtmartial is *The Ordeal of Samar* by Joseph L. Schott (1964).

Useful general works about this early colonialist period are *In the Days of McKinley* by Margaret Leech (1959) and *The Philippine Islands* by former governor W. Cameron Forbes (1928). The U.S. military government of the Philippines is expertly examined in the unpublished Ph.D. thesis for the Harvard Graduate School of Public Administration, September 1948, "Between War and Peace" by Robert Neville Ginsburgh, now Major General, U.S. Air Force, Retired. *A Nation in the Making* by Peter W. Stanley (1974) treats Filipino political and economic development and contains an extensive bibliography.

The Boxer Rebellion has received more attention. Peter Fleming's *The Siege at Peking* (1959) is a fascinating account of the events in North China, with special orientation to the British viewpoint. It is valuable for details about the siege and the expeditions that tried to lift it. Henry Leonard's report on the relief expedition, which he read before the Military Historical Society of Massachusetts on December 4, 1900, is published in its papers, Volume XIV, 1918. Pvt. James J. Sullivan's diary was published in the *Marine Corps Gazette* in November 1968.

Fleming's account is complemented by William Reynolds Braisted's *The United States Navy in the Pacific, 1897–1909* (1958), which explains the rivalries among the great powers and their naval activities in the Western Pacific.

As for the Marine Corps' part in the Boxer Rebellion, three accounts in the *United States Naval Institute Proceedings* are essential sources. An article by Capt. John T. Myers, USMC, "Military Operations and Defenses of the Siege of Peking" (September 1902), is especially valuable. "The Seymour Relief Expedition" by Lt. Daniel W. Wurtsbaugh, USN (June 1902) deals firsthand with that part of the story. "Experiences During the Boxer Rebellion" by Capt. J. K. Taussig, USN (April 1927) provides an eyewitness account of the final relief expedition. The biographical files at Marine Corps Headquarters are also useful, particularly that of John Twiggs Myers.

APPENDICES

Part IX
Imperialism in the Caribbean 1901–1934

One of the better studies of the extension of United States influence and power southward into the Caribbean is *The United States and the Caribbean* by Dexter Perkins (1947). *The Era of Theodore Roosevelt and the Birth of Modern America 1900–1912* by George E. Mowry (1958) also treats the period during which the Marines first became deeply involved in the area.

For the specific Marine Corps interventions the following are recommended: *The United States Marines in Nicaragua* by Bernard C. Nalty (1958, revised 1961) is a superb photocopied Marine Corps report. *Garde d'Haiti 1915–1934* compiled by James H. McCrocklin (1965) is detailed but focuses primarily on the Garde rather than the Corps itself. *The United States and Mexico* by Howard F. Cline (1953) puts the 1914 invasion into the perspective of the Mexican revolution and of U.S.-Mexican relations. *Marines in the Dominican Republic 1916–1924* by Capt. Stephen M. Fuller and Graham A. Cosmas was published by the Marine Corps Historical Division in 1974. *The Dominican Intervention* by Abraham F. Lowenthal (1972) deals chiefly with the 1965 intervention but includes some background material on the earlier one. The Cuban situation is fully explained in Allan Reed Millett's *The Politics of Intervention, the Military Occupation of Cuba, 1906–1909* (1968).

Among the best personal accounts are: *Old Gimlet Eye, the Adventures of Smedley D. Butler* by Lowell Thomas (1933); *Reminiscences of a Marine* by John A. Lejeune (1930); *The Big Yankee, The Life of Carlson of the Raiders* by Michael Blankfort (1947); *Marine! The Life of Lt. Gen. Lewis B. (Chesty) Puller* by Burke Davis (1962), and *The White King of La Gonave* by Faustin Wirkus and Taney Dudley (1931). *—and a Few Marines* by Col. John W. Thomason, Jr., (1943), who also wrote *Fix Bayonets!* (1926) about World War I, re-creates the spirit of the Marines of his era. Merritt A. Edson's series of articles, "The Coco Patrol," in the *Marine Corps Gazette* (August and November 1936 and February 1937), is an excellent report on those expeditions and on guerrilla warfare, well-written, filled with detail and touches of humor.

The basic source for the changes in the Marines' role during this period is the official *Progress and Purpose: A Developmental History of the U.S. Marine Corps 1900–1970* by Lt. Col. Kenneth J. Crawford (1973). Dion Williams' paper can be found in the *United States Naval Institute Proceedings*, June 1902. "The Lauchheimer Controversy: A Case of Group Political Pressure during the Taft Administration" by Wayne A. Wiegand was published in *Military Affairs* for April 1976. A modern appraisal of the prolonged turn-of-the-century controversy over the Marine Corps' mission will be found in "William Freeland Fullam's War with the Corps" by Lt. Col. John G. Miller, USMC, in the November 1975 issue of the *United States Naval Institute Proceedings*.

Part X
World War I 1914–1919

Surprisingly, there is no superlative overall account of the Marines in World War I. Despite the fact that this experience introduced the Corps to modern warfare and was germinal to its modern role, information about the Marines during the nation's first effort at virtually total war must be retrieved from scattered sources. The only official account is a fascimile reprint (1968) of a monograph first published in 1920: *The United States Marine Corps in the World War* by Maj. Edwin N. McClellan, USMC. This 108-page account is a highly factual skeleton of names, dates and figures.

There is considerable reportage on the 4th Brigade in the exceptionally well-written *The American Heritage History of World War I* by S. L. A. Marshall (1964). *World War I* by Hanson W. Baldwin (1962) offers a brief, readable framework through which more detailed examinations can be fitted into perspective. *The American Army in France* by James G. Harbord (1936) details with care the period when the author commanded the Marine Brigade. And Clyde Metcalf's basic 1939 history of the Corps devotes many pages to World War I.

The battle for Belleau Wood, which stopped the Germans' 1918 offensive toward Paris and revolutionized Allied morale, has been treated in many versions, which often disagree on specific details. *At Belleau Wood* by former Marine Robert B. Asprey (1965) is the most extensive report and is sprinkled with accounts by participants. Anyone interested in that crucial battle will find this volume invaluable, as I did.

Decisive Battles of the U.S.A. by J. F. C. Fuller (1942) has a chapter on the Meuse-Argonne.

Activities at Vladivostok are presented in "American Marines in Siberia during the World War" by Major McClellan in the *Marine Corps Gazette* for June 1920.

The early days of Marine aviation are summarized in the *History of Marine Corps Aviation in World War II* by Robert Sherrod (1952).

There is a variety of personal accounts of the war. Most valuable is *The Reminiscences of a Marine* by Maj. Gen. John A. Lejeune (1930), who commanded the 2d Division after Soissons for the duration. Capt. John W. Thomason, Jr.'s *Fix Bayonets!* (1926) is a vivid personal account that captures the flavor of life on the front. *And They Thought We Wouldn't Fight* by Floyd Gibbons (1918) deals effectively with Belleau Wood. *With The Help of God And A Few Marines* by A. W. Catlin and Walter A. Dyer (1918–19) is regrettably overwritten. *A Marine Tells It To You* by Frederic M. Wise and Meigs O. Frost (1929) is well written but not always accurate in detail. An unpublished oral-history transcript by former Gunnery Sgt. Don V. Paradis is available at the Marine Corps Historical Division. "The First To Fight: Marine Corps Expansion, 1914–18" by Jack Shulimson in *Prologue* (Spring 1976) tells authoritatively the story of the Corps' World War I expansion and its drive to fight in France. Of course, the files at the Marine Corps Historical Division contain much biographical and other essential information.

Part XI
Getting Ready 1919–1941

For the Marines in China, one of the best background studies is *20th Century China* by O. Edmund Clubb (1964). *A Brief History of the 4th Marines* by James S. Santelli (1970) is official and particularly valuable. Smedley Butler's autobiography is especially relevant here. And *The Big Yankee, The Life of Carlson of the Raiders* by Michael Blankfort (1947) is enthusiastic and detailed about Carlson's experiences with the Chinese Communists.

Several periodical sources are important: "Shanghai Emergency" by Maj. Richard B. Rothwell in the *Marine Corps Gazette* for November 1972; "China Marine" by Robert M. Leventhal in the same issue, and "Shanghai Duty 1937–1938," a picture portfolio with brief text in the *United States Naval Institute Proceedings* for November 1974. *The Walla Walla*, the intriguing newsweekly published by the Marines in Shanghai, is on file at the Marine Corps Historical Division.

The Marines' evolution toward amphibious assault is thoroughly reported in *Progress and Purpose: A Developmental History of the United States Marine Corps 1900–1970* by Lt. Col. Kenneth J. Clifford (1973). A superb analysis of the transition is contained in *The U.S. Marines and Amphibious Warfare* by Jeter A. Isley and Philip A. Crowl (1951). This study was sponsored by the Marine Corps, but the opinions are the authors' own. The most valuable official source is Volume I of the History of the U.S. Marine Corps Operations in World War II, *Pearl Harbor to Guadalcanal* by Lt. Col. Frank O. Hough, Maj. Verle E. Ludwig and Henry I. Shaw, Jr. The third volume of the epic history of the United States Naval Operations in World War II, *The Rising Sun in the Pacific 1931—April 1942* by Samuel Eliot Morison is magnificently readable. Robert Sherrod's *History of Marine Corps Aviation in World War II* has some material on the pre-war period.

Among the many personal accounts that touch on this crucial time are: *Once a Marine, The Memoirs of General A. A. Vandegrift* as told to Robert B. Asprey (1964); *Coral and Brass* by Gen. Holland M. Smith and Percy Finch (1948); and *The Amphibians Came To Conquer, The Story of Admiral Richmond Kelly Turner* by Vice Adm. George Carroll Dyer (1969). Lejeune's autobiography is not very helpful for his years as Commandant, and Butler's is, necessarily, on the periphery of the main thrust of amphibious developments.

Part XII
World War II 1941–1949

The story of the Marine Corps in World War II has been told more fully than any other part of the Corps' history. Much of the telling has been superb.

Although the source material available in the Historical Division at Marine Corps Headquarters is voluminous and essential, the reader wishing to pursue the story can well start with the published works.

Three overviews are basic: The five-volume *History of the U.S. Marine Corps Operations in World War II*, published by Marine Corps Headquarters, is the official history. Enormously detailed and for the most part clearly written, it is a comprehensive operational account of battles and units. Its chief limitations are that it tends to be impersonal and, of course, restrained in its criticism.

Almost equally useful is Samuel Eliot Morison's excellent fifteen-volume *History of United States Naval Operations in World War II*. Morison puts campaigns and battles into broader context. Although his main focus is on the Navy's engagements at sea, his work contains considerable material about the Marines' amphibious assaults, emphasizing again the inseparable relationship between the Navy and its Marine Corps.

Third, *The U.S. Marines and Amphibious Warfare* by Jeter A. Isely and Philip A. Crowl (1951) was sponsored by the Marine Corps; but the authors claim their conclusions as their own. It is a meaty, valuable analysis of the development and usage of amphibious warfare by the Marines.

The *History of Marine Corps Aviation in World War II* by Robert Sherrod (1952) is a highly readable study of a part of the Marine Corps' story too often neglected.

Blacks in the Marine Corps by Henry I. Shaw, Jr., and Ralph W. Donnelly (1975) is the Corps' own candid history of the black Americans who have been Marines and the Corps' evolving attitude toward them.

Among the more popular volumes telling the overall story of the Marines in World War II are *Strong Men Armed* by Robert Leckie (1962), an anecdotal account of Marines in combat; *The United States Marine Corps in World War II* edited by S. E. Smith (1969), an anthology of usually eyewitness accounts of Marine actions; and *The Big War* by Anton Myrer (1957), a novel that captures what it was like to be an enlisted Marine in this war.

Each of the six Marine divisions published a history of its own campaigns. The best is *The Old Breed* by George McMillan (1949). It tells not only the combat story but includes much on the periods that the Marines of the 1st Division spent in Australia and on Pavuvu. The *History of the Sixth Marine Division* edited by Bevan G. Cass (1948) also contains interesting details and biographies. The Corps' Historical Division has published as a monograph *Special Marine Corps Units of World War II* by Charles L. Updegraph, Jr. (1972).

There are many useful books on individual battles. *Into the Valley* by John Hersey (1943), a report of one patrol on Guadalcanal, and *Tarawa* by Robert Sherrod (1944) are classics. *The Battle for Guadalcanal* by Samuel B. Griffith (1963) is a professional's account. *Iwo Jima* by Richard F. Newcomb (1965) tells well the story of the Marines' costliest battle. George P. Hunt's *Coral Comes High* (1946) is an exciting personal report by a rifle company commander on Peleliu. *Day of Infamy* by Walter Lord (1957) is a well-written account of the opening attack on Pearl Harbor.

Among the innumerable personal accounts of the war are the memoirs of

Vandegrift and Holland Smith, Burke Davis' story of "Chesty" Puller, Michael Blankfort's book on Evans Carlson and George Dyer's two volumes on Richmond Kelly Turner—all referred to in the bibliography of Chapter 11. Others include *Admiral Halsey's Story* by William F. Halsey and J. Bryan III (1947), *Baa Baa Black Sheep* by Gregory "Pappy" Boyington (1958) and *Wake Island Command* by W. Scott Cunningham (1961).

The Marines' role in the opening of the war is presented in detail in three particularly useful accounts: In the Marine Corps Historical Division's Pearl Harbor file is the unpublished manuscript "Marine Barracks, Navy Yard, Pearl—December 1941" by Brig. Gen. Samuel R. Shaw (1972). In the Posts and Stations, Hawaii file is "The Japanese Attack of 7 December 1941 on the Marine Corps Air Station at Ewa, Oahu, Territory of Hawaii" by 2d Lt. Billie Hollingshead, USMCWR (1945). And in the *Marine Corps Gazette* for April 1946 is "Action Report: Bataan" by 1st Lt. William F. Hogaboom.

The story of John F. Kennedy's rescue of Marines at Choiseul is dramatically told in *PT-109: John F. Kennedy in World War Two* by Robert J. Donovan (1961) and *The Search for J.F.K.* by Joan and Clay Blair, Jr. (1976). The ambush at Anping is reported in detail in *The North China Marine*, August 3, 1946, published in Tientsin.

Part XIII
The Korean War 1946–1953

Although the United Nations' military actions in Korea have been intensively reported, the causes, issues and implications of this pivotal conflict, in which the United States first engaged in major battle with a Communist power, have not yet received adequate comprehensive and objective attention. One searching for an understanding of the war's significance and the decision-making process at its critical turning points must investigate a variety of often contradictory sources.

The following summary is limited to published sources available to most interested readers. As always, the files of the Marine Corps' Historical Division are indispensible.

For the problems discussed in Section One of this chapter during the period between World War II and Korea, the Washington battles over the unification of the armed services are dealt with in a number of studies. Most graphic are *The Forrestal Diaries* edited by Walter Millis (1951) and, from the Corps' point of view, *Once A Marine: The Memoirs of General A. A. Vandegrift* as told to Robert B. Asprey (1964).

Blacks in the Marine Corps by Henry I. Shaw, Jr., and Ralph W. Donnelly (1975) is a unique official effort to filter out the participation of blacks in the Corps. The early and Korean development of helicopters by the Marine Corps is told in *Cavalry of the Sky* by Lynn Montross (1954).

The causes of the Korean war, the divergent views in Washington and

Tokyo and finally the firing of MacArthur are portrayed in two intriguing personal accounts: the two-volume *Memoirs of Harry S Truman* (1955, 1956) and *Present at the Creation* by Dean Acheson (1969). Many of the documents involved will be found in the two-volume official *American Foreign Policy 1950–1955* (1957).

The crucial account of the Marines in the war is the official five-volume *U.S. Marine Operations in Korea* (1954-1972). This is thorough and interesting military history, despite the necessary detailing of the movement and activities of the various units involved. The story of the Marine air arm is relatively neglected in the earlier volumes but well covered in Volume V.

Allen S. Whiting expertly analyzes the Chinese entry into the war in *China Crosses the Yalu* (1960). *The Hidden History of the Korean War* by I. F. Stone (1952) discusses the political puzzles in a rather conspiratorial tone. *The Chinese People's Liberation Army* by Samuel B. Griffith II (1967) is highly professional and readable.

The overall military story of the war and the Marines' part in it are variously told in *Soldiers of the Sea* by Robert Debs Heinl, Jr., (1962); *Conflict* by Robert Leckie (1962); *The New Breed* by Andrew Geer (1952), and *The War in Korea* by Matthew B. Ridgway (1967). The former three authors were all Marines.

The early months of the war are effectively described in *South to the Naktong, North to the Yalu* by Roy E. Appleman (1960), the second volume of the official U.S. Army history of the war. The Navy's story is told by the *History of United States Naval Operations—Korea* by James A. Field, Jr., (1962); *The Sea War in Korea* by Malcolm W. Cagle and Frank A. Manson (1957), and *Battle Report, The War in Korea* by Walter Karig, Cagle and Manson (1952).

Two crucial Marine campaigns are related in enthusiastic detail in Heinl's *Victory at High Tide: The Inchon–Seoul Campaign* (1968) and Leckie's account of the Chosin Reservoir campaign, *The March to Glory* (1960). *This is War!* by David Douglas Duncan (1951) is a vivid eyewitness word-and-picture account of specific actions and the Marines in them by a superb combat photographer. Burke Davis' biography *Marine! The Life of Lt. Gen. Lewis B. (Chesty) Puller* (1962) continues with the Korean chapter of the career of this colorful Marine leader.

The record of Marine close air support is summarized in the series of articles by Kenneth W. Condit and Ernest H. Giusti in several issues of the *Marine Corps Gazette* in 1952.

For an understanding of the treatment and conduct of the American POWs see *In Every War But One* by Eugene Kinkead (1959) and *Turncoat* by the author (1968).

The Marine Corps Historical Division has also published *An Annotated Bibliography of the United States Marine Corps in the Korean War* by Michael O'Quinlivan and James S. Santelli (revised 1970).

My understanding of the topography of this war was improved by going over the Marines' battlefield from Inchon to Seoul and in some areas of western Korea while in South Korea on assignment for *Look* magazine.

Part XIV
Tumultuous Times 1953–1965

A Marine's view of the Ribbon Creek tragedy and trial will be found in *Ribbon Creek: The Marine Corps on Trial* by William B. McKean (1958).

Details of the Lebanon landing are in Jack Shulimson's official monograph *Marines in Lebanon 1958* (1966) and in the appropriate chapter of *The Meaning of Limited War* by Robert McClintock (1967).

For more on the Dominican intervention of 1965 see "Ubique" by Maj. Gen. R. McC. Tompkins, a well-written account in the *Marine Corps Gazette*, September 1965; "Dominican Diary" by Capt. James A. Dare, USN, in the *United States Naval Institute Proceedings*, December 1965; *Overtaken by Events* by John Bartlow Martin (1966); *The Dominican Intervention* by Abraham F. Lowenthal (1972), and *The United States in World Affairs 1966* by Richard P. Stebbins (1967).

Part XV
The Vietnam War 1954–1975

The Vietnam war was fought under unprecedented public exposure to mass-media coverage. Any account of the war must depend in large part on this voluminous and variegated reporting until time shapes the story into the perspective of history.

Research for this chapter was greatly aided by the author's three working trips to Vietnam during the war—two to South Vietnam (1967 and 1969) and one to North Vietnam (1970)—as the Foreign Editor of *Look* magazine. During the first two trips, he interviewed Ambassadors Henry Cabot Lodge and Ellsworth Bunker and Generals Abrams, Walt and Krulak, as well as many Marines and American and South Vietnamese officials. In Hanoi, he interviewed North Vietnamese leaders, under much more restricted conditions, for an article entitled "Report from Hanoi" (*Look*, December 29, 1970).

The Marine Corps' own report of its activities in Indochina during this war is being compiled in a series of nine monographs. The first volumes are *U.S. Marines in Vietnam 1954–1964* by Capt. Robert H. Whitlow (1976) and *Marines in Vietnam 1965, The Landing and the Buildup* by Jack Shulimson and Maj. Charles Johnson. Until all the volumes are published, a useful introduction is *The Marines in Vietnam 1954–1973*, published by the Corps' History and Museums Division in 1974. It contains reprints of thirteen professional articles from the *United States Naval Institute Proceedings*, *Naval Review* and *Marine Corps Gazette*. In addition to articles by Col. Victor J. Croizat, Lt. Col. Archie J. Clapp, Lt. Gen. Keith B. McCutcheon and others, the heart of this anthology is a series of four valuable articles on Marine Corps operations in Vietnam by Brig. Gen. Edwin H. Simmons, who served two tours in Vietnam and later as Director of Marine Corps History and Museums.

BIBLIOGRAPHY

Other published sources dealing with the military side of the war begin with *Hell in a Very Small Place: The Siege of Dien Bien Phu* by Bernard B. Fall (1966). *Strange War, Strange Strategy* by Lewis W. Walt (1970) offers an excellent overview of the period during which Walt commanded III MAF. To understand what it was like for Marines to fight in Vietnam, one must read the vivid Marine Corps monograph *Small Unit Action in Vietnam: Summer 1966* by Capt. Francis J. West Jr. (1967). Its equal in visual terms is *War Without Heroes* by David Douglas Duncan (1970), whose photographs depict the tension, grime, pain and death of Marines in combat.

Tet! by Don Oberdorfer (1971) is an expert journalistic account of the 1968 attacks and their aftermath. The Marine Corps Historical Branch published *The Battle for Khe Sanh* by Capt. Moyers S. Shore II, an extensive monograph, in 1969. And the Office of Air Force History published *Air Power and The Fight for Khe Sanh* by Bernard C. Nalty (1973), a detailed report with emphasis on the contribution of air power and a reasonably balanced presentation of the "single manager" dispute. The controversial incident in Cam Ne is detailed in the Marine Corps' now-declassified file: Cam Ne Village, August 1965.

The evacuations of Phnom Penh and Saigon in 1975 are recounted in a *Marine Corps Gazette* series by Brig. Gen. Richard E. Carey and Maj. David A. Quinlan, in the issues of February through May 1976. The series was followed by an article on the Marines' Koh Tang–Mayaguez operation by Col. John M. Johnson, Jr.; Lt. Col. Randall W. Austin; and Major Quinlan. Roy Rowan's *The Four Days of Mayaguez* (1975) is a fine job of on-the-spot reporting by an experienced *Time-Life* editor; it focuses on the ship's crew, not the Marines involved in the incident. The Comptroller General of the United States published a report, *Seizure of the Mayaguez Part IV* in October 1976.

Dissenting views on the military aspects of this war are numerous. Three pertinent to Marines are: *The Winter Soldier Investigation* by the Vietnam Veterans Against the War (1972), which contains too many tales of Marine atrocities to be ignored; *The Betrayal* by Lt. Col. William R. Corson (1968), an angry report on the pacification program; and *Militarism, U.S.A.* by Col. James A. Donovan with a foreword by Gen. David M. Shoup (1970).

The political side of the war has been interpreted by many participants and observers. For the views of varied concerned individuals see the author's interviews in *Look* with Dean Rusk (September 6, 1966), Walt W. Rostow (December 12, 1967), Gunnar Myrdal (December 24, 1968), Arnold Toynbee (March 18, 1969) and Daniel Ellsberg (October 5, 1971).

Two of the best studies available so far are, from the perspective of Vietnam, *Fire in the Lake* by Frances FitzGerald (1972) and, from the perspective of Washington, *The Best and the Brightest* by David Halberstam (1972). *The Pentagon Papers*, as published by *The New York Times* (1971), is indispensable for understanding the decision-making process through mid-1968. A readable academic analysis is *The United States in Vietnam* by George McTurnan Kahin and John Wilson Lewis (1969). *The Arrogance of Power* by J. William Fulbright (1966) effectively states the case against American involvement.

Part XVI
"In Step and Smartly" 1975–

Until now, the histories of the Marine Corps have all been written by Marines or former Marines. The 1875 *History of the United States Marine Corps* by M. Almy Aldrich was edited on the Corps' centennial from official reports and documents and a draft written by Capt. Richard S. Collum. It is most valuable for its Register of Officers 1798–1875. Collum himself wrote another version, *The History of the United States Marine Corps*, in 1890. Maj. Edwin N. McClellan compiled an extensive and unfinished history of the Corps' early years in the 1920s and 1930s. It was never published but can be found in mimeograph and microfilm form at the Marine Corps History Division and the New York Public Library. *One Hundred Eighty Landings of United States Marines 1800–1934* by Capt. Harry A. Ellsworth was mimeographed in 1934 and published as a Marine Corps monograph in 1974.

The first standard modern history, *A History of the United States Marine Corps* by Col. Clyde H. Metcalf (1939), is thorough but pedestrian. *The Compact History of the Marine Corps* by Lt. Cols. Philip N. Pierce and Frank O. Hough was published in 1960. Extremely readable though ardently partisan is Col. Robert D. Heinl, Jr.'s, excellent *Soldiers of the Sea* (1962). Capt. William [Bill] D. Parker wrote the official *A Concise History of the United States Marine Corps 1775–1969* (1970). The professional *The United States Marines* by Brig. Gen. Edwin H. Simmons was published in Great Britain in 1974 and in the United States in 1976, while Simmons was Director of Marine Corps History and Museums. Professor Allan R. Millett of Ohio State University is preparing an organizational history of the Corps. The Marine Corps History and Museums Division has developed over a span of years a series of chronologically arranged pamphlets entitled *A Chronology of the United States Marine Corps* through June 1970.

The Corps' mission and development are usefully traced in two official monographs: *Progress and Purpose: A Developmental History of the U.S. Marine Corps 1900–1970* by Lt. Col. Kenneth J. Clifford (1973) and *A History of Marine Corps Roles and Missions 1775–1962* by Col. Thomas G. Roe, Maj. Ernest H. Giusti, Maj. John H. Johnstone and Benis M. Frank (1962).

Over the years, the Marine Corps has produced a host of monographs, unit histories and other historical reference pamphlets. Many of these are invaluable for those with special areas of interest. A complete list of these publications can be obtained from the History and Museums Division of Marine Corps Headquarters.

A reference book of inestimable value for anyone interested in the major awards won by individual Marines and much other Marine Corps lore is *Heroes: U.S. Marine Corps 1861–1955*, published by Jane Blakeney (1957). The Corps' History and Museums Division has also prepared and reproduced a Reference Information Pamphlet of all Marine Corps recipients of the Medal of Honor (1974). And the U.S. Government Printing Office has published for the U.S. Senate Committee on Veterans' Affairs *Medal of Honor Recipients*

1863–1973 (1973). This work covers all the services and therefore includes the Navy corpsmen, chaplains and other personnel who served with the Marines.

The post-Vietnam discussion of the Marine Corps' future is treated in "The Marines: Now and in the Future" by Brig. Gen. Simmons in the *United States Naval Institute Proceedings* of May 1975 and "To the Limit of Our Vision—And Back" by Gen. Robert E. Cushman, Jr., in the *Proceedings* of May 1974. The entire issue of the *Proceedings* for November 1975 was devoted to the Marine Corps. Most of Commandant Louis H. Wilson's statement before the Senate Armed Services Committee on Marine Corps Posture, Plans and Programs can be found in the *Marine Corps Gazette* for March 1976. The Haynes Board *Report on Marine Corps Manpower Quality and Force Structure* was published as a monograph by the Corps. "Missions and Force Structure" by William S. Lind appeared in the *Gazette* for December 1975. The Brookings Institution study by Martin Binkin and Jeffrey Record was published as *Where Does the Marine Corps Go from Here?* (1976).

Source Notes

MCH–This designation, frequently used in the following documentation, means that the indicated source material is located in the archives of the History and Museums Division, Headquarters, U.S. Marine Corps.

Part I
The Continental Marines 1775–1784/*pages 1–40*

1 JOHN TREVETT, "Journal of John Trevett," *Rhode Island Historical Magazine*, vol. 7 (1887), p. 38. Original is in the Newport Historical Society, Newport, Rhode Island.
2 M. ALMY ALDRICH, *History of the United States Marine Corps* (Boston: Henry L. Shepard and Co., 1875), p. 33.
3 CHARLES OSCAR PAULLIN, *The Navy of the American Revolution* (Cleveland: Burrows Brothers Co., 1906), p. 53.
4 GARDNER W. ALLEN, *A Naval History of the American Revolution*, 2 vols. (Boston: Houghton Mifflin Co., 1913), p. 97.
5 JOHN TREVETT, "Journal of John Trevett," *Rhode Island Historical Magazine*, vol. 6 (1886), p. 73.
6 PAULLIN, *The Navy of the American Revolution*, p. 36.
7 ALFRED T. MAHAN, *The Major Operations of the Navies in the War of American Independence* (Boston: Little, Brown and Co., 1913), p. 9.
8 CHRISTOPHER WARD, *The War of the Revolution*, 2 vols. (New York: Macmillan Co., 1906), p. 390.
9 MAHAN, *The Major Operations of the Navies in the War of American Independence*, p. 7.
10 *Ibid.*, p. 18.
11 *Ibid.*, pp. 3–4.
12 ALDRICH, *History of the United States Marine Corps*, p. 33.
13 LIONEL CASSON, *The Ancient Mariners—Seafarers and Sea Fighters of the Mediterranean in Ancient Times* (New York: Macmillan Co., 1959), p. 100.
14 G. W. M. GROVER, *Short History of the Royal Marines* (Aldershot, England: Gale and Polden Ltd., 1948), p. 22.
15 ALDRICH, *History of the United States Marine Corps*, p. 16.
16 *Early Records of the First Marine Company*, pamphlet (Philadelphia: The Historical Society of Pennsylvania, 1961; photocopy MCH).

17 JAMES ALTON JAMES, *The Life of George Rogers Clark* (Chicago: University of Chicago Press, 1928), p. 108.

18 ALLEN, *A Naval History of the American Revolution*, p. 427.

19 WILLIAM B. WILLCOX, ed., *The American Rebellion, Sir Henry Clinton's Narrative of his Campaigns, 1775–1782, with an Appendix of Original Documents* (New Haven: Yale University Press, 1954), p. 136.

20 JOHN TREVETT, "Journal of John Trevett," *Rhode Island Historical Magazine*, vol. 6 (1886), p. 278.

21 *Ibid.*, pp. 272–73.

22 JOHN TREVETT, "Journal of John Trevett," *Rhode Island Historical Magazine*, vol. 7 (1887), pp. 39–40.

23 PAULLIN, *The Navy of the American Revolution*, p. 206.

24 Saltonstall Letters dated June 14 and 19, 1780, *Records and Papers of the New London County Historical Society*, Part IV, vol. 1 (New London, Connecticut, 1893).

25 ALLEN, *A Naval History of the American Revolution*, pp. 344–45.

26 ALBERT BUSHNELL HART, *American History Told by Contemporaries*, vol. 2: *1689–1783* (New York: Macmillan Co., 1896; reprint ed. New York: Macmillan Co., 1906), pp. 587–90.

Part II
Establishing the Corps 1798–1815/*pages 41–94*

1 WILLIAM RAY, *Horrors of Slavery: or, the American Tars in Tripolitan Slavery* (Troy, New York, 1808; reprinted in *The Magazine of History*, Extra No., no. 14, 1911), p. 207.

2 *Ibid.*, p. 27.

3 *Ibid.*, p. 118.

4 GEORGE R. CLARK, et al., *A Short History of the United States Navy* (Philadelphia: J. B. Lippincott Co., 1910–30), p. 84.

5 *Biographical File on Franklin Wharton* (MCH).

6 THEODORE ROOSEVELT, *The Naval War of 1812*, 2 vols. (New York: G. P. Putnam's Sons, 1882), p. 46.

7 GLENN TUCKER, *Poltroons and Patriots, A Popular Account of the War of 1812*, 2 vols. (Indianapolis: Bobbs-Merrill Co., 1954), pp. 549–50.

8 DAVID PORTER, *Journal of a Cruise made to the Pacific Ocean by Captain David Porter in the United States Frigate Essex, in the Years 1812, 1813 and 1814* (Philadelphia: Bradford and Inskeep, 1815), pp. 68–69.

9 *Ibid.*, p. 186.

10 DAVID PORTER, *Journal of a Cruise Made to the Pacific Ocean by Captain David Porter in the United States Frigate Essex, in the Years 1812, 1813 and 1814*, 2nd ed., vol. 2 (New York: Wiley and Halsted, 1822), p. 21.

11 *Ibid.*, p. 15.

12 *Ibid.*, p. 79.

13 ROOSEVELT, *The Naval War of 1812*, p. 28.

14 PORTER, *Journal of a Cruise*, 2nd ed., p. 28.

15 EDWIN NORTH MCCLELLAN, "John M. Gamble," *Thirty-fifth Annual Report of the Hawaiian Historical Society for the Year 1926* (Honolulu: Advertiser Publishing Co., Ltd., 1927), p. 50.

16 *Army and Navy Chronicle*, 22 September 1836, p. 181.

Part III
Archibald Henderson and the Indian Wars 1817–1842/*pages 95–134*

1 *Biographical File on Franklin Wharton* (MCH).
2 Letter dated 2 December 1799, *Biographical File on Anthony Gale* (MCH).
3 *Biographical File on Anthony Gale* (MCH).
4 Letter dated 30 March 1818, *1818 File* (MCH).
5 Letter dated 4 October 1818, *1818 File* (MCH).
6 *1818 File* (MCH).
7 ALEXANDER SLIDDELL MACKENZIE, *The Life of Commodore Oliver Hazard Perry*, 2 vols. (New York: Harper and Bros., 1840), p. 132.
8 *1812 File* (MCH).
9 Letter dated 11 November 1835, *Biographical File on Archibald Henderson* (MCH).
10 CHARLES S. FOLTZ, *Surgeon of the Seas—The Adventurous Life of Surgeon General Jonathan M. Foltz* (Indianapolis: Bobbs-Merrill Co., 1931), pp. 37–47.
11 PHILIP N. PIERCE AND LEWIS MEYERS, "The Seven Years War," *Marine Corps Gazette*, September 1948, p. 32.
12 *1836 File* (MCH).
13 M. ALMY ALDRICH, *History of the United States Marine Corps* (New York: G. P. Putnam's Sons, 1939), p. 71.
14 ANNIE HELOISE ABEL, "The History of Events Resulting in Indian Consolidation West of the Mississippi," vol. 1, *American Historical Association Annual Report 1906*, p. 330.
15 ROBERT S. COTTERILL, *The Southern Indians* (Norman: University of Oklahoma Press, 1954), p. 204.
16 EDWIN C. MCREYNOLDS, "*The Seminoles*," The Civilizations of the American Indian Series, vol. 47 (Norman: University of Oklahoma Press, 1957), p. 179.
17 *1836 File* (MCH).
18 ALDRICH, *History of the United States Marine Corps*, pp. 73–74.
19 GRANT FOREMAN, *Indian Removal* (Norman: University of Oklahoma Press, 1932), pp. 166–76. This note covers all direct quotations from John T. Sprague in the rest of Section 4.
20 *Ibid.*, p. 176.
21 Extract from Archibald Henderson journal, dated 13 April 1837, *Biographical File on Archibald Henderson* (MCH).
22 MCREYNOLDS, *The Seminoles*, p. 181.
23 Letter to Brig. Gen. R. Jones, dated 5 June 1837, *1837 File* (MCH).
24 *1837 File* (MCH).
25 Letter from Jesup to Henderson, dated 4 July 1837, *1837 File* (MCH).
26 Letter dated 25 July 1837, *1837 File* (MCH).
27 JOHN T. SPRAGUE, *The Origin, Progress, and Conclusion of the Florida War (New York: D. Appleton and Co., 1847), p. 216.*
28 MCREYNOLDS, *The Seminoles*, p. 200.
29 Report dated 2 December 1837, *1837 File* (MCH).
30 Letter dated 11 February 1838, *1838 File* (MCH).
31 Address by Henderson to "Soldiers" on 24 July 1838, *1838 File* (MCH).
32 MCREYNOLDS, *The Seminoles*, p. 243.
33 FOREMAN, *Indian Removal*, p. 366.

SOURCE NOTES

Part IV
The Mexican War 1842–1847/*pages 135–187*

1 HERMAN MELVILLE, *White Jacket or the World in a Man-of-War* (Boston: L. C. Page & Co., 1892), p. 263.

2 *Ibid.*, p. 63.

3 *Ibid.*, pp. 349–50.

4 HERMAN MELVILLE, *Billy Budd, Foretopman* (New York: Bantam Books, 1959), p. 210.

5 CHARLES WILKES, *Narrative of the United States Exploring Expedition*, vol. 5 (London: Wiley and Putnam, 1845), p. 74.

6 Log of frigate *United States, 1842–45 Files* (MCH).

7 ALLAN NEVINS, ed., *Polk, The Diary of a President, 1845–1849* (New York: Longmans, Green and Co., 1929), entry of 30 October 1845.

8 *The Century*, April 1891, p. 923.

9 *Ibid.*, pp. 928–29.

10 *Ibid.*, p. 922.

11 *Ibid.*, p. 924.

12 *Ibid.*, p. 923.

13 *Biographical File on Archibald Gillespie*, 1860 (MCH).

14 BERNARD DeVOTO, *The Year of Decision 1846* (Boston: Little, Brown and Co., 1943), p. 21.

15 *The Century*, April 1891, p. 924.

16 *The Century*, March 1891, p. 781.

17 Letter to Secretary of the Navy, dated 8 July 1848, *Biographical File on Archibald Gillespie* (MCH).

18 J. M. ELLICOTT, "Comedy and Tragedy in Our Occupation of California," *The Marine Corps Gazette*, March 1951, pp. 49–53.

19 *The Century*, April 1891, p. 926.

20 ALLAN NEVINS, *Frémont—The West's Greatest Adventurer* (New York: Harper and Brothers, 1928), p. 275.

21 U.S. Congress. Senate. *Frémont Courtmartial*, S. Exec. Doc. 33, 30th Cong., 1st sess., 1847–48, p. 181.

22 Letter to Bancroft dated 16 February 1847 from Los Angeles, *Biographical File on Archibald Gillespie* (MCH).

23 *Ibid.*

24 Letter to Secretary of the Navy, dated 8 July 1848, *Biographical File on Archibald Gillespie* (MCH).

25 DWIGHT L. CLARKE, *Stephen Watts Kearny: Soldier of the West* (Norman: University of Oklahoma Press, 1961), p. 176.

26 Letter to Bancroft, dated 16 February 1847, from Los Angeles, *Biographical File on Archibald Gillespie* (MCH).

27 *Ibid.*

28 *Ibid.*

29 *Ibid.*

30 Eyewitness account by Joseph W. Revere, *1848 File* (MCH).

31 *Ibid.*

32 U.S. Congress. Senate. *Frémont Courtmartial*, S. Exec. Doc. 33, 30th Cong., 1st sess., 1847–48, p. 181.

33 M. ALMY ALDRICH, *History of the United States Marine Corps* (Boston: Henry L. Shepard & Co., 1875), pp. 92–93.

34 WILLIAM ELLIOT GRIFFIS, *Matthew Calbraith Perry, A Typical American Naval Officer* (Boston: Cupples and Hurd, 1887), p. 212.

35 PHILIP S. P. CONNER, *The Home Squadron Under Commodore Conner in the War with Mexico* (Philadelphia: n.p., 1898), p. 28.

36 *Ibid.*, p. 20.

37 *Ibid.*, p. 42.

38 GRIFFIS, *Matthew Calbraith Perry, A Typical American Naval Officer*, p. 249.

39 RAPHAEL SEMMES, *Service Afloat and Ashore* (Cincinnati: William H. Moore & Co., 1851), p. 321.

40 ULYSSES S. GRANT, *Personal Memoirs of U. S. Grant*, 2 vols. (New York: Charles L. Webster & Co., 1885), 1:154.

41 WINFIELD SCOTT, *Memoirs of Lieut. General Scott, L.L.D.* (New York: Sheldon & Co., 1864), p. 518.

42 J. F. H. CLAIBORNE, *Life and Correspondence of John A. Quitman* (New York: Harper & Brothers, 1860), p. 367.

43 Letter to Secretary of the Navy, dated 25 October 1847, *Biographical File on Archibald Henderson* (MCH).

44 Letter dated 25 October 1847, *Biographical File on George H. Terrett* (MCH).

45 CLAIBORNE, *Life and Correspondence of John A. Quitman*, p. 386.

46 GRANT, *Personal Memoirs of U.S. Grant*, 2:49.

47 DEVOTO, *The Year of Decision 1846*, p. 495.

Part V
The Civil War 1857–1865/*pages 189–277*

1 M. ALMY ALDRICH, *History of the United States Marine Corps* (Boston: Henry L. Shepard & Co., 1875), p. 120.

2 Letter to Henderson, *Biographical File on John Harris* (MCH).

3 *Biographical File on John Harris* (MCH).

4 Lee's Report to Adjutant General U.S. Army, dated 19 October 1859, *Harpers Ferry File* (MCH).

5 Greene's Letter, *Marine Corps Gazette*, September 1929.

6 *Ibid.*

7 U.S. Congress. Senate. *Message of the President of the U.S. to the Two Houses of Congress at the Commencement of the Second Session of the Thirty-seventh Congress*, S. Exec. Doc. 1, 1861, p. 792. Harris Report to Welles, November 23, 1861.

8 *Confederate Marine File* (MCH).

9 BRUCE CATTON, *Grant Moves South* (Boston: Little, Brown & Co., 1960), p. 27.

10 RICHARD S. WEST, JR., *Mr. Lincoln's Navy* (New York: Longmans, Green & Co., 1957), p. 8.

11 MARGARET LEECH, *Reveille In Washington 1860–1865* (New York: Harper & Bros., 1941), p. 4.

12 ALDRICH, *History of the United States Marine Corps*, p. 131.

13 ROBERT V. BRUCE, *Lincoln and the Tools of War* (Indianapolis: Bobbs-Merrill Co., 1956), p. 204.

14 *Official Records of the Union and Confederate Navies in the War of the Rebellion*, 30 vols. (U.S. Government, 1880–1901 and 1897–1927), series 1, vol. 2, serial 2, p. 385.

15 *Ibid.*

16 U.S. Congress. Senate. *Message of the President*, p. 793.

17 ALDRICH, *History of the United States Marine Corps*, p. 134.

18 HENRY STEELE COMMAGER, ed., *The Blue and the Gray: The Story of the Civil War as Told by Participants* (Indianapolis: Bobbs-Merrill Co., 1950), p. xvi.

19 Report of Flag Officer William Mervine, *1861 File* (MCH).

20 U.S. Congress. Senate. *Message of the President*, p. 792.

21 *Ibid.*, p. 706; Aldrich, *History of the United States Marine Corps*, pp. 142–43.

22 U.S. Congress. Senate. *Message of the President*, p. 707.

23 *Ibid.*, p. 688.

24 BRUCE CATTON, *This Hallowed Ground—The Story of the Union Side of the Civil War* (Garden City, N.Y.: Doubleday & Co., 1956), p. 130.

25 JANE BLAKENEY, Heroes: *U.S. Marine Corps 1861–1955* (Washington, D.C.: By the Author, 1957), p. 5.

26 ALDRICH, *History of the United States Marine Corps*, pp. 17–18.

27 CATTON, *This Hallowed Ground*, p. 120.

28 *Diary of Oscar Smith, U.S. Marine Corps, Aboard Flagship Hartford, 1861–1862* (Library of Congress: Transcript with foreword by Carl Smith, dated 24 August 1937).

29 R. U. JOHNSON & C. BUEL, eds., *Battles and Leaders of the Civil War*, 4 vols. (New York: Century Co., 1887), vol. 2, p. 91.

30 CATTON, *This Hallowed Ground*, p. 202.

31 Broome's Report, 16 March 1863, *1863 File* (MCH).

32 *Biographical File on Charles Heywood* (MCH). *Harper's*, August 1891.

33 U.S. Congress. Senate. *Message of the President*, p. 722.

34 GIDEON WELLES, *Diary of Gideon Welles*, 3 vols. (Boston: Houghton Mifflin Co., 1911), vol. 2, p. 31.

35 Letter to Speaker of the House Samuel Randall, dated 26 March 1877, *Biographical File on Ward Marston* (MCH).

36 WELLES, *Diary of Gideon Welles*, entry of 20 August 1862.

37 Welles letter to Harris, dated 21 August 1862, *Biographical File on John Harris* (MCH).

38 WELLES, *Diary of Gideon Welles*, vol. 2, p. 51.

39 Porter's General Order No. 81, quoted in "The Capture of Fort Fisher" by Edwin N. McClellan, *Marine Corps Gazette*, March 1920.

40 ROBLEY D. EVANS, *A Sailor's Log: Recollections of Forty Years of Naval Life* (New York: D. Appleton & Co., 1901), p. 84.

41 *Ibid.*, p. 88.

42 Fagan Report, *1865 File* (MCH).

43 DAVID D. PORTER, *The Naval History of the Civil War* (New York: Herman Publishing Co., 1886), p. 733.

44 EVANS, *A Sailor's Log*, p. 92.

45 *Ibid.*, p. 93.

46 JAMES M. MERRILL, "Fort Fisher and Wilmington Campaign: Letters from Rear Admiral David Porter," *North Carolina Historical Review*, October 1958, p. 472.

47 PORTER, *A Naval History of the Civil War*, p. 720.

48 *Ibid.*, pp, 733–34.
49 Dawson Report from USS *Colorado*, N.Y., to Commandant, dated 27 January 1865, *1865 File* (MCH).
50 PORTER, *A Naval History of the Civil War*, p. 799.
51 *Biographical File on James Forney* (MCH).

Part VI
Sweep toward Empire 1848–1894/*pages 279–300*

1 FRANCIS L. HAWKS, *Narrative of the Expedition of an American Squadron to the China Seas and Japan Performed in the Years 1852, 1853 and 1854* (Washington, D.C.: A.O.P. Nicholson, 1856), p. 261.
2 SAMUEL ELIOT MORISON, *"Old Bruin": Commodore Matthew C. Perry* (Boston: Little, Brown & Co., 1967), p. 335.
3 HAWKS, *Narrative of the Expedition of an American Squadron to the China Seas and Japan*, p. 346.
4 MORISON, *"Old Bruin": Commodore Matthew C. Perry*, p. 429.
5 M. ALMY ALDRICH, *History of the United States Marine Corps* (Boston: Henry L. Shepard & Co., 1875), pp. 18–19.
6 MARGARET LEECH, *In the Days of McKinley* (New York: Harper & Bros., 1959), p. 587.
7 *Biographical File on Louis Fagan* (MCH).
8 *Ibid.*
9 Letter dated 1 October 1875, *Biographical File on Henry Clay Cochrane* (MCH).
10 C. F. W. Coker, "Register of the Henry Clay Cochrane Papers 1809–1957 and Undated in the United States Marine Corps Museum, Quantico, Va.," Manuscript Register Series No. 1, USMC, p. 8.
11 Commandant's Report, dated 1 October 1882, *Biographical File on Charles G. McCawley* (MCH).
12 Article in the *Washington Post*, dated 31 July 1892, *Biographical File on John Philip Sousa* (MCH).
13 Interview in *The Washington Times* dated 26 April 1903, *Biographical File on Francis M. Scala* (MCH).
14 *Biographical File on Charles Heywood* (MCH).
15 W. H. RUSSELL, "The Genesis of FMF Doctrine: 1879–1899," *Marine Corps Gazette*, April–July 1951, part IV, p. 58.
16 Letter dated 21 June 1871, *Biographical File on McLane Tilton* (MCH).

Part VII
The Four-Month War with Spain 1898/*pages 301–313*

1 CHARLES H. BROWN, *The Correspondents' War* (New York: Charles Scribner's Sons, 1967), p. 281.
2 STEPHEN CRANE, *Wounds in the Rain* (New York: Frederick A. Stokes, 1900), p. 179.
3 BROWN, *The Correspondents' War*, p. 286.

4 *New York Herald*, 23 June 1898; *Biographical File on John H. Quick* (MCH).
5 *Ibid.*
6 CRANE, *Wounds in the Rain*, p. 189.
7 HENRY CABOT LODGE, *The War with Spain* (New York: Harper & Bros., 1899), pp. 105–6.
8 BROWN, *The Correspondents' War*, p. 115.
9 BERNARD C. NALTY, *The United States Marines in the War with Spain*, monograph, 2nd printing (Marine Corps Historical Branch, 1959), pp. 3–5.
10 MARGARET LEECH, *In the Days of McKinley* (New York: Harper & Bros., 1959), p. 172.
11 *Ibid.*, p. 206.
12 Haines' report dated 28 July 1898, *Biographical File on Henry C. Haines* (MCH).

Part VIII
On Imperial Duty 1899–1902/*pages 315–343*

1 MARGARET LEECH, *In the Days of McKinley* (New York: Harper & Bros., 1959), p. 401.
2 Elliott's report in Secretary of Navy, *Annual Report 1900*, p. 1107.
3 *Ibid.*, p. 1108.
4 LEECH, *In the Days of McKinley*, p. 406.
5 As told to Lowell Thomas, *Old Gimlet Eye: The Adventures of Smedley D. Butler* (New York: Farrar & Rinehart, 1933), p. 36.
6 "The Diary of Pvt. Sullivan," *The Marine Corps Gazette*, November 1968, p. 70.
7 *Ibid.*, p. 72.
8 CLYDE H. METCALF, *A History of the United States Marine Corps* (New York: G. P. Putnam's Sons, 1939), p. 283.
9 Waller's report, dated 22 June, 1900, in Secretary of Navy, *Annual Report 1901*, p. 1149.
10 JOHN T. MYERS, "Military Operations and Defenses of the Siege of Peking," *United States Naval Institute Proceedings*, September 1902, p. 544.
11 Secretary of Navy, *Annual Report 1901*, p. 1269.
12 FREDERIC MAY WISE, as told to Meigs O. Frost, *A Marine Tells It to You* (New York: J. H. Sears & Co., 1929), pp. 50–51.
13 THOMAS, *Old Gimlet Eye*, p. 69.
14 PETER W. STANLEY, *A Nation in the Making: The Philippines and the United States, 1899–1921* (Cambridge, Mass.: Harvard. U. Press, 1974), p. 65.
15 Waller letter, dated 22 November 1901, to Adjutant General, 1st Marine Brigade, Cavite, *Philippine Islands 1898–99 File* (MCH).
16 *Ibid.*
17 Waller's report, *Philippines Islands Samar File* (MCH).
18 Waller's report, Basey, dated 25 January 1902, *ibid.*
19 *Ibid.*, Porter's report from Balangiga, dated 8 February 1902.
20 *Ibid.*
21 JOSEPH L. SCHOTT, *The Ordeal of Samar* (Indianapolis: Bobbs-Merrill Co., 1954), p. 140.

22 *Ibid.*

23 *Ibid.*, p. 188.

24 *Biographical File on Littleton W. T. Waller* (MCH).

Part IX
Imperialism in the Caribbean 1901–1934/*pages 345–401*

1 As told to Lowell Thomas, *Old Gimlet Eye: The Adventures of Smedley D. Butler* (New York: Farrar & Rinehart, 1933), p. 170.

2 DEXTER PERKINS, *The United States and the Caribbean* (Cambridge, Mass.: Harvard U. Press, 1947), p. 139.

3 *Ibid.*, pp. viii–ix.

4 GEORGE E. MOWRY, *The Era of Theodore Roosevelt and the Birth of Modern America 1900–1912* (New York: Harper & Row, 1958), p. 155.

5 THOMAS, *Old Gimlet Eye*, p. 168.

6 HOWARD F. CLINE, *The United States and Mexico* (Cambridge, Mass.: Harvard U. Press, 1953), p. 144.

7 CLYDE H. METCALF, *A History of the United States Marine Corps* (New York: G. P. Putnam's Sons, 1939), p. 413.

8 WILLIAM L. ROPER, "Air Action in Nicaragua," *Marine Corps Gazette*, November 1972, p. 54.

9 MERRITT A. EDSON, "The Coco Patrol," *Marine Corps Gazette*, November 1936, p. 41.

10 ROBERT L. DENIG, "Native Officer Corps, Guardia Nacional De Nicaragua," *Marine Corps Gazette*, November 1932, p. 77.

11 THOMAS, *Old Gimlet Eye*, p. 184.

12 *Ibid.*, p. 186.

13 *Ibid.*, p. 209.

14 JAMES H. MCCROCKLIN, comp., *Garde d'Haiti 1915–1934* (Annapolis: U.S. Naval Institute, 1956), p. 74.

15 *Ibid.*, p. 79.

16 *Ibid.*, p. 141.

17 CARL KELSEY, "The American Intervention in Haiti," *Annals of the American Academy of Political and Social Science*, March 1922, p. 138.

18 MCCROCKLIN, *Garde d'Haiti 1915–1934*, p. 154.

19 *Biographical File on Hiram I. Bearss* (MCH).

20 METCALF, *A History of the United States Marine Corps*, p. 356.

21 ABRAHAM F. LOWENTHAL, *The Dominican Intervention* (Cambridge, Mass.: Harvard U. Press, 1972), p. 10.

22 *The New York Times*, 1 June 1961.

23 PERKINS, *The United States and the Caribbean*, p. 154.

24 WAYNE A. WIEGAND, "America's Dreyfus Affair?" *Biographical File on Charles H. Lauchheimer* (MCH).

25 *Biographical File on George Elliott* (MCH).

26 KENNETH J. CLIFFORD, *Progress and Purpose: A Developmental History of the United States Marine Corps 1900–1970* (Washington, D.C.: USMC, 1973), p. 10.

27 ROBERT DEBS HEINL, JR., *Soldiers of the Sea* (Annapolis: U.S. Naval Institute, 1962), p. 155.

28 DION WILLIAMS, "The Defense of Our New Naval Stations," *United States Naval Institute Proceedings*, June 1902, p. 185.

29 *Ibid.*, p. 187.

Part X
World War I 1914–1919/*pages 403–444*

1 FLOYD GIBBONS, *And They Thought We Wouldn't Fight* (New York: George H. Doran Co., 1918), p. 304.

2 JAMES G. HARBORD, *The American Army in France 1917–1919* (Boston: Little, Brown & Co., 1936), p. 290.

3 ROBERT B. ASPREY, *At Belleau Wood* (New York: G. P. Putnam's Sons, 1965), pp. 182–83.

4 Lecture, May 21, 1915, quoted in Jack Shulimson, "The First to Fight: Marine Corps Expansion, 1914–1918," *Prologue*, Spring 1976, p. 6.

5 JACK SHULIMSON, "The First to Fight, A Study of the Marine Corps Expansion to Meet the Exigencies of War during the Commandancy of George Barnett 1914–1918," undated manuscript (MCH), p. 17.

6 Eds. of American Heritage, narrative by S. L. A. Marshall, *The American Heritage History of World War I* (New York: American Heritage Publishing Co., 1964), p. 280.

7 *Ibid.*

8 HARBORD, *The American Army in France 1917–1919*, p. 283.

9 FREDERIC MAY WISE, as told to Meigs O. Frost, *A Marine Tells It to You*, (New York: J. H. Sears & Co., 1929), p. 204.

10 *Ibid.*, p. 202.

11 A. W. CATLIN with collaboration of Walter A. Dyer, *With the Help of God and a Few Marines* (Garden City, N.Y.: Doubleday, Page & Co., 1918, 1919), p. 103.

12 WISE, *A Marine Tells It to You*, p. 217.

13 *Ibid.*, p. 222.

14 ASPREY, *At Belleau Wood*, p. 251.

15 *Ibid.*, p. 258.

16 WISE, *A Marine Tells It to You*, pp. 233–34.

17 ASPREY, *At Belleau Wood*, p. 307.

18 HARBORD, *The American Army in France 1917–1919*, p. 298.

19 DON V. PARADIS, "Memoirs of Don V. Paradis, Former Gunnery Sergeant, USMC," unpublished transcript of oral history report, 17 September 1973 (MCH), pp. 208–9.

20 GIBBONS, *And They Thought We Wouldn't Fight*, p. 299.

21 PARADIS, "Memoirs of Don V. Paradis," p. 87.

22 HARBORD, *The American Army in France 1917–1919*, p. 337.

23 *Ibid.*, p. 336.

24 General Orders No. 16, quoted in John A. LeJeune, *The Reminiscences of a Marine* (Philadelphia: Dorrance & Co., 1930), p. 284.

25 *Biographical File on Daniel J. Daly* (MCH).

26 HARBORD, *The American Army in France 1917–1919*, p. 452.

27 PARADIS, "Memoirs of Don V. Paradis," pp. 161–62.

28 LEJEUNE, *The Reminiscences of a Marine*, p. 402.

29 ROBERT SHERROD, *History of Marine Corps Aviation in World War II* (Washington, D.C.: Combat Forces Press, 1952), p. 17.

30 CLYDE H. METCALF, *A History of the United States Marine Corps* (New York: G. P. Putnam's Sons, 1939), p. 521.

31 Letter from Rheinbrohl, Germany, 14 December 1918, in Paradis, "Memoirs of Don V. Paradis," p. 224.

32 JOHN W. THOMASON, JR., *Fix Bayonets!* (New York: Charles Scribner's Sons, 1926), p. 232.

33 *Ibid.*, p. 239.

Part XI
Getting Ready 1919–1941/*pages 445–467*

1 BENIS M. FRANK, "The Relief of General Barnett," *Records of the Columbia Historical Society of Washington, D.C.*, 1971–72, pp. 679–93.

2 As told to Lowell Thomas, *Old Gimlet Eye: The Adventures of Smedley D. Butler* (New York: Farrar & Rinehart, Inc., 1933), p. 276.

3 O. EDMUND CLUBB, *20th Century China* (New York: Columbia U. Press, 1964), p. 52.

4 ROBERT SHERROD, *History of Marine Corps Aviation in World War II* (Washington, D.C.: Combat Forces Press, 1952), p. 28.

5 CLUBB, *20th Century China*, p. 214.

6 MICHAEL BLANKFORT, *The Big Yankee, The Life of Carlson of the Raiders* (Boston: Little, Brown & Co., 1947), p. 223.

7 Memorandum from Commandant dated 2 April 1924, *Biographical File on Earl H. Ellis* (MCH).

8 WAITE W. WORDEN, "Lt. Col. Earl Ellis," p. 3, *Biographical File on Earl H. Ellis* (MCH).

9 HOLLAND M. SMITH AND PERCY FINCH, *Coral and Brass* (New York: Charles Scribner's Sons, 1948), pp. 64–65.

10 JOHN L. ZIMMERMAN, "The Marines' First Spy," *The Saturday Evening Post*, 23 November 1946, p. 100.

11 "Advanced Base Operations in Micronesia," quoted in Jeter A. Isely and Philip A. Crowl, *The U.S. Marines and Amphibious Warfare* (Princeton: Princeton U. Press, 1951), p. 27.

12 KENNETH J. CLIFFORD, *Progress and Purpose: A Developmental History of the United States Marine Corps 1900–1970* (Washington, D.C.: USMC, 1973), p. 30.

13 *Ibid.*

14 *Ibid.*, p. 36.

15 ISELY AND CROWL, *The U.S. Marines and Amphibious Warfare*, p. 4.

16 GEORGE CARROLL DYER, *The Amphibians Came to Conquer—The Story of Admiral Richmond Kelly Turner* (Washington D.C.: GPO, 1969?), p. 203.

17 ISELY AND CROWL, *The U.S. Marines and Amphibious Warfare*, p. 67.

Part XII
World War II 1941–1949/*pages 469–657*

1 WALTER LORD, *Day of Infamy* (New York: Bantam Books, 1958), p. 121.

2 FRANK O. HOUGH, VERLE E. LUDWIG, HENRY I. SHAW, JR., *History of U.S. Marine Corps Operations in World War II*, vol. 1: *Pearl Harbor to Guadalcanal* (Arlington, Va.: Headquarters, USMC, undated), p. 70.

3 SAMUEL ELIOT MORISON, *History of United States Naval Operations*, vol. 3: *The Rising Sun in the Pacific 1931–April 1942* (Boston: Little, Brown & Co., 1958), p. 132.

4 *Ibid.*, p. 232.

5 *Ibid.*, p. 234.

6 *Ibid.*, p. 253.

7 HOUGH, LUDWIG, SHAW, JR., *Pearl Harbor to Guadalcanal*, p. 189.

8 *Ibid.*, pp. 188–89.

9 MORISON, *The Rising Sun in the Pacific*, p. 204.

10 S. E. SMITH, ed. & comp., *The United States Marine Corps in World War II* (New York: Random House, 1969), p. 101.

11 WILLIAM F. HOGABOOM, "Action Report: Bataan," *Marine Corps Gazette*, April 1946, pp. 25–33.

12 S. E. SMITH, *The United States Marine Corps in World War II*, p. 108.

13 ALEXANDER A. VANDEGRIFT as told to Robert B. Asprey, *Once a Marine* (New York: Norton & Co., 1964), p. 100.

14 SAMUEL B. GRIFFITH II, *The Battle for Guadalcanal* (Philadelphia: J. B. Lippincott Co., 1963), pp. 23–24.

15 VANDEGRIFT, *Once a Marine*, p. 122.

16 S. E. SMITH, *The United States Marine Corps in World War II*, p. 166; Marine Corps Historical Division files. Pfc. Ahrens was awarded the Navy Cross.

17 JETER A. ISELY AND PHILIP A. CROWL, *The U.S. Marines and Amphibious Warfare* (Princeton: Princeton U. Press, 1951), p. 129.

18 VANDEGRIFT, *Once a Marine*, p. 129.

19 HOUGH, LUDWIG, SHAW, JR., *Pearl Harbor to Guadalcanal*, p. 260; Samuel Eliot Morison, *History of United States Naval Operations in World War II*, vol. 5: *The Struggle for Guadalcanal August 1942–February 1943 (Boston: Little, Brown & Co., 1949), p. 17.*

20 GEORGE CARROLL DYER, *The Amphibians Came to Conquer—The Story of Admiral Richmond Kelly Turner* (Washington, D.C.: GPO, 1969?) p. 358.

21 VANDEGRIFT, *Once a Marine*, p. 142.

22 MORISON, *The Struggle for Guadalcanal*, p. 73.

23 VANDEGRIFT, *Once a Marine*, p. 153.

24 *Biographical File on John Basilone* (MCH).

25 VANDEGRIFT, *Once a Marine*, p. 153.

26 HOUGH, LUDWIG, SHAW, JR., *Pearl Harbor to Guadalcanal*, p. 357.

27 MORISON, *The Struggle for Guadalcanal*, p. 287.

28 HOUGH, LUDWIG, SHAW, JR., *Pearl Harbor to Guadalcanal*, p. 372.

29 HENRY I. SHAW, JR., AND DOUGLAS T. KANE, *History of U.S. Marine Corps Operations in World War II*, vol. 2: *Isolation of Rabaul* (Arlington, Va.: Headquarters, USMC, 1963), p. 138.

30 SAMUEL ELIOT MORISON, *History of United States Naval Operations in World*

War II, vol. 6: *Breaking the Bismarcks Barrier 22 July 1942–1 May 1944* (Boston: Little, Brown & Co., 1950), p. 224.

31 *Ibid.*, p. 370.

32 *Ibid.*, p. 378.

33 SHAW, JR., AND KANE, *Isolation of Rabaul*, p. 370.

34 S. E. SMITH, *The United States Marine Corps in World War II*, p. 490; Robert Leckie, *Strong Men Armed* (New York: Random House, 1962), p. 264.

35 ROBERT SHERROD, *Tarawa, The Story of a Battle* (New York: Sloan & Pearce, 1949), pp. 47, 108; Isely and Crowl, *The U.S. Marines and Amphibious Warfare*, p. 236.

36 SAMUEL ELIOT MORISON, *History of United States Naval Operations in World War II*, vol. 7: *Aleutians, Gilberts and Marshalls June 1942–April 1944* (Boston: Little, Brown & Co., 1951), p. 148.

37 HENRY I. SHAW, JR., BERNARD C. NALTY, EDWIN T. TURNBLADH, *History of U.S. Marine Corps Operations in World War II*, vol. 3: *Central Pacific Drive* (Arlington, Va.: Headquarters, USMC, 1966), p. 61.

38 *Ibid.*, p. 79.

39 ISELY AND CROWL, *The U.S. Marines and Amphibious Warfare*, pp. 251–52.

40 HOLLAND M. SMITH AND PERCY FINCH, *Coral and Brass* (New York: Charles Scribner's Sons, 1948), pp. 119–20, 142.

41 SHAW, JR., NALTY, TURNBLADH, *Central Pacific Drive*, p. 71.

42 SHERROD, *Tarawa, The Story of a Battle*, p. 35.

43 VANDEGRIFT, *Once a Marine*, p. 242.

44 ISELY AND CROWL, *The U.S. Marines and Amphibious Warfare*, pp. 255–56.

45 MORISON, *Aleutians, Gilberts and Marshalls*, p. 265.

46 *Ibid.*, p. 298.

47 SAMUEL ELIOT MORISON, *History of U.S. Naval Operations in World War II*, vol. 8: *New Guinea and the Marianas March 1944–August 1944* (Boston: Little, Brown & Co., 1953), p. 159.

48 H. M. SMITH AND FINCH, *Coral and Brass*, p. 161.

49 SHAW, JR., NALTY, TURNBLADH, *Central Pacific Drive*, pp. 240–41; Isely and Crowl, *The U.S. Marines and Amphibious Warfare*, p. 341.

50 SHAW, JR., NALTY, TURNBLADH, *Central Pacific Drive*, p. 295.

51 MORISON, *The Rising Sun in the Pacific*, p. vii.

52 *Ibid.*, p. 318.

53 SHAW, JR., NALTY, TURNBLADH, *Central Pacific Drive*, p. 313.

54 H. M. SMITH AND FINCH, *Coral and Brass*, p. 181.

55 *Ibid.*

56 ISELY AND CROWL, *The U.S. Marines and Amphibious Warfare*, pp. 346–47.

57 *Ibid.*, pp. 342–47; Shaw, Jr., Nalty, Turnbladh, *Central Pacific Drive*, pp. 302–20; H. M. Smith and Finch, *Coral and Brass*, pp. 176–88.

58 H. M. SMITH AND FINCH, *Coral and Brass*, pp. 196–97.

59 SHAW, JR., NALTY, TURNBLADH, *Central Pacific Drive*, p. 346.

60 H. M. SMITH AND FINCH, *Coral and Brass*, p. 189.

61 *Ibid.*, p. 210.

62 MICHAEL BLANKFORT, *The Big Yankee, The Life of Carlson of the Raiders* (Boston: Little Brown & Co., 1947), p. 337.

63 H. M. SMITH AND FINCH, *Coral and Brass*, p. 212.

64 SHAW, JR., NALTY, TURNBLADH, *Central Pacific Drive*, p. 392.

65 *Ibid.*, p. 448.

66 MORISON, *New Guinea and the Marianas*, p. 380.

67 Medal of Honor citation.

68 ISELY AND CROWL, *The U.S. Marines and Amphibious Warfare*, p. 376.

69 WILLIAM F. HALSEY AND J. BRYAN III, *Admiral Halsey's Story* (New York: McGraw-Hill Book Co., 1947), p. 199.

70 *Ibid.*, p. 195.

71 SAMUEL ELIOT MORISON, *History of United States Naval Operations in World War II*, vol. 12: *Leyte June 1944–January 1945* (Boston: Little, Brown & Co., 1958), p. 47.

72 GEORGE W. GARAND AND TRUMAN R. STROBRIDGE, *History of U.S. Marine Corps Operations in World War II*, vol. 4: *Western Pacific Operations* (Arlington, Va.: Headquarters, USMC, 1971), p. 285.

73 *The New York Times*, 22 September 1943, quoted in Robert Sherrod, *History of Marine Corps Aviation in World War II* (Washington, D.C.: Combat Forces Press, 1952), p. 264.

74 *Ibid.*, p. 265.

75 MORISON, *Leyte*, p. 6.

76 Letter by Chaplain Edgar E. Siskin in *Hebrew Union College Bulletin*, April 1945, pp. 7–8, quoted in Garand and Strobridge, *Western Pacific Operations*, p. 109.

77 *Ibid.*, p. 110.

78 GEORGE P. HUNT, *Coral Comes High* (New York: New American Library, 1957), p. 29.

79 *Ibid.*, pp. 72–73.

80 S. E. SMITH, *The United States Marine Corps in World War II*, p. 675.

81 Medal of Honor citation; Garand and Strobridge, *Western Pacific Operations*, pp. 157–58.

82 *Ibid.*, p. 161.

83 S. E. SMITH, *The United States Marine Corps in World War II*, p. 680.

84 BURKE DAVIS, *Marine! The Life of Lt. Gen. Lewis B. (Chesty) Puller, USMC (Ret.)* (Boston: Little, Brown & Co., 1962), p. 226.

85 GARAND AND STROBRIDGE, *Western Pacific Operations*, p. 161.

86 SHERROD, *History of Marine Corps Aviation in World War II*, p. 325.

87 *Ibid.*, p. 303; Garand and Strobridge, *Western Pacific Operations*, p. 347.

88 RICHARD F. NEWCOMB, *Iwo Jima* (New York: Holt Rinehart & Winston, 1965), p. 46.

89 ISELY AND CROWL, *The U.S. Marines and Amphibious Warfare*, p. 485.

90 *Ibid.*, p. 487.

91 S. E. SMITH, *The United States Marine Corps in World War II*, p. 748.

92 H. M. SMITH AND FINCH, *Coral and Brass*, p. 270.

93 GARAND AND STROBRIDGE, *Western Pacific Operations*, p. 647.

94 Medal of Honor citation.

95 Medal of Honor citation.

96 GARAND AND STROBRIDGE, *Western Pacific Operations*, p. 681.

97 *Ibid.*, p. 710.

98 *Ibid.*, p. 712.

99 *The New York Times*, 26 February 1945, p. 1 quoted in *Ibid.*, p. 713.

100 ISELY AND CROWL, *The U.S. Marines and Amphibious Warfare*, p. 475.

101 H. M. SMITH AND FINCH, *Coral and Brass*, p. 245.

102 ISELY AND CROWL, *The U.S. Marines and Amphibious Warfare*, p. 558.

103 SAMUEL ELIOT MORISON, *History of United States Naval Operations in World War II*, vol. 14: *Victory in the Pacific 1945* (Boston: Little, Brown & Co., 1960), p. 217.

104 *Ibid.*, p. 172.

105 ERNIE PYLE, *Last Chapter* (New York: Henry Holt & Co., 1946), pp. 139–40.

106 Letter by Lt. M. H. Jaffe dated 14 April 1945.

107 VANDEGRIFT, *Once a Marine*, p. 291.

108 MORISON, *Victory in the Pacific*, p. 273.

109 Medal of Honor citation.

110 BENIS M. FRANK AND HENRY I. SHAW, JR., *History of U.S. Marine Operations in World War II*, vol. 5: *Victory and Occupation* (Arlington, Va.: Headquarters, USMC, 1968), p. 213.

111 Medal of Honor citation.

112 ISELY AND CROWL, *The U.S. Marines and Amphibious Warfare*, p. 575.

113 SHERROD, *History of Marine Corps Aviation in World War II*, p. 397.

114 BEVAN G. CASS, ed., *History of the Sixth Marine Division* (Washington, D.C.: Infantry Journal Press, 1948), p. 120.

115 Letter by Lt. M. H. Jaffe dated 17 June 1945.

116 ISELY AND CROWL, *The U.S. Marines and Amphibious Warfare*, p. 547.

117 CASS, *History of the Sixth Marine Division*, p. 157.

118 GEORGE MCMILLAN, *The Old Breed, A History of the First Marine Division in World War II* (Washington, D.C.: Infantry Journal Press, 1949), p. 413.

119 Quoted in Frank and Shaw, Jr., *Victory and Occupation*, p. 337.

120 Letter by Lt. M. H. Jaffe, 17 June 1945.

121 ROY E. APPLEMAN, et al., *Okinawa: The Last Battle* (Washington, D.C.: Historical Division, Department of the Army, 1948), pp. 384–86.

122 MCMILLAN, *The Old Breed*, pp. 423–24.

123 Quoted in Frank and Shaw, Jr., *Victory and Occupation*, p. 401.

124 JAMES S. SANTELLI, *A Brief History of the 4th Marines* (Arlington, Va.: Headquarters, USMC, 1970), p. 36.

125 ROBERT DEBS HEINL, JR., *Soldiers of the Sea* (Annapolis, Md.: U.S. Naval Institute, 1962), p. 519.

126 MCMILLAN, *The Old Breed*, pp. 428–29.

127 FRANK AND SHAW, JR., *Victory and Occupation*, p. 564.

128 *Ibid.*, p. 572.

129 *Ibid.*, p. 573.

130 Quoted in O. Edmund Clubb, *20th Century China* (New York: Columbia U. Press, 1964), p. 263.

131 Quoted from *The North China Marine*, Tientsin, 28 September 1946, p. 1 in Frank and Shaw, Jr., *Victory and Occupation*, p. 618.

132 *Ibid.*, p. 625.

133 *Ibid.*, p. 633.

134 CLUBB, *20th Century China*, p. 290.

135 *Ibid.*, p. 295.

136 FRANK AND SHAW, JR., *Victory and Occupation*, p. 649.

137 HENRY I. SHAW, JR., AND RALPH W. DONNELLY, *Blacks in the Marine Corps* (Washington, D.C.: History and Museums Division, Headquarters, USMC, 1975), p. 1.

138 *Ibid.*

139 *Ibid.*, p. 3.

140 *Ibid.*, p. 35.

141 FRANK AND SHAW, JR., *Victory and Occupation*, pp. 446–47.

142 ISELY AND CROWL, *The U.S. Marines and Amphibious Warfare*, p. 12.

Part XIII
The Korean War 1946–1953/*pages 659–815*

1 ALEXANDER A. VANDEGRIFT as told to Robert B. Asprey, *Once a Marine* (New York: Norton & Co., 1964), p. 295.

2 *Ibid.*, p. 308.

3 LYNN MONTROSS, HUBARD D. KUOKKA, NORMAN W. HICKS, *U.S. Marine Operations in Korea 1950–1953*, vol. 4: *The East-Central Front* (Arlington, Va.: Headquarters, USMC, 1962), p. 187.

4 HENRY I. SHAW, JR., AND RALPH W. DONNELLY, *Blacks in the Marine Corps* Washington, D.C.: History and Museums Division, Headquarters, USMC, 1975), p. 59.

5 HARRY S TRUMAN, *Memoirs by Harry S Truman*, vol. 2: *Years of Trial and Hope* (Garden City, N.Y.: Doubleday & Co., 1956), p. 46.

6 October 25, 1945, quoted in Vandegrift, *Once a Marine*, p. 301.

7 *Ibid.*, p. 316.

8 *Ibid.*, p. 301.

9 *Ibid.*, p. 316.

10 WALTER MILLIS, ED., *The Forrestal Diaries* (New York: The Viking Press, 1951), p. 224.

11 Quoted in G. C. Thomas, R. D. Heinl, Jr., A. A. Ageton, *The Marine Officer's Guide* (Annapolis, Md.,: U.S. Naval Institute, 1956), p. 70.

12 MERRITT A. EDSON, "Power-Hungry Men in Uniform," *Collier's*, 27 August 1949.

13 ROBERT S. ALLEN, "Too Much Brass," *Collier's*, 6 September 1947.

14 ROBERT LECKIE, *Conflict: The History of the Korean War, 1950–53* (New York: G. P. Putnam's Sons, 1962), p. 34; and Lynn Montross and Nicholas A. Canzona, *U.S. Marine Operations in Korea 1950–1953*, vol. 1: *The Pusan Perimeter* (Arlington, Va.: Headquarters, USMC, 1954), p. 14.

15 TRUMAN, *Years of Trial and Hope*, p. 329.

16 U.S. Department of State, *American Foreign Policy 1950–1955*, Basic Documents, vols. 1 & 2, July 1957, pp. 2317–18.

17 MALCOLM W. CAGLE AND FRANK A. MANSON, *The Sea War in Korea* (Annapolis, Md.: U.S. Naval Institute, 1957), p. 31.

18 ROY E. APPLEMAN, *South to the Naktong, North to the Yalu* (Washington, D.C.: Office of the Chief of Military History, Dept. of the Army, 1961), pp. 207–8.

19 ROBERT DEBS HEINL, JR., *Soldiers of the Sea* (Annapolis, Md.: U.S. Naval Institute, 1962), p. 539; and Lynn Montross and Nicholas A. Canzona, *U.S. Marine Operations in Korea 1950–1953, vol. 2: The Inchon–Seoul Operation* (Arlington, Va.: Headquarters, USMC, 1955), pp. 10–11.

20 ANDREW GEER, *The New Breed: The Story of the U.S. Marines in Korea* (New York: Harper & Bros., 1952), p. 56.

21 APPLEMAN, *South to the Naktong, North to the Yalu*, p. 308.

22 JAMES A. FIELD, JR., *History of United States Naval Operations Korea* (Washington, D.C.: GPO, 1962), p. 152.

23 R. L. MURRAY, "The First Naktong," *Marine Corps Gazette*, November 1965, pp. 84–85.

24 MONTROSS AND CANZONA, *The Pusan Perimeter*, p. 186.

25 *Ibid.*, pp. 203–4.

26 Escort carrier *Sicily* action report quoted in Cagle and Manson, *The Sea War in Korea*, p. 65.

27 APPLEMAN, *South to the Naktong, North to the Yalu*, p. 453.

28 MONTROSS AND CANZONA, *The Pusan Perimeter*, p. 236.

29 *Congressional Record*, 16 May 1952, pp. 5446–47, quoted in Heinl, Jr., *Soldiers of the Sea*, p. 547.

30 MONTROSS AND CANZONA, *The Pusan Perimeter*, p. 239.

31 WALTER KARIG, MALCOLM W. CAGLE, FRANK A. MANSON, *Battle Report: The War in Korea*, vol. 6 (New York: Rinehart & Co., 1952), p. 169.

32 FIELD, JR., *History of United States Naval Operations Korea*, p. 179.

33 MONTROSS AND CANZONA, *The Inchon–Seoul Operation*, p. 90.

34 *Ibid.*, p. 92; Robert Debs Heinl, Jr., *Victory at High Tide: The Inchon–Seoul Campaign* (Philadelphia: J. B. Lippincott Co., 1968), p. 93.

35 Medal of Honor citation.

36 MONTROSS AND CANZONA, *The Inchon–Seoul Operation*, p. 161.

37 *Ibid.*, p. 214.

38 Interview with Lt. Gen. Robert H. Barrow, Headquarters, USMC, Arlington, Va., 27 May 1976.

39 MONTROSS AND CANZONA, *The Inchon–Seoul Operation*, p. 251.

40 APPLEMAN, *South to the Naktong, North to the Yalu*, p. 527.

41 HEINL, JR., *Victory at High Tide: The Inchon–Seoul Campaign*, pp. 212–13.

42 MONTROSS AND CANZONA, *The Inchon–Seoul Operation, p. 247;* Appleman, *South to the Naktong, North to the Yalu*, pp. 524–25; Geer, *The New Breed*, pp. 156–62.

43 APPLEMAN, *South to the Naktong, North to the Yalu*, p. 525.

44 MONTROSS AND CANZONA, *The Inchon–Seoul Operation*, pp. 256–57; Karig, Cagle, Manson, *Battle Report: The War in Korea*, vol. 6 pp. 258–59.

45 BURKE DAVIS, *Marine! The Life of Lt. Gen. Lewis B. (Chesty) Puller, USMC (Ret.)*, (Boston: Little, Brown & Co., 1947) p. 272.

46 *Special Action Report*, night of 25–26 September 1950, from Supporting Arms Coordinator to Battalion Commander, 3rd Battalion, 1st Marines, 27 September 1950 (MCH).

47 MONTROSS AND CANZONA, *The Inchon–Seoul Operation*, p. 264.

48 NORMAN R. STANFORD, "Road Junction," *Marine Corps Gazette*, September 1951, p. 19.

49 MONTROSS AND CANZONA, *The Inchon–Seoul Operation*, pp. 297–98.

50 CAGLE AND MANSON, *The Sea War in Korea*, p. 75.

51 DEAN ACHESON, *Present at the Creation* (New York: W. W. Norton & Co., Inc., 1969), p. 447.

52 *Ibid.*, p. 451.

53 Joint Chiefs of Staff message 92801, 27 September 1950, quoted in Lynn Montross and Nicholas A. Canzona, *U.S. Marine Operations in Korea 1950–1953*, vol. 3: *The Chosin Reservoir Campaign* (Arlington, Va.: Headquarters, USMC, 1957), pp. 5–6.

54 U.S. Department of State, *American Foreign Policy 1950–1955*, pp. 2576–77.

55 ACHESON, *Present at the Creation*, p. 454.

56 Quoted in Appleman, *South to the Naktong, North to the Yalu*, p. 270.

57 ALLEN S. WHITING, *China Crosses the Yalu: The Decision to Enter the Korean War* (New York: The Macmillan Co., 1960), p. 118.

58 APPLEMAN, *South to the Naktong, North to the Yalu*, p. 757.

59 MONTROSS AND CANZONA, *The Chosin Reservoir Campaign*, p. 131.

60 APPLEMAN, *South to the Naktong, North to the Yalu*, p. 670.

61 MONTROSS AND CANZONA, *The Chosin Reservoir Campaign*, p. 39.

62 *Ibid.*, p. 67.

63 *Ibid.*, p. 98.

64 Medal of Honor citation; Geer, *The New Breed*, p. 233.

65 Medal of Honor citation; Geer, *The New Breed*, p. 234.

66 Medal of Honor citation; Phillips "Wound Card" on file MCH.

67 Medal of Honor citation; Montross and Canzona, *The Chosin Reservoir Campaign*, p. 119.

68 APPLEMAN, *South to the Naktong, North to the Yalu*, p. 772.

69 Quoted in Montross and Canzona, *The Chosin Reservoir Campaign*, p. 133.

70 APPLEMAN, *South to the Naktong, North to the Yalu*, pp. 772–73.

71 Medal of Honor citation; Geer, *The New Breed*, pp. 262–63.

72 Medal of Honor citation; Robert Leckie, *The March to Glory* (Cleveland: The World Publishing Co., 1960), p. 65.

73 Myers' Medal of Honor citation; Montross and Canzona, *The Chosin Reservoir Campaign*, pp. 216–18.

74 LECKIE, *The March to Glory*, p. 80.

75 Medal of Honor citation.

76 LECKIE, *The March to Glory*, p. 118.

77 Medal of Honor citation.

78 U.S. Department of State, *American Foreign Policy 1950–1955*, p. 2585.

79 MONTROSS AND CANZONA, *The Chosin Reservoir Campaign*, p. 255.

80 HEINL, JR., *Soldiers of the Sea*, p. 561.

81 Medal of Honor citation.

82 Medal of Honor citation.

83 Interview with Lt. Gen. Robert H. Barrow, Headquarters, USMC, Arlington, Va., 27 May 1976.

84 MONTROSS AND CANZONA, *The Chosin Reservoir Campaign*, p. 317.

85 Quoted in *ibid.*, p. 350; quoted in Ernest H. Giusti and Kenneth W. Condit, "Marine Air Covers the Breakout," *Marine Corps Gazette*, August 1952, p. 27.

86 *Time* (Pacific edition) 18 December 1950, pp. 18–19, quoted in Montross and Canzona, *The Chosin Reservoir Campaign*, p. 333.

87 *Newsweek*, 11 December 1950, p. 11, quoted in *ibid.*, p. 334.

88 *Time* (Pacific edition) 11 December 1950, p. 9, quoted in *ibid.*

89 *Ibid.*, p. 334 footnote.

90 Letter dated 4 December 1950 quoted in Davis, *Marine! The Life of Lt. Gen. Lewis B. (Chesty) Puller, USMC (Ret.)*, p. 312.

91 *Ibid.*, p. 325.

92 McArthur letter dated 17 October 1956 quoted in Montross and Canzona, *The Chosin Reservoir Campaign*, p. 346.

93 TRUMAN, *Years of Trial and Hope*, p. 442.

94 *Ibid.*, p. 416.

95 ACHESON, *Present at the Creation*, p. 527.

96 LYNN MONTROSS, HUBARD D. KUOKKA, NORMAN W. HICKS, *U.S. Marine Operations in Korea 1950–1953*, vol. 4: *The East-Central Front* (Arlington, Va.: Headquarters, USMC, 1962), p. 150.

97 Medal of Honor citation.

98 Medal of Honor citation.

99 Medal of Honor citation.

100 MONTROSS, KUOKKA, HICKS, *The East-Central Front*, p. 186.

101 *Ibid.*, p. 190.

102 *Ibid.*, p. 193; Medal of Honor citation.

103 Quoted in Montross, Kuokka, Hicks, *The East-Central Front*, p. 199.

104 PAT MEID AND JAMES M. YINGLING, *U.S. Marine Operating in Korea 1950–1953*, vol. 5: *Operations in West Korea* (Washington, D.C.: Headquarters, USMC, 1972), p. 36; Medal of Honor citation.

105 *Ibid.*, p. 83; Medal of Honor citations.

106 *Ibid.*, pp. 91–92, Medal of Honor citation.

107 *Ibid.*, p. 95.

108 *Ibid.*, p. 93.

109 *Ibid.*, p. 127; Medal of Honor citation.

110 *Ibid.*, p. 138.

111 *Ibid.*, p. 147; Medal of Honor citation.

112 *Ibid.*, p. 163; Medal of Honor citation.

113 *Ibid.*, p. 168; Medal of Honor citation.

114 *Ibid.*, p. 206–7; Medal of Honor citations.

115 MORRIS R. WILLS as told to J. ROBERT MOSKIN, *Turncoat* (New York: Prentice-Hall, 1966, 1968), pp. 1–17.

116 Medal of Honor citation.

117 MEID AND YINGLING, *Operations in West Korea*, p. 287; Medal of Honor Citation.

118 *Ibid.*, p. 294; Medal of Honor citation.

119 *Ibid.*, p. 296; Medal of Honor citation.

120 *Ibid.*, p. 311.

121 EUGENE KINKEAD, *In Every War But One* (New York: W. W. Norton & Co., 1959), p. 163.

122 MEID AND YINGLING, *Operations in West Korea*, p. 442.

123 KINKEAD, *In Every War But One*, pp. 163–64.

124 *Ibid.*, p. 16.

125 Quoted in Meid and Yingling, *Operations in West Korea*, p. 440.

126 *Ibid.*, p. 483.

127 *Ibid.*, p. 513.

128 CAGLE AND MANSON, *The Sea War in Korea*, p. 270.

129 MATTHEW B. RIDGWAY, *The War in Korea* (London: Barrie & Rockliff, 1967), p. 244.

130 MEID AND YINGLING, *Operations in West Korea*, p. 496.

131 *Ibid.*, p. 519.

132 S. L. A. MARSHALL, *Pork Chop Hill* (New York: William Morrow & Co., 1956), p. 211.

SOURCE NOTES

Part XIV
Tumultuous Times 1953–1965/*pages 817–841*

1 WILLIAM BAGGARLEY MCKEAN, *Ribbon Creek: The Marine Corps on Trial* (New York: The Dial Press, 1958), p. 266.
2 BURKE DAVIS, *Marine! The Life of Lt. Gen. Lewis B. (Chesty) Puller, USMC (Ret.)* (Boston: Little, Brown & Co., 1962), pp. 382–84.
3 J. ROBERT MOSKIN, "Revolution in the Marine Corps," *Look*, 28 May 1957, pp. 35–43.
4 JACK SHULIMSON, *Marines in Lebanon 1958* (Washington, D.C.: Historical Branch, Headquarters, USMC, 1966), p. 12.
5 Quoted in *ibid*, p. 14.
6 *Ibid.*, p. 36.
7 ROBERT MCCLINTOCK, *The Meaning of Limited War* (Boston: Houghton Mifflin Co., 1967), p. 109.
8 Quoted in Shulimson, *Marines in Lebanon 1958*, p. 17.
9 ABRAHAM F. LOWENTHAL, *The Dominican Intervention* (Cambridge, Mass.: Harvard U. Press, 1972), p. 1.
10 *Ibid.*, p. 10.
11 JOHN BARTLOW MARTIN, *Overtaken by Events* (New York: Doubleday & Co., 1966), p. 40.
12 LOWENTHAL, *The Dominican Intervention*, p. 93.
13 Quoted in Eric F. Goldman, *The Tragedy of Lyndon Johnson* (New York: Alfred A. Knopf, 1969), p. 395.
14 R. McC. TOMPKINS, "Ubique," *Marine Corps Gazette*, September 1965, p. 37.
15 LOWENTHAL, *The Dominican Intervention*, p. 124.
16 RICHARD P. STEBBINS, *The United States in World Affairs 1966* (New York: Harper & Row for the Council on Foreign Relations, 1967), pp. 306, 314.
17 DAVID M. SHOUP, "The New American Militarism," *The Atlantic*, April 1969, p. 54.
18 MARTIN, *Overtaken by Events*, p. 705.
19 J. WILLIAM FULBRIGHT, *The Arrogance of Power* (New York: Vintage Books, Random House, 1966), p. 84.

Part XV
The Vietnam War 1954–1975/*pages 843–914*

1 GEORGE McTURNAN KAHIN AND JOHN WILSON LEWIS, *The United States in Vietnam* (New York: The Dial Press, 1969), p. 31.
2 FRANCES FITZGERALD, *Fire in the Lake* (New York: Vintage Books, Random House, 1972), pp. 342–43.
3 *Ibid.*, p. 310.
4 KAHIN AND LEWIS, *The United States in Vietnam*, p. 175.
5 *The Marines in Vietnam 1954–1973, An Anthology and Annotated Bibliography* (Washington, D.C.: History and Museums Div., Headquarters, USMC, 1974), p. 38.
6 *Ibid.*, p. 43.
7 *Ibid.*, p. 53.

8 FitzGerald, *Fire in the Lake*, p. 384.

9 Lewis W. Walt, *Strange War, Strange Strategy* (New York: Funk & Wagnalls, 1970), pp. 125–30.

10 Medal of Honor citation; Walt, *Strange War, Strange Strategy*, pp. 161–63; Francis J. West, Jr., *Small Unit Action in Vietnam: Summer 1966* (Washington, D.C.: Historical Branch, USMC, 1967), pp. 15–30.

11 Medal of Honor citation; Walt, *Strange War, Strange Strategy*, pp. 157–59.

12 West, Jr., *Small Unit Action in Vietnam: Summer 1966*, p. 119.

13 *The Marines in Vietnam 1954–1973*, p. 58.

14 Quoted in Bernard Fall, *Hell in a Very Small Place: The Siege of Dien Bien Phu* (Philadelphia: J. B. Lippincott Co., 1966), p. 28.

15 *The Marines in Vietnam 1954–1973*, p. 59.

16 FitzGerald, *Fire in the Lake*, p. 449.

17 Document 118, 14 October 1966, *The Pentagon Papers*, as published by *The New York Times* (New York: Quadrangle Books, 1971), p. 555.

18 Interview with Lt. Gen. Lewis W. Walt, Da Nang, 1 February 1967.

19 *The Marines in Vietnam 1954–1973*, p. 65.

20 Medal of Honor citation.

21 *The Marines in Vietnam 1954–1973*, p. 71.

22 Medal of Honor citation; Walt, *Strange War, Strange Strategy*, pp. 147–49.

23 *The Marines in Vietnam 1954–1973*, p. 89.

24 Edwin H. Simmons in *ibid.*, p. 96.

25 Bernard C. Nalty, *Air Power and the Fight for Khe Sanh* (Washington, D.C.: Office of Air Force History, 1973), p. 21.

26 Medal of Honor citation.

27 *The Marines in Vietnam 1954–1973*, p. 102.

28 Quoted from speech of 19 October 1968 in *Nixon Speaks Out*, (New York: Nixon-Agnew Campaign Committee, 1968), p. 231.

29 FitzGerald, *Fire in the Lake*, p. 556.

30 Medal of Honor citations.

31 Medal of Honor citation.

32 Medal of Honor citation.

33 E. H. Simmons, *The United States Marines* (London: Leo Cooper, Ltd., 1974), p. 178.

34 Henry I. Shaw, Jr., and Ralph W. Donnelly, *Blacks in the Marine Corps* (Washington, D.C.: History and Museums Div., Headquarters, USMC, 1975), p. 72.

35 *Ibid.*, p. 73.

36 Edward L. Green, "Equal Opportunity," *United States Naval Institute Proceedings*, June 1974, pp. 40–41.

37 *The New York Times*, 6 May 1975, p. 1; *Newsweek*, 21 April 1975, p. 33.

38 Department of Defense, *Table 1051: Number of Casualties Incurred by U.S. Military Personnel in Connection with the Conflict in Vietnam Cumulative from Jan. 1, 1961–Dec. 31, 1975* (15 January 1976).

39 David M. Shoup, "The New American Militarism," *The Atlantic*, April 1969, p. 55.

40 James A. Donovan, *Militarism, U.S.A*, with a foreword by David M. Shoup (New York: Charles Scribner's Sons, 1970), p. xi.

41 *Ibid.*

42 Interview with Chaplain Lester L. Westing, Jr., of Oakland, California, Da Nang, 1 February 1967.

43 Interviews with Cpl. Andre A. Williams, Vietnam, February 1967.

44 WALT, *Strange War, Strange Strategy*, p. 66.

Part XVI
"In Step and Smartly" 1975–/*pages 915–938*

1 MARTIN BINKIN AND JEFFREY RECORD, *Where Does the Marine Corps Go from Here?* (Washington, D.C.: The Brookings Institution, 1976), p. 69.

2 Interview with Lt. Gen. Victor H. Krulak, Hawaii, 9 January 1967.

3 BINKIN AND RECORD, *Where Does the Marine Corps Go from Here?* p. 30.

4 THOMAS G. ROE, et al., *A History of Marine Corps Roles and Missions 1775–1962*, Marine Corps Historical Reference Series No. 30 (Washington, D.C.: Historical Branch, Headquarters, USMC, 1962), p. 10.

5 *Ibid.*, p. 8.

6 Gen. Clifton B. Cates quoted 1951 in *ibid.*, p. 25.

7 Statement by Gen. Louis H. Wilson on "Marine Corps Posture, Plans and Programs" before U.S. Senate Armed Services Committee, 2 February 1976.

8 J. ROBERT MOSKIN, "Our New Western Frontier," *Look*, 30 May 1967, pp. 36–46.

9 JAMES A. DONOVAN, *Militarism, U.S.A.*, with a foreword by David M. Shoup (New York: Charles Scribner's Sons, 1970), p. xii.

10 BINKIN AND RECORD, *Where Does the Marine Corps Go from Here?* p. 35.

11 All quotations by Gen. Louis H. Wilson in this chapter are from an interview at USMC Headquarters, Arlington, Va., 27 May 1976, unless other sources are cited.

12 W. R. BALL, "Brookings Defense Study," *Marine Corps Gazette*, March 1976, p. 7.

13 BINKIN AND RECORD, *Where Does the Marine Corps Go from Here?* p. 7.

14 Interview with Lt. Gen. Leslie E. Brown, USMC Headquarters, Arlington, Va., 28 May 1976.

15 DAVID M. SHOUP, "The New American Militarism," *The Atlantic*, April 1969, p. 55.

16 Transcript of Press Conference by Maj. Gen. Fred E. Haynes, Jr., Washington, D.C., 24 March 1976, p. 7.

17 *Ibid.*, p. 12.

18 *The Defense Monitor*, October 1975, p. 6.

19 Haynes Press Conference Transcript, p. 4.

20 *Ibid.*, p. 7.

21 *Ibid.*, p. 5.

22 Interview with Lt. Gen. Lawrence F. Snowden, USMC Headquarters, Arlington, Va., 28 May 1976.

23 *The New York Times*, 9 July 1975.

24 ROBERT E. CUSHMAN, JR., "To the Limit of Our Vision—And Back," *United States Naval Institute Proceedings*, May 1974, p. 112.

25 Interview with Maj. Gen. Fred E. Haynes, Jr., USMC Headquarters, Arlington, Va., 27 May 1976.

APPENDICES

26 *Report on Marine Corps Manpower Quality and Force Structure* (USMC, 1975), p. 4.
27 "Training the Marines," *The New York Times*, 14 April 1976, p. 36.
28 *The New York Times*, 30 June 1976.
29 *The Wall Street Journal*, 16 June 1976.
30 Interviews with Lt. Gen. Robert H. Barrow, USMC Headquarters, Arlington, Va., 28 May and 30 September 1976.
31 Unpublished paper by Lt. Gen. Robert H. Barrow.
32 WILLIAM SHAKESPEARE, *King Henry V*, Act IV, Scene iii.

Commandants of the U.S. Marine Corps

COMMANDANT	YEARS	BIRTHPLACE
Samuel Nicholas	1775–1781	Philadelphia
William Ward Burrows	1798–1804	Charleston, South Carolina
Franklin Wharton	1804–1818	Philadelphia
Anthony Gale	1819–1820	Dublin, Ireland
Archibald Henderson	1820–1859	Colchester, Virginia
John Harris	1859–1864	East Whiteland, Pennsylvania
Jacob Zeilin	1864–1876	Philadelphia
Charles G. McCawley	1876–1891	Philadelphia
Charles Heywood	1891–1903	Waterville, Maine
George F. Elliott	1903–1910	Utah, Green County, Alabama
William P. Biddle	1911–1914	Philadelphia
George Barnett	1914–1920	Lancaster, Wisconsin
John A. Lejeune	1920–1929	Pointe Coupee, Louisiana
Wendell C. Neville	1929–1930	Portsmouth, Virginia
Ben H. Fuller	1930–1934	Big Rapids, Michigan
John H. Russell	1934–1936	Mare Island, California
Thomas Holcomb	1936–1943	New Castle, Delaware
Alexander A. Vandegrift	1944–1947	Charlottesville, Virginia
Clifton B. Cates	1948–1951	Tiptonville, Tennessee
Lemuel C. Shepherd, Jr.	1952–1955	Norfolk, Virginia
Randolph McC. Pate	1956–1959	Port Royal, South Carolina
David M. Shoup	1960–1963	Battle Ground, Indiana
Wallace M. Greene, Jr.	1964–1967	Waterbury, Vermont
Leonard F. Chapman, Jr.	1968–1971	Key West, Florida
Robert E. Cushman, Jr.	1972–1975	St. Paul, Minnesota
Louis H. Wilson	1975–	Brandon, Mississippi

(The term Commandant was not used until 1800. Nicholas was the senior officer of the Continental Marines.)

U.S. Marines Who Have Received the Medal of Honor

The Medal of Honor is the United States' highest award for military valor. During the century from its first presentation in 1863 to the departure of the Marines from Vietnam in 1973, 291 Marines have received 298 Medals of Honor. A number of Navy corpsmen, chaplains and other personnel serving with Marine Corps units in combat have also earned the Medal.

Only two Marines have earned the Medal of Honor for two separate courageous acts: Daniel J. Daly in 1900 and 1915 and Smedley D. Butler in 1914 and 1915. Five Marines received both the Navy and Army Medals of Honor for the same act during World War I, when separate medals existed.

Of the 291 Marines, 69 were officers and 222 enlisted men. Of the total, 119 were killed as a direct result of the action for which they were cited. The posthumous awards are indicated in this listing by an asterisk following the Marine's name.

NAME	PLACE	DATE	UNIT
	The Civil War 1861–1865		
Sgt. Richard Binder	Fort Fisher	1864–65	USS *Ticonderoga*
Sgt. J. Henry Denig	Mobile Bay	1864	USS *Brooklyn*
Orderly Sgt. Isaac N. Fry	Fort Fisher	1865	USS *Ticonderoga*
Sgt. Michael Hudson	Mobile Bay	1864	USS *Brooklyn*
Cpl. John F. Mackie	Drewry's Bluff	1862	USS *Galena*
Sgt. James Martin	Mobile Bay	1864	USS *Richmond*
Sgt. Andrew Miller	Mobile Bay	1864	USS *Richmond*
Orderly Sgt. Christopher Nugent	Florida	1863	USS *Fort Henry*
Cpl. Miles M. Ovaitt	Mobile Bay	1864	USS *Brooklyn*
Cpl. John Rannahan	Fort Fisher	1865	USS *Minnesota*
Sgt. James S. Roantree	Mobile Bay	1864	USS *Oneida*
Pvt. John Shivers	Fort Fisher	1865	USS *Minnesota*
Cpl. Willard M. Smith	Mobile Bay	1864	USS *Brooklyn*
Orderly Sgt. David Sprowle	Mobile Bay	1864	USS *Richmond*
Pvt. Henry A. Thompson	Fort Fisher	1865	USS *Minnesota*
Cpl. Andrew J. Tomlin	Fort Fisher	1865	USS *Wabash*
Sgt. Pinkerton R. Vaughn	Port Hudson	1863	USS *Mississippi*
	Korean Campaign 1871		
Cpl. Charles Brown			USS *Colorado*
Pvt. John Coleman			USS *Colorado*
Pvt. James Dougherty			USS *Carondelet*
Pvt. Michael McNamara			USS *Benicia*

NAME	PLACE	DATE	UNIT
Pvt. Michael Owens			USS *Colorado*
Pvt. Hugh Purvis			USS *Alaska*

Interim 1872–1881

NAME	PLACE	DATE	UNIT
Cpl. John Morris	France	1881	USS *Lancaster*
Cpl. James A. Stewart	France	1872	USS *Plymouth*

Spanish American War 1898

NAME	PLACE	DATE	UNIT
Pvt. Daniel Campbell	Cuba		USS *Marblehead*
Pvt. Oscar W. Field	Cuba		USS *Nashville*
Pvt. John Fitzgerald	Cuba		1st Marine Battalion
Pvt. Joseph J. Franklin	Cuba		USS *Nashville*
Sgt. Philip Gaughan	Cuba		USS *Nashville*
Pvt. Frank Hill	Cuba		USS *Nashville*
Pvt. Michael Kearney	Cuba		USS *Nashville*
Pvt. Hermann W. Kuchneister	Cuba		USS *Marblehead*
Pvt. Harry L. MacNeal	Cuba		USS *Brooklyn*
Pvt. James Meredith (name changed to Patrick F. Ford, Jr.)	Cuba		USS *Brooklyn*
Pvt. Pomeroy Parker	Cuba		USS *Nashville*
Sgt. John H. Quick	Cuba		1st Marine Battalion
Pvt. Joseph F. Scott	Cuba		USS *Nashville*
Pvt. Edward Sullivan	Cuba		USS Marblehead
Pvt. Walter S. West	Cuba		USS Marblehead

Period of the Philippine Insurrection 1899–1902

Capt. Hiram I. Bearss	Samar	1901	1st Regiment
Pvt. Howard M. Buckley	Luzon	1899	USS *Helena*
Sgt. Bruno A. Forsterer	Samoa	1899	USS *Philadelphia*
Sgt. Harry Harvey	Benictican	1900	1st Regiment
Pvt. Henry L. Hulbert	Samoa	1899	USS *Philadelphia*
Pvt. Joseph Leonard (enlisted as Joseph Melvin)	Luzon	1899	USS *Helena*
Sgt. Michael J. McNally	Samoa	1899	USS *Philadelphia*
Capt. David D. Porter	Samar	1901	Marine Barracks, Cavite
Cpl. Thomas F. Prendergast	Luzon	1899	USS *Helena*

Boxer Rebellion 1900

Sgt. John M. Adams (born George L. Day)	Tientsin	1st Regiment
Cpl. Harry C. Adriance	Tientsin	1st Regiment
Cpl. Edwin N. Appleton	Tientsin	USFS *Newark*
Pvt. Erwin J. Boydston	Peking	USS *Oregon*
Pvt. James Burnes	Tientsin	USFS *Newark*
Pvt. Albert R. Campbell	Tientsin	1st Regiment
Pvt. William L. Carr	Peking	USFS *Newark*
Pvt. James Cooney	Tientsin	1st Regiment
Cpl. John O. Dahlgren	Peking	USS *Oregon*
Pvt. Daniel J. Daly	Peking	USFS *Newark*
Pvt. Harry Fisher*	Peking	USS *Oregon*
Sgt. Alexander J. Foley	Tientsin	1st Regiment
Pvt. Charles R. Francis	Tientsin	1st Regiment

987

NAME	PLACE	DATE	UNIT
Pvt. Louis R. Gaiennie	Peking		USFS *Newark*
Pvt. Henry W. Heisch	Tientsin		USFS *Newark*
Pvt. William C. Horton	Peking		USS *Oregon*
Pvt. Martin Hunt	Peking		USS *Oregon*
Pvt. Thomas W. Kates	Tientsin		1st Regiment
Pvt. Clarence E. Mathias	Tientsin		1st Regiment
Pvt. Albert Moore	Peking		USS *Oregon*
Drummer John A. Murphy	Peking		USFS *Newark*
Pvt. William H. Murray			
(served under the name of Henry W. Davis)			
Pvt. Harry W. Orndoff	Peking		USFS *Newark*
Cpl. Reuben J. Phillips	Relief Expedition		USFS *Newark*
Pvt. Herbert I. Preston	Relief Expedition		USFS *Newark*
Pvt. David J. Scannell	Peking		USS *Oregon*
Pvt. France Silva	Peking		USS *Oregon*
Gunnery Sgt. Peter Stewart	Peking		USFS *Newark*
Sgt. Clarence E. Sutton	Relief Expedition		USFS *Newark*
Pvt. Oscar J. Upham	Tientsin		1st Regiment
Sgt. Edward A. Walker	Peking		USS *Oregon*
Pvt. Frank A. Young	Peking		USS *Oregon*
Pvt. William Zion	Peking		USFS *Newark*
	Peking		USFS *Newark*

Interim 1901

Sgt. John H. Helms	Montevideo		USS *Chicago*

Name	Location/Campaign	Unit
Pvt. Louis F. Pfeifer (served as Louis F. Theis)	Pacific Ocean	USS *Petrel*

Vera Cruz 1914

Maj. Randolph C. Berkeley	2d Advance Base Regiment
Maj. Smedley D. Butler	2d Advance Base Regiment
Maj. Albertus W. Catlin	3rd Regiment
Capt. Jesse F. Dyer	2d Advance Base Regiment
Capt. Eli T. Fryer	2d Advance Base Regiment
Capt. Walter N. Hill	2d Advance Base Regiment
Capt. John A. Hughes	2d Advance Base Regiment
Lt. Col. Wendell C. Neville	2d Regiment
Maj. George C. Reid	3rd Regiment

Haitian Campaign 1915

Name	Location	Unit
Maj. Smedley D. Butler	Fort Riviere	CO, detachments
Gunnery Sgt. Daniel J. Daly	Fort Dipite	2d Regiment
Pvt. Samuel Gross (real name: Samuel Marguiles)	Fort Riviere	USS *Connecticut*
Sgt. Ross L. Iams	Fort Riviere	USS *Connecticut*
1st Lt. Edward A. Ostermann	Fort Dipite	1st Brigade
Capt. William P. Upshur	Fort Dipite	2d Regiment

Dominican Republic 1916

Name	Location	Unit
Cpl. Joseph A. Glowin	Guayacanas	Artillery Battalion

NAME	PLACE	DATE	UNIT
1st Lt. Ernest C. Williams	San Francisco de Macoris		4th Regiment
1st Sgt. Roswell Winans	Guayacanas		4th Regiment
	World War I 1918		
Sgt. Louis Cukela	Forest de Retz		5th Regiment
Gunnery Sgt. Ernest A. Janson (served under the name of Charles Hoffman)	Belleau Wood		5th Regiment
Pvt. John J. Kelly	Blanc Mont Ridge		6th Regiment
Sgt. Matej Kocak	Soissons		5th Regiment
Cpl. John H. Pruitt*	Blanc Mont Ridge		6th Regiment
Gunnery Sgt. Robert G. Robinson	Pittham, Belgium		Northern Bombing Group
Gunnery Sgt. Fred W. Stockham*	Belleau Wood		6th Regiment
2d Lt. Ralph Talbot	Pittham, Belgium		Northern Bombing Group
	Haitian Campaign 1919		
Cpl. William R. Button	Grande Riviere		Constabulary Detachment
Sgt. Herman H. Hanneken	Grande Riviere		Constabulary Detachment
	Interim 1921		
Pvt. Albert J. Smith	Pensacola, Florida		Marine Barracks
	Second Nicaraguan Campaign 1928–1932		
1st Lt. Christian F. Schilt	Quilali	1928	Observation Squadron 7-M

Name	Unit	Year	Campaign
Cpl. Donald L. Truesdale (name changed to Truesdell)	Nicaraguan National Guard Detachment	1932	Coco River

World War II 1941–1945

Name	Unit	Year	Campaign
Pfc. Harold C. Agerholm*	10th Marines	1944	Saipan
Pfc. Richard B. Anderson*	23rd Marines	1944	Kwajalein
Maj. Kenneth D. Bailey*	1st Raider Battalion	1942	Guadalcanal
Sgt. John Basilone	7th Marines	1942	Guadalcanal
Lt. Col. Harold W. Bauer	VMF-212	1942	Guadalcanal
Cpl. Lewis K. Bausell*	5th Marines	1944	Peleliu
Cpl. Charles J. Berry*	26th Marines	1945	Iwo Jima
1st Lt. Alexander Bonneyman, Jr.*	18th Marines	1943	Tarawa
Staff Sgt. William J. Bordelon, Jr.*	18th Marines	1943	Tarawa
Maj. Gregory Boyington	VMF-214	1943–44	Central Solomons
Cpl. Richard E. Bush	4th Marines	1945	Okinawa
Pfc. William R. Caddy*	26th Marines	1945	Iwo Jima
1st Lt. George H. Cannon*	6th Defense Battalion	1941	Midway
Lt. Col. Justice M. Chambers	25th Marines	1945	Iwo Jima
Sgt. Darrell S. Cole*	23rd Marines	1945	Iwo Jima
Maj. Henry A. Courtney*	22d Marines	1945	Okinawa
Cpl. Anthony P. Damato*	22d Marines	1944	Eniwetok
1st Lt. Jefferson J. De Blanc	VMF-112	1943	Solomons
Capt. Robert H. Dunlap	26th Marines	1945	Iwo Jima
Lt. Col. Aquilla J. Dyess*	24th Marines	1944	Kwajalein
Col. Merritt A. Edson	1st Raider Battalion	1942	Guadalcanal
Capt. Henry T. Elrod*	VMF-211	1941	Wake Island

NAME	PLACE	DATE	UNIT
Pfc. Harold G. Epperson*	Saipan	1944	6th Marines
Cpl. John P. Fardy*	Okinawa	1945	1st Marines
Capt. Richard E. Fleming*	Midway	1942	VMSB-241
Capt. Joseph J. Foss	Guadalcanal	1942	VMF-121
Pfc. William A. Foster*	Okinawa	1945	1st Marines
Maj. Robert E. Galer	Solomons	1942	VMF-224
Pvt. Harold Gonsalves	Okinawa	1945	15th Marines
Sgt. Ross F. Gray	Iwo Jima	1945	25th Marines
Pfc. Henry Gurke*	Bougainville	1943	3rd Raider Battalion
Pvt. Dale M. Hansen	Okinawa	1945	1st Marines
1st Lt. Robert M. Hanson	Rabaul	1943–44	VMF-215
Sgt. William G. Harrell	Iwo Jima	1945	28th Marines
Cpl. Louis J. Hauge, Jr.*	Okinawa	1945	1st Marines
1st Lt. William D. Hawkins*	Tarawa	1943	2d Marines
Pfc. Arthur J. Jackson	Peleliu	1944	7th Marines
Pfc. Douglas T. Jacobson	Iwo Jima	1945	23rd Marines
Platoon Sgt. Joseph R. Julian*	Iwo Jima	1945	27th Marines
Sgt. Elbert L. Kinser*	Okinawa	1945	1st Marines
Pfc. Richard E. Kraus*	Peleliu	1944	8th Amphibian Tractor Battalion
Pfc. James D. LaBelle*	Iwo Jima	1945	27th Marines
2d Lt. John Harold Leims	Iwo Jima	1945	9th Marines
Pfc. Jacklyn H. Lucas	Iwo Jima	1945	26th Marines
1st Lt. Jack Lummus*	Iwo Jima	1945	27th Marines
1st Lt. Harry L. Martin*	Iwo Jima	1945	5th Pioneer Battalion
Pfc. Leonard F. Mason*	Guam	1944	3rd Marines
Gunnery Sgt. Robert H. McCard*	Saipan	1944	4th Tank Battalion

Capt. Joseph J. McCarthy	Iwo Jima	1945	24th Marines
Pvt. Robert M. McTureous, Jr.*	Okinawa	1945	29th Marines
Pfc. John D. New*	Peleliu	1944	7th Marines
Sgt. Robert A. Owens*	Bougainville	1943	3rd Marines
Pvt. Joseph W. Ozbourn*	Tinian	1944	23rd Marines
Platoon Sgt. Mitchell Paige	Guadalcanal	1942	7th Marines
Pvt. Wesley Phelps*	Peleliu	1944	7th Marines
Pvt. George Phillips*	Iwo Jima	1945	28th Marines
Capt. Everett P. Pope	Peleliu	1944	1st Marines
1st Lt. John V. Power*	Kwajalein	1944	24th Marines
Pfc. Charles H. Roan*	Peleliu	1944	7th Marines
2d Lt. Carlton R. Rouh	Peleliu	1944	5th Marines
Pfc. Donald J. Ruhl*	Iwo Jima	1945	28th Marines
Pfc. Albert E. Schwab*	Okinawa	1945	5th Marines
Col. David M. Shoup	Tarawa	1943	2d Marines
Pvt. Franklin E. Sigler	Iwo Jima	1945	26th Marines
Pfc. Luther Skaggs, Jr.	Guam	1944	3rd Marines
Maj. John L. Smith	Solomons	1942	VMF-223
Pvt. Richard K. Sorenson	Kwajalein	1944	24th Marines
Cpl. Tony Stein*	Iwo Jima	1945	28th Marines
1st Lt. James E. Swett	Solomons	1943	VMF-221
Sgt. Herbert J. Thomas*	Bougainville	1943	3rd Marines
Sgt. Clyde Thomason*	Makin Island	1942	2d Raider Battalion
Sgt. Grant F. Timmerman*	Saipan	1944	2d Tank Battalion
Maj. Gen. Alexander A. Vandegrift	Solomons	1942	1st Marine Division
1st Lt. Kenneth A. Walsh	Solomons	1943	VMF-124
Gunnery Sgt. William G. Walsh*	Iwo Jima	1945	27th Marines

NAME	PLACE	DATE	UNIT
Pvt. Wilson D. Watson	Iwo Jima	1945	9th Marines
Cpl. Hershel W. Williams	Iwo Jima	1945	21st Marines
Capt. Louis H. Wilson, Jr.	Guam	1944	9th Marines
Pfc. Robert L. Wilson*	Tinian	1944	6th Marines
Pfc. Frank P. Witek*	Guam	1944	9th Marines

Korean War 1950–1953

NAME	PLACE	DATE	UNIT
Cpl. Charles G. Abrell*	Hill 1316	1951	1st Marines
Capt. William E. Barber	Toktong Pass	1950	7th Marines
Pfc. William B. Baugh*	Hell Fire Valley	1950	1st Marines
Pvt. Hector A. Cafferata, Jr.	Toktong Pass	1950	7th Marines
Cpl. David B. Champagne*	Tumae-ri Ridge	1952	7th Marines
Pfc. Stanley R. Christianson*	Seoul	1950	1st Marines
1st Lt. Henry A. Commiskey, Sr.	Yongdungpo	1950	1st Marines
Cpl. Jack A. Davenport*	Songnae-Dong	1951	5th Marines
Lt. Col. Raymond G. Davis	Toktong Pass	1950	7th Marines
Cpl. Duane E. Dewey	Panmunjom	1952	5th Marines
Pfc. Fernando L. Garcia*	Outpost Bruce	1952	5th Marines
Pfc. Edward Gomez*	Hill 749	1951	1st Marines
Staff Sgt. Ambrosio Guillen*	Hill 119	1953	7th Marines
Sgt. James E. Johnson*	Yudam-ni	1950	11th Marines
Pfc. John D. Kelly*	Tumae-ri Ridge	1952	7th Marines
Pfc. Jack W. Kelso*	Outpost Warsaw	1952	7th Marines
Staff Sgt. Robert S. Kennemore	Yudam-ni	1950	7th Marines
Pfc. Herbert A. Littleton*	Horseshoe Ridge	1951	7th Marines
1st Lt. Baldomero Lopez*	Inchon	1950	5th Marines

Sgt. Daniel P. Matthews*	Outpost Vegas	1953	7th Marines
Sgt. Frederick W. Mausert III*	Hill 673	1951	7th Marines
Pfc. Alford L. McLaughlin	Outpost Bruce	1952	5th Marines
1st Lt. Frank N. Mitchell*	Hansan-ni	1950	7th Marines
Pfc. Walter C. Monegan, Jr.*	Sosa-ri	1950	1st Marines
Pfc. Whitt L. Moreland*	Yanggu	1951	5th Marines
2d Lt. Raymond G. Murphy	Ungok Hill	1953	5th Marines
Maj. Reginald R. Myers	Hagaru	1950	1st Marines
Pfc. Eugene A. Obregon*	Seoul	1950	5th Marines
2d Lt. George H. O'Brien	The Hook	1952	7th Marines
Cpl. Lee H. Phillips	Sudong	1950	7th Marines
Sgt. James I. Poynter*	Sudong	1950	7th Marines
2d Lt. George H. Ramer*	Hill 680	1951	7th Marines
2d Lt. Robert D. Reem*	Funchilin Pass	1950	7th Marines
Staff Sgt. William E. Shuck, Jr.*	Outpost Yoke	1952	7th Marines
Pfc. Robert E. Simanek	Outpost Irene	1952	5th Marines
Capt. Carl L. Sitter	Hagaru	1950	1st Marines
2d Lt. Sherrod E. Skinner*	The Hook	1952	11th Marines
Staff Sgt. Archie Van Winkle	Sudong	1950	7th Marines
Cpl. Joseph Vittori*	Hill 749	1951	1st Marines
Staff Sgt. Lewis G. Watkins*	Outpost Frisco	1952	7th Marines
Tech. Sgt. Harold E. Wilson	Horseshoe Ridge	1951	1st Marines
Staff Sgt. William G. Windrich*	Yudam-ni	1950	5th Marines

Vietnam War 1965–1973

Pfc. James Anderson, Jr.*	Cam Lo	1967	3rd Marines
Lance Cpl. Richard A. Anderson*	Quang Tri Province	1969	3rd Reconnaissance Battalion

NAME	PLACE	DATE	UNIT
Pfc. Oscar P. Austin*	Near Da Nang	1969	7th Marines
Lance Cpl. Jedh C. Barker*	Con Thien	1967	4th Marines
1st Lt. Harvey C. Barnum, Jr.	Ky Phu	1965	9th Marines
2d Lt. John P. Bobo*	Quang Tri Province	1967	9th Marines
Pfc. Daniel D. Bruce*	Quang Nam Province	1969	5th Marines
Pfc. Robert C. Burke*	Le Nam	1968	27th Marines
Pfc. Bruce W. Carter*	Quang Tri Province	1969	3rd Marines
Pfc. Raymond M. Clausen		1970	HMM-263
Pfc. Ronald L. Coker*	Quang Tri Province	1969	3rd Marines
Staff Sgt. Peter S. Connor*	Quang Ngai Province	1966	3rd Marines
Lance Cpl. Thomas E. Creek*	Cam Lo	1969	9th Marines
Sgt. Rodney M. Davis*	Quang Nam Province	1967	5th Marines
Lance Cpl. Emilio A. De La Garza, Jr.*	Near Da Nang	1970	1st Marines
Pfc. Ralph E. Dias*		1969	7th Marines
Pfc. Douglas E. Dickey*	Gio Linh	1967	4th Marines
Sgt. Paul H. Foster*	Con Thien	1967	4th Marines
1st Lt. Wesley L. Fox	A Shau Valley	1969	9th Marines
Sgt. Alfredo Gonzalez*	Hue	1968	1st Marines
Capt. James A. Graham*	Quang Tin Province	1967	5th Marines
2d Lt. Terrance C. Graves*	Quang Tri Province	1968	3rd Reconnaissance Battalion
Staff Sgt. Jimmie E. Howard	Chu Lai	1966	1st Reconnaissance Battalion
Lance Cpl. James D. Howe*	Quang Nam Province	1970	7th Marines
Pfc. Robert H. Jenkins, Jr.*	Fire Support Base Argonne	1969	3rd Reconnaissance Battalion
Lance Cpl. Jose F. Jimenez*	Que Son Valley	1969	7th Marines
Pfc. Ralph H. Johnson*	Quan Duc Duc Valley	1968	1st Reconnaissance Battalion

Name	Location	Year	Unit
Lance Cpl. Miguel Keith*	Quang Ngai Province	1970	Combined Action Platoon 1-2-3
Staff Sgt. Allan J. Kellogg, Jr.	Quang Nam Province	1970	5th Marines
Capt. Howard V. Lee	Cam Lo	1966	4th Marines
Capt. James E. Livingston	Dai Do	1968	4th Marines
Pfc. Gary W. Martini*	Que Son Valley	1967	1st Marines
Cpl. Larry L. Maxam*	Cam Lo	1968	4th Marines
Staff Sgt. John J. McGinty III	Cam Lo	1966	4th Marines
Capt. Robert J. Modrzejewski	Cam Lo	1966	4th Marines
Cpl. William D. Morgan*	Quang Tri Province	1969	9th Marines
Pfc. Melvin E. Newlin*	Nong Son	1967	5th Marines
Lance Cpl. Thomas P. Noonan, Jr.*	A Shau Valley	1969	9th Marines
Cpl. Robert E. O'Malley	Van Tuong Peninsula	1965	3rd Marines
Lance Cpl. Joe C. Paul*	Chu Lai	1965	4th Marines
Cpl. William T. Perkins, Jr.*	Quang Tri	1967	3rd Marine Division (combat photographer)
Sgt. Lawrence D. Peters*	Quang Tin Province	1967	5th Marines
Pfc. Jimmy W. Phipps*	An Hoa	1969	1st Engineer Battalion
Lance Cpl. Richard A. Pittman	Near Demilitarized Zone	1966	5th Marines
Capt. Stephen W. Pless	Quang Ngai	1967	VMO-6
Lance Cpl. William R. Prom*	An Hoa	1969	3rd Marines
1st Lt. Frank S. Reasoner*	Da Nang	1965	3rd Reconnaissance Battalion
Sgt. Walter K. Singleton*	Gio Linh	1967	9th Marines
Cpl. Larry E. Smedley*	Quang Nam Province	1967	7th Marines
Staff Sgt. Karl G. Taylor, Sr.*	Near Da Nang	1968	26th Marines
Capt. M. Sando Vargas, Jr.	Dai Do	1968	4th Marines
Lance Cpl. Lester W. Weber*	Quang Nam Province	1968	7th Marines
Lance Cpl. Roy M. Wheat*	Quang Nam Province	1967	7th Marines

NAME	PLACE	DATE	UNIT
Pfc. Dewayne F. Williams*	Quang Nam Province	1968	1st Marines
Pfc. Alfred M. Wilson*	Quang Tri Province	1969	9th Marines
Lance Cpl. Kenneth L. Worley*	Quang Nam Province	1968	7th Marines

Primary source: Reference Information Pamphlet, History and Museums Division, USMC.

"The Club Is Out of Beer"

(From all the documents in the voluminous files of the Marine Corps Historical Division, the following letter is shared with the reader as a reminder that life in the Corps overseas had its lighter side. —*J.R.M.*)

UNITED STATES MARINE CORPS
HEADQUARTERS, ELEVENTH REGIMENT, SECOND BRIGADE,
OCOTAL, NICARAGUA.

22 March 1929.

Dear Berkeley:

Reference your note of 19 March, the first request for a shipment of beer for the Club was made 31 January, this shipment was received during February, and has been consumed, at the Club by members of the Brigade, only.

On 16 February, the second request was mailed; this called for 54 cases of Silver Spray and 42 cases of Tüborg, but to date this beer has not been received although the radios followed original request. Ocotavio Love, the steward, requested his man in Leon to send up two bull-cart loads, pending authority for release of second shipment. Two bull-cart loads of beer for the Club came in this morning so presumably these two are the ones requested by Love.

I have attached a new request, addressed to Collector General of Customs, as you suggest, this to take the place of third request dated March 18, 1929. You will see from the above that we make new requests as shipments are needed, and that there are no undrawn amounts. In fact it is not being released fast enough to insure a continuous supply.

Kindly do what you can to have this beer released, so that immediate shipment may be made. The Club is out of beer, making it necessary for the men to go elsewhere and pay the old price of forty cents, then, I would like to take advantage of the dry season, and get a good supply in; also, price of bull-cart hire is lower now than it will be later.

Sincerely,

[COL. ROBERT H.] DUNLAP

Acknowledgments

During the twenty years since the Ribbon Creek tragedy first involved me in the U.S. Marine Corps' story, many people have helped me to know and understand the Corps, its past and its present, and to turn my ideas and manuscript into this book.

The accuracy of the facts and the validity of the opinions presented here are totally my own responsibility. Although Marine Corps historians have willingly and thoroughly read the entire manuscript for accuracy, any errors that remain are mine, not theirs.

I want to thank the Marine Corps itself and a great many Marines for the cooperation and helpfulness I received. They have opened their records and made themselves available for interviews unhesitatingly. No effort was ever made to limit my access to unclassified material, to hide the warts or to attempt to censor either facts or opinions. As I have discovered again and again in reporting and researching, those closest to a story are usually the most candid about it. This is certainly true of the Marine Corps leadership I have come to know over these years. And I have received the personal encouragement of a number of Commandants, most notably Generals Pate, Shoup, Greene and Wilson.

At the McGraw-Hill Book Company, the publishers, I want particularly to express my appreciation to Frederic W. Hills, Mrs. Lou Ashworth and the late Albert R. Leventhal for seeing the book through its final years with good judgment and patience.

Since much of the early research was done during the years I worked for *Look* magazine, the book would never have been written without the support of William B. Arthur, the late Daniel D. Mich and, of course, Gardner Cowles, who published a magazine on which reporters were allowed to report precisely what they found. On *Look* also, photographer James Hansen made many trips with me around the globe, including visits to Vietnam, Korea and Cuba, and Robert Lerner photographed my first Marine Corps article back in 1957.

For their special contributions to this book, I want to thank George Buctel, who created the maps; Devorah Cohen, who did the extensive picture research; Stan Harvey, who oversaw the book's linguistic accuracy; art director Robert Mitchell; designer Jules Perlmutter; production supervisor Matthew Kardovich; John Hendry, who suggested cuts in much of the manuscript; and Doris Moskin, who shared the book's years of growth and meticulously prepared the source notes. Mrs. Vivien Lyons did the voluminous typing with patient skill and personal interest, Benis M. Frank prepared the Index.

I want to express particular appreciation to Phyllis Jackson, who persevered as my counselor and agent over all these years; to Robert L. Bernstein, who reinforced my original idea, and to Mark, David and Nancy Moskin, who contributed in their own ways.

For their help, encouragement and guidance in their fields of expertise, I would like to thank A. Doak Barnett, the late Bennett Cerf, Maj. Gen. Robert N. Ginsburgh, Martin Goldman, the late Henry Hillman, Donald W. Klein, Myrick Land, Paula Mattlin, Gladys McPartland, Anton O. Myrer, Col. Donald R. Nugent, the late Michael O'Quinlivan, Brig. Gen. Hamilton D. South, Col. Richard S. Stark and Woodrow Wirsig. Marcus Jaffe made available to me his letters as a young Marine in World War II, and David Douglas Duncan generously permitted me to include some of his magnificent pictures of Marines in combat.

Among the many Marine Corps historians who have helped with professionalism and enthusiasm, foremost has been Brig. Gen. Edwin H. Simmons, Director of Marine Corps History and Museums. My appreciation also to Col. Herbert M. Hart, Henry I. Shaw, Jr., Col. F. Brooke Nihart, Lt. Col. Russell B. Tiffany and Dr. Graham A. Cosmas, Ralph W. Donnelly, Benis M. Frank, Roland P. Gill, Dr. Martin K. Gordon, Gabrielle M. Neufeld, Maj. David A. Quinlan, Lt. Col. Lane Rogers, Jack Shulimson and Charles R. Smith. Brig. Gen. William R. Maloney, Marine Corps Director of Information, and Col. Mark J. Gravel, Deputy Director, were vitally helpful on the current Marine Corps.

In addition to the library and archives of the Marine Corps Historical Division, research was done with the help of the National Archives, the Library of Congress, the New York Public Library, the Widener Library of Harvard University, The New York Society Library, The Newberry Library, the Chicago Public Library, the University of Chicago Library, the Harvard Club of New York City Library, the Scarsdale (New York) Public Library and the British Information Services Library in New York.

Index

INDEX

INDEX

About the Author

J. Robert Moskin is a historian and an award-winning journalist. Formerly the Foreign Editor and member of the Editorial Board of *Look* Magazine, he has reported from around the world, including Moscow, Berlin, Warsaw, Jerusalem, Manila, Guantanamo, Seoul, Da Nang and Hanoi. He has written extensively about military and foreign affairs here and abroad. His reporting has received awards from the Overseas Press Club, the National Headliners Club, the Newspaper Guild of New York and the Sidney Hillman Foundation. A contributor to many magazines, he has written several books, including *Morality in America, Turncoat* and *The Decline of the American Male* (co-author). He holds degrees in American history from Harvard and Columbia universities and during World War II served with the U.S. Army in the Southwest Pacific. Mr. Moskin has researched *The U.S. Marine Corps Story* for nearly twenty years. In addition to studying thousands of documents in archives and libraries, he interviewed numerous Marines at Headquarters, from coast to coast and overseas.

ASIA

Bering Sea 1891

NOR

Puget Sound 1856

Chosin Reservoir
1950
Tsingtao 1946   Vladivostok 1919
Peking 1900   Seoul
Tientsin 1900, 1945   1950
Inchon 1950   Monterey 1846
Korea 1871   La Mesa 1847
Shanghai 1927, 1948   Tokyo Bay 1853, 1945
Pusan 1950
Okinawa 1945
Formosa 1867   Iwo Jima 1945   Hawaii 1874   San Jose 184
Canton 1856   Wake Island   Mexico City
Khe Sanh 1968   1941   Pearl Harbor
Hue 1968   Manila Bay 1898   Saipan 1944   1941   Vera Cruz 1
Thailand 1962   Guam 1944
Da Nang 1965   Sohoton Cliffs
1901   PACIFIC
Koh Tang 1975   Corregidor   Leyte   Peleliu 1944   Kwajalein 1944
Saigon   1941   1944   Makin 1942   OCEAN
1975   Tarawa 1943
Quallah Battoo   New Britain 1943
1832   Bougainville 1943   Marquesas Islands 1813
INDIAN   New Georgia   Guadalcanal 1942
1943
OCEAN   Samoa 1899

AUSTRALIA   Fiji Islands
1840   N

UNITED STATES
MARINE CORPS